The Soviet System

REVISED EDITION

The Soviet System

From Crisis to Collapse

edited by

ALEXANDER DALLIN
Stanford University

GAIL W. LAPIDUS
Stanford University

WESTVIEW PRESS
Boulder • San Francisco • Oxford

Copyright © 1991, 1995 by Westview Press, Inc.

Published in 1995 in the United States of America by Westview Press, Inc., 5500 Central Avenue, Boulder, Colorado 80301-2877, and in the United Kingdom by Westview Press, 36 Lonsdale Road, Summertown, Oxford OX2 7EW

Library of Congress Cataloging-in-Publication Data
The Soviet system : from crisis to collapse / edited by Alexander
  Dallin, Gail W. Lapidus.—Rev. ed.
    p.   cm.
  Rev. ed. of: The Soviet system in crisis. 1991.
  Includes bibliographical references.
  ISBN 0-8133-1876-9 (pbk.)
  1. Soviet Union—Politics and government—1985–1991.   2. Soviet
Union—Economic conditions—1985–1991.   3. Perestroĭka.   I. Dallin,
Alexander.   II. Lapidus, Gail Warshofsky.   III. Soviet system in
crisis.
DK286.5.S685   1995
947.085'4—dc20   94-37941
                                                                            CIP

Printed and bound in the United States of America

The paper used in this publication meets the requirements
of the American National Standard for Permanence of Paper
for Printed Library Materials Z39.48-1984.

10   9   8   7   6   5   4   3   2   1

CONTENTS

PREFACE TO THE REVISED EDITION

The dissolution of the Soviet Union in December 1991 and the emergence of fifteen independent states in its territory brought to a dramatic conclusion the historical era that began with the Bolshevik Revolution of October 1917. When Mikhail Gorbachev came to power in 1985, few observers—either here or there—anticipated that in the space of six or seven years what began as a modest attempt to reform the Soviet system would result in its total collapse.

This new edition of *The Soviet System in Crisis,* now retitled *The Soviet System: From Crisis to Collapse,* is intended to cover the entire Gorbachev era and to include some of the postmortems on the causes of the collapse. To provide a more extensive treatment of the coup of August 1991 and its aftermath, we included a number of new documents; it was therefore necessary to delete or shorten some of the selections included in the first edition.

Given the pace of events, their variety across the Soviet Union, and the obstacles to comprehending them, it has been difficult for specialists as well as students and casual observers to keep up. Many of our standard accounts of the Soviet system and of contemporary history have inevitably become obsolete. Those teaching courses on the Soviet Union have been frustrated by the lack of up-to-date readings. Moreover, the events of the last several years have raised fascinating new problems of analysis and interpretation that have divided Soviet as well as Western observers and commentators.

This collection is intended to remedy some of these problems by providing both source materials on and scholarly interpretations of key issues and developments during the Gorbachev years. We selected the most insightful analyses and the most interesting documents and sought to capture something of the diversity of points of view. It is our hope that, within the limits of what can be placed between two covers, the selections in this volume help to convey the substance and flavor both of the events and of the arguments surrounding them.

We considered it essential to preserve something of the uncertainty and tentativeness of the times during which the commentaries were written, when the outcomes were still uncertain, and to avoid insofar as possible imposing on the material the kind of judgment that could come only from hindsight. By the same token, we sought to bring together both documentary materials and contending interpretations of events in an effort to illuminate the controversies that not only accompanied these events but are certain to continue in the years ahead.

In fairness to the authors, we should remind the reader that one consequence of this decision is the inclusion of articles written at different degrees of immediacy to or distance from the events described, and we encourage the reader to consult the Credits for a more precise indication of the original dates of publication.

We would like to add to the list of acknowledgments our thanks to the many colleagues and students who gave us the benefit of their judgment concerning the original edition and to Jeffrey Robins for his research assistance. We would particularly like to express our appreciation to Rebecca Ritke at Westview Press, who cheerfully managed the difficulties of producing this edition and skillfully shepherded it through to publication.

Alexander Dallin
Gail W. Lapidus

PREFACE TO THE FIRST EDITION

This book was inspired by a conversation with Frederick Praeger, then publisher of Westview Press, that began with his apparently innocent question about how Soviet specialists taught the contemporary history of the Soviet Union when all standard textbooks had been overtaken by recent events. It was only a short jump from agreement that a collection of new materials was needed to the idea that we should undertake the task of assembling it—testimony to Fred's enthusiasm and powers of persuasion. We are very grateful for all the work and wise counsel of Susan McEachern, Beverly LeSuer, and their staff at Westview Press. As usual, the book's development turned out to be more complicated and time-consuming than we had thought—in part because we were shooting at a moving target.

Our thanks go to all the authors, editors, and publishers of books and journals who gave permission to reproduce the titles included here. Some pieces, mercifully, were in the public domain. Special thanks go to those who updated their papers for this collection and to those journals that seem to have made themselves indispensable by carrying a large number of seminal pieces central to intellectual debates among Sovietologists.

In a number of instances we have been obliged to reproduce only selections from longer articles, papers, or books. This reflects no judgment regarding any shortcomings of these works but merely an awareness of the limitations of available space. Some of the cuts and omissions were indeed painful to make. And—because we do indicate the source from which our text was taken—we would urge all those who would like to consider the fuller, uncut argument and documentation to consult the original text. We would have loved to include a number of other interesting pieces, but there simply was no room. The rule we tended to follow was to make selections in such a way as to give the reader a fair sampling of diverse opinions—both American and Soviet—as well as the more important contributions to the public debate.

Perfectionists will (properly) complain that this book uses several different citation styles and systems of transliteration from Cyrillic to Latin characters. The general rule we followed was to keep the pieces reproduced in this volume as close as possible to the original. As a result readers will find the same person spelled Yeltsin, Eltsin, and Yel'tsin in different articles. Only in the most outrageous cases have we felt free to alter the spelling or citation form used. Likewise, one conse-

quence of deletions from within certain chapters is the unusual sequence of footnote references, and we can only plead with the reader not to be troubled by having note 14 followed by note 23. These blemishes are regrettable, but (as they used
to say in Moscow) what is this compared to the world revolution?

In the process of selecting, assembling, and translating the items reproduced in
this volume we were helped by several graduate students at Berkeley and Stanford.
We are delighted to express our appreciation for the knowledgeable assistance
and dedication of Joseph Brandt, Philip Goldman, Oleg Kharkhordin, Corbin
Lyday, Semion Lyandres, Kira Reoutt, Kelly Smith, Amy Weisman, and David
Woodruff.

The events in the Soviet Union are as complex as they are fascinating. No single perspective can capture the drama and the promise, the chaos and the collapse. Perhaps this collection can help make them more real—and also convey
something of the variety of perspectives with which outsiders observe and analyze
the Soviet scene.

A.D.
G.W.L.

CREDITS

The chapters in this book are taken from the following sources. Permission to reprint is gratefully acknowledged.

Chapter 2: Reprinted by permission from S. Frederick Starr, "A Usable Past," *The New Republic* (May 15, 1989), pp. 24–27.

Chapter 3: Excerpted from Richard Pipes, *Survival Is Not Enough* (New York: Simon & Schuster, 1984), pp. 17–24.

Chapter 4: Reprinted from Seweryn Bialer, "Domestic and International Factors in the Formation of Gorbachev's Reforms," *Journal of International Affairs* (Spring 1989), pp. 283–297. Published by permission of the *Journal of International Affairs* and the Trustees of Columbia University in the City of New York.

Chapter 5: Excerpted from Peter Hauslohner, "Politics Before Gorbachev: De-Stalinization and the Roots of Reform," in Seweryn Bialer, ed., *Politics, Society, and Nationality: Inside Gorbachev's Russia* (Boulder, Colo: Westview Press, 1989), pp. 41–90, by permission of the publisher.

Chapter 6: Reprinted by permission from Stephen F. Cohen, "The Friends and Foes of Change: Reformism and Conservatism in the Soviet Union," in Stephen F. Cohen et al., eds., *The Soviet Union Since Stalin* (Bloomington: Indiana University Press, 1980), pp. 11–31. Copyright © Stephen F. Cohen. An expanded version of this article, carrying the analysis into the 1990s, appears in Stephen F. Cohen, *Rethinking the Soviet Experience: Politics and History Since 1917*, 2nd ed. (New York: Oxford University Press, 1991).

Chapter 7: Excerpted from Andrei Sakharov, Roy Medvedev, and Valery Turchin, "Letter to the Soviet Leaders," in George Saunders, ed., *Samizdat: Voices of the Soviet Opposition* (New York: Pathfinder Press, 1974), pp. 399–409. Copyright © 1974 by Pathfinder Press. Reprinted by permission.

Chapter 8: Reprinted with permission from David Remnick, "The Pioneers of Perestroika: Back to the Intellectual Roots of Soviet Reforms," *The Washington Post National Weekly Edition* (March 19-25, 1990). Copyright © 1990 *The Washington Post*.

Chapter 9: Reproduced from Chapter 1 of Geoffrey A. Hosking et al., *The Road to Post-Communism* (London: Pinter Publishers, 1992), by permission of Pinter Publishers Ltd., London. All rights reserved.

Chapter 10: Excerpted with permission from Archie Brown, "Political Change in the Soviet Union," *World Policy Journal* (Summer 1989), pp. 469–501.

Chapter 11: Excerpted from Gail W. Lapidus, "State and Society: Toward the Emergence of Civil Society in the Soviet Union," in Seweryn Bialer, ed., *Politics, Society, and Nationality: Inside Gorbachev's Russia* (Boulder, Colo.: Westview Press, 1989), pp. 121–148, by permission of the publisher.

Chapter 12: Reprinted by permission from Steven Fish, "The Emergence of Independent Associations and the Transformation of Russian Political Society," *Journal of Communist Studies* 7, no. 2 (September 1991), published by Frank Cass & Company, 890/900 Eastern Avenue, Ilford, Essex, England. Copyright Frank Cass & Co. Ltd.

Chapter 13: George W. Breslauer, "Evaluating Gorbachev as Leader," was first published in *Soviet Economy* (October-December 1989), pp. 299–340. Copyright © V. H. Winston & Sons, Inc. Reprinted by permission.

Chapter 14: Peter Reddaway, "The Quality of Gorbachev's Leadership," was first published in *Soviet Economy* 6, no. 2 (1990), pp. 125–140. Copyright © V. H. Winston & Sons, Inc. Reprinted by permission.

Chapter 15: Reprinted by permission from Jerry F. Hough, "Gorbachev's Endgame," *World Policy Journal* (Fall 1990), pp. 639–672.

Chapter 16: Excerpted by permission from Josephine Woll, "*Glasnost'* and Soviet Culture," *Problems of Communism* (November-December 1989), pp. 40–50, by permission of the publisher.

Chapter 17: Excerpted from Thomas Sherlock, "Politics and History Under Gorbachev," *Problems of Communism* (May-August 1988), pp. 16–42, by permission of the publisher.

Chapter 18: Excerpted and translated from Nikolai Shmelev, "Avansy i dolgi," *Novyi mir,* no. 6 (1987). Published in English by *The Current Digest of the Soviet Press* 39, no. 8 (1987), pp. 1–7. Translation copyright 1987 by *The Current Digest of the Soviet Press,* published weekly at Columbus, Ohio. Reprinted by permission of the Digest.

Chapter 19: Translated from Vasily Selyunin, "Istoki," *Novyi mir,* no. 5 (1988). Published in English by *The Current Digest of the Soviet Press* 40, no. 40 (1988), pp. 14–17. Translation copyright 1988 by *The Current Digest of the Soviet Press,* published weekly at Columbus, Ohio. Reprinted by permission of the Digest.

Chapter 20: Excerpted and translated from Aleksandr Tsipko, "Khoroshi li nashi printsipy?" *Novyi mir,* no. 4 (1990), pp. 173–204.

Chapter 21: Mikhail Gorbachev's speech at the Conference of the Aktiv of the Khabarovsk Territory Party Organization, July 31, 1986, published in English by *The Current Digest of the Soviet Press* 38, no. 31 (1986), pp. 1–5. Translation copyright 1986 by *The Current Digest of the Soviet Press,* published weekly at Columbus, Ohio. Reprinted by permission of the Digest.

Chapter 22: Translated from Nina Andreyeva, "Ne mogu postupat'sia printsipami," *Sovetskaya Rossiya* (March 13, 1988). Published in English by *The Current Digest of the Soviet Press* 40, no. 13 (1990), pp. 1–6. Translation copyright 1990 by *The Current Digest of the Soviet Press,* published weekly at Columbus, Ohio. Reprinted by permission of the Digest.

Chapter 23: Reprinted from Aleksandr Prokhanov, "Tragedia tsentralizma," *Literaturnaya Rossiya,* no. 1 (January 5, 1990), pp. 4–5. Published in English by *The Current Digest of the*

Soviet Press 42, no. 4 (1990), pp. 1–4. Translation copyright 1990 by *The Current Digest of the Soviet Press*, published weekly at Columbus, Ohio. Reprinted by permission of the Digest.

Chapter 24: Reprinted from Oleg T. Bogomolov, "I Can't Absolve Myself of Guilt," *Ogonyok*, no. 35 (1990). Published in English by *The Current Digest of the Soviet Press* 42, no. 38 (1990), pp. 1–4. Translation copyright 1990 by *The Current Digest of the Soviet Press*, published weekly at Columbus, Ohio. Reprinted by permission of the Digest.

Chapter 25: Excerpted by permission from Boris Yeltsin, *Against the Grain* (New York: Summit Books, 1990). Copyright © 1990 by Boris Yeltsin.

Chapter 26: Translated from "Demokraticheskaia platforma k XXVIII s"ezdu KPSS," *Pravda* (March 3, 1990); "Programmnoe zaiavlenie 'Demokraticheskoi platformy' v KPSS," *Leningradskaya Pravda* (June 1, 1990).

Chapter 27: Ed A. Hewett, "Is Soviet Socialism Reformable?" was presented as the Ernst Sture Memorial Lecture on November 1, 1989, at the Paul H. Nitze School of Advanced International Studies of The Johns Hopkins University. Published by permission.

Chapter 28: Reprinted from a report prepared by the Central Intelligence Agency and the Defense Intelligence Agency for presentation to the Technology and National Security Subcommittee of the Joint Economic Committee, Congress of the United States, May 14, 1991.

Chapter 29: Marshall Goldman, "The Effort Collapses," reprinted from Chapter 6 of *What Went Wrong with Perestroika* by Marshall I. Goldman, by permission of the author and W. W. Norton & Company, Inc. Copyright © 1991 by Marshall I. Goldman.

Chapter 30: Ronald G. Suny, "State, Civil Society and Ethnic Cultural Consolidation in the USSR: Roots of the National Question," is the text of a lecture delivered at King's College, Cambridge University, in June 1990. Published by permission.

Chapter 31: Excerpted from Gail W. Lapidus, "Gorbachev's Nationalities Problem," *Foreign Affairs* (Fall 1989), pp. 92–108. Copyright © 1989 by the Council on Foreign Relations, Inc.

Chapter 32: Excerpted from Roman Szporluk, "Dilemmas of Russian Nationalism," *Problems of Communism* (July-August 1989), pp. 15–35, by permission of the publisher.

Chapter 33: Translated and excerpted from "Perspektivy demokratizatsii (kruglyi stol po problemam politicheskoi reformy v SSSR)," *Polis*, no. 2 (1990), pp. 88–103, by permission of the publisher.

Chapter 34: "Declaration on the State Sovereignty of the Russian Soviet Socialist Republic" is translated from *Argumenty i fakty*, no. 24 (June 16-22, 1990). "Declaration on the State Sovereignty of Ukraine Adopted by the Ukrainian SSR Supreme Soviet on July 16, 1990" is translated from *Argumenty i fakty*, no. 29 (July 21-27, 1990). Both are reprinted by permission of the publisher.

Chapter 35: Translated from Boris Yeltsin's speech to the Russian Federation Congress of People's Deputies, Moscow, May 22, 1990. Published in English by FBIS (May 23, 1990).

Chapter 36: Giulietto Chiesa, with Douglas T. Northrop, "The National Dimension," reprinted from *Transition to Democracy: Political Change in the Soviet Union, 1987–1991* (Hanover, N.H.: University Press of New England, 1993), copyright © 1993 by Giulietto Chiesa, by permission of University Press of New England.

Chapter 37: Excerpted from Robert Legvold, "The Revolution in Soviet Foreign Policy," *Foreign Affairs* (*America and the World*, 1988–1989), pp. 83–98, by permission of *Foreign Affairs*. Copyright © 1988–1989 by the Council on Foreign Relations, Inc.

Chapter 38: Georgii Shakhnazarov, "East-West: The Problem of Deideologizing Relations," was published in *Kommunist*, no. 3 (1989). This translation is from an offprint by the International Center for Development Policy, Washington, D.C.

Chapter 39: Translated from Mikhail Gorbachev's address at the Forty-Third UN General Assembly Session, December 7, 1988. Printed in English by FBIS (December 8, 1988).

Chapter 40: Based on a report by Alexander Dallin to the National Council for Soviet and East European Research, Washington, D.C., "Whatever Happened to World Revolution?" (1990).

Chapter 41: Excerpted from Hannes Adomeit, "Gorbachev and German Unification: Revision of Thinking, Realignment of Power," *Problems of Communism* (July-August 1990), pp. 1–19, by permission of the publisher.

Chapter 42: Excerpted from David E. Albright, "The USSR and the Third World in the 1980's," *Problems of Communism* (March-June 1989), pp. 50–70, by permission of the publisher.

Chapter 43: Excerpted from Bruce Parrott, "Soviet National Security Under Gorbachev," *Problems of Communism* (November-December 1988), pp. 1–36, by permission of the publisher.

Chapter 44: Reprinted from David Holloway, "State, Society, and the Military Under Gorbachev," *International Security* 14, no. 3 (Winter 1989-1990), by permission of The MIT Press, Cambridge, Massachusetts.

Chapter 45: Translated and excerpted from Yuri Katasonov, "Arkhitektory kartonykh sten," *Molodaya Gvardiya*, no. 7 (1990), pp. 219–232, by permission of the publisher.

Chapter 46: Translated from Edvard Shevardnadze, "Speech to the Congress of People's Deputies," December 20, 1990.

Chapter 47: From Kremlin files.

Chapter 48: "An Open Letter to the People," *Sovetskaya Rossia* (July 23, 1991). Published in English by *The Current Digest of the Soviet Press* 43, no. 30 (1991), pp. 8–10. Translation copyright 1991 by *The Current Digest of the Soviet Press*, published weekly at Columbus, Ohio. Reprinted by permission of the Digest.

Chapter 49: Oleg Moroz, "Interview with Aleksandr Yakovlev," *Literaturnaya gazeta*, no. 34 (August 28, 1991). Published in English by *The Current Digest of the Soviet Press* 43, no. 34 (1991), pp. 44–48. Translation copyright 1991 by *The Current Digest of the Soviet Press*, published weekly at Columbus, Ohio. Reprinted by permission of the Digest.

Chapter 50: "A Coup Chronology" excerpted from compilation by *The Current Digest of the Soviet Press* 43, nos. 33 and 34 (1991) from various Soviet publications. Copyright 1991 by *The Current Digest of the Soviet Press*, published weekly at Columbus, Ohio. Reprinted by permission of the Digest.

Chapter 51: John B. Dunlop, "Anatomy of a Failed Coup," excerpted from Chapter 5 of Dunlop, John B., *The Rise of Russia and the Fall of the Soviet Empire* (Princeton, N.J.: Princeton University Press, 1993). Copyright © 1993 by Princeton University Press. Reprinted by permission of Princeton University Press.

Chapter 52: Excerpted from Gavriil Popov, "August 1991," *Izvestia* (August 21-26, 1992). Published in English by *The Current Digest of the Soviet Press* 44, no. 34 (1992), pp. 1–6. Translation copyright 1992 by *The Current Digest of the Soviet Press*, published weekly at Columbus, Ohio. Reprinted by permission of the Digest.

Chapter 53: Boris Yeltsin, speech to the RSFSR Congress of People's Deputies and to the citizens of Russia, October 28, 1991. Published in English by *The Current Digest of the Soviet Press* 43, no. 43 (1991), pp. 1–5. Translation copyright 1991 by *The Current Digest of the Soviet Press*, published weekly at Columbus, Ohio. Reprinted by permission of the Digest.

Chapter 54: Stanislau Shushkevich, Boris Yeltsin, and Leonid Kravchuk, "Agreement on the Creation of a Commonwealth of Independent States," *Izvestia* (December 9, 1991). Published in English by *The Current Digest of the Soviet Press* 43, no. 49 (1991), p. 10. Translation copyright 1991 by *The Current Digest of the Soviet Press*, published weekly at Columbus, Ohio. Reprinted by permission of the Digest.

Chapter 55: "The Alma-Ata Declaration," *Izvestia* (December 9, 1991). Published in English by *The Current Digest of the Soviet Press* 43, no. 51 (1991), p. 4. Translation copyright 1991 by *The Current Digest of the Soviet Press*, published weekly at Columbus, Ohio. Reprinted by permission of the Digest.

Chapter 56: Mikhail Gorbachev's resignation speech on Soviet television, December 25, 1991. Published in English by *The Current Digest of the Soviet Press* 43, no. 52 (1991), pp. 1, 3. Translation copyright 1991 by *The Current Digest of the Soviet Press*, published weekly at Columbus, Ohio. Reprinted by permission of the Digest.

Chapter 57: Excerpted from "Z," "To the Stalin Mausoleum," *Daedalus* (January 1990), pp. 295–344, by permission of the publisher.

Chapter 58: Reprinted from Alexander Dallin, "Causes of the Collapse of the USSR," *Post-Soviet Affairs* 8, no. 4 (1992), pp. 279–302.

Chapter 59: Excerpted by permission from Daniel Deudney and G. John Ikenberry, "Who Won the Cold War?" *Foreign Policy*, no. 87 (1992). Copyright © 1992 by the Carnegie Endowment for International Peace.

Chapter 60: Eduard Shevardnadze, "The 'Shadows' Come to Light," abridged and reprinted with the permission of The Free Press from *The Future Belongs to Freedom* by Eduard Shevardnadze, translated by Catherine A. Fitzpatrick (New York: Free Press, 1991). Copyright © 1991 by Eduard Shevardnadze. Будущее принадлежит свободе published by permission of Rowohlt Verlag Gmbh, Reinbek b. Hamburg. English translation, copyright © 1991 by The Free Press.

Chapter 61: Yegor Ligachev, "Inside Gorbachev's Kremlin," excerpted from Yegor Ligachev, *Inside Gorbachev's Kremlin* (New York: Pantheon, 1993). Copyright © 1993 by Yegor Ligachev. Reprinted by permission of Pantheon Books, a division of Random House, Inc.

1   *The Setting:*
An Introduction

ALEXANDER DALLIN
& GAIL W. LAPIDUS

Less than seven years after Mikhail Gorbachev came to power—first as secretary general of the Communist Party, later also as president of the Soviet Union—the dramatic changes in the Soviet system that he initiated culminated in the unraveling of the East European empire, the dissolution of the Soviet state, and the emergence of fifteen independent states in its former territory. Why the attempt at reform was initiated, how it evolved over time, and why it resulted in the collapse of the Soviet system are among the central questions about this era.

THE MARKERS OF CHANGE

What were the main characteristics of the intervening years of reform? A first and far-reaching transformation was the institution of *glasnost*—in substance, a freeing up of access to information, the gradual erosion of censorship, and the progressive elimination of taboos on discussion of certain subjects in the mass media. The abandonment of an obligatory "general line" (and its corollary that all other lines were wrong and hence impermissible) opened the door to a degree of free expression unprecedented in Soviet practice since the 1920s. Once it was acknowledged that the Party was not the only repository of truth, it was possible to encourage a new "pluralism" of opinion, a receptivity to new ideas and to the search for new answers, particularly as it became apparent that the old ideology had neither the hold nor the power that its proponents had claimed. *Glasnost* created major new opportunities for intellectuals (and unavoidably also for charlatans) to challenge old myths and fill the ideological vacuum. Historians could now gather and present the evidence on events that had been off-limits to discussion, such as the purges of the 1930s, and debate the relationship of Stalin to Lenin or the inevitability of the October Revolution; plays that had long been banned could now be performed; forbidden books could be reprinted; foreign broadcasts were no longer jammed; and a rich array of newspapers and journals representing a broad spectrum of political, ideological, and other concerns made their appearance.

This general erosion of inhibitions and fears under the impact of *glasnost* was accompanied by political democratization, an opening of the political system to diversity, and a growing degree of responsiveness to rank-and-file grievances and

1

demands. The same years saw the rapid and widespread mushrooming of grass-roots organizations—the first competition for the Communist Party in the hitherto "mono-organizational" society. Nominally nonpolitical and sometimes indeed dedicated to local, environmental, social, leisure-time or other pursuits, some of these networks of "informal" organizations proved to be the beginnings of social movements; some later registered as bona fide clubs or associations; and others become political parties.

The first competitive elections in Soviet history and, eventually, the Party's reluctant abandonment of its monopoly on power encouraged the emergence of embryonic rival parties. Most important, the opportunity to nominate and elect independent candidates undercut the critical institution of *nomenklatura*, in which the center selected reliable candidates for key positions, both elective and appointive. However, although the Communist Party candidates suffered major setbacks in the elections, the Party remained the single most powerful—and virtually the only nationwide—actor on the Soviet political scene because of its vast organizational network, its dominance in policymaking and implementation, the vested interests of its staff, and the property (such as newspapers and buildings) it controlled across the whole country.

In addition to this effort at democratization, the reformist leadership sought to promote two other changes in the political system: a division of power between the executive and the legislative branches, with the newly constituted Congress of People's Deputies and the smaller Supreme Soviet functioning not as rubber stamps but as real, if inexperienced, political actors; and a division of power between the Party and the state, with the unadvertised transfer of functions from the Party secretary general to the new office of president (first of the legislature and later of the country) and a similar transfer of responsibilities from the Politburo to a new Presidential Council. Needless to say, such changes were typically resisted by the old establishment—in this case, the incumbent Party secretaries and other functionaries of the Party *apparat*. Indeed, the accelerating pace of institutional changes contributed to a growing sense of instability and jurisdictional uncertainty.

An ambitious agenda was tackled by the new legislature—laws on freedom of the press and freedom of individual conscience, a broad human rights bill, various economic and price reforms, new tax laws, the creation of procedures for a "law-governed state," and congressional oversight of military and security affairs. Even though in practice a combination of inexperience, political foot-dragging, and the control of the agenda from above seriously undermined its effectiveness, the frank discussions in the new legislature and its telecast proceedings served to educate a nationwide audience about serious shortcomings of Soviet life.

Glasnost and democratization had a particularly dramatic impact in the non-Russian republics. The delegitimation of Stalinist policies and practices opened the door to an outpouring of long-suppressed resentments and gave official sanction to newly emerging cultural and political movements devoted to national revival. Initially taking the form of "popular fronts," these umbrella organizations in turn gave birth to a variety of new political parties committed to an expansion of national as well as civil rights. The explosive growth of their public support in a number of republics undermined the Communist Party and contributed to its fragmentation along ethnic as well as political lines. The process of democratization also made possible political initiatives at the republic level, where newly assertive parliaments viewed themselves as the defenders of republics' interests. Assertions of republic autonomy, sovereignty, and independence took on added significance as the Russian republic itself, under the leadership of Boris Yeltsin, became a powerful challenge to Union control.

In the initial plans for *perestroika*, the effort to revitalize the Soviet economy and to overcome economic stagnation occupied a central place. Indeed, the following years witnessed a broadening debate over the sources and remedies for economic decline that itself provided an education in elementary economics. But incoherence and blunders in economic policy and failure to adopt, let alone implement, the major shift toward a market economy that had been so widely discussed accelerated the deterioration of economic performance and confronted the leadership with an increasingly severe economic crisis.

Finally, Soviet relations with the outside world underwent equally—if not more—dramatic changes. On the level of ideas and strategies, the "new political thinking" marked a basic departure from traditional Leninist assumptions. It meant the abandonment of class analysis and therefore of class struggle in the understanding and conduct of world affairs, the renunciation of the use of force in favor of political settlements, and a downgrading of Soviet expectations of Third World revolutions. It introduced a new emphasis on interdependence, common human values, and the need to solve global problems cooperatively.

On the level of foreign policy behavior, the implications of the new thinking pointed to ending the Soviet military intervention in Afghanistan, negotiating significant arms reduction agreements with the United States—both nuclear and conventional—that included far-reaching provisions for verification, reducing its support to a number of allies and client states, and assisting in the settlement of regional conflicts from Namibia to Cambodia. Most dramatically, it meant a Soviet decision not to intervene when a mounting tide of protests and demonstrations in East European Warsaw Pact countries brought down the ruling Communist regimes, ending more than forty years of Soviet domination in Eastern Europe and opening the door to the unification of East and West Germany in 1990.

What was ultimately responsible for Soviet acquiescence to these conditions was the perceived weakness and backwardness of the Soviet system, its economy and society. Recognizing the need to concentrate all resources and attention on domestic restructuring and to avoid a costly and potentially unrewarding escalation of the arms race, Moscow sought a stable and benign international environment, even though this might exact a heavy price.

Without any doubt, the normalization of Soviet foreign relations, the restraint and statesmanship shown by Moscow in its dealings abroad, and the seeming abandonment of its erstwhile messianic ideology earned the Soviet Union considerable goodwill internationally and helped dispel lingering anxieties about the Soviet threat. The Nobel Peace Prize awarded to Mikhail Gorbachev in 1990 symbolized the global significance of these changes and the personal contribution of Gorbachev to initiating them.

THE LIMITS OF CHANGE

In the process of formulating, adopting, and implementing the reforms, those committed to changing the Soviet system faced a variety of obstacles and handicaps, some inevitable and others self-created. As a Soviet wit remarked, it was easy to make fish stew out of an aquarium, but the task of creating an aquarium out of fish stew strained the limits of the possible.

There was, first of all, the intrinsic difficulty of the task of transforming the Soviet system, a task unprecedented in magnitude: to undo totalitarian institutions, habits, and values; to decentralize a command economy based on state ownership; to rationalize a vast and often ossified bureaucracy; to hold together a diverse multinational empire in the face of powerful centrifugal forces; and to offer a new set of ideals and visions that could inspire a cynical and tired society.

Adding to the difficulties were the inexperience and often the ignorance of the reformers. They lacked a master plan, and improvization ranged from brilliant to disastrous. After three generations of Leninism, Stalinism, and Brezhnevism, there were few Soviet officials who had a serious acquaintance with alternative political systems; who understood the principles of a market economy or a convertible currency; who knew the rules of procedure of a legislative body; who sensed how Soviet foreign policy was perceived abroad; and who—in spite of all censorship and falsification of statistics—had acquired an instinctive understanding of the society's massive needs, from the quest for human dignity to syringes, from minicomputers to contraceptives.

The task was further complicated—and at times sabotaged—by the resistance of all those who either saw themselves as the losers from the contemplated changes or considered reforms as threats to their institutions and ideology. This resistance came from the Party secretaries who sought to avoid or delay being ousted by their hitherto silent and obedient followers, from the ideologues who saw the reformers as traitors who needed to be exposed and dismissed before it was too late, and from the military and secret police alarmed at the betrayal of the highest interests of state and at the danger of the disintegration of the country. Although Gorbachev was remarkably successful in defeating and deflecting resistance in the upper echelons of the Party machine, he either did not see or could do little to combat resistance in the military-industrial complex, in the bloated central ministries, in the lower ranks of Communist officialdom, among the commanders of the armed forces, and in the secret police.

Popular attitudes and values provided another set of constraints. Many were prepared to welcome the relaxation of controls, the reassertion of dignity, the opening to the West, and the ideological erosion, yet the reforms also ran into a wall of popular cynicism and mistrust, the legacy of decades of hopes disappointed and betrayed. Pervasive values and attitudes, above all deeply embedded welfarist and egalitarian orientations in large parts of the Soviet population, rural and urban alike, were challenged by the ethos of the reforms, which encouraged individual initiative, choice, and competition.

Finally, the relaxation of controls inevitably permitted the surfacing of socially undesirable activities and phenomena along with the good; and conservative voices called for a return to law and order, identifying crime and corruption, prostitution and pornography, with the spirit or reform and Western influence.

All this took place amid a bitter political struggle that was only partially visible to the outside world. For some five years, Gorbachev played a central role as protagonist of reform and time and again managed to overcome resistance, to strengthen his position, and to broaden still further the scope of change. But by 1989 events were already outrunning his capacity to control them, and he increasingly came to be viewed as a brake on the process of reform. One Soviet observer described him as trying to be "both Luther and the Pope." Caught between the pressures for increasingly radical change and the growing resistance to it, Gorbachev vacillated. On economic reform he hesitated and reversed himself several times because he was unable unequivocally to endorse a market economy and private ownership. On political reform, his support for democratization stopped short of submitting his presidency to popular election or of making common cause with more radical reformers prepared to split the Communist Party and repudiate its conservative wing.[1] On the national question, his failure to appreciate the impact of his political and economic reforms on national identities impeded a serious reform of the federal system. In the end, the polarization of political forces dissolved the center on which Gorbachev had tried to rest his power.

A major decision point came in the fall of 1990 when, repudiating a plan for radical economic reform and a looser federation that he had earlier seemed to endorse, Gorbachev swung to the right and brought several reactionary figures into positions of political influence, precipitating the dramatic resignation of his close associate, Edvard Shevardnadze, as foreign minister.

The disastrous attempt at a crackdown in the Baltic states that followed in January 1991 and the growing tide of reaction in Russia itself prompted a belated revival of the democratic forces under the leadership of Boris Yeltsin. When Gorbachev attempted once more to make common cause with the democrats and prepared to sign a Union Treaty that key elements of the establishment viewed as tantamount to dissolving the Soviet Union, a coalition of powerful opponents of reform took advantage of his absence from Moscow to stage the abortive coup of August 1991.

The attempted coup and its defeat precipitated the final unraveling of the Soviet Union. It discredited the all-Union institutions and leaders associated with the coup—the Communist Party, the KGB, the military high command, the government—and ultimately Gorbachev himself, who bore the responsibility for having appointed all the figures who had turned on him. It confirmed the ascendancy of the democrats and of the Russian Federation under Boris Yeltsin. It compelled recognition of the independence of the Baltic states and contributed to the vote for independence in Ukraine in December 1991. And it set the stage for the resignation of Gorbachev, the dissolution of the Soviet Union, and the emergence of fifteen independent states, most of which joined in a new and amorphous Commonwealth.

LOOKING BACK

The changes in Soviet politics and foreign policy precipitated by Gorbachev's reforms and the even more dramatic reconfiguration of the region that resulted from the collapse of the Soviet system challenged all the prevailing academic paradigms as well as the underlying assumptions of Western policy. The initial Western reaction to the Gorbachev program was one of profound skepticism, given the widely held belief that basic change in the Soviet system was impossible and that it surely could not be carried out by people who had themselves grown up in and benefited from the system.

But in the following years a clear evolution took place. Within the Bush administration the pejorative description of Gorbachev as "drugstore cowboy" yielded to a new image of the Soviet leader as a uniquely skillful and wise reformer and prompted an optimistic search for pathways of cooperation with the Soviet leadership in the pursuit of a new world order. Among journalists and academics, the changes (perhaps more than the obstacles and the distortions) understandably attracted considerable interest. Historians and economists, social scientists and system analysts became increasingly fascinated by the unprecedented transitions they witnessed in the USSR. Focusing on what was new and unexpected, many observers tended to neglect the obstacles and difficulties of the attempted transformations.

The collapse of the Soviet Union unleashed a new debate over whether *perestroika* had been doomed from the start or whether its failures reflected errors of strategy and leadership that might have been avoided. A heated controversy engaged not only Western specialists but leading Soviet participants in the drama as well.

Whatever the judgment about *perestroika*, it launched a process of transformation that will extend far into the future. The disintegration of an old system and the emergence of a new one are processes that can be expected to take many years, if not decades. Counterrevolutions and deformations of all sorts are part of the natural history of such transformations, whether or not in the end they "succeed."

With the benefit of hindsight, it is clear that the victory of the democrats and the rout of the old establishment in late 1991 were far less complete than they initially appeared. The bitter struggles that had characterized the entire Gorbachev era would continue, in varying degrees, in the newly independent states of the region.

NOTES

1. We are adopting the current Russian usage in which "right" and "conservative" refer to persons or groups opposing the reforms or favoring the maintenance of the status quo.

PART 1

The Roots of Perestroika

If Soviet and Western observers alike largely failed to anticipate the inauguration by the Soviet leadership of radical reform from above, a substantial body of writings had nonetheless captured the mounting problems and pressures that ultimately triggered it. Other analysts added their voices once the reform was in progress. These writings reveal important divisions over several issues that relate to the roots of perestroika.

The first involves differing assessments of the condition of the Soviet Union on the eve of the Gorbachev era. One school argues that the protracted failure of the Soviet leadership to come to grips with major festering issues in a changing society—be they a lag in technological innovation or the explosive spread of corruption, an erosion of ideological commitment or a sluggish economy—amounted to a time bomb, and that the system was on the threshold of major crisis that only the succession of a new, activist generation of leaders, aware of the urgency of the problems facing the Soviet Union, could seriously attempt to address.

Others maintain that, whatever its many problems, the country that Brezhnev ruled from 1964 to 1982 was basically stable; that living conditions were improving, if slowly; and that the emphasis of the new leadership on the urgency of change to avert a crisis exaggerated the reality in order to rationalize its own efforts. In this view the destabilization of the system—ideological, political, and economic—was the product of the policies of the Gorbachev regime themselves.

A second controversy surrounds the sources of pressures for reform. Although these perspectives are not necessarily mutually exclusive, some analysts focus on the decisive role of international aspirations, arguing that the costs of playing a superpower role, including the overextension of the Soviet military sector and defense industry (driven partly by Western behavior) as well as the "costs of empire" placed an unsustainable burden on the domestic economy and compelled reforms designed initially to preserve the Soviet Union's superpower status. More recent work has stressed not only the pressures of the international system but also its facilitating role in providing a benign environment conducive to the pursuit of reforms.

Others, on the contrary, emphasize the primacy of domestic concerns in Soviet policymaking, arguing that economic stagnation and bureaucratic immobility contributed to an unraveling of the social contract, a loss of political legitimacy, and the danger of growing popular discontent—factors that, in a "Polish-type" crisis, precipitated a cleavage within the political elite.

9

Granting the existence of such elements, what were the facilitating or propitious circumstances that helped the reformers—and the reforms—prevail? And, in turn, what were the constraining conditions under which they labored? Here too the accents fall on different aspects of the Soviet scene. Among facilitating conditions, some point to the dualism in the Bolshevik tradition itself that has long pitted defenders of the status quo against various advocates of change, with the articulation of reformism going back at least to the 1950s. Others argue that socioeconomic development has served as a critical source of pressure for reforms, triggering a change of values and expectations on the part of a new, better-educated equivalent of an urban middle class. Still others have emphasized the role of the dissident movement in preparing the ground for reform by exposing the brutalities of the Stalinist system, pressing for efforts to deal with the past, and utilizing such international acts as the Universal Declaration of Human Rights and the Helsinki accord as standards by which to judge Soviet behavior.

Many of those stressing the constraints on reform focus on the continuities of Russian (or Soviet) political culture that allegedly prevent, complicate, or doom attempts at meaningful reform. Some emphasize the role of vested interests and conservative institutions, beginning with the vast party and state bureaucracy and the many beneficiaries of the status quo in the armed forces and KGB, as powerful obstacles to any serious reforms.

These arguments have by no means come to an end with the dissolution of the Soviet Union. Debates over the social basis of support for reforms or the role of both pre-Soviet and Soviet political culture raise central questions concerning the future of Russia and the other successor states.

2 *A Usable Past*

S. FREDERICK STARR

"Scratch a Russian and you'll find a Tatar." In 1839 the Marquís de Custine used these dyspeptic words in dismissing all possibility of liberal reform in Russia. A two-month tour had left him convinced that Russia was a land of slaves ruled by knout-wielding bureaucrats. Only the hopelessly naive could imagine that its inhabitants could ever institute a reign of law, parliamentary government, and civic comity.

The view that Russia's political culture has been inhospitable to anything but brute autocracy (whether czarist or Communist) has long been shared by some very thoughtful American scholars all along the ideological spectrum. Among leftists, this view has sometimes been invoked as an implicit apology for authoritarian Soviet rule, and among right-wingers it has been used to fend off claims that the Soviet Union might gradually evolve toward a more open and pluralistic government and economy.

On the left, Leopold Haimson of Columbia University has argued that Russia's liberal movement collapsed before the revolutionary parties did because it was cut off from the masses, extremely narrow in its social base, and hopelessly fragmented. On the right, Richard Pipes of Harvard University emphasizes the "missing bourgeoisie" in Russian history, arguing that the late development of a propertied middle class and of ideas of civil rights and law left the field to radicals and reactionaries, which in turn led to the rise of state-sponsored terror. Similarly, James Billington claims in *The Icon and the Axe* that liberalism took root in Russia only in the 1890s; before that, nearly everyone looked on it with disdain. Constitutional liberalism was "more than any current of ideas in 19th-century Russia the work of college professors," he argues, and was "lost between the frozen Russia of Pobedonostsev and the flaming Russia of social revolution."

If this were the whole picture—if free elections, a free press, the rule of law, and individual economic initiative were truly so alien to Russia's essence as it has existed from Ivan the Terrible through Stalin and his heirs—then Mikhail Gorbachev would be in big trouble. In his efforts to build a more open society he could call on no usable past, invoke no cultural memories, tap no received skills or aspirations. Reform would be foredoomed. There would be little reason to think that the recent elections, and the cascade of other extraordinary events, were more than a flash in the pan. But Russia's heritage isn't so ill-suited to current needs. Russia and the peoples of the Soviet Union possess another tradition as well, a classically liberal heritage in many ways analogous to that of Western Europe and North America.

Always fragile, and dominant only briefly during the reform eras that followed the disastrous Crimean and Russo-Japanese wars, this "other Russia" nonetheless has roots going back hundreds of years. For all its thinness, this strain, which arms the role of law, civil rights, and private property, has proved so hardy that it has survived the most ruthless efforts to suppress it.

Peter the Great, who used Western technology to strengthen czarist autocracy, inadvertently prepared the soil for the "other Russia" by sending students abroad and by opening the country to contemporary ideas. By the end of the 18th century, Russia possessed the beginnings of an independent gentry and of an intelligentsia not subservient to the state. Under Catherine II, it also took the first steps toward building an independent sector in the economy and private institutions to promote social welfare.

Like Jefferson, Catherine II could quote Montesquieu's *Spirit of the Laws* from memory. Unlike Jefferson, she refused to take most of the steps necessary to create a society based on law. Nonetheless, educated Russians were intrigued by the vision of such a society. When the *Moscow News* in 1799 conducted a poll to determine the most significant figures of the waning century, George Washington and the American Founders headed the list. A generation later, the leaders of Russia's first revolution, the abortive Decembrist uprising of 1825, made their goals the abolition of serfdom, reform of the courts, a free press, the establishment of a constitutional monarchy with an elective legislature, and the creation of a federal system based on 13 states. Their rebellion was easily suppressed. But many of the ideas underlying it were perpetuated by young intellectuals in the bureaucracy, much as educated Russians kept alive ideas from the Khrushchev thaw during the somber Brezhnev years. The Decembrists' ideas burst to the surface after Russia's humiliation in the Crimean War and provided the impetus for the so-called Great Reforms of 1855–65.

That Russia peacefully abolished serfdom two years before Lincoln issued the Emancipation Proclamation attests to the vitality of the reformist impulse. Czarist Russia created independent courts and a jury system, set up elective local councils (but not yet a parliament), and allowed the press a degree of *glasnost*. Like James Madison in the Federalist Papers, Russia's 19th-century reformers took a dim view of political parties but—as in the United States—political parties grew up anyway, as Terence Emmons has described in *The Formation of Political Parties and the First National Elections in Russia*. (And recent news about the formation of a reformist "block" in the newly elected Soviet Congress of People's Deputies suggests that Gorbachev, too, will have trouble if he tries to keep pluralism at bay.)

Viewers of late movies are familiar with the image of Russia under the last czar as a dying regime led by weaklings and challenged by irresolute reformers and wild-eyed revolutionaries. The truth is more interesting. Private industry and trade boomed in the two generations before the revolution. Investments flowed in from abroad, and Russian capitalists formed thousands of joint stock companies. It's true that there were many large syndicates with close ties to the government, but many small enterprises proliferated as well. Meanwhile, peasants rushed to gain full title to their land after 1906, creating for the first time a class of independent farmers.

The rise of a strong voluntary sector and private philanthropy showed the Russians' readiness to take social betterment into their own hands. Recent research by Adele Lindenmeyr of Villanova University shows that a staggering 4,801 philanthropic societies were created in the years 1906–09 alone. They operated in areas as diverse as health care, famine relief, and the arts. These are the direct forebears of similar "informals" that have proliferated in recent years.

To be sure, Russia's parliament, the Duma, was limited. But it went beyond Gorbachev's in allowing all seats to be filled by legal political parties, with none reserved for official organizations. The franchise was restricted, but so was America's at the time. Meanwhile, a flourishing Russian press approached general European standards in both freedom and range of coverage, and legal thinking developed sufficiently to attract to law school such bright young men as Vladimir Ulyanov (Lenin) and Alexander Kerensky (not to mention Tchaikovsky, Diaghilev, and Stravinsky). Calls for revolution abounded, of course, and legalized labor unions mounted strikes in increasing numbers before 1914. But Lenin was expressing a widespread view when he declared in 1916, "We'll not live to see the revolution."

The existence of a private sector in the economy and a serious liberal reform movement put the autocracy increasingly on the defensive. The czar's forces beat back every assault from radical revolutionaries until 1917, but they were far less successful in opposing liberal reformers and patriotic capitalists, to whom they made concession after concession, beginning with the Great Reforms. Together, these changes placed Russia squarely on the path that countries of Western and Central Europe had been moving along for centuries—a path leading toward a system based not on royal will but on law, with guaranteed rights against the state, institutional pluralism, and a mixed economy.

Obviously, Russia's direction differed from Britain's and America's, especially in its greater centralization and in the larger role in the economy reserved for government. In these respects it more closely resembled Prussia or France. But it is clear that Russia had moved far beyond the world of serfdom and the knout by World War I. The revolt that brought down czardom was engineered not by radical revolutionaries but by liberal reformers seeking a full constitutional regime.

Why then was all this swept away by the Bolshevik coup? It is not enough simply to affirm that the old regime collapsed under the pressure of world war, or that Lenin seized power "from above," for this overlooks Bolshevism's appeal to millions who had suffered under the autocracy and had not benefited from the semiconstitutional regime. To this extent Bolshevism was a popular movement. Even so, Trotsky's Red Army had to wage a ruthless war that killed millions simply to maintain the Communists in power. And by the end of the Civil War, Lenin was forced to acknowledge that popular resistance—especially in the countryside—had stymied most of his plans, including the collectivization of agriculture. Notwithstanding Gorbachev's claims today, Lenin's New Economic Policy was less a principled compromise between Marxism and capitalism than a concession to necessity. Stalin realized this, and sacrificed the lives of millions to obviate the need for more such concessions.

Those who hold up Stalin's savagery as proof of the absence of any real counterforce to autocracy in Russia ignore one crucial point: however weak the civil society that had grown up in late imperial Russia may have been, to suppress it required greater force than any modern government had every before used against its own people. No regime confident of its own legitimacy would have declared war on its own population as Stalin did and as Lenin had done until he was forced to back off.

Even after the sacrifice of millions of lives, the reformist values that had grown up before 1917 continued to haunt the Bolsheviks. After all, such views were enshrined in the works of many of Russia's finest writers from Pushkin through Turgenev and Chekhov. They were embodied in the rich juridical writing of people like Boris Chicherin, uncle of Lenin's foreign minister, and in the magisterial vision of Russian history created by Vasilii Kliuchevsky before 1917. Unable to obliterate such giants of Russian culture, the Bolsheviks reissued their writings while pathetically trying to explain away or delete their worst "errors." As a result, Russia's liberal tradition survived the darkest days of Stalinism.

Two years ago Gorbachev called on Soviet citizens to fill in the "blank spots" of their history. But Russians and other peoples of the U.S.S.R. had already been preoccupied with this task for a generation. Throughout the post-Stalin years, to be a cultural innovator was to forge links with Russia's past, including not only Orthodox Christianity and moderate populism but also the country's liberal and reformist heritage. Long before Gorbachev chose to allow publication of banned books, those same works were circulating from hand to hand among thousands, even millions. The process by which such books were unofficially disseminated forged independent, horizontal networks through Soviet society, breaking the monopoly of institutions created by Lenin and Stalin to control information. This process grew slowly, much the way someone who has suffered a stroke struggles to renew or replace blocked circuitry within the brain. But in the end the state's monopoly was broken.

Basic changes in Soviet society in the 1960s and 1970s greatly facilitated this process in both its economic and its political dimensions. Independent-minded entrepreneurs set up unsanctioned "businesses" in garden produce and service industries, spanning the country with a twilight "second economy." Operating on (or over) the edge of illegality, these guerrilla marketeers demonstrated that the Soviet public had huge unmet needs that could be satisfied most efficiently outside the state's economic bureaucracy. In the process they proved that Soviet rule had by no means obliterated entrepreneurial skills and initiative.

Politics underwent a parallel development. Unsanctioned, informal groups and networks sprang up in many fields. Tens of thousands were in existence by the mid-1980s, some founded only to provide voluntary services but others existing to influence public policy. The rise of such voluntary associations was greatly facilitated by technologies new to the U.S.S.R. Cassette tape recorders, home photo labs, private home telephones, VCRs, and private automobiles all promoted the horizontal communication essential for a civil society. Initially branded dissident or illegal, the voluntary associations moved swiftly to break the state's monopoly in field after field. Thus, in the very years when intellectuals were rediscovering and laying claim to the many forgotten streams of Russian reformism, other Soviet citizens were unconsciously putting such ideas into practice by creating a set of economic, social, and quasi-political institutions independent of state control.

All of this ferment began prior to Gorbachev's rise to power in 1985. He neither created it nor did much to encourage it, at least initially. Instead, he put his hopes in a campaign for worker discipline and sobriety. When this failed, Gorbachev faced a momentous choice. Either he could try to revive a stagnant economy and an alienated public through further applications of typical Bolshevik controls, or he could seek to draw to his side the new economic and social forces that had brought themselves to life through autonomous action and intellectual contact with Russia's long-suppressed tradition of liberal reform. He chose the latter course. He moved to co-opt the "second economy" (and tax its profits) with his new law allowing private—nominally cooperative—businesses. He recognized the voluntary associations when his then-KGB head Chebrikov acknowledged that they had a legitimate place in Soviet society. Gorbachev's genius is not to have created the elements of *perestroika* but to have taken them from the society around him and championed them with so much conviction as to lead many observers, especially those abroad, to think he had actually fashioned them.

The Soviet Union today is a society in turmoil. Nearly all the institutions created by Lenin and Stalin, including the Communist Party, remain intact, their formal powers undiminished. Tens of millions of Soviet citizens work for these institutions and know their personal fate is tied to the survival of the institutions. Many Russians, both within the government and outside it, look longingly to a romanticized communal past dominated by Orthodoxy and patriarchal institutions. Meanwhile, a very different institutional and social order has grown up in the midst of all this, giving rise to frontal conflict.

All parties are mobilizing their full resources for the battle. While the outcome is far from clear, those advocating the rule of law, civil rights, a free press, constitutional democracy, a working federal system, and an expanded private sector clearly dominate the public agenda. Of course, this has been easier because champions of the old agenda were discredited by a series of crises in both foreign and domestic policy. Nonetheless, the momentum of the social crusade at whose head Gorbachev has placed himself suggests that it has successfully tapped impulses that are deeply ingrained in the minds of many Soviet citizens. It would be an exaggeration to say that Gorbachev has scratched a Russian and found a classical liberal. But he certainly has found no Tatar.

NOTES

ABOUT THE AUTHOR: **S. Frederick Starr**, formerly president of Oberlin College, is currently president of the Aspen Institute.

3   *The Communist System*

RICHARD PIPES

THE HISTORIC BACKGROUND

In its present form, the Communist system of the Soviet Union and its dependencies is the product of two factors: the Russian political tradition and the ideology of Marxism-Leninism. Neither of these factors, taken by themselves, can explain the structure and the behavior of Communist regimes. This hybrid has been produced by the grafting of a modern ideology on the ancient stock of Russian statehood.

The Russian state came into being early in the fourteenth century and developed under conditions very different from those familiar to Western readers.[1] Its home lay in the forest regions of northwestern Eurasia, a territory with an unlimited supply of land but poor soil and a climate unfavorable to agriculture. For many centuries the Russians carried on a semi-nomadic form of cultivation which involved ceaseless movement in search of virgin soil. Because of their mobility, they could not develop advanced forms of social and political organization, which demand a sedentary population with territorial roots. Such social institutions as they did develop were of a rudimentary kind. State and society led separate existences; in medieval Russia, the former represented primarily a military force that protected the land from foreign assaults and went on the offensive to conquer new territories for settlement whenever it felt stronger than its neighbors. This background exerted strong influence on the character of the Russian monarchy, which developed in the fifteenth and sixteenth centuries with a capital in Moscow.

1. Russia had no feudalism which, in the West, enabled powerful lay and clerical figures to usurp monarchical authority; instead, it experienced a dispersion of authority among numerous independent princes. While in Western Europe the creation of the modern state required the kings to retrieve the authority that had been taken away from them, in Russia it called for conquest and absorption of in-

dependent principalities under a single ruler. Thus, from early times, territorial expansion became in Russia a hallmark of sovereignty.

2. The northwestern regions where the Russian state was formed were sparsely populated. They were subsequently colonized by the princes, who provided the settlers with protection and the means with which to transform wilderness into habitable land. Because of this role, Russian rulers came to regard their realms as private property. A regime in which sovereignty and property—that is, political authority and ownership—are fused is known as "patrimonial." Russia was a classic patrimonial regime until the middle of the eighteenth century, when, with the introduction of the concept of private property, it began to undergo a gradual evolution toward governmental forms of the Western type.

3. Russia adopted Christianity not from Rome, as did Western Europe, but from Byzantium. After Byzantium had fallen to the Turks in 1453, Russia was for all practical purposes the only state left in the world professing Orthodox Christianity. Separated from the heretical Latins and the infidel Muslims, who surrounded Russia in the west and east, its rulers, clergy and common people developed a sense of national-religious uniqueness rather than one of belonging to a broader, supranational community. This tended to produce in Russians a feeling of being isolated and under permanent siege, even though their relatively inaccessible location ensured them of a high degree of protection from foreign invasions.

From this historic legacy flow a number of consequences of great importance for the understanding of Russian political culture—a culture that greatly influences Russian political behavior, whatever the declared objectives of the government in power.

- Until quite modern times (the end of the eighteenth century) Russia was unfamiliar with the distinction between political authority and the rights of private ownership, a distinction fundamental to the Western political tradition. Professor Charles McIlwain, in his survey of Western political thought, concluded that if he were asked to produce one maxim that best reflected the political thought of the West in the late Middle Ages, he would choose an aphorism of Seneca's: "To kings belongs authority over all; to private persons, property." This crucial distinction has very shallow roots in Russian political thought and practice, which accounts for some of the greatest differences between the behavior of Russian and Western governments.

- The lack of a feudal tradition meant, among other things, the absence in Russia of the concept of law as a force superior to human will, binding alike on rulers and subjects. Russian governments have always tended to regard law as a device for controlling the population—that is, as a tool of administration, rather than as a principle regulating relations between themselves and their people.

- Because they viewed the population under their control as private property, Russian rulers of premodern times imposed on all their subjects ties of bondage.

They required the landowning gentry to render the monarchy lifelong military or civil service and enserfed virtually all the commoners, compelling them to work either for the rulers or for their service class. Until the middle of the eighteenth century, there were in Russia, for all practical purposes, no freemen endowed with rights; there were only bondsmen endowed with duties who directly or indirectly served the Crown. As recently as the middle of the eighteenth century, in the central provinces of Russia, 85 percent of the population consisted of people bonded either to the state or to landlords; they enjoyed neither legal status nor rights of any kind.

The political culture of Russia is thus very short on the notions of private property, law and human rights, and long on everything that serves to enhance the might of the state. The state, for its part, tends to be expansionist and to feel no allegiance to any supranational community, such as was common among the peoples of Christian Europe or the Islamic world.

The evolution of Russia from the patrimonial tradition to the Western began in the late seventeenth century and accelerated after the accession of Peter the Great. The impetus toward Westernization came largely from the awareness that the West was richer and stronger, and that if Russia hoped to attain the rank of a first-rate European power it had to model itself on the West. The initial motive for Westernization was military—namely, the inability of Russian troops in the seventeenth century to stand up to the better organized and equipped forces of Sweden and Turkey. Awareness of this inferiority led Peter the Great to carry out major reforms. Subsequently, in an effort to keep up with Europe in other than military respects, still more fundamental changes were introduced. In 1762 the gentry were freed from compulsory state service, and ninety-nine years later serfdom was abolished. The principle of private property was introduced in the late eighteenth century; as the Russian economy developed, the traditional fusion of sovereignty and property began to break down. Legal codes, trials by jury, and other judiciary reforms, enacted in the middle of the nineteenth century, introduced into Russia the law as a force regulating relations among citizens (though not relations between the state and citizens, for the state continued to stand above the law).

Even while Westernizing, the Russian monarchy clung tenaciously to the monopoly on political power. It refused to share legislative authority with society long after the other European governments, including Turkey, had introduced constitutional and parliamentary institutions. Russia was governed by a bureaucracy responsible only to the tsar until October 1905, when humiliating defeats in a war with Japan and the nationwide civil disorders that followed compelled the monarchy to concede to the country a constitution and a legislative parliament. But old habits died hard, and in the few years that it had left before its collapse, the monarchy regularly contravened the constitution. The absence of political institutions effectively linking the Crown with its own people contributed greatly to the downfall of tsarism in 1917 and to the chaos that ensued.

Political culture, shaped by a nation's historic experience, enters the nation's bloodstream and changes as slowly and reluctantly as does language or customs. Revolutionary governments may attempt by means of decrees to reshape this culture to their liking, but in the end they are invariably defeated: the fate of revolutions everywhere indicates that instead of traditions changing to suite revolutions, revolutions sooner or later accommodate themselves to traditions. The fate of Marxism in Russia provides an excellent illustration of this rule.

Socialism, of which "Marxism-Leninism" is an offshoot, originated in the West. Formulated in France and Germany, it was imported into Russia in the middle of the nineteenth century and promptly attracted support among the country's educated, public-minded elite, the so-called intelligentsia. Because it is an ideology imported from abroad, many Russian conservatives, both before 1917 and since, have blamed it for Russia's revolutionary excesses. This argument enables them to ascribe to the West their country's misfortunes; this is the position taken by Dostoevsky one hundred years ago, and by Solzhenitsyn today. The position, however, is unconvincing, because the very same socialist ideology that in Russia has come to be identified with totalitarianism has had no such result in the West which suggests that the decisive factors are not the ideas but the soil on which they happen to fall. In Western Europe, socialism quickly shed its authoritarian and revolutionary elements, transforming itself into a movement for social reform. Nowhere in the West has it led to totalitarianism. It is only in Russia and in Asian, African and Latin American countries—which, while receptive to European ideas, lack European traditions—that socialist ideology has given rise to extremely repressive forms of government.

In view of this evidence, the explanation for Soviet totalitarianism must be sought not in socialism but in the political culture which draws on socialist ideas to justify totalitarian practices. In the West, with its strong traditions of private property, law and human rights, socialism has evolved into a movement for social justice and a supplement to political democracy. Where such traditions are lacking and the state is viewed primarily as a means of enriching the ruling class, socialist theory is automatically harnessed in the interest of the government, allowing it to lay claim to the property and labor of its people. Thus it happened that, while in the West the ideology of socialism had the effect of broadening the concept of democracy by augmenting political democracy with the goal of social justice, elsewhere it provided a rationale for the destruction of customs and traditional institutions that in the past had restrained the power of the state.

Like their Western counterparts, Russian socialist intellectuals were committed to democratic ideals; they wanted their country to become a model of political freedom and social equality. It was an axiom among them that the Russian people had to emancipate themselves from oppression by their own efforts and that the role of intellectuals in this struggle would be confined to rendering them assistance. But they quickly learned that the "masses," mainly peasants, did not share either their political or their social idealism, and this caused them to wonder whether a revolution in Russia had any chance of succeeding as a mass movement. In 1879 a small band of radicals who called themselves the "People's Will" launched a campaign of terror against the monarchy, which culminated in 1881 in the murder of the tsar. The People's Will was the parent organization of all subsequent terrorist organizations in Russia and in other parts of the world. It represented a perversion of the original ideal of democratic revolution, because its aim was the forceful overthrow of government for the purpose of enabling a small band of revolutionaries to seize power and carry out a revolution from above.

The so-called Marxists, or Social Democrats, who gained popularity in Russia in the late nineteenth century, opposed terror, counting on industrial development to produce a revolutionary proletariat. But they too experienced disappointment as factory workers showed no more revolutionary spirit than the peasants. As a result of this experience, in the early years of this century, a group of Social Democrats, led by V. I. Lenin, split off from the main body of the party to form a separate faction, which later became the Bolshevik Party. Observing the behavior of industrial workers at home and abroad, Lenin concluded that the working class was not at heart revolutionary and, if left to follow its own inclinations, would make an accommodation with capitalism. To counter this development (Lenin was interested mainly in revolution, not in improved conditions for workers), he formed a small conspiratorial party, whose members were to devote themselves full time to the revolutionary cause. Their task was to wait for an opportune moment to seize power and use the resources of the state to carry out a revolution from above. The masses were relegated to a subsidiary role—a genuine industrial worker obviously could not belong to a party that demanded of its members full-time commitment. Lenin's Bolsheviks were from the outset an elitist body of middle-class intellectuals who appointed themselves to speak and act on behalf of the working class. In their internal organization, they followed a strictly authoritarian model; the Party's administration and theoretical authority were concentrated in the person of Lenin, the infallible *vozhd'* (*Führer*), who claimed to embody the historic mission of the proletariat. This is Marxism-Leninism—that is, Marxism divested of its democratic component and adapted to Russian political conditions. It is the forerunner of all modern totalitarian, one-party movements whether of the left or of the right variety.

The penchant of Russian socialists for violence, conspiracy and undemocratic methods can be justified by the difficult conditions under which they had had to operate: an arbitrary regime and a population among whom survived strong traces of serf mentality. Unlike Western socialists, who were able to agitate in the open and participate in elections, they were harassed, imprisoned or exiled. This explanation, however, only serves to show that an undemocratic political culture twists democratic ideologies out of shape and that undemocratic environments breed antidemocratic socialists.

Until 1917, Lenin's party was a fringe phenomenon in Russia's political life. As soon, however, as tsarism collapsed and anarchy spread, its influence rose. In the Russia of 1917, the Bolsheviks constituted the only disciplined party willing and able to take power. Notwithstanding their small size—in February 1917 they had a mere 30,000 members in a country of some 160 million—they and they alone disposed of the personnel able to fill the administrative vacuum produced by the dissolution of the tsarist bureaucracy. The so-called October Revolution in Petrograd, which secured for them control of the central governmental machinery, was not a revolution at all but a classic *coup d'état*, carried out swiftly and almost bloodlessly.

Observing the birth of the Communist regime, the historian is struck by the ease with which Lenin and his lieutenants slipped into the role so recently vacated by the imperial sovereign. Lenin arrogated to himself not merely the powers of the constitutional monarchy of Nicholas II, nor even the semipatrimonial authority of nineteenth-century emperors, but those of patrimonial autocracy in all its seventeenth-century splendor. The violence of 1917–1920 resulted in the wholesale destruction of the upper and middle classes, which happened to have been the principal Westernized groups in Russia. The disappearance of that relatively thin Westernized layer permitted the unregenerate Muscovite Russia, which had survived intact underneath the veneer of European influences, to float to the surface. Nationalizing, in the name of socialism, the means of production in land and industry had the effect of once again placing all the resources of the country at the disposal of the government; as in medieval Muscovy, sovereignty and ownership came to be fused. The introduction of the principle of compulsory labor for the state, the sole employer, rebonded the entire population of the country in the service of the state. Laws and courts were swept aside to be replaced by summary justice. Lenin himself assumed with perfect ease the role of a Muscovite autocrat, issuing on his personal authority ordinances and decrees, abolishing old institutions and introducing new ones, condemning people to death, without feeling the need either to obtain concurrence from representatives of the "masses" in whose name he claimed to rule, or to observe legal norms of any kind. The Bolsheviks acted in this high-handed manner not only because their situation as a minority party striving for dictatorial power called for rough-and-ready methods, but also because they believed that such were the wishes of the Russian people. When a few days after the Bolshevik power seizure, the Central Executive Committee of the Soviets, in whose name the Bolsheviks theoretically governed, protested Lenin's autocratic methods, Trotsky responded as follows:

> This whole bourgeois scum which presently is incapable of committing itself either to this or to that side will be with us when it learns that our authority is strong. ... The petty bourgeoisie looks for a power to which it must submit. He who does not understand this understands nothing in the world, and less in affairs of government.[2]

The fusion of traditional Russian autocracy and Marxism, adapted to Russian conditions and mentalities, produced a regime that was quite outside the experience of the West but that the West nevertheless has ever since sought to explain in Western categories. It pushed to the forefront in Russia those elements that had remained unaffected by Western culture. Here no sociological or other "scientific" theories are of much help. The Revolution threw Russia back to its pre-Western origins, to patrimonialism, to lawlessness, to human bondage, to the sense of uniqueness and isolation. In the words of the novelist Boris Pilniak:

> The Revolution pitted Russia against Europe. More than that: right after the first days of the Revolution, in its habits, morals, city life, Russia reverted to the seventeenth century.[3]

All Russian revolutionary movements and parties, the Bolsheviks included, pursued international objectives—that is to say, as Russians they dedicated themselves first and foremost to the overthrow of tsarism, but tsarism to them was an integral part of a worldwide regime of political and economic exploitation. "Socialism in one country" and "peaceful coexistence" between socialism and capitalism were to them unacceptable except as transitional phenomena, until such time as the forces of socialism had gathered enough strength to triumph all along the line. The historic advance of socialism could no more stop at national boundaries than could the changing seasons. ...

One of the salient features of the Russian historical experience has been a propensity for imperialism. Russia, of course, has no monopoly on expansion. Most European states have gone through an imperialist phase. Germany, which in the twentieth century became a byword for aggressive militarism, in the eighteenth century had been regarded as a nation of poets and dreamers. Peaceful Sweden in the seventeenth century devastated Central Europe. Holland and Portugal in their day conquered great empires.

Even when this point is conceded, however, Russian imperialism displays certain unique features. One of these is its persistence. In the history of Russia, expansion is not a phase but a constant. Except for brief intervals when domestic difficulties have forced it to turn inward, the Russian state has been expanding since the early fourteenth century with extraordinary vigor; between the middle of the sixteenth century and the end of the seventeenth, it acquired every year the territorial equivalent of modern Holland for 150 years running. The second distinguishing quality of Russian imperialism is its military character: unlike Western colonial powers, which supplemented and reinforced their military activities with economic and cultural penetration, Russia has had to rely mainly on the force of arms. The third is colonization. Because until very recent times Russia's expansion had taken place along its frontier, the conquest of foreign lands was usually followed (and sometimes preceded) by the influx of Russian settlers. Once colonized, every conquered region turned into Russian "patrimony"—that is, inalienable state property, which was under no circumstances to be surrendered to anyone, including its previous owners.

Expansionism of such persistence and an imperialism that maintains such a tenacious hold on its conquests raises the question of causes.

One can dismiss the explanation most often offered by amateur Russian "experts" (although hardly ever by Russians themselves) that Russia expands because of anxieties aroused by relentless foreign invasions of its national territory by neighboring countries. Those who make this point usually have but the scantiest familiarity with Russian history. Their knowledge of Russia's external relations is confined to three or four invasions, made familiar by novels or moving pictures—the conquest of Russia in the thirteenth century by the Mongols (who are sometimes confused with the Chinese); Napoleon's invasion of 1812; the Allied "intervention" during the Russian Civil War; and the Nazi onslaught of 1941. With such light baggage one can readily conclude that, having been uniquely victimized, Russia strikes out to protect itself. Common sense, of course, might suggest even to those who lack knowledge of the facts that a country can no more become the world's most spacious as a result of suffering constant invasions than an individual can gain wealth from being repeatedly robbed. But common sense aside, there is the record of history. It shows that far from being the victim of recurrent acts of aggression, Russia has been engaged for the past three hundred years with single-minded determination in aggressive wars, and that if anyone has reason for paranoia it would have to be its neighbors. In the 1890s, the Russian General Staff carried out a comprehensive study of the history of Russian warfare since the foundations of the state. In the summary volume, the editor told his readers that they could take pride in their country's military record and face the future with confidence—between 1700 and 1870, Russia had spent 106 years fighting 38 military campaigns, of which 36 had been "offensive" and a mere 2 defensive.[15] This authoritative tabulation should dispose of the facile theory that Russian aggression is a defensive reflex.

More serious explanations of Russian expansionism take account of concrete economic, geographic and political factors.

Russia is naturally a poor country. Located far away from the main trade routes, it was unable to participate in international commerce. It is rich in natural resources, but these are difficult and costly to extract. Above all, neither its soil nor its climate is well suited for agriculture, which until the 1930s had been the main source of livelihood for eight or nine out of ten Russian inhabitants. Scientific estimates indicate that the soil of northern Russia, the homeland of the Russian state, cannot support more than 25 inhabitants per square kilometer; this figure compares with some 250 inhabitants per square kilometer for the climatically more favored Western nations. Population growth has made it necessary to acquire ever new land to accommodate the surplus peasantry, and this requirement, in turn, called for a large army, first to conquer territory and then to protect the settlers who colonized it. Thus, unlike the great European powers and Japan, whose imperialism represented an overflow of national wealth in search of profitable investment outlets or fresh markets, Russian imperialism was an escape from poverty. The whole situation had about it the quality of a vicious cycle—poverty necessitated expansion; expansion necessitated large military outlays; and large military outlays robbed the country of productive resources, perpetuating poverty.

II The second factor is geographic. The same location that has such a negative effect on Russian agriculture affords Russia unique opportunities for aggression. Russia occupies and controls that region which geopoliticians have defined as the "heartland." It is the only country in the world bordering on the regions that contain the bulk of the globe's population and natural resources: Europe, the Middle East and East Asia. Russian infantry can reach any part of the European, African and Asian continents without getting their feet wet (a short crossing of the man-made Suez Canal excepted). This geopolitical position affords Russia opportunities for conquest enjoyed by no other power. It can freely shift military forces inside its 67,000 kilometer (or 41,500 mile) frontier from the Baltic to the Black Sea, and from there to the Pacific, and back again, applying pressures and exploiting opportunities with speed and ease that are beyond the reach of any other power in the world. Opportunity has always offered fresh temptations to advance; and because economic conditions have always encouraged expansion, few Russian governments have been able to resist them.

III. The third factor is the quest for loot and luxuries with which to satisfy the elite. In the tsarist period that loot consisted of agricultural land that was lavishly distributed to the service nobility in the conquered territories. Today it consists mainly of consumer goods and comforts, for which the *nomenklatura* has an insatiable appetite. What this means concretely can be seen from a report sent recently by a Swedish correspondent stationed in Afghanistan, one of the world's more backward countries, where the Soviet elite has nevertheless managed to establish a style of colonial life of a brazenly exploitative nature:

> The poor mountain nation has also been blessed with yet another unwelcome "novelty": the new upper class, consisting of what are popularly called Soviet advisers and their families.
>
> The new rulers live in their own well-protected residential areas in Kabul in prefabricated houses manufactured in a Russian-built factory in the city.
>
> They shop in well-stocked shops at prices far below those considered normal at home in the Soviet Union. Their children go to special schools and since birds of a feather flock together they only have social contacts among themselves.
>
> "The Russian upper class," as the advisers and their dependents are called in Kabul, have the advantage of living in something which can be likened to a free trade zone—and they make the maximum use of this.
>
> Nearly all the products which we in the West have grown used to being able to buy, but which for the normal Russian are unattainable luxuries, are available in Afghanistan, both legally and on the flourishing black market. ...[17]

The fourth and most complex set of factors is political. One of these has been noted already—the tradition of making territorial acquisitions in the course of state building. The others have to do with the relationship between Russian governments and their subjects.

Russian governments have always felt the need to solidify their internal position by impressing on the population the awe which they inspired in other nations. There is a Russian proverb that says, "Beat your own people and others will fear you." The proverb is equally valid in reversed form "Beat others and your own people will fear you." By inspiring respect in foreign governments, by bullying neighbors, by undermining them and distributing their lands and riches among their own subjects, Russian governments have historically enhanced their claims to legitimacy and obedience. This close relationship between external expansion and internal authority has been noted by perceptive observers long before the Revolution. Among them was Friedrich Engels, who like his friend Marx devoted much attention to Russian affairs. In 1890, referring to the Russian diplomatic service, Engels wrote:

> It is this secret society, recruited originally from foreign adventurers, that has elevated the Russian empire to its present might. With iron perseverance, with eyes fixed on the goal, not shrinking from any breach of faith, any treachery, any assassination, any servility, lavishly dispersing bribes, never grown overconfident from victory, never discouraged by defeat, over the corpses of millions of soldiers and at least one tsar, it is this gang, as talented as it is without conscience, rather than all the Russian armies put together, that have contributed to the extension of Russia's borders. ... [It is this gang] that has made Russia great, powerful and feared, and has opened up for it the way to world domination. In so doing, however, it has also strengthened the power of tsarism internally. For the vulgar patriotic public, the glory of victory, the conquests that follow one another, the might and splendor of tsardom fully outweigh all its sins, and its despotism, all its injustices and arbitrariness: the boastfulness of chauvinism fully compensates for all the kicks received.[18]

The argument is emotional but deserving of attention. Governments of every kind seek every now and then to divert their citizens' attention from internal troubles by waging war. In the case of Russia, however, the phenomenon is not episodic. For Russian governments, foreign glory is not merely an escape from transient crises, but a feature of the very constitutional order; permanent conquests serve to justify the permanent subservience of Russian society. Because the bonds linking the Russian people with their government are so tenuous and the chasm separating them so wide, there exists always the danger that a Russian regime that is no longer feared at home and abroad (and the two phenomena are closely connected) will appear to have lost the mandate of heaven and fall apart. Psychologically speaking, the greater the awe in which a Russian government is held by foreigners, the stronger is its claim to rule and the more satisfying the compensation that it offers to its people for their debased status. The poet Lermontov expressed well this sentiment when he had a Russian tell a Muslim of the Caucasus whose land the Russians were about to conquer, that he would soon be proud to say, "Yes, I am a slave, but a slave of the tsar of the universe."[19]

Communist ideology and the interests of the *nomenklatura* have reinforced these expansionist traditions, making Russian imperialism more aggressive and more persistent than ever before.

According to Marx, as interpreted by Lenin (see above), the "dictatorship of the proletariat" is necessary as long—and only as long—as the class enemy, the bourgeoisie, survives to threaten the new socialist order; the "withering away of the state" can and indeed must begin the instant the class enemy has been eliminated. Theoretically speaking, the "bourgeoisie" was destroyed in Russia and its dependencies a long time ago, for which reason the survival of the state and the bureaucracy in Communist countries is an anomaly that can no longer be justified. The Communist state should by now have withered away completely. But, of course, the immense parasitic corps of the Party and state functionaries that had ensconced itself in power and privilege since the Revolution, has not the slightest interest in the state's disappearance. The state is the source of its livelihood; for the *nomenklatura* it provides a style of life that is not inferior to that of the Western middle class in a country where the vast majority of citizens subsist on a Third World standard. It needs to justify its power and privileges, and this justification it can find only in keeping alive the specter of the "bourgeoisie" and arguing that while the "bourgeoisie" has indeed been liquidated in Communist societies, it still survives and continues to threaten the socialist community, this time from the outside. Since the triumph of Communism in Russia, class war, which had once been internal, has been transferred onto the international arena; today the "socialist community" champions the cause of the proletariat, while the "imperialist camp," led by the United States, stands for the cause of the bourgeoisie. In other words, the *nomenklatura* requires the foreign class enemy to legitimize its authority; without him, and without the threat that he allegedly poses, it has no excuse left for holding on to power. For this reason, international tension and the specter of war, in the form of an "imperialist" attack on the Soviet Union, are vital to the interests of the Communist elite. In a world genuinely at peace, its survival as a parasitic class would be in danger.

The best way to demonstrate the need for a powerful Communist state and military establishment is constantly to expand the Communist realm. Each encroachment on the "enemy" camp proves the justness of the cause and its inevitable ultimate triumph. It has been noted by many observers that Soviet aggrandizement. and acts of repression abroad (e.g., against Czechoslovakia and Poland) enjoy popularity with the mass of Soviet citizens; it confirms to them that their own lot, with which, as a whole, they are not very happy, will also be that of the rest of mankind, that those foreigners who boast of freedom and prosperity will not be allowed to do so for long. The situation is, indeed, as Engels has described it in regard to tsarist expansionism: the glory of victory, the ceaseless conquests, the might and the splendor of the Soviet state—all compensate the ordinary people for the injustices, the arbitrariness, and the "kicks received." And for the *nomenklatura* they provide an indispensable rationale for practices that, in terms of its own ideology, have long lost any validity.

The greater its successes abroad, the heavier the blows meted out to the "imperialist" enemy, the greater the security of the *nomenklatura* and the vaster its power. ...

Thus, the negative consideration—the need to justify its authority—combines with the positive one—the desire to enhance this authority—to produce an imperialist drive that would be difficult to duplicate from the historical record.

The essential fact to bear in mind is that Soviet expansionism has little if anything to do with what is sometimes called "legitimate Soviet national interests." In the past, when the Russian peasantry pressed on their country's neighbors in search of new land to colonize, expansion might be said to have served in some ways the interests of the people. But this has long ago ceased to be the case. The Soviet Union presently suffers from rural underpopulation; it has more land than people able to cultivate it. Its aggression is carried out exclusively in the interest of the elite, and because of the immense resources that it absorbs and the risks that it entails, aggression is profoundly contrary to Russia's national interests. Western statesmen who hope to appease Soviet aggressiveness by pledging to respect "legitimate Soviet national interests" are dealing with a phantom. The only interests that count are those of the proprietors of Communist countries, and their interests require permanent international tension and ceaseless territorial aggrandizement. Only if and when the power of the *nomenklatura* will be substantially curtailed and the interests of the people allowed legitimate expression will one be able to speak of the national interests of countries presently in the *nomenklatura*'s iron grip. And that, of course, will require fundamental changes in the Soviet system, away from the Stalinism which constitutes its framework.

"Pragmatists" may consider such an expectation utopian. Time alone will tell. But the record of the past leaves no doubt that it is entirely utopian to expect Communist regimes to abandon aggressive behavior as long as they continue to be organized on the current model. ...

NOTES

ABOUT THE AUTHOR: **Richard Pipes,** who served on the National Security Council during the Reagan administration, is professor of history at Harvard University.

1. A full account of the growth of the Russian state can be found in my book *Russia Under the Old Regime* (New York, 1974).

2. Lev Trotsky, *Stalinskaia shkola falsifikatsii* (Berlin, 1932), 124.

3. Boris Pilniak, "Golyi god" in *Izbrannye proizvedeniia* (Moscow, 1976), 83.

15. N. N. Sukhotin, *Voina v istorii russkogo mira* (St. Petersburg, 1898), 13–14.

17. *Dagens Nyheter* (Stockholm), June 9, 1983, 12.

18. Friedrich Engels, "Die auswärtige Politik des russischen Zarenthums," *Die Neue Zeit,* VIII (1890), 146.

19. M. Iu. Lermontov, "Izmail bey," in his *Izbrannye proizvedeniia v dvukh tomakh,* Vol. I (Moscow/Leningrad, 1938), 271.

4 Domestic and International Factors in the Formation of Gorbachev's Reforms

SEWERYN BIALER

Mikhail Gorbachev is now [1989] nearing the end of his fourth year in office and the Soviet Union is in a state of creative turmoil. What is presently happening in the USSR can best be described as a gigantic experiment that in practical terms touches virtually all fields of endeavor. Intellectually, the very system of Russian and Soviet ideas and traditions is being called into question. This experiment is only beginning. The society and the political system within which the experiment is taking place still remain deeply Soviet in all of this term's negative Stalinist connotations. To make a significant difference, to take hold and to change the Soviet system, the new course initiated by the general secretary needs at least another decade.

What has already happened in the Soviet Union in many areas is very exciting and truly remarkable. Gorbachev hopes to attain the most significant breakthrough in the economic sphere. Indeed, the rationale of his entire policy agenda is subordinated to the goal of modernizing the Soviet Union. Yet the most startling developments of Gorbachev's tenure are not in the economy but in the political and cultural areas where radical action came as a surprise. Unless Gorbachev is forced to reverse them, these measures will profoundly change the nature of the system he inherited.

The changes that are taking place in the Soviet Union have deep sources. In Western writings on Gorbachev's domestic and foreign policies and reforms, there is very often a tendency to ascribe these changes primarily or even exclusively to domestic factors. There is no denying that the domestic factors are fundamental in explaining Gorbachev's reforms. Yet without taking into consideration the international factors that inform his actions, the explanations and analyses remain one-sided. Only by understanding the interaction of domestic and international factors can we begin to grasp the nature of Gorbachev's revolutionary course.

DOMESTIC SOURCES OF SOVIET REFORM

The domestic factors that promoted radical reforms by Gorbachev fall into three categories. They concern first, the domestic performance of the Soviet system during the Brezhnev era, second, the new and necessary conditions of Soviet economic growth under contemporary circumstances; and third, the changed nature of Soviet society and the conditions of its stability. These factors explain the urgency of the actions undertaken by Gorbachev and the direction of his reform agenda. They also bring to light the obstacles that he is facing, and narrow the range of probable outcomes of his efforts.

Systemic Crisis

In the modern era, almost all programs of fundamental reform, let alone revolutionary transformations, have grown out of major crisis situations. The Soviet Union is no exception. The leaders who took power in the mid-1980s knew that they had inherited a country and a system in a state of material and spiritual crisis. A phrase used by the new general secretary at the June 1987 Plenum of the Central Committee sums up this assessment quite succinctly: The Brezhnev era, he said, was characterized by the appearance of "pre-crisis phenomena." The clear implication was that, due to the pattern of Brezhnev's leadership, without the urgent actions undertaken by his successors, the Soviet Union would have found itself at present in a crisis situation. The rector of Moscow State University in a speech published in *Pravda* in November 1987 described the situation more dramatically and more accurately: "We were sliding into the abyss and are only starting to stop the slide."

The speeches of the new leader and discussions in the Soviet press are extraordinarily frank. Their frankness stems from the seriousness of the Soviet predicament and can be explained by the need to shock the party and the masses into action, to mobilize the public for countervailing steps. The new leadership also makes it amply clear that the crisis conditions were, and are, not merely segmental, limited to a specific sphere, but were national in character and present in almost all fields of domestic endeavor. They were also, and are, systemic in character. They were not the outgrowth of any specific faulty policy but of the very nature and structure of the Soviet system as it existed over the last 20 years. To overcome the crisis, therefore, requires from the Soviet leaders not simply new and better policies, but a determination to change many basic characteristics of the Soviet system itself.

This national systemic crisis, which confronted the new leadership as it took over the reins of power in the Soviet Union, could be defined as a crisis of effectiveness. The Soviet Union was running down. Its performance in almost every sphere but the military was below not only world standards, but the standards set by its own leadership. The official reports of how well it was doing were simply complete falsehoods. Without urgent and extensive actions undertaken by the new leadership the "crisis of effectiveness" could have been, and can still become, a "crisis of survival" in which the very existence of the system is put at risk.

By the end of the Brezhnev era, Soviet society was chronically ill according to the standards by which social diseases can be diagnosed. In the political arena, the most significant phenomenon was the alienation not only of the population at large, but also of the party—by definition the political public—from the rulers and from the regime. Political stability was achieved in one of the most politicized societies in the world through mass political apathy, the privatization of citizens' concerns and a lack of civic spirit cemented by coercion. The party-state administration became highly bureaucratized, penetrated through and through by a corporatist spirit, thoroughly corrupted in its particular segments by mafia-like informal associations.

As for culture, even the enforced mask of socialist realism, with its optimism at all costs, could no longer hide the sense of deep cultural pessimism permeating the educated strata. This cultural pessimism of the educated was mirrored by a feeling of hopelessness among the working strata. The Soviet Union was probably the only major country in the world where the youth neither rebelled nor channeled any youthful enthusiasm into creative public endeavors. The heroes of Soviet youth were their own "private" poets and balladeers (especially Vladimir Vysotskii), and their major public expression of satisfaction was associated with the meager artifacts of Western mass culture that were officially tolerated but not encouraged.

Economic Imperatives

With regard to the economy, in a speech given at the Plenum of the Central Committee in February 1988, Gorbachev summed up the state of affairs with a mind-boggling statement: In the 20 years previous to his accession to power, the Soviet national income, with the exception of production of alcohol, did not increase in real terms at all. The Stalinist model of the economy, which served the Soviets fairly well in the first phases of their industrial revolution when the development of heavy industry and military might took absolute precedence, was unfit to promote growth as priorities shifted. The new stage of economic development geared to better diet, mass production of durable consumer goods and high technology demanded a new approach. The functioning of the Stalinist model of the economy depended on administrative activity and regulation (it is therefore sometimes described as a command economy) and not on self-generating and self-enforcing economic forces. The Bolshevik fear of political spontaneity found its extreme economic expression in the Stalinist model; a model which stifled initiative and creativity, discouraged development, and with its expansion became more and more cumbersome and unmanageable. The Polish economist Oscar Lange aptly characterized this economic model as a war economy. One should note that this definition has found its way into Soviet economic discussions in the Gorbachev years.

The confining Stalinist model of the economy went hand in hand with the continuation, long after Stalin's death, of an extensive strategy of economic growth totally unsuited to the new Soviet circumstances. Using this model, Soviet leaders tried to achieve economic expansion by continually increasing inputs of labor, capital and land in the production and distribution process.

early 70s - econ probs

It was becoming clear by the early 1970s that the extensive model of growth had its absolute physical and economic limits and that its effectiveness was diminishing. The influx of new labor resources hit a steeply diminishing curve. Cheap sources of raw materials, so abundant in the past, were being exhausted, and costs began to increase exponentially when their extraction and production moved from the easily accessible European parts of the country to the vast wastelands of Siberia. The expansion of land under cultivation was no longer possible, for this required very costly investments. The input of ever-expanding capital expenditures was becoming increasingly difficult. The declining ratio of capital formation to the size of GNP in turn strengthened the tendency towards stagnation. The monumental neglect of the economic infrastructure created extraordinary bottlenecks in the Soviet economy and accounted for an unbelievable waste of materials and labor. For example, more than 20 percent of the agricultural harvest and more than half of the vegetables and fruits do not reach the consumer due to lack of roads, storage facilities and sufficient railroad capacity.

The Soviet political leadership, to say nothing of Soviet economists, was aware of the unsustainability of the extensive strategy of growth for Soviet economic progress long before Gorbachev came to power. They knew, in a general sense, that the Soviet economy had to switch to an intensive strategy of growth, where the following elements necessarily would play a decisive role: (i) increased productivity of labor and capital through technological progress and better incentives; (ii) declining relative costs of production; (iii) conservation of raw materials and energy; and (iv) improved quality of products and a buildup of the infrastructure. Yet, even as they were making efforts to stress intensive factors of growth, they were determined, for reasons of inbred ideological and political conservatism, to do so without any serious changes in the Stalinist model of the economy. A complete dismantling was, under the circumstances, impossible. But so too was the achievement of intensive growth under the Stalinist economic model.

Even before taking power, the new leadership had already recognized elements of the unhappy economic reality hidden behind Brezhnev's bombastic phrases regarding "advanced socialism." After achieving political control, they recognized that they were faced with a fundamental economic crisis of major proportions. They soon reached the conclusion that what was required was a simultaneous change on both sides of the economic equation—a change in the strategy of growth from extensive to intensive, and a change in economic organization from the Stalinist-administrative model to an as yet undefined model where economic instruments and forces, such as the market, would play a much more determining role. They embarked on long-range solutions meant to synchronize the strategy of growth with the model of the economy.

Social Imperatives

The social sources of the Soviet systemic crisis can be defined very simply: In the post-Stalin period, Soviet society in all its segments and its aspirations has changed very significantly while the antiquated political order of a different era has remained largely unchanged. First, the Soviet social system of stratification that rewarded power and was indifferent to performance killed the work ethic of the population and was counterproductive to modernization. Second, official corruption and unfulfilled promises led to far-reaching political alienation of the society as a whole from the party and the regime. Third, in the post-Stalin era the phenomenal growth of the Soviet middle class, and particularly its professional component, was not reflected in the official arena with power sharing and professional and political autonomy of any kind. Fourth, the expansion of the enormous Soviet welfare state combined its two worst possible characteristics—where it was necessary, its productivity was low and declining (e.g., the medical service), and where its existence in an efficient and well-functioning society would have been superfluous, it expanded beyond reason (e.g., subsidies of food prices).

INTERNATIONAL SOURCES OF SOVIET REFORM

The political, cultural, economic and social phenomena that led to the crisis of the Soviet system, and made the new Soviet leadership opt for intervention instead of orthodoxy, were domestic in their origin and nature. It is my contention, however, that their virulence alone would not have been sufficient to cause the Soviet leadership to embark on the radical path of *perestroika* if they were not combined with two international factors of prime importance. The first factor, which is psychological in nature, concerns the Soviet leadership's deeply ingrained tendency to evaluate their domestic accomplishments and global standing against the background of economic and technological trends and developments in the capitalist world. The second and related international factor deals directly with structural limitations imposed by declining Soviet capabilities in the global arena.

Soviet Perceptions and the International Environment

The recognition of the virulence of the Soviet domestic crisis, and of the urgent need to counteract its harmful domestic consequences, was reinforced dramatically by the new Soviet leadership's perception of its negative correlation with developments outside the Soviet Union. For the Soviet leadership and political elite (as well as larger professional groups), the key measure of Soviet progress was, and continues to be, Soviet accomplishments as compared to that of industrially advanced capitalist countries. This relativism in judging Soviet progress is an internalized principle and a basic Soviet tradition. Starting with Lenin, but especially under Stalin and continuing in the post-Stalin era, the slogan of "catching up and surpassing," economically and technologically, the principal capitalist countries—in particular, the main Soviet adversary, the United States—was at the center of attention of the Soviet leadership and was a driving force behind Soviet policy formation. This "comparativist" attitude resulted primarily from ideological necessities, such as the proof of the superiority of the Soviet system, and from obvious security and foreign policy concerns.

The comparative perspective of Soviet economic standards and achievements is also of great importance to Soviet leaders because it serves as a reference point for their self-evaluation and self-esteem. Sputnik, space stations and intercontinental rockets help their self-esteem but the evaluation of relative progress must be decided on earth, on a much broader national scale, with respect not only to extraordinary, heroic deeds but also to everyday lifestyle standards and patterns.

It is significant and highly relevant, therefore, to pause for a moment and assess the changes that have occurred in the last two decades outside the Soviet Union. In the last 15 years, almost all capitalist countries entered the era of the Third Industrial Revolution. The enormous scope, the headlong (and still increasing) speed, and the deep effects of this revolution went far beyond even the most optimistic projections made in the late 1960s. At the core of the Third Industrial Revolution is the immensely expanded complex of communication systems and the enormous and previously unimaginable expansion of information collection, retrieval and exchange. Industrial and public services have broadened in scope and have increased drastically in productivity. There has been a qualitative change in durable consumer goods through their mesh with electronics and miniaturization, and a growing avalanche of new capital and consumer products entering the market. The fantastic speed with which the new production, managerial and leisure opportunities have permeated entire economies and societies has been made possible by the vastly increased role of science in the production and distribution process. The global nature of the market, and the economic and technological interdependence of all countries, based on the traditional principle of the international division of labor, has promoted the full participation, on a competitive basis, of a number of small and previously non-industrialized Asian countries that were able to grasp the advantages of relative backwardness.

The Soviet Union has yet to create many of the requisites for joining this revolution, from simple and reliable telephone networks to the much more complicated production of such primary electronic components as reliable and superminiaturized microchips. By the end of the 1970s parts of the Soviet political and professional classes were well aware of the revolution that was sweeping the West and the East, but the Soviet leadership apparently did not understand the nature of the challenge and did not contemplate a realistic Soviet response.

The combination of the trends of Soviet economic and technological stagnation with the explosive growth in the capitalist world was potentially, and in part actually, calamitous to the Soviet Union and to the domestic and international aspirations of its ruling circles. Excluding the Second World War, the 1970s to the mid-1980s was the first prolonged period in Soviet history when the Soviet Union was falling behind the major capitalist nations in key comparative economic indicators. Most important, the technological gap between the Soviet Union and advanced capitalist countries was widening sharply and with increased momentum.

These quantitative comparisons, however, do not tell the main story. The most important comparisons concern qualitative factors that can seldom be quantified. The major physical indicators of Soviet production, once the most visible signs of its accomplishment—and a matter of great pride to the Soviet leadership, political elite and people—now suddenly seemed either irrelevant or worse, an expression of backwardness.

The Soviet Union produces, for example, twice as much steel as the United States, with a GNP half the size of the United States, and still encounters chronic shortages of steel. The explanation for this anomaly is quite simple: The Soviet Union wastes steel by engaging in an unnecessary and unproductive enterprise. The amount of steel in Soviet capital and consumer goods is comparatively exorbitant. (This incidentally, is also true of lumber and other primary products, notably the wasteful consumption of electricity and oil.)

What counts economically in the contemporary world is not merely quantity. Rather, it is high labor and capital productivity in the production process; the modernity of the product mix; and the costs, quality and easy availability and serviceability of the products. In all these respects in the last two decades, the Soviet Union has regressed as compared to capitalist nations.

Soviet leaders are well aware of the state of affairs described above. They believe that they and their party's ideological sense of purpose are endangered. Their patriotic pride is hurt. The situation of Japan and the modernity of the newly industrial nations in Asia, which often defy imagination, must be a particularly bitter pill for the Soviets to swallow. More important, what they understand to be their patriotic destiny of international greatness has been called into question. Their sense of urgency in countering the economic-technological challenge is strongly reinforced by fears of its potential military consequences. They recognize that their international aspirations to greatness cannot be reconciled in the long term with their relative economic-technological weaknesses and the narrow range of their foreign policy resources. In the final analysis, it is this psychological motivation that is the deepest source of the present Soviet leaders' commitment to real change in the Soviet Union.

Soviet Capabilities and the International Environment

The second international source of the changes taking place in the Soviet Union is its deteriorating international position. At the end of the 1960s and during the early 1970s the Soviet international position was increasingly strong. To the Soviets it looked as if a qualitative change was taking place, the fulfillment of a dream for which generations had been sacrificed. It seemed to them that the "international correlation of forces," which describes not simply a momentary situation but a trend occurring over a large time segment, was moving solidly in their favor, perhaps irreversibly.

Soviet leaders expected major favorable political-international consequences from the American public recognition of a state of strategic parity with the Soviet Union. The *Ostpolitik* of the late 1960s, followed by détente in the early 1970s, was increasingly considered by Soviet leaders to be an offensive strategy. In their eyes, the United States entered the détente compact from a position of weakness brought on by Vietnam and magnified by the Watergate scandal—all of which paralyzed American political institutions and forced a public retreat from international activism. For the Soviets, in the final analysis, détente looked like a guarantee against dangerous confrontation with the United States. They believed that détente would be accompanied by the stabilization of the situation in Europe including the recognition of Soviet domination of East Central Europe; the expansion of economic relations with the West, including large-scale technology transfer needed by the Soviets; and, at the same time, an almost free hand for the expansion of Soviet power and influence in the peripheral regions of Soviet-American competition.

By the late 1970s and the early 1980s, however, the Soviet international position had deteriorated significantly. While the invasion of Afghanistan in 1979 signified the end of Soviet-American détente, American defense policies in the late 1970s, and particularly in the early 1980s, ended the erosion of the strategic balance against America. The Soviets were faced with an intensive and costly new cycle of the unending arms race and Strategic Defense Initiative (SDI) that they feared could lead to an American technological breakout. The deployment of ss-20s in Europe, one of the most foolish acts of Soviet foreign and security policy, backfired by bringing the Atlantic alliance closer together. The Soviet campaign against intermediate-range nuclear forces (INF) was a textbook example of diplomatic clumsiness following a major military error.

While still weary of international military involvements, the United States largely left behind its nihilistic attitude toward international activism. It regained much of its past sense of confidence, increased significantly its military budget and started a qualitatively new stage in the modernization of its conventional forces.

At the same time, the Soviet Union found itself overextended in its international involvement. International commitments both strained Soviet resources and held no promise of near term victories. As a case in point, the so-called national liberation movements that in the 1970s were a symbol of effective Soviet influence, became by the early 1980s an increasingly anti-Soviet force. The Soviet Union found itself with almost no major friends and with trouble in its empire. In Eastern Europe, the unprecedented events in Poland that began in 1980 brought together the working classes and the intelligentsia in a massive all national movement against the communist regime. Luckily for the Soviet Union, these events were arrested without invasion by an internal security crackdown and martial law. But the problems that led to the creation of Solidarity were not resolved. In fact, Poland became the first non-communist country with an organized and nonviolent opposition.

During the leadership paralysis of the Brezhnev period, and the subsequent power vacuum of the Kremlin interregnum, Soviet supervision of Eastern Europe slackened, giving much greater leeway to the centrifugal tendencies of the native communist leaderships. The economic situation in Eastern Europe deteriorated, increasing the Soviet economic burden and creating potentially destabilizing conditions in the Soviet empire.

The Soviet Union's relative decline on the international scene, combined with its domestic crisis, created a situation that required an urgent reassessment of the strategic direction of Soviet security and foreign policies. It reinforced the previously described feeling among parts of the Soviet leadership, political elite and experts, of the inadequacy of Soviet foreign policy resources as related to Soviet global aspirations. The highly unimaginative Soviet leadership, frozen in old strategic concepts and traditional policies and tactically inflexible, could not even begin to address the situation. The obvious gravity of the existing condition in this respect provided an immensely forceful stimulant for deep change. As Gorbachev and his associates argue, with justification, the most important Soviet foreign and security policy statement consists of the program of domestic renewal and radical reform.

THE INFLUENCE OF DOMESTIC REFORM
ON SOVIET FOREIGN POLICY

These domestic and international factors explain why, in the early 1980s, a powerful pressure for change was building up in the Soviet Union. Yet the change now occurring in the USSR was not at all inevitable. The intense perception of the need for change had to combine with a catalyst. A conscious historical agent was needed to transform the pressures for change from a possibility into a reality. This catalyst emerged through the process of Soviet political succession, confirming once again the central role of leadership in human affairs.

The hope that we are presently witnessing changes that will affect the nature and long-term direction of Soviet foreign policy is based primarily on Gorbachev's effort to transform the Soviet Union domestically. The fiercest critics of the Soviet Union have repeatedly insisted that significant Soviet foreign and security policy changes could occur only if the domestic system itself will begin to change. The domestic changes that the United States hoped for have begun, and the Soviet Union is moving in a positive direction. One should not belittle what already is happening nor derogate the plausibility of further evaluation. However, a sober analysis of the potential impact on Soviet foreign policy must be based upon an understanding that this is only the beginning.

Long-term tendencies in Soviet foreign policy will depend primarily on three factors related to the process of domestic reform: (i) the complexity and timetable of Gorbachev's domestic reforms, (ii) the liberal direction of the reforms and their probable consequences; and (iii) the process of demilitarization of Soviet society (which is already becoming evident). ...

NOTES

ABOUT THE AUTHOR: **Seweryn Bialer** is Richard and Renée Belfer Professor of Social Sciences and International Relations and director of the Research Institute on International Change at Columbia University.

5   Politics Before Gorbachev: De-Stalinization and the Roots of Reform

PETER HAUSLOHNER

From the beginning of Mikhail Gorbachev's rule, Western specialists have been deeply divided about the prospects of state-led change in the Soviet Union. Part of this debate has centered on the scope and ambition of Gorbachev's own objectives, although many of these doubts dissipated in the wake of the General Secretary's extraordinary demands for political and economic reform at the January and June 1987 Plenums of the Communist Party Central Committee.[1] On the other hand, most of the disagreement has always had more to do with judgments about the ability of any Party leader, however skilled or well intentioned he or she might be, to carry through so dramatic a transformation of the Soviet system. Just prior to the June Plenum, Peter Reddaway suggested that Gorbachev would eventually have to curb his radicalism or else up the ante and "risk being removed from office à la Khrushchev." Yet, should Gorbachev "persist in his radicalism, and also fail to produce a steady improvement in the standard of living," Reddaway wrote, "then it is hard to see how he could survive for many more years." Although it was at least conceivable that Gorbachev's reforms might lead to "unprecedented changes," the Soviet system still seemed no more "susceptible of transformation today than it was thirty years ago."[2]

But what *is* the Soviet system that so desperately needs to be transformed? To understand the enterprise that Gorbachev has now embarked on, let alone to gauge its chances, we need a clear sense of the system he inherited. Surely the most popular view among specialists is that reflected in the remarks just quoted, which sees the "essence" of the Soviet political-economic system as largely unchanged from what Iosif Stalin left his successors when he died in March 1953. To be sure, proponents of this position do not maintain that everything is as it was in Stalin's time. On the contrary, virtually everyone agrees that the three decades following the dictator's death witnessed major changes that extended throughout society and often resulted in substantial improvements in the quality of ordinary people's lives. Most striking were the changes in state policy: an end to terror and the curtailment of unbridled police powers; the erection of a genuine, although austere, welfare state; and the shift to a foreign policy of "peaceful coexistence," which reduced the severe isolation of the Soviet public from the outside world. Specialists also acknowledge important changes in the manner in which policies were made: a greater degree of rationality and empiricism in the process and much increased opportunities for participation and influence by loyal specialists and lower-ranking officials. However, when one turns to basic institutions and the structure of power, it was and is the *lack of change* that impresses the most: the Communist Party's unqualified monopoly of power; the publicly owned, bureaucratically run "command economy"; and an omnipresent state that made whatever civil society existed practically invisible to the outside observer. It is, above all else, this astonishing yet persistent concentration of formally unaccountable power in the hands of a very few that makes the Soviet system seem so remarkable even today and that has led some writers to characterize "the transition of the Soviet Union from Stalinism to post-Stalinism as a change in the form of rule, not its basic substance."[3]

Yet the juxtaposition of far-reaching policy changes with an unchanging system seems odd, if not implausible. By way of analogy, suppose that one had an old car that was badly out of tune and getting only 15 to 20 miles to the gallon. If the car went into the shop to be tuned and came back a little peppier, now managing perhaps 25 miles to the gallon, one would not be surprised. But if the same car came back, getting 30 to 35 miles per gallon and accelerating from 0 to 50 miles per hour in six seconds rather than twelve, one would know without even looking under the hood that the mechanic had installed a different engine, for no amount of tuning could have changed the old engine's performance so dramatically. Broadly speaking, the same must be true of post-Stalin Soviet politics. Institutional stability and the cycling of policy changes across different administrations—the repudiation of much of Nikita Khrushchev's reformism by Leonid Brezhnev—may have helped to obscure this fact. On the other hand, an end to terror, the uneven but steady growth of a welfare state, and the pursuit of a foreign policy based on peaceful coexistence all represent dramatic departures from Stalinist practice, the duration of which through three decades of widely fluctuating political conditions makes sense only if one assumes that the equivalent of a new "engine of state" was installed somewhere along the way.

This analysis is not meant to suggest that the performance of the Soviet system under Stalin's successors was different in all important respects. On the contrary, from Stalin to Gorbachev, politics was still largely hidden from public view, censorship severe, official lies common, and dissenters harshly repressed. The economy remained extraordinarily wasteful in its use of resources and backward in much of its technology. Culture was drab and mediocre by world standards. Consumer goods and services were in chronic short supply, and their quality struck visitors as more likely the product of an early developing nation than of one of the world's two military-industrial superpowers. Repeated Soviet invasions of neighboring countries demonstrated that the successors could be as cynical and cruel as Stalin himself when it came to guarding or extending a geopolitical advantage. Yet the discontinuities with Stalinism were no less striking, and a good explanation of the similarities in performance must accommodate the differences as well. The key to constructing such an explanation is to recognize that power although obviously crucial, is not the only thing that matters in politics. The rules according to which power is exercised also matter, as do the methods by which power customarily is applied and the purposes for which power is used. Even in the context of an unchanging distribution of power, little imagination is required for one to see how and why significant changes in the rules, methods, and purposes of power might lead to equally far-reaching changes in the chronic behavior of those who wield power and of the system itself.

In this chapter, I shall argue that despite the stability of major institutions and the structure of power, the Soviet political system changed after Stalin's death in fundamental respects. The differences emerge clearly when one considers three factors that are important for assessing any political system. One is the relative strength of political institutions, or the degree to which relatively constant, visible, and widely shared roles, norms, and expectations, as opposed to largely invisible and ever-shifting personal loyalties, shape the political process. A second is the relative strength and capacity of "the state," or the degree to which public authorities are able to ensure, through public institutions, the security of the state from foreign and domestic threats and to pursue the increasingly numerous and complicated policy objectives that all leaderships accumulate over time. Finally, a third factor is the nature of the relationship between state and society and the extent to which public authorities are able to exercise power without relying on coercion or intimidation to maintain public compliance. The far-reaching changes in policy and policymaking that have marked the post-Stalin era can be traced to important changes in each of these factors: the halting if incomplete institutionalization of politics; the continually expanding but awkward power of the Soviet state; and Soviet leaders' adoption of a more inclusive and conciliatory approach toward managing their relations with society. Taken together, these developments suggest that the political order evolving under Khrushchev and Brezhnev was not Stalinism *redux* but something quite different.

However, my argument is less about taxonomy—indeed, I have no substitute label to offer—than about the causes of political change after Stalin and the prospects for renewed change under Gorbachev. The crucial fact is that Stalin's successors could not have reproduced Stalinism even if they had wanted to: not only because the dictator himself was dead, a fact no less important for its being obvious, but because the circumstances that helped give rise to Stalinism had long since disappeared. The new rules, methods, and purposes of power did not emerge spontaneously but were instead stimulated by pressures and opportunities present in the radically different post–World War II world. These were problems and possibilities with which any of Stalin's successors would have had to contend. Even more important, these "adaptations" worked! Again, the crucial fact is that Soviet rulers coped, by and large successfully, with the great dangers and uncertainties associated with Stalin's passing; with the severe economic and social problems that were also Stalin's legacy; and with the Soviet Union's vulnerabilities in the complicated international situation of the early 1950s. Thereafter, the regime enjoyed more than two decades of uninterrupted domestic tranquility and unprecedented prosperity. But such good fortunes did not—in fact, could not—last. During the final decade of Brezhnev's rule, Soviet power began unmistakably to lose its effectiveness. If there appeared to be many reasons for this, most could be traced ultimately to the growing discordances between the now-entrenched rules, methods, and purposes of post-Stalin politics, on the one hand, and newly emerging challenges, pressures, and opportunities embedded in a permanently changing society and global environment, on the other. These discordances, I shall argue, gave rise to the "precrisis" situation Gorbachev has said was developing in the Soviet Union in Brezhnev's final years. At the same time, these discordances offer clues to the likely nature and direction of a new wave of change in the future.

POLITICS WITHOUT TERROR

In a recent essay, T. H. Rigby argued that the basic "rules" of Soviet politics by which Khrushchev rose to power in the 1950s were essentially the same as when Stalin rose to power in the 1920s and little different, he suggested in an aside at the end of his essay, from those prevailing today.[4] ...

... In fact, Rigby projected a politics largely lacking in rules—a politics based primarily on informal and impermanent personal loyalties and relatively little on formal laws and institutions. His maxims suggest an abiding collective disrespect for rules among the elite and a recruitment system that "selects" for politicians who violate rules with unusual willingness and skill.[6] Yet, although the maxims suggest, correctly enough, that there are powerful forces favoring the persistence of "ruleless" politics, it is clear even to casual observers that Soviet politics today is significantly *less* unruly than it used to be, certainly since Stalin's day, but also since the Khrushchev period.

The most obvious reason for this is that one rule in particular seems to have become well established: the rule that bars the use of violence as a normal instrument of politics. Stalin's increasing reliance on violence and terror, from the early 1930s on, lessened his need for friends and policy coalitions and, consequently, his urge to "deliver the goods" to various constituencies. By comparison, the repudiation of violence by Stalin's successors has had the effect of limiting what a top leader can do to punish rivals—thus limiting his or her ability to intimidate clients, friends, and otherwise neutral peers. Delivering the goods has again become an important element of political strategy. The ban on violence also has had the effect of distributing power resources somewhat more broadly within the leadership, mainly by expanding the amount and quality of information available to its members.[7] As a result, Soviet leadership is more "shared" than it was under Stalin, and leaders are much more constrained in the use of their powers. ...

Although the end of widespread political violence was signaled almost immediately after Stalin's death, it is clear that the elite's internalization of this new norm did not take place at once.[13] For example, Khrushchev claimed that shortly after the 1957 "anti-Party group" crisis was resolved, one of the leaders of the defeated conspiracy, Lazar Kaganovich, telephoned Khrushchev to plead that they "not proceed with him as they had dealt with people under Stalin." These very words, Khrushchev said, were evidence that had Kaganovich and his associates won out instead, they would have resorted to the old methods of settling accounts. But Kaganovich had been mistaken to project these assumptions onto others. "We are observing and will adhere to Leninist principles," responded Khrushchev, who promised his caller a job and the opportunity to live and work peacefully.[14] Subsequently, following Khrushchev's own forced retirement from office, a movement arose urging Stalin's full historical rehabilitation, which evidently enjoyed high-level political support but also aroused widespread anxieties at home and abroad. Khrushchev's successors equivocated but finally decided to reject the idea, and Brezhnev pledged in effect that the time for relying mainly on coercion was past and that there would be no return to the era of "administrative rule."

Nor can it be said with total assurance that the resort to violence has been completely abolished, even at the highest levels, or that widespread political violence will never reappear.[16] Numerous examples from recent world history demonstrate how exceptional circumstances can result in extreme violence, even state-sanctioned terror, in what were previously thought to be relatively stable, institutionalized democracies; and a combination of the Soviet Communist Party's own revolutionary traditions and a powerful secret police perhaps makes internalized elite norms forbidding violence even more fragile than elsewhere. Nevertheless, the ongoing process of generational succession must make the likelihood of a return to mass political violence increasingly remote. One should not be surprised to find leaders who entered politics at a time when political violence was considered "normal" feeling, even decades after the formal denunciation of the practice, somewhat ambivalent at least about the utility of violence, if not about its desirability. Yet by the time Brezhnev died, several new elite generations had been inducted into politics, having been taught that violence was not a legitimate or even an effective instrument of rule under normal conditions. Those persons who were in their twenties at the time of Khrushchev's "secret speech" are now in their fifties and are increasingly the cohort running the system. It is a reasonable assumption that norms forbidding violence have been deeply etched in the minds of these men and women and that only truly exceptional provocations could result in the erosion of these norms in the foreseeable future.

AUTHORITY BUILDING

The main result of the end of terror was the return of "normal" politics and the heightened need for politicians at all levels to "deliver the goods." However, this formulation does not fully capture the ramifications of the requirement that Soviet leaders rely on persuasive methods of rule in place of the intimidation afforded by state-sanctioned violence. Particularly illuminating in this respect is George Breslauer's argument that politicians in the post-Stalin period have been led to devote increasing amounts of their scarce time and energy to expanding their personal "authority" among clients, friends, peers, rivals, and the political-intellectual elite as a whole.[17] Authority, which Breslauer defined as "legitimated power" or the willingness of an audience to acquiesce in a leader's exercise of power, is simply a more reliable means of defending one's position than is the "illegitimate" use of power in conditions in which losing is not necessarily permanent.[18] What is important is that the building of one's authority, while a form of "delivering the goods," is more than that—or rather, it means the delivery of important "public" as well as "private" goods. Breslauer maintained that contenders for leadership and leaders who have been selected must continually persuade others, both in the leadership and in the broader elite, of their competence as "problem-solvers" and as "politicians." That means, in the first instance, convincing onlookers that one has the ability to tackle successfully the "big" issues of national security, economic growth, public welfare, and so forth. It also means projecting the image of someone who will lead and solve problems without sowing so much discord in the process that the regime itself becomes threatened by paralysis or internal disorder. Although authority may initially rest on promises and reputation, eventually claims of competence are tested by reality. If the test is positive, authority is liable to be enhanced. If the test is negative and authority is eroded, leaders may choose to modify their program or style of leadership in the hope of improving their performance and credibility in the eyes of opponents. Or leaders may fall back on the more conventional instruments of patronage, manipulation, and intimidation in order to preserve their office.

There are two important implications that flow from this analysis. One is that competition within the leadership, particularly that associated with successions, has become an important, even routinized, source of political and policy innovation. Competing efforts to accumulate authority seem to precipitate a collective search for novel, or simply more effective, approaches to existing problems of policy and governance. Successions, rather than occasions for political crisis as many scholars used to argue, have evidently become (perhaps in addition) a critical source of *systemic* revitalization or reequilibration and stabilization, depending on one's opinion of the defects of the preceding administration.[20]

Second, despite the absence of democratic institutions, it appears that a certain measure of accountability has now been introduced into the Soviet political process—both accountability of individual leaders to the rest of the leadership whose members may seek to depose them should their authority diminish, and accountability of the leaders and the leadership to ever-growing numbers of the political elite and the population as a whole. ...

REVITALIZING THE PARTY

The end of the terror contributed to the institutionalization of politics in several other ways, one of the most significant being the revitalization of the Communist Party. The strengthening of the Party *qua* institution was, in the first instance, a political result dictated by Khrushchev's concerted effort to build support among regional Party secretaries and by the eventual defeat of his government-centered opposition. Yet at a deeper level, rejuvenation of the Party was probably inevitable once Stalin's successors had decided to abandon the leader cult as an important legitimating symbol. Having renounced terror and one-person rule but unwilling to repudiate Soviet power itself or the major institutions underpinning the regime, the new leaders naturally reemphasized Leninism and the principles of collective leadership.

Revitalization proceeded on several levels. Especially important was the resumption of regular meetings of the Party's most authoritative organs, the Congress and Central Committee, which had been almost completely ignored in the late Stalin period.[22] These meetings again became the locus for the transaction of important business—for example, the approval of membership changes in the Party's leading executive organs (Politburo, Secretariat), the issuance of five-year plan directives, annual reviews of the plan and budget, and so forth—and the occasion for cautious public (and more spirited private) discussions of major policy issues. Equally important were and are the opportunities these gatherings afforded mid-level Party and state officials to confer informally with members of the leadership and to consult and "network" among themselves.[23] Thus, even as it continued to serve as an agent of implementation and control, the Party reacquired its status as an instrument of collective deliberation, with an "opinion" that could be discovered, at least in its approximate form, and that must now play a role in the political calculations of those at the top.

There were other changes as well. Although there is less information available about the activities of the highest executive bodies, it is clear that the three most important executive organs—the Politburo, the Secretariat, and the Presidium of the Council of Ministers—have met on a regular, more or less weekly, basis since at least the start of the 1970s and almost certainly from much earlier.[24] Since the mid-1950s, a much higher proportion of formal Party and government decrees have been published. Although the published documents are far from the universe of decisions made, the publication of some of this material has helped to clarify the different responsibilities of these bodies, while making their exercise of power seem more legitimate.[25] In addition, even as the Party's deliberative functions were expanded, the executive responsibilities of Party officials and staff throughout the system were strengthened, particularly in supervision of the economy and within certain institutions (for example, ministries, research institutes). At the symbolic level, the 1977 constitution proclaimed the Party's "leading role" in directing society in a far more explicit and prominent way than had been done in the 1936 Stalin constitution. In the meantime, Party membership levels rose sharply—by 1981 the Party was 2.5 times the size it had been in 1955—and deliberate affirmative action recruitment policies made the Party significantly more representative, in sociological terms, of the general population. The Party today is literally a mass party—one in ten adult citizens is a member, perhaps one in four of all persons with a college degree—with deep roots in the society it leads.[26]

Perhaps the most far-reaching change associated with the Party's revitalization has been the quasi-formalization of a leadership succession procedure. When Stalin died, there were no rules for choosing a successor, nor was it clear even to insiders what position the leader should occupy—or, to reverse the question, what position carried with it the greatest power or potential authority. These uncertainties were a virtual invitation to conspiracy, unsolicited intervention by the security organs, and the use of violence. Khrushchev's subsequent emergence as *primus inter pares*—first over Lavrenty Beriya, the secret police chief who was eventually executed, then over Georgiy Malenkov, the government Premier who at first was shunted aside to a lesser but still powerful job—had all the earmarks of an entirely unexceptional, small-group power struggle. However, when the First Secretary's rivals in the leadership subsequently tried to engineer his removal in June 1957, in the famous "anti-Party group crisis," and when Khrushchev succeeded in forcing the question into the full Central Committee which supported him and threw out his opponents instead, a watershed was reached. In effect, the Central Committee asserted, or was de facto granted, the right to broker in cases of deep disagreement or deadlock at the top. When a new set of conspirators rose up against Khrushchev seven years later and presented their case before the Central Committee, this time gaining its approval with little if any dissent, it was as if the earlier precedent had been reaffirmed.

Khrushchev's victory suggested another precedent: the unambiguous supremacy of Party First Secretary over the head of government. However, this issue was immediately blurred when, a year later, Khrushchev decided to oust his former ally, Nikolay Bulganin, and take on the post of Premier in addition to his Party job. Once again, the relative power of the head of the Party seemed to be in question. These doubts were reinforced when, at the plenum ousting Khrushchev in October 1964, the Central Committee resolved never again to permit one person to hold both the top Party and government posts simultaneously. Yet, looking back at these events, the precedent now seems clearer cut. At the 1957 Plenum, full-time Party officials finally recaptured control of the Presidium (as the Politburo was then called) from full-time government officials who had long had the dominant voice, and they have never surrendered it since. The decision to prevent the Party leader from occupying the post of Premier has probably had the effect of limiting the former's formal responsibilities, hence vulnerabilities, particularly for performance of the economy, without necessarily limiting his power, especially given the Party Secretariat's capacities for oversight. At the Twenty-third Party Congress in 1966, Brezhnev's first as Party leader, the Party rules were amended in order to reinstate formally the post of General Secretary and to mandate that selection to this position be determined by vote of the Central Committee directly. These rules changes reinforced the Central Committee's formal authority governing the succession process, but they also served to elevate the special role and authority of the top leader within the leadership. Lastly, Brezhnev's eclipse of Premier Kosygin—demonstrated with stunning clarity by Brezhnev's dominant role in the Soviet-U.S. summits of 1972–1974—and more than a decade of unchallenged and widely acknowledged rule as "head of Politburo" reinforced both the fact and the perception of preponderant authority vested in the post of General Secretary.[27]

Thus, when Brezhnev finally died, what had not been obvious, let alone "legitimate" thirty years earlier, was evidently well established and accepted throughout the Party and the nation: that the Party General Secretary is the country's leading executive and that the Politburo reserves the right of nomination to this post, subject always to the Central Committee's formal assent. ...

Although much of the day-to-day bargaining and struggle of politics remains hidden, the revitalization of the Party has lent a certain clarity and regularity to the political process, which before was conspicuously lacking. As a result, certain aspects of timing, location, and participation rights in decisionmaking have become more predictable and perhaps symbolically legitimate, to the point where one must assume that players and spectators alike *expect* these procedures to be followed, even if the results are for the most part orchestrated behind the scenes.[28] To be sure, such procedural rules do not alone amount to a change in the structure of power. Yet such rules can nonetheless prove confining, inasmuch as they force leaders to observe schedules and information routines that, in some instances, they might greatly prefer to ignore. ...

... The rules, it is clear, matter most when the balance of power within the leadership is relatively even and when the competition for authority is most intense. To be sure, it is far from evident that the top leader, even Brezhnev toward the end of his rule, can inaugurate fundamentally new policies while ignoring accepted procedures altogether; the single plenum on Afghanistan may be instructive on this point. But it is clear that these procedures are not an important constraint on the leader who would leave policy unchanged, even when standpattism seems an obvious recipe for failure.

FROM LABEL STICKING TO ARGUMENTATION

The end of terror also contributed to the institutionalization of politics by facilitating the recapture of science from the ideologists and the subsequent spread of empiricism and broad consultation in the discussion stages of policymaking. As in the case of Party revitalization, this development had its immediate roots in politics. Largely to win the sympathy and support of groups severely antagonized by the previous administration, both Khrushchev and Brezhnev promised renewed respect for specialists and empirical methods, the publication of more data, and the creation of new forums for the public discussion of policy. To be sure, Khrushchev talked a better game than he played. He often could not refrain from intervening in technical disputes and insisting that his own views prevail, and in this more than in any other respect, his Stalinist origins shone through. Brezhnev proved much more reliable, although the last decade of his administration witnessed a serious reversal of policy with respect to the publication of data, which was lamented and resented by much of the intelligentsia. In a broader sense, however, there were powerful objective pressures that increased the attractiveness of this strategy and would probably have driven Stalin's successors to consider it regardless of the political implications. Such pressures included the need for more information and better technical advice in an increasingly complicated world as well as the imperatives of a ruling strategy that all the successors seemed to prefer, which involved making peace with society and broadening the regime's underlying base of support.[33]

The most immediate consequence was a vast expansion over time in the sheer amount of consultation, much of it formalized, between decisionmakers and "experts" (by which I mean scholars, policy analysts, and lower-ranking administrators who have practical experience in the area in question.)[34] For example, several studies have shown that policy specialists gained increasing freedom to investigate, and to debate publicly, important and contentious public issues. The specialists' ability to convey their findings and recommendations to relevant decisionmakers also increased, often thanks to formal (and routinized) channels established for precisely that purpose.[35] Under Brezhnev, it became standard practice to form large commissions, composed of a wide spectrum of institutional representatives and area experts, to prepare drafts of new laws and decrees, although always under the supervision of the Party. The penultimate drafts of new legislation were frequently published as a means of stimulating broad public debates. Even though these debates were doubtless orchestrated, with the purpose of educating the population and building consensus in support of the new laws, these debates inevitably became an important source of information for decisionmakers and, just as inevitably, an important mechanism of horizontal opinion formation within the specialist community and among the more attentive members of the mass public—opinion that must today play a growing part in the authority-building process described earlier.[36] Last but hardly least, the politicians took steps to improve their knowledge of the general public's attitudes by giving grudging, but slowly expanding approval to the sociologists to conduct applied research, much of which is simple public opinion polling, and by adopting a series of measures intended to yield a more systematic collection and analysis of the huge number of letters and complaints from disgruntled citizens that are received daily by the media, Party offices, and almost every state agency.

The impact of all this consultation is difficult to document conclusively and thus remains a source of controversy among Western observers. Yet to those who have interviewed leading specialists, whether in Soviet research institutes or in the bureaucracy, a single conclusion seems obvious and unassailable: Leading specialists have come to expect—and, indeed, regard it as entirely unexceptional— that when major decisions are to be made in their area of expertise, they will normally be afforded a chance to communicate their thoughts on the matter, which will be duly recorded if not necessarily taken into account.[37]...

However, while Khrushchev and Brezhnev sought to improve their intelligence and to broaden their support among policy intellectuals, they also took steps to reduce the chance that expanded debate and advice-giving might lead to organized opposition or, more subtly, to the growth of intra-Party factionalism. One obvious manifestation of this effort was the harsh treatment meted out to those dissidents who organized, publicized their protests, or persisted in their activities despite warnings from police and prosecutors to stop, compared with the leniency often shown individual protestors who promptly recanted. Equally important were the severe and continuing limits placed on historiography, which prevented a serious internal examination not only of Stalin and Stalinism but also—and in many respects this was more consequential—of the fundamental policy choices adopted at the start of the 1930s (collectivization, the extreme industrialization targets of the early five-year plans) and of the great factional struggles and policy debates of the 1920s. Also falling into this category was the unwillingness of the Soviet leadership after Khrushchev to publish transcripts of Central Committee Plenums, which has likely made it more difficult to organize and mobilize existing policy "tendencies" within the elite.[39] A final manifestation that warrants mention was (and is) the curious segmentation of policy debates that one observes in the published literature, which has meant that the most empirically detailed treatments of an issue, the frankest assessments, and the most radical ideas have by and large been restricted to the most specialized (and smallest circulation) media outlets and, as a result, to the narrowest audiences.[40]

The widespread consultation currently practiced between decisionmakers and policy specialists has doubtless improved the amount and quality of the information at the government's disposal and thus, potentially at least, the quality of public policy. The regime also has considerably broadened its social base, as hundreds of thousands, even millions, of the country's most educated people have been brought into the system and have become implicated in the regime's policies in a far more intimate way than mere membership in the Party would imply. This includes the vast proportion of the society's "best and brightest," who in other circumstances might be available and disposed to lead a revolutionary opposition.

Yet the leadership's persistent fear of anything that smacks of organized political competition, even within the confines of the Party, has limited the benefits of this development while adding its own special costs. The segmentation of policy discussions has prevented ideas from receiving the critical analysis they need—in particular, this practice has prevented review by specialists with different backgrounds and experience who might see inconsistencies or unwanted consequences that someone from within the field in question might not be aware of or able to appreciate.[41] As a result, many of the ideas one finds circulating in the Soviet literature are simply naive or plainly ineffective, and social learning is often slow. On the other hand, even when there are many novel ideas and considerable learning, these usually involve "small" issues or parts of problems rather than "big" issues or problems in their entirety.[42] Because of the constraints on public debate and the intolerance of factionalism, it remains extraordinarily difficult to devise a comprehensive reform program that cuts across multiple issues and constituencies. As a result, radical political-economic reform *must* be incremental and piecemeal, certainly to a far greater degree than in countries where groups, parties, or factions out of power have time to organize and work out in advance alternative programs of governance.

The limits on debate and political organization have also helped to reinforce the importance of clientelism in politics. This has its own worrisome implications for the prospects of reform because politicians who are more loyal to people than to ideas are more likely to be captured by the bureaucratic interests and perspectives of the organizations for which they work. This means that appointed administrators who are clients are likely to be less successful than ideologues or members of factions in forcing their organizations to change and almost certainly less eager than ideologues and factionalists to persist in the effort in the face of resistance from the people they are administering. In other words, the limits on public debate and the absence of even loosely organized factions must make it exceedingly difficult for someone such as Gorbachev to predict how his appointees (whether clients or friends) are likely to perform on the job—or how loyal they are likely to be in the long run, especially when it becomes clear that his policies are causing them acute, job-related discomfort. If constructing a comprehensive package of radical reforms is difficult, getting it implemented will be doubly so.
…
…

THE SOCIAL CONTRACT

A strong state is not necessarily an efficient or an effective state. The Soviet state today is doubtless more secure than before and more capable in the sense of being able to do more things. But to do more things does not mean to do them well, and during Brezhnev's final years the state's performance, especially in the economic sphere, grew steadily worse. …
…

Brezhnev's unwillingness even to give serious consideration to, let alone to pay the costs of, internal reform is often ascribed to bureaucratic opposition or, more subtly, to the presumed self-interest of the *nomenklatura*. Yet, as already suggested, there had to be more to it than that. Indeed, the price of the Stalinist growth strategy included not only poor growth in productivity and lagging technological performance but also a severely depressed popular living standard and, as required for the implementation of this strategy, institutions that allowed ordinary citizens virtually no influence over the political and economic decisions that shaped their lives. Given the tremendous amount of social flux and upheaval entailed in rapid growth, the paltry material benefits that this strategy left the mass public, and the lack of opportunities for political voice, one might have expected a situation in which there was enormous potential for social disorder and political instability. The question is, How did the government manage to keep the peace?

Stalin maintained social order, although at first not very effectively, perhaps largely through violence and intimidation, but also thanks to the fantastic opportunities for upward social mobility that resulted from forced-pace industrialization and as a result of special privileges offered to outstanding workers and to those who succeeded in entering the tiny but rapidly increasing home-grown, technical intelligentsia.[71] Why the dictator's successors felt it necessary to switch so quickly to a fundamentally new approach is still unclear and a subject deserving further study.[72] One obvious factor was the evidently widespread desire among the elite to be rid of the insecurities with which they had recently lived. There may, in addition, have been some anxiety about the popular response to Stalin's death, exemplified in the oft-noted appeal to the population not to succumb to "disorder and panic."[73] Beyond that, top leaders may also have been coming to doubt the effectiveness and durability of their coercive instruments, bolstered by the knowledge of deteriorating order within the camps of the Gulag.[74] Finally, and in the long run most importantly, the gradual slowing of upward mobility rates in the 1950s and the mounting pressures of a more complicated economy and dramatically transformed social structure undoubtedly increased the attractiveness of a more inclusive and conciliatory strategy, while elevating the costs incurred by holding firm to Stalin's approach.

Whatever the explanation, the change was almost immediate. Within six months of the dictator's death, real incomes were up sharply, the result of significant reductions both in consumer prices and in compulsory bond subscriptions, and large increases in the production of various consumer goods and services had been promised under the auspices of Malenkov's New Course. Although this program did not survive its author's political decline, it did mark a permanent shift in the government's priorities. When Stalin died, average living standards were not much higher than they had been at the start of the First Five-Year Plan, twenty-five years earlier. During the next twenty-five years, however, average living standards more than doubled, and few doubt that this was an important cause of the continuing quiescence of the Soviet public. But improved consumption by itself was not enough. Even though living standards rose steadily under Khrushchev and Brezhnev, they remained far below those in the West, and both the elite's and the public's awareness of, and impatience with, this gap grew with the simultaneous expansion of tourism and other international contacts. Meanwhile, the level of social flux remained high, which was largely the result of continued high rates of rural outmigration and urbanization, while ordinary citizens remained deprived of any significant political or economic power.

Then, in the second half of the 1950s, a more elaborate formula was worked out. The social policy introduced at this time, and for the most part sustained throughout the Brezhnev period, was relatively austere and illiberal by world standards. But it did offer the following promises: (1) to minimize the risks of continued economic growth to individuals, through high levels of job security and stable prices for most basic consumer items; (2) to share widely and relatively evenly the benefits of growth, through a steady expansion of the social wage and a generally egalitarian incomes policy; and (3) while granting no greater power over key political and economic decisions, to allow most citizens considerably greater personal freedom as workers and as consumers. In a phrase, Khrushchev developed and Brezhnev maintained an implicit "social contract" in which the government offered a series of socioeconomic guarantees in exchange for the public's compliance and support even as it continued to deny popular political rights.[75]

...

The social contract worked; even Gorbachev has suggested as much. In spite of the profound changes of the post-Stalin period—the death and subsequent denunciation of the infallible leader, the end of terror, and the social flux associated with continued economic growth—Soviet society experienced remarkably little internal disorder. The exceptions, as previously suggested, tended to cluster in periods in which either the leadership or the society seemed to be having second thoughts about meeting its putative obligations. However, since the mid-1970s, signs of a more substantial weakening of support for the social contract by both sides have accumulated. This time, things could not be reversed or patched up as easily as in the past.[80]

There is evidence on a broad front that the social contract was coming unraveled during the last half dozen years of Brezhnev's rule. Eroding public support was suggested by an apparent deterioration in labor and social discipline, a spreading sense of anomie and pessimism concerning the future, and an increase in open forms of protest—for example, letters of complaint, job actions, and even a few scattered attempts to form independent trade unions.[81] Gorbachev has since alluded to this period as one of "social corrosion," in which a "precrisis situation" was developing. At the same time, elite support also was eroding, as evidenced by a growing public debate in which every component of the social contract was subjected to increasingly sharp criticism.[82] Beneath these overt manifestations of decline, the social contract was losing support on numerous levels. Widespread social norms, which in the past had legitimated egalitarian distribution and a high level of economic security, were now being undermined by corruption, a flourishing black market, and a spreading perception that the actual distribution of rewards no longer measured up to any conceivable standard of "social justice." Those institutions to which had been given primary responsibility for implementing and safeguarding the social contract, such as the labor ministry and the trade unions, had in the years since grown more rigid, less responsive to their supposed constituents, and thus less able to diffuse the conflicts that policy implementation inevitably created. Finally, it was becoming apparent that most of the direct benefits of social policy—which had tended to favor blue-collar workers over white-collar professionals and employees, and persons employed in the production of goods over those in services—were flowing to constituencies that were either shrinking or, from an economic standpoint, becoming increasingly marginal. As I have written elsewhere, one could imagine "a kind of social 'de-alignment' taking shape, as the number of partisans of the old order declin[ed], relatively speaking, and the number of dissatisfied 'independents' [grew], waiting to be mobilized behind a new program."[83]

To some extent, the social contract had become yet another casualty of the economic slowdown and the diminishing resources available for consumption. The culprit fingered by most Western observers was the Stalinist growth strategy, which, as had been long predicted, was turning out to be an increasingly poor performer in conditions of a growing scarcity of resources and rapid technological change. Yet the social contract had brought with it economic costs of its own. For example, wage egalitarianism had required that the economic surplus created at relatively profitable enterprises be reallocated to less-profitable ones, but this had weakened the incentive to produce at both. The promise of security and fairness had required uniformity and a powerful, supervisory center, but that had meant severe restrictions on the flexibility and initiative of producers at the grass roots. Institutions that had been revitalized or had been newly established in order to supervise the implementation of the rules and regulations of the social contract had developed their own stake in defending the policies that mandated those rules, even when they no longer made economic sense. As a result, maintenance of the social contract took an ever-larger share of the economy's surplus. It led to increasing inefficiencies because of its inability to accommodate the growing differentiation of economy and society. And it obstructed or prevented the kinds of economic adjustment that might have slowed the rate of decline or allowed for a smoother, less traumatic transition to a new growth strategy.

...

CONCLUSIONS

...

... If this analysis is correct, many of the structural forces that led George F. Kennan and others in the late-1940s to diagnose (probably correctly) an essentially and exceptionally belligerent Soviet state, and to recommend a Western policy of limited and carefully gauged "containment" in response, had by the late 1970s largely dissolved. Although containment was still practiced in one form or another its original theoretical justification no longer applied.

This conclusion will doubtless be vigorously disputed, although possibly for the wrong reasons. My argument is not that Soviet international behavior grew less belligerent in the post-Stalin era. On the contrary, in some respects Soviet behavior was clearly more belligerent or at least more aggressive. Part of the reason for this is to be found in the steady accretion of Soviet military power, which both encouraged and enabled Brezhnev in particular to look to ever-broader horizons. At the same time, the undeniably wooden character of Soviet foreign policy during most of the post-Stalin period and the regime's continuing preference for the instruments of coercion and intimidation over those of diplomacy probably should be credited to the personal conservatism and idiosyncratic biases of an unusually cohesive, solidary, and long-surviving elite generation led by Brezhnev. Indeed, it is surely true in part that generational stagnation, like the locking of plates in the earth's crust, delayed and otherwise obscured the effects of numerous ongoing and far-reaching subterranean changes in society and in many of the system's institutions.[84]

Yet Kennan's original prescription for containment derived not from assumptions concerning the consequences of power and a conservative elite but rather from a diagnosis of the sources of belligerency that Kennan believed were inherent in the Soviet system itself. These were, above all, the messianic ideology of the Party; the profound insecurity of the Party's leaders, engendered by the presumed illegitimacy of the Soviet state; and the leadership's total freedom from popular accountability.[85] It was these factors, and not power per se, that made the Soviet state seem different from ordinary or aspiring Great Powers and that Kennan cited as the justification for containment. This chapter has tried to show that these same factors, whether or not they ever existed in the extreme form Kennan and others supposed, had toward the end of the Brezhnev period all but disappeared. Perhaps it was because containment had "worked." In any event, although possessed of awesome military might and susceptible still to a sometimes acute if increasingly anachronistic xenophobia, the Soviet state had in most other respects become rather ordinary.

The preceding analysis points to a second conclusion that may also be vigorously contested: that even before Gorbachev's rise to power, much of the ground for radical political-economic reform had already been prepared and, indeed, that far-reaching changes in one form or another could scarcely be avoided. The final passing of the Brezhnev generation is part of the explanation for this, but there are other, more important reasons. One is that the intellectual basis of the old regime has for the most part evaporated. Although there is wide disagreement within the Soviet intelligentsia, broadly defined, concerning the details of what should come next and how to get there, the central elements both of the Stalinist economic growth strategy and of the post-Stalin social contract have been widely and thoroughly discredited. Today one looks in vain for serious theoretical justifications of detailed directive planning or egalitarian wage policies, although this was already becoming the case well before the Brezhnev leadership ended. Indeed one of the least-appreciated aspects of the second half of the Breshnev period is that especially among policy specialists the rethinking of old orthodoxies proceeded apace, something that the conservative politics of this era could hide but not halt. At the same time, the need for a new growth strategy and a new social contract became rooted in inescapable objective conditions that can now be ignored only at steadily increasing cost. Such conditions include the requirements of continued economic growth in conditions of advanced development, widespread resource shortage, and accelerating technological change, and the inherent difficulties in satisfying a population that is more educated, more affluent, more likely than ever before to be doing white-collar and service work, and in general more differentiated in its tastes and circumstances. ...

In sum, by the start of the 1980s, sufficient forces and pressures had been assembled to make probable the institution of fundamental political-economic reforms as soon as a leadership succession was under way and the incentives for innovation and authority building had once again intensified. None of this should be interpreted as suggesting that certain reforms (market socialism or political democracy) are inevitable or that the reforms that are adopted will prove success-ful in rebuilding the state's legitimacy, reversing the economic slowdown, or re-claiming the country's prestige and influence internationally. Numerous out-comes are possible, including, as always, revolutionary collapse. Although I think this is extremely unlikely, it is clear that the skill and courage of leadership, and luck, will count heavily in determining which outcomes prevail, how quickly, and at what cost. However, these cautions should not obscure the larger point that powerful forces are now working to promote yet another transformation of the Soviet regime and that a historical juncture is at hand with potentially far-reach-ing implications for both Soviet domestic developments and world politics.

NOTES

ABOUT THE AUTHOR: **Peter Hauslohner,** who taught political science at Yale University at the time this chapter was written, later served in the U.S. Department of State and at the U.S. Embassy in Moscow.

For useful comments on earlier drafts, I would like to thank all the members of the East-West Forum seminar, but especially Donna Bahry, Joe Berliner, Alexander Motyl, and our chairperson, Seweryn Bialer. Extensive criticism and helpful advice were also provided, as always, by George Breslauer and Blair Ruble. I, of course, remain solely responsible for er-rors of fact and grievously wrong interpretations.

1. *Pravda*, January 28, 1987; and *Materialy plenuma tsentral'nogo komiteta KPSS, 25–26 iyunya 1987 (Materials of the CPSU Central Committee Plenum, 25–26 June 1987)* (Moscow: Politizdat, 1987), pp. 6–70.

2. Peter Reddaway, "Gorbachev the Bold," *New York Review of Books* 34, no. 9 (May 28, 1987), pp. 21–25 (at 25).

3. Seweryn Bialer, *The Soviet Paradox* (New York: Knopf, 1986), p. 6.

4. T. H. Rigby, "Khrushchev and the Rules of the Soviet Political Game," in R. F. Miller and F. Fehér, eds., *Khrushchev and the Communist World* (Totowa, N.J.: Barnes & Noble, 1984), pp. 39–81.

6. This was an important theme of Zbigniew Brezezinski and Samuel P. Huntington's classic, Political Power: USA/USSR (New York: Vintage, 1965), Ch. 3.

7. Grey Hodnett, "The Pattern of Leadership Politics," in Seweryn Bialer, ed., *The Do-mestic Context of Soviet Foreign Policy* (Boulder, Colo.: Westview, 1981), pp. 87–118.

13. Key events in the delegitimation of violence included prompt exposure of the noto-rious Doctors' Plot as fraudulent and the release of the surviving physicians; the June 1953 arrest of Lavrenty Beriya and other high police officials, followed by their trial and execu-tion six months later; the simultaneous curbing of secret police powers, in particular the right to convene extrajudicial tribunals; Khrushchev's famous "secret speech" at the Twen-tieth Party Congress in February 1956, in which he denounced Stalin's terror, and the sub-sequent release or rehabilitation of thousands of surviving prisoners and deceased victims; and the 1957 "anti-Party group crisis," after which those who had led the attempted coup against Khrushchev were not killed or even arrested but were exiled to minor jobs in the provinces. For a readable and still useful history of this period, see Wolfgang Leonhard, *The Kremlin Since Stalin* (New York: Praeger, 1962).

14. This account was included in Khrushchev's closing speech to the Twenty-second Party Congress. See *Pravda*, October 29, 1961, p. 3.

16. See, for example, the puzzling circumstances surrounding the death in October 1980 of candidate Politburo member Petr Masherov, as described by Amy W. Knight, "Pyotr Masherov and the Soviet Leadership: A Study in Kremlinology," *Survey* 26, no. 1 (1982), pp. 151–168. For a recent case of political violence practiced at the regional level, in which the long-time Party leader of the Bashkir autonomous republic engineered the arrest and imprisonment of a subordinate Party leader, see "'To Halt the Persecution,'" *Pravda*, May 6, 1987, p. 2.

17. George W. Breslauer, *Khrushchev and Brezhnev as Leaders* (London: Allen & Unwin, 1982).

18. Power is defined conventionally as the ability, whether by virtue of one's organizational position or through control of resources (including coercive resources), to impose one's preferences on another—"pulling rank," as Breslauer put it. Ibid., p. 3.

20. This argument is made with respect to both democratic and socialist regimes in Valerie Bunce, *Do New Leaders Make a Difference?* (Princeton, N.J.: Princeton University Press, 1981).

22. In the nearly eight years that elapsed between the end of the war in Europe and Stalin's death, there had been one Party congress (in 1952) and only one officially reported meeting of the Central Committee (February 1947). During the first decade following Stalin's death, three Party congresses were held, along with twenty-seven announced Central Committee plenums. In fact, the total meeting time of congresses, Party conferences, and Central Committee plenums in 1955–1962 (information is complete for 1953–1954) averaged 15 days/year, as compared with 11.4 days/year in the decade before World War II. Based on *Spravochnyy tom k vos'momu izdaniyu 'KPSS v rezolyutsiyakh i resheniyakh s"yezdov, konferentsiy i plenumov Tsk' (Index Volume to the Eighth Edition of 'The CPSU in the Resolutions and Decisions of Congresses, Conferences and Central Committee Plenums')* (Moscow: Politizdat, 1973), pp. 28–34.

23. See, for example, Fedor Morgun's account of the December 1958 Central Committee Plenum in his memoirs, *Khleb i Lyudi (Grain and People)*, 2nd ed. (Moscow: Politizdat, 1975), pp. 100–106. Morgun, recently named head of a new USSR State Committee for environmental protection, addressed this plenum in his capacity as a state farm chairperson from the Virgin Lands in Kazakhstan.

24. Archie Brown, "The Power of the General Secretary," in T. H. Rigby et al., eds. *Authority, Power and Policy in the USSR* (New York: St. Martin's Press, 1980), p. 140 (and footnote 23). This should be contrasted with Stalin's habit of doing business over late-night dinners and in various, ever-changing subcommittees of the leadership, as described by Khrushchev and numerous others in their memoirs.

25. The most important documentary series include the weekly *Sobraniye postanovleniy pravitel'stva SSSR (Collected Decrees of the USSR Government);* and the two multivolume sets, *KPSS v rezolyutsiyakh i resheniyakh s"yezdov, konferentsiy i plenumov TsK (The CPSU in the Resolutions and Decisions of Congresses, Conferences and Central Committee plenums),* now in its 9th edition, and *Resheniya partii i pravitel'stva po khozyaystvennym voprosam (Decisions of the Party and Government Concerning Economic Issues),* now in its 3rd edition.

26. These developments are conveniently surveyed in Donald R. Kelley, "The Communist Party," in Kelley, ed., *Soviet Politics in the Brezhnev Era* (New York: Praeger, 1980), pp. 27–54. Also see Jerry F. Hough and Merle Fainsod, *How the Soviet Union Is Governed* (Cambridge, Mass.: Harvard University Press, 1979), Ch. 9.

27. These developments are reviewed, although with a slightly different emphasis, in Brown, "The Power of the General Secretary."

28. Hodnett wrote as follows: "Thus we are talking about informal understandings: that business be conducted in official forums, that information will be accessible to members, that participation will be structured in certain ways, that the general secretary will take the initiative in drawing up reports, and that these reports will be collectively approved." Hodnett, "The Pattern of Leadership Politics," p. 107.

33. The need for more information, better data, and higher quality analyses was emphasized at the Twentieth Party Congress, particularly in the speeches by Khrushchev and his ally Anastas Mikoyan. A seminal theoretical treatment of the shift to an "inclusive" political strategy was presented in Kenneth Jowitt's "Inclusion and Mobilization in European Leninist Regimes," *World Politics* 28, no. 1 (October 1975), pp. 69–96.

34. There have long existed elaborate formal rules designed to ensure collective deliberations and extensive consensus building within most institutions, and a sizable Soviet secondary literature contends that these rules, although not always observed, do have a significant impact. See Ellen Jones, "Committee Decision Making in the Soviet Union," *World Politics* 36, no. 2 (January 1984), pp. 165–188.

35. See the especially well documented case of the criminologists by Peter H. Solomon, *Soviet Criminologists and Criminal Policy* (New York: Columbia University Press, 1978) Also see Thane Gustafson, *Reform in Soviet Politics* (Cambridge: Cambridge University Press, 1981), Chs. 3–6.

36. That the leadership was aware of and sensitive to this opinion can be shown through numerous examples. One of the more interesting instances was when Brezhnev took pains to explain why certain suggestions raised during discussion of the draft of the 1977 constitution–proposals to abolish the union republics and to pursue an even more egalitarian social policy–could not be adopted. L. I. Brezhnev, *Leninskim kursom (On Lenin's Path)* (Moscow: Politizdat, 1978), vol. 6, pp. 524–525.

37. Based on my own interviews with Soviet researchers and on reports from Western colleagues with similar experiences. See, in addition, Solomon, *Soviet Criminologists and Criminal Policy;* and Jerry F. Hough, *The Struggle for the Third World* (Washington, D.C.: Brookings Institution, 1986).

39. "Tendencies" is the label that Franklyn Griffiths preferred for potential interests groups, in part to take account of the official intolerance of organized factionalism. See his "A Tendency Analysis of Soviet Policy-Making," in H. Gordon Skilling and Franklyn Griffiths, eds., *Interest Groups in Soviet Politics* (Princeton, N.J.: Princeton University Press, 1971), pp. 335–377. Khrushchev's willingness to publish plenum transcripts (but only beginning in December 1958) can be attributed partly to his preoccupation with rejuvenating the Party, but probably mostly to his interest in using the Central Committee as a means of bringing leverage to bear over the other members of the Presidium. Two plenum transcripts have been published since Khrushchev's ouster: the March 1965 session on agriculture and the June 1983 session (under Andropov) on ideological questions.

40. See, for example, Hough and Fainsod, *How the Soviet Union Is Governed,* pp. 293–297.

41. This is a central theme in Gustafson, *Reform in Soviet Politics,* esp. Ch. 6.

42. In labor policy, for example, there have been some notable advances in specialists' understanding of labor turnover and the causes of poor labor discipline. But there still is surprisingly little awareness of even the existence, let alone the associated advantages and disadvantages of broadly different stategies for managing the labor market, which give different weights to the roles played by wage policy, training, job placement, and various

forms of direct state intervention. See my Ph.D. dissertation, "Managing the Soviet Labor Market: Politics and Policymaking Under Brezhnev" (University of Michigan, 1984).

71. As a result of efforts to reconstruct the social history of Stalinism, the positive aspects of this formula (Stalin's "carrots") have begun to receive increased attention. See, for example, Sheila Fitzpatrick, "Stalin and the Making of a New Elite, 1928–1937," *Slavic Review* 38, no. 3 (1979), pp. 377–402; and Vera Dunham, *In Stalin's Time* (Cambridge: Cambridge University Press, 1976).

72. For a useful, but now forgotten discussion of this issue, see the symposium "Toward a 'Communist Welfare State'?" *Problems of Communism* 9, no. 1 (1960), pp. 1–22, and no. 3, pp. 44–51.

73. *Pravda*, March 7, 1953, p. 1.

74. The erosion of order in the labor camps, which apparently began even before Stalin's death and accelerated thereafter, is treated at length by Aleksandr 1. Solzhenitsyn, *The Gulag Archipelago, 1918–1956,* trans. Harry Willetts (New York: Harper & Row, 1976), vol. 3, part 5.

75. At times, Khrushchev appeared interested in expanding opportunities for meaningful popular participation and voice in local government and enterprise management. But the First Secretary's behavior was equivocal, and nothing lasting came of it.

80. The following paragraphs draw heavily on my article, "Gorbachev's Social Contract," *Soviet Economy* 3, no. 1 (1987) pp. 54–89.

81. On the rise in worker militancy, see Betsy Gidwitz, "Labor Unrest in the Soviet Union," *Problems of Communism* 31, no. 6 (1982), pp. 25–42.

82. For some of the details, see Hauslohner, "Managing the Soviet Labor Market," pp. 425–445.

83. Hauslohner, "Gorbachev's Social Contract," pp. 62–63.

84. For a broadly similar, albeit more cautiously stated proposition concerning the impact of generational solidarity, see Bialer, *Stalin's Successors,* p. 61. In addition, there is a variety of empirical evidence, apart from the aging of the Brezhnev leadership and its implicit reluctance to admit younger members, that is at least consistent with the hypothesis of an unusually solidary elite generation. See, in particular, Jerry F. Hough, "The Generation Gap and the Brezhnev Succession," *Problems of Communism* 28, no. 4 (1979), pp. 1–16; George W. Breslauer, "Is There a Generation Gap in the Soviet Political Establishment?" *Soviet Studies* 36, no. 1 (1984), pp. 1–25; and Beissinger, "In Search of Generations in Soviet Politics."

85. X [George F. Kennan], "The Sources of Soviet Conduct," *Foreign Affairs* 25, no. 4 (July 1947), pp. 566–582.

6　*The Friends and Foes of Change: Reformism and Conservatism in the Soviet Union*

STEPHEN F. COHEN

> *The combination of conservative institutions with revolutionary ideas meant that the Republic was the first successful attempt to reconcile the conservative and revolutionary traditions in France. But it also meant that in the twentieth century the forces of change were resisted and obstructed to the point of frustration.*
>
> —David Thomson, *Democracy in France*

> *The theme of the meeting, "Tradition and Innovation," offers an occasion to talk about serious things.*
>
> —Mikhail Romm (1962)

Change in the Stalinist system, and stubborn resistance to change, have been the central features of Soviet political life since Stalin's death in 1953. The rival forces of "innovation and tradition," to use the language of the official press, have become "two poles" in Soviet politics and society, which are expressed through "sharp clashes between people standing on both sides of the psychological barrier."[1]

Western students of Soviet affairs were slow to perceive this deep-rooted conflict. Accustomed to seeing only one political tradition and thus only continuity in Soviet history, and to imagining the Soviet Union as a frozen "totalitarian" system, most scholars began to think seriously about change and the large controversies it has engendered only in the mid-1960s.[2] Although a valuable scholarship on the subject now exists,[3] it remains inadequate in important respects. Conflict over change is often treated narrowly—either in terms of high Soviet politics and thus apart from society itself, or, at another extreme, in terms of avowed dissidents and thus outside the official political system. No less important, many treatments of the subject lack historical dimensions; and quite a few are couched in a jargon-ridden or value-laden language that obscures more than it reveals.

I propose to argue that the fundamental division between these "two poles" in Soviet life is best understood as a social and political confrontation between reformism and conservatism in the sense that these terms convey in other countries. In generalizing about different aspects of this great conflict during the quarter of a century since 1953, I shall raise some questions that I cannot answer. My overview of the post-Stalin era should therefore be read also as a proposed agenda for further discussion.

REFORMISM AND CONSERVATISM

The terms "reformist" and "conservative" do not embrace the full diversity of political outlook, ranging from far left to far right, that has emerged so dramatically in the Soviet Union since the 1950s. As in other societies, these terms designate only mainstream, not extremist, attitudes toward the status quo and toward change. Even a spectrum of political outlook inside the Soviet Communist Party, for example, would require at least four categories: authentic democrats, reformers, conservatives, and neo-Stalinist reactionaries.[4] But while full-fledged democrats and neo-Stalinists may respectively share many reformist and conservative attitudes, the policies of either would mean radicalism in the Soviet context today, not reform or conservatism. In times of profound crisis, reformism and conservatism everywhere usually give rise to extremist trends and may even grow into their most extreme manifestations—revolution and counterrevolution.[5] But apart from extraordinary historical moments, reformers and conservatives represent the majority of mainstream antagonists—the friends and foes of change—in the Soviet Union as well as in other countries.

Though most scholars use other words to characterize these antagonists in the Soviet Union,[6] the terms reformer and conservative are preferable in important ways. Unlike "functional technocratic modernizer" and similar contrivances, they are not jargonistic or exotic. Unlike "liberal and dogmatist" or "revisionist and orthodox," they do not prejudge or simplify the nature of Soviet reformism and conservatism, which are complex amalgams of opinion and attitudes requiring further analysis rather than restrictive labels. (It is a serious analytical mistake, for example, to insist that real change or reform in the Soviet Union must mean "liberalization" or "democratization" in our sense of these words.) The terms anti-Stalinist and neo-Stalinist are very important, but they identify components within the larger conflict. Above all, archetypical reformers and conservatives are, as even the reticent Soviet press makes clear, "two popular types" in Soviet life, and the universal meaning of reformism and conservatism corresponds fully to the "partisans of the two directions" in the conflicts of the past twenty-five years. Or as the conservative Molotov put it, "There are ... reforming Communists, and then there are the real Communists."[7]

Reformism and conservatism, therefore, are concepts that require no special definition in the Soviet context. Both tendencies take on certain national characteristics in different countries because they are expressed in the different idioms of those political cultures. (Soviet conservatives today often speak, for example, in a neo-Stalinist or nineteenth-century Slavophile idiom.) Moreover, the full nature of reformism and conservatism everywhere is always historical, changing from one period to another. (Liberalism and conservatism in England, France, and the

United States are not the same today as they were earlier in the twentieth century.) But despite these cultural and historical variations, the basic antagonism between reformers and conservatives is similar in different countries, including the Soviet Union.

Reformism is that outlook, and those policies, which seek through measured change to improve the existing order without fundamentally transforming existing social, political, and economic foundations or going beyond prevailing ideological values. Reformism finds both its discontent and its program, and seeks its political legitimacy and success, within the parameters of the existing order. This distinguishes it from radicalism. The essential reformist argument is that the potential of the existing system and the promise of the established ideology—for example, Marxist socialism in the Soviet Union or liberal democracy in the United States—have not been realized, and that they can and must be fulfilled. The reformist premise is that change is progress. Unlike the conservative the reformer everywhere therefore tends to be agnostic about history and cults of the past. He is opposed to "prejudices inherited from the yesterday of our life," to the "tendency to accept as generally valid many propositions that were appropriate for only one period of our history."[8]

The pivot of conservatism is, on the other hand, a deep reverence for the past, a sentimental defense of existing institutions, routines, and orthodoxies which live on from the past, and an abiding fear of change as the harbinger of disorder and of a future that will be worse than the present as well as a sacrilege of the past. Conservatism is often little more than the sum total of inertia, habit, and vested interests. But it can also be a cogent philosophical justification of the status quo as the culmination of everything good in the historical past and thus the only sturdy bridge to the future.[9] Many conservatives can distinguish between stability and immobilism, and they do not flatly reject all change. But the conservative insistence that any change be slow and tightly controlled by established authority, based on law and order, and conform to prevailing orthodoxies is usually prohibitive. In the end, conservatives usually prefer cults of the past and those authorities (notably, the armed forces and the political police) which guard order against change, native tradition against "alien" corruption, the present against the future.[10]

Authentic reformism and conservatism are always social and political. Both trends are expressed below, in society, in popular sentiments and attitudes, and above, in the middle and higher reaches of the political system, in groups, factions, and parties. And still higher, so to speak, they take the more exalted form of ideological and philosophical propositions.

Both reformism and conservatism have been apparent as antagonists on all three of these levels in the Soviet Union since the 1950s. Although we lack the kind of polling and other survey information available for other countries, we know, for example, from firsthand accounts, that profoundly conservative attitudes are widespread among ordinary citizens and officials alike.[11] Detailed scholarly studies point out the sustained struggles between reformist and conservative groups inside the high political establishment, including the party itself.[12] And, as we shall see, the ideological and even philosophical dimensions of this quarrel have become particularly evident in recent years.

What we do not know, and indeed barely perceive, is the relationship between these trends in society below and in the political apparatus above. Though this is partly a problem of inadequate information, it derives also from the untenable but persistent notion that Soviet party-state officialdom is somehow insulated from society itself. This conception makes no empirical sense in a country where the state employs almost every citizen and the party has 18 million members. All of the trends in society, even those expressed by dissidents, also exist, however subterraneanly, inside political officialdom. There is at best, as one Western scholar argues, a "soft boundary" between the two.[13] Once we abandon the commonplace image of a gulf separating political officialdom and society, and see them instead, in the imagery of a Soviet dissident, as "upstairs" and "downstairs,"[14] the fuller social dimensions of the political conflict between Soviet reformism and conservatism will at least come into view.

At the level of politics and policy the conflict between reformism and conservatism derives its scope and intensity from the fact that it is simultaneously a quarrel about the past, the present, and the future. The historical agnosticism of the reformer and the historicism of the conservative are therefore especially antagonistic in a country such as the Soviet Union, where what its citizens call "living history" has been unusually traumatic. Not only the immediate Stalinist past but also the remote tsarist past are subjects of fierce controversy. Conservatives bitterly protest the reformist "deheroization" of the past and the view in which "the past, present, and future ... turn out to be isolated, shut off from each other." The conservative extols the "continuity of generations", the reformer replies, "If the children do not criticize the fathers, mankind does not move ahead." For conservatives, reformist perspectives "distort the past"; for reformers, conservatives "idealize the past" and try "to save the past from the present."[15]

These historical controversies have been an essential part of almost all policy disputes throughout the post-Stalin era. They reflect the political struggle between the forces of reform and conservatism inside Soviet officialdom from 1953 to the present—from an official reformation to a far-reaching conservative reaction.

FROM REFORMISM TO CONSERVATISM

Because of the unusually despotic nature of his long rule, Stalin's death unleashed a decade-long triumph of Soviet reformism which was disproportionate to its actual strength in society or officialdom. Virtually every area of Soviet life was affected (and improved). Though bitterly opposed, often contradictory, and ultimately limited, the changes of the 1950s and early 1960s constituted a reformation—within the limits of the authoritarian system—in Soviet politics and society, as indicated by a brief recitation of the most important reforms.

The kind of personal dictatorship exercised by Stalin for more than twenty years ended and the Communist Party was restored as the ruling political institution. Twenty-five years of mass terror came to an end and the political police, the main agency of Stalin's dictatorship, was brought under control. Millions of prison camp survivors were freed and many who had perished in the terror were legally exonerated, thereby enabling survivors and relatives to regain full citizenship. Many administrative abuses and bureaucratic privileges were curtailed. Educated society began to participate more fully in political and intellectual life. A wide array of economic and welfare reforms were carried out. Major revisions were made in Soviet censorship practices, in the official ideology of Marxism-Leninism, and in foreign policy.

Insofar as this was official reformism, or reform from above, Nikita Khrushchev was its leader, and his overthrow in 1964 marked the beginning of its political defeat.[16] Khrushchev himself was a contradictory figure. His background and career made him the representative of the old as well as the new; and some of his policies, as in certain areas of science, favored conservative forces. But in terms of his overall administration, Khrushchev was, as Russians say, a great reformer *(velikii reformator)*.

Nonetheless, Khrushchev and his faction at the top were only part of a much broader reformist movement inside Soviet officialdom. During the decade after 1953, the struggle between the friends and foes of change spread to all areas of policy making—to the areas of administration and planning, industry and agriculture, science, history, culture, law, family matters, welfare, ideology, and foreign affairs.[17] In each of these areas, reform found notable spokesmen and important allies.[18] Like conservatism, whose adherents ranged from old-line Stalinists to Tory-style moderates, Soviet reformism must be understood as an amalgam of diverse types and motives. It included technocrats in search only of limited change in their special areas as well as authentic democrats; it derived from self-interest as well as idealism. But in relation to the overarching question of change, something akin to two distinct parties—reformist and conservative—emerged inside Soviet officialdom, and within the Communist Party itself, counterposing rival interests, policies, and ideas over a wide range of issues in all political quarters.[19]

Conservatism, as a defense of the inherited Stalinist order, was more fully formed as an ideological and policy movement in the years immediately following Stalin's death. By the early 1960s, however, reformers had developed a characteristic cluster of reformist policies, historical perspectives, and ideological propositions. Most of these were developed, both as critique and program, in opposition to conservative ones, which still drew heavily upon the Stalinist past. There were many of these reformist ideas by the early 1960s, and they cannot easily be summarized. A few examples must suffice.

While conservatives eulogized the tsarist and Stalinist pasts, and particularly the 1930s when many existing Soviet institutions took shape, reformers rehabilitated the radical intelligentsia of the nineteenth century, the Soviet 1920s, and a generation of old Bolsheviks purged by Stalin. While conservatives accented the authoritarian strands in Marxism-Leninism, the Stalin cult, and the dangers of revisionism, reformers stressed socialist democracy, Lenin himself, the criminality of Stalin, and the dangers of dogmatism. Against the conservative themes of Russian nationalism, Soviet hegemony in the communist world, and xenophobia, reformers emphasized internationalism, different roads to socialism, and an opening to the West. In contrast to the conservative preference for heavy-handed censorship, reformers promoted varying degrees of cultural and intellectual liberalism. As opposed to the overly centralized Stalinist system of economic planning and administration, with its decades of heavy industrialism, agricultural retardation, waste, and austerity, reformers advocated the market, decentralized initiative efficiency, consumer goods, and innovations in order to encourage private initiative in the collective system. Against the Stalinist tradition of terror, reformers called for rule of law and due process.[20]

Soviet reformers won many victories during the Khrushchev years. But reform from above everywhere is always limited in substance and duration, and it is usually followed by a conservative backlash. This circumstance is partly a result of the nature of reformism, which struggles against the natural inertia of people and institutions on behalf of limited goals. Many adherents of reform are quickly satisfied, many allies are easily unnerved, and many who only tolerated reform are soon driven to oppose further change. All become part of a neoconservative consensus, defenders of the new, reformed status quo, and critics of reformist "excess." Indeed, this reformist-conservative rhythm is thought to be axiomatic in American and British politics, where Republicans and Tories are expected to follow Democrats and Labourites.

The overthrow of Khrushchev in October 1964 reflected this swing of the pendulum in Soviet officialdom, and possibly in society as well. His fall ushered in, after an interlude of uncertain direction in 1964–65, a far-reaching conservative reaction, which brought an end to major reform, and even some counterreform in most areas of Soviet society, from economics and law, to historiography, culture, and ideology. Since 1966, and especially since the Soviet overthrow of the reform communist government in Czechoslovakia in 1968, the Brezhnev administration has been a regime of conservatism. It has revived many of the conservative practices noted above as well as the preeminent symbol of the past, Stalin himself. Its antireformist spirit and policies have been expressed in a galaxy of refurbished conservative catch phrases and campaigns—"stability in cadres," "law and order," "the strengthening of organization, discipline, and responsibility in all spheres," "military-heroic patriotism," "developed socialism," "vigilance against bourgeois influences," and more.[21] It has, in short, reasserted conservative views on the past, the present, and the future.

The conservative reaction since 1964, though far-reaching, has not meant a restoration of, or return to, Stalinist policies. With society and politics themselves, conservative attitudes and policies change. Stalinism no longer defines Soviet realities, and therefore mainstream Soviet conservatism, as it did in the early 1950s. The Brezhnev government reversed some reforms of the Khrushchev years;

but, for the most part, it has tempered and administered already accomplished re-forms as part of the new status quo, while deploring earlier "excesses" and setting itself against further change. (Republicans and Tories did the same upon re-turning to office in the United States and England in the 1950s.)

Some ideas and policies once associated with Soviet reformers—consumerism, higher investment in agriculture, welfarism, scientific management, legal proceduralism, detente, repudiation of Stalin's "excesses"—have even been incor-porated into the new conservatism. This does not demonstrate, as some Western observers have thought, the reformist spirit of the Brezhnev government, because these once reformist ideas have been infused with deeply conservative meaning. "Economic reform," for example, has been an official idea intermittently since 1964; but the original reforms have been stripped of their essentials—the role of the market and decentralization—so that, in the words of one reformer, they have become "purely superficial, partial changes which do not affect the essence of the prereform system."[22] The official repudiation of reform since the mid-1960s is clearly understood by people inside the Soviet Union: "We are ruled not by a Communist or a fascist party and not by a Stalinist party, but by a status quo party."[23]

By the late 1960s, the increasingly censorious conservatism of the Brezhnev government had muted reformist voices, and thus explicit conflict, in many pol-icy areas. At the same time, however, and possibly for this reason, the conflict be-tween reformers and conservatives broke out dramatically in a different way in the official press: in an often abstract controversy about the nature of Russia as a historical society. Focusing on philosophical, cultural, and even religious themes, the two rival outlooks have now been openly at odds for more than a decade.[24] This controversy echoes the split between Westerners and Slavophiles in nine-teenth-century Russia, but its real importance is contemporary and intensely po-litical. It is a confrontation, couched in a philosophical and older Russian idiom, between present-day Soviet reformism and conservatism. The traditional idiom of the conservatives, with their advocacy of Russia's "eternal values," has become particularly forthright, leading reformers to protest that their ideas are "bor-rowed, transcribed, taken on hire from the storehouse of conservative literature of the past century."[25]

This neoconservative philosophy, which is in many respects congruent with the policy spirit and Russian nationalism of the Brezhnev government, has spread throughout the Soviet press (and *samizdat*) and demonstrated remarkable appeal to many segments of the population. Its popularity tends to confirm firsthand ev-idence that official conservatism is not a regime-made artifice but a reflection of broad and deep currents in Soviet officialdom and society.[26] It has become clear that the great reforms of the Khrushchev years derived more from unusual histor-ical circumstances than from the actual political and social strength of reformism in the Soviet Union. For a fuller perspective on the post-Stalin era and on the fu-ture, we need, then, at least a brief look at the historical origins of contemporary reformism and conservatism in the Stalinist past.

THE STALINIST ROOTS OF REFORMISM
AND CONSERVATISM

The first great reform in Soviet history was the introduction of the New Economic Policy (NEP) in 1921. Intended to replace the extremist practices of the civil war years, NEP quickly grew into a whole series of policies and ideas which Lenin, the father of NEP, called "a reformist approach."[27] For four years after Lenin's death in 1924, NEP remained official Soviet policy, with Nikolai Bukharin as its interpreter and great defender. Thus, when Stalin forcibly abolished NEP in 1929, he inadvertently created a historical model for future generations of communist reformers. Since that time, and especially after 1953, NEP—with its dual economy, concepts of market and plan, cultural diversity, more liberal politics, and Leninist legitimacy—has exercised a powerful appeal to anti-Stalinist party reformers everywhere, from Moscow to Eastern and Western Europe. Soviet reformers have revived many NEP economic ideas, reformist historians have studied NEP admiringly; cultural liberals have cited its tolerant censorship; and reform politicians have sought legitimacy in it.[28]

With the defeat of the Bukharinist opposition (or "right deviation"), the end of NEP, and the onset of Stalin's revolution from above in 1929, party reformism became the special enemy and victim of Stalinism. There were at least two serious attempts by high officials to initiate reform from above during the Stalin years. The first involved the so-called Kirov group in the Politburo in 1933–34, which proposed to ameliorate the terrible hardships of forcible collectivization and heavy industrialization. The second was in 1947–48; it apparently involved similar proposals, by the Politburo member Nikolai Voznesensky and others, for change in economic policy. Both attempts to reform Stalinism ended horribly—in the great terror of 1936–39 and in the Leningrad purge of 1949 and Voznesensky's execution.[29]

Nonetheless, this melancholy history of failed reform shows that even during the worst Stalin years, there was a reformist impulse among high party and state officials. These early strivings toward a "Moscow Spring"(as an insider termed them in 1936) were the official antecedents of Khrushchev's reformism, as he tacitly acknowledged by associating his de-Stalinization campaign with the Kirov affair and by rehabilitating Voznesensky. But it also shows that reform from above stood no chance in the conditions of Stalin's terroristic autocracy and in the face of his personal hostility, which remained adamant to the end.[30]

And yet while Stalin martyred reform at every turn, his system and policies were creating the future political and social base of reformism. The historical Stalinism of 1929–53 was an extraordinary composite of dualities. Stalinism began as a radical act of revolution from above and ended as a rigidly conservative social and political system. It combined revolutionary traditions with tsarist ones; humanitarian ideas of social justice with terror; radical ideology with traditional social policies; the myths of socialist democracy and party rule with the reality of

personal dictatorship; modernization with archaic practices; a routinized bureaucracy with administrative caprice.

Reformism and conservatism grew out of these dualities after Stalin in two
general ways. First, the values and ideas of both post-Stalin reformers and conservatives had been perpetuated in Stalinism. Russian nationalism, terror, and privilege came to dominate, for example, but their opposites remained part of the official ideology. They were maintained in an uneasy state of latent conflict, as a kind
of dual Soviet political culture, by the Stalin cult and the terror.[31] After Stalin's
death, these currents went separate political ways into the conflicts of 1953–79, especially into the conflict between anti-Stalinism and neo-Stalinism, which in the
1950s and early 1960s played a special role in the confrontation between reformers
and conservatives.

The second way in which the Stalinist system prepared its own reformation
was, as Marxists say, dialectical. Stalinism created within itself an alternative
model of political rule.[32] The agent of this potential change was not, as Marxist
critics of Stalinism had hoped for so long, an activist working class, but Stalin's
own political-administrative bureaucracy. Having grown large and powerful under his rule since the 1930s, the leading strata *(nachal'stvo)* of the party-state bureaucracy gained almost everything—income, privilege, status, power over those
below. But what they lacked was no less important: security of position and, even
more, of life. Stalin's terror inflicted one demographic trauma after another. And
no one was more vulnerable after 1934 than the party-state *nachal'stvo*.

The history and ethos of Stalinism made this bureaucracy profoundly conservative in most political and social ways.[33] It yearned, however, for one great reform that would free it from the capricious, terroristic regime at the top, and allow it to become a real bureaucracy—that is, a conservative force based on
stability, personal security, and predictability. While Stalin lived, even the highest
officials felt themselves to be "temporary people" and sought protection against
the abnormality of the terror in various legalisms.[34] But normality in this sense
could come only with the end of the autocrat.

Both reformism and conservatism were thus already in place when Stalin's
death finally came in March 1953. The first words of his heirs, imploring the population to avoid "panic and disarray," revealed them as fearful conservatives (who
always imagine disorder below) in important respects. But fear of retribution
from below and another terror from above led them quickly to major reforms,
from which others followed: the dismantling and curtailment of Stalin's primary
institutions (his secretariat, the terror system, and the cult) and the restoration of
party dictatorship and collective leadership.[35] Restoring the party to political primacy was in itself a major change that had far-reaching ramifications. It proved
to be remarkably easy, reformist rather than revolutionary, partly because it
promised at last protection from terror to high officials throughout the system.
Indeed, this was the essential reformist meaning of Khrushchev's "secret" speech
against Stalin in 1956. For most high officials, this may have been not only popular but also sufficient.

These circumstances help to explain the success of Khrushchev's initial reforms, even though reformism probably was, and remains, a minority outlook in Soviet officialdom. His successes and rise to power in 1953–58 were based on a kind of reformism, or de-Stalinization, which had broader appeal in these special historical circumstances. The majority of Soviet officials and elites wanted, it seems clear, an end to terror, a diminishing of the police system, some historical revisionism, relaxation of international tensions, and certain welfare reforms (in pensions, for example) which benefited them as well. They wanted and got, a thaw—but not a spring.

After 1958, Khrushchev's reformism and renewed de-Stalinization campaign began to mean something different. They came to include quasi-populist policies, or ideas, that impinged directly upon the nature of the central party-state bureaucracy and its relations with society, rather than with the regime above.[36] The quiescent conservative majority emerged and began to resist. Khrushchev became an embattled leader. That he managed to achieve as much as he did after 1958, despite the opposition, his many ill-conceived policies, and his personal inadequacies as a reform leader,[37] is probably explained partly by the momentum and political appeal of anti-Stalinism. When this cause was spent in the early 1960s, so, too, were Khrushchev's great reforms.

SOVIET CONSERVATISM
AND THE FUTURE OF REFORM

The real obstacle to future reform in the Soviet Union is not this or that institution, group, faction, or leader, but the profound conservatism that seems to dominate them all, from the ordinary family to the Politburo, from local authorities to the state *nachal'stvo*. It can be argued that the Soviet Union has become, both downstairs and upstairs, one of the most conservative countries in the world.[38] Real discussion of the prospects for further change therefore must await fuller scholarly study of this political and social conservatism, which manifests itself daily, in all areas of life, as a preference for tradition and order and a fear of innovation and disorder.

It may be argued that a system born in revolution and still professing revolutionary ideas cannot be called conservative, but history has witnessed other such transformations, as well as the inner deradicalization of revolutionary ideologies.[39] Indeed the conservative aftermath of a great social revolution may be a kind of historical law.[40] If so, we might expect this to have been doubly the case in Russia, where revolution from below in 1917 was followed by Stalin's revolution from above in 1929–33. Early Bolsheviks worried that even their own party might end in this way. One warned: "History is full of examples of the transformation of parties of revolution into parties of order. Sometimes the only mementos of a revolutionary party are the watchwords which it has inscribed on public buildings."[41]

There are, in addition, many specific, and mutually reinforcing, sources of Soviet conservatism. Although specialists disagree as to the most important factors in Soviet political life, almost all of these factors have contributed to its conservatism. There is the legacy of tsarist Russia, with its own bureaucratic and conservative traditions. There is the subsequent bureaucratization of Soviet life in the 1930s, which proliferated conservative norms and created a *nomenklatura* class of zealous defenders of position and privilege.[42] There is, in this connection, the persistent scarcity of goods and services, which redoubles the resistance of vested interests. There is the increasing age of Soviet ruling elites. And there is even the official ideology, whose domestic thrust turned many years ago from creating a new order to extolling the existing one.

Underlying all of these factors is the Soviet historical experience with its particular combination of monumental achievements and mountainous disasters. In sixty years, man-made catastrophes have repeatedly victimized millions of ordinary citizens and officials alike—the first European war, revolution, civil war, two great famines, forcible collectivization, Stalin's great terror, World War II, and more. Out of this experience, which is still autobiographical for many people, have come the joint pillars of today's Soviet conservatism: a towering pride in the nation's modernizing and Great-Power achievements, together with an abiding anxiety that the next disaster forever looms and that change is "some sinister Beethovean knock of fate at the door."[43] This is a conservatism at once prideful and fearful, and thus powerful. It appears to influence most segments of the population, even many dissidents, to be a real bond between upstairs and downstairs and therefore the main obstacle to change.

Much would seem to favor, then, only conservatism in Soviet politics. And yet, as we have seen, this has not been the entire story of the post-Stalin years; nor is it now. Advocates of change, however weak their position and however diverse their reformist aspirations, continue to exist in most policy areas and even to hold responsible positions in lower and middle levels of the party-state officialdom.[44] Indeed, one enduring reform of the post-Stalin years has been a broadening of the political system sufficient to tolerate such people even during a conservative regime. Therefore, some of the general factors favoring a resurgence of official reformism must also be taken into account. Leaving aside the possibility of serious domestic crises, and assuming that Soviet reformers stand a chance only in an international environment of diminishing tensions, three weaknesses of Soviet conservatism should be emphasized because they point to permanent sources of reformism in the Soviet system.

Like conservatives everywhere, Soviet opponents of change need a usable past in order to justify and defend the status quo. The relevant past includes, however, the criminal history of Stalinism. Soviet conservatives have coped with this problem in two ways since the fall of Khrushchev. They have selectively rehabilitated the Stalinist past, largely in terms of the great Soviet victory over Germany in World War II, and without fully rehabilitating Stalin himself.[45] And they have groped toward a surrogate past in tsarist history. Neither seems to be a durable solution. Historical de-Stalinization, which is a powerful source of political re-formism, retains its appeal not only because tens of millions died, but because millions of wartime casualties can be blamed directly on the Stalinist government. As for the tsarist past, though partially rehabilitated under Stalin and of consider-able appeal today, its traditions are nonetheless contrary to the ideas of the Rus-sian revolution, which official conservatives still embrace as the main source of their legitimacy. These two traditions cannot be durably reconciled. Ultimately, they inspire rival currents, conflict not harmony in political life, as was the case in post-revolutionary France.[46]

The second conservative weakness, and source of reformism, is the plain dis-crepancy between the official ideology and everyday Soviet realities. Except for a small segment of the population, this is not foremost a discrepancy between democratic ideas and dictatorial practices, but something more fundamental. As an official ideology, Soviet communism has come increasingly to mean, in addi-tion to Russian nationalism, consumer goods plus the welfare state. These com-mitments are exceedingly important to ordinary citizens, to middle-class officials, and to the government. They have been the main domestic pledges of the conser-vative Brezhnev government since the mid-1960s, as well as its most glaring fail-ures.[47] Though elementary welfare provisions were achieved much earlier, low standards of living, chronic shortages of basic foodstuffs and housing, and the scarcity of other consumer goods remain widespread and intractable problems of everyday Soviet life.

As repeatedly expressed ideological commitments, to officialdom as well as to society-at-large, these consumer-welfare promises cannot be easily withdrawn or forever deferred. They are a relentless threat to Soviet conservatives because they attract constant attention to the inadequacies of the centralized economic system and thus keep meaningful economic reform permanently on the agenda. And, as both reformers and conservatives understand, this kind of economic reform, in-volving decentralization and the market, must have reformist implications in po-litical life as well.[48]

The third factor favoring reform also involves official ideology. The role of Marxism-Leninism, or communism, may have declined in recent years, but it re-mains the essential framework for discourse and conflict throughout official So-viet politics. No reformist or conservative movement anywhere can be successful if it is estranged from established political norms and culture. Soviet conserva-tives and reformers must have a Soviet face; they must find inspiration and legiti-macy somewhere within historical Marxism-Leninism. Conservatives are trying, as reformers complain, to fill "Marxist formulas" with their own meanings.[49] But Marxism-Leninism is an unreliable conservative vehicle because it is an ideology, even in its dogmatized version, based upon the very idea, desirability, and inexo-rability of change. Soviet reformers miss no opportunity to make this point: "Any apologetics for things as they are is alien to the materialistic dialectic. ... This applies to any particular form society may have assumed at any stage in its development. To search constantly for new and imaginative ways to transform reality—that is the motto of the dialectic."[50]

In this respect, Soviet reformers have an important advantage over their nineteenth-century counterparts in tsarist officialdom, whose experience may be highly relevant.[51] Struggling against a conservative majority of Russian officials in the decades leading up to the major reforms from above in the 1860s, tsarist reformers were seriously hampered by an official ideology thoroughly hostile to the idea of real change. They had to seek ideological inspiration and legitimacy elsewhere, in suspect "foreign" cultures. Official Soviet reformers do not have this problem, or at least not as acutely. Moreover, they can, and regularly do, point to existing models of communist reform in Eastern Europe as examples which are Marxist-Leninist, and thus fraternal rather than "foreign."[52]

The experience of official reformers under tsarism suggests another important perspective. The growth of reformist sentiments and "enlightened" officials was a slow, cumulative process. It extended over decades and included many setbacks. During the long winters of reform, such ideas could openly circulate only outside the bureaucracy, in circles of nineteenth-century nonconformists, before percolating into the bureaucracy to influence policy. The role of today's Soviet dissidents and their *samizdat* discussions is pertinent to this process. Incapable of effecting reform themselves, since it can come only from above, their real function must be to contribute to the growth of reformist ideas and thus to the "enlightenment" of future officials.[53] Viewed in this way, it could be argued that the sudden, escalating reforms of the Khrushchev years were premature, that the "enlightenment" process was just beginning in officialdom, and that the still ongoing conservative reaction is not the end but only a stage in the history of post-Stalin reform.

This perspective raises a final question. Successful reform is always a result of political coalitions, a fact of special importance to Soviet reformers, who apparently represent a distinct minority of officials. Unable to draw strength directly from protest movements below, as reformers in other societies have done, and advocating economic policies that threaten many petty administrators and even workers,[54] Soviet reformers can find allies only among the conservative majority of officials, who have seemed more attracted by neo-Stalinism in recent years. Is this a real possibility?

"The boundary between progressive and conservative runs through each of us," remarked a Czech official during the Prague Spring.[55] Soviet reformers must appeal to this "progressive" element in moderate conservatives. Historians tell us that conservatives are uncomfortable reformers but that many become reformers to save what they believe is most important in the existing order of things.[56] There is some evidence that in the 1960s a consensus for change was forming between moderate reformers and moderate conservatives, at least among the party intelligentsia. It seemed to center on commonly perceived problems such as the degradation of country life, declining labor productivity, drunkenness, the Stalinist past, and the heavy-handed censorship that frustrated conservatives as well as reformers.[57] The emergence of such a consensus may not yet be in the making, but it is the best, and probably only, hope for reform.

NOTES

ABOUT THE AUTHOR: **Stephen F. Cohen** is professor of politics and director of Russian Studies at Princeton University.

1. A. M. Rumiantsev, "Vstupaiushchemu v mir nauki," *Pravda*, June 8, 1967; "Kogda otstaiut ot vremeni," *Pravda* (editorial), January 27, 1967; and O. Latsis, "Novoe nado otstaivat," *Novyi mir*, no. 10, 1965, p. 255. The theme of innovation versus tradition has been the subject of endless polemics since 1953. It also runs persistently through Soviet fiction, from Vladimir Dudintsev's *Ne khlebom edinym*, published in 1956, to Aleksandr Zinov'ev's *Svetloe budushchee* (Lausanne, 1978).

2. For critical discussion of these habits in Soviet studies, see Stephen F. Cohen, "Bolshevism and Stalinism," in Robert C. Tucker, ed., *Stalinism: Essays in Historical Interpretation* (New York, 1977), pp. 3–29; Carl A. Linden, *Khrushchev and the Soviet Leadership* (Baltimore, 1966), pp. 1–9; and William Taubman, "The Change to Change in Communist Systems," in Henry W. Morton and Rudolf L. Tökés, eds., *Soviet Politics and Society in the 1970's* (New York, 1974), pp. 369–94.

3. Among the most interesting studies are Zbigniew Brzezinski, "The Soviet Political System: Transformation or Degeneration?," in Zbigniew Brzezinski, ed., *Dilemmas of Change in Soviet Politics* (New York, 1969), pp. 1–34; Jerry F. Hough, *The Soviet Union and Social Science Theory* (Cambridge, Mass., 1977), chap. 1; George W. Breslauer, "Khrushchev Reconsidered," *Problems of Communism*, September-October, 1976, pp. 18–33; and George W. Breslauer, *Five Images of the Soviet Future: A Critical Review and Synthesis* (Berkeley, 1978).

4. My categories derive from, though they do not fully correspond to, the following firsthand accounts: Roy A. Medvedev, *On Socialist Democracy* (New York, 1975), chap. 3 and *passim*; Alexander Yanov, *Detente After Brezhnev: The Domestic Roots of Soviet Foreign Policy* (Berkeley, 1977); and Igor Glagolev, "Sovetskoe rukovodstvo: Segodnia i zavtra," *Russkaia mysl'*, August 31, 1978. Considerable information on trends in the party is available in *Politicheskii dnevnik* (2 vols; Amsterdam, 1972 and 1975).

5. Arno J. Mayer, *Dynamics of Counterrevolution in Europe, 1870–1956: An Analytic Framework* (New York, 1971), chap. 2.

6. There are important exceptions. See Sidney I. Ploss, *Conflict and Decision-Making in Soviet Russia: A Case Study of Agricultural Policy, 1953–63* (Princeton, 1965); Linden, *Khrushchev and the Soviet Leadership*, which includes an excellent discussion of this spectrum (pp. 18–21); and Moshe Lewin, *Political Undercurrents in Soviet Economic Debates: From Bukharin to the Modern Reformers* (Princeton, 1974).

7. Alexander Yanov, *Essays on Soviet Society* (*International Journal of Sociology*, vol. 6, no. 2–3; Summer-Fall, 1976), esp. pp. 75–175; G. Kozlov and M. Rumer, "Tol'ko nachalo (Zametki o khoziaistvennoi reforme)," *Novyi mir*, no. 11, 1966, p. 182; F. Chapchakhov, "Pod vidom gipotezy," *Literaturnaia gazeta*, August 16, 1972, which is an attack on, and an inadvertent confirmation of, Yanov's two "types"; and Molotov, quoted in Giuseppe Boffa, *Inside the Khrushchev Era* (New York, 1959), p. 108. The word conservative *(konservator)* is commonly used in the Soviet Union. Various words or expressions are used to express "reformer," though the English word (reformist) is coming into use. See Valentin Turchin, *Inertsiia strakha* (New York, 1977), p. 5. Soviet writers often use these concepts, with obvi-

ous implications for the reader, in analyzing other political societies. See, for example, M. P. Mchedlov, *Evoliutsiia sovremennogo katolitsizma* (Moscow, 1966).

8. V. Lakshin, "Ivan Denisovich, ego druz'ia i nedrugi," *Novyi mir,* no. 1, 1964, p. 230; Medvedev, *On Socialist Democracy,* p. 41.

9. For the range of factors (fear, self-interest, philosophy) that animate conservative opposition to economic reform in the Soviet Union, for example, see the series of articles by A. Birman in *Novyi mir* between 1965 and 1968, and especially his "Sut' reformy," in no. 12, 1968, pp. 185–204.

10. For a summary of the extensive literature on modern conservatism, see Clinton Rossiter, "Conservatism," *International Encyclopedia of the Social Sciences,* vol. 3 (New York, 1968), pp. 290–95.

11. See, for example, Turchin, *Inertsiia strakha;* Medvedev, *On Socialist Democracy;* Yanov, *Essays on Soviet Society,* Andrei Amalrik, *Will the Soviet Union Survive Until 1984?* (New York, 1970); and note 9 above.

12. In addition to the titles cited in note 6, see Michel Tatu, *Power in the Kremlin From Khrushchev to Kosygin* (New York, 1969); and H. Gordon Skilling and Franklyn Griffiths, eds., *Interest Groups in Soviet Politics* (Princeton, 1971).

13. See Lewin, *Political Undercurrents in Soviet Economic Debates,* pp. 262, 298.

14. Alexander Yanov, *The Russian New Right: Right-Wing Ideologies in the Contemporary USSR* (Berkeley, 1978), p. 15.

15. *Politicheskii dnevnik,* I, p. 123; F. Chapchakhov, "Pod vidom gipotezy," *Literaturnaia gazeta,* August 16, 1972; *Politicheskii dnevnik,* no. 66 (samizdat; Moscow, March 1970), p. 36; A. Iakovlev, "Protiv aniistorizma," *Literaturnaia gazeta,* November 15, 1975.

16. See Linden, *Khrushchev and the Soviet Leadership;* and Breslauer, "Khrushchev Reconsidered."

17. In addition to the titles cited in notes 6 and 12 above, see the sections on the 1950s and 1960s in the following works: Nancy Whittier Heer, *Politics and History in the Soviet Union* (Cambridge, Mass., 1971); Peter H. Juviler and Henry W. Morton, eds., *Soviet Policy-Making: Studies of Communism in Transition* (New York, 1967); Peter H. Juviler, *Revolutionary Law and Order: Politics and Social Change in the USSR* (New York, 1976); Gail Warshofsky Lapidus, *Women in Soviet Society: Equality, Development and Social Change* (Berkeley, 1978); Aron Katsenelinboigen, *Studies in Soviet Economic Planning* (White Plains, N.Y., 1978); Timothy McClure, "The Politics of Soviet Culture, 1964–1967," *Problems of Communism,* March-April, 1967, pp. 26–43.

18. Individuals such as Aleksandr Tvardovskii in literature; A. Birman, V. G. Venzher and G. S. Lisichkin in economics; A. M. Rumiantsev and F. M. Burlatskii in the social sciences; M. D. Shargorodskii in law; V. P. Danilov and M. Ia. Gefter in history; and so on. One *samizdat* writer has suggested that "it would be truer to call the epoch of Khrushchev, the epoch of Tvardovskii," because of his editorship of the reformist journal *Novyi mir.*

19. *Pravda* (January 27, 1967) discussed the reformist journal *Novyi mir* and the conservative journal *Oktiabr'* in terms of the "two poles" in Soviet politics. Soviet intellectuals sometimes spoke of them privately in the 1960s as the "organs of our two parties."

20. To give a few more cryptic examples of code words in the conflict, reformers and conservatives emphasized, respectively, the following: bureaucratism as the main danger—anarchy as the main danger; the Lenin of 1921–23—the Lenin of 1918–20; the importance of the intelligentsia—the importance of the worker and the soldier; the 20th and 22nd Party Congresses—the 23rd, 24th, and 25th Congresses; modernism in art—traditionalism in

art; internal problems—external threats; women's rights—the stability of the family; innovation—discipline; renewal of cadres—stability of cadres; social interests—the organic unity of society.

21. See, for example, *Razvitoe sotsialisticheskoe obshchestvo: Sushchnost', kriterii zrelosti, kritika revizionistskikh kontseptsii* (Moscow, 1973); P. M. Rogachev and M. A. Sverklin, *Patriotizm i obshchestvennyi progress* (Moscow, 1974); and the editorials in *Pravda*, February 5 and 24, and October 17, 1978. For discussion of important aspects of these conservative policies, see T. H. Rigby, "The Soviet Leadership: Towards a Self-Stabilizing Oligarchy?," *Soviet Studies*, October, 1970, pp. 167–91; his "The Soviet Regional Leadership: The Brezhnev Generation," *Slavic Review*, vol. 37, no. 1 (March 1978), pp. 1–24; and Breslauer, "Khrushchev Reconsidered."

22. Quoted in Iu. Subotskii, "Upravlenie, khozraschet, samostoiatel'nost'," *Novyi mir*, no. 7, 1969, p. 265.

23. Lev Kopelev, quoted in *The New York Times*, December 3, 1978, p. 14.

24. The controversy began with the rival journals *Novyi mir* and *Molodaia gvardiia*, but it has since spread to many publications. For an excellent survey and analysis, see Frederick C. Barghoorn, "The Political Significance of Great Russian Nationalism in Brezhnev's USSR With Particular Reference to the 'Pseudo-Slavophiles' " (unpublished paper delivered at the AAASS Conference, Washington, October 1977).

25. Yanov, *Essays on Soviet Society*, p. 124. For similar protests, see A. Dement'ev, "O traditsiiakh i narodnosti," *Novyi mir*, no. 4, 1969, pp. 215–35; Iakovlev, "Protiv antiistorizma," *Literaturnaia gazeta*, November 15, 1975; and the running objections in the *samizdat* journal *Politicheskii dnevnik*. Though the idiom is plainly Russian, it is sometimes universally conservative, even Burkean. See, for example, the eulogy of "social authority" and the "continuity of generations" in S. Semanov, *Serdtse rodina* (Moscow, 1977), pp. 92–3.

26. See note 11 above.

27. See Stephen F. Cohen, *Bukharin and the Bolshevik Revolution: A Political Biography, 1888–1938* (New York, 1973), pp. 132–38. Soviet reformers have been eager to identify NEP as "the first reform." See, for example, A. Birman, "Mysli posle plenuma," *Novyi mir*, no. 12, 1965, p. 194.

28. See, for example, Lewin, *Political Undercurrents in Soviet Economic Debates*, chap. 12 and *passim*; G. S. Lisichkin, *Plan i rynok* (Moscow, 1966); M. P. Kim, ed., *Novaia ekonomicheskaia politika: Voprosy teorii i istorii* (Moscow, 1974); and A. Rumiantsev, "Partiia i intelligentsia," *Pravda*, February 21, 1965.

29. Cohen, *Bukharin and the Bolshevik Revolution*, pp. 341–47; Ploss, *Conflict and Decision-Making in Soviet Russia*, pp. 28–58.

30. This was also the case in foreign policy. See Robert C. Tucker, *The Soviet Political Mind* (rev. ed.; New York, 1971), chap. 4.

31. For a cultural approach to Stalinism, see Robert C. Tucker, "Stalinism as Revolution From Above," in Tucker, ed., *Stalinism*, pp. 77–108. For the conservative aspects of Stalinism, see note 33 below.

32. As Moshe Lewin has argued in "The Social Background of Stalinism," in Tucker, ed., *Stalinism*, pp. 133–35.

33. See Vera S. Dunham, *In Stalin's Time: Middleclass Values in Soviet Fiction* (Cambridge, England, 1976); Leon Trotsky, *The Revolution Betrayed* (New York, 1945); Nicholas S. Timasheff, *The Great Retreat* (New York, 1946), and Frederick C. Barghoorn, *Soviet Russian Nationalism* (New York, 1956).

34. Lewin, "The Social Background of Stalinism," pp. 133–35; and Robert H. McNeal, "The Decisions of the CPSU and the Great Purge," *Soviet Studies*, vol. 23, no. 2, October 1971, pp. 177–85. The quote is from *Khrushchev Remembers* (Boston, 1970), p. 307.

35. For the fearful atmosphere surrounding these decisions, see *Khrushchev Remembers*, pp. 315–53.

36. See Breslauer, "Khrushchev Reconsidered."

37. For a critical discussion of Khrushchev's inadequacies by two dissident reformers, see Roy A. Medvedev and Zhores A. Medvedev, *Khrushchev: The Years in Power* (New York, 1978).

38. This does not mean that there are not special bastions of Soviet conservatism such as the elites of the KGB, the Komsomol, the Trade Unions, and the Political Sector of the Army. It does mean, however, that we should not assume that the division between reformers and conservatives is a function of generations. Older people played a major, even leading, role, for example, in the struggles for economic and cultural reform in the 1950s and 1960s. More generally, there is evidence that Soviet youth is no less conservative than its elders. For a discussion of this guestion, see Walter D. Connor, "Generations and Politics in the USSR," *Problems of Communism*, September-October 1975, pp. 20–31.

39. See Robert C. Tucker, *The Marxian Revolutionary Idea* (New York, 1969), chap. 6.

40. This does not mean that the revolution must be repudiated. Often it is simply reinterpreted in a conservative fashion, as has happened in the Soviet Union and the United States. See Michael Kammen, *A Season of Youth: The American Revolution and the Historical Imagination* (New York, 1978).

41. Cohen, *Bukharin and the Bolshevik Revolution*, p. 186.

42. See Bohdan Harasymiw, "*Nomenklatuta*: The Communist Party's Leadership Recruitment System," *Canadian Journal of Political Science*, vol. 2, no. 4 (December 1969), p. 512; and Mervyn Matthews, *Privilege in the Soviet Union: A Study of Elite Life-Styles Under Communism* (London, 1978).

43. The phrase is Yanov's, used in another context. *Essays on Soviet Society*, p. 85. The Soviet press sometimes asks, "Where do the conservatives come from?" (R. Bakhtamov and P. Volin, "Otkuda berutsia konservatory?," *Literaturnaia gazeta*, September 6, 1967.) Although this historical explanation may not be sufficient, it is essential.

44. The sources cited in note 4 relate to the post-Khrushchev period. See also Abraham Brumberg, "A Conversation With Andrei Amalrik," *Encounter*, June 1977, p. 30. Reform proposals, though of a lesser sort, continue to be expressed by responsible officials in the Soviet press.

45. See, for example, C. A. Deborin and B. S. Tel'pukhovskii, *Itogi i uroki velikoi otechestvennoi voiny* (2nd ed.; Moscow, 1975).

46. David Thomson, *Democracy in France* (London, 1960).

47. For the importance of this contract, see George W. Breslauer, "On the Adaptability of Welfare-State Authoritarianism in the USSR," in Karl Ryavec, ed., *Soviet Society and The Communist Party* (Amherst, Mass., 1979), pp. 3–25. Interviews with Soviet emigres over a thirty-year period suggest the great importance citizens place on the welfare provisions of the Soviet state. See Alex Inkeles and Raymond A. Bauer, *The Soviet Citizen* (Cambridge, Mass., 1959), esp. chap. 10; and Zvi Gitelman, "Soviet Political Culture: Insights From Jewish Emigres," *Soviet Studies*, vol. 29, no. 4, October 1977, p. 562.

48. Lewin, *Political Undercurrents in Soviet Economic Debates*, chaps. 6–9.

49. Iakovlev, "Protiv antiistorizma," *Literaturnaia gazeta*, November 15 1975.

50. P. Kopnin quoted in Yanov, *Essays on Soviet Society,* p. 76. Similariy, see A. M. Rumiantsev, "Vstupaiushchemu v mir nauki," *Pravda,* June 8, 1967; and A. Bovin, "Istina protiv dogmy," *Novyi mir,* no. 10, 1963, pp. 180–87.

51. My comments here are based on a reading of S. Frederick Starr, *Decentralization and Self-Government in Russia, 1830–1870* (Princeton, 1972); Richard S. Wortman, *The Development of a Russian Legal Consciousness* (Chicago, 1976); and W. Bruce Lincoln, "The Genesis of an 'Enlightened' Bureaucracy in Russia, 1825–1856," *Jahrbücher für Geschichte Osteuropas,* vol. 2, no. 3, June 1972, pp. 321–30.

52. The connection between East European and Soviet reformers has been very important since 1953. Since the Soviet overthrow of the reform communist government in Czechoslovakia in 1968, Soviet conservative literature on the dangers of "right-wing revisionism" has grown into a virtual industry aimed implicitly at domestic reformers as well. Nonetheless, reformers continue to make the point. See, for example, P. Volin, "Liudi i ekonomika," *Novyi mir,* no. 3, 1969, pp. 154–68. For the reform movement in Eastern Europe, see Vladimir V. Kusin, "An Overview of East European Reformism," *Soviet Studies,* July 1976, pp. 338–61.

53. This perspective has been adopted by some dissidents. See, for example, Medvedev, *On Socialist Democracy;* and, for a more systematic statement, L. Okunev, "Slovo-tozhe delo," *Politicheskii dnevnik,* no. 68 (Moscow: Samizdat, May 1970). But many dissidents have lost all hope of reform in recent years and now address their activities and thoughts not to Soviet officialdom but to Western governments.

54. See Karl W. Ryavec, *Implementation of Soviet Economic Reforms* (New York, 1975), pp. 299–300.

55. Quoted in H. Gordon Skilling, *Czechoslovakia's Interrupted Revolution* (Princeton, 1976), p. 495.

56. Rossiter, "Conservatism," pp. 292, 294.

57. For example journals with different outlooks began to emphasize the same social problems. *Novyi mir* is of particular interest in this connection. Well-known as a kind of reformist community, the journal published, or favorably reviewed, conservative writers such as Efim Dorosh and Vladimir Soloukhin. It also published many newer fiction writers who identified with conservative rural values, but whose writings depicted a post-collectivization countryside in need of reform. The new *samizdat* publications *Pamiat'* and *Poiski,* which include authors of different political outlooks, may be a sign of a similar development in dissident circles.

7 Letter to the Soviet Leaders, March 19, 1970

ANDREI SAKHAROV, ROY MEDVEDEV & VALERY TURCHIN

To L. I. Brezhnev, Central Committee of the CPSU; A. N. Kosygin, USSR Council of Ministers; N. V. Podgorny, Presidium of the Supreme Soviet of the USSR:

Dear Comrades,

We are appealing to you on a question of great importance. Our country has made great strides in the development of production, in the fields of education and culture, in the basic improvement of the living conditions of the working class, and in the development of new socialist human relationships. Our achievements have universal historical significance. They have deeply affected events throughout the world and have laid a firm foundation for the further development of the cause of communism. However, serious difficulties and shortcomings are also evident.

This letter will discuss and develop a point of view which can be formulated briefly by the following theses:

1. At the present time there is an urgent need to carry out a series of measures directed toward the further democratization of our country's public life. This need stems, in particular, from the very close connection between the problem of technological and economic progress and scientific methods of management, on the one hand, and the problems of freedom on information, the open airing of views, and the free clash of ideas, on the other. This need also stems from other domestic and foreign political problems.

2. Democratization must promote the maintenance and consolidation of the Soviet socialist system, the socialist economic structure, our social and cultural achievements, and socialist ideology.

3. Democratization, carried out under the leadership of the CPSU in collaboration with all strata of society, should maintain and strengthen the leading role of the party in the economic, political, and cultural life of society.

4. Democratization should be gradual in order to avoid possible complications and disruptions. At the same time it should be thoroughgoing, carried out consistently in accordance with a carefully worked-out program. Without fundamental democratization, our society will not be able to solve the problems now facing it, and will not be able to develop in a normal manner.

There are reasons to assume that the point of view expressed in the above theses is shared to one degree or another by a significant part of the Soviet intelligentsia and the advanced section of the working class. This attitude is also reflected in the opinions of student and working youth, as well as in numerous private discussions within small groups of friends. However, we believe it is urgent and advisable to set forth this point of view in coherent written form in order to facilitate a broad and open discussion of these most important problems. We are in search of a positive and constructive approach that will be acceptable to the party and government leadership of the country; we seek to reduce certain misunderstandings and unfounded apprehensions.[96]

Over the past decade menacing signs of disorder and stagnation have begun to show themselves in the economy of our country, the roots of which go back to an earlier period and are very deeply embedded. There is an uninterrupted decline in the rate of growth of the national income. The gap between what is necessary for normal development and the new productive forces being introduced is growing wider. A large amount of data is available showing mistakes in the determination of technical and economic policy in industry and agriculture and an intolerable procrastination about finding solutions to urgent problems. Defects in the system of planning, accounting, and incentives often cause contradictions between the local and departmental interests and those of the state and nation. As a result, new means of developing production potential are not being discovered or properly put to use and technical progress has slowed down abruptly. For these very reasons, the natural wealth of the country is often destroyed with impunity and without any supervision or controls: forests are leveled, reservoirs polluted, valuable agricultural land inundated, soil eroded or salinized, etc. The chronically difficult situation in agriculture, particularly in regard to livestock, is well known. The population's real income in recent years has hardly grown at all; food supply and medical and consumer services are improving very slowly, and with unevenness between regions. The number of goods in short supply continues to grow. There are clear signs of inflation.

Of particular concern regarding our country's future is the lag in the development of education: our total expenditures for education in all forms are three times below what they are in the United States, and are rising at a slower rate. Alcoholism is growing in a tragic way and drug addiction is beginning to surface. In many regions of the country the crime rate is climbing systematically. Signs of corruption are becoming more and more noticeable in a number of places. In the work of scientific and scientific-technical organizations, bureaucratism, departmentalism, a formal attitude toward one's tasks, and lack of initiative are becoming more and more pronounced.

As is well known, the productivity of labor is the decisive factor in the comparison of economic systems. It is here that the situation is worst of all. Productivity of labor in our country remains, as before, many times lower than that of the capitalist countries, and the growth of productivity has fallen off abruptly. This situation causes particular anxiety if one compares it with the situation in the leading capitalist countries, in particular with the United States. By introducing elements of state regulation and planning into the economy, these countries have saved themselves from the destructive crises which plagued the capitalist economy in an earlier era. The broad introduction of computer technology and automation assures a rapid rise in the productivity of labor, which in turn facilitates a partial overcoming of certain social problems and contradictions (e.g., by means of unemployment benefits, shortening of the work day, etc.). In comparing our economy with that of the United States, we see that ours lags behind not only in quantitative but also—most regrettable of all—in qualitative terms. The newer and more revolutionary a particular aspect of the economy may be, the wider the gap between the USSR and the USA. We outstrip America in coal production, but we lag behind in the output of oil, gas, and electric power; we lag behind by ten times in the field of chemistry, and we are infinitely outstripped in computer technology. The later is especially crucial, because the introduction of electronic computers into the economy is a phenomenon of decisive importance that radically changes the outlines of the production system and of the entire culture. This phenomenon has justly been called the second industrial revolution. Nevertheless, our stock of computers is 1 *percent* of that of the United States. And with respect to the application of the electronic computer, the gap is so great that it is impossible to even measure it. We simply live in another age.

Things are no better in the sphere of scientific and technological breakthroughs. Our role in this area has not advanced either. Rather, the contrary has been true. At the end of the 1950s our country was the first in the world to launch a satellite and send someone into space. By the end of the 1960s we had lost our lead in this area (as in many others). The first people to land on the moon were Americans. This fact is one of the outward manifestations of the gulf that exists and is continually growing between us and the Western countries all along the line in scientific and technological work. ...

... The source of our difficulties does not lie in the socialist system, but on the contrary, it lies in those peculiarities and conditions of our life which run contrary to socialism and are hostile to it. The source lies in the antidemocratic traditions and norms of public life established in the Stalin era, which have not been decisively eliminated to this day.

Noneconomic coercion, limitations on the exchange of information, restrictions on intellectual freedom, and other examples of the antidemocratic distortion of socialism which took place under Stalin were accepted in our country as an overhead expense of the industrialization process. It was believed that they did not seriously influence the economy of the country, although they had very serious consequences in the political and military arenas, in the destinies of vast layers of the population, and for whole nationalities. We will leave aside the question of the extent to which this point of view is justified for the early stages of the development of a socialist national economy, the decline in the rate of industrial development in the prewar years rather suggests the opposite. But there is no doubt that since the beginning of the second industrial revolution these phenomena have become a decisive economic factor; they have become the main brake on the development of the productive forces in this country. As a consequence of the increased size and complexity of economic systems, the problems of management and organization have moved to the forefront. These problems cannot be resolved by one or several persons holding power and "knowing everything." These problems demand the creative participation of millions of people on all levels of the economic system. They demand the broad interchange of information and ideas. In this lies the difference between modern economics and economics, let us say, in the ancient Orient.

However, we encounter certain insurmountable obstacles on the road toward the free exchange of ideas and information. Truthful information about our shortcomings and negative manifestations is hushed up on the grounds that it "may be used by enemy propaganda." Exchange of information with foreign countries is restricted for fear of "penetration by an enemy ideology." Theoretical generalizations and practical proposals, if they seem too bold to some individuals, are nipped in the bud without any discussion because of the fear that they might "undermine our foundations." An obvious lack of confidence in creatively thinking, critical, and energetic individuals is to be seen here. Under such circumstances the conditions are created for the advancement up the rungs of the official ladder not of those who distinguish themselves by their professional qualities and commitment to principles but of those who proclaim their devotion to the party but in practice are only worried about their own narrow personal interests or are passive time-servers. ...

Our economy can be compared with the traffic moving through an intersection. When there were only a few cars, the traffic police could easily cope with their tasks and traffic flowed smoothly. But the stream of traffic continually increases, and a traffic jam develops. What should be done in this situation? It is possible to fine the drivers and replace the traffic police, but this will not save the situation. The only solution is to widen the intersection. The obstacles hindering the development of our economy lie outside of it, in the social and political sphere, and all measures that do not remove these obstacles are doomed to ineffectiveness.

The vestiges of the Stalin era are having a negative effect on the economy not only directly, because they preclude a scientific approach to the problems of organization and administration, but no less so indirectly, because they reduce the creative potential of people in all fields. But under the conditions of the second industrial revolution, it is precisely creative labor that becomes increasingly important for the national economy.

In this connection the problem of relations between the state and the intelligentsia cannot be left unmentioned either. Freedom of information and creative work are necessary for the intelligentsia due to the nature of its activity and its social function. The intelligentsia's attempts to increase these freedoms are legitimate and natural. The state, however, suppresses these attempts by employing all kinds of restrictions—administrative pressures, dismissals from employment, and even courtroom trials. This all gives rise to a social gulf, an atmosphere of mutual distrust, and a profound lack of mutual understanding, making fruitful collaboration difficult between the party and state apparatus, on the one hand, and the most active layers of the intelligentsia, i.e., the layers that are most valuable for society, on the other. Under the conditions of modern industrial society, in which the role of the intelligentsia is constantly increasing, such a gulf can only be described as suicidal. ...

We propose the following draft program of measures which could be realized over a four-to-five-year period:

1. A statement from the highest party and government bodies on the necessity for further democratization and on the rate and means of achieving it. The publication in the press of a number of articles containing a discussion of the problems of democratization.

2. Limited distribution (through party organs, enterprises, and institutions) of information on the situation in the country and theoretical works on social problems which at the present time would not be made the object of broad discussion. Gradual increase of access to these materials until all limitations on their distribution have been lifted.

3. Extensive, planned organization of complex industrial associations with a high degree of autonomy in matters of industrial planning, technological processes, raw material supply, sale of products, finances, and personnel. The expansion of these rights for smaller productive units as well. Scientific determination after careful research of the form and degree of state regulation.

4. Cessation of interference with foreign radio broadcasts. Free sale of foreign books and periodicals. Adherence by our country to the international copyright convention. Gradual expansion and encouragement of international tourism in both directions (over a three-to-four-year period), expansion of international postal communications, and other measures for broadening international communication with special emphasis in this regard on member nations of Comecon.

5. Establishment of an institute for public opinion research. The publication (limited at first but later complete) of materials indicating public attitudes on the most important domestic and foreign policy questions, as well as other sociological materials.

6. Amnesty for political prisoners. An order requiring publication of the complete record of all trials of a political character. Public supervision of all prisons, camps, and psychiatric institutions.

7. Introduction of measures to improve the functioning of the courts and the procuracy and to enhance their independence from executive powers, local influences, prejudices, and personal ties.

8. Abolition of the indication of nationality on passports and questionnaires. Uniform passport system for the inhabitants of cities and villages. Gradual elimination of the system of passport registration, to be accomplished simultaneously with the evening up of economic and cultural inequalities between different regions of our country.

9. Reforms in education: increased appropriations for elementary and secondary schools; improving the living standard of teachers and increasing their autonomy and leeway to experiment.

10. Passage of a law on information and the press. Guaranteeing the right of social organizations and citizens' groups to establish new publications. Complete elimination of prior censorship in every form.

11. Improvement in the training of leadership cadres in the art of management. Introduction of special managerial training programs on the job. Improvement in the information available to leading cadres at all levels, increasing their autonomy, their rights to experiment, to defend their opinions, and to test them in practice.

12. Gradual introduction of the practice of having several candidates in elections to party and Soviet bodies on every level, even for indirect elections.

13. Expansion of the rights of Soviets; expansion of the rights and the responsibilities of the Supreme Soviet of the USSR.

14. Restoration of the rights of those nationalities deported under Stalin. The reestablishment of the national autonomy of deported peoples with the opportunity for them to resettle in their homeland (in those cases where until now this has not been realized).

15. Measures directed toward increasing public discussion in the work of governing bodies, commensurate with the interests of the state. Establishment of consultative scientific committees to work with the government bodies at every level, such committees to include highly qualified specialists in the different disciplines. ...

NOTES

ABOUT THE AUTHORS: **Andrei Sakharov,** a prominent scientist and a Nobel Prize winner, was perhaps the leading Soviet dissident. **Roy Medvedev,** a historian, and **Valery Turchin,** a physicist, joined him in this letter to the Soviet leaders.

96. Since January 1970 a "Letter to Brezhnev" signed with the name "Sakharov" or "Academician Sakharov" has circulated widely in Moscow. Various versions of this letter were later published in the Western press. In issue no. 1 of the anti-Soviet emigre journal *Posev* in 1970 an article with the pretentious title "The Truth About the Present Time" was published signed with the name "R. Medvedev." This article, full of absurd fabrications, was later broadcast in the Russian language by Radio Liberty (West Germany). We hereby declare that none of us were the authors of the letter or the article. These "documents" are clearly forgeries and are apparently being circulated for purposes of provocation.

8   The Pioneers of Perestroika: Back to the Intellectual Roots of Soviet Reforms

DAVID REMNICK

Fifteen years ago, at a remote academic institute in central Siberia, a young econo-mist named Abel Agenbegyan began his evening meals with a toast: "We shall outlive them!" At times, when he was even less sure that the Kremlin's aged lead-ers would ever step aside, he lifted his glass and said to his liberal young col-leagues, "Comrades! To our noble and hopeless work!"

Agenbegyan, a rotund scholar whose bookshelves bulge with the works of Vla-dimir Lenin and Milton Friedman, is representative of the generation of intellec-tuals and party reformers who were inspired by the brief liberalizing "thaw" of the Nikita Khrushchev era of the late 1950s. They are now the leaders of both the intelligentsia and the liberal, reformist wing of the Communist Party—the "*perestroika* army."

Suddenly, the dreams of Agenbegyan and the small core of progressives within the Communist Party are taking shape. The party, led by Mikhail Gorbachev, took its most dramatic step last month, abandoning its monopoly on power in hopes of restoring its own credibility in an increasingly pluralistic political sys-tem.

Gorbachev's decision was the result of outside pressure—the start of multi-party systems in Eastern Europe, the rise of popular independent political groups in the Soviet Union—and the evolution and evident triumph of the liberal wing of the party.

The intellectual roots of last month's drama go back decades. Scholars such as Agenbegyan and party officials such as Gorbachev survived the post-Khrushchev era of "stagnation" under Leonid Brezhnev in the 1970s and early '80s by leading double lives, working quietly on their plans and dreams, always hoping that a period of reform would come.

Couching some of their best ideas in the vague language of Aesop fables and leaving other ideas for another day, they never took the risks of dissidents. Some compromised themselves completely and, according to journalist Len Karpinsky "lost their souls forever."

Gorbachev, who spent nearly a quarter-century as a party official in the pro-vincial city of Stavropol, was one of the few party officials who were intellectually and morally receptive to ideas that contradicted the dogmas of Stalinism.

"Mikhail Sergeyevich did not just drop out of the sky. There are historical, intellectual reasons that he is who he is," says Oleg Bogomolov, a liberal economist who once worked in a reformist circle of advisers under future Soviet leader Yuri Andropov in the Central Committee apparatus in the 1960s. "The current of reform never ran completely dry."

This is the story of those years of double lives, and of the way Gorbachev pulled together his generation of reformers to provide himself with both an education and a supporting structure of reform intellectuals and politicians.

The world knows a great deal about the brave Soviet dissidents, prophetic figures such as Andrei Sakharov, who insisted on essential human rights and values in the 1960s and '70s despite the unimaginable pressures of the KGB and the party apparatus. Few others had the moral courage to put themselves, their jobs and their families at such risk.

"We all led double lives, not only scholars but a few progressive-minded politicians, like Gorbachev. Except for Sakharov, maybe, there was not a single one among us who could say we never made a single compromise," says Tatyana Zaslavskaya, one of Agenbegyan's colleagues in Novosibirsk and now one of Gorbachev's favorite intellectuals.

The bitterness of such double lives, the need to advance and then retreat, forever holding a finger to the political wind, is evident not only in the published works of the intellectuals who surround Gorbachev, but in Gorbachev himself.

In May 1978, the year he was brought to Moscow by the Kremlin, it was easy to see the duality of the man.

That month, at an ideological conference in Stavropol, Gorbachev extolled Brezhnev's "talent for leadership of the Leninist type"—the supreme compliment. He even praised Brezhnev's torpid, ghost-written memoir "The Little Land," as a work of "great philosophical penetration" and "spiritual and moral strength." The speech was a required act of subservience.

And yet that same May, Gorbachev wrote an astonishingly open report on agriculture for the Central Committee in Moscow. The report made its argument on economic rather than ideological grounds, proposing faster agricultural development, new pricing mechanisms, the return of peasants to their own land.

Those notions are now the basics of perestroika, or restructuring, but 12 years ago, when Gorbachev was summoned to Moscow to serve on the Central Committee, such ideas were close to heresy.

The crucial formative event for Gorbachev's generation was Khrushchev's denunciation of Joseph Stalin's "cult of personality" at the 20th Party Congress in 1956. "It was like a rocket across the sky," says Karpinsky, a columnist at the weekly Moscow News. Bogomolov says Khrushchev's speech was "the official start of perestroika."

In those first years of "The Thaw," as novelist Ilya Ehrenburg called it, Gorbachev's generation saw a world of possibilities. That sense of hope and breakthrough was captured in the literature of the time: Vladimir Voinovich's "I Want to be Honest," Alexander Solzhenitsyn's "One Day in the Life of Ivan

Denisovich," Yevgeny Yevtushenko's "The Heirs of Stalin" and Vladimir Dudintsev's "Not by Bread Alone." The literary journal Novy Mir, under Alexander Tvardovsky, was the closest thing the country had to an opposition press.

But in the later years of Khrushchev's tenure, the climate hardened. And following the overthrow of Khrushchev in 1964, Brezhnev began an era of retrenchment. The currents of reform were forced underground. The dissident movement stirred.

For the rest, an era of double lives had begun.

Yuri Andropov, who one day would lead the country and groom Gorbachev as his successor, was the Central Committee secretary in the 1960s charged with relations with Communist-ruled countries. He was a careful man, steeped in the orthodoxies of the time, but he was more intelligent than most of his colleagues in the Kremlin leadership.

In the early '60s he acquired a young circle of advisers, party intellectuals who were brighter and more progressive than the rest of the party apparatus on Staraya Square. Many of those young Andropov advisers are now key figures in the "perestroika army": political commentator Alexander Bovin, Foreign Ministry spokesman Gennadi Gerasimov, economist Oleg Bogomolov, journalist and legislator Fyodor Burlatsky, Central Committee adviser Nikolai Shishlin and Gorbachev's personal aide and adviser, Georgi Shakhnazarov.

"In the other offices there were just little Marxes and Engelses, only with less hair," says Bovin, now the main foreign policy voice of the government newspaper Izvestia. "Our group was a bunch of white crows, strange birds, in the Central Committee. I was just 33, a kid, walking around the halls of the Central Committee in my flannel shirt without a necktie."

Says Bogomolov, "Andropov is being idealized now. If he had lived, he probably would have changed things some, but he would not have touched the underlying structures of society. He was careful, conservative, maybe a bit like [Politburo member Yegor] Ligachev.

"But Andropov in the days we worked for him was distinguished from the rest. He spoke well and he had a flexible mind."

Andropov kept his distance from his more liberal young aides and never promoted them. When they crossed the street to a local cafeteria to gossip about Kremlin politics and argue policy, Andropov never joined them. But at the office he listened carefully to his young aides, and, through them, was connected firmly to the generation of Gorbachev.

Under Khrushchev, Andropov and his staff were capable of small victories. When Khrushchev had the notion in 1962 of creating a "super-international planning ministry" controlling economies throughout the socialist world, the Andropov circle saw it as just another layer of control and bureaucracy, a potential disaster. They managed to dissuade the leadership from including it in a major address.

The latter years of Khrushchev's rule were marked by inconsistency. At first Andropov thought that Khrushchev's downfall might lead to a resumption of the thaw. "Now we are going to be more persistent in following the course of the 20th Party Congress," Andropov told his staff triumphantly, according to both Burlatsky and Bogomolov.

Just days after Khrushchev's downfall, Andropov and his staff began writing the domestic policy section of the leadership's traditional speech for the anniversary of the Bolshevik Revolution. Brezhnev would deliver the speech, but his ideology chief, Mikhail Suslov, known in Andropov's office as "The Gray Cardinal," had full power over its contents.

"When our draft came back from Suslov, everything about 'peaceful coexistence' and 'democratization' had been slashed," Bogomolov says. "It was a great leap backward, and we were crushed."

In the coming years, Andropov's circle fought other Kremlin factions over the rehabilitation of Stalin. "I think we accomplished another small victory and kept if from becoming an open, full-blown rehabilitation," Bovin says.

Andropov tried to bring more liberal opinions to Brezhnev and even took steps to set up a meeting between Brezhnev and Sakharov, who was beginning to publish his dissident essays in 1967 and 1968. But Suslov and adviser Sergei Trapeznikov, the keepers of the neo-Stalinist orthodoxies, vetoed any such plans.

Although Andropov tried to subtly expand the limits of the possible, he also was content to retreat and play politics. Bovin recalls a night at Brezhnev's dacha in the Moscow suburb of Zavidovo when, after dinner and wine, Brezhnev, Andropov and a few others sang songs.

"Yuri, you sing so well, maybe you ought to be a soloist," Brezhnev said.

"No," Andropov answered, "I've always preferred to sing in the chorus."

That exchange, Bovin says, "reflected something more than just musical preferences."

A few days later, Bovin sat on a bench outside the Bolshoi Theater and read a copy of the party newspaper Pravda. To his horror he read the announcement: Andropov had been put in charge of the KGB. The young circle of advisers was shocked, and they saw Suslov's imprint. "Obviously they wanted Andropov moved over, because our tradition was that once you are KGB chief you can't go any higher," Bogomolov says. "Of course, it didn't quite work out that way."

The final blow for the small group of reformers in the Central Committee apparatus was the decision to invade Czechoslovakia in 1968. Bovin was one of the few aides to write a memo advising against intervention.

"We had even been preparing a Central Committee plenum at the time on— believe it or not—democratization. Not like what we are seeing today, but a step forward," Bovin says. "Then came the reforms in Czechoslovakia and everyone around Brezhnev started telling him, 'Look, Leonid Ilyich! Look at Czechoslovakia, is that the road we want to take? Uncontrolled freedom of the press? Everything, including the party, being criticized?' And so it all came tumbling down."

Bovin did not resign. "I had to go along. There was party discipline to observe," he says. "I thought about leaving but then I thought if I do, someone worse will just come and take my chair. If I could have explained my views to Pravda, then that might have made an impact, but that was not possible."

The decision hardly mattered. The "Andropov Circle" was shattered. The young aides went to institutes and newspapers, all waiting for another day.

A decade later Andropov, despite all his ugly work as KGB chairman, would contribute to reforms once more and bring Mikhail Gorbachev to Moscow.

Len Karpinsky was a Communist golden boy. His father, Vyacheslav, was a revolutionary and a friend of Lenin. The Karpinsky family lived in the most elite apartment building in Moscow, "the house on the embankment." Len went to privileged schools, ate the finest foods, summered at the best dachas. Some of Karpinsky's relatives disappeared in Stalin's purges but his Communist faith was restored and emboldened by Khrushchev's reforms.

By the early '60s, he was one of the national leaders of the Communist Party's youth branch, the Komsomol. He got to know powerful people such as KGB chief Vladimir Semichastny and men who would one day serve in Gorbachev's Politburo, including Alexander Yakovlev, Boris Pugo and Eduard Shevardnadze.

At one meeting, Suslov turned to the young star and said, "Keep up the good work. We have high hopes for you."

Karpinsky was drafted to write for Pravda—a job that transcended mere journalism in the party's eyes—and he aligned himself quickly with the paper's few liberal writers. In 1967, however, Karpinsky lost his job for writing for the youth paper Komsomolskaya Pravda an article that was ostensibly on theater but was really an attack on censorship and the cultural bureaucracy. That was a key moment for Karpinsky, who began to realize he could no longer guard himself, that he could no longer live in privileged privacy.

"Many people had become convinced that we were destined to live in this awful way for centuries, and they retreated into family life, their salaries and jobs that were somehow apart from politics," Karpinsky says. "I was among the people who thought that change was inevitable." The question was when.

"My friends and I, many of whom you see now in the legislature and the Moscow intelligentsia, had a dream that was both pragmatic and romantic. We could not create too much, but we did want to prepare certain intellectual currents and keep them alive."

Only a few heroic figures could abide by Solzhenitsyn's credo, "Live Not by Lies." Karpinsky's circle took a less exalted route but tried to maintain a part of their souls and minds, tried to speak the truth when they could. To go the "complete dissident route," Karpinsky says, meant living the life of a saint and putting yourself and your family perpetually at risk.

"I used vague language and paragraphs of orthodoxy and then tried to make certain progressive hints," he says, describing the balance of the "double life" in a "counter-society" of liberal intellectuals who did not join the dissidents. "I concluded that one could adapt to certain conditions and at the same time, resist them."

Working now apart from the party and Pravda, Karpinsky became even more daring. He became what he calls "a half-dissident." Under the pseudonym "L. Okunev," he wrote in 1969 a manifesto, "Words Are Also Deeds," that anticipated the "inevitability" of *glasnost*—openness—and the intellectual revolution of perestroika a decade in advance.

Karpinsky's thesis was that Khrushchev had set in motion an "irreversible" attack on Stalinism and that the Brezhnev regime and its apparatus were engaged in a futile attempt to battle ideas, technology, democracy and "our future."

The dissident historian Roy Medvedev published Karpinsky's essay in his underground journal, Political Diary. During a KGB search of Medvedev's apartment, agents discovered the manuscript.

In 1975, Karpinsky, Suslov's golden boy, was expelled from the party. His ideas had been arrested. But only temporarily. Under Gorbachev, Karpinsky was readmitted to the party and made a prominent columnist at the liberal Moscow News.

About a half hour's drive from the industrial city of Novosibirsk is Akademgorodok, or Academic City, an ivory tower on the Siberian plains.

In the 1960s and '70s, when the Communist party kept a tight grip on the major institutes in Moscow, Abel Agenbegyan, at age 33, assembled a team of young, liberal economists and sociologists to do in Siberia the work that could not be done in Moscow.

"We could work more easily there," Agenbegyan says. "We were a bunch of like-minded people and we had nothing else to do there but work. It was perfect." Zaslavskaya says she left her job in Moscow for two reasons: In Siberia, she and her family got a larger apartment, and "finally I could stop writing books that did nothing but summarize the statistics in 12 other books. The intellectual freedom in Novosibirsk was like a miracle. I felt 10 years younger there."

Agenbegyan, Zaslavskaya and the Siberians were relatively protected from the compromises of Moscow politics. But they could not always express themselves the way they wished. And when they refused to do the Kremlin's hack work, they suffered. Both Zaslavskaya and Agenbegyan were called upon by Brezhnev's science secretary, Sergei Trapeznikov, to "update" his book on collectivization, which extolled a policy that had led to the starvation and death of millions.

"I refused and Tatyana begged off, saying she was ill," Agenbegyan recalls. "We switched off the telephone for a while after that, but they got their revenge. We received our reprimand."

The main goal of the economists in Siberia was to see the economy plain, to ignore the lies of the official statisticians and the orthodoxies of the ideologists and to examine what worked and what did not. Like Gorbachev years later, they investigated periods of reform in Russian and Soviet history for clues to the Soviet future. In their unpublished reports they toyed with heresies such as "the market" and "pluralist forms of property."

"Economic perestroika did not start on a completely fallow field," says Agenbegyan, adding that these reforms have their roots in Lenin's New Economic

Policy of the early 1920s. "When the program actually started ideas began to crystallize and with time they grew more and more radical."

In 1983, with Andropov now general secretary, the world discovered Novosibirsk. Zaslavskaya and her colleagues held a seminar on the conflicting interests of classes and social groups in the economy. The "Novosibirsk Report," as it was known after it was leaked to the Western press, was essentially a sociological framework for what would one day be known as perestroika.

But the regional committee of the Communist Party condemned the group for "disclosing government documents." Two years later, Agenbegyan and Zaslavskaya would play a major role in the political education of the man who would lead the Second Russian Revolution. ← Very interesting to how he refers to Gorbachev's term.

NOTES

ABOUT THE AUTHOR: **David Remnick** was a Moscow correspondent of the *Washington Post* and more recently the author of *Lenin's Tomb: The Last Days of the Soviet Empire.*

PART 2

Reform and the Political and Social System

What began as an attempt at limited reforms, emphasizing discipline and "accelera-tion," by 1987 had begun to move in the direction of glasnost and what was labeled democratization. Soviet politics was gradually transformed in the process, as the ex-pansion of public debate brought with it a new political "pluralism," the emergence of a public arena permitting spontaneous, grassroots political organization, and ulti-mately the sanctioning of competitive elections and of the principle of a multiparty system.

In the process the Soviet political system itself underwent a variety of institutional changes. Existing structures, such as local soviets, were transformed; paper institu-tions, such as the national and republic legislatures, became real ones; the media ac-quired an important new role; some Communist Party functions were shifted to the state; other institutions, such as the Communist Youth League, withered; and some needed organs, such as the judiciary branch, remained sadly inadequate. Meanwhile an array of new political actors, activities, and arenas came into improvised exis-tence, not always neatly fitting into the existing structures. The prestige and legiti-macy of different organizations and individuals proved to be highly volatile.

It remains a matter of some controversy just why the reformers became committed to democratization to begin with—scarcely the obvious direction to pursue for a lead-ership reared on the notion of a centrally directed and controlled "vanguard party." If it was out of a recognition that it was essential to galvanize the public and to mobilize it in support of reform, against the presumably recalcitrant incumbents, did this strategy pay off?

Some contend that it opened the door to centrifugal processes over which the gov-ernment lost control. As participation outran institutionalization and precipitated a novel defiance of authority, it unwittingly contributed to the backlash demanding limits on free speech and on political activity, and a return to "law and order."

Others question the decision (contrasting with the Chinese experience) to give po-litical democratization priority over economic reform: In their view, this amounted to an invitation to destabilization, making economic reform impossible, and post-poned the time when some tangible payoff of the reforms could be demonstrated to the public at large.

The developments of the past few years have also revealed limitations and weaknesses of democratic institutions in the Soviet context: of legislatures, political

89

parties, and media. Those underscoring their failure to function optimally point to the virtual abdication of the Supreme Soviet in granting the president extraordinary powers; to the proliferation of small parties without a mass following, often sacrificing effectiveness to their self-styled leaders' egos and unable to compromise around a common program; and to the interminable exercises in rhetoric from which no actions ensue.

Others argue that under the circumstances a learning process was bound to be required, that after decades of political repression time was needed to crystallize procedures, create and identify new political leaders with a modicum of professional experience, assemble the resources for the conduct of unfamiliar business, and gain control over the implementation of decisions. Still, it would be hard to deny that over five years the emergent democratic institutions failed to devise an effective defense against intimidation and the use or threat of brute violence, whether by the uniformed services or from the outside.

A topic of particular fascination, which several of the chapters address from various perspectives, is the role of Gorbachev himself in this process—his remarkable skills and his tragic shortcomings. As the new political spectrum evolved, Gorbachev's role changed over time—he went from being on the cutting edge of reform to acting as a centrist balancer to imposing stability in alliance with authoritarian forces against the democratic opposition. To what extent Gorbachev became the hostage of a conservative coalition, and to what extent he was hostage to the limitations of reform communism itself remain key issues to be addressed in a later chapter.

9 The Beginnings of Independent Political Activity

GEOFFREY A. HOSKING

To all appearance, the Soviet Union in the mid-1980s offered a very unpromising soil for the development of civil society—of institutions and associations independent of the state and the ruling party. It was a uniquely centralised polity, in which the party-state apparatus governed not only the aspects of society normally associated with authority, but also the economy, culture, science, education and the media. Everyone's employment depended on the state, and senior appointments in all walks of life were decided under the nomenklatura patronage system controlled by the party.

This made the Soviet Union very different from Spain, Portugal, Greece or any of the Latin American countries feeling their way from authoritarianism to democracy in the 1970s and 1980s. In all those countries, there were social strata which long pre-dated the authoritarian regime and did not owe their existence to it; there was a market economy, distorted perhaps by the state but not entirely dominated by it; there were autonomous churches and religious associations, interest groups and ethnic movements, even sometimes opposition political parties, albeit underground. Such bodies either did not exist in the Soviet Union, or were totally dependent on the state.

Even this list does not quite grasp the peculiarity of the Soviet system (and other communist systems), for its essence lay not in the tightness and pervasiveness of its bureaucratic controls, important though they were, but rather in it adoption of a degenerated utopianism as an ideological adhesive to hold the system together. The fanaticism, brutality and terror of the Stalinist system had largely disappeared, to be replaced by a political charade. The population did not believe in the ideology, but signalled symbolic assent to it in a variety of public rituals. Václav Havel once summarised the spiritual consequences in the person of the greengrocer who displays in his shop-window a placard reading 'Workers of the World, Unite!', not because he believes in workers uniting, but because he wishes to convey to all and sundry that he is willing to assent to the system in order to stay out of trouble. Aggregated individuals acts of this kind confirmed and consolidated the system;, indeed, in a sense they *were* the system.[1]

Against such a regime the normal methods of political struggle—the formation of oppositional parties and the drawing up of alternative programmes—were impracticable or futile. Social interest groups had no identity separate from the nomenklatura hierarchy, so there was no question of their formulating their distinct interests, let alone of forming associations in order to defend them. That constituted the strength of the system.

Its weakness was the brittleness of the structure of simulated assent. A paradoxical fruit of the ascendancy of ideology was that it conferred high status on people whose profession was ideas—that is, those who were the most thoroughly integrated into the system but who were also the most likely to be aware of the emptiness of its public charade. It was, then, among intellectuals and professional people that the first stages of self-detachment from the system took place. Once enough of them had become convinced that the emperor was not only scantily clad but was also failing to deliver the goods—in the form of food, housing, basic services, even (the regime's great specialty) armaments—then the whole integument of deceit suddenly looked remarkably flimsy. This is what happened in much of Eastern Europe in the autumn of 1989.

What intellectuals did publicly has been characterised by Solzhenitsyn and Havel as 'living in the lie'. What they did privately, among close friends and trusted colleagues, might be quite different, as we shall see. The problem was to find a way of transferring honesty from their private to their public lives.

...

'Dissent', then, represented all that it was possible to achieve in the narrow framework of the Brezhnev regime. It was a vital breakthrough by comparison with the past. Yet it had drawbacks as the basis for a civil society. Its activists were usually isolated from the mass of the population whose concerns they were or claimed to be articulating, and indeed they were sometimes viewed askance by their colleagues for 'rocking the boat' and attracting persecution where otherwise the authorities turned a blind eye. Their network of contacts was inevitably restricted by the primitive and laborious technology of samizdat, even if the results of their activities were more widely known, thanks to foreign radio stations. Above all, the tangible political rewards of their activities were minimal: there seemed to be little practical that dissenters could accomplish beyond the repeated assertion of principle in the wilderness. This was discouraging in itself, and also sometimes caused trivial disagreements within the movements to escalate into bitter disputes fuelled by personal antipathies.

For all that, the contribution of the human rights movement to the later emergence of independent political associations was vital. With the widespread freeing of political prisoners, beginning with the release of Andrei Sakharov from administrative exile in December 1986, former human rights activists returned to the scene, some of them ready to resume their work, first of all to obtain the release of their less fortunate colleagues, then in the name of political freedoms generally. In Armenia and Georgia in May–June 1987, committees were formed for the release of named political prisoners, and both were led by prominent Helsinki watch group figures of the 1970s: the Armenian group's chairman was Robert Nazarian, while both Zviad Gamsakhurdia and Merab Kostava were members of the Georgian one.[5] Somewhat later the Ukrainian Helsinki Group announced that it was resuming its existence, including its surviving members Viacheslav Chornovil and Mikhail Horyn', within the framework of the Ukrainian Culturological Club, which from August 1987 began organising public meetings on ecology, culture, historical monuments and the 'blank spots' of recent history. They sponsored, for example, a memorial gathering for Vasyl' Stus, one of the leading 1960s generation poets, who died in a labour camp in 1985, and evenings of testimony and discussion on the famine of 1932–4. The evocation of Helsinki in their name was important not only because it provided a link with the past, but also because it plugged the new movement into an international diplomatic and juridical process.[6]

Together the three Helsinki groups formed an International Committee for the Defence of Political Prisoners, which issued its first statement on 14 January 1988. This noted that most of those still 'inside' were participants of national liberation movements, and adumbrated a whole programme of ethnic rights, much of which was soon to become the working fare of the Popular Fronts: the right to an official language, to education, publication and the conduct of public business in it, the right of each republic to plan its economy in accordance with its own needs and to avoid environmental degradation.[7]

The first national liberation movement to hold mass demonstrations was that of the Crimean Tatars. Deported from their homeland by Stalin in 1944, and resettled in various parts of Central Asia, they had begun as early as 1956 to address loyal petitions to the government asking to be allowed to return. During the 1960s and 1970s they were able to collect hundreds of thousands of signatures for such petitions, and also occasionally held mass meetings, invariably broken up by the police. This unusual tenacity in such a difficult period was undoubtedly due to the fact that they were the largest deported people not permitted to return home in the late 1950s: they thus had one simple overwhelming grievance on which all were agreed.[8]

During the summer of 1987 their Initiative Group held meetings with the Presidium of the USSR Supreme Soviet in Moscow. Frustrated by the outcome, they began to hold regular meetings in Izmailovsky Park, and then finally, on 25 July, a demonstration on Red Square, where some 500 Tatars paraded with banners, chanting 'Homeland! Homeland!' and 'Gorbachev! Gorbachev!'. The police tried to ease them off the square without using force, since foreign correspondents were present, but failed and the demonstration continued till the following afternoon, when those remaining were induced to disperse by the promise of a meeting with Gromyko (then President of the USSR). They gained nothing but vague promises from that meeting, and subsequently members of the Initiative Group and other participants were arrested, put on planes and sent back to Tashkent, where they were warned they might be charged with 'group activities disturbing public order'. In spite of that, they subsequently organised a number of other demonstrations in Central Asian towns.[9]

Like the Crimean Tatars, the Jews had kept their ethnic awareness alive during the 1970s by political campaigns. In their case, since they had no Soviet homeland and felt that Jewish national life was impossible in the USSR, they focused on the right to emigrate. They had occasional small-scale demonstrations of "refuseniks' (those refused an exit visa), which were invariably broken up by the police.[10] From 1987 the emphasis of Jewish political activity changed. Refusenik demonstrations continued,[11] but as the number of exit permits increased emigration ceased to be the single dominant issue; instead, the development of Jewish culture within the USSR, and the protection of Jews from *Pamiat'* and other anti-Semitic movements, now publicly active, came to the fore.[12] The change of mood was marked by a demonstration at Vostriakova cemetery on 26 April 1987 to commemorate the Jews murdered in the Holocaust.[13] The first Jewish Cultural Society was set up in Moscow in May 1988, and it was soon followed by others, in Kiev and L'viv (where their initiative was explicitly supported by Ukrainian activists), in Vil'nius, Riga, Tallinn and Minsk. Their aim was to commemorate the Jewish past, to spread knowledge of Yiddish and Hebrew (the latter hitherto forbidden in the USSR), to perform Jewish plays, music and dance, and generally to bring Jews together in celebration of their diverse and ancient culture. A first all-Union congress of these cultural associations was held in Moscow in March 1989.[14]

In Moscow the Press Club Glasnost' (not to be confused with the unofficial journal of the same name) was the first organisation to espouse publicly the cause of human rights. Set up in July 1987, its initiators contained a number of former human rights activists and editors of samizdat journals: Larisa Bogoraz, Sergei Kovalev, Reshat Dzhemilev, Aleksandr Ogorodnikov, Iosif Begun, Viktor Brailovskii, Sergei Grigor'iants and Lev Timofeev.[15] In December it organised an international human rights seminar, the first time such an event had ever been held on Soviet soil. The attitude of the authorities towards this unprecedented gathering was ambivalent: they did not prevent it meeting altogether, but obstructed the journeys of many of the participants, both from abroad and from inside the Soviet Union, and blocked the hire of any premises large enough to accommodate the whole event. As a result, no plenary sessions could be held, and the occasion was reduced to its various sections meeting separately in private apartments scattered all over Moscow. In spite of the difficulties, about 400 Soviet citizens took part, together with about thirty from abroad, including representatives of the International Helsinki Federation.[16] The occasion was significant in that it made possible the resumption of human and organisational links broken off in the 1970s, as well as the creation of new ones.

The heritage of the former human rights movement was also revived in the new unofficial journals which now started appearing to provide an information and communications base for the emerging political movements. The journal *Ekspress-khronika*, for example, launched in August 1987 by Aleksandr Podrabinek, was consciously modelled on the *Khronika tekushchikh sobytii*. It aimed to get its information to readers much faster by appearing weekly but, like its model, it recorded baldly and without editorial comment violations of human rights within the Soviet Union. Podrabinek had had experience of this kind of work, having in the 1970s edited an information bulletin on psychiatric abuse, and published a book on the subject, for which in 1978 he was charged with slandering the Soviet state and sentenced to five years' exile.[17] Now his latest journal rapidly built up a network of informants around the country, relying partly on older communications links, partly on the new ones now being created. Its editors would meet every Saturday morning to sift the items of information they had received during the week. On Saturday afternoons the typists would get to work, usually carrying on far into the night, at this stage without benefit of word-processing technology. Then on Sunday morning, *Ekspress-khronika* would be sold on Gogol Boulevard in the centre of Moscow, along with a gradually growing gaggle of other unofficial publications, whose editors would come along to meet each other and to distribute their wares under the watchful eye of the militia. By April 1988, 200 copies of *Ekspress-khronika* were being typed out and dispatched to fifty-three towns, in eleven of which they would be retyped and distributed further. Taking part in such a venture could be dangerous: Podrabinek was frequently followed and more than one attacked in the street in circumstances which the police subsequently refused to investigate.[18]

Another former political prisoner, Sergei Grigor'iants, started a journal at about the same time. In March 1983 he had been arrested and sentenced to ten years for editing a human rights periodical called simply *Bulletin V* (short for *vesti* or 'news'). This had appeared roughly twice a month from 1980 to 1983 to supplement the information given in the increasingly sporadic *Khronika tekushchikh sobytii* or to speed up its dissemination. *Bulletin V* had only a very limited circulation and was not known at the time outside the Soviet Union. But it did fulfil its function of keeping informational channels and personal connections open, and Grigor'iants was able to use some of them again after his release in 1987.[19]

The title of his new journal, *Glasnost'*, made adroit use of Gorbachev's own catchword. Grigor'iants conceived *Glasnost'* not only as a bearer of information about the human rights movement, but also as a forum for new political movements to announce their existence and make their aims known, and also for them to expound and discuss their ideas about what was wrong with the Soviet Union and how it might be changed. Within a few months, *Glasnost'* enjoyed such a high reputation that Grigor'iants was able to attract senior members of the official intelligentsia (hitherto cautious about involvement in informal politics) to write for it. Registration of it was, however, refused on the grounds that there was a paper shortage and already quite enough newspapers and journals. Moreover, on 9 May 1988, the police arrested Grigor'iants at his out-of-town dacha, and confiscated all his equipment, including a recently acquired computer. He was released a few days later, but the equipment was not returned.[20]

A third journal which began to appear shortly afterwards (December 1987) was *Referendum*, whose editor, Lev Timofeev, had been arrested in 1985 for circulating in samizdat and publishing abroad his books, which gave a frank picture and a sociological analysis of the state of the Soviet countryside. The journal reflected the thoughtful and scholarly nature of its editor: it was a purveyor of opinion and discussion, allowing its authors space to expound and develop their ideas, and to contest those of their opponents.[21]

Another strand of social protest, quite distinct from the human rights movement, though parallel with it, was the burgeoning youth movement. During the 1960s the situation of young people in Soviet society had begun to change, in paradoxical fashion. Up to that time they had always been in the thick of events, in demand for the urgent tasks of war and peace; often they had been able to win high promotion on the basis of minimal education. Now their lives had become materially more comfortable, and they were no longer threatened by war, revolution or social upheaval; they were also better educated and more sophisticated, with a wider range of interests. By comparison with the past, however, society could no longer offer them an obvious role. Their sometimes impressive qualifications were often not matched by the work they could find, and their promotion was typically blocked by much less able nomenklatura appointees from the past. These changes generated a deep conflict of generations, awaking in the young (and not so young) a sense of alienation and of belonging to a limbo called 'youth', which often considerably outlasted the maximum Komsomol age of 28.

In these dispiriting circumstances, an autonomous youth culture began to form in the 1960s and 1970s, and made its influence felt beyond what one would conventionally term 'youth'. In a sense it was an intense expression of the outlook of a society infantilised by its own rulers. The origins of this culture can be traced back to the 20th Party Congress, with its questioning of the Stalinist past, and to the International Youth Festival of 1957, when young Soviet citizens were able to communicate with their foreign contemporaries for the first time for more than a generation. Its early beginnings were in the Komsomol volunteer brigades and 'communards' of the Khrushchev period.[22] But quite soon, especially under western influences, it became independent of the official Soviet youth movement. In the words of a Soviet sociologist, young people were seeking 'self-fulfillment and sociability, the feeling of belonging to one's age-group, to one's town, district, courtyard, school, social stratum, that is, the sense of having one's own circle which is associated with the word "we"'.[23]

Some young people found the focus of their sociability in supporting sports teams, forming fan clubs which would accompany their heroes, wear their colours and emblems, and sometimes get into fights with their rivals.[24] Others were attracted by rock music (the universal symbol of youth culture), becoming rockers, punks, metallists or breakers according to inclination and circumstance. Some became religious seekers, of Christian or non-Christian persuasion. Some experimented with drugs and with other means of exploring one's social and personal identity.[25] Yet others stood out against the general westernising trend, reaffirming traditional proletarian values in a coarse and sometimes violent form: such were the *Liubery*, militant suburbanites from near Moscow, who would dress in slim-cut jeans and highly coloured shirts, and go into the city in bands, to cut off long hair, tear off jewellery, or even beat up young people of stylish or western appearance.[26] Already here some of the characteristic features of 'informality' can be discerned: the absence of any legal status, the introversion, the search for alternative life-styles, the intense personal relations. Such groups did not struggle against the existing social and political system, but ignored or passively resisted it, while carving out for themselves little niches within it.

Where they formulated a philosophy of life, they did so in reaction against what they saw as the artificial and insincere adult world. The hippies of the so-called 'Older Generation', which appeared in the late 1960s, took as their basic principle that 'in a world deprived of freedom, one can acquire it only in one's own soul'. They conducted the search by means of Yoga, Buddhism, and various forms of mysticism, sometimes accompanied by the use of drugs.[27] The 'people of the System', who came somewhat later, preached a gospel of the reconciliation of all people by the force of universal love: 'The hippy ideal is a society of equality and brotherhood, where there will be no distinction between nations, and where love will be the basic factor in the relationships between people.'[28]

These ideals led naturally on to pacifism and to concern for the urban and natural environment. The 'people of the system' rejected nuclear deterrence and urged increasing contact between ordinary people of east and west, with freedom to travel to make that possible. They also condemned the Afghan war, which they considered made 'moral cripples' out of those who had to fight in it and threatened to revive the fascist mentality. On the environment, the group 'Free Initiative', which grew out of the 'System', proclaimed: 'We want harmony with Nature, not the raping of it for the satisfaction of unnatural needs ... In harmony with nature we will resurrect the gods, who have died of cancer or suffocated in the fumes of factories.'[29]

By the mid-1980s, as a result of continual friction with society and police, some of the hippies had become politicised, and were forging links between groups in different towns, even bringing out manifestos and journals, and organising Union-wide assemblies (in Tallinn, where the authorities were more tolerant than elsewhere).[30]

The hippies' worries about the military and ecological threat were widely shared in society, and not only among young people. They had formed a major part of Andrei Sakharov's arguments in his memorandum of 1968, and had been much discussed among scholars in private and semi-public seminars. Together with the protection of historical monuments, these themes became the principal arenas on which, after 1985, it proved possible to begin challenging official policies and to form a more broad-based political movement. Even before the advent of glasnost' some young people, impatient with the sluggishness of officially approved organisations like VOOPIK, had on occasions formed informal detachments for the defence of specific monuments or natural sites.[31] Now it became possible to communicate with a wider public and mobilise them for action.

One of the first examples of such action came in the autumn of 1986, when the Mossovet decided to demolish the seventeenth-century mansion of the merchant Shcherbakov to make way for a motorway. An action group of students and schoolchildren, led by Kirill Parfenov, occupied the building for two months, while Parfenov himself appeared on a popular television programme to explain the need to protect the capital city's historical heritage.[32]

In Leningrad a similar proposal, to demolish the hotel Angleterre, provoked a number of disparate informal groups to get together and agitate publicly. Leningrad had long possessed a 'second culture', centred around the Klub-81, which had several years earlier concluded an informal agreement with the authorities that they would be allowed to hold unofficial poetry readings and bring out a samizdat journal, provided they did not attempt foreign publication.[33] Klub-81 and its associates linked up with several ecological and preservation societies led by *Spasenie,* which in the previous year had organised a successful campaign to save the house of the poet Del'vig on Vladimir Square. Together they set up a picket outside the hotel and started collecting signatures from passers-by for a petition to the city soviet.

They failed to save the hotel. The soviet moved in its demolition workers suddenly one morning when the pickets were absent.[34] But this failure had a positive effect: it provoked the protesters into a realisation of their need to work more closely together, and to be more systematic in their appeals to the public. In other words, what had happened was a course of political education for them: a question of environmental protection had also become a question of human rights, and one to be pursued by political means.

The informal groups established an umbrella organisation, the Cultural Democratic Movement, or Epicentre, and stationed an information kiosk on the square in front of St Isaac's Cathedral, to hand out leaflets and answer questions. Epicentre started to issue a journal, *Merkurii,* with the watchword 'Claws and teeth for public opinion!', reflecting the lessons learned. It continued its self-politicisation by nominating a candidate, Alexei Kovalev, for the forthcoming local Soviet elections. The authorities, however, refused to register him, and indeed barred him from a graduate course he wished to begin.[35]

Some Russians drew very different conclusions from the progressive degradation of the natural and historical environment. The organisation *Pamiat'* was founded in the late 1970s or early 1980s as a literary and historical society attached to the Ministry of the Aviation Industry: its members carried out voluntary restoration work at weekends. By 1985 some at least of its leaders had decided that the fundamental reason for the disastrous environmental situation, as well for Russia's other afflictions, lay with an international conspiracy of freemasons and Zionists aiming to undermine Russia, and working through Jewish leaders of the Soviet Communist Party was well as through the imperialists. Those who thought this way even dug up the notorious Okhrana forgery, *The Protocols of the Elders of Zion,* as evidence for their view. Thereafter *Pamiat'* became radically opposed to the emerging liberal and reformed socialist current in society. During May 1987 it organised a number of demonstrations in Moscow, which assembled some hundreds of people, and one of which was received by El'tsin, then the first secretary of the city's party committee.[36]

Ecological concerns drew ordinary citizens into the first examples of mass political agitation in a number of republican and provincial towns during 1986–7, encouraged perhaps by the success of scientists and writers in having the planned diversion of northern rivers called off in summer of 1986. In Latvia in the autumn of 1986 a public petition attracted 30,000 signatures in a call to abandon plans for a hydroelectric power station on the Daugava River, which would have drowned a good deal of arable land and several villages. The republican authorities supported the protest, and Gosplan revoked the scheme.[37]

...

At about the same time, another concern of youth culture, international peace, was making itself felt. The 'Group for establishing trust between the USSR and the USA' had a comparatively long history: it was set up in 1982. It grew out of an unofficial seminar, Peace and Social Research, which at that time was being held at Dolgoprudnoe, just outside Moscow, and attracted scholars from a number of disciplines as well as people from the hippy movement concerned about the seemingly unstoppable drift towards nuclear war between the superpowers. In 1982 some of the seminar's members became dissatisfied with the academic nature of their deliberations, and decided to 'go public' in an attempt to undertake more practical and fruitful work. Having formed the Trust Group, they invited Soviet and western journalists to a press conference—the Soviet ones did not come—at which they launched an 'Appeal to the Governments and the Public of the USSR and the USA'. Renouncing criticism of any particular government, they called upon members of the public in all countries to draw up proposals for keeping the peace and to meet in order to discuss them and decide on ways of putting pressure on their governments to implement them. They called this process 'four-sided dialogue.'[40]

...

... In 1986, the Trust Group handed out leaflets in Gor'kii Park, providing facts about the Chernobyl' nuclear explosion and passing on recommendations about precautions to be taken; in this they carried out a public service which the government had neglected on a matter which caused most people deep and legitimate worries.[42]

...

In addition to the human rights movement and the youth movement, a third stream was also preparing, if in more urbane and cautious style, to make its contribution to the swelling flow of informal politics. In universities and academic institutes, groups of scholars had been studying subjects not at all envisaged in the Marxist-Leninist world outlook. Some had been investigating the history, folklore, religion and culture of their peoples, reassembling the fragments of a lost world. Much of their work was officially sanctioned, but some of it was conducted in private or informal seminars. They were restoring the disrupted memory of whole nations, and their labours, once their fruits became widely known, did much to underpin the ethnic revival which burst to the forefront of politics during and after 1988, bringing to prominence such unlikely figures as the musicologist Vytautas Landsbergis in Lithuania, the orientalist Levon Ter-Petrosian in Armenia, and the literary scholar Zviad Gamsakhurdia in Georgia.

More modestly, other scholars had been cultivating among themselves awareness of a world beyond the Soviet frontiers, of political, economic, legal, philosophical and religious alternatives to the society in which they lived. Some of their work later bore fruit in the post-1985 reform process, beginning with the theoretical study of market economics in Novosibirsk, which generated the Zaslavskaia memorandum of 1983. Social science and humanities faculties and institutes, which had long been centres of discreetly cultivate non-conformism, gave high intellectual status to the search for post-totalitarian structures.

It was from this milieu that proposals began to come forth concerning not just single issues but the whole range of politics. On the whole, however, leading scholars were reluctant to jeopardise their establishment status by becoming involved in unauthorised political activities. The most they were prepared to do was to extend discreet protection to younger colleagues who were ready to take more risks.

It was in this fashion that the Klub Perestroika emerged from an ongoing seminar at the Central Economic-Mathematical Institute in Moscow. During the early months of 1987 this seminar had been bringing together young economists, jurists, sociologists, political scientists and others, most of them in their late 20s and 30s, initially to discuss the drafting of a new enterprise law (eventually promulgated in July). The discussions at it were expert, yet also wide-ranging and spontaneous; question and answer soon outgrew the original theme of the seminars, raising problems which affected the whole of Soviet society, and stimulating in many participants the aspiration to move beyond discussions and do something practical. Specialist sections were formed to give shape to these aspirations: one, for example, to discuss models of socialism, another for 'self-administration', another for 'citizens' diplomacy'. One, called *Memorial,* set itself to solicit support for the idea of a memorial centre dedicated to Stalin's victims.[46]

As the debates broadened and draw in more young scholars, Klub Perestroika faced a problem which was to become paradigmatic for all informal movements over the next few years. Growing numbers and looseness of membership criteria raised the questions: should we not have a tighter organisational structure if we are to achieve anything? Should we not have a definite political programme? What should our relationships be with the Institute which shelters us and, beyond that, with the authorities in general?

A political kernel was emerging around four members in particular: Andrei Fadin, Boris Kagarlitskii, Pavel Kudiukin and Gleb Pavlovskii. Fadin, Kudiukin and Kagarlitskii had been arrested in 1982 for editing an unofficial journal propagating unorthodox socialist ideas. The main point of their arguments was the same now as it had been then: that a fundamental restructuring of Soviet society was needed to revive local self-administration through genuinely elected soviets and workers' committees, guided and helped where necessary by a 'new socialist' party of trained intellectuals. Ideas which had been considered criminal in 1982 were accepted in 1987 in one of the most prestigious institutes as a basis for action.[47]

This programme not only posited 'socialism' as an acceptable ideal, but also implied cooperation with reformist elements in the party-state apparatus as a way of bringing it about. Not everyone in Klub Perestroika accepted either the ideal or the means. In November 1987 a debate was held, explicitly on the 'socialist choice', and as a result of it the club split into two groups. Those who wanted to include the word 'socialism' in their programme and were prepared to work with the authorities called themselves Democratic Perestroika and continued to hold meetings at the Institute. Those who rejected the 's-word' and identified the apparat unequivocally as the enemy, who must be confronted, renamed themselves Perestroika-88 and had to look for other premises.[48]

Before this split took place, Klub Perestroika had already made the first moves to coordinate its efforts with those of other informal political clubs in organising an 'informational meeting-dialogue' of informal political associations. One of those it associated with was the Club for Social Initiatives, which had originated in a youth discussion group, *nash Arbat*, held regularly from the spring of 1986 in the *krasnyi ugolok* of a block of flats in central Moscow. Its members had decided to move beyond discussion and become an enabling group to help people with practical proposals for social work to get them realised. Among the early activities they helped launch were a theatre studio, a computer club, and a construction brigade to build a home for the deaf and dumb in Zagorsk.[49]

The club's constitution talked of 'involving broad strata of the population in the process of self-government'. As with the ecological initiative groups of the same period, only on an even wider front, the Club for Social Initiatives was trying to convert ideas into action and also to fill some of the glaring gaps in the social provision afforded by the Soviet state. In this endeavour it was encouraged by the Committee for Social Initiatives of the Soviet Sociological Association, which provided it with premises more appropriate to its ambitions than the *krasnyi ugolok*. This élite patronage was crucial to its survival. The Club was also involved to some extent in defending human rights: in May 1987 it investigated an incident when the police beat up some hippies on the Gogol' Boulevard. The documents it laid before the procuracy provided enough evidence for an acquittal of the hippies.[50]

Another partner in the organisation of the 'meeting-dialogue' was the 'historical-political club' *Obshchina*, the first roots of which went as far back as 1982, when a student discussion circle in the History Faculty of Moscow University began to study the Marxist-Leninist heritage and its application to the contemporary Soviet Union. The circle was still going in the winter of 1986–7, when dissatisfaction among the students with the University's Komsomol organisation came to a head. The circle produced a set of recommendations which would have turned the all-Union Komsomol into a federation of self-governing youth organisations, whose delegates would be subject to recall at any moment. This was both a reassertion of the principle underlying the workers' soviet of 1905 and a return to the ideas of Bakunin, Kropotkin and Proudhon on the optimum structure of society. To underline their debt to the *narodniki* the circle renamed itself *Obshchina:* a reference to the traditional village commune which was finally destroyed by Stalin. The recommendations were spurned by the Komsomol, but they provided the keynote for *Obshchina* as a political club, and later on for the Confederation of Anarcho-Syndicalist (KAS) of which it became the leading member. Its aim was to reactivate soviet democracy through the peaceful undermining of the party-state apparatus and its replacement by a network of democratically elected soviets, while the economy would be run by self-governing workers' councils within each enterprise.[51]

Another organisation involved in the early stages of the organisation of the 'meeting-dialogue' was the All-Union Socio-Political Correspondence Club. This originated from a letter written in the autumn of 1986 by Aleksandr Sukharev, a young scholar from Orenburg, to *Komsomol' skaia pravda* about social problems in the Soviet Union. The editors passed on to him several hundred letters which they received in reply: as a result, an extensive correspondence came into existence on the theoretical problems of socialism. In May 1987 some forty of these correspondents met in Moscow, gave their association its name and charter, and decided that they would organise a conference of independent socialist clubs later that summer. For reasons which are not clear, the Club for Social Initiatives regarded this group as a rival rather than a potential partner, and in the end the Correspondence Club held its own conference at the same time as the Moscow one, but in Taganrog, with about a hundred delegates representing fifty or so towns. The Club remained organisationally sickly, but its network of correspondents helped later to fill the membership lists, especially in provincial towns, of FSOK and KAS.[52]

The 'meeting-dialogue', when it finally took place in Moscow on 20–3 August 1987, was a major turning-point, for it brought together individuals and groups from diverse backgrounds and geographical origins and it established a communications network. It also began the process of differentiation among the 'informals', laying down the main political tendencies and thus preparing the way for later parties. It was held in the House of Culture 'Innovator' with the permission of the party committee of Moscow's Brezhnev raion (soon after renamed Novye Cheremushki). One can only speculate as to the reason why this permission was granted: but some party officials wanted to encourage and maintain links with informal groups of a socialist orientation supporting perestroika from below, and this approach may well have been encouraged by El'tsin, who was head of the Moscow party organisation at the time. At any rate, two conditions were imposed on the organisers of the conference: that all participants should be oriented towards socialism, and that foreign correspondents should not be told of the conference before it was over.[53]

Some fifty-two groups were represented. Apart from *Obshchina*, the Club for Social Initiatives and the Klub Perestroika, there were the Trust Group and the seminars *Demokratiia i gumanizm* and *Druzhba i dialog*, the Leningrad ecological and cultural groups allied in Epicentre, the hippy association 'the System', some romantic socialist groups like the *Kommunary,* the Che Guevara Brigade and the Farabundo Marti Brigade.[54]

In spite of the diversity of the participants, everyone agreed on certain negative statements: no to violence and the propaganda of violence; no to racial and national discrimination; no to any pretension to a monopoly on the truth. Everyone also rejected the Russian chauvinism and anti-Semitism of *Pamiat'.* But that was as far as the unanimity went.[55] Hitherto protest had of itself been a sufficient qualification: to declare openly for radical reform of the system had been enough to distinguish the 'goodies' from the 'baddies'. Now the question arose: what kind of reform and with what ultimate aim in view? It turned out that not everyone shared the commitment to some kind of socialism which had animated the conveners of the meeting. The seminar *Demokratiia i gumanizm,* and in particular its most flamboyant member, Valeriia Novodvorskaia, attracted a good deal of criticism, and there was even a proposal (rejected by the majority) that they be excluded from the conference. Their total rejection of the Soviet experience and of any kind of socialism, their call for a return to the principles of the liberal-democratic February revolution, met with a good deal of support from the floor, but not from the organisers. There was talk of the authorities closing the meeting, since anti-socialist ideas were being expressed.[56]

In the end, the participants decided to accept the fact that there was an unbridgeable division of opinion. Nine clubs agreed to ally themselves as the Federation of Socialist Clubs (FSOK), which envisaged a fairly tight organisation making an explicit commitment to socialism, acknowledging the 'constitutional role of the Communist Party', and declaring a readiness to support its 'healthy and progressive elements' in the 'the course towards developing socialism and democracy which was proclaimed at the 27th Party Congress'. FSOK reaffirmed the notion of the 'withering away of the state' and added: 'we see the formation of independent social groups and associations, and an increase in their influence, as one way of developing a self-managing society and eliminating administrative and bureaucratic structures.'

The other clubs, who remained outside FSOK, envisaged a looser, more noncommittal alliance, for mutual information and support, and were disinclined to compromise with the Communist Party. They called themselves the Social Initiatives Circle (KOI) and claimed their ideal to be 'the renewal of social practice in the spirit of the ideals of socialism, democracy, humanism and progress.'[57] In practice, KOI was so loosely organised that it was stillborn, but FSOK played a leading role in the later move to Popular Fronts, as we shall see below.

One Leningrad delegate exclaimed hopefully, "This is the start of perestroika's "going to the people"".[58] This was over-optimistic as yet, but it is true that out of the working sections of the 'meeting-dialogue' came discrete initiative groups (some of them started initially by Klub Perestroika) which planted the roots of later single-issue movements. The most important off-spring was *Memorial* (see below), but it was not the only one. *Obshchestvennoe samoupravlenie* (Social Self-Government) began to hold seminars to train workers to exercise effectively the new powers envisaged for their representatives in the new enterprise law: their proposed system for electing councils of workers' collectives was tried out at two Moscow factories and three publishing houses.[59] *Sotsial'nyi mir* (Social Peace) began to conduct public workshops on conflict resolution and the maintenance of social peace. *Grazhdanskoe dostoinstvo* (Civic Dignity) was formed to advise and aid people whose legal rights had been violated by the authorities. *Miloserdie* (Charity) undertook to provide counselling and practical help for the old, sick, handicapped, poverty-stricken or lonely.[60]

The most important of the working sections of the 'meeting-dialogue' was *Memorial*, which had its origins in Klub Perestroika. Conference delegates from Klub Perestroika started to collect signatures calling for a thorough examination of the illegal repressions of the past and the erection of a memorial to Stalin's victims. The campaign continued in the streets through the autumn and winter of 1987–8 and attracted sporadic police harassment. Along with Perestroika-88, Democracy and Humanism and the Trust Group, *Memorial* organised a demonstration in memory of Stalin's victims, despite an official ban, on October Square in Moscow on 6 March 1988: many of the participants were detained, but speedily released. By the time Gorbachev lent the idea of a memorial official legitimacy at the 19th Party Conference in June 1988, some 30,000 signatures had been collected.[61]

At this stage the organisers took to the streets again, in provincial towns as well as major cities, this time to find out who the public thought should head an organisation dedicated to erecting a memorial. This was an important new development, for it was the first time for nearly seventy years that the Soviet peoples had been invited to take a genuine vote, even in so rudimentary a form, on personalities or issues. The particular 'election' was of course both eccentric and makeshift, but it did constitute a crude indicator of the moral standing of public figures, at least among the urban population. Significantly, nearly all those who stood highest were either scholars or creative artists. They included Sakharov and Solzhenitsyn, the writers Ales' Adamovich, Vasil' Bykau, Evgenii Evtushenko, Grigorii Baklanov, Lev Razgon, Bulat Okudzhava, Mikhail Shatrov and Anatolii Rybakov, the literary scholars Dmitrii Likhachev and Iurii Kariakin, the actor Mikhail Ul'ianov, the historians Iurii Afanas'ev and Roi Medvedev, the new-style journal editor Vitalii Korotich, and—the only politician—Boris El'tsin. Amongst the organisations which declared themselves sponsors of *Memorial* were a number of creative unions (writers, theatre workers, cinematographers, designers, architects, artists), as well as the weekly journals *Literaturnaia gazeta* and *Ogonek*.[62]

During the signature campaign and the vote for public figures, *Memorial* began to build up an impressive organisation. By January 1989, when its founding congress was held, it had 180 or so branches (103 of which were represented at it), with perhaps 20,000 active members.[63] At this stage the significance of *Memorial* as a formative influence on public attitudes and as a nursery for future political movements can scarcely be overstated. It lent the name of prestigious establishment figures to demands and ideas which until very recently had been officially condemned as subversive and which had brought down persecution on those who professed them. It offered constructive engagement and therefore catharsis for the very powerful feelings of Russians (mainly, since other peoples had other chan-nels) about the unfinished business of their recent past. Its programme of action embraced a whole variety of concerns, which were well articulated by Iurii Afanas'ev at its founding conference:

> The most important task of *Memorial* is to restore to this country its past. But the past is alive in the present. Therefore *Memorial* is a political movement, in so far as today has not yet settled accounts with yesterday.
>
> Our problem is the human being in history. But for us history is not just politics projected into the past, for man's historical habitat is culture. Therefore *Memorial* is also a cultural movement.
>
> By talking about terror and lawlessness, we help to form a notion of legality in the public mind. Therefore *Memorial* is also a movement concerned with the rule of law (*pravovoe dvizhenie*).[64]

Memorial was endeavouring to reconstitute the historical, cultural and legal consciousness of the Soviet peoples, and above all of the Russians. In November 1988 it held a 'week of conscience' in a number of towns. In Moscow a 'wall of memory' was erected, where thousands of photographs of the repressed were ex-hibited. People came to it to seek out relatives they had lost, and to leave forlorn notes of the kind 'Does anyone know my father?' In front of a huge map of the USSR marked with the 'islands' of the Gulag Archipelago was a convict's wheel-barrow in which visitors could place their donations towards a memorial to the victims.[65]

Memorial thus undertook a very ambitious and all-embracing formative role. In most of the non-Russian republics Popular Fronts had already taken up the challenge (often growing out of movements like *Memorial,* for example, the Ukrainian Culturological Club, *Martirologiia* in Belorussia, and the Heritage So-ciety in Estonia). In Russia, however, no single movement had shown itself equal to the task, for the enemy could not be identified as a simple ethnic target: the op-pressors and murderers of Russians had usually been Russians, which much com-plicated the emotional equation. (Those who persuaded themselves otherwise be-longed well outside *Memorial* in the political spectrum, close to the organisation which appropriated to itself an analogous name in Slavonic clothing: *Pamiat'.*) In that sense *Memorial,* at least for a time, came close to fulfilling the role of a Rus-sian Popular Front: it drew prestigious intellectuals and cultural figures for the first time into openly sponsoring and even leading 'informals' and it accustomed broad ranks of the urban population to confrontation with the party-state appa-ratus over fundamental issues of civic consciousness.

However, although it did play a political role in putting forward and agitating for candidates in the elections of 1989–90, *Memorial* never claimed for itself the status of an oppositional party. Instead, since early 1989, with the growth of elec-toral alliances and other political movements, it has devoted itself more especially to its historical and juridical functions: investigating the past, assembling archival materials, preparing plans for a memorial complex which will contain libraries, archives and exhibitions. It has also been working to prevent the creation of 'memory holes' in the present, sending observers to tense regions, such as Baku and the Armenian-Azerbaijani border, where human rights violations are occurring today.[66]

The role of actual political opposition, then, has fallen to other movements. By early 1988 the 'new socialists' of FSOK looked like the most energetically purposeful of these. But there was another, forthrightly non-socialist alternative.

Rejecting what they considered FSOK's compromise with the party-state apparatus, *Demokratiia i gumanizm* left the 'meeting-dialogue' of August 1987 determined to proceed instead by confrontation, forming what they styled an 'opposition party'. Their main partners in this enterprise were the Trust Group (E. Debrianskaia), the juridical commission of Perestroika-88 (V. Kuzin, Iu. Skubko) and the Society of Young Marxists (A. Griaznov).[67] What united this assortment of *neformaly* was not any particular political tendency (there were both liberals and socialists among them), but rather the determination not to cooperate with the communist party or to compromise with the existing system.

The founding conference of the Democratic Union was held in May 1988, and was attended by some 150 delegates from fourteen cities. They were harassed by the police, and the dacha where they were intending to hold their final session was raided, so that the organisational and programmatic arrangements were not entirely clear.[68] There were also disagreements among the participants about whether they envisaged an actual party or merely an alliance of informal groups. The statutes finally issued after its second congress in January 1989 described the Democratic Union as being 'a political party in opposition to the totalitarian structure of the USSR, aiming to bring about its non-violent transformation and the construction of a law-governed state on the principles of humanism, democracy and pluralism'. Being a party of 'the transitional period between totalitarianism and democracy and bringing together people of a variety of democratic convictions', it announced that it had a 'fractional structure and is built on the confederative principle'. Among the fractions which could be identified were Social Democratic, Liberal Democratic, Christian Democrat and Euro-Communist.[69]

In practice, though, the Democratic Union usually described itself as a party, even if one drawing on a wide variety of political outlooks: what united them all was forthright opposition to totalitarianism. During the summer and autumn of 1988 it demonstrated this opposition by a number of demonstrations, notably the one on Pushkin Square in Moscow on 21 August, held to commemorate the twentieth anniversary of the invasion of Czechoslovakia. The police broke it up, arresting one hundred or so demonstrators, forty of whom were given short jail sentences. Soldiers beat some of them up in a police station with the apparent connivance of the authorities.[70]

The Democratic Union's strategy was to refuse to be drawn into the soviets or to cooperate with the party-state apparatus, in order to preserve moral and political purity. It adopted instead a course of non-violent civil disobedience and of campaigning in the streets—'political theatre', as Valeriia Novodvorskaia calls it—seeking gradually to build up parallel alternative institutions of a civil society, until it became possible to convene a Constituent Assembly and establish a fully democratic parliamentary system.[71] There was a daunting moral purity about this, but also a certain sterility. The strategy meant boycotting soviet elections, through participation in which other informal groups were able to extend their public appeal and make a real input into the political system. As a result, though the Democratic Union proved a fertile source of ideas, vitality and campaigning devices, it seemed more a fringe group of martyrs than a real opposition, a little like the Old Believers in Tsarist Russia, and it continually lost individuals and groups to other movements.

...

... On 29 July 1988, twenty-five informal groups met in the information centre of Bauman raion, announced the foundation of the Moscow Popular Front and elected an 'information and coordination committee' to 'extend the maximum practical, informational, theoretical and coordinating assistance to activists of perestroika and participants in the spontaneous democratic movement in other regions of the country, and to support the creation of an All-Union Popular Front.'[84] Two days later, at a mass meeting which gathered about 1,000 people at the Olympic sports complex, the new Front proclaimed the need to ensure that the radical political reform foreshadowed at the 19th Party Conference was transformed into a reality by mass action from below. They welcomed the conference's call for a 'broad patriotic movement in support of perestroika', and claimed that the Popular Front, 'standing for the revolutionary renewal of socialism', should assume this role.[85]

It proved impossible, however, to set up an all-Union Popular Front. ...

...

The real importance of the embryonic Popular Fronts was that they showed that mobilising the public of large cities against the unreformed party-state apparatus was not hopeless (though it required, at least initially, the tolerance of part of that apparatus), and thereby shattered a taboo which had paralysed Soviet political life for nearly seventy years. The way was open for the electoral blocs of 1989–90 to initiate a process of real and fundamental political change.

However, the mould chosen by FSOK, and especially by *Sotsialisticheskaia initsiativa*, as the most energetic and best organised proponents of the Popular Front idea, was too narrow. 'Socialism' was not a word designed to appeal to most urban voters; at the very least it was divisive. All that most voters wanted was opposition to domination by a self-perpetuating nomenklatura élite: to seek agreement on anything more was to invite conflict. It was on that minimal basis that the following year the more successful Associations of Voters were set up. For the moment the exclusive loyalties and doctrinaire proclivities of *kruzhkovshchina* limited the success of the new movements. Nevertheless, by the autumn of 1988 it had been shown that mass mobilisation against the party-state apparatus had a chance of success, and some of the country's leading intellectuals had been drawn into the struggle. For all their failings, the *neformaly* had that achievement to their credit.

NOTES

ABOUT THE AUTHOR: **Geoffrey A. Hosking,** the author of a widely acclaimed history of the Soviet Union, is professor of Russian history at the School of Slavonic Studies of the University of London.

1. Václav Havel, *The Power of the Powerless: Citizens Against the State in Central-Eastern Europe,* London, Hutchinson, 1985, pp. 27–8.

5. *Glasnost',* nos. 2–4, June 1987, published as a supplement to *Russkaia mysl',* 11 September 1987, p. 3.

6. Bohdan Nahaylo, 'Informal Ukrainian Culturological Club helps to break new ground for glasnost', *Radio Liberty Research Report,* 57/88, 8 February 1988; interview with Viacheslav Chornovil and Oles' Shevchenko, 25 April 1988.

7. *Materialy samizdata,* vypusk 13/88, 25 March 1988, AS 6172, pp. 5–10.

8. Alexeyeva, *Soviet Dissent,* Chapter 7.

9. *Vesti iz SSSR,* No. 14, item 4 (henceforth 14–4 etc.), 15/16–4, 1987; Edward J. Lazzerini, 'Crimean Tatars', in Graham Smith (ed.), *The Nationalities Question in the Soviet Union,* London, Longman, 1990, pp. 332–7.

10. Alexeyeva, *Soviet Dissent,* Chapter 10.

11. They were held weekly outside the Lenin Library in Moscow in the early months of 1988. I witnessed one myself on 21 April: the participants were peacefully marched off to waiting police buses and driven away.

12. Yoram Gorlizki, 'Jews', in Smith, *Nationalities,* pp. 339–59.

13. *Vesti iz SSSR,* 8–31, 1987.

14. L. Hirszowicz, 'Breaking the mould: the changing face of Jewish culture under Gorbachev', *Soviet Jewish Affairs,* vol. 18, no. 3, winter 1988, pp. 25–45; the associations which existed by the time of the first congress are listed in ibid., vol. 19, no. 2, summer/autumn 1989, pp. 51–3.

15. *Glasnost',* nos. 2–4, June 1987, in *Russkaia mysl',* 11 September 1987, p. 3; *Vesti iz SSSR,* 13–3, 1987.

16. *Vesti iz SSSR,* 23–3, 1987; *Ekspress-khronika,* no. 19, 13 December 1987, pp. 3–4, no. 20, 20 December 1987, p. 1.

17. Alexeyeva, *Soviet Dissent,* pp. 348–9.

18. Interview with Aleksandr Podrabinek, 18 April 1988; *Ekspress-khronika,* no. 15, 15 November 1987, p. 5, no. 14, 3 April 1988, p. 2.

19. Alexeyeva, *Soviet Dissent,* pp. 373–4; interview with Sergei Grigor'iants, 23 May 1991.

20. Interview with Sergei Grigor'iants, 23 May 1991; *Ekspress-khronika,* no. 20, 15 May 1988, p. 6.

21. For a sample of the journal, see issue no. 12 in *Materialy samizdata,* vypusk 37/88, 29 July 1988, AS 6262.

22. V. N. Shkurin, *Neformal'nye molodezhnye ob"edineniia,* Moscow, Ministerstvo Kul'tury, 1990, p. 56.

23. ibid.

24. I. Iu. Sundiev, 'Neformal'nye molodezhnye ob"edineniia: opyt ekspozitsii', *Sotsiologicheskie issledovaniia,* No. 5, 1987, pp. 58–9.

25. I. Iu. Sundiev, 'Samodeiatel'nye ob"edineniia molodezhi', *Sotsiologicheskie issledovaniia,* No. 2, 1989, pp. 56–62; Jane Ellis, 'USSR: the Christian seminar', *Religion in Communist Lands,* no. 8, 1980, pp. 92ff.

26. Shkurin, *Neformal'nye,* pp. 66–7.

27. Sundiev, *Sotsiologicheskie issledovaniia,* No. 5, 1987, pp. 59–60.

28. 'Ideologiia sovetskikh khippi', *Strana i mir,* No. 6, 1987, p. 140; Shkurin, *Neformal'nye,* op. cit., pp. 98–100; *Neformaly: Civil Society in the USSR,* Helsinki Watch Report, February 1990, pp. 128–9.

29. 'Ideologiia sovetskikh khippi', pp. 140–3.

30. ibid., pp. 140–1.

31. Sundiev, *Sotsiologicheskie issledovaniia,* No. 5, 1987, p. 61.

32. S. N. Iushenkov (ed.), *Neformaly: sotsial'nye initsiativy,* Moscow, Moskovskii rabochii, 1990, p. 22; Boris Kagarlitsky, *The Thinking Reed: Intellectuals and the Soviet State from 1917 to the Present,* London, Verso, 1988, p. 334.

33. Alan Bookbinder *et al., Comrades,* London, BBC Publications, 1985, pp. 159–60.

34. Iushenkov, *Neformaly,* pp. 22–3; V. N. Berezovskii and N. I. Krotov (eds), *Neformal'naia Rossiia,* Moscow, Molodaia Gvardiia, 1990, p. 370.

35. A. Ezhelyov, 'Vodnoi lodke', *Izvestiia,* 1 August 1987; M. Nazarov, 'Na nicheinoi zemle perestroiki', *Russkaia mysl',* 18 September 1987, p. 5; *Vesti iz SSSR,* 10–13, 13–27 (1987).

36. Julia Wishnevsky, 'The origins of Pamyat', *Survey,* vol. 30, no. 3, October 1988, pp. 79–91.

37. N. R. Miuzneks, 'The Daugavpils hydro-station and glasnost in Latvia', *Journal of Baltic Studies,* vol. 18, no. 1, spring 1987, pp. 63–70.

40. *Amnesty,* no. 7, February/March 1984, p. 18; Ludmila Alekseeva, 'Obshchestvennye ob"edineniia v SSSR', *SSSR: vnutrennie protivorechiia,* no. 21, 1988, pp. 74–5.

42. Olga Medvedkov, 'The Moscow Trust Group: an uncontrolled grassroots movement in the Soviet Union', *Mershon Centre Quarterly Report* (Ohio State University), vol. 12, no. 1, spring 1988.

46. *Glasnost',* no. 1, in *Russkaia mysl',* 17 July 1987, p. 6; *Materialy samizdata,* AS 6015, pp. 39–45; V. Kardanovskii, 'Klub Perestroika: opyt pervykh mesiatsev raboty', *Otkrytaia zona,* vypusk 2, November 1987, pp. 4–10.

47. Liudmila Alekseeva, 'Novye partii v SSSR?', *SSSR: vnutrennie protivorechiia,* no. 20, 1987, pp. 35–44.

48. *Glasnost',* op. cit.; P. Kudiukin, 'Uroki odnogo krizisa', *Otkrytaia zona,* vypusk 3, view', *Report on the USSR,* 3 May 1991, pp. 4–6. The Klub Perestroika contained many individuals who were later prominent in independent political movements and/or journals. They included Oleg Rumiantsev, Pavel Kudiukin and Leonid Volkov of the Social Democratic Party; Viktor Zolotarev of the Constitutional Democratic Party; Viktor Kuzin of the Democratic Union; Andrei Fadin, political commentator of *Kommersant;* Igor' Chubais of the Democratic Platform; Viacheslav Igrunov of the Moscow Bureau of Information Exchange; Iurii Samodurov of *Memorial;* and Sergei Stankevich, deputy mayor of Moscow.

49. Interviews with Grigorii Pel'man, 18 April and 5 May 1988; Nick Lampert, 'Russia's new democrats: the club movement and perestroika', *Detente,* nos. 9–10, 1987, p. 10.

50. Grigorii Pel'man, 'Neformal'nye kluby Moskvy', *Forum*, no. 20, 1989, pp. 108–10; Viacheslav Igrunov, 'O neformal'nykh politicheskikh klubakh Moskvy', *Problemy vostochnoi Evropy*, nos. 27–8, 1989, p. 63; V. N. Shkurin, *Neformal'nye*, pp. 199–20.

51. Berezovskii and Krotov (eds). *Neformal'naia Rossiia*, p. 260. A Shubin, 'Politika i pedagogika: ot "obshchiny" k konfederatsii anarkho-sindikalistov', in Iushenkov, *Neformaly*, op. cit., pp. 101–6; interview with Andrei Isaev, 20 September 1990.

52. Berezovskii and Krotov (eds), *Neformal'naia Rossiia*, pp. 239–41; Igrunov, 'O neformal'nykh', op. cit., pp. 69–71; I. Sundiev, 'Nashestvie marsiian', in Lushenkov, *Neformaly*, op. cit., p. 19.

53. Alekseeva, 'Novye partii', p. 52.

54. ibid., pp. 45–6.

55. V. Iakovlev, 'Proschanie s Bazarovym', *Ogonek*, no. 36, 1987, p. 4.

56. Alekseeva, 'Novye partii', p. 56.

57. *Guardian*, 12 September 1987; Iakovlev, 'Proshchanie', p. 5; Pel'man, 'Neformal'nye', pp. 110–12; 'Dokumenty pervoi informatsionnoi vstrechi-dialoga', *Otkrytaia zona*, vypusk 1, October 1987, pp. 2–19.

58. Gleb Pavlovskii, 'Khoziaeva vozvrashchaiutsia', *Kul'turno-prosvetitel'naia rabota*, 11/87, p. 22.

59. *Nyeformaly: Civil Society in the USSR*, Helsinki Watch Report, February 1990, op. cit., p. 60.

60. Pel'man, 'Neformal'nye', pp. 111–12; Iakovlev, 'Proshchanie', p. 5; *Nyeformaly*, Helsinki Watch Report, op. cit., p. 25; *Materialy samizdata*, vypusk 9/88, 22 February 1988, AS 6154.

61. Berezovskii and Krotov (eds), *Neformal' naia Rossiia*, pp. 282–5; *Vesti iz SSSR*, 21–38 (1987); 5/6–4 (1988); interview with Arsenii Roginskii, 16 April 1991.

62. Berezovskii and Krotov (eds), *Neformal' naia Rossiia*, p. 283; Julia Wishnevsky, 'Conflict between state and *Memorial* society', *Report on the USSR*, 20 January 1989, pp. 8–9.

63. Interview with Arsenii Roginskii, 16 April 1991.

64. A. V. Gromov and O. S. Kuzin, *Neformaly: kto est' kto?* Moscow, Mysl', 1990, p. 107.

65. Soviet television report of 27 November 1988, in *Summary of World Broadcasts*, SU/0331, 10 December 1988, B/5; *Guardian*, 22 November 1988; *Moskovskie novosti*, no. 48, 1988, pp. 8–9.

66. Interviews with Dmitrii Leonov, 16 September 1990, and Arsenii Roginskii, 16 April 1991.

67. Berezovskii & Krotov (eds), *Neformal' naia Rossiia*, p. 250.

68. It belonged to Sergei Grigor'iants: see above, p. 7.

69. *Guardian*, 9 May 1988; *Partiia demokraticheskogo soiuza: vtoroi s"ezd: dokumenty*, Riga-Moscow, 1989, p. 6; Jonathan Aves, 'The Democratic Union: a Soviet opposition party?', *Slovo*, vol. 1, no. 2, November 1988, pp. 93–4.

70. Aves, 'Democratic Union', p. 94.

71. Interview with Eduard Molchanov, 11 June 1991.

84. 'Rezoliutsiia soveshchaniia samodeiatel'nykh ob"edinenii Moskvy – uchastnikov dvizheniia Narodnogo Fronta', *Otkrytaia zona*, vypusk 7, August 1988, p. 88.

85. 'Rezoliutsiia mitinga Moskovskogo Narodnogo Fronta', *Otkrytaia zona*, vypusk 7, August 1988, p. 89.

10 *Political Change in the Soviet Union*

ARCHIE BROWN

A new Soviet political system is being created from day to day. At the moment, the new sits uneasily alongside the old, and the old is not giving way without a fight. The changes call into question a great deal that has been taken for granted throughout much of Soviet history, and it has become more difficult than ever before to predict what the system will look like a decade from now. But even those who as recently as 1987 were arguing—wrongly—that nothing of consequence had changed in the Soviet Union must now recognize that dramatic and fundamentally important change is taking place.[1]

Political reform is, of course, proceeding much faster and more successfully than economic reform. So long as material shortages get worse rather than better and there is no improvement in the standard of living of the average Soviet citizen, the continuation of political reform cannot be taken for granted. But many Western commentators, even once they belatedly accepted that Gorbachev was serious about radical reform, have underestimated his staying power and the prospects for *perestroika* moving forward. It has been argued, for example, that the opposition of the party and state apparatus represents an insurmountable obstacle, or that conservative forces are able to draw strength from popular grievances and disappointed expectations.[2]

The combination of freedom to criticize and lack of economic progress is undoubtedly an important factor in the Soviet political equation. But so far, while it has reduced Gorbachev's *popularity* at home as compared with the early days of his leadership in 1985, it has not undermined his *power*.[3] On the contrary, Gorbachev has skillfully used both old and new institutions—on the one hand, the powers of the party general secretaryship and, on the other, the outcome of the elections to the Congress of People's Deputies and the first meeting of that legislative body—to reduce the numerical weight and political influence of conservative Communists in the highest echelons of the party and state apparatus.

The energetic part being played by radically reformist journalists, social scientists, and writers has helped to create a political climate in which it is far from easy for conservative party and state bureaucrats to exploit domestic economic and social problems to their advantage. There are many differences between the present period of Soviet history and Khrushchev's time of attempted reform. One, of course, is the greater political insight and subtlety of Gorbachev, but no less important is the far greater sophistication of the political analyses appearing now in many (though not all) Soviet journals and newspapers and on some radio and television programs. There has been a dramatic increase in the circulation of the most liberal and forward-looking weeklies and monthlies, and the enhanced political education of their readers is now a factor to be reckoned with. (The most spectacular example of this trend is the weekly *Ogonek* which, since Vitaly Korotich became its editor in 1986, has increased its circulation from a few hundred thousand to almost three-and-a-half million. The monthly journal *Znamya*, now under the editorial direction of Georgy Baklanov and Vladimir Lakshin, has a circulation of 980,000 copies today as compared with 175,000 in 1985; and *Novy Mir* currently has a print run of 1,573,000 copies monthly as compared with approximately 496,000 as recently as late 1987. *Novy Mir*'s announcement that it would serialize George Orwell's *Nineteen Eighty-Four* in 1989—which it has, indeed, now published—was one reason for the substantial rise in the number of subscriptions taken out for the present year.)

New ways of thinking and speaking about Soviet politics as well as new ways of behaving have emerged in Gorbachev's Soviet Union, especially since 1987. In an article written for this journal at the end of 1986, I emphasized the significance of the political developments already under way but described the change (in itself far from insignificant) in the postwar Soviet Union as one "from quasi-totalitarianism to authoritarianism to the beginnings of a more enlightened authoritarian regime."[4] In the past two-and-a-half years, the Soviet system has developed beyond that. It is now indeed a more enlightened authoritarian regime and one, furthermore, that already contains some significant elements of political pluralism and of democratization. ...

It is not only ... what is happening in other Communist states that is now influencing the top Soviet leadership. The sources of learning have been extended to include certain aspects of the political systems of "bourgeois democratic" countries and not merely, as in the past, technical or managerial features of their economic systems. Both Gorbachev and Vadim Medvedev, a Politburo member and the secretary of the Central Committee with responsibility for ideology, have stressed the necessity of learning from the nonsocialist world as well as from other socialist countries.[11] Medvedev has appeared to call for a reinterpretation of the achievements of European social democracy, a shift of which there have been numerous other signs in Soviet publications (and on Soviet television), including sympathetic discussion of Sweden and other Scandinavian countries.[12] Indeed, on the reform wing of the Soviet Communist Party the long-standing barrier between communism, on the one hand, and social democracy or democratic socialism, on the other, is crumbling. In a dramatic break with the past, it is not uncommon now to hear prominent Soviet party intellectuals and some of the more enlightened officials say that they regard Sweden not only as an example of socialism but as the best model currently on view.

At the inaugural meeting of the Congress of People's Deputies, held at the end of May and beginning of June [1989], the prominent Soviet writer Chingiz Aitmatov went further. Aitmatov made two major speeches to the congress. In the first, it was he who proposed Mikhail Gorbachev for the post of chairman of the Supreme Soviet.[13] The very fact that Aitmatov was preselected to do this by the overwhelming majority of deputies who are members of the Communist Party and that he was, furthermore, one of the 100 deputies chosen by the party to represent it at the congress is evidence enough that he is in good standing with the party leadership and in the mainstream of reformist thinking rather than on its radical fringes. Yet Aitmatov, in the second of his speeches to the congress, stretched the meaning of socialism in ways unimaginable a few years ago. His address was a long way from traditional socialist theory, in almost any of its variants, but a good example of the importance of understanding the changing meanings of concepts politically and not merely from a theoretical or doctrinal standpoint.

Instead, said Aitmatov, of making an idol of socialism as "the holy of holies of our theoretical doctrine," and instead of laying down the law on what did and what did not constitute socialism, it was necessary to reach an understanding whereby it was judged by its fruits—that is, by its contribution to people's creativity and prosperity. He suggested that the Soviet Union could learn from other countries for whom the Soviet example had performed the service of demonstrating how *not* to go about constructing socialism:

> I have in mind the flourishing law-governed societies of Sweden, Austria, Finland, Norway, the Netherlands, Spain and, finally, Canada across the ocean. About Switzerland I don't even speak—it's a model. The working person in those countries earns on average four to five times more than our workers. The social protection and the level of welfare of those societies are something we can only dream about. This is real and, if you like, worker trade-union socialism, although these countries do not call themselves socialist, but are none the worse for that.[14]

The comparisons important Soviet reformers now make both with the Soviet past and with Western countries are remarkable. Aleksandr Yakovlev, Gorbachev's closest ally on the Politburo, said in response to the questions of a Soviet television journalist on May 27, "For the first time in the history of our country we have a platform of conscience, a platform of morality."[15] When he was asked whether the Congress of People's Deputies could be compared with parliaments abroad, Yakovlev did not argue for the superiority of the new Soviet legislature, though until very recently Soviet officials routinely suggested that even the unreformed Supreme Soviet was vastly more democratic than Western parliaments. Instead, he emphasized the comparative underdevelopment of Soviet parliamentary theory and practice:

> Parliaments in other countries have existed for decades and they have entirely different traditions. They have written many volumes about procedural matters there. We do not have that. Of course, we must learn professionalism in the economy and politics; above all we must learn democratic professionalism. We must learn democracy, tolerance of others' opinions and thoughts. That's not easy. I believe that the

work of the Soviet parliament will demonstrate where we are right and where we are wrong; what we must continue and what must be corrected.[16]...

As James Farr has noted in a recent essay, "Where there are different concepts, there are different beliefs, and so different actions and practices," even though political practice is only partly constituted by concepts.[17] But while acting politically "for strategic and partisan purposes," people do so "in and through language" and "language is an arena of political action." Accordingly, "political change and conceptual change must be understood as one complex and interrelated process."[18]

In the Soviet context, three new concepts in particular deserve special emphasis, for they help to open up space for new political activity and provide a theoretical underpinning for some of the concrete reforms that the more radical interpreters of *perestroika* are attempting to implement. It is worth noting that within a period of 18 months—between the summer of 1987 and the end of 1988—all three received the endorsement of Gorbachev.

The first of these concepts is that of "socialist pluralism," and its adoption represents a radical break with past Soviet doctrine. It is of interest that whereas many reformist concepts are to be encountered first in the writings of scholarly specialists and only later in the speeches of party leaders, in this instance it was Gorbachev who took the bold step of embracing the concept of "pluralism" in public before anyone else had done so.[19]...

... Gorbachev's adoption of the concept of "socialist pluralism" and the positive reference made to a "socialist pluralism of opinions" in the resolution on *glasnost* adopted by the party conference represented a considerable boost for the more radical Soviet political reformers. These endorsements provided a legitimacy previously lacking for political debate and diversity of opinion on political and social issues in Soviet publications, even though the fact that "pluralism" was qualified by the adjective "socialist" indicated that there were still limits on what was deemed fit to print. ...

The second concept adopted in recent times that is of great importance for the advancement of the cause of political and legal reform is that of the *pravovoe gosudarstvo,* or the state based upon the rule of law. While there is nothing new about an emphasis on "socialist legality," the idea of the *pravovoe gosudarstvo* goes beyond that. The "socialist legality" introduced under Khrushchev meant an end to the excesses and extremes of arbitrariness of Stalin's time, but lawyers and the legal system remained firmly subordinated to the party leadership. ...

The idea of the law-governed state is part of a much more profound analysis of arbitrary rule and the abuse of power than took place in Khrushchev's time. It reflects a consciousness of the extent to which powerful individuals and institutions have been able to bend the law to their own purposes, as well as a concern with the inadequacy of the rights of attorneys and of the independence of judges in cases where the interests and views of well-connected officials are involved. ...

As with other innovative concepts that have been accepted by the Soviet leadership, different leaders and theorists can interpret the idea of the law-governed state in different ways. But adoption of the concept marks a considerable step forward in the advancement of the *role* of law—even if there does not yet exist in practice a full-fledged *rule* of law—in Soviet society.

The third concept that is quite new in the Soviet context is that of "checks and balances." Its adoption is a remarkable departure from previous patterns of Soviet thought and it, too, is part of the breakthrough in thinking about the Soviet political system that took place in 1987 and 1988. In the past, the notion of checks and balances, insofar as it was referred to at all, was viewed as part of the deceptive screen behind which the ruling class exercised untrammeled power in bourgeois states. But the more serious Soviet study of foreign political systems in recent years, as well as the contemplation of some of the horrendous results of unchecked power within the Soviet Union (especially in the Stalin period), have led to a reevaluation of the theory and practice of checks and balances. The idea that the concept might have something to offer reformers of the Soviet political system was first broached in print in Moscow as short a time ago as July 1987,[26] and it was adopted by Gorbachev even more recently—at the end of November 1988, in his speech commending the first phase of political reform to the Supreme Soviet.[27]

This is one instance where the influence on Gorbachev's thinking can be traced with some confidence. It was at a meeting of the Soviet Association of Political Sciences presided over by Georgy Shakhnazarov in February 1987 (reported in the monthly journal *Sovetskoe gosudarstvo i pravo* in July of that year) that the call for the development of a "socialist theory of checks and balances" was first heard.[28] To assist in the elaboration of this, it was advocated that the development of bourgeois states should be studied from the standpoint of the creation within them of checks and balances and that relevant Western theoretical writings should also be examined. All this was linked to the necessity of "preventing the concentration in the hands of one organ (or individual) of all political power."[29]

Shakhnazarov was already at that time—while still first deputy head of the Socialist Countries Department of the Central Committee—an informal adviser of Gorbachev, but in early 1988 he became one of his four *pomoshniki,* or full-time personal assistants. He is now an influential figure whose judgment Gorbachev clearly respects. Accordingly, when Gorbachev concluded a discussion of the proposed Committee for Supervision of the Constitution by commenting, "Thus, one may say, comrades, that our own socialist system of 'checks and balances' is taking shape in this country, designed to protect society against any violation of socialist legality at the highest state level,"[30] it was not difficult to detect the influence of Shakhnazarov and of scholars in the reform-minded Soviet Association of Political Sciences, whose presidency Shakhnazarov still combines with his senior political advisory functions. For the leader of the Soviet Communist Party and head of the Soviet state to accept the need for checks and balances, albeit *socialist* checks and balances, is a significant illustration of the "new thinking" that has emerged on Soviet political institutions as well as on foreign policy.

THE PROCESS OF INSTITUTIONAL CHANGE

The most important point about reform of the Soviet political system is that it is not an event but a *process* and, in all probability, a *long-term* process if the reform wing of the Communist Party continues to prevail, as it has increasingly done since Gorbachev became general secretary (and especially since 1987). Gorbachev himself has emphasized that the reforms adopted by the old Supreme Soviet at the end of November 1988 represent only the first phase of reform of the political system. It is impossible to say where they will end, for Soviet reformers themselves do not know. There was much less serious thinking about reform of the political system than about reform of the economy (inadequate though that was) prior to *perestroika,* and ideas on institutional change are being elaborated all the time. It is entirely possible that reform of the Soviet political system will go very much further than it has already if the balance of influence continues to shift in favor of "new thinkers," as it has over the past few years.

The institutional change that has already taken place is far from inconsequential. On the one hand, some major existing institutions are functioning in a significantly different way from before. This is true of the Communist Party as a whole and of some of its constituent institutions. On the other hand, a number of essentially new political institutions have been created. Thus, for example, Soviet elections in 1989 were so different from what were called "elections" in the Soviet Union in the past that they have little in common except the name. Similarly, the new Supreme Soviet is likely to be a much more serious legislature than the body that carried that name previously, and it has been elected by a novel (and already important) institution, the Congress of People's Deputies. There is a new-style presidency, and there is to be a Committee for Supervision of the Constitution. Though it is not possible to provide here an exhaustive survey of the changes in Soviet political institutions, three aspects of this process particularly merit closer examination: electoral reform, the evolving legislature, and the changing structure and role of the party.

Elections. As early as 1987, by way of "experiment," Soviet voters were offered a choice of candidates in elections to local soviets in approximately 5 percent of the constituencies.[31] But the big breakthrough in the Soviet electoral system came with the elections to the new Congress of People's Deputies in late March of [1989]. Of the 2,250 members of the congress, 1,500 are drawn from territorial constituencies, with 750 seats distributed among the various parts of the country on the basis of population density and 750 divided equally among the national-territorial units from union republics to autonomous regions (thus giving disproportionate representation to the smaller nationalities, since tiny Estonia and the enormous Russian republic return the same number of deputies on this "nationality slate"). Approximately three-quarters of the territorial elections to the congress were competitive ones,[32] but even running in a single-candidate district was no guarantee against defeat, as a number of party officials discovered to their dismay when they failed to secure 50 percent support from those who voted.

A negative vote could be cast by crossing out the names of the candidate or candidates a voter wished to reject. However, all voters had to mark their ballots, even if they wished to support the prospective deputy in a single-candidate election. This was an important change from previous Soviet electoral practice, whereby voters were not obliged to enter the voting booth at all. To drop an unmarked ballot in the ballot box counted as support for the candidate and was the normal way of voting. To make any mark at all on the ballot was, up until the most recent elections, to draw attention to oneself as a probable negative voter. Thus, the 1989 national elections were the first in Soviet history to combine universal adult suffrage with secrecy of the ballot and the competitive principle in at least a majority of seats.

The electoral process varied widely from one part of the country to another and had many imperfections. The party apparatus was, for example, much more successful in Soviet Central Asia than in the major European cities in getting its favored candidates selected. But elsewhere the attempt of party officials to foist themselves or their nominees on the electorate provoked, in many cases, an effective backlash. Thus, with the entire Moscow party apparatus opposed to the election of the maverick populist Boris Yeltsin and putting its resources behind his factory manager opponent, Yeltsin won a landslide victory with approximately 90 percent of the votes in a constituency comprising the entire city of Moscow. In fact, the three major Soviet cities—Moscow, Leningrad, and Kiev—all returned deputies who were chosen by the electorate in defiance of their city party bureaucracies. In Moscow, they included not only Roy Medvedev but also the radically reformist director of the Moscow Historical-Archival Institute, Yuri Afanasev, who was elected in a working-class district of Moscow where the overt hostility to him of the local party machine evidently counted in his favor with the electorate. In Moscow, Leningrad, and Kiev there was an easily detectable "anti-apparatus" vote, of which the most highly placed victim was Yuri Solovev, the first secretary of the Leningrad regional party organization and a candidate member of the Politburo.

Not surprisingly, the election results (even though they included a comfortable majority of successful candidates who could be relied upon to follow the lead of the top party leadership at the Congress of People's Deputies) sent shock waves of alarm and anger through the party apparatus. At a Central Committee plenary session held on April 25, many of the regional party secretaries who spoke blamed shortages, the mass media, insufficient party unity, and the central party leadership for their lack of electoral success. The first secretary of the Krasnodar regional party committee, Ivan Polozkov, said it was getting harder to answer people's questions as to why there was no butter, children's shoes, baby carriages, or bicycles for sale. He added sarcastically: "They listen, but they do not understand very well. And as for the absence of soap, they do not wish even to listen."[33] Aleksandr Melnikov, a former Central Committee department head and now a regional party secretary, complained that ordinary people had been led astray by "massive onslaught from the mass media."[34]

The defeated Leningrad party chief, Yuri Solovev, noted that "not one of the six leaders of the party and soviet in Leningrad and its region assembled the necessary number of votes."[35] This, as he pointed out, was not unique to Leningrad, and the only pattern he detected in such votes against the local official establishments was that they had been cast in "major industrial, scientific and cultural centers."[36] That was hardly an encouraging postmortem for the Central Committee.

The 750 deputies who were chosen by public organizations—ranging in size and political weight from the Communist Party itself to the Soviet Culture Foundation and the Soviet Peace Foundation, and including such important bodies as the Academy of Sciences, the Komsomol, and the creative unions (writers, artists, etc.)—produced a still clearer majority of people who could be relied upon not to rock the boat too much.[37] At the same time, though, these organizations provided a minority who were among the most radical people to attend the inaugural session of the Congress of People's Deputies. This was especially true of the Academy of Sciences, whose Presidium produced a list of only 23 candidates, out of which the membership was to choose 20 representatives—and left off the list some of the country's most talented and politically outspoken scientists and scholars, including Academician Andrei Sakharov, who had been nominated by some 60 scientific institutes. In response, the Academy voters struck out 15 of the names presented to them, giving the required 50 percent support to only eight of the candidates. These results necessitated a second round of voting, this time for a list that included the names of some of the Soviet Union's most prominent reformers (the Presidium had learned its lesson). In the end, practically every deputy elected from the Academy was close to the liberal or radical reformist end of the Soviet political spectrum. In the second round, Sakharov was elected comfortably and one of the boldest of economic reformers, Nikolai Shmelev, topped the poll.[38]

The move from elections without choice, in which the social composition as well as the political conformity of the deputies could be determined in advance, to competitive elections and opportunities for citizens to nominate candidates from below (though still within the framework of a one-party system) had a number of consequences probably unintended by the top party leadership. One was that in certain republics, especially the Baltic ones, only those candidates—whether party or nonparty—who were prepared to take a strongly national line and defend the interests of the titular nationality of their republic could hope to be elected. Another was the radical shift in the occupational and class composition of the Congress of People's Deputies as compared with that of its predecessor, the unreformed Supreme Soviet "elected" in 1984. The proportion of industrial and farm workers, for example, went down from 49.5 to 23.1 percent. The representation of employees with higher education and of intellectuals went up. Heads of higher educational institutions, who were entirely unrepresented in the 1984 Supreme Soviet, made up 4.1 percent (83 deputies) of the 1989 Congress of People's

Deputies. The representation of senior KGB officials went down between 1984 and 1989 from 1.1 percent to 0.5 percent, while entirely new categories of occupations to be represented in the list of deputies included those of scientific workers (61 deputies: 3 percent), journalists (28 deputies: 1.4 percent), attorneys (two deputies: 0.1 percent), and clergymen (five deputies: 0.2 percent).[39]

In practice, these changes meant a strengthened representation of highly articulate deputies; not surprisingly, though, the decline in worker representation was strongly attacked by opponents of reform. The growing importance of initiative from below, as opposed to control from above, also led to a sharp fall in the proportion of women deputies as compared with the old Supreme Soviet. This may be a backhanded tribute to the vastly greater significance of the new legislature, given the generally weak position of women in Soviet political life; there has for many years been an inverse relationship between the power of an institution in the Soviet political system and the percentage of women to be found in that body.

Taking the elections as a whole, they must be seen as a remarkable landmark in the process of the democratization of the Soviet political system. The fact that they were still held within the framework of a one-party system did not, as many Soviet citizens feared, mean that there was nothing to choose from among different candidates in terms of their policies and principles. The political reality that the Soviet Communist Party itself (a 20 million–strong body comprising approximately 10 percent of adult citizens) is a coalition of very diverse viewpoints and interests became clearer than ever. In a number of the major cities, there was a lively clash of opinions in the course of the election campaign. This was notwithstanding the fact that 85.3 percent of candidates nominated and 87.6 percent of those actually elected to the Congress of People's Deputies were party members.[40] Short of a "counterrevolutionary" reversal of the entire process of *perestroika*, it is difficult to see any return to the sham elections of the past. In view of the evident dissatisfaction of many of the electorates presented with only a single candidate in the 1989 elections, it is much more likely that movement will be in the direction of electoral choice in *all* constituencies. ...

The New Legislature. Just one of many unique features of the First Congress of People's Deputies was that no one (not even Gorbachev) knew how long it was going to last. As originally conceived, it appeared that the main task of the 2,250 deputies was to elect the inner body, the bicameral, 542-member Supreme Soviet. It is the Supreme Soviet that is to be the more or less permanently functioning part of parliament, meeting for more than half of the year (unlike the old Supreme Soviet, which met for only a few days annually). But the First Congress of People's Deputies itself was in session for far longer than was the pattern with the unreformed Supreme Soviet; it began its deliberations on May 25, and ended them on June 9. If the elections that brought the deputies to the Palace of Congresses in Moscow were a milestone on the road to a form of democracy in the Soviet Union, the congress itself broke new frontiers in public freedom of speech. And it was quite a public. What made the impassioned debate and the breaking of one taboo after another of far greater political consequence than would otherwise have been the case was the live broadcasting on Soviet television and radio of the congress proceedings. The speeches were heard by an estimated audience of between 90 and 100 million people.[43] Some of the addresses, if they had been distributed even in 90 or 100 copies five years ago, would undoubtedly have earned their authors a spell in a labor camp.

A public opinion poll conducted on the eve of the convening of the Congress of People's Deputies showed that there were relatively high hopes for the congress, as well as a new popular willingness to distinguish between the role to be played by the hierarchy of elected soviets and the activity of the party.[44] Asked with which institutions people linked their hopes for an improvement in the state of affairs in the country, respondents mentioned the Congress of People's Deputies more often than any other institution. The soviets at all levels came next, and the general secretary, as a source of hope, was in third place (but, significantly, enjoying a higher level of support than all other party institutions, such as the Politburo, the Central Committee, and party congresses).[45]

The atmosphere at the First Congress of People's Deputies was characterized by one Soviet commentator, Vitaly Tretyakov, as "*glasnost* galore." Even more important, the congress had, in Tretyakov's words, "reduced to a minimum the distance between the canonized *glasnost* and freedom of speech."[46] And this was, said the same author, a "selfless *glasnost*" because "as is very well known, the legal and political guarantees of any *glasnost* are pretty weak in our country still."[47]…

Intraparty Change. The Communist Party is undergoing significant change as a result of the reform of its internal structure, the personnel changes that have reduced the decision-making power of conservative Communists, and the creation of new state institutions. In particular, the introduction of competitive elections and the formation of a new legislative assembly have helped to bring to life dormant political forces within the Soviet Union and have compelled the party to become more responsive to that society as a whole, if it is to retain authority and, perhaps, even its power.

In a memorandum to the Politburo dated August 24, 1988 (but published in a new Soviet journal only in 1989),[63] Gorbachev put forward concrete proposals for the restructuring of the Central Committee apparatus. By authorizing its subsequent publication, he revealed publicly for the first time the precise size of that body immediately prior to its radical reorganization, which was implemented in October. "Today," Gorbachev wrote in the memorandum, "the apparatus of the Central Committee numbers 1,940 responsible workers and 1,275 technical staff."[64] Western estimates of the number of officials working in the Central Committee apparatus have generally varied between 1,000 and 1,500, whereas the actual figure was close to 2,000, excluding support staff. By the beginning of 1989, the numbers were closer to what Western observers had imagined they were before. Gorbachev was aiming at a 50 percent cut in the size of the central apparatus, and by the end of 1988 approximately 40 percent of Central Committee officials had moved either into retirement or to other posts.

The most important feature of this party restructuring was the reduction of the number of Central Committee departments from 20 to nine[65] and the creation of six new Central Committee commissions. ... The creation of the new commissions represented a considerable strengthening of Gorbachev's personal position and of the commitment to *perestroika* within the leadership.[67]

It involved, however, some compromises on Gorbachev's part. The price he paid for moving Chebrikov out of the chairmanship of the KGB was, in effect, to promote him, for Chebrikov became a secretary of the Central Committee alongside the full membership of the Politburo he already enjoyed. Moreover, his 21 years in a senior position in the KGB did not make him the most obvious person to head a commission with responsibility for advancing the cause of the state based on the rule of law. Similarly, by cutting back on Ligachev's supervisory responsibilities within the Secretariat—which had previously included agriculture, but also much more—and confining him to agriculture, Gorbachev forced Ligachev to concentrate his attention on an area crucial to the success of reform, and one that might have benefited from being in the hands of someone less suspicious of marketization. Given, however, Gorbachev's knowledge of and personal interest in agriculture and his degree of commitment to the introduction of a leasehold system granting greater autonomy to groups of farmers (including family groups), Ligachev's new post gave him fewer possibilities to apply a brake to the process of reform than he had previously enjoyed.

Gorbachev's skill and determination in using both his authority and power to the full to advance the cause of reform were shown again in April, when the first Central Committee plenum after the elections for the Congress of People's Deputies took place. While many of the current members of the Central Committee took the opportunity to voice their discontent about the new insecurity of their positions generated by the elections and the changed political climate, the plenum accepted the resignation of 74 full members of the Central Committee, 24 candidate members, and 12 members of the Central Auditing Commission.[68] At the same time, it promoted 24 candidate members of the Central Committee to full membership. Taking into account both the resignations and the promotions, the number of voting Central Committee members was reduced from 303 to 251.[69]

This was an unprecedented degree of turnover to occur between party congresses. Since it is only at these congresses, held every five years, that regular elections for the Central Committee take place, Gorbachev's chances of achieving a Central Committee more attuned to the spirit of the times (that of 1989 rather than 1986, when the present Central Committee was elected) seemed slim. But by *persuading* those Central Committee members who had lost the jobs that justified their membership in that body in the first place (a fact that itself made them a disgruntled and potentially dangerous group within the Central Committee) that they should resign in April rather than wait to be removed at the next regular elections (at the 28th Party Congress due to be held in early 1991), Gorbachev was able at a stroke to reduce substantially the conservative deadweight within that important party institution. Those who departed included such former members of the top leadership team as Gromyko, Nikolai Tikhonov, Dolgikh, and Boris Ponomarov, as well as Petr Fedoseev—the man who, in his capacity as vice-president of the Academy of Sciences with special responsibility for the social sciences, bore a good deal of personal responsibility for the sorry state of those disciplines in Brezhnev's time.[70]

As general secretary, Gorbachev has played a major role in the radicalization of the political reform agenda, but at every stage he has had to carry his Politburo colleagues with him. He began as the most radical member of the Politburo he inherited and, quite apart from the extent to which some of his own views have developed, could not have proposed to that body in 1985 some of the things he advocated in 1987, 1988, and 1989. With the emergence of *glasnost,* competitive elections, and a legislature in which radicals have been given a forum for public protest, Gorbachev and the progress of *perestroika* now have liberal as well as conservative critics. While in some ways this makes life even tougher for the Soviet leader, on balance it is to his political advantage. He can play the role of a centrist, albeit one clearly leaning to the liberal side of center, while taking on board more of the policies of the liberal critics than of their conservative counterparts. The conservatives, in any event, suffer from their lack of a viable alternative policy or program. There are those who would wish to turn the clock back only 15 years and others who would be happier turning it back 40 years, but none of them has a vision remotely relevant to the 21st century. Gorbachev, by contrast, has in mind a Soviet Union that in the year 2000 will be far more democratic and markedly more efficient economically than ever before. His problem is getting from here to there, for the problems of the transition period are horrendously difficult. ...

How long the Soviet population will give credence to a leadership that does not produce concrete economic results remains a moot point. The relevance of political reform in this context is that it provides institutional forums for pressure, criticism, and debate and enough freedom of information and expression to make it hard for conservative Communists to sustain the argument that the problems could be solved by returning to the status quo ante. Gorbachev's consolidation of his power at the top of party and state hierarchy, together with the process of institutional change, have probably secured for the reformers in the Soviet leadership several more years in which to make some improvements in living standards to accompany and reinforce political progress. ...

NOTES

ABOUT THE AUTHOR: **Archie Brown** is professor of politics at Oxford University and a fellow of St. Antony's College, Oxford University.

1. I have, from the outset of Mikhail Gorbachev's general secretaryship, suggested that he was a reformer by disposition and that he would be an agent of significant change. See, for example, my articles, "Gorbachev: New Man in the Kremlin," *Problems of Communism,* Vol. 34, No. 3 (May-June 1985); and "Can Gorbachev Make a Difference?" *Detente,* No. 3

(May 1985). By 1987, change—especially in the political climate and reform agenda—was proceeding faster than anyone had foretold, though it has gone still further in the two years since the June Central Committee plenum of that year. Yet in 1987 there was still a blinkered inability on the part of many observers to understand what was happening in the Soviet Union. A review article of mine on Soviet politics, "Change and Challenge," published in the *Times Literary Supplement* (March 27, 1987) that should, with the benefit of hindsight, have been criticized for its excess of caution, was vehemently attacked for its excessive optimism in a series of readers' letters published between May 15 and July 10. One of the letter-writers (and by no means the most virulent), Françoise Thom, was the co-author with Alain Besançon of a rather extreme contribution to a symposium entitled "What's Happening in Moscow?" published in *The National Interest*, No. 8 (Summer 1987). The symposium embraced a wide spectrum of views, including my own, but in their almost total misunderstanding of Soviet developments, Besançon and Thom were in a class apart. Gorbachev's policy, these authors tell us, "consists of an all-out attack on civil society" (p. 27), and the Soviet Union remains "a uniform, atomized and voiceless society" (p. 29).

2. In the above-mentioned symposium in *The National Interest*, Peter Reddaway did not make the mistake of thinking that Soviet change was merely cosmetic, but he was pessimistic about the prospects for Gorbachev and for *glasnost:* "If Gorbachev is trying to square the circle by embarking on the democratization of the Soviet system, as he shows every sign of doing, then, in my view, he is unlikely to remain in power for many more years. Sooner or later, the *nomenklatura* will surely remove him. And in that case *glasnost* would be bound to suffer in the inevitable conservative reaction" (p. 26).

3. I have discussed Gorbachev's consolidation of his power at some length in my contributions to Archie Brown, ed., *Political Leadership in the Soviet Union* (Bloomington, IN: Indiana University Press, 1989). See also Seweryn Bialer, ed., *Politics, Society and Nationality Inside Gorbachev's Russia* (Boulder, CO: Westview Press, 1989), especially Bialer's final chapter; the symposium, "Gorbachev and Gorbachevism," in *The Journal of Communist Studies*, Vol. 4, No. 4 (December 1988), especially the contributions of Ronald J. Hill, Alex Pravda, and Stephen White; and Patrick Cockburn, "Gorbachev and Soviet Conservatism," *World Policy Journal*, Vol. 6, No. 1 (Winter 1988–89).

4. Archie Brown, "Soviet Political Developments and Prospects," *World Policy Journal*, Vol. 4, No. 1 (Winter 1986–87).

11. Gorbachev's speech to the United Nations in December 1988 was notable for its insistence that the time of "closed societies" was over. See *Pravda*, December 8, 1988, pp. 1–2. See also Vadim Medvedev, *Pravda*, October 5, 1988, p. 4.

12. Medvedev (fn. 11). For a variety of interesting views on the contemporary meaning of socialism, including some that do away with the distinction between socialism of a "Marxist-Leninist" type and "democratic socialism," see the symposium on the concept of socialism in *Voprosy filosofii*, No. 11 (November 1988).

13. *Pravda*, May 26, 1989, p. 3.

14. *Izvestiya*, June 4, 1989, p. 2. In the most recent issue of this journal, the director of the Institute of Economics of the World Socialist System, Oleg Bogomolov, is quoted, in answer to a question about what he hoped the Soviet Union would look like 20 years from now, as replying, "Sweden ... Sweden or perhaps Austria." See Richard Parker, "Assessing Perestroika," *World Policy Journal*, Vol. 6, No. 2 (Spring 1989), p. 294.

15. BBC Summary of World Broadcasts, SU/0473 C/1, June 3, 1989.

16. *Ibid.*

17. James Farr, "Understanding Conceptual Change Politically," in Terence Ball, James Farr, and Russell L. Hanson, eds., *Political Innovation and Conceptual Change* (Cambridge: Cambridge University Press, 1989), p. 29.

18. *Ibid.*, pp. 30 and 32.

19. On Gorbachev's expanding use of the notion of "socialist pluralism," see also Archie Brown, "The Soviet Leadership and the Struggle for Political Reform," *The Harriman Institute Forum*, Vol. 1, No. 4 (April 1988).

26. S. E. Deytsev and I. G. Shablinsky, "Rol' politicheskikh institutov v uskorenii sotsial'no-ekonomicheskogo razvitiya," *Sovetskoe gosudarstvo i pravo*, No. 17 (July 1987), p. 120.

27. *Pravda*, November 30, 1988, p. 2.

28. Deytsev and Shablinsky (fn. 26), pp. 118–120.

29. *Ibid.*, p. 120.

30. *Pravda*, November 30, 1988, p. 2.

31. For an interesting account of these elections and of some of the surrounding discussion, see Jeffrey Hahn, "An Experiment in Competition: The 1987 Elections to the Local Soviet," *Slavic Review*, Vol. 47, No. 2 (Fall 1988).

32. See G. Barabashev and V. Vasilev, "Etapy reformy," *Pravda*, May 7, 1989, p. 3.

33. *Pravda*, April 27, 1989, p. 5.

34. *Ibid.*, p. 6.

35. *Ibid.*, p. 4.

36. *Ibid.*

37. For a list of the public organizations designated to elect deputies, their quota of representatives, and the number of candidates who competed to represent each organization in the elections to the Congress of People's Deputies (and for a useful brief discussion of the elections themselves), see Dawn Mann, "Elections to the Congress of People's Deputies Nearly Over," *Radio Liberty Report on the USSR*, Vol. 1, No. 15 (April 14, 1989).

38. *Izvestiya*, April 21, 1989, p. 3.

39. *Izvestiya*, May 6, 1989, p. 7.

40. *Ibid.*

43. Telephone polls of respondents in major Soviet cities suggested that, in fact, the overwhelming majority of these urban dwellers were watching or listening to the congress proceedings all or most of the time, whether at home or at work. Thus, for example, a poll conducted on May 29 found 81 percent of Muscovites following the proceedings constantly or almost constantly, a figure that had dropped only to 78 percent by early June. The other cities included in these polls were Leningrad, Kiev, Tallin, Tbilisi, and Alma-Ata, and other questions put to the respondents brought out wide differences in the reaction of the inhabitants to some of the major issues discussed at the congress. See *Izvestiya*, May 31, 1989, p. 7; and *Izvestiya*, June 4, 1989, p. 1.

44. *Izvestiya*, May 24, 1989, p. 6.

45. *Ibid.*

46. Vitaly Tretyakov, "Congress of People's Deputies: Whose Hopes Will It Justify?" *Moscow News*, No. 24 (June 11, 1989), p. 7.

47. *Ibid.*

63. *Izvestiya TsK KPSS*, Vol. 1, No. 1 (January 1989), pp. 81–86.

64. *Ibid.*, p. 85.

65. For a list of the new departments and their heads, see *ibid.*, p. 86.

67. For a full list of the leadership personnel changes made at the September 30, 1988 plenary session of the Central Committee, see *ibid.*, p. 3.

68. *Izvestiya TsK KPSS*, Vol. 1, No. 5 (May 1989), pp. 45–46.

69. *Ibid.*, p. 47.

70. Fedoseev's valedictory speech damned "socialist pluralism" with faint praise and called for the ideological unity of the party. See *Pravda*, April 27, 1989, p. 4.

11   *State and Society: Toward the Emergence of Civil Society in the Soviet Union*

GAIL W. LAPIDUS

> There is a difference between reform and quasi-reform. If quasi-reform is a reor-
> ganization at the top, purely a reorganization of the apparatus, reform is a more
> serious matter. Reform vitally changes the organizational relationships between
> the state apparatus and members of the society, collectively and individually,
> and this is what its main substance lies in.[1]
>
> —B. P. Kurashvili

Western analyses of the contemporary Soviet scene frequently portray Mikhail Gorbachev as but the latest in a long line of reforming tsar-autocrats, from Peter the Great to Iosif Stalin, who have sought to impose radical and coercive programs of modernization on a passive, backward, and recalcitrant society. Although this analogy is not entirely off the mark, it fails to capture the extent to which the process of reform now under way in the Soviet Union is also a long-delayed response by the leadership to fundamental social changes that are altering the relationship of state and society. The current attempt at reform is only in part a renewed effort at mobilization from above; this process of reform is also a far-reaching and highly controversial effort to adapt a set of anachronistic economic and political arrange-ments to the needs of an increasingly complex modern society.

THE ROOTS OF GORBACHEV'S REFORMS

Gorbachev's initial reform strategy was animated by the need for serious and comprehensive economic reform to arrest the deterioration of Soviet economic performance that jeopardized both domestic stability and international power. But Gorbachev and his associates increasingly came to recognize that economic stagnation had its roots in deeper social and political problems and that far-reaching changes were necessary if these problems were to be successfully addressed. Gorbachev's sweeping attack, made at the January 1987 Plenum of the Communist Party's Central Committee, on the cumulative effects of economic stagnation, social corrosion, political conservatism and inertia, the spread of apathy and cynicism, and the absence of legal and political accountability (an analysis remarkably similar to that of many Western Sovietologists in the late 1970s and early 1980s) demonstrated a clear recognition that sociopolitical change was a prerequisite for successful economic reform. His remarks expressed a realization that in the environment of the 1980s the "human factor" had become decisive.[2]

This growing recognition of the social sources of stagnation was in turn reflected in the evolution of Gorbachev's conception of *perestroika* (restructuring). From a narrower focus on economic acceleration it expanded to encompass, in Gorbachev's words, "not only the economy but all other sides of social life: social relations, the political system, the spiritual and ideological sphere, the style and work methods of the Party and of all our cadres. Restructuring is a capacious word. I would equate restructuring with revolution ... a genuine revolution in the minds and hearts of people."[3]

To accomplish this revolution, in Gorbachev's view, it is essential to stimulate the initiative and the creativity of the Soviet population by attacking the institutions and social norms that have long stifled it. As Nikita Khrushchev had done some thirty years earlier, Gorbachev has sought to mobilize popular support to carry out structural and policy changes, to curb the powers of officialdom, and to bring abuses of power under public scrutiny. But the novelty and significance of Gorbachev's strategy lie in its realization that Soviet society has reached a level of maturity that requires a new approach to its governance; and that the Soviet people, and above all the educated middle classes, can no longer be treated as the objects of official policy but must be treated as genuine subjects.

Khrushchev had launched this process of inclusion—a shift, however erratic, from the centralized, coercive statism of the Stalinist system to a more conciliatory and flexible approach to social forces.[4] Gorbachev has sought to extend the process of inclusion further. By contrast with Khrushchev's focus on the working class and peasantry, Gorbachev's strategy aims at incorporating the new social strata and values that are a product of the Soviet scientific-technological revolution as well as appealing to the skilled, the energetic, and the creative in every walk of Soviet life. His efforts seek to overcome the alienation of key segments of the Soviet population—from Andrei Sakharov to avant-garde writers and artists, from the entrepreneurs of the unofficial "second economy" to disaffected workers, peasants, and youth—and to enlist their talents and energies in the revitalization of the Soviet system.

Gorbachev's reforms involve a redefinition of socialism itself in an effort to tap the sources of vitality, dynamism, and innovation that have increasingly developed outside the framework of official institutions. By widening the boundaries of legitimate economic, social, political, and cultural behavior, the reforms seek to draw back within these boundaries individuals and activities that had deserted them or been excluded. In short, Gorbachev's reforms are an effort to substitute "voice" for "exit" in Soviet sociopolitical life.[5]

In broadening the boundaries of legitimate social activity, Gorbachev's strategy draws on many of the ideas of leading Soviet intellectuals who in the 1960s and 1970s were considered dissidents. Some twenty years ago, three distinguished members of the Soviet intelligentsia—Andrei Sakharov, Roy Medvedev, and Valery Turchin—addressed a letter to the Soviet leadership appealing for a gradual democratization of the Soviet system and outlining a series of measures for reform. Sakharov, Medvedev, and Turchin compared the Soviet economy to an urban traffic intersection, observing that when only a few cars were present, traffic police could easily cope with their task, but when the stream of traffic increased, fining the drivers and replacing the police no longer guaranteed a smooth flow of traffic. "The only solution," these three intellectuals argued, "is to widen the intersection. The obstacles hindering the development of our economy lie outside it, in the social and political sphere, and all measures that do not remove these obstacles are doomed to ineffectiveness."[6] Gorbachev's policies not only echo many of these recommendations; the policies stem from a similar understanding that economic development and the growing maturity of Soviet society demand fundamentally new approaches to its management.

The thrust of Gorbachev's strategy is to alter the basic premise of the Stalinist system from "all that is not permitted is prohibited."[7] But an expansion of the public arena that broadens the scope of legitimate activities and permits a greater degree of social self-regulation involves a significant redefinition of the role of the Party-state. In political and economic life as in culture, expansion of the public arena would diminish the role of central controls and expand the role of market forces, offer increased autonomy and resources as well as responsibility to a wide range of organizations and individuals, and introduce a degree of "socialist Darwinism" in promoting greater reliance on competition and self-regulation rather than on state-sponsored protection. In short, this expansion would give new impetus, and lend official support, to the emergence of an embryonic civil society.

But these changes confront Soviet reformers with an acute dilemma: the tension between the need to increase social initiative to revitalize the Soviet system and the fear that increased social autonomy will threaten central control. By simultaneously encouraging greater discipline as well as greater autonomy, and more effective central control as well as wider democratization, the current process of reform has set in motion contradictory pressures and opportunities in Soviet social life and policies, and contributes to major cleavages within the political elite.

In this exploration of the social dimensions of the process of reform, I will focus on three broad issues: the way in which broader changes in Soviet social structure and values made reform both urgent and possible; the new perspectives on

Soviet society that inform the reformist program; and how societal reactions affect the prospects for a fundamental transformation of the Soviet system.

THE POLITICAL IMPACT OF SOCIAL CHANGE

Seventy years after the victory of the Bolshevik Revolution, Mikhail Gorbachev asserts that the Soviet system stands at a crossroads, confronted by a set of choices that will determine whether the Soviet Union will enter the twenty-first century "in a manner worthy of a great power." That such an issue can even be raised is not only a measure of the gravity with which an important part of the Soviet leadership views the present situation; it also reflects a virtual revolution in consciousness within the Soviet elite. The growing conviction that domestic stability as well as international security was increasingly jeopardized by the economic stagnation, social corrosion, and political immobility of the Brezhnev era, and that only radical departures from the prevailing policies and norms would serve to avert further deterioration, reflects profound discord within the Soviet political establishment about the urgency of mounting problems, their causes, and the measures required to address them.

By the late 1970s, the erosion of confidence in the Soviet regime within the broader society, and in Leonid Brezhnev's political leadership within the broader elite, was apparent to Soviet citizens and foreign observers alike. This erosion was the product of two mutually reinforcing trends: an objective deterioration in the performance of the Soviet economy, which brought with it a mounting array of social and political problems, and a growing sense of demoralization within the Soviet elite, which reflected a shift in perceptions of regime performance.

The deteriorating performance of the Soviet economy was the key catalyst in the growing perception of failure, both in and of itself and because economic failure compounded other sociopolitical problems. But the economic slowdown and diminished international competitiveness might not have generated a sense of urgency had their presence not coincided with and contributed to a change in attitudes: an increasingly negative assessment of regime performance, which reflected a change in the criteria used to evaluate it; a growing sense of failure; and heightened pessimism about the future—in effect, a crisis of confidence within the Soviet elite. By the early 1980s, not only Western observers but key Soviet officials were, in a fashion unprecedented since the early 1920s, beginning to speak of a "crisis" in order to convey the urgency of the situation.[8]

In this respect, the Soviet case resembles that of a number of authoritarian regimes that, beginning in the 1970s, underwent a series a transitions from authoritarian rule. The critical catalyst in many such cases was a deterioration of regime performance. This deterioration contributed to a loss of confidence within the ruling elite and to the development of major cleavages within it, often combined with the alienation of a growing segment of the population. In Latin America, Spain, Portugal, and Greece, authoritarian systems evolved (in however erratic and uncertain a fashion) in the direction of liberalization if not always democratization, redefining and extending the rights of individuals and groups and providing them increased protection from arbitrary state action. In the Soviet case, however, the totalitarian legacy of the Stalin era, as well as the weak development of liberalism and constitutionalism in the Russian political tradition, placed distinctive constraints on the potential for economic and political liberalization.[9] To what extent these can be overcome in the years ahead is the fundamental question of Soviet politics.

The inauguration of the process of reform in the USSR was in large measure a function of elite politics and cleavages, in which leadership succession served as a major catalyst. But the impetus for reform and the direction it is taking are a product not only of a deteriorating Soviet international position, but of fundamental changes in Soviet social structure and values in the post-Stalin period that altered the aspirations, resources, and behavior of key social groups. By undermining traditional forms of social control and motivation, these changes helped to delegitimize traditional policies and political formulas, and to provide a rationale for fresh approaches.

The social and demographic changes from the mid-1950s to the mid-1980s transformed the passive and inarticulate peasant society of the era of Stalin into an urban industrial society with a highly differentiated social structure and an increasingly articulate and assertive middle class. The society over which Khrushchev ruled in the 1950s was still predominantly rural. By the mid-1980s, by contrast, two-thirds of the Soviet population lived in cities, and a growing percentage had been born in them. In 1959, only three Soviet cities had populations larger than 1 million; by 1985, that figure had reached twenty-two. Modernization was transforming the quality of urban life as well, while the spread of television brought urban lifestyles and values to the remotest corners of Soviet territory. When Khrushchev was dismissed in 1964, fewer than one in three Soviet families owned television sets. By 1988, television was almost universal and had not only brought a vast new universe of events and images into the Soviet household, but had rendered obsolete the system of agitation and propaganda through which the Party had for decades conveyed its message to the Soviet people.

Rapid urbanization was accompanied by a dramatic increase in the educational levels attained by the Soviet population. In 1959, two-thirds of the Soviet population over the age of ten had no more than a primary education; by 1986, almost two-thirds had completed secondary education. The combined effects of urbanization and rising levels of educational attainment transformed the Soviet working class from a relatively homogeneous body only recently drawn from the countryside to a differentiated one whose working-class membership has now increasingly become hereditary. Moreover, rising educational and skill levels among younger cohorts of the working class increasingly distinguished them from older generations of workers who were relegated to the ranks of the less skilled and enjoyed correspondingly lower status and pay. Younger workers also displayed a different set of orientations and values from their predecessors: a declining interest in work itself and a growing focus on family and leisure activities, including increased absorption in consumption, in the amenities made possible by the shift from communal and dormitory housing to private apartments, and by the greater range and availability of leisure activities.

Expanded educational opportunities have also sharply increased the percentage of the Soviet population with higher education. In 1959, only 5.5 million Soviet citizens had higher education; by 1986, the figure had reached 24 million. The growth in the number of "scientific workers" was particularly dramatic: from 1.5 million in 1950 to 15 million in 1986.[10] In short, not only was an increasing percentage of the Soviet working class becoming better educated; by the mid-1980s, a large urban middle class, including a substantial professional, scientific-technical and cultural intelligentsia with new cultural as well as material requirements, had emerged as a major actor on the Soviet scene.

This urban middle class, moreover, occupied an increasingly important place in both the membership and the leadership of the Communist Party itself. More than one-third of all urban males with higher education were Party members, and higher education had become the norm rather than the exception within the upper ranks of the Party, and even the Politburo itself.

The revival of Soviet sociology in the 1960s and 1970s brought the tools of social science to the study of these changes and of their likely impact on the aspirations, attitudes, and behavior of the Soviet population. Inhibited as they were by ideological and bureaucratic constraints, primitive methodological approaches, simplistic formulas about social reality, and the absence of adequate data, these sociological studies were nonetheless able to capture what was becoming a major source of social strain: the increasing tendency of the rising aspirations of the Soviet population for improved material well-being, upward social mobility, and occupational satisfaction and autonomy to outstrip the realistic possibilities for their fulfillment.[11]

For some, the demand for better and more varied food, consumer goods and services, and for higher quality education and health care, found outlets in the burgeoning second economy. For others, material dissatisfaction and frustration at limited opportunities for upward social mobility were expressed in low labor productivity, high turnover and absenteeism, rising alcoholism, and other social pathologies. The "double shift" of the female labor force, burdened by heavy household duties as well as full-time employment, took its own toll in declining birthrates. For others, disaffection took the form of emigration. Although tacit official acquiescence in these various forms of "exit" during the Brezhnev era afforded a safety valve, it offered no serious promise of future improvements.

A wide range of Soviet sources, from sociological studies to Soviet films and fiction, offered evidence that a significant shift in values was taking place in the Brezhnev era: growing pessimism about the Soviet future, increasing disillusionment with official values, and an accompanying decline in civic morale. The sources of alienation differed for different social groups and individuals, but their common thrust was a shift in the standards by which the regime's performance was evaluated. Traditional explanations of failure—the survival of capitalist rem-

nants, growing pains, the aftermath of war, the machinations of unseen enemies—had lost their persuasiveness to a generation reared in the expectation that
the Soviet Union was about to overtake the West and disillusioned by the chasm
that separated myth from reality.

Indeed, it was precisely among the younger and best-educated segments of the
Soviet population, including the inhabitants of its largest and most developed cities, that dissatisfaction appeared to be highest and the rejection of official norms
most pronounced. This shift was a striking and new development, for these
groups had traditionally provided the staunchest support for the Soviet system.
By the 1980s, however, it was among young people and the better educated that
new attitudes and values were taking root, and these included a more critical view
of state control over economic life, greater openness to private economic activity,
and greater commitment to personal freedom and individual rights.[12]

The evidence of alienation from official norms was not confined to the social
science writings; it was equally apparent in Soviet cultural life. The most widely
read novelists and poets and the most popular artists among the intelligentsia
were not those favored by the Party and cultural establishment, but those who addressed universal moral concerns, such as the meaning of truth, the nature of
good and evil, the significance of memory, and issues of national history and
identity, both Russian and non-Russian. It was these themes that provoked intense discussions in Soviet literary and cultural journals and were an expression
of the erosion of traditional ideological commitments and the search for new
values and sources of meaning within the Soviet educated elite.

Other currents, less hospitable to tolerance or liberalization but equally alienated from the ethos of the Brezhnev era, also commanded some support in this
urban milieu. One was a technocratic orientation that sought to solve current
problems by applying new scientific and technological tools and managerial techniques and that saw the military economy as a possible model for emulation. Another was, if anything, antitechnological, identified with a romantic nationalism
that found its symbolism in the Russian past and protested the ravages inflicted
on nature and culture by the unbridled pursuit of industrialism and material progress. Even more extreme forms of nationalism and chauvinism—both Russian
and non-Russian—flourished in the comparative laxity of the time, although they
did not receive public expression until the era of *glasnost*.

The spiritual alienation of important segments of the intelligentsia was further
compounded by its growing exposure to the outside world. As Khrushchev's son-
in-law Aleksei Adzhubei recalled recently, "When Khrushchev went to the exposition in Brussels in 1957, he decided that all the writers, managers, journalists, actors should visit the exhibit. When he visited the United States, representatives of
all the professions went too."[13]

Détente extended this exposure. Scientists and scholars, students and professionals, writers and dancers and journalists took part in the expanding network of
exchange and came into contact with new ideas and approaches, alternative ways
of looking at the world or of organizing professional life, and different standards

of achievement. The desire for international recognition and status among professional peers, as well as the expansion of communication on issues of mutual interest, created a sense of community that transcended differing political and social systems and acknowledged that Western standards of excellence were of universal significance. Foreign radio broadcasts and letters from émigrés to friends and relatives in the USSR further pierced the Iron Curtain, bringing new sources of information about the outside world. Even in Soviet enterprises, the growing presence of Western technologies and machinery operating alongside domestic products encouraged direct comparisons with what the Soviets would later call "world standards of excellence."

These experiences provided new criteria for evaluating Soviet achievements and shortcomings. Judged by these standards, Soviet performance was increasingly found wanting, and earlier official explanations of failure were no longer convincing. Greater contact with the outside world thus contributed to the pessimism and demoralization of an influential scientific-technical and cultural intelligentsia resentful of, and frustrated by, an authoritarian, patronizing, and exclusionary pattern of political rule. This mood provided an important impetus for reform.

This transformation of Soviet attitudes had its counterpart in Soviet behavior as well. Growing alienation and a decline in civic morale contributed to a shift in expectations and energies from the public to the private realm and to the emergence of an intellectual and moral rationale for the increasing privatization of life. "Exit" became an increasingly important option for a small but significant segment of Soviet society, whether in the burgeoning "second economy"; in a blossoming popular culture; or in the emergence of a rich array of informal and unofficial groups pursuing a broad range of cultural as well as sociopolitical activities, from rock music to the preservation of historical monuments. These activities were facilitated by newly available technologies, from automobiles to videotape recorders, not readily amenable to governmental control. Ossified official norms and institutions were thus progressively supplanted by new forms of largely autonomous expression that responded to the preferences of consumers rather than officials. These trends were exemplified by the decline of the Komsomol, the official Soviet youth organization, along with the emergence of a rich and complex youth culture. But the most extreme and dramatic form of "exit" was undoubtedly the emigration of leading writers, artists, and cultural figures from the Soviet Union to escape a stifling cultural orthodoxy or political repression. This "exit" served to accelerate both the erosion of cultural vitality and the growing demoralization of those who remained behind.

What all these trends reflect is the government's decreasing ability to channel and shape the direction of social change. The very image of "revolution from above," with all its connotations of state domination of a passive society, no longer corresponds to a reality where social forces have achieved a degree of autonomy and indeed actively impinge on the political system in unprecedented ways. The erosion of political control of important sectors of Soviet life is abundantly illustrated by the evolution of the "second economy," the very existence of which epitomizes the subversion of centrally established priorities and challenges centralized control of prices, distribution of income, and the allocation of capital and labor. The spread of corruption, particularly within the political elite, threatens the organizational integrity and political legitimacy of the Party and feeds both the resentment of those excluded from patronage and the hostility of those who are critical of it.

A parallel development is visible in the escape of important dimensions of social behavior from official control. People marry, reproduce, and divorce without reference to official demographic policy; they migrate from north and east to south and west in defiance of planners' preferences; and their devotion to religious beliefs and practices resists all efforts to invigorate atheistic propaganda. A whole spectrum of social pathologies, from alcoholism and drug addiction to crime, exemplifies the limits of political control.

This entire trend has complex and contradictory implications, encompassing as it does a whole range of activities and behaviors with varying consequences. The enhanced space for autonomous social behavior allows for increased autonomy as well as corruption in Central Asia. It permits both historical preservationism and nationalistic xenophobia, Christian orthodoxy and punk rock in Moscow. Its manifestations evoke an equally ambivalent reaction within the Soviet elite, where it is welcomed by some as an opportunity for greater social initiative and deplored by others as acquiescence in the weakening of discipline. The tension between these contradictory assessments was reflected in conflicting approaches to the process of reform itself.

TOWARD SOCIALIST PLURALISM:
THE SOCIAL STRATEGY OF THE REFORMERS

Gorbachev's reform strategy involves a significantly new conception of socialism based on a novel set of assumptions about the nature of Soviet society and its relation to the political order. Although the translation of new approaches into policy remains embryonic and somewhat contradictory, support for socialist pluralism, political democratization, and legal reform reflect new ways of thinking about the Soviet system of rule and embrace a new model of socialism.

The point of departure of this new strategy is the view that Soviet development has created an increasingly differentiated, complex, and modern society that remains largely unknown to the Soviet leadership and that it has been trying to govern by methods that are no longer appropriate. The "fictions" of the Stalin era have for too long been accepted as social reality, stereotypes have been a substitute for genuine social research, and unbending dogmatism has stood in the way of necessary policy reassessments. Even the tools required for effective policy-making remain inadequate and undeveloped because of Stalin's mutilation of the social sciences and the ideological and bureaucratic impediments to their revival. The primitive level of economics, not to mention sociology, demography, ethnography, psychology, and the study of public opinion, and the paucity of economic and social statistics have deprived not only policymakers but society as a whole of the self-knowledge that is a prerequisite to genuine progress. The first requirement, in the striking words of Alexander Yakovlev, is that "present-day socialism must become acquainted with itself."[14]

The changes under way in the ideological and cultural sphere and the renewal of selective de-Stalinization express a recognition that the delegitimation of key features of the Stalinist ethos—and above all its continuing legacy in the Soviet mindset—is a necessary first step in clearing the way for new approaches toward society. It has been essential to attack the equation of Stalinism with socialism and to portray Stalinism as a response to specific conditions at a particular historical moment rather than a universally valid approach to economic, social, or political dilemmas.

The renewal of public discussion of the crimes as well as the errors of the Stalin era and the presentation, in Gorbachev's speech on the occasion of the seventieth anniversary of the October Revolution, of a revised framework for the interpretation of Soviet history—one that emphasized those features of the Lenin and later periods that provide doctrinal support for *perestroika*—are an effort to gain enhanced freedom of action for new approaches.[15] The effort at delegitimization focuses on several features of the Stalinist legacy that constitute particular obstacles to sociopolitical reform: ideological dogmatism, lack of trust in Soviet society, the denial of social diversity, and an arbitrary and exclusionary pattern of centralized rule that violates fundamental norms of socialist democracy.

The delegitimation of these deeply entrenched features of Soviet ideology and practice has been accompanied by an attempt to encourage "new political thinking" in a number of areas of domestic as well as foreign policy. These new departures are obviously neither entirely novel nor completely unprecedented; in most cases they involve official endorsement of views and perspectives developed within the scholarly community and cultural intelligentsia during the Khrushchev and Brezhnev eras. In many cases these views had been sharply criticized and explicitly repudiated earlier, and their advocates treated as dissidents and expelled from their positions.[16]

Perhaps the most far-reaching feature of the reformist program is the shift from the notion of a "single truth" to a recognition of the legitimacy and indeed the necessity of divergent opinions. The entire Leninist conception of a vanguard party was premised on the need for Party tutelage over backward masses. Although the post-Stalin era was marked by a considerable broadening of the boundaries of permissible discussion on a wide range of issues, Gorbachev's call for "socialist pluralism," his insistence that open discussion was a prerequisite of scientific progress as well as of cultural vitality and should extend from technical to political issues, directly challenged the traditional claims of Party ideology. ...

The call for socialist pluralism echoed a memorable article that had appeared in late 1986 in *Izvestiya* calling for greater debate and controversy on major issues of the day. "We must get used to the idea that a multiplicity of voices is a natural part of openness," its author had argued.

> We must treat diversity normally, as the natural state of the world; not with clenched teeth, as in the past, but normally as an immutable feature of social life. ... We need in the economy and other areas of Soviet life a situation where multiple variants and alternative solutions are in and of themselves developmental tools and preconditions for obtaining optimal results, and where the coexistence of two opposing points of view on a single subject is most fruitful.

Reminding his audience of the high price paid in the past for intolerance toward other opinions, he concludes, "We must learn to live under democratic conditions."[19]

Official acquiescence in the necessity for, and indeed the desirability of, divergent opinions has not only widened the arena of public discussion; it has also served to legitimize the very notion of debates in Soviet public life. At a meeting with social scientists in spring 1987, Yakovlev proclaimed that "science can develop only in a process of constructive debates, in a clash of opinions. ... We must realize that no one has a monopoly on truth, either in posing new questions or in providing answers."[20] Nor have words remained divorced from deeds. The most visible evidence of this new outlook was the dramatic transformation of the Party's theoretical journal, *Kommunist,* under the editorship of Ivan Frolov and then Nail Bikkenin, from a dreary and sterile custodian of ideological purity to a forum for lively debate on major policy issues.[21]

Formal debate has even found its way to Soviet television. Programs that present diametrically opposed positions on major issues of the day—including a debate about reform itself—and that conclude without an authoritative and final resolution of the issue are a novel departure from long-standing practices.

At the same time, the expression of multiple views is not unlimited in scope, nor does it enshrine full freedom of expression. As Gorbachev himself has affirmed, freedom extends only to those views that serve the cause of socialism. In practice, however, the limits of tolerance remain ill-defined and its boundaries fluid and hotly contested, as the controversy over the Nina Andreyeva letter in the spring of 1988 reaffirmed. But the effort to shed what some Soviets have labeled the "unanimity complex" in favor of socialist pluralism has far-reaching consequences for Soviet society and politics.

The endorsement of *glasnost'* (public disclosure), with its simultaneous connotation of both candor and publicity, constitutes a second major departure in regime-society relations. *Glasnost'* is, needless to say, a policy of preemption intended to reduce the reliance of the Soviet population on foreign and unofficial sources of information—from foreign television and radio broadcasts to gossip—to fill the voids created by Soviet silence. The Chernobyl experience gave enormous impetus to this effort. The fact that the Soviet people first learned of a major domestic catastrophe with far-reaching implications for their own health and welfare from foreign broadcasts, and that the news was initially denied by their own government, was a major political embarrassment. It dramatized as never before the high costs of traditional Soviet secretiveness, both domestically and internationally, and strengthened Gorbachev's determination to expand the flow of information and communication in order to enhance the credibility of the leadership among its citizens.[22]

Glasnost' is also a symbol of trust. It reflects a recognition by the Soviet leadership of the maturity of the Soviet population and a partial repudiation of the patronizing notion that only a small elite can be entrusted with truth. The call for greater openness in place of secrecy, for realism rather than varnishing, is thus a movement toward the normalization of Soviet public life and the potential emergence of a public sphere.

Glasnost' is equally an expression of confidence in the legitimacy of the Soviet system and its leadership, and a recognition that the pretense of infallibility is no longer necessary to command popular allegiance and support. Indeed, greater publicity for shortcomings and problems—whether the shoddy construction of nuclear power plants or the spread of drug addiction—is an indispensable precondition for successfully addressing them.

The case for *glasnost'* and its intimate connection to the prospects for reform was most eloquently put by Tat'yana Zaslavskaya, the reformist sociologist, who argued in a remarkable article in *Pravda,* "If we continue to keep from the people information about the conditions under which they live, say, the degree of environmental pollution, the number of industrial accidents, or the extent of crime, we cannot expect them to assume a more active role in economic or in political life. People will trust and support you only if you trust them."[23] *Glasnost'* is therefore indispensable for genuine feedback and for creating a mechanism for two-way communication between government and society.

Dramatic new departures in Soviet cultural policy—the most far-reaching and tangible of the changes thus far—are another expression of the new orientation toward inclusion and trust.[24] The publication of long-suppressed novels and poems and the screening of controversial films long kept from public view are not only a form of reconciliation with the intelligentsia but also an expression of a more tolerant and inclusive approach to Soviet culture, past and present. The reappraisal of the contributions of such writers and poets as Mikhail Bulgakov, Boris Pasternak, Marina Tsvetaeva, and Anna Akhmatova, once scorned for their deviation from "socialist realism," and the repudiation of measures taken against some of them, extends the boundaries of permissible literature to figures previously outside it. The process of reintegration even extends to selected figures in the emigration, which holds out the prospect of ultimately reuniting the "two streams" of Russian culture at home and abroad.

Finally and of potential significance for the future, *glasnost'* is linked to accountability. An expanded and more independent role for the media—including serious investigative reporting—is an important instrument for exposing abuses of power and position and for holding officials accountable for their actions.

Needless to say, it also offers a convenient weapon for use against political opponents. It is nonetheless of great importance that *glasnost'* has extended, in however tentative a manner, to the first cautious exposés of abuses by the police and the KGB.

Even military and security affairs, traditionally forbidden territory, have begun to be opened, however tentatively, to public discussion and criticism. In a roundtable discussion reported in *Literaturnaia gazeta,* a group of scientists questioned the conscription of university students, arguing "our society does not need soldiers more than it needs ... physicists, biologists, engineers and social scientists."[25] The morality of nuclear weapons has been openly challenged in the Soviet press. A well-known Belorussian writer, Ales' Adamovich, for example, publicly argued that "for me there are no military men more courageous and worthy than those who give their military expertise to the antiwar movement."[26] Even sensitive foreign and security policy issues—from Stalin's contribution to the rise of fascism, to the impact of SS-20 deployments in Europe, to the decision to intervene in Afghanistan, to the size of the Soviet military budget—have begun to be aired. Indeed, Soviet journalists and diplomats have complained publicly that excessive security hinders their work and have called on Soviet defense authorities to provide more information about the country's defense budget and military capabilities so journalists and diplomats will not have to rely exclusively on Western data.[27]

A further novel feature of the reformist program is its explicit recognition of the differentiation and complexity of Soviet society. The fiction of an essentially solidary society (consisting, in Stalinist orthodoxy, of two classes—workers and peasants—and one stratum, the intelligentsia) had already begun to dissolve in the post-Stalin era. But this fiction could not be directly challenged as long as Khrushchev's vision of communism, with its apotheosis of equality, homogeneity, and community, held sway.

With the revival of sociological research in the 1960s and 1970s, a more complex portrait of Soviet social structure began to emerge.[28] It was a portrait that recognized the evolution of a complex pattern of stratification in the Soviet Union; provided evidence of differences in earnings, status, and educational attainments among various social groups; and suggested that new forms of social differentiation might be structurally reproduced in a socialist society. The structure of power and its impact on social stratification remained a closed subject. Nor was it yet possible to acknowledge that different strata and groups might have fundamentally different social interests and that these interests might be a source of serious social antagonisms and conflict. The role of bureaucracy was equally off limits, as was any critical examination of Soviet ideology as an expression of special social interests. ...

The view that Soviet society encompasses diverse and potentially conflicting social interests, a view long held by Tat'yana Zaslavskaya, among others, and circulated in confidential memoranda and reports in the 1970s, has been not only legitimized but given prominence by its publication in *Kommunist.*[32] But the debate has since gone considerably further in focusing on the development of bureaucracy as the key to the emergence of the Stalinist system, and its defense of its ideological and political interests as the main obstacle to economic and political reform, thereby rekindling a debate that Leon Trotsky had launched more than a half century ago.[33]

This new approach to Soviet society is of enormous potential significance as a point of departure for the management of social and political affairs. By explicitly acknowledging the presence of conflicting interests (including bureaucratic interests), rather than obscuring and suppressing them, it not only takes another step toward the legitimation of diversity, it creates the necessary foundation for developing mechanisms for conflict management. It even acknowledges the need for some political expression of diverse views, although not of politically autonomous expression. In an unpublished talk with Soviet writers, Gorbachev himself reportedly acknowledged the need for a functional equivalent of a party opposition,[34] although other Soviet leaders clearly do not share this view. But the recognition of the need for greater political expression of social diversity provides a basis for reformers' efforts to revitalize the system of soviets, introduce competitive elections of officials, reduce the role of the Party, and, above all, of its apparatus in Soviet economic, social, and political life while sanctioning the emergence of a wide range of unofficial and nonparty organizations.

Indeed, the proliferation of informal groups and unofficial organizations concerned with a broad array of cultural, social, and political issues is the most dramatic new departure on the Soviet political landscape. An officially sanctioned conference of unofficial groups in August 1987 brought together the representatives of some forty-seven such groups and generated proposals encompassing a variety of socio-political problems, like providing assistance to invalids and the aged, democratizing the Soviet electoral system, and building a monument to the victims of Stalinism—a proposal adopted a year later following the Nineteenth Party Conference. By 1988, the Soviet press reported that some 30,000 grassroots associations were in existence, provoking major debates about how they should be handled. By the time of the Party Conference in June 1988, a considerable number of unofficial groups and clubs had emerged with distinct political programs of their own, and some were engaged in organizing public demonstrations on environmental and political issues. Proposals were even under discussion to allow selected informal organizations to nominate candidates in local Soviet elections, posing a direct challenge to the existing *nomenklatura* system.[35]

The shift from an emphasis on social homogeneity to a recognition of social diversity and potential for social conflict, and the emergence of increasingly active unofficial organizations in defense of group interests, is especially apparent in the area of nationality problems. Khrushchev's assertion, at the Twenty-second Party Congress in 1961, that "the Party has solved one of the most complex of problems, which has plagued mankind for ages and remains acute in the world of capitalism to this day—the problem of relations between nations,"[36] marked the high tide of

Soviet optimism about the achievements of Soviet nationality policy. In subsequent years the speeches of successive Soviet leaders took an increasingly sober tone. At the Twenty-sixth Party Congress in 1981 Brezhnev acknowledged that although the various nations of the Soviet Union were more united than ever before, "this does not imply that all the problems of the relations among nationalities have been resolved. The dynamics of the development of a large multinational state like ours gives rise to many problems requiring the Party's tactful attention."[37]

This sober reassessment was reaffirmed in even stronger terms by Yuri Andropov in December 1982. Using the occasion of the sixtieth anniversary of the creation of the Soviet multinational system to deliver a major address on the subject, he reminded his audience, "Soviet successes in solving the nationalities question certainly do not mean that all the problems engendered by the very fact of the life and work of numerous nations and nationalities in the framework of a single state have disappeared. This is hardly possible as long as nations exist, as long as there are national distinctions. And they will exist for a long time, much longer than class distinctions."[38]

A growing recognition by the Soviet leadership that successful management of national relations was critical to the stability of the system and demanded patient and delicate social engineering in turn generated increased encouragement and support for empirical social research on ethnic processes. Indeed, Andropov inadvertently testified to the previous shortcomings of such efforts when he called for the formulation of a "well-thought out, scientifically substantiated nationalities policy."[39]

The need for such a policy became painfully urgent following Gorbachev's accession to power. The new pressures and expectations generated by the reform process, as well as the new opportunities and diminished risks for expression of grievances that *glasnost'* appeared to sanction, brought to the surface long-simmering resentments among Russians and non-Russians alike that exploded with stunning force from Alma Ata to the Baltic to Armenia and Azerbaijan. While expressing the usual criticism of national chauvinism and narrowmindedness, Gorbachev's response also acknowledged past mistakes in nationality policy, criticized social scientists for excessively optimistic accounts of Soviet achievements, and explored new approaches for dealing with grievances.[40] Recognizing that national tensions could jeopardize his entire reform program, and ultimately his leadership as well, Gorbachev has called for a Central Committee plenum to be devoted to nationality policy. The seriousness of the issue was further underscored by the Nineteenth Party Conference, which devoted one of six final resolutions to inter-ethnic relations and called for the creation of new institutions to deal with nationality policy.

The central thrust of these emerging perspectives on national and social problems is a gradual retreat from utopia and a growing realization of the limits of social engineering. The Khrushchev era represented the height of the optimism and millenialism inspired by the Bolshevik Revolution and revived again during the era of the First Five-Year Plan. It again stimulated optimistic expectations about the future, the perfectibility of socialism, the malleability of human nature, the merging of nations, and the imminence of full communism.

That optimism has steadily receded in the post-Khrushchev era; Gorbachev's accession dealt it a final blow.[41] The recognition that capitalism has by no means exhausted its potential—and that indeed the gap that Khrushchev so confidently expected to narrow has actually widened in the intervening period—involves a more sober assessment of international as well as domestic realities. The decision to remove from the Party program all concrete targets and explicit goals is a repudiation of a long tradition of exaggerated and unrealistic promises, just as the shift in terminology from "developed socialism" to "developing socialism" extends the time horizon for the achievement of full communism into a remote and indistinct future. Even discussions of the fate of the Soviet multinational system are more likely to emphasize the positive contribution of cultural and national diversity to Soviet life than the aspiration to create a homogeneous Soviet people.

This trend toward greater realism, and indeed outright pessimism, is accompanied by a growing realization that a wide range of social problems may well be structurally rooted in and reproduced under socialism. Where a wide variety of social pathologies—from chauvinism to corruption, from drug addiction and prostitution to crime—were once barely acknowledged and treated as "relics of the past," a phrase that implied a vast chasm would separate the socialist society of the future from its capitalist ancestry, current discussions of a wide range of social problems increasingly accept their universality in all social systems, explore why and how such behaviors are socially reproduced, and focus more on "managing" social problems than on "solving" them.

Moreover, recognizing the limited capacity and resources of the state to address a variety of social needs, and the rigidity and bureaucratization that central control entails, new thinking about social problems is directed to the potential role of voluntary associations and private initiatives in addressing them. Indeed, to the extent that *glasnost'* has focused public attention on a broad range of previously invisible and unacknowledged social problems—from unemployment to homelessness, from abandoned children to the absence of day-care centers for the aged—it has also opened the door to public discussion of how to address them. Terms like "altruism" and "charity" have reappeared in the Soviet lexicon. The campaign for democratization seeks to endow local soviets with enhanced powers and resources that could permit new initiatives in social policy. The emergence of a wide variety of unofficial organizations creates additional frameworks for private initiatives in the name of compassion and charity. Even the Russian Orthodox Church has begun to press for the right to engage in volunteer activities such as nursing. In short, the reforms under way will both require and permit a pattern of provision for social welfare that joins public and private initiatives in novel ways.

All these trends have far-reaching implications for social science as well as for Soviet policy in the Gorbachev era. They involve the admission that Soviet social science is as yet incapable of contributing to a serious understanding of social reality or of helping to generate a suitable strategy for managing a process of reform, particularly one that demands a "civilized" rather than a forcible resolution of contradictions.

The deplorable state of the social sciences has been recognized at the highest level of the leadership. The Politburo itself met in May 1988 to discuss the need to develop serious social research and training, and a subsequent Central Committee decree spelled out a whole range of measures intended to promote serious research and training in sociology on a nationwide scale.[42]

It has become essential to the reform effort to have and to publish accurate economic and social statistics, as well as information about the needs, interests, values, and behavior of diverse social groups and the possible effects of their behavior on social processes.[43] With this objective in mind, a whole series of additional initiatives has been undertaken to give impetus to the development of the social sciences. Following a series of well-publicized criticisms of official economic and social statistics, the Central Statistical Administration was replaced by a new State Committee for Statistics, charged with "increasing the reliability of information, expanding the purview of *glasnost*, and deepening the analysis of processes of economic and social development in the country."[44] New textbooks in social studies are being prepared and annual school examinations in history and social studies had to be cancelled in 1988. Political science as a discipline has made further strides toward institutionalization in the past few years, and its growing legitimation was symbolized by the creation, in the summer of 1988, of a new Center for Political Science Research.[45] Sociology has been given even greater prominence under Gorbachev. Not only will formal training and research be expanded in existing universities and institutes; two new institutes for sociological research have recently been established outside the framework of the Academy of Sciences. An All-Union Center for the Study of Public Opinion, under the leadership of Zaslavskaya herself, will conduct surveys designed to assist the leadership in assessing popular reactions to the reform program while the second will focus on socio-economic aspects of *perestroika*.[46]

Ultimately, the capacity of the Soviet system to develop new mechanisms for the expression of social diversity and for the management of conflict will depend on the successful implementation of political and legal reforms. Political changes that would reduce the concentration of power in the hands of the central ministerial and Party apparatus, and movement toward establishment of the rule of law backed by a judiciary with some degree of independence, are essential to any effort to institutionalize the reform process and to provide some guarantee of its irreversibility. Both within the political leadership and among reform-minded scholars, specialists, and journalists, serious attention is now being devoted to these issues; and the Nineteenth Party Conference provided some impetus to the process.[47] It is the fate of these efforts that will hold the key to the prospects of Gorbachev's reforms more broadly.

THE SOCIAL IMPACT OF THE REFORMS

For the first time since the October Revolution, Soviet society has emerged as a major, through not a unitary, actor on the Soviet political stage. Both its importance and its diversity have been impressed on the consciousness of the political leadership in unprecedented ways. Amorphous yet dynamic, it remains an uncertain weight on the scales of the Soviet future.

Clearly Gorbachev's reforms have been most warmly welcomed among segments of the intelligentsia. The most palpable result of these reforms has been in the cultural sphere, where they have given the cultural intelligentsia considerably enhanced autonomy and have enriched the cultural fare available to consumers of contemporary Soviet culture and the media. A dramatic rise of public interest in political affairs is perhaps the single most visible manifestation of the impact of *glasnost'* and *perestroika*. This is reflected in the soaring circulation of leading newspapers and journals during the past two years, especially those of reformist orientation.[48]

The new atmosphere has also created a degree of trust and perceived reciprocity between the intelligentsia and the regime that had heretofore been missing. Gorbachev's emphasis on the power of ideas and the call for "new thinking" in virtually every domain of Soviet life sets out an agenda that is unprecedentedly dependent on the inputs of specialists and professionals and is more responsive than in the past to their concerns as professionals. Their status and visibility have been correspondingly increased, as have their opportunities for travel abroad. Even within this group, support for the reforms is by no means universal; indeed, the intelligentsia provides leadership for antireformist currents as well. But insofar as we may take Andrei Sakharov as a bellwether of the once dissident, liberal intelligentsia, his supportive stance may be taken as an indication of the relative success of the Gorbachev regime in eliciting "voice" within this milieu.

The benefits of Gorbachev's reform program for other social and occupational groups have been far less apparent. Although the reforms hold out the long-term prospect of improvements in the supply and quality of consumer goods and services, in the short run they have raised expectations that are unlikely to be met. Indeed, the initial impact of the reforms on the economy has been sufficiently disruptive to output and wages to justify the widespread anxieties of Soviet workers. Moreover, discussion of the need for a price reform and the prospect of job insecurity threaten to jeopardize traditional and valued entitlements, whereas the promise of greater workplace democracy is unlikely to offset a real and feared decline in the standard of living. Decades of economic mythmaking have shaped popular expectations in ways that will be politically costly to undo. The simultaneous demand for low prices and abundant supplies of goods and services at those low prices is but one example of the dilemma. For the population at large even *glasnost'* must appear as a mixed blessing because the media no longer offer the comfortable assurance of success and certainty.

The process of reform is at least equally unsettling to important segments of Soviet officialdom and the many millions of state and Party bureaucrats whose role and status under the new arrangements are highly uncertain and whose power is apt to be sharply circumscribed. The widespread skepticism, anxiety, and resistance encountered even at this early stage of reform—and the relatively limited response to the new opportunities it offers for economic initiative—raise troublesome questions about how successfully the process of implementation will proceed.

Fundamental constraints on far-reaching liberalization are also imposed by the structure of the Soviet system itself. The monopoly of political power by the Party could well be maintained even with the new electoral arrangements that require a greater degree of responsiveness to societal forces. Public ownership and the limited development of private property rights limits the resources that can be mobilized by independent social actors. These structural features of the Soviet system highlight the far greater obstacles to a transition from authoritarianism in the Soviet case compared to the situations prevailing in Latin America and Europe.

Gorbachev's program confronts additional impediments that stem from the built-in tensions and contradictions of the reform process itself. The urgent need to overcome stagnation and social alienation by stimulating initiative conflicts with the fear of losing control. The acknowledged need for greater diversity of opinions is widely seen as threatening to the principles of socialism itself. Greater permissiveness and tolerance of various forms of social nonconformity and political protest leave unclear the boundaries of "anti-Soviet" behavior. Finally, while the reformers have come to view political democratization as a condition of economic reform, there are also obvious tensions between the two. Whether within the workplace or at a national level, a substantial expansion of political participation could well create greater constraints on the reform process.

Attitudinal constraints, deeply rooted in Soviet political culture, are a further inhibiting factor. Although neither pervasive nor unchangeable, the widespread attitude toward change appears to reflect an instinctive calculus that the danger of losses outweighs the hope of gains. Moreover, there are remnants of an anticommercial ethos long reinforced by Party ideology that inclines at least a part of the population to be suspicious of private entrepreneurship. There is also a deeply engrained tendency to equate egalitarianism with social justice, which serves as an obstacle to efforts to link rewards to performance.

What is especially striking in the Soviet case is the general poverty of sociopolitical thought, a poverty that extends even to the Soviet emigration. In the absence of more comprehensive sociopolitical programs that would offer viable alternatives to the status quo, vague sentiments that range from romantic nationalism to extreme chauvinism risk to fill the void.

A final set of constraints on potential liberalization is the depth of social and national cleavages. The chasm of mutual distrust between the Russian working class and intelligentsia was mirrored even in the distance between the dissident intellectuals and the attempts at a free trade-union movement, although in some non-Russian republics, from the Baltic to Armenia, the force of nationalism provides precisely such a bond. Ironically but not surprisingly, the extension of *glasnost'* and "democratization" has brought national tensions and antagonisms to the surface. The Gorbachev leadership may well be persuaded that allowing the expression of grievances is a necessary first step in successfully addressing them; but new political and legal mechanisms for conflict management remain to be developed.

NOTES

1. B. P. Kurashvili, in *Sovetskoe gosudarstvo i pravo*, no. 10 (1983).

2. *Pravda*, January 31, 1987. Gorbachev's remarks virtually echo the diagnoses of Soviet political, economic, and social problems in the chapters by Seweryn Bialer, Robert Campbell, and Gail Lapidus in Robert Byrnes, ed., *After Brezhnev: The Sources of Soviet Conduct in the 1980s* (Bloomington: Indiana University Press, 1983). Gorbachev's views are strikingly congruent with those of the reformist Soviet economic sociologist, Tat'yana Zaslavskaya.

3. *Pravda*, August 2, 1986.

4. See Kenneth Jowitt, "Inclusion and Mobilization in Marxist-Leninist Political Systems," *World Politics* (October 1975), pp. 69–97, for an insightful discussion of this issue.

5. Albert Hirschman introduced these terms to describe the options available to a customer faced by deteriorating performance of a firm: to stop buying its products and turn to competitors or to express dissatisfaction to management in an effort to alter its behavior. *Exit, Voice and Loyalty* (Cambridge, Mass.: Harvard University Press, 1970), p. 59.

6. "Appeal for a Gradual Democratization," in George Saunders, ed., *Samizdat: Voices of the Soviet Opposition* (New York: Monad Press, 1974), p. 405.

7. This principle has been advocated by leading Soviet public figures, including academician V. N. Kudryavtsev, director of the Academy of Sciences Institute of State and Law. See *Voprosy filosofii*, 1 (January 1987).

8. See, for example, Konstantin Chernenko, in *Kommunist*, no. 13 (1981), pp. 10–11.

9. For a useful overview drawn from Latin American experiences, see Guillermo O'Donnell et al., *Transitions from Authoritarian Rule: Comparative Perspectives* (Baltimore: Johns Hopkins University Press, 1986).

10. Tsentral'noe statisticheskoe upravlenie, *Narodnoe khoziaistvo SSSR* (Moscow: Finansy i Statistika, 1987), pp. 523, 647.

11. These trends are discussed in some detail in Gail W. Lapidus, "Social Trends," in Byrnes, *After Brezhnev.*

12. Brian Silver, "Political Beliefs of the Soviet Citizen: Sources of Support for Regime Norms," in James Millar, ed., *Politics, Work and Daily Life in the USSR* (Cambridge: Cambridge University Press, 1987). Similar trends by age cohort were revealed in a poll of Muscovites conducted at the Institute of Sociological Research of the Soviet Academy of Sciences for the *New York Times* and CBS News in May 1988. See *New York Times*, May 27, 1988, p. A7. By contrast, among the refugees from World War II interviewed in the Harvard Project of the 1950s, regime support was greater among younger age cohorts and increased with level of education. Raymond Bauer and Alex Inkeles, *The Soviet Citizen* (Cambridge, Mass.: Harvard University Press, 1959). Support for regime norms was higher among those respondents who reported high levels of material satisfaction, but "satisfaction" was highly dependent on subjective perceptions. Recent Soviet research, for example, found that resi-

dents of Moscow and Leningrad were in fact less satisfied with the quality of life they enjoyed than were respondents from seventeen other cities because the former's higher expectations created a wider gap between aspirations and real possibilities. See also Oleg Bozhkov and Valeri Golofast, "Otsenka naseleniem uslovii zhizni v krupnykh gorodakh," *Sotsiologicheskie issledovaniia*, no. 3 (1985).

13. *New York Times*, November 4, 1987.

14. *Pravda*, April 18,1987. Yakovlev's views are more fully developed in his "Dostizhenie kachestvenno novogo sostoianiia sovetskogo obshchestva i obshchestvennye nauki," *Kommunist*, no. 8 (1987).

15. Films such as Abuladze's *Repentance* and novels such as Anatoli Rybakov's *Children of the Arbat* helped reopen the Stalin question. Gorbachev's seventieth anniversary speech reaffirmed elements of the prevailing orthodoxy regarding Lenin and Stalin but was unflinching in referring to Stalin's "unpardonable crimes," broke new ground in defending Lenin's New Economic Policy and his essay "On Cooperation" as precedents for Gorbachev's own reforms. He also presented both Bukharin and Khrushchev in a more positive vein than has been customary. A number of articles have since appeared in the Soviet press offering a favorable appraisal of Khrushchev's contributions.

16. Indeed, a recent article explicitly blames Leonid Brezhnev and his Politburo colleague and party ideologist Mikhail Suslov for the emergence of a Soviet dissident movement because they destroyed the key vehicle for criticism of Stalinism, namely Aleksandr Tvardovsky's journal, *Novyi mir*. Yuri Burtin as cited in Julia Wishnevsky, "A Guide to Some Major Soviet Journals," Radio Liberty Research Bulletin, RL Supplement 2/88 (July 20, 1988).

19. *Izvestiya*, October 28, 1986.

20. *Pravda*, April 18, 1987.

21. See, for instance, the debates over the meaning of social justice, in *Kommunist*, no. 13 (1986). A wide array of Soviet journals now provide an unprecedented forum for discussion and debate on major issues of domestic development.

22. The argument is more fully developed in Gail W. Lapidus, "KAL and Chernobyl: The Soviet Management of Crises," *Survival* (May/June 1987).

23. *Pravda*, February 6, 1987.

24. An editorial in *Kommunist* in October 1987 defended this new orientation, contrasting Lenin's tolerant approach to culture and to the intelligentsia with Stalin's arbitrary effort to impose "bureaucratic regulation."

25. *Literaturnaia gazeta*, May 13, 1987.

26. Ibid., May 13 and June 8, 1987.

27. See, for example, V. Dashichev, in *Literaturnaia gazeta*, May 18, 1988; A. Bovin, in *Izvestiya*, June 16, 1988, V. Berezhkov, in *Sovetskaia molodezh*, August 20, 1987; and A. Bovin, in *Literaturnaia gazeta*, March 16, 1988.

28. See Murray Yanowitch, *The Social Structure of the USSR* (Armonk, N.Y.: M. E. Sharpe, 1986) for a useful collection of translations of important Soviet articles.

32. *Kommunist*, no. 13 (1986). Zaslavskaya's long-standing advocacy of an "interest group" approach to the Soviet political economy is reflected in her editorship of a journal on economic sociology, which focuses on "the analysis of the development of the economy as a social process representing the specific behavior and interaction of classes, strata and groups in Soviet society." T. I. Zaslavskaya and R. V. Ryvkina, *Izvestiia sibirskogo otdeleniia akademii nauk SSSR: seriia ekonomiki i prikladnoi sotsiologii*, no. 1 (January 1984).

33. When Tat'yana Zaslavskaya first referred to entrenched bureaucratic opposition to reiorm (*Ekonomika i organizatsiia promyshlennogo proizvodstva,* 7 [1985], pp. 3–22), it was a striking statement. The discussion of bureaucracy and its interests has now become a staple of the Soviet media. See, for example, Vladimir Shubkin, *Znamya,* April 1987, pp. 162–186, and the roundtable in *Ogonyok,* March 12, 1988.

34. Samizdat Archive "Beseda chlenov soiuza pisatelei SSSR s M. S. Gorbachevym," AS no. 5785 (June 19, 1986).

35. A sharp exchange over the desirability of allowing informal associations to nominate candidates to stand in new Soviet elections was carried in *Izvestiya,* March 20, 1988, p. 3.

36. *Pravda,* October 18, 1961, p. 1. For a more extensive discussion of the evolution of Soviet views, see Gail W. Lapidus, "Ethnonationalism and Political Stability: The Soviet Case," *World Politics* 36 (July 1984).

37. *Pravda,* February 24, 1981.

38. *Pravda,* December 22, 1982.

39. Ibid.

40. The new elements in the present approach involve an unprecedented acknowledgment of past errors in nationality policy, including the treatment of the Baltic states; a fresh approach to bilingualism, which offers more scope for teaching and using national languages; and a search for new procedures and mechanisms for addressing national grievances. See *Kommunist,* no. 3 and no. 13 (1987).

41. For two important treatments of this broad theme, see John Bushnell, "The 'New Soviet Man' Turns Pessimist," in Stephen Cohen et al., eds., *The Soviet Union Since Stalin* (Bloomington: Indiana University Press, 1980), pp. 179–199; and Alexander Dallin, "Retreat from Optimism," in Seweryn Bialer and Sophie Sluzar, eds., *Radicalism in the Contemporary Age,* III (Boulder, Colo.: Westview, 1977), pp. 117–157.

42. *Pravda,* May 13, 1988; *Izvestiya,* June 12, 1988.

43. Zaslavskaya has sharply criticized the suppression of economic and social statistics and has charged that the Soviet Union is in last place among developed countries in the level of publicly available social statistics, a criticism echoed by Gorbachev himself. (*Pravda,* February 6, 1987.)

44. *Pravda,* August 7, 1987.

45. For a useful discussion, see Archie Brown in Alexander Dallin and Bertrand Patenaude, eds., *Soviet Scholarship Under Gorbachev* (Stanford: Stanford University Press, 1988).

46. *Pravda,* March 18, 1988.

47. The need for a socialist *Rechtsstaat* (*sotsialisticheskoe pravovoe gosudarstvo*) was endorsed by the Nineteenth Party Conference, discussed on the front page of *Pravda,* August 2, 1988, and elaborated in *Kommunist,* no. 11 (1988). The inadequacy of Soviet political institutions, and the need for a socialist "theory of checks and balances," was a major theme of the 1987 annual conference of the Soviet Association of Political Sciences (Archie Brown, in Dallin and Patenaude, *Soviet Scholarship Under Gorbachev*).

48. Total subscriptions have increased over 18 million in the past year alone, while the number of subscribers to *Ogonyok* doubled, from 561,415 to 1,313,349. *Novyi mir* reached a record 1,150,000 in January 1988 (*Moscow News,* no. 8 [1988], Wishnevsky, "A Guide to Some Major Soviet Journals"). The letters editor of *Ogonyok* reported that the volume of mail from readers had also increased dramatically, from 15,000 letters in 1986 to 50,000 in 1987 to 20,000 in the first three months of 1988 (*New York Times,* April 24, 1988).

12 The Emergence of Independent Associations and the Transformation of Russian Political Society

STEVEN FISH

The recent, unprecedented emergence of voluntary political associations, independent trade unions and professional associations, and nascent alternative political parties has transformed Russian political society. But have the new organizations yet given birth to a genuine 'civil society' in Russia? ...

... Mikhail Gorbachev's assumption of the general secretaryship marked the beginning of a process of liberalization that made possible an explosion of organized extra-state political activity. ...

PHASE I: EARLY 1985 TO MID-1987

The crucial development of the initial phase of the Gorbachev period was the onset of partial liberalization in official thinking and policy on questions of independent association. The phrase 'socialist pluralism' entered the official Soviet lexicon during this time. This concept was open to a multiplicity of interpretations, but in practice amounted to *de facto* tolerance of the formation of some small citizens' organizations outside the framework of state institutions. Writers known to enjoy contacts with top leaders asserted that diverse and even competing interests existed in Soviet society.[11] The principle of independent, organized intermediation of interests was not affirmed in official thinking, but admission of societal diversity helped provide theoretical justification for limited tolerance of political activity outside the confines of formal state institutions.

Most of the pioneering associations were dedicated to the relatively apolitical tasks of preserving historical monuments, protecting the environment, and fighting alcoholism. More overtly political were Memorial, an association dedicated to investigating the crimes of Stalinism, and Democratic Perestroika, a 'political discussion club' of progressive intellectuals. At their inception, these organizations, like other nascent 'informals', were dedicated to discussion and activism that were not incompatible with the goals of *perestroika,* as defined by top state officials.

PHASE II: MID-1987 TO LATE 1988

This period witnessed a significant expansion in the number of informal groups, the beginning of street demonstrations organized by these associations and the emergence of several groups whose goals and tactics placed them beyond the bounds of official tolerance. One group whose public demonstrations encountered violent repression was the Democratic Union, a diverse conglomeration of tendencies united around the objective of overturning the communist party system and establishing multi-party parliamentary democracy. The group, organized in early 1988, was the first to declare itself an alternative political party.[12]

Though demonstrations by self-proclaimed political parties were not tolerated during this phase, official policy towards 'informal groups' was characterized more by efforts to 'switch' and 'channel' independent activity than to abolish it. In practice, policy often amounted to interference by local officials in the activities of informal groups and condemnation of the groups' 'egoism' in the press.[13] Public discussion of the causes and significance of independent political activity focused on two closely related questions: first, was the emergence of independent groups due to the 'weakness' of official mass organizations, or was it a natural and inevitable consequence of liberalization? Second, were the 'informals' a temporary corrective phenomenon, or healthy, permanent components of political life?[14] Though many regarded some independent activity as normal and progressive, debate in the official press did not yet include challenges to the communist party system of rule.

Despite official ambivalence, a significant growth of new associations, particularly small, progressive discussion clubs, took place during 1987 and 1988, and several umbrella organizations emerged in efforts to unite these groups. For instance, in late 1987 the Soviet Federation of Socialist Clubs was founded in Moscow, bringing together 50 clubs from throughout the Soviet Union.[15] There also occurred a growth of samizdat publications issued by independent associations, but print runs of these papers were very small, and information about independent groups was not widely available.[16] Few of the new groups—the Democratic Union being a notable exception—challenged the communist party's monopoly on power.

PHASE III: LATE 1988 TO LATE 1989

In a number of respects, this period stands out as the crucial take-off phase for independent political activity in Russia. The elections of 1989, and particularly those for the USSR Congress of People's Deputies, served as powerful catalysts to independent action. Election campaigns stimulated the formation of the Moscow Association of Voters, a loosely organized, broad-based citizens' group dedicated to promoting progressive candidates and co-ordinating action among diverse democratic tendencies. The elections only bolstered the self-assurance and radicalism of the new groups, some of which succeeded in having their 'own' candidates elected to the Congress of People's Deputies.[17] Provincial industrial cities such as Sverdlovsk, Yaroslavl' and Kuibyshev experienced a significant growth of independent organizations.[18] Progressive-democratic groups grew particularly rapidly, and tendencies and factions in political discussion clubs evolved in some cases into more coherent formations, some of which clearly resembled parties-in-waiting. The Democratic Perestroika Club and the Moscow People's Front, until this point loose gatherings of progressive intellectuals, spawned the Social Democratic Association, Citizen's Dignity and several other proto-parties.[19] Some associations held all-union conferences, proposing frameworks for future co-operation. Although these gatherings did not prove effective as vehicles for organizational integration, they seem to have emboldened progressive groups and contributed to a radicalization of their demands. For instance, in September 1989 a conference of 100 democratic groups in Leningrad adopted a resolution calling for multi-party democracy, the restoration of private property and the removal from the constitution of Article 6, which guaranteed the 'leading role' of the communist party.[20]

New professional organizations with radical agendas also appeared in 1989. In February, 2,000 lawyers met in Moscow to form an independent union. In July, the Alliance of United Co-operatives was founded, bringing together regional and sectoral co-operative associations in an all-union alliance. The demands of these new organizations were not limited to parochial, particularistic concerns. The lawyers' union demanded the end of the politicization of the advocacy, while the co-operatives' alliance sought 'economic democratization' by means of 'creating conditions favourable for the development of the market and market relations in the economy'.[21]

Perhaps the most remarkable development of 1989 was the sudden organization and radicalization of labour following the summer miners' strikes in the eastern Ukraine. After years of relative quiescence on the part of labour, dozens of strike committees sprang up and quickly assumed the form of independent unions. In July, Sotsprof, a union of workers' and professionals' organizations from ten cities, was founded. In September, representatives of several dozen workers' groups met in Moscow to establish the Congress of Independent Workers' Movements and Organizations. Some of the new independent unions developed goals and asserted demands that went far beyond immediate material considerations. The September congress adopted resolutions calling for a multi-party system and radical reform of the process of election for local soviets. The programme of the United Workers of the Kuzbass condemned the policy of nationalization in effect since 1918 as dehumanizing and economically disastrous. It demanded the restoration of all forms of property, including private.[22]

A substantial growth in independent publications helped give voice to the new unions, professional associations and political groups. During 1989 the number of publications issued by independent organizations tripled, rising to over 600, and print-runs increased significantly.[23]

Discussion to this point has focused mainly on organizations that may be labelled 'progressive'—that is, that favour change in the direction of liberal democracy, as this concept is understood in the West. Noteworthy among the organizations to emerge in 1989 for not fitting this profile was the United Workers' Front (its Russian acronym, OFT, will be used here).[24] The union, which is composed of white- as well as blue-collar workers, favours a dictatorship of the proletariat, strict central planning and full employment, and bitterly opposes private property, co-operatives and the 'young Soviet bourgeoisie'.[25] Evidence suggests strongly that the OFT was the creation of conservative communist intellectuals and conservative fractions of the Leningrad and Sverdlovsk party apparats. Although the union appears to enjoy some genuine working-class support, it possesses only a small fraction of the following enjoyed by progressive workers' organizations.[26]

The foundation of the OFT exemplified a new tactic used by officials during 1989: the establishment or support of ostensibly 'independent' organizations parallel to truly independent radical groups. In June, several months after the founding of the new lawyers' union, the Ministry of Justice announced the creation of the USSR Union of Lawyers, whose stated purpose was to 'create a rule of law state' and promote 'communist self-management' in the legal profession.[27] In August, just weeks after the birth of the Alliance of United Co-operatives, the AUCCTU (the official trade union organization) announced the founding of a new state-sponsored trade union of co-operatives.[28]

The case of the OFT also demonstrates the difficulty of discerning a single state policy or official line on independent organizations during this phase. The impetus for the OFT came not from the 'apparat' as a whole, or even from Moscow, but from a conservative faction of top party officials and communist scholars in Leningrad and several other major cities. Indeed, the OFT has come under criticism in the official press, including newspapers not noted for their unqualified liberalism.[29] The fragmentation of the party and the partial decentralization of authority that began in 1989 undermined to a large extent whatever consistency in policy might have existed earlier.

Yet the urge to obstruct the new organizations' work remained strong. In September 1989, Soviet miners failed to form a national independent trade union after loyalists of the official trade union infiltrated a meeting of representatives of strike committees and voted en masse against the formation of an independent body. In what miners' representatives termed a 'manoeuvre by the hierarchy' of the state organization, at least 300 'activists' unexpectedly joined a meeting in Moscow of 200 genuine members of the Mining Industry Workers' Union and defeated a motion that the union secede from the AUCCTU.[30] The Leningrad party organization adopted a resolution declaring that 'communists working in social organizations and movements must use their authority and influence to draw them into co-operation with the CPSU ... and resolutely reject extremist and anti-socialist elements ... [communists] bear party responsibility for implementing party policy in these social organizations and movements'. Leningrad party leaders appealed time and again to independent groups to pursue 'unity and consolidation' with the party, and blasted conferences of democratic organizations for their advocacy of 'confrontation'. In this respect, Leningrad officials were hardly untypical of their counterparts in other Russian cities.[31]

PHASE IV: EARLY 1990 TO EARLY 1991

This period witnessed further radicalization and some steps towards consolidation of progressive labour. In April 1990 the largest and most comprehensive meeting of radical workers' groups to date convened in Novokuznetsk. The congress declared that 'the time for reform from above has passed', condemned the communist party system of rule as a 'totalitarian dictatorship', and asserted its intention to strive for a united, Solidarity-style alliance of progressive workers and intellectuals.[32] Such attacks and demands were not unprecedented, but they now became the norm among many independent associations. Many groups dropped the word *perestroika* from their lexicon in favour of calls for revolution. Street demonstrations organized by independent groups, which grew in size and frequency during 1990 and early 1991, became more clearly and explicitly anti-party. A perceptible shift occurred in the objects of demonstrators' wrath, away from unpopular individual officials, the KGB and 'opponents of *perestroika*', towards the communist party system as a whole.[33]

As their demands became more radical and their vocabulary more acerbic, and as their capacity to organize mass demonstrations grew, several of the independent political associations declared themselves alternative political parties. Reacting quickly to the repeal of Article 6, the Social Democratic Association became in the early fall of 1990 the Social Democratic Party of Russia (SDP); Citizen's Dignity became the Constitutional Democratic Party; the Democratic Party of Russia (DPR) and several Christian democratic parties came into existence.[34]

Official reactions to the establishment of alternative parties varied greatly. The formation of the Liberal Democratic Party, a self-consciously non-confrontational group whose leader calls for 'co-operation with all parties, including the CPSU', actually received favourable front-page coverage in *Pravda*.[35] The SDP received no such welcome, but neither was its founding obstructed.[36] The DPR encountered considerable harassment, including efforts by the KGB to bully the directors of local community centres in Moscow into denying the group premises for its founding conference and organizational activities.[37] While official newspapers were filled during the first half of 1990 with stories of how local communist party leaders were 'adapting to new political work' with independent groups, and 'enhancing the prestige and leading role of the party' by means of 'boldly establishing contacts' with them, press accounts contained admissions by officials that the independent groups were 'gaining the initiative' in some cities.[38] The growing confusion and even desperation of many local party officials was hardly surprising. They now faced not only growing organized opposition on the part of independent groups, but also deepening fissures in the ranks of the party itself. The division of the party into distinct 'platforms' during 1990, and mass defections from the party, including the formation in October of the Republican Party of Russia (RPR) by former members of the liberal 'Democratic Platform', further reduced the party's capacity for coherent responses to challenges from below.[39]

The autumn and winter of 1990–91 witnessed a dramatic conservative turn in official policy and a partial crackdown by the authorities against independent political activity. Several relatively liberal high officials in Gorbachev's inner circle resigned or were forced out and replaced by hardline conservatives. Official sources of mass information returned to reporting in the style of the Brezhnev era, and a number of publications issued by independent political organizations were shut down. A series of murders of democratic political activists occurred in Moscow under very peculiar circumstances. These events, along with the violent crackdown in Lithuania, the government's decision to place army troops alongside police officers in street patrols in many Soviet cities, and the increasingly arbitrary and authoritarian behaviour of President Gorbachev in general, gave rise to fears of an impending terror against opponents of the regime.[40]

While the crackdown confronted the independent organizations with new challenges and difficulties, it did not arrest their growth, geographical spread and radicalization. Elections for the RSFSR Congress of People's Deputies, which produced electoral victories for many leaders of new independent parties and other organizations and a roughly even split between democrats and conservatives in the Russian Federation's Supreme Soviet, helped bolster the self-assurance and radicalism of the new groups. In October 1990 democratic parliamentarians and leaders of several of the new parties founded Democratic Russia, an umbrella organization intended to foster co-operation among progressive groups at all levels. Although loosely organized and riven even at its inception by internal divisions, the group was united by the common goal of overturning the communist party system and establishing a genuine multi-party system and a legal state. The new wave of miners' strikes that swept Russia and the eastern Ukraine in early 1991, which included demands for Gorbachev's resignation and direct elections for the presidency of the Russian Republic, contributed to the atmosphere of polarization between radical and conservative forces and raised hopes for closer co-operation between workers' movements and democratic political parties.[41]

...

In conclusion, it would seem that the independent organizations in Russia do not score high on any of the indicators employed here. The causes of shortcomings in groups' capacities for aggregating, representing and articulating interests, and influencing policy as interest groups, are found in: vague and undifferentiated agendas and constituencies; a low level of integration of societal interests; weak internal obligatory capacities; narrow or barely-existent channels of access to official sources of power; and underdeveloped mechanisms for exerting leverage over state institutions. Finally, the absence of legal guarantees leaves the autonomy of the new organizations very much in question. In a number of cases, groups have designed novel and even effective strategies for overcoming these difficulties. In general, however, it would appear that independent groups face an uphill struggle in their efforts to acquire the capacities necessary for effective collective action. This analysis does not 'disprove' the existence of a civil society in Russia. It does show that if a civil society exists, its institutional basis is still only weakly developed. And if one regards strong, stable, autonomous interest associations, capable of checking state power, as crucial components of civil society, it suggests strongly that a genuine civil society has not yet been realized in Russia.

Significantly, while the term 'civil society' (*grazhdanskoe obshchestvo*) has entered the lexicon of the independent associations' own publications and debates, few groups appear to believe that a civil society exists in Russia at the present time. Most organizations speak in terms of 'attempting to bring into being' or 'getting started with building' a civil society. In its founding documents, New Forum, a 'citizens' committee' of radical intellectuals, states as a primary goal 'the construction of an infrastructure for civil society', defined as 'a system of self-governing associations of individuals, independent of the state and formed from below, and the establishment of connections between them'. It is precisely this 'infrastructure', according to the group, which is currently lacking, and which must now be created.[79]

AN ALTERNATIVE CONCEPTUALIZATION: THE 'MOVEMENT SOCIETY'

... Russian political society now resembles less a civil society, with its established political parties, unions, professional groups and other interest associations, than a movement society—that is, a myriad of complex, interacting, apocalyptic *political campaigns*.

Analysts of contemporary social movements in the West have discerned several distinct historical stages in organized social movement activity. The 'old' social movements, characteristic of the stage of industrial capitalism, were bound up with the struggle for state power and the extension of political rights. With the achievement of full citizenship, the focus of social movement activity shifted to economic conflict. As Offe has noted, questions of production and distribution then dominated social movement activity in the West until at least the early post–Second World War period. During this phase, socio-economic interest groups often took the form of large-scale representative associations, characterized by a high degree of formal organization. Relations with state agencies and competition among interests assumed the forms of pluralist or corporatist intermediation and political party competition. With the partial 'solution' of the class conflict embodied in the social movement activity of this phase, the 'new social movements', with their looser organizational structures and their emphasis on 'post-class' or 'post-material' issues and values such as peace, the environment and personal autonomy and identity, began to emerge.[83]

What is unique and most intriguing about the birth of Russian political society is the explosive, unprecedented and *simultaneous* emergence of social movements based on all three types of conflict: citizenship, distribution, and 'post-industrial' values. The 'old' and 'new' demands suddenly find expression not only within Russian political society as a whole, but also in the separate, individual programme and set of demands put forward by nearly every major independent association. Few of the new groups, including the unions, fronts and new political parties, fail to demand full voting rights and electoral reform (citizenship), economic reform and an end to the privileges of the apparat (distribution), and major policy changes on issues of the environment and human rights ('post-industrial').

...

In sum, it is the 'full unresolvedness' of even the most basic citizenship and distributive rights, as well as 'post-industrial' societal concerns, that has produced what appears to be a rare, if not unique, historical phenomenon. And it is precisely the sudden and simultaneous emergence of all three types of demands, not only in society as a whole but within many of its individual constituent organizations, that gives the birth of Russian political society its chaotic appearance and its dramatic character.

The Movement Society: Alternative Descriptive Model or Brief Transitional Period?

... Five long-term obstacles to the emergence of civil society in Russia ... give cause for regarding the movement society as something more than a brief phase of transition.

The first, and most complex, factor regards the character of the state. As discussed above, the institutions of state power in Russia so far have demonstrated a striking inability or unwillingness to deal with the new independent organizations as legitimate, autonomous representatives of societal interests. The old socialist hostility to the principle of independent intermediation, and lack of experience in power-sharing and coping with independent challenges, may help explain this inflexibility.[87]

The current disorganization of the communist party may create new opportunities for the emergence of more responsive governing institutions. For the time being, however, the fragmentation and decay of old structures of power and authority may actually *inhibit* the rapid emergence of a genuine civil society. ... A state that lacks effective economic and administrative steering functions, structures permitting the intermediation of interests, and a capacity for the universalization of law, can actually impede the emergence of a 'modern' civil society.[88] Keane and others argue that the strength of state and society do not necessarily stand in inverse relationship: the power of state and societal institutions may even rise or fall together.[89]

Herein lies a central paradox of state-society relations in present-day Russia: while some disintegration of the state is necessary for the emergence of independent *loci* of societal power, the 'too rapid' erosion of governing institutions' power and authority may block the effectiveness of independent organizations. Just as effective intermediation requires that independent groups possess some leverage over the state, so must state institutions hold some resources and values sought by societal organizations.[90] ...

The disintegration of state power not only robs the state of resources needed for effective bargaining with independent groups. It also deprives the groups of something to 'push up against'. Given the current disorganization of formal structures of power and the consequent blurring of lines of authority, it has become difficult to identify even the ministry, agency, department or committee responsible for policy on a given issue. In their efforts to influence policy, independent groups now face state institutions that are not merely intransigent, but that are often not confident in their own authority. Even upon gaining access to given state institutions, political activists often find that power has flowed elsewhere, or that no one actually knows where authority to resolve the issue of concern resides.[91]

... A second barrier to the growth of civil society is found in the enduring political controls on, and backwardness of, communications and information in Russia.[94] State control over the media has not ruled out all coverage of independent political activity, but objective or sympathetic coverage of the new organizations has been sparse, and has become even more so since the conservative turn in official policy that began in autumn 1990. The resourcefulness of the independent associations in gaining access to publishing facilities has broken the state's monopoly on print media. But the alternative press, though growing, still remains comparatively small. Publications issued by independent groups are often difficult to obtain, particularly outside the few largest cities. Expense and bureaucratic restrictions still prevent many organizations from obtaining access to personal computers or even photocopiers. Political strictures constitute only one aspect of the problem: as Fedor Burlatskii has argued, the country's 'mounting technological backwardness' both inhibits the quality of internal communication and slows potentially beneficial 'diffusion effects' of ideas and information from abroad.[95] Such barriers do not, of course, prevent the emergence of independent organizations. But they do, particularly in a country the size of Russia, slow their growth, maturation and integration. Leaders of the new organizations are acutely aware of how problems of communication and information impede their capacity for articulating demands, attracting new members, holding conferences, influencing public opinion and establishing contacts abroad.[96]

A third impediment to the early emergence of civil society in Russia is the absence of large-scale, integrative societal institutions. The historical dependence and weakness of the Russian Orthodox Church, and its consequent inadequacy as a source of independent societal integration, stands in sharp contrast to the Catholic Church in Poland. In Poland, moreover, Solidarity served not only as a framework for the integration of interests, but also for the representation of diverse interests by several discrete organizations that flourished under the Solidarity umbrella. Such an institution is conspicuous by its absence in Russia. Despite the formation of Democratic Russia, and calls by workers' groups for the formation of a Polish-style Solidarity, little vertical integration of groups representing workers' and intellectuals' interests has yet taken place.

The fourth factor concerns the structure of the Russian economy. Above, it was noted that the absence of a free market system reduces the ability of independent groups to obtain needed inputs without reliance on political authorities, and impedes efforts to establish autonomous resource bases. The enduring fusion of polity and economy in Russia, moreover, blocks the emergence of a business class, which in many societies has acted as a powerful counterweight to state power. Nor has the co-operative movement, which initially seemed to hold promise as a vehicle for economic change, yet begun to create genuine markets or spawn an independent business class in Russia. Instead, the partial decentralization of decision-making authority regarding the regulation of the co-operatives led to the near-destruction of the co-operative movement by hostile local and regional officials in several parts of Russia during 1989–90; and the introduction of onerous new rules on taxation and inspection during 1990–91 has added to the co-operatives' difficulties. Co-operatives that survive are often forced into corrupt 'business relationships' with officials, creating 'bureaucratic capital' and a 'racket economy' rather than dynamic capital and competitive markets.[97] ...

... The fifth obstacle is neither structural nor easily tested, and concerns current societal attitudes toward the prospects for political and social transformation. The explosion of independent political activity examined in this article fully discredits political-cultural theories that attributed the quiescence of Russian society to historically conditioned servility or a longing for authority. But political culture, understood loosely as the way people think about politics, cannot be regarded as entirely inapposite to the current situation in Russia. And the way most Russians now think about politics can be captured in a single word: cynicism. Dedication of substantial time and energy to work in independent political organizations, rather than occasional participation in street demonstrations, calls for at least a shred of idealism, and this commodity is now in short supply. Significantly, only a tiny fraction of the several million citizens of the Russian Republic who withdrew from the Communist Party during 1990 joined the RPR or any other political party. Many have simply withdrawn from political life. Cynicism runs particularly deep among the young. In sharp contrast to political 'revolutions from below' in many other societies, radical student and young people's organizations are conspicuous by their weakness. Judging by activism in the new independent associations, the current rising of Russian society resembles a revolution of the middle-aged. The relative quiescence of the young scarcely precludes the growth of powerful independent groups, but it does rob them of potential sources of energy and dynamism.

CONCLUSION: TOWARDS A POLITICAL SCIENCE
OF RUSSIAN SOCIETY

...

Although the 'movement society' suggests skepticism concerning the existence or early emergence of a civil society in Russia, it does not preclude the possibility of eventual democratic transformation. Indeed, some obstacles to the emergence of a civil society may even hold advantages from the standpoint of democratization and the growth of social movement activity. The lack of progress toward legal guarantees for independent associations, for example, may have helped prevent the erection of a deadening bureaucratic apparatus designed to regulate these groups' activities. Indeed, the movement society may scarcely be regarded as weak and impotent. Even if the new associations have not yet established the institutional infrastructure for a civil society, they have 'rendered power visible'; that is, they have helped expose the illegitimacy, corruption and ineffectiveness of the current system of domination, and in so doing have enhanced the prospects for its eventual demise. Initiative for the formulation of alternatives to the current political system has already shifted from the party to the independent organizations; it remains to be seen whether power will follow.

NOTES

ABOUT THE AUTHOR: **Steven Fish** is assistant professor of political science at the University of Pennsylvania.

The author would like to thank Alexander Dallin, Philippe C. Schmitter, George W. Breslauer, Kelly Smith and Rose McDermott for many helpful comments on earlier drafts of this article.

11. 'Garantiia uspekha—nashi sobstvennye deistviia', *Izvestiia*, 21 April 1987.

12. Moscow World Service, 10 June 1988, translated in *Foreign Broadcast Information Service, The Soviet Union*, 13 June 1988 (hereafter cited as *FBIS*); TASS, 10 May 1988, in *FBIS*, 11 May 1988; Moscow World Service, 23 Aug. 1988, in *FBIS*, 24 Aug. 1988.

13. 'O dialektike razvitiia sotsialisticheskogo obshchestva', *Pravda*, 3 March 1988; 'Samozvantsy i "samodel'shchiki"', *Komsomol'skaia Pravda*, 31 Jan. 1988; 'Obratnyi khod', *Izvestiia*, 9 Sept. 1988.

14. 'Uchenyi idet k "neformalam"', *Komsomol'skaia Pravda*, 11 Dec. 1987.

15. '"Glasnost'" Turns Upside Down', *New Statesman*, 29 Jan. 1988, in *FBIS*, 4 Feb. 1988.

16. 'Posle dolgogo zapreta', *Izvestiia*, 17 May 1988.

17. Interview with Vladimir Bokser (Moscow Union of Voters and Democratic Russia), 30 Jan. 1991, Moscow (all interviews cited here were conducted by the author).

18. 'Public Movements in the USSR', *Moscow News*, 25 Feb.–4 March 1990.

19. Bokser interview, 30 Jan. 1991; interview with Vladimir Kardail'skii (Social Democratic Party of Russia), 11 May 1990, Moscow.

20. Moscow World Service, 25 Oct. 1989, in *FBIS*, 27 Oct. 1989; Paris AFP, 18 Sept. 1989, in *FBIS*, 19 Sept. 1989.

21. TASS, 24 Feb. 1989, in *FBIS*, 9 March 1989; *Trud*, 29 June 1989, in *FBIS*, 13 July 1989; TASS, 12 July 1989, in *FBIS*, 23 July 1989.

22. *Vestnik rabochego dvizheniia* (Moscow), No. 1 (Oct. 1989); *Listok rabochei gruppy* (Yaroslavl'), No. 1 (November 1989); *IV Konferentsiia soiuza trudiashchikhsia Kuzbassa*, 18–19 Nov. 1989 (Novokuznetsk); 'An Alternative Trade Union', *Moscow News*, 25 June–2 July 1989.

23. *Spravochnik periodicheskogo samizdata* (Moscow, 1990), pp. 2–6.

24. I clearly focus on groups that may be labelled 'progressive' or 'pro-democratic', due to the relative difference in the strength of these organizations and those representing con-

servative tendencies. For the most part, progressive organizations represent the dominant and fastest growing tendency in present-day Russia. Conservative communist, 'national-patriotic' and chauvinist groups do enjoy some following, but their influence has been overestimated in the West. Their members and sympathizers have fared extremely poorly in elections for local councils, and their press remains much weaker than that of the progressive organizations. Notably, the most popular of the new groups that espouse Russian nationalism, the Russian People's Front, seeks the rebirth of Russian Orthodoxy and traditional culture but also favours parliamentary democracy, a market system of economy and full freedom of association, while strongly condemning Stalinism and anti-Semitism. 'Presech' pogromshchikov!' and 'Deklaratsiia natsional'no-demokraticheskogo obshchestva "Svobodnaia Rossiia"', *Vozrozhdenie Rossii*, No. 1, 1989; 'Ob opasnosti natsional-patriotizma', *Nevskii kur'er*, No. 3, 5–18 Feb. 1990.

25. *Pervyi (uchreditel'nyi) s"ezd Ob"edinennoggo Fronta Trudiashchikhsia Rossii: Dokumenty i materialy* (Sverdlovsk, 1989).

26. 'Diktatura zdravogo smysla', *Izvestiia*, 8 Dec. 1989; 'Yaroslavskii rabochii klub ob ob"edinennom fronte trudiashchikhsia', *Vestnik rabochego dvizheniia*, No. 1 (Oct. 1989); 'Gavriil Popov v zerkale OFT', *Nash Vybor*, No. 2 (Nov. 1989).

27. 'Zachem nam nuzhen soiuz iuristov', *Komsomol'skaia Pravda*, 20 June 1989.

28. 'Kooperatory ob"ediniaiutsaia', *Izvestiia*, 4 Aug. 1989.

29. 'How a Political Club Cheated a Party Raikom', *Sovetskaia Kul'tura*, 16 Sept. 1989, in *FBIS*, 6 Oct. 1989; 'Rabochee dvizhenie: izderzhki i priobreteniia', and 'Kontakty s "neformalami"', *Pravda*, 18 Jan. 1990.

30. Paris AFP, 14 Sept. 1989, in *FBIS*, 14 Sept. 1989; 'V registratsii otkazano?', *Komsomol'skaia Pravda*, 9 July 1989.

31. 'Chto za slovom "demokratiia"?', *Leningradskaia Pravda*, 26 Oct. 1989; 'Pozitsiia kommunista i pliuralizm mnenii', *Pravda*, 3 Oct. 1989; 'Chestnost' dialoga', *Pravda*, 10 Oct. 1989; 'Ot kogo otstal avangard?', *Sotsialisticheskaia Industriia*, 6 Aug. 1989.

32. *I s"ezd nezavisimykh rabochykh dvizhenii i organizatsii, Deklaratsiia osnovnykh printsipov konfederatsii truda*, 1 May 1990 (Novokuznetsk).

33. This conclusion is based largely on extensive personal observation of street meetings and mass demonstrations in Moscow during the period June 1989–April 1991.

34. O. Rumiantsev in *Argumenty i Fakty*, 10–16 March 1990; 'Multiparty System in Russia', *Moscow News*, 28 May–4 June 1990.

35. 'Sozdana liberal'no-demokraticheskaia partiia', *Pravda*, 1 April 1990. Despite its name, this tiny party is universally regarded by other democratic groups as a creation, or at least a tool, of the communist party apparat. Its choleric leader, Vladimir Zhirinovsky, was expelled from a number of other democratic organizations on suspicion of working for the KGB before founding the Liberal Democratic Party.

36. Kardail'skii interview, 11 May 1990.

37. Interview with Nikolai Travkin (Democratic Party of Russia), 31 Jan. 1991, Moscow.

38. 'Bez barrikad', *Izvestiia*, 10 Jan. 1990; 'Kontakty s "neformalami"', *Pravda*, 18 Jan. 1990; 'Opasnyi vakuum', *Sovetskaia Rossiia*, 17 May 1990.

39. 'Za edinstvo vsekh storonnikov radikal'nogo obnovleniia KPSS', *Moskovskaia Pravda*, 19 April 1990; 'Skol'ko platform nuzhno marksistam?', *Pravda*, 9 May 1990; 'Demplatforma v KPSS', *Novaia Rech*, Sept.–Oct. 1990.

40. 'Litva' and 'Novaia strategiia gosteleradio', *Kommersant*, 7–14 Jan. 1991; 'Prikaz Iazova i Pugo', *Kommersant*, 21–28 Jan. 1991; 'Gorbachev', *Nezavisimaia Gazeta*, 17 Jan. 1991;

Aleksandr Obolenskii, 'Tezisy vystupleniia na mitinge demokraticheskikh sil', Moscow, 23 Dec. 1990 (mimeo).

41. 'Dvizhenie "Demokraticheskaia Rossiia" Sozdano', *Doverie*, Nov. 1990; 'Tak kuda zhe poidut shakhtery?'; *Rossiia*, 23–29 March 1991.

79. 'Osnovnye politicheskie printsipy' and 'Nash put' k svobode i demokratii', *Sbornik dokumentov Grazhdanskogo Komiteta 'Novyi Forum'*; 'Grazhdanskii put' sovety', *Svobodnoe Slovo*, 8, May 1990; 'Deklaratsiia dvizheniia deistviia', *Nevskii Kur'er*, 5–18 Feb. 1990; 'Deklaratsiia Natsional'no-Demokraticheskogo Obshchestva', *Vozrozhdenie*, No. 1, 1989.

83. Claus Offe, 'New Social Movements: Challenging the Boundaries of Institutional Politics', *Social Research*, Vol. 52, No. 4 (1985), pp. 821–38; Alberto Melucci, 'Social Movements and the Democratization of Everyday Life', in [John] Keane (ed.), [*Civil Society and the State* (New York: Verso, 1988),] pp. 245–6.

87. Kenneth Jowitt notes that central features of Leninist parties include their inability to share power and authority and their tendency to draw a rigid distinction between party members and 'outsiders'. *The Leninist Response to National Dependency* (Berkeley, CA: Institute of International Studies, 1978), pp. 34–62.

88. [Andrew] Arato and [Jean] Cohen, ['Social Movements, Civil Society, and the Problem of Sovereignty', *Praxis International*, Vol. 4, No. 3 (1984),] pp. 274–5.

89. [John] Keane, *Democracy and Civil Society* [(New York: Verso, 1988)], p. 61; Alberto Melucci, *Nomads of the Present* (London: Hutchinson, 1989), p. 166.

90. [Philippe C.] Schmitter, ['Democratic Theory and Neo-Corporatist Practice', *Social Research*, Vol. 50, No. 4 (1983),] p. 899.

91. The efforts of independent groups to locate and influence proposed draft laws on the status of their organizations provides a case in point. 'Rule Out Loopholes in the Law', *Moscow News*, 28 May–4 June 1989; 'Unofficial Social Movements: Pros and Cons', *Moscow News*, 15–22 May 1988; 'Movement Left?', *Uchitel'skaia Gazeta*, March 1990, in *FBIS*, 17 April 1990.

94. Many theorists have stressed the importance of free and open communication for the development of civil society: Alberto Melucci, 'The Symbolic Challenge of Contemporary Social Movements', *Social Research*, Vol. 52, No. 4 (1985), pp. 796, 803–6; Rakovski, pp. 86–91.

95. 'An Open Society', *Sovetskaia Kultura*, 21 Oct. 1989, in *FBIS*, 3 Nov. 1989.

96. *Vestnik rabochego dvizheniia*, No. 5, 5 March 1990; interview with Vladimir Lepekhin (Socialist Party), 1 March 1991, Moscow.

97. 'Kooperativnoe dvizhenie v opasnosti', *Literaturnaia Gazeta*, 31 Jan. 1990; 'Co-operatives under Review', *Moscow News*, 28 Jan.–4 Feb. 1990; 'The State, Cooperatives, and Bureaucratic Capital', *Moscow News*, 11–18 March 1990; 'Pravitel'stvo vnosit predlozheniia', *Sovetskaia Rossiia*, 8 April 1990.

13 *Evaluating Gorbachev as Leader*

GEORGE W. BRESLAUER

... The quality of leadership can only be evaluated relative to one's conception of the magnitude of the task, the magnitude and mutability of the constraints on change, and the magnitude of the divergence from the traditional, and currently available, skills and mentality required to carry out the task in the face of those constraints. In sum, to what extent was the exercise of leadership, and of the leadership strategy adopted by the person in question, a necessary (albeit not sufficient) condition for realizing the results witnessed to date?[3]

ESTABLISHING BASELINES FOR EVALUATION

This question sensitizes us to a related methodological concern: the baseline for judging accomplishment. Should we focus on the extent to which the current situation diverges along several value-dimensions from the situation five years earlier? Or should we focus instead (or in addition) on the extent to which the current situation falls short of our (or the leader's) vision of the desired future?

If the past is our baseline, and if we postpone the problem of determining Gorbachev's distinctive contribution to the outcome, it is easy to sum up what has changed in the past five years. This is the least taxing approach to evaluation, and one that predominates in public discourse. Domestically, we have witnessed: (1) desacralization of the Brezhnevite political-economic order, including the official principles and mind-set that underpinned it: the leading role of the Party; the "community of peoples"; pride in the system's achievements; optimism about state socialism's potential; commitment to class struggle abroad; and a national security phobia that justified a repressive, militarized regime; (2) legitimation in principle of movement in the direction of a market-driven economic order, a multi-party system, and the right to secede from the Union; (3) changes in policy and structure that have greatly decentralized political initiative, have created more open and competitive political arenas, have moved far toward disenfranchising the nomenklatura, and have swept radical majorities into power in the governmental councils of major cities; (4) changes in economic policy that have allowed the emergence of a legal private sector (the "cooperatives") that has recently burgeoned and currently employs more than 4.6 million citizens; (5) changes in cultural policy, and in policy toward dissent, emigration, travel, religion, and association that have vastly increased the amount of political freedom within the Soviet Union; (6) changes in foreign policy that have opened the USSR to Westernizing political, cultural, and economic influences; (7) changes in foreign policy that have substantially reduced or eliminated Soviet imperial control in Europe, the magnitude of the Soviet military threat, and the expansionism of Soviet Third World policy, including withdrawal of Soviet troops from Afghanistan; and (8) changes in the institutions and processes of central decision-making that have reduced the power and access of many constituencies that were central to the Brezhnevite political order (the regional party apparatus, the ministries, and the military, in particular).

If one accords primary responsibility for these changes to Gorbachev's leadership (both his initiatives and his unwillingness to suppress initiatives from within society), and if one's approach to evaluation requires that one share attachment to the values advanced, then the man would receive very high marks, both for the direction, magnitude, and breadth of the changes and for the speed with which they have taken place. Perhaps only revolutions from below have historically accomplished more in a shorter period of time.

Using the same methodology, however, one could specify how much has not changed, or has changed for the worse by a short-term humanitarian scale of values: (1) a doleful consumer situation that is perhaps worse than it was in 1985; (2) an economy that is experiencing accelerating negative growth of national income, that is ridden by a huge budgetary deficit and monetary overhang, and that suffers from potentially explosive repressed inflation; (3) widespread intercommunal violence in the southern republics; (4) a sharp rise in the incidence of violent crime throughout the country; (5) growing despair within the population and a crisis of public confidence in the reform process; and (6) continued Soviet military involvement in the Third World. If one believes that these phenomena are reprehensible and collectively outweigh what has been accomplished (either normatively or because one sees their consequences as likely to unravel gains in other realms), and if one attributes these shortfalls to Gorbachev's preferences or myopia, then the man would receive relatively low marks.[4]

If we take as our baseline not the past but the vision of a future new order (be it our own or the leader's), our evaluation of Gorbachev, or of any leader, is likely to be quite different. The easy variant of this approach is simply to measure the shortfall between our preferred vision of a stable democratic polity, a tolerable federation or confederation, and a prosperous marketized economy, on the one hand, and current reality, on the other. By this mechanical standard, Gorbachev has failed—or at least has so far to go that his ability to close the gap between reality and vision must be questioned. Yet, by this very standard, one must return to an issue discussed above: the limits of the possible. It is quite likely that simultaneous democratization and marketization of a Leninist polity and a militarized command economy, set within a huge multinational empire, at a time of economic depression, labor unrest, and both ethnic and ecological militancy is an impossible task. Indeed, even accomplishing the first two elements of this equation without the additional qualifications would be historically unprecedented. If this vision is intrinsically impossible to achieve in the Soviet context, then Gorbachev can hardly be faulted for failing to accomplish the impossible. He can, however, perhaps be faulted as quixotic for believing (if he did) that he could, and for trying to do so.[5]

That these are visions out of reach

...

GORBACHEV: EVENT-MAKING MAN?

In his classic *The Hero in History*, Sidney Hook (1943, p. 153) defines the "hero" as "the individual to whom we can justifiably attribute preponderant influence in determining an issue or event whose consequences would have been profoundly different if he had not acted as he did." A sub-category of the concept is the "event-making man," who accomplishes this as a result of his "outstanding capacities of intelligence, will, and character rather than of accidents of position" (*ibid.,* p. 154). Transformational leaders, then, are event-making men (or women) whose exceptional abilities allow them to overcome constraints on changing the structure and culture of a unit in ways that improve the unit's ability to survive and thrive in a changing environment. Beginning with a retrospective analysis of what Gorbachev has accomplished to date, the question that concerns us is whether Gorbachev has been an event-making man during the past five years. The answer appears to be "yes." *Here is professor Breslauer's theses.*

6 = event-making man

Social determinism can hardly explain the changes we have witnessed. The social, political, economic, and international forces supportive of *perestroyka, glasnost'*, democratization, and "new thinking" in foreign policy constituted factors that encouraged and facilitated the changes. Indeed, they were necessary conditions for the changes in policy to be enacted, implemented, and sustained.[8] But they were not sufficient conditions. The relationship between "social forces" and sociopolitical change was mediated by leadership. *says that G. had a part.*

6 interv. repeatedly to help glasn

Gorbachev's leadership was active and initiatory in the first years after he had consolidated his power (1986–1988). He intervened repeatedly to let the *glasnost'* genie out of the bottle, to encourage social forces to attack the bureaucrats, to hold off the forces of backlash (as reflected, for example, in the Nina Andreyeva letter in *Sovetskaya Rossiya* on March 13, 1988), to recall Andrey Sakharov from exile, to release political prisoners, and to force through a democratization program that began the process of transferring power from the party to the soviets. It was Gorbachev whose doctrinal pronouncements encouraged or tolerated *public* desacralization of the Brezhnevite order. This led social forces to believe that fundamental change was not only desirable and necessary (which many of them had probably believed already), but possible as well (a necessary condition for the development of a revolutionary consciousness [Wolpe, 1970]), while discouraging recalcitrant bureaucrats from thinking that they could hold back the tide.

It was Gorbachev who apparently took the lead on matters of foreign policy, often surprising his domestic audiences with announcements of Soviet concessions on nuclear and conventional arms control, making the fundamental decision to cut losses in Afghanistan, and later pulling the rug from under conservative East European elites by withdrawing the Soviet guarantee of protection against revolutionary forces. It was Gorbachev who articulated a vision of a post–Cold War world, Soviet integration into the European cultural, political, and economic orders, and demilitarization of foreign policy that became the bases for both planning and legitimizing his turnabouts in both domestic and foreign policy.

To be sure, once sufficiently emboldened and organized, social forces pushed to further radicalize Gorbachev's policies. By 1988–1989, it is fair to say, Gorbachev had become a leader who was frequently reacting to degrees of radicalization he had not anticipated, desired, or controlled, such as the political resurrection of Boris Yel'tsin, the Baltic and Transcaucasian secessionist movements, inter-communal violence in the southern republics, the Inter-Regional Group within the Congress of People's Deputies, coal miners' strikes in Siberia, the Ukraine, and the Far North, as well as demands for abrogation of the "leading role of the Party" in both the Soviet Union and Eastern Europe.

But in the face of this society-driven radicalization, Gorbachev had a choice. He could have allied with conservative forces to "draw the line" and enforce strict limits. Instead, with the exception of intercommunal violence, he typically made a virtue of necessity, resisting the temptation to use force, often allying with more radical forces, using tactical surprise to further consolidate his power at the top, and purging or holding at bay those who would have preferred to use such radicalization as justification for reversing or halting the reform process. In this "second," more reactive phase of his leadership, Gorbachev was event-making principally in his ability to prevent the use of state-directed violence against the radicalizing tide. A tragic exception to this trend occurred in Tbilisi in April 1989.

MISSED OPPORTUNITIES?

Of course, Gorbachev must also take responsibility for what has not been achieved during these years: an improvement of the economic situation and a radical reform of the economic system. The pace of economic reform has lagged far behind the pace of change in other realms of policy. Gorbachev has sponsored an assault on the old system of planning, and severely disrupted its operations, without yet putting in place an alternative system for coordinating the economy through market forces. The result is a situation of extreme economic disruption. For this reason, economists evaluating Gorbachev's leadership tend to arrive at conclusions that are, on balance, negative ones (M. Goldman, 1990).

The argument is straightforward: if Gorbachev had launched a real and forceful economic reform in 1985–1986, or if he had chosen to reform agriculture first, or if he had avoided a variety of mistaken policies in earlier years, the economy would not be in the mess it is in today. This counterfactual assertion may be a correct one (though it is not uncontroversial), but linking it to leadership evaluation involves a further logical step: one must argue, not only the likely effectiveness of alternative strategies of reform, but also their intellectual availability and their political feasibility at the time they should have been adopted. To what extent were

Soviet leaders, and Gorbachev in particular, aware in earlier years of the need for such immediate, radical economic surgery? And if they or he were aware, to what extent did the Party leader have the political capacity in 1985–1986 to force its enactment and implementation?

The evidence is ambiguous, but it suggests that Gorbachev was a convinced radical on matters of economic reform when he came to power. The careful kremlinology of Anders Åslund (1989) reveals his differences with others in the leadership at the time. The radicalism of his lengthy December 1984 speech to the Central Committee reveals that he had been influenced by the ideas of Tat'yana Zaslavskaya, and that he was putting himself forward as the candidate to succeed Chernenko on the basis of such a radical platform (Gorbachev, 1984). What's more, during 1985, reform economists who were directors of several institutes and whom Gorbachev had consulted regularly as Secretary of the Central Committee, forwarded to the Politburo programs of radical economic reform (Hewett, 1988, chs. 6–7; Brown, 1990, pp. 186–188; Doder and Branson, 1990, p. 82). Even allowing for the inconclusiveness of the historical record, it seems more than likely that radical economic reform was intellectually available, and was defined by Gorbachev in principle as a necessity for progress, already during 1985–1986.

But was it politically feasible at the time? And if so, at what price? Although Gorbachev consolidated his power faster than any leader in Soviet history, he still had to deal with a challenge that faces any new Soviet leader: to expand his political machine within the bureaucracies and build his political team within the Central Committee apparatus and the Politburo. In the meantime, he has to live with many powerful holdovers from the old regime who do not lose their positions just because the old Party leader has died or been replaced. Even among the Andropovites who replaced Brezhnevites during 1985–1986, the dominant orientations were more technocratic or anti-corruption than radical reformist. It is entirely conceivable that Gorbachev did not push harder for economic reform in 1985–1986 because he was building his political base. This interpretation is substantially reinforced by accumulating evidence of the long-term institutionalization of conventions and norms that served as constraints on leadership initiative within policy-making bodies (Hodnett, 1982; Jones, 1987; Hauslohner, 1989; Breslauer, 1989; Rigby, 1990; Daniels, 1990; Miller, 1990). Of course, even when he began the push for economic reform in 1987, the measures were relatively modest, not compared to the past, but compared to the degree of radicalism required to turn the economy around. New laws on joint ventures, cooperatives, and the Law on the State Enterprise were radical departures, but they constituted a "foot-in-the-door" approach, one that delegitimized old values and justified in principle entirely new approaches to economic organization and the world economy. These policies were revised and, in most cases, made more radical in 1988–1989, but the crucial issues of price reform, privatization of property ownership, and demonopolization of the state sector have still not been tackled as of this writing (June 1990). One could argue, therefore, that the economy might be in better shape today had Gorbachev imposed a much more radical economic reform in 1987–1988—and that he bears responsibility for the failure to do so.

Even if one believes that radical economic reform was necessary and feasible at the time, and that an opportunity was missed, one still has to come to terms with the possibility that the Soviet population might not have tolerated the economic deprivations in the absence of the safety valves Gorbachev has offered them: truly competitive elections and opportunities for authentic political participation at all levels of the political system. And one has to confront the possibility that the Soviet leadership would not have tolerated across-the-board radicalism. We know that the leadership was sharply divided (Åslund, 1989; Doder and Branson, 1990). It is entirely conceivable that, in exchange for greater radicalism in economic policy, Gorbachev would have had to "trade off" some of his radicalism in foreign policy, defense policy, or policy toward cultural and political reform. This in turn could have undermined his efforts to transform the image of the USSR in the eyes of the Western world, which has been at the basis of his efforts to undermine the xenophobic forces resisting reform at home. Thus, both at the level of elite decision-making (the Politburo), and at the level of popular tolerance, it is the interrelationship among issues that matters in constructing a counterfactual argument that Gorbachev could have accomplished more had he tried.[9]

During 1987–1988, Gorbachev was either forced to go slow on economic reform in exchange for a faster pace in other areas, or he chose to do so. If he chose to do so, and had the power to do otherwise, one could retrospectively blame him for lacking the vision, understanding, and strategy required by the economic conditions of the time, or retrospectively praise him for understanding the need for preparatory changes in politics and culture at home and abroad. The choice hinges on one's theoretical beliefs regarding the relationship among political, economic, and cultural change.

This last point is at the heart of current debates about appropriate strategies of transition. It is important to bear in mind that no consensus among specialists exists on this matter. There is disagreement about the workability (not just desirability) of varying mixes of equity and efficiency considerations in the setting of economic policy (Hewett, 1988; Kornai, 1990). There is disagreement as to the proper sequencing of marketization and democratization, with some specialists arguing that the two must proceed simultaneously in order to help break bureaucratic monopolies (thus preventing the development of a racket economy), and in order to build popular support and consensus during a period of disruption and privation (Kornai, 1990, ch. 3; Comisso, 1988).[10] Other specialists argue the opposite: that radical economic reform requires the concentration of political power (a "strong hand") or moral authority (a truly charismatic leader), and that simultaneous political democratization will only undermine economic marketization (Migranian, 1989).

Another grouping of specialists agrees that democratization and marketization must proceed simultaneously, but disputes the forms that each of these should take. Thus, Hankiss (1989) and Yanov (1977) have argued that marketization should be accompanied by a period of elitist ("bourgeois") democracy in order to first institutionalize the rights of managers, entrepreneurs, and a middle-class dominated parliament. In contrast, Kagarlitsky (1990) disputes the character of marketization, arguing that privatization of the Soviet economy will be politically unacceptable in a period of rising labor militancy, and that only municipalization of the means of production, along with mass democratization of local power structures, will allow labor to negotiate its own sacrifices, thereby improving the economic situation while maintaining political stability.

Still others argue that the decisive component of a successful strategy must be international: opening up of the economy to world market forces (Hough, 1988; Hough, 1990; Parker, 1990). To this Kagarlitsky (1990) replies that such an opening will only lead to conditions of dependence, exploitation, and (relative) frustration ("Third Worldization"), creating social and political tensions that will ultimately bring down both reform and democratization (see also Janos, 1989). Sometimes the Japanese strategy of the 1950s is recommended as an alternative to excessive privatization and global integration (Schwartz, 1990).

None of these theories is incorrect on the face of it. It is sobering to recall that development theorists in the 1950s wrote off both Japan and Italy as hopeless cases.[11] *Especially* at a time when Polish "shock therapy" and the virtues of privatization are the Zeitgeist of everyday discourse in parts of Eastern Europe and the Soviet Union, we should be hesitant about conclusions based on the self-evident superiority of one or the other theory.

Similar counterfactual and theoretical arguments can be made regarding Gorbachev's handling of the ethnic crisis. Gorbachev may have been aware that the nationality problem was the most intractable issue on the agenda of Soviet politics (Hough, 1989/1990). But he was apparently not aware of the depth of the secessionist and explosive potential lying just below the surface (Lapidus, 1989). Nor did he anticipate how quickly or fully his policies of *glasnost'* and democratization would release that potential. One could argue that, had he called a constitutional convention and offered the opportunity of a confederation or of an orderly, extended secession process to the leaders of the Baltic republics in 1987–1988, rather than begrudgingly and reactively in 1989–1990, he would have avoided the current crisis that has arisen due to unilateral secessions.[12] Or one could argue that, had he raised the status of Nagorno-Karabakh to that of an autonomous republic when the crisis first began in 1987, he might have averted the current situation of full-scale civil war in the Caucasus.

These counterfactuals rest on the assumption that the issues were ever negotiable on more moderate terms. This assumption may be correct, but the claim is equally plausible that the logic of interaction among political democratization, *glasnost'*, economic reform, and the ethnic issue was inexorable in its reinforcement of centrifugal forces, given the depth of the yearning for independence in the Baltic States, the depth of interethnic hostilities in the Caucasus, and the inevitable disruption and deprivation caused by economic reform. If this is true, the same outcome would likely have materialized by varieties of paths. A different

leadership strategy would have changed the path, not the result. On this set of issues, the argument is strongest that Gorbachev faced an impossible, and irreconcilable, combination of tasks. The burden of argument falls on those who claim
that Gorbachev, or any other leader, can combine democratization and
marketization with maintenance of the federation in its current boundaries. Indeed, jettisoning several republics, and renegotiating terms of association with
the rest, may be prerequisites for realizing the combination of democratization
and marketization that is apparently key to Gorbachev's long-term agenda. Philip
Goldman (1990) may be correct when he argues that "the prospects for successful
democratization of the RSFSR increase as the number of republics decreases."

If the theory underlying this viewpoint is correct (a matter to which I will return below), it has profound implications for our evaluation of Gorbachev's leadership. Recall the earlier point: the flip-side of leadership is opportunity. This theory argues that no opportunity existed; therefore, more skillful leadership would
not have made a difference. Here the argument is different from that which governed the evaluation of Gorbachev's economic leadership. In the ethnic arena, the
argument is that Gorbachev had the political leeway to do things differently, but
faced a no-win situation (I have come across no argument that Gorbachev preferred a different strategy toward the minority republics in 1987–1988, but was
hemmed in by competing preferences within the Politburo). Yet here, as in the
economic arena, if one accepts a pessimistic theory about the nature of the situation, one can still criticize Gorbachev as quixotic for failing to appreciate the
strength of the centrifugal ethnic forces he was facing and unleashing.

The "event-making" man not only makes a difference—a big difference—but
does so because of his outstanding personal capacities. On this score, there does
not appear to be very much controversy in the West or the East, although voices
are heard increasingly that Gorbachev is not up to the task of leading the Soviet
Union to a more radical future (*Newsweek,* June 4, 1990). Yet even those who criticize Gorbachev for failing now to become sufficiently radical view him as an unusual member of the Chernenko-led Politburo. No member of that Politburo has
been portrayed as capable of seizing the initiative on socio-political and international issues the way Gorbachev eventually did. Gorbachev's intellectual capacity
and flexibility, his ability to learn on the job, his powers of argumentation, charismatic appeal, serenity in the midst of social turmoil, faith that turbulence will
"smooth out" in the long run (see Tiersky, 1990, p. 114; *Time Magazine,* June 4,
1990, pp. 27–34), his "sustained, single-minded motivation ... and irrepressible
optimism,"[13] his energy, determination, and tactical political skill have been
noted by observers and interlocutors alike (see Doder and Branson, 1990, pp. 31,
304, and *passim*).[14] By previous Soviet standards, as well as by comparative international standards, he stands out as a man of unusual leadership capacity. It
seems incontestable that, social forces notwithstanding, had Gorbachev not been
selected General Secretary after Chernenko's death, the destruction of the
Brezhnevite political order, the creation and nurturing of new democratic institu-

tions and practices, and the radical concessionary turn in Soviet foreign policy would not have taken place as they did in the 1980s.

Thus far, we have been dealing with the causal-historical criteria for evaluation, concluding that Gorbachev's innovations in the areas of cultural policy, political reform, and foreign policy were products of his initiative and his distinctive event-making capabilities. Our evaluation of his leadership in the areas of economic reform and nationalities policy is less laudatory, but also causally less clear-cut. In economics it hinges in part on one's estimation of how much political leeway Gorbachev enjoyed to act upon the programmatic recommendations of radical economists, and in part on one's theory of transition. In the ethnic realm, it hinges in part on one's theory regarding the ultimate compatibility of diverse objectives within Gorbachev's program, and in part on one's estimation of the extent to which his policies represented bold departures from a preexisting Politburo consensus.

Even if we make allowances for the uncertainties and constraints, Gorbachev's handling of the economic and ethnic issues appears unimpressive compared to his handling of the other issues. He has been an "event-making man" in the economic and ethnic realms only in ways that overlap and interconnect with his innovations in other realms: through his public desacralization and partial destruction of the Brezhnevite political-economic and socio-political orders.[15] Perhaps that in itself makes him an event-maker, given the powerful political and ideological obstacles to radical reform of that entrenched system. But he has been unsuccessful thus far in building an alternative to that order for reintegrating the economy and restructuring interethnic relations. In these issue-areas (but not necessarily in the others), it is fair to say that he has thus far been a better destroyer than creator. ...

GORBACHEV AS TRANSFORMATIONAL LEADER

... If one accepts the notion that cultural and political transformation are preconditions for sustained administrative-organizational transformation, then Gorbachev's strategy of proceeding slowly on economic reform as he moved quickly on *glasnost*, political democratization, and foreign policy change appears defensible.[19] ...

Gorbachev has clearly used the resources of his offices to delegitimize the old order—both its institutional framework and the social values it allegedly protected: social egalitarianism; social security; stable prices; guaranteed employment at the present place of work; autarky; political docility; and insulation from the outside world's political, cultural, and economic influences. He has simultaneously acted to create new opportunities for entrepreneurial initiative, both political and economic: *glasnost*, voluntary associations (the "informal organizations"), multiple-candidate elections, freer travel abroad, and the cooperatives.

He launched *perestroyka* by defining the situation of the USSR in the world as one that demanded emergency surgery, lest the country descend into second-class status (Gorbachev, 1984). And he has played upon unanticipated trigger events (Chernobyl'; Matthias Rust's Cessna landing in Red Square; the miners' strikes) both to purge members of the Old Guard and to dramatize the urgency of the need for cultural and institutional change. He has defined a tight connection between his foreign and domestic policies, harnessing forces in the international environment to further the cause of consciousness-raising within the USSR (see Breslauer, 1989b). In each case, this served organizational-technical ends; but in each case it also served more important goals of transforming identities.

Thus, by opening the Soviet economy to global competition, he not only increases pressure on Soviet managers and draws in foreign capital, but also forces elite and mass alike to define progress relative to the achievements of advanced capitalist countries, rather than relative to the Russian or Soviet past.[20] By opening the country to cultural Westernization, he not only reduces the political, scientific, and international costs of trying to insulate the country from the information revolution, but challenges the idea of Russian or Soviet "originality" (*samobytnost'*) that had underpinned both the Brezhnevite order and the xenophobic strains of Russian national consciousness. By working to reduce international threats to the USSR, he not only creates preconditions for lowering the defense budget, but also dilutes the national security phobia that had been used to justify the Brezhnevite political order. By repudiating class struggle abroad, and by emphasizing the priority of "all-human values," he not only defuses regional crises and paves the way for arms control and other forms of superpower cooperation, but undermines the rationale for the CPSU's continued monopoly on power and truth. Indeed, the extraordinary importance of ideas and ideology in Leninist systems makes it all the more imperative that transformative leaders first neutralize the legitimacy of the traditional political culture if they are to create the political space for new patterns of behavior and organization.

As successful transformational leaders must, Gorbachev has recognized that a precondition for fundamental change is the destruction of old identities, and tolerance of the social conflict that inevitably accompanies such a passage. He has used social and political conflict as occasions for educating citizenry and polity alike to the idea that there is no change without pain, and no democracy without conflict.[21] He has reacted to unanticipated levels of conflict (except for intercommunal violence, and the use of violence against state organs) by claiming them as proof that the old way of doing things was intolerable and, more importantly, was now capable of being changed. He has articulated a vision of the USSR as a "normal," modern country on the model of the social-democratic European welfare state, even as he has fudged the question of whether a market-based pluralist democracy is consistent with "socialism." He speaks the language of evolution, defining change (both at home and abroad) as a long-term process that requires acclimatization to continuous change. While he has not transformed the egalitarian envy of the mass publics, he has fostered a widespread belief in pluralism and markets as the desirable and feasible alternatives to political oppression and economic stagnation.

Related to this concern for cultural transformation has been Gorbachev's effort to create a new legal culture that would depersonalize the legal institutions of the state, and thereby provide a foundation of stable expectations for the protection of person and property. Both Gorbachev's efforts to develop a new legal code, to foster a more independent judiciary, to transfer power from party organs to soviets at all levels, and to turn the soviets into parliamentary institutions that would generate legislation binding on all people push in this direction. These, among other things, are components of his professed commitment to a "law-based state" (*pravovoye gosudarstvo*) to replace the previous order based on arbitrary rule by party officials. Progress in this realm has been slower and less spectacular than in other areas of *glasnost'* and democratization. In part that reflects the nature of the task. Legal reform and institutionalization of new procedures are slow processes, wherever they take place. While much more could perhaps have been accomplished in five years, the institutionalization of a rule of law is not a reasonable expectation in that time frame. What has been accomplished, however, has been delegitimation of "rule by men," legitimation of the search for a procedurally predictable alternative, and practical disruption of party organs' ability to monopolize political initiative.

Gorbachev has been a transformational leader in foreign policy as well, and his basic strategy of "culture first" has been applied there as well. In addition to changing the assumptions underlying Soviet foreign policy in the Brezhnev era, he has sought to undermine the very culture of international relations during the Cold War: the dominant "realist" paradigm that emphasized the balancing of military power; the "enemy image" that fed worst-case planning and weapons procurement; and the "two-camps" mentality that defined superpower competition as a confrontational, zero-sum game. Instead, he has justified a concessionary Soviet foreign policy by propounding an idealist vision of international politics that seeks to transform the enemy image of the USSR into an image of a partner in solving all-human problems. His conviction appears to be that such a transformation in assumptions about the enemy is a prerequisite for ending the Cold War and thereby creating an international environment that would be genuinely supportive of his domestic transformational challenge.[22]

And yet, partly because of the ethnic and economic issues, Gorbachev has presided over a process that, according to some observers, may have brought the country to the abyss of chaos, coup, or worse. He has acted as if possessed of an "insane optimism" (Drane, 1990) that he could simultaneously transform the nation, the empire, *and* the international environment. Perhaps such a degree of optimism is a prerequisite for successful transformational leadership, given the magnitude of the task. Yet there is serious question as to whether he has balanced transformation with stability sufficiently to avoid the "spin out of control." Similarly there is serious question as to whether he has transformed biases sufficiently to maintain the momentum of change in the face of backlash. Are we currently witnessing creative disruption or incipient anarchy and restoration? One's evaluation of Gorbachev's *strategy* of transformation will hinge on the answer to these questions about the future. That is a matter to which we will return later in this essay. But first, let us examine more closely his political *tactics*, in the light of recent literature on the tactical requirements for navigating a successful transition to democracy. Admittedly, some tactical prescriptions for managing politics during the democratization of an authoritarian regime may have to be reconsidered when applied to the simultaneous democratization and marketization of a Leninist empire. But an evaluation of Gorbachev's leadership in light of this recent literature nonetheless provides another basis for making initial judgments.

TRANSITIONS TO DEMOCRACY

The Western literature on transitions to democracy has gone through several stages. The "first generation" of that literature treated democratization as a process that depended for its success on social, cultural, and economic preconditions. Little or no attention was devoted to leadership, which implicitly was treated as a hopeless exercise in the absence of the socioeconomic and cultural prerequisites. The more recent literature, in contrast, is much less deterministic and pessimistic. Its optimism and voluntarism are based on a reexamination of the West European historical experience, and on observation of the recent successful transitions in Southern Europe (Spain, Portugal, Greece), Latin America, and (tentatively) East Asia (see Rustow, 1970; Dahl, 1989, chs. 17–18; O'Donnell and Schmitter, 1986; O'Donnell, Schmitter, and Whitehead, 1986; DiPalma, 1990; DiPalma, 1991).

This body of literature takes many confining conditions as mutable and not as decisive obstacles to democratic breakthroughs and democratic consolidation, even though it does acknowledge that some conditions may frustrate even the most skillful leadership strategy.[23] It focuses on coalition-building strategies within the elites, and on strategies for creating "political space" for new publics being mobilized into politics by the collapse of authoritarian regimes. Hence, it is primarily interested in leadership as a factor that not only facilitates the democratic breakthrough and consolidation, but also guards against the ever-present threat of military coup and other forms of regression. A number of prescriptions for successful leadership tactics can be gleaned from this literature and applied as tests to the Gorbachev administration.

Prescription No. 1: attempt to discredit alternatives to the democratic path, in order to keep them less legitimate in the public and elite consciousness than is the prospective democratic outcome. As Przeworski (1986, pp. 51–52) puts it: "what matters for the stability of any regime is not the legitimacy of this particular system of domination but the presence or absence of preferable alternatives." From this standpoint, Gorbachev's strategy of desacralizing and delegitimizing the Brezhnevite social order, and of discrediting even the alleged accomplishments of Brezhnevism (the welfare-state and military security) makes tactical sense. Similarly, his penchant for arguing that "there is no alternative" to continuing along the reformist path constitutes good politics. His arguments that national security and Soviet competitiveness in the 21st century would be threatened by the failure to join the "modern" world, to become a "normal" country, and to "learn democracy" powerfully advance the message that hypothetical alternatives to *perestroyka* simply are not palatable, from either a livability or a national security standpoint.

Prescription No. 2: mobilize new social forces into politics that will ally with reformist forces within the establishment. This is precisely what *glasnost'* and democratization attempted to do, and apparently what they have accomplished. *Glasnost'* began as an effort to activate new social forces by encouraging them to speak out and engage in self-organization, in order to outflank conservative forces within the bureaucratic and political establishments. When Gorbachev unveiled this populist strategy in mid-1986 (Doder and Branson 1990, pp. 140–141), he probably did not anticipate how far it would go, and it clearly went much farther than he had hoped or suggested. But when faced with the consequences, he did not lead a backlash; rather, he generally accommodated himself to the tide, legitimized its "extremism" (thus making a virtue of necessity), moved himself to the "left" (radicalism) on the elite political spectrum, and sought to create new political institutions that would regulate the conflicts now made manifest. This was an important move. It sent out early signals of an attractive democratic game, in order to avoid the early disillusion so common during failed transitions (DiPalma, 1991; also DiPalma, 1990).

From this perspective, it was fortunate that Gorbachev's speech at the January 1987 plenum of the Central Committee called for multicandidate, secret elections and general pluralization of the political order. It was also fortunate that the June 1988 Party conference, and subsequent meetings of the Congress of People's Deputies and the Supreme Soviet, could be viewed on national television, thus demystifying politics and allowing people to believe that political involvement might be rewarding. Gorbachev also was politically wise in helping to ensure that the elections of March 1989 were conducted reasonably fairly. In sum, Gorbachev simultaneously was mobilizing new social forces, discrediting the old political order, and creating new political institutions to regulate the conflict among the forces unleashed by his policies. This created new political space within which democratic oppositions could develop ties with moderates within the regime.

Prescription No. 3: create opportunities for the cooptation of leaders and activists of opposition groups into new political arenas in which they, and reformist members of the establishment, can pursue and learn the pragmatic and accommodative tactics of a democratic process. Creation of the Congress of People's Deputies, and the Supreme Soviet, along with the persistent transfer of more political authority from party organizations to regional soviets at all levels, have marked Gorbachev's political reform strategy since 1987–1988. At the most general level, these innovations have sought to maintain stability by expanding the opportunities for authentic political participation at a rate equal to or exceeding the rate of political mobilization engendered by *glasnost*.[24] But at the specific level of inter-elite interaction, these institutions have proven to be arenas in which general issues of proceduralism, rule of law, parliamentary practice, and the like, have been forced increasingly to the fore. Although the path has been a rocky one, and littered with conflict, that is unsurprising in any democratic transition. What is significant is that the slow process of institutionalization has begun and gained momentum. A recent comparison of deputies' speeches at the first and subsequent convocations of the Congress of People's Deputies reveals a significant rise in procedural thinking among the deputies (Sergeyev and Parshin, 1990). Equally significant, respect for proceduralism has grown, not only among reformists, but also among fence-sitters and conservatives. As DiPalma (1990) has argued, when conservatives conclude that democratization is the only game in town, they can sometimes become very fast learners.

Prescription No. 4: strip the privileged corporate interests of the old regime of their political *immunity,* but give them enough protection against dispossession that they do not exit *en masse* and seek allies who would help them to violently reverse the democratization process. Democracy is a system based on certainty of procedures and uncertainty of outcomes (Przeworski, 1986). Brezhnevism was a system based on uncertainty of procedures (arbitrariness) and certainty of outcomes. Those whose immunity was guaranteed by the Brezhnev regime had to be both stripped of that immunity and given a sufficient stake in the new order that they would not resort to "breakdown games." The imperative is to "make institutionalized uncertainty palatable" (DiPalma, 1991, manuscript ch. III, p. 7), or at least to make it sufficiently palatable that significant segments of the establishment are more willing to play along than to defect. The idea is that they will not only play the game, but will also come to learn and, eventually, value the new rules. It is imperative both to frighten the conservatives into believing that there is no choice but to join the new democratic game and to reassure conservatives that there is a place for them, protected by the leader, in that game.[25]

From these perspectives, Gorbachev's political tactics look wise. Desacralization of the Brezhnevite political order, abrogation of the Communist Party's constitutionally guaranteed monopoly, and mobilization into politics of anti-official social forces have effectively destroyed the political immunity of the Brezhnevite ruling class. At the same time, Gorbachev has distanced himself from *abolitionist* forces, and thereby maintained his ties with conservative establishment forces, through: (a) his unwillingness to attack the socioeconomic privileges of elites too quickly or fully; (b) his *honorable* retirement of many Politburo and Central Committee members; (c) his willingness to allow many conservative and reactionary forces at Central Committee plenums and meetings of the Congress of People's Deputies or Supreme Soviet to be heard on television and read in the newspapers; (d) his introduction of an electoral system that initially reserved significant proportions of seats to elitist designation by party, trade union, *komsomol,* and Academy of Sciences executive committees; and (e) his apparent alliance with segments of the KGB (on which more below). To many radicals in the Soviet Union and abroad, these concessions appeared to be unacceptable conservatism—evidence of Gorbachev's upbringing as an apparatchik. From the standpoint of those steeped in the comparative literature on transitions, however, it made sense.

At the same time, Gorbachev's deft use of crises (some manufactured, some not) to purge or marginalize conservatives in the leadership both disarmed forces of backlash and encouraged bandwagoning tendencies among the fence-sitters by maintaining high uncertainty about the chances of success if they bucked him. Instead of being discredited by crises, he has used them in ways that have allowed him to actually increase his authority.[26]

Prescription No. 5: disperse or neutralize the means of violent coercion. This is an imperative in all democratic transitions, though it is more urgent in the Third World than in the European Leninist world, where military subordination to the Party has been quite strong. Nonetheless, during his first five years in office, Gorbachev worked to reduce the political status of the military within top-level decision-making arenas, to purge the military command, and to sharply expand the flow of information about military affairs. He has labored to create a benign international environment that would defuse xenophobic claims that one can never spend too much on defense. Indeed, as part of his strategy for delegitimizing Brezhnev's foreign and domestic policies and institutions, he has discredited the use of force at home and abroad as an instrument of policy.

Yet, even as he has challenged military prerogatives, he has taken care to avoid simultaneously confronting the KGB (Rahr, 1989, 1990; see also Alexiev, 1989; Knight, 1989; Reddaway, 1989; Tsypkin, 1989). Although he has purged the party, ministerial, and military apparatuses, he has not purged the KGB apparatus and top command. No large-scale organizational reform or dismantling has been imposed on the secret police. At the level of elite politics, the KGB Chairman is a full member of the Politburo as of this writing, while the Defense Minister is still only a candidate member. Although former KGB chairman Viktor Chebrikov was eventually dropped from the leadership, this did not necessarily reflect a divorce between Gorbachev and the KGB.

While some KGB officials lament the excesses of *glasnost'* and democratization, they have not had to lament any lack of work to occupy their organization. The KGB's functions under Gorbachev have actually expanded in the areas of foreign intelligence and counterintelligence (especially economic), and in the struggles against official corruption, terrorism, narcotics trafficking, and, especially, organized crime within the USSR. It is not insignificant that these are precisely the areas in which Gorbachev can call upon the "forces of rectitude" to perform tasks that are congruent with popular values. The KGB's recent efforts to improve its public image, and to avoid campaigns of retribution against it for past crimes, are furthered by such congruence. It is entirely conceivable that, for many members of the KGB command, this is a source of support for Gorbachev that partially or fully offsets their ambivalence about the new politics. In any case, it is clear that

Gorbachev has consciously followed a policy of deference to KGB institutional interests as a means of coopting and politically neutralizing its leadership.[27] The strategy may be a wise one.

Prescription No. 6: when stalemates appear, up the ante in order to increase the perceived costs of regression. This prescription is based on Robert Dahl's famous dictum that democratic breakthroughs hinge on keeping the perceived price of repression higher than the perceived price of toleration. The issue is not whether the current price of toleration is desirable or enjoyable; the issue is whether it is perceived to be more tolerable than the price of a violent backlash.[28]

On this score, Gorbachev has pursued a consistently successful strategy during his first half-decade as leader. He has been a "radical centrist," seeking to keep the process moving to the "left," while himself dominating, but protecting, the floating center of the political spectrum. By encouraging the activation of social forces pushing for more radical change, or by joining with those social forces when they have surprised him, Gorbachev could more easily argue that the price of restoring the status quo ante had become prohibitive.[29] And by encouraging the public expression of popular views that are so impatient for change, and so enraged by the privilege and corruption of the old order, Gorbachev could more credibly argue that any effort to restore the status quo ante, even if successful in the short run, would only postpone the day of reckoning (as Poland's Jaruzelski discovered in 1989). The higher the level of anti-establishment social activation, the higher the perceived price among conservatives of leading a backlash.[30] And yet, at the same time, Gorbachev's selective protection of moderate and conservative interests has allowed him to dominate the center of the political spectrum by increasing the perception of him among middle-of-the-roaders as their protector against radical disenfranchisement.

Finally, by creating avenues of authentic political participation for released social forces, Gorbachev has disarmed the forces of reactionary backlash by robbing them of an excuse to "crush counter-revolution." Rather than allowing the development of a situation in which social forces might have engaged in anomic outbursts or acts of revolutionary violence, Gorbachev has pursued policies that at once raised the price of repression *and* lowered the price of toleration. In the process, he has dominated the center-left of the political spectrum by increasing the level of felt political *dependence* upon him of most radical reformers, moderate-leftists and middle-of-the-roaders alike. This accounts for the fact that so many reformers criticize Gorbachev's "conservatism," yet fear the prospect of his replacement.

Prescription No. 7: harness forces in the international environment that will help to maintain the momentum of reform while also helping to raise the costs of retrogression. This is precisely what Gorbachev's "New Political Thinking" in foreign policy, his approach to foreign economic relations, and his process of cultural Westernization have attempted to do. By opening the country to economic and cultural Westernization, including travel abroad, he has raised dramatically the price in popular tolerance of efforts to reestablish a closed society, while raising the prospective and actual benefits of openness. By defusing conflicts with wealthy adversaries, he has increased the chance of getting economic assistance for his program, while reducing the prospective cost of defense. As I have argued above, his concessionary foreign policies have sought both to cut losses and to transform the international system, so that foreign countries, companies, and publics would develop a perceived interest in adopting policies that favor the continuation of *perestroyka.*

Furthermore, progress in foreign policy realms is easier and quicker to achieve than is progress, especially economic progress, at home. By simultaneously adopting radical reform in both domestic and foreign policies, Gorbachev has expanded the number of issue-areas within which he can seize the initiative, maintain the momentum of his leadership, and keep prospective challengers off balance. By developing such popularity abroad, Gorbachev has been able to build his authority as a statesman to compensate for lack of economic progress at home. And by delivering on his promise to reduce tensions abroad, he has carved out a realm in which would-be challengers find it difficult to claim that they could do better than he.[31] Thus, just as his foreign policies are central to his strategy of domestic cultural and political transformation, so are they crucial to his tactics for simultaneously expanding his political authority and making *perestroyka* increasingly costly to reverse.

In sum, Gorbachev has gone far to fulfill many of the prescriptions of those scholars who have examined the lessons of success and failure in non-Leninist settings. His strategy comes close to meeting Myron Weiner's (1987, p. 866) pithy summary: "For those who seek democratization the lessons are these: mobilize large-scale non-violent opposition to the regime, seek support from the center and, if necessary, from the conservative right, restrain the left ..., woo sections of the military, seek sympathetic coverage from the Western media, and press the United States for support."

Yet, for many people, both in the Soviet Union and abroad, the current situation is alarming. They claim that, after five years, *perestroyka* is in crisis. Substantial liberalization and democratization have taken place, but a democratic "breakthrough" and consolidation have not been completed (Bunce, 1989). A paralysis of power, and a collapse of central governmental capacity to implement policy, has occurred. Radical economic reform remains on the drawing boards, while leaders of both the party and the state debate heatedly the costs and the risks to be borne in the course of marketization. Minority republics are attempting to secede, defying Gorbachev's constitutionalized procedures and timetable. Russian nationalism has grown stronger and more articulate. The election of Boris Yel'tsin as President of the RSFSR Supreme Soviet has forced the issue of constitutional reform and republic rights. The Communist Party may be on the verge of a split, perhaps into as many as three parties. The international environment appears not to be fully cooperating, as German reunification within NATO threatens to dash

Table 1 Images of the Soviet Future (to the year 2010)[a]

Domestic evolution	Foreign Affairs		
	Expansionist	Isolationist	Collaborative
Fascism	1 *Tragic*	2 *Tragic*	3 *Incompatible*
Ungovernability; chronic instability	4 *Tragic*	5 *Tragic*	6 *Probably incompatible*
Zig-zag path to democratization, dismemberment, and marketization	7 *Probably incompatible*	8 *Transformational*	9 *Transformational*
"Smooth" democratization, dismemberment, and marketization	10 *Incompatible*	11 *Transformational*	12 *Transformational*

[a]Cells indicate evaluation of Gorbachev's role.

Gorbachev's claim that he could transform the international system through con-ciliation. Is all this a sign that Gorbachev's leadership has run its course? Has he led his people out of Egypt, only to see them perish in the desert before reaching the Promised Land? Or is the current turmoil part of a necessarily disruptive pas-sage, the results of which will become visible only during the coming decade? The answer to this question hinges as much on one's theory of transition as on one's reading of the facts of the current situation in the USSR.

GORBACHEV'S CONTRIBUTION: TRAGIC OR TRANSFORMATIONAL?

Table 1 correlates four images of the future of Soviet domestic evolution with three images of the future of Soviet foreign policy. One's image of where things are heading will obviously go far to determine one's midstream evaluation of Gorbachev's general contribution to either Russian or Soviet history. I have indi-cated in the cells those combinations that are likely to be judged by historians as either tragic or transformational.

One image of the Soviet future is apocalyptic: social turmoil, civil war, and the ascendancy of a fascist regime. Those who speak of "Weimar Russia" are inclined toward this viewpoint. They view changes introduced to-date as highly reversible, though only at an enormously high price in blood and death. They perceive the current situation to be hopelessly polarized, with mass toleration at the breaking point. They claim that the political center, which Gorbachev has dominated up to now, has virtually disappeared. Among the masses, they perceive hopelessness and disillusionment with *perestroyka* and with Gorbachev. The economy and the polity are both collapsing. The ethnic situation is out of control. The only result of all this can be a fundamentalist restoration.

A second scenario for domestic evolution is sometimes labeled "Ottomanization." This scenario looks toward gradual disintegration of sociopolitical cohesion and a condition of chronic instability. It predicts swings back-and-forth between partially reformist regimes and military or party-based "junta" regimes. But it predicts no decisive democratic breakthrough. It views the situation in the Soviet Union as a stand-off among conflicting social forces and between a diverse but mobilized society and an establishment that still has an abundance of coercive resources at its disposal. The result will not be a return to Stalinism—the price would be too high—but neither will it be a victory for the forces of "modernity." Instead, the Soviet Union will slip into the pattern of chronic instability so typical of the Third World.

Fascism and Ottomanization are the pessimistic scenarios, though the first is more pessimistic than the second. Two optimistic scenarios envisage a rocky and a smooth road to eventual democratic and market breakthroughs, accompanied in each case by Soviet elite acknowledgment that the empire cannot be sustained in its current boundaries. Optimism is based on a perception that the price of failing to reform and to allow self-determination (or to come back to them after a brief consolidative reaction) is simply too high in the modern world. Optimists perceive an actual or potential social base for pluralistic market systems in the USSR, and political, ideological, and international factors facilitating or determining the transition (for an overview, see Breslauer, 1990). The two optimistic scenarios differ from the pessimistic also in their empirical reading of the situation in the USSR today. Optimists are skeptical of the claim that the Soviet economy is collapsing. They acknowledge considerable polarization and disillusionment, but not the disappearance (or irretrievability) of patience or hope, the collapse of the political center, or delegitimation of the reform process itself.

There are many degrees of optimism to be found among those who fall into this camp. Not surprisingly, Mikhail Gorbachev himself professes to be the most optimistic. As he stated in his March 15, 1990, Presidential inaugural address:

> The principal achievement of perestroika is democracy and glasnost, and this is the decisive factor in the whole course of further reform. ...
>
> Society had to go through all this. We were simply unprepared for sweeping changes, and even now we are still not quite ready for them. In a word, the preparatory phase was a truly indispensable one. ... I understand how dramatic the situation is, how complicated and unusual the problems are, and how emotionally charged society is, but I do not see any grounds for panic, let alone for a change of policy. On the contrary, perestroika must obviously be radicalized. And I shall use my presidential powers above all to this end (Gorbachev, 1990, pp. 3, 4, 5).

Gorbachev also explained his theory of transition to the editors of *Time Magazine* (June 4, 1990, pp. 28, 32):

Perestroika has already awakened our people. They've changed. We have a different society now. We will never slip backward. There's still a question of whether the process will go slower or faster, whether it will be more or less painful. But we will certainly keep moving ahead. There might be certain zigzags along the way. That's unavoidable when a country is undergoing major changes. ...

Once the economic reform really gets under way and millions of people become aware of their places in the new order and pitch in vigorously, they'll become more optimistic and confident of their future.

Although he does not address the issue, Gorbachev presumably intends to complete the work he has finished, to preside over the second stage of *perestroyka*. If he does so, and succeeds in what he has proclaimed to be his goal, he will assuredly go down in history as one of the greatest leaders of modern times.

Most optimists are not as confident as Gorbachev that the process of democratization and marketization is irreversible. Yet they remain optimists because they perceive a social base for still further democratization, even as the regime tackles radical economic reform. And while they perceive potential sources of contradiction between political democratization and economic marketization (be it privatized or municipalized), they do not perceive a live option of choosing between the two, and view the two as capable of being mutually reinforcing.

An increasingly popular theory, developed by Andranik Migranian (1989), combines a pessimistic perception of the current situation in the Soviet Union with an optimistic theory of leadership for avoiding the worst and eventually navigating the rocky path to a democratic market system. Migranian argues that a transition from "totalitarianism" to "democracy" is impossible without going through a stage of "authoritarianism." The optimism of those who study the Spanish and Portuguese transitions, Migranian argues, is a product of the authoritarian, not totalitarian, character of those regimes. The Soviet Union needs first to develop a civil society that is based upon a propertied class that will provide the social base for eventual democratization. Without this propertied class, democratic reforms will be easily reversed.

This theory of transition in turn determines Migranian's evaluation of Gorbachev as leader. He criticizes Gorbachev for not having introduced economic reform before introducing political reform, so as to create a bourgeoisie that would make a democratization program viable. Having failed to do so, he now faces the fruits of his myopia: social turmoil. At worst, he will be swept away by a social catastrophe, consigned by history to a place next to Kerensky in the pantheon of leaders. At best, he still has an opportunity to correct the situation by establishing a Gaullist presidency, declaring martial law, and halting further disintegration of governmental authority. He should use his emergency powers to force through radical economic reform and to repress labor unrest that results therefrom. Eventually, he will be able to relax martial law, expand the social base of his regime by constructing a grand coalition that includes the new bourgeoisie, and further develop a constitutional order. Thus, Gorbachev has a choice: either perform the function of a Jaruzelski or be swept away by a "catastrophe."[32] If he successfully follows this advice, of course, he would be highly praised as a leader who overcame his earlier mistakes, learned on the job, and ultimately steered the Soviet Union from totalitarianism through authoritarianism to an elitist democracy.

The controversial assumption underlying Migranian's historical counterfactual is that Gorbachev could have achieved economic reform earlier without an expansion of mass political participation, which others claim to be necessary to overcoming bureaucratic sabotage of any economic decentralization. The controversial assumption underlying his image of the current situation in the USSR is that the political center has disappeared, the population cannot "learn democracy," and the result of a prolonged stalemate will be a social and political explosion that will favor the fascists. Finally, the assumption underlying Migranian's proposed scenario for the 1990s is that Gorbachev could reassert governmental authority and use coercive powers without unleashing social anarchy, civil war, and a fascist restoration.[33]

In contrast, optimists who do not accept Migranian's assumptions and prescriptions believe that democratization and marketization must proceed in tandem. Following the optimistic literature on transitions to democracy, they would urge upon Gorbachev a very different leadership strategy based upon a different theory of transition: simultaneous movement to the *left* on both political and economic reform. He must preside over the partial dismemberment of the Soviet Union, perhaps by calling a constitutional convention to negotiate secessions, minority rights within seceding units, and the terms of association among the republics that remain within the Union (be it a federation or confederation). He must radicalize his policies, continuously creating new coalitions to his *left*, uniting reformist establishment forces with radical opposition forces that are opposed to playing breakdown games (for example, the A. Sobchaks, G. Popovs, and B. Yel'tsins). He must use his powers to introduce a multiparty system within which competing *national* parties will foster alliances that cut across class and sectoral lines. And he must use those powers to create new national trade unions within which labor can negotiate through organized intermediaries that cut across sectoral and branch lines. Representatives of the national parties and national unions must also be brought into a grand coalition of center-left forces.

DiPalma's (1991) optimistic theory of transitions to democracy treats stalemates not necessarily as precursors of breakdown but instead as potential incubators of creative breakthroughs. Thus, stalemates typically result when the price of restoring the status quo ante is perceived to exceed the price of living with the new turbulence. Crisis, rather than portending breakdown or catastrophe, often becomes psychologically routine or at least more palatable than the price of backlash. But eventually, as stalemate makes stagnation appear dangerous to internal or national security, a majority of the elite comes to the conclusion that the price of living with continuing stalemate exceeds the price of forging a historic compromise that effects a democratizing breakout from the stalemate. From this perspective, stalemate can be creative, especially when society is perceived to be an asset, rather than, as in the pessimistic scenarios, it is typically perceived to be a liability due to its low level of "political culture."

Optimists may differ among themselves as to Gorbachev's role in this prospective radicalization of both economic and political reform. If one views him as a man who has a "great political gift ... for compromise ... but not for decisive radical action" (*The New York Times,* April 15, 1990), or as "a brilliant tactician in the increasingly irrelevant arena of Kremlin politics ... [whose] understanding of Soviet society is incomplete ... [and whose] vision of the future is both narrow and vague" (*Newsweek,* June 4, 1990, p. 18), one will be inclined to see the next radical stage as presided over by new leaders. In that case, one might gravitate to the conclusion that Gorbachev was a brilliant and indispensable transitional leader, whose capacity to destroy the old system without inducing civil war or fascism exceeded his ability to create a new system. But if he is superseded by more "enlightened" leaders who succeed in steering the country toward a marketized democracy, Gorbachev would still go down in history as the man who led the political and psychological breakthrough that made this transformation possible.

Of course, one's evaluation of Gorbachev's leadership will presumably be based on his foreign policy accomplishments as well. Table 1 suggests three directions for Soviet foreign policy in the future: an expansionist restoration; an enduring isolationist retrenchment; and collaborative internationalism. By Gorbachev's reckoning, only the last of these three would qualify as "success," since Soviet isolation, to his mind, would run counter to his goal of broader Soviet integration into the international order. By the reckoning of most Western observers, however, both the second and the third scenarios would be considered progressive, since they each imply an end to Leninist expansionism.

Certain combinations of domestic and foreign policy evolution are so incompatible, and hence unlikely, that we may rule them out prima facie. Cells 3 and 10 clearly fall into that category, while cells 6 and 7 arguably may also. We will therefore dispense with further consideration of them. If the "downstream" consequence of Gorbachev's great experiment is found in cells 1, 2, 4, or 5, his leadership will have failed on its own terms, as well as on the terms of most Western evaluators. He will be praised by historians for his intentions, but will be dubbed a tragic episode in Russian and Soviet history. If, on the other hand, the downstream consequence is found in any of cells 8, 9, 11, 12, Gorbachev's leadership will have succeeded on most of its own terms, as well as on the terms of most Western evaluators. He will then likely go down in history as a successful transformational leader, whether or not he presides over the christening of the edifice he helped to design.

CONCLUSION: IN PRAISE OF GORBACHEV'S LEADERSHIP STRATEGY

During his first five years in power, Gorbachev has been an event-making man, exercising unique leadership skills to break his country out of the preexisting order at home and abroad, and to begin the process of building alternative political and international orders. Although he has had social, political, and international allies in each of these endeavors, overcoming constraints and breaking logjams required from him enlightened acts of leadership. It is doubtful that anyone else in the leadership could have supplied them.

What is more, from a comparative perspective, his strategies and tactics of transformation appear to be enlightened as well. Focusing his attention on cultural transformation through desacralization of the old order, followed by legitimation of alternative assumptions about social, economic, and political life, accords with the thrust of much literature on transformational leadership. So does his creation of new institutions that both channel political activity into new arenas and stack the deck in favor of social groups which share his general vision of the country's future. Gorbachev's leadership deserves very high marks from those who approach leadership evaluation by emphasizing changes in structure and culture, rather than greater efficiency or short-term material accomplishments, in reaching conclusions. Rather than simply focusing on how much particular leaders are able to maximize gains within the game being played, an attempt to evaluate transformational leadership must consider the degree to which the leader has been able to restructure the very game itself to the *eventual* benefit of the unit he leads.

Adopting a political tactic of "radical centrism" also accords with the prescriptions advanced in recent literature on leadership strategies during transitions to democracy. By selectively appeasing or allying with conservative forces, while simultaneously raising the price of backlash, Gorbachev has been able to maintain the political initiative without inducing a conservative or reactionary coup. By releasing radical social forces, but providing them with democratic avenues of political participation, he has been able to keep up the momentum of reform, while reducing incentives for nihilism on the left and repression on the right. By fashioning a foreign policy that mobilizes international forces in support of *perestroyka,* he has increased the attractiveness of staying the course, while raising higher the price to be paid for a backlash. *Centering.*

Let me avoid being misunderstood. Whether Gorbachev's efforts have made reform irreversible remains to be seen; irreversibility is typically only knowable in retrospect, if even then. The guesses that observers put forth typically hinge in part on their perception of the degree of polarization, desperation, and incipient anarchy within Soviet politics and society today. Alternatively, those guesses hinge on observers' implicit theories of transition: assumptions about the types and degrees of disruption that are necessary but containable in the course of democratizing and marketizing a Leninist multinational empire.

Yet, on both empirical and theoretical grounds, both optimists and pessimists should avoid stating their positions too forcefully. The state of public and elite opinion in the USSR today is in evolution and is poorly understood: existing studies have not tapped into attitudes toward "least bad" solutions, or into the relationship between attitudes and behavior. As for theory, while it provides useful, transferable propositions, it remains the case that the task facing the Soviet leadership is unprecedented. This could mean that it is impossible; or it could mean that we have yet to develop a theory of transition that specifies the necessary components of a successful strategy. In this essay, I have sought to indicate why Gorbachev's strategy and tactics have worked to this point, and why the popular claim that they have exhausted their utility should be questioned. I am not prepared to write off their continued capacity to navigate the transition, or Gorbachev's capacity to revise his tactics should radical centrism no longer prove appropriate to the evolving situation. ...

NOTES

ABOUT THE AUTHOR: **George W. Breslauer** is professor of political science and chair of the Center for Slavic and East European Studies at the University of California–Berkeley.

3. "Leadership" is a tricky concept to define. Burns (1978, p. 2) points out that "a recent study turned up 130 definitions of the term." As I employ the concept, it refers to a subcategory of the phenomenon—"transformational leadership" (see Burns, 1978, Part III)—that is most appropriate to the tasks facing Gorbachev. As I use the term, leadership of this kind seeks, through non-tyrannical means, to mobilize and institutionalize support for fundamental change in the structure and culture of a unit (in our case, a state). Evaluation of the quality of leadership must additionally posit that such change succeeds in improving the ability of the unit to deal with environmental threats to its survival and vitality.

4. As Bonner (1990, p. 15) writes: "I would fully share the feelings of the West [adulation of Gorbachev—GWB], were it not for other actions of Gorbachev which overshadowed his positive moves."

5. In an especially poignant passage, Doder and Branson (1990, p. 304) quote a close adviser of Gorbachev: "I know we can't succeed. But when I get in front of that warm and charming man [i.e., Gorbachev—GWB] who wants so much to do something for the country, I have no heart to tell him that we can't succeed." On the other hand, it is important to bear in mind that unprecedented outcomes are not necessarily impossible of achievement (though it helps to have advisers who believe in the feasibility of the project). Also, it may not be possible for social scientists to specify what is intrinsically impossible in social action that does not defy physical principles.

8. For arguments that emphasize social forces as determinants of the origins and irreversibility of reform, see Lewin (1988), Hough (1990), Starr (1988), and Ruble (1990); for further analysis of forces pushing for and against the success of reform, see Breslauer (1990).

9. For this reason, I am skeptical of the utility of attempts to evaluate the quality of Gorbachev's leadership in discrete realms of policy.

10. This raises the question of the success of China in pursuing economic marketization without political democratization. The argument would be that the Chinese experience was not transferable to the Soviet Union because of the relative weakness of Chinese party and state bureaucracies after the Cultural Revolution and the continuing hold of the tradition of decentralization and entrepreneurship in China.

11. Personal communication from Professor Richard Ericson, Columbia University.

12. This hypothetical, of course, assumes he had the power to make such an offer.

13. Doig and Hargrove (1987, p. 19) find this characteristic to be typical of successful leaders of the public bureaucracies they studied.

14. Gorbachev's pragmatism, determination, and high learning capacity come through most forcefully in the impressive, recent book by Doder and Branson (1990, especially pp. 31, 75, 106, 126–128, 157, 163, 218–219 251, 277–280, 282, 290, 332–333, 374–376, 386, 409). Henry Kissinger (1979, p. 54) has argued that "it is an illusion to believe that leaders gain in profundity while they gain experience. ... The convictions that leaders have formed before reaching high office are the intellectual capital they will consume as long as they continue in office." The evolution of Gorbachev's thinking during his first five years in office challenges the applicability to his leadership of Kissinger's generalization. If that challenge is sustainable, it will strengthen a positive evaluation of Gorbachev's leadership. Alternatively, one could argue that Gorbachev's "convictions" were fixed before he came to power, and that his learning has been largely "tactical" within the bounds of his earlier convictions.

15. The notion of public desacralization requires a word of explanation. One could argue that, for most of the Soviet population, the Brezhnevite order was not "sacred." That is probably true. The significance of Gorbachev's desacralization was that it *publicly* rejected the sacred, thereby stripping the apparat and the official classes of immunity from systemic criticism, and thereby also emboldening the intelligentsia and the masses to believe that such forceful criticism could now be safely advanced in public. In a Leninist polity, such public desacralization is a crucial political act, as Khrushchev's anti-Stalin campaign demonstrated at an earlier stage of Soviet reformist history.

19. Indeed, whether or not he had the political elbow-room to proceed rapidly on all fronts in 1985–1987 (which I doubt), Gorbachev appears to have concluded that cultural change ("the human factor") was a prerequisite for successful economic reform: "We have to begin, first of all, with changes in our attitudes and psychology, with the style and method of work. ... I have to tell you frankly that, if we do not change ourselves, I am deeply convinced there will be no changes in the economy and our social life" (Gorbachev speech, April 8, 1986, as quoted in Doder and Branson, 1990, p. 137).

20. Sanders (1990) notes that on-the-ground introduction of competitors' products and symbols (such as the opening of McDonald's in Moscow) serves to focus the attention of Soviet managers and workers alike on both the object of emulation and the distance between that object and existing production processes in the Soviet Union. This is analogous to the strategy of some American automobile manufacturers in bringing models of Japanese automobiles into their factories to highlight the competition and legitimize changes in local production processes and organization. For the same reasons, Gorbachev has used television to broadcast images of Western living standards and of the progress of Chinese economic reforms (Doder and Branson, 1990, pp. 293, 363).

21. "Gorbachev was right in believing that national argument was the way to dispel national apathy and to focus attention on problem-solving. The people, he said, 'are emerging from a state of social apathy and indifference.' ... The Russia of the spring and summer of 1988 was quite different from the Russia of the previous year. The country had come alive again, groping for its future" (Doder and Branson, 1990, pp. 317–318). One cause of this change was Gorbachev's decision to televise nationally the debates among Politburo and Central Committee members before and during the Party Conference of June 1988.

22. For his most recent statements, see Gorbachev's speeches in Stanford and San Francisco, California (*New York Times*, June 12, 1990). For a stimulating and skeptical interpre-

tation of Gorbachev's "New Thinking," interpreted as a "Gramscian strategy of counter-hegemony," see Kubalkova and Cruikshank (1989).

23. This is an important point, and one that bears on my earlier argument that simultaneous democratization and marketization of a Leninist multinational empire and command economy at a time of rising labor and ethnic militancy may well prove to be impossible. Rustow (1970), for example, while rejecting earlier claims that certain socioeconomic conditions are prerequisites for successful democratization, nonetheless treats one confining condition as necessary: the definition of the national community being reformed, which is precisely what is lacking in the Soviet empire. Similarly, Przeworski (1986, p. 63), who writes in the same optimistic vein about the ability to construct democracies in diverse milieux, nonetheless claims that "it seems as if an almost complete docility and patience on the part of organized workers are needed for a democratic transformation to succeed." And Levine (1988, p. 389), who is not a member of the optimistic school, argues that inter-elite trust and a valued relationship between leaders and followers are necessary conditions for "pacts" and "garantismo" to regulate the transition. See also Lyday (1990).

24. According to Huntington (1968), maintaining a balance between the rate of mobilization and the availability of opportunities for political participation is key to maintaining political stability.

25. This power tactic is applicable to pluralist leadership more generally. Thus, writing about presidential power, Richard Neustadt (1960, p. 64) advises the leader "to induce as much uncertainty as possible about the consequences of ignoring what he wants. If he cannot make men think him bound to win, his need is to keep them from thinking they can cross him without risk, or that they can be sure what risks they run. At the same time (no mean feat), he needs to keep them from fearing lest he leave them in the lurch if they support him."

26. On the importance of creating incentives for bandwagoning by fence-sitters, see Breslauer (1989a). On the importance of using power in ways that simultaneously increase one's legitimacy as leader, see Neustadt (1960).

27. Most recently, Gorbachev is reported to have stripped of his military rank and decorations a retired KGB major general, Oleg Kalugin, who had publicly revealed details of his life as an operative and had lambasted the KGB's current role in Soviet politics and society (see *The Washington Post*, July 1, 1990, pp. A1, A28). In the same issue of *The Washington Post* (p. A30), KGB Maj. Gen. Alexander Razhivin speaks of his support for the rehabilitation of Stalin's victims and his belief in the inevitability of a multi-party system, adding: "I refuse to answer for Beria's crimes. Now there is a new generation in the KGB. These are completely new people." Of course, others within the KGB have recently mobilized against the "excesses" of *glasnost*, democratization, and demilitarization (see Rahr, 1990).

28. Note the parallel here with Przeworski's (1986) theory of relativity regarding legitimacy. In each case—mass legitimacy and elite toleration–the issue is not whether the situation is perceived to be "the best," or even "desirable," but whether it is perceived to be the "least bad" among the alternatives defined as realistically possible. Note also that, in each case, we are dealing with an assumption of reasonably rational calculation on the part of the actors involved. For a critique that emphasizes the passion and rage in the Soviet Union that makes such rational calculation unlikely, see Lyday (1990).

29. Hough (1989) argues that Gorbachev has been following a conscious tactic of creating "controlled chaos" to justify the further radicalization of reform. I perceive important elements of this, especially in 1987–1988, but I suspect that Gorbachev has also been exer-

cising "planful opportunism" in response to unanticipated levels of social radicalization in 1989–1990. A good example was his response to the miners' strikes of summer 1989.

30. "Gorbachev was not a man to be underestimated; he was mastering a certain kind of power that his opponents did not fully understand, going public when traditional party men expected him to operate behind the scenes. He exercised power differently. When they refused to hear his arguments for political reforms, he announced that he would convene a party conference to seek approval for the reforms" (Doder and Branson, 1990, p. 192; see also p. 344).

31. This is how Doder and Branson (1990, p. 210) characterize Gorbachev's calculations in convoking a three-day meeting of international intellectual and social elites in Moscow in February 1987: "The occasion, as he fully realized, offered an opportunity to enhance his authority, not just in foreign politics but on the domestic front. His enemies, he knew, were lying in wait, ready to turn on him the moment he blundered on security moves or some other issue. But he was becoming increasingly confident in his diplomatic skills, regarded with respect in the West. He demonstrated to the bureaucracy that he was the day-to-day captain of Soviet foreign policy. ... His mastery of detail and the quality of his reflections on display before a glittering audience in the Grand Kremlin Palace proved that the Soviet leader was a forceful figure, commanding the respect of the outside world and thus deserving respect at home."

32. As Roman Szporluk once put it (personal communication), the Soviet leader could become a "Gorbazelski" or a "Gorbacescu"!

33. DiPalma (1991) forcefully echoes Juan Linz in arguing that parliamentarism rather than presidentialism is crucial for sustaining the transition from authoritarianism to democracy, for it gives the broadest array of social forces a perception of representation in the policy-making process and, therefore, an incentive to transfer their loyalties to the democratic order. However, Migranian implicitly rejects the applicability of this analogy by arguing that the contradictions between democratization and marketization, and the greater constraints on change posed by Leninist "totalitarianism," dictate a temporary combination of strong presidentialism and limited parliamentarism.

REFERENCES

Alexiev, Alex, "Commentary [on Rahr]," *Radio Liberty Report on the USSR*, 1, 51:20–22, December 22, 1989.

Åslund, Anders, *Gorbachev's Struggle for Economic Reform*. Ithaca, NY: Cornell University Press, 1989.

Bonner, Yelena, "On Gorbachev," *The New York Review of Books*, XXXVII, 8:14–17 (May 17, 1990).

Breslauer, George W., "Thinking About the Soviet Future," in George W. Breslauer, ed., *Can Gorbachev's Reforms Succeed?* Berkeley, CA: Center for Slavic and East European Studies, University of California at Berkeley, 1990.

Breslauer, George W., "From Brezhnev to Gorbachev: Ends and Means of Soviet Leadership Selection," in Raymond C. Taras, ed., *Leadership Change in Communist States*. Boston: Unwin, Hyman Inc., 1989a.

Breslauer, George W., "Linking Gorbachev's Domestic and Foreign Policies," *Journal of International Affairs*, 2:267–282, 1989b.

Breslauer, George W. and Philip Tetlock, "Introduction," in George W. Breslauer and Philip Tetlock, eds., *Learning in U.S. and Soviet Foreign Policy*. [Westview: 1991].

Brown, Archie, "Power and Policy in a Time of Leadership Transition, 1981–1988," in Archie Brown, ed., *Political Leadership in the Soviet Union*. Bloomington: Indiana University Press, 1990.

Browne, Angela and Aaron Wildavsky, "Implementation as Exploration (1983)," in Jeffrey L. Pressman and Aaron Wildavsky, eds., *Implementation*, third edition, expanded. Berkeley, CA: University of California Press, 1984.

Bunce, Valerie, "The Transition from State Socialism to Liberal Democracy," typescript, Evanston, Illinois, October 1989.

Burns, James McGregor, *Leadership*. New York: Harper and Row, 1978.

Comisso, Ellen, "The Political Conditions of Economic Reform in Socialism," typescript, San Diego, California, April 1988.

Dahl, Robert, *Democracy and Its Critics*. New Haven, CT: Yale University Press, 1989.

Daniels, Robert V., "Political Processes and Generational Change," in Archie Brown, ed., *Political Leadership in the Soviet Union*. Bloomington, IN: Indiana University Press, 1990.

DiPalma, Giuseppe, *To Craft Democracies*, forthcoming, University of California Press, 1991.

DiPalma, Giuseppe, "Transitions: Puzzles and Surprises From West to East," paper presented at Conference of Europeanists, Washington, D.C., March 23–25, 1990.

Doder, Dusko and Louise Branson, *Gorbachev: Heretic in the Kremlin*. New York: Viking, 1990.

Doig, Jameson W. and Erwin C. Hargrove, eds., *Leadership and Innovation*. Baltimore: Johns Hopkins University Press, 1967.

Drane, Melanie, "Can Gorbachev's Reforms Succeed?" seminar paper, Berkeley, CA: May 1990.

Fearon, James D., "Counterfactuals and Hypothesis Testing in Political Science," paper prepared for presentation at the American Political Science Association Meetings, San Francisco, August 30–September 2, 1990.

Goldman, Marshall I., "Gorbachev the Economist," *Foreign Affairs*, 2:28–44, 1990.

Goldman, Philip, "Some Thoughts on the Question 'Can Gorbachev's Reforms Succeed?'" Seminar paper, Berkeley, California, May 1990.

Gorbachev, Mikhail S., *Zhivoye tvorchestvo naroda* (The Living Creativity of the People). Moscow: Politizdat, 1984.

Gorbachev, Mikhail S., *Speech by USSR President Mikhail Gorbachev*. Moscow: Novosti, 1990.

Gustafson, Thane, "The Road to Anarchy?" *Sovset*, January 31, 1990.

Hankiss, Elemer, *East European Alternatives: Are There Any?* manuscript, Budapest, Hungary, September 1988.

Hauslohner, Peter, "Politics Before Gorbachev: DeStalinization and the Roots of Reform," in Seweryn Bialer, ed., *Politics, Society, and Nationality Inside Gorbachev's Russia*. Boulder, CO: Westview, 1989.

Hewett, Ed A., *Reforming the Soviet Economy*. Washington, DC: Brookings Institution, 1988.

Hodnett, Grey, "The Pattern of Leadership Politics," in Seweryn Bialer, ed., *The Domestic Context of Soviet Foreign Policy*. Boulder, CO: Westview Press, 1982.

Hoffmann, Stanley, "Heroic Leadership: The Case of Modern France," in Lewis J. Edinger, ed., *Political Leadership in Industrialized Societies*. New York: John Wiley & Sons, Inc., 1967.

Hook, Sidney, *The Hero in History.* Boston: Beacon Press, 1943.

Hough, Jerry F., *Opening Up the Soviet Economy.* Washington, DC: Brookings Institution, 1988.

Hough, Jerry F., *Russia and the West: Gorbachev and the Politics of Reform,* second edition. New York: Simon and Schuster 1990.

Hough, Jerry F., "The Politics of Successful Economic Reform," *Soviet Economy,* 5, 1:3–46, 1989.

Hough, Jerry F., "Gorbachev's Politics," *Foreign Affairs,* 68, 5:26–41, 1989/90.

Huntington, Samuel, *Political Order in Changing Societies.* New Haven, CT: Yale University Press, 1968.

Janos, Andrew C., "Social Theory and the Dynamics of Political Change in Communist Societies," typescript, Berkeley, California, 1989.

Jones, Ellen, "Committee Decision-Making in the Soviet Union," *World Politics,* 36, 2:165–188, 1984.

Kagarlitskiy, Boris, *The Dialectic of Change.* London: Verso, 1990.

Kissinger, Henry, *White House Years.* Boston: Little-Brown, 1979.

Knight, Amy, "Commentary [on Rahr]," *Radio Liberty Report on the USSR,* 1, 51:22–24, December 22, 1989.

Kornai, Janos, *The Road to a Free Economy.* New York: Norton, 1990.

Kubalkova, V. and A. A. Cruickshank, *Thinking New About Soviet "New Thinking."* Berkeley, CA: Institute of International Studies, University of California at Berkeley, 1989.

Lapidus, Gail W., "Gorbachev and the 'National Question': Restructuring the Soviet Federation," *Soviet Economy,* 5, 3:201–250, 1989.

Leuchtenberg, William E., "Franklin D. Roosevelt: The First Modern President," in Fred I. Greenstein, ed., *Leadership in the Modern Presidency.* Cambridge, MA: Harvard University Press, 1988.

Levine, Daniel H., "Paradigm Lost: Dependence to Democracy," *World Politics,* XL, 3 377–394, 1988.

Lewin, Moshe, *The Gorbachev Phenomenon.* Berkeley, CA: University of California Press, 1988.

Lyday, Corbin, "The Gorbachev Interregnum and Multiethnicity: A Soviet Time of Troubles," seminar paper, Berkeley, California, May 1990.

March, James G. and Johan P. Olsen, *Rediscovering Institutions: The Organizational Basis of Politics.* New York: The Free Press, 1989.

Migranian A., "Dolgiy put' k yevropeyskomu domu" (The Long Road to the European Home), *Novyy Mir,* 7:166–184, 1989.

Miller, John H., "Putting Clients in Place: The Role of Patronage and Cooption into the Soviet Leadership," in Archie Brown, ed., *Political Leadership in the Soviet Union.* Bloomington: Indiana University Press, 1990.

Naylor, Thomas, *The Gorbachev Strategy.* Lexington, MA: Lexington Books, 1988.

Neustadt, Richard, *Presidential Power.* New York: John Wiley & Sons, Inc., 1960.

Newsweek, "Why Is He a Failure?" (cover story) June 4, 1990.

O'Donnell, Guillermo and Philippe C. Schmitter, *Transitions from Authoritarian Rule: Tentative Conclusions about Uncertain Democracies.* Baltimore: Johns Hopkins University Press, 1986.

O'Donnell, Guillermo, Philippe C. Schmitter, and Laurence Whitehead, eds., *Transitions from Authoritarian Rule: Comparative Perspectives.* Baltimore: Johns Hopkins University Press, 1986.

Parker, Richard, "Inside the 'Collapsing' Soviet Economy," *The Atlantic Monthly*, 4:68–80, June 1990.

Przeworski, Adam, "Some Problems in the Study of the Transition to Democracy," in Guillermo O'Donnell, Philippe C. Schmitter, and Laurence Whitehead, eds., *Transitions from Authoritarian Rule: Comparative Perspectives*. Baltimore: Johns Hopkins University Press, 1986.

Rahr, Alexander, "Gorbachev and the Post-Chebrikov KGB," *Radio Liberty Report on the USSR*, 1, 51:16–20, December 22, 1989.

Reddaway, Peter, "Is the Soviet Union on the Road to Anarchy?" *Washington Post*, August 20, 1989a, p. B1.

Reddaway, Peter, "Life After Gorbachev: The Soviets' Grim Future," *Washington Post*, November 26, 1989b, p. C1.

Reddaway, Peter, "Commentary [on Rahr]," *Radio Liberty Report on the USSR*, 1, 51:24–27, December 22, 1989c.

Reddaway, Peter, "The Road to Anarchy Revisited," *Sovset*, April 24, 1990.

Rigby, T. H., "The Soviet Political Executive, 1917–1986," in Archie Brown, ed., *Political Leadership in the Soviet Union*. Bloomington, IN: Indiana University Press, 1990.

Ruble, Blair, "The Soviet Union's Quiet Revolution," in George W. Breslauer, ed., *Can Gorbachev's Reforms Succeed?* Berkeley: Center for Slavic and East European Studies, University of California at Berkeley, 1990.

Rustow, Dankwart, "Transitions to Democracy," *Comparative Politics*, 2:337–363, 1970.

Sanders, Brian, "The Path to Change: Managing the Process of Transformation," seminar paper, Berkeley, California, May 1990.

Schwartz, Andrew, "Japanese Neomercantilism: An Agenda for Soviet Development?" seminar paper, Berkeley, California, May 1990.

Selznick, Philip, *Leadership in Administration*. New York: Harper and Row, 1957.

Sergeyev, Viktor and Pavel Parshin, "Process-Oriented and Procedural Thinking as Reflected in Political Texts," paper presented at Third U.S.-Soviet Workshop on "Models and Concepts of Interdependence Between Nations," Berkeley, California, January 26–29, 1990.

Starr, S. Frederick, "The Changing Nature of Change in the USSR," in Seweryn Bialer and Michael Mandelbaum, eds., *Gorbachev's Russia and American Foreign Policy*. Boulder, CO: Westview, 1988.

Tichy, Noel M. and Mary Anne Devanna, *The Transformational Leader*. New York: John Wiley & Sons, 1986.

Tiersky, Ronald, "Perestroika and Beyond," *Problems of Communism*, XXXIX, 2:109–114, 1990.

Tsypkin, Mikhail, "Commentary [on Rahr]," *Radio Liberty Report on the USSR*, 1, 51:27–30, December 22, 1990.

Weiner, Myron, "Empirical Democratic Theory and the Transition from Authoritarianism to Democracy," *PS*, 10, 3:861–866, 1987.

Wolpe, H., "Some Problems Concerning Revolutionary Consciousness," in Ralph Miliband and John Saville, eds., *The Socialist Register 1970*. London: The Merlin Press, 1970, pp. 251–280.

Yanov, Alexander, *Detente After Brezhnev*. Berkeley, CA: Institute of International Studies, University of California at Berkeley, 1977.

Yel'tsin, Boris, *Against the Grain*. New York: Summit Books 1990.

"Z" (anonymous), "To the Stalin Mausoleum," *Daedalus*, 119, 1:295–344, 1990.

14 *The Quality of Gorbachev's Leadership*

PETER REDDAWAY

George Breslauer's article on Gorbachev's leadership qualities (Breslauer, 1989) is an extremely stimulating, formidably argued matching of theory against practice. Its many fruits deserve a longer response than can be given here. If he had written it in early 1989 rather than so much later in 1990, I would have been impressed and persuaded by almost all his points, rather than by just many of them. As it is, I believe that Gorbachev's vision of the future has increasingly proved uninspiring or off-target to many Soviet people, and, combined with certain apparent mistakes on his part, has led to a crippling and irreversible decline in his authority. This makes impossible, in my view, the kind of continuing success of his leadership that Breslauer thinks plausible. Although disagreement with Breslauer is not the structural focus of this essay, an attempt is made here to marshal selected arguments supporting conclusions which Breslauer's paper tended to deflate.

GORBACHEV IN HISTORICAL PERSPECTIVE

If Gorbachev were voluntarily to relinquish the presidency in the near future, he would probably still receive good marks from historians—first for the dazzling skill with which (as Breslauer rightly demonstrates) he has undermined Party rule, the "administrative-command system," and the traditional political culture, without (until things changed in the fall of 1990) provoking a sharp conservative backlash, and second for opening up the system to new political and economic forces. For historians may well judge that conducting a relatively peaceful transition from totalitarianism to democracy and the market was *in itself* an impossible task, let alone one which could be achieved from start to finish under a single leader.[3]

After all, profound upheavals such as the French revolution of the late 18th century, the Russian revolution of 1917–1921, or the Iranian revolution of the late 1970s, produce, perhaps invariably, a degree of turnover in the revolutionary leadership, especially early on. Thus, even if Gorbachev leaves the stage sometime soon, historians may be impressed by the *longevity* of his tenure—and attribute it primarily to the leadership skills that Breslauer documents. He has, after all, already survived nearly two years since his "revolution from above" began to slip out of his control, under pressure first from the incipient revolution from below and later from the conservative reaction which both these revolutions provoked.

The current danger, as I shall argue, is that Gorbachev may, despite his now minimal domestic authority, cling to office by trying to use his declining and increasingly uncertain power before it becomes *completely* unusable. This could all too easily slow down, sabotage, halt, or even reverse urgently needed economic reform, and could also increase the already serious danger of major domestic strife or even civil war.

But whether or not Gorbachev clings to office, an important question posed by Breslauer remains: What are the criteria for judging a transition to be successful? Would it be a success if, by the year 2000, Russia (with or without the Ukraine and Belorussia) had embraced democracy and the market, but, in the meanwhile, civil war had killed a million people? Historians might reckon that such a tragedy could have been avoided if, for example, in the early years, Gorbachev's leadership strategy had been less (or, alternatively, more) radical. Or they might conclude that his strategy was probably the best one possible, and any other would only have led to even more deaths. The purpose of this brief paragraph is only to stress, somewhat more than Breslauer does, the importance of historical perspective for arriving at solid, rather than tentative, interim judgments about the quality of Gorbachev's leadership.

At the root of Gorbachev's aforementioned mistakes, in my view, is the political conditioning he received as a young apparatchik in the USSR of Khrushchev's time. This led him to believe, with Khrushchev, that if one trusted the people, loosened political controls, increased incentives, created opportunities for political participation, strove for social justice, and conducted a more peaceful foreign policy, the people would be grateful, would work harder, would overcome bureaucratic resistance to their newly released creativity, and would "make socialism work" rather than challenge it by supporting nationalism, regionalism, anti-communism, or multi-party democracy. Both leaders failed (or did not want) to see that within Soviet society lay the seeds of potential anti-Russian and anti-communist revolutions. Doubtless Gorbachev had more of an inkling of this than Khrushchev, since he could not be completely unaware of the public appearance and growth of these seeds, i.e., of dissident movements, from the mid-1960s until the temporary suppression of most of them in the early 1980s. Such an inkling may help to account for the notable "schizophrenic" but characteristic swings in his rhetoric between supreme optimism about the success of *perestroyka* and increasingly frequent anxiety that *perestroyka* is threatened from various quarters by "disaster," "catastrophe," or "civil war."

GORBACHEV'S VISION: A CRITICAL APPRAISAL

In any case, for a transformational leader to be successful, he needs, as Breslauer suggests, to have charisma, or at least a broad and compelling vision of where he is leading his people. In the USSR, unlike abroad, Gorbachev has never in my opinion had significant charismatic appeal.[4] But he has had a broad vision which, from January 1987 and for about three years, he expounded repeatedly and at length. This vision has understandably had much appeal in the West, especially to people of social democratic orientation. But its appeal in the USSR is less broad, and has declined with the passage of time as it has come to seem increasingly utopian or off-target, or both.

Gorbachev's vision of those three years focused on an entity which has scarcely existed in an organic sense, namely the "Soviet people." It posited the following: (a) a strong central government; (b) limited powers for the republics; (c) an economy based on market socialism, with strong regulation from the center, an enlarged but still small private sector, and harder work from everyone; (d) a polity much more flexible and open than before, based on the rule of law (*pravoporyadok*), but still controlled by a Communist Party which would remain the only party permitted to function freely in the political arena; (e) greatly expanded freedom of expression and association, but with limits still imposed on the mass media (*glasnost'*); (f) social justice for all; and (g) a peaceful, conciliatory foreign policy which would permit the defense budget to be steadily reduced.

Apart from the last component, which has been successfully pursued and has met with popular approval and only—until recently—limited resistance from military leaders and hard-liners, all the other components of this vision have proved to be either problematic or unpopular. The broad reason for this is that as *glasnost'* progressively articulated what previously had been more sensed emotionally than understood by the mind, namely the seemingly comprehensive failures and brutality of the entire system, most of the main features of that system consciously became increasingly repugnant. Thus extreme centralism, big government, Russification, the Communist Party, the KGB, Marxism-Leninism, official trade unions, even Lenin and the military, have for many become objects of distaste and revulsion. Conversely, their opposites have become increasingly, if sometimes irrationally, attractive—decentralization, small government, nationalism, regionalism, political pluralism, the right to strike, isolationism, even tsarism and pacifism. Most of this has diverged sharply from Gorbachev's vision. In addition, few people have wanted to work harder, as inflation has gathered pace and the economic future has darkened, and social justice has remained largely on paper.

None of this might have been so serious if Gorbachev had been adroit to the degree Breslauer suggests at redefining goals and norms as events unfolded. However, on the big confrontational issues of 1989–1990—the mounting demands for confederalism, a multi-party system, disestablishment of the Communist Party, and radically privatizing economic reform—Gorbachev was at first strongly and on principle opposed, and only gave way slowly, grudgingly, and in most cases partially or (as on economic reform) highly ambiguously. All this has made his vision uncertain and therefore ineffective.

Part of his motivation in this growing reluctance to redefine goals has clearly been, as Breslauer shows, his desire to continue to bring the traditional party-state apparatus along in his wake, moving unhappily but steadily to the left, i.e., his desire to neutralize its political power if he cannot reform it. But another part has been what Bialer (1990, p. 53) calls the "strategic rigidity" and "commitment to basic ideological 'truths'" that exist beneath his flexibility. And yet another part may be his desire to maintain viable relations with the powerful organizations—the Party, military, KGB, and MVD—which he might decide to call on in a future attempt to save his own political skin.

In any case, while his vision was clear in seeing the need for cultural change at the start, he has not been able to adjust easily to the outcomes of that change. And while he has succeeded in breaking up the old traditions of government, he has not met the Schumpeter-Breslauer prescription about creating "new tradition." He has found this task much harder than that of allowing the progressive removal of political controls and presiding over what often seems, especially to Soviet conservatives, to be *samotyok,* or the spontaneous unfolding of social processes. Indeed, he has clearly been uneasy about some of the destruction of the old culture, and his vision of the future has differed greatly from that of the more dynamic social forces.

All this helps to account for the growing indecisiveness and erratic behavior which Bialer and others have observed in Gorbachev over the last year. Instead of focusing on his mistakes and weaknesses and devising bold new strategies to overcome them, he has either vacillated or acted much too late. When chided for this, he has insisted on the need for patience in finding political solutions, but also indicated that he will use a big stick if all else fails. ...

A COMMENT ON MIGRANYAN

Before moving on from a discussion on Gorbachev's mistakes, a brief comment on Andranik Migranyan's (1989) analysis of Gorbachev's first few years is in order. In the abstract, I agree with him that it would probably have been much better to have achieved, as a first stage, a radical marketing reform and only a limited shift toward democracy. Legislatures without strong representation of autonomous interests (farmers, trade unionists, businessmen, professional people, etc.), as Aleksandr Tsipko (1990) has also pointed out, will inevitably lack cohesion and be too easily swayed by populist passions. However, Breslauer is certainly correct to question whether radical economic reform was politically feasible in the early Gorbachev years, given the strong anti-market forces in the Politburo and Central Committee, whom it probably would have been impossible to dislodge or override.

By contrast, Migranyan's second assumption—that the political center has eroded, that the people cannot assimilate democracy fast enough, and that a prolonged stalemate would lead to social explosions which will favor the forces of reaction—strikes me as reasonable. But his third assumption—that Gorbachev can still successfully reassert central authority and force through economic reform by adopting authoritarian methods—seems much more implausible in November 1990 than it must have seemed in early 1989, when Migranyan was writing, even though Gorbachev has in the meantime persuaded the legislature to give him the power (on paper) to act in this way.[8] This point is elaborated below.

GORBACHEV'S EVAPORATING SUPPORT

I have several interrelated reasons for believing it implausible that Gorbachev could reassert his authority. First, Gorbachev's popular authority, i.e., popular approval of him (as measured by the All-Union Center for the Study of Public Opinion), has sunk from 52 percent in December 1989 to 21 percent in October 1990 (*Moscow News*, No. 45, November 18–25, 1990, p. 7). Second, the conditions of daily life—not much discussed by Breslauer, partly on the reasonable grounds that their deterioration does not *necessarily* compromise either Gorbachev's leadership or an eventually successful transition—have deteriorated very rapidly in the last year or two. Shortages and rationing of goods, social aggression, crime, bloody ethnic clashes, administrative chaos, bewilderment as to where authority lies, real anxiety about the future—all these phenomena have become progressively more acute.

If there were still hope, rather than deep anxiety, none of this might be critical. But for most citizens Gorbachev no longer provides hope. Indeed many of those who constitute his 21 percent support base may do so not because they really approve of his performance, but more because they are fearful of the unknown future: What may follow may well be even worse. Bialer (1990) is almost certainly right: Gorbachev is probably becoming, if he has not already become, part of the problem, not part of the solution. And seemingly he cannot escape. Maneuver as he may, too many people put most of the blame for their dashed hopes of *perestroyka* on him. Hence his plummeting popularity.

More dangerous for him still has been the incipient collapse of support for him in the now enlarged polity, a polity in which passions have grown steadily more intense and the main institutions of the center have lost almost all their authority. Gorbachev has been commendably frank about what, in a speech of November 16, he called the "vacuum" and the "paralysis" of power. Whenever he issued decrees, he said, "debates begin: 'What sort of decree is this? Do we have to carry it out, or not?'" To this he commented in disgust: "This way we'll never get an executive that functions properly" (*Izvestiya*, November 17, 1990, p. 2). While most of the pervasive ignoring of presidential decrees has been silent in nature, in some cases it has not. For example, A. Gorbunovs, Chairman of the Latvian Supreme Council, rejected the authority of such decrees, and explained: "I am not subordinate to the President, since it was not the President who appointed me. I was elected to the republic's Supreme Council, and evidently it will … determine my future" (TASS, November 16, 1990).

The all-Union legislature, too, had, by fall 1990, become almost impotent. Its laws were not implemented; the President had persuaded it to hand over many of its powers to him, especially those regarding the economy and law and order; and its very legitimacy was disappearing, as relatively freely elected legislatures were voted in by now sovereign republics.[9] The Supreme Soviet even failed by a wide time margin to observe the Constitution and rotate its membership on time, i.e., to replace 20 percent of its members with new representatives from the Congress of People's Deputies.[10]

At lower levels, too, most political institutions either lost authority or became impotent, including the Moscow and Leningrad city soviets,[11] which both have a majority of democratic deputies. As Moscow's Mayor Gavriil Popov said, "The fact that 'democrats' are in power does not mean that they wield any power. I essentially have no real power. I don't command anything. I cannot provide a building, I can't ensure protection for privately run shops. I can't do a lot of things" (*The Washington Post*, November 25, 1990, p. A20). The reasons for this paralysis of power throughout the country have been obstructionism by central government ministries, sabotage and de facto usurpation of power by Communist Party organizations, conflicting laws, and, in some places like Leningrad, extreme behavior by radical democrats.

Within this increasingly angry, frustrated, and dislocated polity, then, it is scarcely surprising that patience with the President has been wearing thin.

MOUNTING PRESSURES FROM THE RIGHT

On the right, conservative Leninists increasingly view Gorbachev as having passively allowed an anti-communist revolution to begin. With his authority so low and the likelihood of him effectively restoring order now apparently minimal, they are fast losing faith in his ability to protect them from the volatile wrath of the people.[12] Many conservative Russian nationalists and military leaders are angered even more by Gorbachev's failure to halt the trend toward dismemberment of the country.[13]

Thus, the divided right has been gradually developing some cohesion, basing itself ideologically on the writings of such publicists as Karem Rash (Tsypkin, 1990a) and the editor of *Soviet Literature,* Aleksander Prokhanov. The latter, often dubbed "the nightingale of the General Staff," sums up much of his diagnosis of the situation in this passage from a recent essay. For the first time in world history, he writes, "a state is collapsing not as a result of external blows, plague, or elemental disasters, but as a result of deliberate actions by leaders who received their authority from structures devised by themselves. It's not important what moves them—a Herostratus complex,[14] catastrophic incompetence, or service to interests alien to the fatherland. They will go down in history. For millennia they will be praised abroad and damned in the fatherland. The king of *perestroika* is naked, blindingly naked, and the tailors sewing his morning dress are packing their bags" (Prokhanov, 1990, p. 7).

A more moderate ideologist of the right, the novelist Valentin Rasputin, was appointed to the Presidential Council, but this muzzled him only to some extent. He still lamented in an interview, for example: "The inert powerlessness of the authorities leads to people losing their last remnants of faith and hope. The wooliness and feebleness of the actions of those from whom they await definite decisions and actions—this is one of the main causes of the present situation" (*Moskovskaya pravda*, October 21, 1990, p. 2).

The main political threat that Gorbachev has felt from the right has come from the military conservatives. The Russian Communist Party is conservative and hostile to him, but as yet only a potential threat, since it is young and still forming its identity. The most direct flexing of its muscles to date came in the report by First Secretary Polozkov to its expanded Central Committee plenum of November 1990. In this the Party called on Gorbachev "to take the most decisive measures to create order in the country. If the dystrophy of authority should go still further, then we will be compelled to review our attitude to the actions of the center" (*Sovetskaya Rossiya*, November 16, 1990, p. 2).

Evidently more worrying to Gorbachev than this, though potentially connected to it, has been the growing militancy of respected military leaders like his personal advisor and former Chief of the General Staff, Sergey Akhromeyev. Akhromeyev argued at length in a recent article that while the military would act internally only on the orders of the Supreme Soviet and the President, "in the summer of 1990 a united offensive of the destructive forces [of separatists and capitalists] began against all-Union state and public structures. Thereby an offensive began also against our federated state with the aim of dismembering it, and against our socialist system with the aim of destroying it. Today this is not seen only by people who do not want to see it." This passage led directly into his final sentence—a call for immediate action: "The time has come actively and decisively, within the framework of our Constitution, to defend our federated socialist state, the cause of our lives, and the future of our children" (*Sovetskaya Rossiya*, November 14, 1990, p. 6).

Akhromeyev would appear to be acting on behalf of many military leaders and to be exerting strong pressure on Gorbachev to declare presidential or martial law, all from a politically loyal position. At the same time the Soyuz faction in the all-Union legislature, which claims that over 500 deputies belong to it, has become the base from which other military officers like its chairman V. Alksnis and N. Petrushenko (see *Izvestiya*, November 24, 1990, p. 1) have pushed for the same thing by more confrontational and threatening means. Thus Lieutenant-Colonel Alksnis gave a lengthy interview to *Sovetskaya Rossiya* (November 21, 1990, p. 1) demanding that Gorbachev declare presidential rule in the republics. Also, if he failed to assert his authority within a month, Alksnis said he would press for Gorbachev's resignation. What must worry Gorbachev is that this direct challenge to him has not to date met with strong, high-level rebuttals. Hence his heightened concern in November 1990 to be very solicitous to the military.[15]

Gorbachev seems, in fact, to be increasingly concerned about possible direct military intervention in politics. Apparently this has strengthened his resolve to try to overcome the political and economic crisis by using authoritarian methods. If he rules forcefully by decree, as he seemed to be calculating in late November, he will be able to appease the military and use them in the ways *he* wants, and will not have to share political authority with them. It will be presidential rule, not martial law. And if presidential rule does not work, he will have martial law "in reserve" as a last resort.

...

that would be suicide. ↑

GORBACHEV'S OPTIONS

Thus, unless Gorbachev summons all his courage and embraces the left, he appears trapped. If the left breaks with him, it could perhaps (and despite its fears of its own increasing impotence) use the power that Yel'tsin (with an approval rating still around 50 percent) has over "the street" to organize demonstrations which would force his resignation. But if he at last heeds the right's calls to impose presidential or martial law he would face other hazards. The military, KGB,[22] and MVD are sufficiently divided politically that they might refuse to obey some of his orders. Here lie the seeds of civil war. Also, the right distrusts him so deeply that it might not keep him in power for long, once he was its captive.

The danger now, then, is that Gorbachev will either turn right, despite the obvious danger that this could provoke civil war, or, less likely, go on maneuvering in the vanishing political center, using his skill at infighting to ward off both left and right. In the latter case the trend toward *mnogovlastiye* (many [competing] powers)[23] and anarchy would accelerate, as Moscow and the republics, notably the RSFSR, fought more and more for control over economic institutions, police, natural resources, taxation, military draft, and so on, in the now widely denounced "war of laws," a war which shows that little solid progress toward the rule of law has yet been made.[24]

If, however, Gorbachev were to embrace the left, and then to step down soon as President, the optimistic scenario would have him replaced by a president who would persuade as many republics as possible to adopt an updated version of the Shatalin plan, then assist them to implement it, each under a "strong and tough" (*sil'nyy i zhestkiy*) leadership of the sort Shatalin believes (in tune with the approach of Migranyan and Klyamkin) that his plan requires.[25]

Even under these circumstances, though, longer-term dangers in abundance would remain, which could easily threaten or derail the process of transition. In general terms the main danger would probably be that radical reform would be sufficiently sabotaged by conservative forces and popular culture and that a reactionary coalition based on an ideology of conservative Russian nationalism and primitive welfare socialism would gather strength.[26] This coalition, the embryo of which can be seen already, would consist of the following:

(1) a new unemployed or semi-employed *Lumpenproletariat,* created by marketization;

(2) a strong Leninist contingent from the old Party-state apparatus;

(3) conservatives from the military, KGB, and MVD;

(4) people from military units returning, humiliated, to bad housing from Eastern Europe; and

(5) disgruntled Russian colonists (possibly millions of them) escaping to Russia from the anti-Russian nationalism of the republics in a militant right-wing mood similar to that of the *pieds noirs* returning to France from Algeria around 1960.

Such a coalition could accuse the left of massive failure with a "non-Russian" reform. It could then take power, either at the polls or through a coup. Civil war all too easily could result.

predicting what, to a large extent, is occurring right now.

CONCLUDING NOTE

In conclusion, let me try to sum up Gorbachev's central dilemma, then quote the suggestive thoughts of a historian, General Dmitriy Volkogonov, about Gorbachev's leadership to date. Gorbachev is a leader who has ever less real authority in the eyes of the Soviet polity and people, has no hope of recouping any, and is facing deepening problems of an economic, constitutional, and social nature which could only be turned around by a leader with very great authority. At the same time he possesses so much formal authority that he is widely described as having "taken all power on himself," he has military leaders demanding that he take drastic action to restore order, and he has some cover from foreign criticism, because the West would probably react mildly to a declaration of presidential rule for which he is apparently preparing, so as not to lose his support in the world-wide coalition against Iraq. A declaration of presidential rule could easily be rationalized by him as the only way to salvage reform from chaos. But under a leader of minimal authority, repression of either a systematic or stop-go variety would almost certainly produce more chaos and much more death.

General Volkogonov's analysis is less focused on the present. Stressing his respect for Gorbachev "as a person," he made these main points in a speech to the RSFSR Supreme Soviet.[27] Gorbachev, he said, "has played a large, historic role in the collapse of the totalitarian system, both in our country and in the countries of Eastern Europe. If, though, we are honest, he did not so much play a role, did not so much do things—he did not hinder the process. Did not hinder, because the system itself had come to the point of breakdown, of collapse. This too was very praiseworthy, but we should not say that he foresaw it."

Volkogonov went on: "The President, unfortunately, does not have new ideas. Put in front of yourself 10 to 15 of the President's speeches. They are all similar: Without fail each of them speaks of a decisive stage, of a decisive phase, of new approaches, about the necessity to move forward. But there are no new ideas. This is very sad. I have to say that the absence of new ideas illuminates very well that indecisiveness, that marking of time, those attempts at innumerable compromises which, in the final analysis, always come out to the right of center."

that the system was going to break down anyway

Volkogonov believes that Gorbachev "does not possess the capacity for vision, ... yet today a man of vision is exactly what is needed. Right now the first fundamentally great decision we've approached in five and a half years is the market. ... How much indecision, how much delay and procrastination! If two years ago we had prepared for this gradually, we would now already be on our feet."

Volkogonov's criticism of Gorbachev is not, he says, a prelude to any "radical" suggestions: "I would simply like to recall from history that a person who tries to accommodate everyone may, in the end, not accommodate anyone."

NOTES

ABOUT THE AUTHOR: **Peter Reddaway** is professor of political science at George Washington University in Washington, D.C.

3. On the day that Gorbachev's compromise program for economic reform was approved by the USSR Supreme Soviet, Leonid Abalkin expressed the view at a press conference that "to create a real market ... will require at least ten years, perhaps an entire generation" (*The Washington Post,* October 20, 1990, p. A1).

4. Breslauer seems to disagree on this point. My view is that working people were at first either cautiously supportive of him or skeptical because he sounded like a better educated, though not necessarily otherwise better, version of Khrushchev. Their opinion of him has clearly worsened in the last two years. Relatively few educated people seem to have been captivated by him, as opposed to appreciating and supporting many of his policies.

8. Igor Klyamkin (1990) takes a similar view, believing that in all likelihood authoritarian rule will be needed to maintain political stability while marketization reforms are forced through. Without it, the unemployed and the marginally employed (*marginaly*) would be successfully exploited by populist politicians.

9. On all this see the interview with an influential USSR deputy, Yuriy Ryzhov, in *Moscow News,* No. 44, November 11, 18, 1990, p. 7. Ryzhov believes the Union legislature "has already played its role, and now it's time to move on."

10. See the scathing article about this by Yelena Bonner (1990).

11. On the role of radical democrats in paralyzing power in the Leningrad city soviet, see Andrey Chernov (1990).

12. On Revolution Day in 1990, for example, several hundred hard-line communists infiltrated the official parade in Moscow and displayed banners with slogans like "Anti-communist Gorbachev—Get Out of the Communist Party!" (*The Washington Post,* November 8, 1990, p. A64).

13. For evidence of pervasive military anger with Gorbachev, see the report of his meeting with 1,100 military deputies in *Krasnaya zvezda,* November 16, 1990. Also, the mysterious military maneuvers near Moscow in September, which have caused a long furor in the press, suggest to me contingency planning for some sort of intervention. See especially the letter from Deputy S. Shatalov in *Sovetskaya Rossiya,* October 21, 1990.

14. Herostratus was the Greek who burned down the temple of Artemides in Ephesus in order to immortalize his own name.

15. See, for example, his speeches of November 16 and 17, both in *Izvestiya,* November 17, 1990. However, in the latter speech (p. 2), he rebuked Alksnis for claiming that he had "lost the army." Evidently this rebuke provoked Alksnis's threat to demand his resignation.

Presidential measures to increase the military's security in the minority republics were announced on November 27.

22. See Tsypkin (1990b). See also a remarkable letter of dissent from four serving KGB officers in *Komsomol'skaya pravda*, October 10, 1990, p. 2.

23. See an especially forceful denunciation of the paralysis caused by *mnogovlastiye* by Sergey Alekseyev, chairman of the USSR Constitutional Oversight Committee, in *Literaturnaya gazeta*, No. 44, October 31, 1990, p. 1. For his equally strong argument that only speedy and wholesale privatization on property can "avert the developing ferocious struggle between the Union and the republics over the dividing up of state property," see *Moskovskiye novosti*, No. 42, October 21, 1990, p. 6.

24. Gorbachev's frequent exhortations that this pervasive "legal nihilism" must stop have had a tragic quality about them, as did the empty prescription with which Aleksandr Yakovlev [interview in *Die Welt*, November 19, 1990, trans. in *Foreign Broadcast Information Service: Daily Report: Soviet Union*, November 20, 1990, p. 53] concluded his frank analysis of this profound problem: "Democracy presupposes, above all, fulfillment of the law. But we do not yet have any real laws that would correspond to the building of democracy. That is a deficiency. One of our country's leading politicians said that the Russian laws are characterized by the fact that they are not observed. This state of affairs must be ended." Such exhortations are spoken as though they could be implemented by extra will-power and administrative action.

25. *Meeting Report* (Vol. VII, No. 1) of the Kennan Institute, summarizing Shatalin's address to the Institute, October 2, 1990.

26. Prokhanov in his above-quoted article argues the need, if Russia is to survive, for a coalition between the Russian patriotic movement and the only major political organization which shares many of its concerns, the Russian Communist Party.

27. The speech was delivered on October 25 and extracted in the new RSFSR newspaper *Rossiya*, No. 1, November 1990, p. 2.

REFERENCES

Breslauer, George, "Evaluating Gorbachev as Leader," *Soviet Economy*, 5, 4:299–340, October–December 1989.

Bialer, Seweryn, "The Last Soviet Communist," *U.S. News and World Report*, October 8, 1990, pp. 53–54.

Bonner, Yelena, "Zakon—ne vorota, mozhno i ob'yekhat' (The Law Is Not a Gate—It Can Be Circumvented)," *Mogkovskiye novosti*, No. 43, October 28, 1990, p. 11.

Chernov, Andrey, "In Favor of the 'Strong Hand'," *Moscow News*, No. 41, October 21–28, 1990.

Klyamkin, Igor, interview in *Moskovskiy komsomolets*, June 7, 1990.

Kroncher, Allen, "What Sort of Market Does Gorbachev Want?" *Soviet Analyst*, 19, 21:4–6, October 1990.

Migranyan, Andranik, "Dolgiy put' k yevropeyskomu domu (The Long Road to the European Home)," *Novyy mir*, 7:166–184, 189.

Prokhanov, Aleksandr, "Ideologiya vyzhivaniya (The Ideology of Survival)," *Nash sovremennik*, 9:3–9, 1990.

"Supporters and Opponents of *Perestroyka:* The Second Joint *Soviet Economy* Roundtable," *Soviet Economy*, 4, 4:275–318, October–December 1988.

Tsipko, Aleksandr, lecture at George Washington University, Washington, DC, November 1, 1990.

Tsypkin, Mikhail, "Karem Rash: An Ideologist of Military Power," *Radio Liberty Report on the USSR*, 2, 31:8–11, August 1990a.

Tsypkin, Mikhail, "A Split in the KGB?" *Radio Liberty Report on the USSR*, 2, 39:6–9, September 1990b.

Vyzov, L. and G. Gurevich, "O doverii soyuznogo rukovodstvu (On Trusting All-Union Leadership)," *Argumenty i fakty*, 42:1, October 1990.

15   Gorbachev's Endgame

JERRY F. HOUGH

For most of the first two years of the Bush administration, liberals and moderates criticized the president for failing to support Mikhail Gorbachev and his reform efforts more vigorously. Gorbachev, these critics argued, faced a serious threat from the Soviet right. Conservatives, bureaucrats, Russian nationalists, the military, Yegor Ligachev—these had all purportedly forced Gorbachev to sacrifice his closest ally, Boris Yeltsin, in November 1987, and were continuing to threaten the general secretary and especially his program of *perestroika*. How could we not help him?

The liberal position was naturally criticized by the American right, still too wary of the Soviet Union to countenance active support of Gorbachev. But the proposed program of support for Gorbachev's reforms had a more fundamental problem: the liberals' definition of *perestroika* was quite vague. Originally *perestroika* had been part of a trio of concepts Gorbachev introduced—along with *demokratizatsiia* and *glasnost*—and referred fairly specifically to economic reform. But Westerners, following the lead of Moscow radicals—who were assumed to be Gorbachev's leading supporters—gradually began to equate *perestroika* with democratization.

This image of Gorbachev involved a good deal of deception or self-deception. However democratic his pretensions, Gorbachev was engaged in a very methodical and ruthless consolidation of power. And his only serious opposition came from the left (those who favored more radical reforms) rather than the right (those who resisted such reforms). The radicals, who in their more honest moments acknowledged a dictatorial side to Gorbachev, publicly identified the general secretary with their own program for tactical reasons. It served the short-term interests of American liberals, too, to say that the United States could support Gorbachev and democratization at the same time. In practice, however, this meant that we would be supporting both Gorbachev and the noncommunist radicals who wanted to overthrow him.

Now this game is no longer possible. The 1989 elections to the Congress of People's Deputies and the 1990 elections to the local soviets showed that the conservative right has very little electoral support. The radicals, meanwhile, have begun to leave the Communist Party that Gorbachev continues to dominate, choosing to distance themselves from him. As a result, it has become clear that Gorbachev is not the consummate democrat we had imagined and that support of the democratic radicals is tantamount to opposing the Soviet president. The radicals are calling loudly for U.S. support and are painting a picture of revolutionary disintegration in the Soviet Union that makes this policy seem the only viable alternative.

Many Western analysts agree with this assessment. This year, for instance, Columbia University professor Seweryn Bialer—one of the most influential Sovietologists of the 1980s—changed his already pessimistic assessment of Soviet prospects and began to predict imminent collapse:

> By 1989, Gorbachev had lost control over events in all spheres of Soviet life. The economy is totally destabilized. ... Fragmentation in the political sphere ... has become significantly pronounced [with a] progressive disintegration of the Soviet multinational state. ... The party apparatus in many republics ... cannot be effective if it is not on the side of the nationalities. It seems increasingly probable that a point of no return is being reached and that the world is witnessing the passing of the Soviet order.[1]

A number of other prominent Sovietologists and correspondents have adopted a similar line, combining it with strong attacks on Gorbachev. Those who echoed the Moscow radicals when the latter pretended to support Gorbachev are echoing these same radicals now opposed to Gorbachev. Harvard University's Marshall Goldman, who once saw Gorbachev as perhaps the only true reformer, today criticizes him for his ill-conceived economic policies, arguing that "[Russian Republic President] Yeltsin and his plan seem to be the Soviet Union's best hope." Dimitri Simes, a Soviet émigré and analyst at the Carnegie Endowment for International Peace, has become an open supporter of Yeltsin, who has emerged as one of Gorbachev's most vociferous critics.[2]

Paradoxically, at a time when President George Bush regards Gorbachev's cooperation as vital to a satisfactory resolution of the Persian Gulf crisis, a flood of articles has appeared stressing the Soviet leader's "irrelevance." In an op-ed published in the *New York Times* on the eve of the recent Helsinki summit, Martin Malia, author of the celebrated "Z" article, took the Bialer position to an extreme:

> It is manifest that the Soviet Union ... is no longer a superpower. Less obviously, this is so because "the Soviet Union has ceased to exist," as one now hears in Moscow, either as a coherent polity or economy. ... In the past six months the Soviet Union has gone the way of Central Europe during six weeks last year. It has been a

slow-motion implosion, just as portentous as the collapse of the Berlin Wall. ... Mr. Gorbachev [is left] somewhat in the position of the Empress Dowager of China amid local warlords.[3]

Malia's advice is to support the democratic forces represented by Yeltsin—a position also advocated by William Safire of the *New York Times* in an adjoining column and then, six days later in the same newspaper, by Mark M. Lowenthal, the senior specialist in U.S. foreign policy at the Congressional Research Service. The same argument was also made by Simes in the lead article of the *Washington Post's* opinion section on the morning of the Helsinki summit. "The Mikhail Gorbachev who comes to Helsinki with his army in disarray, his empire disintegrating and his economy on the edge of collapse is no longer the leader of a superpower colossus," Simes argued.[4]

Presumably this analysis flows from a desire to support Yeltsin by undercutting Gorbachev's international status, making it impossible for the Soviet leader to maintain that he has increased Russia's standing in the world. This, in turn, would undermine Gorbachev's claim to represent Russian nationalism. Both Soviet radicals and their U.S. supporters are aware that Moscow rumors and American analysis often travel back to the Soviet Union on foreign radio; they are attempting to exploit the Voice of America in their efforts to bring about Gorbachev's fall.

Yet it would be very unwise for the United States to get pulled into supporting the radicals against Gorbachev, as these analysts urge. In the short run, it makes no sense to undercut Gorbachev at a time when the Soviet president is supporting the United States in an extremely dangerous crisis—one in which thousands of Americans could come home in body bags. Indeed such a policy, if adopted, would have the effect of undercutting Bush's effort to persuade Saddam Hussein that there is a united phalanx of powerful and resolute states lined up against him.

Nor would such a policy serve our longer term interests. We are within reach of ending the conflict between the Soviet Union and the other members of the "Common European Home"—a development we must be careful not to undermine. But if the Europeans are settling their centuries-old conflicts, it is not because history has ended; it is because they look to the Third World with quiet foreboding. Only the most incredibly optimistic—or naïve—can believe that the strains of industrialization and the pressures of ethnic conflict on national borders that produced centuries of war in Europe will not at times have the same effect in Asia and Africa. Saddam Hussein's "border rectification" may be matched many times over in coming decades—and by countries far larger and more dangerous. If so, Soviet cooperation will be needed again, as will the stability of a community stretching from Vladivostok across the Atlantic to San Francisco.

Beyond its weakness from a policy point of view, the argument for supporting the democrats against Gorbachev suffers from an even more fundamental flaw: it is premised on a profound misunderstanding of the Soviet Union. Wishful thinking on the part of Moscow radicals and their American supporters has led them to grossly exaggerate the severity of the Soviet Union's problems. In fact, the real story of the past year has been the further consolidation of Gorbachev's political position, major progress toward radical economic reform, and, recently, early signs that the most volatile national hot spots are settling down. (The marketization of cotton farming in Central Asia, on the other hand, will create truly serious problems, but that is several years away.) Much of the apparent chaos is either the intended result of policy measures or the kinds of developments we take for granted in many other countries—India, for example—that we consider stable. What all of this suggests is that a more sophisticated understanding of Soviet politics is sorely needed.

*   *   *

Ethnic riots, strikes, public denunciations of the general secretary, and the toleration of elections that have led to the defeat of party leaders—these and other developments have created a Soviet politics that is dramatically different from anything seen since the 1920s. For many Americans—and certainly for most Soviet citizens—the unpredictable nature of recent Soviet history has been such a shock that it seems like uncontrolled chaos. Surely, we think, Gorbachev must be as shocked as we are, and surely he is riding a rampaging tiger that will eventually consume him.

We have, however, lost all sense of proportion. We forget that we have been talking about Gorbachev riding a tiger for four years. We forget that we anticipated an impending wave of uncontrolled strikes when the coal miners first struck, and that was over a year ago. We found the unrest in the Baltic States and the deaths in the Transcaucasus and Central Asia the harbinger of certain disintegration. Yet the same American newspapers that reported these events also reported far larger numbers dead from ethnic conflict in Kashmir, Sri Lanka, Liberia, and South Africa. We forget that, despite all the irrationalities of Third World borders, only one ethnic group has managed to secede and form its own country in the postwar period, and that extraordinary event—the creation of Bangladesh—was facilitated by the Indian army. We do not ask why the Soviet Union will disintegrate more easily than the weak states of Africa and Asia. Our poor sense of history blinds us to the fact that nearly all revolutionary bursts are like the protest movements of the 1960s in the United States; they usually last only a few years and then tend to lose force if they do not succeed.

Perhaps most important, we find it very difficult to accept what we know—namely that Mikhail Gorbachev is not merely a good politician but a great one. When we think about politics in the West, we take for granted that a politician has a political strategy and that part of a good strategy is to mask it. Successful politics has a strong element of theater. Today we use terms like "spin control" to disguise a fact long recognized by voters: you cannot really trust what politicians say, especially when they are saying things that might affect their political support.

Yet, despite the fact that Gorbachev was a radical reformer who was wily enough to thrive in the Brezhnev era—indeed, he has clearly been on the fast track since the early 1970s[5]—we refuse to give him credit for any strategy, political or otherwise. We suppose that he is always as surprised by events as the majority of our analysts and that he is forever reacting to events over which he has no control (though, for unexplained reasons, he always lands on his feet). Some of the things he is supposed to have been surprised by—national unrest when he let up on the controls—suggests that he is a man of unusual naïveté.

Without any question, Gorbachev must have been surprised sometimes, and sometimes he must have improvised. His views have most certainly evolved during his tenure in office. This, of course, is true of any leader in any country. But this should not suggest that Gorbachev has had no strategy. In fact, those analysts who have been most successful in their predictions about Gorbachev have assumed that he did have a conscious strategy.[6] And where this analysis has been wrong, it has been in the assumption that emotion and fear of the unknown would prevent Gorbachev from carrying his foreign policy or his determination to consolidate power to a logical conclusion. Even though, for instance, it was quite clear for several years that the liberation of Central Europe and the unification of Germany were a logical part of Gorbachev's strategy, I for one could not believe until early last year that Gorbachev would actually accept such an outcome. Thus my own early predictions on this question were much too conservative.

It seems crucial therefore to start from the recognition that Gorbachev has had a strategy and then to determine what that strategy has been. Otherwise we must assume that he has been lurching from crisis to crisis when in fact things have been flowing quite smoothly—to some extent, one could even say, according to plan.

Dealing w/ misconceptions and assumptions by nmor. towards & politics and (g. as a leader.

*   *   *

Gorbachev came to power with several major goals. A primary objective, of course, was to secure his personal power, but he was also determined to introduce radical change into domestic and foreign policy. The reforms he had in mind were truly far-reaching; they would require major changes in ideology and would lead both to an influx of "subversive" Western ideas and to the kind of inflation in food prices that had produced revolution in Poland in 1980. Gorbachev knew, therefore, that party officials were going to be worried about his policies; more important, he knew that he would face a serious potential danger in the streets. As a result, he could not limit himself to the normal steps of a Brezhnev in consolidating his power.

The problem many American analysts had—and still have—in understanding Gorbachev's strategy is that they misread his basic political problem. They accepted Stephen Cohen's 1979 view of the Russian people ("The Soviet Union has become, both downstairs and upstairs, one of the most conservative countries in the world"[7]) and assumed, as a consequence, that any serious effort at reform and reversal of the "social contract" would produce conservative social unrest. This assumption led to repeated errors in anticipating Gorbachev's policies and the popular reaction to them. Initially, most analysts believed that Gorbachev would be content to muddle along with half-hearted reforms rather than risk antagonizing the Russian masses. Then, when Gorbachev made it clear that he was actually a radical reformer, American analysts worried incessantly that he would be undermined by conservative opposition—both from within the party and from the population. As *New York Times* correspondent Bill Keller was to write as late as September 1990:

> Not too many months ago, it would have been hard to imagine the Russian Republic as a magnet for the young democrats of the Soviet Union, let alone the pacesetter of Soviet reform. Russia, with its willful backwardness [and] its slavish population ... was the heart of the problem Gorbachev was supposed to solve.[8]

Gorbachev was aware of the eventual danger of a backlash as people felt the painful effects of radical reform. We should not, however, assume that he shared the prevailing American view of the Russian people as hopelessly conservative and therefore opposed to reform. During Gorbachev's lifetime, the Soviet people had become vastly more sophisticated, urban, and educated. In 1926, only 7 percent of the population lived in cities with more than 100,000 inhabitants, but this figure had risen to 38 percent by 1979. In 1939, only 11 percent of the population had at least some high school education; by 1979, 63 percent of the population had attended high school.[9] As a peasant boy born in 1931 who went on to graduate from the elite Moscow University, Gorbachev symbolized this transformation. From the beginning of his tenure as general secretary, he based his policies on what Bill Keller and the vast majority of analysts could hardly imagine five years later— namely, the Russian people's receptivity to radical reform.

Even before becoming general secretary, Gorbachev apparently understood the implications of these enormous demographic changes. In December 1984, as Central Committee secretary for ideology under Konstantin Chernenko, he gave a speech in which he referred not only to the changed values of the Soviet population—especially of the youth—but also to the need for fundamental change in Soviet society. He used Marxist language that is arcane for most of us, but that was crystal clear to the insider. Fundamental change had occurred in the "productive forces," he argued, yet outmoded "productive relations" were being preserved. To a Westerner, it might have seemed that Gorbachev was talking about economic reform. He was, but the choice of words was highly significant, since Marx had argued that conflict between "productive forces" and "productive relations" would inevitably bring revolution.[10] Serge Schmemann of the *New York Times* was the first to call attention to this speech even before Gorbachev was elected general secretary, rightly noting that Gorbachev "seemed to be calling for a transformation of the nation as radical as the one wrought by Stalin in the brutal industrialization drive of the 1930s."[11]

Gorbachev had good reason to believe that the Soviet Union was ripe for dramatic political change. Historically, when a country achieves a high level of urbanization and education, the democratic pressure against dictatorship becomes irresistible. The mid-1970s saw the collapse of dictatorial regimes in countries such as Spain, Portugal, and Greece, followed in the 1980s by Argentina, Brazil, and then South Korea. If Russians revolted in the face of higher bread prices, Gorbachev understood that they, like the Poles in 1980, would be demanding free trade unions and other aspects of democracy—not a return to Brezhnevism.

As a Soviet leader well versed in the dynamics of revolution and power politics, Gorbachev had a clear understanding of where the threats to his own position might arise. He knew that in most countries, there are only a few groups that can remove a leader without elections: palace insiders who are willing to assassinate the leader, the military (or a competing military organized outside the established government), and youths in their teens and early twenties—the only group that will face troops and tanks in the street. The Soviet Union, in addition to these, has possessed a somewhat more democratic method of ousting a leader; the general secretary could be removed by a majority in the party Central Committee, a possibility that became a reality in 1964 with the vote against Nikita Khrushchev.

Gorbachev recognized that the transformation of Soviet society had increased the risk of radical popular rebellion relative to the other potential threats to his power. Countries with little industrialization and a poorly educated population are very susceptible to palace and military coups, but their leaders find it relatively easy to suppress popular revolt. As a country urbanizes and education becomes more widespread, however, the threat of popular revolt becomes greater. One key reason is that in an underdeveloped country, the soldiers tend to be uneducated peasants who resent the privileged college students they are ordered to suppress. (The 1989 massacre in Tiananmen Square was a prime illustration of this phenomenon.) In such circumstances, if the military holds strong, the rebellious youth can never prevail. In a more developed country, however, the 18- to 20-year-old soldiers tend to be very similar in their background and values to the 18- to 20-year-olds demonstrating in the streets. As a result, they are much more reluctant to shoot at the demonstrators—at least if they are of the same ethnic group.[12]

As Gorbachev was assessing the relative risks of a Central Committee revolt, a military coup, and a radical popular rebellion, American analysts were focusing on dangers that did not seem to worry Gorbachev nearly as much—conservative opposition and nationalist unrest. In anticipating conservative resistance to perestroika, we focused overwhelmingly on Soviet citizens over 50 years of age, who were comfortable with Brezhnev's status quo–oriented policy and who had every reason to fear inflation-producing reforms, since they were on fixed-income pensions or were moving toward retirement. But we failed to recall that revolutions are almost never conducted by people over 50. We stressed the likelihood of unrest among the non-Russians, but failed to see that such unrest would not pose a real threat to Gorbachev's position, since Russian soldiers would presumably obey orders to fire on them. Meanwhile, we let an almost racist attitude to-

ward Russians and their allegedly authoritarian political culture divert out attention from the revolutionary potential of the young Russians.

Soviet leaders did not make this mistake. When Boris Yeltsin (who clearly has
ambitions of leading the country) decided to break with Gorbachev for personal
and political reasons, he chose to break on the left rather than the right; he knew
which way the political winds were blowing. In 1987, when I gave a book manuscript to a Moscow party secretary to criticize, his first spontaneous comment after reading it was to agree with my assessment that the political dangers to
Gorbachev came not from Ligachev, but from the left.[13]

Gorbachev, as we have seen, understood this as well. He knew, therefore, that
he faced a multipronged problem. He needed to firmly consolidate his power at
the top to avoid the kind of Central Committee revolt that toppled Khrushchev.
He needed to guard against the danger of a military coup if unrest developed too
quickly. He knew that the liberalization, economic reform, and opening to the
West he wanted were going to unleash pent-up resentments in the non-Russian
areas. And he knew that perhaps his most serious challenge would come from the
young Russians who possessed or even exceeded the collective level of education
that had been associated with democratic revolt in the West and in the advanced
Third World countries. To understand Gorbachev's strategy, we must focus on his
attempts to address this multiple challenge.

Any analysis of Gorbachev's early calculations must remain conjectural. Certainly he took all of the usual steps of a Soviet general secretary to consolidate
power. He removed members of the old elite—those who were beholden to Leonid Brezhnev—at the fastest pace of any general secretary in history. He methodi-
cally placed men who seemed beholden to him in key power positions, and he
showed his famous "teeth of iron" when it seemed appropriate (for example, by
removing the minister of defense when a small plane penetrated Soviet airspace
and landed in Red Square). A student of previous leadership consolidations could
only marvel at the skill with which Gorbachev manipulated the traditional levels
of power.[14]

At the same time, Gorbachev's early policies were relatively conservative or at
least gradualist. This led many Western Sovietologists to conclude that he had no
plans for radical reform. The early "Andropov-like" reform was assumed to reflect
his level of thinking at the time. Those who predicted the Soviet future on the basis of Gorbachev's early policy pronouncements—or simply sneered at the ignorance of the Soviet leader—have treated the evolution of his program as the product of an evolution of his thinking.

We must be extraordinarily careful with this line of analysis. It seems far more
likely that Gorbachev's initial caution was rooted in his sense of political timing
than in a failure to see the need for more radical reforms. (Indeed, his chief political adviser Aleksandr Yakovlev specifically emphasized the importance of timing
in an early 1987 interview that was entitled "We will astonish you.")[15] More specifically, Gorbachev knew that he faced multiple political challenges and that he had
to disarm the lesser threats before tackling the potentially greater danger of revolt

from the left. While he could not implement his plans for radical reform at this stage, he nevertheless revealed his intentions on numerous occasions. (For example, Gorbachev told the editors of *Time* in August 1985 that he was thinking of "grandiose" domestic changes and corresponding changes in foreign policy.[16])

Paradoxically, the evidence most often cited as proof of Gorbachev's early lack of understanding—the absence of discussion of certain sensitive topics—is actually the best evidence against this argument. It is true that Gorbachev hardly permitted agricultural reform, let alone nationality problems, to be discussed in print. But this was not because Gorbachev was ignorant of their importance— quite the contrary. If Gorbachev had not fully understood the attractiveness of the economic arguments for beginning reform in agriculture, he would not have prevented these arguments from being published. The reason he did not introduce agricultural reform more quickly, I think, is that he understood its political dangers better than Westerners. The unique problem with agricultural reform is that it runs the risk of alienating both rural and urban constituents. When Western analysts considered the implications of agricultural reform, they focused on the dangers of rising meat prices for urban consumers. But the greater danger arose from the need to attack the collective farm system, which provided a degree of equality and security for rural residents. If Gorbachev had simultaneously attacked the collective farm system and angered the large cities by allowing food prices to rise, he would have dangerously narrowed his base of support.

By the same token, while Gorbachev's failure to discuss the nationality question from 1985 to early 1988 may have made him seem naïve, his actions during that period were those of a man who was quite aware that he had a major problem on his hands. Gorbachev's initial policies in the non-Russian republics were extremely cautious and seemed designed to mute any potential unrest. Except in Central Asia, he did not replace any of the republican first secretaries, and even there his new appointments turned out to be relatively conservative. He kept the old Brezhnevite, Vladimir Shcherbitsky, in charge of the Ukraine until the latter's decline in health forced his retirement. Moreover, Gorbachev's policy in the Baltic republics was quite repressive. When the Pope was invited to Moscow in 1988 for the 1000th anniversary of the introduction of Christianity into Russia, he made his acceptance conditional on the right to visit Catholic Lithuania; Gorbachev adamantly refused. Obviously, he had a clear sense of the explosive mood in Lithuania at that time.

Part of the explanation for Gorbachev's caution can be found in the requirements of coalitional politics and the consolidation of power inside the elite. Realizing that it would take some time to lay the basis for major economic reform in any case, Gorbachev chose a much cleverer way of discrediting his moderate allies. He would allow them to introduce their own economic reform program and try it out; once it was demonstrated that this program would not work, Gorbachev would use them as a scapegoat for its failure.[17]

But Gorbachev was orchestrating a far more sophisticated and complex policy than a mere focus on coalition politics would imply. He understood the complexity of the reform he was undertaking in ways that many of his critics at home and abroad did not. Many observers spoke of a return to the New Economic Policy of Lenin, but Gorbachev was in fact going much further, mounting a challenge to some of the core features of Leninism.[18]

This required the most fundamental changes in ideology. Basic concepts of property, profit, the morality of hiring labor, and the market—not Stalinist concepts, but Leninist ones—had to be modified. While Gorbachev was letting his allies determine economic policy, he concentrated on changing ideology, putting his closest adviser, Aleksandr Yakovlev, in charge of the media.

From the beginning, Gorbachev used ideological language that went much further than the actual policy steps being taken. He seemed to deliberately radicalize his language every few months, first hinting at some profound ideological change and gradually becoming more explicit. In this manner, he would prepare the public for the next step of reform. At the 27th Party Congress in 1986, for example, Gorbachev devoted a great deal of attention to the question of property. The potential of cooperative property has "not been exhausted," he said, and small farmer brigades and families should acquire "the means of production, including land on a contract basis." "The suspicion of money-goods relation should be overcome," he asserted; "prices should become an active instrument of economic and social policy [and] their level should be tied not only with cost, but with … demand."[19] At a time when most thought it impossible that the Soviet Union would move toward a market economy, such language was radical indeed.

Western critics repeatedly scoffed at Gorbachev's early caution, arguing that piecemeal economic reform was like "changing from driving on the left side of the road to the right side by beginning with trucks and then moving to automobiles." This joke certainly illustrated the difficulty of Gorbachev's task, but it was grossly misleading in its suggestion that there was a simple and cost-free way of making the transition all at once. An economy is a very complex set of interrelationships, not a strip of asphalt. Gorbachev assumed that the chaos created by an immediate dismantling of the old system would give rise to political resistance—even revolt. Given the extensive nature of the reforms he favored and the political dangers they raised, he had good reason for introducing these measures in stages.

The method he used—although he never announced it as such—was to start with a very limited and incomplete reform as an experiment, and then strengthen it with successively more radical measures. New policies on individual moonlighting, on the formation of cooperatives, on agriculture, on the management of enterprises, and on joint ventures with foreign firms were first introduced in this fashion. Critics at home and abroad rightly said that these were half-measures that would not succeed, but they did not understand the value of a half-measure in trying out something new for a year or so—and in generating the demand for more radical change in the future. In each of these areas of economic reform, Gorbachev did, in fact, introduce increasingly radical legislation almost every year. The reform process went more slowly than many radicals wanted, but considering that it involved the most profound ideological transformation, its speed was quite remarkable. By 1990, an astounding 5 million people were employed in the cooperative sector.

While Gorbachev had to be concerned about reforms creating too much up-heaval too soon, he clearly had a sense that a certain amount of chaos was inevitable, and even desirable. In the interest of creating a sense of urgency about reform, he allowed concern to mount about the extent of the country's problems. For example, economic performance in the 1980s was not as bad as the vast majority of Russians thought. The production of electricity increased from 1.294 billion kilowatt hours in 1980 to 1.722 billion in 1989. (Ruble figures are highly controversial, but kilowatt hours of electricity produced are generally considered one of the most reliable measures of economic growth.) The amount of the *increase* alone in nine years of "stagnation"—428 million kilowatt hours—was larger than the *total* Soviet output of 369 million kilowatts in 1962, the year of the Cuban missile crisis.[20]

Per-capita consumption of such items as meat and housing also increased substantially. When food shortages occurred, Americans often assumed impending famine, not understanding that the goods were being distributed through a rationing system or that a political game was being played. For example, Moscow city officials required evidence of Moscow residence for the purchase of many consumer goods in Moscow; the agricultural areas that normally supplied Moscow often retaliated against this restriction, producing food shortages in Moscow—but not in the country as a whole. (A colleague who spent last summer in the provincial town of Saratov found conditions quite comfortable.)

Yet Gorbachev and his associates made no effort to emphasize the positive aspects of the economic situation. Instead, they themselves helped encourage a sense of economic malaise, and they gave the most irresponsible radicals virtually free access to the media, which predictably exaggerated problems even more. The Kirghiz party leader summarized the situation in July 1989 when he said, "The impression is being created that someone is skillfully directing popular dissatisfaction with the party."[21] It was obvious that the only "someone" who could be doing it—or authorizing it—was the general secretary himself. Gorbachev answered this criticism bluntly: "Surely it is not necessary to panic when revolutionary processes become a reality. It was *we* who produced them with our policy. Didn't we understand this when we discussed all this?"[22]

Gorbachev's main problem was not an insufficient understanding of the need for radical reform or an inability to predict the consequences of his policies; it was, as suggested earlier, one of timing. For reasons to be discussed in the next section, he was aiming at the summer and autumn of 1990 as the time of crucial decision. In the interim, however, Gorbachev did not want to hand his enemies too many weapons. For example, he did not want to risk nationalist explosions until he was certain his opponents could not use them against him or his economic reform. We sometimes forget that Marxist conservatives in the Soviet Union believe that economic power rests on ownership and that political power rests on economic power. They were likely to believe that policies allowing private property and economic decentralization would have disastrous consequences for Moscow's political power over the republics. This realization undoubtedly would intensify conservative opposition to radical economic reform.

The potential for conservative resistance became very clear in an interview given by Julian Bromley, the top Soviet ethnographer, in March 1990—just a few months before his death. Bromley reported with emotion that he had advised against permitting private property and regional economic autonomy in the Baltic republics because he knew that it would lead to heightened political demands for secession. As he spoke of his World War II military service and his deep dedication to his country, the listener sensed that Bromley spoke for an entire generation, both in his feelings about national unity and in his assumptions about the link between economic power and political power. Gorbachev understood the views of conservatives like Bromley well; he sought to undercut their arguments by acting as if there were no serious nationality question. To have heightened the alarm about unrest in the republics before the resistance to economic reform had been broken would have strengthened that resistance.

*   *   *

It was the encouragement of truly competitive elections and informal antiparty political groups, especially in the republics, that was the biggest surprise of Gorbachev's first five years. By 1987 it was already clear that the general secretary would move away from the uncontested elections of the Soviet past, but it seemed likely that these elections would be similar to those in Central Europe under Brezhnev: workers running against workers, Russians against Russians, Lithuanians against Lithuanians, and all under the banner of the Communist Party. In February 1988, dissidents in Estonia had no hope that another party would be tolerated.[23] When Gorbachev first talked about popular fronts, people with long memories recalled just how little autonomy was enjoyed by the "front" organizations set up abroad by the Communists in the Popular Front period of the 1930s.

Yet the popular fronts that were created in the Baltic republics in June 1988 were soon functioning as independent parties.[24] By August, the Baltic peoples were permitted to hold demonstrations that denounced the Hitler-Stalin Pact of 1939 and questioned the legitimacy of the incorporation of the Baltic republics.[25] All of this pent-up resentment was allowed to burst forth precisely at the moment when the first competitive elections permitted voters to register their anger at official candidates.

If in January 1988 Gorbachev would not permit the Pope to visit Lithuania for fear that he would stir up unrest, why in heaven's name did he permit Sajudis, the Lithuanian national liberation movement, to stir the republic up in the midst of unprecedented free elections a year later? If the worry was that price increases would produce Polish-style riots, why give angry workers the chance to vote party officials out of office in national elections in 1989 and local elections in 1990? In short, if the main danger was from the left, how could Gorbachev dare to liberalize so dramatically and so quickly?

The conventional Western interpretation, which echoed the interpretation of the Moscow radicals, was that Gorbachev needed to mobilize the masses behind economic reform in order to overcome the resistance of the party apparatus and the bureaucrats. In addition, it was said, the population would not work with energy or initiative unless it had the right to vote for the people who were imposing the reforms. Democracy was a condition for economic renewal and growth.

While there are grains of truth in this analysis, the basic explanation seems quite wrong. In the first place, there is no reason to believe the radicals' characterization of the party apparatus as implacably resistant to economic reforms. After all, Soviet dissidents and Western Sovietologists were saying in the early 1980s that the party apparatus contained no reformers.[26] Yet Mikhail Gorbachev, Aleksandr Yakovlev, and Eduard Shevardnadze were all pursuing the careers of typical party apparatchiks at the time.[27]

The party apparatus, moreover, has traditionally—and understandably— tended to support the general secretary in his efforts to attack the Moscow ministries. The apparatus strongly supported Nikita Khrushchev in his creation of regional economic councils in 1957, and it seemed certain that it would support Gorbachev in his plans for economic decentralization as well. Democratization was not necessary to overcome the opposition of the party apparatus; in fact, it was democratization that produced the opposition—on both the left and the right—in the party apparatus.

There is another problem with the argument that Gorbachev needed democratization in order to win the masses' support for economic reform. The people who advanced this interpretation were generally the same ones who spoke of a conservative Russian people obsessed with economic security. But if the Russians were indeed so attached to their "social contract," how could Gorbachev expect them to vote for economic reform?

Indeed, the main effect of the establishment of genuine democratic institutions would be to give increased power to the middle-aged and the elderly—those who have the most reason to fear and oppose economic reform and who would otherwise be powerless. Because of this prospect, some analysts (most notably Marshall Goldman) have seen an insuperable conflict between democratization and economic reform in the Soviet Union. Since democratization, in their view, is essential for economic progress, they have regarded Gorbachev's position as hopeless. However, the very premise of this argument is false. The most rapid economic growth in recent years has come in authoritarian or dictatorial regimes such as Chile, Taiwan, South Korea, and Singapore that have suppressed popular demands, not those that have gone a more populist or Peronist route. Why should the Soviet Union be different?

The only people likely to revolt, the young, benefit enormously from economic reform. As one of the most sophisticated Soviet political observers, *Literaturnaia gazeta* editor Fedor Burlatsky, recently noted, "one-third of society, primarily the youth, thirsts for change."[28] They do not need democratization to convince them of the benefits of radical economic reform, and their professors already report that they are devoting their energies to exploiting economic opportunities rather than to organizing political opposition.

It seems to me that Gorbachev's calculations in democratizing were based not on the imperatives of economic reform, as many Western analysts have argued, but on considerations of political control. Paradoxically, Gorbachev found that democratization was useful in consolidating and expanding his power. This strategy had several components.

In the first place, all the talk about the resistance of the party apparatus and bureaucrats was an attempt on Gorbachev's part to gain support for liberating himself from collective control by the party elite—that is, the Politburo and Central Committee—and consolidating his dictatorial power. To win such support, he played on the Marxist intellectuals' image of the bureaucratic ruling class in the Soviet Union—the old Trotskyite view that the bureaucrats had the same kind of role in the Soviet Union as the owners of the means of production under capitalism.

Second, competitive elections in which a significant number of officials and military officers were defeated—in conjunction with republican unrest, the strikes of 1989, and the rise of Boris Yeltsin—sharply reduced any temptation for the military to think of a coup d'état against Gorbachev. Military officers could have no desire to try to run the country in the new conditions. Even if they thought they had some obligation to restore order, they could have no confidence that they could do so. If Gorbachev and Yeltsin stood together and called for demonstrations in favor of democracy, the military would not be able to count on the soldiers to obey orders. (These doubts must have become particularly strong after the events in Rumania in late 1989.)

The most interesting of Gorbachev's political calculations had to do with the relationship between democratization and the nationality question. American analysts and Soviet intellectuals had correctly sensed in the past that Russians were not ready for a democratic revolution, and this sense had led them to conclude that Russians were peculiarly authoritarian. In fact, the new generations of educated Russians were as ready for democracy and liberalization as other peoples undergoing modernization. What they were not ready for, however, was the breakup of their country.[29]

Gorbachev's central problem in this respect, it seems to me, was that while Soviet propaganda about national harmony had not fooled the non-Russians (or Gorbachev himself), it has been believed by a great many Russians. He knew that full democratization in the Soviet Union would mean a multiplicity of parties, including separatist ones in the republics, but most Russians did not realize this. If Gorbachev could demonstrate to the Russians that total democratization would lead to the disintegration of the country, they might be willing to limit some of their more radical demands; the threat from the left would thereby be diminished.

Gorbachev's basic decision, it seems to me, was to let unrest in the republics—especially the smaller ones—go to an extreme. One purpose was to let off steam in the non-Russian areas. A second purpose was to end any illusions among the Russians about the contentment of the non-Russians and to make them understand the threat to the integrity of the country. Not only would this help dampen demands for complete democratization, but it would also enable Gorbachev to sell decentralization and price reform to the Russians as the price of national unity. If the Russians would not tolerate a rise in meat prices to end shortages, they might accept it as an unavoidable effect of giving economic autonomy to the Baltic republics—and therefore as necessary to preserve the country's integrity.

The odds seem to me well over 50–50 that Gorbachev was applying to the non-Russian republics the lessons that he learned on the Politburo in 1980 and 1981 during the Solidarity revolution in Poland. Clearly, Solidarity was easier to suppress in December 1981, when many Poles were becoming tired of unrest and economic difficulties, than it would have been in the summer of 1980. Gorbachev may have hoped to orchestrate something similar in the non-Russian republics. The lid was let off in the fall of 1988, surely with the understanding that the republican elections of March 1990 would occur at the culmination of 18 months of heated rhetoric—and only a few months before the crucial economic reform decisions were scheduled. By that time, the Russians would all know that they had a nationalities problem to solve. By that time, too, the moderates in the non-Russian republics would have tired of the unrest; they might be prepared to break with the radicals and accept Gorbachev's offer of major economic reform and federal decentralization in the place of independence.

*   *   *

If Gorbachev's strategy is to be understood in these terms, then 1989 and 1990 were years in which the general secretary moved toward the endgame—the completion of his consolidation of power and the preparation of a plan for radical economic reform.

...

In large part, Gorbachev's current strategy was already apparent a year ago. He would use the party congress and the new Central Committee it would elect (and the Politburo the new Central Committee would elect) to break the back of the resistance to radical economic reform in the summer of 1990. Then he would present some radical economic program (such as Yeltsin's 500-day plan) that would be aimed at transforming the planning of production and supply beginning January 1, 1992. (Fundamental agricultural reform has a shorter lead time and presumably would be—and will be—introduced in the winter of 1990–91 after the harvest and before the spring sowing.) He no doubt intended that men like Yegor Ligachev and Nikolai Ryzhkov would be sacrificed as he formally repudiated their policies. Since economic reform and local governmental autonomy are integral to each other, Gorbachev surely planned for the crucial negotiations on radical economic reform to coincide with the beginning of serious negotiations on the federal arrangements of a new constitution.

It is also likely that Gorbachev's policy in Central Europe was part of his strategy of moving toward radical economic reform.[33] The Soviet Union had been sending marketable commodities such as petroleum, natural gas, and cotton to Central Europe and receiving back manufactured goods that were worth some $10 to $15 billion less on the world market. The rationale for such large subsidies was that they were necessary to prevent anticommunist revolts. If, in fact, Gorbachev was unwilling to use troops in the area and such revolts would thus eventually succeed in any case, there was a lot to be said for accelerating the process. Specifically, if Central Europe could be cut loose 15 to 18 months before January 1, 1991, the subsidies could be taken out of the five-year plan. We cannot know whether Gorbachev had such calculations in mind when the communist systems were moving toward collapse in Poland and Hungary in the spring of 1989, but it is clear that he deliberately destabilized East Germany and Czechoslovakia in October 1989 at a crucial stage of the planning process for 1991.

By 1990, Gorbachev seemed to have decided that the consolidation of power he had already achieved was not enough. In a surprise move, he completely junked the changes in party rules proposed in 1988, as well as the constitutional definition of the nature and powers of the chief of state enacted in the winter of 1988–89. Instead of the leader serving as chairman of the Supreme Soviet, he would now be a "president."

...

In short, by the fall of 1990, Gorbachev had achieved virtually absolute power within the central government of the Soviet Union. The Central Committee, the Politburo, and the party apparatus had lost all control over him, and the cabinet (the Presidential Council) was his creature. The official powers of the president vis-à-vis the legislature were enormous, and Gorbachev's informal power was even greater. The conservatives and moderates in the Congress of People's Deputies and Supreme Soviet would vote for his reforms out of party discipline; the Politburo was certain to support his policies because it was dominated by republican first secretaries who favored a decentralization of power. The radicals who had left the Communist Party might sometimes vote against Gorbachev's reforms as half measures, but only when this was a symbolic action. They could never open themselves to the charge of defeating his reforms, be they halfway or otherwise. And in addition to disposing of overwhelming power at home, Gorbachev was using his vast constitutional power in the foreign policy and defense sphere to build up his personal authority as the indispensable representative of the Soviet Union abroad.

*　　*　　*

...

Whatever its origins, the notion of an enfeebled Gorbachev is deeply mistaken. Gorbachev has been deliberately seeking to create an exaggerated sense of crisis in order to force through his reforms and to build support from the democratic intellectuals for his emancipation from the collective control of the party elite. The

Yeltsin radicals, on the other hand, are trying to create an exaggerated sense of Gorbachev's weakness—and of his irrelevance—in order to persuade U.S. foreign policymakers to support them instead of Gorbachev.

Yet the evolution of the Shatalin plan makes clear that Gorbachev has been in firm control of the reform process. The original plan incorporated some of the decentralization provisions that had been contained in an early Gorbachev draft of the treaty for a new Soviet federation. But these provisions were not accepted by Gorbachev when he discussed his economic reform program in the Congress of People's Deputies. When Gorbachev submitted his economic reform program to the parliament, he predictably did not include the provisions that would gut the power of the central government.[35]

The Soviet Union already has "sovereign republics," two of which (the Ukraine and Belorussia) have long been members of the United Nations and all of which have had nominal foreign-affairs ministries since Stalin's time. These republics however, have never had the simple powers of taxation and expenditure enjoyed by American states. Gorbachev's hope is to move the Soviet Union toward a U.S.-style federal nation, with the republics gaining the powers of a California or a New York—but also some of the linguistic and cultural autonomy of a Quebec. It is quite wrong to think the Soviet Union is moving toward something as loosely structured as the Articles of Confederation envisioned, let alone Common Market–style governance—at least not over the next 10 to 20 years.

Moreover, there is no evidence that the republics are in a position to demand more than limited sovereignty, especially now that the Baltic revolt seems to be petering out. In Lithuania the popularity of the Sajudis independence movement has fallen precipitously, particularly in the countryside, and the Estonians are losing interest in politics, with entertainment shows attracting more television viewers than political programming.[36]

In assessing Gorbachev's relative strength, we must be especially careful not to exaggerate Yeltsin's power. After all, Yeltsin was elected chairman of the Russian Supreme Soviet by a margin of four votes against an unattractive candidate—and only a few days after Gorbachev had deliberately (and unnecessarily) announced the "Ryzhkov" rise in bread prices that was certain to create unrest and increase Yeltsin's appeal. A roll-call analysis of votes in the Russian Congress of People's Deputies by Regina Smyth of Duke University shows that Yeltsin and the radicals would have the support of only one-third of the legislators in a showdown.[37] On a number of important votes the radicals have been defeated—most spectacularly on the election of Moscow radicals to the smaller Russian Supreme Soviet, but more subtly on the organization of the Supreme Soviet and election of deputies to it. The subsequent compromises have served Gorbachev's interests.

Indeed, Yeltsin's political position is inherently weak. Because of the centralized nature of the Soviet system, the Russian Republic offers a very weak power base. And in the future, the devolution of power will favor the smaller republics like Estonia and Armenia, which have only a few million people. With its 150 million people, the Russian Republic is too large; power will not remain at the republic level—which is Yeltsin's mooring—but will devolve further to regions and cities such as Lenigrad, Sverdlovsk, and Vladisvostok. The Russian parliament is made up of regional deputies and they will demand such a transfer of power.

Moreover, Yeltsin has to be extremely careful in his efforts to achieve real independence from the central government. Any independence the Russian Republic gains will also have to be given to other republics, where nearly 20 percent of the country's ethnic Russians live. If the Russian Republic is given power to override central laws, then the legislature in Uzbekistan will have the power to introduce Islamic prayers in public schools (including those with local Russians in the classroom) or compel women (including Russian women) to wear the veil. Russians will not tolerate autonomy on these terms, let alone lead the way in forcing it through. Anytime, then, that Gorbachev wishes to turn Russian nationalism against Yeltsin, it will be very easy for him to do.[38]

Yeltsin was right when he said, "If Yeltsin did not exist, Gorbachev would have to invent him."[39] For there have been three abiding elements of Gorbachev's political strategy, and at present Yeltsin is important to each of them.

First, as indicated earlier, Gorbachev has understood that the only nationality that can threaten his rule were and are the Russians. It is only massive riots by Russians that security and military forces will not suppress, and hence it is only such riots that can topple the regime. Gorbachev's policy of transfering power from Moscow to the non-Russian republics has had the potential of producing a Russian backlash. To avoid taking all the blame for what ethnic Russians might perceive as a lack of resolve, he has been extremely eager to associate other Russian leaders—especially radical ones like Boris Yeltsin—with his policy. This is why he initially stacked the Politburo with Russians. But once he downgraded the Politburo and found it useful for other reasons to stack it with non-Russians, he was extremely happy to have Yeltsin and the Russian Republic leading the way on decentralization rather than the Estonians and Georgians, whose "lack of gratitude" the Russians would resent.

Second, Gorbachev has had a near-obsession about positioning himself in the middle. He has wanted left-wing bogeymen to frighten the right, and right-wing bogeymen to frighten the left. He ensured that Yegor Ligachev, on his right, and Aleksandr Yakovlev, on his left, were the two most prominent of his Politburo advisers—and did little to restrain their public duel. He was happy to restore Andrei Sakharov to prominence and to give disproportionate television coverage of the radicals in the Congress of People's Deputies, but at the same time did nothing to suppress groups such as the reactionary Russian nationalist organization Pamyat. His propagandists meanwhile privately briefed Westerners on the threat posed by right-wing nationalists, the military, and, of course, the party apparatus and Ligachev, confident that this speculation would feed into the Soviet political system through the Voice of America and other foreign radio broadcasts. Then when Gorbachev established his Presidential Council, he included not only the major officials of the country, but four lesser figures: the radical economist Stanislav Shatalin and the liberal writer Chingiz Aitmatov on the left, and the village writer Valentin Rasputin and the worker Veniamin Iarin on the right.

Yeltsin fits squarely into this pattern. When Ligachev reached the normal retirement age of 70 in 1990 and Gorbachev needed to replace his "threat" (which never really existed), the new right-wing bogeyman became the new first secretary of the Russian Republic, Ivan Polozkov—a party official from Gorbachev's home base of the Kuban. Yeltsin's rise, in turn, provided Gorbachev with the major figure he needed on the left.

Third, Gorbachev clearly wants the public to perceive that others are responsible for the problems created by economic policy. On questions of foreign policy, by contrast, he deliberately creates a very different image. The chief architect of his foreign policy, Aleksandr Yakovlev, deliberately avoids commenting on the subject. Similarly, Gorbachev has announced the major political reforms without any visible consultation—and with little hint that they are coming. His personal assistant on political affairs, Georgi Shakhnazarov, has been virtually invisible. Clearly Gorbachev has assumed that his changes in foreign policy and political reform are popular and has wanted to associate only himself with them.

Gorbachev has no less power in the economic sphere, but there is much pain and suffering to be produced by economic reform. Not by coincidence, the Soviet president has preferred to give very visible ideological leadership, to define the goals and provide the vision—to use his office as a "bully pulpit," in Theodore Roosevelt's words—and then to have others claim and get the credit for the detailed plans that implement Gorbachev's broad goals. It was "Ryzhkov's economic plan," "Leonid Abalkin's proposals," and "Ligachev's agricultural policy," and most recently either "Yeltsin's" or "Shatalin's" 500-day plan. Gorbachev shows no hesitation at all in giving others the credit for plans in areas where there are certain to be problems—and, likewise, does not hesitate to give them the blame later. ...

... Gorbachev hopes—indeed, assumes—that Yeltsin will be the scapegoat for the problems of the next few years just as Ryzhkov has become the scapegoat for those of the past few years.

In short, Gorbachev has maneuvered the situation to precisely where he wanted it. He is betting that by the time of the next national elections, in 1994, he will get credit for the vision and the achievements of reform and that Yeltsin and the radicals will get the blame for the problems produced by the specific measures of reform. It is possible, of course, that Gorbachev has miscalculated. Yeltsin, after all, is playing the same game—seeking to get credit for himself and to shift the blame for problems onto Gorbachev's "indecisiveness" and "halfway measures." Nevertheless, those Westerners who have consistently underestimated Gorbachev from the beginning of the early 1980s and have bet against him in the past should exercise caution in their criticism of his political judgment now.

...

NOTES

ABOUT THE AUTHOR: **Jerry F. Hough** is professor of political science at Duke University and a senior fellow of the Brookings Institution.

1. Seweryn Bialer, "The Passing of the Soviet Order?" *Survival,* Vol. 32, No. 2 (March-April 1990), pp. 107–120.

2. Marshall I. Goldman, "Boris Yeltsin: At Least *He* Has A Plan," *New York Times,* September 16, 1990; Dimitri Simes in *Washington Post Book World,* May 13, 1990, p. 1.

3. *New York Times,* August 31, 1990.

4. *Washington Post,* September 3, 1990.

5. In 1971, when Gorbachev was Stavropol's first secretary, he was the youngest official elected a full member of the Central Committee. In 1978, when he was elected a Central Committee secretary, he was 19 years younger than the average age of the other 10 secretaries (six months later the next youngest was removed, and Gorbachev was 21 years younger than the average). In 1980, when he was elected a full member of the Politburo, he was 21 years younger than the average age of the 13 Politburo members and only one member was within 10 years of his age and two within 15 years.

6. For my early attempts, see Jerry F. Hough, "Gorbachev's Strategy," *Foreign Affairs,* Vol. 64, No. 1 (Fall 1985), pp. 33–55; "Managing the U.S.-Soviet Relationship," *World Policy Journal,* Vol. 3, No. 1 (Winter 1985–86), pp. 15–22; and "The End of Russia's 'Khomeini' Period," *World Policy Journal,* Vol. 4, No. 4 (Fall 1987), pp. 583–604.

7. Stephen F. Cohen, "The Friends and Foes of Change: Reformism and Conservatism in the Soviet Union," *Slavic Reviw,* Vol. 38, No. 2 (June 1979), p. 198.

8. Bill Keller, "Boris Yeltsin Taking Power," *New York Times Magazine,* September 23, 1990, p. 84.

9. Jerry F. Hough, *Soviet Leadership in Transition* (Washington, DC: Brookings Institution, 1980), pp. 18–22.

10. "At a certain stage of their development the material forces of production come into conflict with the existing relations of production. … From forms of development of the forces of production, their relations turn into their fetters. Then comes the period of social revolution." See Lewis S. Feuer, ed., *Marx and Engels: Basic Writings on Politics and Philosophy* (New York: Doubleday, 1959), pp. 43–44.

11. "The Emergence of Gorbachev," *New York Times Magazine,* March 3, 1985, p. 45. Archie Brown also put great emphasis on this speech just after Gorbachev was elected. "Gorbachev: New Man in the Kremlin," *Problems of Communism,* Vol. 34, No. 3 (May-June 1985), pp. 1–23.

12. Jerry F. Hough, "The Logic of Collective Action and the Pattern of Revolutionary Behavior," *Journal of Soviet Nationalities,* Vol. 1, No. 2 (Summer 1990), pp. 46–54.

13. For this point in the published version of the manuscript, see Jerry F. Hough, *Russia and the West: Gorbachev and the Politics of Reform* (New York: Simon & Schuster, 1988), pp. 180–181.

14. For a description of these steps, see the 1990 revised edition of *Russia and the West,* pp. 156–176.

15. The interview was conducted by Nathan Gardels, *New Perspectives Quarterly,* Spring 1987, p. 34.

16. *Time,* September 9, 1985, p. 29.

17. Eduard Shevardnadze described this strategy—except for the third point—quite clearly in a 1990 speech published in *Literaturnaia gazeta,* April 8, 1990, p. 9.

18. This was the theme of Hough, "The End of Russia's Khomeini Period" (fn. 6).

19. *Pravda*, February 26, 1986, p. 4.

20. *Narodnoe khoziaistvo SSSR v 1964 g.; Statisticheskii ezhegodnik* (Moscow: Statistika, 1965), p. 157; *Narodnoe khoziaistvo SSSR v 1988 g.: Statisticheskii ezhegodnik* (Moscow: Finansy i statistika, 1989), p. 379; *Pravda*, January 28, 1990.

21. *Pravda*, July 21, 1989.

22. *Ibid.*, p. 1.

23. *New York Times*, February 10, 1988.

24. *New York Times*, June 21, 1988.

25. *New York Times*, August 24, 1988.

26. George Feifer, "Russian Disorders," *Harper's*, February 1981, p. 53.

27. Gorbachev and Shevardnadze worked for several decades in Stavropol and Georgia respectively, while Yakovlev was appointed to the propaganda department of the Central Committee in the last year of Stalin's life after working in the party apparatus of Yaroslavl, and he worked with the Central Committee's propaganda department for the next 20 years.

28. *Literaturnaia gazeta*, September 5, 1990, p. 2.

29. This argument is not an ex-post explanation but has been the basis for 10 years of successful prediction. See Jerry F. Hough and Merle Fainsod, *How the Soviet Union Is Governed* (Cambridge, MA: Harvard University Press, 1979), pp. 561–572. See also Hough, *Russia and the West* (fn. 13), pp. 181–182.

33. It is really time to stop talking about Poland, Hungary, etc., as Eastern Europe. "Eastern Europe" geographically is Moscow, Gorki, and Sverdlovsk, and the application of the term to the countries of Central Europe was a Cold War way of saying that the Russians were Asiatic barbarians. Let us move toward a "Common European Home" by admitting that the Russia of the Greek Orthodox Church, of Tolstoi, and of Tchaikovsky is part of Europe.

35. *Washington Post*, September 15, 1990, p. 13.

36. One poll found that Sajudis had become less popular than the Lithuanian Communist Party. Letuvos Ritas (Vilnius), July 9–14, 1990, translated in *FBIS Daily Report-Soviet Union*, August 1, 1990, p. 60. A Carnegie fellow at the Duke East-West Center, Mark Koenig, who is writing his dissertation on Soviet television, reports the change in Estonian television and the hostility toward Sajudis among Lithuanians in the countryside.

37. For this analysis, see Regina Smyth, "Ideological vs. Regional Cleavages: Do Radicals Control the RSFSR Parliament?" *Journal of Soviet Nationalities*, Vol. 1, No. 3 (Fall 1990).

38. For an example of his problems, see Bill Keller, "Yeltsin's Response to the Separatists: Feel Free," *New York Times*, September 3, 1990.

39. *Corriere Della Sera*, June 16, 1989, cited in *FBIS Daily Report-Soviet Union*, June 19, 1989, p. 44.

PART 3

Soviet Political Debates

One of the most significant developments of the years of glasnost was the widening scope of cultural, historical, and political debates; the progressive erosion of long-standing inhibitions and taboos; and the increasingly critical assessment of the Soviet experience.

It has been aptly remarked that throughout Russian history recurrent challenges to the status quo could often be subsumed under two questions—"Who is guilty?" and "What is to be done?" This was remarkably true in the years of perestroika as well. The reassessment of the entire Soviet experience was perhaps crucial to the gradual delegitimation of the old system in the eyes of a vast part of the population.

While perestroika initially emerged as a reaction against the stagnation of the Brezhnev era and an attempt at intrasystem reform, the discussions of the sources of contemporary problems soon took on a momentum of their own. Under Khrushchev, Stalin himself had been obliquely attacked; now Stalinism as a system was assailed and indicted, with a stream of new revelations appearing in the press concerning deportations, purges and terror, and the forcible collectivization of agriculture and terror, and the forcible collectivization of agriculture and the famine that ensued. The concept of totalitarianism was increasingly utilized to describe the "command-administrative system," which was held responsible for all the shortcomings.

If the revelations regarding the Stalin years initially focused on the departures from Leninist norms, the debate—by journalists, scholars, and "survivors"—expanded to include a reassessment of Leninism itself. The scrutiny quickly extended to the Revolution of October 1917—was it inevitable? was it wise?—and ultimately encompassed Marx and Marxism as well. The debate concerned not only abstract questions of historiography but also explosive issues of personal responsibility, complicity, and integrity in the years of Stalinism and stagnation.

A wide range of political orientations, from anarchist and "pure" socialist to advocacy of a free market and a free marketplace of ideas, found expression in Soviet media. The whole wealth of the political and intellectual debate that developed in the non-Russian republics of the Soviet Union, in which a reconsideration of these issues was joined to distinctive national themes, is not even sampled in this section.

To be sure, the revisionists' were not the only voices to be heard. Their views were challenged by articulate and impassioned defenders of a familiar orthodox Marxist-Leninist litany, at times with xenophobic, anti-Semitic overtones; the "open letter" by Nina Andreyeva is the most celebrated example of a larger genre. A variety of Russian national cultural figures also railed against the "Westernizing" thrust of the dominant values of the reformers. By 1990 a sharp and at times threatening tone had been injected into the public dialogue, with charges and countercharges flying fast and furious, especially over the resentments voiced by the self-styled patriotic defenders of national (not to say imperial) interests, who accused the reformers of betraying the integrity and security of the state.

These trends in turn contributed to a deepening ideological and moral crisis that Soviet society and a substantial part of its elite found itself in, once the previously obligatory creed lost its monopoly status. They also contributed to a growing cleavage within the Party itself over the scope and direction of reform. While one group, organized around the Democratic Platform, deplored the Party's failure to embrace a more far-reaching program of social and political change—including a transformation of the Party itself—others accused the reformers of undermining the foundations of Party—and Soviet—rule.

16   Glasnost' *and Soviet Culture*

JOSEPHINE WOLL

In the past two years, the nature of cultural politics in the Soviet Union has changed dramatically. The uncomfortable intimacy of politics and culture, bed-fellows for so many decades, continues, but the relationship is not what it once was. New institutions are functioning, and unexpected material is available in print and on the air waves. Certain trends emerging two years ago have become more pronounced, while others have diminished.[1] This essay attempts to discern and analyze some of the processes and patterns of cultural politics in the last two years—a tumultuous and exciting kaleidoscope of complicated and often contra-dictory trends, reflecting an altered cultural universe. ...

... I shall concentrate on the two unions that have undergone restructuring and on the USSR Union of Writers, which has not.[2]

THE CREATIVE UNIONS

What, then, has happened in the theater and cinema unions, from the start strong supporters of Gorbachev and *perestroyka?* After forcing the retirement of their conservative old-guard leaderships at the earliest opportunity (in April-May 1986), both unions implemented a series of roughly parallel decisions to increase decentralization and to encourage democratization of decision-making. Most of the country's film studios and a number of theaters have become essentially self-financing.

Theater. Eighty-three theaters all over the country are participating in an ex-perimental agreement with the state by which they have gained much greater ar-tistic autonomy (for instance, in the choice of repertory) as well as financial re-sponsibility. A variety of new organizational forms were introduced to support existing theaters and to encourage the creation of new theaters. To give one exam-ple, under the sponsorship of the Moscow City Executive Committee, several "theater-studios"—that is, less well-established or more experimental groups—signed two-year collective contracts entitling them to a public space and making them fully commercial. Formerly such theater groups had to mount their produc-tions wherever they could, on makeshift and borrowed temporary stages; public-ity spread by word-of-mouth, and well-informed friends comprised the audience. Now they have a place to work; if they lose money, they will have to close.

The director of one of the most prominent of these groups, Mark Rozovskiy, has explained that he receives no state subsidy and pays 5 percent of his profits into the state budget. He has full control over 80 percent of the profits his theater earns, as well as full control over the works he stages.[3] The freedom he now enjoys compensates for a number of problems he did not have when his group was outside official control: maintaining, in his words, "ethical purity," because the absence of wage-leveling invites ambition and self-aggrandizement; tackling a mountain of daily bureaucratic paperwork, including restrictions on renovations within his theater; and having no right to set ticket prices, which obviously affects profits.[4]

A newly-created Agency of Amateur Theaters, sponsored by a variety of organizations (among them the USSR Cultural Fund), underwrites amateur troupes. Independent local theaters are funded by party committees, the Komsomol, and other groups and are fueled by the enthusiasm of theater fans. The All-Russian Association of Artistic Workshops, created in the fall of 1987 by the RSFSR Theater Union, acts like a Western producer, funding directors to stage plays and organize troupes.

The "democratization" of theater has had mixed results. Theaters like Rozovskiy's have obviously benefited. By contrast, Georgiy Tovstonogov, artistic director of the Leningrad Bol'shoy Drama Theater, pointed to one of the pitfalls: the incompatibility of "democracy" and talent:

> I'm for [democratization of the theater] in the sense of freeing the arts from the pressure brought to bear on them by bureaucracy. I'm all for the open appraisals of our work, for the joint discussion of the future of the contemporary Soviet theater, for the foundation of a creative union of theatrical workers. ... [But] the majority principle doesn't work in the arts. The majority vote cannot decide the value and profundity of an artist's ideas. A director must be a dictator in his theater, but his rule must be willingly accepted by the actors. It should be a rule based on artistic authority, but never on the fear that he might sack everyone he doesn't like.[5]

Nor has there been an explosion of significant new work. Except for Mikhail Shatrov's plays, particularly "Further ... Further ... Further," few plays have stimulated much excitement. (Shatrov's play, in which he charges Stalin with ordering Sergey Kirov's murder and Trotsky's execution, was extremely controversial, eliciting attacks in *Pravda* and elsewhere. In May 1988, the monthly journal *Znamya,* which had published Shatrov's play in its January issue, printed 30 [out of some 300] letters, most of them defending Shatrov.[6])

Soviet critics continually lament the state of Russian theater, and Yale Drama School's Richard Gilman, after a month's stay recently as part of a cultural exchange program sponsored by the American-Soviet Theater Initiative, concurs: "I went," he writes, "with high expectations stemming from the reputed new energy and openness that *glasnost'* has brought about in the theater, as elsewhere. ... Those expectations were only partly fulfilled. There is energy and openness on the Soviet stage these days, but with few exceptions I found little imaginative vigor."[7] Good politics, he was told by Soviets and saw for himself, but bad art.

Cinema. Like theaters, film studios now have virtual autonomy in all artistic matters—selection of scripts, casting, contractual hiring of directors and actors, freedom of expenditure, etc.—and are financially accountable. Those that fail to show a profit will, at least theoretically, have to shut down. The USSR Cinematographers' Union (which comprises all film workers, and not only cameramen) was the first to introduce these changes, beginning with its blackballing of the entire old-guard of the filmmaking industry at its May 1986 Congress. Elem Klimov, a director whose films released in the West include "Rasputin" and "Come and See," was chosen to lead the union in place of hard-liner Lev Kulidzhanov. In January 1988, Klimov resigned in order to work on a film and was replaced by Andrey Smirnov. (Klimov is slated to return as chair in January 1990.) Filip Yermash, the conservative head of Goskino (the official overseer of the film industry) was replaced in December 1986 by the more professional and open-minded Aleksandr Kamshalov.

To prevent the domination of purely commercial considerations—a sensitive issue vigorously debated at creative union conferences and in the press—the Cinematographers' Union has reserved 1 percent of all profits for films by beginners and for projects undertaken by established artists who wish to experiment with commercially risky films. Predictably, the ensuing competition for desirable contracts has been fierce. A commission of writers, directors, critics, and representatives of Goskino created in August 1986 by the union to handle disputes, and to investigate the fate of "repressed" movies, has succeeded in releasing some 80 of the more than 100 films held back from distribution over a period of 20 years for all kinds of political reasons. They include several films by Aleksey German ("Roadcheck" and "My Friend Ivan Lapshin"); Gleb Panfilov's 1979 "Theme," once unacceptable because of its allusion to Jewish emigration and its portrayal of a successful literary hack; and Aleksandr Askoldov's 1968 "Commissar," in which a pregnant Red Army commissar during the Civil War lives out her confinement and bears her child in the home of a poor Jewish family, leaving the baby with them when she goes back to fight.[8]

Bureaucratic roadblocks continue to exist: a proposed filmmakers' newspaper was vetoed, as was a new film magazine. Student demands for a more creative approach to teaching and the replacement of certain individuals at the All-Union Institute of Cinematography were rejected by the Moscow Party Committee. And within the union, some members feel that those now in powerful positions, who tend to obtain the money and resources for making new movies, have become as hard to budge as their predecessors were.[9]

Nevertheless, in several respects, the filmmaking industry looks much healthier than it did several years ago. The critical disdain for theater plays is not manifested by film-goers or film critics, in part because of the release of previously shelved films and in part because of an explosion of documentary films, often broadcast on all-Union television to enormous audiences. In such feature films as "Little Vera" and Nikolay Gubenko's "Restricted Zone," and in such documentaries as "Is It Easy to be Young?," "Are You Going to the Ball?," and "Solovetskiy

Power," contemporary social and ecological problems and legacies from the Stalinist past are depicted with an honesty that was not possible even a few years ago. "Solovetskiy Power" (its Russian title, *"Solovetskaya vlast'*," is a pun on "Soviet power" [*Sovetskaya vlast'*]) is a documentary on the history of the Solovki labor camps. It includes interviews with seven former inmates of the Gulag, the most prominent among them being Academician Dmitriy Likhachev, as well as an interview with a former Chekist, who was a guard at Solovki between 1923 and 1925.[10] Footage censored from earlier films has been restored, and in some instances reshot. And film distribution has improved markedly: it now bears a reasonable correlation to viewer preferences as determined by, for instance, surveys and questionnaires. Somewhat surprisingly, there seems to be a hunger even for "avant-garde" films: when Riga's self-financing Video Center and the Union of Latvian Cinema Workers organized a six-day film forum in the autumn of 1988, almost 70,000 people paid high prices to see supposedly "non-commercial" films made both within the Soviet Union (early Dovzhenko and Kuleshov, recent work by Paradzhanov, Peleshyan, the brilliant animator Yuriy Norshteyn) and abroad (from classics like "The Cabinet of Dr. Caligari" and "Un chien andalou" to recent Czech, Hungarian, and "underground" American films).[11]

Belles-Lettres. The USSR Writers' Union, like the Composers' and Artists' Unions, presents a rather different picture. It remains largely unreconstructed, dominated by a coalition of *apparatchiks* and ideologues. The former comprise the majority of active members of the influential RSFSR branch of the Writers' Union. Many of them are relatively unknown provincial writers, and while their work rarely penetrates the pages of the large-circulation literary journals, it continues to appear in book form thanks to networks of patronage. These writers were badly frightened by the announcement, in late 1988, that publishing houses might introduce commercial criteria into their 1989 decisions—which might well signal the end of their careers. So, as one observer dryly explained, they took the high moral ground, rejecting such reforms as antithetical to "the sacred principle of 'social justice' and ... to the true interests of culture."[12]

An enormous amount of power, and a formidable range of perquisites and privileges, are at stake.[13] Natal'ya Il'ina, a writer (primarily of satire) well-placed in and extremely knowledgeable about the literary bureaucracy, caused a furor in early 1988 with an article she published in the weekly *Ogonek*. She ascribed the death-grip these *apparatchiks* have on the unions, and on the Soviet literary establishment in general, to human nature rather than to politics. Greed, she claimed, is responsible for much of their resistance to any changes that might threaten their positions.[14] Indeed, the tangible rewards of power within the cultural establishment, which rarely correspond to talent or even genuine popularity, extend far beyond such relative—if desirable—trivia as rooms in exclusive sanatoria or vacation spots. Major financial benefits are involved. In book publishing, Il'ina explains, royalties are based not on the number of copies of a work sold, but on the number of copies of a work printed. Moreover, in the past at least, publishing houses were not responsible for their financial losses. Thus, the system steadily encouraged inflated lists having little to do with merit or the interest of the readers, in turn producing a large number of remaindered books while preventing those of real interest to readers from being printed.[15] All this was going on against the backdrop of a serious paper shortage.

Il'ina illustrates her argument with specific examples. In one case of egregious corruption, the director of the publishing house Sovetskiy pisatel' compiled a volume of prose. It was his first book: before being appointed to that post, he had published only a few short articles. The volume came out under the imprint of 11 different publishing houses, with a print-run in Moscow alone of more than 1 million. By way of quid pro quo, his house published the work of fellow-directors of other publishing houses. (To no one's surprise, both Il'ina and her editor, Vitaliy Korotich, were vehemently attacked by the two main publications of the Writers' Union, in *Literaturnaya Gazeta* [Moscow], No. 3, 1988, and in *Literaturnaya Rossiya,* No. 3, 1988.)

I do not mean to suggest that ideological differences play no role in the Writers' Union disputes. But the bureaucratic resistance to *glasnost'*, and especially to translating *glasnost'* into structural and institutional change, is rooted as much in venality and vanity as in disagreement over matters of principle, and the power of such resistance should not be underestimated.

"LIBERALS" VERSUS "CONSERVATIVES"

What does it mean, in today's Soviet Union, to consider oneself or one's opponent "liberal" or "conservative"? What ideas and values does each rubric signify on the Soviet cultural scene? Do the terms correspond in any meaningful sense to the way they are used in the West? These questions are critical to understanding Soviet cultural politics, and they require careful answers. While I will inevitably simplify the issues, and thereby do some injustice to the "sides" in this cultural civil war, I will attempt to characterize them here.

The terms themselves must be used with extreme caution. The British political vocabulary from which they are derived is hardly relevant either in theory or in practice, to Soviet reality. In the Soviet Russian cultural (and political) world, "conservative" does suggest the disposition to maintain existing institutions. It almost always encompasses a regard—and sometimes nostalgia—for traditional culture, architecture, life-styles, religious values and artifacts, and a profound concern with ecological devastation and cultural damage. In its extreme manifestations, at the far end of the "conservative" spectrum, Russian nationalism fulminates as chauvinism, with decidedly xenophobic tendencies. Its broad appeal, however, derives from its ability to articulate a genuine sense of Russian national grievance, and from its attempts to restore and rebuild destroyed churches, implement legislation to protect the autonomy of the Russian Orthodox Church, and reverse the increase in pollution that has rendered well water undrinkable and rivers and lakes lethal. But "nationalism" is not a synonym for "conservatism," nor is "conservatism" a prerequisite for concern about issues like ecological destruction. Dunlop correctly identified a subgroup, which he called "liberal nationalists," who share Gorbachev's agenda generally but whose priorities differ from those of the "liberals" because of their emphasis on environmental issues and the recovery of the prerevolutionary past.[16] The medievalist Dmitriy Likhachev, an early and consistent supporter of Gorbachev's program who now heads the Cultural Fund, is the most prominent and most popular member of that group.

Similarly, not all economic "conservatives" who disagree with the tenets of *perestroyka* belong together with "nationalists" and "traditionalists." People genuinely disagree on the kind of economic reforms best suited to the Soviet Union, and how they should be implemented, although most people, whatever they think, feel obliged to offer at least token support to Gorbachev's reform package.[17] But the theoretical resistance to the reforms—as distinguished from the obfuscation and obstructionism thrown up by tenacious bureaucrats and *apparatchiks* fearful for their positions and power—tends to come from those economists and social commentators who align themselves, explicitly or by association, with the political conservatives.

"Liberals" form an equally complicated and more fractious bloc. The liberals can fairly be said to favor democratic reforms, although they are not necessarily in favor of abolishing privilege, at least if privilege is construed as earned reward for initiative in one's workplace, as an incentive toward privatization. In all the artistic organizations of Soviet society, the "liberals" have been in the vanguard of the support for *glasnost'*, Gorbachev, and *perestroyka*. They have tended to seek a loosening of the existing strictures on freedom of expression.

"Liberals" and "conservatives" may productively be distinguished from each other on the basis of their respective approaches to issues that have dominated public discussion and the press in the last two or three years. Thus, for example, the legacy of Stalinism is a matter of interest and concern to both groups.[18] Liberals have generally wished to examine the entire Stalin period, while conservatives often try to exempt Stalin's war-time role, because of a reluctance to destroy people's memory, real or fictitious, of what was virtually the only unifying (rather than divisive) event in Soviet history. Liberals make no bones about blaming Stalin for the number of war casualties, especially in the first months after the Nazi invasion; conservatives prefer to emphasize his symbolic importance to the nation as *vozhd'*, ruler, and standard-bearer. As part of their efforts to find alternatives to Stalin within Soviet history, liberals have eagerly reclaimed Old Bolsheviks purged by Stalin (most notably Nikolay Bukharin). By contrast, conservatives have been at pains to show the responsibility such Old Bolsheviks bear for Stalin's rise to power, and how their own efforts created the system that ultimately devoured them. (Few liberal historians deny this complicity, despite what conservative critics like Anatoliy Salutskiy and Vadim Kozhinov imply.)

Inclusiveness as opposed to selectivity distinguishes the two groups on other issues as well. Liberals tend to support the fullest possible disclosures about the past, and the widest rehabilitation of both artistic and historical figures; conservatives tend to urge a more "balanced," that is, less negative analysis of Soviet history. They want more attention paid to the Russian victims of the Stalinist purges and to the Russian peasants who perished during collectivization, and less attention given to the ethnic minorities (Crimean Tatars, Meskhetians, etc.) deported during the war, the political victims of the Great Terror, and the victims of the postwar anti-cosmopolitan campaign.[19]

One example of this disagreement occurred in connection with a letter signed by many well-known writers endorsing the construction of a monument to the victims of the Great Terror. The prominent conservative Vladimir Soloukhin refused to sign. He explained that he refused because the letter mentioned none of the earlier victims of Stalin.[20] A liberal opponent, Benedikt Sarnov, commented: "I, like Soloukhin, also consider that the lawlessness began not in 1937, and that it is no less important to memorialize all the innocents who perished long before the bloody debauch of Stalinism. But I must honestly say that I don't consider this a sufficient basis for not signing a letter asking to memorialize those who died in the 1930's. Particularly since those who perished in the '30's were by no means exclusively residents of the 'House on the Embankment' [an apartment complex mostly occupied by high-level party and government families, including many Old Bolsheviks]."[21]

The same inclusiveness characterizes the liberals' approach to Russian émigré culture.[22] They are willing to reclaim all of it—from post-revolutionary émigré writers like Georgiy Ivanov to recent exiles like Andrei Sinyavsky and Joseph Brodsky, from Marc Chagall to the contemporary painter Mikhail Shemyakin. The conservatives are more selective in their attitude toward émigré culture: Aleksandr Solzhenitsyn interests them far more than Sinyavsky, and Shemyakin interests them not at all.[23]

Sinyavsky is a particular *bête-noir* because of his *Progulki s Pushkinym* (Strolls with Pushkin), a brilliant but iconoclastic appreciation of Pushkin. It was published abroad in 1975, and a small excerpt appeared in *Oktyabr'* in April 1989. *Oktyabr's* editor, Anatoliy Anan'yev, was raked over the coals by the Secretariat of the Writers' Union and by *Literaturnaya Rossiya*. Nearly apoplectic with rage over Sinyavsky's "desecration" of Russia's beloved Pushkin, the editors of *Literaturnaya Rossiya* reprinted an indignant review by Roman Gul', editor of the émigré magazine *Novyy Zhurnal*, and appended a comment.

> The dubious work of Sinyavsky's was judged by the literary community long ago, and the work of our former compatriot long ago sank into oblivion, like all the other spiteful pasquinades that followed the great Russian poet during his lifetime and after. That is why we were so surprised by the appearance of anti-Pushkin attacks on the pages of a Russian literary journal. ... Though like the majority of White émigrés, [Gul's] political views are ambiguous, in his view of Pushkin as the genius of Russia he is decidedly nobler and on a higher level than Sinyavsky and his defenders.[24]

Indeed, because conservatives tend to idealize the Russian past at the expense of modernism and Western influences, they disapprove of virtually all manifestations of Western art and pop culture in Soviet life—abstract painting, the beauty contests introduced in Moscow last summer, the rock concerts now tolerated by the authorities, Soviet-style punk clothing. In his speech at the Congress of People's Deputies, the novelist Valentin Rasputin used some of the time allotted for his address to express his disdain for such manifestations of Western pop culture, and while his distaste for "beauty queens" competing with a minute of silence for the victims of the April 9, 1989, events in Georgia is understandable, his call for a law "to consolidate and protect morality," and to "ban the propaganda of evil, violence, and vice" is frighteningly normative.

The conservatives now dominate the Writers' Union. They did not always do so: at the eighth congress of the union, in July 1986, supporters of reform took the reins, and many of the liberal editors of journals were appointed in the aftermath of the congress. In the last two years, however, the more conservative writers have steadily managed to concentrate more power in their hands. Despite occasional intervention by Gorbachev himself, this wing of the Writers' Union, seemingly undaunted, continues to issue imprecations and threats again its liberal colleagues. At the March 1987 meeting of the secretariat of the Board of the RSFSR Writers' Union, the floor was dominated by angry conservatives, as was the plenum the following month.[25] A year later, at the March 1988 plenum, the same pattern was repeated, with some of the speakers (Stanislav Kunyayev, Vladimir Krupin) defending *Pamyat'* against the (liberal) likes of poet Yevgeniy Yevtushenko, novelist Fazil Iskander, journalist Yelena Lesota, and economist Gavriil Popov. Yuriy Bondarev blamed the liberals, with their undifferentiated "mourning over" Russian history, for the loss of artistic direction in the country—and for sexual promiscuity among young people.[26]

Conservative wrath surfaced at the meeting of the secretariat of the Board of the RSFSR Writers' Union, held in Ryazan' from September 28 to October 2, 1988, and at the plenum of the Board of the RSFSR Writers' Union, held in Moscow in December 1988. The former gave the floor almost exclusively to contributors to *Nash Sovremennik,* who voiced their disapproval of changes in the political and cultural spheres using language deliberately reminiscent of Andrey Zhdanov's 1946 tirades. "Cosmopolitan enemies of Russia," they said, were corrupting its youth and would ultimately destroy the country's independence.[27] The December meeting, supposedly devoted to nonfiction writing on social and economic themes, turned into an all-out attack on the most prominent spokesmen and theoreticians of *perestroyka:* sociologist Tat'yana Zaslavskaya, economists Leonid Abalkin and Nikolay Shmelev, and journalist and deputy editor of *Kommunist* Otto Latsis. (*Kommunist* came in for a disproportionate share of abuse, probably because it had published an editorial in late November criticizing the Ryazan' speeches as anti-democratic, anti-Western, and, implicitly, anti-Semitic.[28]) Novelist Vasiliy Belov voiced his regret that the jamming of Western radio broadcasts had been stopped.[29]

The "mobilization" of the conservatives continued in March 1989, with a conference of the Union for the Spiritual Rebirth of the Fatherland and the establishment of the Foundation for Slavic Writing and Slavic Culture to foster greater historical and cultural knowledge about and cohesion among Russians, Ukrainians, and Belorussians.[30] Though theoretically a common initiative among representatives of all these peoples, it is compromised by the participation of a large number of the most extreme Russian nationalists. (The same people formed, in November 1988, an Association of Russian Artists in Moscow, in order to "awaken, illuminate, and strengthen the national self-awareness and spiritual powers of the Russian people."[31]) Their goals include encouraging Russian folksongs and folklore (rather than rock), preserving Russian library and archival materials, restoring Russian historical and cultural monuments, and improving "the education of the people in the spirit of respect for Russian history and the traditions of military duty." They sponsored a series of rallies under the rubric "The Voices and Colors of Russia," some of which took on a decidedly anti-Semitic tinge.[32]

POLITICAL DEBATE IN THE JOURNALS

The liberals' inability to wrest even a measure of control over the Writers' Union from the conservatives, the organization's relative stagnation, and its deeply-rooted resistance to reform of either itself or the publishing industry, had shifted the battleground of this aspect of the cultural war to the media, in particular to the journals.[33] Editors have traditionally had great power over Soviet literature, acting as first-line censors and in some instances slipping manuscripts into print through briefly-opened windows of opportunity. Now that prior censorship, especially of *belle-lettres,* has virtually ceased, editors have even more power than before. Conservatives continue to control three main journals, *Nash Sovremennik, Molodaya Gvardiya,* and *Moskva,* as well as the newspaper *Sovetskaya Rossiya* (where the infamous Nina Andreyeva letter appeared on March 13, 1988) and the in-house paper of the Moscow chapter of the USSR Writers' Union, *Moskovskiy Literator.* Liberals run the flagship publications of *perestroyka* and *glasnost',* the weeklies *Ogonek* and *Moscow News,* the monthlies *Novyy Mir, Druzhba Narodov, Znamya, Oktyabr',* and *Neva.* (At the First Congress of People's Deputies, in June 1989, Vasiliy Belov, whose recent novel *Vse vperedi* [Everything Lies Ahead] is markedly anti-Semitic, spoke of the concentration of real power in the hands "of those who control the media," who reflect the interests of "certain groups" from the capital.[34] This allegation is often repeated at meetings of extreme nationalists.)

Accusations of "elitism," regularly leveled against the editors of liberal journals who supposedly do not publish what "most people" want to read, are belied by the circulation figures: *Novyy Mir's* print-run for 1988 exceeded 1 million, more than twice that for 1987; *Ogonek's* print-run shot up past 3 million; *Druzhba Narodov* more than quintupled, from 150,000 in 1987 to 800,000 in 1988. *Znamya* and *Neva* both doubled their print-runs for 1988. These are hardly "elitist" magazines, particularly when one considers that (conservatively) three or four readers read every printed copy. This figure is certainly higher for the most popular issues of these journals, like those of *Druzhba Narodov* containing Anatoliy Rybakov's *Children of the Arbat. Molodaya Gvardiya's* circulation went up as well, although by a much smaller percentage (1987: 640,000; 1988: 700,000); so, marginally, did the figures for *Moskva* and *Nash Sovremennik.*

What has developed in the last two years is a process at once reassuring and distressing. Polarization has intensified. Attacks in the conservatives' periodicals on certain individuals identified with *glasnost'* and *perestroyka,* and on artistic works that symbolize them, have increased in frequency and venom. Tat'yana Zaslavskaya is a favorite target, especially of *Nash Sovremennik* economics writer Anatoliy Salutskiy. In a number of articles, Salutskiy distorts and on occasion blatantly falsifies Zaslavskaya's stated views; when challenged, he temporarily backs off but then resumes his disinformation campaign.[35] *Ogonek* and its editor Vitaliy Korotich are constant targets. An egregious example of an attack on Korotich was a letter of denunciation to *Pravda* published on January 19, 1989, and signed by seven prominent conservatives (Mikhail Alekseyev, editor of *Moskva;* Petr Proskurin, chairman of the RSFSR Cultural Foundation; Sergey Vikulov, editor of *Nash Sovremennik;* novelists Viktor Astaf'yev, Vasiliy Belov, and Valentin Rasputin; and film director Sergey Bondarchuk). The signators object to *Ogonek's* criticism of the Ryazan' meeting referred to above, and to its publication of readers' letters criticizing Rasputin, Belov, and the others; such letters, they charged, besmirched "our spiritual values." Korotich is regularly accused of being an unscrupulous careerist who was ready to praise Leonid Brezhnev when that was useful and now supports Gorbachev out of expedience as well. Vasiliy Grossman's novel *Life and Fate* is often lambasted for its "Russophobia" (Vikulov's indictment at the December 1988 plenum); his *Forever Flowing,* published in *Oktyabr'* last spring, is deemed even worse.[36] Anatoliy Rybakov's *Children of the Arbat* supposedly slanders Siberians as "wild, stupid, and promiscuous" (Rasputin, in print and on prime-time television[37]), and falsifies history (A. Baygushev[38]).

One reader to the monthly journal *Literaturnoye Obozreniye* described the journal war last summer:

> It turns out that to come out for democracy means to come out against something. *Perestroyka* has no open opponents, but it seems that it has supporters with whose help democracy can be turned into its very opposite. Nowadays they prefer to obstruct from a position of reactionary romanticism, advocating a patriarchal stance and isolation from the world at the end of the 20th century. Revealingly, some of the "neoslavophile" slogans—the struggle with the forces of foreigners and intellectuals—are close to the positions of the neo-Stalinists. The approach espoused today by *Nash Sovremennik* and *Molodaya Gvardiya* is a form of neo-slavophilism, nationalist utopianism behind which arrant bureaucratic conservatism finds it easy to hide.[39]

At the same time, what is reassuring is the fact that discussion, if at times on a primitive and personally offensive level, is open, public, and continuous. Statements do not go unanswered; prejudices are not allowed to stand unchallenged. Nothing is swept under the rug. Let Salutskiy defame Zaslavskaya in *Nash Sovremennik;* she is quickly defended in *Sovetskaya Kul'-tura.* Let Baygushev attack Anatoliy Rybakov in *Moskva;* Alla Latynina refutes him in *Literaturnaya Gazeta.* A vibrant intellectual pluralism holds sway, and although the extreme conservatives, far from hospitable to the very notion of pluralism, would probably wish to curtail it, their moderate colleagues and their liberal opponents fully appreciate its value.[40] Again to quote the wise *Literaturnoye Obozreniye* reader, "As for journals of another [more conservative] cast ... probably we can't do without them. If there are people who think that way, then let them express themselves." And he points out that when *Novyy Mir* prints, as it has done in the last two years, the work of "conservatives" such as Belov, Astaf'yev, and Feliks Kuznetsov, it signals its tolerance of a variety of views—so long as its aesthetic criteria are maintained—and not a sudden conversion to the position of *Nash Sovremennik.*[41]

In this same spirit of pluralism, on November 22, 1988, Soviet television broadcast a documentary about the slander suit brought against the writer Ales' Adamovich and the newspaper *Sovetskaya Kul'tura* by Ivan Shekhovtsov. Shekhovtsov, an investigator in the Ukrainian republic prosecutor's office in the early 1950's, accused Adamovich and the paper of slandering post-1930 Soviet history, and "blackening and spurning" what patriotic Soviets hold dear. In response, Adamovich and other witnesses spoke of Stalin's genocidal policies as having cost more lives than Hitler's invasion. A documentary called "The Purification," like an earlier documentary called "The Trial," counterposed critics and defenders of Stalin; each justification of or apologia for Stalin was challenged, often by survivors of the purges. In "The Trial," Vladimir Tikhonov, a member of the Academy of Agricultural Sciences and a critic of collectivization, traced the tyranny of Stalinism to the prior ban on dissenting opinion and on the formation of factions.[42]

Moreover, no longer can any decision in the cultural sphere be construed as irrevocable. The vicissitudes of publishing Solzhenitsyn are instructive in this regard.[43] In 1988, the debate was intense. Most editors, journalists, and readers clamored for publication; official spokesmen and a few liberal voices argued against Solzehnitsyn's "anti-Leninist" stance. In June 1988, *Moscow News* ran a piece on *One Day in the Life of Ivan Denisovich* and its significance for Russian literature and Soviet society; two months later, in *Knizhnoye Obozreniye,* Yleena Chukovskaya urged the full rehabilitation of Solzhenitsyn, restoration of his citizenship, and publication of his books. However, the October issue of *Novyy Mir,* whose back cover promised the publication of Solzhenitsyn in 1989, was held back. When the magazine finally appeared, its future contents page made no such commitments. (It also was to have contained Sergey Kaledin's *Construction Brigade.* According to Vyacheslav Kondrat'yev, writing in *Komsomol'-skaya Pravda,* the military censors banned Kaledin's novella, which only came out in the April issue of *Novyy Mir.*) The opponents appeared to have the upper hand, especially when Ideology Secretary Vadim Medvedev explicitly rejected the possibility of publishing Solzhenitsyn, because of his views on Lenin and the October Revolution. Yet only a few days later, on December 11 and 12, Solzhenitsyn's 70th birthday was celebrated by large crowds. The festivities occurred in places like the House of Medical Workers and the House of Architects: in other words, they must have had official sanction, however tacit. At the House of Cinema more than 1,400 people applauded Vladimir Lakshin's call for Solzhenitsyn's return and his praise of Solzhenitsyn as the original trailblazer; the critic Yuriy Koryakin remarked, "Let him be an anti-Communist. So was Dostoevsky. Is he an enemy?"[44]

In 1989, the "Solzhenitsyn case" was happily resolved. After several "deep discussions" with Gorbachev himself,[45] Sergey Zalygin, *Novyy Mir's* editor, made good on his promise of the previous year. In the July issue he published Solzhenitsyn's "Nobel Lecture," and in issues 8, 9, and 10 substantial portions of *The Gulag Archipelago. The First Circle,* and *Cancer Ward* will run (in *Novyy Mir*) in 1990, as will *March 1917* (in the Leningrad journal *Neva*), *August 1914* (in *Zvezda*), and *October 1916* (in *Nash Sovremennik*). The publishing house Sovetskiy pisatel' has announced a forthcoming seven-volume collection of Solzhenitsyn's works in a substantial print-run of 300,000.[46] Back in July, the chief Soviet censor told Bill Keller: "Regarding Solzhenitsyn, all debates are over";[47] the past few months have shown the truth of his words.

In his short prefatory note to the first installment of *Gulag*, Zalygin wrote: "Aleksandr Solzhenitsyn, with his unyielding obduracy, is absolutely necessary to us now—we must know and listen to him, we have neither the moral nor the intellectual right to fail to know and listen to him."[48] Three months later, Igor Vinogradov echoed Zalygin's emphasis on the "up-to-date and ... burning significance" of *Gulag*. Describing it as "the most complete, the most fundamental, truly encyclopedic description of the history and geography, of the laws and customs, of the state structure and population of the prisons, annihilating labour, penal-servitude camps and exile regions of this fantastic country," Vinogradov insisted on its importance for understanding the present and "not los[ing] our way in the future. ... [Solzhenitsyn] offers his diagnosis not only to your reason but also to your conscience, to your behavior today, to your moral responsibility."[49]

PRODUCTS OF *GLASNOST'*

What have readers found in the "thick" journals of the last two years, apart from the always-engrossing letters to the editors? Broadly speaking, essays on social, historical, economic, and political issues; poetry and prose held back for years and sometimes for decades; new poetry and prose. I can only suggest the wide range of works, with no attempt at offering a comprehensive list. 1988 began with two major publications, Grossman's *Life and Fate*[50] (which was one of the books even optimistic observers believed, as recently as two years ago, would not be published) and Pasternak's *Doctor Zhivago*.[51] *Druzhba Narodov* published a work widely accepted in the West as one of the masterpieces of Soviet literature, Andrey Platonov's *Chevengur,* in its third and fourth issues for 1988, and Boris Pilnyak's classic *Mahogany* in its second issue for 1989.

Pleasure in the reclamation of Russian literature is widespread but by no means universal. Dmitriy Urnov, the editor of the leading journal of literary scholarship *Voprosy Literatury,* finds books like *Doctor Zhivago,* Zamyatin's *We,* Platonov's *Chevengur,* and Grossman's *Life and Fate* overrated. "I had and still have the impression," he wrote in response to a *Literaturnoye Obozreniye* survey, "that nearly all these works are without exception weak from a literary point of view, and I think that if works like *We,* for example, were artistically stronger, they would have broken down the wall, overcome all obstacles in their way. ... Precedent tells us that there is always some kind of internal obstacle in the 'unrecognized' work itself to prevent its reaching its readers."[52] Urnov neglects to explain how KGB confiscation qualifies as an "internal obstacle," or for that matter what the aesthetic weakness of *We* had do to with the 60-year ban on its publication in the Soviet Union.

Poetry by writers who could not publish until two or three years ago—Semen Lipkin,[53] Aleksandr Kushner,[54] Inna Lisnyanskaya,[55] Yevgeniy Reyn,[56] and Boris Chichibabin[57]—shares pages with once-taboo émigré poets of various eras, from the 1920s emigre Don Aminado[58] to émigré of the 1970's like Naum Korzhavin[59] and Joseph Brodsky.[60] Readers' thirst for information and analysis of Soviet history is reflected in Dmitriy Volkogonov's biography of Stalin (serialized in *Oktyabr',* Nos. 10–12, 1988) and Fedor Burlatskiy's controversial recollections of the Khrushchev era (in *Novyy Mir,* No. 10, 1988); in the correspondence of Boris Pasternak and Ol'ga Freydenberg (in *Druzhba Narodov,* Nos. 7–10, 1988); and in memoirs by both émigrés (Nina Berberova, Aleksandra Tolstoy) and Soviets (Anatoliy Nayman on Anna Akhmatova in *Novyy Mir,* Nos. 1–3, 1989, and Konstantin Simonov on Stalin, in *Znamya,* Nos. 3–5, 1988). All the thick journals have been running articles by Andrey Nuikin, Nikolay Shmelev (whose short stories are also now printed), Igor' Klyamkin, Vasiliy Selyunin, and a raft of other economists, historians, and social commentators.

It is true that unknown, younger, previously-unpublished writers face stiff competition in getting their work into journals crowded—some say over-crowded—with names from the past. As the critic Aleksey Zverev commented, "It's by no means simple for today's writers to present themselves in such company. The impression made by their work is rather pallid. But this is hardly their fault: who indeed could survive comparisons—which are unavoidable—with the likes of Grossman, Pasternak, Zamyatin, and Nabokov! And that's who they are rubbing shoulders with in the journals!"[61] (Also with George Orwell, Arthur Koestler, and Ken Kesey.) Zverev's point is important: more than 70 years' worth of the best literature written in Russian is being crammed into journals in the span of two to three years—tough competition indeed for even the best contemporary writers. Nevertheless, some new names have emerged: Sergey Kaledin,

Tamara Nabatnikova, Sergey Alekseyev. Most notable, perhaps are Mikhail Kurayev, whose first two novellas *Captain Dikshteyn* and *Night-time Interrogation* (in *Novyy Mir*, No. 9, 1987, and No. 12, 1988, respectively) were warmly received, and Tat'yana Tolstaya, whose stories ran in several issues of *Novyy Mir* and are now available in English (*On the Golden Porch*, published in 1989).

In conclusion, Soviet writers, filmmakers, and intellectuals may occupy "two warring camps," their divisions more sharply etched than ever. At the same time, they maintain a dialogue with each other, sometimes civil, sometimes vicious, but ongoing. Those who profit most from that dialogue are Soviet readers, viewers, and listeners, who have themselves become participants in the dynamic process *glasnost'* signifies.

NOTES

ABOUT THE AUTHOR: **Josephine Woll** is associate professor of Russian literature at Howard University in Washington D.C.

1. See John Dunlop, "Soviet Cultural Politics," *Problems of Communism* (Washington, DC), November-December 1987, pp. 34–56.

2. The Composers' Union, *glasnost'* notwithstanding, has continued to be led by the re- doubtable and seemingly immortal Tikhon Khrennikov (aged 76), whose career began ig- nominiously more than 40 years ago. On September 29, however, Radio Moscow an- nounced that a plenum of the Board of the Union had dissolved the union and created a federation of independent composers' organizations. In February 1988, the Congress of So- viet Artists chose as the chairman of its union an artist, Andrey Vasnetsov, whose paintings had not been exhibited since the notorious 1962 Manezh exhibition that so offended Nikita Khrushchev. One of his goals as chairman is to "show everything there is to show," and though his own work is far from modernist in style, he speaks with tolerance of other schools of painting. See Natalya Kraminova. "The Times of Andrei Vasnetsov," *Moscow News*, No. 6, 1989.

3. Professional theaters in the USSR have always been heavily subsidized by the state, in part because of the traditional view of the theater as an educational and ideological institu- tion. Whether that view will not be superseded by one that sees the theater as an enter- prise—and hence as financially self-supporting—is moot. Given its importance for the fu- ture of Soviet theater, it is a subject hotly debated in the press.

4. *Izvestiya* (Moscow), Aug. 12, 1988.

5. "Democracy and Proficiency," *Moscow News*, No. 3, 1988. Interview with Oleg Kuprin.

6. For an illuminating discussion of Shatrov's work, see David Joravsky, "*Glasnost* The- ater," *The New York Review of Books*, Nov. 10, 1988.

7. *The New York Times*, June 4, 1989.

8. See Anna Lawton, "Toward a New Openness," in Daniel J. Goulding, Ed., *Post New Wave Cinema in the Soviet Union and Eastern Europe*, Bloomington, IN, Indiana University Press, 1989, esp. pp. 36–46.

9. See, for instance, Stanislav Govorukhin, "March of the Envious," *Sovetskaya Kul'tura* (Moscow), June 13, 1989.

10. See Vera Tolz, "Soviet Film Describes Birth of Gulag System," Radio Liberty, *Report on the USSR* (Munich), Apr. 21, 1989, pp. 9–13.

11. As reported by Andrei Vasiliev in *Moscow News*, No. 44, 1988.

12. Julia Wishnevsky, "*Nash Sovremennik* Provides Focus for 'Opposition Party,'" Radio Liberty, *Report on the USSR*, Jan. 20, 1989, p. 5.

13. See Carol and John Garrard, *Inside the Soviet Writers' Union*, New York, Free Press, 1989.

14. Natalya Il'ina, "Welcome, Young and Unknown Tribe ...," *Ogonek* (Moscow), No. 2, 1988, pp. 23–26.

15. Between 1976 and 1980, a reported 500 million out of 700 million new books received by Soviet libraries were removed from shelves *for lack of a single borrower*. See *Literaturnaya Rossiya* (Moscow—the weekly newspaper of the RSFSR Writers' Union), No. 19, 1986, p. 16. A comparable situation exists in the visual arts, according to one art historian. He claims that some 115,000 pieces of art, costing the state over 60 million rubles, are immured in closed depositories and have never been seen by the public. They are, he implied, artistically worthless, and were bought by the Artists' Union for reasons that had little if anything to do with aesthetic merit.

16. Dunlop, "Soviet Cultural Politics," loc. cit., p. 36.

17. Not all, however, Anatoliy Salutskiy, who dubs himself and those of his political cast "radicals," explicitly rejects the reforms. In many articles, he mounts a head-long attack on the "architects of *perestroyka*," especially Abel Aganbegyan and Tat'yana Zaslavskaya. His colleague Mikhail Antonov is equally outspoken, arguing for a "patriotic" rather than "efficient" economy. For an excellent analysis of this dispute, see Wishnevsky, "*Nash Sovremennik* ...," loc. cit.; and idem, "Architects of Perestroika Defended," Radio Liberty, *Report on the USSR*, Mar. 17, 1989, pp. 4–6.

18. Indeed, the first characteristic of the "liberals" that Dunlop identifies is their unfinished agenda, left over from the Khrushchev thaw, "to continue the interrupted process of de-Stalinization—the uncovering and publicizing of Stalin's crimes—and the publication of works suppressed under Stalin or in subsequent periods of 're-Stalinization.' In confronting and attacking the specter of Stalin, the 'liberals' sought to ensure once and for all that a return to a Stalinist system would become impossible." See Dunlop, "Soviet Cultural Politics," loc. cit., p. 36.

19. One peculiar contribution to the recent literature on collectivization (generally accepted by the conservatives as a national tragedy and trauma) came from the deputy chief editor of *Molodaya Gvardiya*, Vyacheslav Gorbachev. He wrote that collectivization had been "different in different parts of the country," and suggested that the dispossession and exile of kulaks was justified. See *Molodaya Gvardiya* (Moscow), No. 7, 1987, pp. 227–28. For *Molodaya Gvardiya's* role in these polemics, see Julia Wishnevsky, "*Molodaya Gvardiya*: A Leading Voice of Opposition to Restructuring," Radio Free Europe-Radio Liberty, *Radio Liberty Research* (Munich), RL 1/88, Jan. 5, 1988.

20. "Why I Did Not Sign That Letter," *Nash Sovremennik*, No. 12, 1988.

21. "On 'The Silent Ones' and 'The First Pupils,'" *Ogonek*, No. 16, 1989, p. 30.

22. See Nancy Condee and Vladimir Padunov, "The Outposts of Official Art: Recharting Soviet Cultural History," *Framework* (London), No. 34, 1987, pp. 61–71 for an analysis of what they call the "recuperation of the émigré heritage."

23. In 1987, for instance, *Molodaya Gvardiya* sharply condemned exhibits of work by Wassily Kandinsky and Marc Chagall. See Nos. 7 and 9.

24. See Anatoliy Anan'yev, "Criticism or Accusation?" *Literaturnaya Rossiya*, No. 35, Sept. 1, 1989; a response to the "Letter of the Secretariat of the Writers' Union of the RSFSR" (from Mikhail Antonov, V. Klykov, and Igor' Shafarevich), which had appeared in *Literaturnaya Rossiya* on Aug. 4, 1989; and the editors' reply to Anan'yev.

240 PART 3: SOVIET POLITICAL DEBATES

25. For details of these two meetings, see Dunlop, "Soviet Cultural Politics," loc. cit., pp. 46–50; also Walter Laqueur, *The Long Road to Freedom*, New York, Charles Scribner's Sons, 1989, pp. 78–90 and passim. Laqueur devotes a separate chapter of his book to the reemergent Russian Right.

26. The proceedings of the plenum were published in *Literaturnaya Gazeta*, No. 10, 1988, pp. 2–10.

27. *Literaturnaya Rossiya*, No. 43, 1988, pp. 2–9.

28. See *Kommunist* (Moscow), No. 17, 1988, pp. 22–26.

29. Julia Wishnevsky properly notes that the non-Russian writers present at the plenum strongly objected to the prevailing Russian nationalist tone. Also, a few days after the plenum, the Moscow Writers' Organization asked the USSR Writers' Union to grant it republican status, which would end its subordination to the RSFSR Writers' Union. See Wishnevsky, "*Nash Sovremennik* ..." loc. cit., pp. 5–6.

30. "A Noble and Beneficial Task," *Literaturnaya Rossiya*, Mar. 17, 1989, pp. 4–5. See Douglas Smith, "Formation of New Russian Nationalist Group Announced," Radio Liberty, *Report on the USSR*, July 7, 1989, pp. 5–8; idem, "Moscow's 'Otechestvo': A Link between Russian Nationalism and Conservative Opposition to Reform," ibid., July 28, 1989, pp. 6–9.

31. *Moskovskiy Literator* (Moscow), Nos. 49–50, Dec. 16, 1988, p. 3. See John Dunlop's analysis of these two organizations in "Two Noteworthy Russian Nationalist Initiatives." Radio Liberty, *Report on the USSR*, May 26, 1989, pp. 1–4; Julia Wishnevsky offers another view in "Ligachev, 'Pamyat'," and Conservative Writers," ibid., Mar. 10, 1989, p. 14.

32. For one version of these rallies see *Sovetskaya Rossiya* (Moscow), Jan. 17, 1989, and *Literaturnaya Rossiya*, Nos. 2–4, 1989. For another, see *Moscow News*, No. 6, 1989, p. 15, and *Ogonek*, No. 7, 1989, p. 11.

33. For a recent summary of changes in Soviet television, see Viktor Yasmann, "Zigzags of *Glasnost*' and Soviet Television," Radio Liberty, *Report on the USSR*, Mar. 31, 1989, pp. 12–17.

34. *Pravda* (Moscow), June 3, 1989.

35. For a review of Salutskiy's recently-published works, see Aleksandr Volkov, "At the Forefront of *Perestroyka*," *Literaturnoye Obozreniye* (Moscow), No. 8, 1988, pp. 72–75.

36. For the "conservatives," the publication of *Forever Flowing* was Anan'yev's chief transgression, worse than Sinyavsky and Alexander Yanov. See the exchange referred to in fn. 24. As of early December 1989, Anan'yev has reportedly been removed from his post as editor of *Oktyabr*' and has been replaced by a staunch nationalist.

37. *Knizhnoye Obozreniye* (Moscow), No. 22, 1988, p. 4. His TV remarks were part of an hour-long program featuring 14 *Nash Sovremennik* editors and regular contributors. See Julia Wishnevsky, "*Nash Sovremennik* Talks to Soviet TV Viewers," *Radio Liberty Research*, RL 346/88, July 28, 1988.

38. Baygushev's piece appeared in *Moskva* (Moscow), No. 12, 1988. Rybakov's defenders include the critic Alla Latynina (*Literaturnaya Gazeta*, Dec. 14, 1988), and he himself replied in a letter to the editor of *Ogonek*, No. 5, 1989.

39. Gennadiy Kuznetsov. "From the Viewpoint of a 'Neophyte'," *Literaturnoye Obozreniye*, No. 8, 1988, p. 93.

40. Valentin Rasputin, at the Congress of People's Deputies: "Pluralism is possible as a variety and multiplicity of public and political opinion. You have imposed on the country a pluralism of morality. That is more dangerous than any bomb." *Izvestiya*, June 6, 1989.

41. Natalya Ivanova, poetry editor of *Druzhba Narodov* and a significant force in the liberal camp, said much the same thing in "Journals in the Focus of Opinion," *Literaturnoye Obozreniye*, No. 4, 1988, p. 98. See also two "dialogues" between Alla Latynina and Sergey Chuprin, "Key to What?" *Literaturnaya Gazeta*, Apr. 12, 1989, and "Left, Right: Which Side?" ibid., Apr. 19, 1989. Other references can be found in John Dunlop, "Alla Latynina: A Self-Proclaimed Centrist Calls for Political Realignment," Radio Liberty, *Report on the USSR*, June 23, 1989, pp. 8–10.

42. On "The Trial" *(Protsess)*, see Julia Wishnevsky, "Soviet Television Discusses Stalin's Legacy," *Radio Liberty Research*, RL 205/88, May 17, 1988. On "The Cleansing" *(Ochishcheniye)*, see idem, "A Stalinist's Lawsuit," ibid., RL 524/88, Nov. 23, 1988. The actual hearing took place on September 20, 1988.

43. For a full description, see John B. Dunlop, "Solzhenitsyn Begins to Emerge from the Political Void," Radio Liberty, *Report on the USSR*, Sept. 8, 1989, pp. 1–6. In the same issue, see also Douglas Smith, "Reappraisal of Solzhenitsyn in the USSR," pp. 6–9.

44. *The New York Times*, Dec. 13, 1988. Lakshin's comments were particularly significant for several reasons. First, he was Aleksandr Tvardovskiy's assistant editor in *Novyy Mir* when the latter won publication approval from Khrushchev for *A Day in the Life of Ivan Denisovich* in 1963. Second, he sharply disputed Solzhenitsyn's portrait of Tvardovskiy (in *The Calf and the Oak*) in his own *samizdat* essay, "Tvardovskiy, Solzhenitsyn, and *Novyy Mir*." Third, he is one of the leading liberals today, in his own writing and as assistant editor of *Znamya*, and as such disagrees with (and is disliked by) virtually all of the conservative critics who claim Solzhenitsyn as their own.

45. Those were Zalygin's words in describing his meetings with Gorbachev. See *The Washington Post*, Apr. 21, 1989.

46. V. Yakimenko in *Komsomol'skaya Pravda* (Moscow), July 13, 1989.

47. *The New York Times*, July 18, 1989.

48. *Novyy Mir*, No. 8, 1989, p. 7.

49. Igor Vinogradov, "Do Not Trust, Do Not Be Afraid, Do Not Ask for Anything," *Moscow News*, No. 45, 1989, p. 12.

50. *Oktyabr'* (Moscow), Nos. 1–4, 1988, with an exemplary afterword by the literary critic Anatoliy Bocharov explaining, among other things, the KGB's confiscation of the manuscript in 1961. The poet Semen Lipkin goes into much greater detail in "The Life and Fate of Vasiliy Grossman," *Literaturnoye Obozreniye*, No. 7, 1988, pp. 98–108.

51. *Novyy Mir* (Moscow), Nos. 1–4, 1988, with a preface by Academician Dmitriy Likhachev; *Novyy Mir* followed up with another notable retrieval: Yuriy Dombrovskiy's *Fakul'tet nenuzhnykh veshchey* (The Faculty of the Superfluous), in Nos. 8–11, 1988.

52. In "Lessons for Tomorrow," *Literaturnoye Obozreniye*, No. 1, 1989, p. 16. For more on Urnov, see Julia Wishnevsky, "Dmitrii Urnov: A Learned Stalinist?" Radio Liberty, *Report on the USSR*, Mar. 17, 1989, pp. 11–13.

53. In, for instance, *Oktyabr'*, No. 8, 1988, pp. 118–20.

54. Ibid., No. 6, 1988, pp. 82–85.

55. Ibid., No. 11, 1988, pp. 130–32; in *Novyy Mir*, No. 6, 1988, pp. 6–7; and *Druzhba Narodov* (Moscow), No. 2, 1989, pp. 108–13.

56. In *Novyy Mir*, No. 2, 1988, pp. 93–95.

57. In *Druzhba Narodov*, No. 4, 1988, pp. 197–219. Publication references for Chichibabin and the previously-mentioned poets are by no means exhaustive.

58. In *Oktyabr'*, No. 9, 1988, pp. 143–46.

59. Ibid., No. 8, 1988, pp. 143–50; *Druzhba Narodov,* No. 12, 1988, pp. 186–89.

60. *Druzhba Narodov,* No. 8, 1988, pp. 226–36; *Novyy Mir,* No. 12, 1987; Neva (Leningrad), No. 3, 1988; *Raduga* (Tallinn); No. 2, 1988; *Literaturnoye Obozreniye,* No. 8, 1988.

61. Zverev's comments are part of a survey of literary critics in "Lessons for Tomorrow," *Literaturnoye Obozreniye,* No. 1, 1989, p. 7.

17   *Politics and History Under Gorbachev*

THOMAS SHERLOCK

The use of Soviet history as a tool of reform has emerged over the past two years as an essential element of Mikhail Gorbachev's political strategy.[1] At first unwilling to address divisive historical issues, particularly those of the Stalin years, the General Secretary has come to countenance and even encourage wide-ranging de-Stalinization and a search for reformist predecessors and precedents in early Soviet history. Although the phenomenon still has an instrumental cast to it, political leaders, writers, social scientists, and other commentators have reopened a number of pages of Soviet history and subjected them to a more objective reading. There is considerable hesitancy in some circles, however, to advance a process that ultimately runs the risk of placing in question the legitimacy of the October Revolution and rule by the communist party.

Gorbachev's own initial caution was evidenced in the new party program approved at the 27th CPSU Congress in early 1986, which devoted only part of a single line to criticism of the Stalin period.[2] When asked, in an interview with *L'Humanité* on February 4, 1986 (shortly before the congress), whether "various circles in the West" were correct in doubting that the "vestiges of Stalinism" had been overcome in the Soviet Union, Gorbachev replied that "Stalinism" was a concept invented by the opponents of socialism to discredit the Soviet Union and socialism as a whole. The USSR, he asserted, had already applied the lessons learned at the 20th Party Congress (where Khrushchev launched his de-Stalinization campaign).[3]

Yet, already, prominent voices were being raised rejecting a cautious approach to the past. In September 1985, the historian Yuriy Afanas'yev, then head of the history section of the party's theoretical journal, *Kommunist,* published an article entitled "The Past and Ourselves." He said that an inadequate understanding of history was "extremely dangerous," and argued that only by rejecting attempts to idealize and manipulate the past could Soviet society understand the present and come to grips with its problems.[4] Another such voice was that of poet Yevgeniy Yevtushenko. At the December 1985 congress of the Soviet writers' union, he condemned the "blank spots" in Soviet history and its periodic rewriting and observed that only "fearlessness in the face of the past" would offer solutions to the problems of today.[5]

Toward the middle of 1986, as Gorbachev came to perceive the need for broad social and political reform in the Soviet Union, he apparently began to perceive the utility of a broad re-examination of Soviet history. This shift was suggested by the July 1986 call in *Pravda* for publication of a new party history, one that would deal openly with "negative phenomena" of the past, including those of the Stalin years.[6]

One can discern three intertwined political calculations that may account for Gorbachev's willingness to allow a re-opening of the Soviet past and a revived de-Stalinization campaign. The first was recognition that, as Afanas'yev argued, the socio-economic and political dysfunctions of Soviet society are in part due to the loss, through excessive controls over the arts and the social sciences, of a collective ability to evaluate the health and coherence of the Soviet system. In effect, Gorbachev gradually came to realize that innovation and adaptation to changing circumstances required the existence of what Hugh Heclo calls "men collectively wondering what to do."[7]

A second factor was the perceived need to undermine bureaucratic, as well as popular, resistance to reform. Gorbachev's program originally sought to reinvigorate the economy through a new "discipline" campaign, moderate decentralization of administrative functions, and the introduction of technological innovation. Yet, even these relatively modest measures were resisted by important segments of the party and state "administrative class," which out of personal interest as well as ideological conviction, were committed to the maintenance of the hierarchically-organized economic mechanism that had survived relatively intact from the Stalin period.[8]

... Gorbachev has unleashed a new de-Stalinization campaign designed to review the past, to delegitimize the cultural and ideological supports of the Stalinist "command economy" and of its political defenders, thereby paving the way for the introduction of "new thinking." This campaign recalls J. H. Plumb's observation that "warring authorities" often produce "warring pasts."[10]

The third factor, closely related to the reformers' unwillingness to base the success of their program entirely on the state and party bureaucracies, was the decision to appeal to the creative and technical intelligentsia as an alternative base of social support. The binding element of this alliance—the removal of many of the existing bureaucratic restrictions on freedom of speech and association—has permitted the intelligentsia, particularly the liberal creative intellectuals, to launch a broad attack on the Stalin era.[11]

The alliance with the intelligentsia has doubtless extended the de-Stalinization campaign beyond limits originally envisaged by Gorbachev. Although the liberal intellectuals are Gorbachev's most fervent supporters, they are also intent on pursuing their own agenda. Their assault on Stalinism is due in part to the fact that the intelligentsia, as Gorbachev himself has acknowledged, "suffered enormous, at times irretrievable, losses because of the violations of socialist legality and the repressions of the 1930's."[12] The intellectuals also view themselves as the moral conscience of their society, as did their 19th-century counterparts.[13] Finally, they perceive the need to sustain the liberal spirit of "restructuring" by destroying the political and cultural conditions that support bureaucratic controls over intellectual inquiry.

The re-opening of the past was set in motion by the extensive personnel changes carried out during Gorbachev's first two years in office. ...

As a whole, renovation in the media and cultural spheres during Gorbachev's first two years was dramatic. As a consequence of changes in key personnel, an increasing number of anti-Stalinist works, particularly literary works, began to appear.

DOMINANT THEMES

Three broad, overlapping themes have emerged on the Gorbachev-era works of Soviet writers, economists, and historians examining the Stalin period: (1) the criminal nature of Stalin; (2) the perversion of Leninist socialism by Stalinism; and (3) the continuing damage inflicted by Stalinism on Soviet society.

In the first case, examination of Stalin as a political figure has placed particular emphasis on political terror. Anatoliy Rybakov's *Deti Arbata* (Children of the Arbat) highlights Stalin's role in engineering the December 1934 assassination of Leningrad party leader Sergey Kirov, as a prelude to nation-wide terror. Regarding Stalin's ruthlessness, one of Rybakov's characters recalls Stalin's words in Tsaritsyn in 1918. "'Death resolves all problems. There is no longer a man or a problem,'" and concludes that "Stalin proved to be right."[18] In his November 2, 1987, speech, Gorbachev openly referred to Stalin's "crimes."[19]

The second theme, Stalinism's perversion of Leninist socialism, is understandably sensitive. Under Gorbachev, the issue of collectivization and the fate of the peasantry under Stalin has received particular attention, in part because Soviet agriculture remains the most intractable of the economic problems inherited from the Stalin era. ...

Turning to the Gorbachev period, the first notable example of the re-examination of the fate of the peasantry was the December 1985 speech by Yevtushenko cited above. Referring to the years of building socialism, the poet stated that "... contrary to Lenin's legacy, the precious agricultural wisdom of many peasants, undeservedly branded as kulaks, was crushed under foot."[25]

The central difference between the Khrushchev and Gorbachev periods in terms of re-examining collectivization and, indeed, the entire Stalin period is the scope and degree of criticism. Under Gorbachev, prominent politicians, academics, and writers—in a wide variety of forums—have offered a comprehensive critique that often explicitly rejects the political, economic, and ideological rationale of Soviet rural policy in the late 1920's and early 1930's. While in power, Khrushchev had continued to defend strongly the agricultural and industrial policies of that epoch, offering little information on the human toll of the "revolution from above." Only late in life would he admit that the "Stalin brand of collectivization brought … nothing but misery and brutality."[26]

By contrast, Abel Aganbegyan, Gorbachev's chief economic adviser, has graphically described the "misery and brutality" of rural life under Stalin, stating that collective farm workers lacked the basic rights of citizens, while payments in kind by the state for agricultural production often failed to "ensure the reproduction of human power."[27] Gorbachev himself has severely criticized the methods used in the collectivization, acknowledging that force, not persuasion, was the primary means used to implement the program.[28]

Although the General Secretary reverts to the conventional justification of collectivization as a necessary response to a threatening international environment, others, particularly reformist economists, have rejected this standard explanation. Indeed, although Soviet historiography has traditionally implied a continuity in the "building of socialism" from Lenin's New Economic Policy (NEP) through forced collectivization,[29] the current materials attack the initiation of collectivization in 1929 as a clear turning point in Soviet history—a point at which the Leninist NEP was overthrown and Stalinist "bureaucratic socialism" took root. For example, Nikolay Shmelev argues that collectivization was not a response to the rise of fascism, but rather the result of irrational pricing policies in 1927, which forced the peasants to reduce production. The decline in output, Shmelev states, led to the decision by the government to resort to "state grain acquisition through force."[30]

Shmelev has also provided figures on the human and economic toll of collectivization. In a lecture at a research institute attached to the party Central Committee, he stated that collectivization had created a "monstrous machine" that brutalized and impoverished the Soviet countryside, leading to a 40 percent drop in agricultural production. According to Shmelev, five million families were branded as kulaks and deported—a figure exceeding the highest estimates appearing in the West.[31] Other Soviet social scientists, too, have examined the human toll of collectivization, particularly the starvation of millions of deportees and villagers.[32]

The academician and influential agricultural specialist Vladimir Tikhonov has openly questioned the class justification for collectivization and the drive to eliminate the kulaks in the countryside. Although it was widely acknowledged prior to Gorbachev that Stalin's blows against the kulaks often fell on the middle peasant, Tikhonov goes further, to argue that very few kulaks remained after the village-led expropriations of 1917–18, and that "millions" who were "de-kulakized" during collectivization were in fact simply peasants who produced somewhat more than their neighbors. As for the then-prevailing assumption that only highly concentrated production units can produce "positive results," Tikhonov observed, "the world of economics does not work like this."[33] ...

Other writers have led the way in rejecting Stalin as Lenin's heir, thereby bringing into question the ruling party's claim to legitimacy based on continuity of leadership. Their portrayal of the Stalin era is one of unrelieved political, cultural, and economic oppression. The works of Tengiz Abuladze, Vasiliy Grossman, and Daniil Granin liken the Soviet Union under Stalinism to Nazi Germany.[36]

The plays of Mikhail Shatrov are particularly critical of Stalin and Stalinism. A figure in *Diktatura sovesti* (Dictatorship of Conscience), staged in February 1986, describes socialism as a system of masters and of slaves. The obedience of the latter is secured by having them spy on one another, by a hierarchical and militarized social structure (the *"mundir"*), and by the shame that the slaves have been made to feel for their own opinions. In this play, Lenin is absolved of blame for the distorted view of socialism held by others.[37] Shatrov's *Dal'she ... Dal'she ... Dal'she!* (Onward ... Onward ... Onward!), completed in August 1987, directly condemns Stalin for undermining Lenin's authority, for complicity in the murders of Kirov and Trotsky, and for fabrication of the Moscow purge trials. Here, Shatrov's Lenin applauds Rosa Luxemburg's observation that "with no general elections, no freedom of the press and assembly, no free conflict of views in every social institution, public activity will be extinguished. ... The bureaucracy will become the sole active element." For his crimes and betrayal of socialism, Stalin is condemned by Shatrov's Lenin.[38]

The third theme of the anti-Stalinist writings—the continuing cost of the Stalinist legacy—has been developed in numerous ways. At the conclusion of both *Diktatura sovesti* and *Dal'she ... Dal'she ... Dal'she!* the audience is left with little doubt that Shatrov is referring not only to the political and socio-economic pathologies of the Stalin period, but also to the "vestiges" of Stalinism. Others have been more explicit. For political scientist Nikolay Butenko, the Stalinist party of "another kind" survives today, possessing only the patina of genuine "democratic centralism," while Aleksandr Gel'man of the Cinematographers' Union asserts that the party, particularly its leading organs, has been the primary force opposing democracy.[39]

In his foreword to Mozhayev's *Muzhiki i baby*, Tikhonov links the past and the present by arguing that both the method of collectivization and the bureaucratic institutions imposed on the countryside at the time continue to cripple the work ethic of the peasantry. Only reforms designed to restore the peasant as master of his own land, he argues, will provide a corrective.[40]

Although Gorbachev himself has addressed each of the three themes of the de-Stalinization campaign, he has concentrated on the second and third. In his November 2, 1987, speech, Gorbachev traced the roots of the Stalinist system to the process of accelerated collectivization and industrialization of the late 1920's. Belief in the "universal effectiveness" of centralized administration spread to the "superstructure," excluding meaningful public participation in political, social, and economic life. The weakening of the role of the soviets and other organs of popular will, he argued, created a "shortage of democracy" and a fertile soil for Stalin's dictatorship and the repressions of the 1930's. Elsewhere, the General Secretary stated that public and state structures remain "bureaucracy-ridden," and the Soviet citizen remains alienated from his "constitutional right" to participate in the "affairs of the state."[41]

For Gorbachev and the reformers, this bureaucratization is sustained by a mindset promoted by "dogmatism and scholasticism" in teaching. In an October 1986 speech to heads of social science departments, Gorbachev called for the revision of academic lectures, textbooks, and programs, in order to foster independent judgment and "creative thinking."[42] At the Central Committee plenum of January 1987, Gorbachev returned to the damage wrought by the "personality cult" in its absolutizing of the conceptualizations of economic and social organization in which the role and interests of the party-state and its regulatory organs were paramount.[43]

According to the reformers, the arid dogmatism of the Stalin period, reflected in such works as Stalin's *Short Course* history of the party and his *Economic Problems of Socialism in the USSR*, socialized generations into viewing Soviet politics and economics as static and unchanging.[44] Hence, Soviet society was stripped of the collective ability to ponder and question which values and principles should be considered socialist, and to adapt to changing circumstances, through such measures as expansion of individual labor and cooperative activity, decentralized economic management, and the competitive elections of enterprise leaderships and of deputies to soviets.

POLITICAL REHABILITATIONS

The logic of reform has influenced the decision to re-open the cases of many individuals purged under Stalin. The historian Nikolay Maslov, in mid-July 1987, observed that:

> many party functionaries well merit a civic rehabilitation since they had not been spies, assassins, or agents of foreign intelligence services, but all of them had been convicted on such charges.[45]

Gorbachev, in his November speech, also stated that many party and nonparty persons had suffered in the 1930's as a result of falsified accusations, and he criticized the Brezhnev leadership for failing to continue the "process of restoring justice" begun under Khrushchev. Moreover, he reported that the October 1987 CC plenum had re-opened the issue of the purges and that the Politburo had subsequently established a commission to "comprehensively examine new facts and documents" relating to the Stalinist repressions. The purges and the rehabilitation process, he stated, would be an important part of a "treatise" on the history

of the CPSU to be prepared by a special commission of the Central Committee.[46]
...

The rehabilitation process serves the Gorbachev reform program in several important ways. It strengthens the appeal of liberal reform by undermining the contention of many Soviets that Stalinism was based on order, justice, and purpose and remains an entirely appropriate model for revitalizing the Soviet system.[51] It is also a means through which the regime seeks to communicate to the population its commitment to thoroughgoing reform and its respect for legal norms. In addition, the regime hopes the rehabilitation process will increase its moral authority and reduce the alienation of many individuals, particularly intellectuals, who have long viewed the Soviet system as an "inauthentic society"—to use Amitai Etzioni's term.[52]

Gorbachev and the reformers are well aware that there remains widespread skepticism and fear that the extensive legislative program of *perestroyka*, which devolves new rights to both individuals and social groups, will remain "just another campaign." For example, numerous Soviet sources confirm that prospective or existing members of the new urban and rural cooperatives are unwilling either to begin new ventures or to expand existing ones due to a pervasive fear that they will suffer the same fate as the "NEPmen" of the 1920's, who "found themselves a long way from home" after the anti-cooperative campaign of the first Five-Year Plan.[53] The rehabilitation policy is designed in part to demonstrate graphically to Soviet citizens that the powers of the state will be confined by the law and that legally-sanctioned social initiative, whether in the economy, politics, or culture, will not bring arbitrary bureaucratic interference.

Moreover, many of the beneficiaries of "posthumous justice" have been individuals whose ideas provide important ideological support for *perestroyka*. In July 1987, it was announced that the Military Collegium of the USSR Supreme Court had rehabilitated, "due to the absence of an event or crime," the economists and scientists convicted of leading the fictitious Labor Peasant Party.[54] Prominent among those rehabilitated was Aleksandr Chayanov, a specialist on rural cooperatives and the small family farm. One of Chayanov's early works influenced Lenin's article "On Cooperation," which outlined the New Economic Policy. Opposed to Stalin's "all-out collectivization *(sploshnaya kollektivizatsiya),*" Chayanov and others were arrested in the early 1930's on charges of "wrecking" the Soviet system. Since the rehabilitation of Chayanov and his colleagues, appeals have appeared in the press to study their works for answers to the "needs and concerns of today." In particular, the works contain evidence that supports Gorbachev's efforts to broaden the use of the "family contract" form of farming.[55]

The civic rehabilitation in February 1988 of Nikolay Bukharin and other defendants at the 1938 purge trial is of much broader significance. Bukharin's rehabilitation has placed his conciliatory rural program, as well as his advocacy of moderate cultural and political lines, in direct opposition not only to the Stalinist "revolution from above," which dramatically expanded the bureaucratic reach of the state, but also to the terror of the 1930's, which destroyed the party as an autonomous political institution. The resurrected image of Bukharin is seen as a powerful antidote to the prevailing "Stalinist" relationship between the Soviet party-state and society and to "bureaucratic centralism" in the party.[56]

RE-IMAGING OF THE PAST

The return to the ideas of Bukharin and Chayanov in Soviet political discourse is part of a broader re-imaging of Lenin and his New Economic Policy as a means of strengthening the ideological foundation for reforms that seek to loosen state controls over society and provide a measure of autonomy for individuals and enterprises alike. This reworking of conventional historical wisdom seeks to blunt the criticism by conservatives that the Gorbachevtsy are departing from the "principles of socialism" and undermining the foundations of the Soviet system.[57]

Gorbachev himself has publicly encouraged the depiction of the NEP as a model of reform, and justified his own turn to "radical" reform by comparing it to Lenin's decision to reject the coercive policies of War Communism and embrace the NEP. At the 27th Party Congress, Gorbachev invoked the *"prodnalog"* (tax-in-kind) of the NEP to describe elements of his agricultural policy, and in November 1987, he called Lenin's last writings on the NEP an "immense theoretical asset for the party," noting that they stressed the advancement of socialism through a consistent reduction of bureaucracy and the enlistment of the working masses "to a man" in running the state.[58] Party-history courses reportedly now focus on the lessons to be derived from the NEP for the contemporary period of reform.[59]

The selective invocation of Lenin's works by the reformers has not been limited to the leader's late writings. The reformers also seek ideological grounding for their efforts to recast the relationship between state and society in his earlier works, in particular the semi-anarchist utopian tract, *State and Revolution,* written immediately prior to the October Revolution. An assault on the traditional state as a bureaucratic "excrescence" on society, this study modeled the future proletarian society after Marx's description of the Paris Commune of 1871 in his *The Civil War in France.* Lenin approvingly quoted Marx's perception of the key features of the commune: a reduction of the pay of officials to the level of workmen's wages, the right to recall elected officials at any time, and the gradual "withering away" of the state through the participation of the people in popular assemblies. Historian Afanas'yev and others have argued that this Lenin tract is entirely relevant to Gorbachev's efforts to generate popular initiative and support for the system by protecting civil society from the bureaucracy's efforts to stifle economic innovation and exclude authentic political participation.[60]

There has also been of late a partial rehabilitation of Nikita Khrushchev as a symbol, and of his period as a model, of reform. After his ouster in 1964, Khrushchev slipped into historical obscurity, his policies condemned under the euphemism of "voluntarism." Under Gorbachev, the creative intelligentsia—particularly those who were students in the 1950's and 1960's—have led the way in reviving interest in the Khrushchev period. In recently published reminiscences, novels, and political commentaries, the period is remembered as a time of optimism, debate, and intellectual vigor that replaced the fear and conformity of the Stalin years. The Khrushchev period is valued by reforming intellectuals and politicians alike for its various efforts to dislodge entrenched bureaucracy, decentralize economic controls, and "democratize" the political process. As such, the period is portrayed as largely analogous to the cultural freedom and reforming atmosphere witnessed under Gorbachev.[61]

Although Khrushchev is still criticized for policy caprice and millenarianism, for allowing his own personality cult to form, and for erratic behavior toward intellectuals, his decision to launch the de-Stalinization campaign at the 20th Party Congress has been praised by Gorbachev as an act of personal courage aimed at liberating the country from the "negative aspects of socio-political life engendered by the Stalin personality cult," in particular, the Stalinist "command-bureaucratic" method of administration and the spiritual and material neglect of the people. Gorbachev has observed that Khrushchev's efforts failed in large part because they were not fully supported by the development of "democratization processes."[62]

The positive re-evaluation of Khrushchev has brought an intensified denigration of the Brezhnev period, which is now labeled the "period of stagnation." At the January 1987 plenum, which introduced Gorbachev's "democratization" program, the Soviet Union's loss of "momentum" and decline of economic growth was traced to the late 1970's and the failure of the leadership to enact timely political and economic reforms.[63] Two months later, Georgiy Smirnov "moved" the origins of the "braking mechanism" back to the October 1964 plenum that removed Khrushchev from office:

> The measures taken by the party leadership after the October 1964 plenum were directed against the democratization of the party and government apparatus that had been earlier implemented, although it had not been systematic and clear in purpose. For example, certain democratic principles that had been introduced into the party rules were altered.[64]

Smirnov's comments clearly suggest that the Central Committee moved against Khrushchev not simply to stabilize a nation disrupted by ill-conceived and rash policies—which was the official explanation—but also to protect political position and privilege. This indictment of virtually the entire party leadership is unprecedented, and underlines the desire of the reformers to reject most of the Brezhnev legacy in the domestic sphere. Through his approval of Khrushchev's political reforms, Smirnov also offers precedent and ideological grounding for the broadly similar proposals favored by Gorbachev, which under the rubric of "democratization" envisage the establishment of what one influential political analyst calls a "constitutional state" based on provisions that would limit the period an individual could hold a party or state position.[65] ...

HISTORIANS AND HISTORY

One of the anomalies of the current Soviet de-Stalinization campaign is that its primary exponents have been largely journalists, writers of fiction, economists, and others within the creative and technical intelligentsia, and not professional historians. The "restructuring" of historical science, particularly that relating to party history, has, in the words of Academician Aleksandr Samsonov, "barely begun":

> Criticism is heard of historians that they, in contrast to writers, have shown themselves unequal to the needs of the time; that writers have already published several works on the complex prewar decades, on the life of the country in the era of the personality cult. [But] there has yet to appear serious works by historians on the same periods. It is a just criticism. ...[81]

Several factors explain the lack of "renewal" in Soviet historiography. Of obvious importance is the nature of the historian's craft. It requires considerably more time to research and write a history than to produce a publishable article for the mass media.[82] Furthermore, unlike writers of fiction, historians apparently have few innovative manuscripts "in the drawer" ready for publication.[83] The historians also work in an environment that is removed from the pressures of "full cost accounting," a condition that has induced many editors and directors to publish deliberately provocative historical works in order to strengthen the financial position of their journals, theaters, and newspapers.

Also important is the fact that conservative scholars and administrators of the Brezhnev period remain in control of most of the institutes of history and the related scholarly journals. The absence of creativity and of freedom of research is largely due to the continuing influence of this group, which presided over the imposition of harsh controls after Khrushchev's ouster and fears loss of authority and professional standing.

An example of such a conservative figure is the chief editor of the Central Committee journal *Voprosy Istorii KPSS* (Questions of CPSU History), Vasiliy Kas'yanenko, who is the leading "official" authority on the Stalin years. Similarly, Fedor Vaganov, chief of the Main Archives Administration, is the author of a strong attack on Bukharin.[84] He has been accused of opposing "restructuring" in Soviet history and the use of new documentary evidence, and, implicitly, of impeding access to critical archival material.[85] Conservative historians have been openly accused of stopping the advance of learning for 20 years, and even of engaging in the wholesale falsification of history.[86] Not surprisingly, these historians resist publication of such criticisms, and consequently such views have surfaced largely in "restructured" journals such as *Kommunist* and *Nauka i Zhizn'* and in "liberal" newspapers such as *Moscow News* and *Sovetskaya Kul'tura.*

Yuriy Afanas'yev has been particularly outspoken about this group. In a 1987 article, he stated:

> There were and are specific people who directly "created" the stagnation. They must at least be made known, especially because their way of thinking and means of operating are working in the same direction even today. The campaign to curb scientific explorations in history in the early 1970's was headed by S. P. Trapeznikov [the head of the Central Committee Science and Education Institutions Department], who enjoyed unlimited freedom of action in managing our science and placed in all positions people who were dependent on him, and, on this basis were bound together by "business" ties.[87]

The sources of inertia, however, extend even beyond the control of journals, institutes, and archives by the conservatives. Even when provided a forum for their views, most historians have remained silent. According to reformers both within and outside the historical sciences, it is "tremendously difficult" to find scholars willing to produce even newspaper articles on sensitive issues of Soviet history.[88]

Three factors may explain this silence in the face of opportunities to express one's views. First, many Soviet historians today may simply not be competent to offer complex historical re-evaluations. According to one observer, the aridity of the social sciences under Brezhnev led to a mass exodus of the most promising history students from the profession, leaving it seriously depleted of talented researchers.[89] It is argued that those who remained failed to develop appropriate analytical skills and are unable to go beyond "commenting on the decisions that had been made by political authorities."[90]

Second, most historians have been conditioned to wait for signals from "above" before attempting to venture into risky areas of research.[91] In this context, the signals from Gorbachev remain somewhat contradictory as to how Soviet history, particularly that relating to the Stalin era, should be treated. A clear party "line" on the matter has yet to appear: existing texts have been withdrawn from use, and a competition is being held for contributions to a new party history, which will serve as a guide for historians to the permissible limits of research and debate.[92] But until the new text appears, most historians—lacking authoritative explanations and directives to guide them—prefer to sit on the fence.[93]

Third, many historians submit to self-censorship despite the circumstances of relaxation under Gorbachev due to memories of widespread reprisals suffered in the past by innovative historians. According to Yuriy Afanas'yev:

> everyone has known that theory and new knowledge in historical science are encouraged only provided that they do not diverge from "generally accepted" opinions. Departure from the "norm" has threatened a historian with many consequences—up to and including removal from the community of scholars. I will cite

only the fates of the historians V. V. Adamov, E. N. Burdzhalov, and P. V. Volobuyev—one could continue on through the alphabet.[94]

The prominence now given such liberal and long-eclipsed historians as Volobuyev is in part designed to reassure cautious historians that "socialist pluralism" is the order of the day and that political criteria will no longer serve as the arbiter of professional opinions.[95] Yet, historians are acutely aware of the unstable political situation under Gorbachev, and remain uncertain as to how long the campaign for *glasnost'* in history will survive. It, therefore, takes considerable personal courage to challenge previously accepted versions of Soviet history or to take on the power structure in the institutes.[96] ...

...

EXTERNAL FACTORS

Changing Soviet views of the international environment are also contributing to the broadening of the limits of what is permissible in the examination of history. International events and the world view of Soviet politicians have long influenced their willingness and ability to allow historians to conduct a more objective examination of the past, particularly the Stalin era. For example, Khrushchev maintained that he withheld the rehabilitation of the purge trial victims of the 1930's because the "representatives of the fraternal communist parties [had] testified ... to the justness of the sentences" and he did not want to "discredit" them.[124] His de-Stalinization campaign was also dealt a set-back by the upheavals in Eastern Europe that followed his "secret speech" of 1956, and later, was cut short at least in part by the domestic and international uproar created by the Cuban missile crisis.[125]

Soviet perceptions of Western "ideological propaganda" and "bourgeois falsification" of Soviet history have also influenced historical inquiry. The fall of Khrushchev brought to power individuals who were deeply concerned with the restoration of political stability and ideological orthodoxy. The banning of anti-Stalin works in belles-lettres and the social sciences was justified in part as a measure to deprive the West of a potent propaganda weapon that could be used to undermine the legitimacy of the Soviet system, of its Eastern Europe satellites, and of Soviet leadership of the international communist movement. ...

...

The return of cold war rhetoric under Ronald Reagan strengthened for a time the argument of conservative politicians and academics that orthodoxy in historiography and the social sciences in general should remain in place. For example, in March 1985, an extraordinary plenum of the party's Central Committee directed the History Department of the Academy of Sciences to increase its "ideological work" in response to "anti-Marxist conceptions of the global historical process" that were being promoted by the capitalist West. According to Academician Sergey Tikhvinskiy:

in conditions where imperialism, in its offensive against socialism, is trying to distort the essence of the processes at work in socialist society and to falsify human history, it is the duty of Soviet historians to give a timely and effective rebuff to anti-Marxist conceptions.[130]

"Counter-propaganda groups" formed by the department's institutes were authorized to produce publications that addressed the ideological concerns of the Central Committee.

Matters have changed dramatically under Gorbachev. The General Secretary's stress on *glasnost'* has clearly strengthened the arguments of intellectuals like Nekrich and Medvedev that refusal to engage in open examination of the Stalinist past only serves to "delight our enemies." In *Let History Judge* (pp. xxviii–xxix), Medvedev stated:

> The longer we keep silent or vacillate, the more successfully will bourgeois propagandists use the cult of personality for their own ends ... only resolute and honest communist self-criticism and resolute and honest correction of Stalinist perversions will cut the ground from under bourgeois propagandists, who have long used these perversions in their fight against socialism. By identifying the Stalinist regime with socialism in general, they have long tried (and not without success) to represent socialism as a system in which there is no respect for law, where the rights and freedoms of the individual are violated and suppressed. Silence and vacillation about Stalin's many crimes repel rather than attract friends abroad.

At a February 1987 meeting with heads of the media and propaganda organs convened at Central Committee headquarters, Gorbachev encountered the argument that critical analysis of Soviet history was like "indulging in a striptease for the whole world to see. ..." Disagreeing, the General Secretary called for the removal of "blank spots" in Soviet history.[131] His renewed intervention at the end of 1987 further tilted the balance in favor of the liberals. Echoing the reforming intellectuals, Gorbachev railed against the "many" officials who still attempt to frighten authors of critical analyses by:

> warning of the possible reaction on the part of the West. The West, they claim, is eager to hear our self-criticism in order to turn it against us, to discredit the socialist way of life. ... I myself do not fear criticism. A critical review of our own experience is a sign of strength, not weakness. Such an approach accords with the principles of socialist ideology.[132]

...

PROSPECTS

The reformers are aware of the corrosive effects that historical myth and historical silence have in an educated and socially complex society.[178] They seem convinced that a more truthful examination of the past will generate ideological renewal and restore the deeply eroded moral authority of the party among alienated or apathetic segments of the population. So, one can expect "historical *glasnost'*" to yield still other unorthodox treatments of the Soviet past, particularly as Gorbachev seeks to accelerate the process of political reform.

But historical *glasnost'* is a fragile blossom, and it is unclear whether the professional historians and their counterparts in the mass media and belles-lettres will ultimately be able to join the "vast wandering enterprise" of objective historical analysis. For one thing, it remains an open question whether or not radical assaults on the historical image of the party will increase the party's authority or mobilize support for *perestroyka*. Moreover, innovative historical analysis has largely been confined to belles-lettres and the mass media. The struggle of liberal historians for professional autonomy is just beginning. Perhaps most important, the charged atmosphere of reform is not conducive to objective historical analysis. Doors to previously taboo topics have been opened, but others remain closed, being viewed as counterproductive to the reform program. Many within the reform movement value historical *glasnost'* for its instrumental aspects and do not view it as an end in itself.

At the same time, it would be unwise to underestimate the forces unleashed by the reformers. If the Gorbachevtsy remain in power, there is reason to expect the emergence, within the increasingly elastic limits of "socialist principles," of a stable culture of debate that ensures competing approaches to controversial topics in Soviet history. Such a development would be convincing evidence that the reformers, perhaps beyond their intentions, have succeeded to some degree in reforming the relationship between state and society in the Soviet Union.

NOTES

ABOUT THE AUTHOR: **Thomas Sherlock** wrote this paper while studying at the Harriman Institute of Columbia University.

1. On the topic of history and politics under Gorbachev, see Stephen Wheatcroft, "Unleashing the Energy of History, Mentioning the Unmentionable, and Reconstructing Soviet Historical Awareness: Moscow 1987," *Australian Slavonic and East European Studies* (Parkville, Victoria), Vol. 1, 1987, pp. 85–132; R. W. Davies, "Soviet History in the Gorbachev Revolution: The First Phase," *The Socialist Register 1988*, London, Merlin Press, 1988, pp. 37–38; and Mark von Hagen, "History and Politics Under Gorbachev: The Struggle for Professional Autonomy," *Harriman Institute Forum* (New York), forthcoming.

2. The sentence read: "Displaying Bolshevik principledness and self-criticism, relying on the masses' support, the party performed a large amount of work to eliminate the consequences of the personality cult and deviations from Lenin's norms of party and state leadership and to rectify errors of a subjectivist and voluntarist nature." From the "CPSU Program New Edition Adopted by the 27th CPSU Congress," as printed in *Pravda* (Moscow), Mar. 7, 1986, and translated in Foreign Broadcast Information Service, *Daily Report: Soviet Union* (Washington, DC—hereafter, *FBIS-SOV*), Mar. 10, 1986, p. O/2.

3. Reproduced in M. Gorbachev, *Izbrannyye rechi i stat'i* (Selected Speeches and Articles), Vol. 3, Moscow, Politizdat, 1987, pp. 162–63.

4. *Kommunist* (Moscow), No. 14, September 1985, pp. 107–09, 112–13.

5. *The New York Times*, Dec. 19, 1985. According to this account, Yevtushenko's more intemperate remarks were censored from the published version of his speech.

6. *Pravda*, July 8, 1986. Already in January, the party newspaper had published a favorable review of a Yevtushenko poem, *FUKU!*, which condemned history's cruel rulers, who shed "seas of blood" in pursuit of their goals (ibid., Jan. 12, 1986—the poem had appeared in *Novyy Mir* [Moscow], No. 9, September 1985).

7. Hugh Heclo, *Modern Social Politics in Britain and Sweden*, New Haven, CT, Yale University Press, 1974, p. 305, cited in Timothy Colton, "Gorbachev and the Politics of System Renewal," in Seweryn Bialer and Michael Mandelbaum, Eds., *Gorbachev's Russia and American Foreign Policy*, Boulder, CO, Westview, 1988, p. 156. The émigré historian Alexandr Nekrich describes the loss of Soviet collective memory and its replacement with "artificial memory" in his memoir, *Otreshis' ot strakha* (Renounce Fear), London, Overseas Publication Interchange, 1979, pp. 293–94. For Gorbachev's views on the importance of "understanding our history" in order to solve current problems, see his speeches of January 8 and February 18, 1988, in *Pravda*, Jan. 15 and Feb. 19, 1988.

8. This opposition was stressed by Anatoliy Butenko in an interview with *Moskovskaya Pravda* (Moscow), May 7, 1987.

10. J. H. Plumb, *The Death of the Past*, London, Macmillan, 1969, p. 40.

On the issue of archaic norms and institutions dating from the Stalin period, see Gail Lapidus, "State and Society: Toward the Emergence of Civil Society in Russia," in Seweryn Bialer, Ed., *Politics, Society, and Nationality Inside Gorbachev's Russia*, Boulder, CO, Westview, [1989].

11. For Gorbachev's comments on the easing on censorship, see M. Gorbachev, *Perestroika: New Thinking for Our Country and the World* (hereafter, *Perestroika*), New York, Harper and Row, 1987, p. 81.

12. Ibid.

13. This point is also made by Sheila Fitzpatrick in "Sources of Change in Soviet History: State, Society, and the Entrepreneurial Tradition," in Bialer and Mandelbaum, op. cit., p. 55.

The Leningrad writer Daniil Granin stresses the "civic responsibility" of the intelligentsia and the need for a "great cleansing" of Soviet society. See *Literaturnaya Gazeta*, Feb. 12, 1986. See also, A. Volodin, "On the Traditions of Our Country's Intelligentsia," *Pravda*, Mar. 10, 1987.

18. As published in *Druzhba Narodov* (Moscow), No. 6, 1987, pp. 80–81.

The fictional and nonfictional portrayals of Stalin's brutality and criminality are voluminous. One of the most dramatic is the article by historian Vasiliy Polikarpov containg excerpts of letters written to Stalin by the Old Bolshevik Fedor Raskol'nikov in 1938 and 1939, when the latter was in Paris. Stalin's list of crimes and victims are described as "endless," the dictator is termed a "traitor" to socialism who forced his followers to "wade ... through pools of blood. ..." *Ogonek* (Moscow), No. 26, June 1987.

19. From the text, as published in Mikhail Gorbachev, *October and Perestroika: The Revolution Continues* (hereafter, *October and Perestroika*), Moscow, Novosti, 1987, p. 26.

25. Loc. cit.

26. *Khrushchev Remembers*, tr. and ed. by Strobe Talbott, Boston, Little, Brown, 1970, p. 74.

27. Abel Aganbegyan, *The Economic Challenge of Perestroika*, Bloomington, IN, Indiana University Press, 1988, pp. 50–53 (pagination from galleys).

28. Gorbachev, *October and Perestroika*, pp. 24–25.

29. For the "standard" view of the NEP under Brezhnev, see Yu. Polyakov, V. P. Dmitrenko, and N. V. Shcherban, *Novaya ekonomicheskaya politika: Razrabotka i osushchestvleniye* (The New Economic Policy: Its Elaboration and Implementation), Moscow, Politizdat, 1982.

30. "Advances and Debts," *Novyy Mir*, No. 6, 1987, p. 144.

31. Shmelev's lecture was summarized in *The Christian Science Monitor* (Boston), June 16, 1987. In addition, see G. Shmelev (also an economist), "Do Not Dare to Command," in *Oktyabr'* (Moscow), No. 2, 1988, pp. 3–25.

Moshe Lewin concludes that at least 2 million families were deported, while Robert Conquest speculates that the number may have reached 3 million households. See Lewin, *Russian Peasants and Soviet Power, A Study of Collectivization*, New York, Norton, 1975, pp. 507–08; and Conquest, *Harvest of Sorrow: Soviet Collectivization and the Terror Famine*, New York, Oxford University Press, 1986, p. 126.

32. The famine in the countryside is examined by sociologist Vladimir Shubkin in *Znamya* (Moscow), No. 4, 1987, p. 183, and by the historian Yegor Bestuzhev-Lada in *Nedelya* (Moscow), No. 15, Apr. 11–17, 1988. Economist Yevgeniy Ambartsumov suggests that forced collectivization resulted in 10 million deaths (*Moscow News*, No. 25, June 26–July 3, 1988).

33. *Literaturnaya Gazeta*, Apr. 8, 1987. Tikhonov's argument has since been taken up in print by others. See, for example, G. Shmelev, loc. cit.; Vasiliy Selyunin, "Sources," in *Novyy Mir*, No. 5, 1988, p. 167; and writer Sergey Antonov, in *Moscow News*, No. 51, Dec. 27–Jan. 3, 1988.

The writer Vasil Bykov, in an interview in *Literaturnaya Gazeta* of May 14, 1986, recounts how peasants were branded as kulaks in order to satisfy the directives of the political authorities. De-kulakization was also driven by personal animosity and the desire to acquire the jobs and property of others (see Bestuzhev-Lada, loc. cit.).

36. Abuladze's film *Pokayaniye* (Repentance) was released in late 1986; Grossman's novel *Zhizn' i sud'ba* (Life and Fate) appeared in *Oktyabr'*, Nos. 1–3, 1988; and Granin's novel, *Zubr* (Aurochs), in *Novyy Mir*, Nos. 1 and 2, 1987.

37. It was published in *Teatr* (Moscow), No. 6, 1986.

38. *Znamya*, No. 1, 1988, pp. 21, 22, and 49.

39. See the interview with Butenko in *Borba* (Belgrade), Sept. 1987, trans. in *FBIS-SOV*, Oct. 23, 1987, p. 46. Gel'man's comments appear in *Sovetskaya Kul'tura* (Moscow), Apr. 9, 1988.

40. *Don*, No. 1, 1987, pp. 18–21. Writer Anatoliy Strelyanyy argues that the rural procurement system founded in the 1930's continues to impoverish the countryside and serves no social purpose beyond the satisfaction of the power interests of local party officials. See "Rural Everyday Life," *Novyy Mir*, No. 12, 1986, pp. 231–41.

41. From the text of the November speech as published in *October and Perestroika*, pp. 24–26; also *Perestroika*, pp. 45–46, 112.

42. *Pravda*, Oct. 2 1986.

43. Moscow Tass, Jan. 27, 1987, in *FBIS-SOV*, Jan. 28, 1987, pp. R/5, R/22, R/24, and R/25.

44. For a critique of *Economic Problems of Socialism in the USSR*, see Boris Bolotin in *Moscow News*, No. 34, Aug. 30–Sept. 6, 1987. The author argues that the ideological heritage of Stalinism, particularly the refusal to accept the market in conditions of socialism, has left a deep impression on the thinking of those who are now over 50, among whom are the

vast majority of mid- and higher-level administrators and scholars. These individuals form the core of the group that views Gorbachev's economic reforms as a "retreat from the principles of socialism."

For a psychological portrait of a high party official who resists Gorbachev's reforms, see Fedor Burlatskiy, "Polemical Dialogue on Restructuring," *Literaturnaya Gazeta*, Oct. 1, 1986, trans. in *FBIS-SOV,* Oct. 8, 1986, pp. R/6–19. Also see the results of a poll that revealed that 79 percent of party secretaries in the polled region were unable to comprehend the difference between old and new methods of economic management, *Pravda,* June 17, 1987.

45. *Moscow News,* No. 29, July 26–Aug. 3, 1987.

46. *October and Perestroika,* p. 27.

51. Popular support for Stalin and Stalinism is not confined to the Stalin generations but is also present among younger members of Soviet society whose idealization of the period often represents an indirect protest against moral malaise and corruption. It is also rooted in the negative reaction of many to the emergence under *glasnost'* of social "permissiveness" and elements of disorder, hippies and punkers, demonstrations on Red Square, and "radical" unofficial groups calling for a multi-party system. See Vladimir Bykov in *Moscow News,* No. 48, Nov. 29, 1987; and Pavel Volobuyev in ibid., No. 51, Dec. 27–Jan. 3, 1988.

52. According to Etzioni, a "relationship, institution, or society is inauthentic if it provides the appearance of responsiveness while the underlying condition is alienating." See Etzioni, *The Active Society: A Theory of Societal and Political Processes,* New York, Free Press, 1968, pp. 619–22, 633–48. The disparity between "words and deeds" that concerns the reformers closely approximates such a state of affairs.

53. Interview with historian Vladimir Dmitrenko in *Izvestiya* (Moscow), Oct. 3, 1987, trans. in *Current Digest of the Soviet Press* (Columbus, OH—hereafter, *CDSP*), Nov. 11, 1987, p. 4.

54. Lev Voskresenskiy, "Posthumous Justice," *Moscow News,* No. 33, Aug. 16, 1987.

55. Ibid.

56. The rehabilitation of Martemyan Ryutin, author of the well-known anti-Stalin platform of 1932 (which called for the dictator's removal), has been employed to underline the expanded limits of intra-party debate. The Politburo's special commission on the purges referred to the document as falling within the acceptable limits of intra-party discussion. See *Pravda,* Aug. 5, 1988.

Official approval of Bukharin's views was reflected in the re-publication of his 1929 speech, "The Political Testament of Lenin," in *Kommunist,* No. 2, January 1988, pp. 93–102.

57. Gorbachev has felt compelled to return to this criticism after he initially addressed it at the 27th Party Congress. See, for example, his speech to the June 1987 Central Committee plenum in *Pravda,* June 26, 1987, trans. in *FBIS-SOV,* June 26, 1987, p. R/ 8; his speech before media, cultural, and ideological workers on January 8, 1988, in *Pravda,* Jan. 13, 1988; and his speech before the CC plenum of February 18, 1988, in ibid., Feb. 19, 1988.

58. *Pravda,* Feb. 26, 1986, and *October and Perestroika,* p. 16.

59. A. Shirokov, "Some Questions of Method in Teaching CPSU History," *Vestnik Moskovskogo Universiteta* (Moscow), No. 1, 1987, pp. 82–89, espec. p. 89.

60. Afanas'yev in *Sovetskaya Kul'tura,* Mar. 21, 1987; E. Kuzmin in *Pravda,* Aug. 8, 1987; B. Lazarev, "The Apparatus of State Administration: Lenin's Ideas and the Contemporary Scene," *Kommunist,* No. 8, May 1987; and V. Gavrilov, *Lenin's "The State and Revolution"—The Main Tasks of the Proletarian Revolution,* Moscow, Progress Publishers, 1988.

In arguing for reform of the political system at the 19th Party Conference in June 1988, Gorbachev himself invoked the model of the Paris Commune. He recalled Lenin's "well-known" definition of the socialist state as one "'which is not a state in the proper sense of the word'" or even a "'half-state,'" *Moscow News*, No. 27, July 10–17, 1988, Supplement. The General Secretary was quoting from Lenin's "The Tasks of the Proletariat in Our Revolution," first published as a pamphlet in September 1917, and included in V. I. Lenin, *Collected Works*, Vol. 24, Moscow, Progress Publishers, 4th printing, 1980, pp. 68, 85.

61. For one of the first positive references under Gorbachev to the Khrushchev period as a time of cultural and spiritual renewal, see the article by the poet Bulat Okudzhava in *Izvestiya*, Mar. 14, 1986. Khrushchev's name was not, however, mentioned. See also Alexandr Bovin in *New Times* (Moscow), No. 5, 1987; and Igor Dedkov, "A Discourse About One Generation," in *Moscow News*, No. 16, Apr. 19, 1987.

Of considerable interest are the novels of Vladimir Makanin, which describe the transitory hopes and enthusiasm of the generation socialized under Khrushchev's reforms: *Odin i odna* (A Lone Man and Woman) in *Oktyabr*, No. 3, 1987, and *Ostavshiye* (Those Left Behind) in *Znamya*, No. 9, 1987. The memoirs of Aleksey Adzhubey, Khrushchev's son-in-law and editor of *Izvestiya* under Khrushchev, were to be published in *Znamya* in the summer of 1988 under the title of "Remembering Khrushchev and His Times." An excerpt appeared in *Moscow News*, No. 20, May 15, 1988.

62. *Perestroika*, p. 43; and *October and Perestroika*, pp. 34–35.

Others continue to criticize Khrushchev's lack of concern for "theory and political strategy," his willingness to allow his own cult to be created, and his erratic behavior toward the intellectuals. The Khrushchev period is portrayed by liberal intellectuals as a cautionary tale, demonstrating not only the pitfalls of poorly planned and poorly executed reforms, but also the weakness of change if progressive forces in society do not apply pressure on the leadership and help shape the process of reform. See Burlatskiy in *Literaturnaya Gazeta*, Feb. 24, 1988; V. Z. Drobyzhev in *Argumenty i Fakty* (Moscow), No. 12, 1988, trans. in *FBIS-SOV*, Mar. 23, 1988, pp. 69–72; and Yuriy Levada and Viktor Sheynis in *Moscow News*, No. 18, May 1, 1988.

63. M. Gorbachev speech to CPSU CC Plenum, as issued by Moscow TASS, Jan. 27, 1987, in *FBIS-SOV*, Jan. 28, 1987, p. R/8.

64. G. Smirnov, "The Revolutionary Essence of Renewal," *Pravda*, Mar. 1, 1987. Smirnov was referring to Article 25 of the new Party Rules introduced at the 22nd Party Congress in 1961, which stipulated that all party committees, from the Central Committee to that of the primary party organization, be extensively renewed at each election. The figure for the Presidium (Politburo) and Central Committee was to be 25 percent. After Khrushchev's ouster, at the 23rd Party Congress in 1966, the institutional changes embodied in Article 25 were repealed and replaced with an informal commitment to virtual lifetime tenure of office—the policy of "stability of cadres." See Leonard Schapiro, *The Communist Party of the Soviet Union*, New York, Vintage, 1971, pp. 597–99.

65. See interview with Aleksandr Bovin in RFE-RL, *Radio Liberty Research*, RL 455/87, Nov. 11, 1987. In the resolutions adopted by the 19th CPSU Conference, a uniform five-year term of office was adopted for all elective party bodies from the CPSU Central Committee down to the district party committees. Limits on the number of terms in elective posts were placed on *members of bureaus and secretaries of party committees* (apparently not on all members of committees), including members of the CC Politburo and the party general secretary. No more than two consecutive terms are to be allowed. *Pravda*, July 5, 1988.

81. *Nauka i Zhizn',* No. 6, 1987, p. 51. Also see Aleksandr Samsonov's comments in the round table discussion in *Kommunist,* No. 12, August 1987, p. 76; and Yuriy Afanas'yev's lecture as recorded in *Nauka i Zhizn',* No. 9, 1987, pp. 56–60.

82. Yu. Polyakov in the round table discussion in *Kommunist,* No. 12, August 1987, p. 74.

83. Samsonov in ibid., p. 76.

84. *Sovetskaya Kul'tura,* Mar. 21, 1987, trans. in *CDSP,* Apr. 22, 1987, p. 4. For more on Trapeznikov, see historian Petr Rodionov in ibid., June 14, 1988; also, the numerous references in Nekrich, *Otreshis' ot strakha;* and Andrey Sakharov, *Progress, Coexistence, and Intellectual Freedom,* New York, Norton, 1968, pp. 56–67.

85. *Pravyy uklon v VKP (b) i yego razgrom* (The Right Deviation in the RKP[b] and Its Defeat), 2nd ed., Moscow, Politizdat, 1977.

86. Genrikh Volkov in *Sovetskaya Kul'tura,* July 4, 1987, trans. in *FBIS-SOV,* 1987, p. R/15. For the conservatives' opposition to the use of new documentary evidence to reassess the past, see the letter of four party historians in *Moscow News,* No. 19, May 10, 1987. An extended treatment of this letter and of Yuriy Afanas'yev's response may be found in Wheatcroft, loc. cit.

87. *Sovetskaya Kul'tura,* Mar. 21, 1987, trans. in *CDSP,* Apr. 22, 1987; and Afanas'yev in *Nauka i Zhizn',* No. 9, 1987, p. 59.

88. *Izvestiya* editor Ivan Laptev's speech to a Journalists' Union plenum, published in *Sovetskaya Kul'tura,* June 20, 1987, trans. in *FBIS-SOV,* June 30, 1987, p. R/28.

89. Historian Yu. Polyakov in *Kommunist,* No. 12, August 1987, p. 74.

90. Historian V. Z. Drobyzhev in ibid., p. 77.

91. Historian Kozlov in *Voprosy Istorii KPSS,* No. 5, 1987, pp. 118–22; see also John Keep, Ed., *Contemporary History in the Soviet Mirror,* New York, Praeger, 1964, pp. 21–23.

92. In conversations with the author in August 1987, Soviet university students and teachers reported that the existing one-volume party history and most of the multivolume party history supervised by P. Pospelov had been withdrawn from use in Soviet schools. Only the second part of Pospelov's *Istoriya Kommunisticheskoy Partii Sovetskogo Soyuza* (History of the Communist Party of the Soviet Union—Moscow, Politizdat, 1980) remained in circulation. It covers the period 1945–59.

93. See historian Stanislav Tyutyukin in *Izvestiya,* May 3, 1987.

94. *Sovetskaya Kultura,* Mar. 21, 1987, trans. in *CDSP,* Apr. 22, 1987; also see Samsonov in *Nauka i Zhizn',* No. 6, 1987, p. 51.

Volobuyev was attacked and censured in 1972 for his views, particularly on the nature of the February 1917 revolution, and was later removed from his post as director of the Institute of USSR History. For one of the attacks on Volobuyev, see P. A. Golub, V. Ya. Laverychev, and P. N. Sobolev, "On the book 'The Russian Proletariat: Profile, Struggle, Hegemony'," *Voprosy Istorii KPSS,* No. 9, 1972, pp. 120–32. E. Burdzhalov suffered a similar fate under Khrushchev for his departure from the "norm." See Nancy W. Heer, *Politics and History in the Soviet Union* (Cambridge, MA: MIT Press, 1971), pp. 87–88, 91–93, 195–97, and 200–01.

95. Volobuyev has figured prominently in news conferences organized by the government and has himself become outspoken in condemning Trapeznikov and his surviving clients. This is noted by Afanas'yev in *Sovetskaya Kul'tura,* Mar. 21, 1987, trans. in *CDSP,* Apr. 22, 1987.

96. See, for example, comments of Samsonov in *Nauka i Zhizn',* No. 6, 1987, p. 51. As if to confirm these fears, *Moscow News,* No. 19, May 10, 1987, published a letter from four historians criticizing Afanas'yev's views and pointedly recalling Volobuyev's fate.

124. *Khrushchev Remembers*, p. 353.

125. See Heer, op. cit., Chap 3; Michel Tatu, *Power in the Kremlin*, New York, Viking, 1970, p. 249; Carl Linden, *Khrushchev and the Soviet Leadership, 1957–1964*, Baltimore, Johns Hopkins University Press, 1966, pp. 147, 158, 180; Roy Medvedev, *On Soviet Dissent, Interviews with Piero Ostellino*, New York, Columbia University Press, 1980, p. 57; and Keep, op. cit., pp. 25, 34.

130. *Voprosy Istorii*, No. 7, 1985, pp. 3, 10, as noted and translated by John Keep, *Moscow's Problems of History: A Select Critical Bibliography of the Soviet Journal "Voprosy Istorii,"* Ottawa, Carleton University, 1986, p. 6.

131. See Yegor Yakovlev's report in *Moscow News*, No. 8, Feb. 22, 1987, p. 8. Gorbachev's speech was printed in *Pravda*, Feb. 15, 1987.

132. Gorbachev, *Perestroika*, p. 80.

178. Soviet surveys have revealed the weak attraction of Marxist-Leninist ideology for much of the population, particularly the young. See *Sotsiologicheskiye issledovaniya* (Moscow), No. 4, 1987; and *Sobesednik* (Moscow), No. 39, 1987. It is not accidental, then, that much of the anti-Stalinist literature has appeared in publications such as *Yunost'* and *Sobesednik*, which are aimed at Soviet youth.

18 *Advances and Debts*

NIKOLAI SHMELEV

The state of the economy satisfies no one. Its two central defects, its built-in defects, so to speak—a producer's monopoly in conditions of universal shortages and enterprises' lack of interest in scientific and technical progress—are doubtless clear to everyone. But it is equally clear that no one is prepared to claim that he has a workable prescription for ridding us of those defects in practice rather than in theory. We all have more questions than answers, and it will take a lot more argument and discussion before we can grope our way to those sorely needed answers.

In terms of the hopes that they have aroused and in terms of their depth, frankness and boldness, the past two years' discussions of our problems have constituted a genuine rebirth of our public thought and national self-awareness. The 27th Party Congress marked the start of revolutionary changes in the life of our society. And the forthright and honest discussion of urgent economic questions is a most important manifestation of that process.

The causes for the economy's blocked arteries and reduced blood flow have already been made clear. The principle that administrative methods must be replaced by economic ones has been put forward. One can say, no doubt, that the road to common sense is open—at least on the ideological-theoretical plane. It is clear, however, that a reconstruction on that scale will not be accomplished with the wave of a hand. Our economy has been command-based rather than ruble-based for too long—so long, in fact, that we have all but forgotten that there was a time when the ruble and not the command (or, in other words, common sense and not arbitrary rule based on armchair speculation) held sway in economic matters.

I understand the kind of reproofs I'm inviting, but the question is too vitally important for me to soften my expressions or pass over some question or other in silence. If we do not admit that the rejection of Lenin's New Economic Policy imposed severe difficulties on the building of socialism in the USSR, we will doom ourselves once again—as in 1953 and 1965—to half-measures, and half-measures, as we know, are often worse than no measures at all. The "administered" economy that replaced the NEP was by its very nature unable to address questions of quality and efficiency and achieved its quantitative results in spite of the laws of economics, and therefore at great cost in material and human resources.

It is still widely believed in our country that the existing system of economic relations, including the property structure, is the very embodiment of Marxism-Leninism and is fully in keeping with the nature of socialism as a social system. It can be improved or modified slightly, so the story goes, but its basic principles are inviolable. But if one's scientific conclusions are guided by facts and not received truths, by an honest desire for revolutionary changes and not by a nostalgia for the recent past, then the question of our economic model's historic roots is by no means resolved.

It's a known fact that when the revolution emerged victorious in Russia, none of its acknowledged theoreticians or authoritative practitioners had (or indeed could have had) a more or less finished notion of the shape of socialism's future economic system. Lenin's prerevolutionary writings, like those of Marx and Engels, had nothing of practical value to say on the subject. There are grounds for believing, however, that Lenin gave the problem very serious thought. That was when he formulated his famous idea that socialism is Soviet power plus Prussian order on the railroad, plus American technology and corporate organization, plus American public education, etc. Initially, in other words, he proceeded from the notion that capitalism had already created all of the economic forms that socialism needed and that the latter had only to fill them with its new, socialist content.

The events that followed, however, produced the policy of "war communism," with its tough, exclusively administrative methods of organizing the economy. At some point Lenin himself, engrossed in that fatal struggle, came to believe that command methods were basic to a socialist economy. He was doubtless heavily influenced by the belief that Russia would not long be the sole socialist system and that the rich industrial West would pave the way to the new economic system—that revolution in the West would help resolve many of our most severe economic problems. As we know, that was not to be. And the NEP constituted a revolution in economic thinking: It was the first time that anyone had asked what a socialist economic system should be like in normal human conditions rather than in an emergency situation. Many people feel that the NEP was just a maneuver, no more than a temporary retreat. A retreat of sorts it was, of course, but its enduring significance lies elsewhere: It was the first effort at formulating the basic principles of a scientific and realistic approach to the tasks of socialist economic construction. It marked the transition to a system that would mobilize, rather than suppress, all of the working people's creative energies—the transition from "administrative socialism" to "economic-accountability socialism." Three practical ideas were central to Lenin's plan for putting the economy on a normal, healthy basis. First, commodity-money and market relations were to be developed to the utmost, a start was to be made on self-support and self-financing, and preponderant use was to be made of cost levers in managing economic processes. Second, economic-accountability trusts, voluntarily organized into associations (syndicates) were to be the economy's basic operating units. Third, cooperative property and cooperative relations were to be developed not merely in the countryside, but in urban areas as well—in industry, construction, retail trade and in what we now call consumer services.

It is a known fact that Lenin and those who implemented the new policy waged a fierce struggle against hypercentralization, bureaucratism and monopoly on the part of any departmental units. They viewed the trusts' and syndicates' economic and organizational independence as the principal guarantee against monopoly and as the principal instrument for gearing production to the market's constantly changing demands.

Even today, people still link the dismantling of Lenin's policy of "economic-accountability socialism" with the rise of fascism and the clear threat of war that emerged in the 1930s. That is not the case: The dismantling began in 1927–1928. Arbitrarily understated grain-procurement prices forced farmers not only to reduce grain sales to the state, but also to reduce grain production. It was then decided to ensure state grain procurements by forcible means. That marked the beginning of the return to an administered economy and to "war communism." It assumed its most graphic form in the collectivization of agriculture. But equally arbitrary relations were very quickly extended to the urban areas as well. Industry began receiving fantasy plan targets and, not surprisingly, did not fulfill its basic assignments in a single prewar five-year plan.

At the cost of extraordinary efforts the country survived the 1930s, the most terrible war in its history and the difficulties of the postwar restoration of the economy. One can understand those who feel that it is pointless today to compare that cost and those results. But one thing is obvious: It can be explained, though not justified, only in terms of extraordinary, inhuman conditions that no longer exist and have not existed since at least the mid-1950s. Meanwhile, the consequences of having renounced the NEP have not only not gone away, but have mounted; the economy's ills have not been cured but have merely been driven deeper below the surface.

The objective demands of modern scientific and technical progress and the new conditions and new tasks of economic competition with capitalism have still further laid bare the historic impracticability of this voluntarist system of managing the economy, a system that is sometimes merely the work of armchair theorists' invention. From the very outset this entire system was marked by economic romanticism, heavily larded with economic incompetence, and by incredible exaggeration of the effectiveness of the so-called administrative and organizational factor. Not only is that system not germane to socialism, as many still believe, but on the contrary, in normal circumstances it is contraindicated for it.

It is necessary to understand clearly that the reason for our difficulties is not merely the heavy burden of military expenditures and the very costly scope of the country's global responsibilities. It is the persistent and prolonged attempts to circumvent the objective laws of economic life and to suppress established, age-old work incentives that has ultimately led to results opposite from those being sought. Today we have a shortage-plagued economy that is actually out of balance in all categories, that is largely unmanageable and, to be completely honest, that is barely amenable to planning and still does not accept scientific and technical progress. Today's industry refuses about 80% of all new and approved technical solutions and inventions. The Soviet Union has one of the lowest labor-productivity levels of any industrial country, particularly in agriculture and construction, since during the years of stagnation the bulk of the working people has lost practically all interest in doing a solid, conscientious day's work.

Apathy, indifference, theft and lack of respect for honest work are rampant, as is aggressive envy toward those who enjoy high earnings—even in cases where the earnings are honestly come by. There are signs of an almost physical degradation of the Soviet people as a result of drunkenness and sloth. And finally, there is distrust of announced goals and intentions, and skepticism about the possibility of organizing economic and social life in a more sensible fashion.

It would obviously be unrealistic to assume that all of this can be quickly changed. It will take years and possibly even generations. In view of today's domestic and international realities, there is no going back to "administrative socialism," but there is also not time for marching in place or for half-measures. But the thing that worries us most of all today is precisely the lack of resolve in moving toward common sense. Appeals can't change the outlook of many executives who have mastered nothing but the technical skills of administration and the running of administrative apparatuses. By the same token, no amount of explanatory work will overcome people's mistrust of words and of the leadership's intention to carry the intended changes through to completion—will convince them that a half-step forward will not be followed once again by two steps back. Only actions will suffice.

In order to instill belief in the restoration of a sound economy, an early success is needed—palpable signs of a better life that are visible to all. The first need is to saturate the market with goods and to saturate it as soon as possible. This will not be easy, but it's possible—though only on the path of "economic-accountability socialism," on the path of developing the market itself.

Consistent economic accountability doesn't require substantial capital outlays. All it takes is boldness, resolve and consistency in freeing up the economy's internal forces. What impedes this? Above all, ideological overinsurance against the fear that we will lose the evil genie of capitalism from the bottle. The groundlessness of these fears is apparent to anyone who understands that management decisions of one kind or another have nothing at all to do with why the classes that make up a society arise, exist and then depart the historical arena.

When people cite the likely increase in uncontrolled phenomena, it is necessary to keep in mind the fact that attempts to establish 100% control over everything lead to such anarchy and lack of control that, by comparison, any normal anarchy seems the very mother of order. But progress and economic revival are what will distinguish this new environment and its uncontrolled elements from the old and accustomed kind that the people see and feel, but that many simply prefer not to notice.

The market must be saturated. And healthy, normal commodity-money relations in the agrarian sector offer the earliest pay-off in this regard.

For a long time now the rate of growth of farm output has amounted to less than 1% a year in our country, despite billions of rubles in capital investments by the state. One can't help wondering why we are willing to pay such a high price for so little. Can it really be out of fear of market relations? Or is it, in fact, to provide work to the very thin stratum of management personnel in the agrarian sector, and thereby justify their existence?

The decision on the new economic mechanism in agriculture is a half-measure. We need to go the rest of the way. First, the law should categorically forbid any outside orders to collective and state farms and any outside interference in their production arrangements. Second, purchase prices for all types of farm output must be brought into line in order to eliminate the unprofitability of many agricultural branches (animal husbandry and potato growing, for example). The wherewithal to do this can be obtained by reducing state food subsidies, which currently amount to more than 50 billion rubles a year. Third, we must resolve on a simple formula for relations between the state and agricultural collectives: hard-and-fast, progressive income-tax rates and absolutely no plan assignments in physical units (there isn't the least need for them). Collective and state farms must have the right to sell their output freely to state and cooperative organizations and to consumers. Fourth, personal auxiliary farming must be put fully on a par with collective farming in terms of both economic and social rights.

Balanced procurement prices are a precondition for contractual arrangements in farming. And the form that the contracts take—be it collective, brigade or family—should depend entirely on local conditions.

The Russian Non-Black-Earth Zone requires special measures. The degradation of the village is so advanced in that area that, in the context of the existing system of agrarian relations, there doubtless are no measures that will help. Only a gradual cure, through an individual approach to each district and each farm, can succeed. Family contracts and rental may be the only salvation for many farms that have long been "unworked." This is indeed a crucial moment for our agriculture. If people's hopes for a return to common sense are disappointed again today (for the nth time!), the apathy could become irreversible.

At one time, the elimination of the kulaks as a class was put forward as the motto. But what was abolished, in fact, was the peasant class. Today we still have the last generation of that class—a none-too-numerous generation of proprietors who love the land and peasant labor. If this generation does not pass its baton to the next generation, an irreparable loss could occur. Contradictory policies are a threat in this area. The most frantic leftist sentiment and bungling have come to the fore under the banner of fighting for social justice and against nonlabor earnings. How is one to justify, for example, the fact that a virtual campaign against personal auxiliary farming broke out again in the press? How is one to understand the signs that became evident in the summer of 1986 indicating that a new pogrom was brewing against personal orchards and hothouse operations and against personal livestock fattening? Wasn't the antistate character of that campaign immediately apparent? We must finally decide once and for all what is most important to us: to have an abundance of food or to eternally indulge an assortment of irresponsible loudmouths and proponents of equality in poverty. We need to call stupidity, incompetence and active Stalinism by their proper names. We need to do whatever it takes to ensure an ample supply of foodstuffs, for without that the idea of activating the human factor will go nowhere. We need to do these things even if it means losing our ideological virginity (which exists, incidentally, only in fairy-tale editorials in the newspapers). In that "virginal" state, there is more theft and self-enrichment than ever before. I'm talking about people who earn money without creating anything—without wanting or being able to create anything at all. Better to let the people flourish who want to and who can give society real products and services. After we solve the problem of meeting our own feed needs, there will be time enough to decide whether the large earnings of the most industrious and enterprising have resulted in threatening accumulations of capital.

Tax levers can and must ensure sensible control over yet another means of saturating the consumer-goods market: personal, family and cooperative production in the service sector and in small manufacturing. Expanding the personal and cooperative sector in urban areas will also serve to wake up our state-run light industry, trade and consumer services, which currently operate in a competition-free environment.

The equipment and materials stored "just in case" at state enterprises' warehouses—billions of rubles' worth!—would more than suffice, if sold on the open market, to meet the initial needs of small individual and cooperative enterprises. And to avert a rash of thefts and corruption, two things would be necessary: wholesale trade in producer goods and materials, and full legal and economic equality of the individual-cooperative sector (both as buyer and seller) with state enterprises and organizations. ...

In contemplating various kinds of medicine for our economy, we cannot fail to consider external economic ties. I have in mind such things as the obvious—but unfortunately, long-term and costly—tasks of restructuring our exports in favor of science-intensive output or cutting our average capital-construction times from their present 11–12 years to the prevailing world standard of one and a half or two years (our "protracted" construction methods keep us from attracting extensive foreign investment credits).

Isn't it time we thought about what to do with the substantial debt that's owed us by CMEA countries? It we gave them unrestricted access to our stable and limitless market, they would surely be willing to leave behind a part of the resulting earnings as payment on their debt. And the mass of competing foreign goods on our market would keep our producers on their toes.

Naturally, opening the Soviet market and creating a CMEA "common market" would not be possible without changing the ruble's present exchange rate and making it freely convertible within the framework of the CMEA. We would have to gradually abandon today's innumerable, industry-specific currency coefficients, shift to a single exchange rate for the ruble, and permit free circulation of national currencies within the CMEA. This is a measure whose time has long since come—an absolutely inevitable measure.

We have decided to permit jointly owned Soviet-foreign enterprises in our country. Perhaps we should also think about creating "free economic zones." Success in this area would both speed the saturation of our domestic market and improve our export position. But the conditions imposed by the new law—particularly the roughly 45% tax on foreign partners' income—is seen abroad as an unattractive feature.

Consistent economic accountability can't simply be created by decree. It requires specific conditions, many of which have yet to be created. The State Planning Committee needs to deal exclusively with its strategic concerns—planning production in physical units for some 250–300 types of strategic output, allocating investment capital by branch and republic, setting rates for taxes, depreciation, bank interest, land use, etc. A 1980s-style new economic policy would also have to deal with the industrial ministries, which are so outrageously numerous and have such bloated staffs that they often simply are forced to look for something to do and inadvertently make difficulties for the enterprises.

It's possible that we will be forced to return to Lenin's scheme for managing the economy: State Planning Committee—syndicate—trust (or "association" in today's terminology). The syndicates, for example, could readily play the role of today's ministries, with one highly valuable and absolutely fundamental distinction: The syndicate is a voluntary association of independent production entities. It is subordinate to them and is supported by the voluntary contributions. Its function is to deal with the questions that the individual enterprise is ill-suited to handle: sales, marketing, managing the common fund for bolstering weak production facilities, and encouraging scientific and technical progress in the branch.

But the toughest problem in organizing full economic accountability lies in bringing basic price relationships into line. The highly subjective and arbitrary pricing decisions that have accumulated since the late 1920s are a truly terrible legacy. Until we do away with them we will never have objective criteria for comparing costs and benefits—and therefore never have true economic accountability.

Virtually identical price proportionality exists today not only in capitalist countries but in many socialist countries as well. In order to quickly and reliably restore our economy to good health, we need to gradually bring our prices—first wholesale, then retail—into line with established world proportionality. Our prices for fuel and for mineral and agricultural raw materials are unduly high. They are unjustifiably low for food, housing and public services and unduly high for consumer durables. Soviet prices should correspond as closely as possible to world prices.

Bringing prices into line is an exceptionally delicate operation, particularly since it will require marked increases in food prices and in charges for housing, utilities and other communal services. But it's something that must be done, after persistent, methodical and—most important—honest and frank preparatory work.

At present the Soviet consumer gets more than 50 billion rubles in the form of subsidized prices for basic foods. But is there any reason why he couldn't get the same amount in the form of an increase in base pay? In the final analysis, why should a person underpay for meat and overpay for textiles and footwear, rather than buy them all at real prices?

Enterprises' and associations' economic situation should depend directly on profits, and until we bring wholesale prices into line and get rid of planned subsidies, profit will not be an accurate gauge of performance. In Lenin's thought, profit is a basic principle of economic accountability. A half century's experience with attempts to manage the economy by administrative means, using plan targets expressed in physical units, has only served to give this idea greater relevance.

The extreme suspicion where profit is concerned is a historical misunderstanding of sorts—the price to be paid for economic ignorance on the part of people who believe that once you have socialism there can be neither profits nor losses. A similar prejudice is the one against stock ownership. Why shouldn't people's and enterprises' available funds be enlisted in building new production facilities and expanding existing ones? Our well-known economists P. Bunich and V. Moskalenko put the question correctly when they said that the present shortfall in investment capital "could be made up in part if the enterprises in question would sell debt obligations to enterprises with surplus funds." One need only modify that to read: "to enterprises and individuals with surplus funds."

I am convinced that our economy today is in need of a financial reform at least as deep and extensive as the one in the early 1920s. Money, prices, taxes, credit, the budget, state loans, state indebtedness—these are all questions that we haven't even begun to discuss seriously. But the defects in our financial system are obvious, ranging from deferred consumer demand to the conversion of credit into what are basically nonrepayable loans (in the agricultural area alone, loans with no hope of repayment are already approaching the 100-billion-ruble mark).

External economic ties will assume increasing importance in the future. To make our products more competitive and to rationalize our imports, it's not enough to simply turn part of our import-export activities over to industrial ministries. We need a direct tie between external and domestic prices. Without such ties and without the possibility of exchanging rubles and foreign currencies (of buying, selling and loaning them) directly at our banks, we will hardly be able to truly interest our enterprises in external economic activities. While bringing wholesale prices into line in our country, we must concurrently establish a single, realistic exchange rate for the ruble and gradually make it as exchangeable as the dollar or the pound sterling. As long as the armchair thinkers pretend that no such problem exists, no transition to universal, thoroughgoing economic accountability will succeed.

The time is also ripe for deciding the fate of the transferrable ruble. This stillborn child has long since been reduced to a simple counting device. Now that its inventor is no longer among the living, there is simply no one who can say what there is about this artificial construct that makes it better than a real live ruble.

A word about quality. The resolution on State Product Acceptance is a step in the right direction. But it would be a serious mistake to think that it is some radical, long-sought method for sharply improving output quality. Its effect will be limited because quality control at the finished-output stage can only slightly influence the production process. American specialists estimate that a product's quality is determined 75% by the designing of the product and production technology, 20% by control of the production process proper, and just 5% by the final check on the finished product. In Japan, just 1% of quality is attributed to this final check.

Quality output is less a question of conscientious work than of production and management—areas for which top executives bear responsibility. The Americans believe that 15%–20% of all mistakes are attributable to those directly involved in doing the work; the rest are attributable to management.

To date, according to the most "patriotic" assessments, only 17%–18% of our manufacturing output is up to world standards, and according to the most cautious and pessimistic assessments, the figure is 7%–8%. We have set ourselves the goal of bringing 80%–90% of our output up to world standards by the end of the present five-year plan. Is it attainable? The roots of this problem are too deep, and we have treated it for too long as a matter of secondary importance.

Many theoreticians and many people working in industry agree that the guaranteed market, the "rationing" of output, the strict and, in fact, forcible binding of customers to suppliers—in other words, the monopoly of the producers—are the main reasons why most of our branches' output doesn't measure up. And this,

of course, is something that will be unaffected by the State Product Acceptance.
...

Of course the market is not the entire answer. Social conditions also play a role in quality. The fact that engineers and designers are paid less than unskilled workers does not bode well. And the low salaries of the majority of people in the decisive research area gives rise to mass apathy. Research has drawn third-rate higherschool graduates. We know what the problem is and how to fix it, but for some reason we can't make up our minds to discuss it fully and openly.

A radical economic reform naturally makes corresponding demands on those who carry it out. In simplified form, one can say that in the former conditions, management at all levels basically performed two primary tasks: They met plan assignments at all costs and ensured their employees a living wage—or at least a subsistence wage—as decreed from on high. And in most cases this wage had nothing to do with work results, as can be seen from a host of ills. Executives were answerable neither to their customers nor their employees, but exclusively to their administrative higher-ups. Personal relations meant practically everything. At the same time, the executive's incentive package was (and still is) quite special. To this day, even a large bonus ranks in something like 10th place in the executive's scheme of things. His professional success is measured in different coin—in awards, public offices and perquisites, including preferential access to consumer goods, travel abroad, etc.

In conditions of full economic accountability, the executive's job changes radically and becomes far more complex. He needs to sell his output as well as produce it, ship on time, meet contractual obligations, finance his own investment program, pursue technical progress and improvements, give priority attention to his employees' social needs, and personally take responsibility for the entire operation. In short, he must be a no-nonsense, competent, economically literate and enterprising person who scrupulously observes business ethics, keeps his word always and in all things, and understands people and their concerns. He must be a well-intentioned, independent and self-confident person who, by virtue of that self-confidence, is unafraid of democratic accountability, either to higher authority or (particularly important today) to his own employees and colleagues.

It will take time and a certain climate in the country to produce a person of that sort, but we must get started immediately—otherwise there will simply be no one to build "economic-accountability socialism" or to run it.

Who will disabuse our present management personnel—particularly the top executives—of their feudal mentality, their managerial-caste arrogance, and their belief in their own unassailability, in their "God-given right" to command and in the idea that they are above the law and above criticism? Whole generations of our executives were schooled in dangers of all sorts save one—dangers from below. Even today, interference in their affairs by the press, by voters or by their own coworkers is not normal for them, but a vexing and extraordinary event.

NOTES

ABOUT THE AUTHOR: **Nikolai Shmelev** is an economist at the Institute of USA and Canada Studies of the Russian Academy of Sciences and served as a member of the Soviet Congress of People's Deputies.

19 *Sources*

VASILY SELYUNIN

Wealth is created by work and work alone. But what force makes people work when everything is held in common? In his "Utopia," Sir Thomas More dealt with the problem by proposing the institution of public overseers whose sole job was to make sure that no one remained idle. Thus the Utopian hit on an important truth: The only alternative to personal gain as a stimulus to work is noneconomic compulsion.

The founders of scientific socialism were somewhat less simple and clear in dealing with this problem. While Engels denied that there would be any differences in remuneration for work in a socialist society, he never dealt with the problem of what would replace previous incentives for work. Marx, on the other hand, admitted differences in pay in accordance with the quantity and quality of people's work, but he observed that as long as such arrangements existed, "equal rights are, in principle, still bourgeois rights."

Many thinkers of the past have assumed that the need for extrinsic incentives for work would eventually disappear as work became people's primary need in life and a matter of the play of their physical and spiritual forces. The strength of such theories is that they cannot be refuted, since the hypothetical conditions on which they are based are only supposed to arise in the future. History, on the other hand, provides the purely negative example of the Jacobins. Some of the harshest measures of the Reign of Terror were motivated by a misguided attempt to impose economic equality by outlawing market relations.

Whereas the Jacobins represented a temporary deviation from the main direction of the French Revolution, the situation is more complex when it comes to socialist revolutions, for which the elimination of market-based production [*tovarnoye proizvodstvo*] is not just a deviation from the goal but the goal itself.

Following the victory of the October Revolution, Lenin insisted that the elimination of big capital was not sufficient by itself to suppress the bourgeoisie. Thus, he wrote: "Anyone who has studied the rudiments of Marxism knows ... that the bourgeoisie arises from the market-based production; under these conditions of market-based production, the peasant who has 100 poods of surplus grain [a pood is about 36 pounds—*Trans.*] that he doesn't need for his family and doesn't turn over to the workers' state on loan to help the hungry worker, and who speculates—what is that? Isn't that the bourgeoisie? Isn't that where it arises? That's what is frightening; that's where the danger for the socialist revolution lies."

On Nov. 10, 1917, speculators were declared enemies of the people, and three months later a decree signed by Lenin ordered that they be shot on the spot. In fact, any sale of foodstuffs was considered to be speculation. Anyone who had surplus grain that he did not turn in to the state was to be brought before a revolutionary court and, if convicted, was to be sentenced to at least 10 years' imprisonment and have his property confiscated.

While it has been customary to attribute these harsh measures to famine and economic devastation, in actuality they had a theoretical basis—Lenin's fear that unless market-based production and the accompanying market were destroyed, the October Revolution might degenerate to the level of a mere bourgeois revolution. It was not famine that occasioned the grain requisitions, but just the other way around: The mass requisitions caused the famine. The peasants were asked to feed the country without deriving any benefit for themselves, and they responded by reducing or even eliminating their plantings.

Lenin's goal was to eliminate market-based production in the countryside, and he launched an all-out attack on the kulaks as the strongest obstacle to that goal. The historical facts irrefutably prove that the liquidation of the kulaks occurred then, during the postrevolutionary years of War Communism, rather than in the late 1920s and early 1930s. However, the middle peasant also wanted to sell the products of his labor, and even that trade was regarded as leading straight to capitalism. The true realization of the socialist revolution's goals was believed to lie in enlisting the entire peasantry to work on common land. Lenin's views on agrarian policy were embodied in the February 1919 "Statute on Socialist Land-Use Policy and Measures to Accomplish the Transition to Socialist Agriculture." It stated that all forms of individual land use should be viewed as transitional and obsolete, and that they would be replaced by state farms, production communes and other such collective-farming associations.

Despite the obvious benefits the new state farms and collective farms offered (the best land, free tools and equipment), the peasants were not eager to join them, and they proved completely unsuccessful. From our historical vantage point we can see that the reason these farms failed was not their lack of modern machinery, as many people thought at the time, but their failure to appeal to the peasants' self-interest. Instead, reliance was placed on crude force to compel peasants to join the new associations.

But the peasantry was not the only object of noneconomic compulsion at that time. In 1918 the government gave Dzerzhinsky's Cheka the power to administratively incarcerate, without trial, persons who were deemed parasites or who otherwise violated labor regulations, i.e., who refused to work voluntarily. The boundaries of coercion were endlessly expanding.

The usual, sanitized version of history holds that the Ninth Party Congress in 1920 turned down Trotsky's plan for the militarization of the economy and mobilization of peasants and workers. In actuality, the Congress's main resolution, "On the Next Tasks in Economic Construction," called for a series of measures to force people to work. Furthermore, another resolution, "On the Transition to a Militia [*militsionnaya*] System," stated that the essence of such a system "should consist in bringing the Army as close as possible to the production process, so that the manpower of certain economic regions is simultaneously the manpower of certain military units."

These two documents lay bare the connection between the economic mechanism and individual rights. Under market-based capitalist production, a person has complete freedom to either get rich or freeze to death. Individual rights are the obverse side of merciless economic liberties. Conversely, under total state ownership, the temptation arises to expropriate the individual himself, his physical and spiritual energies, in order to organize work according to a single plan and uniform procedures. Under such conditions, the individual can be viewed as merely a cog in a gigantic machine, and it is strange to speak of the individual rights or civil liberties of a cog.

The miserable economic results of War Communism left no doubts that the "bourgeois axiom" concerning the inefficiency of compulsory labor was correct. In contrast to Trotsky, Lenin quickly realized the bankruptcy of War Communism. In March 1921, at Lenin's insistence, the 10th Party Congress made a key decision to replace grain requisitions with a fixed tax on peasants. Yet peasants were still not authorized to freely sell the grain they had left over after paying the tax. Lenin still warned that free trade would lead inevitably to the restoration of capitalism. Then, just two months later, a May 1921 Party conference set forth the NEP [New Economic Policy] as a serious, long-term policy. Within a year the entire War Communism economic mechanism had been dismantled and replaced by an economic policy whose main features are similar to those of the new economic mechanism that is being born today.

The speed with which the main provisions of the NEP were implemented is an encouraging lesson for us today, since it demonstrates the possibility of introducing revolutionary changes from above in a matter of months. This is important since we have no time today for the gradualness that some people, even ardent supporters of restructuring, favor in implementing democratization and economic innovations. According to estimates, if drastic changes are not made, our economy will collapse in the mid-1990s.

The NEP achieved impressive results throughout the economy. Not only did private peasant farms meet the country's agricultural needs, from the mid-1920s right up until collectivization the country exported up to 150 million poods of grain annually. Currency acquired real value, and the state was able to use its revenues to invest in industry, especially heavy industry, which grew at an average annual rate of 28.5% in 1923–1928. Noneconomic compulsion was not required as a stimulus for work in either the private or the state sector.

The economic successes of the NEP went hand in hand with democratization: Coercion was sharply curtailed, the rule of law was strengthened, and personal liberties were greatly expanded.

It is true that the small urban entrepreneur still sensed the impermanence of the laws permitting private enterprise and was therefore wary of investing in industrial enterprises. And peasants, too, were afraid of investing in their farms for fear of being declared kulaks. In 1925 Nikolai Bukharin, whose search for answers to real-life problems had led him to evolve rapidly from a "Left Communist" advocating the complete elimination of money into a proponent of the NEP, urged that all strata of the peasantry be encouraged to enrich themselves and develop their farms. He believed that a more prosperous countryside would increase the demand for industrial goods and stimulate industrial growth, and that peasants' bank deposits would provide an additional source of funding for economic development.

In fact, many restrictions on the peasantry were lifted at that time. In early 1925 peasants were allowed to rent land and hire manpower, and all obstacles to free trade were removed. Production for the market inevitably led to a stratification of the countryside—some farms collapsed and others grew stronger. Objectively, the situation was moving toward the development of highly efficient farms, like those in the US.

In a Sept. 30, 1928, *Pravda* editorial Bukharin wrote: "We should put to use and mobilize the maximum number of economic factors that serve to advance socialism. That presupposes an extremely complex combination of personal, group, mass, public and state initiative. We have *over-centralized* everything." Thus, on the very eve of the First Five-Year Plan Bukharin was still trying to influence events.

Bukharin's view (i.e., to all intents and purposes, Lenin's concept of the NEP) had been fiercely opposed from the very outset. Leftist opponents believed that the socialist system had no place for market-based private production, and they wanted to finance industrial growth by taxing the peasantry directly or indirectly (through nonequivalent exchange, by setting artificially high prices for industrial goods and artificially low prices for agricultural goods) at a level that would inevitably result in its ruin.

Once Stalin had consolidated power, he began to implement the leftist policy. The turn toward industrialization began with the savage destruction of the NEP mechanism. Forced collectivization completed the destruction of market-based agricultural production. A series of vigorous measures destroyed the market model in state industry as well.

On Jan. 7, 1933, Stalin declared that the First Five-Year Plan had been fulfilled in four years, even though industrial production in 1928–1933 had grown by only 100%, rather than the 180% called for in the maximum version of the plan that Stalin himself had insisted on adopting. Moreover, the average annual increase in industrial production had declined to 19.4%, down from the NEP period's 23.5%. While it might be argued that doubling industrial production in four years was still not bad, the problem is that the official statistics on which these figures were based were expressed in ruble values, rather than physical terms. Since wholesale prices had skyrocketed during the plan period, official figures overstated actual industrial growth. If industrial production during the first five-year plan period is figured in physical terms, the picture is quite different. For example, compared to the NEP period, the average annual increase in steel production dropped from 670,000 tons to 400,000 tons in 1929–1932, while fabric and sugar production, which had been increasing annually by 400 million meters and 179,000 tons respectively during the NEP, suffered absolute declines during the first five-year plan period.

The economist G. Khanin has recently used new methods to recalculate the most important indices of economic development in 1928–1941, and they show much slower growth than that which is reflected in official statistics. Moreover, while fixed production assets nearly doubled during the period, the output-capital ratio fell by 25%, and the use of materials per unit of final product simultaneously rose by 25%–30%. This period saw the beginning of the disproportions that continue to torment our economy today: disproportions between heavy and light industry, between transportation and the other branches of material production, between monetary income and available goods, etc.

But the gravest legacy of the 1930s was the destruction of agriculture. Not until 1950 did the grain harvest finally surpass the NEP level, and not until the end of the 1950s did the number of cattle and sheep regain the 1926 level—and that was thanks to personal auxiliary farming. The true number of peasants who were physically annihilated during collectivization is still unknown.

By temperament, Stalin favored the classic form of compulsory labor—prison gangs. Convict labor developed Kolyma and the Ural region above the Arctic Circle, Siberia and Kazakhstan; it built Norilsk, Vorkuta and Magadan, and it built canals and northern roads. One could go on and on. Since not enough proper warm clothing was available for prisoners working above the Arctic Circle, a prisoner there was typically used for two weeks—as long as he could last in the clothing he had brought from home—and then sent frozen to rot to death in a camp. While remembering the tragedies of the peasants who suffered during collectivization, we mustn't forget the sufferings of Ivan Denisovich. A people that forgets its history is doomed to repeat it.

Today we are seeking incentives for work based on the correct assumption that personal interest is more dependable in this regard than fear and crude coercion. Yet some people still believe that personal interest, on the one hand, and public, state interests, on the other, are two entirely different things. According to this view, central planning must be preserved as a means of reflecting state interests and properly curbing personal interests. It can be argued, however, that historical experience has failed to demonstrate any particular advantages of directive planning. To the contrary, we all know the disastrous losses society has sustained in strict accordance with the plan. For example, billions of rubles was spent building the Baikal-Amur Railroad, yet there is nothing to haul on it, and it is falling into disrepair without ever having served us. One could cite numerous other examples. The problem here lies not in individual mistakes but in the mistaken idea that you can prescribe from above, more or less in detail, the proportions and priorities of economic development and the scale of production of even the most important products. Our planners themselves belie this idea when they carefully study world trends, which are determined by market forces, in order to plan what we should produce. Thus they tacitly admit that there is a better means than ours for the regulation, or rather self-regulation, of the economy.

The national economy should be a combination of three sectors, each enjoying equal rights: state enterprises operating on the basis of economic accountability, cooperatives, and small-scale private enterprises. The working people themselves would decide in which sector they wanted to work. The state sector would remain the principal sector, but it, too, should operate under conditions of market-based production. That would mean following several simple rules: The production program would be drawn up on the basis of customers' orders, and prices would not be set but agreed upon by seller and buyer. Once an enterprise had paid its taxes and repaid its loans, it would decide on its own what to do with its profits.

In other words, the new economic thinking assumes that everyone would do what he wanted to with his earnings once the taxes on personal or collective income had been paid. Far from causing anarchy, this model would make real centralism possible. The state could use such means as tax rates and the terms of loans to indirectly stimulate the production it deemed desirable. As it is, what we have is pro forma plan dictatorship and growing anarchy in actual economic development. The US economy today has more centralized direction than ours.

Unfortunately, people still have trouble accepting this radical—and the only feasible—version of restructuring. The prejudiced belief that state power over productive forces is an unqualified good and the direct imperative of the historical process is still too deeply rooted. In fact, this prejudice goes back far beyond 70 years.

War Communism had roots in our country's history. The first major step in the assumption of state control over productive forces [ogosudarstvleniye proizvoditelnykh sil] occurred under Ivan the Terrible. During the century before his reign, prebourgeois production relations had begun to develop in our country. This process was especially pronounced on the hereditary estates [votchiny] of the boyars, which were usually leased to free peasant farmers—for payment, preferably, in money rather than in kind. The successful peasant farmers invested their profits in industry and trade, and cities began to grow rapidly. However, in addition to the hereditary estates, there were also nonhereditary estates [pomestya] that princes granted to nobles for the latters' lifetimes. Rather than leasing their land to peasants, the proprietors of the nonhereditary estates preferred to rely on the corvee [barshchina] system of obligatory peasant labor as a means of realizing faster short-term profits. But, as the scholar N. Nosov has pointed out, the corvee system resulted in the destruction of individual peasant farms and undermined the peasant's interest in raising his productivity and marketing his products. In expropriating the major hereditary landed estates (a means of strengthening his autocracy), Ivan the Terrible turned the country's economic development onto a course in which state-owned nonhereditary estates and compulsory serf labor predominated. Prof. Nosov concludes that this critical turn backward toward feudalism and away from incipient capitalism was the principal "objective" reason for the subsequent economic and cultural backwardness of tsarist, serf-owning Russia. In the short run, Ivan the Terrible paid for this reactionary turn with key military losses and economic ruin.

Contrary to the traditional view that Peter I reformed Russia along European lines, it was under Peter that the establishment of state control over productive forces reached its apogee. At the end of his reign the country had 191 factories, and half of the 178 built under Peter had been financed by state funds. Not only did Peter begin the practice of attaching serfs to state enterprises, he issued a decree extending the right to own serfs (previously restricted to the state and landholders) to merchants. Thus his reign gave rise to something unprecedented in history: a serf working class.

While the Russian metallurgical industry developed rapidly under Peter, this development was not subsequently sustained. Whereas Russia and England were both producing 8 billion poods of iron annually at the end of the 18th century, within 50 years England had raised its production to 234 million poods a year, while Russia had only doubled its production. In his novel-essay "Memory" [Pamyat], the late V. Chivilikhin, whose deification of Peter went logically hand-in-hand with his faithful devotion to Stalin, blames the Russian iron industry's failure to sustain the impetus Peter had given it on the failure of Peter's successors to continue his strong leadership in this area. But in his book "The Russian Factory" [Russkaya fabrika], the highly qualified scholar M. Tugan-Baranovsky offers just the opposite explanation. According to Tugan-Baranovsky, it was precisely an excess of government supervision and support that prevented the Russian metallurgical industry from sustaining its growth. With state-built mills, unpaid manpower and an apparatus of compulsory labor, Russian industrialists had no incentive to pursue technical improvements. Moreover, serf iron workers had no incentive to improve their productivity.

An examination of the Russian textile industry in the 18th and 19th centuries demonstrates that mills that employed free labor and could sell their output on the free market at market prices were far more successful, even without state subsidies, than state-subsidized and state-directed mills.

Once the great reforms of the 1860s had created the chief condition for industrial development—a manpower market—Russian industry took off. The metallurgical industry shifted from declining Urals mills to new mills established in the South on a purely capitalist basis. In 1887–1899, the production of cast iron in Russia quintupled, and rates of railroad construction at the end of the 19th century stagger the imagination. By 1913 our country had reached fifth place in the world in industrial output, and its growth rates promised continued gains. Moreover, industry had been growing mainly by relying on the intensive factors characteristic of a market economy. Thus, from 1887 through 1908, industrial production nearly quadrupled, while manpower less than doubled. In industry, we received a fairly decent legacy from old Russia.

In contrast to industry, Russian agriculture continued to stagnate after the reforms of the 1860s. The famous Russian peasant commune [*obshchina*] played a negative role here. Imposed from above as a means of discouraging peasants from concentrating on their own land at the expense of the landlord's, the system of collective land use clipped the wings of the energetic and enterprising peasants and imposed a depressed and impoverished equality. After the emancipation the peasant commune was preserved as a system that both landlords and the state bureaucracy found convenient for the collection of redemption fees and taxes. Yet it proved senseless to combine industrial development with the stagnation of agriculture. Realizing this, Pyotr Stolypin launched [in 1906—*Trans.*] an agrarian program that encouraged the creation of small private farms by making it realistic for peasants to withdraw from the communes. Stolypin's reforms took hold, and by the summer of 1917 62.5% of peasant land was privately owned and controlled, i.e., outside of communes. On the eve of World War I, Russia had attained second place in the world in grain exports, and economic success was increasingly inclining public opinion toward Stolypin's policies.

History, however, decided otherwise. Following the October Revolution the victorious revolutionaries turned to the peasant commune, which had been idealized by the conservative Slavophiles, as the embryo of future socialist collective agriculture. Under War Communism the 50 million hectares confiscated from kulaks was not divided among the peasants but put primarily into communal use. Even at the 10th Party Congress, where the New Economic Policy was taking shape, Lenin insisted on moving from small farms, "to socialized, collective, communal labor." Subsequent researchers have repeatedly emphasized the connection between the peasant commune and the collective farm. Yet history teaches us that it was never possible to create a zeal for work or economic success through the peasant commune. Moreover, commune-type equality and social justice invariably resulted in the suppression of the individual. To this day, the advantages of "socialized, collective, communal labor" have never been demonstrated, although it would seem that every possible variation of such labor has been tried.

The legacy of the prerevolutionary Russian bureaucracy continues to be the chief obstacle to reforms. Since industry under Peter I was mainly state industry, from the very outset the authority of the Russian bureaucracy was far broader than that of government bureaucracies in the West. Peter left behind a vast, overcentralized and inefficient bureaucracy. The breakup of the old state machinery in 1917 failed to sever the bureaucracy's roots. To the contrary, bringing the entire economy into the sphere of government management increased the dangers of bureaucratism, since the management apparatus now had to take over all the functions that are performed by the market in a market economy. The situation was exacerbated by the fact that the economic model of War Communism eliminated all independence of individual economic entities.

Lenin was the first to realize the danger of the bureaucracy and declare war against it. By turning the country abruptly in the direction of the NEP, he fostered the development of objective conditions that would limit the bureaucracy.

With the destruction of the NEP economic mechanism, central directives once again took the place of self-interest in guiding the economy. Since the 1930s the administrative apparatus has grown faster than any other group of working people. In 1976–1983 alone the number of managerial personnel increased by 3 million persons and topped the 17-million mark.

Today this uniquely large and uniquely impotent apparatus is engaged in translating the Party's decisions on restructuring into the language of various instructions and directives. Since bureaucrats' chief concern is self-preservation and, therefore, the preservation of administrative management methods, it is not hard to guess what the results of this process will be.

The existing bureaucratic machine cannot be incorporated in restructuring. It can be broken up and eliminated, but not restructured.

The other side of bureaucratism is social inertia. The bureaucrat's attitude that all revenues belong to the state to dispense or not dispense as it sees fit is complemented by the public's view that all benefits come from the state. The conservativism of the bureaucracy feels a sentimental nostalgia for the past, for order and a strong boss, as instinctive preference for what is familiar, and a corresponding hostility toward innovation. Ordinary people fear independence and look for manna from heaven. Both the bureaucracy and ordinary people share a fear of life and of harsh economic realities. In that sort of situation one serious failure—it doesn't matter whether it be an economic failure, foreign-policy failure, or some other—is enough to morally isolate the reformers.

That is where the chief danger for restructuring lies. Losing time means losing everything. Any economic-management system possesses tremendous inertia and will reject alien elements, no matter how progressive they might be. That is why it is useless to gradually introduce new rules into the existing system. The only thing that can be accomplished that way is to discredit restructuring: "You see, years have been wasted on talk, and one can't see any changes."

History will not forgive us if we miss our chance. An abyss must be crossed in a single leap—you can't make it in two.

NOTES

ABOUT THE AUTHOR: **Vasily Selyunin** is a Soviet economist and journalist.

20 Are Our Principles Any Good?

ALEKSANDR TSIPKO

... Time has no power over our Russian, Soviet "orthodox" [believers in Marxism]. At present, 73 years after the Revolution, they are convinced that the Marxist principles are good from all points of view. ... At present even people standing in queues say that rejection of competition and of the market economy destroyed our economy and our country, that socialist monopoly production is a graveyard for advanced technologies and scientific-technical progress, that socialized property will always belong to no one, that theft and waste are caused by the absence of an owner, that no one is responsible for anything. But our philosophers and publicists prefer not to hear or see anything and insist that the Marxist theory of socializing the means of production is the truth. G. Lisichkin, O. Lacis, G. Vodolazov, A. Butenko, I. Kliamkin, N. Simonia and even G. Popov are trying to persuade their readers that mankind has thought of nothing more clever than the Marxist theory of socializing the means of production. Their chorus warns in unison not to reject Marx's theory but to follow it to the end, to make perestroika according to Marx.

At present, especially after the uprising against the Ceausescu dictatorship in Rumania and other, comparatively more peaceful, events in Eastern Europe, it would seem that it has to be admitted that everywhere and in all cases proletarian dictatorship, ruling communist party monopoly lead to totalitarianism or authoritarianism, and turns out to be a new cruel oppression of the individual and of the working class. ... Stalinism, Rakosiism, Maoism, the Pol Pot regime, the Ceausescu family clique—that is only a short list of political monsters raised on the ideas of a socialist revolution. Communist ideology in its seventy years has given birth to so many more monsters than the old private property civilization could give rise to in three hundred years. But this striking fact is also neglected by the present Soviet "orthodox." They write in ecstasy how democratic and humane Marxism is, how it promises miracles of freedom and the ideological emancipation of the individual.

No doubt the policy of glasnost' and openness brought on by perestroika started and speeded up the process of de-Stalinization in Eastern Europe. But evidently the same democratic processes, common to all socialist countries, lead to unexpected, unpredictable ideological results in the USSR. ... We do everything backward because of our fatal peculiarity. We associate de-Stalinization with a return to the Marxist ideas of October [1917], with a return to the "original truth."

Not only the party leaders write and speak about de-Stalinization, but also "unengaged" persons, including many of our "creative intelligentsia." This is a big problem. ...

Many scholars are convinced that the more fiercely they expose the vices of the Stalin regime or of stagnation society [the Brezhnev years], the more their readers will be persuaded that Marxism, its ideas and principles have nothing to do with all that happened in our country in the 1930s and 40s. ...

In this new ideological situation the present-day "orthodox" have really only one way out: reject the October Revolution, reject Lenin in order to keep faith in true Marxism, thus preserving the opportunity for a new communist offensive on the old world, the opportunity to build a new life in accordance with Marx's predictions. The Bolsheviks' incompetence, according to philosopher N. Simonia, is due to the fact that "in 1917 there was no or nearly no basis for socialism in Russia," and that is why Marx's theory could not have been implemented there. The attempts to make a political explosion without material preconditions to create a new society without classes was quixotic, comments N. Simonia. ...

But why does our society have such a strong affection for Karl Marx, for his ideas? Why can we not step away from the ideas that other people have already abandoned? Is it possible that the reason for our strong adherence to Marxism lies in the striking gullibility of Russian people, the Russian intelligentsia? Is it possible that it was not by accident that many historians, writers, leaders of the October Revolution described Lenin as typically Russian? N. Ustrialov, L. Trotsky, M. Berdiaev, and many others tried to understand the Lenin phenomenon long before V. Grossman did.

It turns out that looking for the sources of Marxist orthodoxy in the Russian character is not a good idea. We should not forget that before the Revolution orthodox Marxists were a negligible minority among the Russian intelligentsia. Many people were influenced by Marxism but as a rule the most intelligent, the most talented overcome Marxist truths, having realized that they were wrong. How can we call a person intelligent if this person is convinced that everything that is done in the name of the working class is moral, that laws, morals, and religion are nothing but bourgeois prejudices? It is no accident that the best of the Russian intelligentsia had to leave Russia after the Civil War. It was also no accident that in the Bolshevik Party itself well-educated people were an insignificant minority.

Lenin is undoubtedly an outstanding figure, not only in Russian but in world history as well. But what makes us think that Lenin is more typically Russian than the leaders of the Duma? Only one thing: Lenin won and they lost. But not everyone has the courage to use the hatred and anger of the neglected and the oppressed for the sake of one's own political triumph. As a rule the Russian intelligentsia could get interested in Marxism only abstractly because the teachings of class struggle and violence as the midwife of history do not coincide with the Christian tradition, with the cultural heritage of Tolstoy and Dostoyevsky on which they were brought up. ... Even if sensible, honest people surrendered their souls to Marxism, this did not last long. It cooled down upon the first contact with real life. ...

I don't like to commit this sin, but it appears that I have to; somebody has to say this at last. The position of most advocates of the "purity" of Marxist teachings can be explained not by their irresponsible faith in it but by their cunning and doublethinking. ...

In his essay, "Tragedy of Centralism," [Aleksandr] Prokhanov describes the idea of communism as a utopia; he adds that the attempt to implement it in Russia cost our people sixty million lives. Prokhanov compares Lenin's and Stalin's dragging Russia into socialism to trying to pull a camel through a needle's eye. It is natural that nothing but dust would be left of old Russia after such an operation.

It is not clear when Prokhanov is sincere: in the first case, when he writes that Marxism with its communist ideas is good and there is nothing else to be desired, or in the second case, when he calls Marxism a utopia that has destroyed the old Russia. ... [But] Prokhanov's twofold position on Marxism is the most harmless cunning compared to the tricks our "orthodox" undertake when they try to save the situation but have nothing to do but grieve that the country no longer believes in the principles of communism. ...

For example, Sergei Chernyshov is cheating when he states that the Russian Marxists misunderstood the spirit of the "Communist Manifesto," that Marx did not call for revolutionary violence, that he did not call for the violent extermination of landowners and capitalists, that he did not call for terror. It is unlikely that the author, writing for the multimillion readership of *Znamya* magazine, does not know that the proletarian revolution, the call for the violent overthrow of capitalist society, is the essence of the outlook of the creator of *Das Kapital.* Marx was not talking about Hegel's *Aufhebung,* or transcendence. He was talking simply of expropriating the expropriators. ...

We can find hardly any of Karl Marx's economic ideas that were not used in the process of building socialism in our country or in other socialist countries and which wouldn't turn out to be a waste of effort and money, and which wouldn't be an economic failure as a result. All socialist countries paid a high price for the Marxists' passion for maximum centralization and concentration of production, for the Marxists' love of big forms. No need to dwell on the sad story of Stalin's big grain factories, the Soviet state farms. ...

Our pathological economic and political situation created dozens of ideological myths which helped Soviet people sincerely believe that their life was really good and that they were the happiest people in the world. That's how the general conviction was reinforced that revolutions are real holidays in history and that the peoples who did not live through terrible, bloody civil wars (as our people did) are simply unfortunate and do not know real happiness. As children we were glad that practically nothing was left of old pre-revolutionary Russia—no landowners, no intelligentsia, no clergy, merchants, prosperous peasantry. We sincerely believed that other peoples would never be happy until they did what we did, until they followed us, until they demolished the cathedrals, did away with merchants, private enterprises, rich farmers, until they became exactly as we did. ...

Some authors still cannot understand why, as soon as it became clear that we would not use the authority of tanks and guns, the East European countries in no time threw away the communist happiness that had been forced upon them and are now returning to normal human life, to the high road of human development.

We tortured by gulags and prisons, by fear and hunger, by rationing cards and never-ending lines, at least three generations of Russians so that they would not realize—but only approach the point of realization—what had been evident to many serious scholars at the turn of the century. Did not Eduard Bernstein warn that Marx was mistaken in his predictions on the prospectives of growth and concentration ... ? Did we have to spend a hundred years to realize that the best form of farming, approved by the whole world's experience, is a farmer on his own land? Did we need a hundred years to realize that eliminating the peasantry brings about hunger? Did not Peter Struve warn at the beginning of the 20th century that there was no serious, scientific proof that the contradictions between the productive forces of capitalism and its juridical expression would be solved according to Marx's formula, by revolutionary explosion (this idea was sacred for the Russian Marxists)? Struve thought that it was much more likely that the contradiction would lead to a change in the quality of capitalism. ... Proudhon warned Marx in his letters that the economic doctrine based on non-competitive monopoly production would inevitably lead to despotism, to a dictatorship of central organs of the commune over its members. ... The Russian revolutionary Mikhail Bakunin said that a society is not a rabbit, and no one is allowed to experiment on it. ... S. N. Bulgakov correctly pointed out that "Marx does not deal with the problem of religion; he is not worried about the individual; he is interested in what is common to all individuals and therefore in a non-individual, and he abstracts this non-individual into a general formula, easily dispensing with the residue that is left in a personality after you subtract the non-individual element and consider the residue to be zero." ...

Now it is evident that without intensive shock therapy by truth our society will not become mentally sound. The coming re-evaluation is bound to have a global character. This is understandable: no people in the history of mankind was ever enslaved by myths as our people was in the 20th century. We had thought that we had tied our lives to a great truth, only to realize that we entrusted ourselves to an intellectual fantasy which could never be realized. We thought we were pioneers leading the rest of mankind to the real of freedom and spiritual blessing, but realized that our way is the road to nowhere. We thought that building communism in the USSR was the greatest deed of our people but we were purposefully engaging in self-destruction. We thought that capitalism was a sick old man sentenced to death but it turned out that capitalism was healthy, powerful, and only beginning to realize its potential. We thought that we were surrounded by people with the same ideals, greateful to us for saving them from capitalist slavery, that all together we formed a powerful socialist bloc, but it turned out that our friends and neighbors were only waiting for a chance to return to their old lives. We thought that our national industry organized like one big factory, with one omnipotent director and with one omnipotent dispatcher's office, was the ultimate achievement of human wisdom, but it all turned out to be an economic absurdity which enslaved the economic and spiritual energy of the peoples of Russia.

It is true that not everyone can withstand such a powerful wave of all-destructive truth. It is easy to get disoriented, but is it better to hide the truth? Are new lies any better? What kind of ideals do we have if we have to hide them from the people? Is it not better to admit the truth, however terrible it is? Is it not better to calm our minds and get ready for the future toils and troubles? Life goes on. We have a lot to do. ...

NOTES

ABOUT THE AUTHOR: **Aleksandr Tsipko** worked for the Central Committee of the Communist Party, was deputy director of the Russian Academy's Institute of International Economic and Political Studies, and has been associated with the Gorbachev Foundation.

21 Speech at the Conference of the Aktiv of the Khabarovsk Territory Party Organization, July 31, 1986

MIKHAIL S. GORBACHEV

... None of us can continue living in the old way. This is obvious. In this sense, we can say that a definite step toward acceleration has been made.

However, there is a danger that the first step will be taken as success, that we will assume that the whole situation has been taken in hand. I said this in Vladivostok. I want to say it again in Khabarovsk. If we were to draw this conclusion, we would be making a big mistake, an error. What has been achieved cannot yet satisfy us in any way. In general, one should never flatter oneself with what has been accomplished. All of us must learn this well. Such are the lessons of the past decades—the last two, at least. And now this is especially dangerous.

No profound qualitative changes that would reinforce the trend toward accelerated growth have taken place as yet. In general, comrades, important and intensive work lies ahead of us. To put it bluntly, the main thing is still to come. Our country's Party aktiv, the entire Party, should understand this well. ...

No one, not only in Khabarovsk but also in Moscow, in the ministries, in the State Planning Committee, in the government or in the Politburo, has any ready-made recipes as to how we should accomplish the task of acceleration.

We should learn as we go along, accomplishing new tasks. And we must not be afraid of advancing boldly, of doing things on the march, in the course of the active accomplishment of economic and social tasks. ...

Restructuring is a capacious word. I would equate the word restructuring with the word revolution. Our transformations, the reforms mapped out in the decisions of the April plenary session of the Party Central Committee and the 27th CPSU Congress, are a genuine revolution in the entire system of relations in society, in the minds and hearts of people, in the psychology and understanding of the present period and, above all, in the tasks engendered by rapid scientific and technical progress.

There is a common understanding in the CPSU and in the country as a whole—we should look for answers to the questions raised by life not outside of socialism but within the framework of our system, disclosing the potential of a planned economy, socialist democracy and culture and the human factor, and relying on the people's vital creativity.

Some people in the West do not like this. There everyone lies in wait for something that would mean a deviation from socialism, for us to go hat in hand to capitalism, for us to borrow its methods. We are receiving a great deal of "advice" from abroad as to how and where we should proceed. Various kinds of provocative broadcasts are made, and articles are published, aimed at casting aspersions on the changes taking place in our country and at driving a wedge between the Party leadership and the people. Such improper attempts are doomed to failure. The interests of the Party and the people are inseparable, and our choice and political course are firm and unshakable. On this main point, the people and the Party are united.

But we also cannot allow ingrained dogmas to cloud our eyes, to impede our progress and keep us from creatively elaborating theory and applying it in practice, in the given, concrete historical stage through which our society is passing. We cannot allow this, either.

I am saying this also because among us there are still, of course, people who have difficulty in accepting the word "restructuring" and who even sometimes can pronounce it only with difficulty. In this process of renewal, they often see not what it in fact contains but all but a shaking of foundations, all but a renunciation of our principles. Our political line is aimed at fully disclosing the potential and advantages of the socialist system, removing all barriers and all obstructions to our progress, and creating scope for factors of social progress.

I want to say something else. The farther we advance into restructuring, the more the complexity of this task is revealed, and the more fully the enormous scale and volume of the forthcoming work is brought out. It is becoming clearer to what extent many notions about the economy and management, social questions, statehood and democracy, upbringing and education and moral demands still lag behind today's requirements and tasks, especially the tasks of further development.

We will have to remove layer by layer, the accumulated problems in all spheres of the life of society, freeing ourselves of what has outlived its time and boldly making creative decisions.

The Central Committee understands that this will require a great deal of effort and considerable time. But it is impermissible to delay, and even more to be inactive, in this situation. For this reason, we return again and again to the need for comprehensive restructuring, and we will do so until a fundamental shift is ensured, above all in the thinking of our leadership cadres and in the thinking and psychology of all the working people and all of society.

Incidentally, and this has been confirmed once more here, on Far Eastern soil, our Soviet people are solidly behind restructuring. The main thing that they express anxiety about in the letters that I receive—and they have been doing so now, during my meetings with people—is that we might slacken the pace in some area or other. ...

Sometimes people ask: Well, just what is this odd business, restructuring? How do you understand it, "what do you eat it with," this restructuring? Yes, we're all for it, some say, but we don't know what to do. Many say this straight out. ...

Restructuring proposes the creation of an atmosphere in society that will impel people to overcome accumulated inertia and indifference, to rid themselves, in work and in life, of everything that does not correspond to the principles of socialism, to our world views and way of life. Frankly, there is some work to be done here. But in this instance everyone must look first of all at himself, comrades—in the Politburo, in the primary Party organizations—and everyone must make a specific attempt to take himself in hand. In past years, we got used to some things in an atmosphere of insufficient criticism, openness and responsibility, things that do not at all correspond to the principles of socialism. I apply this both to rank-and-file personnel and to officials. ...

I will use a good word from the history of our Party, applying it to the present situation, to the place and role of our cadres and the Party aktiv. Today, they are the commissars of the present stage of the struggle for the development of socialism. (*Applause.*) ...

There are quite a few things that are good in the practice, in the activity of the Party in past years. This must be taken into account. But, comrades, now the times and the tasks are quite different. There will be no progress if we seek answers to new questions in the economy and in technology in the experience of the 1930s, the 1940s, the 1950s, or even of the 1960s and the 1970s. ...

...

In general, comrades, we must change our style of work. It should be permeated with respect for the people and their opinions, with real, unfeigned closeness to them. We must actually go to people, listen to them, meet with them, inform them. And the more difficult things are, the more often we must meet with them and be with them when some task or other is being accomplished. In our country, people are responsive; they are a wonderful people, you can't find another people like them. Our people have the greatest endurance. Our people have the greatest political activeness. And now it is growing. This must be welcomed and encouraged in every way. Let us consider that we have come to an agreement on this in the Khabarovsk Party organization. (*Applause.*)

In this connection, some words about public openness. It is sometimes said: Well, why has the Central Committee launched criticism, self-criticism and openness on such a broad scale? I can tell you that so far we have lost nothing, we have only gained. The people have felt an influx of energy; they have become bolder and more active, both at work and in public life. Furthermore, you know that all those who had been trying to circumvent our laws immediately began to quiet down. Because there is nothing stronger than the force of public opinion, when it can be put into effect. And it can be put into effect only in conditions of criticism, self-criticism and broad public openness. ...

Incidentally, it looks as if many local newspapers in cities and provinces are keeping quiet. The central newspapers are speaking out in full voice, supporting everything good and criticizing blunders and shortcomings. But the local papers are silent. When a group of editors assembled in the Central Committee's offices, they said bluntly: "Well, you tell this to our secretaries in the city and district Party committees." And indeed, why shouldn't people know what is going on in the district or the city? Why shouldn't they make a judgment on it and, if need be, express their opinion? This is what a socialism is, comrades. Are there any editors present? (*A voice:* Yes, we're here.)

I hope that the secretaries of the city and district Party committees will take our talk into account. They are the managers. These are their newspapers. We must not be afraid of openness, comrades. We are strong, and the people are in favor of socialism, the Party's policy, changes and restructuring. In general, it is impermissible to approach openness with the yardsticks of traditional short-term campaigns. Public openness is not a one-shot measure but a norm of present-day Soviet life, a continuous, uninterrupted process during which some tasks are accomplished and new tasks—as a rule, still more complicated ones—arise. (*Applause.*)

I could say the same thing about criticism and self-criticism. If we do not criticize and analyze ourselves, what will happen? For us, this is a direct requirement, a vital necessity for purposes of the normal functioning both of the Party and of society. ...

NOTES

ABOUT THE AUTHOR: **Mikhail S. Gorbachev** was first secretary of the Communist Party of the Soviet Union from 1985 to 1991 and was president of the USSR from 1990 to 1991.

22　*I Cannot Forgo My Principles*

NINA ANDREYEVA

I decided to write this letter after a great deal of thought. I am a chemist, and I teach at the Leningrad Soviet Technological Institute in Leningrad. Like many others, I am an adviser for a group of students. In our days, after a period of social apathy and intellectual dependence, students are gradually beginning to be charged with the energy of revolutionary changes. Naturally, debates arise— about the paths of restructuring and its economic and ideological aspects. Openness, candor and the disappearance of zones closed to criticism, as well as emotional fervor in the mass consciousness, especially among young people, are frequently manifested in the posing of problems that, to one extent or another, have been "prompted" by Western radio voices or by those of our compatriots who are not firm in their notions about the essence of socialism. What a wide range of topics is being discussed! A multiparty system, freedom of religious propaganda, leaving the country to live abroad, the right to a broad discussion of sexual problems in the press, the need for the decentralization of the management of culture, the abolition of compulsory military service— Among students, a particularly large number of arguments are about the country's past. ...

So much has been written and said about the Great Patriotic War and the heroism of those who took part in it. But recently a meeting took place in one of our Technological Institute's student dormitories with Hero of the Soviet Union V. F. Molozev, a retired colonel. One of the things he was asked about was political repressions in the Army. The veteran replied that he had not encountered any repressions, and that many of those who had started off the war with him and seen it through to the end had become major military commanders. Some of the students were disappointed with his answer. The now commonplace subject of repression has become excessively magnified in the perception of some young people, pushing an objective comprehension of the past into the background. Examples of this sort are not rare.

It's very gratifying, of course, that even "technos" [*tekhnari*] have a lively interest in theoretical problems of the social sciences. But too many things have turned up that I cannot accept, that I cannot agree with. The constant harping on "terrorism," "the people's political servility," "uninspired social vegetating," "our spiritual slavery," "universal fear," "the entrenched rule of louts"— It is from these mere threads that the history of the period of the transition to socialism in our country is often woven. Therefore, it comes as no surprise, for example, that in some students nihilistic views are intensifying, and ideological confusion, a dislocation of political reference points and even ideological omnivorousness are appearing. Sometimes one hears assertions that it is time to call to account the Communists who supposedly "dehumanized" the country's life after 1917.

At the February plenary session of the Central Committee, it was emphasized once again that it is urgently necessary for "young people to learn the class vision of the world and gain an understanding of the connection between common human and class interests. This includes an understanding of the class essence of the changes taking place in our country."[1] This vision of history and the present day is incompatible with political anecdotes, base gossip and the highly dramatic fantasies that one can frequently encounter today.

I read and reread the much-talked-about articles. What, for example, can they give young people except disorientation and revelations "about the counterrevolution in the USSR at the beginning of the 1930s" and about Stalin's "guilt" for the coming to power of fascism and Hitler in Germany? Or a public "counting" of the number of "Stalinists" in various generations and social groups?

We are Leningraders, so it was with special interest that we recently viewed the excellent documentary film about S. M. Kirov. But the text accompanying the shots at some points not only diverged from the film-document but also gave it a certain ambiguity. For example, shots in the film show an explosion of enthusiasm and joie de vivre and the élan of people who were building socialism, while the narrator's text speaks of repression and lack of information.

Probably I am not the only one who has been struck by the fact that the calls of Party leaders to turn the attention of the "unmaskers" back to the facts of real achievements at various stages of socialist construction are drawing, as if on command, more and more flare-ups of "exposés." A noteworthy phenomenon in this, alas, unfruitful field is the plays of M. Shatrov. ... In "The Peace of Brest" [Brestsky mir], Lenin, at the will of the playwright and the director, kowtows to Trotsky. What a symbolic embodiment of the author's conception. It is developed further in the play "Onward, Onward, Onward!" [Dalshe, dalshe, dalshe!]. A play is not a historical treatise, of course. But after all, in a work of art the truth is ensured by nothing so much as the author's position. Especially if what we're talking about is political theater.

The playwright Shatrov's position has been analyzed in a detailed and well-reasoned way in reviews by historians that were published in *Pravda* and *Sovetskaya Rossia*. I would like to express my opinion as well. In particular, I can't help agreeing with the contention that Shatrov deviates substantially from the accepted principles of socialist realism. In elucidating an extremely crucial period in the history of our country, he elevates the subjective factor of the development of society to the status of an absolute and clearly ignores the objective laws of history that are manifested in the activity of classes and of the masses. The role of the proletarian masses and the Party of Bolsheviks is reduced here to the "background" against which the actions of irresponsible politicians unfold.

Guided by the Marxist-Leninist methodology for studying concrete historical processes, the reviewers convincingly showed that Shatrov distorts the history of socialism in our country. ...

[handwritten note: It seems like she's dealing w/ what was being portrayed in art.]

Unfortunately, the reviewers did not succeed in showing that, for all his authorial pretensions, the playwright is not original. It seems to me that, in the logic of his evaluations and arguments, he is very close to the themes of B. Souvarine's book ["Stalin: A Critical Survey of Bolshevism"—*Trans.*], which was published in Paris in 1935. In his play, Shatrov puts into his characters' mouths what was asserted by opponents of Leninism concerning the course of the Revolution, Lenin's role in it, relations among members of the Central Committee at different stages of the inner-Party struggle— That is the essence of Shatrov's "new reading" of Lenin. I will add that even A. Rybakov, the author of "Children of the Arbat" [*Deti Atbata*], has frankly admitted that he borrowed certain plot elements from emigre publications.

While I have not yet read the play "Onward, Onward, Onward!" (it has not been published), I have read laudatory reviews of it in some publications. What could such haste mean? Then I learned that a stage production is being hurriedly prepared.

Shortly after the February plenary session, *Pravda* published a letter headed "A New Round?" signed by eight of our leading theater people. They warn against what, in their opinion, are possible delays in the staging of M. Shatrov's latest play. This conclusion is drawn from critical assessments of the play that have appeared in the newspapers. For some reason, the letter writers exclude the authors of critical reviews from the ranks of those "to whom the fatherland is dear." Just how does this harmonize with their desire to have a "stormy and impassioned" discussion of the problems of our history, some of it recent and some rather old? What does it come down to—are they the only ones who are allowed to have an opinion of their own? ...

[handwritten note: that through these acts are only one sided views.]

In talking with students and pondering crucial problems with them, I automatically come to the conclusion that a good many distortions and one-sided views have piled up in our country, notions that obviously need to be corrected. I want to devote special attention to some of these things.

Take the question of the place of J. V. Stalin in our country's history. It is with his name that the entire obsession with critical attacks is associated, an obsession that, in my opinion, has to do not so much with the historical personality itself as with the whole extremely complex transitional era—an era linked with the unparalleled exploit of an entire generation of Soviet people who today are gradually retiring from active labor, political and public activity. Industrialization, collectivization and the cultural revolution, which brought our country into the ranks of the great world powers, are being forcibly squeezed into the "personality cult" formula. All these things are being questioned. Things have reached a point at which insistent demands for "repentance" are being made on "Stalinists" (and one can assign to their number whomever one wishes). Praise is being lavished on novels and films that lynch the era of tempestuous changes, which is presented as a "tragedy of peoples."

Let me note at the outset that neither I nor the members of my family have any relationship to Stalin or his entourage, retainers or extollers. My father was a worker in the Leningrad port, and my mother was a mechanic at the Kirov Plant. My older brother worked there, too. He, my father and my sister were killed in battles against the Hitlerites. One of my relatives was repressed and was rehabilitated after the 20th Party Congress. Together with all Soviet people, I share the anger and indignation over the large-scale repressions that took place in the 1930s and 1940s through the fault of the Party and state leadership of that time. But common sense resolutely protests the monochromatic coloring of contradictory events that has now begun to prevail in certain press organs.

I support the Party's call to uphold the honor and dignity of the trailblazers of socialism. I think that it is from these Party and class positions that we should assess the historical role of all Party and state leaders, including Stalin. In this case, one must not reduce the matter to the "court" aspect or to abstract moralizing by people far removed from that stormy time and from the people who lived and worked then. Indeed, they worked in such a way that what they did is an inspirational example for us even today.

For me and for many other people, the decisive role in assessing Stalin is played by the firsthand testimony of contemporaries who came into direct contact with him, on both our side of the barricades and the other side. Those in the latter group are not without interest. For example, take Churchill, who in 1919 was proud of his personal contribution to organizing the military intervention of 14 foreign states against the young Soviet Republic but who, exactly 40 years later, was forced to use the following words to characterize Stalin—one of his most formidable political opponents:

"He was a man of outstanding personality who left an impression on our harsh times, the period in which his life ran its course. Stalin was a man of extraordinary energy, erudition and inflexible will, blunt, tough and merciless in both action and conversation, whom even I, reared in the British Parliament, was at a loss to counter. ... His works resounded with gigantic strength. This strength was so great in Stalin that he seemed unique among leaders of all times and peoples. ... This was a man who used his enemies' hands to destroy his enemy, who made us, whom he openly called imperialists, do battle against imperialists. ... He found Russia with a wooden plow, but he left it equipped with atomic weapons" [retranslated from the Russian—*Trans.*]. This assessment and admission on the part of a faithful guardian of the British Empire cannot be attributed to dissimulation or political expediency.

The basic elements of this characterization can also be found in the memoirs of De Gaulle and in the reminiscences and correspondence of other European and American political figures who dealt with Stalin, both as a wartime ally and as a class adversary. ...

From long and frank discussions with young people, we draw the conclusion that the attacks on the state of the dictatorship of the proletariat and on the leaders of our country at that time have not only political, ideological and moral causes but also their own social substratum. There are quite a few people who have a stake in broadening the staging area of these attacks, and not just on the other side of our borders. Along with the professional anticommunists in the West, who long ago chose the supposedly democratic slogan of "anti-Stalinism," there live and thrive the descendants of the classes overthrown by the October Revolution, by no means all of whom have been able to forget the material and social losses of their forebears. One must include here the spiritual heirs of Dan, Martov and others in the category of Russian Social Democratism, the spiritual followers of Trotsky or Yagoda, and the descendants of the NEPmen, the Basmachi [participants in armed resistance to Soviet rule in Central Asia in 1918–1924—*Trans.*] and the kulaks, who bear a grudge against socialism.

As is known, any historical figure is shaped by specific social, economic, ideological and political conditions, which have a determining influence on the subjective and objective selection of aspirants who are called upon to solve various social problems. Having come to the forefront of history, such an aspirant, in order to "remain afloat," must satisfy the requirements of the era and of the leading social and political structures and must realize an objective pattern in his activity, inevitably leaving the "imprint" of his personality on historical events. In the final analysis, for example, few people today are disturbed by the personal qualities of Peter the Great, but everyone remembers that the country rose to the level of a great European power during his rule. Time has condensed the result that is now contained in our assessment of the historical personality of the Emperor Peter. And the ever-present flowers on his sarcophagus in the cathedral of the Peter and Paul Fortress embody the respect and gratitude of our contemporaries, who are far removed from the autocracy.

I think that, no matter how contradictory and complex a given figure in Soviet history may be, his true role in the construction and defense of socialism will, sooner or later, receive an objective and unambiguous assessment. Needless to say, it will be unambiguous not in the sense of being one-sided, of whitewashing or eclectically summing up contradictory phenomena, of an assessment that makes it possible, with qualifications, to create any kind of subjectivism, to "forgive or not forgive," to "discard or keep" elements of history. An unambiguous assessment means above all a historically concrete, nonopportunistic assessment that manifests—in terms of historical result!—the dialectics of the conformity of a given individual's activity to the basic laws of the development of society. In our country, these laws were also connected with the resolution of the question "Who will win?," in its domestic and international aspects. If we are to follow the Marxist-Leninist methodology of historical research, then we must first of all, in M. S. Gorbachev's words, vividly show how millions of people lived, how they worked and what they believed in, and how victories and setbacks, discoveries and mistakes, the radiant and the tragic, the revolutionary enthusiasm of the masses and violations of socialist legality, and sometimes even crimes, were combined.

For me, there is no doubt that, in the question of assessing Stalin's activity, the Party Central Committee's resolution on overcoming the personality cult and its effects, adopted in 1956, and the report of the General Secretary of the CPSU Central Committee devoted to the 70th anniversary of the Great October Socialist Revolution remain the scientific guidelines to this day.

Recently, one of my students startled me with the revelation that the class struggle is supposedly an obsolete concept, as is the leading role of the proletariat. It would be all right if she were the only one maintaining such a thing. But, for example, a furious argument broke out recently over a respected academician's assertion that the present relations between states of the two different social and economic systems are devoid of class content. I admit that the academician did not deem it necessary to explain why for several decades he had written the exact opposite—that peaceful coexistence is nothing other than a form of class struggle in the international arena. It turns out that the philosopher has now repudiated that notion. Well, views do change. However, it seems to me that the duty of a leading philosopher does enjoin him to explain, at least to those who have learned and are learning from his books: What—does the international working class today, in the form of its state and political organs, really no longer act as a countervailing force to world capital?

It seems to me that the same question—which class or stratum of society is the guiding and mobilizing force of restructuring?—is at the center of many current debates. This was talked about, among other things, in an interview with the writer A. Prokhanov in our city newspaper *Leningradsky rabochy* [Leningrad Worker]. Prokhanov proceeds from the premise that the special nature of the present state of social consciousness is characterized by the existence of two ideological currents or, as he says, "alternative towers" that are trying, from different directions, to overcome the "socialism that has been built in battle" in our country. While he exaggerates the significance and acuteness of the mutual confrontation between these "towers," the writer nevertheless rightly emphasizes that "they agree only on exterminating socialist values." But both, their ideologists assure us, are "in favor of restructuring."

The first, and deepest, ideological current that has already revealed itself in the course of restructuring claims to be a model of some kind of left-liberal dilettantish socialism, to be the exponent of a humanism that is very true and "clean" from class encrustations. Against proletarian collectivism, the adherents of this current put up "the intrinsic worth of the individual"—with modernistic quests in the field of culture, God-seeking tendencies, technocratic idols, the preaching of the "democratic" charms of present-day capitalism and fawning over its achievements, real and imagined. Its representatives assert that we have built the wrong kind of socialism and that only today, "for the first time in history, has an alliance come about between the political leadership and the progressive intelligentsia." At a time when millions of people on our planet are dying from hunger, epidemics and imperialism's military adventures, they demand the immediate drafting of a "legal code for the protection of animal rights," ascribe a singular, supernatural intelligence to nature, and claim that cultivation is not a social but a biological quality, transmitted genetically from parents to children. Tell me: What does all this mean?

It is the champions of "left-liberal socialism" who are shaping the tendency to falsify the history of socialism. They suggest to us that in the country's past only the mistakes and crimes are real, in doing so keeping quiet about the supreme achievements of the past and the present. Laying claim to complete historical truth, they substitute scholastic ethical categories for social and political criteria of the development of society. I would very much like to understand: Who needs, and why, to have every prominent leader of the Party Central Committee and the Soviet government compromised after he leaves office and discredited in connection with his actual or supposed mistakes and miscalculations, made while solving some very complex problems on roads uncharted by history? Where did we get this passion for squandering the prestige and dignity of the leaders of the world's first socialist country?

Another special feature of the views of the "left-liberals" is an obvious or camouflaged cosmopolitan tendency, a sort of nationality-less "internationalism." I have read somewhere that when, after the Revolution, a delegation of merchants and factory owners came to the Petrograd Soviet to see Trotsky "as a Jew," complaining of oppression by Red Guards, he declared that he was "not a Jew but an internationalist," which thoroughly bewildered the supplicants.

For Trotsky, the concept of the "national" meant a kind of inferiority and narrowness in comparison to the "international." That's why he emphasized the "national tradition" of October, wrote about "the national element in Lenin," maintained that the Russian people "had received no cultural legacy," etc. For some reason, we are ashamed to say that it was the Russian proletariat, which the Trotskyists slighted as "backward and uncultured," that carried out, in Lenin's words, "the three Russian Revolutions," or that the Slavic peoples were in the vanguard of mankind's battle against fascism.

Of course, what I have said does not signify any disparagement of the historical contribution of other nations and nationalities. It only, as the current saying goes, ensures a full measure of historical truth. When students ask me how it could have happened that thousands of villages in the Non-Black-Earth Zone and Siberia have become deserted, I reply that this, too, is the high price paid for victory [in World War II] and the postwar rehabilitation of the national economy, as is the irretrievable loss of large numbers of monuments of Russian national culture. I am also convinced that the pacifist erosion of defense and patriotic consciousness, as well as the desire to list the slightest manifestation of national pride by Great Russians under the heading of great-power chauvinism, stem from disparagement of the significance of historical consciousness.

Here is something else that alarms me: Militant cosmopolitanism is now linked with the practice of "refusenikism"—of "refusing" socialism. Unfortunately, we suddenly think of this only when its neophytes plague us with their outrages in front of Smolny or under the Kremlin's walls. Moreover, we are somehow gradually being trained to see this phenomenon as an almost inoffensive change of "place of residence," not as class and nationality betrayal by persons most of whom have been graduated from higher schools and graduate schools at public expense. In general, some people are inclined to look at "refusenikism" as some kind of manifestation of "democracy" and "human rights," feeling that the talents of those involved have been prevented from blossoming by "stagnant socialism." Well, if over there, in the "free world," their tireless enterprise and "genius" aren't appreciated and selling their conscience doesn't interest the special services, they can come back— ...

Whereas the "neoliberals" are oriented toward the West, the other "alternative tower" (to use Prokhanov's expression), the "guardians and traditionalists," seeks to "overcome socialism by moving backward"—in other words, to return to the social forms of presocialist Russia. The spokesmen for this unique "peasant socialism" are fascinated with this image. In their opinion, a loss of the moral values that the peasant community had accumulated through the dim haze of centuries took place 100 years ago. The "traditionalists" have rendered undoubted services in exposing corruption, in fairly solving ecological problems, in combating alcoholism, in protecting historical monuments and in countering the dominance of mass culture, which they rightly assess as a psychosis of consumerism.

At the same time, the views of the ideologists of "peasant socialism" contain a misunderstanding of the historical significance of October for the fatherland's fate, a one-sided appraisal of collectivization as "frightful arbitrary treatment of the peasantry," uncritical views on religious-mystical Russian philosophy, old tsarist concepts in scholarship relating to our country's history, and an unwillingness to see the postrevolutionary stratification of the peasantry and the revolutionary role of the working class.

In the class struggle in the countryside, for example, there is frequently an overemphasis on "village" commissars who "shot middle peasants in the back." There were, of course, all kinds of commissars in our enormous country, which had been stirred to new life by the Revolution. But the basic tenor of our life was determined by those commissars who were themselves shot. It was they who had stars cut into their backs or were burned alive. The "attacking class" had to pay not only with the lives of commissars, Chekists [state security personnel], village Bolsheviks, members of poor peasants' committees and "twenty-thousanders" [industrial workers who helped in the collectivization of agriculture in the early 1930s—*Trans.*], but also those of the first tractor drivers, rural correspondents, girl-teachers and rural Young Communists, with the lives of tens of thousands of other unknown fighters for socialism.

The difficulties in the upbringing of young people are deepened still more by the fact that unofficial [*neformalny*] organizations and associations are being created in the pattern of the ideas of the "neoliberals" and "neo-Slavophiles." In some cases, extremist elements capable of provocations are gaining the upper hand in the leadership of these groups. Recently, the politicization of these grassroots [*samodeyatelny*] organizations on the basis of a pluralism that is far from socialist has been noted. Frequently the leaders of these organizations talk about "power-sharing" on the basis of a "parliamentary regime," "free trade unions," "autonomous publishing houses," etc. In my opinion, all this makes it possible to draw the conclusion that the main and cardinal question in the debates now under way in the country is the question of recognizing or not recognizing the leading role of the Party and the working class in socialist construction, and hence in restructuring—needless to say, with all the theoretical and practical conclusions for politics, the economy and ideology that stem therefrom. ...

Today, the question of the role and place of socialist ideology has taken on a very acute form. Under the aegis of a moral and spiritual "cleansing," the authors of opportunistic constructs are eroding the boundaries and criteria of scientific ideology, manipulating openness, and propagating an extra-socialist pluralism, which objectively impedes restructuring in social consciousness. This is having an especially detrimental effect on young people, something that, I repeat, we higher-school instructors, schoolteachers and all those who deal with young people's problems are distinctly aware of. As M. S. Gorbachev said at the February plenary session of the CPSU Central Committee: "In the spiritual sphere as well, and perhaps in this sphere first of all, we must be guided by our Marxist-Leninist principles. Comrades, we must not forgo these principles under any pretexts."

We stand on this, and we will continue to do so. We have not received these principles as a gift: We have gained them through suffering at decisive turning points in the history of the fatherland.

NOTES

ABOUT THE AUTHOR: **Nina Andreyeva,** a Leningrad schoolteacher, emerged, in part thanks to this article, as a leading figure in the movement challenging Gorbachev's reforms.

1. [The quotation is from Ye. K. Ligachev's report on education at the plenary session. See *Current Digest of the Soviet Press,* Vol. XL, No. 8, p. 11.]

23 *The Tragedy of Centralism*

ALEKSANDR PROKHANOV

For the second time in a century we are experiencing a tragedy of centralism. In the space of an hour the monarchy crumbled through the Party's efforts, and the empire rained down on our heads in a pile of shards. In the Civil War, in the crucible of a social utopia, and in the attempts to refashion elementary administrative structures across our vast expanses, we lost the aristocratic elite, a fragile, inchoate civil society and a refined culture, and we recreated a centralism on the total, Stalinist model. In destroying the centralist idea and then recreating it, we lost 60 million of our fellow countrymen. Today, for a second time, through the will of providence and its earthly disciples, we find ourselves in this razor-sharp spiral, offering our shaven and defenseless necks.

The destruction of centralism, and of the state along with it, is occurring in accordance with a proven algorithm, as if the entire program had been entered on a computer punch card and the sequence of operations—their rate of execution and timing—were the result of rational efforts based on an immense potential.

Here are the paragraphs of that program:

Paragraph One.—The integrating socialist ideology has been cast off, the communist ideal has been excluded from development, and the strategic goals that fashioned our present out of the future have been repudiated, goals that united us as a social whole and reconciled the contradictions inherited from the past. ... The ideology's destruction has deprived the peoples of a common future and caused an instantaneous growth in national ideas and beliefs, which are tearing us apart in irreversible centrifugal efforts. Today, we are a galaxy that has exploded and is flying off in all directions, with a black emptiness at its center.

Paragraph Two.—An attack has been mounted and successfully carried out against the centralist structures, whose tough, unbending joists held together the state's immense expanses, supported the inordinate weight of the outlying areas and made possible the concentration of colossal potential at times of crisis. Today, those structures have been smashed. ...

The "scrapping of the command-administrative system" has led, in practice, to the destruction of the economy by making it absolutely unmanageable; it has given rise to managerial chaos and led to the degradation of entire branches of the economy. ...

The Army—the multinational Army—is a single pot of interests, cares and tasks, a single technosphere, and a single form of service that permeates the entire state. The Army, which links past and present, old and young with its tradition, is the guarantor of stability and sovereignty. It is a school of precious centralist experience that made it possible not only to win the most terrible of wars and withstand the pressures of the great American empire, but also to carry out colossal scientific-technical programs that are impelling us into the 21st century. The Army today is being destroyed like so many columns in an Afghan ravine. ... The paralysis of the general-officer ranks and reduction of the enlisted ranks and junior officers to a state of distraction are turning the Army into a motionless, demoralized mass and depriving it of its basic defensive functions.

The Party, which seemed united and which suffused all the country's immense brawn with its nerve tissue, reconciling contradictions based on ethnic origins, social rank, occupation or world view—that Party cannot serve as a consolidating force today, because it is itself in need of consolidating; it is itself cut into rump factions and filled with internecine strife. ... The Party, disconnected from power, deprived of a world view, and cast into philosophical chaos, is being held answerable for the failures of the past and for the present crisis; it is being sold out to fomented public hysteria and removed before our very eyes from the political arena.

Such is the fate of the three important centralist structures, which are burning like fuses, turning into long ashen veins from ocean to ocean.

Paragraph Three.—The attack on the "Russian factor," on Russia and things Russian. ... Efforts are being made to instill an inferiority complex in Russians; ... a rigged trial is being staged of Russian history and the Russian character, in which they are charged with responsibility for universal disaster. Russophobia is a political instrument for destroying the multinational state, which is in large measure nourished by the Russian ability to unify.

Paragraph Four.—The emergence, in economic life, of immense riches concentrated in private hands. The legalization of criminal wheeler-dealers. ... The headlong growth of social inequality; the legitimation of that inequality as an ideal; a sold-out, nongoverning government and a sold-out, idiocy-inducing culture—all these things are making us a country of millionaires and poor people, sowing hatred, depriving us of civic unity, and tearing us apart with suspicion and enmity.

Paragraph Five.—We are being hooked into the world economic system, into world currencies, and into world financial energy, which, through concessions and joint businesses, is supposed to flow into our moribund tissues and sprinkle us with life-giving water. This money is pouring into our birch-bark and bast economy in tiny, red-hot streams and reducing it to ashes. ... By hitching ourselves to world money we are putting ourselves in the hands of the world's true bosses. ...

Paragraph Six.—The strapped economy, poverty, life at the semistarvation level, the dismal outlook, moral and psychological depression, and anarchy are causing the people to hold strikes. They are still industry-specific strikes, hitting now mines, now railroads, now taxis. But they are ready to cross industry lines, shutting down motors and engines in whole regions and bringing the entire country to a standstill. Crafty politicians who know the laws of mass psychosis are squeezing the trigger of popular disturbances with their calls for an all-Union strike. ...

Today, strikes at nuclear power stations, chemical factories, oil pipelines and munitions plants threaten Chernobyls of unprecedented force. Cities aflame on the horizon, refugees fleeing exploded nuclear reactors, unintended ballistic-missile launches, destruction of the biosphere over immense areas—those are the dangers lurking in an all-Union strike.

Paragraph Seven.—The final chord in the apocalyptic symphony is a civil war in the USSR, with all the mercilessness of the previous war, plus the new nightmarish components offered by a military-technical civilization. … There's no ruling out a collective attempt by the countries of the world to stabilize the process in the USSR in the interests of mankind's safety—of saving the planet and the human race. This new entente would attempt to occupy a helpless and unarmed country. …

Those are the steps in the destruction of centralism, steps of which only the last one and a half have yet to be carried out.

The seismic waves of these terrible blows are spreading beyond the USSR's bounds, into the external world. The entire geopolitical architecture of Eastern Europe, created by our country at an immense price, was destroyed in no time. The balance of forces within Europe has been upset, with unforseeable consequences. The sentimental theory of "our common European home" has led to the collapse of East European communist parties, a change in state systems, and the inevitability of the reunification of Germany. The end of the 20th century will see the rise of a German industrial giant in the center of Europe, a giant filled with energy, inspired by a pan-Germanic idea, and encompassing the age-old German lands in its gravitational field. …

The "philosophy of the new thinking" and "the primacy of universal human values over class values" have developed, in fact, into a disregard for the interests of the socialist state, and the satisfaction of the imperialist oligarchies' ambitions. The American invasion of Panama marks a new stage in international relations in which a weakened Soviet Union that is being withdrawn from whole regions of the world is no longer able to serve as a restraining factor for the expansion of bourgeois empires. …

Today, the Soviet Union is weaker than ever before. The crisis of 1917 occurred against the backdrop of worldwide crisis and destruction. Our present crisis is occurring against the backdrop of a flourishing world.

The blame for the failure of this five-year-long policy lies with the liberals, who mindlessly repeated the experience of destroying centralism. They—the liberal economists, writers and historians who are spiritually and intellectually oriented toward the democratic West and have been in opposition to their own state for decades—knew too little about their own people, about its psychology and subconscious. … For a second time, liberal thought, reared on a different culture and different politics, has disdained the country and people's genetic experience and is conducting an irresponsible experiment. …

The immense Eurasian land mass of the USSR cannot be inserted into the world community. The doctrine of insertion implies the dismemberment of the USSR into republics, regions, and separate zones, cities, towns, and farms—into separate individuals. …

Such insertion presupposes the use of force. The people, having once gone through the needle's eye of socialist construction, having ground away layers of their culture and faith and lost tens of millions of their fellow countrymen, are now supposed to make that passage a second time, but in the opposite direction, and they will do so only with the application of force. ...

The other model that has traits indicative of real thought is that of a neo-Stalinist breakout from the backwardness, degradation and chaos. ... Present-day neo-Stalinist policy presupposes a second round of requisitions, a second fleecing of the people in order to fill our impoverished treasury, to muster resources from our granaries and, in those areas of development where there is still intellectual and technological vitality, to achieve breakthroughs into a post-industrial society—to come within reach of Japan and America in the most important areas, while turning the rest of the country into a destitute but organized camp. ... That move, that program of development, like the first, presupposes the use of force, a totalitarian system, and the strict, simplified organization of all aspects of life.

Those are the actions that our in-a-hurry intellectual leaders have in mind in proposing their prescriptions for getting out of the catastrophe. ...

Alas, the people can't stand any more violence—either from the one side or from the other. ...

There is a third, utopian-like picture that is repugnant to active natures by dint of its limpidity, nonmathematical grounding and lack of concreteness. A third model of development that excludes dictatorship and death. ...

The future idea of our development and the future formula for our existence are latent in the future, yet-to-mature woodland of our destroyed culture. ...

We must consciously stop hurrying. We must accept losses of time in the social sphere. We must spend the entire next century nurturing our culture. We must stop thinking in terms of five-year plans and campaigns, thinking from congress to congress and leader to leader, and learn once again to think in centuries. ...

The principal, basic type of human individual must dispense with the traits of the iron leader, the spendid warrior, and the strong-willed commander and manager, and must acquire the traits of a gardener, forester and shepherd. ...

The basic and most vital task of present-day public consciousness is to immediately declare civil peace, to work out a theory of civil reconciliation, and to prevent the outbreak of civil carnage. ... We must, at long last, bury Red and White bones together in a common, fraternal grave. ... It is precisely on that fraternal grave that today's general and priest, today's Party member and unofficial-organization member will come together. ...

Utopia is the glittering shadow of catastrophe. If we are destined to remain intact and if the destruction of the state and society is to be stopped, then let the government's first act be one of ecumenical reconciliation, proclaimed from the *Lobnoye mesto*[1] ...

If the terrible calamity, unthinkable for the Russian mind, should occur—if the state should split apart, and the people, robbed and deceived by their thousand-year history, should find themselves alone (if the recent "brothers" should gather up their belongings, rush into their "national launches" and cast off from the listing ship)—then so be it: We have no other place to go. ...

The Russian state system, which embodies the "Russian idea" politically, economically and spiritually, will be built anew. It brings together all that is best from both the thousand-year monarchy and the momentary, fleeting 70 years of Soviet history. Even today, minds unclaimed by perestroika have put together a conception of our future economy, education system and public institutions, and of Russians' global ties with the world. ...

NOTES

ABOUT THE AUTHOR: **Aleksandr Prokhanov** is a leading journalist and political activist on the far right of the Russian political spectrum.

1. The *Lobnoye mesto* is a slightly elevated structure, dating from the 16th century, near St. Basil's cathedral in Red Square from which important Russian government proclamations and decrees were read.—*Trans.*

24   *I Can't Absolve Myself of Guilt*

OLEG T. BOGOMOLOV

... A conscious choice was made in the fall of 1917, a choice that, as we can see today, has led us down a blind alley despite all the sacrifices borne and the heroic efforts made. The other options were discarded because of an unshakable faith in the scientific validity of the only correct, though still unbeaten, path. One can, of course, argue over whether the lamentable results were caused by deformations of socialist doctrine and practice or whether the initial premises themselves were wrong, and therefore the system built in accordance with them needs not reform but replacement. The truth will eventually be established. But that isn't what torments me. Another question is constantly on my mind. Who bears responsibility (in either case) for the countless victims, the poverty and the backwardness with which we have paid and continue to pay for the mistakes or deformations? ...

No matter how hard I try, I can't comprehend why there is no one specific to be held responsible for what has been done, why those to blame for major miscalculations even during the present era of restructuring are unknown, and why the moral problem of repentance and atonement has been utterly rejected. ...

Everything in our life—both the good and the bad—was done under the leadership of the Party. ...

The CPSU was termed the honor, conscience and mind of our era. Well, to my understanding, maintaining one's honor requires accepting blame for the grave consequences of one's actions and atoning for one's guilt. It must be openly confessed that the Party has led the country to the brink of disaster, and now we must all act together to save ourselves. ...

The 28th CPSU Congress ... granted Party members an indulgence for all the sins of the leaders of former times, but I cannot absolve myself of my share of responsibility.

After all, if those who inwardly protested against the squelching of the Prague Spring of 1968 had not remained silent and done nothing, it's possible that there would not have been any invasion of Afghanistan, which was also swallowed in silence for the most part. And could a significant fraction of Party members really have failed to notice that for 18 years the Party was headed by a dull-witted individual who ended up in the position by dint of chance? Didn't we feel like turning off the television set at the sight of another parade of our leaders crowning this nonentity with a new award? And what about the raptures and prizes over what passed for memoirs, penned for the author by obliging writers? We should have plucked up our courage and shouted, "The emperor has no clothes!" Restructuring might well have begun much sooner. Let's also recall the many billions spent senselessly on land reclamation. And what about the economic reform of 1965, which was killed in defiance of common sense, and many other things? Can one really say that Party members had nothing to do with all of this and so there is no point in talking about repentance? They wrote apologetical books and articles, and uttered congratulatory speeches and slogans. The social sciences, art, literature and television served official policy. Party cells unanimously approved everything that came down from above. The directives came from a mere handful of leaders, but those who carried them out numbered in the millions. I was among them; I don't deny it. Along with like-minded colleagues, I wondered many times what was more honorable: to prolong the political life of the inglorious leaders, inserting into their speeches sensible ideas that would make it possible to take even a single step away from dead dogmas, or to renounce any participation at all in this, at the same time probably giving up the chance to head an institute and engage in research and politics? Unfortunately, I chose in favor of the first option. We faintheartedly deceived ourselves, believing that the scientific notes we sent "upstairs" were progressive and that they would help correct policy and avert grave consequences. In actuality, our notes about the erroneousness of the invasion of Afghanistan, the true nature of the Ceausescu regime, the progressiveness of the Hungarian economy's market orientation and the true reasons for and objective nature of the events in Poland; our proposals on restructuring foreign economic activity in the USSR; our theoretical workups on crises under and antagonisms within socialism; our conclusions that the German question could not be considered closed, etc., played a very, very limited role, although they did not disappear without a trace. The greatest thing that I and some of my colleagues proved capable of was, heeding A. I. Solzhenitsyn's call, to refuse to participate in

a lie. And we didn't always manage even that, I'm afraid. But there is still no justification for our lack of Sakharov's courage. The arguments we made then on the
need to preserve some scientific groundwork and some independently thinking
scholars and scientists for the future, when a need for them would arise, today
don't look very convincing. We should have protested openly against deception,
untruth and violence. *should of, could of, would of — but didn't*

Of course, our submissiveness and passivity could be explained in large part by *was it b-lc*
fear of the all-encompassing grinder of the totalitarian system. *they*

But nevertheless, the main root of evil is cowardice and slavish submission to *didn't*
fate. All those who kept silent and reconciled themselves to the situation are *want*
themselves to blame for the fact that they lived a significant portion of their lives *to give*
in vain and that our country has turned into a country of missed opportunities. *up*
Repentance is necessary, not for the sake of punishment, as a ritual, but for self- *what*
purification, so that all of our souls can finally awaken. Otherwise we will remain *they*
blind forever, seeing nothing and understanding nothing. ... *had.*

Unfortunately, [the 28th Party Congress] missed the last opportunity to break
with the past and revive the Party's moral authority. It assigned it[self] the role of
the continuer of previous policy—perhaps not all of it, but its main components.
And for me personally, this makes it impossible to remain in the Party any longer.
As a scholar who tries to take nothing on faith, I can't live any longer in expectation of a communist miracle, closing my eyes to past and present realities.

It's time to stop swearing allegiance to the dogmas of the Marxist faith and to
turn toward common sense, universal human experience and age-old moral precepts, which have never yet let people down. Aren't they the key to salvation and a
way out of our impasse?

NOTES

ABOUT THE AUTHOR: **Oleg T. Bogomolov**, a prominent economist, is director of the Institute of International Economic and Political Studies of the Russian Academy of Sciences
and a member of parliament.

25 *Elite Privileges*

BORIS YELTSIN

... The party leadership is obsequious, obedient, and unchanging. An intelligent,
independent-minded official of the Central Committee is a combination of words
so paradoxical that one's tongue cannot even utter them.

Obsequiousness and obedience are rewarded in turn by privilege: special hospitals, special vacation retreats, the excellent Central Committee canteen, the equally excellent service for home delivery of groceries and other goods, the Kremlin telephone system, the free transportation. The higher you climb up the professional ladder, the more comforts surround you and the harder and more painful it is to lose them. Therefore the more obedient and dependable you become. It has all been most carefully devised: A section chief does not have a personal car, but he has the right to order one from the Central Committee car pool for himself and his immediate staff. The deputy head of a department already has his personal Volga, while the head has another and better Volga, fitted with a car phone.

But if you have climbed all the way to the top of the establishment pyramid, then it's full communism! ...

... Their needs are so great that so far it has only been possible to create real communism for a couple of dozen people—communism is created for them by the ninth directorate of the KGB, and this all-powerful directorate can do anything. ... A dacha behind a high green fence encircling spacious grounds alongside the Moscow River, with a garden, tennis courts, and playing fields, a bodyguard under every window and an alarm system. Even at my level as a candidate member of the Politburo, my domestic staff consisted of three cooks, three waitresses, a housemaid, and a gardener with his own team of assistant gardeners. ...

It was almost impossible to meet anybody or do anything in the ordinary normal way. If you wanted to go to the cinema, the theater, a museum, indeed any public place, a whole squad of heavies was sent there in advance. They would check and cordon off the whole place, and only then could you go yourself. But the dacha had its own cinema, and every Friday, Saturday, and Sunday a projectionist would arrive, complete with a selection of films.

As for medical treatment, the medicines and equipment are all imported, all of them the last word in scientific research and technology. The rooms in the Kremlin hospital are huge suites, also surrounded by luxury: porcelain, crystal, carpets, and chandeliers. Afraid of taking responsibility, an individual physician never makes an independent decision, and diagnoses and treatments are invariably agreed upon by a group of five to ten doctors, sometimes including the most highly qualified specialists. ...

...

The Kremlin ration, a special allocation of normally unobtainable products, is paid for by the top echelon at half its normal price, and it consists of the highest-quality foods. In Moscow, a total of some forty thousand people enjoy the privilege of these special rations, in various categories of quantity and quality. There are whole sections of GUM—the huge department store that faces the Kremlin across Red Square—closed to the public and specially reserved for the highest of the elite, while for officials a rung or two lower on the ladder there are other special shops. And so on down the scale, all organized by rank. All are called "special": special workshops, special dry cleaners, special polyclinics, special hospitals, special houses, special services. ...

When the elite want to go on vacation, they can choose virtually any place in the warm south. There is bound to be a special dacha there. For the rest of the year these dachas are empty. There are other opportunities to go on leave too, because a two-week winter holiday supplements the summer break. Excellent sports facilities exist for "special" use only, for example on the Lenin Hills—indoor and outdoor tennis courts, a large swimming pool, and a sauna. Then there are the personal airplanes, an IL-62 or a TU-134 in which a Central Committee secretary, a candidate member, or a full member of the Politburo flies alone, except for his bodyguard and the cabin crew.

... Within this system nothing belongs to the individual. Stalin cunningly brought this machinery to such a state of perfection that even the wives of his immediate colleagues did not belong to them. They, too, belonged to the system. The system could take those wives away and imprison them, just as Stalin imprisoned the wives of Kalinin and Molotov, and neither man dared to utter so much as a squeak of protest.

...

... Every Central Committee secretary, every member or candidate member of the Politburo, is assigned an officer in charge of his bodyguard; this man is his aide-de-camp and organizes his life. ...

Do you want a new suit? Precisely at the appointed hour comes a discreet knock on the door of your office. In walks a tailor, who takes your measurements and returns the next day for a fitting. Soon you have an elegant new suit.

Do you need a present for your wife for March 8, International Women's Day in the USSR? No problem: You are brought a catalog with a choice of gifts to satisfy even the most sophisticated taste. All you have to do is choose! The attitude toward families is most considerate. There is a Volga for their use, bearing prestigious Kremlin license plates, with drivers working in shifts, taking your wife to work or the children to and from the dacha. The big ZIL, of course, is reserved for the father of the family.

Sometimes this essentially cynical system will exhibit an equally cynical lapse where the immediate family members of the head of the clan are concerned. When, for instance, the chief bodyguard was instructing my wife and children that they must not feed me fruit and vegetables bought in the market because they might be poisoned, one of my daughters asked timidly whether she and my wife might eat market-bought produce. She was told that they could but that I must not. In other words, you can go ahead and be poisoned, but he is sacred.

...

... The dacha is a story in itself. As I mentioned earlier, before it was assigned to me, it had been occupied by Gorbachev, who had moved into another, specially built for him.

When I drove up to the dacha for the first time, I was met at the door by the commander of the bodyguard, who introduced me to the domestic staff. Then we began our inspection of the house. Even from the outside I had been over-whelmed by the size of the place. I entered a hall measuring about thirty by fifteen feet, with an enormous fireplace, marble paneling, parquet floor, large carpets, chandeliers, and luxurious furniture. We went on, passing through first one room, then a second, a third, and a fourth, each of which sported a television set. Also on the ground floor was an enormous veranda with a glass roof, and a small movie theater–cum–billiard room. I lost count of the number of bathrooms and lavatories. There was a dining room with an incredible thirty-foot-long table and behind it a kitchen big enough to feed an army, with a refrigerator that consti-tuted a separate underground room. We went up the steps of a broad staircase to the second floor. Again there was a vast hallway with an open fireplace, and a door opened into the solarium, furnished with rocking chairs and chaise longues. After that came the study, the bedrooms, two more rooms, intended for I know not what, more lavatories and bathrooms. Everywhere was crystal, antique and mod-ern chandeliers, oak and parquet floors.

When we finished the tour of inspection, the commander of the bodyguard, beaming with delight, asking me what I thought. I mumbled something inarticu-late; my wife and daughters were too overcome and depressed to reply. We were shattered by the senselessness of it all. I will not even bother to discuss such no-tions as social justice, the stratification of society, and the huge differences in standards of living; all that goes without saying. But what was the point of the whole thing? Why was it thought necessary to give expression to such an absurd degree to the fantasies of property, pleasure, and megalomania harbored by the party elite? No one, not even the most outstanding public figures of the contem-porary world, could possibly find a use for so many rooms, lavatories, and televi-sion sets all at the same time.

And who pays for all this? The KGB. ...

26   Democratic Platform Program of the CPSU, Statement of June 1, 1990

This is the second draft program document dedicated to the setting out of the views and suggestions of "Democratic Platform" on the fundamental problems of perestroika. As a part of the party-wide discussion they are presented for the wide debate of all members of the CPSU, non-party persons, and members of [other] movements and organizations.

I. IDEOLOGICAL PLATFORM

The party bases its activity on the priority of general human values over the interests of classes and social groups.

We support the cooperation of various social groups and political forces on the basis of mutual respect for interests and equal rights. We oppose social and national confrontation in society.

We reject the monopoly of any ideology and the subordination of theoretical thought to political dictates.

All the attempts to bring to life visions of Communist society with the help of violence, liquidation of the market economy and political pluralism have brought us to a social impasse and caused the tragedy of millions of people and whole nations.

We feel that the striving of the people to a life worthy of man can most fully be satisfied on the path of democratic socialism.

For democratic socialism is constant motion, a ceaseless perfection of society by means of the historic creativity of the people itself.

II. POLITICAL REFORM

The basic goal of radical political reform, and simultaneously the most important precondition for and means of carrying out all the other transformations, is the dismantling of the totalitarian system of power and a transition to a parliamentary, multi-party, law-based state.

For movement toward this goal it is essential to condemn irreversibly and in a principled way the mistakes and crimes of the past, and bring their initiators and participants to justice.

The place and role in society of parties and public organizations is determined by their authority and support among the people. The main indicator of this is mandates received in democratic elections.

PART 4

The Economy

The urgency of restoring economic dynamism was a central motivation in the inauguration of perestroika. *In this light the failure to stem and reverse the continuing deterioration of the Soviet economy was a most dramatic failure. It is scarcely an exaggeration to say that, although in politics and foreign affairs the reformers could point to signal successes, in economic policy* perestroika *proved to be an unmitigated disaster.*

Some of the difficulties of economic reform were intrinsic to the enormous task itself. The shift from a highly centralized command economy to a market system based on private property (or a mix of private, cooperative, and public enterprises) was a task for which there were neither models to copy nor theoretical guidelines to follow. But the Gorbachev leadership was by no means unequivocally committed to such a fundamental transition, and the intrinsic difficulties of economic reform were compounded by the low level of economic understanding in high places, by the confusion and hesitation of decisionmakers, and by resistance and opposition both within the establishment and in the population at large.

As far as the scope and sophistication of economic discourse are concerned, the Gorbachev years provided considerable evidence of learning. This was demonstrated by the shift of attention from the initial interest in "acceleration" to the later quest for "marketization" and finally to a focus on the issue of private property, especially of land. Growing exposure to Western economic theory and practice was supplemented by extensive consultation with foreign economic specialists. A series of personnel changes brought to the fore economists with greater professional expertise who were charged with elaborating programs of economic reform. At the same time, the adoption and execution of these programs was seriously distorted and blocked by officials at various levels and agencies on ideological, economic, and technical grounds or as a means of protecting their turf. In particular, the central ministries, which would have lost their functions and power as a result of decontrol and decentralization, and the sizable and influential military-industrial sector vocally and tacitly obstructed reforms.

Faulty governmental policies also contributed to counterproductive patterns of economic behavior across the country. The breakdown of work discipline, itself a product of the absence of effective incentives, impeded both production and distribution and exacerbated the alienation of the population. Mounting inflation and the declining value of the ruble resulted from the government's increasing resort to deficit spending. Some of Gorbachev's policies inadvertently strengthened regionalism and localism by transferring greater responsibility to local officials while at the same time depriving them of resources to meet these responsibilities. Inevitably, opening up a once autarchic and insulated system dominated by state monopolies to the outside world was bound to create vast opportunities for speculation, corruption, and the rise of "mafias."

These problems were exacerbated by popular attitudes born of a habitual acceptance of what has been called a "nanny state." Moreover, an improvement in the quality of goods and services that would enable Soviet products to compete on the world market presupposes incentives for better workmanship as well as management—the latter through the prospect of profits and ownership. Yet popular attitudes toward "profiteering" remain generally confused and are typically hostile to rewarding a minority of activist entrepreneurs. More generally, the trade-offs between efficiency and equality are still inadequately understood. Corruption, pilfering, and outright theft of government property—from spare parts and edibles to military equipment—and an ethos of ignoring authoritative orders further undermine the functioning of the economy.

Ultimately, the economic crisis was greatly compounded by the vacillation of the Gorbachev leadership between preserving a centralized economy and radically reforming it. In addition, plans for reform were caught up in the broader struggle over the future of the Union itself. Deteriorating economic performance fed growing demands for greater autonomy or sovereignty by the Union republics. At the same time, officials at the center resisted transferring control of resources to the republics during an increasingly bitter struggle between Moscow and the peripheries over the future of the federal system. All these issues were joined in the fall of 1990 in the struggle over the "500 days" program, which Gorbachev appeared to endorse and then repudiated. The so-called Shatalin Plan, which combined a transition toward a market economy with a project to reconstitute the USSR as a confederation, ultimately remained untried.

There were no rapid or simple solutions to the Soviet Union's economic problems, particularly at a time of growing determination by republics, regions, and cities to control their own resources and establish their economic policies in response to local needs. A key dilemma was the very compatibility of a socialist system, however loosely defined, with a market. The Gorbachev leadership sought to incorporate market principles into the existing framework but stopped short of sanctioning full-scale privatization.

27 Is Soviet Socialism Reformable?

ED A. HEWETT

... The Soviet Union began the decade in a state of political paralysis and economic stagnation, both of which posed an unmistakable threat to the basic foundations of the Soviet system. It ends the decade in the midst of a revolution beyond our wildest dreams, and certainly well beyond the hopes of virtually all Soviet citizens, whether they be Russian, Estonian, or Uzbek.

And yet, the political renaissance—however breathtaking its pace and scope—has left the economy virtually untouched, the result being continued economic stagnation which threatens support for *perestroika*. It is clear to all now that the fate of *perestroika*, and the future course of East-West relations, rest on the ability of Soviet leaders to radically, but peacefully, transform the Soviet system. It is for that reason that I have chosen for my topic the question, "Is Soviet Socialism Reformable?" This is what Soviets like to call the "question of all questions."

The conventional wisdom on this question, inside and outside the Soviet Union, is increasingly pessimistic. The core of what might be called "*perestroika-pessimism*" is a gloomy assessment of the prospects for economic reform which—possibly too briefly and unfairly—might be summarized in the following way:

1.) Mikhail Gorbachev and his advisors have made terrible blunders, by underestimating the depth of the economic crisis, and by introducing half-hearted, inconsistent, and ultimately counter-productive economic reforms.

2.) Now they are coming to their senses, having finally come to appreciate the need to throw away the old system and start over again.

3.) But it is too late: the population has lost both its enthusiasm for reform and its faith in Gorbachev. They want results now.

I understand the roots of this pessimism. It is indeed tempting to give in to it. However, I am reluctant to embrace the pessimistic view, not because it is without foundation, but because it seems premature.

We and the Soviets are on poorly charted territory. No country has yet successfully dismantled a Soviet-type system, thus there is no experience to refer to in judging a particular approach. On such unfamiliar territory, judgements about whether things are going well or badly are hazardous, based, as they must be, on weak analogies, or on an analysis of the process itself, neither of which can support more than tentative conclusions.

In this situation even the economics of the economic reform can be tricky. Apparent "setbacks" to the reform process may in fact be progress, while apparent signs of progress may in fact represent setbacks. A retreat on price reform or a partial crackdown on cooperatives—both taken in conventional wisdom as "bad" signs for Soviet reform—may, for example, be good signs, a point to which I return below.

The politics of the economic reform are no easier to gauge. Developments which appear on first glance to be "retreats" from economic reforms—such as statements proclaiming a continued commitment to socialism and an opposition to private property—may ultimately prove to be critical to their successes by providing a smoke-screen for radical change.

Mikhail Gorbachev is writing a textbook on the political economy of transitions—the first textbook of its kind. And, given the startling pace and scope of changes so far under his leadership, I certainly am not ready to predict what the last chapters will say. In the meantime it is clear that our uneven knowledge about what works, and what does not work, in transitions of this sort suggests the need for a large dose of humility. ...

TRANSITION TO WHAT?

One of the most commonly-voiced criticisms of Soviet economic reforms is the inability or unwillingness of the leadership to articulate the nature of the new system they wish to create. Obviously an economic transition is potentially dangerous if the final goal is left unspecified or vague. The likelihood of costly errors rises dramatically as steps are taken which must later be reversed. Moreover, there is a good chance that the reforms will go nowhere at all for lack of a final goal. As one Chinese wag reportedly put it, "If you don't know where you are going, any road will get you there."

This is a legitimate criticism for an *economist* to raise. From the very beginning of the Gorbachev reforms it has been true that the only point of true consensus in the Soviet Union has been over the need to change the system, by decentralizing decision-making powers to state enterprises. Beyond that very general proposition there is, as yet, no consensus. Statements on the nature of a reformed system are full of huge "black holes" regarding critical components of the new system: property rights, acceptable income and wealth distributions, the nature of economic security guarantees in the new system, and so on. There is, as yet, no authoritative statement by the leadership which outlines in detail acceptable to an economist the nature of the new system.[1]

But a *political* economist would be somewhat more cautious in condemning the reform process for commencing without an explicitly agreed-upon end. A full-blown debate leading to clarity on the final outcome of a reform process could easily make it impossible to develop the consensus necessary to embark on the reforms. The populace would see clearly that socialism as they know it is disappearing, to be replaced by something suspiciously similar to the capitalism so recently vilified in the press. The party would see quite clearly that its role in the new system would be modest, at best, and possibly nil. Even those leaders who are "reform-minded," but basically moderates, could well lose courage if they were told at the beginning how far they would eventually have to go to achieve the economic goals they have set for themselves.

I am not suggesting that in the Soviet case the ambiguity about the new system is a conscious part of Gorbachev's strategy, namely, that he knows precisely where all of this will lead, and that he is simply waiting for the right time to reveal his full intentions to the party and the population at large. There may be elements of this strategy in Gorbachev's thinking, but it is clear that he himself has been, and may still be, unclear on how far these reforms should finally go. Rather, the point is that at the beginning of such a radical reform, there is a trade-off between seeking the clarity of purpose which will make the economics go as smoothly as possible, and holding back, allowing ambiguities which may ease the politics of the reform.

Even from a strictly economic point of view one can overdo criticism over ambiguities about the character of the new system. Whether the eventual goal of a reform is the full restoration of a capitalist market economy, or any of a number of variants of market socialism, the early stages of the transition will be almost identical. It is possible, therefore, to analyze the course of the transition, even in the context of an ambiguous final goal. And in the Soviet case there has been substantial criticism, some of it justified, of the course of the transition to date.

HOW TO GET FROM HERE TO THERE?

…

…Western economists know a great deal about how to manage a market economy, but very little about how to create one. Much of what supposedly comprises western economists' "advice" for reformers boils down to a recommendation to create a market economy, and then—if the society survives the trip—to call on us for guidance on how to manage the newly-created system. I am reminded of an East European friend who had taught economics to many young economists from developing countries. Some years ago he was awakened from a sound sleep by a long-distance phone call in which one of his best students proudly announced, "The revolution has succeeded; we've just taken power. Now what?" His first temptation was to say, "You've reached a wrong number!" Many western economists receiving an analogous "call" nowadays are sorely tempted to give precisely that answer.

But instead we must give an answer. And in fact we are not without some guidelines for the transitions now under way.

Decentralization Is the Key

Virtually anyone working in or on socialist centrally planned economies can see plainly that the basic guiding principle in the reform must be decentralization of considerable authority over economic decision-making to individual economic units. The basic idea here is simple common sense: give the power to make decisions to those who have information about production possibilities and consumer preferences, and create an economic environment which will compel them to act on that information.

That economic environment is critical to the success of the entire operation. Decentralization in and of itself, without changes in the economic environment, is outright dangerous. Prices paid and received by economic units exercising their newly-granted decision-making powers must be generally accurate reflections of supply and demand for products, capital, and foreign currency. Decentralization in the context of distorted prices leads inexorably to distorted economic decisions, which in turn can lead to calls for a recentralization of economic decisions.

At the beginning, the right prices can be approximated by central revisions of fixed prices, since it is not terribly difficult to estimate in a gross sense how relative prices should be changed. But if the decentralization is to be self-sustaining, and self-validating, then the price system itself must be flexible, so that prices can move automatically, first to correct the mistakes in the initial price revisions, and then to reflect changing conditions in supply and demand.

But even price flexibility in and of itself is not sufficient to guarantee a smooth, or even an economically acceptable, reform process. Prices will only be an accurate reflection of supply and demand if markets are sufficiently competitive that producers are compelled by the economic environment to pay attention to consumers. This means that institutions must be operating to insure free entry, including (as much as possible) foreign competition for domestic producers.[2] Ultimately the competitive environment must operate not only in the market for products, but also those for capital, labor and foreign exchange. It can do as much harm as good to increase the competitiveness of product markets, but then tie the hands of individual enterprises by retaining administrative mechanisms for allocating capital, foreign exchange, or labor. Markets come in a package, and introducing part of the package may make matters worse, not better.[3] Without such a competitive environment, buttressed by a commitment from the government to do all it can to foster such an environment, it is dangerous to simply free up product prices.

But the competitive environment itself will be difficult to create if the government is not firmly committed to a tight money policy, to make sure that the market is limited by the incomes (and ultimately the productivity) of the population. If prices are free, but at the same time government printing presses pour out money to subsidize insolvent firms or to keep a lid on politically-sensitive prices, then the competitive market will never get off the ground. Markets work because money is difficult to earn without productive labor. Easy money weakens the link between productivity and income, ultimately undermining the effort to foster a competitive environment.

In the final analysis, then, the decentralization will work well only if a full set of markets is in operation. But that then suggests that the only feasible transition strategy will be an "overnight" change in which the system is rapidly transformed into a new, and very tough, economic environment, with attendant bankruptcies and other disruptions. This, of course, is not so much a theory of transition, as it is an argument for a great leap, with all the uncertainties that implies.

Soviet reforms to date have a mixed record on addressing the complexities of decentralization. They violated the most elemental common sense in 1988 by giving enterprises more economic decision-making authority without even a partial effort to tighten up money, reform prices, or increase competition. The result—which Soviet leaders now ruefully admit was totally predictable—was an acceleration in hidden inflation as Soviet enterprises used their monopoly power to shift the product mix towards high-priced, high-profit, products which Soviet consumers lined up to buy for lack of alternatives.

On the other hand, that mistake led to an increasingly sophisticated understanding of the cost of partial reforms, one of the consequences being a growing opposition from the most radical reform economists to a price reform without an accompanying anti-monopoly policy, and a commitment to tight money. This strong opposition to price reforms in 1988—taken by some as a sign that the ardor for reform was cooling—was in fact a good sign, providing one example of how an apparent "retreat" can in fact be an advance.

Property Rights

Those of us who have studied socialist centrally planned economies have tended to underestimate the importance of property rights to the success of reforms. The implicit assumption has been that, while private ownership clearly provides the best incentive system for high efficiency and high growth driven by innovation, it might still be possible to implement a decentralization of decision-making rights to lower-level units which could improve economic performance even though the state retains ownership rights over assets.

But the East European experience in the 1970s has suggested that in fact property rights issues are central to the success of a reform effort. Capitalist market economies, when they are working well, institutionalize pressure on individuals who own their own assets to try to increase the value of those assets, in the process producing goods and services in demand, at low cost. No socialist incentives scheme has yet been discovered which can replicate the incentives inherent in private ownership.

Hence, first in Eastern Europe, and now in the Soviet Union, there are unmistakable signs of an increasing emphasis on denationalization as a critical component of the reform. This is by no means full-scale, Thatcherite, privatization. However, *de facto* privatization through liberal leases of land and factories and the legalization of cooperatives (which are in fact private enterprises), can go a long way towards expanding property rights, while retaining for society some control over the distribution of wealth and income.

This is surely one of the most encouraging aspects of the evolution in public debates and policy on economic reform in the Soviet Union. A few years ago the discussion of property rights was limited and generally conservative. Now it is at center stage as Academician Leonid Abalkin, newly appointed as Deputy Prime Minister chairing a commission on economic reform, advocates "de-statization" (*razgosudarstvlenie*) of the bulk of productive assets by the mid-1990s.[4] Hungary and Poland are going much further, pursuing wide-scale privatization, including the sales of local factories to foreign investors. And it is likely that Soviet thinking will continue to evolve in that direction.

A corollary of this new emphasis on property rights is that small private and cooperative enterprises will play an important role, providing the foundation for a pro-competitive policy, particularly in the supply of consumer goods and services. The Soviet Union and Eastern Europe lack the myriad of small enterprises we take for granted in the West, and the governments must create conditions which will encourage them.

Soviet leaders have understood this basic point, and by 1988 cooperatives were legalized in a wide range of fields, focused on consumer goods and services. But cooperatives have gotten off to a shaky start, having developed a reputation as a haven for price-gouging criminal elements intent on making an easy ruble through speculative activity, rather than on producing a low-cost, high-quality, good or service. This has led to tremendous popular resentment, channeled through the new Supreme Soviet, which in turn has forced the government to institute new controls on cooperative pricing, and the products they can produce. That, not surprisingly, is taken as a retreat from the commitment to radical reforms.

But here, once again, one must be careful. The introduction of cooperatives in 1988 provides a text-book example of how not to expand property rights during the early phases of a reform. The cooperatives were legalized, but were given virtually no legal access to material inputs, capital, or foreign exchange. Moreover, they began operation in a system where retail prices for many basic consumer goods were subsidized, and the products were in short supply. Not surprisingly, some of the cooperatives found they had to raise their capital, or obtain their supplies, through black-market channels. And they discovered it was easy to make money by selling the scarce products they obtained relatively cheaply, at market-clearing prices. It is not the cooperatives' fault this happened; the economic environment pushed them in the direction of speculation and illegal activity. Even then it is far from clear that the majority of the 130,000 cooperatives operating in mid-1989 were actually breaking laws. Even operating legally, but somewhat more efficiently, can be very profitable in the current Soviet economy.

In sum, the new administrative restrictions on cooperatives may make sense until, and if, prices are reformed to remove the most tempting targets for speculation. The real test for the strength of commitment to reforms will be in the willingness of the government to create that competitive environment which will permit cooperatives and other economic entities to operate freely, constrained by competition, not regulations.

Sequencing

Even when governments commit themselves to decentralization in the context of a competitive environment, facilitated by a dramatic expansion in property rights, the issue still remains of what sequence the liberalization should follow. Are there some sectors which logically should "lead" the decentralization? Are there some which logically should come last?

The most venerable piece of conventional wisdom in this regard, which might be called the "China-theorem," holds that agriculture should go first. Liberalizing agriculture, or—more precisely—rural economic activity, is easiest and can bring quick results. Production cycles are short; the large number of producers leads naturally to strong competition; overcentralization in this sector does the most harm; and links to the remainder of the economy are relatively limited, allowing decentralization to proceed apace without unduly influencing, or being influenced by, the slower pace of change in the remainder of the system. The short production cycles can lead to a rapid expansion in the supply of food and consumer goods and services, creating popular support for the tougher reforms to follow in industry.

This was basically the Chinese strategy, with impressive results. It surely should have been the Soviet strategy, but was not, for reasons still not fully apparent. For reasons we have yet to learn, Mikhail Gorbachev—the man who rose to national prominence as the party secretary in charge of agriculture—chose to begin his reform in industry. Now, five years later, with no visible improvements in the supply of food or consumer goods, the cost of that miscalculation is painfully evident.

Aside from the "China-theorem" there is rather little practical advice from economists on where to start, in particular whether there is a preferred sequence for the various industrial sectors in a reform. Mario Nuti probably offers the most sensible advice, suggesting that reformers should move in steps, beginning by liberalizing the production and pricing of consumer goods; then liberalizing interenterprise transactions, while retaining control over the share of inputs devoted to consumer and to other uses (defense, investment); then freeing up investment in consumer sectors, while retaining control over the share of investment going to consumer and capital goods; and then finally decontrolling decisions on the level and structure of investment.[5]

The common-sense of this approach is appealing: one begins liberalizing pricing and the general economic conditions for those products closest to consumers (which includes food products), then moving by stages back into the basic sectors and the basic decisions determining the level and structure of capital investment. As a practical matter, the major difficulty is that—at least in the USSR—most large enterprises produce goods that cover the entire spectrum of commodities and services from consumer goods to basic capital goods. Piece-meal liberalization by product will mean that most enterprises will be operating in a combination of a liberalized, free-price, environment, and an administratively-controlled, fixed-price environment. The chances for games here—for example using fixed-price inputs to produce freely-priced consumer goods—are endless, and so therefore are the dangers to the success of such a strategy.

A more sensible strategy might involve agriculture first, and then liberalization by enterprises (not products) in the rest of the economy beginning with those enterprises whose product mix is focused primarily on consumer goods and services. This could be done either by leasing state enterprises, or—preferably—selling them off. Enterprises outside the state sector would be neither controlled, nor subsidized; they would have to make a go of it without access to administratively-allocated materials, relying on markets for their inputs. The possibilities for arbitrage would still be there as long as some enterprises are operating in a controlled environment and others are not, but if the sequence of liberalization moves quickly enough, the benefits from this approach might outweigh the costs.

How Quickly Should Reforms Be Introduced?

The issue of how quickly the reforms should be introduced is, of course, one of the most difficult ones, where economic and political considerations come into direct conflict. The economic argument favors a quick, comprehensive reform; anything else will lead to contradictions among partial reforms. One of the more commonly-stated pearls of wisdom among Soviet and East European reformers now is that "... one can't cross a chasm in two jumps."

On the other hand, there are strong political arguments, and even some economic arguments, against a quick reform. The economic risks stem from the fact that a quick transition in the USSR (or Eastern Europe) would constitute a first-ever social experiment, since nothing like it has been attempted before. The results are unpredictable, but it is at least conceivable that the shock would be so great as to throw the system into a long-term, and very costly, depression in which many enterprises would go under which—given a little bit of time to adjust—could have survived.

That possibility supports the fears of politicians that such a transition would destroy their power base, leading to an overthrow of the government, and the party. Economists who have a theory of chasm-jumping, but no experience, can hardly comfort politicians with a compelling desire to survive the jump.

The logic of these fears seems to argue for gradual reforms. However, there are some powerful economic and political arguments against gradualism. From the economic point of view, gradual reforms will mean selected, declining subsidies to enterprises to allow them time to adjust. But how can the government choose between those enterprises which are potential winners deserving subsidies, and those which are hopeless, and therefore should be told to "sink or swim?" The answer is that there is no satisfactory way, *a priori*, to make those choices. If central authorities knew enough to sort out sinners from losers, they would not need a reform in the first place. It is the center's inability to micromanage the economy for lack of sufficient information which leads to reforms; and that same inability means that it cannot possibly choose intelligently among the inevitably universal requests of firms for transition subsidies. That argues for a quick transition with a very stingy subsidy policy, but a tight safety net to manage high, if short-term, transitional unemployment.

From the political point of view the argument against gradualism is the time it allows for opposition forces to build up, eventually diluting the reform beyond recognition. Reforms are wars without bullets, but nevertheless with high casualties. And like wars, it might be best from the political point of view to get the economic carnage out of the way quickly to cut off what could otherwise be an endless debate over how to minimize the inevitable pain.

On balance, these arguments for and against quick, comprehensive reforms, suggest that the quicker the better. Certainly that is the lesson from the Gorbachev years, in which the reforms have been so agonizingly gradual, so partial, and so ineffective that the credibility of the entire economic reform process is now threatened. The problem here is that politicians have, at least until recently, been the gatekeepers deciding how rapidly a reform would proceed; and they have tended to be cautious.

Politics and Economic Reforms

The role of politicians, and politics in general, is now coming to the fore as one of the most interesting dilemmas in reform strategy, a matter about which academic specialists have had very little to say. In comparing the course of reforms in the USSR and China over the last few years, one must ask whether political reforms are a necessary prerequisite for economic reforms? The (rather recent) conventional wisdom seems now to be that indeed without political reforms, economic reforms will ultimately fail. Events in China the last few years seem to provide one piece of confirming evidence that the lack of political reform can lead to an explosion, a retreat on economic reform. The other bit of evidence is from the USSR, where the political reforms have clearly provided (through the new legislative institutions) a safety valve to the populace, as well as a form of popular pressure to remove bureaucrats opposing change.

It is in fact too early to say much about this supposed requirement that political and economic reforms go hand in hand. Certainly the Soviet experience so far seems to support it. Democratization combined with *glasnost'* has seriously undermined local and mid-level bureaucratic opposition to reforms, leading to the removal of many "old-thinkers." The local elections in early 1990 should move that process ahead considerably. The Congress of People's Deputies, and the new Supreme Soviet, also seem to have a generally positive influence on economic policy and economic reform as they bring an accountability to those processes hitherto missing.

But inevitably the negative side of this new democratization will emerge in the next few years. Economic difficulties are likely to encourage a form of economic "populism" in which elected officials look for simple solutions to complex problems, in the process diluting some of the key elements of the reform (most likely beginning by resisting a much-needed reform of retail prices). No doubt these populist pressures will arise; the only question is how Soviet leaders will deal with them.

Likewise, democratization is leading naturally to pressure for increased regional autonomy, which could interfere directly with the need to impose austerity via a tight money policy, and with the efforts to create a competitive economy. Without going into the details, I would only note that the drive for regional autonomy, while potentially a threat to the reforms, also holds within it the possibility to support an acceleration of the reforms by allowing some regions to go out ahead of the remainder of the system. But that is an economic point and of course there are important political considerations here as well. We shall simply have to wait and see how political leaders handle this very complex issue.

IS SOVIET SOCIALISM REFORMABLE?

Is Soviet socialism reformable? Yes, it is reformable, and it is already being reformed at a pace far greater than the conventional wisdom would suggest. In the first place, Mikhail Gorbachev got some things right. He used *glasnost'* to discredit the past, which is critical in undercutting the credibility of conservative arguments favoring retreat. Moreover, he has constantly acted to radicalize the debate, through his own words, and also through the open press which has allowed a wide range of sometimes extraordinarily radical views to receive a complete and highly-visible hearing.

For those who see some of Gorbachev's moves in the last year as "retreats"— the crackdown on cooperatives, the slowdown on price reform, and so on—my answer is that they are thinking of a comprehensive process in terms of bits and pieces. Looking at the process as a whole, some of the "retreats" in fact can be interpreted as signs of a growing sophistication so necessary to move ahead.

What is most impressive about Mikhail Gorbachev and those around him is their ability to learn, something which is unmistakable this fall as they set out under the leadership of Leonid Abalkin to once again set the course for a radical reform. What is always true, is particularly so in poorly-charted territory; mistakes are not important, but learning from them is. Soviet leaders are learning.

Nevertheless, there have been serious mistakes in the first four and a half years under Mikhail Gorbachev, and the question now is whether he can recover and move ahead with the reform. In principle, I do not see why he cannot manage that, but he will have to move quickly, and with a much stronger reform than he has been able to manage so far. The basic philosophy of that new reform must focus on the creation of an economic environment which encourages innovation and cost-cutting, which will require that the government pursue a pro-competitive industrial policy, and a tight-money macro policy of the sort it has not yet been able to manage. Early on the government will have to build a reputation that it will be tough but fair, holding firm in a very stingy subsidy policy and a very liberal policy on prices, in order to begin the painful process of the transition. It will have to do this as quickly as possible to avoid the pitfalls of gradual reforms.

This fall, Leonid Abalkin, with the full support and urging of Mikhail Gorbachev, is putting together just such a program, and in 1990 the initial implementation phase should begin. It is far too early to predict the final details of the program even on paper, let alone its character as implemented, or its impact on the economic system. Furthermore, it is impossible to predict now the outcome of conflicts in the USSR over how local autonomy will work out, and their final resolution will have a major impact on the reform process. What is clear now is that Soviet leaders are aware of the magnitude of their problems. Moreover, they admit even their most recent mistakes, and they are learning from them.

Under the best of circumstances Soviet economic reform will be a long process, involving several governments, and probably more than one Soviet leader. And the circumstances will probably not be the best, so the road to reform will be quite rocky; its outcome, unpredictable. All I know for certain is that the Soviet Union of 1989 is a far more interesting and promising country than the Soviet Union of 1984. Because of that, and because of the inherent uncertainties in this reform process, it is far too early to write off *perestroika*.

NOTES

ABOUT THE AUTHOR: The late **Ed A. Hewett** was a senior fellow in foreign policy studies at the Brookings Institution of Washington, D.C.

1. This is true even of Leonid Abalkin's new reform program, introduced and discussed the week after this year's Sturc lecture. While that program provides the most radical, and complete, version of the new system, it still leaves much to the imagination on the important issues mentioned here. See Ed A. Hewett, "Perestroika-'Plus': The Abalkin Reforms," *PlanEcon Report*, December 1, 1989.

2. In small economies, such as those in Eastern Europe, competitive imports are indispensible to the success of the reform. But the USSR is a large and diverse market, one it might be possible to successfully reform without immediately opening up markets—say, a Japanese-type approach; although things would obviously go faster if competitive imports were used as one device for disciplining enterprises. Clearly this is yet another issue where the economics of the reform are fairly clear, but the politics may suggest the need for compromise. In the early stages of a reform the Soviet population will be far more prepared (albeit still quite reluctant) to accept plant closings forced by competition among Soviet enterprises, than to accept plant closings because Soviet enterprises could not compete with German, Japanese, or American firms.

3. Marton Tardos provides a very interesting argument in this regard with respect to bankruptcy laws, which are frequently taken as one of the "litmus" tests of the serious intentions of reformers. He argues that tough bankruptcy laws in a system with weak or nonexistent capital and labor markets (and even with socially-imposed restrictions against layoffs) can actually destroy enterprises which, in a market economy, could use their ability to lay off workers or borrow capital at high rates to make it through a difficult period. See Marton Tardos, "How to Create Markets in Eastern Europe: The Hungarian Case," in Josef C. Brada, Ed A. Hewett, and Thomas A. Wolf (eds.), *Economic Adjustment and Reform in*

Eastern Europe and the Soviet Union. Durham and London: Duke University Press, 1988, 259–284.

4. See Hewett, "Perestroika-'Plus'."

5. Domenico Mario Nuti, "Remonetization and Capital Markets in the Reform of Centrally Planned Economies," Paper presented to the Third Annual Conference of The European Economic Association, Bologna University, 27–29 August 1988. Those who are familiar with the literature on economic systems will recognize this as basically an "unravelling" of the various possible zones of influence between state and individual preferences discussed by Jan Drewnowski in "The Economic Theory of Socialism: A Suggestion for Reconsideration," *Journal of Political Economy*, Vol. LXIX, No. 4 (August, 1961), 341–54; reprinted in Morris Bornstein (ed.), *Comparative Economic Systems: Models and Cases*, Homewood, Ill.: R.D. Irwin, Revised Edition, 1969, 110–127.

28   Beyond Perestroyka: The Soviet Economy in Crisis

THE SYSTEM IN CRISIS

After six years under Mikhail Gorbachev, the Soviet economy is in crisis. This crisis has several elements: an accelerating decline in production, worsening inflation, a breakdown in interregional trade, and a fierce political struggle between the center and the republics over the future of the multinational state. Rather than responding to these problems with reforms, since last fall the union authorities have attempted to reassert central control over the economy and politics. This approach has been counterproductive. Although a new approach to the country's economic and political ills may be in the offing if a center-republic accord signed in late April bears fruit, previous agreements of this sort have proved fragile and fleeting.

SHARP DETERIORATION IN ECONOMIC PERFORMANCE

The Soviet economy had a bad year in 1989, but the period since January 1990 has been much worse. For the first time since World War II, the Soviets have acknowledged that overall output is declining—by 2 percent in 1990 and by a startling 8 percent during the first quarter of 1991 compared to the same period last year. Our own estimates, while subject to greater uncertainty than in years past, continue to indicate that the decline has been greater than officially claimed. Also, inflation is accelerating sharply, with retail prices rising by an estimated 14 percent in 1990, a reported 24 percent in the first quarter of 1991, and an average of more than 60 percent on 2 April of this year as a result of a presidential decree.

Measures of output and inflation alone do not fully reflect the extent to which imbalances between supply and demand have worsened or indicate how explosive the economy's problems have become. Shoppers with huge accumulations of excess rubles have swept store shelves clean. And rising prices and proliferating shortages have made consumer frustration a growing liability for leaders at all levels of government—especially as the population becomes increasingly aware of how poorly Soviet living standards compare with those in other countries.

Shortages of energy and basic industrial materials such as steel and chemicals have also intensified, and their impact has spread rapidly across the economy. Shortfalls in production of metallurgical coal, for example, have contributed to a reduction in steel output, which in turn has left machine builders short of materials. Factory managers, who can no longer rely on ministry and party officials to help them find supplies, have spent more and more time searching for crucial inputs and arranging barter deals. Even the defense industries appear to be less insulated than in the past from difficulties experienced in the rest of the economy. In an open letter in *Pravda* last September, for example, 45 high-level defense industry managers complained that the USSR's economic problems have caused increasing disruptions in their enterprises and "massive losses" of skilled workers.

Regional Fragmentation

The regional fragmentation of the Soviet state and economy is also proceeding at an increasingly rapid rate. Some republics—Estonia, Latvia, and Lithuania in the Baltic region, Armenia and Georgia in the Caucasus, and Moldova on the border with Romania—are bent on independence regardless of what happens in the rest of the USSR. The central leadership and the other republics have been locked in disagreement over a wide range of issues: the shape and content of a union treaty, the strategy and pace of market-oriented economic reforms, and control over natural resources, budget revenues, banks, the money supply, and earnings from hard currency exports. This political gridlock has impeded the efforts of leaders at all levels of government to address the economy's problems.

The nationwide breakdown of distribution has been aggravated by the efforts of republic and local authorities to insulate their own territories from the effects of ubiquitous shortages. Republics producing large amounts of food and other consumer goods have tried to keep their own populations supplied by withholding deliveries to central stocks and customary trading partners. The Ukraine and Kazakhstan failed to meet targets for grain deliveries to the state last year, and Georgia restricted shipments of citrus fruit and tea—its primary exports to the rest of the USSR. Many republics held back on deliveries of livestock products, which have been especially valuable in barter transactions. The main losers as a result of these disruptions in food deliveries have been industrial cities, other nonagricultural regions, and the food processing industry.

Regions producing key raw materials—such as oil, coal, and cotton—have also begun to ignore centrally mandated delivery targets in an effort to deal for supplies the center cannot guarantee. The Bashkir autonomous republic in Russia, for example, bartered oil for Estonian consumer goods last year, while Azerbaijan concluded a similar deal with Turkey. Uzbekistan withheld cotton from the state in hopes of increasing hard currency exports.

As these problems spread across the USSR, few regions escaped the decline in output last year. Official Soviet statistics indicate that in 1990 only three republics—Estonia, Turkmeniya, and Uzbekistan—registered increases in national income (a Soviet measure of total output excluding services). Some of the steepest declines occurred in republics experiencing interethnic violence or striving for independence—Armenia, Azerbaijan, and Lithuania.

In an ominous sign for future inflation, the dispute over the transfer of budget revenues from the republics to the central government has escalated sharply. Shortfalls in republic contributions reportedly left the union budget with a deficit of 27 billion rubles in the first quarter of this year—more than double the expected amount of 11 billion rubles.

Problems in Foreign Economic Relations

As a result of the ills afflicting the domestic economy, Soviet foreign economic relations are suffering, and the problems in foreign economic relations in turn are magnifying the domestic economy's problems. Hard currency imports, which jumped by more than 50 percent from 1987 to 1989, continued to climb in the first half of 1990. The Soviet leadership's efforts to ease shortages of consumer goods were largely responsible for this import surge, and enterprises exercising newly acquired rights to buy directly from Western businesses also played a role. Hard currency exports also rose but could not keep pace with imports, and the trade deficit for the first half of last year reached a record $4 billion.

The USSR got some breathing space in the second half of 1990. Heightened tensions in the Middle East led to a rough doubling of the hard currency prices of oil exports, and a reassertion of central control brought down hard currency imports. Many of the import cuts, however, came from supplies—particularly of steel products and chemicals—that were badly needed for domestic production.

To finance their burgeoning import bill, the Soviets nearly doubled their total borrowing from the West from 1987 to 1989. In late 1989 they also began to run up an unprecedented backlog of late payments to Western suppliers. With these arrears coming on top of mounting domestic political and economic turmoil, the Soviets found Western banks unwilling to provide new loans last year. To alleviate the resulting credit crunch, the USSR has drawn down cash reserves in Western banks, stepped up gold sales, and obtained financial assistance from Western governments. Nonetheless, its hard currency position remains weak.

The Soviets' economic problems—and the profound transformation under way in the region—have taken an especially heavy toll on Soviet-East European trade. The USSR ran a deficit in trade with Eastern Europe last year, when oil exports fell and imports remained about the same as in 1989. In the first quarter of 1991, when most of these longstanding trade arrangements changed to a hard currency basis, the Soviets slashed imports. Because they cut exports by much less than imports, the Soviets ran a trade surplus with Eastern Europe and earned badly needed hard currency. The costs have been high, however. The Soviets have lost badly needed imports of industrial supplies and consumer goods, and East European exports have suffered a severe blow.

In another dramatic change this year, the USSR will become a recipient of significant aid from the rest of the world. The Soviets have lined up about $14 billion in grants, loans, and credits backed by non-Communist governments that they must rely on during 1991 to maintain imports of needed goods. Italy and Germany are the largest donors of overall financial assistance, but about one-third of the aid to be disbursed this year will come from Arab states and South Korea. Moreover, Soviet economic aid to the less developed world is dropping sharply. Longtime clients such as Mongolia and Vietnam are slated to be virtually stricken from the aid roster this year.

Erosion of Living Standards

Since late 1988, the Soviet leadership has attempted to improve living standards by shifting resources from investment and defense to consumption. This policy has produced few benefits for Soviet consumers, who have complained with increasing frequency that inflation and shortages have sharply reduced their welfare. Although estimated consumption of goods and services adjusted for inflation registered a small per capita increase in 1990, much of this increase reflected higher output of alcohol and expensive household appliances and consumer electronics. Moreover, the imports and drawdowns of inventories that helped boost consumption last year cannot be sustained.

Problems on the supply side, in any event, have been only partly to blame for the erosion of living standards. Personal money incomes leaped by 16 percent per capita in 1990, according to official Soviet statistics, overwhelming the small improvement in supplies of consumer goods and services. One result was a surge of inflation. Our estimates indicate that retail prices of consumer goods sold in state stores and on farmers' markets climbed by about 14 percent last year—roughly twice as fast as in 1989. Black market prices almost certainly went up even faster. In addition, because controls still kept most prices from rising enough to balance supply and demand, some inflation was repressed, resulting in shortages and a scramble for goods. According to one Soviet report, for example, the "availability"—not further defined—of basic food items declined from 90 percent in 1983 to 22 percent in 1989 and 11 percent in mid-1990.

With shortages leaving state store shelves bare, some lucky consumers have had access to special distribution channels, such as workplace sales of food and appliances. Arrangements of this kind have spread rapidly in recent years, helping some segments of the population—especially workers at large factories—but reducing supplies of consumer goods available to the general public.

In an effort to protect residents of their areas from shortages, first local and now republic-level authorities throughout the Soviet Union have introduced a rapidly growing number and variety of rationing schemes. More and more cities have issued coupons for consumer goods in short supply, such as meat and sugar. In the Baltic republics and in many cities, including Moscow and Leningrad, consumer goods are sold only on proof of residence. The most extensive rationing scheme to date—introduced by the Ukraine in November 1990 and adopted by Moldova in March 1991—requires purchasers to provide coupons distributed along with their pay or pensions, in addition to money, for the vast majority of their purchases from state stores. Also, as mentioned earlier, several republics have banned the shipment of consumer goods outside their borders, in what one Soviet economist has called a "bacchanalia of local protectionism."

Consumers whose needs are not covered by special distribution channels or rationing have been left to rely to an ever greater extent on black market purchases, if they can afford the higher prices, or on potluck in state stores. Press reports indicate that many shoppers buy goods they do not want themselves and barter with family members and friends for what they do need, and almost everyone stocks goods for future use. One Soviet survey found that 9 out of 10 respondents maintained such stocks in 1989, up from 1 out of 4 in 1988. In November 1990, a deputy trade minister placed the value of household hoards at 120 to 130 billion rubles—roughly one-fourth of the value of retail sales last year.

As miserable as the consumer's lot was in 1990, it has worsened since the beginning of this year. Official Soviet statistics indicate that output of manufactured consumer goods in the first quarter of 1991 was 3 percent lower than in the same period last year, while money incomes went up by 24 percent. Two presidential decrees implemented in January also added to rising consumer frustration. A 5 percent sales tax was imposed on all goods—even the most basic consumer necessities—and a currency changeover resulted in the confiscation of 50- and 100-ruble notes that could not be proved to have been earned.

Probably the greatest blow to consumers occurred on 2 April 1991, when much of the repressed inflation that has built up in recent years was transformed into open price increases. The retail prices of consumer goods were raised by 60 to 70 percent on average—with larger increases in food prices that were particularly alarming for the low-income population. Despite the compensation payments accompanying these price hikes, we estimate that the purchasing power of people's incomes has fallen by 15 to 20 percent on average.

Cutbacks in Investment

Although the regime's shift of resources toward consumption has done little to improve living standards, it has taken a substantial bite out of investment at a time when the Soviet economy is in dire need of modernization. According to official Soviet statistics, state investment in 1990 was 4 percent less than in 1989, reflecting a sharp drop in centrally financed investment that was partly offset by an increase in investment funded by enterprises. Completions of investment projects also declined, and only two-fifths of the high-priority projects included in state orders were finished—down from one-half in 1989. This decrease in project completions included infrastructure intended to benefit consumers, such as housing, schools, preschools, hospitals, and clinics. Meanwhile, the backlog of unfinished construction reportedly swelled by 11 percent.

The investment downturn last year reflected a decrease in domestic output of machinery and an especially sharp drop in construction activity. Inadequate supplies of construction materials and equipment such as bulldozers, cranes, and excavators were part of the problem. In addition, state construction organizations lost workers to cooperatives, where wages reportedly were nearly one-third higher.

Defense Spending Down

Defense program reductions last year followed the same general trends that developed in 1989. Our estimates indicate that the overall annual decline in defense spending was about 6 percent in both years. The driving forces behind these cuts have been the poor state of the economy and the leadership's desire to reduce the budget deficit and shift resources to civilian production. On the arms control front, the Soviets have tried to ease requirements for new weapons by constraining Western force modernization while posturing their forces for Strategic Arms Reduction Talks and Conventional Forces in Europe agreements.

We estimate that procurement outlays, which account for almost half of total defense spending, fell by about 10 percent in each of the last two years. Percentage reductions were almost equally distributed between strategic and general purpose forces. The heaviest cuts in both 1989 and 1990 came in procurement of land arms—artillery, light armored vehicles, and particularly tanks. Aircraft procurement declined as well.

Expenditures on the other major components of defense also have fallen over the past two years, although not quite as steeply as procurement. Personnel outlays reflect a decrease of about 500,000 in the number of troops since 1988. The decline in spending on operations and maintenance results primarily from a downturn in space launch activity, as well as from shrinking inventories and a slower pace of training and exercises. The available evidence suggests that outlays on research and development leveled off in 1989 and declined in 1990, although our estimates for this category are much more uncertain than for the other components of defense spending.

chronological type of outline explaining what went wrong.

SOURCES OF DIFFICULTIES

The Soviets' current economic problems stem from a variety of sources: an accelerating breakdown of the traditional system of managing the economy from the center, a progressive loss of control over financial flows, a mismanaged shift of resources from investment and defense to consumption, and rising political and social tensions.

Breakdown of Traditional System

especially one they ignored. basic market structure and they didn't like & were capitalist

The traditional Soviet economic system—with central planners setting output targets for all sorts of products and allocating the supplies needed to produce at these levels—was always inefficient. Its allocation procedures and excessive secrecy also condemned the USSR to technological backwardness. In short, it was a system that was relegating the USSR to the status of a developing country. Nonetheless, it was a functioning system with fairly stable rules. In 1988 and 1989, however, it was seriously weakened by partial economic reforms, and, since early last year, its erosion has accelerated rapidly and developed a regional dimension. The country went from stagnation into decline.

Early in the *perestroyka* years, enterprises were instructed to earn profits, but most prices—which did not reflect supply and demand accurately—were not changed until 1991. Even the realigned prices now in effect take little account of demand, although they do better reflect current production costs. Under these conditions, prices have not stimulated increases in production of the goods that are needed most urgently. Moreover, controlled prices have combined with inflationary pressures— fueled by the excessive budget deficits discussed below—to create steadily worsening shortages.

Another problem is that the development of the "direct links" between buyers and sellers that were supposed to reduce the need for central planning has run into difficulties. The lack of progress stems partly from the continuing efforts of bureaucrats in ministries and supply organizations to cling to their old functions. It has been exacerbated by the longstanding monopolization of industry and by the recent plague of regional protectionism.

monopoly was encouraged

Many Soviet industries are dominated by monopoly producers, whose development was actively encouraged by central planners. For example, the USSR's entire output of potato, corn, and cotton harvesting machinery comes from single factories—all in different republics. Single factories also account for more than half of all production of automobiles, freezers, and oil and gas drilling rigs. Under these conditions, shortfalls of output at one plant cannot be made up elsewhere and spread rapidly across the economy.

The efforts of republic and local authorities to protect factories and consumers on their territories from the general deterioration of the economy became a major factor in the erosion of the traditional system last year. In the past, Soviet economic development policy encouraged most republics to specialize in certain kinds of production and trade with each other rather than become self-sufficient. The Ukraine is a major center of heavy industry, for instance, while Uzbekistan specializes in cotton. Given these circumstances, republic bans on shipping goods outside their borders have been particularly disruptive. On a more positive note, the republics have moved quickly to sign economic agreements with each other in efforts to assure deliveries of needed supplies. The terms of most of the basic agreements are vague, however, and often cannot be enforced.

Loss of Financial Control

For all but the first year of Gorbachev's tenure, the Soviet government has been running large budget deficits, and the 1990 deficit further fueled inflationary pressure. We are skeptical of official claims that the deficit last year was slightly below the limit approved by the Supreme Soviet, partly because the claimed figure for total budget revenues appears inflated compared with the information available on individual revenue categories. In addition, a thorough examination of the Soviet budget by the International Monetary Fund indicates that off-budget expenditures to support agricultural prices should be added to the official deficit.[1] Whatever the actual deficit was, the government's efforts to finance it by selling interest-bearing securities fell far short of plan. As in the past, therefore, the deficit was funded almost entirely by adding to the money supply, which increased by an estimated 15 percent in 1990. The excessive budget deficit and rapid growth of the money supply, in turn, made a major contribution to the leap in personal money incomes.

Fiscal and monetary problems multiplied rapidly in the first quarter of 1991. Budget outlays on subsidies rose sharply when wholesale prices were raised on 1 January while retail price hikes were delayed, pending negotiation of a center-republic agreement, until 2 April. The subsidy burden shifted to the republics starting this year, and perhaps partly to cover that bill, they withheld budget revenues from the central government. The center was then forced to finance its expenditures by creating money. Now that retail prices are up, subsidies will be reduced sharply, but compensation payments to the population—financed by a combination of budget and enterprise funds—are so generous that they will add new fuel to inflationary fires.

Mismanaged Shift of Resources

The leadership's policy of shifting resources toward consumption is a move that was badly needed and long overdue, but the mismanaged implementation of this policy has led to disarray and confusion in investment and the defense industry. Skimping on investment in basic industrial materials has contributed to declining output and shortages of these vital supplies. Centralized investment in these industries was cut last year, and producing enterprises—whose profit margins were dwindling rapidly before wholesale prices were raised this January—had few funds of their own to invest. Moreover, investment in transportation has been neglected for years. Premier Pavlov recently recommended an adjustment of priorities to maintain adequate investment in output not directly used by consumers.

Soviet officials have said that only part of the drop in military production is being offset by increases in the defense industry's output of civilian goods. Moreover, many defense industry managers are now worried that the speed with which they have had to increase civilian production is causing them to lose valuable technical expertise acquired over years of working for the military. A number of these managers have expressed interest in developing export markets and spin-offs of their traditional output that would allow them to maintain military production capacity and remain solvent financially.

Moreover, efforts to improve supplies of consumer goods quickly by stepping up imports have left the USSR with a rising hard currency debt, which must now be serviced in spite of falling oil production and the reluctance of commercial creditors to extend new loans. Hard currency problems led to some reductions last year in imports of materials and equipment needed to sustain domestic production and much sharper cutbacks in the first quarter of 1991.

Political and Social Tensions

Another reason for the economy's decline is that mounting political and social tensions have interacted with—and worsened—Soviet economic difficulties. Center-republic clashes over the republics' efforts to achieve independence, for example, have sparked labor protests and blockades as well as entailing violence and loss of life, as in Lithuania in January 1991. Ethnic disputes, too, have fueled a variety of conflicts—many of them violent—between and within republics, and these conflicts have at times played havoc with the economy. The clashes between Armenia and Azerbaijan in early 1990, for example, dealt severe setbacks to economic performance in both republics.

Strikes—sparked partly by worsening consumer shortages and inflation—have also become an increasingly serious problem. According to Soviet statistics, losses of work time as a result of strikes amounted to 10 million worker days in 1990—easily surpassing the previous record of 7 million in 1989. This year, the coal miners' strikes that began in March have aggravated energy shortages and contributed heavily to the sharp drop in output.

Finally, popular concern over the environment has forced plant closures that have made a substantial dent in industrial output. The impact on the chemical and wood products industries last year was particularly severe. A series of closings and partial reopenings of the Nairit chemical factory in Armenia, for example, cut supplies of plastics, synthetic rubber, and chemicals used to produce medicine. The shutdown of the Sloka pulp plant in Latvia removed the USSR's sole source of paper for computer punch cards, book and magazine covers, and cigarette packaging. In addition, public protests about the safety of nuclear power plants in the last several years have contributed to delays in the construction of electric power stations. Nuclear plants accounted for more than half of the shortfall in completing new electric power generating capacity in 1990.

LITTLE PROGRESS TOWARD A MARKET ECONOMY

Although advocates of markets can take some consolation from important legislation passed last year, the Soviet central leadership has concentrated on stabilization since last November while putting market-oriented economic reforms on the back burner. In response, some republics, especially Russia, have attempted to seize the initiative from the center by proposing alternative reform programs. At the grass roots level, moreover, private economic initiative remains alive despite cumbersome and frequently changing regulations.

The Reform Debate

As the Soviet economic crisis deepened last year most economists and politicians came to realize that the reform and stabilization plan approved in December 1989 had been overtaken by events and was simply inadequate to the task at hand. The consensus ended there, however, and most of the year was consumed by bickering over which of several proposed new game plans to adopt.

The debate over a new economic program began in May 1990 when Premier Ryzhkov first presented the government's version to the Supreme Soviet. Ryzhkov's plan called for a five-year transition to a "regulated market" economy and emphasized the need for price revisions as a first step toward deregulation. Legislators rejected the increase in bread prices he proposed for July, questioned the wisdom of other price hikes scheduled for January 1991, and remanded the program for further work.

Meanwhile, Boris Yel'tsin, elected head of the Russian republic's legislature in May, began promoting an alternative program that would give first priority to supplanting state control of assets with private ownership and shorten the time allotted for the transition to a market economy from five years to "500 days." To keep Yel'tsin from moving ahead on his own, Gorbachev reached an agreement with him to cosponsor a working group, chaired by Presidential Council member Stanislav Shatalin, that would come up with a "synthesis" of the Yel'tsin and Ryzhkov programs. Ryzhkov and other members of his government, however, were totally unwilling to cooperate with Shatalin, and Gorbachev himself may have developed doubts as he realized the loss of central power the Shatalin plan would entail.

Gorbachev's Program:
A Pledge to Implement Real Reforms ...

Gorbachev directed the preparation of another program that replaced Shatalin's link between stabilization and reform with an emphasis on stabilization now, reform later. That program, which was approved by the legislature in October, still called for the eventual replacement of Marxist by market economics. ... If strictly implemented, it would deregulate most prices, sell off a substantial portion of state assets to joint-stock companies, labor collectives, cooperatives, and individuals, and introduce an element of genuine competition to an economy long dominated by monopolies.

... but with Potentially Fatal Flaws

The Gorbachev economic program, however, contained a number of fatal flaws:

- Like past reform programs, all of which have failed, it placed considerable responsibility for implementation on the central government bureaucracy—the very institution that stands to lose the most from the dismantling of a command economy.
- The increased economic autonomy it gave the republics fell far short of their demands, reducing the prospects for unionwide adherence.
- The vagueness of its provisions and timetables made it subject to selective implementation and delay by the political leadership.

The plan's malleability predictably has proved a curse for reform. The regime's initial implementing decrees have given a clear priority to stabilization, with much of this to be accomplished by administrative measures and a new reliance on the police and KGB to enforce the center's economic decrees. This emphasis has come largely at the expense of fundamental reforms the economy so urgently needs. Moreover, stabilization by administrative decree has proved elusive at a time when the center's commands carry increasingly less weight with republic leaders and enterprise managers.

The regime's retreat from reforms has not been confined to the economic arena. Powerful groups—notably the Communist Party, the military, and defense industrialists—felt seriously threatened last fall by the devolution of power to the republics proposed in the Shatalin program. To placate these groups, Gorbachev has used the expanded presidential powers he requested and received in November to fight reformist efforts being pursued by the republics.

Some Remaining Bright Spots on Reform Front

Economic reform legislation passed last year, however, remains on the books and could provide a framework for the development of private economic activity and markets at some future date, if the political climate improves. The USSR Supreme Soviet approved a wide array of laws on such fundamental issues as property rights, land use, enterprise rights, taxes, and banking. Most were drawn up in 1989 but became the subject of prolonged and divisive debate that stretched well into 1990. While the final package is a product of political compromise, it still breaks new ground in establishing the legal basis for a more market-oriented system.

The growing self-assertiveness of the republics and their willingness to pursue policies different from the center's also have given reformers reason to believe that their cause is no longer completely hostage to changes in the commitment of the union authorities. Market-oriented reform efforts in the republics during the past year have been closely intertwined with efforts to promote economic independence from the central government. All of the republics have issued declarations of sovereignty that proclaim authority over natural resources on their territory and control over their tax collection and banking systems, but republic reform efforts have varied greatly in pace and scope.

The reform climate has been most favorable in the Russian and Baltic republics. Russia has passed key legislation on property and land reform as part of a professed commitment to the Shatalin program rejected by the center. In addition, the government's most recent reform initiative calls for stepped up privatization and a phased decontrol of prices within six to eight months. The Baltic republics also have begun implementing ambitious plans to privatize property, reduce budget subsidies, and create their own banks and convertible currencies. In addition to these reform efforts, Russia and all three Baltic republics are actively promoting trade with the outside world and foreign investment on their territory.

Meanwhile, at the grass roots level private economic initiative continues to expand and find new outlets. According to Soviet statistics, production by cooperative businesses increased by 75 percent last year, even though the number of restrictive regulations also grew. In agriculture, the formation of independent farms has continued, albeit slowly, with a minimum of official encouragement. One of the most promising recent developments is the sprouting of "commodity exchanges" in cities from the Baltics to Siberia. So far, these exchanges bear little resemblance to the sophisticated Western organizations of the same name, but they do provide a source of badly needed supplies for factory managers who can no longer rely on the crumbling central distribution system. In addition, they are much more efficient than barter deals arranged one at a time.

Given several years to develop in a political environment conducive to their growth, these exchanges and other fledgling market institutions could contribute greatly to economic recovery. The Soviet economy's problems are currently so severe, however, that our assessment of its prospects must have a shorter-term focus.

GRIM PROSPECTS IN NEAR TERM

The Soviet economy is in such turmoil that it is impossible to estimate its performance by relying totally on the methods used when the economic system was relatively stable. All things considered, we believe real Soviet gross national product (GNP) declined by about 4 to 5 percent in 1990. Given the great perturbation in the economy, however, GNP numbers alone tell much less of a story than usual.

There is no doubt that 1991 will be a worse year for the Soviet economy than 1990, and in all likelihood it will be sharply worse. Despite renewed expressions of support for market-oriented reforms by the union leadership and an agreement by the center and nine republics to implement anticrisis measures, the politics of both reform and stabilization likely will continue in turmoil, and the economy likely will continue to suffer from sharp shifts in government policy. Most unofficial Soviet forecasts place the likely decline in output at 10 to 20 percent, and, according to some estimates—which we consider extreme—output could fall by as much as 40 percent. Declining output will not be the only problem, moreover. The Soviets also will have to face the consequences of excessive budget deficits, rapid expansion of the money supply, rising inflation, and deteriorating external economic relations.

The Leadership's Anticrisis Program

The central leadership recently responded to the accelerating deterioration of the economy with yet another effort at stabilization—this time called an "action program for leading the economy out of crisis." The draft anticrisis program issued in early April includes a host of measures aimed at stabilizing the production and distribution of goods—especially food and other consumer necessities—and bringing the budget deficit and money supply under control. Some of these measures have been tried before with little success, but others—for example, the removal of restrictions on overtime work and the reopening of factories closed for environmental reasons—are as yet untested. In an effort to enhance its appeal to reformers, the program also calls for speeding up the privatization of housing, retail trade, consumer services, and small industrial enterprises, as well as for completing the transition to "primary free price formation" by 1 October 1992.

The prospects for the anticrisis program depend less on these provisions, however, than on whether the center and the republics can resolve the impasse in their political and economic relations and on whether the promises in the program will be followed by concrete actions. The agreement reached on 23 April 1991 by Gorbachev and the leaders of nine republics may be a promising sign for future cooperation and could give new momentum to economic reform. Although not all the details of this accord are known, it appears that Gorbachev consented to a devolution of political and economic power to the republics in return for their support of the center's stabilization measures and agreement to sign a new union treaty soon. Reportedly the republics will be free to pursue economic reform at their own pace. If so, they will be given a chance to demonstrate that their claims of being more committed than the center to free market principles are more than empty boasts. If the accord is to be sustained for more than a few months, however, the center will have to permit a much larger republic role in central decision-making.

Falling Output and Rising Inflation

The course Gorbachev was pursuing prior to 23 April—trying to stabilize the economy and maintain the union through a mixture of administrative measures and intimidation—has already led to a sharp drop in output. If this course is maintained, real Soviet GNP is likely to decline by 10 to 15 percent in 1991, and the annual rate of inflation could easily exceed 100 percent.

If the regime resorts to more repressive policies—such as the introduction of presidential rule in the republics and severe punishment for failure to comply with central orders—the results would depend on the population's response. Acceptance of such a step back toward the old system probably would help stem the decline in output and the rise in prices in the short run. The regime would run a serious risk, however, of popular resistance in the form of demonstrations, strikes, and possibly outright rebellions. Under these conditions, real GNP would fall by at least 15 percent, and inflation could spiral out of control.

Another possibility is that the 23 April agreement could serve as a basis for sustained improvement in center-republic relations and a renewal of reform. This would help to reduce confusion over lines of authority, promote interrepublic trade and thus ease supply bottlenecks, and facilitate center-republic cooperation on efforts to reduce the budget deficit. The decline in real GNP this year probably would still be close to 10 percent, but inflationary pressures could ease. In the next few years, prospects for stabilizing output would improve, but the freeing of prices that serious reform efforts would require probably would lead to extremely high inflation.

Hard Currency Crunch

Whatever course the center pursues, the USSR will face tough choices this year in trying to halt the deterioration of its external financial position. Oil exports will continue to decline as a result of problems in domestic production and the soft world market. Depending on world prices, hard currency revenues from oil exports could fall by 25 to 60 percent. Markets will remain weak for Soviet exports of manufactured goods, including arms. Meanwhile, demand for imports, especially of agricultural products, is likely to remain high.

The Soviets will also face a rising debt service burden in the form of interest charges and scheduled payments of principal on medium- and long-term debt. Some short-term credits that Western lenders have been refusing to roll over also will have to be repaid, and the pressure to eliminate arrears in payments to Western firms will be great. Some of the credits already pledged by Western governments have been disbursed slowly—probably as a result of Western displeasure over center-republic confrontations and a lack of progress on economic reforms. Moreover, the Soviets have not drawn heavily on credits tied to nonfood goods. Instead, the drastic import reductions in the first quarter of 1991 indicate that the USSR has chosen to limit expenditures rather than face comprehensive debt rescheduling. These import cuts have hurt domestic production, however, and the Soviets will have difficulty continuing along this course.

Tighter Belts All Around

Given the sharp drop in output that appears all but inevitable this year, nearly everyone will be left with fewer resources. Rising pressure to reduce the budget deficit but still improve the social safety net is likely to mean continued reductions in both investment and defense. Indeed, defense cuts are likely regardless of the direction center-republic relations take. If the center resorts to more repressive tactics, the most likely result would be a drop in output so sharp that it would necessitate lower military spending. A center-republic accord, in contrast, would improve economic prospects generally. At the same time, it would likely give the republics a greater share of tax revenues and reduce the funds available for defense and other programs financed by the central government.

After the erosion in the quality of life that has occurred during the past two years, Soviet consumers are reluctant to endure further hardships. Unfortunately, no relief is in sight. The drop in output in the first quarter extended to manufactured consumer goods, and the defense conversion program has not provided the benefits the leadership hoped for. Moreover, tight limits on the availability of hard currency will make it increasingly difficult to boost imports. Perhaps worst of all are the twin threats of rising unemployment and accelerating consumer inflation.

Under these circumstances, it is no surprise that consumer hardships have become a severe liability for political leaders at all levels of government. The recent prolonged strikes by coal miners and sporadic protests by other workers were directed at the policies of the central government and played a role in moving the center back toward a dialogue with reform-minded republic leaders. But these demonstrations were also an indication of popular impatience with all levels of government for not improving standards of living. It will take great political skill to retain—and, in the case of the central government, regain—popular trust and to put through effective but often initially painful reform measures. The alternative, however, is a completely bleak Soviet future.

NOTES

ABOUT THIS CHAPTER: This report was prepared by the U.S. Central Intelligence Agency and the Defense Intelligence Agency. The data presented presumably do not include the so-called second economy, whose activities are by definition not covered in any official statistics. It is likely that the relative role of the second economy increased in recent years. It is equally likely that estimates of its contribution to the Soviet economy would change figures somewhat, but would scarcely invalidate the findings presented in this report.

1. International Monetary Fund, The World Bank, Organization for Economic Cooperation and Development, European Bank for Reconstruction and Development, *A Study of the Soviet Economy* (Paris, February 1991), Volume 1, p. 54.

29   *The Effort Collapses*

MARSHALL GOLDMAN

Once having stumbled, Gorbachev found it virtually impossible to regain his balance. By mid-1987, possibly even beginning in late 1986, the damage had already been done. After two years or so of poor results, he had lost much of his credibility, at least on economic matters. Thereafter, the crisis began to build. By mid-1988 the decline was becoming evident and important economic institutions were beginning to disintegrate. Even if he had an ideal program at that point, he would have had a great deal of difficulty redressing his past mistakes. By that time only massive radical surgery could have rescued the economy.

At the core of his problem was a macroeconomic difficulty of his own making. Heretofore Soviet officials, including Gorbachev and his economic advisers, thought only in terms of central plans and administrative decision making. Macro- and microeconomics were capitalist system-type issues that had no relevance for a centrally planned economy. Stalin in effect had decreed null and void the impact of taxes, expenditures, monetary policy, interest rates (macroeconomics), and supply and demand, and competition (microeconomics) played little or no role. Unaccustomed to paying attention to such matters, they ignored signs of runaway inflation until it was too late.

For decades Soviet officials had insisted that the national budget was in balance. Even though this was not true, they did not worry about such things. And as we saw, when even a Politburo member like Gorbachev asked Andropov if there were budget deficits, he was told that it was nothing he should worry about. More important to the Soviet leadership was whether or not the five-year plans were in balance. This approach was a natural reaction from engineers who predominated in Gosplan's offices. They understood the need to balance physical supplies, but not revenues and expenditures. Consequently an unbalanced budget in their eyes would not have made much difference.

When unexpectedly in October 1988 it was announced as part of glasnost that the Soviet budget had been running a deficit since 1976, the reaction was initially more one of bemusement than one of great concern.[1] That there had been budget deficits for a long period of time and that the public had not been informed apparently seemed to have made little difference. As far as most economists could ascertain, the economy in that period operated much as it usually did. Moreover, this was not the only time the government had lied. [Even Gorbachev, as we saw earlier, was denied a full accounting by Andropov when he tried to find out if the Soviet Union had a budget deficit.]

According to official but untrue statistics, Boris Gosteev, the minister of finance, reported in October 1985 that the Soviet Union had generated a budget surplus of 4.1 billion rubles.[2] Belatedly in 1988, he corrected himself to reveal that on the contrary, the 1985 budget had not run a surplus but a deficit of 37 billion rubles, or about $59 billion.[3] Conditions apparently had not changed much in the early years of the Gorbachev era. Gosteev anticipated that in 1989 there would be a budget deficit of 35 billion rubles or about $56 billion, not much different from the deficit ultimately reported in 1985.[4] ...

It became quickly apparent, however, that the deficit and its magnitude involved more than a debate among Sovietologists. Some important economic issues were involved, affecting not only how the Soviet economy had been operating, but how it would operate in the future. The sudden acknowledgment of a deficit suggested there might be a cover-up on other economic matters as well. In his confession, Minister of Finance Gosteev, for example, continued to insist that the Soviet Union would spend only 20.2 billion rubles (about $33 billion), or almost 2 percent of the Soviet GNP, on the maintenance of Soviet armed forces.[6] Given that military expenditures constituted the largest single budget item in the Soviet budget, this seemed a ridiculously low figure. Subsequently Gorbachev himself acknowledged that the military budget amounted to 77 billion rubles, or some 7 percent of the Soviet GNP. Since so much more was being spent on the military, how could Gosteev report that the budget deficit in 1989 was only 35 billion rubles? Most observers in the West, including the CIA, agreed that the defense budget was closer to 15 to 20 percent of the Soviet GNP, and some Soviet critics said the military expenditures may have been as high as 25 percent of the Soviet GNP.[7]

This absence of a full accounting revealed the limits to glasnost. Equally important, because of continued quirks in the Soviet pricing system, Soviet officials really do not know how to price their military equipment. Traditionally, the military sector has received special treatment. There is a strong sense among many Soviet and Western economists that because of the subsidies provided to enterprises producing military goods, the Soviet military industrial complex claims a larger share of the country's resources than is reflected in the statistics. That means that machinery used for military production is priced more cheaply than comparable machinery used for civilian production. Soviet soldiers and also draftees receive a very low salary. Reinforcing that skepticism is the fact that the Soviet economists assigned to official commissions to design some of the reform programs that have been officially commissioned are also unable to obtain the official data.[8]

What had caused the rapid increases in the budget deficit? Since Ministry of Finance officials acknowledged that the budget had moved into the red in the early 1970s before Gorbachev was summoned to Moscow, it is evident that deficits are not solely due to faulty decision making on Gorbachev's part.[9] The deficit fluctuated in a relatively narrow range between 1978 and 1985.

But the increases in the deficit beginning in 1986 are mainly Gorbachev's doing. In one year, from 1985 to 1986, the budget deficit increased almost threefold from 17–18 billion rubles to 48–50 billion. [Gosteev's figure for 1985 is 37 billion rubles.] Of course the public was given no hint at the time, but the increase in the deficit can be attributed to Gorbachev's approach to perestroika. … Gorbachev's first version of perestroika involved an increased emphasis on the role of heavy industry and machine tools, or what the Soviets call sector A. His fetish with machine tools also had a double-barreled impact on Soviet foreign trade. On the one hand, he and his advisers deliberately set out to increase imports of Western machine tools. On the other hand, to pay for these imports, Gorbachev found it necessary to reduce imports of consumer goods. This resulted in shortages and lost sales tax revenue.

… By 1988, the Soviet Union had increased imports of machinery by approximately 2.5 billion rubles over 1984. This was done despite the fact that due to the fall in the world price of oil, petroleum export sales to both hard and soft currency buyers fell from a high of 30.9 billion rubles in 1984 in the pre-Gorbachev period to about 20.7 billion rubles in 1988. This loss constituted a staggering drop of 10 billion rubles, or one third of the total of the Soviet Union's export earning capacity.

Fortunately, two good harvests in 1986 and 1987 made it possible for the Soviet Union to reduce grain imports. This allowed a reduction of 2–3 billion rubles in import expenditures, making up for some of the shrinkage in export earnings. But poor harvests in 1988 and 1989 made it necessary to increase grain imports by 50 percent in 1988 and again in 1989, thereby increasing hard currency expenditures on imports. When it became clear that oil export revenues had fallen off sharply, Gorbachev's advisers would have been prudent to recommend reducing machinery imports by a substantial amount as early as 1985 and certainly before 1987. … However, Gorbachev and his staff did just the opposite; rather than cut back on machinery imports, they actually increased them.

To compensate, Soviet officials cut imports of consumer goods. This began in 1986 and continued each year into 1989, so that by 1988 Soviet consumer goods were about 1.5 billion rubles less than they had been in 1985. … With sales tax and exchange rate supplements included, these imported consumer goods would have been marked up about sixfold by the time they were sold to Soviet consumers. This explains why Soviet authorities report that under Gorbachev, food and consumer good imports fell by the equivalent of 8.5 billion rubles in retail prices.[10] This slashing of consumer good imports and the resulting loss of sales tax revenue had serious fiscal implications.

The fetish with industrial machinery was further reflected in the domestic budget. Budget expenditures on capital investment for both factory construction and machinery (particularly sector A—heavy industry) continued to rise steadily throughout the Gorbachev years, with a particularly notable surge in 1986.[11]

Taken alone, the increase in budget expenditures for machine tools would probably not have been enough to precipitate the breakdown in fiscal discipline that has proven to be so difficult to control. However, when this expenditure was combined with a decision about social policy, the problem was compounded. The May 1985 crackdown on vodka sales, while regarded primarily as a laudable social policy, had serious economic implications.

The curb on the sale of vodka combined with the sale of fewer consumer good imports resulted in a drop in turnover tax receipts, the Soviet counterpart of a sales tax. From a high of 103 billion rubles in 1983 and 1984, turnover tax collections fell by nearly 13 percent to a low of 91.5 billion rubles in 1986. Overall the anti-alcohol drive was said to cost 200 billion rubles.[12]

The impact of higher budget expenditures on machine tools combined with lower turnover tax collections was dramatic. It was the main reason for the increase in size of the deficit to 48 billion rubles in 1986. Once the 17 billion ruble deficit was breached, what little economic discipline was left seemed to dissipate. Thereafter the deficit increased each year and continued to grow. By 1989, the budget deficit was not the 35 billion rubles that Gosteev anticipated, but at least 90 billion rubles. A new minister of finance, Valentin Pavlov, reported that the deficit in 1989 actually totalled 120 billion rubles, or 10–12 percent of the Soviet GNP.[13] Again the disparity probably reflects the continuing inability of Soviet statisticians to determine what the figures actually were.

Because of strenuous and determined efforts to cut budget subsidies, it was predicted that the deficit of 1990 would be reduced to 60 billion rubles.[14] Similar to efforts in the United States, that proved to be wishful thinking. Unofficial estimates in October 1990 indicated that instead of a shrinkage, the 1990 Soviet budget deficit had actually increased to over 150 billion rubles and maybe even 200 billion rubles.[15] Some officials in the Ministry of Finance insist the deficit was closer to 100 billion rubles, but as of 1990 most Soviet economists acknowledge in private conversation that with the size of the military budget in doubt and the various republics acting as if they are sovereign countries, no one really knows what the deficit is. Led by the Russian Republic, the republics began to withhold three quarters of the 1991 tax collections which the center had expected to collect. This caused Vladimir Orlov, then the minister of finance, to warn that the first quarter budget deficit already exceeded the planned deficit for the whole year.

Gorbachev's well-intended but misguided economic strategy was in itself enough to cripple any chance to bring about the economic revitalization he wanted so badly. But the macroeconomic implications of his budget deficit eventually came to have their own impact. Whatever their commitment to socialist economic planning, Soviet officials by 1989 and certainly by 1990 belatedly came to understand that macroeconomics and budget deficits, particularly large ones, do matter. As Gorbachev himself admitted in an October 19, 1990, speech to the Supreme Soviet of the USSR, "We lost control over the financial situation in the country. This was our most serious mistake in the years of perestroika. ... Achieving a balanced budget today is the number one task and the most important one."[16] But Gorbachev's disregard of macroeconomics and the conventional wisdom that planning was what mattered had taken its toll. Because it had been ignored, the budget deficit had become so large that it set in motion forces that made the malfunctioning of the system all the harder to remedy. The magnitude of the deficit began to threaten the continued functioning of the national economic system.

One of the most serious consequences of the growing budget deficit was a sharp jump in inflation. For the most part, these deficits and debts were financed the old-fashioned way—by turning on the printing presses, which in turn caused the sudden inflation and goods shortages. Inflation is not an entirely new phenomenon in the Soviet Union. Because of the persistent emphasis on military expenditures and heavy industry, there has always been a tendency to pay out a wage bill that was larger than the value of the consumer goods and services available for purchase with those wages. And since most prices were carefully controlled in state shops, the result was a steady form of suppressed inflation. But the increasing size of the budget deficit and the legalization of cooperative ventures with considerably more power to set their own prices made inflation overt even in official Soviet statistics. In 1988, for the first time since World War II, prices of virtually all Soviet goods began to rise. The impact was immediate. According to the Soviet journalist-economist Vasilii Seliunin, the emphasis on heavy industry, combined with the outpouring of newly printed rubles, explained why "we have fewer goods than planned and twice as much additional money. What happens in this case? During the second half of last year [1988] trade began to fall to pieces before our eyes."[17] By 1989, many prices were increasing at a rate of 20 percent or more—that is, when one could find the goods to buy. Some Soviet economists even began to warn of hyperinflation.[18] The reports that prices on the collective farm markets had increased by almost 70 percent in early 1991 over 1990 and the threefold April 2, 1991, increase in the price of basic consumer goods in state stores seemed to validate such warnings.[19]

Gorbachev's decision to curb the sale of alcohol was particularly unpopular. From 1985 and 1986, production of alcoholic beverages was cut in half, from 600 million deciliters to 325 million deciliters.[20] No matter how laudable the decision seemed at first, the crackdown had several unintended consequences in addition to the loss of state revenues. To the working class, this was a direct assault on their main escape from socialist reality. Gorbachev's attack on vodka effectively alienated him further from the proletariat. It also engendered a shortage psychology. After a few months of effective enforcement, thousands of enterprising Russians realized that there was much money to be made in distilling home-produced vodka, moonshine, or *samogon,* as the Soviets call it. Distilling became a massive business. Moonshiners, however, found they needed large quantities of sugar for their work. In a short time it was not only vodka but sugar that had disappeared from the country's shops, even in Moscow. For the country as a whole, sugar consumption increased from 42 kilograms per capita in 1985 to 50 kilograms per capita in 1990. But the demand grew even faster and so did the sugar shortage, an almost unknown event in the pre-Gorbachev era.

The unprecedented sugar shortage combined with the decision to reduce consumer good imports, plus the surge of newly printed rubles and resultant inflation, triggered a buyers' panic. To protect themselves from any future fall in the value of the ruble, Soviet consumers began to seek out tangible items to buy in exchange for the increasingly worthless ruble. People started to hoard. One Moscow friend acknowledged that there was no more room to store the sugar that she had to buy with ration coupons. As she put it, "It has reached the point where I can no longer squeeze into my kitchen." Nonetheless, she continued to buy for fear that sugar would not available when she needed it or that the price would be even higher. When I saw her a few months later and asked if conditions had changed any, she replied, "No. Now I have another problem. I can't move around my bedroom. It's filled with soap." In this kind of environment it was difficult to keep much on the store shelves. By mid-1991 conditions had deteriorated so that her kitchen and bedroom were empty, and even with ration coupons there was almost nothing for her to buy. Most Soviet stores at various times were empty of such products as jewelry, furniture, milk products, sausage, soap, laundry detergent, pasta, tea, matches, and even salt.

...

I

Gorbachev's efforts at reforming state-owned industry have been equally counterproductive. To many observers, the keystone of Gorbachev's reform effort was his June 1987 reform, the Enterprise Law. Of course, in 1985, intensification, *uskoreniie*, superministries, and Gosagroprom were keystones. The Shatalin Five Hundred Day Plan of 1990 and the anti-crisis plan of 1991 were other examples. Each year Gorbachev seemed to come up with at least one more final solution. But at the time, the Enterprise Law seemed to promise a solution to the most intractable sector of the Soviet economy, the big state enterprises controlled by various industrial ministries. By 1987, Gorbachev came to understand that unless these industrial enterprises acted more independently, there could be no economic reform. Under the Enterprise Law, the role of the ministers in Moscow was to be curbed and the role of the plant managers out in the field to be expanded. Within broad limits, managers were given authority to set wages, determine product mix, and finance the operation and expansion of the enterprises with bank loans and deductions from profits. To ensure that this new initiative would win the support of the work force, the enterprise workers were allowed to elect their own managers.

Most important, managers as we saw were promised that each year they could set aside a larger and larger share of production, which they could sell on their own at whatever price they could negotiate in the market. It was assumed that the attraction of higher prices and therefore higher profits would make managers eager to respond to these new opportunities. The share of output retained by the state in the form of state orders or *goszakazy* was to shrink to 70 percent. It was assumed that the opportunity to sell their output outside the control of the state plan would appeal to enterprise managers because the prices customers would be willing to pay for goods that were usually in short supply would be higher than official state prices. These prices would generate higher profits and bonuses for the managers and workers, which in turn would stimulate increased output that would serve to establish a market equilibrium at lower prices. Eventually, as the state's share continued to shrink and the freely marketed share expand, economic planning would cease to play a meaningful role. *Goszakazy* would not disappear completely; they would be available to respond to some government needs, just as the Department of Defense orders equipment in the capitalist world.

It was a good idea, but it did not work. The Enterprise Law went part of the way, but not far enough, and as usual it was too little, too late. Unwilling to attempt too much too soon, it was decided that enterprises producing 50 percent of the country's output would shift to the new guidelines as of January 1, 1988, and that the rest of the country's industries would shift a year later, in January 1989. Not surprisingly, this staggered approach caused confusion. ...

Confusion was caused not only because some enterprises were allowed to reduce their share of *goszakazy*, but also because essential parts of the traditional market infrastructure were missing. There were no wholesalers available for industrial managers to turn to for needed supplies when they wanted to go beyond the product mix authorized by the plan. Nor were there wholesalers for them to sell to. Manufacturers had to establish their own trading relations with potential suppliers and customers. There were no middlemen available to perform that function for them. Since very few manufacturers had access to the necessary information (even the ministries were not completely informed), only a few of the more venturesome enterprise managers were willing to risk setting off on their own. It was much safer to adhere to the old system. Most enterprise managers were delighted therefore when their ministries continued to insist on control of not 70 percent, but often 90 percent or even 100 percent of the factory's output. And for those ministries that tried to operate with a 70 percent share of *goszakazy*, more often than not the enterprises themselves insisted that the ministers take a larger share. It might mean lost profit opportunities, but offsetting that enterprise managers freed themselves from having to worry about finding customers, disposing of output, or obtaining adequate supplies. All of this suited the ministries, which were equally reluctant to see the enterprises become more independent. Were they to take up the challenge, there would be no need for the ministries or their bureaucrats.

Not only did the Enterprise Law fail to facilitate the move to a market system and reduce the role of planners and ministries, in many ways it contributed to the magnitude of the macro and monetary problems. This law was one of the factors that helps explain why the economic situation actually began to deteriorate under Gorbachev. With increased authority to choose their own product assortment, the managers invariably opted to increase the share of expensive goods they produced. While this provided them with higher profits, it also guaranteed the disappearance of cheaper products, thereby exacerbating the problem of shortages.

At the same time that the Enterprise Law was adding to the shortage of certain types of goods, it was fueling an increase in overall demand. To curry favor with the workers to whom they owed their jobs, managers responded readily to pressure for higher wages. As a consequence, wages rose rapidly. In 1988 average wages rose by 8 percent, and in 1989 they rose 13 percent.[21]

With hard budget constraints and rigorous self-financing limitations, there might have been fewer problems. The managers would have had to act with more restraint or face bankruptcy. But the enterprise managers knew that the state would not tolerate bankruptcy, with its resulting unemployment and abandonment of capital. As expected, the state continued to provide subsidies when asked. Because of the increased distortion in the product mix and the newly aggravated wage inflation, the subsidies required were greater than before the introduction of the Enterprise Law. Recognizing that the law had been a mistake, Gorbachev on June 11, 1990, amended it by taking away the workers' right to elect their own managers.[22] The intention was to reduce wage inflation, which may have helped somewhat; but most of the damage had already been done.

II

Despite his reluctance to turn to the market and his lack of an effective strategy, Gorbachev achieved one thing: the gradual dismantling of the planned and administrative economic system. This dismantling was not entirely intentional. As we saw, in 1985, when Gorbachev established superministries, his original goal was to strengthen the planning system by making it more effective and efficient. However, as he merged, created, and abolished a dizzying array of ministries and planning organizations, the effect was to create confusion, disarray, and ultimately ineffectiveness. Ministries and their ministers were here today and likely to be gone tomorrow. While it had never been easy, it now became increasingly difficult to find someone who could answer relevant questions. And if answers were given, there was no guarantee that they would not be reversed a few days later.

It was not that Gorbachev completely dismantled or destroyed the planning system. He did not. Nor was it certain that he wanted to destroy it completely. That became evident in the summer of 1990 as he struggled to decide on yet another reform effort. As we shall see, he could not make up his mind whether to support the far-reaching Shatalin Five Hundred Day Plan or alternative plans that were considerably less radical in scope and retained some elements of planning. Whatever Gorbachev's intentions, this continued bombarding of the planning mechanism resulted in the increased weakening of planning effectiveness. At the same time, little was being done to establish an alternative mechanism such as more reliance on the market. An inevitable result of Gorbachev's flip-flopping was that the Soviet Union had neither an effective market nor a planning system. Just as he had his doubts about central planning, he was uncertain about too much reliance on the market and private ownership. As late as April 1990, he gave a speech in Sverdlovsk in which he complained, "They say, 'let's have free enterprise and give the green light to all forms of private ownership. ... But I cannot accept such ideas. ... They are impossible ideas."[23]

Had he been more committed to the market and private property, however, there was still little likelihood that Gorbachev could have produced an overnight transformation. Even in countries like Poland, where the market is the goal, it takes time for the market to develop in its full complexity. ... Creating a market is a bit like trying to build a forest. The market, like a forest, is easy to destroy: just chop it down. But planting twenty trees does not create a forest, nor does opening several retail stores create a market. A forest, like a market, is an organic phenomenon, with an infrastructure of insects, animals, and underbrush, which serve as forms of supportive life, sources of supply, and servicing systems.

Once legalized, private trade can immediately provide certain basic functions, especially at the retail level. But it is too much to expect that wholesaling, let alone sophisticated banking, credit, and ultimately fiscal and monetary processes, will emerge quickly enough to produce a relatively balanced, efficient economy. It takes decades, for example, to evolve a Federal Reserve-type banking operation or a reasonably fair and operational tax system. The difficulty in creating a host of new and highly complex institutions from scratch is compounded by the absence of qualified personnel. Not only were the most innovative and productive farmers destroyed as a class by the early 1930s, but for decades Soviet authorities punished or suppressed anyone who demonstrated entrepreneurial instincts. Nor did the Soviet Union train a cadre of technocrats in the mysteries of monetary and macro policy. To assign Soviet officials bred in the environment of central planning the task of fine tuning the economy by manipulating the money supply and adjusting tax policies would be like assigning a railroad engineer who has never flown before the task of flying a Boeing 747. It is not impossible, but it has its risks.

...

VIII

Much as he tried to change things, Gorbachev himself invariably reverted to the old habits of "experimenting" and "campaigning." ... By trying to solve all the country's problems with one stroke, such campaigns are almost always a recipe for failure.

Some of Gorbachev's experiments such as allowing joint ventures have been daring, even heretical in terms of Marxist doctrine and Soviet traditions. But despite his initiatives, he always seems to be holding one hand behind his back, for as bold as some of his reforms have been, in almost every case he has been reluctant or unable to push that "experiment" far enough so that it could make a difference. In part this is a consequence of Gorbachev's coalition-building approach to politics. As we have seen, he invariably seeks to surround himself with representatives from the conservative political spectrum, such as Yegor Ligachev,

Veniamin Yarin, and Valentin Rasputin. Eventually he ends up purging many of these conservatives; but for a time at least, he uses their implicit acquiescence to give his innovative changes the appearance that they are backed by conservatives as well as the radicals. But this comes at a price. Indeed, Gorbachev can introduce previously unprecedented reforms such as private enterprise and joint ventures, but then he ends up circumscribing the scope of their operations as a compromise with the conservatives. Private enterprise and cooperatives, for example, at first could only be opened by pensioners and students, thus having a minimal impact on the regular work force and state enterprises. Similarly, foreign partners in joint ventures were limited to a 49 percent ownership and peasants who set up their own farms could not sell the land they had leased to other private owners. Such limits made it inevitable that initially relatively few people would risk involving themselves in such ventures, thereby guaranteeing that the numbers attracted to these new opportunities would not be able to generate any significant increase in supplies. Sooner or later criticisms will be heard about the ineffectiveness of such initiatives, which always seem to precipitate increases in prices but not increases in goods.

Most likely, even an all-out reform would not have increased supplies significantly. After seventy years of bureaucratism, the Soviet people have learned to weather the various storms of reforms that blow in from different directions. Sooner or later they pass, without making too much of a mark. Unfortunately, each failure leads only to increased cynicism, which in turn compromises other efforts in the future.

NOTES

ABOUT THE AUTHOR: **Marshall Goldman** is Kathryn Wasserman Davis Professor of Russian Economics at Wellesley College and associate director of Harvard University's Russian Research Center.

1. *The New York Times,* October 28, 1988, p. 1; November 31, 1988, p. A1; *Pravda,* October 28, 1988, p. 4.

2. Tsentral'noe Statisticheskoe Upravlenie SSSR, *Narodnoe khoziastvo,* 1985 g; *Finansy i Statistiki,* 1986, p. 559.

3. *The Boston Globe,* November 2, 1988, p. 3.

4. *The Wall Street Journal,* November 2, 1988, p. A17.

6. *The New York Times,* August 28, 1988, p. 85.

7. *The New York Times,* April 24, 1990, p. A14; *Moscow News,* no. 32, 1990, p. 3; *Pravda,* December 30, 1989, p. 2; *Business in the USSR,* no. 8 (January 1991), p. 31.

8. Personal conversation with Revold Entov of the Institute of World Economics and International Relations, who served on one such commission, July 18, 1990, in Cambridge, Mass.

9. *Ekonomicheskaia gazeta,* no. 44, 1989, p. 6.

10. *Ekonomicheskaia gazeta,* no. 1, 1989, p. 10; *Literaturnaia gazeta* (January 1989), no. 3, p. 11.

11. *Narodnoe khoziastvo,* 1988, pp. 624–625.

12. *Narodnoe khoziastvo,* 1984, p. 573; 1988, p. 624; FBIS, June 18, 1991, p. 25.

13. *Ekonomika i zhizn'*, no. 25 (June 1980), p. 7; *Pravda*, June 9, 1989, p. 2; *The Wall Street Journal*, August 7, 1989, p. A15; *FBIS*, August 7, 1989, p. 60; *Pravitel'stennii vestnik*, no. 18, 1989, p. 6; *FBIS*, July 27, 1990, p. 50; September 26, 1989, p. 85.

14. *Sovset*, October 15, 1990, p. 43; *FBIS*, September 26, 1989, p. 49; May 29, 1990, p. 77.

15. *The New York Times*, March 15, 1990, p. 20; *Moscow News*, no. 22, 1990, p. 4.

16. *Pravda*, October 20, 1990, pp. 1–2.

17. *Sotsialisticheskaia industria*, April 6, 1989, p. 1.

18. E. Gaidar, "Trudnyi vybor," *Kommunist*, no. 2, 1990, p. 25.

19. *Rabochaia tribuna*, November 29, 1990, p. 1.

20. *Robitnycha gazeta*, September 9, 1990, p. 2; March 23, 1991, p. 1.

21. *Pravda*, January 28, 1990, p. 2; *Narodnoe khoziastvo*, 1988, p. 77.

22. *Izvestiia*, June 12, 1990, p. 1.

23. *The Washington Post*, September 13, 1990, p. A31.

PART 5

Nationalities and Federation

The Gorbachev reforms not only brought the "national question" to the top of the political agenda; they transformed the very premises of the discussion. The "national question" in the form in which it was inherited from the past ceased to exist; its place was taken by a major political struggle over the nature and future of the Soviet federation itself. It is therefore striking to recall that the national question was never initially part of the reformist agenda. Neither the reform-oriented intelligentsia nor the Gorbachev leadership anticipated the emergence of national movements, and both groups underestimated the potential explosiveness of the entire issue. Because they saw reform as an all-Union project, they responded to these movements with considerable ambivalence. On the one hand, they recognized that these movements shared a common stake in reform and were valuable political allies. On the other hand, the "separatist" tendencies among some of the non-Russian groups split the reformist coalition along national lines and, in the view of some of Gorbachev's supporters, jeopardized perestroika *itself.*

How and why the nationality problem was transformed from a marginal concern to the central issue on the Soviet political agenda and why it posed an unmanageable challenge and precipitated the dissolution of the Soviet Union are the themes of the chapters included in this part.

These chapters raise a number of controversial and unresolved issues. The first question involves the extent to which the reforms unleashed an already existing set of tensions and the extent to which they actively helped create them.

A second set of issues explores the slow and largely ineffective response of the leadership to the succession of ethnic conflicts and crises, from Alma-Ata and Nagorno-Karabakh to Novyi Uzen and Tbilisi and from Baltic assertions of independence to the series of proclamations of sovereignty by one republic after another. To what extent was the aggravation of the situation a product of the unpreparedness and incompetence of the center in handling these crises, and to what extent were the accumulated problems intrinsically unmanageable and the increasingly radical demands for autonomy and independence inherent in the logic of national revival itself?

A third issue examines the critical role of the Russian republic in this process. The emergence of Russia, long conflated with the Union, as an increasingly assertive political actor in opposition to the Union and of Boris Yeltsin in opposition to Mikhail Gorbachev bestowed a mantle of legitimacy on the demands of all republics for new federal or confederal arrangements. Was the political rivalry of Yeltsin and Gorbachev a central cause of or merely the trigger for the collapse of the Soviet state?

A final set of issues involves the inevitability of the dissolution of the Union. Although some observers argue that the forces of nationalism set in motion by the process of reform inevitably led to the disintegration of what was in effect an empire and the emergence of independent states across its territory, others argue that the breakup of the Soviet system could have been avoided. Some place the blame on Gorbachev's espousal of glasnost *and democratization and on his failure to suppress incipient nationalist activism. Others argue that, on the contrary, had the Gorbachev leadership acquiesced more quickly in the independence of the Baltic states and moved more rapidly to accommodate demands for greater autonomy and a new federation, the interdependence of the republics and the advantages of integration would have proven sufficiently powerful to sustain a union, albeit a less centralized and monolithic one.*

30 *State, Civil Society and Ethnic Cultural Consolidation in the USSR: Roots of the National Question*

RONALD G. SUNY

The recent explosions of ethnic nationalism and separatism in Gorbachev's Soviet Union seem to confirm the metaphor of empire as appropriate to the Soviet regime. A century and a half ago the European traveller, the Marquis de Custine, called the tsarist empire "the prisonhouse of nations," and that term has enjoyed a long run as a description of the imperialism of tsardom's Soviet successor. The Soviet slogans that masked ethnic tensions and inequalities, the rhetoric of internationalism and *Druzhba narodov,* have been overwhelmed by the rainbow of national flags that proclaim the self-assertion of peoples whose identities had long been contained within prescribed formulae. Nations have emerged within the empire, and in that emergence the empire has begun to die. Whether it will miraculously spring back to life, or in its death agony transform itself into a new democratic multinational state, or simply disintegrate is, of course, one of the key political questions of our time. In exploring how that empire was made and how nations grew within it to overwhelm it is the subject of this talk tonight.

Conventionally, empire is understood to be a large state made up of many peoples or nationalities, ruled by a central power that usually represents one people holding a privileged position in the political and social hierarchy of the empire.[1] Thus, empire is inherently an inequitable political arrangement, a relationship of subordination and superordination, hierarchical, and usually exploitative of the subordinate ethnicities. Since few peoples willingly accept a subordinate role as exploited subject, at least in the age of nationalism, the imperial relationship is one that is ultimately maintained more by force and violence than by consensus. Given freedom of choice, subject nationalities would opt for either equality within the reformed state, a degree of autonomy based on ethnicity, or separation and independence. In this way, a multinational state is pulled between imperial, centralizing tendencies and disintegrating ones that include self-expression, autonomy, equality, and sovereignty.

Empire is understandably contrasted to nation, and the two often are seen as mutually exclusive, and subversive to one another, as in the Hapsburg or Ottoman Empires where the rise of nationalism and the formation of ethnic nations undermined the imperial, dynastic principles on which the multinational empires had been built. But equally threatening to empire is democracy, the legally guaranteed popular participation in the choosing of government. The more democratic a state becomes, the less it can maintain inequitable imperial relationships within the state. A truly democratic state would involve, not only majority rule, but legal protection for the rights of minorities.

If one accepts these introductory notions, it appears that the Soviet Union has been moving in the last half decade—and indeed even longer—from a centralized Russian-dominated empire toward a more decentralized multinational state with more democratic features. Not only within the state but in its inter-state relations with the formerly subordinate states of East Central Europe, Moscow under Gorbachev has gradually been surrendering its former position of dominance and exploitation. But as relatively peaceful as the transformation of inter-state relations in Eastern Europe has been to date (with the notable exception of Rumania), the parallel metamorphosis within the Soviet Union has been marked by interethnic violence, an explosion of national chauvinism and anti-Semitism, and a desperate drive by several Soviet republics toward national independence, no matter what the consequences for Gorbachev, his program of *perestroika,* and the Soviet Union they wish to leave behind.

What I would like to explore with you today are the long-term and more immediate causes of the swelling wave of nationalism in the Soviet Union and some consideration of the prospects for the near future.

In a most interesting article on "Post-Communist Nationalism," published in *Foreign Affairs,* one of the classic theorists of totalitarianism, Zbigniew Brzezinski, argues that "communism in fact intensified popular nationalist passions." Though in the current daily barrage of news of nationalist expression in the Soviet Union, such an announcement may not seem startling, it in fact marks a reversal of a long and powerful tradition in sovietological thought. For the original model of totalitarianism, so influential during the long years of the Cold War consensus, not so much denied the relevance of nationality, ethnicity, or nationalism in discussing the Soviet Union as it simply did not notice the multinational potential for resistance. When Brzezinski and Friedrich listed the "islands of separateness" that potentially offered some resistance to totalitarian rule, they mentioned family, churches, universities, writers and artists, but not nationalities. Indeed for much of the last four decades the study of nationality has been marginalized in Soviet studies, the appropriate field for discontented emigrés nostalgic for a lost homeland, bitter over the conquest by communists. The mainstream of the profession dealt with the USSR as if it were monolithic, not only politically and socially, but ethnically as well. And even in his reassessment of the course of Soviet history, Brzezinski brings to his review a top-down approach, beginning with politics and ideology that was so characteristic of the totalitarian school of thinking. In Brzezinski's view, Gorbachev's decentralization "created an opportunity for long-suppressed national grievances to surface." Popular nationalism is the natural response to communist oppression:

... communism in fact intensified popular nationalist passion. It produced a political culture imbued with intolerance, self-righteousness, rejection of social compromise and a massive inclination toward self-glorifying oversimplification. On the level of belief, dogmatic communism thus fused with and even reinforced intolerant nationalism; on the level of practice, the destruction of such relatively internationalist social classes as the aristocracy or the business elite further reinforced the populist inclination toward nationalistic chauvinism. Nationalism was thereby nurtured, rather than diluted, in the communist experience.[2]

Without question the real historic experience of the non-Russian peoples in the Soviet Union has shaped the present forms of action and discourse in which they are engaged. But the actual generation of the centrifugal nationalisms of the Soviet peoples, including that of the Great Russians, is not so easily explained as the result of natural impulses long suppressed and released by a new dawn of relative freedom. Instead of what might be called the "sleeping beauty" approach to nationalism—nationalism as the essential and authentic expression of ethnic communities—I would like to suggest what I would like to call the "making of nations" approach—the idea that nationality as well as nationalism, like other social and cultural formations, is the product of real historical conjunctures in which ethnic communities, activist intelligentsias, and political imperatives have worked together to create a new level of national coherence, consolidation, and consciousness. One of the central ironies of Soviet history is that a regime dedicated to effacing nationality and creating a supraethnic community and a party that posited that class rather than nationality was the key determinant of social structure have presided over a long historic process in which modern nations have been formed within the union they governed. These Soviet nations, though built on earlier ethnic communities and elite nationalist movements, are largely the result of the complex history of the last seventy years.

...

Before the revolutions of 1917, most of the constituent peoples of what now makes up the Soviet Union were not yet fully formed, self-conscious nations. Though ethnolinguistic communities with distinct religious and ethnic cultures had existed on what is now Soviet territory since prehistoric times, few of the peoples of the Russian empire had coalesced around the more modern notions of a secular, territorial nation. Most had never had a state in the past, and nationalist ideas expressed by urban intellectuals had not yet spread to the less educated, either in towns or the countryside. Even during the years of revolution and civil war (1917–1921), when independent and semi-independent national states appeared on the borders of ethnic Russia, nationalism was still largely a phenomenon centered in the educated townspeople, students and the lower middle classes, with only an unstable following in the countryside.

With the end of the Civil War several major nationalities found themselves independent of the Soviet Union. As a result of Soviet weakness, effective resistance to native Bolshevik adherents, and Western intervention, the Poles, Finns, Lithuanians, Estonians, and Latvians created their own independent states. Those left under Soviet rule—Russians, Ukrainians, Belorussians, Moldavians, Armenians, Georgians, Azerbaijanis and other Muslim peoples—were organized in a new federal state, the first ever to base its political units on ethnicity. Marxist theory at the time proposed that nationalism and national exclusivity could eventually be eliminated through the real development of socialism, but even this simplistic reduction of ethnic culture and national formation to the economic base recognized the contemporary power of the appeal of nationality. Consistently a defender of "national self-determination," Lenin proposed a post-revolutionary compromise: to maximize national political and cultural autonomy within a federation dominated by the Communist Party and to condemn the over-centralizing tendencies of more Russian chauvinist members of the Party (among whom he included Stalin).[6] Committed ideologically to Lenin's idea of national self-determination (to the point of separation!), the Bolsheviks at the same time believed that Soviet power was an historically advanced stage beyond parliamentary democracy and that the rule of the working class through its vanguard, the Communist Party, was a sufficient guarantee of the interests of the population as a whole. The Soviet Union had been formed in the Civil War by the victories of the Red Army and the defeats of the ethnic nationalists. The rhetoric of internationalism and the federalism of the new state ultimately did not prevent the rapid establishment of inequitable, hierarchical, imperial relationships between the center and the peripheral peoples. Power rather than persuasion was the final arbiter.

Although the republics quickly lost real state sovereignty, each nationality maintained its own republic or autonomous district in which the national language and culture were to be encouraged and where native cadres were to dominate in administration. This policy of "nativization" (korenizatsiia in Russian), encouraged by Lenin (and even supported by Stalin for a time), was sincerely carried out in the 1920s with spectacular results. The ethnic republics became demographically and culturally more ethnic. In Ukraine, as in other republics, a cultural renaissance blossomed. Russians seeking higher education there had to learn in Ukrainian.[7] Many smaller peoples who had never had a written language were provided alphabets, and campaigns for literacy promoted both socialism and national culture simultaneously. Even the Jews, who did not have a republic of their own, benefitted from this policy, enjoying a revival of Yiddish learning and culture, the formation of a Jewish section of the Communist Party, and a new security from a state that legislated against manifestations of anti-Semitism.[8]

At the same time, however, the Bolshevik program of modernization had a more ambivalent effect on the nationalities, at one and the same time undermining various traditions and cultural institutions, often brutally attacking the church, campaigning against patriarchy, and subverting traditional patterns of leadership and deference. At the same time the shift from village to town, farm to factory, gave millions of ethnic peasants greater social mobility, higher education, and broader cultural and intellectual horizons. The legacy of October for millions of Soviet citizens, regardless of their ethnicity, was upward mobility, access to education, and the promise of material improvement.[9]

By the early 1930s, once Stalin had consolidated the hegemony of his faction within the party, the imperatives of rapid industrialization and the massive effort of forcing peasants into collective farms carried the party leadership toward a more expedient nationality policy. Nativization as a deliberate state policy almost immediately suffered from the Stalin revolution of the 1930s and the revival under his personal autocracy of Russian chauvinism. Stalin had never reconciled himself to Lenin's notion of federalism, and though he preserved the form he created a unitary state, highly centralized, with little political autonomy left to the peripheries. Through the instrument of police terror he destroyed the last vestiges of "national Communism," imprisoning or executing tens of thousands of ethnic Communist leaders in the Great Purges. All hints of small-nation nationalism were severely punished, and Russian culture was promoted as the most advanced in the USSR. At the end of the 1930s study of the Russian language was made compulsory in all schools—though the non-Russian languages continued to be taught in the ethnic areas. Industrialization led to the migration of hundreds of thousands of Russians and other Slavs to Central Asia and (after their annexation to the Soviet Union in the early 1940s) to the Baltic republics. Even when some accommodation was made to national and religious feeling, as during the struggle against the Nazis in the Second World War, the new emphasis on Russian patriotic themes and national heroes subordinated the non-Russian peoples to the state's primary efforts to defend and develop the country economically. Several small peoples—the Crimean Tatars, Meskhetians, Volga Germans, Karachai, Kalmyks, Balkars, Ingush and Chechens—were condemned as traitors to the Soviet state and forcibly removed from their homelands and sent into Central Asian exile.[10] During the years of Stalinism the Soviet Union most closely resembled the ideal type of an empire—centralized, ruled by force and a unitary ideology, with the dominant nationality, the Russians, gaining a distinctly superior position in the state and in public perception.

Nevertheless, despite the political repression of the Stalin years and the abandonment of much of the cultural program of *korenizatsiia,* the non-Russians managed to maintain their demographic and cultural hold on several of the republics. By the time of Stalin's death the so-called titular nationalities dominated in numbers in most of the republics, even though they had been unable to establish any real political autonomy or carry on any nationalist expression for nearly a quarter of a century. When the worst excesses of Stalinism were eliminated by Khrushchev in the early 1950s, tentative national expression reappeared—first in the form of reprinted writers, rehabilitated victims of the *Stalinshchina,* and new themes in art, film, and literature. A part of the national heritage of non-Russians was officially sanctioned, promoted, and, in a sense, appropriated as part of the collective Soviet past. At the same time significant historical figures, even whole movements central to historical understanding, were beyond the newly-established limits of discussion. Armenian Dashnaks, Georgian Mensheviks, national-

ist poets or those who had fled abroad were ritualistically condemned by officialdom. Yet in the atmosphere of increased freedom the border between the
forbidden and the acceptable was constantly crossed by emboldened writers and
principled dissidents.

Khrushchev also established a more decentralized political and economic system, though this limited political autonomy was far from democratic. With less
control from the center, but in the absence of any real democracy, limited political
autonomy resulted in the strengthening of local elites, most of them carryovers
from Stalin's time. In Transcaucasia and Central Asia particularly, local ethnic
"mafias" gained control of the economy and political patronage systems. Corruption, bribery, the advancement of friends or relatives into positions of power became the norm for local administrators. As long as the Communist leaders in the
republics could placate Moscow by maintaining stability, keeping some restraints
on nationalism, and showing economic growth, they remained relatively free
from reprisals from the center. The perverse result of the end of Terror and centralization was the strengthening of already powerful ethno-political machines
that ripped off the state economic sector, patronized the "second economy," and
satisfied significant parts of the local population who either benefitted from the
spoils system or enjoyed the usually freer way of life in their homelands. "Diamond" Anton Kochinian, First Secretary of the Communist Party in Armenia,
and the rapacious Vasilii Mzhavanadze, his counterpart in Georgia, were matched
in their venality and brazen disregard of the law by petty party potentates in Central Asia, most notoriously Uzbekistan's Sharaf Rashidov.

For nearly a decade after the fall of Khrushchev in 1964, little changed for the
national elites. The conservative cadre policy of "the chairman of the board," Leonid Brezhnev, encouraged the corruption until it enveloped all parts of the Soviet
Union and reached into the family of Brezhnev himself. No attempt was made at
structural reform, however. The problem of the non-Russian regions was dealt
with administratively and only very rarely by changes of the top leadership. In
Central Asia and the Baltic republics party chiefs stayed in power for decades.[12]
In Transcaucasia, where the "second economy" had grown to gargantuan proportions by the early 1970s and economic indicators dipped ever lower, attempts were
made to bring in personnel from outside the patronage system. In 1969 Heidar
Aliev, a career KGB officer, was named first secretary of the Azerbaijani Communist Party. Three years later Eduard Shevardnadze, also from the security apparatus, became head of the Georgian party, and in 1974 Karen Demirjian, an engineer
educated outside of Armenia, was brought in to head the Armenian party. Their
mandates were similar: to end the corruption and system of favoritism in personnel decisions, to contain the growing nationalism, and to stimulate the local economies. Success was mixed. Purges of thousands of officials only temporarily affected "business as usual." The "second economy" was too deeply imbedded in
kinship networks and local cultural prohibitions against betrayal of friends, patrons, and clients to be eradicated or even seriously injured by changes at the
top.[13] As Brezhnev, ever more feeble, clung to power, the local "mafias" held sway

in the border republics and former reformers, like Aliev and Demirjian, became the beneficiaries of their own power networks. Cynicism, disillusionment, and a growing pessimism marked the dominant mood in the population. Economic and political stagnation eroded the last vestiges of faith in socialism. Some gave up on the Soviet Union altogether and sought refuge abroad. Many retreated into the details of daily life. And still others turned away from the mundane burdens of a spiritless modernization toward nationalism as an internal refuge.

The uneven and contradictory development of nations in the Soviet Union— at the same time consolidating ethnically in some republics while threatened by assimilation, in-migration, and linguistic Russification elsewhere—gave rise to a variety of nationalist responses in the 1960s and 1970s. Some of the deported peoples who had lost their homelands under Stalin, most courageously the Crimean Tatars, organized daring demonstrations in the heart of Moscow. Newly inspired by Israeli military victories and encouraged by supporters abroad, Soviet Jews agitated after 1967 to emigrate to Israel or the West. At first defiantly and later with permission, Armenians marched year after year, beginning in 1965, to commemorate the Genocide of 1915. When in April 1978 the Georgian party tried to remove a clause in the republic's constitution that established Georgian as the official state language, thousands marched to the party headquarters and forced Shevardnadze to reverse the decision. That same year Abkhazians protested against poor treatment by their Georgian overlords and petitioned to join the Russian federated republic. Karabagh Armenians repeatedly raised objections to Azerbaijani restrictions on Armenian culture and learning but with no results. Ukrainian writers, teachers, and journalists protested against Russian inroads in their republic and suffered a cruel repression. Lithuanians rallied around the Catholic Church, protesting restrictions on religious observance. In Kaunas a student immolated himself by fire. In Muslim Central Asia there was generally little open protest, but many Western observers believed that Islam presented a potential source of cultural resistance to Soviet authority.[14] And perhaps most ominously of all, the same economic, social, and cultural discontents that gave rise to non-Russian nationalisms also affected the Great Russians as well.

Like the national consciousness of smaller nations, that of the Russians was centered on a perception of national danger, of the erosion and irreplaceable loss of culture, of a sense of the past. Like the Armenian, Estonian, and other national movements, the Russian was deeply concerned with environmental destruction, with threats to Russian nature, and with the brutal treatment of cultural and religious monuments. This relatively benign affection for the village and the church was molded by some groups into a vicious xenophobic, anti-Semitic chauvinism that pictured the Russians as a disadvantaged nation victimized by foreigners and the non-Russians of the USSR. Religious nationalists, neo-Slavophiles emphasizing the innate virtues of Slavic peoples, National Bolsheviks combining Russophilia with Great Power chauvinism, and outright fascists emerged on the right wing of underground Russian nationalism in the Brezhnev years, and less virulent versions of their Russocentric ideas could be read in official journals like

Molodaia gvardiia and *Nash sovremennik.* When a prominent party official (now a close advisor to Gorbachev), Aleksandr Iakovlev, strongly criticized the ideology of the nationalists, he was "exiled" to Canada as ambassador. Clearly Russophilia, so alien to Lenin, had deeply penetrated his party in the six decades since his death, and much of the Russian intelligentsia openly admired the sensationalist depictions of tsars and priests of the painter Ilia Glazunov or the religious nationalism, with its explicit authoritarianism, of Aleksandr Solzhenitsyn. With the coming of *glasnost*, the Russian nationalist organization *Pamiat* (Memory), suspiciously protected by highly-placed officials, combined Russophilic themes, a xenophobic sense of national danger, and the now fashionable anti-Stalinism to blame Jews, Latvians, and other non-Russians for the repressions of the Stalinist past and the evident degeneration of Russian life.[15]

The first signs of nationalist resistance to central state policy in the Gorbachev years occurred in December 1986 when the long-serving Kazakh party chief and close friend of the late Leonid Brezhnev, Dinmukhammed Kunaev, was dismissed by Moscow and replaced with a Russian. Young people streamed into the streets in protest at this affront to Kazakh pride and privilege. The protests were condemned, and no concessions were made to the demonstrators. A little over a year later, however, as *perestroika* and *glasnost'* accelerated, much more sustained and massive nationalist demonstrations were organized by Armenians in Karabagh, an ethnically Armenian enclave within the Azerbaijani republic. Within a few days the gradualist politics of early *perestroika* was transformed into the ethnopolitics of national self-determination and democratization. In February of 1988, tens of thousands of Armenians marched through the streets of Erevan in support of their compatriots in Mountainous Karabagh in neighboring Azerbaijan, who wished to join their region to the Armenian republic. Even in their defiance the Armenians proclaimed themselves loyal to Soviet power and to the ideals of *perestroika.* Then, tragically, Azerbaijani youth, incensed at the perceived threat to their republic, went on a rampage in Sumgait in the last days of February, killing their Armenian neighbors indiscriminately.

The events in the Caucasus were followed a few months later by a broad-based, all-class national protest in the Baltic republics over Russian dominance. Demands for greater national autonomy led to the creation of alternative political fronts and to concessions by the Communist parties. While in the Baltic new party leaders found a common language with the nationalists, in Azerbaijan and Armenia martial law and the arrest of the leaders of the protests brought the movements to a temporary halt by the end of 1988. In Moldavia, Belorussia, and Ukraine issues from the unburied past, fears about the threat to the native languages, and anxiety about demographic and linguistic Russification brought intellectuals together with their ethnic compatriots in common protests. Peaceful marches, mass meetings, and hunger strikes became daily challenges to the monopoly of power by national communist parties. In early April 1989 hundreds of demonstrators in Tbilisi were hurt (and at least eighteen killed) when Soviet troops acted swiftly and brutally to quell demands for Georgian independence.

Just as each mobilized republic raised its own national flag and resurrected its particular national symbols and myths, so each of these movements developed their own agendas—some consonant with the plans of the Kremlin reformers, others a deadly challenge to the more tentative process of democratization initiated from the top.

In retrospect it is clear that several new elements had been introduced into Soviet politics in 1988: the public display of "people power"; the reluctance of the Gorbachev government to use armed force against public expressions of nationalism; the eruption of interethnic hostilities that quickly degenerated into pogroms (Sumgait); and the steady displacement of Communist Party influence by informal nationalist committees and popular fronts. As ethnic expression took bolder form and expanded out from ethnic intellectuals to include broader strata of the population, it metamorphosed into something both deeper and more inclusive than a simple cultural nationalism. Besides the issues of democracy and openness, the Gorbachev initiative had raised questions of the limits of central authority and local autonomy and had given a new political significance to persistent frictions caused by a central state perceived as Russifying. Suddenly, the consequences of attempting to democratize a multinational empire were thrown into high relief. Gorbachev would later admit publicly that "we had underestimated the forces of nationalism and separatism that were hidden deep within our system and their ability to merge with populist elements creating a socially explosive mixture."[16]

The new mass nationalist movements stemmed from both an increased capacity of ethnic populations to act in their own interest (and not only because of a freer political atmosphere but also because of greater coherence and consciousness of the nationalities themselves) and palpable perceptions of non-Russians (and Russians!) that their nations are in danger, either demographically, linguistically, or culturally. These massive ethnic expressions represented the emergence of civil society and were far more the product of Soviet history than any primordial ethnicity or natural striving for self-determination. Whatever the intentions and predictions of self-styled Marxist internationalist officials and theorists, the actual history of most of the major Soviet peoples has been one of greater consolidation of ethnic nations, heightened national consciousness, and increased capacity to act in defense of their perceived national interests. Even the processes that had been understood by Marxists and liberals to undermine nationality—urbanization, industrialization, mobility, secular education—worked in complex ways to make nationality stronger within the pseudo-federal Soviet state. Gorbachev provided an opportunity, by pulling back state power, for the open expression of nationalist agendas, which had been shaped both by the experience of peoples in the Soviet period and by the possibility of recovering histories that had been broken off seventy (or forty) years earlier.

Beginning with Karabagh, the first year of the new nationalist movement, however, proved to be only the first round in an intensifying struggle of nationalities for greater power and autonomy. The chronic economic stagnation fed the discontents of all Soviet citizens, which were often expressed in the language of nationalism. At the same time the political demands of the nationalists and the conflicts between ethnicities accelerated the economic decline of the country.

The axes of conflict within the USSR are not only between Russians and non-Russians but between various non-Russian peoples who have had long religious, cultural, or territorial disputes. The Abkhaz-Georgian hostility of 1977–1978, which revived in 1989, was a foretaste of the more tragic Azerbaijani-Armenian clashes a decade later. In Central Asia the expectations of many Western observers of a unified Muslim response to Soviet colonialism evaporated as Uzbeks attacked Meskhetian Turks and clashed with Tajiks and Kirghiz. But particularly vexing was the bleeding wound of Karabagh, the first major ethnic challenge to Gorbachev and one that resisted solution. Rather than granting the Armenian demand for the incorporation of Karabagh into Armenia—a political impossibility after the killings in Sumgait—a program of reforms was set out that implicitly recognized the long record of Azerbaijani discrimination against the Karabagh Armenians. Even more importantly, Azerbaijani sovereignty over Karabagh was replaced de facto by the appointment of a commission from Moscow to oversee the implementation of reforms in the autonomous region. Expectations were raised that Karabagh might be elevated to the level of an autonomous republic, though the precise rights of autonomous regions, autonomous republics, and union republics have not yet been legally elaborated. In his interventions in the Supreme Soviet debate on Karabagh, the General Secretary made it clear that both stability and progress, the goals of *perestroika,* were undermined by nationalism and ethnic conflict. Only political compromise offered a solution. Repeatedly affirming that there could be no winners and losers at the expense of another ethnic group, Gorbachev pushed hard for satisfying some grievances of each of the parties. But as the authority of the local Communist parties evaporated and the nationalist fronts grew in influence, in frustration and anger Gorbachev attempted to crack down on the emergent social forces.

Following the devastating earthquake of December 7, 1988, the Soviet authorities arrested the Karabagh Committee and leading Azerbaijani militants in an attempt to restore authority to the discredited Communist parties and to gain time for the implementation of a solution from above. In January 1989 Karabagh was placed under the direct rule of Moscow. Though this compromise satisfied neither the Armenians nor the Azerbaijanis, it was thought that it permitted some "breathing space" for the passions and hostilities of the past year to settle. Compromise and calls for calm, however, failed.

By the fall of 1989 the renewed Azerbaijani Popular Front (APF) gained enormous popularity and power in the republic. On September 4, the APF called a general strike in the republic, demanding recognition and a declaration by the Supreme Soviet of Azerbaijan that the republic was sovereign. Six days later the Communist Party of Azerbaijan capitulated to the Front and signed an agreement recognizing its legitimacy. Through the fall the Front organized a rail and road blockade of Soviet Armenia and Karabagh, thus cutting off over 80% of fuel and food to the Armenians. Rebuilding of the earthquake-damaged areas came to a halt. At the September plenum of the Central Committee, which was dedicated to the nationality question, Gorbachev spoke out in no uncertain terms: "We will not depart from the path of solving all problems by means of political methods, but where the critical nature of the situation dictates it, where there is a threat to people's lives and safety, we will act decisively, using the full force of Soviet laws." The reference to Azerbaijan was clear to all. But at the same time he once again reiterated his view that the forms and borders of national entities should not be changed. His proposed alternative was the creation of a true federation in which the nationalities would have real guarantees of autonomy and local power.

Fighting continued through the fall and winter in Azerbaijan and Karabagh. At the same time there were flare-ups of nationality violence in Georgia, Moldavia and Central Asia. The Baltic republics moved decisively toward declaring their independence from the Soviet Union. For reasons that remain a mystery, the Supreme Soviet of the USSR decided to return Karabagh to the jurisdiction of Azerbaijan (November 28). Neither side had been satisfied with the administration from Moscow, and the Kremlin hoped to end the continuing blockade of Armenia by making a major concession to Azerbaijan. The Soviets showed extraordinary restraint in the face of growing militancy in Baku and Nakhichevan. Azerbaijanis tore down border guard posts and walked into Iran. Soviet power essentially no longer functioned in the republic. The local communist party was either impotent or actively collaborating with the nationalists.

The Armenian Supreme Soviet declared Karabagh to be part of the republic of Armenia. In all but name the two republics were at war. While Gorbachev was preoccupied with the secession of the Lithuanian Communist Party from the CPSU, violence exploded in Baku. On January 13, militants broke away from the large demonstration led by the Popular Front and began killing and burning the bodies of Armenians. At least 25 people died the first night. Leaflets called for the expulsion of all Armenians from the city. Moscow began sending reinforcements of internal security troops by the 14th. The next day a state of emergency was declared, and the army was sent in. Within the week Baku was occupied and an uneasy calm was imposed on the republic. The party chief, Vezirov, was dismissed, and the Soviet authorities attempted to negotiate with the local nationalists. At the same time those considered too militant were arrested.

The dramatic mobilization of Armenians and Baltic peoples in 1988 ended the long period of benign neglect of the nationality question. While Moscow might have preferred that this "problem" await its considered solution in the repeatedly delayed Central Committee plenum on the nationality question (finally held in September 1989), the contours of the issues were being shaped by people in the streets, by ad hoc committees and their intellectual leaders, and by sensitive Communist leaders, like Vaino Valas in Estonia and Brazauskas in Lithuania, who worked with rather than against the local popular fronts. The Baltic strategy of cooperative competition between party and popular front contrasted with the harsher policy of martial law, arrests, and shootings in Transcaucasia. Eventually in Transcaucasia as well the regime was forced to accommodate the popular fronts. Yet in neither the Caucasus nor the Baltic were state policies able to end the national movements, and as the country entered the 1990s the very survival of the Soviet Union was being called into question.

The thrust of the more mobilized peoples is simultaneously toward a recovery of the past, the removal of local mafias, the end of demographic and linguistic Russification, a struggle against environmental pollution, greater local autonomy, republic-level *khozrashchet* (self-financing), sovereignty and democracy. The interests of the non-Russians could no longer be sacrificed on the altar of economic development. For Estonians this meant an end to placing plants in their republic and importing Russian workers without the agreement of the local people. For Uzbeks it could mean the end of exclusive planting of cotton, so necessary for Soviet independence from foreign cotton, but ruinous to the land, resources, and diversity of the economy in Uzbekistan. Though ethnic conflict and nationalism cannot be crudely reduced to economic causes, part of the toxic mix that produced ethnic discontent was prepared by the chronic material shortages and slow economic development of the whole country. At times Kremlin leaders appear to hope wistfully that their policies of economic stimulation, if blessed by the fruits of prosperity, will dampen the ardor of the nationalists. In his visit to Vilnius to convince Lithuanians that their best future lies within the Soviet Union, Gorbachev spoke of the integration of the Soviet and Lithuanian economies while Lithuanian demonstrators held their national flag aloft and sang patriotic songs. While economic progress certainly might help, the transition to a market economy promises only greater dislocations in the near future and a greater danger that material and psychological discontents will be expressed in ethnic struggles.

Though predicting the future of the USSR has become a dangerous though popular practice for Sovietologists and journalists, any discussion of the origins and contours of the emergence of Soviet nationalism must include some analysis of the possible scenarios that exist for the Soviet Union. The first—and in my opinion, the least likely—would be a return to the pre-Gorbachevian order, a return to party oligarchy, centralization, and an imperial relationship between Moscow and its constituent nations. Though this scenario remains a utopian dream for many Communists, who have imbibed the deeply conservative legacy of Stalinism, without a coup d'état supported by the army and the police a return to the recent past remains impossible. The popular mobilization, the loss of faith in the old ideology, and the lack of any program of the Right to restore the Soviet economy make a Stalinesque or Brezhnevian vision completely unrealistic.

A second possible scenario is the one increasingly being predicted in the West and by many Soviet nationalists—the breakup of the Soviet Union, independence for the non-Russian republics, the creation of a dozen or more sovereign states. This would mean the end of empire, though not necessarily the triumph of democracy. In several of the non-Russian republics authoritarian and national chauvinistic tendencies are paramount, and the minorities that live in Georgia or Uzbekistan, Azerbaijan or even Lithuania, are fearful about their future in countries dominated by the majority nationality. This scenario is a real possibility, though, in my opinion, not a very probable one. Much neglected in many Western analyses has been the appreciation of the forces that bind the extremities of the Soviet Union together into one country—not only the party, police, and army, but also the interdependence of the economy, the far-flung Soviet diaspora (25 million Russians live in the non-Russian republics; 60 million Soviet citizens live outside their home republic), the multinationality of many of the Soviet republics (Armenia is most homogeneous at over 90% Armenian, Lithuania is also quite homogeneous at about 70% Lithuanian, but most republics are more varied in composition).

A third scenario is the partial breakup of the Soviet Union: independence for the Baltic republics, possible unification of Moldavia with a more democratic Rumania, but the unity of the three Slavic republics with Central Asia and Transcaucasia on the basis of confederation. Here empire would be combined with democracy. The new, smaller Soviet Union would be a voluntary union, based on shared powers, with great internal political, cultural, and economic autonomy for the republics and regions of the new state.

The fourth scenario is related to the third but is perhaps the most optimistic of all the possible solutions: the renewal of the USSR as a democratic confederation. This is, of course, Gorbachev's preferred solution, and one he might have achieved had he been able to act earlier, more consistently, and more courageously on the national question. Karabagh was, as the demonstrators proclaimed on their signs, a "test for perestroika," but it was one that so far Gorbachev has failed.

Full democratization is the only real alternative to empire in the Soviet Union. The consequences of that democratization, it is clear, is the threat of dissolution, but there is no turning back without ending *perestroika*. Time, unfortunately, is not on Gorbachev's side, even if history is. He must quickly create a new constitutional order that guarantees full democratic rights and autonomy to the republics, including the RSFSR, and on the basis of a new state treaty recreates the Soviet Union as a democratic confederation. Gorbachev's problems in this area are not unique in the world today, as any Canadian can tell you, but the simultaneous economic crisis and political threat to his control of the Communist party make his position particularly vulnerable. He must act soon. He must provide a positive model of a future state that would attract nations that grew up within the Soviet Union and now see their future outside what is left of the empire.

NOTES

ABOUT THE AUTHOR: **Ronald G. Suny** is Alex Manoogian Professor of Modern Armenian History at the University of Michigan Center for Russian and East European Studies.

1. For discussions of the concept of empire, see S. Eisenstadt, *The Political Systems of Empires* (1963); his essay "Empires," in *The New International Encyclopedia of the Social Sciences* (New York, 1968), pp. 41–49.

2. Zbigniew Brzezinski, "Post-Communist Nationalism," *Foreign Affairs*, LXVIII, 5 (Winter 1989/90), p. 2.

6. Moshe Lewin, *Lenin's Last Struggle* (New York: Pantheon Books, 1968).

7. James E. Mace, *Communism and the Dilemmas of National Liberation: National Communism in Soviet Ukraine, 1918–1933* (Cambridge, Mass.: Ukrainian Research Institute, 1983).

8. Zvi Y. Gitelman, *Jewish Nationality and Soviet Politics: The Jewish Sections of the CPSU, 1917–1930* (Princeton: Princeton University Press, 1974).

9. This point has been made most effectively in the work of Sheila Fitzpatrick.

10. Aleksandr M. Nekrich, *The Punished Peoples: The Deportation and Tragic Fate of Soviet Minorities at the End of the Second World War,* trans. by George Saunders (New York: W. W. Norton, 1978).

12. The long tenure of first secretaries in the Central Asian republics encouraged illegal activity and cronyism. In Uzbekistan Sharaf Rashidov ruled from 1959 until his death in 1983; in Tajikistan Jabar Rasulov ran the party from 1961 until his death in 1982; Turdakun Usubaliev was party chief in Kirghizia from 1961 to 1985, Dinmukhammed Kunaev headed the Kazakh party from 1964 until his removal by Gorbachev in December 1986; and Mukhamednazar Gapurov headed the Turkmen Communist Party from 1969 to 1985. In the Soviet West the situation was not dissimilar: Petr Maskerov in Belorussia (1965–1983), Ivan Bodyul in Moldavia (1961–1980), I. G. Kebin in Estonia (1950–1978), August Voss in Latvia (1966–1984), and P. P. Grishkiavichius in Lithuania (1974–1987).

13. Yochanan Altman, "A Reconstruction, Using Anthropological Methods, of the Second Economy of Soviet Georgia," Ph.D. dissertation, Centre of Occupation and Community Research, Middlesex Polytechnic, 1983; Gerald Mars and Yochanan Altman, "The Cultural Bases of Soviet Georgia's Second Economy," *Soviet Studies,* XXXV, 4 (October 1983), pp. 546–560.

14. "In the USSR today there is a Moslem society which is united by the bonds of history, culture, and tradition. The fact that Homo Islamicus asserts himself in Daghestan or Tashkent, in the city or the country, raises a serious problem for the Soviet regime. ... Homo Islamicus is not an adversary. He does not set himself up as an enemy of the Soviet system, which he does not even criticize. But simply by his existence, by his presence in the whole area where the Moslem civilization has existed, he bears witness that the Soviet people has at least two components: the Soviets and the Soviet Moslems." [Helene Carrere d'Encausse, *Decline of an Empire: The Soviet Socialist Republic in Revolt,* trans. by Martin Sokolinsky and Henry A. La Farge (New York: Newsweek Books, 1979), p. 264.] Michael Rywkin disputes this sharp dichotomy: "The Soviet *Homo islamicus* does in fact display some characteristics of his Russian counterpart, unless he is among the minority who live in the most remote villages with no contacts with the Russians and practice Islam in the most traditional way, with all its rituals. For the bulk of Soviet Muslims, it is impossible to remain totally unaffected by Soviet Russian reality, and this results in multiple social identities. Thus, for example, an Uzbek may view himself as Uzbek, as Turkestani, as Muslim, and as Soviet depending on circumstances and the person (or persons) with whom he deals or converses." [*Moscow's Muslim Challenge: Soviet Central Asia* (Armonk, N.Y.: M. E. Sharpe, 1982), p. 106.]

15. *Izvestiia*, August 14, 1988, p. 6; Current Digest of the Soviet Press, XL, 33, September 14, 1988, pp. 7–8.

16. Francis X. Clines, "Gorbachev Assails Foes of His Plans," *The New York Times,* June 20, 1990, p. A6.

31   *Gorbachev's Nationalities Problem*

GAIL W. LAPIDUS

Mikhail Gorbachev's reforms have unleashed an unprecedented tide of protests and demonstrations across the U.S.S.R. in which national grievances occupy a central place alongside economic unrest. From Alma Ata to Abkhazia, from Tallinn to Tbilisi, virtually no region of this vast and complex multinational society appears immune to the rising tide of national self-assertion. Whether in the form of anti-Russian demonstrations, as in Kazakhstan and Georgia, or in the emergence of new sociopolitical movements demanding greater economic and political autonomy, such as the Popular Fronts of Estonia, Lithuania and Latvia, or in more volatile outbursts of communal violence that have resulted in a tragic loss of lives and many thousands of refugees, as in Armenia, Azerbaijan and Uzbekistan—all pose a growing threat to Gorbachev's leadership and to the future of his reforms.

The increasing intensity of ethnonationalism among Russians and non-Russians alike, sometimes taking extreme and chauvinistic forms, has not only provoked increasing alarm among Soviet citizens and leaders, it has also precipitated a sharp controversy over Soviet policy toward the "nationalities question" and over the nature and future of the Soviet federal system itself.[1]

The complacent official assertion that the victory of socialism in the U.S.S.R. created a new historical community in which national antagonisms were obliterated has been exposed as a myth. A gamut of sensitive issues previously closed to discussion is the subject of heated public debate: the extent to which the national republics that comprise the Soviet federation should enjoy real sovereignty; the legal status of the Baltic republics, annexed as a result of the Molotov-Ribbentrop pact; the criteria for resource allocation among the regions of the U.S.S.R., and the degree to which more developed areas should subsidize the less developed; the representation of different nationalities in leadership positions; the language and cultural rights of different national groups; the role of Russian as a *lingua franca;* and finally the question of where the right to make such decisions should reside.

Traditional assumptions and approaches are being directly challenged in public discussions unprecedented in their scope and frankness, as well as in the confusion, uncertainty and anxiety they bring to the surface. By injecting passionately emotional issues into what is already a contentious political struggle, rising ethnonationalism exacerbates other cleavages and further complicates the effort at political and economic reform.

Two competing visions of the Soviet system contend with each other in these debates. The first seeks to give greater political recognition to national diversity; it views the U.S.S.R. as a confederation of sovereign national republics that should enjoy substantial economic and political autonomy in shaping their own historical destinies. The second vision gives increased priority to economic and political integration; it argues—by analogy with the American model—that the individual rather than the group should be the subject of political rights, views the Soviet Union as "our common home," and insists there should be no corner of the territory of the U.S.S.R. where any Soviet citizen cannot feel at home.[2] Although the Soviet leadership seeks to straddle the issue, difficult policy choices will have to be made.

II

To Gorbachev's critics, including members of the top party leadership itself, the growing tensions and controversies surrounding national relations are yet additional evidence that glasnost and democratization have gone too far. Soviet achievements, they have charged, are regularly maligned in the media, unofficial political groups are challenging the leadership and the very legitimacy of the party, and national movements are taking advantage of an excessively tolerant political environment to marshal forces that will ultimately challenge Soviet rule. In the view of these critics, current developments are exacerbating inter-ethnic relations in general, posing a growing threat to the Russian settler communities dispersed throughout the non-Russian regions of the country and ultimately threatening the cohesion and very stability of the Soviet system.[3] ...

In the view of Soviet reformers, by contrast, glasnost and democratization—compounded by sharply deteriorating economic conditions—have simply brought to the surface long-simmering resentments and grievances and provided legitimate outlets for their expression. The eruption of national tensions in the past few years is for them dramatic evidence that traditional ways of managing the multinational Soviet system have reached a dead end and demonstrates the urgency of a fundamental restructuring of nationality policy. Echoing Gorbachev's own words, they insist that turmoil is inseparable from revitalization, and that some degree of instability is a necessary condition of any far-reaching change. Resort to political repression will not only provoke popular explosions of increasing scale and ferocity and strengthen separatist tendencies, they argue; it would also entail the demise of the reform process itself, cause further economic decline and lead to a return of a more authoritarian system.

The effort of the Soviet leadership to cope with this rising tide of national unrest is complicated by the fact that it embraces at least two distinct, though mutually reinforcing, currents. The first is the growing assertiveness of national elites (and above all, their cultural intelligentsia) in challenging the extreme centralization of the Soviet system and demanding greater economic, political and cultural autonomy. The second current is a more amorphous and unorganized but intense and potentially explosive sense of resentment. It is particularly strong among unskilled workers and underemployed or unemployed youth, whose economic and political grievances are in effect displaced onto ethnic hostility directed against "outsiders."[4] Coping with both dimensions of this problem therefore requires not only far-reaching changes in a broad range of attitudes, institutions and policies connected with national relations, it also demands that a clear line be drawn between legitimate political and economic protest and impermissible communal violence.

The Soviet leadership, and Gorbachev in particular, clearly failed to anticipate that the process of reform would inevitably reignite the "nationalities question," and then they underestimated its potential explosiveness. In this as in other areas, Gorbachev's education was rapid; in two short years, between 1986 and 1988, swiftly moving events propelled the nationalities question to the top of the Soviet political agenda. The decision to convene a special plenum of the Communist Party Central Committee to address critical problems of national relations was clear recognition of both the urgency of the challenge and the need for new departures. The fact that the plenum, as of this writing, has been postponed four times is testimony to the issue's complexity. Whether the Soviet leadership will succeed in containing and managing the complex and contradictory pressures created by national aspirations, demands and conflicts is critical to the prospects for political stability, as well as reform, in the months ahead.

III

The complexity of the nationalities question in contemporary Soviet politics stems from the fact that the key actors are not merely dispersed ethnic groups, as in the United States, but nations and nationalities inhabiting or laying claim to historical territorial homelands. Over one hundred such national groups—differing in language, culture, historical experience, religion, and level of economic and social development—make up the Soviet population today, with Russians comprising just over half the total. By contrast with the American pattern, political-administrative boundaries in the U.S.S.R. tend to coincide with ethnic boundaries, infusing center-periphery relations with heightened emotional intensity and injecting the nationalities question into virtually every aspect of Soviet policy.

Gorbachev's dilemmas have their roots in the Bolshevik Revolution of 1917, which established Soviet power on the ruins of the tsarist imperial state. ...

A fundamental tension was thus built into the Soviet system from its very origins: the federal structure offered an organizational framework and political legitimacy for the protection and advancement of the interests of national groups, but at the same time Soviet ideology anticipated the ultimate dissolution of national attachments and loyalties and sought the creation of an integrated political and economic community based on universal Soviet citizenship. What balance to strike between these two orientations has remained an enduring dilemma in Soviet politics.

The Stalin era was marked by a dramatic shift toward greater centralization, cultural Russification and the repression of non-Russian national elites. The rights of republics and autonomous regions were whittled away, their boundaries arbitrarily redrawn, and the populations of some liquidated or forcibly resettled during World War II, as in the cases of Crimean Tatars, Kalmyks, Chechen-Ingush, Volga Germans and Meskhetian Georgians. National histories were re-written to emphasize the progressive character of Russian imperialism, and criticism of Great Russian chauvinism came to an end. Central economic ministries treated the entire territory of the U.S.S.R. as a single complex, establishing new industries and relocating workers without concern for republic boundaries. The cultivation of national languages and cultures was replaced by a process of Sovietization that was sometimes indistinguishable from Russification. The imperial features of the Soviet system were further strengthened during World War II with the forcible annexation of the Baltic states, the western Ukraine and Byelorussia, and part of Moldavia.

While repression served as a critical mechanism in maintaining central domination, the Stalinist system of rule also depended on the cultivation and cooperation of indigenous political elites whose loyalty was rewarded by significant opportunities for advancement. Moreover, the economic and social changes launched in the Stalin era—industrialization, urbanization and the spread of educational opportunities—far from obliterating national identities and loyalties, served to strengthen them. The emergence of modern urban elites in the national republics, in which the cultural intelligentsia occupied a dominant and prestigious place, provided critical leadership in the process of national revival in subsequent decades.

Stalin's death in 1953, and the process of de-Stalinization initiated by Khrushchev, began to unravel the system of controls and challenge the myths that sustained it. Cautiously and selectively, a reassessment of Stalin's legacy in nationality policy, as in other areas, was launched. While Brezhnev's policies sought to mute the reformist impulse, by the early 1980s it was becoming clear that traditional instruments for managing the Soviet multinational system were largely exhausted.

...

IV

Gorbachev came to power relatively ill prepared—both by personal temperament and by previous political experience—to deal with the nationalities question. He was clearly impatient that such intensely emotional, indeed irrational, sentiments could divert attention from the larger struggle over reform. By contrast with his predecessors, his political career had not included a stint in a non-Russian republic, and his early speeches contained little beyond the customary platitudes on the subject.

In his initial preoccupation with rationalizing the economic and political system, and his focus on efficiency and control, he demonstrated little sensitivity to how key decisions would impinge on national relations. He was taken by surprise, for example, when the appointment of Gennadi Kolbin, a Russian, to succeed Dinmukhamed Kunayev, the ethnically Kazakh first secretary of the Kazakhstan party organization, triggered massive disturbances in the capital city of Alma Ata in December 1986.

In succeeding years a series of upheavals and demonstrations in other national areas, culminating in the bloody Armenian-Azerbaijani confrontations over the Nagorno-Karabakh region, forced the issue to the center of attention. The tenor of Gorbachev's own speeches on national relations shifted from his initial complacency to increasing concern. They contained a growing acknowledgment of errors and distortions in the party's nationalities policy, and a recognition that the nationalities question was not a peripheral one but stood at the heart of (and was inextricably entwined with) the issue of reform itself.[5]

Three aspects of Gorbachev's reform program played critical roles in bringing nationalities problems to the forefront of politics. First and foremost was the impact of glasnost, which gave an enormous impetus to the expression of long-simmering grievances by legitimizing public discussion of issues that were previously taboo, and allowing the Soviet media to become settings for genuine public debate. Gorbachev himself gave explicit encouragement to this trend when he complained that for years social scientists had depicted national relations in an excessively rosy light, and that the absence of frank discussions of the problems had in fact exacerbated them. Social scientists, he asserted, should stop depicting national relations in terms "reminiscent ... of complimentary toasts rather than serious scientific studies."[6]

The leadership's increasingly radical critique of Stalinism, and its call for the development of a new model of socialism, gave further impetus to a fundamental reassessment of the nationalities question. By explicitly criticizing Stalin's deviations from and distortions of Lenin's nationality policy the leadership was, in effect, officially sanctioning a broader public assault. A growing number of articles, letters and roundtable discussions in the Soviet media began to speak out against an overcentralization that undermined the very principle of federation, against economic ministries that rode roughshod over local needs and interests, against language and cultural policies that were tantamount to forced Russification and threatened the extinction of national identities, against the mutilation of national histories and the repression of national elites.

... The revival of national self-consciousness extended to Russians themselves, and found expression in complaints that the greatest hardships in the course of Soviet development had been borne by the Russian Republic, the well-being of which had been sacrificed to the progress of the backward regions of the country. In this view, the existing federal system—far from reflecting the domination of Russians over the rest of the union as many non-Russians were now alleging—in fact revealed their victimization. The absence of a separate Russian Republic party organization, or a specifically Russian academy of sciences, some argued, demonstrated the inferior position of Russians within the federation.

Increased official tolerance for the revival of national consciousness (and indeed of religious belief, as the handling of the millennium of Orthodox Christianity illustrated) among Russians and non-Russians alike reflected a broader normalization of regime-society relations, and a growing appreciation of the value as well as the reality of social pluralism. Gorbachev explicitly endorsed this attitude in a meeting with journalists in July 1987 when he asserted: "Every people has its own language and its own history; it wants to understand its roots. Can this be at variance with socialism? Of course not."[7]

The effects of glasnost were given additional impetus by the political "democratization" that by 1988 had come to occupy a central place in Gorbachev's reform program. His reforms radically transformed the Soviet political landscape by encouraging greater grass-roots political activism, expanding the boundaries of permissible political activity and curtailing the activities of the KGB. Where once the effort of a small handful of dissidents to demonstrate against Soviet policy resulted in prison terms, exile or confinement in psychiatric institutions, now mass meetings and public demonstrations numbering many thousands of participants became a regular feature of the Soviet scene. Informal and unofficial organizations devoted to a variety of political and social causes (with environmental issues high on many agendas) proliferated, aided by new communications technologies—above all, personal computers—that facilitated the production and circulation of a myriad of newsletters, communiqués and documents.

While these new political movements embraced a broad spectrum of causes and orientations, common nationality and shared historical grievances were among the most powerful of all potential bonds, and the scale of the national republics and density of contacts among their intellectual elites offered a natural basis for organization. The emergence of popular fronts in the three Baltic republics, the most organizationally and programmatically cohesive of all the new political movements, served as both inspiration and model to other groups, not only in a number of non-Russian republics, including Byelorussia, Moldavia and Georgia, but in many cities of the Russian Republic itself. At the same time, these new movements provoked counter-organizations among the increasingly alarmed and hostile Russians who had settled in non-Russian republics. They saw their own interests and status threatened by developments in the Baltic republics, and they appealed to their own patrons in the central party leadership for support.

Political democratization also altered the status and attitudes of local leaders. Once almost exclusively dependent on political superiors, their careers now depended as well on their perceived responsiveness to local constituencies, as measured by success or failure in competitive elections.

The dilemma of maintaining central control over local officials while encouraging them to be responsive to local constituencies is best illustrated by the dispute over Nagorno-Karabakh—a predominantly Armenian enclave within the

Azerbaijan Republic. In June 1988 virtually the entire political leadership of the Armenian Republic supported the transfer of Nagorno-Karabakh to Armenia. The Azerbaijani leadership voted to retain the territory.

This division marked a watershed in Soviet political life. For the first time in its history, the Communist Party itself had fragmented along clearly national lines. Growing national divisions were creating tensions within other republic party organizations as well, prompting repeated appeals from the Baltic leadership to maintain party unity and organizational discipline.

By mid-1989, while the newly elected Congress of People's Deputies was debating the virtues of a multiparty system, many Soviet citizens were claiming that, de facto, one already existed. In virtually every republic, embryonic political organizations had emerged, embracing a broad spectrum of political positions, from explicitly separatist parties in several of the non-Russian republics, to extreme Russian chauvinist organizations like *Pamyat,* to the progressive Popular Fronts, to Christian, Social-Democratic, "Green" and other movements. Local authorities displayed equally varied attitudes toward these new movements: in the Baltic republics many officials had close ties with the Popular Fronts, whereas in the Ukraine and Byelorussia the authorities sought to suppress them.

Finally, economic stringency—compounded by the disruptions caused by the very process of economic reorganization—was itself a major source of rising discontent, just as economic growth had earlier contributed to political stability. Emboldened by a political climate that tolerated increasing outspokenness and expression of discontent, striking miners in Siberia and the Ukraine in July extracted major concessions from the leadership and set an example that was likely to have widespread repercussions. Their grievances could be directed against local officials and used to promote more radical reform. In more volatile multiethnic settings, however, economic grievances were increasingly spilling over into communal violence.

In sum, a complex and volatile process of political mobilization was under way in the U.S.S.R. which thrust the nationalities question to the top of the political agenda.

V

The decision to convene a special plenum of the party Central Committee to formulate new directions for Soviet nationality policy was both a response to growing tensions and demands and a catalyst in eliciting alternative proposals. The discussions leading up to the plenum revealed some profound shifts in the very understanding of the problem. But they also made clear both the difficulty and the danger of the task, and the depth of disagreement over what directions Soviet policy should take.

The point of departure of much of the commentary about national relations— and the one area in which a virtual consensus appeared to prevail—was the explicit abandonment of the myth that the nationalities question could be once and for all time "solved." For several decades Soviet policy was based on the expectation that modernization and socialism would automatically erode national identities and loyalties and that a new multinational community, based on the equality, prosperity, harmony and increasing uniformity of all its members, would be the outcome. Such illusions have largely vanished, and in Soviet rhetoric the focus on "solving" the nationalities question has been replaced with a concern over "managing" it.

Yet another staple of earlier discussions that is also vanishing from the pages of Soviet publications is the view that the disappearance of national differences is a possible or desirable object of policy. While Soviet scholars and officials have acknowledged for a number of years that national identities are less malleable and more enduring than classical socialist theory posited, what is novel in current Soviet discussions is the considerable value now attached to national distinctiveness and the notion that its disappearance would constitute an irreparable human loss.

...

... If diversity is to be cultivated—both at home and abroad—rather than eradicated, reformers now argue, the fundamental challenge is to reduce the potential for conflict and to create mechanisms for managing it non-repressively.

A third element in the emerging "new thinking" about national relations involves the recognition that a country as vast and diverse as the U.S.S.R. cannot be treated as a monolithic whole. Differentiated policies are required, suited to the distinctive problems and needs of different regions of the country, and increasingly varied patterns of economic, political and cultural life are likely to be the outcome. How such variations can be accommodated within the framework of a single political, economic and legal universe has now emerged as a major subject of controversy.

Changes in the present federal structure to expand the rights and responsibilities of union republics are likely to be adopted in the months ahead. Constitutional changes have been proposed that would distinguish those areas that are appropriately subject to all-union jurisdiction (e.g., foreign affairs, defense, overall economic planning) from those that can be more effectively managed by local authorities (e.g., economic and social policy, ecology, education and cultural affairs). The precise balance to be struck, however, is the subject of considerable disagreement, and this, in turn, reflects a more fundamental struggle over the nature of the federal system. Moscow sees these changes as a devolution of power from the center, by contrast with some of the radical defenders of republic sovereignty who would limit the powers of the central government to those explicitly delegated by the republics. Indeed, a potential constitutional crisis has already been created by decisions affirming republic sovereignty over the territory of Lithuania, Latvia and Estonia and insisting that no all-union legislation can take effect without explicit approval by republic organs.

The present state structure of the U.S.S.R.—which comprises 15 union republics, 20 autonomous republics, 8 autonomous provinces and 10 autonomous regions (all of which are themselves multinational)—in itself gives rise to new demands. The higher a unit stands in this hierarchy, the greater the advantages it tends to enjoy. But the rationale for many of these arrangements no longer seems persuasive. Several sizable nationalities are demanding that their status be upgraded. Other groups are demanding the restoration of their state structures abolished by Stalin. Disputed territories, like Nagorno-Karabakh, present an additional set of problems. And the prospect of enhanced republic autonomy has in turn triggered violent protests from minority nationalities within these republics who fear that their own rights might be curtailed. Protests in the autonomous republic of Abkhazia (in the republic of Georgia), for instance, touched off the demonstrations in Tbilisi that led to at least 20 deaths in April 1989 and violent outbreaks in subsequent months that have proved difficult to control. The Soviet leadership thus faces a difficult trade-off between correcting what are perceived as grave historical injustices and opening up a Pandora's box from which redress of the grievances of one national group can be achieved only at the expense of another.

Pressures for restructuring the federal system focus particularly sharply on altering the economic relationships between center and periphery. The central economic ministries have been the target of harsh criticism for arrogantly ignoring the social, cultural and ecological interests of local communities. They are accused of siting industrial plants without serious consultation with local authorities; importing large numbers of workers from outside many regions without provision for social and cultural infrastructure, forcing overburdened municipalities to deal with the consequences; and of polluting rivers and poisoning the air without regard for the health and welfare of future generations. These built-in features of what has come to be called the "command-administrative system" provoke particular resentment when they are perceived to threaten vital republic interests, as, for example, when massive immigration threatens to make the titular nationality a minority in its own republic.

While a special government commission headed by Yuri Maslyukov, chairman of the State Planning Commission, has prepared draft legislation that would enhance the economic powers of the republics, the Estonian and Lithuanian republics have moved ahead with even more far-reaching plans for economic autonomy. Considerable sympathy for their approach can be found among reformist intellectuals and political figures. Academician Leonid Abalkin, a distinguished economist and now a vice premier of the U.S.S.R., has argued, for example:

> It is necessary to recognize a union republic's sovereign right to solve any problems associated with the construction of new enterprises, regardless of whether they are detrimental to nature or not. After all, when we talk about a territory we mean more than just a shaded area on a geographical map. It means a people's habitat, a social and cultural sphere within which a people's history evolved. And these very sensitive factors, which are impossible to translate into the language of economic calculations, must without fail be taken into account when solving problems of republic self-management.[10]

Although the recently elected Supreme Soviet has approved the Baltic plan in principle, a number of delegates and officials have expressed concern that republic economic autonomy is incompatible with a unified economic system and with a social policy requiring redistribution of resources across the entire U.S.S.R. Indeed, some view these proposals as a thinly disguised step toward secession. Although critics acknowledge that greater local control could conceivably yield economic benefits, they fear it would increase tendencies toward autarky at the republic level, which Moscow would be loath to sanction. They point out that at a time when Europe is moving toward greater political and economic integration, pressures for local economic autonomy in the Soviet Union represent a step backward.

Finally, significant changes are already under way with regard to language policy. The Soviet Union is officially committed to bilingualism, but in practice this policy has been one-sided and asymmetrical. The entire population of the Soviet Union has been obliged to study Russian, which serves as the language of international communication in the country as a whole. At the same time, Russians and other non-titular nationalities residing in the non-Russian republics have not been under an equal obligation to learn the languages of the republics in which they live and work.

Following heated public discussions, six union republics have now adopted legislation that makes their national language the official language of the republic and mandates its use in a variety of contexts. This may seem a reasonable solution to members of the titular nationality of the republic, but others perceive it as a grave threat. Not only does it have great symbolic importance, but language policy has a decisive influence on the educational and career opportunities of different groups. Because the Russian settler communities or other nationalities residing in these republics will be obliged to adjust to these changes in their status if they choose to remain, many of their members have understandably been in the forefront of resistance to these measures. Moreover, during the long term these changes—which will enhance the cultural distinctiveness of the various republics—will increase the obstacles to mobility throughout the U.S.S.R.

These developments have focused new attention on how to guarantee the rights of all Soviet citizens against infringements by local as well as central authorities. They have also provoked a discussion of how to address the language and cultural needs of the large number of nationals living outside their titular republics—some 55 million Soviet citizens, by recent count. New opportunities for the creation of voluntary associations and cultural institutions have emerged in the past few years, and these might well supplement state institutions in serving the needs of ethnic minorities. Nonetheless, it is safe to assume that controversy over language and cultural rights will be a continuing feature of the Soviet scene, whatever measures are adopted.

All these policy dilemmas point up the need for new political mechanisms in which conflicting demands can be expressed and managed in a noncoercive way. The Supreme Soviet (in particular its Council of Nationalities) is emerging as a major forum for addressing problems of national relations. But a whole range of new institutions—from research centers, to government agencies, to judicial institutions—will have to be created to manage the complex issues that lie ahead.

VI

The Gorbachev coalition is caught between contending forces pressing for and against major changes in nationality policies. Moving forward on these issues without violently antagonizing any major constituency will tax the considerable political talents of the Soviet leader. His strategy appears to be to build a coalition between reformist elements at the center and the moderates in the various republics and regions around the country (reaching out to distinguished members of the intelligentsia of different national groups) to avoid a polarization of political alternatives along national lines. At the same time, he has been careful not to open himself to charges that he is presiding over the dismantling of the Soviet Union.

Only a short time ago one of Gorbachev's problems was how to stimulate initiative on the local level. Now he faces the challenge of containing and channeling local forces. The rapid tempo of events and the limited instruments available to the central leadership (short of a potentially disastrous resort to coercion to enforce "law and order") make this a particularly daunting task.

The mounting tide of national tensions in the Soviet Union also poses a challenge to Western observers. The events of the past few years call into question earlier predictions that identified Islamic fundamentalism as the critical source of potential destabilization, urging Western policymakers to exploit it. Recent developments also reveal the limitations of other conventional paradigms—that the fundamental cleavage in Soviet society pitted Russians against non-Russians or that Great Russian nationalism had captured the Soviet elite.

All this underscores the complexity as well as the volatility of the Soviet scene and the difficulties in assessing—let alone predicting or influencing—political developments there. Under the circumstances the United States would be well advised, while reaffirming the principle of national self-determination and cognizant of the special legal status of the Baltic states, to refrain from aligning itself in support of one or another national group. What the United States should do is to broaden its knowledge of the diverse nations and territories that make up the Soviet Union and to expand the spectrum of political, cultural and economic contacts with them.

NOTES

1. The term "nationalities" is used here to refer to the entire range of nations, nationalities and ethnic groups in the Soviet Union.

2. Both positions, and numerous variations on them, have been elaborated in a number of Soviet publications including the party's theoretical organ, *Kommunist,* in 1988–89.

3. The view that opponents of reform will be the main beneficiaries of increasing national unrest is a continuing theme in major speeches and publications. As a recent article

in *Pravda* warned: "Nationalistic ideas and manifestations ... only strengthen the position of the opponents of perestroika." (May 22, 1989, p. 2.)

4. Azerbaijan and Uzbekistan, both scenes of considerable ethnic violence, also have the highest rates of adults not employed in socialized production—23 percent and 27 percent, respectively, compared to 8 percent in the Russian Republic. (From "Ideologicheskiye problemy mezhnatsionalnykh otnoshenii," in *Izvestiya TsK KPSS*, no 6, 1989, p. 79.)

5. On July 1, 1989, responding to spreading ethnic violence in Georgia, Uzbekistan and Kazakhstan, Gorbachev delivered a somber speech on national television appealing for an end to ethnic strife. Warning that those who sought to stir up national hatreds were playing with fire, Gorbachev stated: "The present generation and our descendents will curse both those who pushed us onto this path and those who did not wam in time and halt the madness." (*Pravda*, July 2, 1989.)

6. *Pravda*, Jan. 28, 1987.

7. *Pravda*, July 15, 1987.

10. *Ekonomicheskaya gazeta*, Apr. 15, 1989, pp. 4–5.

32 *Dilemmas of Russian Nationalism*

ROMAN SZPORLUK

The present state of ethnic relations in the Soviet Union, writes Aleksandr Zharnikov in the June 1989 issue of *Kommunist*, results from the literal collapse of the "command-administrative system." This system had consistently undermined the principle of self-determination of nations, replacing it with the concept of the Russians as "elder brother" of the other Soviet peoples. This substitution lies at the root of recent expressions of anti-Russian sentiments. It is not surprising, argues Zharnikov, that the sins of the compromised command-administrative system tend to be attributed in some degree to the "elder brother," i.e., to the Russian people. Unfortunately, there are also people who deliberately "speculate" on the problems of their nations—"and which nation has no problems?"—and try to make the "elder brother" responsible for all their troubles.[1]

Zharnikov's is only one of many voices that have explicitly or implicitly argued recently that the relationship between the Russian nation and the Soviet state—let us call it the Russian national problem—is *the* central ethnic problem in the Soviet Union today, not least because it also defines the nature of the other nationality problems in the USSR. For the non-Russians tend to formulate their own agendas in light of their perception of the status and role of the Russian nation in the Soviet state.

If this is the case, then the roots of the Russian problem go deeper than the bankrupt command-administrative system or Stalinism. After all, it is commonplace to view Stalinism, and by extension the present Soviet system, as a continuation of the tsarist, imperial pattern of inter-nationality relations. Thus, the search for solutions to current nationality problems must go back to the relationship established in tsarist times between the state and the Russian nation. Moreover, a genuine normalization or "regularization" of the Soviet nationality situation requires above all that the Russian national problem be properly defined—and resolved. ...

EMPIRE OR NATION-STATE

The Bolshevik victory in the Civil War stopped what in 1917–19 looked like the natural process of disintegration of the Russian Empire into a number of independent nation-states that had started following the February (March) Revolution of 1917. As we see now, this victory also prevented Russia's evolution into a "normal" nation and state.[9] ...

This legacy makes the question "What is Russia?" even more complex. But the present map of Soviet and Russian politics will become much clearer if one distinguishes between two basic responses from the Russian people to the question—that of "empire-savers" and that of "nation-builders."

"Empire-savers" regard the present Soviet Union in its current boundaries as the proper and legitimate national "space" of the Russian nation. Indeed, some of them may extend it to the Soviet bloc. They may and indeed do differ profoundly about how they would like to see that country governed, how non-Russians should be treated in it, and so forth. But they all share the conviction that the USSR is in essence a synonym for Russia and consider the preservation of its political unity as a Russian (or Russian-dominated) state to be their primary political goal. That they may include extreme right-wingers and no less extreme left-wingers is not as important as the fact that they all agree on this fundamental point.

On the other side are those Russians who think of Russia as something very different from the USSR—as a geographical, historical, and cultural entity that does not encompass what they themselves recognize to be non-Russian lands and nations, even if these are part of the USSR. The geographical extent of Russia is not identical for all "nation-builders." Unlike the empire-savers, some nation-builders exclude the Baltic states from Russia but include the Caucasus; others exclude both of these but include Ukraine and Belorussia, and so on. What unifies them is a basically national position and the political goal of establishing a Russia that is a *nation-state*. Their goal is not to save, reform, transform, or modernize the empire but to establish in its place a Russian and a number of non-Russian nation-states. Insofar as nation-builders envisage close ties between Russia and some or all of the other "successors"—and some Russian nation-builders are in favor of such ties—they want *Russia*, and not the imperial center, to be a party to such arrangements.

It is impossible to determine how many Russians prefer empire-saving to nation-building or vice versa. But it is remarkable that in a recent article called "Preservation of the Empire or Self-Preservation by Way of National Sovereignty— The Main National Problem of the Russian People," Vladimir Balakhonov formulates the Russian national dilemma in these same terms,[10] which suggests that the issue is entering the political agenda.

"EMPIRE-SAVERS"

It is essential to keep in mind that this broad designation encompasses ideas and programs, individuals and organizations, which in most other respects have little in common, and may disagree and oppose one another on some fundamental matters. But this fact does not make "empire-saving" a meaningless concept. When the chips are down, all empire-savers (it would be much simpler to call them "imperialists," but this term has now become one of abuse) agree that the preservation of the territorial integrity of the state is more important than anything else.

The classical expression of this approach is to be seen in the post-1917 phenomenon of "National Bolshevism," a designation describing those Russian anticommunists in the Civil War who opted for the Bolsheviks because they saw the latter as the only force capable of saving the empire. Private property, independent courts, freedom of religion, representative government—all these could be given up in exchange for "Russia's" retention of Ukraine, the Caucasus, or Central Asia. For the National Bolsheviks, a smaller but democratic Russia was no consolation for the loss of the empire.

Among today's most obvious empire-savers are the military and the police, the state and party bureaucracies, members of other "all-Union" structures and apparatuses, such as foreign ministry or cultural officials engaged in foreign relations. Imperial nationalism offers an ideological justification for the dominant position of the central bureaucracy (and its departmental and territorial subdivisions). For the Moscow bureaucracy, the whole of the USSR, be it Estonia or Armenia, Russia "proper" or Moldavia, Ukraine or Uzbekistan, represents the canvas for its "creative" undertakings. The ministries of nuclear power stations and of water irrigation, not to mention the State Planning Committee, embody this imperial perspective and vision. A song that was popularized by the official media during the era of "stagnation" (and now is criticised for its wrong attitude) reflects "artistically" the same imperial outlook, especially in this much-quoted refrain: "Not some house, not some street—my address is the Soviet Union."

Some of today's empire-savers may continue to believe that the political system established by Lenin and Stalin is the best for the Soviet Union. As a matter of principle, they may question whether political freedom is a desirable goal in any circumstances, and they are certain to oppose political freedoms when these threaten the unity, and thus indirectly the territorial integrity, of the Soviet state. Indeed, some may go even further and favor some kind of military or fascist-style dictatorship that would abandon Marxist-Leninist ideology openly and completely. For our purposes, they are empire-savers, because they consider the USSR to be a Russian state. But right-wing extremism is not the only "empire-saving" outlook today. It may even be the least important, although it is very vocal.

Other empire-savers seem to favor Western, liberal-democratic, and constitutional institutions for the Soviet Union. Indeed, when some of those "liberals" think of their ideal Russia, they envisage a polity closely resembling what they imagine the United States to be. That their empire would be a liberal one, would have independent courts, would accept equality of all citizens before the law (without regard to ethnic origins, national background, religion and so forth), is of course praiseworthy. But what is decisive in this outlook is that it treats the non-Russian peoples—and the Russians too—as subject to decisions made in Moscow—and not by those peoples themselves. Some of these "imperial" admirers of America are prepared to allow local and regional autonomy in their state, and they even discuss the possibility of basing such autonomy on what they see as the most significant aspect of the American model: dissociation of ethnicity *from territory*.

Some of the "Westernizers" go even farther. They openly proclaim their own desire for a total separation of ethnicity from politics and the state, for making nationality, as it were, a private matter of concern only to individuals, rather than having it be a factor affecting the state structure. Again, some Soviet scholars seem to think that this idea is realized in the United States.[11]

There are grounds to surmise that the current line of the center in the face of rising ethnic nationalisms is to defuse the threat coming from the larger nations by having Moscow assume the role of defender of smaller nations, and especially of scattered national and religious groups living among the non-Russian peoples. This policy would serve two purposes. It would weaken union republics by granting their citizens the right to go to Moscow for justice, and it would create a new mission for the old apparat—which would become the protector of ethnic and human rights all over the USSR, in the same old centralized way to which it became accustomed while admittedly doing other things. The newly appointed head of the Ethnography Institute of the USSR Academy of Sciences, Valeriy Tishkov, for one, is on record against "absolutizing" the rights of the union republics over the rights of other entities such as autonomous republics or national districts.[12] Indeed, the center seems, in self-defense, to be advocating the granting of broader rights to the subdivisions of the union republics, presumably in order to give Moscow more things to do, and not because the Moscow bureaucracy now consists of converts to libertarianism and individualism.

Whether empire-savers are fascist or liberal, extremist or moderate, atheist or Orthodox, their "geography" is the same—it is an imperial geography, and their Russia is co-extensive with the empire. But why should the hoped-for liberal empire be called Russian? Why should it not have the "Soviet" or some other non-ethnic designation? Recent Soviet discussions help answer this question.

The historic failure of the Soviet system is openly conceded today. The declaration of the Congress of People's Deputies issued in June 1989 speaks about the present "crisis" of the Soviet Union. It is admitted that the Soviet system has failed to defeat capitalism in their historic "great contest." This failure has called into question the concept of a "Soviet people." If a new Soviet civilization has not been created, as is also being admitted, then in what sense are the peoples living in the USSR a *Soviet* people?[13]

The empire-savers are noticeably concerned to preserve the concept of a "Soviet people." But when one examines their arguments closely, one discovers that the "Soviet people" they defend is a form of the Russian nation. Academician Yulian Bromley (until 1989 director of the Ethnography Institute) defined the "Soviet people" as a real community that is held together by common socialist features. He called it a "meta-ethnic community."[14] In a January 1989 article, Bromley recognized that demands for greater use of "national"—which in the Soviet usage means subnational or local or regional—languages in the non-Russian republics of the Soviet Union are legitimate. But he stressed the necessity of a continuing and expanding use of Russian throughout the USSR. Revealingly, Bromley referred to the publication of fiction and poetry in the non-Russian languages as indicating the growth of the "nationally-specific" as opposed to the "general," which means that he considers the publication of fiction and poetry in Russian to represent "the general," that is, the integrating or internationalizing tendency.[15]

Bromley attributes "international" qualities to the Russian language, and by extension to the Russian ethnos, even though to an outsider there would appear to be no more internationalism in the Russian language than there is in Georgian or Abkhazian. One may well ask whether a poem praising Lenin in Armenian would be "nationally specific," while one written in Russian, praising Nicholas II, would be "general and integrating" just because it was written in Russian. Absurd as this may be, such categorizations lay at the root of imperial thinking in Stalin's time—and seem to be alive today. The Estonian scholar Jaan K. Rebane has recently made the point that in this view, the "internationalist" (i.e., Soviet) or "general" means one ethnically specific aspect—the Russian.[16]

Bromley's reference to the non-Russian languages as expressing "the specific" and his assumption that Russian stands for "the general" shows quintessential Russian imperial thinking, and makes it clear why it is a Russian, and not a Soviet, imperial thinking. It is based on the assumption that Russian ethnicity is not in the same category as all the other ethnicities in the USSR: it is above them, it is a distinguishing feature of the "universality" of Sovietism. This approach holds that the unity of the USSR is based on the non-Russians' submergence in—not their integration as equals with—Russia.

What some other prominent figures understood by "internationalization" became clear from a speech by Yevgeniy M. Primakov given at the 19th Party Conference in June 1988. Primakov proposed the establishment of "international structures" by means of a "rotation of cadres along horizontal lines in the whole country," a move made imperative by "the lessons from recent events in Azerbaijan and Armenia." Primakov argued:

> Only through such a horizontal transfer of party and economic personnel will it be possible to create a single international fusion in the Soviet Union, one that will be more monolithic than the sum of national [i.e., ethnic] formations that gravitate toward seclusion.[17]

Academician Primakov did not explain who would implement such a transfer of cadres. The new political reforms in the USSR seem to make the decision as to who shall head a given party or economic organization subject to elections. This would mean that Moscow could no longer appoint or transfer leading cadres from one republic or region to another. It is obvious that Primakov's plan would require the retention of the power of appointment by the center.

Exchange of cadres between republics was a standard theme in the Brezhnev and Andropov times, and Mikhail Gorbachev himself also used to endorse it, at least until the January 1987 plenum of the Central Committee, after which this topic seems to have disappeared from his public pronouncements. But in April 1989, Abdul-Rakhman Bezirov, first secretary of the Azerbaijan Central Committee, spoke strongly in favor of an exchange of party officials between republics and the center, although from a different perspective than Primakov's. His complaint was that for years no party officials from his republic had been called to serve in Moscow.[18]

Academician S. L. Tikhvinskiy, an influential historian, insisted at an academic conference in 1987 that it was necessary to develop new forms of inter-republic cooperation in the scholarly sphere. Tikhvinskiy stressed the need to "resolutely overcome the harmful tendency to divide science (*nauka*) into Ukrainian or Azerbaijani, central or peripheral." According to him, only one, Soviet, historical science existed, and it was "firmly grounded" in Marxism-Leninism and socialist internationalism.[19] It is worth noting that Tikhvinskiy spoke about Soviet scholarship and about internationalism, but did not deny the existence of a Russian historical science. One suspects that he identified Russian with Soviet or "internationalist" scholarship, even though it was hard in 1987, and impossible in 1989, to ignore the fact that Russian historical writing is not firmly grounded in either Marxism-Leninism or in socialist internationalism.

Some scholars do not have Tikhvinskiy's or Primakov's inhibitions about explicitly identifying "Soviet" with "Russian." Examples of uninhibited Russian imperial thinking may be found in the symposium "Democracy is Conflict" published in the monthly magazine *Vek XX i Mir*. Doctor of Philosophical Sciences A. Prigozhin was refreshingly open in characterizing the Russian nation as the "patron-nation" (*narod-patron*) of all the Soviet peoples. Prigozhin thought it quite self-evident and normal that the Russians should form the highest leadership of the country (i.e., of the USSR), and should predominate among the heads of the state's central agencies, in the USSR Academy of Sciences, the Central Committee of the CPSU, and so forth. He even thought that in the non-Russian national republics, Russian leaders should "also occupy a special position."[20] Clearly, for Prigozhin, being "Russian" means embodying and personifying the general or universal, the "Soviet," in the Soviet Union. By the same token, the other ethnic elements in Prigozhin's scheme of things represented the "specific," or particular, in other words, something local, subordinate, and unessential.

"NATION-BUILDERS"

One of the consequences of the Soviet Union's identity crisis is the current rise of ethnic assertiveness in many regions of the country. Dissatisfaction with the Soviet system, general disillusionment with the empty promises of a better Soviet way of life," and the search for alternative explanations of the current problems and ways of solving them lie behind the present processes in which ethnic communities "construct" and "reconstruct" themselves.

Among the nations in search of an identity and purpose are the Russians. They are increasingly asserting themselves—and defining themselves—as a *Russian nation* and, especially important, as a nation that exists independently of the state, which in this case means the empire. Some of the emerging Russian nationalists take pains to dissociate the Russian nation from the Soviet state's record not only in the 1930's, but also in the 1920's. Indeed, some are repudiating even the immediate post-revolutionary years. The process of reevaluation of history has assumed sufficiently large proportions to raise the possibility of a "divorce" or secession of Russian nationalism from the Soviet state and Marxist-Leninist ideology. If the trend continues and gains in scope, it may lead to the dissolution, "ungluing," or coming apart of what has been called by some Russia's "national communism."

More than 20 years ago, Mark G. Field defined national communism as "the search, on the part of a nation that has recently emerged as a major world power on the world scene, for a national and cultural identity." National communism, he wrote, rested on "the fusion of the doctrinal bases of the communist movement and identification of the interests of that movement (which is, in essence, supranational) with the interests of the Russian nation." Field saw the sources of that "fusion" in the recognition by the Soviet leaders that "no proletarian revolution was in sight and the resulting decision (primarily Stalin's) to build 'socialism in one country'." Stalin considered Russia the bastion of the communist movement and held that "anything that added to the strength of Russia as a nation (industrialization, for example) was good for the movement."[21]

It is a separate question whether Stalin ultimately proved to be "good" for the world communist movement; what is relevant here is that more and more people say openly now that Stalin's regime was very bad for Russia. Bad not just for the Russian "landlords and bourgeoisie," for kulaks or even peasants in general, but also bad for Russia in the sense of the entire people and country. This theme has long been heard from declared anti-communists, for example, Aleksandr Solzhenitsyn, who in the early 1970's, when he was still in the USSR, used to be the most prominent spokesman for this assessment of communism's relationship to Russia. While Solzhenitsyn criticized communism on behalf of the old, Orthodox Russia, certain extremist chauvinist elements among the dissidents criticized the Soviet past and present from another vantage point. They blamed the Soviet state's negative aspects on the Jews, Zionists, Freemasons, and so on, but professed their profound loyalty to "genuine" Soviet socialism (under which term they also understood Stalinism).[22]

Today, many people are convinced that Russia is hopelessly behind when compared with the other Soviet republics (not to mention foreign countries), and it is frequently said or implied that the ruling party, the state, and the ideology are to blame. Many examples can be cited to illustrate this pervasive mood, but a few will have to suffice. The well-known "village" writer Vasiliy Belov, speaking as a candidate for the USSR Congress of People's Deputies, said: "The ill-considered collectivization of the '30's inflicted great losses not only on the peasantry but also on the whole Russian people [narod]. According to my information, the Russians now constitute less than one half of the country's [population]." Belov complained that despite this fact, some scholars claimed that the Russians were characterized "by some special kind of aggressiveness." Those unnamed scholars even "dare to say that there exist special medical means to treat this aggressiveness. I was deeply angered to hear such a statement at one very representative conference."

Belov was no less critical of the government's conduct of foreign trade under the terms of which, he said, the Soviet Union exports its best goods, which are not accessible to the Soviet population, and buys industrial machinery from abroad, thus perpetuating the country's traditional role as a backward nation dependent on the foreigners' "technology of yesterday." (Belov assumed that foreigners do not sell their most up-to-date products.) If such practices continue, the country risks becoming "a colony."[23]

In an article in a series remarkably called "Who Is to Blame or What Is to be Done?" Yuriy Chernichenko referred to Russia (meaning the RSFSR, not the USSR as a whole) as a country that was the dirtiest in all of the USSR and in all of Europe, being dirtier in the Soviet era than in the early 19th century when the poet Mikhail Lermontov had called Russia *"nemytaya Rossiya"* (unwashed Russia). Chernichenko said it was time to "wash up" Russia *(otmyt' Rossiyu),* and he drew a direct connection between the sorry state of Russia and the rule by party bureaucrats who headed a "purely totalitarian regime, an administrative regime."[24]

It is not unusual to identify Russian nationalism with the most extreme, fascist, or racist ideas and groups. This point of view is erroneous. Fascism, racism, and extremism are not the only Russian-proposed alternatives to the ideology of communism and the present Soviet political system. There are many diverse currents in Russia, and it would be an impossible task to classify them without crude oversimplification. For the purposes of this discussion, however, let us rather consider several different models envisaged for Russia, each of which has at its source its proponents' sense of alienation from the present system.

First, there are those Russians who reject communism and Sovietism and who look for an alternative in a nationalism rooted in culture, especially in religion. The second model of Russia proposes a democratic, liberal, Western-style modern nation-state. A third model is advanced by those who are critical of the imperial structure of the Soviet Union and expect a change for the better if the RSFSR were to become a full-fledged republic. Their opposition to "Moscow"—read the Stalinist bureaucratic and centralized machine—leads these Russians to call for a basic change in the status of the Russian Soviet Federated Socialist Republic within the Soviet Union. They seem to believe that the national needs of Russia might be addressed and met if the RSFSR acquired an identity that was separate from the USSR and its governmental, party, and other organizations.

RSFSR-Nationalism. Let us begin with the third model, which is anti-empire but is not anti-socialist or anti-Soviet in principle. It calls for an institutional rearrangement for the RSFSR that would amount to the removal of the Russian nation from the position of imperial nation in the USSR. An interview given recently by the secretary of the Moscow Writers' Union, Anatoliy Zhukov, to *Literaturnaya Rossiya* conveys well the mood of those "RSFSR-Russians." Zhukov cited some of the ethnic problems arising in Central Asia, the Baltic states, Armenia and Azerbaijan, as well the rise of "Russophobia" in Kazakhstan and elsewhere, and attributed them to neglect of the specific conditions in those particular regions. These republics could not deal with their problems adequately because they lacked the freedom to run their own affairs. When asked if this was also true of the Russian Federation, Zhukov responded:

> Of course. Why should we be an exception? But we are an exception. In Russian schools, for example, Russian history is not being taught, there is only the history of the USSR. We do not have our own republic academy of sciences, we do not have our own republic party or Komsomol central committee, there are no [republic-rank] trade union organs, and no congresses are held. The Russians are last in the number of specialists with college education and in the number of scientists per 1000 of population, our countryside has been ruined, our birth rates have fallen, our national culture has been almost destroyed. What is this if not an exception? We do not even have a capital of our own—we "share" one with the whole country.[25]

It goes without saying that Zhukov's statements are not always accurate. For example, he seems not to know that Ukrainian schools do not teach a subject called "Ukrainian history." What is more interesting is that Zhukov—and other Russian critics who complain that Russian history is not taught in Russian schools—do not think that what is being presented as the "history of the USSR" is a history of Russia. What is called "history of the USSR" in Soviet textbooks is principally the history of the tsarist state. When critics of this kind of history say they want a history of the Russian people, the Russian nation, they are revealing a belief that the story of the grand princes and tsars is not real Russian history. Indeed, some dispute the propriety of calling the pre-1917 history a history of the "USSR" (which is what Soviet historians do, and not only in textbooks but also in scholarly works). Thus, in a letter to the journal *Nash Sovremennik*, Colonel (Ret.) I. A. Zaichkin and Major-General of the Air Force I. N. Pochkayev called it absurd to have book titles like "History of the USSR: Feudal Epoch." On the pre-1917 era, they said, there should be histories of Russia and of other nations.[26]

Admittedly, there is nothing politically subversive in such proposals. However, Russian demands of this kind are frequently presented by individuals who combine them with chauvinistic, including anti-Semitic, views. Thus, a letter to the 19th Party Conference signed by a group of Russian cultural figures contained a demand for ethnic quotas in those RSFSR institutions that the letter-signers wanted to have established.[27] (Incidentally, like Zhukov, the authors of this letter seem convinced that in the non-Russian republics, the histories of the respective nations are taught. This, as mentioned above, is certainly not the case now in Ukraine, and it seems most unlikely to be the case in Belorussia and a number of other republics.) The Russian "cultural figures" charged that the absence of RSFSR structures (they also included in their list the KGB and academies of the sciences and of the arts) perpetuates a "Zionist-Trotskyist program," which they described as follows: "A federation for the 'nationalities' with separate centers for them, but without one for the Russians." They said that Lenin had protested this program—evidently without success. "And so the Russians have now proved to be without rights in their own country!"[28]

The support for some of the Russian national desiderata by professed anti-Semites and reactionaries should not obscure the fact that not all of these desiderata are objectionable. While it would obviously be wrong to restrict employment in a Russian academy of sciences by ethnic quotas, the idea of establishing such a new academy is not discriminatory per se. Indeed, if realized, it might help to develop Russia and at the same time help to dissociate "Sovietism" from the Russian people as the Soviet Union's allegedly dominant master nation, or "patron-nation" in Prigozhin's phrase. Indeed, some years ago similar Russian demands circulated in *samizdat* and were then supported by leftists.[29]

One such idea that constantly reappears and seems to bother Russians of all political persuasions is the dual role of Moscow as capital of the USSR and the RSFSR. Many Russians also complain that Leningrad has fallen from the rank of an imperial capital to that of a regional center. The question of the status of Leningrad was again raised quite recently in *Literaturnaya Gazeta* and *Literaturnaya Rossiya*. Writing in the latter, the Leningrad writer Feliks Dymov recalled that one of Stalin's charges against the Leningrad party leaders in 1949–50 was their proposal to move the capital of the RSFSR to that city. (Stalin regarded this as separatism.) Although Dymov did not take a definite stand in favor of such a move, he deplored the low ranking of the former capital, which, he said, in population, scientific potential, and industrial output, was far ahead of the 14 union-republic capitals.[30]

Nation as Culture. No current of contemporary Russian opinion, whether unofficial or "legal," has attracted Western scholars more than the complexities of Russian national-religious and "culturalist" thought. Indeed, there are Russian thinkers who want to explore and affirm the importance of the Orthodox religion and the Orthodox Church in the history of Russia, and who consider this spiritual aspect a formative influence on modern Russian identity. These thinkers disagree profoundly among themselves in their specific assessments of individuals and events in Russia's spiritual history, and even more profoundly on the implications of Russia's past for its present spiritual and political problems. Their ideas deserve attention.

Until very recently, most of those cultural and national debates were conducted among the intelligentsia on the pages of "thick" journals. In the past year or two, however, formal organizations have emerged seeking to promote their respective visions of a culturally-defined Russia among the general public. One might see in these emerging structures initial attempts to give an institutional shape to the different ideas of Russia. It is evident that these organizations are characterized by diverse approaches to the questions of Russian national identity, the territorial shape of "Russia," and the empire.

Remembering that such distinctions lack precision, especially because a certain overlap is evident in the positions of the groups in question, let us first mention those that concentrate their attention on Russian culture broadly defined but make it clear that they do not claim for Russia any special position in relation to the other nationalities in the Soviet Union.

One such organization was founded in June 1989 under the name of "National [or People's] Home of Russia" *(Narodnyy dom Rossii).* The "National Home" expressly limits its sphere of operation to the RSFSR, and its program aims at "the revival of the spiritual, social, cultural, and socio-economic life of the Russian Federation." It wants to achieve this goal by freeing the energies of a society that had for long lived under "the oppression of a totally prohibitive system."[31]

Another Russian national initiative that emphasizes its autonomy from the state is the "Russian Encyclopedia Cultural Center." The projected Russian encyclopedia is to be devoted to all aspects of Russian history, culture, and civilization, and will not attempt to be a universal encyclopedia of the kind represented by the *Great Soviet Encyclopedia* or the comprehensive encyclopedias published in the union republics. The Russian encyclopedia planners insist on their independence from the state.[32]

John Dunlop draws attention to two other recent nationalist initiatives in the cultural area. Both are remarkably political—not to say "imperial"—in their "cultural" concerns. One of these is called "Foundation for Slavic Writing and Slavic Cultures" *(Fond slavyanskoy pis'mennosti i slavyanskikh kul'tur)* and includes among its founders individuals whom Dunlop calls "conservative Russian nationalists." As he puts it, the Foundation is "pan-Slavic in orientation."[33] Dunlop notes that the Foundation, launched in March 1989, has among its more than 80 sponsoring organizations the Writers' Union of the RSFSR as well as those of Ukraine and Belorussia, the academies of sciences of Ukraine and Belorussia, as well as numerous Russian and general Soviet organizations. He thinks that the "de facto goal of the new organization appears to be to cement relations among Russians, Ukrainians, and Belorussians." Only secondarily, according to Dunlop, is the Foundation concerned with Slavic and/or Orthodox nations abroad.

Dunlop quotes from a statement by Dmitriy Balashov, "the well-known Russian nationalist historical writer," who expressed this view: "The question of the day … is whether the 'supra-ethnic' state created by ethnic Russians can be preserved." It would be lamentable, Balashov said, "if the miracle of Russian statehood should be consumed by 'chaos'." This and similar statements led Dunlop to the following general observation: "Conservative Russian nationalists are concerned about the future political fragmentation of the Soviet empire. They are attempting to shore up the Eastern Slav nucleus of the USSR."[34]

The other organization discussed by Dunlop is the "Association of Russian Artists," also organized in early 1989. Dunlop notes that the Association's primary aim is to "combat separatist minority nationalist tendencies threatening the unity of the Soviet Union," and he quotes from a declaration of the Association to support his assessment:

> The once-powerful union of the peoples of Russia, joined together by the idea of steadfast unity, is experiencing a difficult period, during which, under the guise of demagogic slogans, nationalist groups are seeking to break up and destroy the unity of peoples.[35]

Recently, Boris Tsarev, the Association's business manager, declared that the organization supported the free development of all nationalities even though its own focus was on Russian culture. The Association firmly defends the unity of the USSR, which it views as a product of historical development that has produced a "brotherhood" of all peoples living in a common state. Tsarev warned the non-Russian nationalities against (unnamed) elements who work for the destruction of the USSR and aspire to establish their domination "over all nations."[36]

At least two other Russian nationalist organizations also began their existence in the spring of 1989. The Union for Spiritual Rebirth of the Fatherland (*Soyuz dukhovnogo vozrozhdeniya Otechestva*) was officially organized in Moscow on March 16–17, 1989. According to *Moskovskiy Literator*, the organizing session was attended by some 200 delegates from "patriotic associations and organizations" of Moscow, Leningrad, the Volga region, the Urals, Siberia, Belorussia, Ukraine, and Kazakhstan, as well as by representatives of the Russian Orthodox Church. The organization's listed "founders" included the *Sovetskaya Rossiya* Publishing House, the Lenin Library, the Scientific Council for Problems of Russian Literature in the USSR Academy of Sciences, a kolkhoz in Chuvashia, and "eight patriotic associations from regions of the Urals and Siberia."[37]

One week after the initial announcement, M. Antonov, president of the Union for Spiritual Rebirth, publicly explained the Union's goals. The Union expects resolution of the country's crisis "only on the condition that there is a moral rebirth of every nation of our great Fatherland." Only those patriotic organizations that have actually shown by deeds that they support socialism and the preservation of the independence of the country, and that support the party in its *perestroyka* policies, may join the Union. The manifesto of the Union, which was published next to Antonov's article, was directed to "Our compatriots, fellow Russian (*rossiyane*) brothers and sisters, all nations which have flourished in our Fatherland."[38]

Judging by the text of the Manifesto and Antonov's article, the Union is a strongly nationalistic, anti-Western, and anti-liberal body that appeals simultaneously to communist and Russian nationalist slogans. It would not be unfair to call the Union a national-socialist organization, envisioning the "Fatherland" as a multinational country led by the Russians. As if one such Union were not enough, many of the same organizations that sponsored the Union for Spiritual Rebirth were behind the establishment, also in March 1989 and also in Moscow, of yet another body, namely, the "Moscow Russian Patriotic Society 'Fatherland'" (*Moskovskoye russkoye patrioticheskoye obshchestvo "Otechestvo"*). The Moscow Society clearly sees itself as an ethnic organization, as shown by its use of the adjective *russkoye*, not *rossiyskoye*, the former being an ethnic or personal designation, the latter a territorial one in which non-Russian citizens of the Russian Republic can also be included. Its program advocates the establishment of a Russian (meaning the RSFSR) television network and a Russian academy of sciences, and several other causes. It stresses "military-patriotic education" and includes on its board at least one military officer.[39] In its stronger emphasis on Russian ethnicity, the Association differs from the Union for Spiritual Rebirth, which is clearly interested in extending its activities throughout the entire Soviet Union.

This brief and of necessity superficial review of recent Russian initiatives nevertheless reveals a rise in nationalist sentiment and concerns and testifies at the same time to the continuing confusion about what kind of country it is that the Russians are envisaging. Some of the positions mentioned here closely parallel those of empire-savers, although the empire-savers prefer to call themselves Soviet rather than Russian, even when they really mean Russian. Other positions are more clearly concerned with Russia proper, the RSFSR. But those "culturalist" nationalists who stress the Orthodox religious factor and who emphasize the Russians' ties to their fellow Slavs appear to be rather oblivious to the fact that the Russian Republic is the homeland of several Muslim nations, including the Volga Tatars, who form a large nation not only by RSFSR but also by all-Union standards. The culturalists' neglect of the non-Slavs within Russia, and their accenting of Ukrainian and Belorussian affinity with the Russians—some of them imply that the three nations are really one—seem to betray an "empire-saving" rather than a "nation-building" orientation.

Russia as a Democratic Nation-State. The third model of Russia is that which is beginning to take shape in the thinking of the activists and theorists of the national democratic movement of Russia. As of the summer of 1989, the Russian democratic movement has not created all-Russia structures comparable to those already existing in the Baltic states or even those emerging in Ukraine and Belorussia. But "popular" or "national" fronts have already been created in the Urals, in Yaroslavl', Leningrad, and most recently, in Moscow. It is only a matter of time, one imagines, before they coalesce into a *Russian* popular front.

It is also conceivable that these fronts will unite to proclaim the establishment of an "all-Union"—rather than a Russian—popular front, thus setting up the Russians in a position of leadership once again. If this happens, Russian democrats will be following in the footsteps of the Bolsheviks as well as of their democratic predecessors in pre-1917 Russia, who until the very last declined to identify themselves simply as "Great Russians." On this subject, the recollections of Paul Milyukov, written in the 1920's, are very revealing. He recalled how before the 1917 revolution, non-Russian nationalists asked the Russian democratic intelligentsia to redefine its national identity as a precondition for cooperation. In asking the Russians to become "Great Russian," i.e., to define themselves in ethnic terms rather than as a group representing the whole empire, the non-Russians argued that this redefinition would make it possible for all parties to act as equals. But by defining themselves as "Russian" in an imperial rather than a national sense, in the view of the non-Russians, Russian democrats were making a claim to superiority and leadership *(pervenstvo)* over the other nationalities. In Milyukov's retrospective view, the Russian intelligentsia could not have acted other than it did, since yielding to those demands required "undoing" Russian history.[40] In other words, it required denying legitimacy to that product of Russian history that Milyukov and his fellow intellectuals really valued—the empire.

Will the Russian intelligentsia in the 1990's agree to do what its predecessors refused to do in the 1900's? The article by Balakhonov mentioned earlier is remarkable for addressing, in the most explicit manner possible, the necessity to dissociate the Russian nation from imperial ambitions, thereby possibly giving the answer that Milyukov was unable to give.[41] If Balakhonov's proposal for the solution of the "Russian question" were implemented, it would not only allow the non-Russian peoples of the USSR to become free but, in the words of Milovan Djilas, would also mean "the emancipation of the Russian nation from the present (and often unwillingly borne) burdens of empire." In a conversation with George Urban, Djilas put his view of the Soviet-imperial versus Russian-national problem in the following way:

> We are talking about the natural expiry of an unnatural tyrannical regime which is bound to come, as surely as the British and French empires had to face their demise when the time was ripe. The Russian people would benefit the most. They would gain a free and more prosperous life and yet remain, undoubtedly, a great nation. You see, the Communist system has forced the Russian people into a state of sulking

introspection which seeks outlets in xenophobia, petulant demonstrations of national superiority—or, at the opposite end, maudlin admissions of national inferiority. I firmly believe that a reduced but self-confident, opened-up democratic Russian state would induce much less brooding in the Russian people and make them a happier race, to the extent that Russians can be happy. Imagine what would it mean for free men and women everywhere to see this last bastion of universal unfreedom go the way of all tyrannies.[42]

Let me summarize the most important points of the Balakhonov proposal—bearing in mind that at least some of his ideas are also being debated and presumably shared by the Democratic Union, which may well be the first major Russian political force that is both national (or "nationalist") and liberal, pro-Western, and democratic. For complex and deep historical reasons, Balakhonov argues, Russian national consciousness has become tied to the idea of empire (which also happens to be an autocratic, centralized state). In these deep historical recesses he sees the source of the most recent expressions of "imperial ideology." Balakhonov also thinks that the extremist positions of *Pamyat'* are rooted in an imperial-statist outlook.

The primary task of the Russian nation, Balakhonov writes, should be to reshape its national consciousness. The Russians need to fathom the value of democracy and to see that Russia's "voluntary withdrawal from the 'large empire' of the USSR" will be beneficial to the Russian people. The Russians ought to understand, too, that the "'small empire'—the RSFSR," which he says forms the core of the "large empire," should also be dismantled.

Specifically, Balakhonov proposes the formation of three or four Russian-speaking states out of those parts of the RSFSR where the Russians predominate. Those democratic and sovereign states would include: (1) Russia proper, embracing Moscow and historic Russian lands to the west of the Urals, where the Great Russians and the Russian state were originally formed; (2) West Siberia; (3) East Siberia (although he takes into account the possibility that there would be a single Siberian state); (4) the Russian Far East. Balakhonov thinks that the creation of independent states in Siberia and the Far East would enable the Russian nation to participate in, and benefit from, the development of the "Pacific Community" in the 21st century. In any case, he is sure that the dismantling of the empire would benefit both the non-Russians and the Russians themselves. Indeed, he thinks that some Russians already acknowledge this possibility: "Both in Russian Siberia and in the Far East, voices are already heard in favor of their economic, state-political, and cultural autonomy, in favor of reducing their dependence on the supercentralized administration."[43]

But Balakhonov recognizes that his plans are not likely to win mass support in the foreseeable future. He therefore thinks that the most urgent task is to advance a restructuring of the Russian people's consciousness, because most Russians still remain under the influence of an imperial mentality. "The imperial instinct of the Russians is exceptionally strong, and as yet, we simply do not imagine a form of existence other than the framework of the present empire from Brest to Vladivostok." Because the Russians themselves have not been under foreign rule for many centuries, they do not understand what national oppression means and accordingly do not sympathize with the national-liberation movements of dependent nations. Nevertheless, the Russians will have to accept the fall of the empire as a result of which they will become free themselves—or they can try to preserve the empire but in doing so they will deprive themselves of freedom. The latter course might ultimately lead to the rise of a "great-power Russian Nazism."[44]

Balakhonov's is not a lone voice. *Atmoda,* the newspaper of the National Front of Latvia, recently published a speech before the Baltic Assembly by Boris Rakitskiy, vice-president of the Soviet Sociological Association. As quoted in *Literaturnaya Rossiya,* Rakitskiy said:

> The Russian democratic movement, I assure you, is concerned now precisely with its inability to penetrate into the thicket of popular consciousness in order to try to root out its imperial component. This consciousness is great-power consciousness in form, but slavish in content. But we are working, we are trying on our part to support your efforts.[45]

In his article "To Russian Society on Russian Problems," Aleksandr Kazakov called upon his compatriots to stop identifying their fatherland with the state and "the authority." The Russian people have to learn, Kazakov said, not to mistake their love for their native land with love of the state and its political, military, and economic might. The Russians should work above all for "the revival of a national Russia" *(natsional'naya Rossiya).*[46]

It is impossible to determine at this stage how widely ideas like Balakhonov's, Rakitskiy's, or Kazakov's are supported. Balakhonov himself began to speak out in the 1970's in favor of dismantling the Soviet empire and replacing it by a Russian democratic nation-state as one of the empire's successors—and was punished for it at the time. Irrespective of how widely his ideas are shared, he is certainly right in paying attention to the political prospects of regional movements within the Russian Republic, including those in the ethnically-Russian core of the RSFSR.

If the Russian nation ever frees itself of its "imperial mentality," by which Balakhonov and his fellow-thinkers claim it is dominated, this will not happen as a consequence of some kind of massive intellectual revolution originating in Moscow or Leningrad. It is more realistic to suppose that the change will begin along the path that many are apparently already taking in "the provinces," where regional "popular fronts," like those already formed in the Urals, various Siberian centers, and in European Russian provincial capitals, are being established.

Some signs point to a democratic Russian nationalism—a democratic Russian national consciousness—taking shape in organized form. The Democratic Union appears to be a Russian, not an "all-Union," organization. On March 12, 1989, it held a demonstration in honor of the first Revolution of 1917, and the participants, according to *The New York Times,* carried Russian flags of a pre-Soviet vintage. Just as the Balts and the Ukrainians celebrate various dates in 1918 as their national independence days, so democratic Russians seem to have adopted the March 1917 anniversary as a Russian national holiday to mark their nation's emancipation from tsarism.[47]

March 1917 is not a date Russian nationalists in the RSFSR Writers' Union (not to mention the *Pamyat'* Society or its fellow travelers) would choose for a Russian national holiday. Some of them are more critical of those who overthrew the tsar in March 1917 than they are of those who seized power in November 1917.[48] It is easy to understand why this should be so: the liberals, radicals, and democrats inaugurated the disintegration of the empire; the Bolsheviks restored it.

CONCLUSIONS

There is no question that the Russian intelligentsia is giving much thought to the problems of Russian national identity, including the political issues involved in those problems. It is also clear that the non-Russians are pressing for a solution of the Russian problem by means of an institutional separation of Russia from the USSR as a prerequisite for overcoming "imperial thinking" and imperial practices in the Soviet Union.

What do "ordinary" Russians—the *russkiy narod*—think about the matter? Sergey Grigoryants started his recent article on "The Russian National Movement" in the following way: "As yet, a Russian national movement that could become the support of a future democratic state, does not exist in our country."[77] Although democratic organizations do exist among the Russians, they are relatively weak and often lack a clearly defined national outlook. Grigoryants, who thinks that *Pamyat'* represents the statist or imperial version of Russian national consciousness taken from the tsarist past, concedes that no counterweight to it has yet emerged that would be both democratic and national. In his view, the political spectrum lacks a force that would promote the cause of a democratic Russia, and focus on the fact that the Russians too are one of the nationalities of the Soviet Union and that their national needs should be met as well. ...

... The rise of the "interfronts," or "international fronts," consisting mainly of Russians and other Russian-speaking immigrants, says Grigoryants, should be seen as an expression not of Russian national sentiment but of an "unquestionably Soviet" sentiment.[82] In other words, most Russians in Latvia or Estonia view themselves as representatives of the state, of the Soviet-imperial principle, and feel they are living in a potentially rebellious province. They do not view themselves as a (Russian) national minority living in a country that is different from Russia.

It would seem, therefore, that a democratic, "normal" Russian national consciousness has a better chance of emerging in Russia proper, perhaps by developing from some regional autonomist grass roots. There may be reason to see the workers movement in Siberia in the summer of 1989 in this light. It is evident that the striking miners objected not only to intolerable material conditions but equally strongly to the entire way of life to which they are condemned. They spoke up against bureaucracy, "colonialism," "domination by Moscow," and similar enemies. This would suggest that at stake there are relations between an imperial center and its dependent province.

What role did the intelligentsia have in this conflict? It so happens that in April 1989, there appeared an announcement of the establishment in Novosibirsk of a "Siberian Independent Information Agency." (That announcement was not printed in the official Soviet media.) The inaugural meeting of that "Agency" was attended by representatives of independent journals from Novosibirsk (three publications) and Omsk, as well as by "independent journalists" from Irkutsk, Krasnoyarsk, Novokuznetsk, Kemerovo, and Yakutsk. The declaration adopted at the meeting contains phrases that reveal a sense of a distinct Siberian identity and suggest that it may be assuming a political form. Thus, the declaration protests that Siberia, "which finds itself in a colonial dependence on Moscow authorities," has no mass media of its own and is subject to an "information *diktat*" by the all-Union publications. Siberia has to make do with regional media, but lacks media covering Siberia as a whole. It was in order to correct this lack of specifically Siberian media that the Siberian information agency was founded. The agency's organizers said they would be willing to cooperate professionally with international and national news services interested in covering Siberian affairs. They also hoped that the new agency would be supported by the "Siberian people" (*Sibirskiy narod*) as well as the authorities.[83]

Speeches at the April 1989 plenum of the CPSU Central Committee supplied another kind of evidence that social and economic problems are being perceived in Siberia as in essence problems of *regional* dependence on the center, which is viewed as the embodiment of the bureaucratic, command-administrative system. The plenum agenda was devoted to assessing the results of the March elections to the Congress of People's Deputies. The elections resulted in defeats of numerous party officials and regional bosses, notably in Leningrad, Moscow, and Kiev, the three largest cities of the Soviet Union. But as one of the losers, the Kemerovo oblast first secretary, noted, the biggest defeats of party officials happened in Siberia and the Far East, "from the Urals to the ocean." The secretary, A. G. Mel'nikov, noted that the whole area—with 30 million inhabitants—suffered from profound social tensions, that "people have come to live much worse," and that the problems were "critical." Mel'nikov cited coal and oil output figures on Siberia's contribution to the economy and complained that despite its importance Siberia was not treated as a single unit but that its regions were separately managed by central agencies from Moscow, all employing administrative-command methods "because we still do not know of any other way" to manage. The only way out of the critical situation was to give Siberia its own rights, its economic and administrative autonomy, and to treat it as an economic partner—and so assure its contribution to the national economy.[84] The appropriateness of these warnings was confirmed by the Siberian strikes.

The key issues for Russian democratic nationalism are also key for all currents of Russian national consciousness. The one to which most attention has been devoted in this article is the attitude toward the state. The second issue, whose urgency and potential destructiveness is daily becoming more apparent, is the social and economic question broadly defined. This somewhat general and academic term covers the most serious and pressing matters of daily life for millions of people: health, ecology, food supplies or rather food shortages, education, wages, housing, work safety—the list goes on. The realization that in all these respects, the Soviet Union lags behind most of the developed world, even certain parts of the Third World, is universal in the Soviet Union. Among the Russians, this awareness is increasingly assuming the form of injured national feelings: "We, the Russians, who have suffered most, we who helped the others in the USSR, in Eastern Europe, Asia, Cuba, Africa, we are now poor and backward."

The resulting anger is directed against many targets. One obvious target is the state and party bureaucracy—"Moscow." Another—the nationalities, such as the Balts and the peoples of the Caucasus. Some elements are explaining the plight of Russia by accusing the "Jews, the internationalist Zionist conspiracy," or "the Masons." These extremists do not blame the state for the present crisis—and for the most part also not the communist ideology per se. Rather, they attribute the sins of the Soviet regime to the Jews who at one time or another occupied important posts in it, and by extension—to Jews as a people.

In such a situation it would seem imperative for the liberal and democratic Russian intelligentsia to make sure that the specifically national or nationalist Russian concerns and issues are not left to extremists of the *Pamyat'* kind. Against the right-wing models of Russia, which so prominently feature anti-Semitism and other forms of prejudice, the democrats and liberals need to propose their own democratic, tolerant, and progressive model of *Russia*. They cannot afford to ignore the specific Russian problem as they concern themselves with general social, economic, or political issues in somewhat abstract terms. In this regard, the Russian intelligentsia would do well to ponder the circumstances that in the 1920s had allowed the Fascists in Italy and the Nazis in Germany to capture considerable popular support by appealing to national sentiments and traditions.[85]

Clearly, the situation is very critical; and the intellectual and political confusion, overwhelming. The second question, therefore, that Russian nationalists, and everybody else in the Soviet Union, have to ask is: which ideology and program currently on "the market" will the masses accept as their own? Like so many thinking Russians are doing these days, Balakhonov quotes in his article the famous Pushkin lines expressing the poet's dread of "Russian mutiny, senseless and merciless." To prevent such a "mutiny," the intelligentsia will have to find a common language with the workers, the likes of whom struck the mines in Siberia. Will the Russian intelligentsia prove capable of accomplishing what Polish intellectuals accomplished in the 1970's? As the world knows, the Polish strikes of 1980 produced Solidarity, not a "senseless and merciless mutiny."[86]

One of the most insightful analyses of the Solidarity phenomenon was provided by Alain Touraine, the French sociologist. Touraine sees the historical meaning of Solidarity, whose rise he believes to signal "the end of communist society," in "setting an alternative agenda of historical action," thereby challenging a major prerogative that the communist regime had reserved for itself.[87] To follow Solidarity in this respect will require that the Russian nationalist intelligentsia put aside its more abstract debates about Orthodox tradition and forget about Zionist plotters. Instead, the intellectuals in Russia (and in other republics) will have to think of ways in which they can help construct a new agenda, an alternative vision of the future. How they perform this task will help determine the shape of any new national identity or identities that are likely to emerge in the USSR. ...

NOTES

ABOUT THE AUTHOR: **Roman Szporluk** is M. S. Hrushevskyi Professor of Ukrainian History at Harvard University.

1. Aleksandr Zharnikov, "National Self-Determination in Theory and Practice," *Kommunist* (Moscow), No. 9, June 1989, p. 62. Zharnikov is the scientific secretary of the scientific communism section in the Institute of Marxism-Leninism in Moscow.

9. Alain Besançon, "Nationalism and Bolshevism in the USSR," in Robert Conquest, Ed., *The Last Empire: Nationality and the Soviet Future,* Stanford, CA, Hoover Institution Press, 1986, pp. 12–13.

10. See *Russkaya Mysl'* (Paris), June 23, 1989, pp. 6–7. Balakhonov's article was originally published in issue No. 13 of *Svobodnoye Slovo,* the independent publication of the Democratic Union.

11. See the various "liberal" views expressed in the round-table discussion entitled "Democracy Is Conflict. A Search for a Correct Resolution of National Problems in the USSR," *Vek XX i Mir* (Moscow), No. 12, 1988, pp. 8–17.

12. Valeriy Tishkov, "Nations and the State," *Kommunist,* No. 1, January 1989, pp. 49–59.

13. For a fuller discussion of this problem, see Roman Szporluk, "The Imperial Legacy and the Soviet Nationalities Problem," in Lubomyr Hajda and Mark Beissinger, Eds., *The Nationalities Factor in Soviet Politics and Society,* Boulder, CO, Westview (forthcoming).

14. Yu. V. Bromley, "Being a Cohesive Force," *Sovetskaya Kul'tura* (Moscow), June 25, 1988, p. 8.

15. Yu. V. Bromley, "National Problems under Restructuring" *Voprosy Istorii* (Moscow), No. 1, 1989, p. 40.

16. J. K. Rebane, "Let Us Build Together Reasonable Relations," *Kommunist,* No. 4, March 1989, p. 85. This argument is not new, of course, as the title of Ivan Dzyuba's book written a quarter of a century ago—*Internationalism or Russification?*—reminds us.

17. *Pravda* (Moscow), July 2, 1988.

18. Ibid., Apr. 27, 1989.

19. S. L. Tikhvinskiy, "Tasks of Coordination in the Area of Historical Science," *Istoriya SSSR* (Moscow), No. 1, 1988, p. 119.

20. "Democracy Is Conflict ...," loc. cit., p. 10.

21. Mark G. Field, "Soviet Society and Communist Party Controls: A Case of Constricted Development," in Donald W. Treadgold, Ed., *Soviet and Chinese Communism: Similarities and Differences,* Seattle, WA, University of Washington Press, 1967, p. 196.

22. Alexander Yanov's and John B. Dunlop's many publications provide full documentation and analysis of those currents.

23. G. Sazonov, "Vasiliy Belov: Do Not Be Afraid of *Glasnost'*," *Pravda*, Mar. 5, 1989.

24. *Znamya* (Moscow), No. 2, 1989, pp. 168–69.

25. Interview in *Literaturnaya Rossiya*, June 2, 1989.

26. "For Objectivity in the History of the Fatherland," *Nash Sovremennik* (Moscow), No. 5, 1988, pp. 186–88.

27. "Letter to the Soviet Government," *Literaturnyy Irkutsk*, December 1988, pp. 4 and 7.

28. Ibid. The authors refer to Lenin's *Polnoye sobraniye sochineniy* (Complete Collected Works), Vol. 22, pp. 229–30, to support their assertion. The Soviet scholar, G. I. Kunitsyn, in "Self-Determination of Nations: The History of the Problem and Our Times," *Voprosy Filosofii* (Moscow), No. 5, 1989, pp. 66–86, argues that the Stalinist conception of the role of the Russian nation as the ruling nation of the Soviet state was put into practice after 1917, and that this was done in direct violation of Lenin's view. By depriving the RSFSR of the normal state structure of Soviet republics, and by placing Russia directly under central authorities, Stalin restored the pre-revolutionary great-power, imperialist concept, but he disguised it under revolutionary terminology. (See especially pp. 76–78.) There is not a word about "Zionists" or "Trotskyists" in Kunitsyn's balanced and well-documented account.

29. Roy Medvedev wrote more than 10 years ago: "It is a fact that the national life of Russians is hampered to a far greater degree than that of, say Armenians, Georgians, and the Uzbek peoples."

"Thus, for example, the villages and hamlets of basically Russian districts are in an immeasurably more neglected condition than the villages of Ukraine, Moldavia, the Transcaucasus, and the Baltic. Furthermore, Russians are basically deprived of their capital. As the capital of a multinational Union, Moscow has almost lost its traits of a national Russian city, a capital of Russian lands such as it was prior to the Revolution. The more European, industrial, and bureaucratic Petersburg was the capital of the Empire. This transformation of Moscow into an international center devoid of clear national lines is by no means a positive consequence for the whole Russian nation."

"At present, the weakening of the national foundations of Russian life is neither legal [*zakonomernyy*—meaning, a natural process], nor progressive."

"How could not only the preservation but also the development of the distinctive originality of the Russian people be furthered? This is a question that demands social analysis. Let us note, first of all, that the old proposal of separating the capitals of the USSR and the RSFSR, for which many people were condemned under Stalin, is not so fruitless. Similarly, it is necessary to undertake wide-ranging and urgent measures for upgrading agriculture and culture in the basically Russian districts, especially in the center and the north of the European area of the RSFSR." See "What Awaits Us in the Future? (Regarding A. I. Solzhenitsyn's Letter)," in Michael Meerson-Aksenov and Boris Shragin, Eds. *The Political, Social, and Religious Thought of Russian "Samizdat"—An Anthology*, Belmont, MA, Nordland, 1977, pp. 77–78.

30. Feliks Dymov, "Permit Whatever Is Not Forbidden!" *Literaturnaya Rossiya*, No 24, June 17, 1988, p. 3. See also a report on the symposium (whose participants included D. S. Likhachev and N. A. Tolstoy), "A Great City with a Provincial Fate?" *Literaturnaya Gazeta* (Moscow), Mar. 2, 1988, p. 10.

31. S. Galayeva, "National Home of Russia," *Literaturnaya Rossiya*, No. 25, June 23, 1989, p. 18.

32. See the interview with the chairman of the board, corresponding member of the USSR Academy of Sciences Oleg Trubachev, in *Literaturnaya Gazeta,* Mar. 22, 1989, p. 5: and a report entitled "Plans for a Russian Encyclopedia," *Literaturnaya Rossiya,* Apr. 14, 1989, p. 3.

33. John B. Dunlop, "Two Noteworthy Russian Nationalist Initiatives," RFE-RL, *Report on the USSR* (Munich), No. 21, May 26, 1989, p. 3.

34. Ibid., pp. 3–4.

35. *Moskovskiy Literator,* Dec. 16, 1988, p. 3, as quoted by John B. Dunlop.

36. Boris Ivanovich Tsarev, "By the Force of Russian Brotherhood," *Literaturnaya Rossiya,* June 16, 1989, p. 11.

37. *Moskovskiy Literator,* Mar. 24, 1989, p. 1; and *Literaturnaya Rossiya,* Mar. 31, 1989, p. 10.

38. M. Antonov, "From the Standpoint of Socialism," *Moskovskiy Literator,* Mar. 31, 1989; and "Appeal of the Union of Spiritual Rebirth of the Fatherland," ibid.

39. "Thinking of the Homeland, of Russia," *Literaturnaya Rossiya,* Mar. 31, 1989, p. 10; and "Fatherland—the Highest Good," ibid., June 23, 1989, p. 14. The former source calls the organization a "movement" (*dvizheniye*); the latter, a "society" (*obshchestvo*).

40. P. N. Milyukov, *Natsional'nyy vopros—Proiskhozhdeniye natsional'nosti i natsional'nyye voprosy v Rossii* (The National Problem—The Origins of Nationality and National Problems in Russia), no place of publication, Biblioteka izdatel'stva "Svobodnaya Rossiya," 1925, pp. 116–17.

41. Vladimir Balakhonov, "Preservation of the Empire or Self-Preservation by Way of National Sovereignty—the Main National Problem of the Russian People," *Russkaya Mysl',* June 23, 1989, pp. 6–7.

42. "Djilas on Gorbachev (II): Milovan Djilas and George Urban in Conversation," *Encounter* (London), November 1988, p. 30.

43. Balakhonov, loc. cit., p. 6. Suggestions about subdividing the RSFSR have appeared in an official Moscow weekly, *Literaturnaya Gazeta.* See Vladimir Sokolov, "Democracy and Borders: Concepts," Aug. 2, 1989.

44. Ibid., p. 7.

45. *Literaturnaya Rossiya,* June 30, 1989, p. 14.

46. Ibid.

47. *The New York Times,* Mar. 13, 1989.

48. Julia Wishnevsky, "*Nash Sovremennik* Provides Focus for 'Opposition Party'," *Report on the USSR,* Jan. 20, 1989, p. 30.

77. Sergey Grigoryants, "The Russian National Movement," *Russkaya Mysl',* No. 3775, May 12, 1989, p. 6.

82. Grigoryants, loc. cit., p. 6.

83. "Creation of a Siberian Independent Information Agency," *Russkaya Mysl',* Apr. 14, 1989, p. 2.

84. *Pravda,* Apr. 27 1989.

85. See Geoff Eley's chapter "What Produces Fascism: Preindustrial Traditions or a Crisis of the Capitalist State?" in *From Unification to Nazism: Reinterpreting the German Past,* Boston, London, and Sydney, Allen and Unwin, 1986, pp. 254–82; see also Roman Szporluk, *Communism and Nationalism: Karl Marx versus Friedrich List,* New York and Oxford, Oxford University Press, 1988, pp. 189–90.

86. According to Bill Keller writing from Moscow on the strikes in the Ukrainian SSR, "miners who walked out today in the western Ukrainian city of Chervonograd included in

398 PART 5: NATIONALITIES AND FEDERATION

their demands the creation of an independent national coal-miners' union explicitly modeled on the Polish union Solidarity." ("Soviet Strikers Hint at Forming a Free Union like
Solidarity," *The New York Times*, July 21, 1989.) Future events will show whether these demands will acquire substance and whether the workers of Siberia and Donbas will organize
unions modeled on Solidarity.

The original Solidarity in Poland had many dimensions—religious and national as well
as social and economic. Just as it is too early to tell whether the workers of Siberia feel any
definite regional Siberian or national Russian identity, so it is impossible to detect any specific regional or national Ukrainian identity in the workers' consciousness in the Donbas
or Western Ukraine. This brings to mind Ukrainian writer Yuriy Shcherbak's recent remark that unlike elsewhere in the USSR, in Ukraine there have emerged not interethnic
conflicts but rather a conflict between Ukrainians and those whom Shcherbak calls "Little
Russians." (Interview with Yuriy Shcherbak, interview in *Literaturnaya Gazeta*, Jan. 18,
1989, p. 3.) The latter term would describe those ethnic Ukrainians who prefer to consider
themselves members of a larger Russian nation while preserving some specific regional
Ukrainian features. Thus, the "Little Russians" represent Ukrainian supporters of an "all-
Russian" national identity discussed earlier. It would seem, therefore, that in contemporary Ukraine, especially in such heavily Russified areas as Donbas. at least three identities
are competing for popular support: Russian, Ukrainian, and "Little Russian." Conceivably,
there is a fourth one too—some form of *Soviet* identity. The possibility of such an identity
actually taking shape should not be dismissed a priori, even though the concept itself was
originally "manufactured upstairs." For ample evidence on how national traditions and
national identities were being "invented," that is, consciously produced (not to say manufactured) in 19th-century Europe and elsewhere, see Eric Hobsbawm and Terence Ranger,
Eds., *The Invention of Tradition*, Cambridge, Cambridge University Press, 1988.

87. Alain Touraine, *Return of the Actor: Social Theory in Postindustrial Society*, tr. by
Myrna Godzich. Minneapolis, MN, University of Minnesota Press, 1988, p. xix.

33   The Russian Question:
In Search of an Answer
(a Roundtable)

"Independence in the Name of Democracy"—that was the title of an article by V.
Chichkanov, the director of the Institute of Economics of the Urals branch of the
USSR Academy of Sciences and a corresponding member of the Academy, which
was printed by the newspaper *Soviet Russia* at the end of last year. That publication marked perhaps the first time that a very well defined conclusion was overtly
expressed: the restriction of the rights of Russia is vitally necessary for the persis-

tence of the administrative-bureaucratic system. Furthermore (the quote is a bit long, but it is worth citing): "In the existing administrative-bureaucratic system, Russia fulfilled a threefold function: a function of guaranteeing that system (by its military, industrial and natural resource potential); a function of compensating for the economic incapacity of the bureaucratic apparatus (the mass sale of natural resources); and a function of 'large-scale allocation'—dissatisfaction with the operations of the organs of power was frequently turned against Russia. Without such a buttress the administrative system would not have been able and will not be able to exist. Thus, all the efforts aimed at strengthening the sovereignty of Russia meet with almost insurmountable counter-action."

Here only one perplexity springs up: why is the threefold function of Russia spoken of in the past tense? The dismantling of the administrative-bureaucratic system is far from concluded, and the best witness of this as before is the dependent, humbled, and profaned colonial position of Russia and the disastrous condition of the Russian people. The bitter fate of our long-suffering Homeland has changed little until now. As before, oil and natural gas flow away abroad—that same natural gas of which the Russian village has been dreaming for dozens of years. The broad sale of our natural wealth continues, and traces of Russian gold remain inscrutable. To satisfy the demand of other union republics, billions of rubles are raked out of Russia's budget without the permission or will of those people who, by heavy labor, earned it. ...

... In domestic prices seven republics export more products to other republics than they import: the RSFSR by 3.65 billion rubles; the Ukrainian SSR by 1.56 billion rubles; the Belorussian SSR by 3.15 billion rubles; the Georgian SSR by 0.58 billion; the Azerbaijanian SSR by 2.04 billion; the Moldavian SSR by 0.63 billion; and the Armenian SSR by 0.59 billion. The other republics have a negative balance, that is, they import more than they export.

Now, if this situation were evaluated in terms of world-market prices, it would turn out that a positive balance in inter-republic exchange is maintained by only two republics: the RSFSR and the Azerbaijanian SSR. According to this, all the republics (except the Azerbaijanian SSR) should have to pay the Russian Federation for its goods 25 billion rubles more, if the calculation were in terms of world-market prices. If we were to take into account that the difference came about only as a result of the distortion of prices on the domestic market, it is the pure profit of Russian enterprises which actually goes into the budget of other republics. They win by acquiring raw materials from Russia at lower than world-market prices and exporting food and products of light industry at higher prices. ...

After all this, should we be surprised that the inhabitants of Russia find themselves at the lowest position in terms of standard of living, provision of national consumer goods (including both food and non-food products), and social development, and that they cannot build roads, restore the demolished country villages, small towns and cultural monuments, mend spiritual life, bring the ecology back to a normal state, raise the level of wages for labor, free women from excessive toil, nor create conditions for the normal development and raising of children?

In 1988 101 billion rubles of profits, or 61 percent, was confiscated from Russia. By all accounts it is evident that what the Union republics think about least of all is moderating their appetites. This year the Central Asian republics are receiving from the Russian budget 8.5 billion rubles of so-called subsidy. Armenia is receiving 100 million rubles. Therefore, when it comes to the correct slogan, "The better we work, the better we live," in actuality the opposite is true for Russians and the slogan is but base demagoguery and cannot provoke anything but mockery and revulsion. Under these conditions the people respond in the only manner available to them—with extremely low labor productivity. They "respond" also with the fact that today 58 percent of the families in Russia have only one child. The demographic situation has intensified to the extent that the historical existence of the Russian nation is in question. Every year three thousand country villages disappear off the map of Russia, farm lands are left empty, and fields become overgrown with weeds. And unsanctioned by any democratic decisions, the redistribution of age-old Russian land to people of Central Asian extraction continues.
...

... These and other questions were discussed at a meeting of USSR People's Deputies with writers and editorial members of the journal *Moskva*. ...

G. LITVINOVA, PROFESSOR OF LAW. One can trace a distinct pattern: the higher the proportion of the industrial working class of one or another ethnic group, the slower the pace of its development in social, demographic, economic, and other spheres.

Russians have the highest proportion of industrial workers. Therefore, here the national question intertwines with the social. The problem of the industrial working class is foremost a Russian problem, in so far as the working class is not only in Russia, but is represented to a significant extent specifically by Russians in many republics, if not in the majority of them.

And, vice versa, the lower the proportion of the industrial working class, the higher the percentage of academics, directors, and creative intelligentsia. This correlation suggests the idea that, seemingly, either the slogans which we proclaimed 70 years ago about the leading role of the working class are basically a sham or else our social experience is not following that path, which should have formed the basis of Marxist-Leninist views on the role of the working class. That is why our vital task consists in raising the political role of the working class.

N. BYKOVSKIKH, DEPUTY (OLD OSKOL, BELGOROD REGION). Most importantly, the working class has understood that if they do not, let's say, take power in their own hands, that means that they cannot count on the success of *perestroika*. And power needs to be seized literally: not in words, but in deeds in order to help the government extricate itself from the quagmire in which it now finds itself. And the workers demand from us, their deputies, that we clearly define our positions and actively defend their interests. Because now there is candid and honest discussion in the vein of: "either the mafia gets us or we get the mafia." This is how the working class now thinks.

E. VOLODIN, PROFESSOR OF PHILOSOPHY. ... The main problem consists of the fact that in the course of many years Russia did not give its billions even to the budget of the Union. It simply transferred them to the budget of the Union republics. That is why the Uzbek Supreme Soviet, for example, can adopt decisions to the effect that first through fifth grade school children receive free breakfasts, while students renting living quarters from other individuals receive monetary aid. We Russians for whatever reason, cannot allow ourselves such things.

The multi-billion tribute which for some reason Russia pays its republics under the name of a state subsidy is not only leading to a serious drop in the standard of living of the people of the Russian Federation, but is also generating a certain psychology for the people of the Union republics—the psychology of dependency.

G. DEMIDOV, DEPUTY (PENZA). ... Of course, we cannot forget about the millions of Russians who are located outside the bounds of the Russian Federation, that is, in other republics. These are for the most part industrial workers, who number about 20 million people. Their fate cannot but worry me as both a person and as a People's Deputy. It is too bad that the lashing out against the Russian people has not met with any rebuff—and that includes us deputies. This, in my opinion, allows even more unbridled antagonism to be unleashed against Russia, as when crowds of extremists can yell out anti-Russian slogans, call Russians occupiers, and so on.

G. LITVINOVA. Now the question of a capital is being very seriously discussed, and it is already beginning to be debated in all circles and at all levels. It has been suggested that Moscow be separated from the Russian Federation and be set apart, that is, be given the status of a Union republic. Now, it should not be forgotten that, in contrast to the Soviet Union, which is a bit over sixty years old, Russia has existed for thousands of years and Moscow was the capital for many centuries. Therefore, as soon as the Soviet Union, for all my preference for it, becomes a new state, permit its capital to be a new city as well, as is done in some Latin American countries. But Moscow must remain the capital of Russia. We do not need to build another Nagorno-Karabakh, and enough with doing whatever people please without asking Russians how they react to it! After all, Moscow does not belong only to Muscovites, it belongs to Russia. And no one should dare separate it from Russia without asking the opinion of every Russian. ...

O. MIKHAILOV. "Well, anyway, what is going on with Russia?" This question of questions we ask ourselves again and again, not without a glimmer of hopelessness. Its half-cured sickness was reflected from the very beginning—either in a mass hunger, which was evidently organized from above in the largest grain-producing region, where, it happened, Russians ate each other; or it was reflected in the bareness of prehistoric atheism (which went to the point of erecting a statue of

Judas of Iscariot in one of the provincial cities of New Russia), then it was reflected, let's say—already closer to our time—in national unrest, as in Novocherkassk, where people were crushed by tanks with stone-like indifference. All the means were proper to use—if only the thieving was conducted quietly.

Meanwhile, for dozens of years of forcibly raising the level of the outlying areas at Russia's expense, zealous experimentalist-internationalists did not see that by the planned destruction of the center, the core, they are destroying the very field of force of gravitation of the state. And so, the power of attraction wore out. Russia no longer exists as the center, like the Sun, and today the planets are ready to break away from their republican orbit and fly apart. Only in what form will the prodigal children later want to return (this, I think, is also possible)? Are they not in the position of free-floating asteroids? Hangers-on, who will require being clothed and shoed anew? In such a situation the variant of the forestalled exit of Russia from the Union becomes not so anecdotal with the transfer of the republic capital to Petersburg-Leningrad. Then the first-enthroned would at least find the hope of ridding themselves of hard-currency prostitutes, Caucasian battlers, anti-Zionist and Zionist centers, gallant racketeers, fatal tumors of the ministry, porno-video salons for minors, caddish, arrogant drivers in black Volgas, billionaires from shady economic practices who buy up houses on the Arbat, beggars in the underground passageways, and the other charms of *perestroika*. To begin speaking about these things yesterday by all accounts is already too late. The waves of a growing tornado are covering us.

Perestroika has been going on for not five years, it has been going on since 1917, and its end is not in sight. Newer and newer experiments are being conducted, even though conducting experiments on people is a crime. Even in medicine, drugs (not for healthy and sound people, but for sick ones) are tried first on animals. But when a theory, even a brilliant one, is thought up in a study through book learning and is employed in order to make millions upon millions of people happy, it is easy to harm the gene of nationality itself and to destroy the genetic code of the people. ...

M. ANTONOV. A situation is taking shape whereby the Soviet Union is turning more and more into a colony of multi-national corporations, while Russia within the Soviet Union remains a colony of our other republics. And we poorly conceive of the extent to which we quite insufficiently counter the arguments of our opponents. Let's say, certain forces in the Baltic Republics speak out for leaving the Soviet Union and as their strongest reason refer to the fact that before entering the Union, their economy was developing successfully. But this reason appears convincing only when uninformed. In actuality, the well-being of the Baltic Republics in many ways was based on profiteering activities. As is known, Soviet Russia when it came into being, was economically blockaded. However, our country at that time bought a lot in the West and sold to it. It was carried out like this: that very same Estonia bought raw materials at low prices from us and sold it at significantly higher prices in the West. An opposite process went on with Western goods: they were bought cheaply and sold to us at three times the price. And with similar operations the Baltic Republics secured their relatively high economic potential.

As to strictly Russian problems, our main drama is spiritual impoverishment. We stopped being a people because we lost our culture, our traditions. I think that in our spiritual re-birth the church should play a big role. Ordinary clergymen could now do an unusually great deal. And if our deputies scorn contact with the church, they are making a very big mistake.

Another aspect of culture. Polish sociologists in their research have shown that 30 percent of any people can fully master a university-level course. In this respect nature turned out to be democratic. This index is the same for Yakuts, blacks, Russians, and Jews. If any nationality has more diplomas than its allowed allotment of 30 percent, then that means that they have somebody else's diplomas and as a result propagate incompetency. If any nationality in our country has too high an allotment of people with a higher education, not even speaking about Ph.D.'s and academics, then today this turns into simply a threat for all humanity. It is namely this incompetency, besides everything else, that is to blame for the tragedy of Chernobyl, for the destruction of the Aral Sea, and for many other catastrophes which occurred, are occurring, and will occur. And the Russian people need to speak out about this threat. ...

34   *Declarations of the State Sovereignty of the Russian and Ukrainian Republics*

DECLARATION ON THE STATE SOVEREIGNTY OF THE RUSSIAN SOVIET FEDERATION SOCIALIST REPUBLIC

The first RSFSR Congress of People's Deputies,

—conscious of its historical responsibility for the fate of Russia,

—testifying to its respect for the sovereign rights of all peoples within the Union of Soviet Socialist Republics,

—expressing the will of the peoples of the RSFSR,

solemnly proclaims the state sovereignty of the Russian Soviet Federated Socialist Republic over its entire territory and declares its resolve to create a democratic law-based state, part of a renewed USSR.

1. The Russian Soviet Federated Socialist Republic is a sovereign state, created by the peoples that have historically united in it.

2. The Sovereignty of the RSFSR is the natural and essential condition for the existence of Russian statehood, which has centuries of history, culture, and accumulated traditions.

3. The bearer of sovereignty and the source of state power in the RSFSR is its multi-national people. The people wield state power directly and through representative organs on the basis of the RSFSR Constitution.

4. The state sovereignty of the RSFSR is declared in the name of higher goals— the guaranteeing to each person of the inalienable right to a worthy life, free development and use of his native language, and to each people the right to self-determination in the national government structure and cultural forms it chooses.

5. In order to secure the political, economic and legal guarantees of RSFSR sovereignty the following are established:

full power of the RSFSR in decisions on all questions of state and public life, with the exclusion of those which it voluntarily transfers to the discretion of the Union;

the priority of the RSFSR's Constitution and Laws on the entire territory of the RSFSR; the effect of laws of the Union that contradict the sovereign rights of the RSFSR are suspended by the Republic on its territory. Disagreements between the Republic and the Union are resolved through a procedure established by the Union Treaty;

the exclusive right of the people to ownership, use and disposal of the national riches of Russia;

authorized representation of the RSFSR in other Union republics and in foreign countries;

the right of the Republic to participate in the exercise of the authority it transfers to the Union.

6. The Russian Soviet Federated Socialist Republic unites with other republics in the Union on the basis of the Union Treaty. The RSFSR recognizes and respects the sovereign rights of the Union republics and the Union.

7. The RSFSR reserves the right of free exit from the USSR according to a procedure established by the Union Treaty and legislation based upon it.

8. The territory of the RSFSR cannot be changed without the people expressing its will by means of a referendum.

9. The RSFSR Congress of People's Deputies affirms the need for a significant widening of the rights of the autonomous republics, autonomous provinces, and autonomous districts in the RSFSR, as well as those of territories and districts of the RSFSR. Concrete questions of the exercise of these rights must be determined in RSFSR legislation on the structure of the Federation's territorial administration and nationality government formations.

10. All citizens and persons without citizenship living on the territory of the RSFSR are guaranteed the rights and freedoms set out by the RSFSR Constitution, the USSR Constitution and the norms of international law.

Representatives of nationalities living outside the borders of their nationality's government structures or who do not have them within the RSFSR are guaranteed their legal political, economic, national and cultural rights.

11. Citizenship of the republic is established on the entire territory of the RSFSR. Each citizen of the RSFSR preserves USSR citizenship.

12. The RSFSR guarantees all citizens, political parties, public organizations, mass movements and religious organizations that act in the framework of the RSFSR Constitution equal legal opportunities to participate in the conduct of state and public affairs.

13. The division of legislative, executive and judicial power is the most important principle for the functioning of the RSFSR as a law-based state.

14. The RSFSR declares its adherence to generally accepted principles of international law and its readiness to live with all countries and peoples in peace and harmony and to take every measure to prevent confrontation in international, inter-republic and inter-nationality relations while defending the interests of the peoples of Russia.

15. The present Declaration will serve as the basis for developing a new RSFSR Constitution, a Union Treaty and the perfection of the republic's legislation.

DECLARATION ON THE STATE SOVEREIGNTY
OF UKRAINE ADOPTED BY THE UKRAINIAN
SSR SUPREME SOVIET ON JULY 16, 1990

The Supreme Soviet of the Ukrainian SSR,
    expressing the will of the Ukrainian people,
    undertaking to create a democratic society,
    proceeding from the need fully to secure human rights and freedoms,
    esteeming the national rights of all peoples,

concerned for the full political, economic, social and spiritual development of the Ukrainian people,

PROCLAIMS

the state sovereignty of Ukraine to be supreme; the autonomy, totality, and indivisibility of the Republic's power within its territory; and its independence and equal status in foreign relations.

I. SELF-DETERMINATION OF THE UKRAINIAN NATION

The Ukrainian SSR as a sovereign national state develops within its existing borders on the basis of the exercise by the Ukrainian nation of its inalienable right to self-determination.

The Ukrainian SSR conducts the defense and protection of the national statehood of the Ukrainian people.

Any violent acts against the Ukrainian national state on the part of political parties, public organizations, other organizations or individuals are punishable by law.

II. POPULAR POWER

Citizens of the Republic of all nationalities make up the Ukrainian people.

The Ukrainian people is the only source of state power in the Republic.

The full power of the Ukrainian people is realized on the basis of the Republic's Constitution both directly and through people's deputies elected to the Supreme Soviet and local Soviets of the Ukrainian SSR.

Only the Supreme Soviet of the Ukrainian SSR may speak in the name of the entire people. No political party, public organization, other grouping nor individual may speak in the name of the entire Ukrainian people.

III. STATE POWER

The Ukrainian SSR is independent in deciding all questions of its state life.

The Ukrainian SSR guarantees the priority of the Constitution and laws of the Republic on its territory.

State power in the Republic is exercised according to the principle of its division into legislative, executive and judicial power.

The supreme supervision over the exact and uniform fulfillment of laws is carried out by the Attorney General of the Ukrainian SSR, who is named by the Supreme Soviet of the Ukrainian SSR, is accountable to it and reports only to it.

IV. CITIZENSHIP OF THE UKRAINIAN SSR

The Ukrainian SSR has its own citizenship and guarantees every citizen the right to preserve USSR citizenship.

The bases for acquiring and losing Ukrainian SSR citizenship are determined by a Ukrainian SSR Law on citizenship.

All citizens of the Ukrainian SSR are guaranteed the rights and freedoms that are established in the Ukrainian SSR Constitution and those norms of international law that are recognized by the Ukrainian SSR.

The Ukrainian SSR ensures the equality before the law of all citizens of the Republic without regard to their origin, social and economic status, race and nationality affiliation, gender, education, language, political views, religious convictions, type and character of employment, living place or other circumstances.

The Ukrainian SSR regulates immigration processes.

The Ukrainian SSR shows care for and takes measures to secure and protect the interests of Ukrainian SSR citizens living outside the Republic's borders.

V. TERRITORIAL SUPREMACY

The Ukrainian SSR exercises supremacy on its entire territory.

The territory of the Ukrainian SSR in its present borders is inviolate and cannot be changed nor used without its agreement.

The Ukrainian SSR independently determines the territorial administrative structure of the Republic and the procedure for forming nationality administration units.

VI. ECONOMIC INDEPENDENCE

The Ukrainian SSR independently determines its economic status and conforms to it in law.

The Ukrainian people have an exclusive right to ownership, use and disposition of the national riches of Ukraine.

The land, what lies below it, air space, water and other natural resources located within the territory of the Ukrainian SSR, the natural resources of its continental shelf and exclusive (ocean) economic zone and the entire economic and scientific-technical potential accumulated on Ukrainian territory are the property of its people, the material basis for the Republic's sovereignty and are used to fulfill the material and spiritual requirements of its people.

The Ukrainian SSR has the right to the share of the general Union wealth, including the general Union diamond and hard-currency stores and gold reserve, that was created through the efforts of the Republic's people.

Resolution of questions about Union-wide property (the general property of all republics) is done on the basis of agreement between the republics that own this property.

Enterprises, institutions, organizations and objects of other states, their citizens, and international organizations may locate on the territory of the Ukrainian SSR and use its resources according to the laws of the Ukrainian SSR.

The Ukrainian SSR independently forms banking (including foreign-trade banking), price, financial, customs, and tax systems. It sets the state budget and if necessary introduces its own currency.

The highest credit institution of the Ukrainian SSR is the national Ukrainian Bank, subordinated to the Supreme Soviet of the Ukrainian SSR.

Enterprises, institutions, organizations and production units located on the territory of the Ukrainian SSR pay a tariff for the use of land and other natural and labor resources, a tax on their hard-currency income, and also pay taxes to local budgets.

The Ukrainian SSR ensures the defense of all forms of property.

VII. ECOLOGICAL SECURITY

The Ukrainian SSR independently establishes the procedure for the organization of nature conservation, the use of natural resources on the Republic's territory.

The Ukrainian SSR has a national commission for radiation protection of the people.

The Ukrainian SSR has the right to forbid construction and to stop the operation of any enterprises, institutions, organizations and other objects that threaten ecological security.

The Ukrainian SSR shows concern for the ecological security of its citizens, the people's gene stock, and the young generation.

VIII. CULTURAL DEVELOPMENT

The Ukrainian SSR is independent in resolving questions of science, education, and the cultural and spiritual development of the Ukrainian nation, and guarantees to all nationalities that live on the republic's territory the right to the free development of their national culture.

The Ukrainian SSR endeavors to create a national cultural renaissance of the Ukrainian people, to preserve its historical consciousness and traditions and its national and ethnographic character traits, and to ensure the use of the Ukrainian language in all spheres of public life.

The Ukrainian SSR manifests concern for the satisfaction of the national cultural, spiritual and linguistic needs of Ukrainians living outside the Republic's boundaries.

National, cultural and historical valuables on the territory of the Ukrainian SSR are the exclusive property of the Republic's people.

The Ukrainian SSR has the right to return to the property of the Ukrainian people national, cultural and historical valuables located outside the boundaries of the Ukrainian SSR.

IX. EXTERNAL AND INTERNAL SECURITY

The Ukrainian SSR has the right to its own Armed Forces.

The Ukrainian SSR has its own internal forces and organs of state security, subordinate to the Supreme Soviet of the Ukrainian SSR.

The Ukrainian SSR determines the procedure for military service by citizens of the Republic.

Citizens of the Ukrainian SSR carry out their active military duty, as a rule, on the territory of the Republic and cannot be used for military purposes outside its borders without the agreement of the Supreme Soviet of the Ukrainian SSR.

The Ukrainian SSR solemnly proclaims its intention to become in the future a constantly neutral state that does not take part in military blocs and adheres to the three non-nuclear principles: not to accept, not to produce, and not to acquire nuclear weapons.

X. INTERNATIONAL RELATIONS

The Ukrainian SSR as a subject of international law maintains direct relations with other states, concludes treaties with them, and exchanges diplomatic, consulate, and trade representatives. It takes part in the activities of international organizations to the extent necessary effectively to protect the national interests of the Republic in the political, economic, ecological, informational, scientific, technical, cultural, and sporting spheres.

The Ukrainian SSR is an equal participant in international relations, actively facilitates the strengthening of general peace and international security, and directly participates in the general European process and European structures.

The Ukrainian SSR recognizes the priority of general human values over class values, and the priority of generally recognized norms of international law over the norms of internal state law.

The relations of the Ukrainian SSR with the other Soviet republics are built on the basis of treaties based on the principles of equal rights, mutual respect and non-interference in internal affairs.

This Declaration is the basis for a new Constitution and laws of Ukraine and determines the position of the Republic while concluding international agreements. The principles of the Declaration on Ukrainian Sovereignty are used for concluding a union treaty.

35 Speech to the Russian Federation Congress of People's Deputies, Moscow, May 22, 1990

BORIS YELTSIN

Esteemed people's deputies! The years of imperial policy of the center have led to the uncertain nature of the current situation in the Union republics, and the vagueness of their rights, obligations and responsibilities. First and foremost, this applies to Russia, which has suffered the greatest damage from the command-administrative system, which has become obsolete but is still clinging on for dear life. There can be no reconciling with a situation where in labor productivity the republic finds itself in third place in the country, and in ratio of expenditure for social needs is 15th and last. The unanimous vote of the people's deputies to include the question under discussion in the agenda shows that it is abundantly clear to all of us that one of the most important tactical ways out of the crisis is that of ensuring real democracy in Russia. A means of achieving this objective is by ensuring the real sovereignty of Russia on equal terms with the Union republics. We need the kind of sovereignty which would not mean carrying over power and privileges from Union bureaucrats to Russian ones.

The problems of the republic cannot be solved without full-blooded political sovereignty. This alone can enable relations between Russia and the Union and between the autonomous territories within Russia to be harmonized.

The political sovereignty of Russia is also necessary in international affairs. The following fundamental principles should be included in the political basis of the new republican constitution, which is due to be adopted before the new Union Constitution, this year, I believe.

1. The Russian republic is a sovereign democratic law-based state of peoples enjoying equal rights who have voluntarily joined together within it.
2. All power in the republic belongs to the people who implement it direct]y and through the soviets of people's deputies.

3. Relations between Russia and the other Union republics are regulated by separate treaties, and with the Union also by a special separate treaty. The center is for Russia today the cruel exploiter, the miserly benefactor, and the favorite [vremenshchik] who does not think about the future. We must put an end to the injustice of these relations. Today it is not the center but Russia which must think about which functions to transfer to the center, and which to keep for itself.

Is it not also time to raise the question of what sort of center Russia and the other republics of the Union need? [applause]

4. Acts adopted by the Union must not contradict Russia's new Constitution and the treaty with the Union.
5. Apart from the powers delegated to the Union, the republic implements its domestic and foreign policy independently.
6. Relations between subjects of the federation within Russia are regulated on the basis of a federative treaty, under which they are guaranteed sovereignty, the economic independence of autonomous formations, their distinct cultural and national characteristics, and the right to just and equal representation in all bodies of the Federation.
7. A single republican citizenship is established in Russia. Nobody can be stripped of that citizenship.
8. The republic's Constitution guarantees political pluralism and a multi-party system operating within the framework of parliamentary democracy. The monopoly on power of any part is excluded. Parties and social organizations operate within the framework of a special law. [applause]
9. Citizens of Russia and citizens of other Union republics resident on its territory are guaranteed all civil, political, and property rights.
10. All forms of ownership by citizens of Russia are protected by law.
11. Complete and unconditional separation of legislative, executive, and judicial powers is implemented in the republic.
12. Elections to the representative bodies of state power are universal, equal, direct, and secret.
13. A review of Russia's symbols, envisaging, in particular, the creation of an anthem for the republic.

The economic sovereignty of Russia is possible only on condition that republican ownership is formed, whose basis must be the land, the soil beneath and the air above, forests, water and other natural resources, enterprises, all produced output and its scientific-technical and intellectual potential. It is necessary to guarantee in law that they are used exclusively in the interests of Russia. The transfer of natural and other resources belonging to the republics can be carried out, on the basis of payment favorable to the republic, only by Russia's parliament. It is obvious that the same principle must also be spread downwards, to the subjects of the Russian Federation.

Subjects of the Federation may be not only national autonomous entities, but also territorial and economic formations. I consider it necessary to guarantee real economic independence for enterprises, regardless of their form of ownership. In other words, the topic is this: The most important, primary sovereignty in Russia is the person and his rights; further on, the enterprise, the collective and state farm and other organizations—that is where the primary and strongest sovereignty must be, as well as, of course, the sovereignty of the rayon soviet or any other primary soviet. Proceeding on the basis of the specific character of the Russian Federation and its state and political system to sovereignty, the republic must have the right to introduce and cancel economic mechanisms on its territory and conduct cardinal reforms of them, without the obligatory consent of the Union government. Russia's relations with other Union republics are built on the principle of mutual economic interest and on the basis, as a rule, of world prices. Russia determines for herself her partners in relations with foreign countries. Russia's share in financing Union programs and the amounts assigned to the Union budget are implemented strictly according to accounts and the expediency of each program and each type of expenditure in the Union budget. [applause]

Russia must implement an independent foreign trade and currency and finance policy, including the establishment of free enterprise zones on her territory. The republic determines for itself the independence in foreign economic activity of enterprises sited on its territory, and conducts trade in frontier and coastal zones for hard currency. I believe that the protection of the economic interests of the republic, the subjects of the Federation and the enterprises and citizens of Russia abroad must come exclusively under Russia's jurisdiction. The republic's state bank must be separated from the Union state bank and the republican government, have the right of circulation, and be subordinated to Russia's parliament. An independent Russian foreign trade bank must be established. Only the economic sovereignty of Russia will enable us to talk seriously about the technical modernization of production and its real reorientation, primarily toward the person, toward the Russians themselves. Only on that condition will Russia be able to provide a real guarantee for the social sovereignty of the person and his rights and safety from state and local diktat and bureaucratism, and to implement in practice a strong social policy.

But in no case does any of this mean that we are talking about some kind of confrontation with the center. The main thrust is in just one direction—the strengthening of the Union.

What, then, should be the main thing, the prime thing, in the program for the democratic renewal of Russia and the acquisition of its sovereignty? The adoption of the program which has been proposed by the Moscow, Urals, Leningrad and other groups of deputies which I will hand to the presidium; furthermore the voluntary rejection by Russia of its role as guarantor of the existence of the former system of government in the country. The use of Russia's potential in terms of resources and its economic, human, intellectual, and military potential for implementing a policy of diktat and interference in the affairs of other states and peoples both abroad and within the country should be banned through legislation. [applause]

Second, [Yeltsin continues without waiting for applause to subside] Russia's parliament must adopt and address to the parliaments and the peoples of the other Union republics proposing the urgent commencement of negotiations on working out new, mutually acceptable, forms of comity [sodruzhestvo]. It is proposed that these negotiations should be entered into without any prior political or economic conditions.

Third, guarantees that the civil, political, economic, and property rights of that part of Russia's peoples which currently resides in other union republics will be observed must be provided by non-violent methods.

Finally the fourth point: All national and patriotic forces must rally in the struggle for the construction of a democratic and civil society in Russia. Nationwide concord in Russia is an essential condition for this at this time, which is difficult and crucial for Russia: I call upon all people's deputies and all citizens of Russia to display this. No matter how varied the viewpoints of the deputies, I think that we are all united on the fact that Russia must have full-blooded and real state sovereignty. Thank you. [applause]

NOTES

ABOUT THE AUTHOR: **Boris Yeltsin** was president of the Congress of People's Deputies of the RSFSR at the time of this address.

36 *The National Dimension*

GIULIETTO CHIESA
with Douglas T. Northrop

... National and ethnic loyalties, existing independently of other foci of debate (ideological, socioeconomic, cultural, or religious), held the key to the developing Soviet civil society and its democratic structures. We therefore need to use a three-dimensional approach to understand contemporary Soviet (and post-Soviet) politics.

... Soviet sociologists Gordon and Nazimova[1] offer a two-dimensional picture of these politics as they appeared in mid-1989 [Table 11]. Their reasoning may be

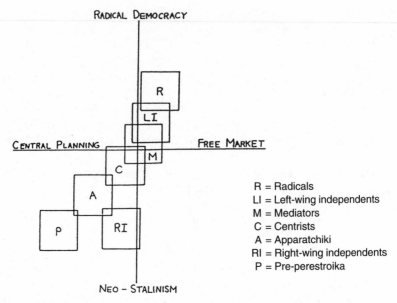

RADICAL DEMOCRACY

CENTRAL PLANNING　　　　　　　　FREE MARKET

R = Radicals
LI = Left-wing independents
M = Mediators
C = Centrists
A = Apparatchiki
RI = Right-wing independents
P = Pre-perestroika

NEO – STALINISM

Table 11. Two-Dimensional (Gordon-Nazimova) View of Soviet Politics in 1989

summarized by positing the existence of a Cartesian plane, with an x-axis and a y-axis.[2] The abscissa defines economic views, moving from a centrally-controlled, planned economy on the left to a completely free, unregulated market on the right. The ordinate represents political views, running from neo-Stalinism at the bottom to radical democratic reform at the top. The plane is split into four regions, and the views of deputies falling into any one of these regions may be summarized as follows:[3]

Zone 1 (upper right): Support for "global *perestroika*," meaning a total change of the politico-economic system towards a multiparty state governed by law and a free-market economy.

Zone 2 (lower right): Support for "technocratic" reform, meaning the modification of economic structures without corresponding shifts in political mechanisms. This group hoped to bring about an economic revival while preserving sufficiently strong central power to maintain discipline and order throughout the USSR.

Zone 3 (lower left): Support for "reactionary" policies; that is, rejecting reform in either the political or the economic sphere and preserving an administrative-command economic system and the one-party state.

Zone 4 (upper left): Support for political democratization but opposition to tampering with the crucial elements of a planned socialist economy.

Subjectively placing our seven groups on this grid, we find that only two are compact and limited to a single zone—the *apparatchiki* and pre-*perestroika* groups, both falling in zone 3—while the other five spill across zones. In their essay, Gordon and Nazimova admit that this method of viewing the Soviet political space is imperfect since, they write, the four groups they describe

> ... do not at all exhaust the possible approaches. It is necessary [also] to consider the enormous importance of the national and national-regional questions. On these issues, each of the specified strategies could be further subdivided. Actually, each (apart from the most reactionary) includes varying opinions, both economic and political, on the question of degrees of permissible autonomy; on the preservation of central powers; and so on.[4]

In this recognition Gordon and Nazimova implicitly realize the need for a third dimension to "stretch" their Cartesian plane [Table 12]. In terms of our seven-group categorization, left- and right-wing independents, along with pre-*perestroika* deputies, particularly require this additional variable in order to be placed accurately. Without this third, national dimension, Soviet politics cannot be understood. As a result, we will modify the simple Cartesian plane by adding a z-axis to represent national feelings. This third axis runs from a high of "nationalist democratic federalism" to a low of "national separatism and neo-Stalinism."[5]

The addition of this axis at a stroke doubles to eight the number of categories into which deputies may be placed, and represents much more fully the variety of political strategies in the Soviet Union of 1989. The first sector, then, represents an entirely new Soviet Union—featuring a federal constitution, a multiparty political system, and a socialist market economy. The centrist group protruded into this sector only slightly. Left-wing independents were located mainly in this area, albeit with a sizable minority below the x-y plane (that is, favoring democratic reforms within their republics but too nationalist to favor the extension of these reforms throughout a preserved Union). The entire radical group, most left-wing independents and mediators, and a few centrists, then, located themselves above the x-y plane, favoring a "reformed confederal" structure for the USSR.[6] These deputies represented the Congress, but also reflected general social and political movements in Soviet society during *perestroika's* fifth year.

This detailed treatment of the national question is not an abstract exercise in political analysis. It is needed to understand why radical reformers both inside and outside the leadership failed to comprehend the importance of the national question. The reformist intelligentsia, while working for a thorough democratic transformation of a colossal *Eurasian* country, reasoned only in *European,* or more accurately *West* European, terms. That is, in conceiving the Soviet Union as a basically unitary state they underestimated the necessity of building, in Gefter's words, "a new house as an unprecedented projection of the entire world community. A sovereign union of completely different people!"[7] As a result they underestimated the strength of particularism and separatism, which grew in tandem with

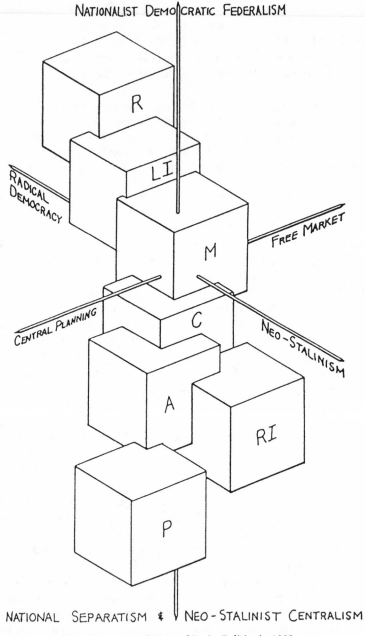

NATIONALIST DEMOCRATIC FEDERALISM

RADICAL DEMOCRACY

FREE MARKET

CENTRAL PLANNING

NEO-STALINISM

R

LI

M

C

A

RI

P

NATIONAL SEPARATISM & NEO-STALINIST CENTRALISM

Table 12. Three-Dimensional View of Soviet Politics in 1989

three other developments: the extension of democratization, the creation of new, pluralist institutions, and the end of decades of attempts to use repression to prevent national cultural and linguistic self-expression.

Unfortunately, Gefter's was only one voice, and in pointing out the impossibility of a unitary, pan-Soviet approach to reform and democratization it was in a tiny minority. Few shared his opinion that the problem was one of "carrying out gradual transformations, at different paces, with a full range of different priorities and different forms," at all times remaining conscious of local peculiarities and conditions.[8] Only a minority understood that the processes of *perestroika* and democratization resembled the Copernican revolution in science. Centuries of strong centralist rule in Russia, where even the great reformers—Peter the Great, Alexander II, even Lenin—had acted from positions of central power, had to be cast off in an attempt to construct a democratic polity and civil society. Hence, Gorbachev's indecision on national issues, probably the only area in which his policy was so seriously deficient, is understandable. His ability to forge compromises, to sense instinctively the proper tactical course, proved dangerously inadequate to cope with the depth of ethnic and national passions. He constantly sought the center of political debates, in order to control the situation, but too often defined this center in terms of political and economic issues, to the exclusion of ethnic and national concerns. Defining a two-dimensional "center" meant that he often found himself "above" or "below" the true political center. This lack of recognition of the national dimension more than once endangered Gorbachev's own political position.

NOTES

ABOUT THE AUTHOR: **Giulietto Chiesa** has been Moscow correspondent for the Italian newspaper *La Stampa* and is the author of several books on the Soviet Union.

1. Leonid Gordon and Alla Nazimova, "Perestroika: Vozmozhnye Varianty?" *Kommunist* 13 (1989).

2. See table 11.

3. These summaries of deputy positions are original, and cannot be blamed on Gordon and Nazimova if faulty.

4. *Kommunist* 13 (1989): 41.

5. See table 12.

6. The "reformed confederation" position is represented by the area of zone 1 in table 11, projected above the x-y plane.

7. See Mikhail Gefter, "Zaslon smute—v kom on?" *Moskovskie Novosti* 52 (31 December 1989).

8. See Gordon and Nazimova, p. 41.

PART 6

Foreign and Security Policy

In the first years of the Gorbachev regime there was a good deal of uncertainty among Western analysts and policymakers concerning the fundamental intentions of the new leadership with respect to Soviet foreign and defense policy. Too often in the past, many commentators recalled, seeming concessions had proved to be only tactical or short-term maneuvers that obscured fundamental continuities of Soviet objectives and behavior abroad. But gradually such doubts were dispelled as Soviet behavior passed all the "mental litmus tests" devised by Western analysts—on arms reduction agreements, on withdrawing from Afghanistan, on assisting with the settlement of regional issues from Namibia to Nicaragua to Kuwait, on normalizing relations with China, and ultimately on ending the sources of the cold war by permitting the countries of Eastern Europe to change governments and leave the Soviet bloc and by acquiescing in the unification of the two Germanies.

All these and other changes in Soviet conduct abroad were related to a profound conceptual revolution in foreign affairs. The urgency of the domestic economic, social, and political crises demanded a more stable and predictable international environment and a sharp reduction in the enormous military burden that traditional Soviet policies entailed. At the same time, the foreign affairs experts—the so-called mezhdunarodniki, with new foreign minister Edvard Shevardnadze in the lead—expressed a powerful desire to reduce if not end the sense of antagonism and isolation that had long characterized Soviet relations with the noncommunist world. The new political thinking was the centerpiece of the effort to normalize the Soviet approach to, and the Soviet role in, the international system. With its stress on interdependence, on shared human values, on the search for political rather than military solutions to international problems, and on the renunciation of the use of force in the pursuit of political objectives, the new thinking radically broke with the traditional Soviet outlook.

The new policies, which included a sharp cutback in military spending, and the new theories repudiating class analysis in international relations were not welcomed by significant elements of the Soviet establishment. By 1990 a new coalition had formed, with military figures prominently in the lead as self-styled defenders of national interests, that challenged the foreign and security policies of the Gorbachev regime. This coalition not only triggered the resignation of Shevardnadze but openly challenged the Soviet "retreat" from Eastern Europe, Soviet consent to the united Germany's membership in NATO, and Soviet agreement to asymmetrical arms reductions. The Soviet retreat from its globalist role in the Third World, including the abandonment of clients abroad, was attacked as well. Soviet endorsement of the United Nations policy and the U.S.-led campaign against Iraq in 1990–1991 was portrayed as a particularly egregious example of kowtowing to the West.

The same "patriotic" alliance also sought to undo what it saw as the pernicious effects of glasnost and democratization on the armed forces and the security apparatus. The sharp criticisms and controversies within the military and security elites over many of these issues were themselves an important indicator of the far-reaching scope of the changes in the Soviet system. By November–December 1990, a group of military officers, in cooperation with the conservative apparatus of the Party and the KBG, had chosen to play a virtually unprecedented role in Soviet politics by putting extreme pressure on the country's president to reverse many of his policies.

Some of the policies, at home and abroad, that the Soviet authorities began to pursue in the winter of 1990–1991 reflected serious concessions to this coalition, be they the crackdown in the Baltic republics, the restraints imposed on the media, the use of the military to patrol the streets of Soviet cities, or the obstruction of the arms reduction agreements. Some of its sponsors saw the bloody crackdown in Vilnius as a dress rehearsal for a similar assertion of power in the capital.

But it remained uncertain to what extent the changes introduced into Soviet foreign policy from 1985 to 1990 had become irreversible. Clearly some of them could not be undone: Soviet troops would not reenter Afghanistan, and Eastern Europe would not be restored to its former satellite status. But the edge of antagonism toward the West that had been blunted in the Shevardnadze days—a major accomplishment— now threatened to get a new lease on life, and substantial parts of the military and security establishment—and part of the civilian elites, as well—were manifestly unhappy with the drift of Soviet policies at home and abroad.

37 The Revolution in Soviet Foreign Policy

ROBERT LEGVOLD

A revolution is under way in Soviet foreign policy greater than any in the postwar period, indeed greater than any since Lenin in the early years of his regime accepted the failure of the pan-European revolution and allowed the Soviet Union to join the game of nations. The current upheaval is on a scale with the other dramatic foreign policy reorientations of the last half-century: comparable to the 1940s when U.S. foreign policy moved from isolation to global engagement; greater, in fact, than the 1950s when French policy passed from the modest aims of the Fourth Republic to the grand enterprises of de Gaulle's Fifth Republic; and greater, too, than the 1960s in Chinese policy, a ten-year transition from a troubled alignment with the Soviet camp to an emerging realignment with the West.

Steadily but chaotically, with a lurching, creative energy, the transformation has cut wider and deeper into the rudiments of Soviet foreign policy. For three and a half years, changes have accumulated, spreading from one sphere to the next, altering not merely the workaday calculations that trapped Mikhail Gorbachev's predecessors in their Afghan imbroglio and in their leaden approach to the Euromissile challenge, but altering the assumptions by which the Soviets explain the functioning of international politics and from which they derive the concepts underlying the deeper pattern of their actions. Revolutions of this kind do not make states into saints nor do they remove them as preoccupations in the policies of other nations, but they do leave a vastly different challenge. Once understood by the outside world, such revolutions create new imperatives and often new opportunities.

Why now? Why, when only a few years ago Soviet policy seemed so menacing in its rigidity? A part of the answer lies in the fact that radical circumstance often stirs radical change, and the Soviet circumstance these days is surely radical. Rarely, if ever, has a leadership under the duress of a basic failure of its system attempted so much. It would be difficult to do what Gorbachev wants to do to the Soviet economic and political order and not also affect the foreign policy order, to focus on massive problems in one sphere and ignore those in another, to turn society upside down but leave the external stakes of the country untouched, or to reexamine the entire Stalinist experience but give no thought to the lessons of the last twenty years in foreign affairs.

When a foreign policy has diminished national welfare and weakened the state's ability to influence or control external change, as so many Soviet spokesmen now freely admit has been true of Soviet policy, the price of not responding mounts. Moreover, no country, least of all a superpower such as the Soviet Union, can disregard the constraints and requirements of a changing international environment, one less and less amenable to old formulas and presumptions. In the Soviet case, intellectuals and various parts of the foreign policy establishment have known this for some time, and over the last decade they have slowly created the foundation of a substantially different Soviet approach to international politics. When all these influences converge, especially in the presence of a leader like Gorbachev, great, even revolutionary, departures come more naturally.

Revolution is not a word to be used lightly. To qualify, change must be of historic proportions. It would not be enough for the Soviet leadership to alter its actions in this or that respect, even if some of those shifts represented important breaks with the past. Even far-reaching modifications in strategy would be insufficient.

What must change is thinking. Real revolutions are, ultimately, conceptual. Unless the national leadership's understanding of the realities of the world undergoes a modification, no initiative, no matter how surprising, carries sufficient depth or conviction. Therefore, to assume that only deeds, and not words, count, as cautious Western audiences have so often done in reacting to Gorbachev, ignores what deeds owe to words, when words represent the concepts by which leaders come to terms with reality. Before behavioral revolutions come conceptual revolutions.

II

Since Gorbachev came to power in March 1985, Soviet ideas about international politics and how the Soviet Union should perform as a superpower have been in constant flux. No aspect of policy, no dimension of the intellectual underpinning of policy, remains untouched. In the process the tumult has slowly engulfed the whole of policy, from the mechanisms of its formulation to the core assumption on which it rests. Indeed, the sheer sweep of the drama is what should have first caught our eye.

There is, however, a good deal more. What gives such power to the conceptual revolution currently under way is its appearance on three different and critically linked levels. Change at any one level would be important enough. Take, for example, change in what might be called *basic concepts*, or the key notions by which the Soviet leaders and foreign policy elites make sense of the opportunities and problems posed for them by the world outside. These have not been so thoroughly reconsidered for more than sixty years—not since the wrenching adaptations to the Treaty of Brest Litovsk, the civil war and the Rapallo accords. Literally every dimension of Soviet policy is being touched.

First, Gorbachev has radically altered the Soviet concept of national security, or, at least, the framework within which it is discussed. He has raised the most fundamental questions: What constitutes national security in these waning years of the twentieth century? How is a superpower like the Soviet Union to pursue it without becoming its own worst enemy? His answer, boiled down to its two essential parts, stresses, as the answer of no Soviet leader has before, (1) the insufficiency of military power as the way to national security, and (2) the link between national and mutual security.

As early as the 27th Party Congress in February 1986, Gorbachev began to convey an unusually complex appreciation of what constitutes national security. The military dimension, he has since said over and over, is but one aspect of the problem—almost certainly not the main one. It is not merely, to use his words from the party congress, that "the character of contemporary weapons leaves no country with any hope of safeguarding itself solely with military and technical means, for example by building up a defense system, even the most powerful one." More to the point, in the present era, according to Gorbachev, most threats to national well-being are not military but economic and political—and the possession of military power, let alone its use, provides little or no solution to these threats.

The second theme emerged in the fall and winter of 1985. After that year's Geneva summit Gorbachev went out of his way to emphasize his "deep conviction" that, were the United States to possess less security than the Soviet Union, only bad could come of it, because inevitably only mistrust and greater instability would follow. No nation's security, he has repeated often since, can be achieved at the expense of another country. Thus national security cannot be divorced from mutual security. "To think otherwise," he said in August 1986, "is to live in a world of illusions, in a world of self-deception."

Of still greater significance, Gorbachev has also helped to reorder a second basic concept. From Lenin's day it has been an article of Soviet faith that the struggle between two social systems, capitalism and socialism, creates the core dynamic of international politics. The notion is not simply hollow cant. What the Soviets have thought about the possibilities of East-West relations and what they have felt obliged to do for Third World revolutions derive from it.

No longer, say Gorbachev and the many who take their cue from him. Not the struggle between classes but the common plight of man forms the central imperative. Not a Manichaean contest between good and evil, but the entangling effect of interdependence, holds the upper hand. Aleksandr Yakovlev, Gorbachev's alter ego in the Politburo, spoke last August of a "planet compressed to an unprecedentedly small size," a world whose history can end with "the touch of a button," a world in which "any event becomes the property of five billion people within hours," a world needing not the primacy of "individual countries or classes, people, or social groups," but ways of countering "the forces of separation, of opposition, of confrontation, and of war, which have already delayed the development of civilization by whole countries."[1] The Soviet foreign minister, Eduard Shevardnadze, third among the most powerful Soviet foreign policy figures, views as "anti-Leninist" the Khrushchev-Brezhnev thesis of peaceful coexistence as a specific form of class struggle.

The third change concerns the place of the Third World in international politics, and of the superpowers in the Third World. Soviet thinking in this respect no longer resembles what prevailed in the pre-Gorbachev era. Hardly anyone pretends any longer that the woes and turmoil in Asia, Africa, the Middle East and Latin America are part of some grand, heroic "national liberation struggle," once the excuse for Soviet commitments and intrusions. Instead, Third World conflicts are portrayed more as a vast drain on the pitiful resources of developing countries and a "catalyst to local and international tensions."[2] Or, as Gorbachev proclaimed in his speech before the U.N. General Assembly this past December: "The bell of every regional conflict tolls for all of us." There is a corollary: not so long ago Soviet leaders and elites treated their own country's role in the Third World imperiously (beyond reproach and none of the United States' business); now they agree that any future agenda of detente with the Americans must set limits to superpower intervention.

Finally, the concepts by which Soviet leaders order their relations within the world of socialism—with Eastern Europe, China and nonruling communist parties—are no less in flux. Considering the importance and scope of the conceptual categories already discussed, to add this fourth one is to say that no piece of the foundation of Soviet foreign policy remains unaffected.

From the late 1940s, when Stalin made over Eastern Europe in his own image, according to the Soviet catechism, the socialist world has been a universe unto itself: Soviet leaders have refused to admit that within it relations could be anything other than harmonious, built as they were on the "general laws" (or imperatives) of socialist development, laws validated first and foremost by the Soviet model. Assuming a natural, even preordained, unity, Soviet leaders and their proconsuls in Eastern Europe presumed not merely a need, but a right to discipline any serious deviation from it.

Under Gorbachev, the catechism has changed. Those who reflect deeply on the power of the Soviet Union in its relations with Eastern Europe (and, in the long run, in Sino-Soviet relations), including Gorbachev, Yakovlev and Shevardnadze, now acknowledge that socialist international relations are no different from those of any other type of polity. They are as prone to conflicts, including armed engagements arising from self-interest and ambition, as are relations among and with other systems. In light of this, Soviet leaders now ask: Why pretend, let alone demand, that a "single truth," a single shared wisdom, should prevail within what until recently was called the socialist commonwealth?

III

The revolution in Soviet foreign policy is occurring on yet another level, where notions more directly inform practical choice, the level of *policy concepts*. The change is stunning and portentous. If Soviet leaders are rethinking the very notion of national security, they are also revising the concepts that guide their defense decisions and their negotiating posture in arms control settings. Three new ideas form the core of this transformation.

The first is the notion of "reasonable sufficiency," an idea Gorbachev himself first introduced at the 27th Party Congress in 1986. By these words, he and other nonmilitary commentators mean something less than parity, not to mention superiority. In simple terms, they are advocating that the Soviet Union cope with, rather than keep up with, the Joneses. Rather than imitate every new U.S. program, such as the Strategic Defense Initiative, it would be better, in their view, if the Soviet Union were to take the cheaper and simpler route of developing means of foiling the weapons the Americans field. And rather than match the capabilities of each and every country whose arms could threaten the Soviet Union, they would ask of Soviet defenses only that they meet threats that might be plausibly imagined.

Gorbachev has not provided specifics, doubtless because he does not yet have them in mind. But others, beginning with his foreign minister, are filling in the blanks, and their thoughts have far-reaching implications for the Soviet approach to the military competition with the West.[3] In the strategic nuclear realm "reasonable sufficiency" would end the quest for a Soviet arsenal designed to overmatch the United States at every rung up the ladder of nuclear escalation—including, in the end, a force designed to devastate the nuclear arms of the other side—and replace it with a secure retaliatory force capable of ensuring some essential but minimal level of deterrence. In conventional arms the concept would leave the Soviet Union with forces capable of defending against a surprise attack but not of launching one or, more important, of conducting a large-scale, extended offensive. As for Soviet military power usable at great remove, according to the new doctrine there should be enough to help discourage outside interference in local crises, but not to make revolutions or save clients too feeble to defend themselves.

The other two ideas are strategic stability and defensive defense, the latter with its corollary of asymmetrical arms reductions. Strategic stability incorporates the technical, and narrower, American notion of crisis stability (namely, a structured nuclear balance that reduces the temptation for hair-trigger response in crisis situations) but goes much further. For more than a year, Soviet experts working on the problem have struggled to imagine a more stable nuclear regime at drastically reduced levels of armament, one that takes into account not merely the characteristics of weapons systems, but also the effects of strategic doctrine and even of political context.

Defensive defense embodies the simple idea that in no sphere of military power, conventional or nuclear, should either side be able to launch and maintain a vast frontal offensive. The idea is simple; figuring out how to achieve it is another matter. Gorbachev, however, in summer 1986 did introduce a new, albeit vague, guideline for proceeding, one that has since become a standard Soviet formula: let the side with an edge be the one to sacrifice more in order to create a more stable balance at lower levels.

The knowledgeable reader is no doubt protesting: "But these notions have not been embraced by much of the Soviet professional military—and is that not a complication of some consequence?" Indeed it is, yet not one to be overestimated. First, to say that the military by and large does not use the same concepts is not to say they have consciously chosen against them. Second, where their preferences are clearly in conflict with the new ideas, that is not to say they will fight to have their way. And, third, in those instances where they do choose to fight, this is not to say that they will win, given their current comparative political disadvantage.

Other new policy concepts parallel Gorbachev's reformulated insight into the basic dynamic of contemporary international politics, an insight that exalts interdependence and devalues class struggle. Reduced to their essence, these concepts stress multilateralism in place of great-power unilateralism and substitute responsibility of the many for the arrogated duty of the two superpowers. This in turn means strengthening international institutions, such as the United Nations, to give them a larger role with all manner of tasks, from facilitating communication during crises to providing aid in environmental emergencies, from managing regional violence to policing the fragile settlements by which such violence is ended. However, it also means altering Soviet institutions and practices that make the U.S.S.R. an unfit participant in other international institutions, such as the General Agreement on Tariffs and Trade (GATT) and the International Monetary Fund.

The Soviet leadership has not been as successful at developing policy concepts to go along with shifts in its thinking about the place of the Third World in international politics. Since late summer 1987 Soviet speakers have begun favoring political over military settlements and suggesting the notion of "national reconciliation" as the way out of the chaos in places like Afghanistan, Angola and Cambodia—and this might be taken as a new policy concept. But it may only represent a recoiling from the ardors of these particular entanglements, rather than a more durable new approach to regional instability as such. In the last year or so, however, Soviet academics have urged that the United States, the Soviet Union and other great powers begin designing an explicit code of conduct regulating their intrusions in the Third World. The outlines of such a code remain foggy and, at times, distinctly prejudicial to the far-flung basing of U.S. military power.

Of the transformations in basic concepts, the gravest and most traumatic is the process of rethinking Soviet relations within the socialist world, particularly with Eastern Europe. Not surprisingly, therefore, Soviet leaders are not having an easy time generating concrete concepts to guide policy in this area. Two departures, however, have enormous implications. First, the old notion of "socialist internationalism," for decades a euphemism for Soviet tutelage, has been replaced by something far closer to laissez-faire. East European regimes are to be left essentially alone to solve their own problems and make their own mistakes. Second, the Brezhnev Doctrine, while not actually lifted, no longer sets the same limits to change. Put differently, doubtless there are still circumstances in which the Soviet

Union would intervene with force, but they would probably not include those of 1968 and 1981.

In sum, we are witnessing significant changes in basic concepts and operational policy. What makes all of these changes on the two levels still more momentous, however, is the passage occurring on a third level.

To a degree particularly difficult for Americans to understand, *fundamental assumptions,* on which the entire edifice of Soviet foreign policy beliefs ultimately rests, are at stake. Never, not even in the 1940s or as a result of the Vietnam War, have Americans been forced to reexamine the basic premises of their worldview. In the Soviet Union, today, people are engaging in such a reexamination. No two matters are more fundamental to the Soviet mind than revolution and capitalism, and the view of each has come to a remarkable pass.

Twice before, the Soviet conception of revolution has undergone profound change. The first time was in the years following 1917, when Lenin's rationalization of the Russian Revolution as the "spark" for a European revolution died, and Soviet leaders were left to fend for themselves. The second time was in the 1950s, when the advent of the nuclear era forced them to rethink the relationship between war and revolution, and, therefore, accept the argument for peaceful coexistence.

Now comes a third transformation: the end of revolutionary faith. Its last repository had been the Third World, but nothing any longer convinces most Soviet observers that revolution is the probable fate of most developing countries (not, at least, the kind of revolution that they would wish to see); more likely their fate is either political vagrancy or, for those that escape into the ranks of the newly industrializing countries, something more akin to capitalism.

Capitalism, too, is coming to represent something vastly different for Gorbachev and his supporters. They are more attentive to the durability of capitalism, as the twentieth century draws to a close, than to its predicted doom. More of their sensitivity is concentrated on its dynamism than on its crises, a dynamism that some openly, others by implication, acknowledge has shamed socialism. For capitalism has successfully made the transition from the industrial to the technical-information age, while socialism has yet to prove that it can—an admission that one finds in Soviet journals these days. (Hence, not so incidentally, the "crisis" of communist parties in the West, to put it as Soviet commentators now do.) And the discovery that certain ills, such as militarism, are not in fact intrinsic to capitalism engages more attention now than do the features which the Soviets continue to regard as capitalism's flaws.

When Gorbachev can come to New York and deliver a speech in praise of tolerance and diversity and "the universal human idea," raise the revolution of 1789 to equality with that of 1917 as a source of "a most precious spiritual heritage," identify "freedom of choice" as "a universal principle that should allow for no exceptions," reject force or the threat of its use as an instrument of policy, and call for a more open international order, he may risk being "a little too romantic"— and Gorbachev has acknowledged that some of his own people think he is. But his words should not be regarded as mere bluster. Not when values, assumptions and prescriptions are being recast at every turn, at every level, in every dimension of policy.

IV

Is the revolution in Soviet foreign policy really so radical? What evidence might be offered to the skeptic? The evidence is threefold: first, the nature of the process Gorbachev has set in motion; second, the opposition to it; and, third, the actions accompanying the process.

First, what is the nature of the process? It seems reasonable to suspect that something so comprehensive cannot be easily scripted by one oligarch—or even by a score. When literally every dimension of policy is affected, an invisible, not a human, hand is at work. What is more important, the process has been from the start unsystematic in its essence, far too much so to be simply a clever contrivance. In a less natural process, the progression would be more logical: first, the affectation of a shift in fundamental assumptions, then the supposed adjustment of basic concepts, and from these an appropriately modified array of policy concepts.

But that is not at all what has been happening. On the contrary, change has come piecemeal and out of any logical order. It has tumbled forth on all levels at once. The process has been like some great random sewing machine, stitching back and forth, slowly exposing the pattern. Gorbachev starts by acknowledging, at last, the interconnection of national and mutual security, or maybe simply by coming forward with a new negotiating position in the Strategic Arms Reduction Talks (START), or maybe by vaguely suggesting a new standard for defense, which he calls reasonable sufficiency, all of which did happen between October 1985 and February 1986. Others then seize the opening and push the argument forward, taking a notion like reasonable sufficiency and spelling it out, adding as well other logically related new ideas, such as strategic stability or defensive defense. Within months these accumulating notions make their way back into the next Gorbachev or Shevardnadze pronouncement.

Meanwhile, each part of the establishment—the policy leaders in a vague and sweeping fashion, the policy intellectuals in a more elaborate and specific fashion—attacks one issue, only to find itself led to another still more fundamental conclusion. Thus, someone sets out to elaborate an idea, say the notion of "reasonable sufficiency." He then begins to question the role of military power in Soviet policy and finally to admit, as did Americanologist Georgi Arbatov, that "in the past we did not realize, as we realize now, the limited possibilities of the use of military power"; as a result "our national security policy overemphasized military means."[4] Such questioning of the place of military power in Soviet foreign policy prompts others to challenge the whole Soviet concept of what threatens the U.S.S.R., a question that began to emerge in academic articles by early 1988 and now threads its way through leadership speeches.

We were wrong, these Soviet policymakers say, to conceive of the threat in thoroughly military terms, to represent the military threat as one of war, and to imagine the war would likely break out in central Europe. In fact, they argue, the real threat has increasingly become the deformation of the Soviet economy produced by a preoccupation with military power, a debilitating order of priorities consciously imposed on the Soviet Union by a richer West. Indeed, they ask, how is it that Soviet military power grew throughout the 1970s, while Soviet national security, when thought of in terms of the country's economic, social and political stability, shrank?

The process continues. It is not enough to stop with a rethinking of the nature of the threat, a growing number of Soviet leaders contend; the need is to grapple with the larger question of where Soviet national interests lie. Shevardnadze referred explicitly to this problem in an important address to a foreign ministry conference last July, and since then a number of writers have offered bold responses.[5] Their common theme is that the mindless willingness to make commitments in the past, the reflexive jockeying for international position and the struggle for spheres of influence scarcely corresponded to the nation's real national interests. They urge instead that foreign policy be corralled and made to serve the interests of society, not a disembodied "bureaucratic internationalism," as one of them puts it.

Although paradoxical, a second reason to take the process seriously is the opposition to it, or at least to certain aspects of it. (Of course, opposition is also a reason to fear for the future of the process.) When Yegor Ligachev, thought to be the second-ranking member of the Soviet Politburo until recently, argues on behalf of a class-based view of international politics and defends the notion of class struggle, as he did last summer, it is a reasonable deduction that he regards the new ideas as more than an artifice.

But, if the misgivings of more traditional minds give us further reason to believe something real is afoot, are they not also reason to avoid overrating its chances of success? If there is indeed a struggle under way, who is to say the architects of the new concepts will prevail? In the abstract this is a perfectly prudent concern. In reality, it gravely miscalculates the current state of affairs.

Gorbachev, Yakovlev and the others are not locked in a furious battle with critics of their foreign policy program. Ligachev obviously worries about the potential loss of self-identity and ballast when old and familiar ideological frameworks are abandoned. But to compare the 28 lines in one of his speeches with a virtual avalanche of pent-up new ideas seems less than judicious. Conservative skepticism over what is being said and done by Gorbachev in foreign policy certainly must exist but, to keep matters in proportion, one has to look long and hard to find traces of it in the public record, quite unlike the case with criticism of his domestic reforms. Moreover, with the important exception of the military, when we consider the ranks of those who make or influence Soviet foreign policy— whether the dominant figures in the foreign ministry or the international apparat of the party, the personal advisers to key Politburo members, senior figures in the media or the most powerful personalities within the Academy of Sciences—an overwhelming proportion are part of the revolution, not a threat to it.

Finally, Soviet actions over the last three years, particularly in the last year and a half, suggest that the churning in Soviet minds is genuine. Some of the evidence lies in a wide range of what might be called symptomatic behavior. Releasing Andrei Sakharov from internal exile in Gorky in December 1986 was an early illustration. Paying long-owed obligations for U.N. peacekeeping operations in May 1988 was another. Handling the hijacking of a Soviet cargo aircraft in November 1988 as Washington itself might have was a third. This behavior is symptomatic because, while none of these actions is crucial, taken together they represent something qualitatively different from the Soviet Union's past demeanor.

By now the list is long: the end to the jamming of foreign broadcasting; the bid for observer status in GATT, the Asian Development Bank and the Pacific Economic Cooperation Council; collaboration with British law-enforcement agencies against drug trafficking; cooperation with the International Atomic Energy Agency investigating the Chernobyl disaster; the vote in favor of keeping Israel and South Africa in that agency; the creation of a commission to examine the so-called blank spots in Polish-Soviet history—and so the list swells. It is already too long and too diverse to be only a nondescript series of random occurrences.

The same can be said of Soviet actions in areas that truly count. For a long time after Gorbachev came to power, skeptics had a point when they reminded audiences that the deeds of the Soviets were less inspiring than their words. But this case is harder and harder to make. The agreement to eliminate intermediate-range nuclear forces (INF), largely on NATO's terms, could be explained as a hard-headed, albeit courageous, corrective to a politically and materially expensive mistake. So could the decision to withdraw from Afghanistan. One realizes, however, that even these decisions carry more profound implications. Leaving an agony like Afghanistan by cutting and running, as others like the French and Americans know too well, sets limits to future interventions. Making a deal with the West on INF involving the destruction of a whole generation of modern weapons (without the destruction of the threat for which they were designed) and allowing the most intrusive forms of verification is an impingement on defense decisionmaking such as has not been allowed under any Soviet leader since Khrushchev.

From the start, there have also been other actions that broke more clearly with the past. One such action was the decision in October 1985 to offer 50-percent reductions in strategic nuclear forces, including subceilings that could greatly lessen the Soviet threat to U.S. fixed land-based missiles (at one time the essence of the American fear of a "window of vulnerability"). The acceptance of on-site verification in the INF agreement is another. A third is the effort to address China's three "obstacles" to better Sino-Soviet relations by initiative rather than rhetoric, including since late 1987 the active cajoling of Vietnam to pull its troops out of Cambodia.

In December 1988 in New York came a fourth break—one which almost no one was prepared to pass over. A unilateral decision to cut Soviet active military forces by 500,000 troops, or almost 15 percent, and to withdraw more than 40 percent of Soviet tank divisions from Eastern Europe, together with 50 percent of Soviet tanks, is a giant shift in the Soviet approach. Only some very basic adjustment of Soviet thinking can explain it. If, in fact, a less-publicized but more significant pledge in the Gorbachev speech comes about, a very real revolution in behavior will have occurred. "All Soviet divisions remaining, for the time being, on the territory of our allies are being reorganized," he said. "Their structure will be different from what it is now; after a major cutback of their tanks it will become clearly defensive." ...

... Whatever happens to Gorbachev or to his effort at perestroika, the same pressures will be there. He has most assuredly accelerated and deepened the process of adjusting, and his passing would slow its momentum—but not end it. The conceptual revolution I have been describing can be undone only by leaders who plan to disregard powerful and unforgiving realities (and the failures of past policy).

No one should conclude from all this that the Soviet Union will soon cease to be a concern of U.S. policy. Talk of what it will do to the United States and the Western alliance to lose the Soviet Union as an enemy is wildly premature. Nothing in what I have laid out implies that the Soviet Union will soon embrace Western ways, foreswear great ambitions abroad or cease to be a military superpower. Nothing guarantees that Soviet leaders will never again offend the West by the use of force at home or in Eastern Europe, or worry it by their involvements far from their own borders.

But a historic opportunity now presents itself to the United States and its allies, and neither timidity nor old ways of framing the issue are the right response. It is fashionable these days to say the cold war is over and the West has won. What many people do not realize is that we in the West are in danger of ending it on Soviet terms. For it would end on Soviet terms if Moscow finally established itself in the eyes of the world, including those of our own people, as the leadership with the greater vision and the more compelling foreign policy values, as the leadership more willing to run risks for a safer and less militarized international order, as the leadership more committed to strong and effective international institutions, and as the leadership more ready to free us from the contests of the past. ...

As the new Soviet leadership has begun to stir interest in the West, the closest thing we have had to statesmanship is the urging that we "test" Gorbachev, by which is meant that we take him seriously and probe to see how far he is willing to alter Soviet policy. It seems increasingly irrelevant advice, as Gorbachev meets more and more tests we have not yet collected ourselves to pose. Increasingly the test is for the West: Do we have the imagination, creativity and courage to respond to the very revolution in Soviet foreign policy for which we have waited half a century?

NOTES

ABOUT THE AUTHOR: **Robert Legvold** is professor of international relations at the Harriman Institute, Columbia University.

1. From *Vremya* broadcast, Aug. 12, 1988, as reported in *Foreign Broadcast Information Service,* Aug. 16, p. 52.

2. A. Kislov, in the journal *Mirovaya ekonomika i mezhdunarodnye otnosheniya,* August 1988, p. 39.

3. A particularly compelling example is Aleksei Arbatov, "Parity and Reasonable Sufficiency," *International Affairs,* October 1988, pp. 75–87.

4. "Perestroika, Glasnost and Foreign Policy," unpublished paper, 1988.

5. For one of the boldest, see Igor Malashenko, "Ideals and Interests," *New Times,* November 1988, pp. 26–28.

38 East-West: The Problem of Deideologizing Relations

GEORGII SHAKHNAZAROV

The new political thinking, the core of which consists of recognizing the integrity of a contradictory but interdependent world, compels us to examine anew a number of concepts having to do with theoretical and practical activity in the international sphere. It is especially important that we bring our views concerning interrelations between the states of today's two fundamental social systems—socialism and capitalism—into accord with today's objective realities, with the idea of an integral world. To an enormous extent, solving the problem of East and West is a matter on which depend not just the fates of both sides, but the very survival of humanity. And a solution to this problem is ultimately impossible without surmounting the profound ideological confrontation which is the basis of the present-day division of the world. Not economic, not intellectual, and not even political, but precisely ideological. It is entirely out of the question to eliminate the ideological differences arising from the conditions of existence, interests, and positions of modern society's principal classes and social groups. No one has the power to abolish the perpetual dispute carried on between the various ideologies of social, national, and religious origin. The question is only whether this dispute should lead to unlimited confrontation and end in a universal Bartholomew's Night.

The objection can be made that ideological struggle does not in and of itself hinder peaceful coexistence, collaboration, or cooperative efforts in solving today's global problems, first and foremost in averting nuclear carnage. As evidence one can cite the experience of detente in the 1970's, and especially the favorable changes in the international climate resulting from the policy of the CPSU's Twenty-Seventh Congress, with its application of the new thinking to world affairs.

These are weighty arguments. But they fail to consider one circumstance: in both cases we are dealing with incomplete processes. Detente was broken off precisely because it encompassed only the "tip of the iceberg," only the foreign policy sphere of interrelations between the states of the two systems. As for the present abrupt warming, it became possible to a decisive degree only because of our perestroika [restructuring], and further progress in this direction will correspond to social processes in the East and West, to their ideological reflections and interpretations.

I.

First of all, one should establish whether the confrontation is really rooted in the very conditions of social development, and thus comprises one of its objective regularities. If so, one might somehow soften its effects and accommodate oneself to it, but can man really have power over the iron tread of history, over fate? Here, in essence, is the idee fixe which has turned into a kind of constant of modern social existence, an article of faith. It has not been thought necessary to prove this self-evident truth, to cast doubt upon it.

It is of some use, in our view, to examine once again the justification for the idea of confrontation. It is based on the idea that our era is a revolutionary epoch of transition from capitalism to socialism, and that this transformation will be achieved in a brutal struggle between the world proletariat and the world bourgeoisie. After October, 1917, this idea took on concrete form, with the difference that in place of a struggle of world proletariat and world bourgeoisie there took place a struggle between revolutionary Russia and the counterrevolutionary imperialist powers. Thus, right from the beginning, the conflict, which was conceived of theoretically as a class struggle, took the form of a struggle between states. From that moment up to, in effect, the present day, the clash between socialism and capitalism as social systems was embodied and one might even say substantiated as the confrontation of the Soviet state, and then all the socialist states, with the states of the capitalist world.

This "substitution," although to some degree answering the logic of the historical events of the first post-revolutionary period, greatly simplified the picture of social development. Just as within the country the sectarians saw only two warring classes—the proletariat and bourgeoisie—so in the international arena only two opposing systems remained in the field of view. Henceforth, everything on "our side" was declared socialist, and everything on the "other side" bourgeois.

Any phenomenon could fit into this category, from the natural sciences (cybernetics or genetics) to clothing fashions.

A speculative division into bourgeois and socialist took place in practically all areas of activity: architecture and medicine, music and theater, etc. Everything originating in the West was branded bourgeois. Meanwhile, the fact was essentially ignored that "the West" is heterogeneous, that there is a bourgeoisie there, but also a working class, a peasantry, an intelligentsia, and other strata on which depend the possibility of socialist transformations. And strata persist in socialist states, especially in the transitional period, which are not organically linked to socialism by their conditions of existence, even less their views and aspirations.

Even more important is the circumstance that the basic content of international relations comprises interrelations between states, and not these or those social strata or political currents. It stands to reason that certain classes and parties are in power in these states and determine their political course. But nevertheless, the subjects of international relations are still sovereign nation-states. Therefore, it is wrong in principle to identify relations between states or groups of states with relations between systems. Those relations which can be termed "intersystemic" belong entirely to the realm of ideology, of theoretical and political principles. Relations between states, however, are substantive. States conduct negotiations and make agreements with one another, but systems cannot do this; they are not able to exchange memoranda and seek compromises. The concept of a "social system" is essentially a high degree of abstraction, and to transplant it to the soil of political struggle is to do violence to reality.

It can be objected that ideological principles exert an enormous influence on the material world, and that doctrinal disputes very often become the source of bloody clashes. This is a fact, although, for example, behind almost all religious wars lurks the perfectly mundane desire to seize another's goods. And one can trace the following regular pattern through history: conflicts of the "intersystemic" variety, for all their significance and keenness, have not as a rule been in the foreground, and have not in any case been an insurmountable obstacle to cooperation between states. For example, the bourgeois revolution and the execution of Charles I did not prevent Cromwell from establishing good relations with the majority of European monarchs of the time. Absolutist Russia and France aided the American colonists' struggle for independence.

One could say that all this happened in the context of relations between the exploiting classes. But what of the Second World War? Naturally, the ruling circles of the US, England, and France did not renounce their anticommunist convictions when they allied with the USSR in the war with Hitler's Germany. But that is just the point: in that critical situation they made a choice, seeing the primary danger in Fascism. The conflict between democracy and totalitarian reaction turned out to be much keener than the conflict between socialism and capitalism.

In my opinion, however, the correct conclusions have not been drawn from this fact. In so far as the idea of confrontation became central to the Stalinist interpretation of international relations, so everything that did not correspond to it was treated as a chance event, a temporary anomaly. Of course, official theoretical positions were not entirely indifferent to changes in the world arena. The severe formulations of the period when the Soviet Union was the lone socialist island in a sea of capitalist encirclement gave way to more restrained formulations at times of comparatively positive developments in our relations with the countries of the West. The concepts of "struggle," "confrontation," and "stand-off" were replaced by the words "competition," "rivalry," and "contest." The prognosis changed for the outcome of the struggle between the two systems: while at first it was believed that the collapse of capitalism would take one or two decades, subsequently a more realistic approach prevailed.

But only recent documents have overcome attempts to mark the starting date of the worldwide socialist era on the calendar of history. By loosing the fetters from our socio-political thought, perestroika spurred a reconsideration of interrelations between the states of the two systems under present-day conditions. Of special significance in this regard are fundamental ideas on the priority of universal human values and the unity of civilization. The logical working out of these ideas, begun by the Twenty-Seventh Congress of the CPSU, led naturally to the conclusions that the peaceful coexistence of states with differing systems should not be considered a "special form of class struggle," and that the struggle between these systems is not the most characteristic tendency of the modern epoch.

In the end, both conclusions are based on the recognition that life on Earth, apparently eternal like nature itself, can end at any moment as a result of nuclear war or ecological catastrophe. Both in our theoretical consciousness and throughout the world, a scale of priorities has taken shape in which the struggle for survival stands higher than the struggle for class, national, or other interests. But it is still not completely recognized that these value positions cannot be arranged one after another in a "waiting line." (First we will survive, and then we will take up class considerations and the preservation of national interests.) Nor can they be the object of singular preference, since they simultaneously contradict and are firmly linked to one another. We cannot say: for the sake of peace we will give up social progress and the rights of nations to freedom of choice. Not just because oppressed social strata and hapless nations will never give up struggling for their interests, but also because a peace based on unjust principles cannot be stable and longlasting. Accordingly, the problems of social progress and national development can only be considered as organic constituents of the problem of survival. The quite genuine conflict between these goals can be eliminated by excluding armed methods. All just goals in a world facing global threats should be attained by political means.

But being satisfied with this criterion would mean stopping halfway, recognizing, as already noted, no more than the possibility of the coexistence of states hostile to one another by nature. Such an objectively compulsory confrontation, while not capable of completely preventing a joint solution of global problems, enormously complicates and delays this process. And humanity does not have great reserves of time. A delay of this sort could play a fatal role.

What is to happen? Certainly, no social movement or political current will renounce its ideology or beliefs. But there is no need for that. It is enough to throw off the blinders from our eyes and look carefully at reality in order to be convinced of the incorrectness and one-dimensionality of the thesis of the opposed nature of the two social systems.

"There are classes, and they are antagonistic—that is reality," states M. S. Gorbachev. "But a one-dimensional division of the world community into poles opposed on the basis of class, to which gravitate various social and national differences and oppositions, no longer aids a correct and complete explanation of events in the modern world. This is not because this division and the policy resulting from it were wrong from the start. On the contrary, for decades after 1917 it was precisely class struggle which, both in theory and practice, operated on a global scale to change the world, and which changed it radically. But the social consequences of this struggle, together with the scientific and technical revolution which began to roll over humanity in waves, one stronger than the other, have changed, at the end of the century, both the nature and criteria of progress, as well as the actors who play a role in it."

...

The thesis of the fated confrontation (and the resulting irreconcilable enmity) between socialism and capitalism is, in our view, refuted by the changes which have occurred in the capitalist system itself.

In the words of V. I. Lenin, "the dialectical process of development actually introduces elements of the new society, and its material and intellectual elements, while still within the framework of capitalism." (*Collected Works*, v. 11, p. 370). True, Lenin then criticizes those who cannot distinguish a piece from the whole, and says that socialism should make a slogan of the words: the whole and not a piece. But this does not alter the principal point. The "consumer cooperative," local government, and much else were considered by the founders of Marxism to be elements of socialism in capitalism.

...

It stands to reason that all this does not change the class nature of private ownership, nor provide grounds for abandoning the socialist demand that it be surmounted. However, all the experience of the period since the October Revolution, and all the realities of the modern era, support the conclusion that private ownership should be eliminated by economic means. And this will happen when we find the optimal variant of social ownership, permitting the attainment of higher results with fewer costs for society and nature.

The next question deserving attention in the context of the theme under consideration is the possibility of the convergence of the two systems. Galbraith's theory, popular at one time, was relegated to the background by the exacerbation of the struggle between East and West. It would seem that it has recently found its second wind. Many theorists see signs of it in the present on-going process of strengthened trust, joint steps to limit the arms race, settlement of conflicts, and economic cooperation.

I have already shown, in the work, "The Fiasco of Futurology," why the convergence of the systems is impossible. Capitalism and socialism, different social entities, cannot converge, no more than can geographical poles. They exist only in the form in which they exist. These are abstract characteristics, attributed by us to certain phenomena; if they begin to draw together, they would lose their original qualities, and thus would cease to represent them in our consciousness. In short, as Kipling wrote, West is West, and East is East, and never the twain shall meet.

The countries, however, of East and West not only can but must draw together, borrowing the best from one another. This is perfectly in keeping with human nature and rationalist policy in the modern, interconnected world. And the best way to further this rapprochement in the interests of all peoples is to concentrate on specific tasks: how to guarantee the survival of civilization; how to raise peoples' living standards; ensure individual rights; raise the standard of social justice; protect nature; organize more effectively the utilization of scientific and technical progress, and so on.

Such an approach, it seems to me, eliminates the abstract ideologizing which advances arguments for confrontation between the two systems. Moreover, the endless ideological dispute unwittingly gives rise to the need to achieve victory over the other side. Accordingly, the other side is inevitably seen as an enemy, and problems of rivalry, and not the interests at hand, assume priority. And in so far as the systems are identified with states, the world is again divided into opposing blocs, even if they have learned to control their behavior so as to avoid nuclear war.

Meanwhile, the best way to deal with an enemy is to turn him into a friend, or, at the worst, an ordinary neighbor. In our interdependent world, subject to nuclear, ecological, and many other threats, such an approach becomes not just desirable, but an imperative demand, a condition of survival and development. Rivalry is something suitable and necessary for artists, master craftsmen, and athletes. Competition permits the comparison and selection of the best forms of organization of social existence and political structure. But, I repeat, in my opinion it is necessary to overcome the idee fixe of the struggle between systems being the "axial line" of social development.

But what of the comparative advantages of this or that system? It seems we must again avoid a "general system" approach and see in the achievements of East and West, of this or that group of countries linked by economic or political alliances, the result of a number of factors grounded in historical conditions. If the Western societies still outstrip the Eastern countries in labor productivity, this is primarily because they are in a region where industrial development began much earlier, and where a powerful scientific and technical potential was created.

Experience has repeatedly shown the wrongness of attempts to link all achievements or failures solely to social structure. For example, after the launching of the first Earth satellite it was written here that "socialism is the launching pad for the conquest of space." Meanwhile, it was already clear at that time that any state with a mature science and industry was capable of participating in the "cosmic odyssey" if it obtained sufficient means and considered it to be in its interest to do so.

It stands to reason that peculiarities of social structure have an influence of one kind or another on all areas of social existence, and in many ways predetermine the choice of goals, methods of achieving them, mobilization of resources, etc. We are convinced that socialism is far from uncovering its inherent possibilities, and this task will be resolved in the course of the appearance, and comparisons made between, its different forms and models as a result of explorations on a world-wide scale.

At the same time, the Western propagandists who try to attribute all their countries' achievements to contributions of capitalism should remember that they were forced into many of these achievements by the existence of socialism. Without the Soviet Union, without its pioneering example in the area of the planned economy and the broad introduction of the socialist rights of the individual, without the wave of workers' and democratic movements raised by the October Revolution, they would not, of course, be what they are today. Or: the liberation of colonies and dependent countries created the preconditions for the rapid expansion of the world market and thus opened up new possibilities for the development of economic ties. Moreover, the development of the liberation process originated to a great extent because of that same impulse from the October Revolution, and then the succeeding support of the Soviet Union and other socialist countries for the struggle of the peoples for national independence.

And, finally, the very progress of a large group of states along the socialist path, with all its pluses and minuses, revealed to the world the nature of social progress in our era, and clearly proved both the creativity of socialism and the need for a rational combination of social, collective, and individual elements. The results of our development might have been incomparably greater if it had not been deformed by Stalinism. Perestroika offers the chance of reviving in full the values of scientific socialism, enriching them with accumulated national and world experience, and creating on this foundation a new, much more viable and effective model of socialist social structure.

III.

Thus, the contemporary world, seen from the standpoint of social structure, is at the stage of establishing a new, non-exploitative socio-economic structure, and in this sense the basic prognosis of K. Marx and F. Engels has shown itself to be irreproachable. And not just their forecasts—the same was predicted for humanity by Fourier, Owen, Chernyshevsky, and many other prophets.

But actual development followed a much more complicated path than any of them could have supposed. In evaluating the more important features of the present transitional state of society in its global dimensions, one can present, for purposes of discussion, the following problems.

First, the process of socialization acquires a universal character, although it moves forward in an extremely uneven fashion, depending on its driving force (revolution or evolution), the level of economic development and culture, histori-cal traditions, the correlation of class forces, and many other factors. What are its horizons under the conditions of the continuing stormy development of the sci-entific and technical revolution (in particular, the automation and intellectualiza-tion of production)?

Second, in place of the epoch when the problem of a progressive and just social structure applied to individual societies (at best, on a European scale), an epoch has arrived in which this problem must be dealt with and solved on a world scale. Judging by many signs, we are now at the very beginning stage of a new civiliza-tion, in which the processes of internationalization and socialization will be inter-woven.

Now for the conclusions which, in my view, follow from this situation in inter-national relations.

Above all, it is necessary to exclude from social and political consciousness the idea of the confrontation between countries on the basis of their adherence to dif-ferent social systems. We really are different, but not opposed, and, I repeat, the specific character of social structure has no more significance than that originat-ing in differences in level of economic development or political regimes.

Achieving such an admittedly difficult, but quite attainable, change in con-sciousness promises to be an enormous victory for all humanity. The solving of global problems, strengthening of mutual trust, settlement of conflicts, building of a new international order—all that we are attaining at the cost of huge efforts with a fragmented consciousness and divided world—will be achieved in a much simpler, faster, and more thorough fashion. An objective process of international-ization and integration, reductions in spontaneity, and increased degrees of man-agement of world affairs will develop in the incomparably more positive ideologi-cal and political atmosphere. All this, of course, does not mean that in the blink of an eye the world will turn into a blessed paradise of universal unity and agree-ment. It has had and will unavoidably have certain alliances of states based on in-terests, arguments, disputes, and competition. But now without blind impatience, and with the understanding and acknowledgement of the priority of universal hu-man interests above all others.

The surmounting of "intersystemic confrontation" would also facilitate the resolution of another historic task, by eliminating the basis of the confrontation between the two principal branches of the workers' movements, and by establish-ing the prerequisites for broad cooperation and providing the prospect of the re-unification of left-wing forces.

It should be emphasized that a big step in this direction is the CPSU's policy of perestroika, at the core of which is the joining of socialism and democracy. Glasnost [openness]; self-management of labor collectives; the realistic ensuring of political freedoms together with the socialist rights of the individual; radical re-form of the political system as determined by the Nineteenth Party Conference and the laws adopted by the USSR Supreme Soviet in December, 1988; the nascent process of harmonization in international relations—all this has been widely acknowledged in the world. The establishment of a socialist rule-of-law state means the elimination of one of the main sources of disagreement among the adherents of socialism. Major transformations in the direction of democratization are taking place in other socialist countries.

But this is not all. The fact of the matter is that the differences between the two basic currents of socialist thought and activity, in addition to attitudes regarding democracy, concern yet another question of principle: attitudes regarding the development of socialism.

Contemporary social-democracy, as a matter of fact, chose for its theoretical credo and political aim the method of spontaneous self-development of socialization, with attainable objective and subjective circumstances as the governing measure, or rather an orientation toward this process. Social-democratic party programs do not set themselves the task of building socialism as a whole according to a plan worked out ahead of time, but define specific methods of progress and concrete goals. The weak aspects of such an approach are obvious, and they are subject to criticism from the left wing of the socialist movement itself.

Communist doctrine and politics are marked by the conceptual method of social development and a preference for deliberateness over spontaneity. It is precisely the deviation from these principles that explains the failure of attempts at reform made after the Twentieth Congress. The pledge of perestroika's success is in its all-embracing approach, encompassing not only economics, but also politics, intellectual life, and international affairs, linking urgent tasks with the prospect of the revolutionary renewal of our socialist society.

However, while noting the strong points of communist doctrine, one must also see a positive side to social-democracy. It is quite solidly tied to real life, is more pragmatic, and is directed at achieving direct results from these or those social measures or political actions. Our adoption of these positive elements and acknowledgement of the very phenomenon of evolutionary socialism would eliminate the essential disagreement between communists and social-democrats.

In speaking of the possibility of consolidating the adherents of socialism while preserving a natural diversity of views and approaches to these or those problems of social progress, one must take into account that the concept of an integral and interdependent world requires the formation of as broad a social agreement as possible, at least regarding the key questions of social development. The preconditions for this are being established. Now a consciousness of cooperation and universal human solidarity is forming, based on such values as the rights and liberties of the individual, concern for the world, for man's natural and intellectual environment, help for the unfortunate, and aid to development.

It is understood that universal human interests should first of all be apprehended in this form so as to be defended and implemented. And this is impossible without a combined search, without the surmounting of the division in the realm of scientific knowledge. While among us the epithet "bourgeois," when applied to the social sciences, meant that they were not sciences at all, but utter magic or even charlatanism, on "the other side" the same meaning was put on the term "Marxist." Both sides lost something, but the biggest loser was science itself, which is in essence unitary and undivided, existing objectively for the sake of understanding the truth.

If one discards the intolerance inculcated for decades, the question remains: is it possible to have a unitary science, the object of which is at the epicenter of a class struggle? The answer will be negative if one sticks to sectarian positions, and certainly positive if one remembers that the goal of socialism is the good of the entire society, and that the interests of universal human development stand higher than any other interests. In rehabilitating this fundamental Marxist-Leninist position, the new political thinking has also opened the way for surmounting the "great divisions" in science.

This, of course, does not mean renouncing the originality of the basic currents of contemporary social-science thinking, Marxist and non-Marxist, not to mention the various schools and trends existing within both or in "no man's land." Competition between ideas and concepts is the natural condition of science, without which it is doomed to sterility. But this should just be scientific polemic, and not the terrible clash of warring sides intent on destroying one another.

We touched in passing only on the important probable results of surmounting the "intersystemic" political and ideological confrontation of states, of the transfer of disagreements from the realm of intolerance and enmity to the realm of theoretical and political dialogue and interaction. Returning to the starting point of our reflections, it should be emphasized that the concept according to which the principal pivot of world development is the struggle of two opposing systems no longer reflects reality. It does not follow, however, that it should simply be discarded. The whole point is that the competition between the systems (I repeat once more: not countries, but systems), has changed from being the principal conflict to being one of the conflicts giving impetus to the progress of humanity and determining its future.

In other words, the analogy is appropriate here of the "swallowing" of Euclidean geometry by that of Lobachevsky and Riemann, or of the mechanics of Newton and Galileo by Einstein's theory of relativity. The discovery of general laws did not abolish the particular laws, but only allotted them a more modest role and fixed the boundaries of their operation.

All the aforesaid can be summed up and expressed in one image: East and West, just as North and South, face the task of not merely bridging the abysses now separating them, but of endeavoring to eliminate those abysses.

NOTES

ABOUT THE AUTHOR: **Georgii Shakhnazarov** is president of the Soviet Political Science Association and was personal adviser to President Gorbachev.

39   *Address at the Forty-Third UN General Assembly Session, December 7, 1988*

MIKHAIL S. GORBACHEV

... Two great revolutions, the French revolution of 1789 and the Russian revolution of 1917, have exerted a powerful influence on the actual nature of the historical process and radically changed the course of world events. Both of them, each in its own way, have given a gigantic impetus to man's progress. They are also the ones that have formed in many respects the way of thinking which is still prevailing in the public consciousness.

That is a very great spiritual wealth, but there emerges before us today a different world, for which it is necessary to seek different roads toward the future, to seek—relying, of course, on accumulated experience—but also seeing the radical differences between that which was yesterday and that which is taking place today.

The newness of the tasks, and at the same time their difficulty, are not limited to this. Today we have entered an era when progress will be based on the interests of all mankind. Consciousness of this requires that world policy, too, should be determined by the priority of the values of all mankind.

The history of the past centuries and millennia has been a history of almost ubiquitous wars, and sometimes desperate battles, leading to mutual destruction. They occurred in the clash of social and political interests and national hostility, be it from ideological or religious incompatibility. All that was the case, and even now many still claim that this past—which has not been overcome—is an immutable pattern. However, parallel with the process of wars, hostility, and alienation of peoples and countries, another process, just as objectively conditioned, was in motion and gaining force: The process of the emergence of a mutually connected and integral world.

Further world progress is now possible only through the search for a consensus of all mankind, in movement toward a new world order. We have arrived at a frontier at which uncontrolled spontaneity leads to a dead end. The world community must learn to shape and direct the process in such a way as to preserve civilization, to make it safe for all and more pleasant for normal life. It is a question of cooperation that could be more accurately called "cocreation" and "codevelopment." The formula of development "at another's expense" is becoming outdated. In light of present realities, genuine progress by infringing upon the rights and liberties of man and peoples, or at the expense of nature, is impossible.

The very tackling of global problems requires a new "volume" and "quality" of cooperation by states and sociopolitical currents regardless of ideological and other differences.

Of course, radical and revolutionary changes are taking place and will continue to take place within individual countries and social structures. This has been and will continue to be the case, but our times are making corrections here, too. Internal transformational processes cannot achieve their national objectives merely by taking "course parallel" with others without using the achievements of the surrounding world and the possibilities of equitable cooperation. In these conditions, interference in those internal processes with the aim of altering them according to someone else's prescription would be all the more destructive for the emergence of a peaceful order. In the past, differences often served as a factor in pulling away from one another. Now they are being given the opportunity to be a factor in mutual enrichment and attraction. Behind differences in social structure, in the way of life, and in the preference for certain values, stand interests. There is no getting away from that, but neither is there any getting away from the need to find a balance of interests within an international framework, which has become a condition for survival and progress. As you ponder all this, you come to the conclusion that if we wish to take account of the lessons of the past and the realities of the present, if we must reckon with the objective logic of world development, it is necessary to seek—and to seek jointly—an approach toward improving the international situation and building a new world. If that is so, then it is also worth agreeing on the fundamental and truly universal prerequisites and principles for such activities. It is evident, for example, that force and the threat of force can no longer be, and should not be instruments of foreign policy. This applies, in the first instance, to nuclear weapons, but it goes further than that. Everyone, and the strongest in the first instance, is required to restrict himself, and to exclude totally the use of external force. That is the first vital component of a nonviolent world as an ideal we declared, together with India, in the Delhi Declaration, and which we invite others to follow. Moreover, it is clear today that the stepping-up of military force does not make any single power all-powerful. Moreover, a one-sided emphasis on military force, in the final analysis, weakens other components of national security.

The compelling necessity of the principle of *freedom of choice* is also clear to us. The failure to recognize this, to recognize it, is fraught with very dire consequences, consequences for world peace. Denying that right to the peoples, no matter what the pretext, no matter what words are used to conceal it, means infringing upon even the unstable balance that is has been possible to achieve.

Freedom of choice is a universal principle to which there should be no exceptions. We have not come to the conclusion of the immutability of this principle simply through good motives. We have been led to it through impartial analysis of the objective processes of our time. The *increasing varieties* of social development in different countries are becoming an ever more perceptible feature of these processes. This relates to both the capitalist and socialist systems. The variety of sociopolitical structures which has grown over the last decades from national liberation movements also demonstrates this. This objective fact presupposes respect for other people's views and stands, tolerance, a preparedness to see phenomena that are different as not necessarily bad or hostile, and an ability to learn to live side by side while remaining different and not agreeing with one another on every issue.

The self-assertion of the world's diversity makes attempts to look down on others and teach them "one's own" democracy untenable, not to mention the fact that democratic values "made for export" often lose their value very quickly. Thus, the question is of unity in diversity. If we state this in the political sphere, if we confirm that we adhere to freedom of choice, then the idea that certain people live on Earth by "divine will" while others are here purely by accident and will be discarded. It is time to get rid of such complexes and to construct one's political line correspondingly. Then prospects for strengthening world unity also will open up.

The de-ideologization of interstate relations has become a demand of the new stage. We are not giving up our convictions, philosophy, or traditions. Neither are we calling on anyone else to give up theirs. Yet we are not going to shut ourselves up within the range of our values. That would lead to spiritual impoverishment, for it would mean renouncing so powerful a source of development as sharing all the original things created independently by each nation. In the course of such sharing, each should prove the advantages of his own system, his own way of life and values, but not through words or propaganda alone, but through real deeds as well. That is, indeed, an honest struggle of ideology, but it must not be carried over into mutual relations between states. Otherwise we simply will not be able to solve a single world problem; arrange broad, mutually advantageous and equitable cooperation between peoples; manage rationally the achievements of the scientific and technical revolution; transform world economic relations; protect the environment; overcome underdevelopment; or put an end to hunger, disease, illiteracy, and other mass ills. Finally, in that case, we will not manage to eliminate the nuclear threat and militarism.

Such are our reflections on the natural order of things in the world on the threshold of the 21st century. We are, of course, far from claiming to have the infallible truth, but having subjected the previous realities—realities that have arisen again—to strict analysis, we have come to the conclusion that it is by precisely such approaches that we must search jointly for a way to achieve the *supremacy of the common human idea* over the countless multiplicity of centrifugal forces, to preserve the vitality of a civilization that is possibly the only one in the universe.

Is there not here a certain romanticism, an exaggeration of the potential and maturity of public awareness in the world? We hear such doubts and questions both at home and from some of our Western partners. I am convinced that we are not losing touch with reality. Forces already have formed in the world which one way or another are inducing the *start of a period of peace*. The peoples, broad circles of the public, really and earnestly want a change for the better in the state of affairs. They want to learn to cooperate. Sometimes it is even striking how strong this trend is. It is important for this sort of mood to begin to be transformed into policy. The change both in philosophical approaches and in political relations is an important prerequisite, providing a powerful spur to efforts directed at establishing new relations between states by relying on objective processes on a world scale. The corresponding conclusions are being made even by those politicians whose activity was at one time connected with the "cold war," sometimes at its most acute stages. From their experience of those times, they, of all people, find it especially difficult to renounce stereotypes. And if even they are making such an about-turn, then it is obvious that with the coming of new generations, the possibilities will be greater still.

In short, understanding the need for a period of peace is making a way for itself and becoming the dominant trend. As a result, the first real steps in improving the international situation and in disarmament have become possible. What arises from this on a practical level? The natural, wise thing would be not to renounce that which is positive, which we have already attained, but to advance all that is positive, that has been achieved in recent years, created by joint efforts. I mean the process of talks on the problems of nuclear weapons, conventional weapons, chemical weapons, the search for political ways of halting regional conflicts. And, of course, first and foremost, political dialogue, which is more intensive, more open, and targeted at the heart of problems and not on confrontation, at an exchange not of accusations but of constructive ideas. Without political dialogue, the talks' process will not proceed. In our view, there are sufficiently optimistic prospects for the near and the more remote future. Look how our relations with the United States have changed: Little by little mutual understanding has started to be built up, elements of trust have arisen, without which it is very difficult to move forward in politics. There are even more of these elements in Europe. The Helsinki process is a great process; in my opinion it remains fully in force. It must be preserved and deepened in all aspects—the philosophical, political, and practical aspects—but must take into account the new circumstances.

The realities are now such that to have a dialogue which ensures the normal and constructive progress of the international process requires the constant, active participation of all countries and regions of the world, of those of great magnitude such as India, China, Japan and Brazil, and of others, large, medium, and small.

II.

In this specific historical situation, the question of the new role of the UN Organization is also arising. It seems to us that it is necessary for states to rethink somewhat their attitude to such a unique instrument as the United Nations Organization, without which world politics is no longer imaginable.

The recent galvanization of its peacemaking role has again demonstrated the United Nation's ability to help its members in coping with the threatening challenges of the times, and in following the path of the humanization of relations. [Moscow Television Service, in its broadcast of this speech at 1607 GMT on 7 December, omits the passage starting in the last sentence of the previous paragraph from "without which world" through "United Nation's ability" in the preceding sentence.] Unfortunately, right after it was set up, it found itself under the onslaught of the "cold war." It became for many years a field for propaganda battles and for cultivating political confrontation. Let historians argue about who is more and who is less to blame for this, while the politicians today must learn the lessons of this chapter in the history of the United Nations Organizations, which has contradicted the actual essence and intention of the United Nations Organizations.

One of the bitterest and most important lessons is the long list of missed opportunities and, as a consequence, a reduction at some stage in the prestige of the United Nations Organizations, the failure of many of its attempts to act. What is very indicative is that the rebirth of the UN Organization's role is connected with improvements in the international climate. The UN Organization is absorbing, as it were, the interests of various countries. It is the only organization which is able to combine in one stream their bilateral, regional, and all-embracing efforts. New opportunities are opening up for it in all spheres, which become naturally part of the UN Organization's competence: Military-political, economic, scientific and technical, ecological, and humanitarian opportunities.

Take, for example, the *problem of development*. This is a problem which is truly common to all mankind. The living conditions of tens of millions of people in a number of regions in the "Third World" are simply becoming dangerous for all mankind. No closed formations or regional groups of states, however important they are, are able to untie the main knots which have formed on the principle lines of world economic ties: North-South, East-West, South-South, South-East, and East-East. Combined efforts are needed here. The interests of all groups of countries needs to be taken into account, and only such an organization as the United Nations is capable of ensuring this.

Foreign debt is one of the most acute problems. Let us not forget that, at the cost of incalculable losses and sacrifices in the colonial era, the developing world aided the prosperity of a considerable part of the world community. The time has come to give compensation for the deprivations which accompanied its historic and tragic contribution made to world material progress. The way out—we are convinced—lies also in *internationalizing the method of approach*. Looking at things realistically, we must recognize that the accumulated debt cannot be either repaid or recovered on the original conditions. The Soviet Union is prepared to establish a lengthy moratorium—right up to 100 years—on the repayment of debts from the least developed countries, and in a whole series of cases to write them off entirely. ...

International economic security is unthinkable outside a link not only with disarmament but also with *identifying the worldwide ecological threat.* The ecological situation in a number of regions is simply appalling. A conference on the environment within the UN framework is planned for 1992. We welcome this decision and are preparing for such a forum to produce results corresponding to the scale of the problem. But time does not wait, and a great deal is being done in various countries.

Here I should like yet again, and most forcefully, to stress the opportunities that are being opened up for ecological revival in the process of disarmament— above all, of course, nuclear disarmament. Let us also ponder whether a center for urgent ecological aid ought to be set up under UN auspices. Its functions would be to send international groups of specialists promptly to areas where there is a sharp deterioration in the ecological situation.

The USSR is also ready to cooperate in the creation of an international space laboratory or manned orbiting station which would be exclusively engaged in monitoring the environment.

Altogether the features of a future space industry are appearing ever more distinctly *in the conquest of space.* The USSR's position is well known: activity in space must rule out the placing of weapons there. This also requires a legal basis. The foundation for this already exists: the 1967 treaty, and other agreements. However, the need to elaborate an all-embracing regime for peaceful work in space has already come to a head; and verifying [Kontrol] the observation of the regime would be a matter for a world space organization. We have already suggested setting up such a body more than once. We are also prepared to include our Krasnoyarsk radar station within the system of that organization. The decision has already been taken to transfer that station to the USSR Academy of Sciences. Soviet scientists are prepared to receive foreign colleagues and to discuss with them how to reequip it as an international center for peaceful cooperation, dismantling and altering individual facilities and structures and also providing it with equipment which it lacks. This whole system could function under the aegis of the United Nations.

The whole world welcomes the efforts by the UN Organization and by Secretary General Perez de Cuellar and his representatives to solve *regional problems.* Allow me to dwell on this theme a while. Rephrasing the verse by the English poet that Hemingway took as the epigraph for his famous novel, let us say this: The bell of each regional conflict tolls for all of us. This is particularly true because these conflicts are occurring in the "Third World," which even without this has many troubles and problems on a scale which cannot fail to concern all of us.

The year 1988 brought a ray of hope in that area of our common concerns, too. It affected almost all regional crises and there are improvements in some places. We welcome them; we have encouraged them to the extent possible. I will dwell specifically just on Afghanistan. The Geneva Accords, the fundamental and practical importance of which was rated highly throughout the world, provided the opportunity to complete a settlement even this year, but that did not happen.

This regrettable fact again recalls the political, legal, and moral significance of the ancient roman maxim: pacta sunt servanda—treaties must be fulfilled. I do not want to use this platform for reproaching anyone, but it seems to us that within the competence of the United Nations, the November resolution of the General Assembly could have some specific measures added to it.

In the words of the resolution "For the Immediate Achievement of an All-Embracing Solution by the Afghans Themselves of the Question of a Broad-Based Government," the following should be undertaken:

> A full cease-fire everywhere, beginning I January 1989, and a halt to all offensive operations or shellings, with all territories occupied by opposing Afghan groups to remain under their respective control for the duration of the talks;
>
> Linked to this and beginning on the same date, a halt to arms deliveries to all belligerent parties;
>
> For the period of the establishment of the broad-based government envisaged in the General Assembly resolution, the sending to Kabul and other strategic centers in the country a contingent of UN peace-keeping forces.

We also appeal to the UN secretary general to foster the speediest possible implementation of the idea of holding an international conference on the neutrality and demilitarization of Afghanistan.

We will continue in the future to help in the most active way to heal the wounds of war. We are ready to cooperate in this matter both with the United Nations and on a bilateral basis.

We support the proposal to set up under UN auspices a volunteer international peace corps to assist in the rebirth of Afghanistan.

In connection with the problem of settling regional conflicts, I cannot fail to express my judgement on a serious incident that occurred very recently with regard to the work of this session. The representative of an organization having permanent-observer status at the United Nations was not admitted to New York by the U.S. authorities to speak at the General Assembly. I am talking about Yasir 'Arafat. And that took place at a time when the PLO has made an important and constructive step which facilitates the search for a solution to the Middle East problem with the participation of the UN Security Council. That happened at the moment a positive trend toward a political settlement of other regional conflicts had taken shape, and in a number of cases with assistance from the United States and the USSR. We express great regret over what has taken place, and also express our solidarity with the PLO.

Gentlemen, the concept of all-embracing international security is based on the principles of the UN charter, and proceeds from the obligatory nature of *international law* for all states. In favoring the demilitarization of international relations, we want to see politico-legal methods dominating in the solution of emerging problems. Our ideal is a world community of states based on the rule of law, which also make their foreign policy activity subordinate to the law. The attainment of this would be facilitated by an accord within the UN framework on a uniform understanding of the principles and norms of international law, and their codification, taking account of new conditions, and also the formulation of legal norms for new spheres of cooperation. In the conditions of the nuclear age, the efficacy of international law must rely not on coercion of execution, but on the norms reflecting the balance of interests of states.

Together with an increasing awareness of the objective commonality of fate, this would create a sincere interest for every state in restricting itself within the bounds of international law. The democratization of international relations is not only the maximum internationalization of the solution of problems by all members of the world community; it is also a *humanization* of those relations. International links will fully reflect the real interests of the peoples and reliably serve the cause of their common security only when man's concerns, rights, and liberties are at the center of everything. In this context, I would like to add my country's voice to the high assessments of the significance of the General Declaration of Human Rights adopted 40 years ago on 10 December 1948. This document is still topical today. It also reflected the universal nature of the aims and tasks of the United Nations. The most suitable way for a state to mark the declaration's anniversary is to improve its own conditions at home for the observance and defense of citizens' rights.

Before telling you precisely what we have done in this sphere recently, I would like to say the following: Our country is undergoing a truly revolutionary upsurge. The process of restructuring is gaining pace. We started by elaborating the theoretical concepts of restructuring; we had to assess the nature and scope of the problems, to interpret the lessons of the past, and to express this in the form of political conclusions and programs. This was done. The theoretical work, the reinterpretation of what had happened, the final elaboration, enrichment, and correction of political stances have not ended. They continue. However, it was fundamentally important to start from an overall concept, which is already now being confirmed by the experience of past years, which has turned out to be generally correct and to which there is no alternative.

In order to involve society in implementing the plans for restructuring it had to be made more truly democratic. Under the badge of democratization, restructuring has now encompassed politics, the economy, spiritual life, and ideology. We have unfolded a radical economic reform, we have accumulated experience, and from the new year we are transferring the entire national economy to new forms and work methods. Moreover, this means a profound reorganization of production relations and the realization of the immense potential of socialist property.

In moving toward such bold revolutionary transformations, we understood that there would be errors, that there would be resistance, that the novelty would bring new problems. We foresaw the possibility of braking in individual sections. However, the profound democratic reform of the entire system of power and government is the guarantee that the overall process of restructuring will move steadily forward and gather strength.

We completed the first stage of the process of political reform with the recent decisions by the USSR Supreme Soviet on amendments to the Constitution and the adoption of the Law on Elections. Without stopping, we embarked upon the second stage of this, at which the most important task will be working on the interaction between the central government and the republics, settling relations between nationalities on the principles of Leninist internationalism bequeathed to us by the great revolution and, at the same time, reorganizing the power of the Soviets locally. We are faced with immense work. At the same time we must resolve major problems.

We are more than fully confident. We have both the theory, the policy, and the vanguard force of restructuring, a party which is also restructuring itself in accordance with the new tasks and the radical changes throughout society. And the most important thing: all peoples and all generations of citizens in our great country are in favor of restructuring.

We have gone substantially and deeply into the business of constructing a socialist state based on the rule of law. A whole series of new laws has been prepared or is at a completion stage. Many of them come into force as early as 1989, and we trust that they will correspond to the highest standards from the point of view of ensuring the rights of the individual. Soviet democracy is to acquire a firm, normative base. This means such acts as the Law on Freedom of Conscience, on glasnost, on public associations and organizations, and on much else. There are now no people in places of imprisonment in the country who have been sentenced for their political or religious convictions. It is proposed to include in the drafts of the new laws additional guarantees ruling out any form of persecution on these bases. Of course, this does not apply to those who have committed real criminal or state offences: espionage, sabotage, terrorism, and so on, whatever political or philosophical views they may hold.

The draft amendments to the criminal code are ready and waiting their turn. In particular, those articles relating to the use of the supreme measure of punishment are being reviewed. The problem of exit and entry is also being resolved in a humane spirit, including the case of leaving the country in order to be reunited with relatives. As you know, one of the reasons for refusal of visas is citizens' possession of secrets. Strictly substantiated terms for the length of time for possessing secrets are being introduced in advance. On starting work at a relevant institution or enterprise, everyone will be made aware of this regulation. Disputes that arise can be appealed under the law. Thus the problem of the so-called "refuseniks" is being removed.

We intend to expand the Soviet Union's participation in the monitoring mechanism on human rights in the United Nations and within the framework of the pan-European process. We consider that the jurisdiction of the International Court in the Hague with respect to interpreting and applying agreements in the field of human rights should be obligatory for all states.

Within the context of the Helsinki process, we also are examining an end to jamming of all foreign radio broadcasts to the Soviet Union. On the whole, our credo is as follows: Political problems should be solved only by political means, and human problems only in a humane way.

III.

Now about the most important topic, without which no problem of the coming century can be resolved: *disarmament.*

International development and contacts have been deformed by the arms race and militarization of thinking: On 15 January 1986 the Soviet Union put forward, as is known, a program for building a nuclear-free world. Its embodiment in real negotiating positions has already provided material results. Tomorrow is the first anniversary of the signing of the treaty scrapping intermediate and shorter-range missiles. With still greater satisfaction, I say that the implementation of that treaty—the destruction of the missiles—is proceeding normally, in an atmosphere of trust and efficiency. It would seem that a breach has been made in the impenetrable wall of suspicion and hostility. Before our eyes we are seeing a new historic reality arising, *a turnaround from the principle of over-abundance of weaponry to the principle of reasonable sufficiency for defense.* We are present to see the first glimmers of the formation of a new model of ensuring security, not with the help of increasing weapons—as was almost always the case—but on the contrary through reducing them on the basis of compromise. The Soviet leadership has decided once again to demonstrate its readiness to strengthen this healthy process, not only in words, but in *deeds.*

Today I can inform you of the following: The Soviet Union has made a decision on reducing its armed forces. In the next 2 years, their numerical strength will be reduced by 500,000 persons, and the volume of conventional arms will also be cut considerably. These reductions will be made on a *unilateral basis,* unconnected with the negotiations on the mandate for the Vienna meeting. By agreement with our allies in the Warsaw Pact, we have made the decision to withdraw six tank divisions from the GDR, Czechoslovakia, and Hungary, and to disband them by 1991. Assault landing formations and units, and a number of others, including assault river-crossing forces, with their armaments and combat equipment, will also be withdrawn from the groups of Soviet forces situated in those countries. The Soviet forces situated in those countries will be cut by 50,000 persons, and their arms by 5,000 tanks. All remaining Soviet divisions on the territory of our allies will be reorganized. They will be given a different structure from today's, which will become unambiguously defensive, after the removal of a large number of their tanks.

At the same time, we will also cut the numbers of the personnel of our forces and the quantity of arms in the European part of the USSR. Altogether, in that part of our country and on the territory of our European allies, the Soviet Armed

Forces will be reduced by 10,000 tanks, 8,500 artillery systems, and 800 combat aircraft.

Over these 2 years we will substantially reduce the grouping of armed forces in the Asian part of the country, too. By agreement with the Government of the Mongolian People's Republic, a considerable part of the Soviet troops temporarily present there will return home. In adopting these decisions of fundamental importance, the Soviet leadership is voicing the will of a people engaged in an in-depth renewal of its entire socialist society. We will maintain our country's defense capability on a level of reasonable and reliable sufficiency, so that no one should find themselves tempted to infringe upon the security of the USSR and its allies.

By this act, just as by all our actions aimed at the demilitarization of international relations, we would also like to draw the attention of the world community to another topical problem, the problem of changing over *from an economy of armament to an economy of disarmament.* Is the conversion of military production realistic? I have already had occasion to speak about this. We believe that it is, indeed, realistic. For its part, the Soviet Union is ready to do the following. Within the framework of the economic reform we are ready to draw up and submit our internal plan for conversion, to prepare in the course of 1989, as an experiment, the plans for the conversion of two or three defense enterprises, to publish our experience of job relocation of specialists from the military industry, and also of using its equipment, buildings, and works in civilian industry. It is desirable that all states. primarily the major military powers, submit their national plans on this issue to the United Nations.

It would also be useful to form a group of scientists, entrusting it with a comprehensive analysis of problems of conversion as a whole and as applied to individual countries and regions, to be reported to the UN secretary general, and later to examine this matter at a General Assembly session.

IV.

Finally, being on U.S. soil, but also for other, understandable reasons, I cannot but turn to the subject of our relations with this great country. I was able to fully appreciate its hospitality during my memorable visit to Washington exactly a year ago. Relations between the Soviet Union and the United States of America span 5 and 1/2 decades. The world has changed, and so have the nature, role, and place of these relations in world politics. For too long they were built under the banner of confrontation, and sometimes of hostility, either open or concealed. But in the last few years, throughout the world people were able to heave a sigh of relief, thanks to the changes for the better in the substance and atmosphere of the relations between Moscow and Washington.

No one intends to underestimate the serious nature of the disagreements, and the difficulties of the problems which have not been settled. However, we have already graduated from the primary school of instruction in mutual understanding and in searching for solutions in our own and in the common interests. The USSR and the United States created the biggest nuclear missile arsenals, but after objectively recognizing their responsibility, they were able to be the first to conclude an agreement on the reduction and physical destruction of a proportion of these weapons, which threatened both themselves and everyone else.

Both sides possess the biggest and the most refined military secrets. But it is they who have laid the basis for and are developing a system of mutual verification with regard to both the destruction and the limiting and banning of armaments production. It is they who are amassing experience for future bilateral and multilateral agreements. We value this.

We acknowledge and value the contribution of President Ronald Reagan and the members of his administration, above all Mr. George Shultz. All this is capital that has been invested in a joint undertaking of historic importance. It must not be wasted or left out of circulation. The future U.S. Administration headed by newly elected President George Bush will find in us a partner, ready—without long pauses and backward movements—to continue the dialogue in a spirit of realism, openness, and goodwill, and with a striving for concrete results, over an agenda encompassing the key issues of Soviet-U.S. relations and international politics.

We are talking first and foremost about consistent progress toward concluding a treaty on a 50 percent reduction in strategic offensive weapons, while retaining the ABM Treaty; about elaborating a convention on the elimination of chemical weapons—here, it seems to us, we have the preconditions for making 1989 the decisive year; and about talks on reducing conventional weapons and armed forces in Europe. We are also talking about economic, ecological and humanitarian problems in the widest possible sense.

It would be absolutely incorrect to credit the USSR and the United States alone for the positive changes in the international situation.

The Soviet Union highly appreciates the large and original contribution of the socialist countries to the process of improving the international situation. In the course of negotiations we constantly experience the presence of other major states, nuclear and non-nuclear. An indispensably important and constructive role is being played by many, including medium-sized and small countries, and of course by the Nonaligned Movement, as well as the intercontinental "Group of Six."

We in Moscow are delighted that an ever growing number of state, political, party, and public figures are ready to shoulder the burden of universal responsibility, and in particular I would like to mention the scientists, cultural figures, representatives of mass organizations and various churches, and activists of what is termed people's diplomacy. In this regard I think the idea of a regular convening of an assembly of public organizations under UN auspices merits attention.

We are not inclined to oversimplify the situation in the world. Yes, the tendency toward disarmament has received a strong impetus, and this process is gaining its own momentum, but it has not become irreversible. Yes, the striving to give up confrontation in favor of dialogue and cooperation has made itself strongly felt, but is has by no means secured its position forever in the practice of international relations. Yes, the movement toward a nuclear-free and nonviolent world is capable of fundamentally transforming the political and spiritual face of the planet, but only the very first steps have been taken. Moreover, in certain influential circles, they have been greeted with mistrust, and they are meeting resistance.

The inheritance and the inertia of the past are continuing to operate. Profound contradictions and the roots of many conflicts have not disappeared. The fundamental fact remains that the formation of the peaceful period will take place in conditions of the existence and rivalry of various socioeconomic and political systems. However, the meaning of our international efforts, and one of the key tenets of the new thinking, is precisely to impart to this rivalry the quality of sensible competition in conditions of respect for freedom of choice and a balance of interests. In this case it will even become useful and productive from the viewpoint of general world development; otherwise, if the main component remains the arms race, as it has been till now, rivalry will be fatal. Indeed, an ever greater number of people throughout the world, from the man in the street to leaders, are beginning to understand this.

Esteemed Mr. Chairman, esteemed delegates: I finish my first speech at the United Nations with the same feeling with which I began it: a feeling of responsibility to my own people and to the world community. We have met at the end of a year that has been so significant for the United Nations, and on the threshold of a year from which all of us expect so much. One would like to believe that our joint efforts to put an end to the era of wars, confrontation and regional conflicts, aggression against nature, the terror of hunger and poverty, as well as political terrorism, will be comparable with our hopes. This is our common goal, and it is only by acting together that we may attain it. Thank you.

40 *New Thinking About World Communism*

ALEXANDER DALLIN

... While the reformists in the saddle had other priorities, by 1987 senior independent publicists like Aleksandr Bovin were taking advantage of the new glasnost' to write derisively of the customary communist attempts to depict the course of events—whatever the course, whatever the events—as being in harmony with the predicted unfolding of the inevitable. History, he wrote, "mocks attempts to control its course." Thus, it had to be admitted that the prospects of socialist revolution were not at all what had been expected.

> Above all, it should be acknowledged that the ability of capitalism to adapt to the new historical setting has surpassed our expectations. The prospect of socialist transformations in developed capitalist countries has receded indefinitely.

As for the Third World,

> In a number of countries of socialist orientation, the situation remains unstable, fraught with the possibility of regression.

More generally,

> Both in capitalist countries and in Third World countries, the communist parties, with few exceptions, have failed to become mass organizations, to win for themselves the support of the bulk of the working class, of the toilers.

One of the reasons for these failures had been the failure of the Soviet Union and other socialist countries to provide an attractive model.

> The society that, by all indications, should have been an example, a model to be imitated, a stimulus in the struggle for the socialist reordering of society, has not been created in the Soviet Union.

The same had been true of China as well. Here, too, the equivalent of a perestroika, Bovin argued, at least held out a hope for the future.[3]

Such articles set out many of the themes that were to be developed in the following years. Typically the journalists spoke out first. After them came the diplomats and other practitioners, then the scholars, and finally the ideologues. In March 1988, the journal *MEMO* [*Mirovaya ekonomika i mezhdunarodnye otnosheniia*] published a major article by its editor, German Diligensky, which went a good deal further and deeper in questioning traditional assumptions concerning revolutions abroad, but still from a Leninist perspective.[4] By early 1990 a communist party journal could devote a remarkably candid roundtable to the same subject.[5]

THEMES AND ARGUMENTS

While they tended to become more radical and outspoken over time, most such analyses could be fitted into the same general framework. They tried to provide answers to three questions: (1) In what ways have we (or our predecessors) been wrong about the prospects of revolution (whose inevitability and ultimate success Marxists had been taking for granted)? (2) What are the sources of our errors? (3) What follows from this realization?

There was little argument about the first proposition. In the major capitalist countries—indeed, the most highly developed ones—such as the United States, Britain, and Germany, the communist parties were a pitiful joke; in France and even Italy, where they had a mass following, they were losing support. In the Third World, countries of allegedly socialist orientation were turning elsewhere instead. Well before the crisis in Eastern Europe in the fall of 1989, Moscow recognized that even within the "socialist commonwealth" there were serious problems that required study and reform. But in regard to (2) and (3) opinions varied. Moreover, while the gloves were off, for some time there remained the prudential convention that no one turned overtly against the very idea of a socialist revolution (although its essence and meaning could be, and were widely, questioned, and it no longer needed to be equated with "proletarian" revolution or indeed any violent revolution at all).

The search for the sources of erroneous past (and present) analyses led the writers into the labyrinth of Marxism-Leninism.[6] This reopened the linked issues of the nature of capitalism, the socialist model, and the future of the Third World. It was no longer a matter of ritual or dogma that the infallibility of the "classics" of Marxism-Leninism needed unquestioningly to be reaffirmed. Soviet writers now condemned the "stereotype of bipolarity"—socialism and capitalism as the only alternatives—that was the product of vulgar Marxism. Others questioned the "myth" of the victorious "historical mission of the working class." Now it could be acknowledged that for decades the class struggle and class antagonisms had been "absolutized" by communist analysts and mechanically given undue importance. Historians were arguing against the previously mandatory stress on *zakonomernost'*—the insistence that history proceeded in conformity with immutable laws of social development—and instead pleaded for *al'ternativnost'*—room for choices and alternative paths.

It turned out that nationalization did not in itself give workers a sense of ownership and identification with their enterprise. Another axiom that was likewise challenged concerned the equation of the interests of the international proletariat and those of the Soviet Union.

We are being greatly harmed [declared a professor at the Central Committee's training school for foreign communists] when we try to strengthen our [international] position by referring to the fact that we, as it were automatically, represent the interests of the entire international proletariat—all 670 million people. That is simply incorrect. The scope and the diversity of the interests of the working class cannot be represented by any one party or movement. ... One must not automatically arrogate to oneself the ability to represent all the aspirations of the international working class, especially those beyond the borders of our country.[7]

Soviet publications convey, to a greater degree than personal interviews do, an instrumental, utilitarian approach: what of the old ideological baggage must be jettisoned to rescue the essence of the cause? At least in print authors—especially those in official Soviet positions—will reaffirm that, in spite of all, the class struggle is not just fading away; that the working class remains essential as the architect of historical change; that sooner or later it must pass from defense to offense; that since current conditions favor evolution rather than revolution and "global" rather than "class" objectives, international communism must stress working together with others, such as social-democrats and "greens."

Others, however, will much more candidly admit the bankruptcy of communist thinking. After the many years of glossing over all unpleasantness and the repetition of abstractions and stereotypes removed from real life, it is not too much to speak of "pessimism, disappointment, and disorientation" among communist analysts, of a "crisis" in world communism (words used in recent Soviet publications on the subject). ...

On the other hand, the working class in the West (and that is where most of the attention of Soviet analysts was) had undergone important structural changes—and here different Soviet analysts had their own explanations, be it the inclusion of "scientific workers" and the vast expansion of white-collar workers or the qualitative stratification within the working class(es). Some analysts found it hard to say what interests all types of labor had in common that distinguished them from all other strata of society.

At the same time, capitalism was no longer the brutal exploiter. Soviet observers, it was commonly agreed, had underestimated the vitality of Western capitalism and the ability of the state to introduce reforms that seemingly went against the interests of the ruling class. The areas of alienation and exploitation had been reduced, and so consequently had the workers' hostility to the system. The government had typically imposed elements of social responsibility, welfare, and security that mitigated the potential effects of economic crises. Moreover, internationalization of production and international cooperation among capitalist states rendered the old images of intra-capitalist conflict obsolete. (Soviet authors have been more reluctant to tinker with the Leninist notion of imperialism, but some—including Bovin—have cast it overboard, if only, they argue, because imperialism has changed fundamentally since Lenin's days.)

There was some implicit disagreement over the question whether or not the changes had an "objective" basis that could somehow be integrated into a Marxist perspective. Some commentators attributed the change in the working class primarily to the "scientific-technological revolution" that had recently intervened. Others associated the priority of global values with the advent of nuclear weapons.

More cruel critics, by contrast, candidly stressed the basic error of communist categories and axioms. One result, once this was recognized (a historian suggested) was that communists now had no answers other than reformism, i.e., they now found themselves groping for political space already occupied by others. The working class in advanced societies, another argued, had changed qualitatively, including its culture and values, and had no use for communists as they had come to know them in the past. No, others argued, the problem was more basic: at root, the error was the Marxists' assumptions, to begin with. A. I. Volkov, a historian, declared at a roundtable on this subject:

> A realistic assessment of contemporary capitalism, its development, its vitality, is in fundamental conflict with the assumptions of communists—so to speak, with our genetic code, which consists of the notion that human happiness can be achieved only by means of revolution, which is understood as the forcible redistribution of property and power. This is an illusion, since hopes can be tied not to redistribution but only to some higher form of production. Today's developed societies have demonstrated the possibility, in principle, to solve social problems far more painlessly and more effectively, permitting these societies to rise to a higher level of development not by means of destruction but by building and assimilating the best of the achievements of earlier generations and forms of organization of social life. ...[8]

...

TYPES OF RESPONSES

While the positions of different commentators are still in flux, and some public statements may not represent their actual views fairly, one may suggest an emerging typology of responses to the shared recognition of a crisis in the "international labor movement" or, more properly, in the communist world. In simplest terms, they divide into those who believe one of the following propositions:

(1) In all essential respects Marx and Lenin were right and their theories remain largely valid, though their application has at times been faulty.

(2) Marxism-Leninism was correct in its day, but the world has changed in significant ways, which requires a fresh look and a new political orientation. Thus, instead of appealing to the working class, communists should now appeal to the entire society. Though Lenin attacked social-chauvinism and social-opportunism, this must not mean the rejection of reformism for all times. Similarly, a fresh look is in order with regard to the Third World (a topic on which Soviet observers divide and which by its complexity exceeds the bounds of this chapter, but on which increasingly Soviet observers acknowledge their disappointment and a recognition that developments in even "progressive" societies have scarcely lived up to Soviet expectations).

(3) In a number of fundamental respects, Marxism-Leninism turns out always to have been in error. Serious doubts are in order about the whole notion of historical inevitability. Marxism is deficient in lacking moral categories. It is impossible effectively to direct a world movement from a single center, just as it is impossible for Gosplan effectively to direct the entire Soviet economy. Or putting it more gently, there were in Marxism serious contradictions that needed to be highlighted, exposed, and amended, though they did not require socialism in toto.[10]

(4) Never mind the theory, which can always be manipulated; what is needed is new guidance to practice—e.g., an appeal to the Socialist International to work together (i.e., neither to ostracize it nor to merge with it). The narrowest, most utilitarian approach is to argue that, since communists abroad were doing so poorly, what was needed was a broad coalition of social forces (read: political parties and movements).

(5) International communism has been a vast failure—misleading and expensive at that—and it will be wise for the Soviet authorities to disengage from it as undramatically and as elegantly as possible, writing it off as the product of an earlier era.

All in all, world communism and world revolution have receded, in the minds of most Soviet observers and policy makers, to a distant, dubious, and dependent role—compared to urgent and immediate needs, compared to domestic priorities, and compared to international security, economics, and diplomatic tasks, in a general atmosphere of "de-ideologization."[11] In all these regards, the place assigned to world communism and world revolution in the context of the New Political Thinking represents the logical though important next step in a process of evolution that began with the first doubts soon after the October Revolution. Not so the dominant reaction to events in the "socialist camp."

THE SOCIALIST CAMP

Curiously, the New Political Thinking—focussing first and foremost on Soviet-American relations—had little to say about Soviet relations with "socialist countries." True, Mikhail Gorbachev in his UN General Assembly speech in December 1988 stressed freedom of choice for all countries—presumably, including allegiance and development path. In November 1986 he had distributed to his colleagues a memorandum, discussed at a working meeting of the leaders of ruling communist parties in Moscow, which dealt with equalizing relations among the "fraternal countries." Gradually a sense developed that the tolerance of diversity—pluralism—within the Soviet Union also applied to relations within the socialist camp (provided that diversity was limited to "socialist" systems and did not jeopardize security relations).[12]

A large part of the Soviet elite perceived that there were troubling aspects to Soviet relations with Eastern Europe; especially the Polish events of 1980/81 had caused concern. But the general feeling, in the 1980s, was that the East European governments had gained or were gaining legitimacy at home; that there was no crisis at hand; and that problematic issues (such as the Nazi-Soviet deal of 1939, or Soviet responsibility for the Katyn massacre) were finally being addressed. In the words of a leading Soviet Party official,

> The elements of 'paternalistic' relations, in which we, as it were, played the role of patron, are gone. The need for strictly observing the equality principle, which was advanced before, has been reaffirmed in the spirit of New Thinking by the conclu-

sioń that no party has a monopoly on the truth of socialism, and only the strengthening of socialism in practice can serve as criteria of this truth. It is no longer viewed as harmful to the unity of socialist countries that there exist different ideas of how to build a new society and that individual socialist countries may have their specific national and state interests. In light of New Thinking we have fully realized that the most reliable way to unity lies not in the mechanical unification of these countries, but in the persistent search for solutions based on a balance of their interests, and our common socialist foundation provides the most favorable conditions for this.[13]

True, "it is obvious that the increasing democratization of mutual relations brings out more clearly than before the existence of certain contradictions between socialist countries because at times their national interests do not coincide on some specific issues." In fact, "an analysis of the situation indicates that cooperation with our friends has not yet reached a true turning point."[14] A few months later Vitali Zhurkin, director of the Europe Institute at the USSR Academy of Sciences, could recall:

> ... Some time in the past we arrived at a consensus on the inevitability of reform in Eastern Europe. But we all believed quite sincerely that they would take 10 to 15 years and would come about gently, advancing at a leisurely pace. Yet what happened was explosions. ...[15]

In 1989 Soviet officials, from Gorbachev on down, had made public declarations that what in the West was called the "Brezhnev Doctrine" was no longer in force. While this was a bit of a charade (if only because there never had been a Brezhnev Doctrine), it was nonetheless significant in marking the Soviet renunciation of the use of force in regard to Eastern Europe—and was so understood.[16]

By all indications, the sequence of events in Eastern Europe that led to the ouster or replacement of governments from East Berlin to Bucharest surprised the masters in Moscow as much as it did observers in the West—and this, in spite of the fact that it was Soviet signals that were crucial in triggering the whole chain of events. What is of particular interest in the context of this chapter is the conceptual response. The reformist wing in Moscow did not hesitate to express their approval. What took place in Eastern Europe, wrote Vladimir Lukin, a prominent foreign affairs specialist and more recently chairman of the International Relations Committee of the RSFSR Supreme Soviet, was "the result of a series of sweeping antitotalitarian democratic revolutions."

> The Soviet Union's reaction to the events in Eastern Europe has been most reassuring. We seem to be learning—better late than never—to tell the interests of genuine national security from a desire to keep 'our people' in power in neighboring European capitals.[17]

True, events in Eastern Europe went further than even Soviet reformers would have wished, but consistent commentators dismissed this as within the range of the tolerable: once Moscow had agreed not to intervene, the consequences had to be worked out without an active Soviet role. For some people, another commentator explained, the events in Eastern Europe were a cause for euphoria; for others they were a source of pain and bitterness. "To my mind, what happened had to happen. A positive process is taking place, mirroring a world-wide tendency. Its essence is the transition from totalitarianism to parliamentary pluralism, civil society, and a state of law."[18]

And yet, a good many members of the Soviet foreign-affairs community seemed to have lost their power of speech. No doubt it was a serious ideological and political embarrassment to be obliged to acknowledge that the inevitable course of history had been reversed and communist governments were forced from office, from the Baltic to the Black Sea. Indeed, it took some months for serious theoretical treatments of the events to appear; Soviet journals acknowledge that "regrettably, no coherent conceptual analysis" of the events has as yet been offered.

But the bitterness ran deep. After being variously hinted at for months, an overt attack on the policy—and the outlook—that had brought about the collapse of the East European bloc, and with it, of the Warsaw Pact, came in June 1990 from the same quarters who had attacked other elements of the New Political Thinking and now found a responsive audience at the founding congress of the Russian Communist party; it was repeated at the XXVIII CPSU Congress, the following month. Yegor Ligachev charged the new thinkers—presumably, including Gorbachev and certainly, including Shevardnadze—with selling out the comrades and betraying the principles of communist solidarity. General Albert Makashov dwelt on the security implications of the setback. Both voiced alarm at the prospect of a formidable new united Germany that the Soviet people had fought so hard to defeat. If this was the result of the New Thinking, it was a danger to the health of the Soviet Union (as was, the hardliners argued, Gorbachev's policy toward the Soviet nationalities).[19] Curiously, most of the arguments—on both sides—were couched in terms of national security and patriotism, not in the traditional jargon or rhetoric of "proletarian internationalism."

Perhaps the most powerful reply to the various charges came from Shevardnadze, who likened the innuendo of Soviet criticism to Sen. Joseph McCarthy's campaign in the United States that had asked, forty years earlier, "Who lost China?"

> Strange as it may seem, recently we too have had similar accusations. One gets the impression that some people would love to conduct an investigation on "Who lost Eastern Europe?" Some people seem to look on Eastern Europe as spoils of war, with chauvinistic and insulting remarks, for which I must apologize to the peoples of Eastern Europe.
>
> It is high time to understand that neither socialism, nor friendship, nor good-neighborly relations, nor respect can be built on a foundation of bayonets, tanks, and blood. Relations with any country must be based on taking account of mutual interests, mutual benefit, and the principle of free choice.[20]

Shevardnadze managed to fight off his critics, but characteristically did not even seek to be re-elected to the CPSU Central Committee; having been made a member of the Presidential Council and remaining at the head of the Foreign Ministry, his fate reflected the shift in power at the apex of the Soviet pyramid, as well as the malaise in Communist Party circles increased by the East European events.

The Soviet view of the remaining "fraternal countries" was no less confusing. Presumably all—from China to Yugoslavia, from Albania to Cuba, from North Korea to Laos—were now acknowledged to be socialist (though what this meant was another question—as Nikolai Shishlin remarked, "You know, we wonder whether we ourselves are a socialist state").[21] But by what criteria that determination was made—and whether it any longer mattered—was left unclear. For those planning to sort out Soviet concepts and perspectives, on ruling as well as nonruling communist parties, a lot of work remained to be done.

DISORIENTATION: ORGANIZATIONAL COSTS

Compared to the general propositions of the New Political Thinking, official Moscow showed far greater disarray and defensiveness with regard to the communist world. If previously the growth of the Soviet bloc had been proclaimed inevitable, now its collapse was, a bit shamefacedly, presented as equally inevitable.[22] As for the "fraternal" parties elsewhere in the world, the Soviet establishment seemed to be giving them less thought, attention, or resources than ever before.

The clearest expression of this unprecedented sense of failure and depression concerning world communism was to be found in the area of "organizational consequences." In the spring of 1990 the one "international" Soviet-sponsored publication aimed at all foreign communist parties, *Problems of Peace and Socialism* (also published in English as *World Marxist Review*) ceased publication.[23] The monthly journal sponsored by the Institute on the International Labor Movement, *Rabochii klass i sovremennyi mir* [The Working Class and the Contemporary World], was about to become a political-science journal under the title, *Polis,* presumably as part of the general scramble by those who had taught or propagated Marxism-Leninism now to find legitimacy in the newly-sanctioned field of "politology." ...

FROM 1917 TO 1990

At the time of the October Revolution, Lenin had described world revolution as "essential" for the survival of the Soviet state. Three generations later, there was not a word of protest or excitement when, in a discussion of a new flag in the RSFSR Supreme Soviet, a woman deputy (an editor of *Molodaya Gvardiya*) declared on May 22, 1990, "The formula, 'Workers of the World, Unite' on our flag has long been—you will agree—an absurdity."

An outside observer might describe the process that had intervened as a slow though characteristic response to cognitive dissonance "when prophecy fails" (to borrow the title of a familiar monograph). Another way to characterize it would be to think of it as a protracted learning process in which ideological axioms and imperatives are gradually overridden by a perceived need for realism. In either case, the expectation of world revolution is either abandoned or else removed into so distant a future as to lose all operational significance. Similarly, belief in the inevitability of the victorious march of the "working class movement" through history is either tacitly cast aside or else so attenuated as to become a (shaky) article of faith that requires neither validation nor individual exertion.

Thus, while Soviet analysts had managed to face the real world of diplomacy and international security with a well-ordered (though at times improvised) system of precepts, the vision of world revolution had been all but eroded, the future of world communism proved strikingly fuzzy, and—amidst unprecedented candor in the atmosphere of *glasnost'*—a virtual lack of new concepts characterized the Soviet approach to *fin de siècle* communism.

NOTES

3. Aleksandr Bovin, "Perestroika i sud'by sotsializma," *Izvestiia,* July 11, 1987. See also Evgenii Plimak, "Novoe myshlenie i perspektivy sotsial'nogo obnovleniya mira," *Voprosy filosofii,* 1987, no. 6: "Even relatively recently, communists believed that the 20th century would be the century of the worldwide triumph of socialism. Now, however, it is clear that—no matter how great the natural desire of revolutionaries to bring nearer the hour of victory, this goal is receding into the distant future. The truth is that we underestimated the ability of capitalism to adapt to new conditions, ... and at the same time we overestimated the speed with which the influence of socialism might spread."

4. German Diligensky, "Revolyutsionnaya teoriya i sovremennost'," *MEMO,* 1988, no. 3, pp. 15–25; Engl. trans. also in Steve Hirsch, ed., *MEMO* (Washington, D.C.: BNA, 1989), pp. 30–45. Another paper by Diligensky is his "Theory of Revolution Today," in Institute of World History, USSR Academy of Sciences, *Revolutions and Reforms in World History* (Moscow: Nauka, 1990), pp. 236–253. On the same general topic, see also interview with Vladlen Sirotkin, professor at the Diplomatic Academy of the Foreign Ministry, Revolyutsiya v soznanii," in *XX vek i mir,* 1988, no. 7, pp. 17–24; also Sirotkin in *50/50: Opyt slovarya novogo myshlenya,* Yuri Afanas'yev and Marc Ferro, eds. (Moscow: Progress, 1989), pp. 70–72, 86–89.

5. *Dialog,* 1990, no. 3, pp. 91–98, with the participation of Vadim Zagladin, Yuri Krasin, Aleksandr Galkin, et al.

6. This and the following paragraphs are based on the sources cited in the preceding footnotes as well as some forty interviews conducted by the author in Moscow in April-May 1990. There are few other Western analyses of this subject. See, however, Steven Kull, "Dateline Moscow: Burying Lenin," *Foreign Policy,* no. 78 (Spring 1990), pp. 172–191.

7. Yu. Kuznets, in "Novoe myshlenie v mezhdunarodnykh delakh: kruglyi stol ... ," *Kommunist,* 1989, no. 8, p. 100.

8. *Dialog,* loc. cit.

10. For an "authoritative" version of this position, see Igor' Pantin and Evgenii Plimak, "Idei K. Marksa na perelome chelovecheskoi tsivilizatsii," *Kommunist,* 1990, no. 4, pp. 28–45.

11. On the latter point, see e.g. Georgii Shakhnazarov, "Vostok—Zapad: k voprosu o deideologizatsii mezhgosudarstvennykh otnoshenii," *Kommunist*, 1989, no. 3, pp. 67–78; Igor' Malashenko, "Interesy strany: mnimye i real'nye," *ibid.*, 1989, no. 13, pp. 114–23; Evgenii Stepanov, "Ponyatie 'interesy' vo vneshnei politike," *Problemy dal'nego vostoka*, 1990, no. 3, pp. 63–72.

12. For earlier Soviet approaches to Eastern Europe, see e.g. Sarah Terry, ed., *Soviet Policy in Eastern Europe* (New Haven: Yale University Press, 1984); Zbigniew Brzezinski, *The Soviet Bloc* (rev. ed., Cambridge, MA: Harvard University Press, 1967); also Margot Light, *The Soviet Theory of International Relations* (Wheatshead, 1988), pp. 145ff, 305ff. For a detailed account of the changing Soviet policy, see Karen Dawisha, *Eastern Europe, Gorbachev, and Reform: The Great Challenge,* Second edition (Cambridge University Press, 1990).

13. Alexander Kapto, "Priority will be given to our Relations with Socialist Countries" [summary of a conference at the Ministry of Foreign Affairs], *International Affairs* (English ed.), November 1988, p. 29.

14. Deputy Foreign Minister Ivan Aboimov, "Development of USSR Relations with the Socialist Countries," *ibid.* (English ed.), October 1988, pp. 38–39.

15. *Ibid.* (English ed.), March 1990, pp. 33–34. See also Diligensky, *op. cit.*, pp. 23–25.

16. See, e.g., Andranik Migranyan, "An Epitaph to the Brezhnev Doctrine," *Moscow News*, 1989, no. 34, p. 6; and Evgenii Ambartsumov, interview, *La Repubblica* (Rome), August 13/14, 1989.

17. Vladimir Lukin, "1989: The Crossroads of History," *Moscow News*, 1989, no. 52, p. 3. See also Evgenii Ambartsumov, "Not Agony but Turn to Life," *Moscow News*, 1989, no. 445, p. 7. For an interesting discussion of the East European experience and its possible lessons for the Soviet Union, see "Ternistyi put' k politicheskomu plyuralizmu: problemy, konflikty, perespektivy," in *Voprosy istorii KPSS*, 1990, no. 8 (August), pp. 15–25.

18. Evgenii Shashkov, "Vostochnaya Evropa—vospominaniya i realii," *Kommunist*, 1990, no. 10, pp. 113–119. See also Valerii Musatov "Peremeny v Vostochnoi Evrope i nasha perestroika," *Pravda*, May 14, 1990. Musatov was deputy chief of the International Department of the CPSU Central Committee.

19. *International Herald Tribune,* June 27, 1990.

20. *Pravda*, June 26,1990. For the charges and Shevardnadze's replies, see also *Sovetskaia Rossiia,* June 22, 1990; *Pravda*, July 5 and 11, 1990; USSR Ministry of Foreign Affairs, *Vestnik,* no. 13(71) and 14(72) (July 15 and 31, 1990). See also Shevardnadze's interview in *Argumenty i fakty*, 1990, no. 2, p. 2.

21. Paris *Libération,* September 11, 1989, p. 4.

22. The new political parties and fronts (other than the CPSU) emerging in the Soviet Union have been singularly lacking in interest in the communist world beyond the USSR, except for an occasional barbed comment about Cuba and North Korea.

23. The journal had been established in 1958, appeared as a monthly in a number of languages, and had had its editorial offices in Prague. Its internal politics, and the experience of its Soviet staff members, present an interesting topic that remains to be studied.

41 Gorbachev and German Unification: Revision of Thinking, Realignment of Power

HANNES ADOMEIT

History had decided. It has proven Stalin right in his prediction that, in the long run, it would be impossible to keep Germany down and divided. But Stalin himself failed to draw the right political lesson from his own insight. He permitted, and even actively promoted, the slide toward the division of Germany and hence the partition of Europe. Nikita Khrushchev and Leonid Brezhnev then turned this slide into deliberate policy. They attempted to transform the eastern part of Germany into an economically efficient, politically viable, and militarily effective ally. Lest it be forgotten, until the first half of the 1980's, it appeared as if their policy was and would continue to be successful.

Mikhail Gorbachev has now abandoned this policy. In fact, he has done more than abandon it. He has embarked on a course of action that is unprecedented in modern history: comprehensive withdrawal from what until recently were considered, in both the East and the West, areas of paramount strategic significance for the Soviet Union. He has accepted not only the establishment of non-communist regimes in East-Central Europe, including East Germany, but also German unification and even membership of a unified Germany in the North Atlantic Treaty Organization. ...

Certainly, there are a number of objective indications that a basic shift in the "correlation of forces" has occurred to the disadvantage of the Soviet Union. First, the power base of the Soviet Union has eroded. This development is characterized by the deterioration of economic conditions, the disintegration of the social fabric, the increase in political conflict, and the spreading of secessionism and ethnic violence. Second, the importance and global influence of the "world socialist system" (or what remains of it) has declined. This decline is indicated by the disintegration of the system's binding glue, Marxist-Leninist ideology; the withering away of the socialist system's appeal as a model of development in the Third World; the loss of power and effectiveness of its institutions, including the communist parties, the Warsaw Treaty Organization, and the Council for Economic Mutual Assistance; and the system's inability to keep up in the technological (and military-technological) competition with the Western industrialized countries. Third, Western ideas and institutions have shown themselves to be more resilient and responsive to challenges than expected. This has been demonstrated, among

many other ways, by the West's continued economic growth and technological innovation and the accelerated process of its economic integration, most notably by
the European Community's commitment to create a single, integrated market by
the end of 1992. But it is also revealed by the (re)constitution (with the exceptions
thus far of Romania and Bulgaria) of political systems in East-Central Europe
based on conservative and social-democratic principles. Fourth, West German influence in European affairs has been rising steadily since the 1960's; with the addition of East Germany to the West German state, a potentially powerful united
Germany is reemerging.

Concerning the last factor, it would be irresponsible and ahistorical for any Soviet or Russian leadership to proceed on the assumption that the consummation
of German unity will somehow spell the "end of history." With the passing of the
postwar German problem, a new chapter of history will have to be opened. Policies for coping with German power and influence will have to be designed. This
requirement is clearly dictated by the memory of several centuries of Russian and
Soviet conflict and competition with Germany—with the Teutonic Order, the
Hanseatic League, Prussia, Imperial Germany, and the Nazi Reich. Therefore,
Gorbachev has to devise a new policy, if only for domestic political reasons.

This is not to say that the future power and influence of Germany will depend
on its military strength. Indeed, it is questionable whether military power automatically enhances security and promotes political power. Among other things,
nuclear weapons have largely invalidated such propositions. Nevertheless, Soviet
civilian and military specialists, as well as traditional Marxist-Leninist and
neorealist analysts, agree on one proposition: economics, politics, and security
are still closely intertwined. They recognize that only a modern, efficient economy
can provide modern, effective armed forces; that economic decline weakens the
foundations of military power and political influence; and that economic power
ultimately translates into political power.

If one were to grant the argument that military power is destined to become
obsolete as a "currency" in the "common house" of Europe, and that a civilian
and civilized society is emerging in that geographic area, complex problems of
transition still would have to be solved. Foremost among them, Gorbachev and
his adherents would have to answer a crucial question to the satisfaction of both
benign and hostile critics at home: with the possible or projected obsolescence of
military power as the primary basis of Soviet influence in Europe, and the failure
thus far of *perestroyka*, how can the Soviet Union succeed in retaining an influential role in Europe? ...

GORBACHEV'S GERMAN POLICY, 1985–90

Gorbachev's policy on the German problem evolved on four different but interacting levels: (1) change in the Soviet Union; (2) redefinition of the Soviet–East
European relationship; (3) events in East Germany, notably the Honecker regime's refusal to embark on reform; and (4) Soviet *Westpolitik,* that is, the reor-

dering of Soviet relations with the United States and Western Europe, including West Germany. It is also useful to divide Gorbachev's German policy chronologically into three main stages.

The first stage can be said to extend roughly from March 1985 to October 1988, when Chancellor Helmut Kohl visited the Soviet Union and a return visit by Gorbachev to Bonn was arranged. In this stage, the German Democratic Republic appeared basically stable, German reunification a long way off, and Soviet–West German relations vacillated between cool and correct.

The second stage covers the interval from October 1988 to January 1990, during which time significant improvements in Soviet–West German relations occurred. These improvements, however, were at risk of being undercut by the emergence and rapid acceleration of crisis symptoms in the GDR. The collapse of the Honecker and communist successor regimes and the unification of Germany became distinct possibilities during this time, but their realization had to be delayed.

The third stage begins with Gorbachev's public acknowledgement, at the end of January 1990, that the unification of Germany was inevitable, and ends with his consent, in the name of *Realpolitik*, in mid-July 1990 to the membership of a united Germany in NATO. This period witnessed the collapse of the GDR as a socialist state and ally of the Soviet Union, renewed Soviet attempts to slow down the process of unification, a plethora of proposals on how to bind Germany in a European security framework, and, finally, the Soviet consent to Western proposals.

Stage One: Safeguarding Stability and the Status Quo. The first level, Soviet domestic affairs, had top priority in the first stage (as, indeed, it did in all three stages). The Soviet Union was to be transformed into a modern, efficient, and prosperous state. Soviet foreign policy was to be designed in such a way as to create the most advantageous framework for a fundamental reform of Soviet society, economics, and politics. Initially, however, Gorbachev seemed to believe that a second New Economic Policy could be successfully implemented. Somehow, plan and market were to be harmoniously combined. Modernization was to be achieved through "acceleration," exhortation, and discipline, including the campaign against alcoholism, as well as mobilization of hidden "reserves" in the socialist system and the "utilization of the achievements of the scientific-technological revolution." When this approach did not produce the desired results, Gorbachev proclaimed a further "radicalization" of the reform effort.

On the second level, quite in accordance with his assumptions about the likely evolution of events in the USSR, Gorbachev appears to have been genuinely convinced of the theoretical and practical possibility of a "third road" in Eastern Europe. He envisaged an evolutionary path between the neo-Stalinist, centralized, bureaucratic "socialist" system in the East, and the pluralist, social-democratic, market-oriented "capitalist" system in the West. There was, from Moscow's perspective in 1985–88, no reason for ruling out such an evolution in Poland, Czechoslovakia, Hungary, and, above all, in East Germany. The model adumbrated by Alexander Dubček in Czechoslovakia in 1968 may have loomed large in Gorbachev's mind. Indeed, it is unclear even today whether Gorbachev has given up the idea of change in the Soviet Union within a modified "socialist" framework.[1] The spring 1990 elections in Romania and Bulgaria, which returned to power communists with a refurbished "socialist" program, demonstrated that such change, rather than explosive upheaval, was in the realm of the possible.

Turning to events in the GDR, the third level in the evolution of events, the country and its regime appeared to be basically stable during this stage. A separate East German national consciousness (*Nationalbewusstsein*) may have been lacking, but there seemed to be a considerable degree of identification among East Germans with the state (*Staatsbewusstsein*). There also appeared to be no potential for revolution. Indeed, since the failure of the communist revolution in Germany in 1918–21, communists in the Soviet Union and elsewhere have often mused, in sorrow and in anger, that "you can't have a revolution in Germany because people would have to step on the lawn." The East German economy was also in good shape in comparison to the economies of its Eastern neighbors. In Moscow's view, the GDR's stability would be even further strengthened once East Germany undertook some unquestionably necessary reforms and aligned itself with the processes of *perestroyka, demokratizatsiya,* and *glasnost'* in the USSR. No need, then, artificially to raise the issue of German unity.

Gorbachev's policies at the fourth level closely corresponded with his perceptions of the GDR. Contrary to the grand fanfare about the "common house of Europe," from November 1985, when the Gorbachev-Reagan summit took place in Geneva, to October 1988, when Kohl visited Moscow, the Soviet leader concentrated on the reordering of relations with the United States. Europe played a subsidiary role in Soviet *Westpolitik,* and West Germany was given the cold shoulder. The "new page in the book of Soviet-West German relations," a phrase used several times in that period, ended up having little substance.[2] Moscow, in essence, continued its previous policy of attempting to isolate and circumvent West Germany, and presumably to "punish" it for its role in legitimizing the stationing of US medium-range nuclear missiles in Western Europe and supporting the idea of space-based strategic defense. It took one visit by the president of the Federal Republic of Germany to Moscow (July 1987), three visits by Chancellor Kohl (July 1983, March 1985, and October 1988), five by Foreign Minister Hans-Dietrich Genscher, and one by the prime ministers of Bavaria and Baden-Württemberg finally to elicit sufficient interest for Gorbachev to schedule a visit to Bonn.

How is one to explain this astonishing refusal to respond favorably to Bonn's overtures to improve relations in the period before October 1988? And how, too, can one explain the lack of content in the "European house" slogan? Gorbachev obviously realized that he faced a dilemma. If his policy of opening up the Soviet Union internally and internationally was to succeed, inclusion of the Federal Republic in the approach to the West as a whole was, of course, essential. But inclusion of the Federal Republic in wider East-West cooperation was likely to lead to greater West German penetration of the East and a reduction of Soviet influence and control in "Eastern Europe." At this stage, this was a risk that Gorbachev was willing to take.

Just how intense Moscow's reluctance was to deal with Bonn, let alone address the German problem, is indicated by Gorbachev's statements during this period. For instance, when Richard von Weizsäcker, president of the FRG, raised the issue of one "German nation" during his visit to Moscow in July 1987, Gorbachev was reported by TASS as not having wanted to "theorize" about it. In his view, only the political aspect, the existence of two German states with different socioeconomic systems was relevant. He stated that what things would look like "*in a hundred years,* history will decide." He further pointed out that one could "hear time and again" that the "German problem remains open," and that this gave rise to doubts as to whether the FRG still intended to adhere to the 1970 Moscow treaty.[3]

Similarly, when Chancellor Kohl visited Moscow in October 1988, Gorbachev complained that he had already "spoken several times about the so-called 'German problem,'" but that the matter apparently still needed clarification. "The current situation," he warned, "is the result of history. Attempts at overturning what has been created by it or to force things by an unrealistic policy are an incalculable and even dangerous endeavor."[4]

The Soviet refusal at this stage to turn to a new page on German unity could not have been stated more clearly. "History," not Gorbachev, would decide. Yet, conceptual shifts in Moscow were to steer history inexorably in the direction of German unity.

Stage Two: The New Conceptual Approach. In the period from October 1988 to January 1990 the basis for the disappearance of the GDR as a separate state was laid—both conceptually and practically. Western observers and certainly many critics in Moscow feel that the key to understanding this turn of events can be found on the first level, namely, domestic developments in the Soviet Union. In this view, the state of crisis in the Soviet Union and the tilt of the "correlation of forces" in favor of the West was such that Gorbachev had no other option but to consent to the changes of system and foreign-policy alignment of his erstwhile allies in East-Central Europe.

This argument, however, fails to take into account that, militarily, the Soviet Union was and still is a superpower. No one would have been able to force the USSR out of Eastern Europe unless the Soviet leadership itself had been inclined to change its relationship to the region. Thus, at the very least, changes in the power relationship *in conjunction with conceptual reinterpretation* ("new thinking") would seem to explain the shift in Soviet policies toward Eastern Europe and with regard to the German issue.

At the second level—that of change in East-Central Europe and Soviet relations with what used to be the "socialist community"—there are clear indications that such conceptual innovations did occur. The most important innovation is the principle of "freedom of choice."[5] First articulated at the 19th All-Union

CPSU Conference in June 1988, this principle was clarified by Gorbachev in his December 1988 speech at the United Nations. Gorbachev stated that for the Soviet Union, "the obligation of the principle of freedom of choice is above every doubt. Freedom of choice is a general principle that does not admit any exceptions."[6] In February 1989, in Kiev, Gorbachev maintained that Soviet relations with the socialist states should be based on "unconditional independence (*bezuslovnaya samostoyatel'nost'*), full equality, and strict non-intervention in internal affairs."[7] This, in turn, presupposed "responsibility of the party and government of each socialist country toward its own people."[8] In other words, the local party leaderships could no longer rely on the Brezhnev doctrine and Soviet military intervention to keep them in power. They themselves had to establish their own political legitimacy and viability.

The principle of "freedom of choice" had tremendous implications for the third level of policy, namely, relations with East Germany. A crucial question needs to be asked here. Was the Honecker regime exempted from the obligation to establish its own legitimacy and viability? Did Gorbachev disingenuously imply that "freedom of choice" should apply to the GDR state and government but *not* to the people of East Germany?

On this issue, ambiguity can quickly be dispelled. The Soviet–West German Joint Declaration, signed by Gorbachev during his visit to West Germany in June 1989, clearly spoke of the "right of all peoples and states" freely to determine their destiny.[9] It went even further by endorsing the "precedence of international law in domestic and international politics" and "unqualified respect for the norms and principles of international law, *especially respect for the right of peoples to self-determination*."[10] This wording is the international legal counterpart of "freedom of choice." As used in four decades of political and legal discussion in the Federal Republic, it referred to the holding of free elections in East Germany, which, in turn, were the precondition for the reestablishment of German unity. Any third-rate political adviser to Gorbachev, and certainly Valentin Falin, former ambassador to Bonn, head of the CPSU Central Committee's International Department, and adviser to Gorbachev on Germany, would have been able to recognize the significance of this formula. In the six months of careful preparation of the Joint Declaration, the Soviet Union certainly could have objected, if it so desired, to the inclusion of this wording in the document.

The Joint Declaration contains two other important indications of a shift in Soviet thinking on the German problem. One concerns the substitution of a single letter for another—a change in Russian from "i" to "a". The very first sentence of the document refers to the Federal Republic of Germany as *Federativnaya Respublika Germaniya* rather than *Germanii*. This alteration implies that there is only one single Germany (*Germaniya*) with a federal structure rather than two Germanys, with only one having a federal structure. This modification, too, was hardly inadvertent, since the West German foreign office had persistently attempted to get the Soviet Union to agree to it.

The second clue concerns the division of Europe. The Joint Declaration deplores the fact that the European "continent has been divided for decades" and goes on to say that both governments consider it "their paramount objective to contribute toward overcoming the division of Europe." Surely, it was obvious to everyone concerned that the division of Europe could not be overcome without ending the division of Germany.

At about the same time, the conceptual basis for the collapse of the GDR was supplemented by a practical precondition: the removal of the Berlin Wall. This was achieved for all practical purposes, beginning in May 1989, by the dismantling of the Iron Curtain in Hungary. Given the fact that Hungary refused to round up and return the ever-increasing number of East Germans who were attempting to make their way to the West through Hungary, and the fact that other East Germans were attempting to take special trains and buses to the West from the Federal Republic's embassies in Prague and Warsaw, Honecker had to decide on one of two courses of action. He could attempt to prevent the exodus by sealing the borders not just with West Berlin and West Germany but also with Czechoslovakia and Poland, that is, he could build another, even longer, wall to keep the East Germans in. Alternatively, he could try to persuade them to stay. Under the circumstances, this would have meant introducing comprehensive reform measures along Soviet, Polish, and Hungarian lines—with the obvious risk of ultimate dissolution of the GDR and merger with Federal *Germaniya*.

The dilemma facing both East Germany and the Soviet Union in the summer and fall of 1989 was, according to information received by West German intelligence, cogently summarized by Valentin Falin. In a memorandum to the Soviet leadership he is reported to have stated that one had "to be concerned about the possibility that the widely distributed dissatisfaction will, in a relatively short time—by the spring of next year at the very latest—lead to mass demonstrations which would be difficult to control."[11] Falin also reportedly noted that "the leadership of the SED is [reacting to] the exodus, for which it bears responsibility, essentially helplessly, not knowing what to do." Falin did *not* assume that an opposition movement could, in the foreseeable future, be strong enough to compel the party and government to embark on substantial reform. And even though he detected signs that Honecker had "no longer the full and complete support of the party apparatus" and that "a sense of resignation is spreading, putting in question the leading role of the party," he did not think that the party leader was likely to retire even after the SED congress scheduled for May 1990.

Falin also commented on a state of "alienation" between the CPSU and SED. Moscow had little power to exert influence on the party leadership in East Berlin—a state of affairs exacerbated by the "small reservoir of common political views" between the two. Furthermore, East Berlin had cut back on consultations with Moscow, and attempts by the Moscow leadership to induce East Berlin to embark on reforms along Soviet lines had been "harshly rejected."[12]

During his visit to the GDR in October 1989, Gorbachev again tried to exert pressure on Honecker to reconsider. He reminded the East German leader that

"Those who are late will be punished by life itself."[13] The SED party leader still refused. But at the same time he was unwilling to follow the Chinese example and, in a reenactment of Tiananmen Square, ruthlessly suppress the ever-increasing wave of demonstrations. It was not a surprise that Honecker was replaced by his own party in mid-October 1989.

It is in the logic of the Soviet conceptual shift that Soviet spokesmen at this time publicly began to talk about the possibility—not yet openly the desirability—of German unification. On October 27, 1989, Yevgeniy Primakov was quoted as saying he saw "no formidable obstacle to reunification."[14] Questioned about the recent demonstrations and other events in East Germany, an official spokesman of the CPSU Central Committee, Nikolay Shishlin, too, left open the possibility of reunification: "Nobody can predict what will happen. And I am sure that this situation should be changed and will be changed." When pressed as to how he thought the change would come about, he replied: *"By the right of choice.* Everything depends on the Germans. But it is necessary to understand our interests, not to destabilize the situation in Europe. Let us wait for a little bit, and I think that we will find a new situation."[15]

Shishlin did not directly address the issue when asked if the Berlin Wall would be dismantled. But he said, "I hope that everything will be changed. You are seeing these events in East Germany. We do understand the meaning of these events."[16] Thus, even though the Soviet leadership—as its counterparts elsewhere—did not foresee the rapidity with which "these events" were to proceed, it was, even at this stage, fully prepared to accept unity as one of the eventual outcomes of change in the GDR.

The evolution of Gorbachev's policy in "Eastern Europe" and East Germany is complemented by movement at the fourth level. In the fall of 1989, at long last, Soviet policy swung away from its fixation on the United States and brought Western Europe into sharper focus. This shift was indicated by Gorbachev's meetings with Prime Minister Ciriaco de Mita of Italy, Chancellor Franz Vranitzky of Austria, Chancellor Helmut Kohl of West Germany, and President François Mitterrand of France.

More important, however, was Gorbachev's earlier announcement, at the United Nations on December 7, 1988, of unilateral Soviet troop cuts and withdrawals. In addition to a reduction of the Soviet armed forces by 500,000 officers and men, six Soviet tank divisions were to be withdrawn from the GDR, Czechoslovakia, and Hungary. Western intelligence sources estimated that a total of 28 Soviet tank and motorized rifle divisions were then based on those countries. Along with these six divisions, 5,000 tanks and 50,000 troops, including assault-landing formations and river-crossing units, were to be withdrawn. The six divisions were to be disbanded. The 5,000 tanks were to replace older models in the western parts of the Soviet Union, where a total of 10,000 tanks were scheduled to be dismantled.

The significance of this December 1988 initiative for the evolution of Soviet policy on the German problem is difficult to overestimate. Prior to it, one could still legitimately ask whether the agreement on the abolition of intermediate-range nuclear missiles was just a variation on the policy that Leonid Brezhnev had pursued, namely, denuclearization of Europe, erosion of NATO's doctrine of "flexible response," and the separation of Western Europe from the United States. By 1989, however, it was evident that the Soviet Union was serious about making progress toward a reduction of its conventional superiority in Europe, and about limiting its capabilities for surprise attack and invasion. In addition to the announcement of unilateral troop cuts and partial withdrawals, this seriousness was demonstrated by the significant Soviet concessions at the Vienna talks on conventional force reductions in Europe (CFE).

Another facet of new security structures in Europe became visible in January 1989. In talks with his West German counterpart, Soviet Foreign Minister Shevardnadze stated that the Soviet Union had set itself the objective "to withdraw *all* of its military forces from the territories of other countries."[17] Since the bulk of these forces was made up by the Western Group of Forces (WGF), this objective clearly included withdrawal of Soviet troops from East Germany.

In light of the above, to argue that Soviet attitudes and policies on Germany evolved against a backdrop characterized by a complete lack of foresight, conceptual incompetence, and loss of control reinforced by loss of power is to seriously misrepresent the facts. Even though Gorbachev, in 1988 and 1989, did not actively promote the unification of Germany, he did in all probability consider it a possible and, for the Soviet Union, an acceptable consequence of his policy conceptions. Once unity of Germany appeared on the European political agenda, he quickly adjusted to the idea and, as will be seen, was willing to deal with it in a constructive spirit.

Stage Three: Consent to the Unification of Germany. At the Soviet-American summit conference at Malta, on December 3, 1989, Gorbachev had still asserted Moscow's traditional position on the German problem. He reiterated that "there are two German states in Europe today, the Federal Republic and the German Democratic Republic. They are members of the United Nations, sovereign states. This is the bidding of history, this is what history has willed."[18] But only a few weeks later, at a meeting with East German Prime Minister Hans Modrow in Moscow on January 30, 1990, he acknowledged that pressure was building up for German reunification. *"Time itself is having an impact on the process and lending dynamism to it."*[19] In response to a question about the possibility of reunification, Gorbachev replied:

> Basically, no one casts any doubt upon it. However, the development of events in the world, in the German Democratic Republic and in the Soviet Union, requires profound assessment and an analytical approach to a solution of an issue that is an important aspect of European and world politics.[20]

What had happened at the four levels that made the (public) shift come so quickly?

At the *first* level, the decline in Soviet power had accelerated. Five years of *perestroyka* had failed to bring about any significant modernization of the machine-tool industry or an acceleration of the rates of technological innovation. Popular support for *perestroyka* was being undermined by a deterioration in the supply of agricultural and consumer goods. Urgently required price reforms had been postponed several times, and a comprehensive economic reform package still had not been assembled. The deeply entrenched power of the economic bureaucracy and the "military-industrial complex" had not been broken. Internationally, there was lots of goodwill and some interest in economic cooperation with the Soviet Union but insufficient substantive commitment (e.g., to large-scale economic assistance and joint ventures) to promise a rapid change for the better in the economic situation.

The economic predicaments were sharpened by domestic political developments. The authority of the party was beginning to suffer; orders of party officials were increasingly being ignored. Strikes and ethnic violence were taking their economic and financial toll. Secessionism and separatism were beginning to put the very existence of the Soviet Union in question—or at least its survival in the form of a centralized state embracing all 15 republics.

All these developments affected Gorbachev's bargaining position on the German problem. Since the fate of Gorbachev and *perestroyka* were now widely being seen, in the Soviet Union and abroad, as hinging on rapid economic improvement, particularly in the supply of food and consumer goods, the Federal Republic's economic, technological, financial, managerial, and political support in the international community seemed more important than ever before.

These trends were reinforced by events at the *second* level. At the beginning of 1990, the Soviet Union was facing a fundamentally transformed political situation in Eastern Europe. The institutional framework of Soviet influence and control was being rendered illegitimate and irrelevant. East Germany, Moscow's important "strategic ally,"[21] was disintegrating as a socialist state. This will be examined below in more detail. In Poland and Czechoslovakia, Moscow's other two strategic allies in the "northern tier," the main noncommunist opposition movements, Solidarity and Civic Forum, had become the dominant political forces in their respective countries and governments. Hungary had declared itself an independent, democratic state based on democracy, pluralism, the rule of law, and a market economy. In Romania, the Ceauşescu regime had been overthrown, and in Bulgaria, the communist party was engaged in a fundamental revision of its principles and policies.

In Hungary and Czechoslovakia, the moral basis for the presence of Soviet forces was particularly tenuous. Soviet troops had been introduced, or reintroduced, in these countries in the course of military intervention and had been left there as a powerful reminder of Soviet control in East-Central Europe. Predictably, after the systemic changes in the two countries, both Prague and Budapest demanded that negotiations on the withdrawal of Soviet forces be opened. Moscow consented to the discussions and promised to withdraw its forces from both countries by June 1991. Significantly, in both cases the negotiations dealt almost exclusively with the *logistics* of the pullout. No serious effort was made by the Soviet representatives to justify leaving a residual force, other than some initial suggestions that unilateral withdrawals might adversely affect the Warsaw Pact's position at the Vienna conventional arms reduction talks.[22]

But what about the Warsaw Pact itself? Col. Gen. Nikolay F. Chervov of the Soviet General Staff announced at a meeting attended by military chiefs from the CSCE signatory states, that the Warsaw Pact would be thoroughly restructured as a result of the "fast developments in Eastern Europe with the emergence of a multiplicity of parties and with the communist parties no longer leading the states."[23] A Soviet foreign ministry participant in the meeting added that the Pact's future would be shaped by political and regional interests rather than by ideological considerations.[24]

With troops soon to be removed from Hungary and Czechoslovakia, the Soviet forces in the GDR would have been in an exposed position in terms of purely military-strategic considerations, even if no systemic change in that country took place. But once systemic change began to occur, the scales swung decisively toward their removal.

Several trends were coalescing in this final stage to make reunification of Germany and the withdrawal of Soviet forces inevitable. First and foremost, East Germany's economy had reached a critical stage of deterioration, as more and more people were leaving the country. The *Partei des Demokratischen Sozialismus* (PDS—the successor to the East German communist party, the SED) the Modrow government, and probably also some political leaders and analysts in Moscow were all still hoping that the right of unrestricted travel and emigration, combined with the prospect of comprehensive reform, would persuade East German citizens to stay in their country. This assumption turned out to be wrong.

In November 1989 alone, 133,429 East German refugees (*Übersiedler*) had registered in West Germany; this was more than a third of the total for all of 1989 (324,776 persons). In December, the rate of emigration fluctuated between 2,000 and 4,000 persons a day. In the first two weeks of January 1990, 25,550 citizens left the GDR.[25] These rates of emigration surpassed those during the previous peak period, August 1961, when the East German party chief, Walter Ulbricht, saw no other option but to close the borders and build the Berlin Wall. For a country with less than 16.6 million inhabitants as of January 1990, the exodus was a serious drain on the economy and society. In January, the GDR economics minister revealed that the budget deficit had swollen to between 5 and 6 billion East German marks, that hard-currency assets had shrunk to the equivalent of 6 to 7 billion marks; and that the net external debt had risen to 20.6 billion marks.[26] The only remedy that objectively remained was that of rapid reunification.

This objective necessity coincided with a decisive shift in mood in favor of reunification. At the first demonstration of the new year in Leipzig, in which an estimated 150,000 people participated, the calls for "socialist renewal" had practically disappeared. They were replaced by slogans such as *Deutschland, einig*

Vaterland (Germany, united Fatherland) and *SED auflösen, Deutschland vereinen* (Dissolve the SED, Unite Germany).[27] The mayor of Dresden, Wolfgang Berghofer, correctly stated that the demands for unification were providing ample "proof that, despite the emergence of two German states, the unity of the German nation has been preserved" and that "no separate national identity has evolved in the GDR."[28]

Third, the socialist successor of the communist party continued to lose power and influence in the country. Party membership was shrinking. Leading reformers, such as Berghofer and Hans-Joachim Willerding, a secretary of the Central Committee and a non-voting member of the party's Politburo, were leaving the party. Its attractiveness as an electoral force was declining. In an interview in late 1989, Prime Minister Hans Modrow had expressed the fear that the SED would win no more than 20 percent of the vote if elections were held in the GDR.[29] As it turned out, in the March 18, 1990, elections to the East German parliament (*Volkskammer*), the PDS received 16.3 percent of the vote. It thus ceased to be an important political force in the life of the country.

Fourth, the West German government and West German political parties were becoming the dominant force in the GDR. When Chancellor Kohl and Prime Minister Modrow met in Bonn, in mid-February 1990, the atmosphere and outcome of the meeting conformed to the new realities in East Germany.[30] The established political parties of the Federal Republic were closely involved in the organization, financing, and management of their sister parties in East Germany, and their leading members were actively campaigning in the March 1990 electoral campaign. As one of the members of the independent opposition movement New Forum was to remark scathingly, the various East German parties had become "absolute puppets" of their more powerful counterparts in West Germany. "They can't open a boiled egg without first calling their party chairman to ask which end."[31]

The outcome of the March 1990 elections confirmed the dominant role of Bonn and the West German political parties in East German affairs. Approximately three-fourths of the votes were cast for the Federal Republic's sister parties in the GDR. The conservative Alliance for Germany (Christian Democrats, Christian Socialists and Democratic Awakening) won almost an absolute majority of votes. In order to influence events in East Berlin, Moscow now had to deal with Bonn.

This was clearly reflected at the *fourth* level, that of Soviet relations with West Germany and the Western alliance. The Soviet Union rapidly and, for the most part, constructively responded to the new conditions. This became evident during Chancellor Kohl's visit to Moscow in mid-February 1990, which turned into an historic occasion. The German Chancellor received "unequivocal" assurances from Gorbachev that Moscow would respect the right of the two Germanys "to decide for themselves the timing and structure of their reunification."[32] Agreement was also reached on a framework of negotiations. The agreement was to be confirmed a few days later, at the "open skies" foreign ministers' conference in Ottawa. It stipulated that after the elections in the GDR and the formation of a representative East German government, the four principal World War II victors would hold a series of "two-plus-four" meetings with representatives of both German states. This formula was emphasized and clearly distinguished by Foreign Minister Genscher from a "four-plus-two" format, which could have implied that the Germanys were simply to be consulted or informed about four-power decisions.

Both Kohl and Genscher were surprised and visibly moved by the Soviet leadership's attitude toward German unification. They had braced themselves for tough bargaining, stringent conditions, and unpleasant controversy. Instead, they were met with much understanding and a cooperative spirit concerning possible ways to safeguard the security of the Soviet Union and Germany's neighbors.[33]

The Soviet leadership, however, was anxious to dispel the notion that the German problem could be resolved by the Germans alone. Soviet foreign ministry spokesman Gennadiy Gerasimov confirmed that "we have declared that the Germans themselves have to decide the question of the unification of the German nation, including its speed, dates, conditions, and provisions." But this was not the entire picture. Gerasimov also said that the German problem "does not exist in isolation but in a political, historical, geographic, and even psychological context."[34] Nevertheless, the German participants in the Moscow meeting had the distinct impression that the Soviet leadership had not made up its mind what sort of security arrangements it would like to see set up in Europe.[35]

The plethora of proposals, put forward by Moscow in the period from mid-February to mid-July 1990, are convincing evidence of its indecision. The proposals included calls, in rapid succession and often with no compatibility among them, for (1) the dissolution of the two military alliances and their replacement by permanent pan-European security structures; (2) a European-wide referendum on the international and security aspects of German unification; (3) the neutralization and demilitarization of Germany; (4) a military-political status for Germany in NATO similar to that of France; (5) continued, though modified, exercise of four-power occupation rights in Germany; (6) the formation of a center in Berlin to control all military forces in Germany; (7) membership of Germany in both NATO and the Warsaw Treaty Organization; (8) membership of the Soviet Union in NATO; and (9) membership of the Federal Republic in NATO and "associate" status for the eastern part of Germany in the Warsaw Pact.

While these proposals can be interpreted as part of a *genuine* Soviet search for new security arrangements in Europe, they can also be regarded as a tactical device. Gorbachev may have wanted to get the best possible security deal for the Soviet Union in Europe; to retain for his country a significant measure of political influence; and, perhaps most important, to provide as much time as possible for the Soviet public to adjust to new realities.

BUILDING BLOCKS OF SOVIET SECURITY
IN THE 1990's

... Answers can now be suggested concerning near- and medium-term Soviet security policy toward Germany in the form of the following propositions.

- The Soviet leadership has, for the time being at least, *abandoned traditional Soviet objectives on European security and NATO.* It no longer aims at the dissolution of NATO, and the removal of the US military presence and security guarantees from Europe. It has come to accept, perhaps reluctantly, that both NATO and the United States have an important role to play in European affairs.
- The Gorbachev leadership appears to base its revised approach on the assumption that a *united Germany will not be a significant security threat to the Soviet Union in the 1990's.* Nevertheless prudence and domestic considerations demand that safeguards be put in place. But Moscow is no longer looking to new international control machinery for the neutralization of Germany but to the existing institutions into which today's West Germany is integrated, that is, primarily the European Community and NATO.
- Consequently, *NATO membership for Germany is acceptable for the Soviet Union.* The main conditions of this acceptance were codified in the July 16, 1990, accord between Kohl and Gorbachev at the Caucasian spa of Zheleznovodsk. The accord hinges on a close interrelationship among the "two-plus-four" talks on Germany, the CFE negotiations in Vienna, confirmation of the Oder-Neisse line as the permanent border between Germany and Poland, the Soviet-German economic talks, transformation of the Warsaw Pact and NATO, and the creation of permanent institutions under CSCE auspices.
- Foremost among the *specific conditions* to be met by the West on security issues are: NATO's abandonment of the strategy of "forward defense"; prohibition of NATO forces on what is now GDR territory; limitation of the overall size of the German armed forces; significant reduction of the number of US and other foreign forces in the western part of Germany; stationing of Soviet troops in the eastern part of Germany only for a transitional period; no German access to nuclear, biological or chemical weapons; no modernization of US nuclear weapons stationed in West Germany; and (probably) removal of US nuclear weapons from German soil.

These building blocks of Soviet security vis-à-vis Germany need to be analyzed in some detail.

United States in Europe, Germany in NATO. On the issue of NATO and the US military presence on the European continent, it would be an exaggeration to speak simply of a "revision" of Soviet attitudes. Even in the Brezhnev era, there was sufficient ambiguity in Soviet policy to justify doubt as to whether the USSR was absolutely determined to remove the US presence from the continent. But whatever Brezhnev's policies may have been, with the exception of a brief interval, from March to October 1985, Gorbachev's concept of the "common house of Europe" has always included the idea that the United States and Canada not only do but also *should* play an important role in European affairs.

Leading proponents of "new thinking" have provided several rationales as to why this should be so. They have argued that there is a close and inseparable *economic* relationship between the United States and Western Europe and that the ties which bind these two entities ("centers of imperialism" in the orthodox Soviet lexicon) are objectively stronger than the issues that divide them. In *military* affairs, their reasoning is that advances in transport and communications technology have significantly reduced the geographical distance between the United States and Europe. The nuclear age and intercontinental strategic missiles have drastically shrunk the significance of the Atlantic. In security terms, America is now as close to Europe as Great Britain was at the beginning of the century. From a practical *political* perspective, even if it were desirable, the abolition of the US military presence in Europe would be impossible because American policymakers have no intention of disengaging the United States from Europe; the greater attention given to the Asia-Pacific region does not represent a substitute for US involvement in Europe but is merely supplementary. But above and beyond that, binding the United States to security responsibilities in Europe serves to preserve the mostly salutary influence of the European powers on American policy and military strategy. Finally, a withdrawal of the US forces from Europe could create fears and feelings of insecurity in some of the West European countries; such anxieties would not necessarily work in the Soviet Union's favor, because they might induce the Europeans to strengthen their defenses. In sum, participation by the United States in European security affairs had to be viewed as "logical and necessary," while the effects of a withdrawal by the US would be "destabilizing."[36]

It is on the basis of such considerations that—contrary to the time-honored rhetoric invariably contained in Warsaw Pact communiqués about the "dissolution of the blocs"—Gorbachev said to his German hosts during his June 1989 visit to Bonn:

> [the Joint Declaration] does not demand that you, or we, should renounce our uniqueness or weaken our allegiance to the alliances. On the contrary, I am confident that the adherence to [the Declaration] in our policies will serve to consolidate the contribution of each state to the creation of a peaceful European order as well as to shape a common European outlook.[37]

Similarly, after the initial indications that German unity was going to be a major issue in European security affairs, Gorbachev told the visiting French foreign minister, Roland Dumas, in mid-November 1989: "*Now is not the time to break up the established international political and economic institutions. Let them be trans-*

formed, taking into account internal processes; let them find their place in the new situation and work together."[38] Finally, reporting to the Supreme Soviet on the results of the Soviet-American summit of early June 1990, Gorbachev conceded that the two alliances would continue to exist "for longer than might be imagined."[39]

How is one to explain then the fact that, officially, the Soviet leadership continued to advocate as late as June 1990 the "dissolution of the blocs" and to *oppose membership of Germany in NATO?* To take some representative examples, in February 1990 Valentin Falin stated bluntly: "If the Western alliance sticks to its demand for a NATO membership of all of Germany, then there won't be any reunification."[40] CPSU Central Committee expert on German affairs, Nikolay Portugalov, claimed in the same month that the idea of Germany staying inside NATO was a "joke."[41] And two weeks before the Zheleznovodsk accord, Col. Gen. Nikolay F. Chervov wrote that a united Germany in NATO would be "definitely unacceptable, both politically and psychologically, to the Soviet people. It would seriously upset the military balance of strength that has developed in Europe"[42] As for Gorbachev, in an interview with *Time* magazine in June 1990, he expected "major disagreement" with President George Bush on the issue of a united Germany's membership in NATO. He rejected as "just not serious" Western arguments to the effect that in the new phase of international relations, NATO would serve the interests of the Soviet Union. For the Soviet people, he continued:

> NATO is associated with the cold war ... as an organization designed from the start to be hostile to the Soviet Union, as a force that whipped up the arms race and the danger of war. Regardless of what is being said about NATO now, for us it is *a symbol of the past, a dangerous and confrontational past.* And we will *never agree to assign to it the leading role in building a new Europe.* I want us to be understood correctly on this.[43]

Being unwilling to assign the "leading" role to NATO did not preclude the possibility that Gorbachev might be prepared to assign to it an *important* role. Apart from that, it is precisely the "symbolic" significance of NATO that explains some of the extraordinary twists and turns in the Soviet position on the issue. For four decades, NATO was portrayed by Soviet propagandists as the most dangerous and most reactionary executive committee of "imperialism." How, then, in the official image, could one suddenly change the wolf into a lamb? This was obviously difficult to do without loss of face for the Soviet leadership and party. Furthermore, some segments of the political and military leadership were, and still are, genuinely and emphatically opposed to the idea of German membership in NATO. This problem will be discussed below. Last but not least, as suggested earlier, the Soviet contortions on the issue were probably related to bargaining tactics and to the price to be asked for Germany's remaining in NATO. Similarly, the Soviet troops in Germany represented a negotiating asset. But can they be expected to play a role in the transition period until they are finally withdrawn?

Abolition of the Soviet Military Presence in Germany. When Gorbachev announced the unilateral troop cuts in December 1988, a major portion of the cuts in "Eastern Europe" was to come from the Western Group of Forces in East Germany. The WGF, as Soviet spokesmen later clarified, was to be pared down by some 36,000 troops, representing almost 75 percent of the originally projected cuts.[44] In 1989, the first year of the two-year reduction period envisaged by Gorbachev, the USSR withdrew 24,509 troops, 11,416 coming from the GDR.

At the end of 1989 and the beginning of 1990, however, the timetable for the cuts and the Soviet position at the Vienna CFE talks were put in disarray. The East German armed forces, it became evident, would soon no longer be part of the Warsaw Pact. As noted above, Hungary and Czechoslovakia had asked for the complete withdrawal of Soviet forces from their territories. With an additional commitment to withdraw 5,000 troops from Poland, the Soviet General Staff now had to work on plans to pull back not just 50,000 troops from Central Europe, but more than 150,000.

The cuts in Soviet troop levels and the withdrawals from Central Europe were bound to be difficult. The already existing severe housing shortage for Soviet military officers and non-commissioned officers was worsening and having adverse effects on morale. This author was told repeatedly in Moscow in May of this year that the housing problem made it necessary for a number of the units returning "home" to stay in tents through the winter.[45]

Housing is not the only problem. Now that the main outlines of a settlement of the international aspects of German unification have been agreed upon, a more radical reform effort in the Soviet Union appears likely. This will almost certainly entail even more extensive troop cuts, which, in turn, will create the problem of finding jobs for more demobilized troops.

When the Soviet Union halted its partial troop withdrawal from East Germany in spring 1990, it could easily have justified this move by citing technical problems. However, Soviet foreign ministry spokesman Gerasimov stated that a decision on further withdrawals from the GDR depended both on the CFE talks and on "the *political* solution of the German problem."[46] The possibility existed, therefore, that the Soviet leadership would use the remaining 364,000 troops in Germany as a means to impose its will on the "two-plus-four" talks, by invoking existing occupation rights and four-power agreements. Such a move would have made a sham of the sovereignty of a united Germany.

The Soviet leadership rejected this course of action, to repeat, not because it was forced to do so but because of its firm commitment to a comprehensive withdrawal of Soviet forces from Central Europe and its determination to come to a modus vivendi with Germany. In accordance with these political priorities, the former commander-in-chief of the Warsaw Pact armed forces, Marshal Viktor Kulikov, asserted, in late May 1990, that the partial withdrawal schedule would be met.[47] More important, at the 28th CPSU Congress, Shevardnadze explained that "it is not in our interests to drag out the resolution of the external aspects of German unity."[48] Finally, Gorbachev agreed at Zheleznovodsk that all the Soviet forces would be withdrawn from Germany "in three to four years."[49]

In addition to commitment and conceptual reorientation, there are practical political reasons counseling speedy withdrawal. As argued above, the *military* rationale for the presence of Soviet forces in the eastern part of Germany after the projected withdrawal of forces from Hungary and Czechoslovakia by June 1991 was being undercut. Their continued presence for *political* reasons would have been even more difficult. Notwithstanding Moscow's commitment to withdraw its troops, tensions and conflicts between German civilians and Soviet soldiers and their dependents have been rising.[50] There no longer is a communist government to silence open criticism of the Soviet troop presence. Attempts to hang on to outlived occupation rights would almost certainly cause even greater resentment among the Germans and, for the first time since the revolution of 1989, probably lead to widespread nationalist agitation. The damage done to a relationship yet to be built would be enormous.

Thus, the vitally important political function performed by the presence of the Soviet armed forces in Germany has come to an end after 45 years. The USSR has insisted nevertheless that the stationing costs be borne primarily by (West) Germany. In accordance with an agreement reached at the end of June 1990, the Federal Republic has consented to pay 1.25 billion Deutsche mark (US$780 million) by the end of December to defray the stationing costs, and will continue to do so in all likelihood until the completion of the troop withdrawals.[51] Somewhat euphemistically, the Zheleznovodsk agreement refers to a "transition treaty about the consequences of the introduction of the Deutsche mark in the GDR" that "shall be concluded with the Soviet Union."[52]

Finally, it seems almost certain that Moscow's allies in the Warsaw Pact would have failed to support any open-ended retention of Soviet forces and occupation rights in Germany.

Transformation of the Military Alliances. In fact, at the February 1990 "open skies" meeting of the foreign ministers of NATO and the Warsaw Pact in Ottawa, nothing was said about this topic. The meeting, however, did reveal serious differences in the Warsaw Pact. Only two foreign ministers were calling for the neutralization of Germany: Shevardnadze and East German Foreign Minister Oskar Fischel. At the mid-March 1990 Warsaw Pact foreign ministers' conference in Prague, the USSR again found itself in a minority on the issue. At the closing news conference, Czechoslovakia's foreign minister, Jiři Dienstbier, said that neutrality would be "the worst alternative."[53] Polish Foreign Minister Krzysztof Skubiszewski stated that a neutral Germany "would not be good for Europe." Neutrality would "foster some tendencies in Germany to be a great power acting on its own."[54] Only the East German foreign minister still supported his Soviet counterpart. When he was replaced a few weeks later as a result of free elections and the formation of a conservative-led government in East Berlin, the isolation of Moscow on this issue became complete.

Domestic and international politics would be less complicated for Gorbachev if the Warsaw Pact could be transformed into a viable institution. The impression of a semblance of reciprocity and equivalence existing between the two military alliances would then be maintained. Residual allegiances and commitments could also be more easily connected with the special, temporary military arrangement for the eastern part of Germany.

Moscow certainly appears willing to transform the Warsaw Pact from an instrument of Soviet domination and control to a political institution fully respecting the sovereignty of its six (without East Germany) member-states. The Soviet leadership clearly hopes that some aspect of this organization can be salvaged. It apparently bases its optimism on the idea that the "state interests" of the Warsaw Pact members have in essence remained the same. Marshal Sergey Akhromeyev put the matter as follows:

> First of all, there's the stability of the territory and state boundaries. Second, there are the economic interests of the states. After all, they've been linked for many decades. That is why the military-political alliance remains. The state interests of both alliances still remain, and the contradictions remain. And a certain quantity of arms and armed forces will remain. But what matters is that it be such a quantity which would not permit the country to start a war, even if it wanted to.[55]

Such perceptions were put to the test at two meetings of the Warsaw Pact. One was the June 7, 1990, conference of the Political Consultative Committee (PCC) in Moscow; the other was the Military Committee's gathering on June 14–15 in Strausberg, near East Berlin. Despite the differences of view (Hungary predictably taking the most radical position), the trend that emerged from the final document adopted by the PCC and statements of the participants at both meetings was unambiguous. The "character, functions, and activities of the Warsaw Pact" were (and will continue to be) thoroughly reviewed.[56] The organization is (1) to change from a political and military alliance to a political alliance with military consultation; (2) the centralized, Soviet-controlled command structure is to be abandoned, which in practice will mean that a Soviet deputy minister of defense will no longer be the Pact's commander-in-chief, and may mean that the Joint Supreme Command will be dissolved; (3) the member-states will gain control of their own national forces in accordance with the principle of full national sovereignty; and (4) as long as the Pact's multilateral institutions continue in existence, representatives of the member-states will fill positions in them by rotation.

As for national differences over the Pact, mainly because of the reconstitution of a potentially powerful Germany at its western borders, Poland more than any other country has until now remained committed to cooperation with the USSR in a thoroughly revised Pact. Thus, the Polish prime minister, Tadeusz Mazow-iecki, confirmed the validity of Akhromeyev's assessment by claiming:

> We have passed in the alliance with the Soviet Union to the state level from the ideo-logical level. But this does not mean that at the state level we do not see the impor-tance of this alliance for the problem of security for our borders."[57]

Furthermore, he has argued that Soviet troops should remain in Poland as a guar-antee because of "the German problem."[58]

Bulgaria has also supported the Soviet viewpoint. But Czechoslovakia and Hungary have insisted on speedy and complete Soviet troop withdrawals, and the Hungarian parliament has already voted to suspend Hungary's participation in the military organization of the alliance. Nevertheless, tendencies exist in Prague and in Budapest against *unilaterally* forcing the issue of a dissolution of the War-saw Pact in addition to curtailing or abolishing its supranational military func-tions. The governments of both countries are aware that the transition to new se-curity arrangements would be endangered by a collapse of the Warsaw Pact. The organization, they realize, has a role to play in conventional arms-control negoti-ations, in arms production, and in the coordination of regional military policies. But over the medium term, the Pact will probably be dissolved altogether or transformed into a merely political component of a comprehensive, all-European security system.

This seems even more likely in view of the changes in NATO. In fact, it is diffi-cult to imagine the Soviet Union's consent to a unified Germany's inclusion in NATO without an appropriate response by the Western alliance. The PCC's call for "constructive cooperation" between the two blocs and a Europe "without arti-ficial barriers and ideological hostility,"[59] found its equivalent in the declaration adopted by the summit conference of NATO leaders in London on July 6, which extended the "hand of friendship" to the countries of the East. NATO was ready, among other things, "to enhance the political component of our Alliance"; to in-tensify military contacts with "Moscow and other Central and East European cap-itals"; to field, after the conclusion of the CFE negotiations, "smaller and restruc-tured active forces"; to move "away from 'forward defense'", and to reduce its "reliance on nuclear weapons."[60] Clearly, the NATO declaration greatly facilitated Gorbachev's task of placating his domestic critics and of gaining, if not their sup-port of, then at least their acquiescence to, membership of Germany in NATO.

Curtailment of German Military Power. The prospect of the political unity of Germany immediately raised the issue of its potential *military* capabilities. In the new conditions of a reduction in the Soviet threat, none of Germany's future neighbors, east or west, could be expected to welcome the reemergence of a strong, perhaps even dominant, German army on the continent. The Soviet Union is no exception. Typical of Moscow's position was the demand, reempha-sized by Shevardnadze at the "two-plus-four" talks in East Berlin in June 1990, that any final document on the international aspects of German unification include measures to limit the size of the future German armed forces, rendering them structurally "incapable of offensive operations."[61] From Bonn's viewpoint, however, it was important that numerical constraints on the German armed forces not be imposed in the "two-plus-four" talks but be included in an overall agreement at the CFE negotiations. A limitation agreement at the "two-plus-four" talks could have been interpreted as a continuation of international control machinery and, thus, singularization of Germany in the new Europe.

The solution found at Zheleznovodsk was to have the Federal Republic government declare its willingness "to give a binding declaration in the current Vienna talks to reduce the army of a unified Germany within three to four years to a personnel strength of 370,000." This commitment was made conditional on success at the CFE talks, since the reduction of German forces would start only "when the first Vienna agreement comes into effect."[62]

In anticipation of the accord reached at Zheleznovodsk, Shevardnadze asked the delegates to the 28th Party Congress, "What is better for us? To deal with a half-million strong *Bundeswehr* of the FRG, or, say, an army half that size of a united Germany?"[63] Although Shevardnadze's figures do not quite add up,[64] the Foreign Minister did have a strong argument: the overall reductions do amount to a significant constraint on Germany's conventional capabilities.

Furthermore, the future military potential of Germany, and of NATO on German soil, was limited by Chancellor Kohl's assurances that, for the transitional period when Soviet forces remain in eastern Germany, only units of German territorial defense would be stationed there. Moreover, even after the withdrawal of Soviet forces, no nuclear weapons or foreign troops would be stationed in the eastern part of Germany.[65]

If for the Soviet theoreticians and practitioners brought up on the "correlation of forces" credo these were still insufficient guarantees against the reemergence of a German military threat, there was yet another, crucially important safeguard. A terse, matter-of-fact statement in the Zheleznovodsk agreement codified that "A unified Germany will *refrain from producing, owning, or controlling atomic, biological, and chemical weapons,* and will continue to adhere to the Nuclear Non-Proliferation Treaty."[66]

The last constraint can, in fact, be considered the ultimate reassurance. With its panoply of nuclear weapons—battlefield, tactical, and strategic—the Soviet Union will remain a superpower in Europe. Germany will have nothing to match it. In addition, current sentiment in both the Federal Republic and in East Germany is to get rid of all nuclear weapons on German territory, above all, the battlefield nuclear weapons (which could be used on German soil), and in all likelihood also the modernized, longer-range tactical air-to-surface missiles currently under discussion in NATO.

This ultimate reassurance will, of course, not be mentioned publicly in the Soviet Union. Reliance on nuclear weapons for security blatantly contradicts the "new thinking" and, more specifically, Gorbachev's ambitious program for ridding mankind of the scourge of nuclear weapons by the year 2000. In private conversation, however, the ultimate weapon will frankly be acknowledged as the supreme safeguard of Soviet security. Prohibition of German access to nuclear weapons was one inalienable precondition of the Soviet consent to German unification. Another was renunciation by Germany of any territorial claims in the east.

Territorial Issues: Finality of the Oder-Neisse Border. Under the Potsdam agreement, "Königsberg and the adjacent area," i.e., the northern part of East Prussia (today the Kaliningrad oblast and Klaipéda, the latter now a bone of contention between Lithuania and the Soviet Union) were transferred to the Soviet Union. Even though the transfer was defined as provisional—pending "the final determination of territorial questions at the peace settlement"—the signatories also committed themselves "in principle ... to the *ultimate transfer*" of these territories (section VI of the protocol). No such commitment existed in the section dealing with Poland. The German territories, extending from the Baltic (including Danzig) in the north to Czechoslovakia in the south, and from the Soviet portions of East Prussia in the northeast to the Oder and Neisse rivers in the west, were only provisionally placed under the control of the Polish state (section IX of the protocol).

As for Soviet-German territorial issues, they did not really play much of a role in the negotiating process over the unification of Germany. There was nothing to discuss; new realities had been created since the expulsion of the German population and over the subsequent 46 years of Russian settlement. But even though such new realities had also been created in the formerly German areas "under Polish administration," and despite the close interconnectedness of all the eastern border issues (Stalin had compensated Poland for territorial losses in the east with gains in the west), there was considerable Polish sensitivity on the problem.

On the surface, there was not much reason for concern. The GDR had recognized the finality of the East German-Polish border in the Görlitz treaty in 1950. The Federal Republic had reaffirmed, in the Warsaw treaty of December 1970, "the inviolability of the existing frontiers now and in the future," and in the same treaty, the two countries had declared that "they have no territorial claims whatsoever against each other and that they will not assert such claims in the future."[67]

What remained was only Bonn's legalistic argument that (1) "Germany continued to exist as a legal entity in the borders of 1937" and that (2) prior to the establishment of the parliament of a united Germany, neither the Federal Republic nor the GDR could legally act in its name. What the parliaments in Bonn and East Berlin could do, however, was to give pledges that they would settle the border issue in accordance with the provisions of the Görlitz and Warsaw treaties. This they did in March and April 1990 respectively. Such assurances were also made part of the June 1990 treaty on German economic and social union; of the Zheleznovodsk agreement, which states that the unification of Germany "encompasses the Federal Republic, the GDR, and Berlin"; and, one day later, of the "two-plus-five" talks (with Poland included), which specified that the parliament of a united Germany will confirm the Oder-Neisse border with Poland "in the shortest possible time" after unification and remove from its laws any language suggesting that the border is provisional.[68]

Important as legal issues may be, the main reasons for Polish sensitivity are political and economic. They flow from the sheer size of the territories ceded by Germany, the significant number of the German expellees from these territories and their potential or actual political influence in the Federal Republic and the geographical proximity of a strong and powerful Germany to Poland. But there is also the fact that Poles and Germans are probably the least reconciled of all the antagonists of World War II.

Prejudices run deep: *polnische Wirtschaft* in Germany predates the war as a derogatory term for laziness, shoddy workmanship, and inefficiency in economic affairs. West Germans assert that successive Polish communist regimes (and the Soviet Union) have deliberately kept anti-German sentiment alive to justify Poland's allegiance to Moscow. They resent the influx of Poles into Germany under the false premises of being "ethnic German" and "asylum-seekers,"[69] and their allegedly ubiquitous presence in Berlin and East Germany as "black marketeers." And they charge that minority rights are denied to those Germans in Poland who are truly of German origin and want to retain their cultural identity.

Poles, by contrast, remember the partitions of their country among Imperial Germany and Russia (and Austria-Hungary), and between Nazi Germany and Soviet Russia. They have not forgotten Hitler's systematic attempt to eradicate the Polish intellectual, economic, military, and political elite so as to ensure long-term German domination of the country. They are unsure of the current loyalty of the German minority. They consider the German refusal to pay reparations and even compensation for the suffering of hundreds of thousands of Poles in German concentration and labor camps morally reprehensible. And while looking to German financial and economic assistance to rebuild their economy, they are also concerned about German economic power and Polish dependency.

Such complexities in German-Polish relations are matched by those found in relations between the Soviet Union and Germany.

SOVIET-GERMAN POLITICAL
AND ECONOMIC RELATIONS

It would be missing the point entirely if one were to focus exclusively on the elaborate technical machinery and on the constraints, guarantees, limitations, and safeguards that constitute the building blocks of Soviet security. The essence of the Soviet approach is a comprehensively revised conception of security. The "common interests of mankind" are to take precedence over "class struggle." "Dialogue, cooperation, and interaction," Shevardnadze told the delegates to the 28th Party Congress, "allow both ourselves and others to approach boldly a reevaluation of priorities in domestic and external policy, to give preference to peaceful needs and joint endeavors in resolving increasingly acute global problems."[70]

A vision of partnership and close interaction with Germany clearly emerges from the new images evoked by top Soviet leaders. At the press conference with Chancellor Kohl at Zheleznovodsk, Gorbachev spoke of the "great German people" (*velikiy nemetskiy narod*) and Foreign Minister Shevardnadze, at the 28th Party Congress, similarly referred to the Germans as a "great nation" (*velikaya natsiya*). He also called for cooperation "on a broad, large scale of mutual advantage with a united Germany, both in politics and economics, and in all other spheres."[71] ...

NOTES

ABOUT THE AUTHOR: **Hannes Adomeit** is associate professor of international politics at the Fletcher School of Law and Diplomacy, Tufts University.

1. See, for instance, Gorbachev's frequent attacks on Boris Yel'tsin for allegedly wanting to abandon socialism. Earlier, in a speech in Kiev in February 1989, Gorbachev had said that the goal of *perestroyka* in the Soviet Union was to "reveal the human face of socialism." See Pravda (Moscow), Feb. 24, 1989.

2. The metaphor was used for the first time by Gorbachev when West Germany's foreign minister, Hans-Dietrich Genscher, visited Moscow in July 1986. *Frankfurter Allgemeine Zeitung* (Frankfurt-am-Main), July 22,1986. For a detailed treatment of Gorbachev's failure to respond to West German overtures, see the article series by Hannes Adomeit, "Gorbachev's *Westpolitik:* 'The Common European House' or an Atlantic Orientation?" *Osteuropa* (Stuttgart), Nos. 6, 9, 12, 1988.

3. *Pravda*, July 8, 1987 (emphasis added—H.A.).

4. In a dinner speech on Oct. 24, 1988. See ibid., Oct. 25, 1988.

5. As Soviet theoreticians have correctly emphasized, "the principles of new political thinking, including that of freedom of choice, are incompatible with the concept of class struggle." See E. Pozdniakov, *New Political Thinking and International Relations,* Moscow, Allied Publishers, 1989, p. 25.

6. *Pravda*, Dec. 8, 1988.

7. Ibid., Feb. 24, 1989.

8. Ibid.

9. *Izvestiya* (Moscow), June 15, 1989.

10. Ibid. (emphasis added—H.A.).

11. Report by the intelligence agency of the Federal Republic (BND), as quoted in "Moscow Fears Uprising in the GDR," *Die Welt* (Hamburg), Sept. 15, 1989. The BND report reflects information received as of Aug. 16, 1989. The report did not contain the precise date or circumstances of Falin's assessment.

12. Ibid. Indirect confirmation of this state of affairs was provided in a meeting between the top Soviet and East German party officials in Moscow on Feb. 2, 1990. The SED/PDS delegation was led by its party chairman, Gregor Gysi; Soviet participants included Aleksandr Yakovlev and Valentin Falin. According to Gysi, as reported by the East German party newspaper, the participants noted that "after 1985, the relationship between the leaderships of the CPSU and the SED showed ever more irritations"—a situation for which "the previous SED leadership was clearly responsible." See "Gorbachev and Gysi in Moscow: A New Beginning in Relations with the CPSU," *Neues Deutschland* (East Berlin), Feb. 3–4, 1990.

13. Gorbachev in a private meeting with Honecker on Oct. 7, 1989, as quoted by an official Soviet spokesman. See also the confirmation of this warning by Soviet foreign ministry spokesman, Gennadiy Gerasimov, Radio DDR II (in German), Oct. 19, 1989. In a recent interview, a former member of the East German Politburo, Günther Schabowski, claimed that Gorbachev did not put pressure on Honecker (see Serge Schmemann, "A Wistful Glance Back at When the Wall Fell," *The New York Times,* Oct. 17, 1989). However, such pressure referred to the East German leader's possible resignation, not to the introduction of reforms in the GDR.

14. Yevgeniy Primakov, chairman of the Council of the Union, the upper chamber of the USSR Supreme Soviet, and at the time a candidate member of the Politburo (previously head of the World Economics and International Relations Institute [IMEMO]), speaking at the Brookings Institution, quoted in ibid., Oct. 28, 1989.

15. Shishlin speaking on the ABC news program, "This Week With David Brinkley," Oct. 29, 1989 (emphasis added—H.A.).

16. Ibid.

17. On Jan. 18, 1989, in Vienna during a CSCE human rights meeting, quoted in *Süddeutsche Zeitung* (Munich), Jan. 20, 1989 (emphasis added—H.A.).

18. Joint news conference with president George Bush, transcript provided by Federal News Service, Dec. 4, 1989.

19. TASS report (in Russian), Jan. 30, 1990.

20. Ibid. The question was put by an East German television reporter; see also Francis X. Clines, "Gorbachev Sees a German Union But Warns of 'Chaos of Nihillism,'" *The New York Times,* Jan. 31, 1990.

21. Soviet foreign ministry spokesman, Gennadiy Gerasimov, at a press briefing in Moscow after the opening of the Berlin Wall; as quoted by Esther B. Fein, "The Kremlin Reacts Calmly, But Says Border Must Stay," ibid., Nov. 11, 1989, and David Remnick, "Soviets Warn Against Reunification," *The Washington Post,* Nov. 11, 1989.

22. See Douglas L. Clarke, "Soviet Troop Withdrawals from East Europe," Radio Free Europe Research, *Report on Eastern Europe* (Munich), Mar. 30, 1990, pp. 41–46.

23. Alan Riding, "Russians, at Conference, See Broad Changes in Warsaw Pact," *The New York Times,* Jan. 18, 1990.

24. Ibid.

25. According to official figures of the Federal Republic's Ministry of the Interior, as reported in various issues of the *bulletin des Presse-und Informationsamts der Bundesregierung* (Bonn), 1989 and 1990.

26. Christa Luft, at the round-table talks in East Berlin; as broadcast on East German Television evening news, Jan. 3, 1990.

27. Deutsche Welle (Cologne), Jan. 9, 1990.

28. To the Dresden city parliament, as broadcast on East German Television evening news, Jan. 25, 1990.

29. *Der Spiegel* (Hamburg), Dec. 1, 1989.

30. The East German head of government and his delegation of 17 cabinet ministers were met at the airport by low-ranking protocol officials. Delegation members, after their return to East Berlin, complained that the attitude of their West German counterparts had been disdainful, condescending, and high-handed (as reported in *Neues Deutschland,* Feb. 13 and 14, 1990). The FRG government refrained from providing the scale of economic assistance that the Modrow government had requested. It evidently preferred to support the government that was to emerge from the March 1990 elections.

31. Interview with Sebastian Pflugbeil, as quoted by Henry Kamm, "Some East Germans See Their Hopes Eclipsed by Bonn's Ascendancy," *The New York Times*, Jan. 28, 1990.

32. Statement on Feb. 10,1990, by Chancellor Kohl in Moscow, as quoted in *Süddeutsche Zeitung*, Feb. 12, 1990.

33. Interviews conducted by the author in May 1990 at the foreign office in Bonn.

34. Press conference in Moscow, reported by DPA (West German news agency) from Moscow in German, Feb. 12, 1990.

35. Udo Bergdoll and Bernhard Küppers. "The Small Miracle of Moscow," *Süddeutsche Zeitung*, Feb. 12, 1990.

36. These arguments have been made, inter alia, by Sergey Karaganov. See his "America in the Common European Home," *Moskovskiye Novosti*, Nov. 13, 1988; and his statements at a conference held at the Center for European Policy Studies (CEPS) in Brussels, quoted in *Süddeutsche Zeitung*, Nov. 25, 1988, and at the 86th round of the Bergedorfer Gesprächskreis, in *Das Gemeinsame europäische Haus aus der Sicht der Sowjetunion und der Bundesrepublik Deutschland* (The Common House of Europe from the Perspective of the Soviet Union and the Federal Republic of Germany), protocol of the 86th round of talks of the Bergedorfer Gesprächskreis, held in Bonn-Bad Godesberg, Dec. 3–4, 1988, Hamburg, Körber Stiftung, 1989, p. 78. Similar or identical views on these issues have been advanced by Yuriy Davydov, "The Soviet Vision of a Common European House," paper delivered to the International Studies Conference (ISA) in London, Mar. 29–Apr. 1, 1989, (unpubl.), and by V. G. Baranovskiy, *Zapadnaya Evropa: voyenno-politicheskaya integratsiya* (Western Europe: Military-Political Integration), Moscow, Mezhdunarodnyye otnosheniya, 1988, pp. 180–84.

37. "M. S. Gorbachev's Visit to the FRG. Speech of M. S. Gorbachev," *Pravda*, June 13, 1989.

38. Bill Keller, "Gorbachev Urges West to Show Restraint on Turmoil in Eastern Europe," *The New York Times*, Nov. 15, 1989 (emphasis added—H.A.).

39. "M. S. Gorbachev's Speech at the Third Session of the USSR Supreme Soviet," *Pravda*, June 13, 1990.

40. Interview with the Saarländische Rundfunk, the Saar state *(Land)* radio, quoted in "German Ties to NATO Opposed," *The Boston Globe*, Sunday, Feb. 18, 1990.

41. *The Economist* (London), Feb. 10, 1990, p. 49.

42. Col. Gen. Nikolay Chervov, "United Germany Should Not Be NATO Member," *Svenska Dagbladet* (Stockholm), July 1, 1990, translated in Foreign Broadcast Information Service, Daily Report: Soviet Union (Washington, DC—hereafter, *FBIS-SOV*), July 5, 1990, pp. 4–5.

43. *Time* (New York), June 4, 1990 (emphasis added—H.A.).

44. This account of the size and role of the WGF draws on Douglas L. Clarke, "Soviets Halt Troop Pullout from East Germany," Radio Free Europe Research, *Report on Eastern Europe*, June 1, 1990, pp. 28–30.

45. See also Stephen Foye, "Soviet Armed Forces Face Housing Crisis," Radio Liberty, *Report on the USSR* (Munich), Mar. 30, 1990, pp. 5–7.

46. Tass (in Russian), May 17, 1990.

47. In an interview with *Der Standard* (Vienna), Kulikov claimed that the troop withdrawals had been held up because of difficulties in reintegrating the officers and men in the Soviet Union. However, he stated that the USSR had committed itself to the withdrawal of 22,000 troops by July 1 and it would meet this deadline. Thus far, 11,620 soldiers had returned to the USSR; quoted in *Berliner Zeitung* (East Berlin), May 31, 1990.

48. "Reports of Members and Candidate Members of the Politburo, and Secretaries of the CC of the CPSU, E. A. Shevardnadze," *Pravda,* July 5, 1990.

49. "Press conference of M. S. Gorbachev and H. Kohl," ibid., July 18, 1990.

50. See the extensive report in *Der Spiegel,* July 16, 1990, pp. 28–36; see also Craig W. Whitney, "Germans Who Want Russians Out vs. the Russians Who Want to Stay," *The New York Times,* July 31, 1990.

51. "Moscow Receives 1.25 Billion Deutsche Mark for Troops in the GDR," *Frankfurter Allgemeine Zeitung,* June 30, 1990.

52. *Pravda,* July 18, 1990.

53. Celestine Bohlen, "Warsaw Alliance Split on Germany," *The New York Times,* Mar. 18, 1990.

54. Ibid.

55. Interview with Bill Keller, "Gorbachev's Hope for Future: A Common European Home," ibid., Nov. 30, 1989. Marshal Sergey F. Akhromeyev is a former chief of staff of the Soviet armed forces and currently an adviser to Gorbachev on arms control issues. He is also a member of the USSR Supreme Soviet.

56. According to the text of the final communiqué of the Political Consultative Committee meeting, *Pravda,* June 8, 1990.

57. At a news conference in Warsaw, Associated Press, Feb. 21, 1990.

58. Ibid.

59. Communiqué of the PCC's Moscow meeting, *Pravda,* June 8, 1990.

60. Text of the London declaration of NATO, *The New York Times,* July 7, 1990.

61. Quoted by Serge Schmemann, "Shevardnadze Seeks Curbs on Forces in New Germany," ibid., June 23, 1990.

62. *Pravda,* July 18, 1990. "Army" in the accord clearly refers to all the three services, that is, to the total armed forces.

63. Ibid., July 5, 1990. "To have against us" a half-million strong *Bundeswehr* is the FBIS translation of this portion of Shevardnadze's speech on Soviet central television. The translation implies an adversarial relationship (see *FBIS-SOV,* Supplement: *28th Party Congress,* July 5, 1990, p. 9). The *Pravda* version of *imet' delo* (have to deal with), however, does not convey such an adversarial impression.

64. The size of the West German armed forces alone, at present, amounts to about 494,000 men, and the combined total of the armed forces of the two Germanys (discounting that the numerical strength of the East German *Volksarmee* has withered) would be 667,700. The 370,000 men for the future *Bundeswehr* are equivalent to about 55 percent of this total. At the joint press conference of the leaders of the Federal Republic and the Soviet Union, Gorbachev stated that the leadership of the FRG had committed itself to cutting the future size of the *Bundeswehr* "by almost half—42–45 percent—of the combined current number of the army of the two German states." Pravda, luly 18, 1990.

65. Ibid.

66. Ibid., (emphasis added—H.A.). The German term *Verfügungsgewalt* and the Russian *rasporyazheniye* are best translated in this context as "control."

67. *The Treaty between the Federal Republic of Germany and the People's Republic of Poland,* Bonn, Press and Information Office of the Federal Government, 1971, p. 8.

68. *The New York Times,* July 18, 1990.

69. About 200,000 Poles emigrated to West Germany in 1988; more than 250,000 emigrated in 1989. More than 1 million Polish citizens visit West Germany each year, many of whom are working there illegally in order to earn hard currency.

70. *Pravda*, July 5, 1990.
71. Ibid.

42 The USSR and the Third World in the 1980's

DAVID E. ALBRIGHT

Virtually all Western analysts today agree that Soviet policy toward the Third World has changed during the 1980's, but they differ widely in their assessments of the extent and meaning of the policy shifts. One group argues that although Moscow's policy has undergone some modification, the Soviet approach to the Third World remains fundamentally the same as before. However, members of this group disagree as to which factors explain this perceived continuity. Some trace it back to tsarist policies that have been reinforced in the Soviet era.[1] Others view it as the product of lingering ideological commitments on the part of the Soviet elite.[2] Still others see it in terms of recurrent patterns of Soviet behavior toward developing areas.[3]

A second group asserts that the alterations in Soviet policy reflect a basic change in the Soviet approach to the Third World, yet there is also no unanimity within this group about the reasons for the shift. Some maintain that it has resulted from the declining impact of ideology on Soviet perceptions of the Third World.[4] Others contend that it has stemmed essentially from domestic considerations—particularly the need to improve the performance of the USSR's economy.[5]

In addressing these issues, however, analysts tend to ignore some major new developments. In the last decade, the number of distinct Soviet schools of thought about what policy the USSR should pursue toward the Third World has multiplied significantly. The top Soviet leadership, in contrast with earlier periods, has not endorsed a single school of thought exclusively. Finally, the USSR's behavior in the Third World has combined elements of the policy prescriptions of all of the contending schools of persuasion, and the mix has varied substantially from region to region. Each of these developments, it should be stressed, antedates Mikhail Gorbachev's advent to power.

These changes have important implications. Moreover, these implications relate not just to the nature of policy but to the nature of policy formulation as well.

The present article will examine these changes and their likely bearing on future Soviet Third World policy.

CONTENDING POLICY VIEWPOINTS

Controversy in the USSR over policy toward the Third World is nothing new. It has prevailed almost constantly within the Soviet hierarchy since the early 1960's, as a result of differing assessments of circumstances in the Third World. However, prior to the early 1980's, the debate had never involved more than two perspectives on the issue at any given juncture. From about 1962 through the mid-1960's, for example, arguments over policy had focused on the merits of two alternative approaches to trying to expand the USSR's presence and role in the Third World.[6]

Proponents of the first approach held that at least some "bourgeois-nationalist" leaders in the Third World were undergoing radicalization. Not only did these leaders exhibit increased interest in Marxism-Leninism, according to the assessment, but they were also carrying out significant "progressive" reforms in their countries. Therefore, the USSR should enter into close alliances with the states under the rule of such leaders and serve as these leaders' revolutionary mentor. That is, it should help them deepen their understanding of "true" socialism and the measures required to achieve it.

Supporters of the second approach maintained that these leaders, despite their "progressive" attributes, would probably never preside over "real" socialist transformations of their countries. Consequently, the USSR should, while taking advantage of the openings that such leaders offered for enhancing its position in the Third World, pursue a policy of both "alliance" and "struggle" with them and their governments. Specifically, it should cooperate with the leaders to the extent possible in foreign affairs, but it should encourage leftist elements in the countries under the control of these leaders to try to increase their own influence in state affairs and bring about further radicalization of local situations.

By the early 1980's, however, the number of contending Soviet visions of what policy the USSR should follow with respect to the Third World had expanded to four and the ensuing years have witnessed no reduction in that total. These visions have entailed often conflicting judgments about what entities should be the USSR's primary targets of interest, what sort of relationships Moscow should attempt to establish with these entities, what means it should employ to forge such links, and what posture it should strike toward the West in the Third World. As in the preceding years, the views have flowed from contrasting perceptions of conditions in the Third World.

To refer to these policy outlooks, it is useful to have short-hand designations. Thus, the analysis here will label them the "revolutionary-democratic" school, the "pro-military" school, the "national-capitalism" school, and the "economic-interdependence" school.

The "Revolutionary-Democratic" School. Adherents of this perspective insist that a gradual process of radicalization is taking place in Third World areas: these areas, despite some zigs and zags, are bypassing capitalism and advancing directly toward socialism. In the eyes of these individuals, not only have the ranks of Third World "socialist-oriented" states—and particularly the most radical of them, the "revolutionary democracies"—grown over time, but in some "revolutionary democracies" such as the People's Democratic Republic of Yemen, Angola, Mozambique, and Ethiopia, ruling parties of a "new" or "vanguard" type have emerged. As the revolutionary process in the Third World deepens, the estimate goes, the number of "revolutionary democracies" will continue to increase, the circle of "vanguard" parties will expand, and at least some of these parties will transform themselves into full-fledged communist parties.

Partisans of this line do admit that even existing "revolutionary-democratic" regimes with "vanguard" parties have severe faults, and they acknowledge that it is impossible to rule out a reversal of course in all cases. Nonetheless, they still maintain that the Third World is marching inexorably toward socialism and will avoid capitalism. Therefore, they hold that "socialist-oriented," and especially "revolutionary-democratic," governments—however deficient—are the wave of the future and the best available allies for the USSR in the Third World at present.

In keeping with the stress on ties with "revolutionary-democratic" regimes, this school of persuasion urges that the USSR try to build long-term structural relationships with the states that these regimes run. Here proponents of the outlook have in mind joint collaboration in constructing institutions that will enable these regimes to entrench themselves in power. This includes cooperation in building a party apparatus, in establishing or strengthening intelligence and security services, in training military personnel, and the like.

As for instruments, advocates of this viewpoint lean toward reliance on nonmilitary tools. They do not, to be sure, reject military means. Indeed, they have approved Soviet use of military force to ensure the survival of "revolutionary-democratic" governments run by "vanguard" parties, and they have recognized the role of military assistance in the development of close Soviet ties with such regimes. Yet their specific vision of a long-term structural relationship with these governments implicitly pushes them toward stress on nonmilitary instruments, especially political ones.

With respect to posture toward the West in the Third World, backers of this perspective have on occasion evinced readiness to risk confrontation with the West where ruling "revolutionary-democratic" parties of a "vanguard" type have been concerned, but that willingness has declined noticeably over the course of the 1980's. Furthermore, adherents of the school have always discouraged military confrontation with the West in the Third World. Nevertheless, the group has appeared to foresee that Soviet relations with the West in the Third World will inevitably be contentious in nature.

. . .

The "Pro-Military" School. Exponents of this viewpoint emphasize the high percentage of Third World states under military rule, or at least dominated by military elements, and they contend that a substantial number of these military

governments evince a resolve to effect major social transformations in the countries that they run and a willingness to enter into close relations with the USSR. In
light of such factors, the group concludes that the USSR should devote its energies
principally to military-controlled states—especially those with "progressive" regimes.

These Soviet observers do concede that, in the abstract, a "vanguard" party
might constitute a more satisfactory vehicle for carrying out social change and a
more reliable ally for the USSR than military leaderships do, but they point out
that "vanguard" parties have not yet taken shape in most Third World countries
under military domination. Nor does this situation appear to them likely to
change in the years immediately ahead, for many militaries in power in the Third
World see "vanguard" parties as potential competitors for political authority.
Even where militaries have tolerated the formation of "vanguard" parties, the
champions of this perspective assert, the armed forces remain the key institutions
shaping the destinies of their countries. If they decide to act in opposition to local
"vanguard" parties or to do away with such parties altogether, these parties do
not have the mass base and the access to instruments of violence required to meet
such challenges effectively. Hence, those committed to this outlook submit that
ties with Third World militaries, and particularly radical militaries, afford the
USSR the best openings available to advance the revolutionary process in the
Third World and improve the Soviet position there.

...

The "National-Capitalism" School. According to adherents of this school, the
vast majority of Third World states have now chosen the path of development
that they intend to pursue, and the bulk of them have opted for a capitalist, or at
least a nonsocialist, path. Thus, the analysis goes, most Third World countries will
probably pass through a capitalist or non-socialist phase of development before
embarking on a socialist course. This prospect means that "socialist-oriented"
countries will in all likelihood remain in the minority in the Third World for the
indefinite future.

Furthermore, the group argues, the states that have adopted a "socialist orientation" have disturbing faults. Even the most "progressive" of these states—the
"revolutionary democracies" with "vanguard" parties—have displayed a less than
steadfast desire to implement far-reaching social transformations internally and
have vacillated in their foreign policies. As a result, they have substantial deficiencies as Soviet allies.

...

Advocates of this perspective believe that the USSR has little chance of constructing long-term structural links with the great bulk of the states that they consider the prime targets for courtship. And these Soviet analysts accept the probability that over time there will be divergences of interests between the USSR and
many of the countries that they pinpoint for attention. Nevertheless, as they see
things, eclecticism in defining potential allies will tend to offset this difficulty, for

profitable relations with a large and varied circle of states will reduce the impact that a setback in any one of these states can have on overall Soviet fortunes in the Third World. ...

The "Economic-Interdependence" School. Partisans of this viewpoint note that most countries in the Third World, whether they be "capitalist-oriented" or "socialist-oriented," have to date chalked up poor records of economic performance. Not only have they been slipping farther and farther behind the advanced industrial powers, but they have also failed to achieve significant economic growth in absolute terms. Even those states that have done reasonably well economically have encountered difficulties of one sort or another—soaring debts, depressed demand for exports, and so on. Thus, according to this group's assessment, leaders of these diverse countries are seeking ways to improve their local economic situations.

This search, backers of the perspective contend, opens up new opportunities for the USSR to broaden its relations in the Third World, for even the top economic performers among "capitalist-oriented" states are prepared to intensify their dealings with the USSR substantially to further economic development. Moreover, endorsers of the line insist, the USSR has the wherewithal to take advantage of these opportunities. To be sure, the USSR has economic troubles of its own, and it does not possess the resources to solve the economic problems of Third World countries. But these deficiencies do not really matter. The only way of overcoming Third World economic woes anyway is through the working out of a coherent world system of economic interdependence. Within such a system, these Soviet observers maintain, the USSR could play a key part that would enable it to build up ties with a broad spectrum of states.

...

As for the stance toward the West in the Third World, exponents of this policy approach favor a less conflictual posture than do adherents of any of the other schools of thought. The group appears to assume that competition between the USSR and the Western powers will continue in the Third World, but it does not foresee that this competition will inevitably result in military clashes or even political strife. On the contrary, it entertains the possibility of Soviet-Western cooperation in certain situations. For instance, it sanctions close Soviet trade relations with the West, and it contemplates that both the West and the USSR will purchase the minerals and raw materials that Third World states will have to sell as these states attempt to develop economically.

...

STANCE OF THE TOP LEADERSHIP

Up to the early 1980's, the top Soviet leadership had invariably singled out for broad official endorsement one of the positions articulated during periods of controversy over the USSR's Third World policy. ...

But by the early 1980's, the top Soviet leadership had ceased to uphold any single school of persuasion as official Third World policy. General Secretary Brezhnev's political report to the 26th CPSU Congress in February 1981 was indicative. It contained features that reflected aspects of at least three of the perspectives detailed above.[18]

...

Gorbachev's elevation to CPSU general secretary has brought proliferating evidence that no school of thought about Third World policy can claim exclusive top-level support. Gorbachev's discussion of the Third World in his book *Perestroika: New Thinking for Our Country and the World*—comments that represent his most extensive and personal public statement about the Third World to date—is especially revealing in this regard.[20]

In this discussion, the General Secretary shied away from broad references to "socialist-oriented" states, to "revolutionary democracies," and to "revolutionary-democratic" parties of a "vanguard" sort, but he wrote at fair length about a number of the entities that normally show up on the lists set forth by partisans of the "revolutionary-democratic" line. For instance, he declared that "we fully appreciate the formidable tasks facing progressive regimes in Africa." Through "economic and financial means" and even "by resorting to arms," imperialism "is out to retain" the positions that it acquired in African countries during the colonial era. However, he stated, the "progressive" regimes there "are determined to pursue a course toward consolidating gains." For "these efforts and these policies" he expressed firm Soviet backing, and he went on to underscore that "our country has always acted, and will continue to act, in support of the national liberation struggle of African nations."

With regard to Nicaragua, he charged the United States with pursuing "an undeclared war against a small country whose only 'fault' is that it wants to live its own way, without interference from the outside." In addition, he contended that the Nicaraguan revolution had come about in the first place because of "unbearable conditions" there that the United States had created by treating all of Central America as its "backyard." The USSR, he concluded, "sympathized" with "the liberation movements of peoples fighting for social justice," and it believed that "if the United States left Nicaragua in peace, this would be better for the US itself, for the Latin Americans, and for the rest of the world."

Consistent with the "economic-interdependence" perspective, Gorbachev pointed to "the growing tendency towards interdependence of the states of the world community." This tendency, he asserted, produces "global issues" which "become vital to the destinies of civilization" and require solutions "in the framework of the world community." Among the specific issues that he cited was the economic development of Third World states.

Such development, the General Secretary emphasized, did not threaten "traditional links between the United States and Western Europe, on the one hand, and developing countries on the other." He acknowledged "how important the Middle East, Asia, Latin America, other Third World regions, and also South Africa are for American and West European economies, in particular as raw material sources," and stated that "to cut these links is the last thing we want to do, and we have no desire to provoke ruptures in historically formed, mutual economic interests."

In consonance with the "national-capitalism" viewpoint, Gorbachev sought to portray the USSR as a champion of Third World "capitalist-oriented" states trying to shake off the vestiges of Western domination. He began by holding that "economic, political, and ideological competition between capitalist and socialist countries is inevitable," although, "it can and must be kept within a framework of peaceful competition." Then he proceeded to demonstrate his commitment to such competition by arguing that every Third World state "is entitled to choose its own way of development, to dispose of its fate, its territory, and its human and natural resources." Significantly, he did not confine his defense of this right simply to countries that opted for "socialist orientation," but extended it to states on their way to becoming modern industrialized countries of a capitalist type. According to him, even those in this category that were "growing into great powers" confronted "uneven and painful" economic growth, for the "rich Western states" continued "to collect neo-colonialist 'tribute'." He wound up, therefore, calling upon Western leaders to "set aside the psychology and notions of colonial times" and stop treating "capitalist-oriented" as well as other kinds of Third World countries as the West's "sphere of influence."

The General Secretary's ensuing remarks about specific Third World states testified to the importance that he assigned to "capitalist-oriented" ones. He indicated that the USSR was "ready to develop [its] relations with each of the ASEAN nations individually and with ASEAN as a whole." He depicted the USSR's relations with India as "an example for others to emulate," and he saw in these relations "a budding world order in which peaceful coexistence and mutually beneficial cooperation based on goodwill will be universal norms." He avowed Soviet sympathy "with the Latin American countries in their efforts to consolidate their independence in every sphere and to cast off all neo-colonialist fetters," and praised the "energetic foreign policies" and the "responsible stances on disarmament and international security" of Mexico and Argentina, the "peace-making efforts of the Contadora Group. ...."

Indirect yet striking confirmation of the absence of top-level endorsement of a sole school of persuasion about Third World policy emerged at a major conference of the Ministry of Foreign Affairs in late July 1988. It came from Karen Brutents, at the time a deputy director of the CPSU International Department and a key expounder of the "national-capitalism" viewpoint. He told the gathering: "It is ... only fair to say that the problems of developing countries have yet to be worked out in accordance with the concept of new thinking."[21] ...

IMPLICATIONS

What, then, do these shifts suggest about the USSR's policy toward the Third World? Two points stand out. First, from a substantive viewpoint, increased complexity has become the key feature of Soviet policy. Specifically, the policy now reflects several different, often clashing visions of what the Soviet approach to the Third World ought to be. It is true that, as the evidence laid out in the preceding pages attests, a good case can be made that today change outweighs continuity in the content of Soviet policy. Yet elements of continuity persist. More critical, even if these elements of continuity were to disappear, the heightened complexity of policy would still prevail as long as multiple schools of persuasion about desirable policy existed and the USSR's top leadership embraced no one of them exclusively.

The significance of this new complexity in Soviet policy toward the Third World arises from its impact on the predictability of that policy. In any concrete set of circumstances, it is hard to anticipate precisely what mix of the various policy perspectives will shape Soviet behavior. Thus, foreseeing the USSR's response to these circumstances is highly problematic.

From Moscow's standpoint, of course, this development is not necessarily a drawback. Nor is the greater flexibility that the added complexity permits in Soviet handling of the Third World. The absence of a firm official line, for example, gives Moscow more room to adjust its conduct in light of the conditions it may see as relevant in each individual situation.

Second, in terms of process, the formulation of the USSR's policy toward the Third World has also turned into a highly complicated affair. Policy now emerges from competition among a number of groups with diverse policy outlooks in the Soviet hierarchy. ...

Gorbachev's rise to power brought a young, dynamic individual to the top leadership post, but he lacked experience in foreign affairs and had virtually no experience in dealing with the Third World. Perhaps more important, his immediate concerns were domestic in nature, and his need to solidify his political control reinforced this preoccupation. Hence, he devoted little attention to the Third World at the outset.[75]

In addition, until roughly 1987, officials with diverse prescriptions for the USSR's Third World policy were entrenched in those Soviet institutions that had a major hand in shaping the Soviet approach toward the Third World. The CPSU International Department, for example, included among its directing elements representatives of three of the four Soviet schools of thought about Third World policy.[76] Without firm policy guidelines from above, these and other strategically-placed individuals were in a position to affect Soviet conduct at least within their own spheres of responsibility.

Since about 1987, however, the competition has taken on a more structured form, as advocates of each policy line battle to influence the content of the "new thinking." An item published in a leading Soviet academic journal in mid-1988 affords a graphic illustration. Under the headline "Socialist Orientation and New Political Thinking," two prominent specialists on the Third World with long-standing, conflicting outlooks on Soviet Third World policy engaged in a dialogue on "socialist orientation." One expounded a "revolutionary-democratic" viewpoint; the other, a "national-capitalism" viewpoint. Yet both claimed that their arguments accorded with "new political thinking."[77]

The previously cited observation by Brutents at the Ministry of Foreign Affairs conference in July 1988 offers equally revealing evidence. In saying that "the problems of developing countries have yet to be worked out" in light of "the concept of new thinking," he implied that "new thinking" required further refinement. Given his long-term commitment to a "national-capitalism" perspective, there can be little doubt what sort of refinement he had in mind.

This shift in the nature of the competition has come about for a combination of reasons. Over the years, Gorbachev has greatly enhanced his power by engineering a variety of personnel and institutional changes in the USSR, although he still appears to confront strong opposition in some quarters.

The General Secretary has also begun to evince a fair degree of interest in the Third World, and he has even set forth some general principles for Soviet policy toward it. These flow essentially out of his larger political and foreign policy concerns. That is particularly true of the two primary principles. As Gorbachev sees things, Soviet involvements in the Third World must not impede the restructuring of the Soviet economy, and the USSR's behavior there must not undermine Soviet attempts to improve relations with the West in general and the United States in particular.[78]

Aside from insisting on adherence to a few governing principles, however, Gorbachev has shown a willingness to listen to expert advice on how to deal with the Third World. This willingness has legitimized efforts by representatives of all policy persuasions to make inputs on the subject, and despite Gorbachev's shakeup of the personnel and institutions handling Third World matters, diversity of outlook persists among the well-placed experts. Indeed, even Gorbachev's two top-ranking lieutenants in the realm of foreign policy—Yakovlev and Shevardnadze—seem to hold clashing views on desirable Soviet Third World policy.[79]

PROSPECTS

...

... Indications have cropped up since mid-1988 that a fifth vision of policy may be emerging, although these hints still remain scanty enough to leave questions about whether it has enough backing to qualify as a full-fledged school of thought. This perspective accepts a basic premise of the "national-capitalism" outlook—that at least most Third World states will pass through a capitalist or nonsocialist phase of development before arriving at socialism. Yet is sees far less possibility of advance toward socialism under present circumstances than even the "national-capitalism" line does. Not only is this viewpoint skeptical that "capitalist-oriented" countries in the Third World will try to assert their independence vis-à-vis the Western "imperialist" powers in economic and other spheres by expanding their contacts with the USSR, but it is pessimistic about even modest steps toward socialism on the part of "socialist-oriented" states. Worst of all from its standpoint, even the most consistent of the USSR's Third World allies are seeking to broaden their political and economic ties with the West, and the USSR lacks the resources to reverse this situation. In fact, Moscow is even having troubles increasing these resources, for it bears heavy military burdens in the Third World and other areas. As a result, the socialist path of development is losing its appeal in the Third World.

Thus, according to advocates of this possible new school of thought, the USSR must reduce its involvements in the Third World so as to focus on restructuring its own economy and making the socialist path more attractive. In doing so, it should not use political orientation as a basis for retaining close relations; rather, it should adopt pragmatic criteria based on its political interests and goals in each region. Nor should it attempt to maintain or develop links with Third World countries that entail heavy commitments of resources, especially those of an economic character. In addition, it should rely chiefly on political means, instead of more costly military and economic instruments, in pursuing its ends. Finally, it should adopt a nonprovocative posture toward the West; otherwise, it might find itself embroiled in Third World conflicts that would drain off its resources.

So far, we have not been able to identify any high-level individual who has publicly associated himself with this line of argument.[81] Nevertheless, some (unnamed) senior members of the Ministry of Foreign Affairs, including ambassadors and high-ranking staff members of the ministry, did openly call at the ministry's July 1988 conference for a hard-headed reassessment of Soviet undertakings in the Third World. They urged that the USSR develop relations with Third World states "on realistic lines, with due regard to the peculiarities of each particular country and, first and foremost, to our actual possibilities."[82]

What appears beyond doubt is that controversy over Third World policy will continue in the USSR for the foreseeable future. Moreover, it seems highly probable that multiple schools of persuasion on the subject will remain in existence as well. ...

NOTES

ABOUT THE AUTHOR: **David E. Albright** is professor emeritus of national security affairs at Air University, Montgomery, Alabama, and visiting scholar at George Washington University.

1. See, for example, Alvin Z. Rubinstein, *Moscow's Third World Strategy,* Princeton, NJ, Princeton University Press, 1988.

2. A typical illustration is Daniel S. Papp, *Soviet Perceptions of the Developing World in the 1980's: The Ideological Basis,* Lexington, MA, Lexington Books, 1985.

3. See, for instance, the writings of Francis Fukuyama—especially, *Moscow's Post-Brezhnev Reassessment of the Third World,* R-3337-USDP, Santa Monica, CA, RAND Corporation, February 1986; "Gorbachev and the Third World," *Foreign Affairs* (New York), Spring 1986, pp. 715–31; "Patterns of Soviet Third World Policy," *Problems of Communism* (Washington, DC), September-October 1987, pp. 1–13.

4. Both Jerry Hough and Elizabeth Valkenier fall into this category. See Hough, *The Struggle for the Third World: Soviet Debates and American Options,* Washington, DC, The Brookings Institution, 1986; Valkenier, *The Soviet Union and the Third World: An Economic Bind,* New York, Praeger, 1983; idem, "Revolutionary Change in the Third World: Recent Soviet Assessments," *World Politics* (Princeton, NJ), April 1986, pp. 415–34; and idem, "New Soviet Thinking About the Third World," *World Policy Journal* (New York), Fall 1987, pp. 651–74.

5. Jack Snyder, "The Gorbachev Revolution: A Waning of Soviet Expansionism?" *International Security* (Cambridge, MA), Winter 1987–88, pp. 93–131, affords a typical example.

6. For detailed discussion of this particular controversy, see especially Uri Ra'anan, "Moscow and the Third World," *Problems of Communism,* January-February 1965, pp. 22–31. A systematic treatment of all Soviet policy debates since the early 1960's may be found in David E. Albright, *Vanguard Parties and Revolutionary Change in the Third World: The Soviet Perspective and Its Implications,* forthcoming.

18. [*Pravda*], Feb. 24 1981.

20. See specifically Chs. 3 ("How We See the World of Today") and 5 ("The Third World in the International Community") in Mikhail Gorbachev, *Perestroika: New Thinking for Our Country and the World,* New York, Harper and Row, 1987. Other key items providing insight into Gorbachev's position include the new CPSU Program published in draft in October 1985 and approved in slightly revised form at the 27th CPSU Congress in early 1986, and the General Secretary's political report to the 27th CPSU Congress. The draft of the former may be found in *Pravda,* Oct. 26, 1985, while the final version appeared in *Moscow News,* No. 12, Mar. 30–Apr. 6, 1986, Supplement. Gorbachev's report to the 27th CPSU Congress was carried in *Pravda,* Feb. 25, 1986.

21. "Cooperation and Dialogue with Political Parties and Movements," *International Affairs,* November 1988, pp. 38–39.

75. For more extended treatment of these points, see Roderic Lyne, "Making Waves: Gorbachev's Public Diplomacy, 1985–86," in Robbin F. Laird, Ed., *Soviet Foreign Policy,* New York, Academy of Political Science, 1987, pp. 235–53.

76. As already noted, Ponomarev, the head of the department, and Ul'yanovskiy, a deputy chief, subscribed to the "revolutionary-democratic" outlook; Brutents, a deputy director, to the "national-capitalism" viewpoint; and Zagladin, the first deputy chief, to the "economic-interdependence" perspective. For elaboration, see David E. Albright, "The CPSU International Department and the Third World in the Gorbachev Era," in Donald Graves, Ed., *The CPSU International Department and Soviet Foreign Policy,* Washington, DC, Center for Foreign Policy Development, [1990].

77. Vladimir Lee and Georgy Mirsky, "Socialist Orientation and New Political Thinking," *Asia and Africa Today* (Moscow), July-August 1988, pp. 64–70.

78. See his speech to the staff of the Ministry of Foreign Affairs in *Vestnik Ministerstva Inostrannykh Del, SSSR* (Moscow), Aug. 5, 1987, and his *Perestroika: New Thinking for Our Country and the World,* pp. 139–40, 174, 177–78, 188–89.

79. As pointed out previously, Yakovlev, Politburo member and head of the CPSU International Policy Commission, adheres to the "national-capitalism" school, while Shevardnadze, a Politburo member and minister of foreign affairs, identifies with the "economic-interdependence" school.

81. The most expansive statement to data of this vision of policy may be found in Alexey Izyumov and Andrey Kortunov, "The Soviet Union in the Changing World," *International Affairs,* August 1988, esp. pp. 51–56.

82. See the account by Deputy Foreign Minister Leonid Il'ichev of the deliberations of a section on "Policy Toward Developing Countries and Regional Conflicts" at this conference, in ibid., October 1988, pp. 49–50.

43 *Soviet National Security Under Gorbachev*

BRUCE PARROTT

When Mikhail Gorbachev was elected general secretary of the Communist Party of the Soviet Union, few Western observers anticipated major alterations in Soviet external policy; today, most believe that the changes since 1985 have been dramatic, and even spectacular. Gorbachev has elaborated a sweeping vision whose postulates about military power and security contradict the views of recent Soviet leaders. In superpower arms negotiations the USSR has agreed to drastic arms cuts and intrusive verification measures which have no precedent in past Soviet practice. Meanwhile, the party leadership, once apparently under the sway of the military high command, has downgraded the military's public role and encouraged a cadre of civilian defense analysts to propose radical revisions of inherited military policy. In addition, reformist party leaders have begun to reappraise the role of the Committee for State Security (KGB) and have subjected that once sacrosanct institution to public criticism. These changes have been accompanied by a whirlwind of daring foreign-policy innovations that Gorbachev's immediate predecessors could scarcely have imagined, let alone carried out.

The feverish pace and occasional inconsistency of the Soviet initiatives have spawned disagreements among Western analysts. Some view the proclamation of "new political thinking" as a fundamental shift in Soviet security policy, whereas others regard it primarily as a rhetorical exercise designed to lull the West.[1] Analysts also disagree over whether the recent foreign-policy changes are designed to be permanent or are temporary expedients to allow the regime to cope with domestic difficulties before returning to a more confrontational policy toward the West. Closely linked to this issue is the disputed question of whether the professional officer corps has supported or opposed Gorbachev's new approach to security and budgetary priorities.[2] Less often discussed but no less important is the attitude of the KGB. Have KGB views on security matters paralleled or diverged from the military perspective, and how has the relationship between the two hierarchies affected security decision-making? If Gorbachev is indeed pursuing policies that threaten the interests of both the military and the KGB, has he amassed enough political power to avoid a fate like Nikita Khrushchev's in 1964?[3] ...

GORBACHEV AND THE SECURITY AGENDA

The Dual-Track Policy and Its Critics. On becoming general secretary, Gorbachev inherited the dual-track approach to national security hammered out by Leonid Brezhnev at the start of the 1970's. This approach, which Brezhnev had introduced despite resistance from hard-liners opposed to détente with the West, had several features: a nearly reflexive conviction that the continuous expansion of Soviet military power would automatically enhance Soviet security; a belief that diplomatic negotiations, particularly arms-control negotiations, were a valuable complementary means of managing the competition with the United States; a vigorous determination to expand Soviet influence in the Third World; and a desire to draw on Western economic inputs while simultaneously insulating the Soviet domestic system from Western political and cultural influences. By the mid-1970's these policies had become part of a broad political consensus within the party and military elite.

During Brezhnev's final years, however, major international and domestic changes called the dual-track security approach into question. Several Western policies begun under President Jimmy Carter and reinforced under President Ronald Reagan—the new US military buildup, the refusal to ratify the SALT II agreement, and the decision to move toward deployment of American intermediate-range nuclear missiles (INF) in Europe—raised doubts about the security benefits of negotiating with the capitalist powers. The West's vigorous political reaction and economic sanctions against the Soviet invasion of Afghanistan also generated uncertainty about the stability of détente and the wisdom of drawing on Western grain and technology. Soviet difficulties were compounded by a sudden drop in Soviet economic growth and by the Polish explosion, which created the specter of political collapse not only elsewhere in Eastern Europe but possibly inside the USSR itself.

The main public challenge to the dual-track security approach came from the conservative wing of the elite, although soft-line officials and foreign-policy intellectuals apparently lobbied quietly behind the scenes.[4] Questioning the centrist balance between military and diplomatic security instruments struck by Brezhnev, these hard-liners asserted that détente had been permanently eclipsed by a growing American aggressiveness, and that this situation required a large increase in the Soviet defense budget.[5] In addition, they faulted Brezhnev's trade and economic policies for leaving the USSR vulnerable to Western embargoes on technology and grain.[6] Brezhnev, and later his successors Yuriy Andropov and Konstantin Chernenko, countered that détente was a long-term trend that could be revived by tenacious, iron-bottomed diplomacy and that a major increase in defense spending was therefore unnecessary. They also contended that a more militant international posture and higher defense spending would dangerously compound the social and economic problems accumulating at home.[7] An outcome of this acrimonious policy struggle was the 1983 decision to break off the superpower arms talks in retaliation for the INF deployments in Europe—a decision which was followed by intense infighting over whether to return to the bargaining table on US terms. While the controversy yielded no new national-security formula, it indicated that the elite consensus on the dual-track security strategy, like the elite consensus on domestic policy, was disintegrating. ...

After succeeding Chernenko, Gorbachev pledged to continue the existing foreign-policy line and concentrated most of his attention on reshaping domestic policy. Championing economic revitalization and the reestablishment of internal discipline, he quickly stepped up Chernenko's desultory anti-corruption campaign and cracked down on lax labor practices. But Gorbachev also dropped a few hints that he envisioned changes in foreign policy as well. By calling for "civilized relations" with the West, he intimated that East and West had fundamental values in common.[12] It was necessary, he said, not simply to return to the détente of the 1970's but to achieve "much more"—namely, a comprehensive system of international security based on the recognition that the socialist and capitalist worlds both could benefit from cooperation and both be harmed by rivalry.[13] These statements may have reflected unreported deliberations that later led to dramatic changes in Soviet security policy.[14]

Gorbachev's early speeches underscored the dangerousness of current international trends but contended that vigorous political action could reverse those trends. He underscored the alleged desire of hostile American groups to obtain military superiority and promised to safeguard Soviet strategic parity as a reliable means of deterring Western attack.[15] At the same time, he singled out positive elements in the Reagan Administration's pronouncements and stressed the growing influence of the Western antiwar movement.[16] Noting the burden of the arms race for "all" countries, Gorbachev suggested that the current defense budget was adequate and emphasized the primacy of accelerated technological and economic development in assuring the USSR's survival as a superpower.[17] On the crucial matter of SDI, he remarked that the USSR would respond to a US deployment of space-based defenses by expanding its offensive forces, but he did not say that it would build similar defenses of its own.[18]

To buttress his security views, Gorbachev set forth his own reading of the history of Soviet foreign relations. Asserting that the East-West confrontation was a historical "anomaly," he rejected the historical analogy to the 1930's that Soviet conservatives have traditionally brought up to justify a hard-line foreign policy. Rather than draw confrontational lessons from the lack of Soviet military preparedness on the eve of World War II, Gorbachev alluded to a new assessment of the causes of the war and hinted that some of the responsibility for the war belonged to the USSR for following a political line that allowed Adolf Hitler to come to power in the first place. ...[19]

Among the Politburo members who supported Gorbachev's security approach, one of the most important was Andrey Gromyko, the veteran diplomat and party elder statesman. During the final struggle over Chernenko's mantle, Gromyko evidently played a key role in shoring up the pro-Gorbachev coalition inside the party Central Committee and thus helped ensure Gorbachev's victory.[22] While nominating Gorbachev at the March 1985 Central Committee plenum, Gromyko went out of his way to present Gorbachev's foreign-policy credentials in terms that suggested he was trying to allay misgivings among party conservatives concerned about military security.[23] For Gromyko, the main virtue of Gorbachev's program was that it continued the dual-track approach Gromyko had helped Brezhnev to devise and to defend against hard-line criticism in the early 1980's.[24]

...

... Some other Politburo members harbored serious doubts about the General Secretary's security approach. Ukrainian party chief Volodymyr Shcherbytskyi, claiming that adventurist tendencies were becoming stronger in Western policies, warned that the United States was seeking "*decisive* military superiority" over the USSR—a formulation used only by such advocates of stepped-up military spending as Marshal Nikolay Ogarkov.[35] Since Shcherbytskyi also voiced pessimism about the influence of the Western antiwar movement, it can be assumed that he favored a more vigorous Soviet military effort. Having visited the United States and West Germany in early 1985, he remarked that McCarthyite and neo-Nazi tendencies in the two countries "remind world society of similar processes that occurred in the states of the fascist coalition on the eve of the [Second World] War."[36] The parallel drawn by Shcherbytskyi, which was directly at odds with Gorbachev's outlook, was almost certainly intended to bolster a similar parallel drawn by the resilient Ogarkov, who renewed his demand for higher defense spending at this time.[37] Shcherbytskyi also seemed readier than Gorbachev to threaten that the USSR would meet the further development of the SDI program with extensive missile defenses of its own.[38] ...

Defense Minister Sergey L. Sokolov shared some of the same attitudes. Although he echoed Gorbachev's statement that all East-West disputes could be resolved by peaceful means, Sokolov painted a grim picture of deepening US militarism. Implying that the Soviet Armed Forces did not currently have all they needed, he remarked that the "severe lessons" of World War II demanded great vigilance. "*The growing military threat from the US and its NATO allies requires [us] to strengthen the defense capacity of our Motherland and the combat might of the Soviet Armed Forces,*" Sokolov said emphatically.[40] There was also a noteworthy difference between Gorbachev's and Sokolov's descriptions of how the USSR would respond to continued development of SDI. Whereas Gorbachev avoided raising the possibility of deploying a Soviet space-based ballistic missile defense, Sokolov said that one side's deployment of an extensive ABM system would "inevitably" provoke a comprehensive response including not only a strategic offensive buildup but also the creation of a large-scale ABM defense.[41] ...

Economic Acceleration and the Defense Budget. Another point of friction between Sokolov and Gorbachev was the issue of guns versus growth. Gorbachev voiced profound concern about the USSR's future security but highlighted the economic rather than the strictly military aspects of the danger. While promising not to let the United States obtain strategic superiority, he asserted that the future of the Soviet system and of world socialism hinged on accelerated economic development, and he remarked that added increments of military power did not necessarily increase the state's security.[43] Overriding priority, he asserted, must be given to modernizing the machine-building, computer, and other high-technology industries.[44] Although this strong emphasis on industrial modernization offered potential military benefits in the long term, it also created a strong temptation to divert resources from current military programs to industrial research and investment.[45] ...

With Romanov [ousted from the Politburo,] Gorbachev took a firmer line toward the budgetary demands of the Armed Forces. In mid-July 1985, he met in Minsk with the military high command. According to informal accounts of his speech, he announced stringent limits on the growth of military expenditures and also called for some changes of military personnel.[47] The fact that this speech has never been published indicates that its contents were unusually sensitive, and indirect evidence suggests that it caused discomfort in the military leadership.[48]

...

Diplomacy, Summits, and Security. During his first three months as general secretary, Gorbachev implied that the USSR might again break off the superpower arms talks if the United States were not more forthcoming. In the summer, however, he gained greater control over foreign policy and discarded this theme in favor of conciliatory gestures toward the West. In the same shake-up that removed Romanov from the Politburo, Gorbachev managed to shift Gromyko to the chairmanship of the Supreme Soviet and installed Shevardnadze, an exceptionally close political ally, as foreign minister. Although he initially avoided major personnel changes at the foreign ministry in order not to offend Gromyko and Gromyko's Central Committee allies,[53] Gorbachev announced a forthcoming summit with President Reagan and declared a unilateral nuclear-test moratorium that he urged the United States to emulate. Shrewdly gauging the tendency of many recent Soviet military theorists to downgrade the role of nuclear weapons in favor of high-technology conventional arms, Gorbachev replaced Marshal Vladimir Tolubko, a veteran rocket specialist who most likely opposed reductions in the Soviet missile arsenal, with a new Strategic Rocket Forces chief more amenable to the dramatic nuclear cuts that Gorbachev now offered to negotiate.[54] At the Geneva summit, Gorbachev hinted that the INF question, previously linked by the USSR to SDI, might be resolved separately, and he agreed to hold two further summits with President Reagan in 1986 and 1987.[55] Together, these steps marked a distinct shift in diplomatic tactics.

Senior party leaders, however, differed over the wisdom of this shift, particularly in view of the fact that the Geneva summit produced few concrete results.[56] Remarking that the Soviet side had not had "the smallest illusions" about American intentions on the eve of the summit, Gorbachev asserted optimistically that the final joint communiqué was significant because it entailed a recognition that nuclear war was unwinnable, along with a pledge not to seek military superiority. The communiqué was not a formal agreement, he acknowledged, but it nevertheless expressed "a fundamental stance of the leaders of both countries obligating [them] to a great deal." Although serious differences continued to separate the two sides, the differences could be resolved and should not be exaggerated. "Even the smallest chance" to curb the arms race through negotiations should not be lost; "inactivity or slowness in actions" would be "criminal."[57] Obviously, Gorbachev regarded the summit as part of an urgent political struggle against US military programs, especially SDI, and he appeared to be trying to persuade other leaders that the summit had been as successful as he claimed.

Led by Shevardnadze, several Politburo members embraced Gorbachev's arguments. Highlighting the Warsaw Pact members' "exceptionally high evaluation" of Gorbachev's skill at Geneva, Shevardnadze hailed the meeting as "an event of enormous international significance."[58] ...

Gromyko's much more restrained description of the Geneva communiqué as a matter of "importance" apparently signified the onset of tensions with Gorbachev.[61] After the summit, Gorbachev intimated that he was dissatisfied with the objectivity of reports from Soviet diplomats abroad and hinted that these reports might adversely affect the formulation of Soviet policy.[62] Most of the diplomats had been appointed when Gromyko was foreign minister, and Gorbachev may have been complaining about their reporting on the impact abroad of the Geneva summit. A month later, on the eve of his definitive statement delinking INF from SDI—an issue the Soviet side had treated ambiguously since the summit—Gorbachev observed that a Soviet policy based on ultimatums would allow other governments to hide behind the uncompromising Soviet stance and deceive their peoples about their real intentions.[63] By contrast, Gromyko remarked that the restoration of détente had always been the aim of Soviet policy, "including before Geneva, at the Soviet-American summit, and after Geneva."[64] Gromyko's accent on continuity seemed to downgrade the significance of the Geneva meeting and implicitly to justify the handling of foreign policy when he had been foreign minister. Although Gromyko's position on delinking INF from SDI remains unclear, these exchanges suggest that he and Gorbachev were sparring over whether a more flexible diplomatic strategy, including the commitment to hold two more summits, would improve superpower relations. Ligachev's endorsement of the summit also seemed half-hearted.[65]

In comparison, Shcherbytskyi was an outright skeptic.[66] Although he hailed the joint communiqué's statements on nuclear war, he passed over the mutual pledge not to seek military superiority. In a riposte to Gorbachev, he warned against "needless illusions" about the benefits of the summit. Even before the meeting, he asserted, it had been clear that the Reagan Administration intended to continue to pursue military superiority, and recent While House statements demonstrated that superiority remained the administration's goal. At present, possibilities for reaching a superpower understanding on "fundamental questions," particularly SDI and the SALT II agreement, "do not exist," according to Shcherbytskyi.[67] In his view, the US commitment to SDI doomed the world to many years of an arms race and undermined the very basis for limiting or reducing the number of weapons.[68]

... Skeptical responses from Chief of the General Staff Akhromeyev and some military commentators indicated that a significant group of professional officers agreed with this view of the summit's results.[69]

REVAMPING SOVIET DIPLOMACY

This tugging foreshadowed the adoption by Gorbachev of a more daring security policy. In January 1986, he unveiled a sweeping proposal for phased arms reductions and the elimination of nuclear weapons by the year 2000, and at the 27th Party Congress in February he declared that the growing interdependence of the world required a radical improvement of East-West relations. A new level of East-West cooperation was attainable, he asserted, and a rapid transition to constructive action was necessary.[70] Seeking to forestall conservative objections, Gorbachev maintained that this approach did not require the Soviet Union to renounce its principles or ideals.

Although Gorbachev voiced deep apprehension about trends in the East-West military competition, he departed from customary Soviet statements of alarm by identifying political accommodation rather than the expansion of military power as the solution to the problem. With SDI uppermost in his mind, Gorbachev asserted that even the strongest state could no longer protect itself solely by military-technical means; security was increasingly becoming a task that could be solved only by political means. Emphasizing the unpredictability of conflict situations and the increasing encroachment of automated weapons systems on politicians' ability to control events during a crisis, Gorbachev raised the specter of military logic escaping political control and bringing on accidental nuclear war.[71]

In keeping with this picture, Gorbachev expressed skepticism about the utility of military power. A year earlier, he had praised the Soviet achievement of parity and described it as an effective means for deterring Western attack. Now he asserted that in future stages of the arms race, even if superpower parity were maintained, the Soviet policy of deterrence might not prevent a nuclear war.[72] His new pronouncements signalled the public emergence of a liberal critique of the dual-track security strategy that had been formulated under Brezhnev.

The essence of this critique was that the Brezhnev leadership had placed too much stress on military instruments—not too little, as hard-line critics maintained—and had failed to gain the security benefits available through flexible diplomacy and compromise. At the party congress, Gorbachev gave his first unmistakable signal of displeasure with recent Soviet foreign policy, and shortly afterward he spelled out his criticisms in a speech at the Ministry of Foreign Affairs that was not published until the following year. Gorbachev invoked the "Leninist" style of leadership to justify changes in the security policy inherited from Brezhnev and Gromyko. Observing that continuity in foreign policy had nothing in common with mechanical repetition of past practice, he argued that new approaches were needed to avoid confrontation and reach mutually acceptable compromises. Toward this end, he advocated that future Soviet policy aim not to provoke other countries' "fears, even if imaginary, for their security."[73] This statement, obviously at odds with Gromyko's recent stress on continuity in foreign policy, constituted a striking reversal of the traditional Soviet refusal to acknowledge that Soviet military programs might provoke legitimate apprehensions in other countries. It also heralded a far-reaching personnel shakeup at the Ministry of Foreign Affairs.[74] ...

... Evidently some advocates of larger defense budgets believed that a new summit, rather than yielding beneficial advances in arms control, would merely help the Reagan Administration reinforce its domestic support for the US military buildup.

Widening the Diplomatic Agenda. Gorbachev strove to minimize this possibility by unveiling a new four-part security agenda that included not only arms control and economic cooperation with the West but cooperation in political and "humanitarian" matters as well.[79] In negotiations, Gorbachev said in his remarks at the ministry of Foreign Affairs, Soviet representatives must avoid a "senseless stubbornness" that led to impasses and created the image of "Mr. Nyet" for the USSR. Instead of being passive or defensive when the West raises human-rights issues, Soviet diplomats should engage the West in an open dialogue that stresses Soviet accomplishments in the human-rights area, Gorbachev said.[80]

Gorbachev also implicitly downgraded the importance of the Third World and hinted at a less supportive policy toward Third-World revolutions and commitments. At the party congress, he limited himself to a rather perfunctory pledge of "solidarity" with national-liberation movements and the observation that capitalism had succeeded in keeping many liberated countries in a position of economic dependency. He also sounded a new note by calling the war in Afghanistan a "bleeding wound."[81] While he repeated his predecessors' assurance that the USSR would not "export revolution," he omitted the usual accompanying promise that the USSR would struggle against the "export of counterrevolution" by the West, and he cited Lenin's condemnation of left-wing communists who tried to "push" foreign revolutions.[82] Subsequently, he implied that the aggregate economic burden of Soviet Third-World commitments ought to be reduced.[83]

Gorbachev's view of the relationship between diplomacy and military power was vigorously backed by Shevardnadze, who called for "a decisive renunciation of outdated ... doctrines" and remarked pointedly that Soviet foreign policy had not yet tapped important reserves of diplomatic dynamism and scholarly expertise. This attitude evidently provoked private objections from Gromyko and his clients in the diplomatic apparatus, since Shevardnadze made a special effort to counter the charge that any defects in the foreign-affairs bureaucracy were of his own making.[84] In ambiguous comments potentially relevant to Soviet as well as Western military doctrine, Shevardnadze condemned the belief that nuclear weapons were necessary to deter a foreign attack. Hailing the beneficial effects of foreign-policy *glasnost*, he attached special significance to Gorbachev's recent declaration calling for phased arms reductions and the elimination of nuclear weapons by the year 2000.[85] ...

The most thorough exposition of the need to revise security policy came from Anatoliy Dobrynin. Two months before Gorbachev's speech at the Ministry of Foreign Affairs, Dobrynin was recalled from his ambassadorial post in Washington and installed as the Central Committee secretary overseeing East-West relations. Shortly after the speech Dobrynin—who played a key role in the shakeup of the diplomatic corps—published a path-breaking call for a new approach to national security.[87] Soviet passivity in the face of negative international trends was unacceptable, said Dobrynin in a jab at the advocates of stand-pat or hard-line diplomacy. Instead, the USSR must respond with unprecedentedly active diplomacy involving a qualitatively higher level of flexibility and make "reasonable compromises."[88] Flexible diplomacy would put the US on the defensive and create virtually irresistible political pressures that would lead to advantageous arms agreements.[89] The Soviet Union, Dobrynin assured the skeptics, would not let itself be outwitted in the maneuvering over another summit meeting, nor would it allow the United States to achieve military superiority while engaging in negotiations.

Dobrynin clearly thought that the accumulation of Soviet military power was part of the problem rather than part of the solution. In explaining how general war had been avoided in recent decades, he sharply downgraded the role of Soviet military might and highlighted the contribution of Soviet diplomacy, along with the growing influence of reasonable political groups abroad.[90] Looking to the future, Dobrynin, unlike Soviet conservatives, did not focus on the danger of a premeditated Western attack. Instead, he suggested that the current military balance was vulnerable to accidental war and that further advances in military technology would make it more so. In the long term, nuclear deterrence could not prevent general war. Scholars and politicians, said Dobrynin in a slap at military men, had long understood that improved weapons serve merely to make war more terrible, not to avoid it, and nuclear weapons should not be justified on the grounds that they reduced the chances of conventional conflict. Dobrynin also indicated that any future Soviet military response to SDI would probably not be in space.[91]

To spur rethinking of security policy, Dobrynin pushed hard for the creation of new centers of military expertise staffed by civilians. He praised the recent emergence of a "contemporary Soviet school of foreign-policy and military-political research" but noted that many new problems still required scholarly investigation. Dobrynin then listed a series of military-technical topics to which Soviet military theorists and planners had devoted years of careful professional study.[92]

At no point, however, did he refer to any of the military academies and institutes engaged in analyzing these topics. Instead, he singled out the Scientific Council on Peace and Disarmament and the institutes of the Academy of Sciences as the loci of promising new research.[93] The same interest in increasing the role of civilian experts in the formulation of military policy was shown by Aleksandr Yakovlev—himself a former director of one of the Academy's foreign-affairs institutes—after he became a full member of the Politburo.[94]

Dobrynin's glaring omission of any reference to military specialists signaled an attempt to reduce the professional authority of the officer corps in favor of civilian defense specialists. Shortly after being appointed to the Secretariat, Dorbynin organized a military affairs section within the Central Committee's International Department. A small arms-control section was also set up under Yakovlev's Propaganda Department. At about the same time, a research department doing classified work on military and security issues was set up inside the Academy's Institute of the World Economy and International Relations, the think-tank that Yakovlev had once headed.[95] Some of the staff members of these new units were retired officers or military men seconded from regular military assignments. As a rule, however, their views have tended to fall outside the mainstream of conventional military thought, and they have generally functioned as allies of civilian experts working to recast security policy.

Dobrynin's desire to improve relations with the United States led him to endorse the unilateral test moratorium and to advocate a less venturesome Third-World policy.[96] But perhaps most striking was his explicit and positive recognition of the linkage between superpower arms control and human rights. The human rights issue, he granted Soviet conservatives, must be removed from the realm of Western political manipulation (*spekulyatsiya*). To do this, however, it was necessary not simply to rebut Western propaganda but to handle the problem constructively. In his view, cooperation in the "humanitarian" field was possible without compromising socialist principles. Civilized international relations, Dobrynin said, involved not just interstate ties, but a broadening of contacts between people and organizations.[97]

Dobrynin's critique of security policy under Brezhnev implicitly challenged the three main state bureaucracies implementing that policy. Apart from censuring the lack of imaginative diplomacy at the Ministry of Foreign Affairs in Gromyko's time, Dobrynin was asserting that military power, embodied in the Ministry of Defense, had contributed less to Soviet security than previously supposed. He was also suggesting that the handling of human-rights issues by the KGB had obstructed the achievement of the regime's security goals. ...

Several Politburo centrists accepted the need for diplomatic engagement with the West but distrusted Gorbachev's tendency to make dramatic concessions in order to sway Western opinion. Gromyko, for example, continued to advocate arms control and supported summit diplomacy. But the veteran diplomat, who was obviously the target of Gorbachev's barbed remarks about "Mr. Nyet," seemed reluctant to soften the Soviet position on the Middle East and other regional conflicts in order to improve relations with the United States.[99] Gromyko was plainly unreceptive to Gorbachev's idea that the West needed political reassurance about Soviet strategic intentions. Instead, he continued to treat Western expressions of fear about Soviet strategic aims as propaganda calculated to put the USSR on the political defensive.[100] Moreover, he resisted the notion of a more open diplomatic style that might reveal internal policy disagreements and involve making open concessions to the West on human rights.[101]

KGB chairman Chebrikov, though he backed Gorbachev's comprehensive disarmament plan, shared Gromyko's distrust of conciliatory diplomatic and human-rights initiatives. He treated Western expressions of apprehension about Soviet military programs as a myth that Western propagandists knew to be untrue.[102] Along with some military men, the KGB chief seemed wary of the more forthcoming arms-verification approach that Gorbachev apparently initiated at Geneva, and he feared the sort of society-to-society contacts Gorbachev had endorsed there.[103] ...

If such "swing votes" as Gromyko and Chebrikov questioned Gorbachev's diplomatic tactics but still hoped for substantial benefits from superpower arms talks, such hard-liners as Shcherbytskyi harbored serious reservations about the talks themselves. Although Gorbachev had already gone on record as favoring a separate INF agreement, his highly-publicized January 1986 declaration outlining a plan for phased arms reductions was ambiguous on the question of INF-SDI linkage.[106] Three days after the declaration, Shcherbytskyi described it as offering a phased program for the liquidation of nuclear weapons by the year 2000 "on the condition of the prohibition of the creation, testing, and deployment of space-strike weapons."[107] Although accurate in a sense, this description of the declaration differed from the terms used by other leaders, who did not mention SDI in their references to it.[108] Moreover, when Shcherbytskyi mentioned the January declaration at the party congress in February, he remarked only that Soviet citizens could not fail to feel "bitterness and disappointment" at the unforthcoming US response, which was in essence blocking an opportunity for agreement.[109]

In addition, Shcherbytskyi implicitly placed the requirements of the military budget above investments in economic growth. Whereas Gorbachev was touting the geopolitical significance of faster economic development and maintaining that the recent improvement in growth rates was responsible for the upturn in Soviet-American relations, Shcherbytskyi remarked that the realization of Soviet internal tasks depended on the international situation, which remained sharp and complex.[110] In other words, Soviet security demanded that the defense budget receive higher priority than the growth of the economy. ...

...

SECURITY, CREDIBILITY, LIBERALIZATION

Since the beginning of 1987, Gorbachev has pushed harder to upgrade the relative importance of political factors in the Soviet security calculus. This attitude is exemplified by his decisions once again to decouple INF from SDI, to conclude an INF treaty involving asymmetrical Soviet reductions, and to announce a unilateral plan for reducing Soviet military manpower by 500,000 men. On a bureaucratic level, Gorbachev has focused elite attention on the political elements of security by giving a green light to unorthodox civilian defense theorists and stepping up the pressure for a reform of the Armed Forces that encompasses military doctrine as well as organization. He has also encroached on some traditional KGB prerogatives, particularly the blanketing in secrecy of Soviet institutions and decision-making, in order to satisfy the unprecedented verification requirements of the INF and prospective START agreements. Perhaps most significantly, he and his supporters have tried to institutionalize the new security approach by promoting a drastic revision of the traditional assessment of the Western military threat and by proposing reforms that would allow the domestic public to influence the broad contours of security policy.

These steps have been complemented by redoubled efforts to allay Western fears of the USSR. In addition to offering new concessions on arms cuts and verification, Gorbachev has sought to recast the traditional relationship between Soviet domestic politics and external policy. His predecessors tended instinctively to link the pursuit of external security with internal regimentation. In contrast, Gorbachev is attempting to moderate Western military behavior by capitalizing on the dramatic new program of internal political liberalization that he first unveiled before the Central Committee in January 1987. In revising security policy, he has drawn increasingly on the intellectual class for point men and political allies.[136] This tactic, designed to overcome conservative resistance at home, is also intended to reshape Western opinion by appealing to foreign intellectuals and opinion-makers. It is graphically symbolized by Gorbachev's decision to end Andrey Sakharov's six-year banishment, to invite the eminent dissenter to address the international Moscow Forum in February 1987, and, most recently, to allow him to travel to the United States.[137]

Security and Military Power. One indication of the evolution of Gorbachev's policy is his pledge that the USSR will not seek more security for itself than the United States has because this would make the United States feel insecure and thus violate political stability.[138] By emphasizing that strategic stability has a vital political as well as a military component, Gorbachev implicitly gave political relations with the United States a significant role—at least in theory—in determining Soviet military requirements.[139] Previously Gorbachev had confined his criticism of deterrence theory to warnings that in the future the policy of deterrence might lead to war. In the fall of 1987, however, he denied the past contribution of nuclear deterrence to Soviet security and implied that such a policy endangers the country. "Many people," he said, still sincerely believe in the efficacy of nuclear deterrence. In actuality, the possibility of catastrophic technical or human error has risen with the number of weapons, their complexity, and the duration of their deployment. Together these factors constitute "an enormous number of contingencies" that has heightened the likelihood of military conflict.[140]

Clearly the danger of accidental nuclear war triggered by a reflexive commitment to deterrence has worried Gorbachev more than the danger of an unprovoked Western attack. Contextual evidence makes it virtually certain that this critique of deterrence theory was directed at the theory's Soviet as well as Western proponents.[141] During this period, Soviet START negotiators in Geneva were showing an increasing willingness to consider deep cuts in strategic nuclear weapons, and Gorbachev appeared ready to push the logic of such cuts a long way.[142]

Gorbachev also gave a new twist to his contention that Soviet security depended on greater economic dynamism. While playing down the Western military threat, he claimed that reactionary Western circles were trying to slow the USSR's progress by locking it into a policy of military confrontation. However, he asserted, the USSR would not "irrationally and automatically" adopt military programs that imperialism was trying to foist on it through the arms competition.[143] The obvious implication was that a larger Soviet military effort, far from foiling imperialist designs, might play into the West's hands by undermining Soviet economic performance.

Gorbachev's increasingly radical security approach provoked tension. In advancing his sweeping proposals for political liberalization at the January plenum, Gorbachev sought to change the complexion of the Politburo by adding to it the liberal Aleksandr Yakovlev, and he focused on the political and economic "crisis phenomena" inside the Soviet system.[144] Glossing over the military competition with the West, he indicated that the Armed Forces should make more effective use of existing resources rather than press the party for bigger budgets.[145] He also expressed veiled dissatisfaction with the military establishment, which he said "also lives by means of restructuring." His displeasure probably stemmed from military foot-dragging on personnel changes as well as on other aspects of internal military reform.[146]

After hearing Gorbachev's speech, the Central Committee adopted a divergent interpretation of Soviet security needs. Omitting the concept of a domestic crisis, the plenum's final resolution highlighted the efforts of "militant imperialist circles" to attain strategic superiority. Although it stated that the party must "maintain the country's defense capacity on the necessary level"—language Gorbachev probably favored—the resolution also said incongruously that the international situation required "a comprehensive strengthening of the defense possibilities of our country." Moreover, it praised the Armed Forces fulsomely, dropping the undertone of criticism in Gorbachev's speech.[147]

This episode illustrates the obstacles Gorbachev has encountered in trying to recast the bureaucratic hierarchies overseeing the various elements of security policy. His greatest success occurred in the Ministry of Foreign Affairs. At the plenum Gorbachev pressed for the continuation of staff and structural changes at the MFA as a prerequisite for a more active foreign policy. Echoing this theme a few months later, Shevardnadze attacked the diplomatic service for having pursued a distorted definition of the Soviet national interest in the past and voiced his determination to carry out further staff changes.[148]

Marshal Sokolov, on the other hand, was far less receptive to the idea of revamping the Ministry of Defense to pursue a revised interpretation of the national interest and responded coolly to Gorbachev's January plenum speech.[149] Although Marshal Akhromeyev began to treat military personnel and leadership practices as areas requiring serious reform, Sokolov paid only lip service to the idea.[150] Obviously relying on the conservative resistance to Gorbachev within the Central Committee, Sokolov expatiated on the "high evaluation" the Armed Forces had received at the January plenum and played down the need for the rejuvenation of military cadres.[151] In all likelihood, it was Sokolov who instructed the military press to ignore Gorbachev's comments at the plenum about a brewing internal crisis and about the military's shortcomings.[152] ...

Thus Gorbachev launched a campaign to renovate the military high command and, in the process, to install officers with doctrinal dispositions closer to his own.[157] The campaign received a serendipitous boost from the Matthias Rust affair. The ability of the West German youth to pilot his small Cessna to an unhindered landing near Red Square deeply embarassed the Armed Forces and provided a golden opportunity to replace Sokolov with Dmitriy Yazov, an officer more sympathetic to internal military reform.[158] Even before it became fashionable, Yazov had voiced concern about the need to upgrade the personal and professional standards of Soviet military men, and he had been put in charge of personnel policy at the Ministry of Defense shortly after Gorbachev called for *perestroyka* of the military. In selecting the relatively junior Yazov to succeed Sokolov, Gorbachev by-passed a layer of higher-ranking officers and created a defense minister owing a larger than usual political debt to the general secretary.

The drive for military reform was also fueled by an unprecedented wave of articles in which civilian foreign-affairs specialists invaded the domain of the military theoreticians and took stands uncongenial to mainstream military thought. In the pre-Gorbachev days, civilian specialists had tried to influence military policy only indirectly—by offering a more temperate image of the West and its military intentions. Now, in response to the urgings of officials such as Shevardnadze, Yakovlev, and Dobrynin, civilian analysts began to offer opinions on the nature of strategic stability, the scope of arms cuts, and the kinds of weapons that should be eliminated.[159] Although these analysts still lacked access to many varieties of Soviet military data, their outspokenness confronted professional military theorists with an unfamiliar challenge.

Part of the challenge was a growing civilian interest in unilateral military reductions. For example, a deputy director of the USA Institute co-authored an article that recalled Khrushchev's unilateral troop cuts and claimed that the cuts had not harmed Soviet security because "they were accompanied by a broad peace offensive that made it virtually impossible for the West to bring additional military pressure to bear on our country."[160] Disputing this idea, Deputy Defense

Minister Ivan Tret'yak warned that curbing imperialism was more important than reducing the defense budget and asserted that the deleterious effects of Khrushchev's troop cuts had endured to the present day.[161] Nevertheless, some prominent civilian analysts continued to advocate unilateral cuts as a more effective means of promoting the country's security and lightening its military burden than negotiated bilateral arms reductions.[162] Although none of the liberal Politburo members publicly espoused this view, privately it plainly enjoyed high-level backing and foreshadowed Gorbachev's 1988 announcement of planned unilateral cuts.

Breaking the Reykjavik Stalemate. Gorbachev's battle for tighter control of the country's foreign-policy apparatus coincided with his search for a way out of the post-Reykjavik stalemate. At the end of February 1987, in a move that artfully obscured the simultaneous termination of the Soviet moratorium on nuclear tests, Gorbachev once again decoupled the INF issue from talks on strategic offensive and defensive arms and promised to strive for a quick INF accord.[163] As the INF negotiations progressed and the United States pressed for rigorous measures to verify such a treaty, Soviet negotiators began to evince a new willingness to consider measures that previously had been rejected out of hand. Meanwhile, building on his call for political reform at the January plenum, Gorbachev endorsed the "humanization of international relations" and announced a new approach to the human-rights issues subsumed under Basket Three of the Conference on Security and Cooperation in Europe (CSCE). Denying the assertion of "those who assume ... that our position is the result of pressure from the West," he called for a CSCE meeting in Moscow on "humanitarian cooperation," despite the likelihood that such a conference would generate Western pressures for further liberalization of the Soviet system.[164]

In addition, Gorbachev hinted at a relaxation of efforts to promote pro-Soviet regimes in the Third World. The sovereign right of peoples to decide on revolutionary or evolutionary paths of development, including the right to preserve "the status quo," should be observed unconditionally, he said.[165] This statement appeared in a speech advocating a major expansion in the peace-keeping role of the United Nations. Evidently it was intended to signal a new Soviet restraint in regional conflicts and to build up the UN as an umbrella under which the USSR could withdraw from some of its most exposed Third-World commitments, particularly in Afghanistan.

Several of Gorbachev's colleagues backed his diplomacy, including his announcement delinking INF from other arms issues. ...

Other figures reacted more coolly to Gorbachev's emphasis on political gestures and concessionary arms-control initiatives. Ligachev waited almost two months before mentioning and commending the new policy.[170] If the meaning of this delay was ambiguous, Shcherbytskyi's position was more clear-cut. Unlike some liberal politicians, the Ukrainian leader refrained from mentioning the positive effects of the January plenum on Western public opinion. Instead he interpreted the plenum in a way that underscored the comments on military prepared-ness in the plenum resolution. More important, his brief reference to the new policy on INF fell far short of an endorsement, most likely signaling a continuing belief that no INF agreement should be signed in the absence of new limits on SDI.[171]

Minister of Defense Sokolov, not yet under the shadow of the Rust affair, also remained skeptical. After keeping silent for two and a half months about the INF decision, Sokolov finally endorsed it, but he simultaneously emphasized the ag-gressive nature of imperialism and presented a pessimistic gloss on the lessons of World War II, thereby suggesting that a policy of diplomatic maneuver might not suffice to counter the Western military threat.[172] In short, the debate about how to combine political gestures, negotiating concessions, and military preparations was still simmering.[173]

This impression was confirmed by polemics that broke out shortly after Gorbachev announced his decision to delink INF. Aleksandr Bovin, a liberal jour-nalist who had long favored a softer line toward the West and was pushing for more *glasnost'* in the media's treatment of foreign policy, suggested that the origi-nal decision to deploy SS-20 missiles in the European theater had been a mistake. Invoking Lenin's criticism of a diplomacy based on "ultimatums," Bovin justified the recent decoupling of INF from SDI in terms that suggested some people be-lieved the recoupling at Reykjavik should become part of a long-term strategy, rather than merely a short-term tactical maneuver.[174]

Bovin was promptly challenged by Major-General Yuriy Lebedev, a General Staff officer who had served as military advisor at the unsuccessful Soviet-Ameri-can INF negotiations in the early 1980's. According to Lebedev, the original deci-sion to deploy the SS-20's was correct. It had not provoked the American INF de-ployments—as Bovin implied—but had been a response to military moves that the West had already planned.[175] Lebedev was silent about the decoupling of INF, but he was plainly unsympathetic to Bovin's broad hint that Soviet military pro-grams should be curbed to elicit reciprocal Western restraint in areas like SDI. Persistent skepticism about the feasibility of such tactics apparently compelled Gorbachev to defend himself against the charge that his economy-minded em-phasis on opening up and commercializing the Soviet space program was causing the USSR to fall behind the United States in the military competition in space.[176]
...

SECURITY, LIBERALIZATION, AND SUBVERSION

The evolving security debate posed questions not only about diplomatic tactics and military policy but about opening the Soviet system to the outside world. As the superpowers edged closer to agreeing on the weapons to be eliminated under an INF accord, Soviet decision-makers were forced to weigh how much informa-tion and access the USSR would give American arms-control monitors in order to gain American acceptance of the agreement. One hint came in August, when Soviet and American negotiators agreed on a system of compulsory challenge inspections of chemical weapons facilities. Another signal came in September, when several US Congressmen traveling in the USSR were unexpectedly allowed to inspect and photograph the controversial Krasnoyarsk radar facility. These events lent weight to Gorbachev's statement the following week that the USSR was prepared to embrace "previously unheard-of standards" of openness to ensure the monitoring of international arms-control obligations.[179] They also gave some credibility to his implicit acknowledgment that the published Soviet defense budget was misleading and his promise that as the regime carried out internal economic reform, it would publish a defense budget comparable to Western budgets.[180]

The interaction between security policy and political liberalization was also reflected in the shifting Soviet stance on human rights. In September, despite a sharp rise in human-rights protests by some ethnic minorities, Gorbachev followed up his earlier proposal for a Moscow CSCE meeting by stating that national legislation and rules on humanitarian issues must be brought into conformity with international obligations and norms.[181] Shortly before Gorbachev traveled to meet President Reagan in Washington, the press announced the formation of a Public Commission for Humanitarian Questions and Human Rights to "achieve conformity of Soviet legislation with the obligations assumed by the Soviet Union in the Helsinki Final Act and in UN human rights documents."[182] Despite the internal sensitivity of the issue, Gorbachev sought to accommodate Western concerns and played down the possibility that the West might manipulate the issue to undermine the Soviet system. ...

This linking of *perestroyka* and foreign relations struck the more conservative leaders as dangerous. Figures such as Shcherbytskyi had taken a hard line on security policy from the beginning; others, such as Ligachev, were disciplinarian reformers whose views of security now seemed increasingly conservative because of the emerging radicalism of Gorbachev's approach. Although these leaders generally believed that economic revitalization would strengthen the USSR's international position, they were far more skeptical about the benefits of political liberalization.[185] Shcherbytskyi and Ligachev both asserted that the West sought to promote a form of democratization that would destroy the socialist system, and both remained silent about the idea of an international human-rights meeting in Moscow.[186] The connection between domestic political reform and socialism's attractiveness abroad, Ligachev explained, had to be understood "from precise class positions."[187] In other words, the essentials of the party's authoritarian rule must not be sacrificed in a misguided effort to make the USSR politically appealing to the West.

Chebrikov articulated the conservative view most forcefully in a speech commemorating the birth of Feliks Dzerzhinskiy, the first head of the secret police. Liberalized treatment of dissidents, said Chebrikov, would not eliminate Western "ideological speculation" on human-rights issues. Rather, it would give greater influence to antisocialist elements susceptible to being used for subversive ends by Western intelligence agencies.[188] ...

Chebrikov also appeared concerned about the security implications of Gorbachev's diplomatic tactics and approach to arms-control verification. Western intelligence agencies, warned the KGB chief, were stepping up efforts to gain information about Soviet technical research and economic plans, as well as about the USSR's "planned foreign-policy actions."[191] This remark was a clear rebuttal to Shevardnadze and others pressing for more *glasnost'* in the realm of foreign policy. In all probability Chebrikov, who had taken a conservative line on the general issue of *glasnost'* and had warned of intensifying Western efforts to obtain Soviet military secrets, disliked Gorbachev's radically new stance on arms-control verification. Many KGB officials undoubtedly distrusted it because it threatened to breach the secrecy in which the KGB had long cloaked Soviet military activities. ...

The gradual convergence of Gorbachev's revision of security policy with his campaign for domestic political liberalization posed a serious challenge to the country's national-security institutions. As it happened, Yel'tsin had already provided a harbinger of the challenge by launching lacerating public attacks on the Air Defense Forces in the aftermath of the Rust affair. Flaying commanders for "elitism" and for ignoring party recommendations in making military promotions, Yel'tsin complained that the military establishment had ignored the party's call for *glasnost'* out of a mistaken belief that public discussion of military deficiencies would be harmful to national security.[195]

At about the same time, a prominent Belorussian writer actually argued that if the West launched a massive first strike, Soviet nuclear retaliation would be unjustified, and he praised the superior courage of military men who "give their military expertise to the antiwar movement."[196] Leading officers in the Main Political Directorate and General Staff replied with angry denunciations of such "pacificism."[197] Nonetheless, the liberal intellectuals reiterated their position unequivocally, arguing that "the truth of the new thinking is obligatory even for military thought," and some objected to the traditional practice of interrupting the education of promising young specialists by drafting them for military service. A few daring writers even went so far as to argue that the military establishment had a vested interest in opposing peace and was willfully misinterpreting Gorbachev's pronouncements on security.[198]

The anger this provoked among some Politburo members was expressed most forcefully by Defense Minister Yazov. Although willing to agree that organizational and doctrinal reforms could make the Armed Forces more efficient, Yazov clearly resented such wide-ranging attacks on military values. Adopting a cautious attitude toward political liberalization as a whole, Yazov warned that criticism was a very sharp weapon. Sensationalism and a disrespectful attitude toward military cadres should be avoided, he said, and the forthcoming celebration of the Revolution's 70th anniversary should be used to instill a patriotic appreciation of Soviet history.[199] Yazov's remarks about disrespect may have been intended as a rebuttal to Yel'tsin, and the Defense Minister must have been happy to see Yel'tsin publicly humiliated when Gorbachev, carefully weighing the political situation, came down on the side of Yel'tsin's enemies. In December 1987, Yazov met with a group of Soviet writers and again lashed out at the negative depiction of the military in literature that, in his view, threatened the patriotic sentiments needed to maintain a powerful military establishment.[200]

The disagreements about literature clearly overlapped with the debates over security policy. At the meeting with the writers, deputy chief of the Main Political Directorate Col.-Gen. D. Volkogonov complained that although "the term deterrence has been stigmatized, today, *when no political mechanism for curbing war is available,* we ... have no other option but to resort to the military mechanism."[201] Similarly, Aleksandr Prokhanov, a highly conservative writer and author of many articles praising the intervention in Afghanistan, glorified the army for achieving parity with the United States and castigated the "shameful" attacks on the military by liberal intellectuals. Denying that the INF Treaty had come about because of "pacificism" rather than Soviet strategic parity, he contended that the military's special expertise had to make it the central participant in arms control, just as it was central in the military buildup.[202] ...

Reassessing the Western Challenge. Near the end of 1987 Gorbachev began to articulate the idea, latent in his previous speeches, that the Western powers might be adopting a much less aggressive form of international behavior. At the 70th anniversary celebration of the Revolution, Gorbachev noted that members of the Western ruling elite now recognized the existence of a "catastrophic danger to peace," and he asked rhetorically whether heightened world interdependence might not curb the most destructive types of imperialist behavior.[205] In February 1988, he told the Central Committee that current international conditions were substantially different from past conditions because the political balance in Western regimes had shifted from the "party of war" to the "party of peace."[206] Yakovlev echoed this theme, claiming that the USSR had entered an era "entirely different" from the one during which it had been necessary to respond to the West's military challenges with emergency measures.[207] Gorbachev and his Politburo allies obviously felt that the West had ceased to behave in a traditional "imperialist" fashion, although they refrained from saying this directly, and they sanctioned the publication of articles by civilian analysts who spelled out this view with extraordinary bluntness.

The clearest example was an article by three foreign-affairs specialists published in the first issue of *Kommunist* in 1988. Vigorously rejecting analogies between 1941 and the current international situation, the authors categorically denied that the West would intentionally attack the USSR. According to them "today in East-West relations there is not one conflict" that might produce "the temptation to resort to war ... it is difficult to imagine for what goals Western armies might invade the territory of the socialist states ... today there are no politically influential forces in Western Europe or in the USA which would set themselves such a task," let alone launch a surprise nuclear attack. In place of the classic Leninist claim that imperialism's internal dynamics make it inherently aggressive, these authors asserted that "bourgeois democracy serves as a definite barrier on the path of unleashing ... war" between the capitalist and socialist systems. However, they warned, the likelihood of *accidental* nuclear war between East and West was growing: "An outwardly paradoxical situation is therefore developing: the threat of intentional nuclear aggression is declining, but the threat of war can also increase."[208]

The implications of this diagnosis were truly radical. If East-West military conflict was likely to arise not from premeditated Western aggression but from misperceptions and technical malfunctioning of weapons systems, the main goal of Soviet security policy must shift from intimidating the West to reassuring it. This being the case, the accumulation of military power could easily become counterproductive, whereas measures to allay the fears of potential adversaries would acquire a vital role in protecting the USSR against nuclear destruction.

Some party leaders and military men, however, doubted that the trends in Western policy were as benign as Gorbachev and his allies contended. Shcherbytskyi, for example, highlighted the "aggressive nature of imperialism" and underscored the need to keep in mind "the severe experience of the past." In his view, highly influential groups in the West were still pursuing a reckless plan to achieve military superiority through the militarization of space, as well as by fanning regional conflicts and engaging in international terrorism. Apparently Shcherbytskyi, whose reservations about the INF treaty have already been noted, disapproved of Gorbachev's approach to the resolution of regional conflicts. In what was probably a reference to internal deliberations over whether to sign an agreement calling for the removal of Soviet troops from Afghanistan, he declared that the USSR was on the side of "all states and peoples repelling the attacks of international reaction ... [and] defending the sovereign right to select the paths and forms of their development."[209]

The theme of persisting imperialist aggressiveness was also underscored by Defense Minister Yazov. Yazov had displayed considerable flexibility on a number of points of military policy and doctrine. He had endorsed the goal of a 50 percent cut in strategic arms and a "radical, bilateral reduction of conventional forces."[210] He also declared that the avoidance of war had become a governing principle of Soviet military doctrine—thereby implying that the Armed Forces must devote greater attention to confidence-building measures designed to prevent inadvertent war.[211] But Yazov was not ready to dismiss the Western military threat or to contemplate unilateral cuts. "The threat emanating from imperialism," he warned, "must not be underestimated."[212] Asserting repeatedly that military-strategic parity was the decisive condition for preventing war, he maintained that military parity must be a crucial part of any definition of military sufficiency.[213] He also demanded that historians describe the Armed Forces' decisive contribution in the past to the avoidance of war.[214] ...

THE 19TH PARTY CONFERENCE AND AFTER

In the spring of 1988, as preparations unfolded for the 19th national party confer-ence, the "Andreyeva affair" revealed the depth of the political disagreements sur-rounding security policy. Reportedly on the prompting of Ligachev, the newspa-per *Sovetskaya Rossiya* printed a chauvinistic attack by Nina Andreyeva on Gorbachev's political program.[217] In a thinly veiled allusion to Gorbachev's and Yakovlev's accent on the priority of "common human values" in international re-lations, Andreyeva objected to the recent intellectual about-face of "a respected academician" who now asserted that "present-day relations between states from the two different socioeconomic systems apparently lack any class content." In ac-tuality, said Andreyeva, "peaceful coexistence is nothing but a form of class strug-gle in the international arena." Andreyeva denounced "a pacifist erosion of de-fense and patriotic consciousness" that fed such ideas as the abolition of Soviet military service. She also inveighed against emigration, especially of Soviet Jews, and warned that the politicization of unofficial organizations at home was lead-ing to "a by no means socialist pluralism" patterned on Western political liberal-ism.[218] All in all, the article amounted to a defiant restatement of traditional na-tional-security attitudes carried over from the Stalin era, and some military as well as civilian party units called meetings to publicize its contents.[219]

After almost three weeks, *Pravda* delivered a stinging editorial rebuttal. Con-demning persons who failed to understand the depth of the domestic crisis affect-ing the country, the party newspaper accused conservative forces of supporting a brittle ideology that made the Soviet regime more susceptible to foreign propa-ganda. *Pravda* also condemned Andreyeva's "speculation on the concept of patri-otism. A patriot is not one who screams loudly about alleged 'internal threats' to socialism. ... A patriot is someone who, not fearing any difficulties, acts in the in-terests of the country and the benefit of the people."[220] According to one Western press report, after a Politburo confrontation over the Andreyeva letter Gorbachev met with several military district commanders, possibly to shore up his position with the officer corps.[221]

Nevertheless, echoes of the deep anxieties voiced by Andreyeva continued to appear in the statements of political conservatives and military men who were alarmed about the harsh criticism of the military establishment by liberal civil-ians. A military theorist warned against overestimating the influence of the West-ern "peace parties" (which according to Gorbachev now determined Western pol-icy) and challenged the reformers' pet notion of responding asymmetrically to new Western military programs. In the same vein, the conservative writer Prokhanov claimed that military parity was indispensable for the USSR, which was still "surrounded by powerful Western civilizations that have integrated against us." "Amateurish experiments" in arms control, he warned, "can set off an explosion because the present balance is very tenuous."[222]

In response, the liberal reformers, already seeking ways to undermine the theo-retical assumptions of traditional security policy, launched a complementary attack on its historiographical underpinnings. The most dramatic example appeared in the publications of Vyacheslav Dashichev, a historian employed at an institute of the Academy of Sciences. Closely identifying his views with Shevardnadze and the Foreign Ministry, Dashichev faulted Stalin's foreign policies for a political failure to protect Soviet security against the Nazis and for causing the West to unite against a perceived Soviet military threat after World War II. More recently, he said, such ill-considered actions as the intervention in Afghanistan and the deployment of the SS-20's had given the United States a pretext for military expansion, creating a dangerously superior Western potential for generating military power, and had crystallized an anti-Soviet front including the NATO powers, China, and Japan.[223] Dashichev denied that strategic parity with the West was desirable and clearly contrasted the idea of parity with the notion of "reasonable sufficiency." To curb the arms race, he said, a "political modus vivendi" must be found between East and West. Instead of misguided efforts to achieve "small-change" successes in the Third World, the USSR's real national interests required the creation of an international climate favorable to a deep sociopolitical and economic transformation of the Soviet system, which "can and must influence the world social process exclusively by its economic, political, scientific, and cultural successes."[224]

These assertive arguments provoked sharp ripostes from more conservative commentators. No doubt upset by the military establishment's crumbling monopoly over drawing military lessons from Soviet history, Defense Minister Yazov warned that writers on military history bore a "great responsibility" to avoid superficiality and a lack of objectivity.[225] In a similar vein, two foreign-affairs specialists, Valentin Falin and Lev Bezymenskiy, provided a lengthy rebuttal of the liberal line. The reappraisal of Soviet diplomacy, they cautioned, should not yield to "the temptation to seek the truth 'somewhere in the middle' and to metaphysically divide in two the blame for all prewar and postwar complexities ..., let alone to load these sins on Stalin and Stalinism just for the sake of 'breaking' with the past." According to these writers, "the 'cold war' was not our choice" but the result of American machinations.[226]

These disputes foreshadowed developments at the party conference. Gorbachev's keynote speech severely criticized the foreign-policy legacy he had inherited. The past application of "command-administrative methods," he asserted, had produced erroneous foreign-policy decisions made by a handful of people without adequate reflection or consultation. Gorbachev stated that attaining strategic parity with the US had been necessary, but he vigorously questioned the lengths to which this policy had been carried. Although "fundamental changes in the world" had made it possible to employ political methods of ensuring security, he argued, these methods had not always been used, and the USSR had allowed itself to become entangled in an arms race harmful to its socioeconomic development and international standing. Moreover, traditional Soviet political methods of struggling for peace and disarmament had lost their persuasiveness, thereby increasing the danger of military confrontation and requiring new political thinking.

As Gorbachev described it, the heart of the new thinking was the priority of common human values over class values in the nuclear age. Thanks to the new approach, said Gorbachev, "the USSR is, as it were, 'opening' anew for the outside world." From extensive contacts with other societies it was extracting useful ideas and reaching new understandings of the meaning of such values as freedom and democracy.[227] This comment signaled Gorbachev's desire to incorporate Western economic and political ideas into the reform agenda and to use society-to-society contacts with the West to modify the traditional Soviet political culture. At the same time, Gorbachev signaled reduced attention to military requirements. Proclaiming that the share of national income going to consumption must be increased in the upcoming five-year plan, he connected this goal with the need for "deep changes" in the heavy and defense industries. The technological and manpower requirements of defense programs, he said, should now be guaranteed primarily in qualitative rather than quantitative terms.[228]

Gorbachev also advocated basic alterations in the process of formulating and implementing security policy. Calling for much more foreign-policy *glasnost'*, he advocated decision-making arrangements that would reflect the interests and desire of all social groups. In addition, he urged a "radical increase" in the administrative effectiveness of the agencies handling foreign affairs. No agency, he said pointedly, could remain outside the process of democratic renewal, it was necessary to support the work of the KGB, the Ministry of Defense, and the General Staff in bettering their activity in conditions of unfolding democratic processes.[229] Unlike Gorbachev's past criticisms of the management of external policy, this statement did not name the Ministry of Foreign Affairs. Foreshadowing developments later in the fall, Gorbachev's new accent on *perestroyka* in the KGB and the General Staff amounted to a demand for institutional and policy change in these components of the national-security establishment.

This demand dovetailed with Gorbachev's proposal for a governmental reform that would strengthen the legislative organs and vest extensive new powers over external policy in a chief of state elected to chair the Supreme Soviet. Under this new dispensation, the chief of state, in addition to setting the domestic political agenda, would chair the Defense Council and play the central role in deciding major questions of foreign and security policy.[230] Gorbachev plainly intended to occupy this new post himself rather than concede it to Gromyko, the head of state at the time. At the conference one regional party official took the extraordinary step of advocating changes in the Politburo, and after a leading question from Gorbachev, he named Gromyko and Mikhail Solomentsev as members who should be removed.[231]

These maneuvers provoked high-level resistance. Just before the Politburo and Central Committee met to finalize the theses to be discussed at the conference, an angry Gromyko twice warned Gorbachev against forcing the pace of *perestroyka*.[232] Gromyko's objection probably explains why the theses, which were published before the conference, made no mention of restructuring the office of chief of state. The proposal appeared without forewarning in Gorbachev's opening conference address, and the final conference resolutions skirted the question of what powers the chief of state would exercise under a reformed governmental structure. Moreover, Gorbachev's efforts to remove Gromyko were temporarily stymied. Working to shore up the centrist and conservative forces in the Politburo, Ligachev intervened by pointedly reminding the conference that Gorbachev had become general secretary thanks to support from Gromyko, Chebrikov, Solomentsev, and himself.[233] Shcherbytskyi, perhaps reflecting the opinion of some military men, also resisted Gromyko's removal.[234] Gorbachev's bid to use legislative reform to strengthen his power and mobilize public support for his security agenda was momentarily blocked.

Behind the scenes, however, Gorbachev and his allies continued to press their attack. Addressing a large meeting at the Ministry of Foreign Affairs in July, Shevardnadze issued a ringing affirmation of the priority of common human values over class values and urged the "exclusive hegemony" of political over military means in conducting foreign relations. According to the Foreign Minister, the interpretation of peaceful coexistence as a specific form of class struggle was "erroneous" and "anti-Leninist." Glancing back over the history of Soviet external relations, Shevardnadze echoed many of the themes sounded by Dashichev and other liberal publicists. Stalin's mistaken line toward the German Social Democrats, he said, had contributed to Hitler's rise, and the blood purges had undermined the credibility of Soviet foreign policy among potential sympathizers abroad. After the war, the USSR had failed to exhaust all the possibilities for mitigating the Cold War. Arguing for a rethinking of the lessons from World War II in light of "the newest experience," Shevardnadze contended that the war had shown that large standing military forces were not of decisive importance. Any advantage in standing forces enjoyed by an aggressor could be overcome if the victim possessed a developed scientific and industrial base.[235]

Shevardnadze's comments about the current international scene were equally provocative. His suggestive remark about the "peculiar boomerang effect" of the use of military force in the postwar era undoubtedly referred to Afghanistan and probably also reflected a belief that the decision to deploy the SS-20's had been a mistake.[236] In any case, he bluntly criticized the 1983 Soviet walkout from the superpower arms talks as an error that had contributed to the creation of "a second strategic front" against the USSR through the US INF deployments.[237] He also complained that previous Soviet leaders had contributed to the stalemate in the Vienna negotiations on mutual and balanced (conventional) force reductions (MBFR) by failing to conduct the talks with sufficient energy.[238] This sweeping indictment of the past work of many veteran diplomats, chief among them Gromyko, foreshadowed a shift to unilateral cuts as a means of imparting momentum to East-West force reductions.

Shevardnadze coupled his criticism of Soviet diplomacy with barbed complaints about the role of the Ministry of Defense.[239] Calling for the creation of a threat-assessment "mechanism free of arbitrary outside pressures from anyone," he went out of his way to say that past Soviet decisions to produce chemical weapons had been based on "the most primitive and distorted conception about what strengthens and what weakens the country." Shevardnadze criticized the past "compulsory delegation" of diplomatic functions from the foreign ministry to "other command spheres." Ensuring the priority of political means in security, he said, required a rethinking of the "role and place of the Ministry of Foreign Affairs in the structure of executive authority, ensuring its higher activity ... and effectiveness in developing all dimensions of our external policy." Soviet diplomats did not claim the right to know literally everything, but they wanted to know everything related to their sphere of responsibility. Hence "major innovations in the realm of the defense program must pass through an MFA check for their legal conformity with current international agreements and with [the USSR's] declared political positions."[240] In other words, Shevardnadze was asserting his ministry's right to rule on the congruence of new military policies and weapons systems with Soviet treaty obligations and political declarations.

Shevardnadze also complained indirectly about the KGB's handling of human rights and took a position on military secrecy that probably displeased many KGB officials. In comments undoubtedly intended for Ligachev and Chebrikov, he denied that the USSR was paying too much attention to foreign opinion about human rights and argued that domestic political liberalization was inherently desirable. Parrying the charge that legal reform fell outside his ministry's legitimate concerns, Shevardnadze asserted that the USSR must take account of foreign opinion and that its policy toward the rights of citizens was a critical determinant of the Soviet image abroad. In order to defend Soviet foreign-policy interests, he said, it was essential to ensure "irreproachable positions in ... the activity of the law-enforcement departments and their adherence to the laws, which must not contradict our political declarations."[241] Shevardnadze also extolled the recent "giant leap" embodied in the changed Soviet policy toward arms-control verification. "It has turned out," he said, "that our national interests will be better ensured if we open the doors of our nuclear 'foundries' to foreign monitors and in turn ourselves step over the thresholds of foreign nuclear facilities. ... This seems improbable, but it is a fact."[242] KGB handling of dissidents was undoubtedly one target of Shevardnadze's remarks about human rights,[243] and his observations about verification must have grated on the KGB officials responsible for guarding Soviet military secrets against Western espionage.

Shevardnadze's brief for his own ministry tied in with his elaboration of Gorbachev's plan to create a constitutional mechanism for the formulation of security policy. Shevardnadze referred favorably to the idea of having open legislative hearings at which ministers would be required to answer unrehearsed questions from Supreme Soviet deputies, and he asserted that the elected organs should supervise the open discussion of military budgets, plans for military development, and the use of Soviet military forces abroad. He also proposed soliciting the general public's views on basic foreign-policy decisions by means of opinion surveys and referenda. While it is doubtful that Shevardnadze was prepared to grant the public the final word on major foreign-policy decisions, he did envision giving the public a significant role in shaping security policy, and he obviously expected that this would generate pressure for the policies he favored.[244]

Shevardnadze's speech drew a quick rebuttal from Ligachev. Although Ligachev granted that combatting the danger of nuclear war was a vital common human interest, he implicitly denied the priority of common human interests and underscored the class character of international relations. "Any other framing of the question merely introduces confusion into the consciousness of Soviet people and our friends abroad," he said. Plainly upset by Shevardnadze's approach to human rights, Ligachev again warned against the growing enthusiasm for Western political and economic liberalism. Ligachev also took issue with the reformers' increasing inclination to press for compromise settlements of Third-World conflicts as a way of improving relations with the United States. "Active [Soviet] involvement in deciding common human problems," Ligachev cautioned, "by no means signifies any sort of artificial 'braking' of the social and national-liberation struggle."[245] Ligachev sought to buttress his position by stating that Gorbachev's speech at the 19th Party Conference had affirmed the CPSU's solidarity with the workers of the world. He failed, however, to note that Gorbachev had stressed the universality of the principle of self-determination and the impermissibility of using military or other means to force a nation to adopt a particular social system; nor did he mention Gorbachev's depiction of the withdrawal from Afghanistan as a major watershed in the resolution of various regional conflicts. Shortly after Ligachev's speech, Yakovlev reiterated and extended the liberal point of view. Siding with Shevardnadze, Yakovlev asserted that the priority of common human values allowed one to view the theory of coexistence with the West "realistically and healthily."[246] At the time of the party conference Yakovlev had implied that the Soviet system was not yet inherently peaceful and could become so only through further political liberalization.[247] More clearly than ever before, he spelled out the goal of incorporating Western political and economic practices into the radically new model of socialism that, liberals contended, the Soviet Union required.[248]

At the end of September, Gorbachev and his allies won a significant victory in the struggle over security policy. At a hastily called meeting of the Central Committee, Gromyko resigned and Solomentsev was removed from the Politburo, along with two nonvoting members from the Brezhnev years. At the same meeting, party secretary Vadim Medvedev vaulted to voting membership in the Politburo without passing through the nonvoting stage. Medvedev, who had played a key part in developing a more flexible policy toward Eastern Europe, voiced enthusiastic support for the primacy of common human values in international relations and called for the incorporation of Western elements into a new Soviet model of socialism.[249] Following Gromyko's resignation, the Supreme Soviet also elected Gorbachev chief of state. The Politburo balance thus shifted noticeably toward those favoring a more accommodating, less militarized policy toward the

West, and Gorbachev took an important step toward creating a personal power base outside the party apparatus and capitalizing on the projected legislative reforms to strengthen his control over security policy. ...

Chebrikov's transfer appears to be part of a stratagem to reshape the KGB into an institution devoted more to foreign intelligence gathering than to domestic political repression.[251] His replacement as KGB chief is Vladimir A. Kryuchkov, previously head of the KGB's First Chief Directorate, the branch responsible for foreign intelligence gathering and operations. In the past, chairmen selected from the KGB's own ranks came generally from the more numerous and larger branches responsible for domestic political surveillance, whose officers followed a career path separate from those in the foreign intelligence directorate.[252] In contrast to domestic KGB officers, who have traditionally resisted East-West détente because of the disruptive impact on Soviet internal affairs, KGB foreign intelligence officers have a vested interest in better relations with the West. The relaxation of East-West tensions facilitates espionage and the theft of foreign technology, and it upgrades the significance of KGB political operations (in contrast to Soviet military programs) as a means of enhancing Soviet interests abroad.[253]

Circumstantial evidence suggests that Kryuchkov is more closely aligned with Gorbachev than with Chebrikov or other party conservatives. ...

Shortly before his promotion, Kryuchkov made some statements that meshed with the reformist platform and differed from Chebrikov's views. On the eve of the leadership shake-up, Chebrikov voiced resistance to a renovation of police personnel and reiterated the conservative line on human rights and military secrecy.[255] By contrast, Kryuchkov, who attended the July meeting at the foreign ministry, went out of his way to praise Shevardnadze's keynote speech, despite its implicit criticism of the KGB's handling of human rights, and to compliment the Ministry of Foreign Affairs.[256] Kryuchkov strongly underscored the benefits of Gorbachev's flexible approach to arms control and foreign policy. Alluding, perhaps, to Chebrikov's reservations about signing the INF treaty, he remarked that events had answered the people who had recently asked whether further efforts should be expended on disarmament negotiations with the current American administration. Kryuchkov also asserted that the policy of national reconciliation in Afghanistan offered hope and light in the "long and dark tunnel" of that conflict. Although he remarked that foreign intelligence services were continuing their efforts against the USSR, he did not repeat Chebrikov's claim that these efforts were intensifying or that they threatened the existence of the state. Instead, he focused on the benefits of closer East-West ties for Soviet foreign policy—and, by implication, for Soviet intelligence gathering abroad.[257] Further, he suggested that in some respects *perestroyka* had made the job of Western intelligence services more difficult.[258] ...

Gorbachev's December 1988 speech at the United Nations marked a watershed in the internal debate over security policy. By announcing plans for a unilateral reduction of 500,000 troops over the next two years, Gorbachev swung publicly toward the civilians who contend that unilateral Soviet cuts can serve as a political stimulus to Western arms reductions and provide a rapid amelioration of mounting internal economic hardships. Gorbachev's pledge to withdraw some 5,000 tanks and bridging equipment from Eastern Europe was also an important step toward making Soviet military doctrine defensive in an operational rather than merely in a rhetorical sense. Apparently these dramatic policy changes generated civil-military tensions and led to the retirement of Marshal Akhromeyev as First Deputy Minister of Defense and Chief of the General Staff. Although Akhromeyev allegedly retired on grounds of health, the fact that his retirement became known on the day of Gorbachev's speech suggests that it was the product of disagreement about the unilateral reductions Gorbachev announced.[263] ...

CONCLUSION

The Soviet national-security agenda has changed dramatically under Gorbachev. In the five years before he became general secretary, the Brezhnevian dual-track policy was repeatedly attacked by hard-liners who doubted the utility of superpower negotiations and insisted that Soviet military spending must be sharply expanded. By stimulating a new critique of the dual-track approach which charged that too much rather than too little weight had been put on military power, Gorbachev has transformed the two-sided public debate into a three-cornered contest among hard-liners, centrists, and liberals. The story of Soviet security policy since 1985 is a chronicle of the increasing strength of the Politburo forces favoring the liberal approach. Although Gorbachev and his allies have not yet engineered an equally decisive renovation of the party Central Committee, they clearly dominate security decision-making at the present time.

This changing political balance has made Soviet security policy increasingly daring and accommodating. During his first year in office, Gorbachev won domestic acceptance of the principle of negotiated, symmetrical cuts in the Eastern and Western arsenals. Through the INF Treaty, he established a precedent for negotiated but asymmetrical cuts. His recent UN speech validates unilateral reductions as a legitimate method of guaranteeing Soviet security. He and his political allies have shown an unprecedented willingness to accept on-site inspections of military facilities, to respond to Western concerns about human-rights violations, and to open their society to extensive international contacts that previously would have been rejected as a pretext for Western espionage.

Almost all these changes have encountered resistance from significant groups of party conservatives, professional officers, and KGB officials. These groups distrust Gorbachev's emphasis on political instruments of security and his penchant for conciliatory gestures toward the West, and they fear the potential impact of his policies on the Soviet internal order. On occasion, the General Secretary has been forced to backtrack, as the recoupling of INF and SDI at Reykjavik and the temporary postponement of the Washington summit suggest. On balance, however, he and his backers have succeeded in revising security policy along increasingly liberal lines.

Despite this adept orchestration of liberal policy innovations, costly and even dangerous setbacks could easily occur, and the reformers are now seeking to institutionalize their security approach. This effort follows logically from Gorbachev's earlier decisions to use domestic political liberalization not only to defuse Western fears of the USSR but to dismantle the image of imperialism that has long justified a confrontational Soviet policy toward the West. The liberal leaders are pushing internal political reforms, which they link explicitly with the de-militarization and de-ideologization of Soviet foreign policy, and which they believe will make a reversion to confrontational policies impossible. Apart from the crucial effort to elaborate a new conception of the Soviet national interest, their agenda includes steps to publish a meaningful defense budget and give the general public a significant influence on the development and use of military power abroad— measures which, given rising popular dissatisfaction with the standard of living, will generate strong public pressures to cut defense spending. The liberals' agenda also includes a reduction of state secrecy, a shift in the focus of the KGB's activities from internal toward external affairs, and the establishment of legal restrictions on the KGB's domestic role. Taken as a whole, the reform program constitutes an act of extraordinary daring with a potential to change the USSR's international behavior in ways without precedent in Soviet history.

The emerging linkage between security policy and internal liberalization makes it increasingly clear that Gorbachev and the liberal reformers are seeking a permanent alteration in the superpower relationship rather than a temporary respite. That is almost certainly one meaning of the recent polemics over whether "common human values" must enjoy priority in relations between East and West. In 1985, disciplinarian reformers such as Ligachev and Chebrikov could accept Gorbachev's security strategy because it meshed with the idea that a policy of diplomatic conciliation offered a breathing space during which the regime could put its house in order before returning to a more antagonistic policy toward the West. Today, however, liberal reformers are speaking of "common values" between the two camps and implying that there will be a long, open-ended period of East-West cooperation. Even more important, the liberals conceive of these common values not simply as a shared interest in avoiding nuclear war but as the basis for a partial convergence of Soviet political values and institutions with those of the West. Although it remains unclear just how far the reformers are prepared to go, the new emphasis on the rule of law, the creation of an independent judiciary, and public participation in legislatures with real power unquestionably represents a far-reaching effort at political liberalization.

The outcome of this monumental undertaking is completely uncertain. On the positive side of the ledger, Gorbachev has built up tremendous personal power despite the temporary setback of the Yel'tsin affair and the outbreaks of ethnic unrest that appear to confirm some of his critics' warnings. In sharp contrast to the policy-making deadlock of the early 1980's, he has imparted a powerful dynamism to Soviet security policy and has achieved extremely impressive international successes. These successes include four US-Soviet summits, the INF Treaty, substantial progress toward agreement on drastic cuts in strategic arms, and a sea change in Western attitudes toward the Soviet Union brought about partly by the Soviet decision to begin withdrawing from Afghanistan.

At the same time, any balanced assessment must take account of the powerful historical forces that Gorbachev and his liberal backers are seeking to tame. He and his allies are pursuing nothing less than a basic transformation of the Soviet polity and its relationship with the West. In so doing, they are posing profound questions about the troubled historical relationship between a Soviet Union based on a fusion of sectarian ideology with Russian nationalism and Western polities based on more inclusive political and cultural values. Despite the differences separating Gorbachev's generation from its predecessors, it is quite likely that a large proportion of the new generation regards the liberal reformers' efforts with serious misgivings. Xenophobia, dogmatism, and an instinct to fall back on force have deep historical roots in Soviet political culture. Gorbachev and his allies will need finely tuned political timing and an exceptional capacity to persuade the waverers that liberalization represents the correct path. Given the economic hardships and political turbulence already unleashed by the drive for domestic reform, they will probably also need all their political skill to prevent the emergence of a coalition uniting skeptical politicians with soldiers and policemen convinced that the new approach to national security threatens the vital interests and perhaps the survival of the Soviet state. Last but perhaps not least, the reformers will need to be able to produce tangible evidence for their claim that the West can and will respond positively to the prospect of a new era in East-West relations.

NOTES

ABOUT THE AUTHOR: **Bruce Parrott** is professor at the Paul Nitze School of Advanced International Studies, Johns Hopkins University.

1. Compare Raymond Garthoff, "New Thinking in Soviet Military Doctrine," *The Washington Quarterly* (Washington, DC), Summer 1988, pp. 131–58, with Gerhard Wettig, " 'New Thinking' on Security and East-West Relations," *Problems of Communism* (Washington, DC), March-April 1988, pp. 1–14.

2. Compare George G. Weickhardt, "The Military Consensus Behind Soviet Arms Control," *Arms Control Today* (Washington, DC), September 1987, pp. 20–24, and US Congress, Joint Economic Committee, *Allocation of Resources in the Soviet Union and China—1985*, Part II, Washington, DC, US Government Printing Office, 1986, pp. 50, 55, 91, with Jack Snyder, "The Gorbachev Revolution: A Waning of Soviet Expansionism?" *International Security* (Cambridge, MA), Winter 1987/88, pp. 93–131.

3. Compare Jerry Hough, "Gorbachev Consolidating Power," *Problems of Communism*, July-August 1987, pp. 21–43, with Peter Reddaway, "Resisting Gorbachev," *The New York Review of Books*, Aug. 18, 1988, pp. 36–41.

4. Scattered evidence indicates that soft-line criticisms were being made privately. Oleg Bogomolov, director of the Institute of the Economics of the World Socialist System within the USSR Academy of Sciences, recently revealed that in early 1980 his institute sent the party leadership a memorandum warning that the invasion of Afghanistan had weakened

the USSR's geopolitical position and would prevent progress in controlling the arms race. See the weekly *Literaturnaya Gazeta* (Moscow), Mar. 16, 1988, trans. in Foreign Broadcast Information Service, *Daily Report: Soviet Union* (Washington, DC—hereafter *FBIS-SOV*), Mar. 15, 1988, p. 19. In addition, a major article published at a crucial juncture during Konstantin Chernenko's tenure focused on rejecting hard-line forecasts of intensified East-West political and military competition, but it also referred briefly to critics who advocated unilateral Soviet steps in disarmament to "set an example" for the West. See Yu. Molchanov in *Kommunist* (Moscow), No. 13, September 1984, pp. 109–10.

5. Dan L. Strode and Rebecca V. Strode, "Diplomacy and Defense in Soviet National Security Policy," *International Security,* Fall 1983, pp. 91–116; and Bruce Parrott, "Soviet Policy Toward the United States: A Fork in the Road?" *SAIS Review* (Washington, DC), Winter-Spring 1985, pp. 110–15.

6. Thomas N. Bjorkman and Thomas J. Zamostny, "Soviet Politics and Strategy Toward the West: Three Case Studies," *World Politics* (Princeton, NJ), January 1984, p. 196; Bruce Parrott, "Soviet Policy Toward the West: A Fork in the Road?" loc. cit.; and idem, "Soviet Foreign Policy, Internal Politics, and Trade with the West," in Bruce Parrott, Ed., *Trade, Technology, and Soviet-American Relations,* Bloomington, IN, Indiana University Press, 1985, pp. 46–55.

7. Jeremy Azrael, *The Soviet Civilian Leadership and the Military High Command,* 1976–1986, R-3521-AF, Santa Monica, CA, Rand Corporation, 1987, pp. 19–21.

12. *Pravda,* Apr. 24, 1985; see also Mikhail Gorbachev, *Izbrannyye rechi i stat'i* (Selected Speeches and Articles), Moscow, Politizdat, 1987–88, Vol. II, p. 204.

13. Mikhail Gorbachev, *Izbrannyye rechi i stat'i,* Vol. II, pp. 134, 205 (Apr. 7 and May 8, 1985); *Kommunist,* No. 13, September 1985, p. 18.

14. Gorbachev later remarked (see *Izvestiya,* Feb. 26, 1986) that the April 1985 plenum had undertaken a new analysis of the threat of nuclear war. The plenum materials published at the time gave no indication of such a reassessment. However, Marshal Akhromeyev later indicated that the April plenum had initiated a two-year-long reevaluation of strategic doctrine by the Defense Council. See Raymond Garthoff, "Continuity and Change in Soviet Military Doctrine," in Bruce Parrott, Ed., *The Dynamics of Soviet Defense Policy* (forthcoming).

15. *Pravda,* Apr. 24, 1985.

16. Thus, in a move anticipating his discussions with President Reagan at Geneva a few months later, he singled out the "positive aspects" of the President's "very important" statement that nuclear war was unwinnable and the remark that the United States was not seeking military superiority. See *Kommunist,* No. 13, September 1985, p. 25; also Gorbachev, *Izbrannyye rechi i stat'i,* Vol. II, pp. 204–05.

17. See, for instance, Gorbachev, *Izbrannyye rechi i stat'i,* Vol. II, p. 147 (Apr. 16, 1985); and *Kommunist,* No. 17, November 1985, p. 48.

18. Gorbachev, *Izbrannyye rechi i stat'i,* Vol. II, p. 178.

19. Ibid., Vol. II, pp. 136 and 180 (Apr. 7 and May 5, 1985); *Kommunist,* No. 8, May 1985, pp. 13–14. Gorbachev's broad wording suggests that he was referring to Stalin's disastrous orders for the German Communists to concentrate their political attacks on the German Social Democrats rather than on the Nazis—orders that greatly facilitated the Nazis' assumption of power in 1933. As shown below, this criticism of Stalin's early policy toward Germany was later spelled out by several Soviet exponents of foreign-policy reform. At the 27th CPSU Congress, Gorbachev warned against underestimating the danger of a further move to the right in contemporary capitalist politics. See *XXVII s"yezd Kommunisticheskoy*

Partii Sovetskogo Soyuza (The 27th Congress of the Communist Party of the Soviet Union), Moscow, Politizdat, 1986, Vol. I, p. 3.

22. On the dynamics of the succession, see Jerry Hough, *Russia and the West: Gorbachev and the Politics of Reform,* New York, Simon and Schuster, 1988, pp. 156–64. Yegor Ligachev later listed four leaders who had enabled Gorbachev to become general secretary; he also referred to the major contribution made by a group of regional party secretaries, most of whom doubtless belonged to the Central Committee. See *Pravda,* July 2, 1988.

23. *Kommunist,* No. 5, March 1985, pp. 6–7; see also *Pravda,* May 25, 1985.

24. On Gromyko's role in the early 1980's, see Parrott, "Soviet Policy Toward the United States: A Fork in the Road?" loc. cit. pp. 114–16.

35. *Pravda Ukrainy* (Kiev), May 8 and 22, 1985; *Pravda,* Mar. 8, 1985 (emphasis added).

36. *Pravda Ukrainy,* May 8, 1985; see also the account of the Politburo meeting in *Izvestiya,* Apr. 12, 1985.

37. N. A. Ogarkov, *Istoriya uchit bditel'nosti* (History Teaches Vigilance), Moscow, Voyenizdat, 1985, pp. 20, 24, 93. Shortly after his demotion in September 1984, Ogarkov was forced to recant many of his alarmist views (see *Kommunist Vooruzhennykh Sil* [Moscow], No. 21, 1984, pp. 22–25). In the spring of 1985, however, he published a new book. Although it was an amalgam of disparate elements, it set forth most of the alarmist points that Ogarkov had briefly retracted the previous fall. It was sent to the compositor in late February and signed for printing in early April. Ogarkov's views contrasted with the statements by Marshal Akhromeyev made about the same time.

38. In March 1985, Shcherbytskyi told officials in the US that Moscow would respond to the further development of SDI with "both offensive and defensive" measures, a formula that hinted at the possible deployment of extensive Soviet ABM defenses. See *The Washington Post,* Mar. 8, 1985.

40. *Kommunist,* No. 6, April 1985, p. 67 (emphasis in the original). The party, Sokolov remarked, "is working out and realizing … a complex of measures for supplying the army and navy with everything necessary" (p. 69). The implication was that the military would not have all it needed until these measures were fully implemented.

41. *Pravda,* Nov. 6, 1985. This constituted a noticeable hardening of Sokolov's position on SDI (cf. *Krasnaya Zvezda,* May 5, 1985).

43. *Pravda,* Apr. 24, 1985; Parrott, *The Soviet Union and Ballistic Missile Defense,* (Boulder, CO: Westview Press, 1987), Chap. 5.

44. Gorbachev, *Izbrannyye rechi i stat'i,* Vol. II, p. 147 (Apr. 16, 1985); and *Kommunist,* No. 17, November 1985, p. 48.

45. Jan Vanous and Bryan Roberts, "Time to Choose Between Tanks and Tractors: Why Gorbachev Must Come to the Negotiating Table or Face a Collapse of His Ambitious Modernization Program," *PlanEcon Report* (Washington, DC), Vol. II, Nos. 25–26, 1986, pp. 1–16.

47. Dale Herspring, "The Soviet Military in the Aftermath of the 27th Party Congress," *Orbis* (Philadelphia), Summer 1986, p. 311; and Malvin Helgesen, "Civil-Military Relations under Gorbachev," in Bruce Parrott, Ed., *The Dynamics of Soviet Defense Policy* (forthcoming). This interpretation is consistent with the treatment of the speech by Col. Gen. A. Lizichev, the new Main Political Directorate chief installed after Gorbachev's assumption of power. Lizichev bracketed the Minsk speech with two previous national military meetings, in 1982 and 1984, at which the main theme had been the containment of military spending and the justification of this line to restive officers. See *Kommunist,* No. 3, February 1986, p. 97; also *Pravda Ukrainy,* July 17, 1985.

48. For instance, an account of the December 1985 meeting of the General Staff's party *aktiv* implied that Marshal Akhromeyev and other officers were uneasy with the line taken by Gorbachev in the Minsk speech. See *Krasnaya Zvezda,* Dec. 31, 1985.

53. Jerry Hough, *Russia and the West,* p. 169.

54. Marshal Tolubko, who had presided over the large buildup of the Strategic Rocket Forces (SRF), was clearly seeking to preserve preeminent status for his service within the military establishment. His replacement, Gen. Yu. P. Maksimov, was a Ground Forces officer with no previous experience in the SRF. In September, Soviet negotiators in Geneva proposed 50 percent reductions in US and Soviet strategic warheads. See Malvin M. Helgesen, loc. cit.; and Rose Gottenmoeller, "Conflict and Consensus in the Armed Forces," in Bruce Parrott, Ed., *The Dynamics of Soviet Defense Policy.*

55. *The New York Times,* Feb. 6, 1986.

56. This paragraph is based on Parrott, *The Soviet Union and Ballistic Missile Defense.*

57. *Kommunist,* No. 17, November 1985, pp. 17, 35–43, 45.

58. *Pravda,* Dec. 7, 1985.

61. *Pravda,* Dec. 11 and 17, 1985.

62. Gorbachev, *Izbrannyye rechi i stat'i,* Vol. III, p. 121 (Dec. 27, 1985).

63. Ibid., Vol. III, p. 167 (Feb. 4, 1986).

64. *Izvestiya,* Jan. 31, 1986.

65. As one of Gorbachev's most forceful allies in the struggle against Brezhnevite holdovers inside the party, Ligachev presumably had an incentive to express and possibly overstate any favorable attitudes about the Geneva meeting. Seen in this light, his laconic description of the meeting as a "major political event" suggests he was not enthusiastic about the results. See *Bakinskiy Rabochiy* (Baku), Dec. 22, 1985.

66. This paragraph is based on Parrott, *The Soviet Union and Ballistic Missile Defense.*

67. *Ivestiya,* Nov. 28, 1985; *Pravda Ukrainy,* Dec. 22, 1985. Compare with Gorbachev, *Izbrannyye rechi i stat'i,* Vol. III, p. 119 (Dec. 27, 1985).

68. *Pravda Ukrainy,* Dec. 22, 1985.

69. *Izvestiya,* Nov. 23, 1985; *Krasnaya Zvezda,* Nov. 24, 1985.

70. *Izvestiya,* Feb. 26, 1986.

71. Ibid.

72. Gorbachev manifestly had in mind both the Soviet and Western variants of deterrence. Security, he said, could not be built forever on the doctrines of deterrence *(sderzhivaniye)* and intimidation *(ustrasheniye).* Soviet commentators have customarily used the word *"sderzhivaniye"* to describe Soviet nuclear doctrine. They have reserved the pejorative *"ustrasheniye"* to stigmatize Western nuclear doctrine.

73. *Izvestiya,* Feb. 26, 1986.

74. Between January and August 1986, seven of the eight deputy foreign ministers who had served under Gromyko were replaced (see Hough, "Gorbachev Consolidating Power," loc. cit.). In addition to Gorbachev, three recently appointed party secretaries attended the meeting at the Ministry of Foreign Affairs: Anatoliy Dobrynin, head of the International Department; Aleksandr Yakovlev, overseer of the Propaganda Department; and Vadim Medvedev, head of the Department for Liaison with Communist and Workers' Parties of Socialist Countries.

79. *XXVII s"yezd KPSS,* Vol. I, pp. 97–99.

80. *Vestnik Ministerstva Inostrannykh Del SSSR,* No. 1, 1987, pp. 4–6. Although Gorbachev addressed the Foreign Ministry officials soon after the 27th CPSU Congress, his

remarks were not published until over a year later. His speech at a major conference of KGB officials held shortly after the foreign-ministry conference has still not been published. See Viktor Yassman in *Radio Liberty Research Bulletin*, RL 382/88, Aug. 29, 1988.

81. *XXVII s"yezd KPSS*, Vol. 1, p. 92.

82. *Izvestiya*, Feb. 26, 1986, Francis Fukuyama, "Gorbachev and the Third World," *Foreign Affairs* (New York), Spring 1986, p. 716.

83. *Vestnik Ministerstva Inostrannykh Del SSSR*, No. 1, 1987, p. 5.

84. *XXVII s"yezd KPSS*, Vol. I, p. 416.

85. "It would seem that everything is perfectly clear and simple: nuclear weaponry is a terrible, immoral and unnatural thing. However, one has only to call for its complete elimination, and at once 'lawyers' appear who give it out as nearly a universal good. Today they are trying anew to prove that such weaponry is allegedly necessary as a factor of mutual deterrence, that allegedly there is no doing without it." In addition to the elimination of nuclear weapons, Shevardnadze advocated the simultaneous implementation of "stabilizing reductions of conventional weapons." See ibid., Vol. I, pp. 412–13.

87. *Kommunist*, No. 9, June 1986, pp. 18–32.

88. *Kazakhstanskaya Pravda* (Alma-Ata), May 21, 1986; *Kommunist*, No. 9, June 1986, pp. 24–25.

89. The Western antiwar movements, Dobrynin asserted, had, perhaps for the first time in history, become a powerful force of independent importance, and some opportunities to strengthen the political influence of Western workers were not yet being utilized or even recognized. See *Kazakhstanskaya Pravda*, May 20 and 21, 1986; *Kommunist*, No. 9, June 1986, pp. 24–25, and No. 16, November 1986, pp. 23–24.

90. During the nuclear era, Dobrynin said, the US had repeatedly tried to use nuclear weapons as an instrument of military-political blackmail. "And if a nuclear war nevertheless did not break out during the four postwar decades, that is not at all thanks to the 'deterrent' *(sderzhivayushchey)* force of nuclear weaponry. In part, the reason of politicians played a role, and in still larger measure, the efforts of the USSR and other peace-loving states and the rise of the mass antiwar movement." *Kommunist*, No. 9, June 1986, p. 20.

91. Ibid.

92. These included the interaction between offensive and defensive armaments, as well as between nuclear and conventional weapons, the definition of "reasonable sufficiency" in nuclear arsenals, the mathematical modeling of strategic stability, and the verification of arms-control agreements. Ibid., pp. 26–28.

93. Ibid., pp. 19, 27–28. The Scientific Council was a civilian body set up immediately after the signing of the SALT II treaty as an umbrella for research on foreign-policy and security matters (see Bjorkman and Zamostny, loc. cit., pp. 204–05). Dobrynin's article was originally delivered as the keynote address at a meeting of scientists organized by the Committee of Soviet Scientists in Defense of Peace, Against the Nuclear Threat. Chaired by Academician Yevgeniy P. Velikhov, this group was set up in 1983 primarily to lobby Western scientists against SDI, but it gradually became involved in deliberations on Soviet military policy, including the deliberations that preceded the Soviet declaration of a unilateral nuclear test moratorium in 1985. See *Vestnik Akademii Nauk SSSR* (Moscow), No. 12, 1986, pp. 3–84; Parrott, "Political Change and Civil-Military Relations"; and Jeffrey Checkel, "Gorbachev's 'New Political Thinking' and the Formation of Soviet Foreign Policy," in Radio Free Europe-Radio Liberty, *Radio Liberty Research* (Munich) RL 429/88, Sept. 23, 1988, p. 4.

94. *FBIS-SOV*, Mar. 16, 1987, p. G/12; A. Yakovlev in *Kommunist*, No. 8, May 1987, p. 18.

95. Personal communication from Professor Seweryn Bialer, April 1987; *The New York Times*, May 31, 1987; and Jack Snyder, loc. cit., p. 116.

96. *Kommunist*, No. 9, June 1986, pp. 25, 30.

97. Ibid., pp. 29–30; *Pravda*, May 28, 1986; and *Kazakhstanskaya Pravda*, May 21, 1986.

99. For example, where Gromyko had affirmed the necessity for the creation of a Palestinian state, Dobrynin omitted this idea. Compare Gromyko in *Pravda*, Mar. 12 and May 25, 1985, with Dobrynin in *Kazakhstanskaya Pravda*, May 20, 1986.

100. At the 27th CPSU Congress, Gromyko hailed Gorbachev's January declaration on arms control. At the same time, he warned, as he had in March 1985, that the West was seeking to exploit any internal division within the Soviet leadership. By branding Westerners worried about the Soviet military threat as the knowing perpetrators of "a crude deception," Gromyko implicitly dismissed Gorbachev's suggestion that such views might be genuine concerns requiring Soviet concessions. See *XXVII s"yezd KPSS*, Vol. I, pp. 191–92.

101. Ibid., pp. 191–92, 196–97.

102. For example, Chebrikov approvingly quoted Lenin's attack on Westerners who raise the specter of "red militarism," "make a face as if they believe this stupid stuff," and contrive false arguments to deceive the masses. See *Pravda*, No 7, 1985.

103. According to one Soviet source, during the Geneva summit Gorbachev privately informed Soviet arms control experts that the Soviet position on verification must be altered because of its negative impact in the West. See Ye. Primakov in *Pravda*, Jan. 8, 1988, as cited in Jeffrey Checkel, loc. cit., p. 2. A few months later, Deputy Defense Minister Vitaliy Shabanov warned against the danger of espionage through most kinds of on-site inspection. See *Izvestiya*, Mar. 24, 1988, cited in Helgesen, loc. cit.

106. Parrott, *The Soviet Union and Ballistic Missile Defense*, pp. 62–63.

107. *Pravda Ukrainy*, Jan. 18, 1986.

108. By any reading, the declaration required limits on SDI before strategic weapons could be reduced. It was, however, ambiguous about INF reductions, which were part of the "phased" reductions also mentioned by Shcherbytskyi.

109. *XXVII s"yezd KPSS*, Vol. I, p. 136.

110. *Pravda Ukrainy*, July 12, 1986.

136. Gorbachev, *Izbrannyye rechi i stat'i*, Vol. III, p. 416; *Kommunist*, No. 16, November 1986, p. 14.

137. Sakharov's banishment was lifted in December 1986. He travelled to the US in early November 1988 to participate in a meeting of the International Foundation for the Survival and Development of Humanity, a new nongovernmental Soviet-American organization with headquarters in Moscow and Washington, DC.

138. *Pravda*, Sept. 30, 1987.

139. Ibid., Feb. 26, 1987.

140. Taking up a theme sounded earlier by Dobrynin, Gorbachev denied that world war has been avoided in recent decades because of nuclear weapons. Rather, he asserted, world war was avoided despite such weaponry. *Pravda*, Sept. 17, 1987.

141. Ibid. As previously, the word Gorbachev used to describe the idea of deterrence was the neutral "sderzhivaniye," not the pejorative "ustrasheniye," suggesting that he has Soviet policy in mind as well. Moreover, some military men have declined to endorse his critique of deterrence.

142. In the fall of 1987, for example, he referred favorably to a Soviet-American study which suggests that strategic stability could be maintained with only 5 percent of existing

nuclear weapons (*Pravda*, Sept. 17, 1987). Soviet participants in this work apparently included some of the civilian theorists from the Academy of Sciences who have been involved since 1984 in modeling the effects of deep cuts beyond a first stage of 50 percent reductions. For details of this work, see A. A. Kokoshin in *SShA: Ekonomika, Politika, Ideologiya* (Moscow), No. 2, 1988, pp. 3–12.

143. *Pravda*, Feb. 28, 1987.

144. Yakovlev was made a nonvoting member at the January 1987 plenum. He was elevated to voting membership in April.

145. Gorbachev told the plenum that Soviet military cadres has "an enormous responsibility before the people" to protect the country's security. The people and the party, he said, were doing "everything" to strengthen the Armed Forces and had a right to assume that no aggression could catch the USSR unawares. The party was counting on the officer corps in deciding on the tasks for strengthening the state's defense capacity, said Gorbachev, and the Central Committee was sure that all military cadres would act "with the greatest responsibility." *Pravda*, Jan. 28 and Apr. 11, 1987.

146. Dale Herspring, "On Perestroyka: Gorbachev, Yazov, and the Military," loc. cit., p. 101.

147. *Pravda*, Jan. 29, 1987.

148. *Vestnik Ministerstva Inostrannykh Del SSSR*, No. 2, 1987, pp. 30–34, trans. in *FBIS-SOV*, Oct. 27, 1987, pp. 52–53.

149. Employing the same tactics that he and other conservative officials had used earlier, Sokolov played down the significance of Gorbachev's proposals at the January plenum and emphasized that the party's "strategic course" had been set at earlier party conclaves. *Pravda*, Feb. 23, 1987.

150. In particular, Akhromeyev acknowledged the need for a better cadres policy. See *Sovetskaya Rossiya* (Moscow), Feb. 21, 1987. Cf. Sokolov in *Pravda*, Feb. 23, 1987, and Marshal Viktor Kulikov in *Trud* (Moscow), Feb. 22, 1987.

151. According to Sokolov, the central requirement of military personnel policy was "capably to combine young and experienced cadres, to ensure their continuity and the development of everything good that has been accumulated in the activity of commanders … and has passed the test of time." See *Pravda*, Feb. 23, 1987. Shortly afterward, Sokolov attended a meeting of a military party *aktiv* in which several speakers endorsed changes in cadres policy, including the downgrading of seniority and service records in making military appointments. Sokolov addressed the meeting, but his remarks were not published, no doubt because he opposed the changes. See *Krasnaya Zvezda*, Mar. 7, 1987, trans. in *FBIS-SOV*, Mar. 10, 1987, p. V/1.

152. In publishing the "theses" of Gorbachev's speech, *Krasnaya Zvezda* (Jan. 28, 1987) excised his references to "crisis phenomena" in the USSR. The military newspaper accurately paraphrased Gorbachev's demand for better performance from the Ministry of Foreign Affairs, but it omitted his reference to the need for *perestroyka* in the military. Instead, it merely reported that Gorbachev had voiced "our most important concern" about the military cadres who were defending the country. Three days later (Jan. 31), *Pravda* ran an editorial on the plenum that mentioned Soviet "crisis phenomena" and referred to the new demands facing "foreign-policy departments" (presumably including the Ministry of Defense). The next day, *Krasnaya Zvezda*, most likely under pressure from the Gorbachev camp, reprinted the *Pravda* editorial on its front page.

157. See, in particular, *Krasnaya Zvezda*, Mar. 18, 1987. During the preceding two years, the officer corps had responded sluggishly to Gorbachev's calls for "criticism and self-criti-

cism" and institutional *perestroyka*. See Dale Herspring, "On Perestroyka ...," loc. cit., p. 101.

158. Ibid.

159. Robert Legvold, "Gorbachev's New Approach to Conventional Arms Control," *The Harriman Institute Forum* (New York), January 1988; Raymond Garthoff, "New Thinking in Soviet Military Doctrine," *The Washington Quarterly* (Washington, DC), Summer 1988, pp. 131–58; and A. Arbatov in *Mirovaya Ekonomika i Mezhdunarodnyye Otnosheniya* (Moscow—hereafter, cited as *MEMO*), No. 4, 1988, pp. 10–22.

160. Vitaliy Zhurkin, Sergey Karaganov, and Andrey Kortunov in *Novoye Vremya* (Moscow), No. 40, 1987, quoted in Harry Gelman, *The Soviet Military Leadership and the Question of Soviet Deployment Retreats*, Santa Monica, Ca. Rand Corporation, September 1988. I am grateful to Dr. Gelman for allowing me to read this report before its publication.

161. *Moscow News*, No. 8, 1988, quoted in Gelman, op. cit.

162. See, in particular, A. G. Arbatov's presentation of this view to the Scientific Council of the Academy's Institute of the World Economy and International Relations, *MEMO*, No. 5, 1988, p. 152.

163. *Pravda*, Mar. 1, 1987.

164. Ibid., Feb. 17 and 25, Apr. 11, 1987.

165. Ibid., Sep. 17, 1987.

170. *FBIS-SOV*, Apr. 27 1987, p. F/3. When Ligachev did mention the decision, his comments were quite favorable, although still less positive than those of Gorbachev's ardent supporters.

171. Shcherbytskyi remarked that the January plenum "again affirmed the unshakable character of the unity of the CPSU's internal and foreign policy." He left open the question of whether internal requirements or external dangers should receive greater weight in national policy-making, but in view of his past remarks, it would be fair to assume that he continued to assign special significance to external threats. Shcherbytskyi—in contrast to several of the figures discussed above—did not refer explicitly to the decoupling of INF, and he said nothing about future benefits from the step. *Pravda Ukrainy*, Mar. 25, 1987.

172. *Pravda*, May 9, 1987. Like Shcherbytskyi, Sokolov described the Soviet proposal as being for the liquidation of intermediate-range rockets in Europe; he did not refer directly to the decision to delink the issue from other arms matters.

173. For other evidence of continuing debate, see the comments of Gromyko in *Izvestiya*, Jan. 18, 1987; and in *Pravda*, Mar. 14, 1987.

174. *Moscow News*, No. 10, 1987. During this period, Bovin chastised the ministries of foreign affairs and defense for their secretiveness, and Fedor Burlatskiy called on Soviet journalists to present more factual analyses of the West. *Sovetskaya Kul'tura* (Moscow), May 21, 1987.

175. *Moscow News*, No. 11, 1987, as cited in *Radio Liberty Daily Report* (Munich), Mar. 20, 1987.

176. *Pravda*, May 14, 1987; see also "Sales Blitz by Soviet Seeks to Tap Global Market in Space Services," *The New York Times*, Sept. 6, 1987.

179. *Pravda*, Sept. 17, 1987.

180. Ibid., Aug. 27, 1987.

181. Ibid., Feb. 17 and 25, Apr. 11, and Sept. 17, 1987.

182. *Izvestiya*, Nov. 30, 1987, as quoted in Radio Free Europe-Radio Liberty, *Soviet East European Report* (Washington, DC), No. 13, 1988. The head of the commission is Fedor Burlatskiy.

185. Ligachev, for instance, observed that economic revitalization and better consumer goods would enhance the attractiveness of socialism's image abroad. *Ekonomicheskaya Gazeta* (Moscow), No. 22, 1987.

186. *FBIS-SOV,* Mar. 10, 1987, p. R/8; *Pravda Ukrainy,* Mar. 7, 1987.

187. *Problemy Mira i Sotsializma* (Prague), No. 7, 1987, p. 6.

188. *Pravda,* Sept. 11, 1987.

191. Ibid., Sept. 11, 1987.

195. *Krasnaya Zvezda,* June 17, 1987.

196. *Moskovskiye Novosti,* Mar. 8, 1987, as quoted in Stephen Foye, "Intellectuals Attack the Military," *Sovset' News* (3, No. 9) July 30, 1987. The writer, Ales Adamovich, was active in the work of the Committee of Soviet Scientists for Peace and Against the Nuclear Threat. The Committee was set up in 1983 primarily to lobby Western scientists against SDI but began to play a significant role in Soviet security deliberations under Gorbachev. Adamovich also became a member of the human-rights commission established under Burlatsky's chairmanship in the fall of 1987.

197. *Literaturnaya Gazeta,* May 8, 1987, as quoted in Foye, loc. cit.

198. *Literaturnaya Gazeta,* May 22 and June 8, 1987, as quoted in Foye, loc. cit.; and A. Nuykin in *Vek XX i mir* (The 20th Century and Peace), as cited by A. Pavlov and V. Lyashenko in *Kommunist vooruzhennykh Sil,* No. 21, 1988, p. 24.

199. *Krasnaya Zvezda,* July 29 and Aug. 13, 1987.

200. Moscow Television Service in Russian, Jan. 16, 1988, trans. in *FBIS-SOV,* Jan. 22, 1988, pp. 68–69.

201. Ibid., p. 65, emphasis added.

202. "I think that we are now experiencing a moment when culture must come to the aid of ... the Army without delay. Attacks by certain sectors of our culture on the Army are, in my opinion, shameful. This is because our contemporary repentant culture, which has been genuinely repentant for its role in the years of stagnation, cannot be compared with the Army which during the same period of so-called stagnation managed to achieve military-political and strategic parity with the United States. We have nothing to blame the Army for. The Army is now in need of moral support." Ibid., pp. 66–67.

205. *Pravda,* Nov. 3, 1987; see also ibid., Feb. 26, 1987.

206. Ibid., Feb. 19, 1988.

207. Ibid. Nov. 4 and 28, 1987.

208. V. Zhurkin, S. Karaganov, and A. Kortunov in *Kommunist,* No. 1, January 1988, pp. 44–47. See also Stanislav Kondrashov in *Izvestiya,* Apr. 2, 1988, trans. in *FBIS-SOV,* Apr. 6, 1988, pp. 2–3.

209. *Izvestiya,* Dec. 13, 1987.

210. *FBIS-SOV,* Feb. 26, 1988, p. 71.

211. *Krasnaya Zvezda,* July 29, 1987; *Pravda,* Feb. 8, 1988.

212. *FBIS-SOV,* May 13, 1988 p. 16; *Krasnaya Zvezda,* Feb. 23, 1988.

213. *Krasnaya Zvezda,* Feb. 23 1988, *FBIS-SOV,* Feb. 26, 1988, p. 70.

214. *FBIS-SOV,* Feb. 26, 1988, p. 68; *Pravda,* May 9, 1988.

217. Unconfirmed reports suggest that the letter, which appeared over the signature of Andreyeva, a Leningrad chemistry teacher, was originally sent to Ligachev and was carefully revised under his instructions before being printed. After its publication, Ligachev reportedly endorsed it in private as a guideline for party policy, and almost four weeks passed without any public signal to the contrary. Only after heated debate inside the Polit-

buro did *Pravda* repudiate the article. See Michel Tatu, "19th CPSU Conference," *Problems of Communism*, May-August 1988, pp. 1–4, and Seweryn Bialer, "The Changing Soviet Political System: The Nineteenth Party Conference and After," in *Inside Gorbachev's Russia*, Seweryn Bialer, Ed., Boulder, CO, Westview, 1989, pp. 207–208.

218. *Sovetskaya Rossiya*, Mar. 13, 1988, trans. in *FBIS-SOV*, Mar. 16, 1988, p. 51.

219. Helgesen, loc. cit., citing Soviet press sources; Bialer, "The Changing Soviet Political System" loc. cit. p. 207.

220. *Pravda*, Apr. 5, 1988.

221. *L'Unità* (Rome), Apr. 22, 1988, cited in Helgesen, loc. cit.

222. *Literaturnaya Rossiya* (Moscow), May 6, 1988, in *FBIS-SOV*, June 9, 1988, pp. 72–73. See also the article by MPD chief Lizichev in *Izvestiya*, May 29, 1988, trans. in *FBIS-SOV*, June 6, 1988, p. 63; and Colonel G. Mukhin in *Krasnaya Zvezda*, June 7, 1988, in *FBIS-SOV*, June 8, 1988, p. 2.

223. *Literaturnaya Gazeta*, May 18, 1988; *Komsomol'skaya Pravda* (Moscow), June 19, 1988. On Stalin's mistaken policies toward the Nazis and German Social Democrats in the early 1930's, see also Ernst Genri in *Moskovskaya Pravda*, May 19, 1988, in *FBIS-SOV*, June 9, 1988, pp. 63–64.

224. *Literaturnaya Gazeta*, May 18, 1988. Academician Oleg Bogomolov, who directs the institute where Dashichev works, claimed that negotiating strategic parity at lower military levels would "still be a colossal burden for our economy—a burden that will not allow us to breathe and will condemn us to a continued lag." Ibid., June 29, 1988.

225. *FBIS-SOV*, Feb. 26, 1988, p. 68; *Pravda*, May 9, 1988.

226. Lev Bezymenskiy and Valentin Falin in *Pravda*, Aug. 29, 1988, trans. in *FBIS-SOV*, Aug. 31, 1988, pp. 6, 11.

227. *Pravda*, June 29, 1988.

228. Ibid.

229. Ibid.

230. Ibid.

231. Ibid., July 1, 1988; Tatu, "19th CPSU Conference," loc. cit., p. 8, fn. 32.

232. Gromyko first cautioned that an attempt to set a timetable for the completion of *perestroyka* would be "erroneous and not statesmanlike (*ne po-gosudarstvennomu*)." *Pravda*, May 16, 1988. Five days later, he was more pointed: "It is clear that if a certain person declares that it is necessary to complete *perestroyka* by such-and-such a date, then he will place himself under the threat of provoking the most unpleasant commentaries addressed to him." Ibid., May 19, 1988. A few days later, the Politburo met to discuss the draft theses before submitting them to the Central Committee.

233. Ibid., July 2, 1988.

234. Shcherbytskyi, chairing an evening session of the conference, read a note from a delegate defending Gromyko as a committed Communist who should not be mistreated. Had Shcherbytskyi favored Gromyko's removal, he undoubtedly could have ignored the note. The note was from a "Comrade Mamayev," presumably the A. Mamayev who oversaw patriotic education for DOSAAF and who was the only person associated with the military to address the conference. See *FBIS-SOV*, July 5, 1988, pp. 54–55.

235. *Vestnik Ministerstva Inostrannykh Del SSSR*, No. 15, 1988, pp. 32–33. This view was also strongly advocated in a major theoretical article which appeared about the same time (see I. Usachev, "The All-Human and Class [Factors] in World Politics," *Kommunist*, No. 11, July 1988, esp. pp. 110–12, 115–18).

236. *Vestnik Ministerstva Inostrannykh Del SSSR*, No. 15, 1988, p. 35.

237. Ibid., p. 37.

238. Ibid.

239. In the early 1980's, the inability of Soviet diplomatic gambits to block the impending INF deployments had sparked tensions between the two ministries, but the tensions had been expressed indirectly. See the article by Gromyko in *Kommunist*, No. 6, April 1983; and Parrott, "Soviet Policy toward the United States: A Fork in the Road?" loc. cit., pp. 115–16.

240. *Vestnik Ministerstva Inostrannykh Del SSSR*, No. 15, 1988, pp. 29, 37, 36.

241. Ibid., p. 40.

242. Ibid., p. 33.

243. In addition, the comments may have been aimed partly at the Ministry of Internal Affairs for its recent harsh handling of some public demonstrations.

244. *Vestnik Ministerstva Inostrannykh Del SSSR*, No. 15, 1988, pp. 29, 34, 37, and 43. Shevardnadze revealed that the ministry had set up an opinion-survey service with the aid of the Academy's Institute of Sociological Research and had already conducted a series of surveys. Earlier, as republic party first secretary, Shevardnadze had championed the use of public-opinion polling in his native Georgia. As Shevardnadze described it, one use of polling would be to "nourish and form" public opinion.

On the ambiguous treatment of referenda in the current program of legislative reform, see Sergei Voronitsyn in *Ratio Liberty Research*, RL 478/88, Oct. 19, 1988.

245. *Pravda*, Aug. 8, 1988.

246. Ibid., Aug. 13, 1988.

247. *FBIS-SOV,* June 29, 1988, pp. 38–39.

248. During the previous year, Yakovlev's writings had heavily stressed several liberal themes: the expansion of *glasnost'*, the recognition of the supreme value of the individual, the reduction of the state's power over the citizens, the creation of political mechanisms to ensure feedback from society to the political leadership, and the adoption of legislation that would block arbitrary behavior by officials. See, especially, his article in *Kommunist*, No. 8, May 1987.

During the 19th Party Conference Yakovlev observed: "For the first time the question has been raised of a ... practical creation of a political system that would match the nature of a new society and the modern stage of development of socialism" (ibid., p. 38). And later, "Socialism as practice is ... the art of actually taking account of all traditions and the most up-to-date tendencies ... of economics and politics ... both in our country and abroad. At present, when socialism is preparing for the deepest, radical self-renewal ... we again turn to the theory and practice of all world development, both socialist and nonsocialist," *Pravda*, Aug. 13, 1988.

249. Medvedev disavowed the idea of a full convergence between East and West. However, he also remarked that the notion that the capitalist and socialist systems could develop on separate tracks was outdated; rather, the two systems influence each other "within the boundaries of one and the same human civilization." More concretely, Medvedev declared that in creating a new model of socialism, Soviet theorists should look not only inside the socialist bloc but outside it. In particular, he said, it was necessary seriously to study the practices of "contemporary social democracy, its concrete activity, including [its activity] in defending the social and general democratic achievements of the workers." *Pravda*, Oct. 5, 1988. In the budgetary debates of the early 1980's, Medvedev defended a pro-

consumer line against the advocates of heavy industry and military spending. See *Kommunist,* No. 5, March 1980, pp. 22–23.

251. For a different view, see Amy Knight, "The KGB and Soviet Reform."

252. Knight, *The KGB: Police and Politics in the Soviet Union,* p. 122.

253. Ibid., pp. 294–95.

255. Asked by an interviewer to describe *perestroyka* within the KGB, Chebrikov began by recalling the January plenum's judgment that "the state security organs have cadres who are ideologically tempered, devoted to the party and people, and professionally trained. That is a high assessment." Although he acknowledged the need to "restructure our staffers' thinking," he made no mention of any need to bring "fresh forces" into the police establishment. While Chebrikov noted that the KGB was participating in the preparation of security legislation envisaging "a considerable relaxation ... of measures connected with the protection of state secrets," he emphasized that reactionary imperialist circles were still trying to "discredit the CPSU's domestic and foreign policy and undermine ... our state ... security." Soviet observers who believed that this view amounted to " 'spy mania' " and the conjuring up of " 'mythical foreign agents' " were incorrect, he asserted, because foreign intelligence services were expanding their activities against the USSR. See *Pravda,* Sept. 2, 1988. Shortly before the appearance of the Chebrikov interview, *Znamya* had criticized a collection of stories about the KGB for stirring up 'spy mania.' *Znamya,* No. 2, July 1988, as quoted in Knight, "The KGB and Soviet Reform," loc. cit.

256. *Mezhdunarodnaya Zhizn',* No. 10, 1988, pp. 34–37.

257. Past Soviet policy-makers, he said, had not quickly grasped the potential of the Western antiwar movement, and too many stereotypes had afflicted the Soviet perception of Western political and business groups. "We are studying and learning badly about people; we are giving little attention to developing contacts with foreign political and social activists and are ... inadequately struggling for their minds. Apparently it is easier and simpler to create enemies than to win supporters." Ibid.

258. According to Kryuchkov, *perestroyka* had made it harder for Western intelligence agencies to compromise Soviet citizens traveling abroad, because the expression of unorthodox political ideas could no longer be made a basis for blackmail. He cautioned, however, that this meant Western intelligence services would look instead for shortcomings in citizens' moral conduct.

263. See M. Hauner and A. Rahr, "New Chief of General Staff Appointed," *Radio Liberty Research,* RL 546/88, Dec. 16, 1988. According to this report, Akhromeyev had been recently confirmed as military affairs advisor to Gorbachev.

44 State, Society, and the Military Under Gorbachev

DAVID HOLLOWAY

As a result of changes initiated by Mikhail Gorbachev, civil-military relations in the Soviet Union have entered a new stage. Especially since the 19th Party Conference in the summer of 1988, a significant shift has taken place away from the pattern of relations that existed under Leonid Brezhnev, toward a new pattern in which society, through the expression of public opinion, is playing an increasingly important role.

Most Western students of the role of the military in Soviet politics have taken as the focus of their analysis relations within the Party-state apparatus (between the Party leadership and the High Command, or between the Main Political Administration and the officer corps, for example). The central question in Soviet politics today, however, is not how the different elements of the Party-state apparatus relate to one another, but whether the Soviet Union can make the transition from state socialism, in which civil society enjoyed at best a limited autonomy, to a system in which an independent public opinion will play a central role in directing the state and its activities. If this is indeed the central issue in Soviet politics, civil-military relations should be examined in this context, too.

This article argues that the emergence of an independent public opinion (fragile though that is, as yet) has already had an important effect on Soviet civil-military relations, helping to set in motion a process of demilitarization. But this new pattern of civil-military relations in turn has potentially far-reaching implications for the uncertain and difficult process of democratization.

CIVIL-MILITARY RELATIONS
UNDER BREZHNEV AND GORBACHEV

The relations between the Soviet state, society, and military under Brezhnev and Gorbachev contrast in significant ways. The Brezhnev pattern of civil-military relations was in many respects congenial to military interests. By stressing the importance of conflict between states, the Party provided a clear rationale for the armed forces' existence. Gorbachev's "new thinking" on the other hand, has shifted the emphasis from conflict between states to cooperation, thereby giving rise to disagreement about the extent of the military threat to the Soviet Union. Brezhnev gave highest priority to defense, and allocated massive resources to the creation of military power. Under Gorbachev the priority of military power has been undercut by the application of the new thinking abroad, and by pressing economic needs at home.

The Brezhnev leadership by and large accepted the military's monopoly of professional expertise in military affairs (or at least in military-technical affairs), while Gorbachev has allowed military policy to become the subject of public debate and the new Supreme Soviet shows signs of wanting to exercise authority over defense policy. Under Brezhnev the Party took pains to enhance the prestige of the military profession, and promoted an extensive program of military-patriotic education. Now the armed forces have been subjected to wide-ranging criticism in the Soviet press. In the Brezhnev years secrecy helped to preserve the priority accorded to defense and to uphold the authority of military professionalism. Now military *glasnost* has allowed some light to penetrate the veil of secrecy that has hidden military affairs from public gaze.

These changes have become especially apparent since mid-1988. Gorbachev treated the military carefully in the early years of *perestroika*. It was only after the January 1987 Plenum of the Central Committee that the armed forces came in for detailed criticism of the kind that other institutions had already been subjected to. The Mathias Rust affair provided a pretext in May 1987 for the appointment of General Dmitri Yazov as minister of defense, and for further criticism, much of which was directed against sources of ineffectiveness in the armed forces. After the 19th Party Conference in the summer of 1988, and especially after the September Plenum of that year, a new phase began, with a far-reaching public debate of the military's place in society.

By the autumn of 1988 public discussion of the military was touching on themes that even one year earlier had been taboo. In the words of a participant in a round-table discussion: "I fully understand that the army, as an unsociable body, mostly ignores the cries of the 'mob' and looks very skeptically upon antiwar 'amusements' of the nonofficial public. But it seems the time has come— long-awaited and blessed—when the theme 'army and society' might become a topic of public discussion."[1] This topic played a prominent part in the election campaign for the Congress of People's Deputies, and in the early deliberations of the Congress and of the new Supreme Soviet.

Gorbachev has used *glasnost* and political reform to bring into play new political forces that will help him to transform the Soviet system. By relaxing censorship and instituting competitive elections, he has created the opportunity for the public expression of attitudes, opinions and views that hitherto would have had to be uttered in private or would have been considered dissident. Through the process of democratization society has acquired a voice, and that voice has proved to be highly critical of the main institutions in the Party-state apparatus, including the military.

MILITARISM AND DEMILITARIZATION

Some concept of militarism or militarization is needed as a benchmark, if the process of demilitarization is to be explored. The term "militarism" can, as

Stanislas Andreski has pointed out, mean several different things, which may or may not be related: an aggressive foreign policy; preponderance of the military in the state; subservience of the whole society to the needs of the army; or an ideology of military ideals.[2] Militarism takes different forms in different societies. In Andreski's terms, Soviet militarism in the Brezhnev years was characterized by a foreign policy that relied heavily on military power, by the subservience of society to military needs, and by the Party's effort to inculcate military values. The military, however, was not preponderant in the state, in spite of much Western speculation to that effect.

In the 1970s and early 1980s militarism in the Soviet Union was debated by western analysts.[3] The main issue was how to explain those features of Soviet "militarism" characteristic of the Brezhnev years: high priority for military power; heavy reliance on military instruments of foreign policy; military-patriotic education; and secrecy. This debate did not lead to consensus, except on one crucial point. All the participants stressed that, whatever the degree of militarism or militarization might be, it had to be explained not in terms of the influence of the military, but rather in terms of the priorities of the state, which were determined by civilian leaders. Soviet "militarism," in other words, was a secondary aspect of Soviet statism, and could not be explained solely, or even primarily, by reference to the power of the military.

This debate is relevant now because if Soviet "militarism" is to be understood as an aspect of Soviet statism, a changing relationship between state and society should have important implications for the main elements of that "militarism." A weakening of the state and a strengthening of society should be accompanied by a weakening of "militarism," and by a process of demilitarization.[4]

This article examines the effect of democratization on the militarist or militarized features of Soviet society. It focuses on two of Andreski's categories and uses the term "demilitarization" with these two dimensions of social life in mind: the subservience of society to military needs, as reflected in the priority of defense; and the inculcation of military ideals, as reflected in the public debate over "the army and society."

THE CHANGING PRIORITY OF DEFENSE

The Soviet economy in the 1970s and 1980s had been a command economy, designed to enforce priorities set by the leadership and to ignore the economic demands of the mass of the population. The high priority accorded to defense was no secret, but the size and composition of the defense budget were, and this secrecy helped to prevent public discussion of the trade-offs between defense and other priorities. Although economic reform has not yet succeeded in restructuring the economy, political reform has changed the politics of defense spending.

Soviet military power grew rapidly in the 1970s, but the economic and technological basis of that power began to erode in the late 1970s. As the economy stagnated, the military burden grew. Military expenditure which, according to U.S.

Central Intelligence Agency (CIA) estimates, had constituted 12–14 percent of gross national product (GNP) in 1970, had grown to 15–17 percent by 1985.[5]

At the outset Gorbachev tried to "accelerate" economic growth while seeking to restrain the growth of defense outlays; in July 1985 he apparently told a meeting of military leaders in Minsk that there would be strict limits on the resources they could have.[6] It soon became clear that Gorbachev wanted to escape from the old pattern of arms racing, and to deal with the threatening international situation by political rather than by military means. He stressed the need for a stable and peaceful international environment in order to concentrate on domestic reforms, and put forward the "new thinking" as a conceptual framework to guide Soviet foreign and defense policy in a new direction.

In spite of Gorbachev's new thinking, Western governments did not detect any clear signs of a reduction in the rate of growth of military expenditure after 1985. Indeed, estimates by the CIA and the U.S. Defense Intelligence Agency (DIA) indicated a slight increase in the rate of growth under Gorbachev.[7] Nevertheless, the Deputy Minister of Defense for Armament, General V. Shabanov, said in July 1988 that military outlays had begun to decrease slightly in 1986, and Leonard Vid, deputy chief of *Gosplan,* has written recently that "Soviet military production and arms spending started to decline in early 1988."[8]

By the end of 1988 there were clear signs that Gorbachev had decided to reduce defense outlays. In December 1988 he announced a unilateral cut of 500,000 men in the armed forces, and on January 6, 1989, he declared that "we must also review expenditures on defense. A preliminary study shows that we could cut them without weakening our state's security or its defense potential."[9] Several days later he told a visiting Western delegation that "the defense budget will be reduced by 14.2 percent, the production of armaments and military hardware by 19.5 percent."[10]

On May 30, 1989 Gorbachev told the Congress of People's Deputies that the Soviet defense budget in 1989 amounted to 77.3 billion rubles, which is about 9 percent of the Soviet gross national product, and said that it would be reduced by ten billion rubles in 1990–91.[11] A week later Nikolai Ryzhkov, chairman of the Council of Ministers, gave the Congress a breakdown of the budget and said that it was the government's intention to reduce the proportion of national income going to defense by one-and-one-half to two times by 1995.[12]

These figures provided more information about Soviet defense expenditures than had been available before, but they are still difficult to interpret. The main problem is that we do not know whether the prices paid for military goods and services reflect the costs of those goods and services. It has been reported, for example, that raw materials are supplied to the armed forces and to the defense industrial ministries at a lower price than to other customers, and that the military are able to force unrealistically low prices for weapons and equipment on the defense industry.[13] The defense budget may therefore seriously understate the true cost of defense.

Gorbachev has made it clear that, for the first time since Khrushchev, the Soviet leadership intends to reduce defense spending. A number of explanations may be offered for this decision: economic performance has not yet improved under *perestroika,* and 1988 was a very poor year, marked by growing shortages of food and of consumer goods, and by a worsening deficit;[14] the consolidation of Gorbachev's political position at the September 1988 Central Committee Plenum (when he strengthened his hand vis-à-vis the main conservative member of the Politburo, Yegor Ligachev) may have made it possible for him to move ahead with policies he had long had in mind;[15] and the improving international climate, which has been brought about largely by Soviet policies, has made it easier to claim that a reduction of forces would not harm Soviet security.

The decision to reduce the military burden by cutting the armed forces and military production will free productive capacity in the defense sector. The Soviet defense sector has always produced goods for civilian use, and Brezhnev twice publicly urged the defense sector to contribute more to the civilian economy, though to little apparent effect. Gorbachev has put pressure on the defense sector to increase its civilian production. In 1988, for example, the Ministry of Machine Building for Light and Food Industry was dissolved, and its plants were taken over by various defense industry ministries.[16] The Ministry of the Aviation Industry is to produce machines for processing fruit and vegetables, and for producing macaroni. The Ministry of the Defense Industry is to produce equipment and production lines for meat and poultry processing plants. The Ministry of Medium Machine Building (which is responsible for the nuclear industry) is producing milk-processing equipment.[17]

Gorbachev's United Nations speech was apparently followed by further orders to the defense industry to increase civilian production. The general director of the "Kommunar" Machine Building Production Association has said that some people in the Soviet Union took Gorbachev's declaration at the U.N. of unilateral cuts "as a slogan," but "then orders were placed, and we saw that we have to do some serious thinking about how to make ends meet."[18] Forty percent of the output of the defense sector is now for civilian use, and that proportion is supposed to rise to 46 percent in 1990, and to over 60 percent in 1995.[19]

Little preparation for conversion had been made before the present shift in policy. The free capacity in the defense industry is to be used to produce consumer goods and machinery for the food-processing industry in the first instance. Some economists have criticized this decision, arguing that it would have been better to use the defense industry to produce high-technology goods and equipment.[20] Apparently this too will be done, but the need to improve the supply of consumer goods and food to the population has taken priority.

As the priorities of the Party leadership have changed and become more complex, the importance of economic calculation in defense policy has grown. Civilian voices were raised early in 1989 to ask for information about the costs of defense, and for economic considerations to be taken more seriously into account in defense policy-making. Thus S. G. Arutiunov, director of the Tushinskii Machine Building Plant, commented in a discussion of conversion that "we, unfortunately, have become convinced that the spending mechanism (*zatratnyi mekhanizm*) in the hands of the military is in danger of blowing up the economy. Defense expenditures must be put under the control of an authoritative commission of the Supreme Soviet of the USSR."[21] Similarly, E. Shashkov, writing in *Kommunist*, has argued that "now nobody has the right secretly (*neglasno*) to spend the resources of the country, without counting them, as happened in the past."[22] *Glasnost*, he argues, must enter military affairs, and "all departments (*vedomstva*) dealing with military and military-industrial activity" should be brought under the control of the highest electoral bodies in the country.[23]

The Supreme Soviet has established a Committee on Defense and State Security (*Komitet po voprosam oborony i gosudarstvennoi bezopasnosti*) under the chairmanship of V. L. Lapygin, a chief designer of missile guidance systems. The Committee's main task, according to Lapygin, is to strengthen the defense of the country and to exercise oversight (*kontrol'*) over the executive agencies with responsibility for defense. "We will base our work," he said, "on the principles of the new political, military, and economic thinking. Such approaches to Soviet defense construction will make it possible to reduce military expenditure by raising the quality of our armed forces, without damaging the defense capability of the USSR."[24]

By examining defense programs the Supreme Soviet Committee will no doubt encourage public discussion about the priority of defense, about the size and allocation of the defense budget, and about the system of prices for military equipment. For the first time public opinion will have an institutionalized voice in defense policy-making.

THE MILITARY AND SOCIETY

In the 1970s most Western observers regarded the Soviet armed forces (along with the KGB) as one of the two Soviet institutions that worked well. This image was fostered not only by Western defense ministries, which needed to support their claims for more resources, but also by the Soviet press which, although it carried articles on problems in the armed forces, was devoted to inculcating respect for the military.

Now, however, things have changed. The military has come in for widespread criticism. Some of this comes from soldiers and officers who are concerned about conditions in the armed forces; some comes from civilians who are critical not only of social relations in the military, but also of the relationship between the military and society. The armed forces now look less like an exemplary institution than they did in the 1970s. Trotsky was perhaps right when he wrote that "the army is a copy of society and suffers from all its ills, usually at a higher temperature."[25]

The current Soviet discussion of "army and society" ranges over many issues: nepotism and protectionism in the military; housing for officers; military-patriotic education and pacifism; the treatment of veterans of the Afghan War; the arrangements for the 97,000 officers who will be demobilized as a result of

Gorbachev's cuts; the growing number of officers who are seeking early discharge,[26] and the lack of recruits for the officer corps. Four issues are discussed briefly here to illustrate the public attitudes now being expressed towards the military, and the questions that public opinion is raising: *dedovshchina* (the brutal bullying of new conscripts by those who have already completed some of their service), student deferments; military reform; and public attitudes in the Baltic republics.

Dedovshchina

Dedovshchina is not a new phenomenon (it dates back at least to the 1960s, and perhaps earlier), but it is only in the last few years that it has been widely exposed in the press. One of the participants in a round-table discussion on the "Army and Society" remarked that:

> I know hundreds of stories of demobilized soldiers about the so-called nonregulation relations. They are horrible stories about humiliation and the insult of human dignity, about crimes against morality and consciousness. The humiliation of younger soldiers, which we only recently began speaking about, is in fact legalized slavery, very convenient for the brass who's accustomed to having others do its dirty work.
>
> To preserve its prestige and authority, the army itself—through its newspapers, radio and television—should have told about cases of despotism, the breaching of law and regulations. But instead—sugary programmes of the type: "Serve the Soviet Union!" to the accompaniment of cheery clangs of march music.[27]

The military authorities have tried to reassure public opinion by saying that they are working energetically to eradicate *dedovshchina*.[28] They are worried by the fact that unfavorable publicity is making young men reluctant to serve in the armed forces.

The discussion of *dedovshchina* has raised a number of questions. For example, are the causes of "non-regulation relations" to be found in the military, or have the military imported them from the broader society? Civilian critics tend to argue the former point, military spokesmen the latter.[29]

Student Deferments

In the early 1980s, it was decided not to grant students in higher education automatic deferment of military service until after graduation, and after 1984 male students in higher education were drafted in the middle of their studies. The decision not to grant deferments was taken in order to ensure that the armed forces had the manpower they needed when the number of young men available for military service was declining. It caused resentment not only among students, but also among the intelligentsia, and especially in the scientific community. The issue was raised in public in a round-table discussion in *Literaturnaia Gazeta* in May 1987, when two scientists pointed to the harm that military service did to young scientists. Boris Raushenbakh claimed that the young men who become students after military service "are fine executants, very well organized, but they won't become Newtons. Evidently atrophy takes place, a deadening of the creative abilities."[30]

These comments evoked heated replies from the military, and accusations that the critics were unpatriotic. Protests from students and from the scientific community continued, however, and in a number of universities students boycotted the courses offered by the military departments (*voennye kafedry*).[31] Raushenbakh's complaints about the effects of military service on students were amplified by other scientists. The rector of Moscow State University wrote to the Central Committee in 1987 to ask that young scientists not be conscripted during their studies. V. A. Sadovnich, deputy rector of Moscow State University, said in a recent interview that after military service students have more problems with their studies: "*Dedovshchina* leaves its mark for many years."[32] The military rarely use the specialist knowledge that students possess, but rather take the view that they should make "real men" of the students by giving them tough physical assignments.

These protests were successful, for in April 1989 it was announced that deferment would be given to all daytime (i.e., not extra-mural) students at higher educational establishments (VUZy, *Vysshye uchebnye zavedeniia*). Graduates of VUZy and specialized secondary schools who have taken courses in the military departments and training courses in the military will be given the title of reserve officer without further military service. The period of military service for soldiers, seamen and non-commissioned officers with higher education will now be one year.[33] This decision has been presented in the press as a consequence of Gorbachev's decision to reduce the armed forces by 500,000.

The decision to reinstate student deferments has removed a bone of contention between the military and the intelligentsia. The dispute was a bitter one, not merely because military service disrupted higher education, but because the military resented the notion that army life was in some sense antithetical to science and culture, and also because the relative importance to the country of military power and of science and learning was at issue. As one newspaper put it, the decision to reinstate deferments shows official acceptance of the idea that "training highly qualified specialists for the national economy is no less patriotic a task than training soldiers."[34]

Military Reform

The issue of military reform emerged quite suddenly at the end of 1988 when Lieutenant-Colonel Aleksandr Savinkin of the Main Political Administration published an article in *Moscow News* under the title "What Kind of Armed Forces Do We Need?"[35] Savinkin argued that the Soviet Union should adopt a mixed professional-militia system, consisting of "a relatively small, perfectly technically equipped, professionally trained and mainly voluntarily staffed military organization supported by a broad network of local militia formations." This was the kind of system that had been established by Frunze's military reforms of 1924–25, but abandoned by Stalin in the 1930s.

Savinkin argued that a professional-militia system would: create a democratic military structure that would be integrated into society; make it possible to re-shape the army in accordance with the principles of reasonable sufficiency and defensive defense; reduce the military burden; and remove a potential military threat to other countries. The need for reform is urgent, in Savinkin's mind, be-cause although the strength of the armed forces lies in popular support, there is a "certain dislocation of relations between Soviet society and its armed forces." The reasons he gives for this dislocation are: the "state-political estrangement" of the armed forces from the people; the slower pace of *perestroika* in the military; the influence of the war in Afghanistan; and the lack of information in Soviet society about defense policy and life in the armed forces.

Leading military officers were quick to reject Savinkin's proposal. The new chief of the General Staff, Army General M. Moiseev, the chief of the Main Politi-cal Administration, Army General A. Lizichev, and Defense Minister Yazov have all criticized the principle of voluntarism and the proposal for a territorial mili-tia.[36] Savinkin's opponents reject the idea of voluntarism as undemocratic and as a violation of social justice; as requiring a 400–700 percent increase in expendi-tures; and as unlikely to provide sufficient reserves for long-term military actions. Other critics have argued that if voluntary recruitment were introduced there would be no volunteers.[37] Savinkin's critics reject the territorial-militia element as unsuited to the complexities of modern warfare; as divorced from the country's real military needs; as likely to lower military preparedness and disrupt the local economies; and as undermining the goal of social integration in a multinational state.

In spite of these robust criticisms the issue of military reform has not gone away. The General Staff is now deluged with letters about military reform, and ci-vilian critics have challenged the objections to reform that the military leaders have raised.[38] V. L. Lapygin, chairman of the Supreme Soviet's Committee on De-fense and State Security, supports the idea of military reform.[39] Some reformers want an all-professional force, others the mixed system advocated by Savinkin. They argue that, as it is, conscripts are not able to cope with the complex equip-ment they are supposed to handle, and they claim that a professional force would not necessarily be more expensive than the present system.

The Armed Forces and the Baltic Nations

One of the most interesting debates about the military in recent months has been caused by pressure from the Baltic republics for reforms that would take account of national sensibilities. There is widespread popular antipathy in the Baltic to the existing military system, and this has been reflected not only in the programs of the newly-organized popular fronts, but in the statements and appeals of govern-ment and Party leaders too.

In April 1989 Indrek Toome, chairman of the Estonian Council of Ministers, and A. Ryuytel, chairman of the Presidium of the Estonian Supreme Soviet, submitted eight proposals on military service to the authorities in Moscow: conscripts from Estonia must be allowed to serve initially in the Baltic Military District or at least in national units outside the District; 50–60 percent of Tallinn's militia should come from Estonia; at least 30–40 percent of border troops stationed in Estonia should come from the republic; students should have a choice whether to do military studies in one of the VUZy or to go into the military after graduation; alternative labor service should be provided in Estonia for conscientious objectors; military training in schools should be reduced or abolished; commanders in chief of the branches of the armed forces must in future discuss any stationing of additional troops in Estonia with the republic's government; the army must abide by Estonia's environmental laws.[40]

In pressing these claims, the Estonian authorities are reflecting popular concern about the military, and also expressing frustration at their own powerlessness. "The Army is no longer under the control of civilian authorities and this can no longer be tolerated," Toome said in an interview. "The armed forces must be subordinated to both the government and the parliament." Toome made it clear that this letter, which he called the "first real step toward curbing the Army's omnipotence," was the beginning of a long process. He claimed that the Estonian authorities had already had some success in influencing the military: almost 25 percent of conscripts would serve in the Baltic Military District (compared with 2 percent before), while almost 20 percent would serve in the groups of Soviet forces in Eastern Europe; pre-induction military training for girls had been ended; and the next immediate goal was the "final elimination of militarism from the education process."[41]

The situation in the Baltic republics is a special one because the memory of independence is still strong and some people regard the Soviet armed forces there as little better than an army of occupation. The Baltic press has reported that conscripts from those republics suffer especially from *dedovshchina*, and one particular case has aroused widespread indignation. A Lithunian private, Arturas Sakalauskas, shot and killed eight of his fellow-soldiers when they tried to rape him after months of tormenting him and beating him up. A television documentary about the case evoked a wave of sympathy for Sakalauskas, and petitions asking for his acquittal have been organized.[42]

The proposals of the popular fronts in the Baltic republics have come in for sharp criticism in the central Soviet press, and especially in *Krasnaia zvezda*.[43] But the military authorities have made some effort to show that they are willing to respond to public criticisms and demands. Lieutenant-General Kuzmin, commander of the Baltic Military District, proposed during the election for the Congress of People's Deputies that thirty percent of those called up in the Baltic republics serve in the Baltic Military District; he was elected.[44] Defense Minister Yazov promised Algirdas Brazauskas, the Lithuanian party secretary, that starting in the spring of 1989, as many Lithuanians as possible would do their military service close to home, but he also said that a decision on the question of national formations had been postponed.[45]

The response of the Moscow authorities is far from satisfying all the demands put forward by the leaders in the Baltic republics, and pressure on these issues will not dissipate. In May 1989 the Lithuanian Supreme Soviet set up a Commission on Matters of Military Service by the Republic's Young Men. This commission is to "observe the procedure of ... call-up to the Army, to find out about conditions of military service, to maintain contacts with military units and soldiers' parents, to take part in investigations of cases involving non-regulation relations in the Army and acts of violence, and to show concern for soldiers' families."[46] The Estonian premier, Indrek Toome, has said that: "The Army must be brought under the republic's control. The Army's activities must be regulated by the republic's laws. ... Speaking about the law-governed state nobody, neither the army, the security forces, nor the police can remain out of control."[47]

THE MILITARY'S REACTION TO CRITICISM

...

There is little doubt that many officers, including the High Command, find criticism of the military distasteful, and that they regard such criticism as ill-informed and inspired by anti-military motives, even when it comes from other officers.[49] On July 6, 1989, *Krasnaia zvezda* published a joint memorandum by the Central Committee departments for State-Legal Affairs and for Ideology, and by the Main Political Administration of the Armed Forces, accusing some publications of describing military life "in an unobjective and one-sided fashion." Savinkin's article on military reform, for example, was criticized in the memorandum as one of a "series of incompetent publications." The newspaper also published a resolution of the Central Committee Secretariat agreeing with the memorandum and proposing that military officers who are qualified journalists be attached to the editorial offices of central newspapers.[50]

There is also evident in the military press a dislike of the changes taking place in the society at large. It is true of course that under Brezhnev the economic and technological basis of Soviet military power was beginning to erode and that, in spite of the glorification of military life, conditions of service were often difficult. For this reason many officers have embraced *perestroika* and *glasnost,* and the diversity that *glasnost* has revealed should make us careful not to generalize about military attitudes. But it is clear that there is widespread unhappiness in the military with the way in which Soviet society is developing.

A striking example of military disaffection has appeared in the *Journal of Military History (Voenno-istoricheskii zhurnal)*. Published by the Ministry of Defense, this journal has been running a series of articles by the educator and writer Karem Rash on the theme of the "Army and culture." It has always been a highly professional journal and, under a new editorial board, has pursued greater *glasnost* in military history. But the articles by Rash, who is praised effusively in the editorial introduction, betray a very deep dislike of what is now going on in the Soviet Union:

> *Perestroika* is a regrouping of forces before the offensive. Can the army achieve victory if it opposes the enemy not with its advanced units, but by pushing forward the baggage-trains and heroes of the rear, and moves against the enemy with the vanguard of prancing and jerking guitarists who deafen themselves and the enemy with electrical decibels? In advance go the enterprising journalists, the aerobics landing force *(desant)*, the grinning parodists, the effeminate dancers, because "in ballet we are ahead of the whole planet," and the spearhead of the attack is the Ministry of Culture, more precisely the Ministry of Spectacles and Amusements, and the *Komsomol,* which is essentially trying to replace its patronage *(shefstvo)* of the Army and Navy with patronage of leisure and cooperation.[51]

Rash goes on to identify criticism of the Army as a symptom of the sickness of society: "Love for one's Army, loyalty to its traditions is the truest sign of the health of a nation. Attacks on the Army always begin when there is an attempt to hide and leave untouched society's deeper vices. Hostility towards the Army springs most often from an impure conscience and fear of service and duty."[52] He portrays the army as the embodiment of all that is good in Russian culture.

Rash's most striking passage comes, however, in a section in which he notes that it is the soldier who is called on in difficult situations like Chernobyl: "Who recently saved Poland from national chaos, anarchy and humiliation, who held her fast at the last moment on the edge of the abyss? The Polish Army! And so whom is the enemy vilifying? Of course those who guard the socialist fatherland—the people's Army."[53] This hint that the military might be used to halt the current process of change is echoed from the other side of the political spectrum. One of the participants in the round-table discussion asked "whose side will the army be on if someone in this country attempts to forcibly liquidate *perestroika?*"[54] In April 1989 the army was used to break up a demonstration in Tbilisi, using brutal tactics that resulted in the deaths of some young demonstrators. This action provoked intense criticism of the military, and repeated questions, which remain unanswered, about who in Moscow had ordered the troops to be used. Echoing what is evidently a widespread fear, Andrei Sakharov has spoken of the danger of a right wing coup, either by the military or by the Party leadership.[55]

CONCLUSION: DEMILITARIZATION AND DEMOCRACY

Perestroika and *glasnost* have created the opportunity for public opinion to emerge on military affairs. The discussion of military issues was helped by the election campaign for the Congress of People's Deputies. Relations between the military and society were an important issue in the campaign, and the results of the election (in which some senior military officers were defeated) show that the military do not enjoy unquestioned authority in Soviet society.[56]

The Supreme Soviet will become the crucial forum for society's attempt to establish control over the armed forces. General Yazov was subjected to three hours of critical questioning before he was confirmed as minister of defense by the Supreme Soviet on July 3, 1989.[57] The chairman of the Supreme Soviet's Committee on Defense and State Security has already indicated that it will exercise active oversight over defense policy. "The time of careless wastefulness, of departmental 'infallibility' has gone," Lapygin has asserted.[58] How the committee's work will be affected by the fact that half of its members (19 out of 38) come from the military-industrial complex remains to be seen. There were some protests about the composition of the committee in June, and one new member (from Lithuania), was added as a result.[59] The process of establishing democratic control over the armed forces and military affairs may be long and difficult.

The changing relationship between state and society has affected the priority given to defense and the position of the military in Soviet society: the allocation of resources to defense is no longer immune from public questioning; and society, far from being the passive recipient of military-patriotic propaganda, has begun to express its own views about the armed forces. Since Soviet "militarism" has been a secondary element of Soviet statism, the process of democratization, through which public opinion has begun to find expression, has resulted in some degree of demilitarization. Democratization and demilitarization have gone in hand. But the future development of these processes remains uncertain, and the danger exists that the military might be a willing instrument in bringing them to an end. The role of the military in the state and in the society is therefore a crucial issue in the changes now taking place in the Soviet Union.

NOTES

ABOUT THE AUTHOR: **David Holloway** is professor of political science and codirector of the Center for International Security and Arms Control at Stanford University.

1. "Army and Society," *Twentieth Century and Peace*, No. 9 (1988), p. 19.

2. See the article by Stanislas Andreski in J. Gould and W. L. Kolb, eds., *A Dictionary of the Social Sciences* (London: Tavistock, 1964), pp. 429–430.

3. Among the contributions to this debate were William Odom, "The 'Militarization' of Soviet Society," *Problems of Communism*, Vol. 25, No. 5 (September-October 1976), pp. 34–51; Timothy J. Colton, "The Impact of the Military on Soviet Society," in Seweryn Bailer, ed., *The Domestic Context of Soviet Foreign Policy* (Boulder: Westview Press, 1981), pp. 119–138; Richard Pipes, "Militarism and the Soviet State," *Daedalus*, Vol. 109, No. 4 (Fall 1980), pp. 1–12; David Holloway, "War, Militarism, and the Soviet State," *Alternatives*, Vol. 6, No. 1 (March 1980), pp. 59–92.

4. For a good discussion of militarization under Brezhnev, see M. Steven Fish, "The 'Militarized Society' in the Era of Reform: First Steps Toward Demilitarization?" in *Analyzing the Gorbachev Era: Working Papers of the Students of the Berkeley-Stanford Program in Soviet Studies*, Berkeley and Stanford, California, 1989, pp. 117–142.

5. Joint Economic Committee, U.S. Congress, *Allocation of Resources in the Soviet Union and China—1986* (Washington D.C.: United States Government Printing Office [U.S. GPO], 1988), p. 15. The estimation of Soviet defense expenditure is a highly controversial

issue. Some economists argue that the CIA understates the military burden because it excludes activities such as civil defense and military aid. If this broader definition is used, they argue, the military burden rose from about 20 percent in GNP in 1970 to about 25 percent by the mid-1980s. (See Defense Intelligence Agency, *The High Cost of Soviet Defense,* DRC 118–88 [Washington, D.C.: U.S. GPO, December 1988], p. 3). Still other economists argue that even this estimate is too low—that the proportion is about 30–35 percent—not because the CIA has underestimated the size or cost of the defense effort, but because it has overestimated the size of the Soviet GNP. See Richard E. Ericson, "The Soviet Statistical Debate: Khanin vs. TsSU," unpublished paper, February 1988, p. 34. Other economists argue that the CIA estimate is too high. See Franklyn D. Holzman, "Politics and Guesswork: CIA and DIA Estimates of Soviet Military Spending," *International Security,* Vol. 14, No. 2 (Fall 1989), pp. 101–131.

6. His speech has not been published; for comments on the meeting see Bruce Parrott, "Soviet National Security Under Gorbachev," *Problems of Communism,* Vol. 37, No 6 (November-December 1988), p. 7.

7. Joint Economic Committee, U.S. Congress, *Allocation of Resources in the Soviet Union and China—1987* (Washington, D.C.: U.S. GPO, 1989), p. 23.

8. For Shabanov's comments, see R. Jeffrey Smith, "Arms Budget Cut, Soviet Says," *Washington Post,* July 27, 1988, p. A18; for Leonard Vid's comments see his forthcoming article on conversion in *The Bulletin of the Atomic Scientists.*

9. "Narashchivat' intellektual'nyi potentsial perestroiki," *Pravda,* January 8, 1989, p. 2.

10. Bill Keller, "Gorbachev Tells of Military Cuts," *New York Times,* January 19, 1989. These figures were later embodied in a law in March 1989 on the reduction of Soviet armed forces by 1991.

11. "Ob osnovnykh napravlenniiakh vnutrennei i vneshnei politiki SSSR," *Pravda,* May 31, 1989, p. 2.

12. "Sluzhit' interesam naroda," *Pravda,* June 8, 1989, p. 3.

13. A. Isaev, "Reforma i oboronnye otrasli," *Kommunist,* No. 5 (March 1989), pp. 25–26; Hedrick Smith, "On the Road With Gorbachev's Guru," *New York Times Magazine,* April 10, 1988, p. 42. See also Michael R. Gordon, "Soviets Cite 40 Percent Cut in Tank Output," *New York Times,* July 22, 1989, p. 4. When Soviet spokesmen first promised in 1987 that detailed figures on defense spending would be published, they said that this would be done after prices had been reformed, but the price reform has been postponed, so one must suppose that the published figures have been compiled using unreformed prices.

14. Both E. Shashkov ("Skol'ko stoit bezopasnost'?" *Kommunist,* No. 4 [March 1989], p. 110) and Aleksei Kireev ("Skol'ko tratit' na oboronu," *Ogonek,* No. 19 [May 1989], p. 6) stress the importance of the deficit in the decision to reduce defense outlays.

15. It should be noted, however, that it is not clear whether it is Gorbachev's own views on defense expenditure that have changed, or only what he has felt it politically possible to say.

16. A decision was taken to draw 345 plants and 200 research institutes of the defense sector into civilian production. See Kireev, "Skol'ko tratit'," p. 8.

17. For a discussion see "The Soviet Economy in 1988: Gorbachev Changes Course," a Report by the Central Intelligence Agency and the Defense Intelligence Agency presented to the Subcommittee on National Security Economics of the Joint Economic Committee, U.S. Congress, April 14, 1989, pp. 14–21.

18. "Kak perekovat' mechi na orala," *Moskovskaia Pravda,* March 21, 1989, p. 2.

19. N. I. Ryzhkov, "Sluzhit' interesam naroda," *Pravda,* June 8, 1989, p. 3. What branches are being counted as part of the "defense complex" is not clear, but it seems likely to be the nine ministries normally counted as Military-Industrial Commission (*Voenno-promy-shlennaia kommissiia,* or VPK) ministries. Brezhnev mentioned 42 percent in 1971, but perhaps that was for the Defense Industry Ministry alone; the head of that ministry has said that 50 percent of his output is now civilian. Note that increases in production of civilian goods need not necessarily come at the expense of military production, since civilian production may use reserve capacity at military plants.

20. For example, Kireev, "Skol'ko tratit'," p. 8.

21. "Kak perekovat' mechi na orala," p. 2.

22. Shashkov, "Skol'ko stoit," p. 111.

23. Shashkov, "Skol'ko stoit," pp. 113, 114.

24. "S pozitsii novogo myshleniia," *Krasnaia zvezda,* June 22, 1989, p. 1. This is an interview with Lapygin.

25. L. D. Trotsky, *The Revolution Betrayed* (London: New Park Publishers, 1967), p. 222 (first published in 1936).

26. There has been, apparently, a growing number of letters from officers seeking to leave the military before their term of duty is up. The military have dealt with this firmly, evidently afraid that yielding to such requests would merely encourage others to seek the same course.

27. "Army and Society," p. 24.

28. See, for example, the comments by Army General A. Lizichev, head of the Main Political Administration, in *Kommunist,* No. 3 (February 1989), pp. 19–20.

29. I have not, however, seen a serious analysis of this question.

30. "Pochemu u nas malo po-nastoiashchemu obrazovannykh liudei?" *Literaturnaia Gazeta,* May 13, 1987, p. 12.

31. See, for example, the Radio Liberty report by Kathleen Mihalisko on boycotts and protests at Kiev University, January 12, 1989; and the interview with V. A. Sadovnich, "Sokrashchenie armii i studenty," *Literaturnaia Gazeta,* April 5, 1989, p. 13.

32. Sadovnich interview, "Sokrashchenie armii," p. 13.

33. "Studenty i armiia," *Izvestiia,* April 13, 1989, p. 1.

34. Editorial introduction to the interview with Sadovnich, "Sokrashchenie armii."

35. Lt.-Col. Alexander Savinkin, "What Kind of Armed Forces Do We Need?" *Moscow News,* No. 45 (1988), p. 6. Savinkin had already raised this issue in the round-table discussion, "Army and Society," but his article in *Moscow News* provided a more elaborate statement of his views.

36. See, for example, for Lizichev's views, "V tsentre perestroiki—chelovek," *Krasnaia zvezda,* February 3, 1989, p. 2; for Moiseev's views, "S pozitsii oboronitel'noi doktriny," *Krasnaia zvezda,* February 10, 1989, p. 2; and for Yazov's position "Byt' na ostrie perestroiki," *Krasnaia zvezda,* March 7, 1989, p. 2.

37. "Army and Society," p. 22.

38. For example Kireev, "Skol'ko tratit'," p. 8.

39. "Glasnost' i gosudarstvennaia bezopasnost'," *Izvestiia,* June 26, 1989, p. 2. This is an interview with V. L. Lapygin.

40. "Estonian Leadership Sends Note to Soviet Defence Minister," *Homeland* (Supplement to the Estonian *Kodumaa* weekly), April 19, 1989, p. 1.

41. The interview with Toome is in "Vosem' predlozhenii po delam voennym," *Sovetskaia Estoniia,* April 14, 1989, pp. 1, 3. The figure of 25 percent for Estonian conscripts

serving in the Baltic Military District seems to mark an increase from about 2 percent; see "Estonia's Prime Minister and Military Commissar support calls to restructure military service," *Homeland,* April 12, 1989, p. 1. A week after Toome's memorandum to Moscow, the Estonian Women's Congress sent an appeal to Yazov calling for similar changes in the military. In their appeal they wrote that "a system based on despotism and degradation produces cruel people who in civilian life beat women and children, raise their hand against their parents, and taunt the weak. Cruelty in relations between draftees can even arouse base instincts in those young men whose evil inclinations could never have been manifested in other circumstances"; "Ministru oborony SSSR—D. T. Yazovu," *Sovetskaia Estoniia,* April 21, 1989, p. 3.

42. "Baltic Conscripts Have Hard Time in the Soviet Army Now," *Homeland,* April 5, 1989, p. 6.

43. See, for example, Iu. Rubtsov, "Dvizhenie ubezhdeno," *Krasnaia zvezda,* December 22, 1988, p. 2.

44. Reported on Radio Moscow, March 11, 1989; see Foreign Broadcast Information Service (FBIS), *Daily Report—Soviet Union,* FBIS-SOV-89–047, March 13, 1989, p. 119.

45. Radio broadcast from Vilnius, April 16, 1989; FBIS-SOV-89–075, Akpril 20, 1989, p. 71.

46. "V Prezidiume Verkhovnogo Soveta Litovskoi SSSR," *Sovetskaia Litva,* May 6, 1989, p. 3.

47. "Estonia's Prime Minister and Military Commissar Support Calls to Restructure Military Service," *Homeland,* April 12, 1989, p. 1.

49. The round-table discussion in *Twentieth Century and Peace* is followed by an editorial comment that contains this sentence: "Having known about the theme of the discussion, the high military bosses expressed their disapproval, hinting that the so-called 'round tables' of some editorial boards try to find out on whose sides the army will be if *perestroika* gathers a high speed and scope." "Army and Society," p. 28. This round-table was chaired by a military officer, and a number of officers took part.

50. "Ob osveshchenii v tsentral'noi pechati zhizni i deiatel'nosti Sovetskikh Vooruzhennykh Sil," *Krasnaia zvezda,* July 6, 1989, p. 2.

51. Karem Rash, "Armiia i kul'tura," *Voenno-istoricheskii zhurnal,* No. 2 (1989), p. 12.

52. Rash "Armiia i kul'tura" *Voenno-istoricheskii zhurnal,* No. 3 (1989), p. 3.

53. Rash "Armiia i kul'tura" *Voenno-istoricheskii zhurnal,* No. 2 (1989), p. 15.

54. "Army and society," p. 26.

55. "Stepen'svobody," *Ogonek,* No. 31 (July 1989), p. 28. This is an interview with Sakharov.

56. Senior officers make up 3.1 percent of the people's deputies in the Congress, and are also represented in the Supreme Soviet. The 3.1 percent figure is taken from the analysis by A. Nazimova and V. Sheinis, "Vybor sdelan," *Izvestiia,* May 6, 1989, p. 3 This refers, however, to deputy defense ministers and other senior officers; it omits some lower-ranking officers who were elected to the Congress. The corresponding figure for the 1984 Supreme Soviet was 3.5 percent. Out of 121 military candidates (including those from public organizations), 76 were elected (30 of these were unopposed). See V. Nechaev, "Vybory: uroki, vyvody, problemy," *Krasnaia zvezda,* April 9, 1989, p. 2.

57. "Ministry poluchaiut 'dobro'," *Izvestiia,* July 3, 1989, p. 1.

58. "Glasnost' i gosudarstvennaia bezopasnost'," *Izvestiia,* June 26, 1989, p. 2.

59. Bill Keller, "Soviet Deputies, in Show of Power, Block 8 Nominees," *New York Times,* June 28, 1989, p. 1; see also the interviews with Lapygin in *Krasnaia zvezda* and *Izvestiia* referred to above.

45   *The Architects of Card Houses*

YURI KATASONOV

With the growing involvement of the Army in bloody inter-ethnic conflicts in this country and the candid appeals of extremist left-wing radicals to "storm the Kremlin," on the one hand, and with the downfall of the military-political system in Eastern Europe and the prospect of a united Germany as a NATO member, on the other, the task of struggling for the Army has become especially acute and urgent.

The Army has for a long time been the object of attacks by those forces which aim to destroy our state system and transform our great power—the USSR—into a conglomerate of territories dependent on the West, torn apart by inter-ethnic and appanage quarrels. The Soviet Army—united and supra-national, linked to the people by blood, glorious in its combat traditions, and still powerful by present-day standards—remains the last obstacle on the path to the realization of these schemes.

A politically highly active group of persons with Western orientations, united by mercenary interests, are coming out as the ideologues of the campaign against the Army. These people are our homebred compradores, who have seized key positions in international political science, in official "public" organizations dealing with world affairs, and in the majority of mass media. These figures are working closely, and in some instances have actually merged, with a number of political leaders and higher functionaries in party and state organs, through whom a pernicious influence is being exerted on military policy and on the position and activity of the Army.

Simultaneously, through channels of mass information and by other means, the very same group is shaping public opinion so as to convey a negative impression of the Soviet Army, and to stimulate disrespect and animosity towards it and its representatives. ...

This evokes great satisfaction in the political circles of the USA and other NATO countries, which have always looked upon Soviet military power as the main restraint on their "freedom" of action, that is, arbitrary behavior on the world arena, as the warrant of security for the USSR and its allies.

First and foremost, an arbitrary interpretation of the New Political Thinking serves as the "ideological" basis for attacking the Army. It is presented as if an era of universal equality, of international cooperation had actually arrived, in which all the major states of the world renounce reliance on military power. This promotes the growth of complacency and euphoria in society in regard to external security, an indifference to questions of defense, and nihilism toward the Army and anything associated with the military. ...

The greatest blow was delivered upon the Army after April 1985 when the foreign policy of the USSR started being built on a completely different basis than before and different from the way it is built in the majority of governments in the world today, that is, not on the strengthening of one's own military-political position but on the consistent unilateral abandonment of that position. In many ways this policy was being conducted as though the New Thinking was in actuality already accepted by other countries, including our long-term adversaries. Inasmuch as this is not so, a dangerous situation developed when Soviet foreign policy decisions at times began to be based, not so much on the calculation of realities, especially unpleasant ones for us, but on "ideal" conceptions whose practical realization is at least problematic—that is, on a utopia. The situation has a clear resemblance to that which sprung up after October 1917, when for many years Soviet policy was based on the utopian idea of world revolution. The pernicious consequences of this for our country and our people are well known.

Many important Soviet foreign policy moves of the last few years are connected with the unilateral reduction of Soviet military activity. They include the moratorium on nuclear testing, the curtailment of armed forces and armaments, of the military budget and the production of weapons technology, the cutback of Soviet troops stationed in Warsaw Pact countries and the removal of nuclear warheads from their territory, the adoption of a defensive military doctrine which provides for a reduction in the quantity, functions, and combat readiness of the armed forces. ...

The negotiations which the USSR and the Warsaw Pact countries are conducting with the U.S. and its NATO allies, on the reduction of armed forces and armaments in Europe, have from the outset been based on unequal principles: their object includes only a fraction of the elements of the military balance—above all those in which the Soviet Union is strong, and first of all, Soviet ground forces—which is why the other side is interested in their curtailment. In certain aspects of military strength where the USA has a clear advantage—above all, naval forces—they categorically refuse to enter into negotiations because they want to retain their superiority. ... The United States also refuses to negotiate on the reduction of tactical nuclear weapons, since by modernizing them it is planning to compensate for the nuclear rocket potential which was liquidated in compliance with the

Intermediate Range Missile Treaty, that is, to circumvent the treaty by such means.

That is how matters stand with the adoption of the New Thinking in the area of arms reductions, where for all intents and purposes it has assumed the form of unilateral disarmament on our part. The long-term consequences of these actions are hard to predict but they are clearly dangerous. It is already clear today that the defense of our country and the Army as its embodiment have become their victim.

Thus, the most dangerous political illusion of our day is becoming established in our society—an illusion that can turn into a great misfortune for the country, possibly into a new 1941 but in a cosmic-nuclear age which in its consequences is not comparable to the past—or else into total political capitulation and the loss of national independence. These conclusions follow from the following grim realities.

Firstly, the benevolence of official circles in the West toward our country in connection with perestroika is still limited chiefly to rhetoric and approval of those processes that suit them but do not please us in the least (such as the development of economic and political institutions according to Western capitalist models, the unilateral or unequal reduction of our armed forces and weaponry, and so forth). ...

Secondly, the countries of the West do not by any means plan to be guided by the principles of the New Thinking. ... (U.S. intervention in Panama, aggression against Libya in 1986, etc.).

Thirdly, they use our difficulties for strengthening their own superiority over the USSR in all spheres, especially in the military, and continue at an unabated pace to develop and build up their military's technical potential with the goal of creating an insurmountable gap between themselves and the USSR, reducing it to a second-rate power. ...

Fourthly, just as before, the U.S. and NATO consider the Soviet Union their main adversary. ... The possibility of using nuclear weapons remains the foundation of their strategy. ...

Today the most important ideologist of unilateral disarmament is the director of the Institute of USA and Canada Studies of the USSR Academy of Sciences, G. Arbatov, a protegé of Brezhnev's and for many years an "adviser to the Kremlin" (as he is called in the West). At the Second Congress of People's Deputies, Arbatov depicted American politicians as peace-loving and peace-makers (while at that very time they were readying for the invasion of Panama) and portrayed our military as advocates of the arms race, that is, blamed the wrong side, and on those grounds demanded the further unilateral reduction of the Soviet military budget, Armed Forces, and armaments. He even tried to show that the USSR allegedly spends more on military expenditures than the USA. Other deputies immediately rebutted Arbatov's irresponsible demagogy, catching him at juggling facts and figures. Thus, the deputy A. Ovchinnikov recalled that the Soviet military budget amounts to 71 billion rubles, whereas the American is 305.5 billion dollars. One need not be an academician to understand the difference between these two figures, especially since today everybody knows that the exchange rate is one dollar to six rubles and not the other way around. ...

What is behind all this? Perhaps the learned Americanist knew from sources unavailable to the other deputies (for example, from the former Deputy Director of the CIA, A. Cox, with whom Arbatov co-chairs the "joint venture" of a Soviet-American research project on problems of stability) that the Pentagon has taken the "path of peace." No, better than most people, he knew this not to be the case. Already in the mid-1980s Arbatov authoritatively reported that the Pentagon had received the task of working out "plans for inflicting a defeat on the Soviet Union at every level of conflict, from insurgent operations to nuclear war." Not long ago it was officially declared that in 1991 the U.S. military budget will again increase and all the fundamental military programs are safeguarded in this budget. ...

The spiritual and blood-related "children of Arbatov" behave in very much the same manner as he does. They include his deputy Kokoshin, former deputies Zhurkin (today the director of the Institute on Europe of the USSR Academy of Sciences) and Bogdanov (now first Vice Chairman of the Soviet Peace Committee), the former academic secretary of the Institute of USA and Canada Studies I. E. Malashenko (today on the staff of the International Department of the Central Committee of the CPSU), the academician's son, A. Arbatov, who is section head at the Institute of World Economics and International Relations (IMEMO), and others. It would not be out of place to note that the younger Arbatov made swift professional progress under the wing of the directors of IMEMO, A. N. Yakovlev (1983–1985) and E. M. Primakov (1985–1989). As a member of the CPSU Central Committee and a member of the Presidium of the USSR Academy of Sciences, G. Arbatov assisted them both in gaining this position, their academic titles, and other advances. In turn Yakovlev, now a member of the Politburo and secretary of the Central Committee of the CPSU and Primakov, a candidate member of the Politburo, help keep "afloat" G. Arbatov, once the implementor of the policy of stagnation, as he was described at the XIX Party Conference. Someone on Arbatov's staff has gone so far as to recommend the reduction of our strategic forces unilaterally by 95 per cent! And former and present staff members of the same Institute on USA and Canada Studies discuss this proposal in several issues of the *Moscow News* with a serious mien. ...

Where are the other points of view on the military and political aspects of Soviet-American relations? Only recently and infrequently have military officers begun to express them in restrained fashion in the press. As for the other scholarly and other civilian institutions that deal with Soviet-American relations, practically all of them are in the sphere of influence of the "one-view monopoly": different points of view are not allowed and are harshly suppressed. ...

... It's not just a matter of incompetence and not only the opportunism of Arbatov and his associates: we are dealing with quite a specific "line." Today for the first time they are doing openly what they have been doing virtually for many years: they are acting as advocates of the interests of the West in our country, advertising its values and policies and undermining our military doctrine and defensive capability. The American sovietologist Jerry Hough pointed this out and noted that although such scholars and figures in the Soviet peace movement as Arbatov "must earn their bread by supporting Soviet foreign policy" (*Los Angeles Times*, 1986), they are doing work that is useful for the West. Hough considers that for destroying Soviet military doctrine and ideology and constraining the growth of the USSR's military potential, Arbatov deserves the Nobel peace prize. Thus far Arbatov has not received this award—they have found more deserving claimants. But his endeavors in this direction continue to mount. ...

The revived "sufficiency" principle re-emerged during the course of carrying out the aforementioned Soviet-American research project on the problems of stability, which was established in 1985. Its recommendations stated in particular that "the USA and USSR should accept the 'reasonable sufficiency' conception in their military planning. In accordance with this conception, they should reduce their armed forces to much lower levels, while maintaining a stable balance at each level" ("The Requirements for Assuring Stable Co-existence in Soviet-American Relations," p. 23). To date this recommendation has been adopted only by us, and our own military doctrine represents, however paradoxically, the incarnation of an Arbatov-American recommendation. Among the American authors of the latter, besides the aforementioned A. Cox, are also the former director of the CIA, W. Colby, the former deputy secretary of defense T. Hoopes, the former deputy secretary of state, G. Ball, and others; and among the Soviets, besides Arbatov, there are V. V. Zhurkin, F. M. Burlatsky, V. M. Falin, and others. Such are the grimaces of perestroika and the New Political Thinking. ...

The use of the Army to put out inter-ethnic fires, and the blood shed in connection with this, are the most acute expressions of the crisis of our society that cancel out all the well-intentioned declarations about perestroika. ... It is mostly Russians and Russian-speaking soldiers and officers who are being sent to the "hot" spots. For the Russians this turns out to be a great misfortune: in putting out inter-ethnic fires, Russian blood is being shed, and now thousands of Russian refugees have also appeared, in the first place the families of military personnel.

Yes, the Army has many sore spots and problems today. Most of them are the ills which our entire society suffers from or which are rooted in our society. And still, we are greatly indebted to the Army whose representatives fulfill the most responsible, physically difficult and psychologically unique task: to assure the security of our country and to this end to be ready to risk their health and their lives at any moment.

Our sacred duty today is to come to the aid of the Army, to defend it. And it will reliably defend us and defend the Fatherland.

PART 7

From Coup to Collapse

The failed coup of August 1991 dealt a fatal blow to the Soviet system. By forcing a dramatic showdown between the pillars of the old system and the defenders of the "White House," led by Boris Yeltsin, the coup effectively undermined Gorbachev's efforts to preserve a centrist coalition, tilted the political balance decisively toward the democratic reformers, and accelerated the unraveling of the Union. The immediate catalyst for the coup was the planned signing of the Union Treaty on August 20. To secure the crucial backing of the Union republics, beginning with Boris Yeltsin's Russian Federation, Gorbachev had in the end agreed to significant concessions, ceding power over taxation and in effect acquiescing to a loose confederal arrangement.

Meanwhile, the growing frustration of the hardliners at their inability to make Gorbachev their political captive and their alarm at the imminent signing of the Union Treaty, which in their view spelled the disintegration of the country, came to a head. On August 19, with Gorbachev on vacation in the Crimea, a self-proclaimed State Emergency Committee cut off Gorbachev's communications and announced that it had assumed power because of Gorbachev's ostensible illness. Dominated by the head of the KGB, it was a powerful coalition of heads of key government institutions, including the vice president, the prime minister, the minister of defense, and the minister of the interior—ironically, almost all hand-picked by Gorbachev and enjoying his trust. Behind the scenes, the presiding officer of the Supreme Soviet, the head of Gorbachev's personal staff, and high Communist Party officials had been involved. Without a doubt, millions of Soviet citizens were prepared to support it. Why then did the attempted coup fail?

First, the plotters seem to have counted on staging a "constitutional coup," assuming they could secure Gorbachev's acquiescence or, barring that, his resignation and thus the legitimate transfer of power to the vice president. Gorbachev's refusal threw them into disarray.

Second, their planning for the coup was inept and incomplete. Virtually none of the many figures targeted for arrest was in fact picked up. Columns of tanks sent into the center of Moscow were not sent into action. Telephone lines to the White House— Yeltsin's headquarters at the Russian parliament building—were not disrupted. Foreign television companies continued to report. By the second day, the plotters—some of them quite drunk—appeared uncertain what to do.

Third, Boris Yeltsin and his colleagues at the White House galvanized the resistance to the coup by their defiance, labeling the coup an "anticonstitutional act" and calling upon citizens to resist. They rapidly became the nucleus of a courageous vol-

unteer organization that not only built barricades around the White House but made contact with like-minded officials across the country. Though modest at first, popular demonstrations broke out increasingly in many places, including Leningrad (now renamed St. Petersburg).

Finally, the coup attempt precipitated serious divisions within the military and the KGB: A number of officers and units recoiled from the prospect of civil war, and some actually joined the defenders of the constitutional order.

The entire eposide is complicated by unresolved puzzles. The first involves ambiguities in the behavior of Gorbachev himself: Why did he depart from Moscow at a time when there were strong suggestions that a coup was about to be mounted? Had he given the coup plotters reason to believe that they could count on his acquiescence? A second set of puzzles concerns the intentions and behavior of different members of the State Emergency Committee and the explanation for their bungling. It remains unclear to what extent they lacked a coherent plan of action and to what extent their plans were foiled in the execution. Other questions remain about divisions among the military and the secret police and about the rival flights of plotters and loyalists to Foros, where Gorbachev was confined, and back to the capital.

The collapse of the coup attempt had profound consequences. It symbolized the bankruptcy of the old order. It eliminated the leaders of key constituencies opposed to the reforms and laid bare the failure of old beliefs, institutions, and processes. It revealed the irrelevance of communism as a belief system and further discredited the Communist Party. Gorbachev resigned as general secretary, and the Party was suspended from active political work, with some of its records, assets, and archives seized.

The failed coup accelerated the further breakup of the Soviet Union. The three Baltic republics gained recognition of their independence, and separatist pressures in many other Union republics accelerated. Above all, the Russian Federation's leaders emerged with enhanced powers and prestige—if with no clear program—and spearheaded the final struggle with the old Union government.

The referendum of December 1, 1991, in which a majority of voters in Ukraine endorsed full independence, was the final blow to Gorbachev's efforts to preserve the Union. Moving to find a way out—or to take advantage—of the impasse, the Yeltsin government engineered an agreement among Russia, Ukraine, and Belarus to dissolve the old Soviet Union and form a new Slavic Commonwealth. Two week later, on December 21, in deference to the desires of other republics' leaders, it was transformed into the Commonwealth of Independent States, a loose confederation of uncertain powers that embraced all the remaining republics of the Soviet Union except Georgia. Four days later, Mikhail Gorbachev reluctantly resigned his presidency. Over the Kremlin, the red flag was lowered for the last time.

46   Speech to the Congress of People's Deputies, December 20, 1990

EDVARD SHEVARDNADZE

Comrades deputies! I have perhaps the shortest and the most difficult speech of my life. ...

Yesterday there were speeches by some comrades—they are our veterans—who raised the question of the need for a declaration to be adopted forbidding the President and the country's leadership from sending troops to the Persian Gulf. That was the approximate content, and this was not the first or the second occasion. ...

We have no moral right to reconcile ourselves to aggression and the annexation of a small, defenseless country. In that case we would have had to cross out everything that has been done in recent years by all of us, by the whole country and by all of our people in regard to asserting the principles of the New Political Thinking. That is the first thing.

Second, ... nobody is going to send a single military man or even a single representative of the Soviet armed forces there. This has been said. But somebody needed to raise this issue, this problem again. And I know what is happening in the corridors of the Congress.

Third. I have said and confirm it and state it publicly, that if the interests of Soviet people are encroached upon, if just one person suffers—wherever it may happen, in any country, not just in Iraq—yes, the Soviet government, the Soviet side will stand up for the interests of its citizens. I think that the deputies should back up the Soviet leadership on this.

But I would like to raise another question. Excuse me, is it all accidental? Is it an accident that two members of this parliament make a statement saying that the Minister of Internal Affairs was removed successfully and that the time has come to settle accounts with the Foreign Minister? The statement has been circulated literally throughout the world press and our newspapers.

Are they such daredevils, these lads—I will call them that, age permits me to because they are really boys in colonel's epaulets—to address such statements to a minister, to a member of the government? ...

In this connection, I remember the party congress [in July 1990]. Was this really a chance phenomenon? Because at the congress a real struggle developed, a most acute struggle between the reformers and—I will not say conservatives because they have their own views which are acceptable to society—but the reactionaries, precisely the reactionaries. And, it must be stated bluntly, this battle was won with merit by the progressive section, the progressive members, delegates to the congress. ...

I am now going to recall the session of the Supreme Soviet. The same people who are now speaking came out with serious accusations against the Minister of Foreign Affairs, of unilateral concessions, of incompetence, lack of skill and so on and so forth. Not one person could be found, including the person in the chair, to reply and say simply that this was dishonorable, that this is not the way things are done in civilized states. I find this deeply worrying. Things went as far as personal insults. I endured that too.

Comrades, a hounding is taking place. I will not name the publications, all manner of publications—I add the Pamyat society to these publications—but what statements: Down with the Gorbachev clique! And they also add Shevardnadze and several other names. Who are they, the so-called reformers?

Democrats, I'll put it bluntly: Comrade democrats, in the widest meaning of this word, you have scattered. The reformers have gone into hiding. A dictatorship is approaching—I tell you that with full responsibility. No one knows what this dictatorship will be like, what kind of dictator will come to power and what order will be established.

I want to make the following statement. I am resigning. Let this be my contribution—and do not react and do not curse me—if you like, my protest against the onset of dictatorship. I want to express sincere gratitude to Mikhail Sergeyevich Gorbachev. I am his friend and a fellow thinker of his. I have always supported and will support to the end of my days the ideas of perestroika, the ideas of renewal, the ideas of democracy, of democratization.

We did great work in international affairs. But I think this is my duty. As a man, as a citizen, as a Communist, I cannot reconcile myself with what is happening in my country and to the trials which await our people.

I believe nevertheless that the dictatorship will not succeed, that the future belongs to democracy and freedom.

NOTES

ABOUT THE AUTHOR: **Edvard Shevardnadze** was Soviet minister of foreign affairs until January 1991 and more recently has served as head of state of the republic of Georgia.

47   Top-Secret KGB Memorandum to the President of the USSR

VLADIMIR KRYUCHKOV

February 1991
Committee of State Security of the USSR
No. 219-k Moscow

Top Secret
SPECIAL FILE

To the President of the USSR
Comrade Gorbachev M.S.

ON THE POLITICAL SITUATION IN THE COUNTRY

The acute political crisis which has enveloped our country threatens the fate of *perestroika,* the processes of democratization, the renewal of society. The possibility of the collapse of the unity of the USSR, the destruction of the sociopolitical and economic system has become real. Provoked by the decisions of a number of Union republics, the "war of sovereignties" has practically nullified efforts to stabilize the economy and has greatly complicated conditions for the signing of a new Union treaty. Under the influence of well-known decisions of the Congress of People's Deputies and the Supreme Soviet of the RSFSR the confrontations between the Center and the Union republics have received a powerful impetus. The head of the Russian parliament, together with certain forces, circles of shady business, have clearly declared their intention to create a "second Center" as a counterweight to the state political leadership of the USSR. Practically all opposition parties and movements have not failed to make use of it to strengthen their positions. National chauvinistic and separatist tendencies have increased in many regions of the country.

Events have confirmed our evaluation that the policy of appeasing the aggressive wing of the "democratic movement" is not able to forestall the spread of destructive processes and, in fact, allows the pseudo-democrats to realize unhindered their plans concerning the usurpation of power and changing the nature of the social system.

The danger of this tendency is further aggravated by the numerical growth and increasing power of illegal militarized formations. Today they have at their disposal state-of-the-art weapons, from automatic weapons and machine guns down to reactive shells. Taking into consideration this factor, social and national conflicts may assume a new character, turning into numerous hotbeds of civil war.

The outcome of the political battle in the coming months will depend on who wins the support of the bulk of the toiling population. In turn, active support of the leadership of the country, it would seem, hinges decisively on the extent of its success in averting a drastic decline in the living standard of the population. It is impossible not to take into account the fact that large social groups are poorly protected and are frequently impoverished. There exists no real possibility of improving their well-being at this time.

Taking into consideration the peculiarities of the economic structure of the USSR as well as the misapprehension by a significant portion of the population of even primitive forms of market relations, every step in the transition to a market economy demands circumspection, caution, and verification. The commitment to a forced introduction of market relations might turn out to exact an exorbitantly high price from the country.

In these circumstances, the war against economic sabotage assumes special meaning. Clearly, in and of itself, it will not increase production, but it may enable a more just distribution of goods, inflict a blow on shady business [black marketers] and considerably alleviate the grave situation in which the least well-to-do strata of the population find themselves.

Public opinion reacts negatively to the way in which shady businessmen exploit the unfolding situation. The intensifying property stratification evokes an increase in social tensions. The process of enrichment, by its internal logic, draws shady business into the battle for political influence, so that within the framework of privatization it may further broaden the scope for property accumulation. That inevitably leads to the creation of a category of "new bourgeoisie" with all that it entails.

At present, owing to the sharpening of the socioeconomic crisis, a narrowing of the social base of support for the domestic political course of the President and the Cabinet of Ministers of the USSR can be observed. This process is exacerbated by a demonstrative refusal of a part of the scientific and humanitarian [cultural] intelligentsia (basically elite) to support the policies of the President because of the recent events in the Baltics. Under current conditions, such a position on the part of representatives of the intelligentsia is dangerous, also because it may give impetus to a "brain drain" abroad.

The stability of the political situation in the country today also depends to a significant extent on the international position of the USSR.

The reality is such that the United States is working towards the collapse of the USSR as a superpower. In political circles of the United States the predominant opinion is that the weakening of the Soviet Union—down to the secession of a series of republics, above all the Baltics—is in the American national interest. The departure of Lithuania, for example, would in turn make the prospect of losing the Kaliningrad oblast quite real.

Taking into account this situation, we can scarcely count on significant financial and economic help from the United States. According to reliable information, the United States is putting pressure on Japan and Western Europe to limit the possible scale of their cooperation with the USSR. One should also be aware of the fact that even extensive help from the West would not, in itself, be sufficient to extricate this country from its economic crisis.

Proceeding from that premise, in the international arena it is important to do everything possible in order to mitigate the acuteness of the situation that is taking shape around the USSR. The interests of the country would be best served by a policy conducted in such a way as not to give it [sic] a reason for toughening its position in relation to the Soviet Union.

The anticonstitutional forces, acting according to a scenario worked out with the participation of Western experts, view the present moment as favorable for the organization of a frontal attack on the existing governmental and social structures of the Soviet state. The leading role in this belongs to the organizationally formed bloc of opposition forces "Democratic Russia" (DR), whose political precepts the leadership of the Supreme Soviet of the RSFSR [Boris Yeltsin] is trying to realize.

With the formation of the governing organs of DR, the task of "transforming the soviets on all levels into instruments of the opposition" has moved into the realm of practicality, as is the imminent winning to its side of the vast majority of the population. Measures are being taken for the creation of cells of DR in industrial enterprises, in state institutions, and colleges. The attention "Democrats" pay to engineering and technical personnel, as well as to the working class as a whole, is growing, inasmuch as expectations of an "elite coup" by the humanitarian [cultural] intelligentsia have not been fulfilled. Opposition leaders have embarked on the formation of a party built on the foundation of DR that would be capable of pushing the CPSU out of the political arena. It is assumed that it will be headed by the most prominent leaders among the "Democrats" and will become de facto the leading force in the alignment of political forces both in the Supreme Soviet of the RSFSR and in the soviets of a number of large republican centers.

A step in the direction of consolidating the majority of antisocialist forces on the level of the Union was marked by the constituent conference of the so-called "Democratic Congress" (Kharkov, January 26–27).

In recent weeks the tactics of the right radicals underwent a transformation from "constructive opposition" to a total rejection of the actions and initiatives of the President, a refusal to compromise with the Central state organs. The torpedoing of any steps to realize the program of economic reform passed by the Supreme Soviet of the USSR characterizes their propaganda line. In order to add weight to such actions, they are planning to stage a series of "nonviolent actions" and, if absolutely necessary, to conduct a general political strike. The opposition, considering the likelihood of workers' strikes of an economic character, seeks the opportunity to head up the strike movement and channel it into the destruction of existing state structures.

In addition, right-wing circles, conscious of the fact that at any moment the situation in the country may develop in a way unfavorable to them, also foresee the alternative of an ongoing and irreconcilable battle, including the use of illegal structures.

Supporters of the "Democrats" are taking persistent measures to extend their influence in the army, striving to neutralize it as one of the guarantors of the unity of the USSR and the integrity of the constitutional system. On the other hand, the recent events in the Baltic republics have had a very negative effect on the morale of the troops and have strengthened, especially among the officer corps, doubts about the ability of the country's leadership to keep the situation under control.

The escalation of the propaganda war that is being waged by the anti-communists against their own people, and the increased material means at their disposal (including the drawing in of shady capital), are devastating for the unity of the USSR and for Soviet society. The conquest of one propaganda organ after another is under way, and when that fails, they create new ones. Within just the last month in Russia, more specifically in Moscow, four substantial new publications have begun to appear and two radio stations have begun to broadcast. Western specialists are drawn into their activity in the sphere of psychological warfare (Radio Liberty, the NTS publishing company "Posev," etc.).

Official Soviet propaganda unjustifiably delays the unfolding of a powerful propaganda offensive. The question of preparing for the all-Union referendum on the preservation of the USSR reveals most graphically the imbalance in the propaganda war: While the "democratic press" decided to disparage the referendum as soon as it was announced, the central and party-controlled mass media have carried virtually no serious features on its behalf.

The interests of the Soviet constitutional system insistently dictate essential state control over the mass media and the inadmissibility of watering down its personnel, much less its transformation into a mouthpiece for antisocialist forces.

An analysis of the unfolding situation demands serious and critical comprehension of the extent to which the concepts of democratization and *glasnost* formulated six years ago have currently been implemented in practice. It is impossible not to see that antisocialist circles have, at a given stage, succeeded in replacing their contents, imposing upon society a vision of *perestroika,* not as the renewal of socialism but as the inexorable return into the "mainstream of world civilization"—capitalism. The thesis of the "illegality of the October Revolution" [of 1917] is being promoted. Democratization and *glasnost* come to be seen as the elimination of any limitations on political insinuations and unbridled slander under the flag of "freedom of speech." The cynical manipulation of public opinion shows with particular clarity in the firmly established "double standards," in accordance with which even the criminal actions of "democratic leaders" (down to their use of bloody coercion in Lithuania, Latvia, and Georgia) are unconditionally justified or hushed up, whereas the actions of the authorities in restoring order and constitutional norms are decried wholesale as illegal and dictatorial.

According to incoming information, an understanding of the dire consequences that the lingering crisis in the CPSU will have for the country is growing among the population. It is clear that the weakening of ideological work in defense of the socialist ideal cannot be made up by any other political force. Although the opposition is able to appeal to the personal interests of the average person, Party propaganda is still fumbling about for ways to conduct mass agitational work.

The failures of a series of recent provocative actions of the opposition—in the first place, the so-called all-Union political strike—demonstrate that it does not yet have enough reliable support among wide strata of the population. The political timidity of the "silent majority" preserves for the Party the possibility of using its indispensable advantages over the opposition, such as its extensive organizations, the propaganda apparatus, and its high intellectual potential.

With all its drama, the current situation can still be turned around, considering the unused arsenal of constructive measures. There is not a great deal of room in which to maneuver, but there is some. One must not fail to consider that, as is everywhere noted, people are tired of the hardships, stress, and social collisions and are losing their faith in the ability of the leadership to restore order. The danger arises that people will follow those who take it upon themselves to restore order.

The Supreme Soviet and the Congress of People's Deputies of the USSR, as the most constructive political institutions, can and must play an essential role in the search for a way out of the unfolding crisis. This requires protecting these organs of popular government from attacks and activating and strengthening their creative potential.

At the same time, considering the depth of the crisis and the probability of a dramatic worsening of circumstances, one cannot exclude the possibility of forming, at the appropriate moment, temporary bodies within the framework of extraordinary measures to be introduced by the President of the Supreme Soviet of the USSR.

Such a step would require powerful propaganda support, a direct address to the nation with an appeal to unity for the preservation of the USSR and the defense of the public order.

NOTES

ABOUT THE AUTHOR: **Vladimir Kryuchkov** was chairman of the Committee of State Security of the USSR (KGB) when this memorandum was written.

48 *An Open Letter to the People, July 23, 1991*

YURY BONDAREV ET AL.

Dear residents of the Russian Republic! Citizens of the USSR! Compatriots!

An enormous, unprecedented misfortune has befallen us. Our homeland and country, a great state that was given into our care by history, nature and our glorious ancestors, is perishing, breaking up, and being plunged into darkness and nonexistence. And this ruination is taking place with our silence, connivance and consent. Can it be that our hearts and souls have turned to stone, that not one of us has the vigor, courage and love for the fatherland that motivated our grandfathers and fathers, who laid down their lives for the homeland on fields of battle and in gloomy torture chambers, in great feats of labor and in struggles, who shaped a mighty power out of prayers, burdens and revelations, and for whom the homeland and the state were the most sacred things in life?

What has happened to us, brothers? Why is it that sly and pompous rulers, intelligent and clever apostates and greedy and rich moneygrubbers, mocking us, scoffing at our beliefs and taking advantage of our naivete, have seized power and are pilfering our wealth, taking homes, factories and land away from the people, carving the country up into separate parts, embroiling us with one another and pulling the wool over our eyes, excommunicating us from the past and debarring us from the future—dooming us to pitiful vegetation in slavery and subordination to our all-powerful neighbors? How did it happen that, at our deafening rallies and in our irritation and impatience, yearning for changes and desiring prosperity for the country, we admitted to power people who do not love this country, who fawn on their overseas patrons and seek advice and blessing there, overseas?

Brothers, we are waking up at a late hour and noticing the disaster at a late hour, when our home is already burning on all sides, when the fire will have to be put out not with water but with our tears and blood. Will we really permit civil strife and war, for the second time in this century? Will we again throw ourselves between cruel millstones that we ourselves did not set in motion, where the people's bones are ground up and Russia's backbone is broken?

We address you in the most responsible way possible, appealing to representatives of all occupations and classes, of all ideologies and religions and of all parties and movements for whom our differences are nothing in the face of the general calamity and distress, in the face of the general love for the homeland, which we see as a single, indivisible entity that has united fraternal peoples in a mighty state, without which we would have no existence.

Let us wake up, let us come to our senses, let us stand up for the country, young and old. Let us say "No!" to the destroyers and usurpers. Let us set a limit to our retreat at the last line of resistance.

We are beginning a nationwide movement, calling into our ranks those who have recognized the terrible misfortune that has befallen the country.

We summon the working people, whom the present-day Pharisees promised abundance and good pay but who are now being driven out of the factories and mines and doomed to hunger, no rights, and despondent standing in line for financial help, a hunk of bread, and the charity of the wealthy and the bosses.

...

We summon the industrious peasants, who have been worn out by the ignorant authorities and whose current fate is being decided by those who yesterday destroyed the villages and drew up utopian programs, imposing a one-sided exchange on grain growers and dooming plowland to desolation and the surviving farms that feed the country to destruction.

We call on engineers, whose hands, minds and talents have created a unique technical civilization and a mighty industry that has ensured the people's well-being and protection and enabled the homeland to fly into outer space. The equipment they created, already worn out and in need of modernization and renovation, during six years of inaction and profuse verbiage has ground to a halt and broken down, and now we are a country of idled enterprises, silenced power engineering, vanished goods, and bewildered and impoverished engineers removed from creative activity.

We call on scientists, who have advanced the development of Soviet science in a worthy manner, amazed the world with the fruits of their labor, and accumulated in laboratories and institutes discoveries for the next spurt into the 21st century, where we hope to have a fitting place in human civilization. Instead of this, demagogues and malefactors are destroying precious accumulated discoveries, scattering collectives of researchers, closing whole areas of science, obstructing the development of space research, nuclear technology and advanced chemistry, and dooming the best minds to vegetation and to fleeing the homeland for prosperous countries, where their talent will nourish the development not of their own country but of foreign lands.

We turn our voice to the Army, which won mankind's respect for its selfless feat of saving Europe from the Hitlerite plague, to the Army that has inherited the best qualities of the Russian and Soviet Armies and resists aggressive forces. Our glorious defenders are living through difficult times. It is not the Army's fault that it has been forced to hurriedly abandon its garrisons abroad, to be the target of shameless political exploitation, and to be subjected constantly to false and slanderous attacks by irresponsible intriguers. But no one will succeed in turning the Armed Forces into an amorphous mass, in demoralizing them from within and consigning them to desecration. We are convinced that the fighting men of the Army and the Navy, loyal to their sacred duty, will not allow a fratricidal war or

very nationalistic + patriotic

the destruction of the fatherland and will act as a reliable guarantor of security and a mainstay of all the healthy forces of society.

We turn our voice to the artists and writers, who bit by bit created a culture on the ruins of the defeated classics, who came up with images of beauty and goodness for the people and expected a flourishing of the arts in the future but found destitution and a lowering of creativity to the level of a pitiful farce designed to amuse businessmen and the wealthy, in which the people, cut off from spirituality, deprived of an ideal and governed by immoral and sly people, are removed from history and turned into a cheap work force for foreign manufacturers.

We appeal to the Orthodox Church, which, having gone through Calvary, is slowly, after all the beatings, rising from the grave. The church, whose spiritual light shone in Russian history even during dark times, is today, while still gaining new strength, being torn by strife and wounded in the eparchies and parishes, and is not finding proper support from the temporal powers that be. May it hear the voice of the people calling for salvation.

We appeal to Moslems, Buddhists, Protestants and believers of all persuasions for whom faith is synonymous with goodness, beauty and truth; today they are being assaulted by cruelty, ugliness and lies that are destroying their living souls.

We appeal to parties, both large and small, to liberals and monarchists, to centralists and local-autonomy advocates, to bards of the national idea. We appeal to the Communist Party, which bears full responsibility not only for the victories and failures of the preceding 70 years but also for the six most recent years, tragic years, into which the Communist Party first led the country and then gave up its power, turning that power over to thoughtless and inept parliamentarians who embroiled us with one another and brought forth thousands of stillborn laws, of which the only ones that are alive are those that are returning the people to bondage and dividing the country's exhausted body into pieces. Communists, whose leaders are destroying their own Party, giving up their Party cards, are rushing into the enemy camp one after another—playing the traitor, demanding the gallows for recent comrades—let the Communists hear our call!

...

Young people, our hope and flower, who are being corrupted, placed at the service of false idols, and doomed to idleness, lack of talent, drugs and crime.

Old people, our wisdom and pride, reliable toilers and our tireless breadwinners, whose lot has been penury and mockery of the lives they have lived and profanation in printed and televised slop by those who are striving to kill memories and to pit generations against one another.

Young veterans and internationalist fighting men, who have exhibited selflessness and humanism and lofty moral qualities but who have been put in the position of innocent victims.

Women, who are denying themselves the highest natural right—to continue the family by bearing descendants—because of a fear of engendering poverty and filling the army of a civil war with soldiers, afraid of their own love and their own motherhood.

Everyone, no matter who, in the cities and villages, in the steppes and the forests, at the edges of the great oceans surrounding our country—let us awaken and stand up for unity and for a rebuff to the destroyers of the homeland!

Let us start out on the path of saving the state this very minute. Let us create a people's patriotic movement in which everyone, while having his own will and influence, will unite in the name of the supreme goal of saving the fatherland.

Let us unite:

to stop the chain reaction of the ruinous disintegration of the state, the economy and the individual;

to promote the strengthening of Soviet power and its transformation into a true people's power, not a feeding trough for greedy nouveaux riches who are willing to sell off everything for the sake of their insatiable appetites;

to prevent the fires of discord between nationalities and civil war from raging.

We will spare no energy in carrying out reforms that are capable of overcoming people's intolerable alienation from power, labor, property and culture, and of creating fitting conditions for their lives and self-expression. We will give energetic support to progressive innovations aimed at moving our society forward, attaining present-day heights in scientific and technical progress, and emancipating people's minds and energy so that everyone can live according to his labor, conscience and justice. And we will oppose plans that drag the country backward into the darkness of the Middle Ages, where there is a cult of money, strength, cruelty and lust.

Our movement is for those to whom the itch to destroy is something alien, who are burning with a desire to construct and furnish our common home, so that every people—large and small—and every person—young and old—can live harmoniously, comfortably and happily therein.

This is no time to amuse ourselves with illusions, unconcernedly relying on the sagacity of the newly appeared messiahs, who with unwonted ease promise us first one and then another panacea for all our woes. It is time to shake off our torpor and to seek a way out of the present impasse together, as an entire people. Among Russian Republic residents, there are statesmen who are prepared to lead the country into a proud, sovereign future. There are economic experts who are capable of restoring production. There are thinkers and spiritual leaders who are beginning to see the nationwide ideal clearly.

The Soviet Union is our home and bulwark, built through the great efforts of all peoples and nations, which saved us from disgrace and slavery in the times of black invasions! Russia—our only beloved!—is calling for help.—[signed] Yury Bondarev, Yury Blokhin, Valentin Varennikov, Eduard Volodin, Boris Gromov, Gennady Zyuganov, Lyudmila Zykina, Vyacheslav Klykov, Aleksandr Prokhanov, Valentin Rasputin, Vasily Starodubtsev and Aleksandr Tizyakov.

NOTES

ABOUT THE AUTHOR: **Yury Bondarev** is a prominent writer and a leading voice for Russian conservative nationalists.

49 Interview with Aleksandr Yakovlev, August 16, 1991

OLEG MOROZ

Interview on the Eve of the Coup. ... *Literaturnaya gazeta,* No. 34, Aug. 28. ... I spoke with Aleksandr Nikolayevich Yakovlev on Friday Morning [August 16]. And then, on Monday morning— ...

The interview with A. N. Yakovlev was slated to be published in the Aug. 21 issue of *Literaturnaya gazeta.* However, that issue was canceled; along with other democratic publications, *Literaturnaya gazeta* was banned by the junta.

...

*　　*　　*

Question.—You were one of the initiators of perestroika. One can detect a certain symbolism in the fact that the CPSU is now getting rid of you: This party no longer has any use for perestroika; perestroika sticks in its throat. What do you think—is this symbolism being brought out deliberately, or are the people who are expelling you not thinking about this?

Answer.—Of course it's being done deliberately. I think it's deliberate. ...

In principle, of course, they are against perestroika. The apparatus was always against it, never accepted it. The rejection merely varied in degree. Until the January 1987 plenary session, say—until the apparatus's interests were affected—it voted in favor, albeit reluctantly and with dissatisfied grumbling. But once its interests were directly affected, the law of bureaucratology went into effect—hang onto your position no matter what. The apparatus joined open battle—first of all, against those who had actually started perestroika and were defending it. It wasn't the Party that began perestroika, after all. That's just something that was said for public consumption, for rhetorical effect. ...

Q.—Could they have failed to consult with Gorbachev on the matter of expelling you?

A.—... If he knew about it and it was done with his blessing, that will be the greatest disillusionment of my life. However, I still cherish the hope that they did it behind his back [Gorbachev confirmed this on his return from the Crimea—**O. M.**]. These people are immoral, irresponsible and ill-educated. In fact, they've raised the question of his own resignation, too. They've been hounding him at one plenary session after another. It was only at the last plenum that they got scared. Scared not of him but of the possibility that all of a sudden he really would step down, and they would be left naked.

Q.—What are they actually hoping for? What is their strategic objective?

A.—Of course, in my view, they're bolstering their spirits with illusions, but they are making preparations for a revenge match. They hope they can carry off a Party and state coup. Such thoughts occur only to people in a delirious, abnormal state.

Q.—So you think they don't have the potential for such a coup?

A.—They have the potential, all right, but they would have to fight the people, to resort to violence and bloodshed. And I am convinced that it wouldn't end in victory for them. That's exactly what they're afraid of. I think they really aren't confident of victory, although they may try to start some sort of fight—making use of some kind of provocation, some dissatisfaction. Trying to capitalize on it and stirring up emotions. After all, every revolution—in the 20th century, let's say—has started with empty cooking pots.

Q.—If you compare the current situation with the way things were a year ago, what do you think—is the danger of a right-wing, fascist coup greater or smaller?

A.—You know, on the surface it looks smaller. Because the elections in the Russian SFSR, Moscow and Leningrad did frighten a certain number of these people, who were hoping for entirely different results. ... [The outcome] couldn't help but have an effect on the subsequent course of events. But now there's some kind of inexplicable lull. Maybe it has something to do with August vacations. Lulls like this put me on guard. In general, the closer the end, the more dangerous a wounded beast becomes.

Q.—What can you say about the state of affairs in the country? Is Gorbachev in control of the situation? Specifically, are the Army, the Ministry of Internal Affairs and the State Security Committee [KGB] still controllable? The recent events in the Baltics and the Transcaucasus make one doubt this.

A.—You know, I don't have the slightest bit of information on this specific question, but I personally have the idea that some sort of force exists that is seemingly in command of all this. Everyone says it just happened. The OMON special police declare they'll take to the forests if anyone starts putting pressure on them. They'll organize a guerrilla war and fight to the bitter end. This seems to indicate an anarchist mentality, a refusal to submit to anyone but themselves. But on the other hand, if this is true, then any government authority ought to put them in custody immediately, and prosecute them on the basis of the criminal code. Yet everyone is taking a calm view of it, for some reason. Now that puts me on guard.

Q.—Surely it can't be true that as a senior adviser to the President, you didn't talk with him about this?

A.—No, why? Why wouldn't I have talked with him? What gives you that idea? ...

Q.—Doesn't it seem to you that there is a plot against Gorbachev? One element of that plot would be the murders at the Lithuanian customs post, timed to coincide with the meeting between Gorbachev and Bush. ...

A.—I have no facts on the matter, of course, but I have the feeling that a powerful group exists—whether organized or unorganized, I don't know—that has set itself the goal of overthrowing the President. Indeed, they make no particular secret of it.

Q.—Recently Sovetskaya Rossia printed another hysterical "Address to the People." In essence, it contains an appeal to overthrow Gorbachev.

A.—Yes, of course.

Q.—This "Address" was unquestionably cooked up by certain well-known fascist-leaning writers, the inflammatory writers Prokhanov and Bondarev. But besides their signatures, ... it bore the signatures of people "with positions"—General of the Army Varennikov, USSR Deputy Minister of Defense and Commander in Chief of the Ground Forces; and Col. Gen. Gromov, First Deputy Minister of Internal Affairs. Since the "Address" calls for rebellion, for disobedience to the authorities, these generals should have resigned immediately. Or the President should have dismissed them. Yet they remain in their posts.

A.—In any democratic state, that is indeed what happens. But we don't yet have real democracy. ....

Q.—It seems to me that Gorbachev will soon leave the office of General Secretary of the CPSU Central Committee. Things are headed in that direction. ... The two ice floes that Gorbachev is standing on are moving apart in different directions. He will have to jump off one of them.

A.—I think they'll deal with him at the [Party] Congress, and they'll do it painfully and ruthlessly. If he doesn't forestall them.

Q.—From the standpoint of maintaining his prestige, it would probably be better for him to tender his resignation himself, wouldn't it? Not half in pretense, as he did at the April plenary session, but in earnest.

A.—I really don't understand why he puts up with the endless insults, attacks and hounding. After all, the whole point is that it isn't he who needs them, but they who need him.

Q.—But is it really true that he doesn't need them at all? After all, they still have power, especially in the provinces.

A.—No, what do you mean power?! If he weren't the leader, they wouldn't have any power. That's the whole point. They're capitalizing on the fact that the President of the country is the General Secretary of the apparatus.

Q.—So you believe that Gorbachev should have left the office of General Secretary long ago?

A.—Yes, I believe he should have. The 28th [Party] Congress would have been an excellent time to step down. At that point a plenary session like this year's April plenum could already be foreseen. ...

...

Q.—Have you left his team once and for all, or do you think that you and he may yet meet on some road or other?

A.—A lot depends on him. If the line of rapprochement with the democrats that he has now chosen continues, I see no obstacles to working together to further the cause in which I really do sincerely believe. In the final analysis, we have to pull the country onto the track of democratic development! In the final analysis, our people have a right to that! ...

NOTES

ABOUT THE AUTHOR: **Oleg Moroz** was a correspondent for the Moscow weekly *Literaturnaya gazeta*.

50   A Coup Chronology

EDITORS OF CURRENT DIGEST
OF THE SOVIET PRESS

The following chronology has been compiled from three primary sources—the article "Putsch in the USSR, Aug. 19, 20, 21," published in *Komsomolskaya pravda* on Aug. 22 … ; "Chronicle of the Coup and Resistance," published in *Nezavisimaya gazeta* on Aug. 22 … ; and "Chronicle of the Coup and Resistance: How a Besieged Moscow Held Out," carried in *Rossiiskaya gazeta* on Aug. 23, … —with additional items drawn from the special issue of *Kuranty* published Aug. 22 … and from p. 4 of the special *Obshchaya gazeta* [Joint Newspaper] compilation published Aug. 22. … The source of each chronology entry or set of entries is indicated at the end, with the bracketed designations [Kp], [Ng], [Rg], [K] and [Og]. …

AUGUST 19

04:00. The Sevastopol Regiment of USSR KGB troops blockades M. S. Gorbachev's dacha at Foros in the Crimea. Two tractors block the landing strip in Belbek, where the President's aircraft—a TU-134 plane and an Mi-8 helicopter—are located. This is done on orders from Col. Gen. Maltsev, chief of staff of the country's air defense forces and one of the plotters.

...

06:00. USSR Minister of Defense D. Yazov calls a meeting of troop commanders of the various military districts. His instructions boil down to ensuring order and, if the situation warrants it, reinforcing the security of military installations.

"As for the rest," the minister says, "you'll learn of that from radio and television reports."

07:40. KGB personnel enter the editorial offices of the Echo of Moscow radio station, throw the main switches and seal the premises.

08:00. Central TV and radio announcers read the SCSE's [State Committee for the State of Emergency] documents and A. Lukyanov's "Statement by the Chairman of the USSR Supreme Soviet." The impression is created that the coup is sanctioned by Lukyanov. The "Statement by the Soviet Leadership," signed by G. Yanayev, V. Pavlov and O. Baklanov, begins with a barefaced lie: "In connection with the inability of Mikhail Sergeyevich Gorbachev to perform the duties of President of the USSR due to the state of his health."

09:00. B. N. Yeltsin, I. S. Silayev and R. I. Khasbulatov sign an appeal "To the Citizens of Russia." In the Moscow City Soviet, a staff is formed to deal with the emergency situation.

The conspirators' first step is to limit the publication of central and Moscow newspapers to nine that constitute the "chosen few." The forbidden newspapers include even *Pionerskaya pravda*.

09:20. B. N. Yeltsin signs Decree No. 59, consisting of three points. According to Point 3, acts by officials carrying out the decisions of the self-styled committee fall under the provisions of the RSFSR Criminal Code.

10:00. A session of the [Presidium of the] RSFSR Supreme Soviet decides to convene the republic's Supreme Soviet in emergency session on Aug. 21. [Rg]

10:00. The building housing *Komsomolskaya pravda*'s editorial offices is surrounded by armored personnel carriers armed with machine guns. [Kp]

...

12:00. In the "White House," Yeltsin, Silayev and Khasbulatov hold their first press conference for Soviet and foreign journalists. They issue an appeal to Muscovites to gather at the "White House" and protect their legitimate authorities and democracy. They reaffirm the Russian Republic leadership's firm stand with respect to the putschists.

Several thousand people have gathered on Manege Square. Deputies to the Moscow City Soviet call on the people to support Russia's legitimate government with an open-ended general strike. [Rg]

12:30. RSFSR President B. Yeltsin issues a decree declaring the Committee for the State of Emergency to be unconstitutional and terming its organizers' actions a coup d'etat. All of its decisions are deemed to be without force on RSFSR territory, where only legally elected authorities hold sway. Officials obeying the Committee's orders will be prosecuted under the law. [Ng]

13:00. Boris Yeltsin emerges from the House of Soviets and, from atop tank No. 110 of the Taman Division, appeals to Muscovites and all citizens of Russia to respond in a suitable fashion to the putschists and demand that the country be returned to its normal constitutional development. [Rg]

By a subsequent decree of the RSFSR President, all functions of USSR executive power on RSFSR territory are henceforth to be exercised by appropriate Russian Republic bodies. ...

An appeal by B. Yeltsin to military personnel states: "The 'order' that the latter-day saviors of the fatherland are promising us will end in concentration camps, suppression of dissent, and nighttime arrests. 'A better life' will remain a propaganda fraud. Dark clouds of terror and dictatorship have gathered over Russia. But the law will triumph on our soil, and our long-suffering people will regain their freedom, this time once and for all!"

By decree of the RSFSR President, O. Lobov, A. Yablokov and S. Krasavchenko are assigned the task of organizing day-to-day management of the RSFSR's economic complex.

A subsequent decree (the last to be issued Aug. 19) declares G. Yanayev, V. Pavlov, V. Kryuchkov, B. Pugo, D. Yazov, V. Starodubtsev and A. Tizyakov to be outlaws. As justification, the decree cites the grave state crimes committed by them, crimes that violate Art. 62 of the USSR Constitution and that are covered by appropriate articles of the RSFSR Criminal Code. The decree grants prosecutor's-office and state-security employees and members of the Armed Forces the right to "act on the basis of laws and the Constitution" and guarantees them legal protection.

According to a report from the RSFSR Supreme Soviet's press center, a battalion of the Taman Division has gone over to the side of the legal Russian government. Ten tanks have arrived at the Russian parliament building to defend it. [Ng]

17:00. In *Komsomolskaya pravda*'s Blue Room, the editor in chief tells the staff that the newspaper has been banned. The staff is instructed to keep calm and continue working. [Kp]

17:00. G. Yanayev, B. Pugo, O. Baklanov, V. Starodubtsev and A. Tizyakov begin their press conference for Soviet and foreign journalists at the USSR Ministry of Foreign Affairs' Press Center. G. Yanayev says that M. S. Gorbachev "is resting and undergoing medical treatment in the Crimea. Over the past few years he has become very tired, and some time is needed for him to regain his health." As for the state of emergency, it has been declared at a very difficult period for the country, in order to avoid excesses of any sort. "We were forced to take certain measures to ensure the safety of our citizens," Yanayev said, apparently having in mind the internment of the USSR President.

...

22:00. Eight armored scout vehicles (BRDMs) flying the tricolor Russian flag arrive at the "White House." Vice-President Aleksandr Rutskoi announces that these vehicles have appeared by order of Maj. Gen. Lebed, Deputy Commander of the USSR Airborne Forces. After meeting with Yeltsin, Lebed publicly announces that he and the large number of airborne troops accompanying him have arrived, on orders from Commander of Airborne Forces Grachov, to protect the legal Russian authorities. [Ng]

...

Postfactum, Interfax and the Russian News Agency are not yet closed and continue operating. Barricades made out of rocks and metal bars going up around the Russian parliament. Columns of people are constantly arriving to protect the government building. ... [Kp]

23:30. A working group from [the Russian TV program] "News" [*Vesti*], which still exists and is operating with its own equipment, arrives at the "White House."

Copies of materials from the unpublished issue of *Nezavisimaya gazeta* and an underground special edition of the newspaper *Kuranty* are circulated outside the RSFSR Supreme Soviet.

Gavriil Popov, who has returned to the capital, addresses those gathered outside the "White House." He urges Muscovites to picket the editorial offices of the publications that the SCSE has allowed to publish. [Ng]

AUGUST 20

00:00–01:00. Moscow Mayor Gavriil Popov arrives at Russia's Government House. The internal communications system in the Government House building broadcasts radio programs moderated by journalists from Radio Russia, "Viewpoint" [*Vzglyad*] and "Fifth Wheel" [*Pyatoye koleso*].

...

At about 1:20, eight or nine tanks exit through the Kremlin's Borovitskiye Gates and appear to be heading in the direction of Krasnaya Presnya Embankment.

...

02:00–03:00. It is reported that Yeltsin tried to call Yanayev in the morning but was told that the acting President was resting after a sleepless night. Later, when Boris Yeltsin did succeed in speaking with Yanayev, the latter told the Russian President the same thing he had told the entire Soviet people: For health reasons, Gorbachev was not yet capable of carrying out his duties.

The new Soviet authorities ban foreign television reporters from transmitting video images abroad. Only audio reports may be sent abroad. [Kp]

02:45. An amateur radio station located in the House of Soviets begins broadcasting. It carries an appeal from Russian Vice-President Rutskoi to young people and soldiers. "Don't let yourselves be used in this dirty puppet war." Rutskoi calls on military personnel to obey Yeltsin's decree. [Rg]

As of 3 a.m., the number of demonstrators gathered outside the Russian government building has reached 15,000.

03:00–04:00. ... The Leningrad City Soviet calls on residents of the city and province to support Yeltsin's call for a general strike. The following evening, Leningrad Mayor Anatoly Sobchak addresses 5,000 of the city's residents. The mayor announces that he has spoken with the Leningrad military commandant, Gen. Viktor Samsonov, and has warned him of criminal liability should he issue any illegal orders.

...

At 4:30, journalist Vladimir Molchanov takes over from Aleksandr Politkovsky at the microphone of the radio transmitter set up on the ground floor of the "White House." Like many others who speak that night, Molchanov apologizes to Gorbachev, saying "Mikhail Sergeyevich, you are my President!"

...

05:00–06:00. The entire Sakhalin garrison declares allegiance to the RSFSR Constitution.

...

According to a report by Leningrad Soviet Deputy Trubin, nearly 150 military vehicles, tanks and armored personnel carriers are moving toward Leningrad along the Kiev and Moscow Highways. At the Leningrad Soviet's urging, self-defense detachments are formed, consisting primarily of young people between the ages of 16 and 20.

...

10:00. It is reported that Rutskoi, Silayev and Khasbulatov have left for the Kremlin by car with no security guards, to present an ultimatum to Lukyanov. [Kp]

From early morning, thousands of people have been congregating at the House of Soviets on Krasnaya Presnya Embankment. The building of barricades continues.

11:00. The RSFSR Ministry of the Press and Information registers *Obshchaya gazeta*, a joint publication of 11 banned democratic newspapers, of which *Rossiiskaya gazeta* is one. [Rg]

11:30. Rutskoi, Silayev and Khasbulatov return from a meeting with Lukyanov at which they presented to him the Russian Republic leadership's ultimatum to the Eight. A delighted crowd greets them at the entrance to the "White House." ...

12:00. A 200,000-strong rally gets under way at the Russian parliament building. Addressing the crowd, Russian Vice-President Rutskoi announces that the putschists have been given 24 hours to meet the Russian authorities' demands and that Anatoly Lukyanov himself admits the illegality of the SCSE's actions. Addressing the rally, Boris Yeltsin reaffirms the Russian leadership's position. [Ng]

12:00. A. Yakovlev, G. Popov, E. Shevardnadze, S. Stankevich and others address a rally of thousands outside the Moscow City Soviet. They call the members of the SCSE "state criminals."

...

12:30. The Congress of Russian Business Circles, representing banks, exchanges, insurance companies and the entire entrepreneurial sector of the RSFSR, meets in emergency session. Those in attendance condemn the attempted coup d'etat and adopt an appeal to the world community's business circles.

13:00. Mstislav Rostropovich flies from Paris to Moscow to be with his fellow countrymen at this difficult hour.

14:00. Aleksy II, Patriarch of All Rus, appeals to the inhabitants of Russia to avoid bloodshed. [Rg]

16:00. At the conclusion of the rally [outside the Russian parliament], volunteer units are formed to defend the "White House" against a possible assault. [Ng]

...

17:30. Over the RSFSR Supreme Soviet's internal radio net, S. Stankevich asks all women to leave the building, since the putschists plan to begin their assault on the "White House" in half an hour. [Rg]

18:00. There are two divisions in Moscow, an armored and a motorized-infantry division, and two special police units. The troops are deployed at Kuntsevo, the Center, the Kirov Subway Station and Leningrad Prospect. Oleg Poptsov calls on residents of the capital and officials of motor-vehicle transport enterprises to form a ring of heavy equipment around the RSFSR Supreme Soviet in order to block the tanks' advance.

...

Outside the RSFSR Supreme Soviet building, leaders who have emerged from among the people divide the men protecting the building into groups of 10. The people are armed with clubs. They have gas masks and respirators. Over a bullhorn, women are asked to go out to meet the soldiers and persuade them not to fire on the people. The women form a semicircle and carry a sign reading "Soldiers, don't fire on mothers!"

Molotov cocktails appear among the defenders of the RSFSR Supreme Soviet, and people are instructed in how to use them, our correspondent reports. B. Yeltsin issues a decree appointing Rear Admiral V. B. Shcherbakov Commander of the Leningrad Military District and placing all Leningrad units under his authority.

20:00. Boris Yeltsin declares: "I do not believe that Anatoly Lukyanov did not know of the impending coup."

Gen. Kalinin, the Moscow commandant, issues an order imposing a curfew in the city from 11 p.m. to 5 a.m.

The "White House" is being guarded by the Russian Ministry of Internal Affairs, whose men are armed with AKS automatic rifles. Personnel from the Aleks [private detective] bureau move about with black stockings on their heads. ...

The "Time" [*Vremya*] program reports that on the morning of Aug. 19, V. Pavlov suffered a hypertensive crisis.

Yanayev countermands all three of Yeltsin's decrees on the grounds that they are "at variance with the laws and Constitution of the USSR."

Russian Foreign Minister A. Kozyrev says at a press conference in Paris that if the situation in the Soviet Union deteriorates, the possibility of setting up a Russian government in exile is not ruled out. [Kp]

...

22:00. On Manege Square, tanks whose numbers have been painted over are seen moving out. It is believed in the "White House" that they are heading in the direction of Krasnaya Presnya Embankment. [Kp]

People continue arriving at the "White House." There are rumors of an impending assault. [Ng]

All police stations in the city are closed down. Power in the city has been turned over to the military. [Rg]

23:00. The curfew takes effect in the city. Tass reports that in view of the curfew, it is suspending operations for the day.

Minister Kobets addresses RSFSR Deputies in front of the "White House." He declares: "There are plans to have a special police unit surround the government building at 1 a.m. The building will be protected by nearly 2,000 organized defenders, including 300 armed professionals." Kobets also warns that the special units may use so-called psychotropic gas generators. [Kp]

23:00. A group of Deputies leaves to meet with the commanders of the Taman and Kantemirov Divisions ... to persuade them to refuse to take military action.

Gas masks are issued to everyone inside the Russian Supreme Soviet building.

The cadre personnel of a number of Moscow military academies declare their readiness to swear allegiance to Russia.

Maj. Gen. Pavel Cheryshev, had of security for the House of Soviets, receives a report that the assault on the building has been set for 2 a.m.

23:30. ... The situation of democracy's defenders is desperate: 1,500 "people's volunteers," 300 armed professionals, 300 Afghan War veterans, six outposts and 16 barricades. Plus thousands of people surrounding the building who are prepared to block the path of military vehicles. Members of the Russian Republic government have been issued weapons. [K]

AUGUST 21

00:00. ... Ten combat vehicles based on Red Square have come over to the side of the Russian government, according to the "White House" radio station.

The defenders of the government building break up into groups of 100 and turn bulldozers and tractors in the direction of the expected attack.

We learn from the operations duty officer of the Moscow Military District that all tanks have been moved from the bridges to various sites located within city limits.

Burbulis asks all defenders of the "White House" not to throw themselves in the path of the vehicles but to make way for them—"We must win a moral victory." [Kp]

00:00. Helicopter crews refuse to transport the assault groups to seize the parliament. [K]

00:06. The first bursts of automatic weapons fire are heard from the direction of the American Embassy. Five or six tanks and about 20 armored personnel carriers approach the "White House" from various sides.

00:10. Answering bursts of tracer fire from the "White House" pass over the tanks. Lights are doused in the building, and photocorrespondents are forbidden to use their flash attachments.

00:21. A report is received by telephone to the effect that a barge is moving along the Moscow River carrying troops and storage tanks of some sort—presumably for a gas attack or smoke screen. Citing USSR People's Deputies, Radio Liberty broadcasts a report that Lukyanov has said Gorbachev is involved in the plot.

00:32. First casualty. A young man has been run over by an armored personnel carrier on Kalinin Prospect.

00:45. In the vicinity of Insurrection Square, a crowd blocks the road, impeding the movement of armored personnel carriers. The crew opens fire with turret machine guns. The tracer fire is directed vertically upward. The crowd disperses. The column of armored personnel carriers enters the tunnel under the Kalinin Bridge. The impression is created that the troops are not planning a frontal assault. ...

...

01:00. The Russian Supreme Soviet's defense forces are prepared to give battle should a breakthrough occur. The [aforementioned] column of armored personnel carriers is bottled up inside the tunnel by two barricades made of Icarus buses and garbage and street-cleaning trucks. [Ng]

01:00. Demonstrators throw rocks and Molotov cocktails at tanks and infantry fighting vehicles on the approaches to the "White House."

We are informed at 1:03 by the duty office of the USSR Ministry of Internal Affairs that all police posts were shut down at 10 p.m. Authority in the city has been handed down to the military.

...

01:12. A report comes over the government building's internal radio system: Tanks are moving along the embankment.

We again phone the offices of the country's top leaders. We ask just one question: What do you know? Yanayev's office answers that it has no information. Kryuchkov's: We have no information. Yazov's: Go check it out yourselves. At Pugo's office no one answers the phone. At Lukyanov's: We have no information. The duty office at the USSR Ministry of Internal Affairs: No information. The operations duty officer of the Moscow Military District pleads busyness and asks us to call back later.

A spokesman for the strike committees at Vnukovo, Domodedovo and Bykovo Airports informs the newspaper during the night that they will not go on strike for one reason: RSFSR People's Deputies must get to Moscow for the [RSFSR Supreme Soviet] session.

...

01:15. Snipers have been spotted on the rooftops of tall buildings located near the "White House." [Ng]

01:15. A. Rutskoi gives the defense forces the order to fire without warning if those conducting the assault should break through to the building. [Rg]

01:30. A report is received from the headquarters of the Moscow Military District that the Kantemir and Taman Divisions are being withdrawn from Moscow as unreliable. Only KGB and special-forces units remain in the city. [Ng]

01:40. N. Nazarbayev phones B. Yeltsin and informs him that he has spoken with Yanayev, who had "promised not to use forcible measures." [Kp]

...

01:45. About 30 Deputies go out into the street or prevent bloodshed.

...

02:00 The armored personnel carriers attempt to break out of the tunnel by smashing through the barricade but are bombarded with Molotov cocktails. Two of the vehicles burst into flame, and one begins turning in place. One defender of the "White House" is crushed, another shot through the head by a machine gun.

...

02:15. According to rough estimates, the crowd around the "White House" numbers 50,000. There are tens of thousands of others on the distant approaches to Krasnaya Presnya Embankment. [Rg]

02:30. According to information from the defense staff of the "White House," the night's losses total seven killed. The military has lost three combat vehicles. It is also reported that the soldiers opened fire first, and only then did the Afghan

War veterans begin throwing Molotov cocktails at the armored personnel carriers. [Ng]

02:30. The OMON special police leave the Moscow City Soviet.

02:43. River transport crews bring their vessels to the Krasnaya Presnya Embankment of the Moscow River and declare that they support Yeltsin. [Kp]

02:45. A tugboat brings up three old barges to form a barrier across the Moscow River opposite the RSFSR Supreme Soviet building. [Ng]

03:00. Our on-site correspondents ascertain the details of the burning of several armored personnel carriers. The armored vehicles were moving along the Sadovoye Ring, and at the tunnel where it intersects Kalinin Prospect, heavy canvas was thrown over them. The armored personnel carriers tried to break free. Two of the vehicles managed to get out by crushing a trolleybus. The rest were held back by a human wall and [a barricade of] motor vehicles; they were "boxed up" inside the tunnel. ...

...

After prolonged negotiations, the column of armored vehicles moves toward the "White House" under Russian flags. The burned vehicle No. 536 remains at the exit from the tunnel, without a crew.

03:30. ...

Aleksy II, Patriarch of All Rus, has appealed to the Soviet people to stop the bloodshed and demanded that Gorbachev be given an opportunity to address the country, Interfax reports.

03:40. ...

According to information from Gen. Kobets, the Vitebsk Division of the USSR KGB is on its way to Moscow with the aim of defending the interests of the State Committee for the State of Emergency.

Russian Vice-President A. Rutskoi says he has learned from a conversation with Lukyanov that Gorbachev's health is normal, if you don't count high blood pressure and sciatica.

We phone Vadim Bakatin, who tells that he and Yevgeny Primakov are aware that Gorbachev is in normal health and is insistently demanding to address the people of the country. Bakatin refuses to elaborate on details.

...

04:15. Talks are held between a group of RSFSR People's Deputies and V. Polevik, director of the Airborne Forces' political administration. He reports that "H Hour" has passed and everyone can sleep in peace. He also gives assurances that there is not a single paratroop unit in Moscow. A regiment of the Bolgrad Division of the Airborne Forces is at the military airfield in Kubinka, and other airborne units are now based at Tushino. "Rumors of Yazov's resignation are greatly exaggerated; the Defense Minister is in his proper place and is directing the Army," V. Polevik avers. [Kp]

04:30. The SCSE, headed by Yanayev, meets at the Oktyabrskaya Hotel. There are highly varied reports of the meeting's possible results. ...

...

04:40. According to USSR People's Deputy Viktor Minin, the movement of troops around Moscow is explained by the fact that Defense Ministry units are being replaced by units of KGB troops. Also according to Minin, the Alpha group (USSR KGB) made an attempt to break into the RSFSR Supreme Soviet building without using weapons. The attempt failed.

Burbulis contacted Kryuchkov several times during the night about possible movements of KGB troops and warned him of the inadvisability of storming the White House, to which Kryuchkov answered, "I know nothing about movements of KGB troops."

04:47. Rostropovich states in the studio of the "White House's" internal radio station that he has been happy to spend the night among such people—worthy citizens of the country of Pushkin and Lermontov.

. . .

05:25. Two KGB brigades, one moving down Lenin Prospect and the other down Minsk Highway toward the center, are turned back after a phone call from Burbulis to Kryuchkov. In Burbulis's opinion, "a turning point has been passed." [Rg]

05:30. It has been learned at Kobets's headquarters that most units of the Vitebsk KGB Division stopped on the Mozhaiskoye Highway and did not enter Moscow. A report from the RSFSR Ministry of Internal Affairs is broadcast over the "White House's" internal radio: The Bryansk, Orel and Vladimir police schools have come over to the side of the RSFSR Supreme Soviet. [Kp]

. . .

05:50. Deputy Minin reports that Burbulis has spoken twice with Kryuchkov. An ultimatum to the putschists is being drafted. The leaders of all the Union republics will be asked to sign it, and it will be submitted for approval at the RSFSR Supreme Soviet session that is to begin today at 11 a.m. The main idea in the document is that the coup must be ended today, Aug. 21.

Armored personnel carriers and tanks left the Ukraina Hotel 15 minutes ago.

06:15. There is no new information on the whereabouts and health of the President of the USSR. No one answers the phone at M. Gorbachev's various offices in the Kremlin. The only one "on duty" is the General Secretary's office on Staraya Square. However, "the person on duty has no information about Gorbachev."

. . .

Toward morning, Yanayev phones Burbulis and says, "I only wanted to improve the country's economic situation, not knowing what consequences this would lead to." [Kp]

07:00. On the Mozhaiskoye Highway, Deputies and the public succeed in halting the progress of military vehicles from Moldova.

. . .

09:25. Yazov resigns. [Ng]

10:00. The extraordinary session of Russia's Supreme Soviet begins. In an open vote, with 25 abstentions, it is decided to air the session live. An RSFSR Deputy reports that he has managed to telephone Kravchenko, the head of the All-Union

Television Company, who was nonplussed by this decision of the extraordinary session. [Kp]

11:00. The extraordinary session of the RSFSR Supreme Soviet opens at precisely the planned time.

The putsch is bogged down. [Rg]

12:00 (approximately). Yeltsin speaks. He signs a decree "On the Economic Sovereignty of Russia." The session rejects Kryuchkov's proposal to Yeltsin that they fly together to Foros for a meeting with Gorbachev. [Ng]

12:00. According to information communicated to our correspondent at the Russian parliament by Yeltsin's press secretary Pavel Voshchanov, an agreement has been reached with Kryuchkov that the Russian Republic leadership will go to Foros to meet with Gorbachev.

On instructions from the Secretariat of the CPSU Central Committee, Vladimir Ivashko raises with Yanayev the question of a meeting with Gorbachev.

A. Yakovlev reports that the troops are scheduled to be withdrawn from Moscow at 4 p.m.

Since dawn, about 100,000 rubles has been collected near the RSFSR Supreme Soviet building on Krasnaya Presnya Embankment to help the families of the people who were killed.

12:30. There is a report from Petropavlovsk-Kamchatsky that the command of the Kamchatka Nuclear Submarine Flotilla, headed by Adm. Faleyev, supports the government of Russia, while the ships of the Navy's surface fleet are on the side of the SCSE.

Russian Defense Minister Col. Gen. Kobets confirms in a conversation with our correspondents that an order from V. Kryuchkov to take over the "White House" does indeed exist. The plan is for three KGB battalions and two battalions of the Defense Ministry's Chief Intelligence Administration to take part in the seizure.

B. Yeltsin speaks at the extraordinary session of the RSFSR Supreme Soviet. He reports that the entire SCSE has left for Vnukovo Airport. The Russian Defense Ministry and KGB have been given an order to cut them off immediately at the airport.

Yeltsin asks the RSFSR Supreme Soviet to authorize him to take away the powers of the leaders of the provinces and regions that supported the decrees of the Eight. Authorization is granted, with three "no" votes.

USSR presidential adviser G. Shakhnazarov speaks at the extraordinary session of the RSFSR Supreme Soviet at 2:10 p.m. He says, "I was vacationing at a sanatorium on the southern Crimean coast. Mikhail Sergeyevich contacted me several times by telephone. As usual, he continued to work intensively even on vacation. We discussed a number of upcoming events, including his speech at the signing of the Union Treaty on Aug. 20. The last time the President called me was at 4 p.m. on the 18th. I remember the time, because I had just returned from a walk and automatically looked at my watch. He said, 'Well then, we leave tomorrow?' The departure was scheduled for the evening of the 19th.

"Then he asked what was new. He shared his views on some things that had come out in the press. During our conversation I asked how he was feeling, how his health was, because I knew he had sciatica. He said, 'Everything's fine, they've treated it, everything's normal.'"

...

13.20. Pospelov, the duty officer at the Moscow Chief Administration for Internal Affairs, provides revised, more accurate information on the people killed and wounded during last night's events.

Three people were killed. ...

Two were wounded. ...

...

14:55. Col. Gen. N. Kalinin, Commander of the Moscow Military District and Commandant of Moscow, announces that on the morning of Aug. 21 there was a meeting of the collegium of the Ministry of Defense that was not attended by Defense Minister D. Yazov. A decision was made to rescind the curfew in Moscow and to withdraw the troops from the capital and return them to their permanent stations. [Rg]

...

15:40. According the information from the "White House" defenders and the Russian KGB, the members of the SCSE took off from Vnukovo Airport half an hour ago and flew toward the south. The Russian KGB detained members of the SCSE's staff. A plane with I. Silayev on board also left Vnukovo.

At a morning meeting at the USSR Ministry of Defense, D. Yazov said that anyone who did not wish to carry out his orders could promptly resign.

...

16:00. Arkady Volsky, president of the USSR Union of Science and Industry and member of the CPSU Central Committee, holds a press conference. He calls on the CPSU Central Committee to condemn the coup in order to deflect "any and all suspicion" from the Party. [Rg]

...

16:40. An aircraft with Bakatin and Primakov aboard leaves Vnukovo for Belbek. They are presumed to be accompanied by Rutskoi and Silayev. [Ng]

16:50. The radio broadcasts a Tass report to the effect that the restrictions on the work of the press that were established by the former SCSE have been lifted.

17:00. At the CPSU Central Committee's press center the CPSU leadership holds a press conference at which A. Dzasokhov states: "From the very outset of the coup, representatives of the Central Committee's Secretariat have made attempts to contact the SCSE and have insisted on a meeting with Gorbachev. Only today have their efforts met with success." V. Ivashko has flown to the Crimea. [Rg]

17:05. A report is transmitted from the collegium of the USSR Ministry of Defense indicating that all the troops have been withdrawn from Moscow.

The session of the Russian Supreme Soviet is being broadcast live.

We learn from reliable sources that at about 4 p.m. Rutskoi left the parliament building and set out for Vnukovo. There he found out that the SCSE members had already taken off in the direction of the Crimea in one airplane and had taken another plane—an empty one—along with them. Obviously, the latter was for President Gorbachev. Rutskoi boarded a third plane and took off in the same direction.

At the session of the RSFSR Supreme Soviet, Ruslan Khasbulatov suggest shutting down the newspapers that pledged allegiance to the "new" authorities. [Kp]

17:15. In the Kremlin, the Presidium of the USSR Supreme Soviet declares the creation of the SCSE to have been unlawful and resolves to bring charges against its members, Lukyanov included. [Ng]

17:30. There begins an avalanche of press conferences, speeches and statements by state officials of various ranks and by representatives of state institutions and public organizations, hastening to declare their respect for the President of the USSR and to repudiate the actions of the SCSE. Among them is a press conference given by USSR Minister of Foreign Affairs A. Bessmertnykh, who says he was ill until Aug. 21. The USSR Prosecutor's Office issues a similar statement. [Rg]

...

18:00. Telephone service is restored at the USSR President's dacha at Foros. [Rg]

18:00. There is crowd of people around the KGB building on Lubyanka Square. Universal jubilation.

...

At 18:30 M. S. Gorbachev phones B. N. Yeltsin. The content of their conversation is as yet unknown. ...

...

...20:00. An immense rally continues at the "White House." It is decided that the defense of the Russian Republic seat of government will not be removed until complete victory is attained.

20:30. There is a report from the House of Soviets that the Russian Republic leadership has decided to arrest the members of the junta.

20:40. USSR Deputy Prime Minister V. Shcherbakov holds a press conference at the USSR Ministry of Foreign Affairs. He states that V. Pavlov had nothing to do with the conspiracy and that "the USSR Cabinet of Ministers is loyal to the President." According to Shcherbakov, the Cabinet's curious behavior during the days of the crisis can be explained by the fact that it was ill-informed.

21:05. The "Time" [*Vremya*] program broadcasts a brief statement issued by the USSR President for the country's radio and television. The President stresses that he is fully in command of the situation and that his communications with the country, which were interrupted as a result of the rash actions of a group of state officials, have been restored. The President intends to return to Moscow in a matter of hours.

22:00. By this time—as B. N. Yeltsin reports the next day—the conspirators' criminal activities have ceased altogether. [Rg]

23:00. Gorbachev has arrived? [Kp]

51   *Anatomy of a Failed Coup*

JOHN B. DUNLOP

...

In light of the immense political resonance of the coup, it behooves the historian to sift through the testimonies of eyewitnesses and journalists carefully in an attempt to determine what actually occurred, and why. This task is especially important in light of the tendency of many both in Russia and in the West not to take the plotters and their designs seriously. For not a few commentators, the coup perpetrators represented ineffective eccentrics, latter-day Don Quixotes. ...

Questions have been raised as to whether a coup was even attempted. "I know how coups are planned," the influential proto-fascist editor and publicist Aleksandr Prokhanov has commented. "What happened here was a circus. The *spetsnaz* rested, and on the streets they brought out armor which served to agitate everyone greatly, as if a bear had crept into a beehive. But the people who, at first, were afraid learned that the vehicles contained no shells, and they then climbed up and sat upon those vehicles, placing flowers in their empty muzzles and feeding the soldiers from spoons."[4] For Prokhanov, the August coup represented a derisory "quasi-plot" or "pseudo-plot."

Similarly, for "democrat" Leonid Radzikhovskii, writing in the weekly *Ogonek*, the coup was merely a timid "imitation coup" launched by irresolute Gorbachevites fearful of shedding blood. Did the plotters, he asked, seek "to restore a totalitarian system?" "No," he answered. "Their maximum aim was to roll back the video-tape three to four years. ..."[5] They did not arrest Russian president Boris Yeltsin, Radzikhovskii contended, "because there was no reason to."

Such benign or contemptuous views of the coup have been sharply contested by other commentators. Gorbachev himself has stated flatly that "only killers could propose to introduce, reintroduce a totalitarian regime in our country."[6] And historian A. Kiva has observed: "People say that this coup was not serious, that it was almost contemptible. This is an absolute and extremely serious error!

... The plotters succeeded in attracting to their side almost all of the highest officials [of the USSR]. On their side were the vice president, the prime minister, and,
as it turns out, the chairman of the USSR Supreme Soviet, as well as the heads of
three key ministries [i.e., the KGB, MVD, and Ministry of Defense]. The Secretariat of the Central Committee was on their side. ... In short, it is difficult to imagine how to prepare a coup more seriously."[7]

Other commentators have noted that the coup de facto threatened the West as
seriously as it did the citizens of Russia. ...

RSFSR congressman Colonel General Dmitrii Volkogonov has agreed with this
assessment: "For me it was clear that if the putsch ... had succeeded," he told the
newspaper *Estoniya*, "then the country would have sunk into the gloom of neo-
Stalinism, and repressions would inevitably have begun. The winds of a 'cold war'
would have started to blow. ..."[9]

... Volkogonov's opinion is confirmed by the text of a virulently anti-Ameri-
can statement that the coup plotters sent to Foreign Minister Aleksandr
Bessmertnykh for approval on the second day of the putsch. ...

This truculent statement took on added resonance in light of the recently revealed fact that the coup plotters had control of the "nuclear suitcase" during the
period from August 18 through 21.[11]

...

THE GKChP

The State Committee for the State of Emergency, or GKChP, to use the committee's Russian initials, represented a cross section of Soviet elites which felt mas-
sively threatened by the new union treaty which Gorbachev had announced that
he planned to sign on August 20. The "gang of eight," as they became known in
Russia, who attempted officially to take power at 4:00 A.M. on August 19, were vehemently committed to the preservation of a unitary Soviet state. These eight
high-ranking functionaries were:

> Gennadii Yanaev (b. 1937), vice president of the USSR
> Valentin Pavlov (b. 1937), USSR prime minister
> Vladimir Kryuchkov (b. 1924), chairman of the USSR KGB
> Dmitrii Yazov (b. 1923), USSR minister of defense
> Boris Pugo (b. 1937), USSR minister of internal affairs
> Oleg Baklanov (b. 1932), first deputy chairman of the USSR Defense Council
> Aleksandr Tizyakov (b. 1926), president of the Association of USSR State Industries
> Vasilii Starodubtsev (b. 1931), Chairman of the USSR Union of Peasants[31]

In addition to these seven individual—Boris Pugo had committed suicide on
August 22 and so, of course, could not be brought to trial—eight other high-ranking figures were also arrested and charged by the Russian Procuracy with participation in the attempted coup: Anatolii Luk'yanov, chairman of the USSR Su-

preme Soviet; Oleg Shenin, a member of the Politburo and of the Party Secretariat; Valerii Boldin, Gorbachev's chief of staff; two first deputy chairmen of the KGB—Viktor Grushko and Genii Ageev; two KGB generals whose job it had been to ensure Gorbachev's security—Yurii Plekhanov and Vyacheslav Generalov; and, last, General Valentin Varennikov, commander of the ground forces of the Soviet Army.

The Russian Procuracy had also wanted to charge a sixteenth individual, Deputy Defense Minister Vladislav Achalov, with participation in the coup, but, in an obstructionist move, the increasingly conservative Russian parliament has refused to lift Achalov's immunity as an elected member of that body. In addition to the fifteen persons who were arrested and charged, it was clear that scores and perhaps hundreds of other Party, military, and police officials could have been brought to trial for participation in the attempted putsch. Mikhail Moiseev, the Army chief of staff, and Yurii Prokof'ev, a Politburo member and the Party boss of Moscow, were two names that came immediately to mind in this connection.

According to Chief Investigator Lisov of the Russian Procuracy, a core of six future putschists had been planning the coup over an extended period of time.[32] Lisov did not specifically identify who these six individuals were, but, from the context, it seemed clear that he had the following persons in mind: Kryuchkov, Yazov, Baklanov, Shenin, Tizyakov, and Boldin. These six leaders, of course, represented the vital interests of the KGB, Army, military-industrial complex, state industries, and the large conservative wing of the Communist party. Their subsequent decision to include Vasilii Starodubtsev in the membership of the GKChP may have reflected the thinking of Sergei Kurginyan and his center ... concerning the need to enlist Soviet industrialists and agrarians in the effort to preserve the unity of the Soviet Union. (It is noteworthy that MVD chairman Boris Pugo was apparently not apprised of the impending coup until August 18, the day that Gorbachev was "isolated" at his summer house in the Crimea.[33])

Major General Viktor Ivanenko, head of the Russian KGB, which remained loyal to Yeltsin during the attempted coup, has stated that Vladimir Kryuchkov should be considered the "organizer" of the putsch, and Oleg Baklanov and Oleg Shenin (i.e., the military-industrial complex and the conservative wing of the Party), its "clients."[34] Chief Investigator Lisov has similarly maintained: "Without the participation of the KGB, the conspiracy would have been impossible. It was precisely in its bosom that all the coup documents were drafted. ... However, the KGB acted not on its own but in collaboration with the CPSU, the Ministry of Internal Affairs, the Army, and the military-industrial complex."[35] ...

PREPARING THE COUP

As the six investigations into the causes of the August 1991 coup have shown, the roots of the putsch extended back to the year 1989—the year of the First Congress of USSR People's Deputies—when the KGB established tight surveillance over Boris Yeltsin, former USSR Procuracy investigators Tel'man Gdlyan and Nikolai

Ivanov, and in effect "over all members of the Interregional Group of People's Deputies."[36] As the "democrats" increased their influence, the KGB's interest in them increased proportionately. The organization Democratic Russia was singled out for special attention (and was successfully infiltrated) by the KGB.[37]

Among those whose telephone conversations were illegally eavesdropped upon (and taped) were such leading Russian government officials as: Boris Yeltsin, Aleksandr Rutskoi, Ruslan Khasbulatov, Gennadii Burbulis, and Mikhail Poltoranin. Leading Soviet officials who were subjected to the same treatment were: Aleksandr Yakovlev, Eduard Shevardnadze, and Vadim Bakatin. The mayor and deputy mayor of Moscow, Gavriil Popov and Yurii Luzhkov, had their telephone conversations regularly taped.[38] Subject to "total shadowing" by the KGB were such important political activists as Yurii Afanas'ev, Galina Starovoitova, Academician Dmitrii Likhachev, chess champion Garri Kasparov, and (surprisingly) conservative Russian writer Valentin Rasputin.[39] On trips abroad, the following were shadowed and eavesdropped upon by the KGB's foreign espionage network: Afanas'ev, Starovoitova, Academician Stanislav Shatalin, Academician Oleg Bogomolov, leading economist Nikolai Shmelev, Sergei Stankevich, and "about fifty people's deputies, including members of the closest circle around Gorbachev himself."[40]

The Soviet president, Gorbachev, was, along with the Communist party apparatus, a regular reader of these illegal KGB surveillance and wiretap reports. As we have seen, he was in the foolish habit of appending handwritten comments in the margins of the materials that were supplied to him in abundance by the KGB.[41] It was difficult not to agree with Sergei Stepashin, chairman of the Russian parliamentary committee on security and defense, when he argued that "Mikhail Gorbachev must bear full responsibility" for the KGB's illegal surveillance and wiretapping activities because he was a willing recipient of the materials supplied to him in great number.[42]

The materials that were unearthed by investigators in the KGB and Communist party archives after the coup showed that the actual preparation for the future putsch began during the fall of 1990. In September 1990, it will be recalled, several paratroop divisions had mysteriously converged upon Moscow, and Yeltsin had been taken out of action in a suspicious automobile accident during which he suffered a concussion. September 1990, the newspaper *Komsomol'skaya pravda* has concluded, "was the prelude for the August putsch."[43] The attempted coup in the Baltic during January 1991 and the ominous deployment of 50,000 troops in Moscow at the time of the pro-democracy demonstration on March 28, 1991, were also singled out by investigators as key developments preparing the way for the August 1991 coup. "All of that," Sergei Stepashin has underlined, "was staged by the KGB under the pretext of introducing order."[44]

By August 4, 1991 (the day before Gorbachev left on vacation), all the documents for the coup, including a draft declaration for the imposition of a state of emergency, had been prepared by the KGB. On August 7, there began regular meetings of Chairman Kryuchkov and various future coup leaders at the so-called "ABC" KGB safe house in Moscow. On instructions from defense minister Yazov, General Pavel Grachev, commander of Soviet paratroops, worked closely with two KGB officials, Zhizhin and Egorov, in planning the introduction of emergency rule.[45]

The evidence of an impending coup was becoming so strong that, beginning in June of 1991, the Bush administration felt impelled to send three warnings to Gorbachev that it believed a putsch against him was imminent.[46] Similarly, former Politburo member Aleksandr Yakovlev told Austrian television after the August coup had failed that he had been warning Gorbachev of the danger of a putsch since the time of the Twenty-eighth Party Congress, and that he had even given the Soviet president the names of potential plotters, including some of those who ended up as members of the GKChP. Gorbachev, Yakovlev recalled, did not take the warnings seriously, asserting that the persons named "lack the courage to stage a coup."[47] According to the Gosset and Fedorovski book on the putsch, Yakovlev was alerted by a trustworthy veteran KGB employee on August 14 that a coup was impending; Yakovlev issued a warning to the Russian public on August 16.[48]

WHY THE PLOTTERS DECIDED TO ACT

Contrary to what Gorbachev told Yakovlev, the conspirators did not lack the courage to act. Or perhaps their fear of the future was a sufficient motivator to overcome what hesitation they may have experienced. It is now clear that the plotters had a number of cogent reasons for wanting to remove Gorbachev and to replace him with the docile Yanaev. First, of course, there was the fact that the union treaty was due to be signed on August 20. This new treaty would inevitably have reduced the powers of all of the plotters and of the powerful institutions—the KGB, the military-industrial complex, the kolkhoz system, etc.—which they represented. Even worse, from their perspective, the heads of the increasingly powerful union republics had apparently targeted several of the plotters for removal. In an interview with the BBC, Gorbachev asserted that his chief of security, General Medvedev, had placed a bugging device in the presidential dacha outside of Moscow which enabled Vladimir Kryuchkov and the other plotters to learn of a conversation that he had had (on July 31) with Presidents Yeltsin and Nazarbaev of Kazakhstan. During that conversation, Gorbachev recalled, Yeltsin and Nazarbayev had singled out Yazov, Kryuchkov, and Luk'yanov as particularly dangerous men. While defending his team to the two republican presidents, Gorbachev had admitted that after the treaty had been signed, everything would have to be reorganized, "everything: the Army and the KGB."[49] The three men in question, he had added, would have to have their wings clipped. This conversation presumably served to galvanize the coup perpetrators.

Fear for their jobs and for their privileges was but one of the numerous factors inducing the plotters to take action. Oleg Shenin, a member of the Politburo and the Party Secretariat, has provided a detailed explanation of why he joined the conspiracy, contained in a letter to the party Central Committee and published after his arrest in the newspaper *Den*.[50] "I always fully supported the course of April 1985," Shenin declared. "But I am opposed to the course of April 1991, when the country set off toward catastrophe and the complete disintegration of the Soviet Union. ...."

Economic considerations were one key area singled out by Shenin. The rapid growth of market relations in the country, he wrote, had led to "the enriching of small groups of black marketeers (*teneviki*)," and to the "impoverishment of millions of Soviet people." Shenin also underlined spiraling "interethnic conflict" in the country as another factor prompting him to take action.

In his letter to the Central Committee, Shenin also dwelled at some length on Gorbachev's abandonment of the traditional Soviet principle of collective rule. Discussions of "questions vitally important for the fate of the people and the country," he wrote, were decided "behind closed doors by a narrow circle of people." Even the USSR Supreme Soviet and the Soviet Congress of People's Deputies had, he noted, lost any real power, while the results of the March 1991 USSR-wide referendum, in which the populace had voted to retain the Soviet Union, were simply ignored.

Last but certainly not least in Shenin's thinking, was Gorbachev's dismissive attitude toward the Communist party. The Party's general secretary, he complained, had "simply ceased to take it into consideration." As for the Politburo, it lay dormant with almost nothing to do.

Shenin's angry letter shows that the plotters had strong grievances against the man who occupied the posts of Party general secretary and Soviet president. By calling for a return to "April 1985," Shenin signaled that he wanted to go back to what British historian Geoffrey Hosking has termed "*Perestroika* Mark One," i.e., to the policies pursued by Gorbachev during the first year of his period in office.[51]

In his testimony before investigators on August 22, Defense Minister Dmitrii Yazov struck certain of the same notes as had Shenin. "Inevitably," he recalled, "we [the future members of GKChP] came to the conclusion that the guilt must lie with the President [Gorbachev], inasmuch as he had distanced himself from the Party and abandoned the army to misfortune."[52] "Gorbachev," Yazov groused, "traveled a lot in recent years. And often we did not know in general what important matters he discussed there." There was obviously a suspicion on the part of the plotters that the Soviet president was selling out to the West, and especially to the United States. Yazov underlined that he and his fellow putschists were "not prepared to enter into major dependence upon the USA—in political, economic, and military matters."

In a useful analysis of the reasons for the August coup, commentator Simon Kordonskii, writing in the weekly *Novoe vremya*, has listed some of the events and developments that, in his opinion, virtually impelled the plotters to take action. Among these were: the attempt by Boris Yeltsin to nationalize the oil and gas industry in the RSFSR (a step execrated by Soviet prime minister Pavlov); the announced plan of several republics to introduce their own currencies; the poor harvest in 1991; a 50 percent decline in new orders to the defense industry; a rampant commercialization of relations among enterprises in the USSR; Yeltsin's decree on departification of the KGB, MVD, military, USSR enterprises, and other institutions on Russian soil; and, last, the formation of republican organs of state security which would have begun taking power away from the union-wide KGB.[53] Clearly, any one of these developments might by itself have been deemed serious enough to precipitate a coup; taken together, they virtually mandated that the plotters—who represented the vital interests of powerful Soviet institutions—take action.

As well-informed men, the plotters were aware that a Marxist-Leninist restoration would enjoy little support on the part of a deideologized populace. They therefore attempted to tailor their message to address what they thought were festering grievances in the souls of Soviet citizens. The "Appeal to the Soviet People," a document formally adopted by the conspirators on August 18 and released by TASS the following day, provides perhaps the best summary of the message that the GKChP wanted to deliver to the Soviet populace. In measures tones, the authors laid out a plan for rescuing a country that they saw as being in "mortal danger."[54]

...

In summary, the authors of the "Appeal to the Soviet People" obviously believed that a combination of economic and social discipline plus fervent Soviet patriotism would successfully serve to rally the masses around a rigorous program. The plotters would have been reinforced in this conviction by the results of a poll published just five days before the coup took place in the Communist party newspaper *Glasnost*. This poll indicated that 79 percent of respondents in the RSFSR, 86 percent in Ukraine, and 69 percent in Lithuania favored the preservation of state controls over most enterprises in the USSR and reacted "coldly" to the idea of a transition to a market economy.[55] The authors of this poll, which was conducted by the USSR Academy of Social Sciences at the Party Central Committee, may have intentionally skewed the results. The pollsters could well have "cooked" the results to satisfy higher-ups in the Party. Simon Kordonskii has noted that a similar poll conducted by the same organization was utilized in an attempt to "introduce order" within the USSR during the period October–November 1990.

During the three days that it held power, the GKChP focused heavily upon the "war on crime." On August 20, TASS announced that the KGB, in cooperation with the MVD and the Soviet Procuracy, was actively engaged in "unmasking and curtailing the activity of criminal groups in the sphere of the Soviet economy."[56] The authorities were said to be pitted in a fierce struggle with "mafiosi and other criminal elements" which had succeeded in "establishing ties with criminals abroad." An anti-Western element was thus introduced by coup leaders into the war against Soviet crime.

...

The view that the GKChP wished to convey to the public was of a country being overrun by crime. The criminals, moreover, were said to be aided and abetted by confederates in the West.

According to Russian procurator general Valentin Stepankov, the text of a draft decree was found at the homes of two of the coup leaders "according to which patrols were permitted to shoot thieves and hooligans on the spot, without a trial or investigation. ..."[58] It is not difficult to imagine how military and police patrols might have chosen to interpret this call to institute summary justice. Pro-democracy demonstrators could, for example, have been executed "on the spot" as hooligans.

...

THE RIDDLE OF FOROS: PART I

...

Presumably concerned that his place in history might be tarnished by his perceived close affiliation with the coup plotters—a number of whom had constituted his "team"—Gorbachev rushed into print his version of the events that occurred at his summer house at Foros. The result was a slender volume, *The August Coup: The Truth and the Lessons.*[76] Gorbachev's version was backed up by his wife's account of what had transpired, and by published excerpts from a diary kept by his close assistant, Anatolii Chernyaev, who was with him and his family at the dacha in Foros.[77]

Chief Investigator Evgenii Lisov, speaking for the Russian Procuracy, has substantiated Gorbachev's account by affirming: "We say unequivocally: Gorbachev did not give any hints, obliquely or directly, to indicate he was with them [the conspirators]." But Lisov then added: "However, his [Gorbachev's] long contact with the members of the plot, who were his close colleagues, and some aspects of his character, in our view, gave the plotters the right to think that sooner or later, after one, two, or three days [they would bring Gorbachev over to their side]."[78] It should also be noted here that if it could have been shown that Gorbachev had actually authorized the state of emergency, then the Russian Procuracy would have had no case against the coup leaders, because the putsch would then have represented a "constitutional act."[79] The procuracy therefore (and Boris Yeltsin as well) had a genuine stake in absolving the former Soviet president of any legal responsibility for the coup.

In Russia, as opposed to the West, where Gorbachev's version of events has received general acceptance, there has remained great skepticism over whether the former Soviet president is to be believed. The skepticism has generally focused upon the following three questions: 1. Was Gorbachev actually without communications for seventy-two hours, as he claims? 2. Was he in fact under "house arrest" as he maintains? 3. Is his version of what happened on August 18, when he was visited by GKChP leaders Baklanov, Shenin, Boldin, and General Varennikov, and of what occurred on August 21, when Kryuchkov, Yazov, Baklanov, Tizyakov, and

Luk'yanov flew to Foros, to be believed? Elena Bonner, Andrei Sakharov's widow, for one, has asserted, "I am profoundly convinced that Mikhail Gorbachev prepared the state of emergency, probably together with [Anatolii] Luk'yanov."[80] In her opinion, Gorbachev's account of his actions is a deceiving one.

...

Basing himself on the vast information contained in the 140 volumes of material compiled by the Russian Procuracy, former Soviet vice president Gennadii Yanaev has written:

> Despite the heroic description of the Foros "imprisonment" which Gorbachev has written, the materials of the criminal case testify to the fact that there actually took place a "self-isolation" of the President of the USSR. His personal guard remained loyal to him and carried out only his instructions. The dacha's internal guard and the land and naval borderguards also remained on the side of the president. Even more, they gave a signal to the president's personal guard that they were prepared to ensure a safe exit for Gorbachev and his family in any direction. This force represented several hundred men as well as their equipment, their ships, and a fast-moving patrol boat on which to leave for the sea. The radio communications of the border guards, of the militia, and on the ships were cut off by no one, and in fact that would have been impossible. In the garage, the keys to which were held by [Gorbachev's] duty officer, were automobiles with all sorts of communications equipment.[87]

This situation led Yanaev to conclude: "Gorbachev was waiting to see which way events would turn. If the GKChP won, then he would immediately emerge from his 'isolation' and resume work as president in carrying out the decisions of the USSR Supreme Soviet. If they were defeated, then Gorbachev would lose nothing; he would return to his duties and strengthen his relations with the Russian democrats."

In a similar vein, Anatolii Luk'yanov, the former chairman of the USSR Supreme Soviet, has recalled that on August 3 (two days before Gorbachev went on vacation) the Soviet president affirmed at a session of the USSR Cabinet of Ministers that "there was an emergency situation in the country and a need for emergency measures," after which Gorbachev added: "The people will understand this."[88] Elsewhere Luk'yanov has maintained that Gorbachev knew about the coup in advance "and he took not a single step to block it."[89]

...

The question of whether or not Gorbachev was actually blockaded at his summer house is a second issue that will intrigue future historians. In his book, *The August Coup*, Gorbachev has insisted that he was cut off from the outside world: "The plotters," he wrote, "isolated me completely from the outside world, both from the sea and the land, creating what was essentially psychological pressure. I was totally isolated. ... I was left with the thirty-two men of my bodyguard."[92]

...

If Gorbachev was not in actuality isolated at Foros but instead chose to *appear* to be cut off—and this issue is, of course, far from settled—then it suggests that he and KGB chairman Kryuchkov must have come to an agreement: Gorbachev would not approve the coup but would remain incommunicado, while Kryuchkov and the other GKChP leaders would attempt to impose emergency rule on the country. A logical terminus for this "experiment" would have been August 26, the date that Anatolii Luk'yanov had set for a session of the USSR Supreme Soviet.[95]

...

The three days that Gorbachev spent "blockaded" and "without communications" at Foros present a similar riddle of behavior. Perhaps, he, his family, and his entourage did behave nobly, even heroically, as he has described in *The August Coup*. Or perhaps, instead, his actions were dictated by "tactical and unprincipled considerations of the general struggle for power," to employ Sakharov's words. In the latter case, one presumes, Gorbachev would have been playing an exceptionally cunning and risk-ridden game: first, he would have let the GKChP leaders suppress Yeltsin and the Russian "democrats," plus the leaderships of four rebellious states, i.e., the Baltic republics and Moldavia. Then after a unitary Soviet state had been reestablished, he, probably working in concord with cooperative republican leaders like Nazarbaev and Kravchuk, might have attempted to oust Kryuchkov, Pavlov, Baklanov, Tizyakov and certain other GKChP leaders from power and then have sought to form a new "right-centrist" team, perhaps with Arkadii Vol'skii as USSR prime minister, which would have set a reform communist course for the country. In this way, he would have triumphed over both the leftist "democrats" and the coup plotters.

THE KGB ARREST LIST

The first step in the August coup, the "isolation" of the Soviet president, had been accomplished flawlessly. The second step was considerably more complicated: namely, the arrest of seventy persons on a special list prepared by the KGB; the order to bring in these individuals was issued at 7:20 A.M. on August 19 by General Kryuchkov.[100] Although the original arrest lists have been destroyed, the names on them have been painstakingly restored by the KGB officers cooperating with investigators.[101] An examination of this list—which is divided into persons to be seized immediately and those to be arrested when the opportunity arose—can tell us a good deal about the political aims of the GKChP.

First, Boris Yeltsin and virtually his entire team of top advisers were to have been apprehended: the list included the names of Vice President Aleksandr Rutskoi; State Secretary Gennadii Burbulis; State Councilors Sergei Shakhrai and Sergei Stankevich; and acting chairman of the RSFSR Supreme Soviet, Ruslan Khasbulatov. It should be obvious that the seizure of these individuals would have amounted to a "beheading" of the newly sovereign Russian Republic.

In addition, Mikhail Poltoranin, RSFSR minister for the Press and Mass Information, and Oleg Poptsov, chairman of the Russian Television and Radio Committee, were both on the "immediate arrest" list. A primary aim of the coup was to muzzle all RSFSR means of mass communication.

Besides decapitating the political and media leadership of the Russian Republic, the coup plotters wanted to crush the burgeoning democratic movements and political parties of the RSFSR. A number of leading activists of the democratic umbrella organization, *Democratic Russia,* consequently found themselves on the list: Lev Ponomarev, Arkadii Murashev, Fr. Gleb Yakunin (immediate arrest list), Viktor Sheinis (immediate arrest), Il'ya Zaslavskii, Leonid Batkin, V. Bokser (immediate arrest), M. Shneider, and V. Kriger. The leaders of the most dynamic new political parties were also targeted by the plotters: Oleg Rumyantsev and Galina Rakitskaya (as well as her husband) of the Social Democratic party, Nikolai Travkin of the Democratic party, Vladimir Lysenko and S. Sulakshin of the Republican party, Yurii Chernichenko of the Peasants' party, Viktor Aksyuchits of the Christian Democratic movement, and Mikhail Chelnokov, the leader of the Radical Democrats. One individual on the arrest list, Valeriya Novodvorskaya, a leader of the Democratic Union, was already incarcerated, in the KGB's Lefortovo Prison at the time the coup was launched.[102]

Also on the arrest list were a number of well-known former Party and state officials who, in the opinion of the conspirators, were responsible for bringing the country to its present sorry state: Eduard Shevardnadze, Aleksandr Yakovlev, Vadim Bakatin, the mayor of Moscow, Gavriil Popov, and Academician Stanislav Shatalin. Similarly targeted were leading reform editors and publicists who had played a key role in moving the country from the neo-Andropovite "*Perestroika* Mark One" to "*Perestroika* Mark Two": Egor Yakovlev, chief editor of *Moskovskie novosti;* Vitalii Korotich, chief editor of *Ogonek;* and Fedor Burlatskii of *Literaturnaya gazeta.*

… Leading political dissidents from the Brezhnev era once again found themselves singled out by an old nemesis: Valerii Senderov, Lev Timofeev, Sergei Grigoryants, Academician Sakharov's close associate, Sergei Kovalev, Fr. Gleb Yakunin. Not surprisingly, KGB officers that had "gone bad" also found themselves on the list: Oleg Kalugin and Mikhail Lyubimov. So, too, did people's deputies who had showed an unhealthy curiosity concerning the KGB's repressive activities: Sergei Belozertsev and Yurii Shchekochikhin (the latter was also an editor of *Literaturnaya gazeta*).

The military and military-industrial complex leadership was also to be permitted a swipe at their tormentors: Colonel General Dmitrii Volkogonov, an outspoken critic of Soviet military policy and a revisionist military historian, was on the arrest list, as was Academician Yurii Ryzhov, a USSR congressman and co-deputy chairman of Yeltsin's advisory committee, as well as a harsh critic of the military-industrial complex. Pacifist writer and publicist Ales' Adamovich also figured on the list.

The arrest list was also directed against the USSR's growing class of entrepreneurs. The name of the well-known "Soviet millionaire" Artem Tarasov was on the list. On August 20, in the provincial city of Chelyabinsk, Eduard Tenyakov, head of the Moscow Stock Exchange, was seized by the local authorities.[104]

There has been some puzzlement expressed on the part of Russian and Western commentators as to why so few individuals were successfully arrested by the KGB. Only five persons, it emerged, were actually picked up. ...

...

... In their well-informed study, *Histoire secrète d'un coup d'état,* French journalist Ulysse Gosset and Russian political activist Vladimir Fedorovski (who was a spokesman for the Movement for Democratic Reforms led by Aleksandr Yakovlev and Eduard Shevardnadze) interviewed two KGB officers who stated that a "mass repression" was scheduled to begin two weeks after the inception of the coup.[108] This wide-ranging crackdown was to have commenced after the USSR Supreme Soviet had put its imprimatur on a state of emergency. From the beginning, the GKChP and the KGB had wanted to impart an air of legality to the putsch. Gosset and Fedorovski have also reported that Directorate "Z" of the KGB prepared "several thousand" arrest forms which were then signed by the commander of the Moscow Military District, General Kalinin. The place for the names of those to be arrested was left blank.[109] ...

In addition to planning mass arrests, the GKChP had also intended to abolish all structures of legislative rule throughout the country. Chief Investigator Lisov has reported that at the home of one coup plotter a series of documents was found which showed that the GKChP "was planning fully to abolish the existing structures of power and administration, from supreme soviets to village councils. It was also planning to liquidate the executive branch and to create a provisional committee for administering the country, as well as a new cabinet of ministers, whose leader was to be one of the plotters, but not Pavlov—it was to be Tizyakov. ... The economy was to be returned to harsh administrative rule, almost to a wartime system of administration."[110]

Such were the mild changes envisioned by the "Don Quixotes" serving on the GKChP.

THE RIDDLE OF ARKHANGEL'SKOE

The events at Foros constituted the first riddle of the putsch; what happened at Yeltsin's summer house on the morning of August 19 represented the coup's second great mystery. Yeltsin and his entourage were staying at the official Russian government dacha complex located in the isolated village of Arkhangel'skoe, thirty kilometers from Moscow, when the Russian president received a telephone call at 6:07 A.M.—seven minutes after Moscow Radio had announced the putsch—informing him of the existence of the GKChP.[111] Having taking stock of his position, Yeltsin must have concluded that his prospects were poor, if not hopeless. He likely surmised that the secluded village in which he found himself, protected by a mere eight bodyguards, had been surrounded by KGB *spetsnaz*. (It was.) As was his habit, however, Yeltsin reacted calmly to the danger about him.

First, Yeltsin asked the other high-ranking Russian officials staying in Arkhangel'skoe to come to his dacha. Then he had a number of other key officials telephoned. Some, such as Anatolii Sobchak, the mayor of Leningrad, who was visiting in Moscow, and Yurii Luzhkov, the deputy mayor of Moscow, telephoned Yeltsin themselves and were told to come to Arkhangel'skoe. Once these officials had arrived, they set to work drafting an appeal entitled "To the Citizens of Russia," which was completed by 9:00 A.M.[112]

Anatolii Sobchak arrived at Yeltsin's dacha at approximately 7:30 A.M. He has recalled his initial impressions: "As I walked inside, my heart stopped: the entire leadership of Russia was sitting there, and a single commando could have knocked out the whole government."[113] Colonel General Kobets, chairman of the Russian parliamentary commission for military and security affairs and a close Yeltsin ally, was visited by similar thoughts when he arrived at the dacha. "Only my presence had been lacking," he thought, "to garnish the junta's salad bowl."[114]

...

Once the appeal "To the Citizens of Russia" had been completed and its text telephoned to the Russian "White House" by RSFSR Prime Minister Ivan Silaev, the assembled officials confronted a difficult decision. Should they remain at Arkhangel'skoe and make it their headquarters? Or should they chance arrest by leaving the dacha for the "White House"? General Kobets and Anatolii Sobchak have both claimed credit for inducing the others to agree to the latter choice. ...

...

Whatever the reasons for their inaction, the "A" group permitted the Yelstin party to leave the presidential dacha, an ideal secluded spot for it to have been arrested.

Even with this incredible bit of luck, the Yeltsin party may have only narrowly escaped seizure. Ten to fifteen minutes after they had left the dacha, an armored unit swept down upon Arkhangel'skoe. "As we learned later," General Kobets has recalled, "less than a quarter hour later, the village was ringed with armored vehicles, and tough lads arrived to 'take' us."[124]

The Russian Procuracy in its investigation of the coup has concluded that no arrests were made at Arkhangel'skoe because no order to seize Yeltsin and his party was given. But was that in fact the reason for what happened? Or did a miracle of sorts take place in the "village of the Archangel"?

YELTSIN RALLIES RUSSIA

In explaining a cardinal reason for the failure of the coup, RSFSR congressman Anatolii Medvedev has observed that "... they [the plotters] were simply not prepared for the opposition exhibited by the Russian government and the simple people. ..."[125] "The scenario of such a turn of events," Leonid Radzikhovskii has agreed, "was not foreseen [by the conspirators]."[126]

All early commentators on the coup have singled out the central role of Boris Yeltsin in stymieing the designs of the putschists. "Almost by sheer force of will," journalist Bill Keller wrote, "Mr. Yeltsin rallied the resistance."[127] A senior Western diplomat in Moscow put it similarly: "Yeltsin's style is to create the illusion of power with will power."[128] And Radio Liberty's Iain Elliot, who was in Moscow at the time of the coup, commented that Yeltsin "appeared to be the right person in the right place at the right time."[129] This early judgment is one that will likely stand the test of time.

As they gathered inside the Russian "White House"—the building of the RSFSR Supreme Soviet—on the morning of August 19, at a time when hundreds of tanks were investing the city, Yeltsin and his team were aware that they were playing a weak hand. To be sure, they had taken certain precautions against such an eventuality. According to a report by the BBC, the Russian Defense Committee, which had been set up by Yeltsin in late June, had sent secret orders to regional commands of the army and KGB telling them to support the Russian authorities in the event of a coup.[130] A secret "reserve government" had also been set up in the woods some seventy kilometers from Sverdlovsk, to be headed by RSFSR deputy prime minister Oleg Lobov.[131] (It is, of course, difficult to believe that the KGB leadership would have been unaware of such initiatives.) According to General Kobets, he and Yeltsin had worked out a detailed plan, which they called "Plan X," for the defense of the "White House" in case of an attempted putsch.[132] These precautions, however, must have seemed pitifully little on the morning of the nineteenth.

Since late 1987, when he had set out on his "long march" to political power, Yeltsin had, however, consistently been defeating the odds. Unerringly, he and his team decided upon a correct strategy: "We had to act quickly and decisively," Yeltsin recalled on the twenty-second, "in order to seize the initiative from the rebels and not let them grow stronger or pick up the tempo. ... [A] headquarters aimed at neutralizing their criminal activity went into action at the House of the Soviets [i.e., the "White House"]. ... The President of Russia assumed command of all armed forces on the territory of the RSFSR. Colonel General Kobets was named defense minister for the republic."[133]

Attack, attack, attack—this was the strategy that Yeltsin and his followers immediately and instinctively adopted. The splitting of the Soviet military became their number-one priority. A second top goal was to gain expressions of support from Western leaders—especially from President Bush—and from Russians enjoying respect and prestige at home, particularly the patriarch of the Russian Orthodox Church, Aleksii II.

On August 19, at about noon, Yeltsin intuitively chose a symbol that would resonate throughout the country and around the world. Colonel Teselkin of the Tamanskaya Division has recalled that Yeltsin unexpectedly emerged from the "White House" and came up to his lead tank. "Do you come here to kill Yeltsin?" he asked a stunned Teselkin. "No, of course not," the colonel mumbled. Yeltsin then climbed up on Teselkin's tank and delivered a fiery speech of defiance heard (and seen on television) around the world. He was followed by Colonel General Kobets, a pillar of strength and fortitude throughout the coup, who rallied Russian troops to the side of their legitimate government.[134] The Russian people responded to this courageous and unflinching gesture; "the people came to life (*narod ozhil*)," in the words of journalist Mikhail Sokolov.[135]

...

Because the GKChP was taking measured steps to establish its legitimacy—Vice President Yanaev was claiming to be the legitimate replacement for the allegedly stricken Gorbachev—it was essential that Yeltsin and his followers declare their own legitimacy and then get this information out to Russia, to the other republics, and to the world. In light of the information blockade organized by the putschists, this was to be no simple task. Nevertheless, on the morning of the nineteenth, Yeltsin, RSFSR prime minister Ivan Silaev, and Ruslan Khasbulatov, acting head of the Russian parliament, issued their ringing appeal "To the Citizens of Russia."

"On the night of August 18–19," the appeal began, "the legally elected President of the country was removed from power. Whatever reasons are used to justify his removal, we have to do with a right-wing, reactionary, anti-constitutional coup d'état."[137] If the GKChP was unlawful and unconstitutional, the Russian government, by contrast, was fully legitimate—Yeltsin having been elected president in a popular vote in June—and it was therefore incumbent upon all citizens of the republic to side with it. "We are certain," Yeltsin, Silaev, and Khasbulatov wrote, "that the organs of local authority [i.e., the local soviets] will unswervingly follow the constitutional Laws and Decrees of the President of the RSFSR. ... [W]e appeal to the military forces to manifest civic awareness and not to take part in this reactionary coup. Until these demands are carried out, we call for a general, permanent strike. We have no doubts that the world community will give an objective evaluation to this cynical attempt at a right-wing coup."

By firmly setting up a counterlegitimacy to the shaky claims of the GKChP, Yeltsin and this team began to put pressure on regional soviets, the military, and on the world community to make a choice. This appeal and subsequent appeals and decrees soon found their way into the hands of the military personnel moving into Moscow and, via modern communications, they were also flashed throughout Russia and to the West.

An especially bold move of Yeltsin's was to assume full command of all military and police forces located on Russian soil. Vadim Bakatin, a member of Gorbachev's National Security Committee (and also a person featured on the KGB arrest list), was at the "White House" early Monday morning. He has reported that Yeltsin was initially reluctant to issue such a command to the military and police because "he feared that such an order would split the army and perhaps start a bloody civil war." Bakatin and others present, however, "convinced Yeltsin that if no one exercising constitutional authority was willing to countermand orders from the junta, then the army might eventually, if reluctantly, consent to invade the White House and arrest them all, and the coup would succeed."[138] After this moment of uncharacteristic hesitation, Yeltsin never again wavered during the tense three days of the coup.

In his decree to the employees of the organs of the procuracy, of state security, of the interior ministries of both the USSR and RSFSR, and to all military forces "recognizing their responsibility for the fate of their people and of the state," Yeltsin asked for their support "on the basis of the Constitution and of the laws of the USSR and RSFSR." "As the President of Russia," he added, "and in the name of the people who elected me, I guarantee you both legal defense and moral support. The fate of Russia and of the Union is in your hands."[139] Note that Yeltsin was speaking here in the name of USSR as well as of Russian legitimacy—such a tack was intended to appeal to the "Soviet patriotism" characterizing many military and police officers.

As has already been mentioned, the strategy of Yeltsin and his team throughout the coup was—attack, attack, and attack; divide and rule. Although they must have suspected that they were on a KGB arrest list, Vice President Aleksandr Rutskoi, Silaev, and Khasbulatov left the "White House" for a meeting with Anatolii Luk'yanov in his office in the Kremlin at 10 A.M. on the twentieth. The purpose of this visit was to put pressure on Luk'yanov and other plotters; a letter from Yeltsin demanded that Luk'yanov within twenty-four hours organize a meeting of Yeltsin, Silaev, and Khasbulatov with Gorbachev; the letter insisted that Yanaev be present as well. It was also demanded that within three days a medical examination of Gorbachev be conducted, with the participation of specialists from the World Health Organization. Snidely, the RSFSR government pledged to cover the "hard currency expenses" involved in transporting the WHO doctors to Gorbachev's bed.[140]

Pressure was also put on Patriarch Aleksii of the Russian Orthodox Church to issue a statement in support of the Russian government. At considerable personal risk, Vice President Rutskoi traveled to the patriarch's residence on the morning of the nineteenth to hand-deliver Yeltsin's appeal to the patriarch. Rutskoi was told that the patriarch was ill and could not see him. The following day, however, the patriarch did issue a statement in support of Gorbachev, which objectively served to help Yeltsin's cause. The patriarch also appealed to the Soviet armed forces to remain calm and "not to permit fraternal blood to be shed."[141]

The marshaling of support abroad was, as has been mentioned, a key goal of Yeltsin and his followers. At 11:00 A.M. on the nineteenth, the RSFSR foreign minister, Andrei Kozyrev, and other officials held a briefing at the "White House" for foreign ambassadors and the foreign press. After this briefing, Kozyrev has recalled, "the Western embassies in effect began to work for us. Through them, we received and passed on information."[142]

Acting on orders from Yeltsin, Kozyrev also hand-delivered a letter from the Russian president addressed to President Bush, which was personally picked up by the U.S. deputy chief of mission in Moscow and immediately cabled to Washington, whence it was relayed to *Air Force One*, where Bush happened to be in flight. Immediately, President Bush and his national security adviser, Brent

Scowcroft, began to retreat from their earlier ambivalent utterances concerning the coup. In his next public statement, Bush flatly declared that he considered the coup "unconstitutional." The following morning, Tuesday, Bush called Yeltsin at the "White House" and assured him of his support.[143]

Also on the twentieth, in an act of impressive bravery, Kozyrev drove out to Sheremet'evo Airport and purchased a ticket on the first flight out to the West—to Paris. "I went through [passport control]," he has recalled, "together with the other passengers and tried to lose myself in the crowd. ... Probably the border guards did not have my name in their computers. My appearance in Paris produced a stunning effect upon the French."[144] Kozyrev's mission was to fly on to New York from Paris and to present the Yeltsin government's case to the UN. In a worst-case scenario, he was empowered to form a Russian government-in-exile.

... How did the Russian "White House" manage to survive the first night of the coup? Why was it not stormed by special units of the KGB, MVD, and military? According to the Russian Procuracy, it was not assaulted because no order to do so was given (or, alternatively, an order to storm the building was later rescinded). This version could well be true for the first night of the coup, but, as we shall see, there are other possible explanations as well.

...

The assault on the "White House" on the nineteenth may not have occurred because, as the Russian Procuracy has argued, no order to attack was given, or because group "A" and other key units refused to participate in the carnage. Or there may have been yet another reason.

Late on the evening of the nineteenth, several military units located in the vicinity of the "White House" began apparently coming over to the side of the Russian government. At 10:40 P.M., ten tanks under Major Evdokimov of the Tamanskaya Division came over to Yeltsin's side, to the great jubilation of the defenders of the parliament building. The symbolic effect of this defection was enormous, but the military significance, negligible, because the tanks did not have any shells.

At 11:00 P.M., an event of considerably greater significance occurred; a paratroop battalion based in Ryazan' took up a defensive position around the "White House." This force, under the overall command of Major General Aleksandr Lebed', was expanded by twenty-two armored transport vehicles, five trucks, and a field kitchen. Journalist Aleksandr Pogonchenkov may well be right in arguing that the possible defection of this battle-tested battalion to Yeltsin's side late on the nineteenth caused the coup plotters to delay storming the "White House" for a critical twenty-four hours.[261] The prospect of an all-out shooting war in the center of Moscow presumably did not appeal to the plotters.

Joining General Lebed's troops in the deployment around the "White House" was another unnamed unit of paratroopers who had arrived in trucks and who were armed with grenade launchers and automatic weapons.[262] This unit was subsequently identified as a KGB special force under the command of Major General Gusha. On the following night, this unit reportedly refused to participate in the storming of the "White House."[263]

Had these units arrived to storm the "White House" or to protect it? Or perhaps to accomplish a third purpose? In an interview with the pro-democracy Interfax News Service, Lieutenant General Podkolozin of the paratroops stated: "[T]he paratroops are neither against the Russian government nor against the provisional government [i.e., the GKChP]. ... Our task is not to permit disorder, chaos, or hooliganism."[264]

In retrospect, we can see that neither the coup plotters nor the Russian government were certain of the loyalty of these troops that had surrounded and sealed off the "White House." The Russian prime minister, Ivan Silaev, came out of the building and inspected the troops, expressing himself "satisfied" with the way in which they had been deployed.[265] But when asked by a journalist whether these troops had in fact come over to the side of the Russian government, General Kobets, chief of the defenses of the "White House," responded: "I would not draw that conclusion."[266]

There is a prehistory to the mysterious arrival of Major General Lebed's paratroops at the "White House." According to Ulysse Gosset and Vladimir Fedorovski in their book on the coup, Boris Yeltsin called General Grachev, Lebed's commanding officer, shortly after 7:00 A.M. on the nineteenth and directly asked Grachev what he planned to do in case of an order to attack. Grachev, Gosset and Fedorovski reported, "answered him that he would not attack the Russian parliament and promised to send a detachment of paratroops to assure the protection of the White House, headed by one of his deputies, Major General Lebed."[267] Grachev has confirmed that this telephone conversation took place, although he has placed its time at 6:30 A.M.[268]

The paratroops that had been promised to Yeltsin by Grachev arrived sixteen hours late but, perhaps, in the nick of time. Defense Minister Yazov appears to have considered the loyalties of these troops to be problematic. At 7:30 the following morning, he ordered them withdrawn "because he considered the troops unreliable."[269] As for General Kobets, he came to view the troops' unexpected appearance as a marvelous gift. "A battalion of paratroops at the foot of the White House," he enthused, "that was a gift of fate upon which we were not counting."[270]

THE RIDDLE OF NIGHT TWO OF THE PUTSCH

By the morning of August 20, it had presumably become clear to the coup leaders that they had no more than twenty-four hours in which to seize the "White House." If they failed to take it on the night of August 20–21, then the putsch would likely unravel, and their own fates would become highly problematic.

...

General Grachev, the commander of USSR paratroops, has given the following account of the meeting at the Defense Ministry:

On August 20, between 2:00 and 3:00 P.M., a meeting took place in the office of Deputy Defense Minister Achalov. ... Generals Varennikov, Kalinin, Karpukhin, and many civilians whom I did not now know were present. The situation was tense. ... They said: "The Russian government has come out against the GKChP, and negotiations with it have led to nothing. ..." The task was posed to surround the parliament building. I was told to place my paratroops in the area of the American embassy. The MVD was to be placed on Kutuzovskii Avenue, and the "Alpha" special unit, on the embankment. The plan was the following: the MVD would push the people back from around the parliament, and "Alpha" would enter in and storm the building.[273]

...

The available evidence suggests strongly that an attack was in fact launched on the "White House," and at approximately 1:00 A.M. on the twenty-first. It was at that time, it will be recalled, that tanks and armored vehicles began to attempt to break through the barricades that had been erected to defend the various approaches to the parliament building, and it was then that the three young defenders, Usov, Komar', and Krichevskii, were killed. According to a report by correspondents of the Russian Information Agency, who were on the spot, "the first attack on the 'White House' was repulsed." And the report went on: "The military armored vehicles, unable to overcome the barricades constructed out of overturned trolleys, moved back to Novyi Arbat."[287]

This represented, however, only the first wave of a deadly assault. When General Kobets, in charge of the defense of the parliament building, was asked by *Moscow News* what the "most difficult moments" during the coup had been, he replied:

[On August twenty-first] at 2:00 A.M. Precisely then it became clear that a vanguard detachment of the 103d [or Vitebsk] KGB paratroop division had begun its movement along the Novyi Arbat with the goal of seizing the "White House." Simultaneously, three helicopters were prepared for landing paratroopers [on the building's roof]. A ground attack was being prepared from the Mir Hotel.

If the vanguard detachment had succeeded in moving as was required by its orders ... then it would have been all over for us. But it was unable to. We succeeded in stopping them with barricades in whose construction Mikhail Malei, the Russian deputy prime minister, played an enormous role.

And the Helicopters?

There [Kobets went on] one must perhaps say thank you to [Fr.] Gleb Yakunin. Precisely at that time a drenching rain came down, and visibility became so poor that they were unable to storm the building from the air. ...[288]

...

What if the assault force had successfully taken the "White House"? What would have been the fate of the building's defenders? KGB documents show that all surviving defenders would have been arrested. There was also apparently an execution list. General Kobets has stated that his name stood sixth on that list.[298] (He has also noted that Marshal Yazov threatened to imprison his family.) Boris Yeltsin was, if at all possible, to have been captured alive.[299] A special plane with the number 762612 on its side was waiting to whisk him away to a secret location. Later on, he and the surviving democratic leaders would apparently have been brought to trial, presumably on a charge of treason. According to one source, after the original 70 persons on the KGB arrest list had been detained, another 7,000 persons—including hundreds of journalists—were to have been interned.[300] ...

...

THE RIDDLE OF FOROS: PART II

The coup effectively ended where, in a sense, it had begun—at Gorbachev's luxurious summer house in Foros. At 2:18 P.M. on the twenty-first, a plane carrying GKChP leaders Kryuchkov, Yazov, Baklanov, Tizyakov, and Luk'yanov, plus Vladimir Ivashko, deputy chairman of the USSR Communist party, left Moscow for Foros on Gorbachev's presidential jumbo jet, departing only minutes before fifty Russian MVD officers arrived to seize them.[316] Two and a half hours later another plane, carrying Russian vice president Rutskoi and prime minister Silaev and USSR National Security Council members Vadim Bakatin and Evgenii Primakov, took off in chase.

One is justified in wondering why the plotters elected to return to a president whose communications they had supposedly cut off and who had been isolated by KGB forces (if indeed his communications had been cut and he had in fact been isolated). In their book on the attempted putsch, Gosset and Fedorovski have asked why the GKChP leaders did not fly instead to a "friendly" country—to Libya, North Korea, Cuba, or Iraq. "Why not," they have written, "request political exile in a 'people's democracy'? Why go and ask for an audience with the 'tsar' [Gorbachev]?"[317] Perhaps, they speculated, the plotters believed that they could still set Gorbachev against Yeltsin "playing on the menace of Yeltsin as all-powerful, anticommunist, and imperial."

In a post-coup interview with Gorbachev, Yurii Shchekochikhin asked the Soviet president about this curious development:

SHCHEKOCHIKHIN: Even now I don't understand why they flew to Foros.
GORBACHEV: The second time?
SHEKOCHIKHIN: Yes, when everything was clear. Why? To fall down at your feet? Or what? I don't see the logic in their action.
GORBACHEV: I don't either.[318]

Boris Yeltsin, for his part, has interpreted the putschists' arrival in Foros as the result of a "chess game" that he played and won against the "main ideologist and organizer" of the coup, Kryuchkov.[319] His task, Yeltsin recalled, was to get the GKChP leaders out of the well-defended Kremlin where they were ensconced. So he "negotiated" with Kryuchkov, insisting upon written proof that Gorbachev was actually incapacitated, and arguing that the coup leaders should fly to Foros to obtain it. Kryuchkov and Yazov, Yeltsin reported, fell for this ploy, went to Foros, and were arrested by Russian government loyalists.

Yeltsin's explanation seems far too facile. Why should the five GKChP leaders have set off on a mission that one of them could easily have performed? It appears clear that the coup leaders went to Foros because they urgently wanted to talk to Gorbachev. According to Gorbachev's version, however, he firmly refused to meet with them. In his book, *The August Coup,* he has written:

> [A]round five o'clock on the evening of 21 August there in the south I was informed that a group of plotters had arrived in the Crimea in the presidential aircraft. ... When the plotters turned up at the dacha I gave orders that they should be arrested, and I issued my demand that I would not speak to any of them until the government line was reconnected. ... The operator told me that Kryuchkov ... wanted to talk to me. I replied: Let him wait. Then I immediately called Boris Yeltsin [and other republican presidents].

Gorbachev's account continued:

> I was informed that Ivashko and Luk'yanov were begging insistently to be received: they asserted that they were not involved with the plotters. I received them later [in the presence of Bakatin and Primakov] ... the others—Kryuchkov, Baklanov, and Yazov—I did not receive. I did not even set eyes on them. We split up in different aircraft and took them to Moscow where Yazov and Kryuchkov were arrested as they left the aircraft.[320]

If the coup leaders were in fact "arrested" by Gorbachev's loyal guards when they arrived at Foros, why, one wonders, did they have to be taken a second time when they arrived in Moscow? Is Gorbachev to be believed when he asserts that he did not meet with the GKChP figures during the two and a half hours they sat around waiting for Rutskoi and Silaev to arrive? It should also be remembered that for much of this period Kryuchkov apparently intended to have Rutskoi's plane diverted to distant Simferopol' or destroyed.

The book on the attempted putsch written by Russian procurators Stepankov and Lisov sheds valuable light on what transpired at Bel'bek Airport and in Foros on the twenty-first. When Yeltsin learned that the plotters had successfully taken off for the Crimea, the authors write, the Russian president contacted General Shaposhnikov, the commander of the Soviet air force, who had firmly sided with the Russian government, and asked if there were any way of stopping the plane. Shaposhnikov replied that the only way to stop it was to shoot it down. Yeltsin rejected that solution as "unacceptable." Shaposhnikov, Stepankov and Lisov continue, then contacted General Moiseev, the army chief of staff, and asked him to give permission to have the plane diverted to another airfield; Moiseev refused, arguing that it was unacceptable to divert a plane belonging to the president of the USSR.[321]

The plane carrying the GKChP leaders, Stepankov and Lisov report, arrived at Bel'bek Airport at 4:08 P.M., where its party was given a respectful reception. By this time, the airport authorities and the KGB were aware that Rutskoi's plane was also on its way. According to the testimony of Senior Lieutenant Andrei Pulin, "The flight of that plane, it was explained to us, was not sanctioned, and if the people on the plane refused to surrender, then we were to destroy it." KGB *spetsnaz* forces were positioned in the bushes around the airport. At 6:30 P.M., the airport's runways were blocked with heavy vehicles.

Shortly thereafter, Stepankov and Lisov note, Rutskoi's plane was spotted in the air and informed by radio that it could not land at Bel'bek but must divert to Simferopol'. One can well imagine how the intrepid Rutskoi, who had been decorated for bravery in combat, responded to such an ultimatum. The situation appeared to have reached the brink of bloodshed.

At this critical point, Stepankov and Lisov note, Gorbachev's communications were suddenly restored. (According to the CNN book on the putsch, they were restored at precisely 6:38 P.M.[322]) The Soviet president then immediately entered into contact with Rutskoi's plane and asked what the problem was. He was told that the runaway at Bel'bek Airport had been blockaded and that the plane was unable to land. Gorbachev then contacted army chief of staff Moiseev and ordered that the runway be cleared. This was accomplished with maximum speed. At 7:16 P.M., Rutskoi's plane touched down. By this time, the authors add, the KGB *spetsnaz* troops had speedily and as silently as possible vanished from the bushes around the airfield.

Did, one is prompted to ask, Gorbachev finally "crack" when faced with the prospect of the destruction of Rutskoi's plane and the death of a number of high-ranking Soviet and Russian officials, two of whom—Primakov and Bakatin—were his close associates? Does this incident represent yet another, ultimately decisive, example of the Soviet president's visceral abhorrence of bloodshed? Future historians, one suspects, will seek answers to these questions.

At 12:01 A.M. on August 22, procurators Stepankov and Lisov report, a plane carrying Rutskoi, Gorbachev, and Kryuchkov, among others, left Bel'bek for Vnukovo Airport in Moscow. The plan arrived at its destination at approximately 2:30 A.M.[323] Rutskoi, in an account that is highly sympathetic to Gorbachev, and which accepts Gorbachev's version of what transpired at Foros, has recalled that, during the flight, the Soviet president "at first did not agree to arrest Kryuchkov" and that he had "wanted to defend" army chief of staff Mikhail Moiseev.[324] Why would Gorbachev, one is prompted to ask, have resisted approving the arrest of the man, Kryuchkov, who had led the coup to remove him from power? And why had he defended General Moiseev whose activities on behalf of the coup appeared clear?[325] The events at Foros on the twenty-first remain as clothed in mystery as those on the eighteenth had been.

CONCLUSION

The preceding account has had the goal of demonstrating that the coup perpetrators were in fact serious men with ruthless intentions. The "hard" elements among their number, such as KGB chieftain Kryuchkov and Defense Minister Yazov, were prepared to do whatever was necessary to suppress opposition to their bid for power. Their political program was an unambiguous return to Andropovite order and discipline, which was to be emotively underpinned by a "war on crime" and "Soviet patriotism."

The putschists appear in retrospect to have been the victims of a string of bad luck. Yeltsin may have barely eluded a tightening net of KGB *spetsnaz* and army paratroopers on the morning of the nineteenth, which set the scene for the now-fabled defense of the Russian "White House" over the next three days. That development, one suspects, did not at first overly concern the hard-line elements among the conspirators. An elaborate plan was drawn up by Deputy Defense Minister Achalov, a former head of Soviet paratroops, to capture the parliament building, and an explicit order was given to carry out the plan. The apparent planned storming of the Russian parliament at 3 A.M. on the twentieth had to be scrubbed, perhaps because a battalion of paratroops with combat experience in Afghanistan, supported by a number of armored vehicles, had come over to Yeltsin's side, or had assumed "neutrality," four hours previously.

Bad luck also bedeviled the plotters on the pivotal night of August 20–21. Inclement weather meant that a large helicopter-transported unit needed for the scheduled storming of the "White House" did not arrive. In view of this development, "A" group and other elite KGB units apparently refused to participate in an attack. By the time the full Vitebsk KGB paratroop division had arrived in the city at about five in the morning, it was probably deemed too late to put General Achalov's plan into effect, inasmuch as dissident generals like Shaposhnikov, Grachev, Maksimov, and Admiral Chernavin were by then pressing hard for a removal of all troops from the capital. Air force commander Shaposhnikov was apparently prepared to use his planes to defend the Russian parliament. A decision to remove the troops from Moscow was formally taken at a meeting of the Collegium of the Defense Ministry, held at 8:00 A.M. on the twenty-first.

There was especially bad luck for the conspirators in the fact that the three KGB and MVD companies that did succeed in penetrating the outer defenses of the "White House" at about 3 A.M. on the twenty-first were spotted at what may have been close to the last minute by detectives from "Alex." Had these units succeeded in breaking into the building, a much different history of the coup would have had to be written.

Should we conclude, then, that the coup failed because a critical split developed within the Soviet military? This, obviously, was a major reason for the collapse of the putsch, but it should be noted that serious opposition to the coup did not appear to have crystallized within the military until the evening of the twentieth. The firm stand that Yeltsin, Rutskoi, Silaev, Khasbulatov, and their colleagues took on the morning of the nineteenth bought critical time so that the processes of disintegration within the military could begin to occur. Moreover, the courageous actions of a detachment of Moscow oblast OMON, of detectives from "Alex," of intrepid Russian journalists, of young men, women, and *afgantsy,* and all other groups that participated in the defense of the Russian parliament also served to purchase critical hours, because the barricades and other obstacles which they had erected required that an elaborate attack plan be devised by General Achalov and his colleagues to "sweep them aside."

But what if Yeltsin and his team had been successfully apprehended on the morning of the nineteenth? Would not that have spelled success for the coup? Speculation is risky, but, on the basis of the information available, one suspects that large-scale resistance to the coup would soon have broken out in the Russian Republic (as well as in Ukraine). The much feared "Romanian variant" might well therefore have erupted, something that would have required Western policymakers to contemplate the unthinkable: namely, a civil insurrection on the territory of a nuclear superpower. If the Russian "White House" had been successfully stormed, General Kobets has written, "then that would have been the beginning of a civil war."[326]

The failure of the August 1991 coup was a key political event of our century. One feels safe in predicting that Russian and Western scholars will be studying both it and its political aftermath for decades to come.

NOTES

ABOUT THE AUTHOR: **John B. Dunlop,** a senior fellow at the Hoover Institution, Stanford University, is the author of several studies on Russian nationalism and politics.

4. "Propadi ona propadom, eta svoboda! ... ," *Komsomol'skaya pravda,* 3 Sept. 1991, 4.

5. Leonid Radzikhovskii, "Sovetskii Pinochet: Vtoraya primerka," *Ogonek,* no. 41 (1991).

6. *New York Times,* 23 Aug. 1991, A8.

7. Radio Russia, 16 Sept. 1991, in *USSR Today,* 16 Sept. 1991, 801/19–23.

9. *Estoniya,* 14 Sept. 1991, 3.

11. See "Gorbachev Lost Nuclear Control, Russians Report," the *New York Times,* 23 Aug. 1992, A3, and "Did Gorbachev Control the Nuclear Button?" *Newsweek,* 31 Aug. 1992, 46–47. See also the detailed account in *Nezavisimaya gazeta,* 21 Aug. 1992, 1; according to this account, the "suitcase" was flown to Moscow on the evening of Aug. 19. The plotters themselves apparently lost control of part of the "chain of nuclear keys" on Aug. 21. On this, see General Constantin Kobets, *La Vie quotidienne à Moscou pendant le putsch* (Paris: Hachette, 1991), 257–58.

31. For the biographies of these individuals, see *Argumenty i fakty,* no. 33 (1991): 6.

32. See the *Financial Times* (London), 22 Jan. 1992 and the *Wall Street Journal,* 22 Jan. 1992.

33. See the excerpts from Stepankov and Lisov's book in *Komsomol'skaya pravda,* 29 August 1992.

34. See the interview with Ivanenko in *Ogonek,* nos. 12–13 (1992).

35. ITAR-TASS, 4 Feb. 1992, in *CIS Today,* 4 Feb. 1992, 117/15.

36. On this, see "Strana pod kolpakom. V proshlom?" *Moskovskie novosti*, no. 49 (8 December 1991): 15.

37. On this, see the *Times* (London), 5 Feb. 1992.

38. In *Moskovskie novosti*, no. 49 (1991): 15.

39. Russian Radio, 4 Feb. 1992 in *CIS Today*, 4 Feb. 1992, 117/11–12.

40. See *Komsomol'skaya pravda*, 11 Jan. 1992.

41. See *Rabochaya tribuna*, 7 Jan. 1992. For excerpts from the wiretap and surveillance reports which the KGB supplied in abundance to Gorbachev, see *Ogonek*, nos. 36–37 (September 1992).

42. Cited in the *Times* (London), 5 Feb. 1992.

43. In *Komsomol'skaya pravda*, 11 Jan. 1992.

44. ITAR-TASS, 4 Feb. 1992, in *CIS Today*, 4 Feb. 1992, 117/12–13.

45. See *Komsolol'skaya pravda*, 21 Dec. 1991, 3.

46. *Washington Post*, 15 Nov. 1991 and *Novoe vremya*, no. 45 (1991): 91–94. For Gorbachev's comments on Bush's warnings, see *Svobodnaya mysl'*, no. 13 (1992): 4.

47. Radio Free Europe/Radio Liberty, *Daily Report*, 22 Aug. 1991, 3.

48. Ulysse Gosset and Vladimir Fedorovski, *Histoire secrète d'un coup d'état* (Paris: J. C. Lattes, 1991), 234.

49. *Times* (London), 13 Nov. 1991. Vladimir Kryuchkov's defense attorney has vehemently denied that this conversation was eavesdropped upon. See *Pravda*, 12 Sept. 1992, 4. The date of July 31 for the meeting is stipulated in *Komsomol'skaya pravda*, 29 Aug. 1992, 1.

50. See *Den'*, no. 19 (September 1991): 73–74.

51. Geoffrey Hosking, *The Awakening of the Soviet Union*, 2d ed. (London: Mandarin, 1991), 139–41.

52. In *Komsomol'skaya pravda*, 10 Oct. 1991.

53. Simon Kordonskii, "Gosudarstvennyi perevorot: neudacha s posledstviyami," *Novoe vremya*, no. 36 (1991): 7.

54. "Obrashchenie k sovetskomu narodu," TASS, 19 Aug. 1991 in *USSR Today*, 19 Aug. 1991, 687/12–17. For a useful collection of the documents and statements issues by the GKChP, see *Smert' zagovora*, [*Belaya Kniga* (Moscow: "Novosti," 1992),] 5–18, 27–40.

55. Cited by Kordonskii, "Gosudarstvennyi perevorot ..."

56. TASS. 20 Aug. 1991, in *USSR Today*, 20 Aug. 1991, 694/37.

58. Russian Radio, 24 Jan. 1992, in *CIS Today*, 24 Jan. 1992, 79/43. On the subject of these draft decrees, see also the interview with chief Investigator Lisov in *Kuranty*, 17 Sept. 1992, 5.

76. Published in English translation by HarperCollins in 1991. For the Russian original, see *Avgustovskii putch (Prichiny i sledstviya)* (Moscow: "Novosti," 1991). See also Gorbachev's comments on the putsch in *Vechernyaya Moskva*, 20 Aug. 1992. 7.

77. For the interview with Raisa Gorbacheva, see *Trud*, 3 Sept. 1991. The excerpts from Chernyaev's diary appeared in *Izvestiya*, 1 Oct. 1991.

78. Moscow Radio-1, 21 Jan. 1992, in *FBIS-SOV-91–014*, 22 Jan. 1991, 33–34.

79. This point was made by Russian Procuracy investigator A.V. Frolov during hearings conducted by the Russian parliament. See *Armiya*, nos. 7–8 (1992): 31.

80. Cited in Ulysse Gosset and Vladimir Fedorovski, *Histoire secrète d'un coup d'état* (Paris: J.C. Lattes, 1991), 261.

87. In *Novyi vzglyad*, no. 48 (1991): 1 in *Russia and CIS Today*, 6 Dec. 1992, 330/30–47. See also the interview with Yanaev on this subject in *Narodnaya pravda*, no. 46 (November 1992): 7 in *Russia and CIS Today*, 3 Dec. 1992, 325/01–05.

88. In *Narodnaya pravda*, no. 40 (October 1992): 4 in *Russia and CIS Today*, 30 Oct. 1992, 248/39.

89. In *Newsweek*, 31 Aug. 1992, 38. See also *Komsomol'skaya pravda*, 28 Jan. 1993, 1 and Russian Television, 15 Feb. 1993 in *Russia and CIS Today*, 16 Feb. 1993, 0119/16–22. For interviews with other GKChP leaders, see *Novyi vzglyad*, no. 7 (1993) and no. 8 (1993); *Sovetskaya Rossiya*, 23 Feb. 1933, 1; *Smena*, 17 Feb. 1993, 1; and Ostankino Television, 15 Feb. 1993, in *Russia and CIS Today*, 16 Feb. 1993, 0119/14–15.

92. In [Mikhail Gorbachev] *The August Coup* [(New York: HarperCollins, 1991),] 23.

95. On August 26 as an end point for the coup, see *Novyi vzglyad*, no. 14 (1992): 4 and *Chernaya noch' nad Belym Domom* (Moscow: "Rossiya," 1991), 13B.

100. The KGB Directorate "Z" arrest unit was headed by Vitalii Vorotnikov and his deputy, Gennadii Dobrovol'skii. See *Novoe vremya*, no. 8 (1992). On the arrested list, see *Histoire Secrete* … , 75.

101. For the list of names, see *Argumenty i fakty*, no. 38 (1991): 8. A few names may have been omitted from the restored list; Lt. Colonel Aleksandr Kichikhin of the KGB's Department "Z" has recalled, for example, that Yeltsin adviser Galina Starovoitova's name was on the list. (*New Times*, no. 35 (1991): 14–17) Russian Procuracy investigator A.V. Frolov has stated that there were seventy-five names on the arrest list. See *Armiya*, nos. 7–8 (1992): 26.

102. See *Ogonek* no. 38 (1991): 28.

104. *Izvestiya*, 10 Sept. 1991, 2. On Tenyakov, see also TASS, 12 Dec. 1991, in *USSR Today*, 12 Dec. 1991, 1146/47.

108. In *Histoire secrete* … , 237.

109. Ibid., 119. These forms were sent to Kalinin by the KGB at 5:01 A.M. on August 19 (*Newsweek*, 31 Aug. 1992, 45).

110. Russian Radio, 23 Jan. 1992, in *CIS Today*, 23 Jan. 1992, 74/47. According to Stepankov and Lisov's book on the coup, Pavlov was informed by Kryuchkov and Yazov on August 17 that he would be removed as USSR prime minister on August 20; Pavlov is said to have offered no objections to this scenario. See *Komsomol'skaya pravda*, 29 Aug. 1992, 1.

111. In *Histoire secrete* … , 78–79.

112. For the text, see *Smert' zagovora*, 41–42. This volume contains the texts of all decrees issued by Yeltsin and the Russian government during the time of the putsch.

113. Anatoly Sobchak, *For a New Russia* (New York: The Free Press, 1992), 176–77. For Sobchak's recollections of the coup, see also *Korichnevyi putch krasnykh* (Moscow: "Tekst," 1991), 32.

114. Kobets, *La Vie quotidienne* … , 48–52.

124. *La Vie quotidienne* … , 52. On this incident, see also Mikhail Sokolov, "Slovo protiv broni," *Sobesednik*, no. 35 (1991) and Aleksandr Pogonchenkov, "Zagovor dvoechenkov," *Demokraticheskaya Rossiya*, nos. 22–23 (23 Aug.–4 Sept. 1991).

125. Radio Russia, 25 Aug. 1991 in *USSR Today*, 25 Aug. 1991, 712//15–18. Medvedev's comments originally appeared in the newspaper *Moskovskii komsomolets*.

126. Leonid Radzikhovskii, "Sovetskii Pinochet … ," *Ogonek*, no. 41 (1991).

127. *New York Times*, 25 Aug. 1991, A10.

128. *New York Times*, 22 Aug. 1991, A1.

129. Iain Elliot, "Three Days in August: On-the-Spot Impressions," *Report on the USSR*, 6 Sept. 1991, 63–67.

130. Agence France Presse dispatch, 7 Sept. 1991.

131. *Komsomol'skaya pravda*, 27 Aug. 1991, 3.

132. On "Plan X," see *La Vie quotidienne* ... , 61, 92, 150–51.

133. Central Television, 22 Aug. 1991 in *USSR Today*, 21 Aug. 1991, 700/25–30.

134. From the *Los Angeles Times*, 4 Oct. 1991.

135. Mikhail Sokolov, "Slovo protiv broni."

137. In *Rossiya*, emergency edition, 19 Aug. 1991.

138. *Time*, 2 Sept. 1991, 36 and 38.

139. In *USSR Today*, special edition, 26 Aug. 1991, 713/05.

140. Ibid., 713/29.

141. On this episode, see Oxana Antic, "Church Reaction to the Coup," in *Report on the USSR*, 29 Sept. 1991, 15–17, and Vladimir Moss, "The Free Russian Orthodox Church," in *Report on the USSR*, 1 Nov. 1991, 8–12.

142. In *Demokraticheskaya Rossiya*, nos. 22–23, 23 Aug.–4 Sept. 1991.

143. *Time*, 2 Sept. 1991, 48. For a detailed account of the Bush administration's response to the attempted coup, see Michael R. Beschloss and Strobe Talbott, *At the Highest Levels* (Boston: Little, Brown, 1993), chapter 21.

144. In *Demokratichaya Rossiya*, nos. 22–23 (1991).

261. *Demokraticheskya Rossiya*, nos. 22–23 (August 23–September 4, 1991).

262. *Korichnevyi putch* ... , 75.

263. See *Komsomol'skaya pravda*, 21 Dec. 1991, 3.

264. In *Korichnevyi putch* ..., 75.

265. Ibid.

266. Ibid.

267. *Histoire secrète* ..., 85.

268. *Izvestiya*, 4 Sept. 1991, 8.

269. [Stuart H. Loory and Ann Imse, eds.,] *Seven Days* [*That Shook the World* (Atlanta, Turner Publishing, 1991),] 106.

270. In *La Vie quotidienne* ... , 161. For the views of Kobets on this key episode, see also *La Vie*, 127–32.

273. *Izvestiya*, 4 Sept. 1991, 8. See also Grachev's comments cited in *Seven Days* ... , 125.

287. In *Putch* [(Moscow: "Progress," 1991),] 138.

288. In *Moskovskie novosti*, 1 Sept. 1991, 4.

298. In *Moskovskie novosti*, no. 35 (September 1, 1991): 4. Former USSR congressman Sergei Belozertsev revealed during Russian parliamentary hearings that General Varennikov had sent a coded telegram from Kiev to his fellow conspirators in which he demanded that "the group of the adventurist Yeltsin be destroyed as a prophylactic measure." (In *Armiya*, nos. 7–8 [1992]: 32.)

299. Ibid.

300. In Mikhail Sokolov, "Slovo protiv broni."

316. In *Putch*, 179–80, and *Seven Days* ... , 145.

317. *Histoire secrète* ... , 168.

318. In *Literaturnaya gazeta*, no. 48 (1991).

319. In the *Los Angeles Times*, 22 Aug. 1992, A6.

320. *The August Coup*, 36–37.

321. In *Ogonek*, nos. 36–37 (September 1992). Russian Procuracy investigator Frolov has provided an inaccurate and sanitized version of what happened at Bel'bek Airport. He has been criticized for so doing by former USSR congressman Sergei Belozertsev. (See *Armiya*, nos. 7–8 [1992]: 27 and 33.)

322. *Seven Days That Shook the World,* 149.

323. In *Histoire secrète* ... , 188–90.

324. Central Television, 24 Aug. 1991, in *USSR Today,* 25 Aug. 1991, 712/34.

325. It has been claimed by some Russian journalists that the pressure for an assault on the "White House" increased significantly once Moiseev had assumed overall command of the operation on the twentieth. Boris Yeltsin has indicated that he believes that Moiseev bore the chief responsibility for the planned storming of the Russian parliament. (Central Television and Russian Television, 25 Aug. 1991, in *USSR Today,* 25 Aug. 1991, 712/01–07.)

326. *La Vie quotidienne* ... , 218.

52　*The Coup Revisited*

GAVRIIL POPOV

[I.] "USING A VICTORY WELL IS MORE IMPORTANT THAN WINNING."— Plutarch. *Selected Lives,* vol. 2, p. 193.— ... In a political sense, the range of assessments of both the coup and the way events developed after it is exceptionally broad. In one view, it was "a great revolution equal in significance to October 1917." In another, it was "a revolution of missed opportunities." According to a third view, it was "a revolution betrayed." And according to a fourth, "there was no revolution at all."

My overall assessment is that the democrats' victory over the coup plotters did not bring to power the democrats, who were totally unprepared to be in that position, but finally forced the reformist apparatchiks and nomenklatura to do what they had done in 1985, 1989 or 1990—to organize themselves, unite, cleanse themselves of ideological garbage, remove the conservatives and start making reforms. To start slowly, but to start.

A Clash Involving Force Became Inevitable

... I am inclined to think that, for the most part the organizers of the coup were people faithful to an idea, loyal servants of the pyramid that had raised them to great heights. They were thinking about the interests of the country—according to their own, communist understanding. ...

The country was falling apart. Either there had to be a break with the center and each republic had to follow its own path, or the center had to strengthen its authority and try to do something itself. A clash became inevitable. Both the democrats and the conservatives realized this. The conservatives decided to anticipate events, and they acted first.

In a recent interview, Mikhail Sergeyevich [Gorbachev] said again that a normal process was under way that was interrupted by the coup. Over the course of six years Mikhail Sergeyevich tried to convince us dozens of times that a normal process was under way. But in actuality the noose was tightening. Therefore, the signing of the Union Treaty that was coming up on Aug. 20, 1991, was only a new stage in the process of tightening the knot. Or else Gorbachev intended to finally begin destroying the center and its backbone—the CPSU structure—after the treaty was signed, or was prepared to give the republics the opportunity to do this. Possibly. But judging from his speeches during the first hours after he returned to Moscow and from his actions, he wasn't ready to do such things. Consequently, there was no foreseeable prospect of anything "normal" appearing. So one can agree with the coup plotters on one thing: The "process" required radical, surgical intervention.

Therefore, the coup was not something unexpected. The coup plotters had previously had a chance to stage a legal coup in favor of the center—when Pavlov demanded extraordinary powers five days after Yeltsin was elected President of Russia, when Yeltsin was in the US. I was among those who contributed to the collapse of that plan. I will talk about this … sometime. The question of extraordinary powers was dropped at the time.

The conservatives realized that we [the democrats] would give battle in the fall—because, like them, we couldn't wait any longer either. The people were demanding reforms from us, and we would have had to begin them by taking away the center's right to interfere in Russia's affairs. The conservatives tried to forestall us.

In light of what I have said, I have my own attitude toward the idea of putting the State Committee for the State of Emergency on trial. The CPSU, yes. But as for the SCSE, that's debatable. The SCSE was a violation of legality, of course. But we, too, would have had to violate legality (as happened, incidentally, in the dissolution of the USSR). Great turning points cannot be judged by the articles of former laws, since they involve a changeover to a system of new laws. The SCSE can be tried as part of the trial of the CPSU. But the CPSU trial itself—like the trial of National Socialism in Nuremberg in its time—requires the adoption of a special status for the court, special norms, etc., not appeals to the laws of the socialist state. The present "legal" approach will most likely lead us down a blind alley.

The Success of the Democratic President

Only the leaders of the republics could act against the SCSE. And Boris Yeltsin became the key figure. In the hour of trial he proved—as an individual, a citizen and a leader—that millions of voters had not made a mistake in voting for him.

In Russia the importance of the top man is immeasurably higher than his formal functions would indicate, and than that of his counterparts in other countries. The fact that there was a legitimate President in Russia, that his orders had to be obeyed and that opposition to the SCSE was not a rebellion but only compliance with the instructions of the Russian President enabled thousands of administors who were against the SCSE in their hearts but felt very uncomfortable in the role of "resisters" to "rest assured." The orientation toward the will of the authorities that had been fostered during the era of totalitarianism now worked against the coup.

Did the SCSE members know the significance of this factor?

Yes. Without a doubt. ...

[But] they clearly underestimated the special significance to Russia of the emergence of an official center of resistance as a mobilizing and consolidating principle.

Furthermore, they believed that Yeltsin's personal resentment against Gorbachev (for which there were more than ample grounds; they knew what had been done against Yeltsin with Gorbachev's consent or without his opposition) was so great that Yeltsin would rejoice over the fall of "the enemy." The fact that Yeltsin would turn out to be a relentlessly clear-headed politician capable of suppressing his emotions and oriented toward political goals came as a surprise to them. ... In the hour of trial, Yeltsin did not allow personal resentments to overshadow the interests of the cause. ...

The leaders of the other republics were an important consideration. Former or current leaders of the Central Committees of the republic Communist Parties, they yielded, for the most part, to the persuasion of the SCSE members. Evidently the latter promised to give the other republics—not Russia—more than Gorbachev promised them. But the destruction of the chief republic leader would have meant that the SCSE had the right—just as in the good old days—to change the leadership in the republics. Neither Kravchuk nor Nazarbayev could consent to that. And it is not impossible that Yeltsin's freedom was a condition for their reacting calmly to the SCSE: Changes in your own circle, in the center, are one thing. But you can't touch the leaders of the republics. If Russia is treated that way, what can the others expect?

But it seems to me that the most important thing was the following. I call it the Beria syndrome. Some member of the SCSE would have personally had to give the order to destroy Yeltsin. The person who gave such an order, or even failed to prevent it, would have been doomed. He—like Beria in his time—would have been made the scapegoat for all the blood that this option would have involved (and it would have been the blood of thousands of people). ... All the members of the SCSE realized this. It is symptomatic that each of them demanded that the others issue an order concerning Yeltsin, but no one wanted to issue it himself. There were no kamikazes to be found among the SCSE members, even for the sake of the Communists' cause.

This unwillingness was immediately conveyed to the second echelon of leaders, especially in the Army and the State Security Committee [KGB], who then had even less desire to be responsible for an attack and, moreover, seeing the hesitation of the SCSE leaders, began to seek an agreement with Yeltsin.

As a result, Yeltsin remained free and immediately began to act. He chose the following tactic. ...

As his first and chief demand, Boris Nikolayevich called for the restoration of power to the legitimate President. He did precisely what the SCSE least expected. Why would Yeltsin fight for Gorbachev's return? After all, anyone taking Gorbachev's place would certainly be a weaker opponent for Yeltsin. Wouldn't it be better for him to face someone like Lukyanov in the ring and untie his hands for a fight and a victory?

But the removal of Gorbachev was the SCSE's weakest spot, and that is precisely where Yeltsin struck. In so doing, he immediately gained several advantages.

First of all, he knocked the Gorbachev card out of the SCSE's hand. People had doubts: Was the SCSE really against Gorbachev, or was there some sort of plot between them? By demanding Mikhail Sergeyevich's return, Yeltsin immediately, on the one hand, deprived the SCSE of the possibility of reaching an agreement with Gorbachev, and, on the other hand, put Gorbachev himself in a position in which an agreement with the SCSE would have been a betrayal of a Russia that had remained loyal to him. If the SCSE didn't return Gorbachev, that would mean the SCSE was against the Constitution. If it did return him, that would be a point for Yeltsin and a failure for the SCSE. On the whole, the return of Gorbachev became the symbol for the SCSE's failure.

In sticking up for Gorbachev, Yeltsin immediately turned all the West's sympathy toward himself. Now everyone in the West who cared about Gorbachev would have to help Yeltsin.

And finally, Gorbachev's own supporters in the USSR, who at first tried to wait (Primakov, Volsky and others), sooner or later had to show solidarity with Yeltsin. ...

Now to address Yeltsin's strategy. It was to use the coup to turn the SCSE leaders into violators of legality and destroy the CPSU elite.

And, along with the elite, to destroy the structure of the CPSU. ...

And to seize from the CPSU control of the Army, state security, the Ministry of Internal Affairs and the press, and to eliminate the very foundation of totalitarianism.

In sum, to destroy the very center that had proven to be the chief obstacle to reforms.

Behind these strategic objectives, one overriding objective arose—how to govern Russia afterwards.

The chief thing for which Yeltsin deserves credit as a politician is that he completely rejected the idea of turning the victory over the SCSE into an all-out purge of the previous system, into a Leninist-type revolution.

It is to Boris Yeltsin's credit that the storming of the Central Committee buildings in Moscow, unlike the storming of the Winter Palace in Petrograd, did not become the beginning of a wave of riots and anarchy throughout Russia. I can say now that after Aug. 22, groups of democrats from various cities poured into Moscow. There had been no sound out of them during the days of the coup, but now they were bursting to prove their readiness to fight for democracy. There was an influx of groups of curiosity-seekers and outright bandits who expected that there would be something to make a profit off. A crowd of informers besieged the KGB in a fierce effort to be the first to break into the building and burn all traces of the deeds they had done over many years. Without the support of the Russian President, I, as mayor, would never have been able to avert the masses' "revolutionary" wrath.

That the victory over the bureaucratic center did not touch off interethnic slaughter and did not turn the USSR into a Yugoslavia is also to the credit of the Russian President.

Whereas the CPSU leadership deserves the "credit" for the fact that a clash involving force became inevitable, it is to the credit of the first President democratically elected by the people of Russia that—in contrast to 1917—this clash involving force was not the beginning of riots, anarchy and rebellion. The President preserved Russia and opened the way to the possibility of peaceful transformations. That is his contribution to Russia's experience.

And he achieved all these successes alone—he advanced the idea of transferring power from the CPSU to a coalition of democrats and reformist apparatchiks. ...

In the coup situation, why didn't Yeltsin follow Lenin's path? There is nothing accidental about this. Yeltsin's course of making an alliance with part of the overthrown apparatus was the result of many factors.

Boris Yeltsin had left the ranks of CPSU leaders. Like many of us, he had started out with confidence that working actively and honestly within the CPSU system was the main way to improve the situation of the people and the state. Later, after seeing the ineffectiveness of his efforts, he called for a reform of the CPSU. Finally he broke with the CPSU over the reluctance of its leadership and the apparatus that controlled the Party to embark on any kind of significant reforms.

But, after breaking with the CPSU, Yeltsin could see very well how many reformers there were among the apparatchiks. They expressed both overt and, especially, covert support for him. They did not have his inherent courage to break with the CPSU, but in everything else they were very close to him. ... Unlike the leaders of the 1917 Russian Revolution, who personally were totally alien to the class that had ruled Russia before them, Yeltsin could view the reform-minded part of the Party apparatus and other apparatuses of the USSR as a potential reserve . ...

On the other hand, Yeltsin succeeded in arranging his cooperation with the democratic forces in such a way that he could be both declared and elected leader without binding himself by any formal commitments to democratic organizations. He did not commit himself to propose and to secure the approval of personnel or draft laws in any democratic structures. ...

Therefore, when I was besieged by representatives of Democratic Russia who were indignant over certain appointments or decrees, I always answered: Your complaints have no basis; Boris Nikolayevich isn't deceiving anyone. Show me his commitments! I think that Yeltsin would have refused cooperation outright if the democrats had made such demands on him. In this regard, Yeltsin confirmed once again that he is a high-class politician. ...

The democrats, rejoicing during the days after the coup, never even dreamed that the idea of a coalition with the reformist apparatchiks had also triumphed during those days. In the most critical hours, while waiting for the expected attack, I saw Yury Petrov at Yeltsin's side, standing his ground just as firmly as all the democrats. I thought, "It is during these days that the reformist apparatchiks have made their final break with the CPSU leadership and made the most important choice of their lives. Now their future will be linked with Yeltsin, and it isn't hard to foresee how actively they will begin to work beside him." ...

[Yeltsin] did not deceive the democrats: He offered them a place in the coalition and every opportunity to become the chief figures in that coalition. What's more, the President himself was prepared for this to happen. Nothing more could be demanded of him. Who would prevail in the new coalition? It seemed as though after the coup, all the circumstances gave the better chance to the democrats. But the democrats were unable to take advantage of the opportunity offered to them by the President. ...

[II.] ... COULD THE DEMOCRATS HAVE TAKEN POWER?

... [The democrats'] main mistake [was] that they imagined they had taken power in Russia after the coup. Unfortunately, the people believed this, too. ...

But the democrats were thinking only about posts. ...

The idea had become firmly rooted in the minds of the people, the CPSU and its leaders that obtaining power meant obtaining an appointment to a post.

It wasn't even realized that power is a complex mechanism that binds together in tightly knit interaction the rank-and-file functionary who fills out the most trivial form at the borough building-maintenance office, the journalist at a newspaper, the door guard at a ministry, the sales clerk in a state store, old-age pensioners living on state pensions and assistance from sons who are officers in the service of the state, and hundreds of instructions and laws that are comprehensible only to a bureaucrat. The democrats didn't even have a concept of what "taking power" means. ...

If we are going to talk seriously about power, then, besides the problem of taking control of its entire mechanism, there was also the problem of what the democrats actually were before and after the coup. ...

When the coup occurred, the democrats were split by numerous schisms and were characterized by organizational weakness within individual blocs and the movement as a whole. Organizationally, the democrats were not ready to take power.

Added to the organizational weakness was weakness in terms of programs. After all, for a long time we had acted on the assumption that we would be only an opposition. We waited for various government actions and then saw it as our role to form a democratic attitude toward them.

In all the main areas—nationalities policy, the state system, privatization, structural reorganization of the economy, micro-economic policy, agrarian reform, a social program for the USSR, foreign relations—we lacked concrete programs in versions that were suitable for practical application. We had documents on objectives—for an opposition, that was sufficient.

The actual programs—the 500 Days, the law on privatization, etc.—were not programs developed by the democrats but programs developed by reformist apparatchiks, drawn up with a view toward democratic approaches and ideas.

Yeltsin was reproached for the fact that for an entire month after the coup there was no new program from the Russian government, but what could he do if the movement as a whole, though it possessed the country's best minds, had not come up with a program that could become the starting point for the development of a government plan? ...

Even then—though not as clearly as now—I saw in general outlines that we had not taken any sort of power, that we had only entered a coalition, but that we would not be able to be the leaders in it, either. ...

But I ... did not find within myself the strength and resolve to draw all the conclusions stemming from that assessment.

I should have exerted every effort to ensure that, together with the sessions of the Russian and USSR Supreme Soviets, a Forum of Democratic Forces—both of Russia and of the USSR—immediately went into operation as a factor for putting pressure on the authorities.

I should have assisted in organizing a new movement on the basis of Democratic Russia—not a conglomeration of opponents of the CPSU but a movement of forces that were truly democratic by nature.

I had an obligation to insist that Yeltsin agree to become President of the USSR as well as of Russia. ...

I was well enough acquainted with Gorbachev that he would have listened without bias to a suggestion from me that he hand over his post to Yeltsin on the very first day after the coup. On his own he couldn't bring himself to do this; his associates were putting pressure on him. But after all, Mikhail Sergeyevich himself had once let drop the phrase, "Should I perhaps turn everything over to Boris?" ...

I am certain that it would not have been possible to change the course of events in any fundamental way. Power was bound to be transferred to the reformist apparatchiks. But within the framework of that historically inevitable process, it would have been possible to create more conditions conducive to democratic versions of reform, if instead of the two birds in the bush we had thought about the one in our hand.

I will always be proud of the fact that during the days of the coup I tried with all my might to help overthrow the obsolete system that was threatening Russia's future. But I will never forgive myself for the fact that I could have done more but didn't—as a democrat, as an ideologist and theoretician, as a member of the Russian intelligentsia, and simply as a citizen.

III. THE NOMENKLATURA WITHOUT THE CPSU

... In contrast to the democratic movement, the apparatus acted with exceptional skill. Someday historians will write a lot of works on this subject. Here I would like to note what has already become clear during the first year since the coup.

First of all, the apparatus supported the general illusion that the democrats had taken power. This gave it many advantages. It was able to "transfer to the democrats' account" a lot of the past sins of totalitarianism. Whenever anything bad came to light, no matter what and where it was, it was immediately linked with the democrats' being in power. ...

The apparatus had to learn to live without the CPSU. Without running to the Central Committee, province committees or district committees with complaints against someone. Without its own members' being called "on the carpet" there. It needed time to figure out in practical terms how to live: without the CPSU, but still retaining power for itself.

It also needed time to restructure itself. It was necessary to ascertain which people were willing to become reformist apparatchiks; to get acquainted with each other, reach agreements and unite. Simply put, to "sniff each other out." While the democrats were arguing about posts, the apparatus was feverishly reorganizing its ranks.

The apparatus judiciously singled out a minimum that it could not let go of under any circumstances—administration and personnel. ...

Its wisest decision was whom to put in the first row of the presidium. ... It realized that to push forward now would mean to spoil everything. But unlike the democrats, the apparatus, tempered by years of service, knew how to be patient and wait.

So it proposed for the top roles people who officially had the least possible connection with the apparatus but were still its personnel. Those who had been known in the apparatus as "radicals" before all this began. There had always been such reformist apparatchiks in the apparatus. But the apparatus used to keep these intelligent and bright minds as advisers: at institutes and on editorial boards. Now they were put in the front ranks. ...

They were radical reformers, but they were still the apparatus. ...

Then the apparatus began working hard on the democrats who had filled the new posts. It wasn't difficult to prove to them quickly that they didn't have even an approximate notion of the real situation and could not get by without constantly leaning on apparatchiks from "their own" apparatus. While adorning itself with the name of some well-known democrat, the apparatus of one or another ministry or department retained real control over everything. ...

The restructuring of the apparatus, which had been postponed since 1985, proceeded quickly. But the apparatus also had to prove its ability to conduct reforms in the economy.

Here, too, it demonstrated exceptional skill. Given that it was definitely necessary to do something, and that the people thought that power was in the hands of the democrats, it was best of all to begin implementing the measures that were most painful from a social standpoint—to increase prices, reduce incomes, devalue the population's savings, and so on and so forth. And to postpone the most important matters—first and foremost, the dividing up of property—until the apparatus had established itself more firmly in power. ...

Only as its positions grew stronger did it, under pressure from the President and the democratic forces, gradually include the problems of privatization in its action program. ...

[Now] privatization options with a preponderance of apparatus viewpoints are being called a democratic approach. But there is still no agrarian reform. ...

The apparatchiks [also] used [this] time to form their own political vanguard. At first in the form of individual parties and movements. And then they united them in the Civic Alliance. ...

Behind the government's outwardly stormy debates with the Civic Alliance and various Deputies' groups made up of apparatchiks, what is really at issue is not a transfer of power from the democrats to the apparatus, as some people are trying to depict the situation. The apparatus never lost power. What is at issue right now is a redistribution of power among individual groups within the apparatus. ...

The apparatus has thoroughly "purged" its ranks in the past year: It has gotten rid of dogmatists; it has gotten rid of ignoramuses and bunglers. It has shifted the most corrupt people into the ranks of businessmen. It has renewed and rejuvenated itself.

Of course, the conservative group that has its base in the most unpromising parts of the military-industrial complex and of the agrarian sector is still very active in the ranks of the apparatus. Left without the protection of CPSU structures, it is nevertheless still very powerful. ...

In the past year the apparatus, hiding behind the smoke screen of the illusion that the democrats are in power, has succeeded in preparing itself to take into its own hands, not only in actuality but also officially, the process of transforming Russia into a postindustrial society. What's more, it is already conducting this process. ...

There is nothing tragic about the fact that, after the CPSU, power remained in the hands of the apparatus. There was no other way to begin reforms. All the other forces in society were unprepared to conduct reforms on their own. ...

IV. THE POSITION OF A DEMOCRAT

...

A year after the coup we can see that the unprecedented upsurge in the energy of the people, who themselves literally made history in August 1991, has made it possible to accomplish three historic tasks.

One. The dictatorship of the CPSU, with its suppression of the people's initiative, low work efficiency, decreasing prosperity for the masses and increasing prospect of nuclear and ecological catastrophe, a threat that grew greater with every passing year, has been eliminated. ...

Two. Russia rejected the path of a revolution involving a bloody war between the victorious and vanquished segments of society, accompanied by the danger of a new dictatorship as a reaction to the anarchy that would have been inevitable if events had developed in that way. ... Russia chose the path of reforms. This was a critically important event in Russian history, and in world history as well. Reforms have begun and have yielded their first important results.

Three. Leadership of the reforms has been concentrated in the hands of the nomenklatura and the apparatus, now cleansed of CPSU control. I think that this is a guarantee that the reforms will be implemented, since Russia has proven unready for the best thing—a democratic version of reforms. ...

If these three results—the elimination of the CPSU, the beginning of practical reforms, and the consolidation in power of an apparatus that is renewing itself—are augmented by a fourth—the creation of a new democratic opposition—then August 1991 will truly mark not only the end of the past, but the beginning of an era of Russia's transition from totalitarianism to a postindustrial society created by the apparatus under effective pressure from the democratic opposition.

Foros, August 1992

NOTES

ABOUT THE AUTHOR: **Gavriil Popov,** a prominent economist, became a leader of "Democratic Russia" and mayor of Moscow in the Gorbachev years.

53 Speech to the RSFSR Congress of People's Deputies and to the Citizens of Russia, October 28, 1991

BORIS YELTSIN

... The present time is one of the most critical moments in Russian history. It is now that the future of Russia and of the country as a whole in the years and decades to come is being decided. We must unreservedly embark on a path of thoroughgoing reforms, in which the support of all strata of the population is needed. The time has come to adopt the main decision and to begin to act. Specific measures for carrying out a package of reforms have now been worked out. The situation in Russia is difficult, but it is not hopeless. There is no reason for panic. The period of moving in small steps is over. The field for reforms has been cleared of mines. There is a unique opportunity to stabilize the economic situation over several months and to begin the process of improving that situation. Under conditions of political freedom, we must provide economic freedom, lift all barriers to the freedom of enterprises and entrepreneurship, and give people the opportunity to work and to receive as much as they can earn, casting off bureaucratic constraints. However, given the extremely acute crisis, it will not be possible to conduct the reforms painlessly.

If we embark on this path today, we will obtain real results by the autumn of 1992.

...

The most important, most decisive actions will have to be taken in the sphere of the economy. The first area is economic stabilization. It will be based on a tough monetary, financial and credit policy, a tax reform and the strengthening of the ruble. But the most painful measure will be a one-time unfreezing of prices in the current year. *orthodox econ. measure*

The second area is privatization and the creation of a healthy mixed economy with a powerful private sector. Giving greater dynamics to land reform and creating a fundamentally new situation in the agrarian sector by the spring of 1992 are of special significance for Russia.

Free prices are to be an instrument of production growth, something that will put a limit on price increases in the future. Moreover, Russia is a traditional supplier of raw-material resources to the other republics. In the present confused situation regarding prices, we are ending up in an extremely disadvantageous position—we are losing 33 billion rubles a year. To this day, prices for raw materials remain fixed, but the products that are made from our raw materials are more and more often returning to us at different prices. We are trading at a loss. A number of sovereign states that were in the former Union have already moved to free up prices, and the Russian Republic's fixed prices are superattractive to them. This has prompted a special decision to create a Russian Republic customs service, which is now being formed on the basis of the Union customs service.

A one-time changeover to market prices is a difficult and forced measure, but a necessary one. For approximately six months things will be worse for everyone, but then prices will fall, the consumer market will be filled with goods, and by the autumn of 1992 there will be economic stabilization and a gradual improvement in people's lives.

A major review of Russia's expenditures on state needs has begun. Next year's budget will provide for a significant reduction in appropriations for maintaining inefficient production facilities, for defense and for the managerial apparatus. As of Nov. 1, Russia will stop financing Union ministries and other central institutions (there are about 70 of them) whose existence is not stipulated by the Treaty on an Economic Community. The transfer of money to the Union stabilization fund is being terminated. This money will be used to stabilize Russia's economy. Aid and the issuing of credits to all countries will be completely stopped. A list of the most urgent social programs that will be open to financing has been prepared.

It is proposed that Russia's tax system be strengthened in the near future. The reorganization of the tax system is not aimed at increasing the taxes collected from citizens; the primary goal is to bring order into this sphere. Taxes will not stifle but provide an incentive to producers, entrepreneurs, and especially those who produce consumer goods. At the same time, taxes will impede economic actions in which society has no stake. The reorganization of the tax system will have to be conducted in an organized and speedy fashion, so that by the beginning of next year we will have efficient and stable mechanisms for obtaining revenues for the state budget.

The preparation of a package of measure to reform the banking system is nearing completion. The most important area here is the introduction of tough mechanisms against the uncontrolled emission of money and credits. If this is delayed any longer, hyperinflation and the collapse of the entire monetary system are inevitable. We intend in the near future to begin creating a real reserve banking system with hard currency. Two options are possible here. The first is the creation of a single interstate bank for the entire ruble zone. We are prepared to do this if the following conditions are observed. First, clear-cut and unambiguous renunciation by all the republics of attempts to introduce their own monetary units anytime in the near future. Second, parity among the republics in monitoring observance of the bank's charter. Third, conformity between the number of votes each republic has in the bank union and on the bank's board, on the one hand, and its share of the bank's capital, on the other. If an accord on these conditions is not reached in the near future, we will act in accordance with the second option—the Russian Republic State Bank will assume the emission function. If this need arises, Russia will find it possible to establish control over both cash and credit emission of the ruble. In this case, we will be prepared to introduce a new Russian Republic currency.

The freeing up of prices will be accompanied by measures for the social protection of the population. Decrees on reforming the pension system of private social insurance are being prepared now. Our possibilities are such that we will help the neediest social groups first of all. Therefore, a subsistence minimum is now being calculated, based on the real rate of inflation with adjustments for regional conditions. Mechanisms will be activated that provide direct access to the consumer market for socially unprotected groups of the population. I have in mind above all a changeover from monetary to in-kind assistance, free meals, food coupons, and access to inexpensive goods for the weak and the poor.

A new task of our social policy is the creation of a system of social assistance specially targeted toward the most vulnerable strata of the population and children. A network of soup kitchens, shelters and special stores, a mechanism for purchasing prime necessities and a reliable system for delivering them to specific individuals will have to be created. The Ministry of Social Protection for the Population will handle this. With a view of reacting flexibly and quickly to the needs and misfortunes of our citizens, it is necessary to form a republic fund for the social support of the population.

It is planned to conduct a wage reform before the end of this year. All restrictions on increases in individual earnings and a person's opportunities to earn money honestly will be lifted. The main task here is to give working people the opportunity to compensate for price increases on their own, to unleash personal initiative. I consider the trade unions' demand of "market wages for market prices" to be fair, with one addition: market wages for market productivity. Our strategic task is to gradually bring up the fixed incomes of employees in the budget-financed branches to the income level of those employed in the market sector of the economy, including physicians, teachers and others. A month before prices are freed up, we plan to increase the pay of teachers and physicians, raise the minimum wage, and increase pensions and stipends.

We have debated for an impermissibly long time over whether we need private property. Meanwhile, the Party-state elite has been actively engaged in personal privatization. The scope, enterprise and hypocrisy that this involves are simply astonishing. Privatization has been under way in Russia for a long time, but in an ungoverned, spontaneous way, and frequently on a criminal basis. Today it is necessary to seize the initiative, and we intend to do so. First of all, attention will be devoted to so-called small-scale privatization—small and medium-sized enterprises in the sphere of services and trade, in industry and in transportation.

The privatization of housing has already begun in Russia, but a good many citizens have run into difficulties and bureaucratic obstacles. Bribery is flourishing. We intend to set up a rigid barrier to this.

The basic principles of housing privatization in Russia will be published in the press in two to three weeks. We will strive for unswerving observance of these principles by the local authorities.

The situation with respect to the privatization of industrial giants is much more complicated. A good many of them will remain under state ownership. But their activity will undergo substantial changes.

A large-scale and rapid process of transforming state enterprises into joint-stock companies, with shares distributed between the state and the labor collectives, is to begin in the next few months. The second step is the sale of the state's portion of the shares to all those who wish to buy at market prices.

A special question for Russia is its agriculture and peasantry. The current situation in this area is critical.

The agrarian reform that was begun after the second Congress of People's Deputies has not been able to remedy the situation appreciably. The 30,000 private farms created during that time are just a drop in the bucket. The 1992 budget proposes that 6.5 billion rubles be allocated to support private farms, backing up this money with material resources. Some 24,000 tractors, 22,000 trucks and many other types of equipment are to be provided out of existing stocks. The government has prepared a special program for peasant farms, the intent being to draw foreign firms into this endeavor on a broad scale. We will buy $100 million worth of farm machinery and means of transportation abroad.

A network of enterprises to provide services for private farmers and enterprises for the processing, storage and sale of agricultural output will be created in the near future on a cooperative, commercial and state basis.

The main task for the coming winter is privatization of the facilities that provide services to the peasants, above all the trade and supply networks. It is also proposed to begin privatizing the property of collective farms and state farms that have been unprofitable for a long time and chronically fail to fulfill their commitments to the state.

The land of these enterprises—after an analysis of each case, of course—will be transferred to peasants and to those who want to acquire it in order to organize medium-sized or small-scale peasant enterprises.

The President will go to the Supreme Soviet with a package of amendments to the Law on Land Reform that are aimed at strengthening the legislative basis for transformations in this sphere and at resolving, at long last, the problem of the buying and selling of land. A state committee with appropriate structures in the territories, provinces and districts will be created to organize work on the agrarian reform.

A special feature of the Russian Republic economy is the high degree to which it is dominated by monopolies. A large share of all output is produced by gigantic enterprises and concerns that have no competitors. This allows them not to be concerned about the quality of their output or, since the disappearance of the plan, even about its quantity.

An exorbitant price for an item is established by hook or by crook, which makes the consumer pay through the nose.

At the same time, a good many operations are involuntary monopolists. Frequently an enterprise makes a monopolist concern run an overall deficit. The freeing up of prices will put everything in its place. Moreover, we have a package of measures that will be taken to combat monopolism and stimulate competition. We are ready in the near future to begin breaking up a number of concerns and creating competing firms on their basis.

Monopolism will be undermined by the small and medium-sized private enterprises that will appear the first months of privatization and by the development of cooperation between the government and business circles in Russia.

The destruction of the economic "iron curtain" will help establish a climate of competition. The administrative regulation of foreign-economic activity was a powerful source of abuses and corruption. Moreover, we are incurring losses running into billions of dollars due to the uncontrolled transporting of Russian Republic resources out of the country. Our citizens are horrified by the prices at which imported goods are being sold today, and many such goods are simply inaccessible because they can be bought only for foreign currency. The superbureaucratism that is flourishing in the foreign-economic departments is frightening away reputable entrepreneurs and attracting people with a dubious reputation, sometimes outright swindlers.

We intend to immediately implement a number of measures that will begin to remedy the situation. Among them are the competitive sale for rubles of exporting and importing licenses; the authorization of foreign juristic persons to sell goods of social significance to the population for rubles, with the subsequent investment of these rubles; and the competitive sale of rubles to foreign juristic persons for foreign currency, with the subsequent investment of that currency in the Russian economy.

One of the central areas of transformations is the conversion of defense production facilities. Russia is completing the drafting of a program for thoroughgoing conversion. An appropriate committee has been created to implement and monitor it. The conversion program proposes a changeover to a system of direct orders from the Ministry of Defense. These orders have already been set for 1992.

Military and civilian production will be separated.

It is proposed to shut down a certain number of enterprises, as well as to completely reconfigure a number of military plants for the production of civilian output and consumer goods.

...

The time has come to say clearly and precisely that there is one source of power in Russia: the Russian Republic's Congress and Supreme Soviet, the Russian Republic's government and the Russian Republic's President.

A dynamic process of extracting the institutions of power from under the heel of the CPSU is under way. We are not afraid of accusations of being undemocratic, and we will act decisively in this respect. Henceforth, no one party will be the self-styled master in the Russian state.

In conducting the reforms, the principal burden rests with the Russian government. This burden is too heavy for that government's present makeup and cumbersome structure. It can be borne only by a government of popular confidence, one that people will trust, one that will convince them that its actions are correct.

...

The republics within Russia have gained a good deal from the democratic transformations that have occurred in recent years. At the same time, many problems remain unsolved. A number of republics—Tataria, Yakutia and several others—justifiably point out that a large part of their raw-material and economic potential is under the control of central departments and is not yielding a proper return for the republics' inhabitants. These questions should be considered and resolved by the new Russian Republic Cabinet. In this respect, we must accommodate the reasonable and legitimate demands of the republics within the Russian Republic.

At the same time, there is a line that we cannot cross under any conditions. This line is the territorial integrity of Russia, its constitutional-law unity. We cannot permit, and on no account will we permit, the collapse of Russia and its fragmentation into dozens of appanage principalities quarreling with one another. We recognize the right of peoples to self-determination. But this right cannot be exercised to the detriment of the right of other peoples. Any changes in the state status of the republics and territories within Russia should be made in a constitutional manner and on the basis of the law. But the main criterion for resolving such questions should be the will of the citizens, the will of the peoples living in the republic or territory in question, as expressed in a referendum.

The question of Russia's foreign-economic strategy comes up again and again. It is time to introduce clarity here. We are prepared, in cooperation with foreign specialists, to immediately disclose the strategic data necessary for admission into international organizations and to accept the basic principles set forth in the charter of the International Monetary Fund. We will make an official appeal to the International Monetary fund, the World Bank and the European Bank for Reconstruction and Development, inviting them to work out a detailed plan for cooperation and participation in the economic reforms.

...

54 Agreement on the Creation of a Commonwealth of Independent States

STANISLAU SHUSHKEVICH, BORIS YELTSIN & LEONID KRAVCHUK

STATEMENT BY THE HEADS OF STATE OF THE REPUBLIC OF BELARUS, THE RUSSIAN SFSR AND UKRAINE

We, the leaders of the Republic of Belarus, the RSFSR and Ukraine,

—noting that the talks on the drafting of a new Union Treaty have reached an impasse and that the objective process of the secession of republics from the USSR and the formation of independent states has become a real fact;

—stating that the shortsighted policy of the center has led to a profound economic and political crisis, the collapse of production and a catastrophic decline in the living standard for virtually all strata of society;

—taking into consideration the increase in social tension in many regions of the former USSR, which has led to conflicts between nationalities with numerous human casualties;

—aware of our responsibility to our peoples and the world community and of the urgent need for the practical implementation of political and economic reforms, hereby declare the formation of a Commonwealth of Independent States, on which the parties signed an Agreement on Dec. 8, 1991.

The Commonwealth of Independent States, consisting of the Republic of Belarus, the RSFSR and Ukraine, is open for accession by all member-states of the former USSR, as well as for other states that share the goals and principles of this Agreement.

The member-states of the Commonwealth intend to pursue a course aimed at strengthening international peace and security. They guarantee the fulfillment of international obligations stemming from the treaties and agreements of the former USSR and ensure unified control over nuclear weapons and their nonproliferation.

> S. Shushkevich, Chairman of the Supreme Soviet
> of the Republic of Belarus.
> B. Yeltsin, President of the RSFSR.
> L. Kravchuk, President of Ukraine.

Minsk, Dec. 8, 1991.

...

AGREEMENT ON THE CREATION OF
A COMMONWEALTH OF INDEPENDENT STATES

We, the Republic of Belarus, the Russian Federation (RSFSR) and Ukraine, as founder-states of the USSR and signatories to the Union Treaty of 1922, hereinafter called the High Contracting Parties, state that the USSR as a subject of international law and geopolitical reality is terminating its existence.

Based on the historic community of our peoples and the ties that have developed among them, and considering the bilateral treaties concluded between the High Contracting Parties,

seeking to build democratic states based on the rule of law,

intending to develop our relations on the basis of mutual recognition of and respect for state sovereignty, the inalienable right of self-determination, the principles of equality and noninterference in internal affairs, the renunciation of the use of force and economic or any other means of pressure, the settlement of disputed problems through conciliation, and other generally recognized principles and norms of international law,

concerning that the further development and strengthening of relations of friendship, good-neighborliness and mutually advantageous cooperation among our states corresponds to the fundamental national interests of their peoples and serves the cause of peace and security,

confirming our commitment to the goals and principles of the United Nations Charter, the Helsinki Final Act and other documents of the Conference on Security and Cooperation in Europe,

pledging to observe generally recognized international norms on human rights and the rights of peoples,

have agreed on the following:

Art. 1.—The High Contracting Parties are founding a Commonwealth of Independent States.

Art. 2.—The High Contracting Parties guarantee equal rights and liberties to their citizens, regardless of nationality or other differences. Each of the High Contracting Parties guarantees to the citizens of other Parties, as well as to stateless individuals living on its territory, regardless of nationality or other differences, civil, political, social, economic and cultural rights and liberties in accordance with generally recognized norms of human rights.

Art. 3.—The High Contracting Parties, wishing to promote the expression, preservation and development of the distinctive ethnic, cultural, linguistic and religious features of the national minorities living on their territories and of existing unique ethno-cultural regions, take them under their protection.

Art. 4.—The High Contracting Parties will develop equal and mutually advantageous cooperation among their peoples and states in the fields of politics, economics, culture, education, public health, environmental protection, science and trade and in humanitarian and other fields, will further the broad exchange of information, and will observe mutual obligations conscientiously and unswervingly.

The Parties consider it necessary to conclude agreements on cooperation in the indicated fields.

Art. 5.—The High Contracting Parties recognize and respect one another's territorial integrity and the inviolability of existing borders in the framework of the Commonwealth.

They guarantee open borders and freedom of movement for citizens and freedom for the transfer of information within the framework of the Commonwealth.

Art. 6.—The member-states of the Commonwealth will cooperate in ensuring international peace and security and in implementing effective measures for reducing weapons and military spending. They are striving for the elimination of all nuclear weapons and general and complete disarmament under strict international control.

The Parties will respect one another's endeavors to achieve the status of nuclear-weapon-free zones and neutral states.

The member-states of the Commonwealth will preserve and support a common military-strategic space under a joint command, including unified control over nuclear weapons, the procedure for which will be regulated by a special agreement.

They also jointly guarantee the necessary conditions for the stationing, functioning, and material and social support of the strategic armed forces. The Parties pledge to conduct a coordinated policy on questions of the social protection of and pensions for servicemen and their families.

Art. 7.—The High Contracting Parties recognize that the sphere of their joint activity, conducted on an equal basis through the common coordinating institutions of the Commonwealth, includes:

—the coordination of foreign-policy activity;

—cooperation in the formation and development of a common economic space and of all-European and Eurasian markets, and in the field of customs policy;

—cooperation in the development of transportation and communications systems;

—cooperation in the field of environmental protection, and participation in the creation of an all-encompassing international system of ecological security;

—questions of migration policy;

—the struggle against organized crime.

Art. 8.—The Parties recognize the planetary nature of the Chernobyl catastrophe and pledge to unite and coordinate their efforts to minimize and overcome its consequences.

They have agreed to conclude a special agreement for this purpose, one that takes into consideration the gravity of the consequences of the catastrophe.

Art. 9.—Disputes concerning the interpretation and application of the norms of this Agreement are to be resolved through negotiations between the appropriate agencies, and if necessary at the level of heads of state and government.

Art. 10.—Each of the High Contracting Parties reserves the right to suspend this Agreement or individual articles of it after notifying the signatories to the Agreement one year in advance.

The provisions of this Agreement may be added to or changed by mutual agreement of the High Contracting Parties.

Art. 11.—From the moment this Agreement is signed, the norms of third states, including the former USSR, may not be applied on the territory of the states signing the Agreement.

Art. 12.—The High Contracting Parties guarantee the fulfillment of their international obligations stemming from the treaties and agreements of the former USSR.

Art. 13.—This Agreement does not affect the obligations of the High Contracting Parties with respect to third states.

This Agreement is open for accession by all member-states of the former USSR, as well as for other states that share the goals and principles of this Agreement.

Art. 14.—The official location of the Commonwealth's coordinating agencies is the city of Minsk.

The activity of agencies of the former USSR on the territory of the member-states of the Commonwealth is terminated.

Done in the city of Minsk on Dec. 8, 1991, in three copies each in the Belorussian, Russian and Ukrainian languages, all three texts having equal force.— [signed] For the Republic of Belarus, S. Shushkevich and V. Kebich; for the RSFSR, B. Yeltsin and G. Burbulis; for Ukraine, L. Kravchuk and V. Fokin.

NOTES

ABOUT THE AUTHORS: **Stanislau Shushkevich,** a nuclear physicist, became the first head of state of independent Belarus, 1991–1993. **Leonid Kravchuk,** a leading Communist politician, in 1991 became the first president of independent Ukraine.

55　*The Alma-Ata Declaration*

A. MUTALIBOV ET AL.

PROTOCOL TO THE AGREEMENT
ON THE CREATION OF A COMMONWEALTH
OF INDEPENDENT STATES THAT WAS SIGNED
ON DEC. 8, 1991, IN THE CITY OF MINSK
BY THE REPUBLIC OF BELARUS,
THE RUSSIAN FEDERATION (RSFSR) AND UKRAINE

The Azerbaidzhan Republic, the Republic of Armenia, the Republic of Belarus, the Republic of Kazakhstan, the Republic of Kyrgyzstan, the Republic of Moldova, the Russian Federation (RSFSR), the Republic of Tadzhikistan, Turkmenistan, the Republic of Uzbekistan and Ukraine, on an equal basis and as the High Contracting Parties, are forming a Commonwealth of Independent States.

The agreement on the creation of a Commonwealth of Independent States enters into force for each of the High Contracting Parties from the moment of its ratification.

Documents regulating cooperation within the framework of the Commonwealth will be worked out on the basis of the Agreement on the Creation of a Commonwealth of Independent States and with consideration for the reservations made during its ratification.

This Protocol is a component part of the Agreement on the Creation of a Commonwealth of Independent States.

Done in the city of Alma-Ata on Dec. 21, 1991, in one copy each in the Azerbaidzhani, Armenian, Belorussian, Kazakh, Kyrgyz, Moldavian, Russian, Tadzhik, Turkmenian, Uzbek and Ukrainian languages. All texts have equal force. The original will be kept in the archives of the government of the Republic of Belarus, which will send the High Contracting Parties certified copies of this Protocol.

ALMA-ATA DECLARATION

The following independent states

—the Azerbaidzhan Republic, the Republic of Armenia, the Republic of Belarus, the Republic of Kazakhstan, the Republic of Kyrgyzstan, the Republic of Moldova, the Russian Federation (RSFSR), the Republic of Tadzhikistan, Turkmenistan, the Republic of Uzbekistan and Ukraine,

Seeking to build democratic states based on the rule of law, states the relations among which will be developed on the basis of mutual recognition of and respect for state sovereignty and sovereign equality, the inalienable right of self-determination, the principles of equality and noninterference in internal affairs, the renunciation of the use of force and the threat of force and of economic or any other means of pressure, the peaceful settlement of disputes, respect for human rights and liberties, including the rights of national minorities, and the conscientious fulfillment of obligations and other generally recognized principles and norms of international laws;

Recognizing and respecting one another's territorial integrity and the inviolability of existing borders;

Believing that the strengthening of relations of friendship, good-neighborliness and mutually advantageous cooperation, which have deep historical roots, corresponds to the fundamental interests of the peoples and serves the cause of peace and security;

Aware of their responsibility for preserving civil peace and concord among nationalities;

Adhering to the goals and principles of the Agreement on the Creation of a Commonwealth of Independent States,

Declare the following:

Cooperation among the members of the Commonwealth will be carried out on the principle of equality, through coordinating institutions formed on a parity basis and operating in accordance with a procedure determined by agreements among the members of the Commonwealth, which is neither a state nor a suprastate formation.

With a view to ensuring international strategic stability and security, the joint command of military-strategic forces and unified control over nuclear weapons will be preserved; the parties will respect one another's aspirations to achieve the status of nuclear-weapon-free and/or neutral states.

The Commonwealth of Independent States is open, with the consent of all of its members, for accession by member-states of the former USSR, as well as by other states that share the goals and principles of the Commonwealth.

Commitment to cooperation in the formation and development of a common economic space and of all-European and Eurasian markets is confirmed.

With the formation of the Commonwealth of Independent States, the Union of Soviet Socialist Republics ceases to exist.

The member-states of the Commonwealth, in accordance with their constitutional procedures, guarantee the fulfillment of the international obligations stemming from the treaties and agreements of the former USSR.

The member-states of the Commonwealth pledge to unswervingly observe the principles of this Declaration.—[signed] A. Mutalibov, President of the Azerbaidzhan Republic; L. Ter-Petrosyan, President of the Republic of Armenia; S. Shushkevich, Chairman of the Supreme Soviet of the Republic of Belarus; N. Nazarbayev, President of the Republic of Kazakhstan; A. Akayev, President of the Republic of Kyrgyzstan; M. Snegur, President of the Republic of Moldova; B. Yeltsin, President of the Russian Federation (RSFSR); R. Nabiyev, President of the

Republic of Tadzhikistan; S. Niyazov, President of Turkmenistan; I. Karimov, President of the Republic of Uzbekistan; and L. Kravchuk, President of Ukraine.
Alma-Ata, Dec. 21, 1991.

56 Resignation Speech, December 25, 1991

MIKHAIL S. GORBACHEV

Dear compatriots! Fellow citizens! Due to the situation that has taken shape as a result of the formation of the Commonwealth of Independent States, I am ceasing my activity in the post of President of the USSR. I am making this decision out of considerations of principle.

I have firmly advocated the independence of peoples and the sovereignty of republics. But at the same time I have favored the preservation of the Union state and the integrity of the country.

Events have taken a different path. A policy line aimed at dismembering the country and disuniting the state has prevailed, something that I cannot agree with.

Even after the Alma-Ata meeting and the decisions adopted there, my position on this score has not changed.

Moreover, I am convinced that decisions of such scope should have been adopted on the basis of the free expression of the people's will.

Nevertheless, I will do everything in my power to ensure that the agreements signed there lead to real concord in society, make it easier to get out of the crisis and facilitate the process of reform.

Speaking to you for the last time as President of the USSR, I consider it necessary to express my assessment of the path traversed since 1985. Especially since there are a good many contradictory, superficial and unobjective opinions on this score.

Fate ordained that when I became head of state it was already clear that things were not going well in the country. We have a great deal of everything—land, petroleum, gas and other natural resources—and God has endowed us with intelligence and talent, too, but we live much worse than people in the developed countries do, and we are lagging further and further behind them.

The reason was evident—society was suffocating in the grip of the command-bureaucratic system. Doomed to serve ideology and to bear the terrible burden of the arms race, it had been pushed to the limit of what was possible.

All attempts at partial reforms—and there were a good many of them—failed, one after the other. The country had lost direction. It was impossible to go on living that way. Everything had to be changed fundamentally.

That is why I have never once regretted that I did not take advantage of the position of General Secretary just to "reign" for a few years. I would have considered that irresponsible and immoral.

I realized that to begin reforms on such a scale and in such a society as ours was an extremely difficult and even risky endeavor. But even today I am convinced of the historical correctness of the democratic reforms that were begun in the spring of 1985.

The process of renewing the country and of fundamental changes in the world community proved to be much more complex than could have been surmised. However, what has been accomplished should be appraised on its merits.

Society has received freedom and has been emancipated politically and spiritually. This is the most important gain, one that we have not yet become fully aware of, and for this reason we have not yet learned to make use of freedom.

Nevertheless, work of historic significance has been done:

—The totalitarian system, which for a long time deprived the country of the opportunity to become prosperous and flourishing, has been eliminated.

—A breakthrough has been achieved in the area of democratic transformations. Free elections, freedom of the press, religious freedoms, representative bodies of power and a multiparty system have become a reality. Human rights have been recognized as the highest principle.

—Movement toward a mixed economy has begun, and the equality of all forms of ownership is being established. Within the framework of a land reform, the peasantry has begun to revive, private farming has appeared, and millions of hectares of land are being given to rural and urban people. The economic freedom of the producer has been legalized, and entrepreneurship, the formation of joint-stock companies and privatization have begun to gather momentum.

—In turning the economy toward a market, it is important to remember that this is being done for the sake of human beings. In this difficult time, everything possible must be done for their social protection, and this applies especially to old people and children.

We are living in a new world:

—An end has been put to the cold war, and the arms race and the insane militarization of the country, which disfigured our economy and the public consciousness and morals, have been halted. The threat of a world war has been removed.

I want to emphasize once again that, for my part, during the transitional period I did everything I could to preserve reliable control over nuclear weapons.

—We opened up to the world and renounced interference in the affairs of others and the use of troops outside the country's borders. And in response we received trust, solidarity and respect.

—We have become one of the main bulwarks in the reorganization of present-day civilization on peaceful, democratic principles.

—Peoples and nations have received real freedom in choosing the path of their self-determination. Searches for democratic reforms in the multinational state led us to the threshold of concluding a new Union Treaty.

All these changes required enormous effort and took place in an acute struggle, with mounting resistance from old, obsolete and reactionary forces—both the former Party-state structures and the economic apparatus—and also from our habits, ideological prejudices, and a leveling and parasitic mentality. The changes ran up against our intolerance, low level of political sophistication and fear of change.

For this reason, we lost a great deal of time. The old system collapsed before a new one had time to start working. And the crisis in society became even more exacerbated.

I know about the dissatisfaction with the present grave situation and about the sharp criticism that is being made of the authorities at all levels, and of my personal activity. But I would like to emphasize once again: Fundamental changes in such an enormous country, and one with such a legacy, could not proceed painlessly or without difficulties and upheavals.

The August putsch brought the general crisis to the breaking point. The most disastrous aspect of this crisis was the disintegration of the state system. Today I am alarmed by our people's losing their citizenship in a great country—the consequences may prove to be very grave for everyone.

It seems vitally important to me to preserve the democratic gains of the past few years. They were achieved through suffering throughout our history and our tragic experience. Under no circumstances and on no pretext can they be given up. Otherwise, all hopes for something better will be buried.

I am saying all this honestly and straightforwardly. This is my moral duty.

Today I want to express my gratitude to all citizens who supported the policy of renewing the country and joined in the implementation of democratic reforms.

I am grateful to the state, political and public figures and the millions of people abroad who understood our plans, supported them, met us halfway, and embarked on sincere cooperation with us.

I am leaving my post with a feeling of anxiety. But also with hope and with faith in you, in your wisdom and strength of spirit. We are the heirs to a great civilization, and its rebirth into a new, up-to-date and fitting life now depends on each and every one of us.

I want to thank from the bottom of my heart those who during these years stood with me for a right and good cause. Certainly some mistakes could have been avoided, and many things could have been done better. But I am sure that sooner or later our common efforts will bear fruit and our peoples will live in a prosperous and democratic society.

I wish all of you the very best.

PART 8

Reflections

Once they were over, the Gorbachev years were bound to invite not only recrimination and bitterness among some but also jubilation and a sense of liberation and promise among others. They also raised serious questions about both the causes and the consequences of the collapse.

Looking back over those years, some of the key participants reflected on what had gone wrong with perestroika. *Edvard Shevardnadze and Yegor Ligachev came to this question from opposite political perspectives, but what they shared was the belief that it could have worked (though they meant different things by "it") had it not been for the wrong policies pursued. In essence, they both faulted Gorbachev for his political strategy—for one, it was too hesitant, for the other, too radical.*

There is the broader question of whether a liberalization of the Soviet system could have worked under any circumstances. Different observers in the Soviet elite blamed the failure of the whole enterprise on particular features—failure to reform the federal system, failure to reform or split the Communist Party, failure to carry out a fundamental economic reform, failure to oust key officials of the old regime. Others stressed the resistance, even sabotage, by entrenched officials, officers, and managers.

But could the system have been reformed at all? There were those who firmly denied it. Most explicitly and systematically, Martin Malia insisted that the Soviet system needed to be demolished before a new order could be built to replace it: The Bolshevik system could not be transformed in piecemeal fashion because it had been born with an evil "genetic code" from the start.

Others rejected this argument and posited instead more complex and contingent schemes to explain the system's collapse. Some gave particular weight to individual variables, such as the progressive spread of corruption or the impact of economic stagnation; others stressed the cumulative impact of a number of interacting factors from the erosion of ideological commitment to the effects of social change. Some focused on the unintended consequences of Gorbachev's own policies as decisive in bringing about the collapse, given the unreconciled contradictions inherent in glasnost *and democratization from above.*

The question of whether internal causes were crucial or whether the external environment played an important part was also addressed by foreign observers. And although some credited the United States—more specifically, the military buildup un-

der Ronald Reagan, symbolized by the "Star Wars" project—with bringing home the bankruptcy of the Soviet system, others stressed the ways in which a benign international environment and the generally supportive atmosphere during the years of perestroika contributed to its success. However, many observers believed the causes had to be found, first and foremost, within the Soviet Union itself.

57 *To the Stalin Mausoleum*

"Z" [MARTIN MALIA]

> The most dangerous time for a bad government is when it starts to reform itself.
> —Alexis de Tocqueville, anent
> Turgot and Louis XVI

I

The Soviet socialist "experiment" has been the great utopian adventure of our century. For more than seventy years, to millions it has meant hope, and to other millions, horror; but for all it has spelled fascination. Nor does age seem to wither its infinite allure.

Never has this fascination been greater than since Mikhail Gorbachev launched *perestroika* in the spring of 1985: a derivative painting in the Paris manner of 1905, a Beatles' vintage rock concert, or a *Moscow News* article revealing some dark episode from the Soviet past known to the rest of the planet for decades could send tremors of expectation throughout the West if it were datelined Moscow. So conservative-to-centrist Margaret Thatcher and Hans-Dietrich Genscher have vied with the liberal-to-radical mainstream of Anglo-American Sovietology in eulogizing Gorbachev's "modernity." Even though after seventy years, the road to the putative "radiant future" of mankind no longer leads through Moscow, the road to world peace still does. And who is against world peace?

But this is not the whole explanation: Moscow is still the focus of a now septuagenarian ideological fixation. On the Right there is the hope that communism may yet repent of its evil totalitarian ways and evolve into a market democracy of sorts (into the bargain putting down the Western Left). On the Left there is the wish that the "experiment" not turn out to be a total loss (if only so as not to comfort the Western Right) and yet acquire something approximating a human face. So on all sides alleged connoisseurs of the *res sovietica* are anxiously asked: Are you optimistic or pessimistic about the chances for perestroika? Can Gorbachev succeed? Will he survive? Should we help him?

These questions, however, presuppose answers with diverse ideological intonations. To what is no doubt a majority in Western opinion, Gorbachev's reforms mean that Stalinism and the Cold War are over and that democracy is at hand in the East, bringing with it the end of global conflict for all. For a smaller but vocal group, the Cold War is indeed over and the West has won, a victory that presages the global triumph of capitalism, the end of communism, indeed even the "end of history."[1] A third group, once large but now a dwindling phalanx, holds that communism remains communism for all Gorbachev's glitter and that *glasnost* is sim-

interesting theory

ply a ploy to dupe the West into financing perestroika until Moscow recovers the strength to resume its inveterate expansionism.[2]

Yet the two dominant Western perspectives on Gorbachev have one element in common: the implication that our troubles with the East are over, that we are home free, at the "end of the division of Europe" and on the eve of the Soviet Union's "reintegration into the international order," a prospect first advanced by Gorbachev but eventually taken up by a hesitant President Bush. So in an odd way the perestroika pietism of the Gorbophiles and the free-market triumphalism of the Gorbophobes converge in anticipation of a happy dénouement of a half-century of postwar polarization of the world.

And, indeed, in this avalanche year of 1989 we are surely coming to the end of a historical epoch. It is hardly so clear, however, that we are entering a simpler, serener age: decaying superpowers do not go quietly into the night. It is not even clear that we are asking the right questions at all about Gorbachev. Certainly Western Sovietology, so assiduously fostered over the past four decades, has done nothing to prepare us for the surprises of the past four years.

Nor is the predominant Western question about Gorbachev's chances for success the most pertinent one, or at least the first we should ask. The real question is: Why is it that seventy years after 1917—which was to have been the ultimate revolution, the revolution to end all further need of revolutions—Gorbachev proclaims *urbi et orbi* that Soviet socialism urgently requires a "new revolution," a "rebuilding" of its fundamental fabric? What is so drastically wrong as to require such drastic action? And what, after four and a half years of increasingly frenetic activity, has in fact been accomplished?

The most natural way to approach this question is to focus on personalities and policies: on Gorbachev and his "conservative" opponents; on "perestroika," "glasnost," and "democratization." And it is this preoccupation which explains the cult of his personality in the West. But if fundamental revolution is now really on the Soviet agenda, then our focus of inquiry ought to be the *longue durée* of deep structures and abiding institutions. And these, as Gorbachev constantly reminds us, were created "sixty years ago," a euphemism for Stalin's "Year of the Great Break," 1929. For this was the beginning of the forced collectivization of agriculture through "de-kulakization," together with "full steam ahead" in industry for a "First Five-Year Plan in four years," policies that created the Soviet system as it exists in its main outlines to the present day. In short, Gorbachev is calling into question the very basis of the Soviet order and the historical matrix of what until now was called "developed" or "real" socialism. Perestroika is thus not just a reform of a basically sound structure, but the manifestation of a systemic crisis of Sovietism per se.

II

It is precisely because during the past twenty-odd years mainline Western Sovietology has concentrated on the sources of Soviet "stability" as a "mature industrial society" with a potential for "pluralist development" that it has prepared us so poorly for the present crisis, not only in the Soviet Union but in communist systems everywhere.[3] Instead of taking the Soviet leadership at its ideological word—that their task was to "build socialism"—Western Sovietology has by and large foisted on Soviet reality social science categories derived from Western realities, with the result that the extraordinary, indeed surreal, Soviet experience has been rendered banal to the point of triviality.

Much of this was done in the name of refuting the alleged simplifications of the post-World War II "totalitarian model," itself deemed to be the product of the ideological passions of the Cold War. Thus, beginning in the mid-1960s successive waves of revisionists have sought to replace the totalitarian model's emphasis on ideology and politics with an emphasis on society and economics, to move from "regime studies" to "social studies," and to displace "history from above" with "history from below."[4] This reversal of the totalitarian model's priorities of explanation has yielded a Soviet Union where the political "superstructure" of the regime derives logically from its "social base" in the proletariat and a peasantry being transformed into urban workers, with a new intelligentsia emerging from both classes. This inversion of the actual roles of state and society obviously gives the Soviet world a normal, almost prosaically Western, character and a democratic cast as well.

At the cost of some simplification, it is possible to say that this social science approach (with a fair admixture of Marxism) has produced a consensus that the Soviet historical trajectory leads "from utopia to development."[5] In this perspective the key to Soviet history is presented as "modernization" through "urbanization" and "universal education"—a process carried out in brutal and costly form, to be sure, especially under Stalin, but the end result of which was the same as in the West. Often this social science reductionism holds that the Stalinist excesses perpetrated during an essentially creative Soviet industrial transformation represented only a passing phase, an "aberration," which under Brezhnev gave way to "normalcy" and "institutional pluralism" expressed through such "interest groups" as the army, industrial managers, or the Academy of Sciences.[6] Indeed, Stalinism itself has been viewed by the more thoroughgoing revisionists not as an aberration at all, but as an essentially democratic phenomenon, stemming from a "cultural revolution" from below, within the Party and the working class, and resulting in a massive "upward mobility" that produced "the Brezhnev generation." In this view the whole revolutionary process may be summed up as "terror, progress, and social mobility," with the modest overall cost in purge victims falling in the "low hundreds of thousands."[7]

A corollary to this revisionist picture is that Gorbachev's "restructuring" will be the crowning of the edifice of Soviet modernity. Thus, all that is required to humanize the Soviet Union is a measure of "reform" in the ordinary sense of reorganization: that is, a "calibrated" decentralization and a gradual debureaucratization of administrative structures, or more specifically, a reduction of the role of the central plan and the *nomenklatura,* or those administrative and managerial posts reserved for appointment by Party committees.

Such, indeed, was the expectation behind Gorbachev's early policies, as in the new Party program (now forgotten) voted at the [Twenty-seventh] Party Congress in February 1986 and expressed in his book *Perestroika and New Thinking* in the fall of the next year. This was still the expectation two years later of the main line of American Sovietology; indeed, this Sovietology to a degree reflected Soviet thinking in the Moscow social science institutes of the Academy of Sciences.[8] But the border nationalities crisis of 1988 and the union-wide economic crisis of 1989 have made these anticipations, though hardly four years old, already superannuated. As for the blatant fantasies—to use a charitable term—about democratic Stalinism, they are clearly destined for that same trashcan of history to which Trotsky once consigned the Provisional Government of 1917.

As the crisis year 1989 draws to a close, it is—or ought to be—patent that both the Soviet regime and its Western analysts are in for an agonizing reappraisal of long-standing assumptions about Soviet "stability." More precisely, the time has come to take a fresh look at the starting point of Western Sovietological analysis: namely, the two bases of the totalitarian model, ideology and politics, and at the ways in which these factors have modeled the institutions and the mentalities created by seventy years of "utopia in power."[9] For if the fact of glasnost demonstrates the Soviet capacity to return to human "normalcy," the revelations of glasnost prove incontrovertibly that for the past seven decades Russia has been anything but just another modernizing country. As we now know, both from Gorbachev's economists and from televised shots of empty shelves in Moscow stores, the Soviet Union, though clearly a failed utopia, is neither a developed nor a modern nation. It is rather something *sui generis,* a phenomenon qualitatively different from all other forms of despotism in this or previous centuries.

It is for this reason that the term *totalitarian,* coined by Mussolini with a positive connotation to designate his new order and first applied in a negative sense to Stalin's Russia by Trotsky, was taken up by Hannah Arendt to produce a general theory of perverse modernity. And she did so because the blander term *authoritarian,* serviceable, say, for a Salazar or a Chiang Kai-shek, simply would not do for the gruesome grandeur of Stalin, Hitler, or Mao. Contrary to current opinion, Jeane Kirkpatrick did not invent but simply continued this distinction, though she added the corollary that totalitarian regimes are far more permanent than authoritarian regimes, a proposition with which the struggling intellectuals of Eastern Europe thoroughly agree, since as yet no country, not even Poland or Hungary, has successfully completed its exit from communism.

The Sovietological revisionists of the West, however, find Kirkpatrick's distinction scandalous, in part because of the conflation it effects between communism and fascism (though the Soviet novelist Vasili Grossman does exactly this in his enormously popular *Fate and Life*) and in part because Stalin must be presented as an aberration from the Leninist main line of Sovietism, for if he is integral to the system, then the prospects for its democratic transformation are dim indeed.

But this sanitization of the Soviet regime into mere authoritarianism, at least for the period after Stalin, is achieved only at the cost of a fundamental conceptual confusion, if not an outright caricature of the totalitarian concept. Totalitarianism does not mean that such regimes in fact exercise total control over the population; it means rather that such control is their aspiration. It does not mean they are omnipotent in performance, but instead that they are institutionally omnicompetent. It is not Soviet society that is totalitarian, but the Soviet state.

This conceptual confusion results from taking as the defining criterion of a regime the degree or quantity of repression, not its nature or quality. Thus, since Khrushchev shrank the dimensions of the Gulag and Brezhnev killed or imprisoned far fewer people than did Stalin, the Soviet regime is deemed to have evolved from totalitarianism to authoritarianism (or as some would put it, "post-totalitarianism"), say on the model of Greece under the colonels or of Pinochet's Chile. But this view neglects the central fact that the structures of the Party-state, with its central plan, its police, and its nomenklatura, have remained the same—as Gorbachev's more liberal supporters, such as Sakharov, have constantly complained. Consequently, the milder face of Sovietism after Stalin—and the quantitative change is quite real for those who live under it—simply offers us, in Adam Michnik's phrase, "totalitarianism with its teeth knocked out."[10]

Paradoxically, just as the "T word" was being expunged from Western Sovietology around 1970, it became current in Eastern Europe: Hannah Arendt was translated in *samizdat,* and Soviet intellectuals now routinely refer to the whole system, including its Leninist phase, as totalitarian, and to the Brezhnev period as classical or stable Stalinism.[11] Even more paradoxically, it is when communist totalitarianism began to unravel under Gorbachev that the inner logic of the system became most transparently clear to those who have to live under it.[12] To resort, à la Marx, to a quotation from Hegel: in matters of historical understanding "the owl of Minerva takes flight only as the shades of night are falling." It is this twilight, Eastern view of the evolution of the Soviet experiment from 1917 to Gorbachev that will be adopted here, in an effort to present a historicized update of the original, and in truth too static, totalitarian interpretation.

III

It is impossible to understand anything about Gorbachev and perestroika without taking seriously the origins of the Soviet system in a utopia. The utopia, of course, was never realized, but this is not the point. For applied utopias do not simply fail and fade away; the effort to realize them leads rather, through a perverse cunning of reason, to the creation of a monstrous antireality, or an inverted world. So the great Soviet adventure turned out to be, in the words of an early Polish observer, a grim "mistake of Columbus." This unforeseen landfall led to the creation of a new politics, a new economics, and a new Soviet man, which are at the root of the present crisis of perestroika.

The utopia in which the Soviet system originated is integral revolutionary socialism. This is not to be confused with simple egalitarianism, although this is obviously involved under so protean a label as "socialism." Nor is it to be confused with mere social democracy (a term for which both Marx and Lenin had a distinct aversion), for this is clearly compatible with a mixed economy and constitutional government. Rather, integral revolutionary socialism in the Marxist tradition means full noncapitalism. As the *Manifesto* puts it, "The theory of the Communists may be summed up in the single phrase: Abolition of private property." From this it follows that the product of private property—profit—and the means for realizing this profit—the market—must also be abolished. For property, profit, and the market dehumanize man and fetishize the fruits of his labor by transforming both into reified commodities. It was to end this scandal that the most deprived and dehumanized class, the proletariat, received the world-historical mission of bringing about the socialist revolution, whereby mankind would at last be led out of "prehistory" into genuine human existence in the oneness and unity of a classless society. And all of this is supposed to come about through the inexorable logic of history, operating through the self-enriching alienation of the class struggle. This set of beliefs—the core tenets of marxism—has been characterized by Leszek Kołakowski as "the greatest fantasy of our century."[13]

But the logic of history does not work this way (if indeed it exists at all); and although private property and the market can be abolished, their demise will not come about automatically. Therefore, the hand of history must be forced by the creation of a special instrument, "a party of a new type," with which Lenin declared he "would overturn all Russia." Thus, utopia can be achieved only by an act of political will exercised through revolutionary coercion, in short by quasi-military means. Utopians of this ruthless temper, however, can get a chance at power only in extreme crisis, amid the collapse of all structures capable of resisting them. Such an exceptional state of affairs came about in Russia in 1917, when under the impact of modern war, the old order unraveled with stunning rapidity to the point where Lenin's Bolsheviks simply "found power lying in the streets and picked it up." True, they enjoyed a significant measure of worker support at the time and their ranks were largely filled with former workers. But this does not mean that what they themselves called, until well into the 1920s, the October overturn (*perevorot*) was any the less a minority coup d'état staged against a background of generalized, particularly peasant, anarchy, and not a "proletarian revolution" in any meaningful sense of that term.[14]

The Bolsheviks then had to confront their utopia with reality in the form of economic collapse and civil war. Under the combined pressure of the military emergency and the logic of their ideology, between 1918 and 1920 they produced the world's first version of noncapitalism, "War Communism." Nor at the time was this viewed as an emergency expedient. For Lenin, socialism would emerge out of the fullness of capitalism; the "imperialist war" was the highest phase of capitalism; General Ludendorff's militarization of the German economy during the struggle was therefore the supreme form of capitalism and by the same token, the matrix of the new socialist order. So nationalizing the entire urban economy under the Supreme Economic Council (the ancestor of the present Soviet industrial ministries and of "Gosplan"), the Bolsheviks amplified Ludendorff's practices in Russia and abolished profit and the market. To this was added the "advanced" American method of Taylorism for the rational organization of work and an ambitious program for building power stations under the conviction that "socialism equals Soviet power plus electrification." At the same time, the Bolsheviks experimented with rural collectives, or *Sovkhozes,* and thereby adumbrated the extension of their statist model to the countryside and the entire population; and in the meantime they simply pillaged alleged "petty bourgeois kulaks" for grain under the policy of "class warfare" in the villages. In fact, during War Communism the Bolsheviks created the first rough draft of what later would be called a planned, or more accurately a command, economy.[15]

Simultaneously, Trotsky hit upon another essential component of the new system, the political commissar. The vocation of the Party is political and ideological, not technical and professional in any of the activities necessary for the functioning of society. Since the Party was at war, the most important professional expertise at the time was military, expertise the Bolsheviks lacked, while most trained officers in the country were former members of the Imperial Army and hence unreliable. So the new people's commissar for war simply conscripted the officers he needed and flanked them with trustworthy Party monitors, such as Stalin, Kirov, Voroshilov, and Orjonikidze, all future leaders of the 1930s. In this way a dual system of administration was created in the army, but one that could easily be adapted to economic and other civilian tasks, where Party figures would supervise industrial managers, collective farm chairmen, educators, scientists, writers—indeed, everybody and everything. This is the earliest origin of the *apparat* and its nomenklatura right of appointment to all functional posts of importance in society. Dual administration thus adumbrates the end of "civil society," by which Central Europeans and Soviets mean social groups capable of self-organization independent of the state. This mode of control is the essence of the Party-state, a system wherein the functional, governmental, or "soviet," bureaucracy is monitored from behind the scenes by a parallel and unaccountable Party administration that has the real power of decision.

The period of War Communism produced a second monitoring apparatus as well, this time for "enemies" of the whole system—the Cheka, or political police. Conceived by Lenin as early as November 1917 to wage class war against those who were certain to resist the Bolsheviks' unilateral seizure of power, the Cheka was originally directed against "feudal" or "bourgeois" parties, but was soon turned against erring, "petty bourgeois" socialist parties as well as recalcitrant workers and peasants who supported them. But there was no structural reason in the system to prevent the Cheka's eventual use against enemies within Bolshevik ranks themselves. For as the Civil War raged on, it became increasingly apparent that the Party and its leadership represented (to use Kołakowski's language again) not the "empirical proletariat," but a "metaphysical proletariat" that had the world-historical mission of leading mankind to socialism. Thus, whenever workers or peasants rejected the Party's power, as in the Kronstadt revolt of 1921, they were automatically revealed as "petty bourgeois" and disposed of *manu militari*.

And so by 1921 all the essential institutions of Sovietism had either been created or sketched in: the Party-state with its monopoly of power, or "leading role," as it is now called; the dual administration of soviet and apparat, both backed by the Cheka; the central plan and the agricultural collective; and a propaganda monopoly in the service of the dictatorship of the proletariat, with its single "correct" ideology and the cult of technological Prometheanism. It is difficult to believe that a system of such internal coherence and logic should be the passing product of military emergency, although this is now the dominant view in Western Sovietology. In any event, it is this model that, in fact, was to become the main line of Soviet development, from Stalin to the eve of perestroika. And this, as the Soviets used to say in their earlier, more ideological days, is surely "no accident."

But War Communism would become the Soviet norm only after what turned out to be the temporary retreat to the mixed economy of the New Economic Policy (NEP) in the 1920s. For War Communism, though it permitted the Bolshevik victory over the Whites, also produced one of the worst social and economic collapses of the twentieth century. In the course of the Civil War, some 15 million to 19 million people perished from war, terror, famine, and epidemic—or more than in all of World War 1. By 1921 industrial production had virtually halted, money had disappeared, and organized exchange had given way to barter. To be sure, a part of this primitivization was due to six years of war; but it was due in even greater part to the ideological extravagance and incompetence of Bolshevik policy, which continued with fanatical grimness for months after the war had been won.[16]

IV

The limited return to the market under the NEP was a success in reviving the country, but not in leading it to socialism. This contradictory circumstance has given rise to endless speculation and controversy about the true nature of the system in the past, and thus about the proper tasks of perestroika in the present. The central questions are these: Is the "hard" communism of War Communism and Stalin the norm or a deviation in Soviet history? Or is the "soft" communism of the NEP this norm and therefore the model for perestroika—a perspective in which Stalinism, together with its Brezhnevite prolongation, becomes the deviation from which perestroika is the hoped-for recovery? Finally, which of these two communisms, the hard or the soft, is the legitimate heir of Lenin and October? Or to put the whole debate in one classic question, Was Stalin necessary?[17]

In strictly temporal terms there is no doubt about the answer to these questions: three years of War Communism, twenty-five of Stalin, and eighteen of Brezhnev clearly add up to the empirical norm of Soviet history, and it is the eight years of the NEP (together with bits and pieces of the Khrushchev period) that are the "aberration," or, if one prefers, the metaphysical norm of "real" Leninism; and this overwhelming preponderance of hard communism must have something to do with the logic, if not of history, then at least of the Soviet system. Yet these questions are not really about chronology; they are about essences, and through these about present attitudes and policies toward Soviet reformability.

The case for the NEP as essential Sovietism rests on the fact that Lenin inaugurated it and did so with the admission that War Communism had been an error, or at least a premature attempt at attaining socialism. In his dying months, moreover, he gave his blessings to "cooperatives" (a concept he did not flesh out) as the means for arriving at socialism. Nikolai Bukharin then developed these hints into something of a system in the mid-1920s and thereby became the true heir of Lenin. Stalin (attacked by name, moreover, in the founder's "Testament") thus rose to power only as an intriguer and a usurper.

In this view the true Leninist-Bukharinist course, which enjoyed majority support in the Party by mid-decade, drew from the horrors and errors of War Communism the lesson that the regime's first priority should be to preserve the "revolutionary alliance of workers and peasants" allegedly forged in October. To this end, the Party was to conciliate the 80 percent of the population that was peasant by orienting the "commanding heights" of state industry to meet rural consumer needs and thereby to accumulate through the market the capital for the industrial development necessary to achieve mature socialism. In this way the socialist sector, since by definition it would be the more efficient, would out-compete the private, peasant sector; the rural cooperatives would be gradually transformed into genuine collective farms; and the whole nation would thus "grow into socialism," in the sense of the full transcendence of capitalism.[18]

There are numerous objections to this view over and above the puerile fetishization of Lenin involved and the bizarre notion that the supreme achievement of October Revolution was the discovery, in 1921, of the virtues of cooperatives and the market. The first major objection is that never during the NEP and Bukharin's brief ascendancy did the Party play the economic game according to market rules: it constantly resorted to "administrative" means to manipulate both supply and demand since it feared the peasants' power over the economy, and hence the state, through their purchasing power, or more simply their freedom to grant or withhold the supply of grain. The second major objection is that the empirical evidence about the resistance of the peasants to the forced requisition of grain during War Communism, and their refusal even to market it under the NEP, especially after 1927, whenever the price ratio was unfavorable, indicates their inveterate distrust of Bolshevik arbitrariness. Never under a Bolshevik monopoly of power would they have entered collective farms voluntarily. Given these circumstances, a collision between the Party and the peasants was at some point inevitable, and the NEP was inherently unstable. Ultimately, either the Party would have to give up on integral socialism and share economic, and eventually political, power with the peasants through the market—in short, opt for mere social democracy—or it would have to crush peasant independence, and along with it the market, and march toward full socialism by coercive, "administrative" methods. ...

Even when, under Khrushchev, the Soviet Union became the world's "second largest economy," just behind the United States, indeed outstripping it in output of the sinews of modern industry—steel—this number two status was true only in quantitative, not qualitative, terms. Almost all Soviet products were imitative, archaic, crude, or outright defective. Almost nothing the Soviet Union produced, outside of military hardware, was competitive on the international market, and it could sell its products on the internal market only because it had a monopoly that excluded more efficient foreign competition. Even in its most successful decades, therefore, under Stalin and in the early years of Khrushchev, the Soviet Union was never a great industrial power, and still less a "modern" society. The belief that it was such a power is among the great illusions of the century, shared until recently not just by the editorialists of our major newspapers, but by economists of the prominence of John Kenneth Galbraith, and even Wassily Leontief.[22] In reality, however, the Soviet Union in its prime was never more than a great military-industrial complex and a Party-state superpower. ...

IX

Against the background of such a history and the highly constraining structural logic underlying it, the task of reform can only be Herculean. But do the system's constraints permit the emergence of the people, and of the vision, necessary for such a staggering task? In this question lies the whole drama, and the dilemma, of the Gorbachev era.

Awareness that something was seriously amiss with Sovietism first came to the surface in 1983 under Andropov. As head of the KGB, he knew far better than his colleagues the true state of affairs; and he took the novel step of calling on intelligentsia specialists, especially economists and sociologists from the Academy of Sciences, to consult on possible remedies, an enterprise in which his protégé Gorbachev was involved. This endeavor produced the *Novosibirsk Report* by the sociologist Tatiana Zaslavskaia, who argued that the Soviet system of centralized planning had become obsolete, a fetter on production, and that Soviet society, far from being a harmonious unity, was riven by the conflicting interests of both the ruling and the ruled—an analysis that implied the necessity of radical restructuring for sheer survival. This document, leaked to the Western press in the once putatively fatal year of 1984, first alerted the world to the impending end of Soviet stability.[33]

At the beginning of his general secretaryship, Gorbachev may be considered as Andropov redux, though the younger leader was driven by a much more acute sense of crisis and a correspondingly bolder willingness to experiment. His initial program of perestroika as controlled economic reform from above therefore quickly branched out in new directions under the pressure of events. *Perestroika* soon came to stand for "radical reform," then "revolutionary change"; and further policies were added to it: "new thinking," or retrenchment, in foreign relations, and "acceleration," "glasnost," and "democratization" domestically. It is in this historical sequence that its course will be examined here.

When Gorbachev first launched perestroika in April 1985, it had the relatively limited purpose of producing a rapid acceleration, or *uskorenie*, of national economic performance; and his method was similar to Andropov's: reliance on administrative action from above in consultation with intelligentsia experts and operation within the existing structures of the Plan and its attendant ministries. For *perestroika* means, literally and simply, refashioning an existing edifice, or *stroika*, the root also of the Russian term for the "building" of socialism. Thus, while he summoned Zaslavskaia and the Novosibirsk economist Abel Aganbegyan to Moscow and positions in Academy of Science think tanks, his basic approach was to jump-start the stalled Soviet productive mechanism by the classic administrative methods of exhortation and bureaucratic reorganization.

An example of the first tack was his 1986 anti-alcohol campaign. This measure backfired, however, by increasing the budget deficit through loss of sizable vodka sales, which now went to the "black" economy. An example of the second tack was the "quality control" of industrial products by state inspectors, whose power to refuse substandard goods, and hence also to lower enterprise revenues, generated insecurity among both managers and workers. In addition, Gorbachev regrouped ministries and replaced cadres on a scale not seen since Stalin. As a result of this, by the fall of 1986 strong resistance emerged among the apparat to further changes, whether of policy or of personnel.[34]

Gorbachev therefore embarked on a second policy, glasnost. In this he was advised by his chief theoretician, Alexander Yakovlev, who had become a connoisseur of modern, Western ways during a decade as ambassador to Canada, an experience that both sharpened his appreciation of Russia's backwardness and acquainted him with the contemporary television techniques required to stimulate innovation. In choosing this new course, Gorbachev was guided by two considerations. As a question of conviction, he recognized that a dynamic economy could not be built with a passive population, isolated from knowledge of the modern world, ignorant even of real conditions within the Soviet Union—a state of affairs that produced Chernobyl, for example. Glasnost was thus intended to energize the nation. Also, as a matter of political tactics, he now made an all-out wager on the "creative intelligentsia" to bring pressure for reform on the recalcitrant apparat.

To signal this change, and to give the intelligentsia assurance that they could speak up without fear, he made a dramatic telephone call to Sakharov in Gorki in December 1986 to summon him back from exile. During the next eighteen months the liberal intelligentsia, in the press and on television, began to criticize society's ills, and to fill in the "blank spots," in Gorbachev's expression, of the Soviet past, with a fervor born of the twenty years of frustration that had built up since the previous thaw under Khrushchev. They did this with all the more passion since it was only by owning up to the errors of the past that they could attack the problems it had created for the present.[35]

In the course of this glasnost explosion, both Gorbachev and his supporters radicalized as they encountered resistance from "conservative" (or more accurately, old socialist) forces under Ligachev. A note of desperation crept into the dehate, and on both sides. Ligachev and his allies asserted that the liberal intelligentsia's criticism was leading the country to ruin by undermining the institutions and values that had built socialism and won the Fatherland War. Gorbachev and his supporters answered that the situation was so far gone that there was "no alternative to perestroika": to continue the policies of stagnation would lead to the rapid obsolescence of the economy, loss of superpower status, and ultimately the death of the system. As Yakovlev, in early 1989, put it more bluntly than Gorbachev himself would have dared, "We probably have no more than two to three years to prove that Leninist socialism can work."[36] Thus in 1987 and 1988, the initially self-confident campaign for perestroika of 1985 took on the air of an increasingly desperate gamble, an ever more urgent race against time; and by 1989 matters had acquired the aura of a crisis of survival, which recalled, though in different form, the disaster years of 1921, 1932, and 1941.

The flood of candor under glasnost did indeed produce the consequences of which the conservatives complained, and in a form more radical than during Khrushchev's thaw. For each new revelation about past crimes and disasters did less to stimulate the people to new effort than to desacralize the system in their eyes; it did so all the more thoroughly since the Myth was long since dead, especially among the young. Repressed awareness of the Lie poured forth in a flood progressing from the publication of Anatoli Rybakov's mild novel *Children of the Arbat* in 1986 to that of Solzhenitsyn's outright anti-Soviet *Gulag Archipelago* in 1989. In the process, not only were the long decades of Stalin and Brezhnev swept away, but the very foundations of Sovietism, the economic theories of Marx and the political practices of Lenin, were touched. By 1988 Marxism-Leninism was a shambles; and by 1989 it could be openly denounced by leading intellectuals, such as the historian Iuri Afanasiev, as a dead weight on the mind of the nation.[37]

In the midst of the turmoil unleashed by glasnost, the system was threatened by still another danger: the nationalities crisis and the beginning of the breakup of the empire. The leadership had known from the start of perestroika that it faced an economic problem, but in its Russocentric naiveté was quite unaware it had an equally grave nationalities problem. So the mass strikes of February 1988 in Armenia over the issue of Nagorny-Karabakh came as a total surprise, a "moral Chernobyl," as one Soviet leader put it. But soon autonomist, even separatist, agitation spread to the Baltic states, then to Georgia and Azerbaijan, and by 1989 to the vital Ukraine.

These movements, moreover, everywhere assumed the form of "popular fronts," grouping all classes of the population against the Party apparat (or in the Baltic virtually taking the Party over), a pattern reminiscent of the "dual power" that existed between the original "soviets," or workers' councils, and the Provisional Government in 1917. The cause of this sudden explosion lay in the same process of desacralization that was undermining all Soviet institutions. The fiction that the Party-state was a federal "union" was perhaps the most egregious form of the Lie, for all the border "republics" had in fact been conquered by the Great Russian central region beginning in 1920, with the Baltic states and the Western Ukraine added only as recently as 1939–1944, and then only after a deal with Hitler. When the freedom to criticize released these border populations from fear, the result was a national as well as an anti-Party upsurge; for them *perestroika* came to signify "sovereignty," by which they really meant independence.

With this danger added to the other strains produced by glasnost, the old-line socialists, or conservatives, redoubled their efforts to retain control of the apparat, where the general secretary still lacked an unquestioned majority, from the Politburo down to the base. Given the constraints of Party discipline, this resistance could express itself in public only obliquely, but behind the scenes, what liberals called a bloodless civil war in fact was raging. Its most open expressions were the firing of Boris Yeltsin as Moscow Party chief in the fall of 1987 and the national-Communist, anti-Gorbachev manifesto, known as the "Nina Andreeva Letter," published in much of the press in the spring of 1988.

In response to these pressures, the general secretary moved to a third and still more revolutionary policy: democratization. First bruited in early 1987, this meant double or multiple candidacies in elections and fixed terms of office for all Party and state, or Soviet, posts. This policy was first applied to the Party by convening a Special Party Conference (in effect, a mini-Congress) in June 1988 in an effort to gain at last the majority necessary for a renewed attempt at economic reform. Yet this device, like glasnost, overshot the mark assigned to it, while at the same time it fell short of achieving its intended positive function. The conference turned out to lack the necessary majority of proreform delegates for a purge of apparat deadwood yet began the politicization of the hitherto quiescent Russian lower classes, since the partially televised proceedings revealed the once monolithic and mysterious Party to be a fallible and quarrelsome body of self-seeking interests.

Failing to revitalize the Party, Gorbachev then upped the ante of democratization by using it the following year to reanimate the hierarchy of state administrative bodies, the soviets. Taking up the 1917 slogan "all power to the soviets," he sought to give real political life to both halves of the system of dual administration, in which all power, since Lenin, had belonged to the Party. Again his motives were mixed. There was first his Leninism—by no means a mere ritual invocation—which he vaunted as the "pragmatic" capacity to adapt policy rapidly to changing circumstance and the constant willingness to risk a gamble. Then, too, democracy, like glasnost, was necessary to galvanize the population for perestroika. But above all, Gorbachev sought to give himself a structure of power parallel to the regular apparat. He sought this in part so that he could not be deposed by a Central Committee coup as Khrushchev had been in 1964—a precedent on everyone's mind in the perestroika era—and in part to give himself an independent instrument for putting through his stalled economic programs.[38] And, as some Soviets noted, this effort to outflank the old guard by a parallel power was reminiscent, *mutatis mutandis,* of the way Stalin had used the NKVD against the mainline Party.

This second round of democratization overshot its intended mark far more widely than the first. This became apparent during the elections in March 1989 to a Congress of People's Deputies, whose function was to create a strong executive presidency for Gorbachev and to elect a Supreme Soviet, or national parliament, with some measure of legislative power, unlike its rubber-stamp predecessor. An unintended result of these elections, however, was to produce a resounding defeat not just for the apparat, as Gorbachev wished, but for the Party as an institution. For the first time in seventy years, the population had the possibility of saying no to official candidates, and did so, at least in the large cities, on a major scale. As a result, the "correlation of forces" within the country changed radically: the Party which had hitherto inspired fear in the people suddenly came to fear the population, and demoralization spread throughout its ranks.

This effect was compounded at the Congress meetings, televised live for two weeks during May and June. To be sure, Gorbachev got himself elected president and thus secured a buffer against a coup by the Party. He also obtained the selection of a new Supreme Soviet—in effect, a consultative assembly, rather than a genuine legislature—which he felt confident would do his bidding. But the authoritarian way he pushed these elections through the Congress caused his popularity, already low because of the economic and ethnic problems engendered by perestroika, to reach its nadir; he, too, was desacralized and made to appear as just a bigger apparatchik. Moreover, the liberal delegates, though a minority, dominated the proceedings with a barrage of exposés of all the ills with which the country is afflicted: the poverty, the abominable health service, the rising crime rate, the ecological disasters, the economic disintegration, the KGB's "secret empire," as one deputy dared call it, and the Party corruption. The net result of the Congress was, in the words of another deputy, "the demystification of power."

As a result, Gorbachev's initially demagogic slogan "all power to the people" began to acquire some real content. The Congress first of all produced an organized Left opposition to Gorbachev in the form of the Interregional Group, led by such figures as Sakharov, Yeltsin, Afanasiev, and the economist Popov, a loyal opposition to be sure, yet one that nonetheless insisted that real perestroika was still in the future. Even more boldly, this group broke the supreme taboo of communism and demanded an end to the leading role of the Party.[39] Simultaneously, the Congress debates produced a politicalization of the Great Russian and Ukrainian populations almost as intense as that of the border nationalities. And since the Congress had come up with no concrete remedies for the ills its debates had exposed, by July the population began to take matters into its own hands. The country was swept with a wave of self-organization from below; popular fronts and embryonic trade union associations appeared in the cities of Russia and the Ukraine. Thus "civil society", as the opposition called these new formations, began to emerge for the first time since it had been suppressed in 1918; and in some areas this movement edged off into a form of "dual power," as some radicals asserted, a phenomenon of which the Kuzbas and Donbas miners' strikes in July 1989 were only the most visible and spectacular manifestations.

X

While all this was going on, what had been accomplished in the economic sphere to produce the hoped-for "acceleration" that had been perestroika's starting point? The short answer is: nothing much. Or more accurately still, those measures that were taken led to an outright deterioration of the situation.

Gorbachev's economic program has thus far consisted of two main components, both formulated in 1987.[40] The first of these is the creation of small "cooperatives," in reality private ventures, in the service sector. But the impact of this cooperative sector has been derisory, since its services are priced far above the purchasing power of the 200-rouble-per-month average wage of the majority of the population. These enterprises have therefore become the focus of popular hostility to economic reform in general, since any form of marketization is perceived by "the people"—as the miners made clear during their strike—to benefit only "speculators" and the privileged—a reaction quite in conformity with the socialist egalitarianism the regime inculcated in the population for decades. Moreover, the cooperatives are harassed by the state bureaucracy, whose monopoly they threaten, and are often either taken over by, or made to pay protection money to, various Mafias from the "black" economy.

The second component of Gorbachev's economic reform is the Law on State Enterprises, providing for "self-management" and "self-financing." If actually applied, these provisions would significantly reduce the role of Gosplan and the central ministries by using self-interest to correct the predominance of administrative directives. This reform is thus an effort to return to the spirit, if not the precise institutions, of the NEP, and to its policy of *khozraschyot*, or businesslike management and accountability under a regime of state enterprise. In other words, it is a variant of the half-measures of soft communism, put forth periodically in Soviet history from Bukharin to Eugene Varga just after World War II to Kosygin, but never really implemented because they threaten the Party apparat's "leading role." And, indeed, this time too, the Law on State Enterprises has remained a dead letter ever since it took effect in January 1988, because the silent resistance of legions of apparatchiki has kept industry operating at 90 percent on "state orders"—that is, on the old Plan.[41]

In still other domains, Gorbachev's economic perestroika has met with failure, but this time without his having really tried to produce a program. In agriculture Gorbachev has spoken repeatedly of long-term leases of land, indeed up to fifty years, for the peasantry. But this proposal has gone nowhere, in part because of the resistance of the huge kolkhoz bureaucracy, in part because the peasantry has seen so many different agrarian reforms imposed from above that it will not trust the regime to respect leases of any duration and hence will not take up the government's half-offer.

Thus, Gorbachev is in a far more difficult position than his predecessors in communist economic reform. He no longer has the option of Lenin in 1921 at the beginning of the NEP, or of Deng Xiaoping in 1979 of reviving agricultural and artisan production rapidly by granting the 80 percent of the population that is peasant a free market. The Russian peasantry, now disproportionately aged and only 35 percent of the population, is too decimated and demoralized by over sixty years of collectivization to respond to any NEP-type initiatives. In consequence, Gorbachev has been obliged to begin his perestroika with industry, where the transition to marketization is far more difficult than in agriculture. Here the very success of Stalin in urbanizing Russia has created a cast-iron block to progress.

Another such block is financial and monetary policy. Heavy state subsidies to hold retail prices low, to keep unprofitable factories running, to maintain full employment, and to secure the safety net in place—what some Western specialists call the social contract between regime and people—cannot be abolished without unleashing inflation and thus igniting a social explosion. But unless these subsidies are abolished, or at least reduced, the economy cannot move to real prices; and without real prices there can be no dilution of the Plan by marketization or privatization; nor can there be convertibility of the rouble to reintegrate Russia into the international order. And without movement in these directions, there can be no revival of the economy. So the alternative before Gorbachev is either economic stagnation through subsidies or social upheaval through real prices.

And perestroika faces other problems as well; the infrastructure and the capital stock created by decades of extensive development are now approaching exhaustion. In a nationally televised address in October 1989, Prime Minister Ryzhkov warned that the overburdened railway system (Russia still lives basically in the railroad age) was on the verge of collapse. The country's enormous metallurgical plant is outmoded and unprofitable. Housing and administrative buildings are in a state of disrepair often bordering on disintegration. The extraordinary number of industrial "accidents," from Chernobyl to the gas-line and train explosions of June 1989 are usually due to functional breakdown or criminal neglect. All this exhausted equipment must be restored or replaced, and much of the work force retrained and remotivated.

Then, too, the stores must be filled again. Under the present conditions of collapse and penury, available goods are either siphoned off legally by state enterprises to supply their workers, or they disappear illegally into the black economy. But short of massive imports of foreign goods, stocking the shelves is an impossible task, since decades of wasteful investments and subsidies, and of printing money to finance both, have now created an enormous budget deficit and rapid inflation—both "discovered," or admitted, by the government only in late 1988. As a result of this, a movement away from the rouble to the dollar or to barter is well under way, a phenomenon that presages the collapse of the consumer market.

Under such conditions of near breakdown, any transition to real prices, self-management, and self-financing are quite out of the question for the foreseeable future; and the old reflexes of the command-administrative system are sure to persist, if only to ensure a modicum of order. Thus, active consideration of real market reform has been postponed time and again and is now slated, more or less, for the mid-1990s. Indeed, economic perestroika of any type has been stalled since early 1988.

Overall, then, the balance sheet of more than four years of perestroika has been that the half-reforms introduced so far have unsettled the old economic structures without putting new ones in their place. And in this, perestroika resembles earlier failed halfway-house reforms in Central Europe: General Jaruzelski's reforms of self-management in 1982 and of self-financing in 1987 in Poland, and earlier still the failed, halfway New Economic Mechanism in Hungary. Yet, despite this accumulated evidence of failure, Gorbachev intends to stick to the unnatural hybrid of "market socialism," as his chief economic advisor, Leonid Abalkin, made clear in November 1989 in launching an updated plan of alleged "transition" away from statism.[42]

The current impasse of perestroika, furthermore, resembles the Soviet NEP, but in reverse. The NEP saw the progressive stifling of the surviving prerevolutionary market economy by the nascent ambitions of Party-state power. Gorbachev's perestroika has witnessed the tenacious resistance of an ailing but still massive Party-state structure to a fledgling yet corrosive market. Whereas it proved easy to move brutally from a market to a command economy, it is turning out to be inordinately difficult to make the more delicate reverse transition. Between Gorbachev and a neo-NEP stands the mountainous mass of decaying Stalinist success, whereas between Lenin and the first NEP there stood only the failed wreckage of War Communism. So Gorbachev is left with the worst of two possible worlds: an old one that refuses to die and a new one without the strength to be born.

At the same time, this failure of economic perestroika coincides with the runaway success of glasnost and the progress of democratization and popular politicalization. The result is a new kind of "scissors crisis," to appropriate a metaphor used by Trotsky during the unstable NEP to describe the upward curve of industrial prices when charted against the downward curve of agricultural prices. Similarly, under the unstable neo-NEP of perestroika, the curve of glasnost and politicalization is running alarmingly high, and that of economic restructuring is sinking catastrophically low.[43] So perestroika, like its predecessor, risks being destroyed by the widening gap of the scissors unless energetic emergency measures are taken soon.

By late fall 1989, Moscow began to hear rumors of a coup. Other rumors, more plausibly, offered speculation about an imminent state of emergency or of a mitigated form of martial law (*osoboe polozhenie*). To everyone, society seemed to be adrift in disorder. Fear of state authority had almost vanished during the summer after the Congress, and with it, so it seemed, the regime's ability to govern. When the emigré Andrei Amalrik twenty years ago published his *Will the Soviet Union Survive Until 1984?* his question was met with incredulity, even derision.[44] Now it may well turn out that he was only a few years off.

In the midst of all this, what of Gorbachev, on whose person the West concentrates its attention and hopes? To the outside world, he passes for a bold and decisive leader, a mover and a shaker of major stature, especially in international affairs. When seen from Moscow, however, after his first initiative in unleashing the perestroika deluge, he has come to look more like a reactive than an active figure, a man increasingly incapable of staking out strong policy positions on the two make-or-break domestic issues of his reign, the economy and the nationalities. Instead, he appears essentially as a political tactician, fully at home only in Party maneuvering, now pruning the Politburo of conservative foes such as the former KGB chief, Chebrikov, or the Ukrainian Party boss, Shcherbitsky, as in the fall of 1989, now tacking from left to right and back again in the debates of the new Supreme Soviet. Indeed, by giving way totally and immediately to the miners' demands in July 1989, he appeared downright weak. And in all things he acts as if his economic problems could be solved by political means. Yet, since the direct road to economic perestroika is closed to him by structural blockage, this easier political route of glasnost and democratization is the only one left open to him.

Nor does he seem to be able to make up his mind whether he is head of state or head of the opposition. As one Soviet commentator put it, he is trying to be both Luther and the pope at the same time.[45] But in such a contradictory situation, for all his political prowess, he may yet turn out to be no more than the ultimate sorcerer's apprentice of Sovietism.

XI

As 1989 draws to a close, it is clear that it will enter history as the beginning of communism's terminal crisis, the year of the Second Great Break, but in the descending, not the ascending, phase of utopia in power; and this not just in Russia, but from the Baltic to the China Sea, and from Berlin to Beijing. It is also clear that perestroika and glasnost, welcome as they are in their intention, have in their application only aggravated the systemic crisis they were intended to alleviate. And they have done so because like all forms of soft communism, they go against the logic of the system they are trying to save. The internal contradiction of perestroika is that Gorbachev has been trying to promote soft communism through structures and a population programmed for hard communism. But the latter is the only variety of Sovietism that is the genuine article for the essence of all varieties of Sovietism is Party supremacy. Thus, the instrument of Gorbachev's reform—the Party—is at the same time the basic cause of Sovietism's troubles. To adapt a diagnosis of Alexander Herzen regarding earlier revolutionaries, the Party is not the doctor; it is the disease.

And the way out of this contradiction then? As one Soviet reformer put it after the June Congress, "The country now stands at a crossroads. From here we either go the Chinese way or the Polish-Hungarian way." Although the speaker obviously wished for the latter course, the alternative he posed may well be a Hobson's choice. The Chinese way since June 1989 means relative, though now declining, market prosperity under a regime of political and military repression. Repression is certainly a possibility in Russia, but market prosperity is quite out of the question for the indefinite future. Conversely, the Polish-Hungarian way means genuine democracy, but this is being attempted in the midst of economic ruin so severe as to threaten the survival of the new constitutional order. In Russia the economic ruin is even worse than in Poland and Hungary, but real democracy, as opposed to mere democratization, is not even on the agenda. Thus, the Russian way could well combine the worst of the Chinese and the Central European scenarios: economic failure in conjunction with an inexpungeable leading role for the Party.

Indeed, all three paths of communist reform (we may leave out of consideration the frozen Albanias such as Romania, Cuba, and North Korea) seem to end in one or another type of impasse. In this way Leninist totalitarianism shows another facet of its difference from ordinary authoritarianism. As Polish radicals discovered in the early 1980s in looking for possible models of liberation, post-Franco Spain and post-Pinochet Chile could not serve as examples. For those countries were able to make the transition to democracy because they had only been political authoritarianisms, not economic, social, and ideological monoliths. And, of course, they possessed market economies, so when political tyranny was ended, civil society, which had never been destroyed, could emerge fully into the light of day. But Leninist regimes, when they enter their final decline, seem able only either to implode, as in Poland, Hungary, and East Germany, or to dig in their heels militarily to stave off implosion, as under Deng Xiaoping in 1989, or his favorite model, the General Jaruzelski of 1981.

Yet whether they implode or hang on for a last desperate stand, all that they leave behind is economic and social rubble—hardly the foundation for building a "normal" society, as the Poles call their hoped-for post-Leninist order. And the leaders of Solidarity are acutely aware of the enormous risk they are taking in assuming power under such parlous conditions. Yet they have no choice but to try, since after eight years of Jaruzelski's failed attempt at being a Polish Kádár—that is, repression followed by liberalizing economic reform—the Party was as bankrupt as the country.

XII

This grim impasse at the end of utopia in power is the logical outcome of the structures which that power had built. The whole impossible enterprise of Lenin and Stalin was sustainable only as long as the human and material resources on which the system fed retained the vitality to endure the burden of the regime, and as long as some modicum of material success undergirded the Party's monopolistic position. But when these conditions ceased to hold, beginning with Deng

Xiaoping's marketization of 1979 and Solidarity's revolt of 1980, the Communist parties' will to power began to flag and their people's habit of fear began to fade. This soon made necessary, for the Soviet Party-state's survival, the recourse to the expedients of perestroika and glasnost. But these are only pale substitutes for the market and democracy, halfway measures designed to square the circle of making the vivifying forces of a resurrected civil society compatible with the Party's leading role.

But this circle cannot be squared. If marketization and privatization are the economic goals of reform in communist countries, then Party planning becomes superfluous, indeed downright parasitical. If multiple parties, elections, and the rule of law are the political goals of reform in communist countries, then the dual administration of the Party-state becomes supernumerary, indeed positively noxious.

The Party is not a party, in the normal sense of an association for contesting elections and alternating in government under the rule of law. The Party is, rather, a self-appointed society for the monopoly of power. It can tolerate normal parties only as temporary expedients, satellites, or fronts when the political weather is stormy. Likewise, the dual administrative body of the Party-state is not a normal state, but a special instrument created by the Party to act as a transmission belt of its policies to the population through the nomenklatura. Such a state cannot therefore be turned into a normal polity simply by legalizing other parties, since they will not have equal access with the Party to the monopolistic facilities of the state apparatus, from its police to its press. Nor is socialist planning an alternative way to organize the economy; it is the negation of the economy, its death as a separate sphere of human activity through its subordination to politics and ideological imperatives. It is this total amalgam, this whole surreal world, that is summed up by the sacrosanct tenet of the leading role.

This role is in its essence inimical to all the professed goals of reform now echoing throughout the Soviet Union and Central Europe, whether glasnost, democratization, or multiparty elections. All these reforms imply that there is a third way, a halfway house between what the ideological call socialism and capitalism, or what the inhabitants of the East think of as Sovietism and a "normal society." But there is no third way between Leninism and the market, between bolshevism and constitutional government. Marketization and democratization lead to the revival of civil society, and such a society requires the rule of law. But civil society under the rule of law is incompatible with the preservation of the lawless leading role.

At some point, therefore, the redline will be reached where reform crosses over into the liquidation of the leading role and all the structures it has created. And both Russia and Central Europe are now reaching that critical line. The false problem of how to restructure Leninism is now giving way to the real problem of how to dismantle the system, how to effect at last an exit from communism Perestroika is not a solution, but a transition to this exit. As Milovan Djilas fore-

saw early in perestroika: communism is not reforming itself, it is disintegrating.[46]
...

XIV

Let us return now to the questions with which this inquiry began: Can Gorbachev succeed? Should we help him? It is now the official United States position, to quote President Bush, that Gorbachev is a "genuine reformer" and that we all "wish perestroika to succeed," a stance that implies at least moral help. But to answer these questions meaningfully, we must, as with the questions of Stalin's necessity, rephrase them first. Succeed at what? Help him to do what?

If by perestroika's success we mean producing a communist system that is economically effective and politically democratic, then the answer must be no: the empirical record of seventy years shows that the fundamental structures of the Leninist system reached an inextricable impasse at the end of the 1970s; and the mounting contradictions of perestroika indicate that the system cannot be restructured or reformed, but can only either stagnate or be dismantled and replaced by market institutions over a long period of time. In this case, any aid the West might render to the Soviet state to save or improve the existing system would be futile: on this score, Gorbachev is beyond our help. Such aid would also work against the real interests of the restive Soviet peoples and thus of international stability. Like Western credits to Eduard Gierek and the Polish Party-state in the 1970s, aid to the Soviet government would simply prolong the agony of everyone concerned.

Yet if by perestroika's success we mean effecting a transition from a Party-state and a command economy to democracy and the market, then the answer, unfortunately, must still be no. First of all, such a transition is not the aim of Gorbachev's perestroika; its aim, rather, is to salvage what can be saved of the existing system by halfway-house concessions to economic and human reality, concessions moreover that are constantly being revised as new sections of the system give way and as the regime improvises frantically in the hope that something might turn the situation around. Second, and even more important, such a transition would bring the end of the cardinal leading role and hence would amount to the self-liquidation of communism, something Gorbachev clearly does not intend to do.

Still, events are pressing toward the eventual dwindling away of the system, whatever the Soviet leadership's intentions and whoever that leader might be in the future. And here Western help could play a constructive role. First, reducing the mutual burden of armaments, if carried out with due attention to legitimate security concerns, would ease the severity of the Soviet crisis (though it would not alter its structural causes). And Gorbachev has clearly indicated his willingness to engage in arms reductions, while at the same time taking care that the Soviet's international retreat does not turn into a rout.

670 ■ PART 8: REFLECTIONS

Second, although Western aid should not go to shoring up Soviet economic institutions in the state sector, it could be usefully applied to the piecemeal development of parallel structures in a private sector operating on market principles so as to promote economic and eventually, political pluralism. This could take the form, say, of free economic zones operating under IMF conditions in such places as the Baltic states, Armenia, or the Soviet Far East. In this case, the expectation would be that such a parallel sector, perhaps with its own convertible currency, would eventually spread across the Soviet Union. ...

Yet, however the Soviet Union edges toward its particular exit from communism this unchartered process can only be a long and painful one. Nor will it be a unilinear or an incremental progress toward integration in some "common European house." Instead, further crises will most likely be necessary to produce further, and more real, reforms. And a last-ditch attempt to stave off ruin by curtailing destabilizing reform altogether could lead to that military reaction so feared by Moscow liberals. And who knows, in this scenario Gorbachev might be agile enough to become his own successor, or if perestroika ends in another eighteenth of Brumaire, to be his own Bonaparte. Gorbachev would be hard to replace because his international reputation is now the Soviet Union's chief capital asset; yet he could not afford to be a very tough Bonaparte, since he has become the prisoner of his foreign policy successes.

Obviously, none of these prospects is a cheering one, and none would be easy for the West to live alongside. But it is better to look realistically at the genuine options in the East as they have been molded by seventy years of failed utopia than to engage in fantasies about Gorbachev as a demiurge of instant democracy or about the end of conflict in history. Nor should we forget that communism, though a disaster in almost every creative domain, has always been supremely successful at one thing: resourcefulness and tenacity in holding on to its monopoly of power. So the Soviet world's transition to normality will be a long time coming, for the Party, though now dyed with the hues of glasnost and democratization, will cling to the bitter end, like some poisoned tunic of Nessus, around the bodies of nations it has enfolded in its embrace for so many decades.

NOTES

ABOUT THE AUTHOR: **"Z"** was the pseudonym used by **Martin Malia,** emeritus professor of history at the University of California–Berkeley.

1. Francis Fukuyama, "The End of History?" *The National Interest* (Summer 1988).

2. See, for example, Judy Stone, *The Coming Soviet Crash: Gorbachev's Desperate Pursuit of Credit in Western Financial Markets* (New York: The Free Press, 1989)—a bad title for an otherwise good book. The threat of financial crash is quite real, but until now Gorbachev has steadfastly refused to use foreign credit extensively for fear of compromising national independence.

3. See, for example, Frederic J. Fleron, Jr., ed., *Communist Studies and the Social Sciences: Essays on Methodology and Empirical Theory* (Chicago: Rand McNally, 1969); and Susan Gross Solomon, *Pluralism in the Soviet Union* (New York: St. Martin's Press, 1983).

See also the social-science-oriented essays in Erik P. Hoffman and Robin F. Laird, eds., *The Soviet Polity in the Modern Era* (New York: Aldine Publishing Company, 1984). For the thesis of "stability" as the great common characteristic of the Soviet Union and the United States, see Samuel P. Huntington, *Political Order in Changing Societies* (New Haven: Yale University Press, 1968).

4. See notably *Stalinism, Essays in Historical Interpretation,* ed. Robert C. Tucker (New York: Norton, 1977), especially the Introduction and contributions by S. Cohen and R. Tucker.

5. The theme of a seminal, and for the most part penetrating, essay by Richard Lowenthal, "Development versus Utopia in Communist Policy," in Chalmers Johnson, ed., *Change in Communist Systems* (Stanford, Calif.: Stanford University Press, 1970). A revised version of this essay, entitled "Beyond Totalitarianism?" in Irving Howe, ed., *1984 Revisited* (New York: Harper and Row, 1983) could still be presented as the last word on Sovietism on the eve of Gorbachev's accession to power. In the same volume see also Michael Walzer's more categorical rejection of the relevance of the totalitarian concept, in "On 'Failed Totalitarianism.'"

6. Jerry F. Hough and Merle Fainsod, *How the Soviet Union Is Governed* (Cambridge: Harvard University Press, 1979). The book in fact has kept virtually nothing of Fainsod's original *How Russia Is Ruled* (Cambridge: Harvard University Press, 1963), which offered the classic statement of the totalitarian model. For urbanization as the supposed key to Sovietism, see Moshe Lewin, *The Gorbachev Phenomenon: A Historical Interpretation* (Berkeley and Los Angeles: University of California Press, 1988).

7. See *Cultural Revolution in Russia, 1928–1931,* ed. Sheila Fitzpatrick (Bloomington, Ind.: University of Indiana Press, 1978), especially the essays by S. Fitzpatrick and J. Hough; and Sheila Fitzpatrick, *The Russian Revolution* (New York: Oxford University Press, 1982), especially 8, 157, and 159.

8. *Politics, Society and Nationality Inside Gorbachev's Russia,* ed. Seweryn Bialer (Boulder and London: Westview Press, 1989).

9. The theme of Mikhail Heller and Alexander Nekrich, *Utopia in Power,* transl. Phillis B. Carlos (New York: Simon and Schuster, 1985). First published in Russian (London: Overseas Press, 1982).

10. Adam Michnik, "Towards a Civil Society: Hopes for Polish Democracy," *Times Literary Supplement* (4, 429) 19–25 February 1988: 188, 198–99.

11. See especially the essays of Pierre Hassner, Jacques Rupnik, and Aleksander Smolar in *Totalitarismes,* ed. Guy Hermet (Paris: Economics, 1984).

12. Paul Thibaud, "Réflexions sur la decomposition des communismes," *Notes de la Fondation Saint-Simon* (July 1989).

13. Leszek Kolakowski, *Main Currents of Marxism,* transl. P. S. Falla, vol. 3 (Oxford: Clarendon Press, 1978), 523.

14. For a convenient short course in revisionist history on 1917 as a proletarian revolution, see Ronald Suny, "Toward a Social History of the October Revolution," *American Historical Review* 88 (1) (February 1983).

15. See Thomas Remington, *Building Socialism in Bolshevik Russia: Ideology and Industrial Organization, 1917–1921* (Pittsburgh: University of Pittsburgh Press, 1984); and Silvana Malle, *The Economic Organization of War Communism, 1918–1921* (New York: Cambridge University Press, 1985).

16. See Laszlo Szamuely, *First Models of the Socialist Economic Systems* (Budapest: Akademiai Kiado, 1974).

17. Alec Nove, *Was Stalin Really Necessary?* (New York: Praeger, 1965).

18. The classic statement of this position is Stephen Cohen, *Bukharin and the Bolshevik Revolution* (New York: Oxford University Press, 1980[1971]). See also Moshe Lewin, *Lenin's Last Struggle,* transl. A. M. Sheridan Smith (New York: Random House, 1970). The most sophisticated elaboration of this position is Lewin's *Russian Peasants and Soviet Power,* transl. Irene Nove and John Biggard (Evanston, Ill.: Northwestern University Press, 1968).

22. For example, John Kenneth Galbraith, *The New Industrial State* (Boston: Houghton-Mifflin, 1967), and Wassily Leontiev, "The Decline and Rise of Soviet Economic Science," *Foreign Affairs* 38 (January 1960): 261–72.

33. Tatiana Zaslavskaia, "The Novosibirsk Report," *Survey* 28 (1) (1984): 88–108. An early and perceptive Western statement of the growing contradictions of Sovietism is Seweryn Bialer's *The Soviet Paradox: External Expansion, Internal Decline* (New York: Knopf, 1986).

34. The best treatment of the beginnings of perestroika is Michel Tatu's *Gorbachev: L'U.R.S.S., va-t-elle changer?* (Paris: Le Centurion-Le Monde, 1987).

35. The most comprehensive collection of reformist intelligentsia writings was issued for the June 1988 Special Party Conference. See *Inogo ne dano,* ed. Iuri Afanasiev (Moscow: Izdatel'stvo Progress, 1988). A partial translation exists in French under the title *La Seule Issue* (Paris: Alban Michel, 1989). For the geneology of the submerged tradition of soft communism from the 1920s on, see Moshe Lewin, *Political Undercurrents in Soviet Economic Debates: From Bukharin to the Modern Reformers* (Princeton, N.J.: Princeton University Press, 1974).

36. Quoted in *Le Monde,* 20 December 1988.

37. Quoted in *Russkaia Mysl' (La pensee russe)* (Paris), 4 August 1989.

38. Igor Kliamkin, *Moscow News,* 15 April 1989.

39. Sakharov's speech at the Congress launching his idea was reproduced in *The New York Review of Books,* 17 August 1989, 25–26.

40. The best discussion of the background to Gorbachev's economic reforms and the development of his early programs is Ed. H. Hewett, *Reforming the Soviet Economy* (Washington, D.C.: The Brookings Institution, 1987). On the Soviet side see Tatiana Zaslavskaia, in *A Voice of Reform: Essays by Tatiana Zaslavskaia,* ed. Murray Yanovitch (Armonk, N.Y.: M. E. Sharpe, 1989) and especially Nikolai Shmelyov and Vladimir Popov's *Na perelome (At the Breaking Point)* (Moscow: Ekonomika, 1989).

41. The most informed, penetrating and realistic study of economic perestroika's record to date is Anders Åslund, *Gorbachev's Struggle for Economic Reform* (Ithaca, N.Y.: Cornell University Press, 1989).

42. The best general treatments to date of the Gorbachev era overall are: Alec Nove, *Glasnost in Action: Cultural Renaissance in Russia* (Boston: Unwin Hyman, 1989), which is moderately pessimistic, and Walter Laqueur, *The Long Road to Freedom: Russia and Glasnost* (New York: Scribners, 1989), which is distinctly pessimistic. A strong statement of the internal contradictions of Gorbachevism is Vladimir Bukovsky's "Who Resists Gorbachev?" *Washington Quarterly* (Winter 1989).

43. The scissors metaphor was applied to Gorbachev by the historian Sergio Romano, Italian ambassador to Moscow during the last four years. It will be the theme of his forthcoming book, in Italian, on perestroika.

44. Andrei Amalrik, *Will the Soviet Union Survive Until 1984?* (New York: Harper and Row, 1970).

45. Andranik Migranyan, *Literaturnaia Gazeta,* 16 August 1989.

46. Milovan Djilas and George Urban, "Djilas on Gorbachev," *Encounter 71* (September-October 1987): 3–19.

58   Causes of the Collapse of the USSR

ALEXANDER DALLIN

In awe, amazement, and disbelief, the world witnessed the collapse of the Soviet Union, which swept away the Soviet system of government, the erstwhile superpower, the communist belief system, and the ruling party.

Why did the Soviet system disintegrate? In the first year since its collapse, several conflicting and controversial "theories" have been proposed in explanation. A sharp line may be drawn between explanations that focus on particular aspects of the Soviet system—operations (as indicated by the slowdown of the economy, for example), institutions or personalities—and those which find the cause of the collapse in the essence of the Soviet regime.

ESSENTIALIST ARGUMENTS

The "essentialists," whose moral absolutism was at the root of the famous identification of the Soviet Union, barely ten years ago, as the "evil empire," make three claims regarding the origins of Soviet collapse:

(1) The original seizure of power by the Leninists in 1917 was illegitimate, and this illegitimacy and a peculiar "genetic code" remained attached to the ruling party and the regime. And much as a form of original sin, they could not be shed or overcome; thus, the system was in some sense doomed from the start.

(2) Throughout its history, the Soviet system was essentially unchangeable; whatever the alterations in institutions, policies, and personalities, these were relatively trivial, as throughout it was and remained an "ideocracy" and a "partocracy."

(3) The Soviet system was "intrinsically unreformable": efforts to tinker with it, including those of the Gorbachev era, were intended only to rescue and

strengthen it, whereas the system needed to be demolished and a new system built from scratch on a different foundation.[2]

The essentialists themselves break down into those who see the Soviet Union as the quintessence of the worst of Russian political culture and those others who see the source of evil—its totalitarianism— in ideology and organization, that is, in Marxism-Leninism and the Communist Party.[3] In fact, the differences between these two camps are not at all insignificant.[4]

We may take the recent writings of Martin Malia as the most explicit, most elegant, and most systematic exposition of the neo-totalitarian approach, which moreover does claim to provide an explanation for what he calls the "implosion" of the Soviet order.[5] Precisely because this argument risks becoming an ideology of its own—and because it is based on assumptions that this observer considers thoroughly misguided—the following is an attempt to provide a different set of propositions to explain the Soviet collapse.

AGAINST PREDETERMINATION

Identifying the sources of historical events is a notoriously chancy and disputed business. We have no experimental method, nor proof that would stand up in a scientific court of law. Etiology—the search for causes—is not a science, nor is there any reliable technique for weighing the relative importance of different inputs. The archives will reveal no documents that will conveniently spell out the causes of the Soviet collapse. Moreover, the assessment of causes may well change with the distance in time from the events. Finally, as with an earthquake, at times subterranean processes are at work without our being able to track them in advance of their eruption.

Research will help, as will a commitment to making assumptions explicit. At the very least, it is often possible to tell who has gotten it wrong, without being sure who has gotten it right. But, ultimately, we have to rely on an individual analyst's scholarly intuition and empathy, and on his or her implicit philosophy of history. It is only fair to indicate that my own inclination is to distrust both conspiracy theories and flukes, and to be suspicious of all manner of determinism and inevitability, mysterious "essences" and broad a priori philosophical schemes. It is far better, I would maintain, to examine the empirical evidence without prejudging the case.

I find no grounds for arguing that the outcome—the disintegration of the Soviet system—was predetermined, let alone inscribed in the "genetic code" that went back to October 1917 and the origins of that system. How do we know what, if anything, was preordained? More concretely, the system withstood many tests far more severe than what it experienced in the 1980s (for example, in the first Five-Year Plan and in World War II) and survived: its institutions and controls were scarcely brittle then, and popular attitudes—admittedly, difficult to probe in retrospect—scarcely bore out the neo-totalitarian argument that the regime never had any legitimacy in the eyes of the population.

Of course the seizure of power in 1917 was illegitimate. But it is impossible seriously to derive the events of 1991 from that fact. It is far more sensible and far more persuasive to argue that what we see in the Soviet collapse is the product of unintended results, both of socio-economic development and of earlier policy choices. According to the neo-totalitarian argument, the Soviet Union remained totalitarian after Stalin—not because the reality of Soviet life was so, but because of a continued commitment of the decision-makers to a totalitarian vision. By the same token, it is precisely the extent to which Soviet reality diverged from that vision that provides evidence of social autonomy—of what is properly referred to as unintended consequences.[6]

What we are really puzzling over is how as thoroughly controlled, as tightly disciplined, as rigidly programmed, and as heavily indoctrinated a system as the Soviet managed to fall apart, unravel so easily and so completely, and in the process prompt in its citizenry an utter scorn for authority, and a disregard for laws and regulations.

The answers, I believe, have to go beyond social psychology, for they centrally involve political institutions and behavior. They involve both broad secular changes and particular individual choices. There is, I suggest, a cluster of interrelated developments that together, and in their interaction, formed the essential preconditions—necessary but not sufficient—for what occurred in the 1990s. In brief, they are: (1) the loosening of controls; (2) the spread of corruption; (3) the erosion of ideology; (4) the impact of social change on values and social pathologies; (5) the growing impact of the external environment on Soviet society and politics; and (6) the consequences of economic constraints. Against these background conditions, certain decisions of the Gorbachev regime, in turn, appear decisive as catalysts for collapse.

THE LOOSENING OF CONTROLS

One thing that held the Soviet Union together, exacted obedience and compliance, and provided the framework for its *sui generis* development was the sweeping Stalinist system of controls. Stalin died in 1953. In retrospect, what we see during the following 30 years is a gradual, unheralded loosening and then breakdown of these controls.

An essential part of the control structure and process was the terror that had reached unbelievable proportions and exacted such an incredible cost in the Stalin years. In the Khrushchev years it was the abandonment of mass political terror that provided the conditions for reducing the scope of controls. It ended the atomization, the silencing of that society—with an impact that did not become fully apparent until a generation later.[7] As T. H. Rigby (1992, pp. 18–19), an astute analyst of the Soviet scene, observed, in differentiating between active and symbolic, covert and overt elements that presaged the emergence of a civil society a generation later:

> The most interesting developments came in the covert active elements. I am not thinking so much of the shadow economy and clientelist networks, although these also thrived mightily, especially during the Brezhnev years. Of far greater importance for the future of the civil society was the profuse blossoming vastly greater than what was apparent publicly. The key facilitating factor here was the curbing of the political police after Stalin's death. ... People gradually found they could get away with a great deal in the way of unorthodox opinions and behaviour in private—from rock music to listening to western radio broadcasts, from abstract art to passing on forbidden books or samizdat materials. The rehousing program helped here, because tens of millions of city dwellers now acquired some real privacy as they moved from so-called communal apartments to little family flats. The Soviet population was acquiring "freedom of speech in one kitchen."

At the same time, the post-Stalin years unintentionally conveyed to the Soviet citizen a sense of fallibility and uncertainty in the country's leadership. This was suggested both by the tinkering with institutions—Khrushchev's *sovnarkhozy* and the "bifurcation" of the party, for instance—and by the continuous struggle over power and policy within the elite, which found policy expression in, among other things, the anti-Stalin campaign, and which culminated in the ouster of Khrushchev.[8]

In the Brezhnev years a remarkable change in mood became apparent. Whether or not it accurately reflected reality, Soviet observers began to speak— rather more candidly than before—of stagnation and the leadership's failure to come to grips with urgent problems, and foreigners noted the change. Thus the economist Joseph Berliner was struck by the contrast between 1958 and 1967. By the later date,

> there was in fact an air of gloom in the comments of economists I talked to. Perhaps my impression was heightened by the contrast in their tone with that during my earlier visit to the USSR [in 1958] ... the USSR was riding the crest of a period of rapid economic growth. Consumption levels had risen rapidly following Stalin's death, and rates of investment were high. ... There was a mood of exuberance and confidence in the vitality of the Soviet economic system. All this had changed by 1967. One found a candid admission that the economy was facing some nasty problems (Strong, 1971, pp. 50–51).

This is echoed from the perspective of the 1970s as well, when it had become even more apparent. Soon it went beyond the economy. In a very perceptive analysis, based on his own experience, John Bushnell (1980, pp. 179–182) wrote:

during the 1950s the Soviet middle class became increasingly optimistic about the performance of the Soviet system and about its own prospects for material betterment. ... In the 1970s it has given way to pessimism. The rise and decline of middle-class optimism can be linked in part to political developments, but the crucial determinant has been the changing perception of Soviet economic performance.

Bushnell detected "mounting skepticism and cynicism about the values and performance of the regime in other areas as well."[9]

And Dusko Doder (1988, pp. 31, 38) recalled:

When I arrived in Moscow on temporary duty in the summer of 1978, it was apparent that incremental changes had taken place over the past decade. ... In the narrow circle of my friends I found something that was new, or at least more pronounced than before—the quest for the comforts of middle-class life: a car, a place in the country, a tiled bathroom, a Japanese stereo, a chance to travel abroad—at least to Bulgaria.

By the early 1980s it was apparent to him that

Brezhnev's stable regime had produced an amazing proliferation of corruption, a cynicism that undermined all enterprise. An air of stagnation, the timeless inertia of the bureaucracy, a crisis of spirit—all characterized a system that seemed to have accompanied the aging leaders into exhaustion and debility.

These comments touch on the principal arenas in which critical changes were indeed taking place. To what extent the Communist Party itself was affected was not yet apparent, and of course large bureaucratic organizations are capable of conducting routine operations regardless of the morale or enthusiasm, or lack thereof, of their personnel. But something else was becoming evident: what had been aptly described as a "mono-organizational" system (Rigby, 1976) was showing cracks. Party, state, and police officials were working the system for their own benefit.

Blair Ruble (1990) has suggested that (by analogy with Quebec) what was taking place was a sort of "quiet revolution"—with the informal emergence of a second economy, a second culture, even a second politics alongside, and in full recognition of the continuing limits imposed by the official ones.[10] What added to the toleration of the new ambiguities was the fact that the second economy (Grossman, 1977) had its functional aspects insofar as performance was concerned. So, it has been argued, had the crystallization of rival patronage networks cultivated by various Soviet leaders. While the emergence of patron-client relations is a virtually ubiquitous development in all complex societies, John Willerton (1992, pp. 2–8) posits convincingly that, insofar as it promotes individual needs or interests, it undercuts the centrality or priority of government (or party) norms and goals.

THE SPREAD OF CORRUPTION

Far more serious is the massive spread of corruption, in all its many aspects, as a way of life. In a powerful account based on personal experience and replete with well-documented anecdotes, Konstantin Simis, in his *USSR: The Corrupt Society* (1982), is compelled to conclude:

> The Soviet Union is infected from top to bottom with corruption—from the worker who gives the foreman a bottle of vodka to get the best job, to Politburo candidate Mzhavanadze who takes hundreds of thousands of rubles for protecting underground millionaires; from the street prostitute, who pays the policeman ten rubles so that he won't prevent her from soliciting clients, to the former member of the Politburo Ekaterina Furtseva, who built a luxurious suburban villa at the government's expense—each and everyone is afflicted with corruption.
>
> I was born in that country and lived there for almost sixty years. Year after year since childhood and throughout my whole conscious life I watched as corruption ate more deeply into society until it turned the Soviet regime in the sixties and seventies into a land of corrupt rulers, ruling over a corrupted people.[11]

Especially in the late Brezhnev years, scandalous examples multiplied, from the appearance of feudal baronies in Uzbekistan or in the Urals, where high officials were able to operate with impunity, to the involvement of Brezhnev's daughter, Galina, and her lover with a crowd of circus crooks, the theft of jewels, and the entanglement of high secret-police officials.

No doubt, many instances of corruption remained unexposed. But what is known argues strongly that the corruption presupposed a loosening of controls, permitting a wanton violation of law to take place in the interstices. It also implied and fostered a new measure of cynicism about the "radiant heights" of communist morality.

Much of this "quiet revolution" became possible because the end of mass terror also meant an end to the individual's paralyzing fear, and because bureaucratic actors saw opportunities for self-aggrandizement with minimal risk or cost. But in Stalin's time, in addition to both outer constraints and often simply the lack of opportunity for autonomous corruption, there had been psychological inhibitions on many well-placed individuals, rooted in their belief in the system and in the cause in the name of which it was all being done. Later, with a change of generations and apparently a change of values, one began to observe an erosion of ideological commitments and a more single-minded pursuit, and at times also a more explicit articulation, of personal priorities.

Perhaps the most interesting conceptualization of this phenomenon is to be found in Ken Jowitt's (1983) writings. Stressing the disappearance of the party's overriding combat task—or transformation agenda—of earlier years, he remarked in the 1980s: "Today what impresses one about the Soviet Union is the party leadership's inability and/or unwillingness to devise a credible and authoritative social combat task capable of sustaining a distinction between the regime elite's particular status interests and the party's general competence and interest. ..." What is remarkable, he finds, is the increasing tendency of individual members to be "oriented to personal, familial, and material concerns." In Jowitt's post-Weberian vocabulary, "the subordination of office charisma to the incumbents' particular interests" is then identified precisely as "corrupt routinization."[12]

THE EROSION OF IDEOLOGY

Beginning at an earlier point but most explicit and tangible in the post-Stalin years, some of the millions of communists who made up the Soviet elite, and who were slated to become the regime's next generation of leaders, experienced an unadvertised but far-reaching crisis of identity and self-doubt.

One facet of this crisis was the subtle erosion of faith in the future and of the belief that the Bolsheviks alone had all the answers. This disillusionment, greatly intensified by Khrushchev's anti-Stalin campaign, was accompanied by an unheralded transformation in the dominant orientation: a shift from the pursuit of the millennium to compromising with reality. Seweryn Bialer (1987, pp. 54ff.) was one of those who remarked on the withering of utopianism in the Brezhnev years. Wherever the faithful looked, the traditional prophecies had failed to come through: world revolution had not occurred, crime had not vanished, nationalism and religion had not disappeared with the passing of capitalism, as had been predicted. To be sure, the orthodox formulae continued to be reprinted *ad nauseam*, but inspiration had turned into ritual, and especially in the Brezhnev years there was no longer any serious effort made to reconcile conflicting articles of faith and observation.[13]

Strikingly, a similar decline may be noted in the rulers' self-confidence concerning their right to rule. Unwittingly, memoirs such as those of Khrushchev's son Sergei and of others close to the leadership testify to this point.[14] A number of former Soviet academics have privately related their difficulties in coming to terms with the Stalin phenomenon. How had it been possible in the first place, and how could Stalinism now be explained to the next generation? What were the implications for the Soviet experiment? Within the limits of the permissible, serious questions were raised from within the Marxist-Leninist tradition: for instance, on the nature of "contradictions" under socialism, and the phenomenon of bureaucracy.

A good example is also provided by General Dmitriy Volkogonov, who recently recalled that in the 1970s

> I was an orthodox Marxist, an officer who knew his duty. I was not part of some liberal current. All my changes came from within, off on my own. I had access to all kinds of literature. ... I was a Stalinist. I contributed to the strengthening of the system that I am now trying to dismantle. But latently, I had my ideas. I began asking myself questions about Lenin, how, if he was such a genius, none of his predictions came true. The proletarian dictatorship never came to be, the principle of class

struggle was discredited, communism was not built in fifteen years as he had promised. None of Lenin's major predictions ever came true! I confess it: I used my position, I began gathering information even though I didn't know yet what I would do
with it (Remnick, 1992, p. 15).

Yet there can be no doubt about the importance of faith for the cohesion of a
regime that had chosen to make its ideology so central and weighty a core of the
system.

Indeed, it was during the Brezhnev years that we witnessed an unprecedented
surge of dissident literature—not from people who had never shared the regime's
values or goals but from prominent individuals well within the system's elite. In
retrospect, the number of dissidents appears to have been greater than was commonly assumed at the time. In 1970, Andrey Sakharov, Roy Medvedev, and Valeriy
Turchin addressed a letter to the Soviet leadership, arguing in favor of far-reaching democratization.

Over the past decade menacing signs of disorder and stagnation have begun to show
themselves in the economy of our country. ... The population's real income in recent years has hardly grown at all; food supply and medical and consumer services
are improving very slowly, and with unevenness between regions. The number of
goods in short supply continues to grow. ... What is the source of all this trouble?
The source lies in the antidemocratic traditions and norms of public life established
in the Stalin era, which have not been decisively eliminated to this day. Noneconomic coercion, limitations on the exchange of information, restrictions on intellectual freedom, and other examples of the antidemocratic distortion of socialism
which took place under Stalin were accepted in our country as an overhead expense
in the industrialization process (Sanders, 1974, pp. 400–403).

Whether or not this had been justified in the first rush of industrialization,
they wrote, there is no doubt that these had now become serious handicaps.
There is a need, they argued, for free access to information and ideas. Otherwise
the Soviet Union will become a second-rate power. They added:

There are reasons to assume that the point of view expressed in the above theses is
shared to one degree or another by a significant part of the Soviet intelligentsia and
the advanced section of the working class. This attitude is also reflected in the opinions of student and working youth, as well as in numerous private discussions
within small groups of friends (Sanders, 1974, p. 403).

And in 1983 the famous "Novosibirsk memorandum" (Zaslavskaya, 1983)
found its way abroad. In it, Tat'yana Zaslavskaya, was telling the authorities:

Over a number of decades, Soviet society's economic development had been characterized by high rates and great stability. ... However, in the past 12–15 years a tendency towards a noticeable decline in the rate of growth of the national income be-

gan to make itself felt in the development of the economy of the USSR. ... This does not provide for either the rate of growth in living standards that is required for the people, or for the intensive technical retooling of production. ... In our opinion, [the cause of this is] the inability of this system to make provision for the full and sufficiently effective use of the labour potential and intellectual resources of society (p. 88).

While written in a style entirely loyal and conforming to official Soviet norms, the memorandum does point to a number of changes that have occurred in Soviet economy, society, and technology that require recognition and changes in institutions, attitudes, and practices.

In the light of what has been said, we must admit that the social mechanism of economic development as it functions at present in the USSR does not ensure satisfactory results. The social type of worker formed by it fails to correspond not only to the strategic aims of a developed socialist society, but also to the technological requirements of contemporary production. The widespread characteristics of many workers, whose personal formation occurred during past five-year plans, are low labour- and production-discipline, an indifferent attitude to the work performed and its low quality, social passivity, a low value attached to labour as a means of self-realization, an intense consumer orientation, and a rather low level of moral discipline. It is enough to mention the broad scale of activity of the so-called "touts" ["pilferers"—AD], the rampant spread of various "shady" deals made at public expense, the development of illegal output, of irregular registrations, of procuring wages which are not dependent on the results of labour (p. 106).

As discussed below, the increasing acquaintance and fascination with foreign norms, styles, and practices—and goods—would, in their own way, further contribute to the erosion of commitments to official Soviet orthodoxy.

SOCIAL CHANGE

The Soviet era witnessed a remarkable process of social change. In some measure it had begun even before the 1917 revolutions: urbanization and higher educational attainments are the universal by-product of economic development. To a significant degree, this was ideologically welcome to the Leninists as it promoted "proletarianization" at the expense of the peasantry. Later, the "liquidation of the kulaks as a class" was a conscious policy decision buttressed by ideological, economic, and security considerations (whether spurious or not). Similarly, the massive employment of female labor, the wholesale resettlement and migration, as well as the expansion of labor camps and forced settlements, were willed by the regime. And to some extent, the new social stratification was the inevitable by-product of choices made on behalf of rapid industrialization, bureaucratization, and centralization. But, whether willed or not, these developments had unforeseen, unintended, and (from the regime's point of view) often undesirable consequences.

The magnitude of the transformations is suggested by Soviet census figures: the urban share of the population rose from some 18 percent in 1926 to about 65 percent in 1985. The number of "specialists"—the so-called intelligentsia—grew from some 2 million before World War II to over 30 million in the 1980s, of whom more than half had specialized training or higher education.[15] The government, party, police, and military bureaucracies grew at a comparable pace.

The resulting sociography of the Soviet Union still awaits thorough study. For instance, the attitudes and values of the working class—and regional variations— remain to be better understood. What is clear, however, is that, in so far as they involved the formation of a new intelligentsia (the equivalent of an urban middle class), and the crystallization of new values, priorities, and aspirations within it, these transformations had profound effects in generating a new sociopolitical force. So, inevitably, did the appearance of a new, postwar generation of citizens, possessed of rising expectations, and whose members had not shared in the hopes and sufferings of earlier years.

An additional factor in the 1970s and early 1980s was the (accurate) perception, spreading in urban society, that the previously axiomatic opportunities for upward social mobility were no longer there. With the slowdown of economic growth, the more or less stable size of administrative and military cadres, the end of massive purges (and the widespread retention of older officials in office), it was plausible that there should be fewer vacancies to be filled. The resulting effect on morale, especially among ambitious younger people, was obvious.

We find then an unmistakable spread of skepticism and widespread cynicism, particularly in the 1970s. Along with the "weakening belief in ideals," cited above, observers pointed to a career-mindedness and materialism, and a combination of consumerism and consumer pessimism. Moreover, it was pointed out, "because economic performance has been so central to sociopolitical stability, the consequences of this stagnation are potentially serious" (Lapidus, 1983, p 198). There was also a lack of fit between educational opportunities and career needs; and high aspirations combined with a disdain for manual labor to create further tensions. High rates of labor turnover, low productivity, and low worker morale were additional indicators of growing problems (Lapidus, 1983, pp. 204–210).

The loss of optimism and the loss of purpose readily led to a change of attitude. This was reflected, for instance, in the jocular remark, "We pretend to be working, and they pretend to be paying us," as well as in the middle-class view of corruption reported by Bushnell (1980, p. 187): "It's a crime *not* to steal from them," which is revealing also for the use of "them" for the authorities. It easily spilled over into antisocial behavior. Alcoholism, in particular, became even more of a severe problem than before, with manifest consequences from industrial accidents to family life. Lying and cheating seemed to become pandemic in Soviet society.[16]

One conclusion of particular interest, prompted by studies of Soviet refugees, émigrés, and "displaced persons," concerns variation of grievances by age groups. The so-called Harvard study of Soviet refugees in the 1950s (Inkeles and Bauer, 1961) had concluded that young people were more thoroughly indoctrinated and less critical of the Soviet system than their elders. But in the early 1980s a corresponding study of Brezhnev-era émigrés (Millar, 1987) found evidence that, on the contrary, young people (as well as those with more education) now tended to be more negative and more disenchanted with the performance of the system than their elders.[17]

Students of Soviet society concluded, even prior to the accession of Gorbachev, that the potential for instability was greater then than at any time since World War II.

> Possibly the most dramatic change of recent years, and one with profound implications for the legitimacy and stability of the Soviet system, has been a shift in attitudes within the Soviet population during the two decades [i.e., 1960s and 70s]. Most visible within the middle class and intelligentsia but extending to the working class as well, it involves growing pessimism about the Soviet future, increasing disillusionment with official values, and an accompanying decline in civic morale (Lapidus, 1983, p. 233).

As Geoffrey Hosking (1990, pp. 4–5), a well-qualified observer, remarked: "There had been evidence for more than two decades that society and politics were out of phase with one another, that society was starting to outgrow the crude and rigid integument of the party-controlled political system."

These attitudes and values need not have been dangerously incongruent with the existing regime. In fact, in large part the new middle class as well as the workers were dependent on that regime for their own advancement and careers, a circumstance that importantly distinguishes Soviet "classes" from their counterparts in liberal-democratic societies. For better or for worse, Soviet citizens had been accustomed—at whatever price to themselves—to distinguish between their private and their public personae and not to give voice to impolitic desires. Moreover, the existence of unorthodox attitudes does not, and need not, readily translate into political demands or action programs. Yet, it turned out, especially the new middle class—in and out of the Communist Party—provided a fertile breeding ground and, later, a social base, first for the "reformers" and then for the "democrats."[18]

As Zbigniew Brzezinski (1989, pp. 33–34) concluded:

> the Stalinist system endured [in the Brezhnev years] not only because Brezhnev and his immediate comrades benefited from it and remained loyal to it. It survived because it had become a vast structure of overlapping privileges, controls, rewards, and vested interest. ... Most important, Stalinism both endured and stagnated because it was a political system without real political life within it. That stagnation could not be forever ignored. Already by the later years of the Brezhnev era, a sense

of malaise was developing within a portion of the upper Soviet elite. An awareness of decay, of ideological rot, of cultural sterility was setting in. It began not only to permeate the intellectual circles but also to infect some members of the political elite.

THE INTERNATIONAL ENVIRONMENT

There has been discussion in the West, more of it political than scholarly, about the extent to which the international environment, and more explicitly, American policy, can take credit for the collapse of the Soviet system.[19] In regard to explicit policy by Western powers, it is impossible to find direct evidence of its destabilizing impact on Soviet society or polity, though at least three factors can be assumed to have played some role: (1) the unintended consequences of the inclusion of "Basket 3" (on human rights) in the Helsinki accords of 1975; (2) a heightening of the fear of nuclear war; and (3) almost certainly the strains imposed by the defense burden, discussed below.[20] On the other hand, it remains to be studied whether or not a "tough" Western posture tended to reinforce a siege mentality within the Moscow elite. But, quite distinct from Western policy and conduct, there is good evidence of the importance of simply the existence of the outside world as a challenge to and as a reference group for comparisons by Soviet observers.

The years up to 1985, when Gorbachev came to power, saw a significant increase in the Soviet elite's familiarity with alternative political and socioeconomic systems and with life abroad, a result of both technology and détente. While on the surface that early détente was a political failure, it worked certain important changes in information and attitude that are relevant to our discussion, by strengthening pro-reform images.

Thus, after many years of imposed isolation, Soviet specialists were allowed to travel abroad, correspond with professional colleagues, read foreign journals and magazines. Tourists began to visit other countries; we saw Soviet exchange scholars and students in the U.S. wandering through supermarkets and reading books that had been forbidden back home. In fact, at a time of growing middle-class *veshchizm* (crass consumerism), rapidly expanding tourism even to Eastern Europe stimulated provocative comparisons.[21]

What is more, new technology could be enlisted on behalf of the curious citizenry (and not solely, as George Orwell had posited, on behalf of the regime). Direct-dialing telephones put them in easier touch with émigrés and colleagues abroad, gave them a chance to realize how far behind they were, and stimulated questions about regime policies and the assumptions that had prompted them. Audio cassettes, television, and VCRs (video-cassette recorders) made both information and ideas more accessible.

Nor should we dismiss this new acquaintanceship as trivial or marginal. We know the importance of reference groups from numerous studies. And we know of historical instances where exposure to other civilizations wrought havoc, be it China's acquaintance with the West as a result of the Opium Wars, or the intrusion of Islam into the Mediterranean civilization; or for that matter, the impact of television—showing how people lived elsewhere—on the American civil rights movement in the 1960s and on French Quebec.[22]

ECONOMIC DECLINE

Specialists told us that the Soviet economy needed structural reform long before 1985. Above all, the central command economy had failed to keep up its previously impressive growth rate, the GNP plummeting (by Western estimates) from some 6 percent growth rates in the 1960s to perhaps 2 percent or less in the early 1980s. Per capita real income declined as well. One reason was that earlier on, inputs—capital, labor, energy—had been ample and cheap. By the 1970s this was no longer so, and it was necessary to switch from a strategy of extensive development to an intensive one. Moreover, productivity was low, and the system failed to provide adequate incentives for harder work or for technological innovation. If anything, the technological gap and lag behind the West were increasing. Typically, the quality of production and services were substantially below world standards. This reduced Soviet ability to export goods and also added to consumer dissatisfaction, given the rising expectations of the new elite.

This was also the one area where U.S. policy may have had an impact. Given the Soviet leadership's commitment after the Cuban missile crisis of 1962 to catch up with American military might, including R&D in advanced technology, a totally disproportionate share of Soviet GNP (clearly over 15 percent, by some estimates a lot more) was allocated for the arms race—in an economy whose total product was a good deal less than that of the U.S. The result of these investments was to seriously distort the economy at precisely a time when the decline in its growth rate required cuts in allocations to other parts of the economy, including welfare, services, and consumption.[23]

Here then we have a combination of inherent trends and disastrous policy choices by the Soviet leadership. In addition to objective problems that the Soviet economy presented, the trends sketched above were bound to impact subjective perceptions as well. Not only was the unquestioned priority of defense expenditures becoming more apparent, but the resulting "defense burden" no longer went unchallenged. In addition, the implications of the slowdown not only affected other sectors of the economy but also led to questions concerning the axiomatic effect of continued economy growth on the perceived legitimation of the Soviet system. For some years short-term successes (as well as economic and social problems abroad) had concealed the structural inadequacies of the Soviet economic mechanism, but by the early 1980s profound doubts about it had matured, particularly as Soviet observers increasingly tended to judge the system by its performance rather than by its promises.

INTERACTION AMONG THE VARIABLES

All this adds up to a subtle change in the relationship of state and society on the even of the Gorbachev years. Society gains greater autonomy, grievances and expectations become more critical and more overt, and there occurs an implicit shift to some expectation of accountability. If there is an increasing inclination to judge the regime by its performance, in the 1980s the regime falls short. And, more immediately important in 1985, it is essentially this perception of the same trends that shaped the conviction of Mikhail Gorbachev and his friends that "things cannot go on like this."[24]

I have argued that none of the trends we have examined was the prime motor in this process of change. It is precisely the interaction among these variables that was critical. While we cannot "replay" the events with one variable left out, some inferences as to relative weights are plausibly strong. Thus, had the whole control structure not loosened up, much of the articulation of grievances could not have occurred, acquaintance with the outside world would have been far more modest, and the assertion of autonomy in various venues could neither have been undertaken nor succeeded to the degree that it did. Similarly, the effect of the loosening up on the spread of corruption, the perception of stagnation, and contact with the West all facilitated the erosion of ideological commitments. So manifestly did the social pathologies, the value shift and the rising expectations among the new urban middle class erode the faith among officials and non-officials alike.

True, the economic constraints alone should have been enough to engender doubts, comparisons, and grievances. However, the true economic facts were not widely known; indeed, some "derogatory" facts were scarcely known even in the highest leadership circles. Furthermore, at earlier times of economic difficulty— be it 1930 or 1946—there had been no such articulation, essentially because both the actors and the political environment had been so different. We must then conclude that the cluster of trends we have focused on provided a set of necessary conditions for the changes that ensued.

THE GORBACHEV FACTOR

Taken together, the trends and developments discussed above suggest a number of serious flaws and fragilities in the Soviet system. But there are no grounds for arguing that they doomed it. If we had seen them as clearly as we do now in, say, 1984, would we have been led to conclude that a collapse of the Soviet Union was inevitable in the foreseeable future? I think the answer has to be "no."

In that case, do we mean to say that, had Gorbachev and his associates *not* come to power, the Soviet Union would have hobbled along, and might have continued to muddle through without overt instability? That is the only possible conclusion. If we reach that conclusion, based on those premises, then we must give serious weight to the proposition that the much-touted "collapse of communism" was perhaps not nearly so inevitable and surely not necessarily so imminent as it has been made out to be.

There is room for counterfactual speculation, and I think the most responsible answer is that, while we cannot be sure, at the very least Moscow might have gained considerable time, might have avoided the destabilization and delegitimation that the Gorbachev years brought, and might have shaped the domestic and international environment very differently from what in fact occurred. What comes to mind as one scenario is something like the evolution of Turkey or Mexico, which experienced radical regimes and transformations in the first quarter of this century, but where revolutionary zeal petered out without an overthrow of governments.

One could point to problems with this sort of scenario, born of differences between the Soviet Union and Mexico or Turkey. Specifically, the Soviet regime propagated an explicit, mandatory ideology based on the notion of two adversary world systems. That ideology, among other things, provided the justification for the inordinately burdensome effort to match the United States in defense expenditures and weapons research. One could argue, therefore, that drastically cutting the military effort—for a nuclear superpower, at that—would have required a fundamental reorientation of the image of the enemy and the whole ideological mind-set. (Moreover, even such a major restructuring of the Soviet budget probably would not have sufficed to address the structural disorders that ailed the Soviet economy.)

This argument is compelling, though not entirely convincing. True, rational policy choices are constrained by dos and don'ts rooted in beliefs. But was this true under Brezhnev? To some extent, yes; but it was becoming less so. Precisely the Brezhnev years had been a great exercise in fudging issues and overtly denying realities. Such behavior both reflected and deepened the disillusionment and uncertainty about ideological verities within the political establishment. But precisely because of that change in perspectives, the doctrine became even more pragmatically malleable. With a little semantic effort, Brezhnev's successors, had they been so inclined, could surely have managed to cut defense without giving up such parts of the residual communist vision as they wished to protect and preserve. Thus, they could have made policy adjustments while continuing to legitimize their right to rule by reference to other components of the ideology. They would have sacrificed some measure of credibility in the process. But that is not the same as losing the ability to maintain elite unity against challenges to the system.

If my argument has merit, the implication is that the Gorbachev years, and what is now called *katastroyka,* are an essential part of the explanation of the collapse. They are not sufficient by themselves to explain it, but they are, ironically or tragically, a vital link in the chain of destabilization, delegitimation, and disintegration that led from the superpower status of the 1970s to the new, shrunken, confused, and impoverished Russian Federation of the 1990s.

Unlike some of the earlier trends that we can label impersonal or secular, in the Gorbachev period we are dealing with the very distinct acts of will, acts that in retrospect should deaden any temptation to agree with those who seek to transform history and politics into mathematical formulae of rational choice. It did make a lot of difference that these particular individuals, beginning with Gorbachev and soon Yakovlev and Shevardnadze, were the ones taking charge in Moscow. Suffice it to contemplate counterfactual scenarios in which, say, Chernenko remained in office for another five years, or was succeeded by Grishin or Romanov: how different would the country have looked?

Those who see the Soviet period and the dominant Leninist ideology as a seamless web have difficulty explaining how a Gorbachev and his cohort could have emerged in charge of such a system in the first place. Whatever happens elsewhere, here personalities have certainly played a significant part. The fact that they, and not any others, came to power in 1985 also serves to torpedo the "inevitable collapse" argument. To claim that the Soviet system was bound to crash amounts to committing what Reinhard Bendix (1964, p. 13) called "the fallacy of retrospective determinism"—denying the choices (however constrained) that the actors had available before acting.

But what was it about the Gorbachev policies—so many of which were brilliant—that contributed to the system's collapse? First and foremost, Gorbachev put an end to the claim that there was one single truth and therefore one single party that was its carrier. In association with this argument, he fostered *glasnost'*, an end to censorship, an end to widespread political repression, and an end to the official monopoly on rewriting the past. In terms of sociopolitical impact, all this brought about a remarkable sense of having been lied to, of having been deprived of what the rest of the world had had access to, a "desacralization" of the system (Malia, 1990) and delegitimation of the authorities, a transformation of the Communist Party from the unchallenged clan of privilege to a hollow institution without a rational task other than self-preservation. This in turn opened the floodgates to massive and varied grassroots organization and articulation outside the party.

The other major arena in which the new policy of *glasnost'* had an impact was the republics. From Estonia to Azerbaijan, *glasnost'* mobilized opinion around issues of ethnic identity, beginning with language, school, or culture, and ending with national-liberation fronts. And while there had obviously been some sense of national consciousness that had been stifled earlier on, some of its growth was another unintended consequence of the Soviet experience. The organization of the federation by Union republics, each with its dominant nationality, the ethnic identification of all Soviet citizens in their passports, and the promotion of national cultures and histories (in however circumscribed a fashion) all served to nurture memories and identifications that would be mobilized and reshaped later, when conditions permitted.

Yet, one may hypothesize, the big impetus came precisely from the new doubts about, and the newly perceived challengeability of, the Soviet system. For once their identities as Soviet citizens or communists faded, people looked around for alternative loci of loyalty and identity, and the most powerful "imagined communities" (Anderson, 1983) were the ethnonational ones. Thus (to oversimplify a complicated process) *glasnost'* made possible the political mobilization of doubting, contemptuous, and newly emboldened publics, and the invention of new organizations. These acquired an additional ethnic coloration because of the discrediting of alternative identities, which brought to the top of the political agenda the question of the future of the Soviet federal system. That transformation did not come soon enough to avoid the polarization between the centralist "coup plotters" of August 1991 and the separatists at the other end of the center/periphery spectrum.[25] A year later, Gorbachev admitted that his failure fully to recognize the seriousness of the "nationality question" had perhaps been his most serious error in office (*We/My,* No. 6 [June 1–14, 1992]).

In arguing that the liberalization of the system from 1985 to 1991 was part of the explanation for its collapse, I am *not* agreeing with the proposition that the system could not be reformed. That argument comes from both ends of the political spectrum, though it is made with divergent purposes in mind. The Stalinists in Moscow insist that *any* attempt to "reform" the Soviet system—to alter or abandon its Stalinist cast—was bound to subvert it and therefore must at all costs be avoided; Molotov's critique of Khrushchev's policy in the 1950s came close to this view. Likewise, we hear from those at the other extreme that the Soviet system could not be reformed step by step but needed to be totally demolished before a democratic and healthy system could be erected from scratch. The experience of the Gorbachev regime does not answer the question whether its errors—say, on the nationality question or in economic policy—were avoidable or not. I believe they were, as they were errors of individual judgments, not inherent and inescapable trends. While there are many significant differences between the two cases, the "Chinese option" also suggests that—in the regime's own terms—certain reforms could succeed.

Finally we must ask what, in this setting, provided the trigger for the outward collapse of what remained of the Soviet Union. Here Boris Yel'tsin and his successful "second coming" deserve a little credit (or blame). His re-emergence in 1990 in the context of competitive elections was a product of the unraveling of the system and in turn contributed to the shift in the locus of power and popular support away from the old center. His declaration of Russian sovereignty legitimated the other republics' posture against the "center" and momentarily united democrats and nationalists. His election as president of Russia in June 1991 and, two months later, his stand against the "coup plotters" dramatized both his strength and Gorbachev's weakness. Yel'tsin chose to magnify that asymmetry, and in December he decided to torpedo what remained of the "Union" structure and to erect the impoverished "Commonwealth" framework in its place.

Yel'tsin could not have pulled off these changes if the system had not already been badly injured. Still, he made the most of it, for himself as well, and in the process permitted the collapse of the Soviet Union itself. Identifying him as the final catalyst of the collapse may be the easiest part of this exercise.

CONCLUSION

It is perhaps natural for us to seek simple explanations, single causes, and yes-or-no answers. More often than not, in real life, things are far more complex. We must take care not to introduce retrospectively a clarity, let alone inevitability, where there was contingency and complexity. A retrospective view should underscore the dynamic and variable character of many Soviet policies and institutions. While it is no doubt true that "the party" or "the secret police" or "the dictator" was an ever-present power in the Soviet state, the limits of each changed over time. If corruption was a perennial feature, its scope varied greatly. So did dissent and deviance.

And so did legitimacy. From the manifest fact that the Soviet regime, by 1991, was not widely perceived as legitimate by the population, it is important not to draw the inference that the Soviet regime had been perceived as illegitimate at all earlier times—during the NEP, at the end of World War II, or in the 1960s and 1970s, for instance. The recognition of this fact helps us understand why it is not the case that the Soviet system could have collapsed at any given moment during its 74-year history (though, of course, factors other than a lack of legitimacy could have brought about its demise). It turned out that its end required the maturation, as well as the interaction, of the several trends identified above. It also required the particular, albeit understandable, blind spots in the perceptions and policy choices of the Gorbachev leadership.

NOTES

2. On the "essentialist" approach, see Dallin and Lapidus (1989, pp. 199–202) and sources quoted therein. The three points made above are taken from the recent writings of Malia. See "Z" (1990); Malia, 1991, 1992a, 1992b). The words in quotation marks above are drawn from these writings. On the genetic code, see Malia (1992a, p. 103): In 1991 "the genetic code born of the October overturn of 1917 at last worked itself out fully, that is, to the extinction of the organism."

3. Six months before Gorbachev became General Secretary, Richard Pipes wrote that the Soviet Union was "by definition incapable of evolution from within and impervious to change from without" (Pipes, 1984, p. 49). On the "hard-line" outlook and argument, see also Dallin (1988). In all fairness, Pipes has changed his views somewhat in the wake of recent events. The changes, after Stalin, within communist regimes, and the differences among them, stimulated widespread discussion about the utility and accuracy, or otherwise, of the concept of totalitarianism. This is hardly the place to refight that battle. For our purposes, it many suffice to recognize that in large measure this is a matter of definition. Certainly the "classic" definition, as provided by Carl Friedrich and Zbigniew Brzezinski (1956) does not fit. If the concept is to be used, there is merit in the approach outlined by Juan Linz (1975) and others. (See Gleason (1984) for the twists and turns of the argument.) Rather than viewing "soft communism" (as Malia does) as an emergency rescue mode

adopted when things go perilously wrong, it is far more accurate to consider "soft" and "hard" (or better, right and left) communism—reformist and antireformist orientations— as "two worlds in one communist breast," equally legitimate political tempers or tempera- ments. (See Cohen (1980) and Dallin (1969). Also see Gill (1991).) A still different, neo- Marxist perspective is represented by Hillel Ticktin (1992), who sees the Soviet Union as "neither socialist nor capitalist." He concludes, "There is no mature form of the USSR. It is a historical accident, an accident brought about through the defeat of the October revolu- tion in the form of the seizure of power by a bureaucratic ruling group. Just as Neanderthal man could never become man, so the USSR can never reform to become socialism or capi- talism. It is an unfortunate deviation of history, which is now [1991], under Gorbachev, coming to an end" (p. 14).

4. See Malia (1991). Pipes and Malia agree that the October Revolution was an illegiti- mate seizure of power. They also agree that Lenin logically led to Stalin, who was no aber- ration or traitor to the revolution. Where they differ is described by Malia as follows: for Pipes, "the key to sovietism lies in the Russian national tradition and a virtually changeless Russian political culture compounded of despotism above and servitude below, a tradition in which the country and its inhabitants are the property of the ruler, and sovereignty is confused with ownership ... Pipes rides his claims of immutable Russianness to implausi- ble lengths" (pp. 25–25).

5. I do not believe Malia defines what he means by "implosion." The collapse of the So- viet Union, hardly foreseen by any analyst, provides Malia with a springboard for a massive attack on—or rather, caricature of—all Sovietology, in fact on all social science. See Malia (1992a, pp. 94–102).

6. The *locus classicus* on the concept is Merton (1936).

7. See also Dallin and Breslauer (1970).

8. On the politics of the Khrushchev reforms, see Breslauer (1982), Chotiner (1984), Lin- den (1967), Tatu (1969). See also Hodnett (1966).

9. See also Feifer (1981).

10. See also Hauslohner (1989).

11. See also Vaksberg (1991) and Zemtsov (1976).

12. Jowitt (1983, p. 284). He also (p. 288) quotes from Gregory Grossman (1977, p. 37) that "the prevalence of economic illegalities and corruption elevates the power of money [in Soviet society] to rival that of the dictatorship itself, rendering the regime's implements of rule less effective and less certain."

13. See also Kull (1992) and Dallin (1993).

14. See Khrushchev (1990), Burlatsky (1991), and Arbatov (1992a, b).

15. The evidence and its implications are developed further in Lewin (1980). See also Lapidus (1983) and Bushnell (1980).

16. Bushnell (1980, pp. 185–187); Lapidus (1983, pp. 192, 236–238). On consumerism, see also Binyon (1984) and Smith (1976). On alcoholism see Treml (1982). Even by official fig- ures, per capita consumption, not counting various forms of "moonshine" and alcohol not intended for human consumption, more than doubled from 1955 to 1980. See also Jones, et al. (1991).

17. See in particular the chapters by Donna Bahry and Brian Silver in Millar (1987, pp. 61–141). Also see Hankiss (1990).

18. There remains a need to study the social bases of political affinities in Soviet society, and in particular that of the "reformers" (as distinguished from dissidents). One may sur-

mise that, in the period leading up to and including the Gorbachev years, most came from the intelligentsia; many were "insiders." If there were kolkhoz reformers or even worker reformers, they were rarely heard. (The Donbas strike committee in 1990 included a number of *intelligenty* such as engineers who had shifted to physical labor as a better source of income.)

19. For more serious discussions of the role of the international environment, see Bialer (1989), bearing in mind that the sources of reform are not necessarily identical with the causes of collapse. See also Deudney and Ikenberry (1991/1992); and the column by George F. Kennan in *The New York Times*, October 28, 1992.

20. In considering the international environment, some additional weight might be given to the Soviet involvement in, and ultimate withdrawal from, Afghanistan, and to the Soviet perception of instability in Eastern Europe (especially Poland in 1980–1981). It is hard to gauge the impact of these events. Concern over a "workers' movement" such as *Solidarność* was real, it appears, primarily among members of the Soviet establishment, but in subsequent interviews by the author Eastern Europe was mentioned by well-placed Soviet respondents only rarely as a major cause of concern or as a significant influence on their political views.

21. See, for example, Bushnell (1980, p. 192) and Lapidus (1983, pp. 192ff.); also see Starr (1983) for a fine case study of ambivalence and struggle over one form of "cosmopolitan" influence.

22. True, acquaintance with the West was not a *sine qua non* for the development of reformist perspectives. The Gorbachev team would include not only people like Aleksandr Yakovlev, who had studied in New York and later spent ten years as ambassador in Canada, but also others like Eduard Shevardnadze, who had no significant exposure to the outside world.

23. See, for example, U.S. Central Intelligence Agency (1990); Levine and Bergson (1983); Rowen and Wolf (1990); Åslund (1989); Hewett (1989). For a rebuttal, see Bergson (1991). Although some "insiders" may have argued the case for bankrupting the Soviet Union, I know of no evidence that Washington decision-makers adopted the American build-up policy in order to exacerbate these trends and the perceived burden in the Soviet economy rather than to offset a perceived military threat. No attempt is made here to provide precise numerical indicators for the state of the Soviet economy, since, in the Gorbachev years and after, enough has been revealed concerning the witting and unwitting falsification of Soviet statistics to make numbers, especially comparisons with analogous numbers in the U.S., more misleading than helpful. The resulting uncertainty is particularly glaring in regard to the total Soviet "defense burden" and its share in the total annual budget.

24. See Gorbachev's speech to cultural leaders, in *Pravda*, December 1, 1990. For another version, see Shevardnadze (1991, p. 79).

25. See Lapidus (1992). Whether a new "Union Treaty" would have sufficed to stem the centrifugal forces throughout the Soviet Union must remain a matter of speculation. A more extensive discussion would, of course, need to make major distinctions among the successor states.

REFERENCES

Anderson, Benedict, *Imagined Communities*. London: Verso, 1983.

Arbatov, Georgi, *An Insider's Life*. New York: Times Books, 1992b.

Arbatov, Georgi, *The System.* New York: Times Books, 1922b.

Åslund, Anders, *Gorbachev's Struggle for Economic Reform,* Ithaca, NY: Cornell University Press, 1989.

Bendix, Reinhard, *Nation-Building and Citizenship.* New York: John Wiley & Sons, 1964.

Bergson, Abram, "The USSR Before the Fall," *Journal of Economic Perspectives,* 5, 4:29–44, 1991.

Bialer, Seweryn, *The Soviet Paradox.* New York: Vintage Books, 1987.

Bialer, Seweryn, "The Domestic and International Sources of Gorbachev's Reforms," *Journal of International Affairs,* **42,** 2:283–297, 1989.

Binyon, Michael, *Life in Russia,* New York: Pantheon, 1984.

Breslauer, George W., *Khrushchev and Brezhnev as Leaders.* London: Allen & Unwin, 1982.

Brzezinski, Zbigniew, *The Grand Failure.* New York: Scribner's, 1989.

Burlatsky, Fyodor, *Khrushchev and the First Russian Spring.* New York: Scribner's,1991.

Bushnell, John, "The 'New Soviet Man' Turns Pessimist," in Stephen F. Cohen et al., eds., *The Soviet Union Since Stalin.* Bloomington, IN: Indiana University Press, **1980.**

Chotiner, Barbara, *Khrushchev's Party Reform.* Westport, CT: Greenwood Press, 1984.

Cohen, Stephen F., "Friends and Foes of Change," in Cohen et al., *The Soviet Union Since Stalin.* Bloomington, IN: Indiana University Press, 1980.

Dallin, Alexander, "Soviet Foreign Policy and Domestic Politics," *Journal of International Affairs,* **23,** 2:25–265, 1969.

Dallin, Alexander, "The Uses and Abuses of Russian History," in Terry L. Thompson and Richard Sheldon, eds., *Soviet Society and Culture: Essays in Honor of Vera S. Dunham.* Boulder, CO: Westview Press, 1988.

Dallin, Alexander and George W. Breslauer, *Political Terror in Communist Systems.* Stanford, CA: Stanford University Press, 1970.

Dallin, Alexander and Gail W. Lapidus, "Reagan and the Russians," in Kenneth Oye et al., eds., *Eagle Resurgent?* Boston: Little, Brown, 1987.

Dallin, Alexander, "From Faith to Failure: The Erosion of Soviet Optimism," in Dan Caldwell and Timothy McKeown, eds., *Diplomacy, Force and Leadership: Essays in Honor of Alexander L. George.* Boulder, Co: Westview Press, 1993.

Deudney, Daniel and G. John Ikenberry, "The International Sources of Soviet Change," in *International Security.* **16,** 3:74–188, winter 1991/1992.

Doder, Dusko, *Shadows and Whispers,* London: Penguin, 1988.

Feifer, George, "Russian Disorders," *Harper's,* **262,** 1569:41–55, February 1981.

Friedrich, Carl J. and Zbigniew Brzezinski, *Totalitarian Dictatorship and Autocracy.* Cambridge, MA: Harvard University Press, 1956.

Gill, Graeme, "The Sources of Political Reform in the Soviet Union," *Studies in Comparative Communism,* **24,** 3:235–235, 1991.

Gleason, Abbott, "Totalitarianism in 1984," *Russian Review,* **432,** 2:145–159, 1984.

Grossman, Gregory, "The 'Second Economy' of the USSR," *Problems of Communism,* XXVI, 5:25–40, 1977.

Hankiss, Elemer, *East European Alternatives.* Oxford: Clarendon, 1990.

Hauslohner, Peter, "Politics Before Gorbachev," in Seweryn Bialer, ed., *Politics, Society, and Nationality Inside Gorbachev's Russia.* Boulder, CO: Westview Press, 1989.

Hewett, Ed A., *Reforming the Soviet Economy.* Washington, DC: Brookings Institution, 1988.

Hodnett, Grey, "Khrushchev and Party-State Control," in Alexander Dallin and Alan F. Westin, eds., *Politics in the Soviet Union: Seven Cases.* New York: Harcourt, Brace, 1966.

Hosking, Geoffrey, *The Awakening of the Soviet Union.* Cambridge, MA: Harvard University Press, 1990.

Inkeles, Alex and Raymond Bauer, *The Soviet Citizen: Daily Life in a Totalitarian Society.* Cambridge, MA: Harvard University Press, 1961.

Jones, Anthony, et al., eds., *Soviet Social Problems.* Boulder, CO: Westview Press, 1991.

Jowitt, Ken, "Soviet Neotraditionalism: The Political Corruption of a Leninist Regime," *Soviet Studies,* **35,** 3:275–297, 1983.

Khrushchev, Sergei, *Khrushchev on Khrushchev.* Boston: Little, Brown, 1990.

Kull, Steven, *Burying Lenin.* Boulder, CO: Westview Press, 1992.

Lapidus, Gail W., "Social Trends," in Robert Byrnes, ed., *After Brezhnev.* Bloomington, IN: Indiana University Press, 1983.

Lapidus, Gail W., "From Democratization to Disintegration: The Impact of *Perestroika* on the National Question," in Lapidus et al., eds., *From Union to Commonwealth.* New York: Cambridge University Press, 1992.

Levine, Herbert and Abram Bergson, eds., *The Soviet Economy Towards the Year 2000.* London: Allen & Unwin, 1983.

Lewin, Moshe, *The Gorbachev Phenomenon.* Berkeley: University of California Press, 1988.

Ligachev, Yegor, *Inside Gorbachev's Kremlin.* New York: Pantheon, 1993.

Linden, Carl A., *Khrushchev and the Soviet Leadership.* Baltimore: Johns Hopkins Press, 1967.

Linz, Juan, "Totalitarian Systems," in Fred I. Greenstein and Nelson Polsby, eds., *Handbook of Political Science,* vol. III, Reading, MA: Addison-Wesley, 1975.

Malia, Martin, "The Hunt for the True October," *Commentary,* **92,** 4:21–28, October 1991.

Malia, Martin, "From Under the Rubble, What?" *Problems of Communism,* **XLI,** 1–2:89–106, 1992a.

Malia, Martin, "Leninist Endgame," *Daedalus.* **121,** 2:57–75, 1992b.

Merton, Robert K., "The Unanticipated Consequences of Purposive Social Action," *American Sociological Review,* **1,** 6:894–904, 1936.

Millar, James R., ed., *Politics, Work, and Daily Life in the USSR.* New York: Cambridge University Press, 1987.

Pipes, Richard, "Can the Soviet Union Reform?" *Foreign Affairs,* **63,** 1:47–61, 1984.

Remnick, David, "Invitation to a Beheading," *New York Review of Books,* **XXXIX,** 18:12–17, November 5, 1992.

Rigby, T. H., "Politics in the Mono-Organizational Society," in Andrew C. Janos, ed., *Authoritarian Politics in Communist Europe.* Berkeley, CA: Institute of International Studies, University of California, 1976.

Rigby, T. H., "The USSR: End of a Long, Dark Night?" in Robert F. Miller, ed. *The Developments of Civil Society in Communist Systems.* Sydney, Australia: Allen & Unwin, 1992.

Rowen, Henry S. and Charles Wolf, eds., *The Impoverished Superpower: Perestroika and the Soviet Military Burden.* San Francisco: Institute for Contemporary Studies, 1990.

Ruble, Blair, "The Soviet Union's Quiet Revolution," in George Breslauer, ed., *Can Gorbachev's Reforms Succeed?* Berkeley, CA: University of California, Center for Slavic and East European Studies, 1990.

Sanders, George, ed., *Samizdat.* New York: Monad Press, **1974.**

Shevardnadze, Eduard, *Moy vybor (My Choice).* Moscow: Novosti, 1991.

Simis, Konstantin, *USSR: The Corrupt Society.* New York: Simon & Schuster, 1982.

Smith, Hedrick, *The Russians.* New York: Quadrangle, 1976.

Starr, S. Frederick, *Red and Hot.* New York: Oxford University Press, 1983.

Strong, John W., ed., *The Soviet Union Under Brezhnev and Kosygin.* New York: Van Nostrand, 1971.

Tatu, Michel, *Power in the Kremlin.* New York: Viking, 1969.

Ticktin, Hillel, *Origins of the Crisis in the USSR.* Armonk, NY: M. E. Sharpe, 1992.

Treml, Vladimir G., *Alcoholism in the USSR.* Durham, NC: Duke Press, 1982.

U.S. Central Intelligence Agency, *Measuring Soviet GNP: Problems and Solutions—A Conference Report* (SOV 90–10038, September 1990).

Vaksberg, Arkady, *The Soviet Mafia.* New York: St. Martin's Press, 1991.

Willerton, John P., *Patronage and Politics in the USSR.* New York: Cambridge University Press, 1992.

"Z" [pseud. of Martin Malia], "To the Stalin Mausoleum," *Daedalus,* **119,** 2:295–344, 1990.

Zaslavskaya, Tat'yana (anonymous), "The Novosibirsk Report," *Survey,* **28,** 1:88–108, 1984.

Zemtsov, Il'ya, *Partiya ili mafiya (Party or Mafia).* Paris: Editerus, 1976.

59 *Who Won the Cold War?*

DANIEL DEUDNEY AND G. JOHN IKENBERRY

...

In assessing the rest of the world's impact on Soviet change, a remarkably simplistic and self-serving conventional wisdom has emerged in the United States. This new conventional wisdom, the "Reagan victory school," holds that President Ronald Reagan's military and ideological assertiveness during the 1980s played the lead role in the collapse of Soviet communism and the "taming" of its foreign policy. In that view the Reagan administration's ideological counter-offensive and military buildup delivered the knock-out punch to a system that was internally bankrupt and on the ropes. The Reagan Right's perspective is an ideologically pointed version of the more broadly held conventional wisdom on the end of the Cold War that emphasizes the success of the "peace-through-strength" strategy manifest in four decades of Western containment. After decades of waging a costly "twilight struggle," the West now celebrates the triumph of its military and ideological resolve.

The Reagan victory school and the broader peace-through-strength perspectives are, however, misleading and incomplete—both in their interpretation of events in the 1980s and in their understanding of deeper forces that led to the end of the Cold War. It is important to reconsider the emerging conventional wisdom before it truly becomes an article of faith on Cold War history and comes to distort the thinking of policymakers in America and elsewhere.

... Perhaps the greatest anomaly of the Reagan victory school is the "Great Communicator" himself. The Reagan Right ignores that his anti-nuclearism was as strong as his anticommunism. Reagan's personal convictions on nuclear weapons were profoundly at odds with the beliefs of most in his administration. Staffed by officials who considered nuclear weapons a useful instrument of statecraft and who were openly disdainful of the moral critique of nuclear weapons articulated by the arms control community and the peace movement, the administration pursued the hardest line on nuclear policy and the Soviet Union in the postwar era. Then vice president George Bush's observation that nuclear weapons would be fired as a warning shot and Deputy Under Secretary of Defense T. K. Jones's widely quoted view that nuclear war was survivable captured the reigning ethos within the Reagan administration.

In contrast, there is abundant evidence that Reagan himself felt a deep antipathy for nuclear weapons and viewed their abolition to be a realistic and desirable goal. Reagan's call in this famous March 1983 "Star Wars" speech for a program to make nuclear weapons impotent and obsolete was viewed as cynical by many, but actually it expressed Reagan's heartfelt views, views that he came to act upon. As *Washington Post* reporter Lou Cannon's 1991 biography points out, Reagan was deeply disturbed by nuclear deterrence and attracted to abolitionist solutions. "I know I speak for people everywhere when I say our dream is to see the day when nuclear weapons will be banished from the face of the earth," Reagan said in November 1983. Whereas the Right saw anti-nuclearism as a threat to American military spending and the legitimacy of an important foreign policy tool, or as propaganda for domestic consumption, Reagan sincerely believed it. Reagan's anti-nuclearism was not just a personal sentiment. It surfaced at decisive junctures to affect Soviet perceptions of American policy. Sovietologist and strategic analyst Michael MccGwire has argued persuasively that Reagan's anti-nuclearism decisively influenced Soviet-U.S. relations during the early Gorbachev years.

Contrary to the conventional wisdom, the defense buildup did not produce Soviet capitulation. The initial Soviet response to the Reagan administration's buildup and belligerent rhetoric was to accelerate production of offensive weapons, both strategic and conventional. That impasse was broken not by Soviet capitulation but by an extraordinary convergence by Reagan and Mikhail Gorbachev on a vision of mutual nuclear vulnerability and disarmament. On the Soviet side, the dominance of the hardline response to the newly assertive America was thrown into question in early 1985 when Gorbachev became general secretary of the Communist party after the death of Konstantin Chernenko. Without a background in foreign affairs, Gorbachev was eager to assess American intentions directly and put his stamp on Soviet security policy. Reagan's strong antinuclear views expressed at the November 1985 Geneva summit were decisive in convincing Gorbachev that it was possible to work with the West in halting the nuclear arms race. ...

...

Reagan's commitment to anti-nuclearism and its potential for transforming the U.S.-Soviet confrontation was more graphically demonstrated at the October 1986 Reykjavík summit when Reagan and Gorbachev came close to agreeing on a comprehensive program of global denuclearization that was far bolder than any seriously entertained by American strategists since the Baruch Plan of 1946. The sharp contrast between Reagan's and Gorbachev's shared skepticism toward nuclear weapons on the one hand, and the Washington security establishment's consensus on the other, was showcased in former secretary of defense James Schlesinger's scathing accusation that Reagan was engaged in "casual utopianism." But Reagan's anomalous anti-nuclearism provided the crucial signal to Gorbachev that bold initiatives would be reciprocated rather than exploited. Reagan's anti-nuclearism was more important than his administration's military buildup in catalyzing the end of the Cold War.

...

Whether Reagan is seen as the consummate hardliner or the prophet of anti-nuclearism, one should not exaggerate the influence of his administration, or of other short-term forces. Within the Washington beltway, debates about postwar military and foreign policy would suggest that Western strategy fluctuated wildly, but in fact the basic thrust of Western policy toward the USSR remained remarkably consistent. Arguments from the New Right notwithstanding, Reagan's containment strategy was not that different from those of his predecessors. Indeed, the broader peace-through-strength perspective sees the Cold War's finale as the product of a long-term policy, applied over the decades.

In any case, although containment certainly played an important role in blocking Soviet expansionism, it cannot explain either the end of the Cold War or the direction of Soviet policy responses. The West's relationship with the Soviet Union was not limited to containment, but included important elements of mutual vulnerability and engagement. The Cold War's end was not simply a result of Western strength but of mutual weakness and intentional engagement as well.

Most dramatically, the mutual vulnerability created by nuclear weapons overshadowed containment. Nuclear weapons forced the United States and the Soviet Union to eschew war and the serious threat of war as tools of diplomacy and created imperatives for the cooperative regulation of nuclear capability. Both countries tried to fashion nuclear explosives into useful instruments of policy, but they came to the realization—as the joint Soviet-American statement issued from the 1985 Geneva summit put it—that "nuclear war cannot be won and must never be fought." Both countries slowly but surely came to view nuclear weapons as a common threat that must be regulated jointly. Not just containment, but also the overwhelming and common nuclear threat brought the Soviets to the negotiating table. In the shadow of nuclear destruction, common purpose defused traditional antagonisms.

A second error of the peace-through-strength perspective is the failure to recognize that the West offered an increasingly benign face to the communist world. Traditionally, the Soviets' Marxist-Leninist doctrine held that the capitalist West was inevitably hostile and aggressive, an expectation reinforced by the aggression of capitalist, fascist Germany. Since World War II, the Soviets' principal adversaries had been democratic capitalist states. Slowly but surely, Soviet doctrine acknowledged that the West's behavior did not follow Leninist expectations, but was instead increasingly pacific and cooperative. The Soviet willingness to abandon the Brezhnev Doctrine in the late 1980s in favor of the "Sinatra Doctrine"—under which any East European country could sing, "I did it my way"—suggests a radical transformation in the prevailing Soviet perception of threat from the West. In 1990, the Soviet acceptance of the de facto absorption of communist East Germany into West Germany involved the same calculation with even higher stakes. In accepting the German reunification, despite that country's past aggression, Gorbachev acted on the assumption that the Western system was fundamentally pacific. As Russian foreign minister Andrei Kozyrev noted subsequently, that Western countries are pluralistic democracies "practically rules out the pursuance of an aggressive foreign policy." Thus the Cold War ended despite the assertiveness of Western hardliners, rather than because of it.

The second front of the Cold War, according to the Reagan victory school, was ideological. Reagan spearheaded a Western ideological offensive that dealt the USSR a death blow. For the Right, driving home the image of the Evil Empire was a decisive stroke rather than a rhetorical flourish. Ideological warfare was such a key front in the Cold War because the Soviet Union was, at its core, an ideological creation. According to the Reagan Right, the supreme vulnerability of the Soviet Union to ideological assault was greatly underappreciated by Western leaders and publics. In that view, the Cold War was won by the West's uncompromising assertion of the superiority of its values and its complete denial of the moral legitimacy of the Soviet system during the 1980s. Western military strength could prevent defeat, but only ideological breakthrough could bring victory.

...

The ideological legitimacy of the Soviet system collapsed in the eyes of its own citizens not because of an assault by Western ex-leftists, but because of the appeal of Western affluence and permissiveness. The puritanical austerity of Bolshevism's "New Soviet Man" held far less appeal than the "bourgeois decadence" of the West. For the peoples of the USSR and Eastern Europe, it was not so much abstract liberal principles but rather the Western way of life—the material and cultural manifestations of the West's freedoms—that subverted the Soviet vision. Western popular culture—exemplified in rock and roll, television, film, and blue jeans—seduced the communist world far more effectively than ideological sermons by anti-communist activists. As journalist William Echikson noted in his 1990 book, *Lighting the Night: Revolution in Eastern Europe,* "instead of listening to the liturgy of Marx and Lenin, generations of would-be socialists tuned into the Rolling Stones and the Beatles."

If Western popular culture and permissiveness helped subvert communist legitimacy, it is a development of profound irony. Domestically, the New Right battled precisely those cultural forms that had such global appeal. V. I. Lenin's most potent ideological foils were John Lennon and Paul McCartney, not Adam Smith and Thomas Jefferson. The Right fought a two-front war against communism abroad and hedonism and consumerism at home. Had it not lost the latter struggle, the West may not have won the former.

The Reagan victory school argues that ideological assertiveness precipitated the end of the Cold War. While it is true that right-wing American intellectuals were assertive toward the Soviet Union, other Western activists and intellectuals were building links with highly placed reformist intellectuals there. The Reagan victory school narrative ignores that Gorbachev's reform program was based upon "new thinking"—a body of ideas developed by globalist thinkers cooperating across the East-West divide. The key themes of new thinking—the common threat of nuclear destruction, the need for strong international institutions, and the importance of ecological sustainability—built upon the cosmopolitanism of the Marxist tradition and officially replaced the Communist party's class-conflict doctrine during the Gorbachev period.

It is widely recognized that a major source of Gorbachev's new thinking was his close aide and speechwriter, Georgi Shakhnazarov. A former president of the Soviet political science association, Shakhnazarov worked extensively with Western globalists, particularly the New York–based group known as the World Order Models Project. Gorbachev's speeches and policy statements were replete with the language and ideas of globalism. The Cold War ended not with Soviet ideological capitulation to Reagan's anticommunism but rather with a Soviet embrace of globalist themes promoted by a network of liberal internationalists. Those intellectual influences were greatest with the state elite, who had greater access to the West and from whom the reforms originated.

...

On the ideological front, the new conventional wisdom is also flawed. The conservatives' anticommunism was far less important in delegitimating the Soviet system than were that system's internal failures and the attraction of precisely the Western "permissive culture" abhorred by the Right. In addition, Gorbachev's attempts to reform communism in the late-1980s were less an ideological capitulation than a reflection of philosophical convergence on the globalist norms championed by liberal internationalists. And the West was more appealing not because of its laissez-faire purity, but because of the success of Keynesian and social welfare innovations whose use the Right resisted.

...

NOTES

ABOUT THE AUTHORS: **Daniel Deudney** is assistant professor of political science at the University of Pennsylvania. **G. John Ikenberry** is assistant professor of politics and international affairs at Princeton University.

60 The "Shadows" Come to Light

EDVARD SHEVARDNADZE

...

... The problem of truth and deception was central to my resignation. I began to contemplate leaving approximately a year before December 20, 1990. But even at the early stages of my activity as a member of the Politburo and as Foreign Minister, when I constantly encountered throwbacks to the old double standard, backsliding from stated principles, and attempts to operate in the old fashion, I was compelled to reflect upon my role and its limitations. Back in 1986 I asked myself how long I could go on speaking as an exporter of the new thinking while other people and groups inside the country were obviously oriented toward the old thinking.

I am not blaming anyone for adhering to old thinking, and my reason is by no means a desire to come across as the righteous type who overlooks the sins of others. All of us were cut from the same cloth. To put it more accurately, we all meant to be, in words at least. But although some genuinely wanted to throw off the totalitarian mantle, others could not, and still others found it suited them just fine, as if it had been custom-tailored. I remember how they demanded that words about the class struggle be included in the Party's program, and Gorbachev said to them: "We remember about the class struggle when we want to force people to starve." It was naïve to think that generations raised for decades on barracks socialism could quickly adjust their consciousness. But I would like to believe that it is possible, because it is vitally necessary, and I have kept assuring myself and those close to me that the time will come when we will learn how to speak the truth, and speak it in time.

Chernobyl was the first test of glasnost, and it failed. Now it's all up ahead, I told myself, we're just starting. But ahead lay the tragedies in Alma-Ata, Sumgait, Stepanakert, Baku, Tbilisi, Vilnius, and Riga, and the old mechanisms kicked in, simplifying, distorting, or just eliminating the truth about events. I myself ran into a clear attempt to conceal from the country's leadership important details of the April execution in Tbilisi, so I can back Gorbachev's statement that he knew about the events in Vilnius only after they happened. But that means a theory of some "shadow" authority inevitably surfaces, a force operating at cross purposes with the lawful authorities, sending out disinformation along with the tanks. Or there was a desire to "cover for" this power and keep it out of the glasnost zone, something that is harder for me to believe.

*   *   *

...

I well recall October 15, 1990, the day when the announcement was made that Gorbachev had been awarded the Nobel Peace Prize. In the hours when Gorbachev was accepting congratulations, his Foreign Minister was at the podium in the Supreme Soviet, fending off attacks from the Soyuz group, which condemned him for the very thing that had motivated the Nobel Committee to make their award. Knowing this, Supreme Soviet Chairman Lukyanov kept silent.

The next day, I called Gorbachev and congratulated him on the well-earned distinction. He thanked me and said that I shared it with him. I had no need of this private recognition or of any public tribute to my merits, whether real or imagined. The only thing I needed, wanted and expected from the President was that he take a clear position: that he rebuff the right-wingers, and openly defend our common policy.

I waited in vain.

...

... The news about the suicide of Marshal Sergei Akhromeyev shook me. He was a man of duty, and I respect that in him. We were not friends. He said that himself. We were colleagues, and could not be more than that. But he never left me indifferent. He was a fighter with an open visor.

I spent many hours alongside him at the treaty table, and in explaining our positions to each other. He was the co-author of many very important decisions regarding armament. But in the process, he didn't hide his views from us—or almost never. He knew how to underscore his disagreement with a look, with an expression, with a gesture.

One could immediately see that he was a dutiful soldier. To be sure, sometimes people were taken aback that he could deviate from the demands of honor in the name of duty. For example, he could wrap himself in a veil of silence when we were savagely criticized on account of decisions that he himself had helped to make. Or he could claim to have opposed the dispatch of troops into Afghanistan, even though he had simply in fact advised a delay.

On reflection, I would say that the following sort of statement was most typical of him:

"My father disappeared during the period of collectivization. But I don't hold that against the Soviet state, because collectivization was a historical necessity."

Feelings of duty that are set above moral sentiments fill one with horror. What duty instructs you to exterminate your own father, along with thousands of others, in the name of "historical necessity" ... ?

The accomplices in the August conspiracy may have been planning something similar. On my desk there is a copy of a directive from the high command concerning preventive detention—but detention of whom? Of anyone whom the junta considered it necessary to seize? The space for names is blank. Include whomever you want. With totalitarianism, this "whomever" has no limits. There are just as few limits when it comes to executions, deportations, and reprisals. A mass of tanks is worth more than human lives. In the scales of "history," the latter means nothing.

Speaking of tanks, when the Ministry of Defense and the General Staff hid thousands of them behind the Urals in circumvention of the Paris Charter, I lodged a protest with the President. He instructed his advisor, Marshal Akhromeyev, to clarify the matter. Sergei Akhromeyev submitted a memorandum completely justifying the move. My protest withered under the metallic gleam of his argument, along with my distress that the reduction of tanks was accomplished by deceitfully repainting them with Marine Infantry colors.

The country has paid dearly for all of that. The treaty on strategic arms, the trust reposed in us by others and the politics of new thinking, the future of Soviet-American relations and the new world order—all of this was placed in doubt. That's how Akhromeyev fulfilled his duty. Was it fulfilling his duty to serve the President and the top military commanders even though he disagreed with them?

But there is another more pressing question. How could the President bring such people into his circle—people who so unmistakably opposed his policies? Was this generosity? Breadth of vision? Tolerance for those of different viewpoints? Those are magnificent qualities, as long as you do not have to pay the price with plots and putsches. The shadow forces had made themselves at home alongside the legal powers, not even bothering to hide themselves, and undermined their partners.

...

Meanwhile, the anxiety mounted. In November 1990, after the notorious "Declaration of the Fifty-three," it became unbearable. On one occasion I couldn't stand it any longer and called Gorbachev. I was told that he was on his way to work. I phoned his car.

"Acts of violence are the end of perestroika, and of your reputation. ..."

"What are you thinking?," said Gorbachev furiously. "How can it even occur to you that I would allow something like that to happen?"

I believed him. I had to believe him, just as I had to both earlier and later, when Mikhail Gorbachev said that the puppet-masters who were behind the events in the Baltics were unknown to him. But I began to suspect that there were certain hidden forces that were prepared to take criminal actions, lurking behind the President's back. Soon my suspicions began to be certainties.

In my own mind, the events of April in Tbilisi represented the dress rehearsal for a totalitarian anti-utopia. What I had experienced in December 1989 was still sharp in my memory: a powerful chorus raised their voices in support and justification of the organizers of this slaughter. The directors remained hidden, and no one did anything, as if nothing has happened.

This lesson was useless. The President allowed more blows to land and was thereby made all the more vulnerable. Now they dictated their demands to him and imposed ultimatums. I am not speaking here of deputies with epaulets, but rather of men of the highest rank.

...

On July 23, 1991, a little article with the headline "A Word to the People," appeared in the newspaper *Sovietskaya Rossiya* which in my view was a call to rebellion. Among those who signed this incendiary manifesto I found the names of all those who had for many years overtly or covertly acted against the legitimate government, organized smear campaigns against us, slowed down the execution of the decisions we had made, and had called Gorbachev, Yakovlev and myself "the Knights of Malta.'" Heroes of infantry and writers of a chauvinistic bent proposed an overt plan of action. The article even mentioned people who were willing and wound up on the list of dictators, and a third went to Gorbachev in the Crimea with an ultimatum.

The increasingly visible reactionary front, which had united everyone among the ultras from the Party apparatus, the military, and the chauvinist press, was now preparing direct attacks.

What did the President do? He went on vacation.

What did we do, his former friends and comrades who did not want to conceal the activities of the gang surrounding him?

Everything, even resigning from the team, was in vain. The President always remained deaf to the advice of the people genuinely loyal to him. Thus in June 1991, I thought it necessary to call for the unification of the country's democratic forces, and for a legal and constructive opposition. I was motivated by this simple thought: an organized democratic opposition should form the political base for the few reformers still active in the country's government. The elbow with which the President tried to prop himself up on the right was obviously slipping out from under him.

How did he reply to me and my friends? How did the reactionary leadership of the CPSU respond? With threats of a Party inquisition and punishment. New insults and insinuations. Persecution of the most prominent members of the Party devoted to democracy, Alexander Yakovlev, Alexander Rutskoy, Vasily Lipitsky, Nikolai Stolyarov and others.

But the Democratic Reform Movement which we had founded in spite of the President's wishes (and I also knew that for a fact), and even with his frank opposition, did not weaken; on the contrary, it grew and spread. And the right-wingers, seeing it as a threat, concentrated their fire on its initiators and leaders.

We were pummelled from the right, but he was silent. We were supported by those whom he branded as "so-called democrats"—Democratic Russia, and other parties in the RSFSR and other republics.

To be sure, he was busy with the drafting of the New Union Treaty. Yes, he himself suffered attacks and humiliations. But even so, with amazing stubbornness, he refused to see that the circle of the coup was closing in on him.

Did he not see it? Did he not want to see it? Or was it something else? I don't know. Numerous questions are raised for which I don't have any answers. On August 20, upon finding the French TV reporter Ulissa Gosse on TV1, I gave him my "Cry in the Wilderness."

In the interests of truth, it is worth quoting:

"The events of August 19 were not unanticipated. They were foreseen and forecast publicly, not only by me but by my comrades. Both I and they warned the President of them in personal conversations, and warned the country and the world in public statements from the parliamentary tribune, in newspapers, and on television."

"At the moment we know nothing about the fate of President Gorbachev and his family, so we are refraining from any speculation about the degree of his complicity in the plans of the coup plotters. For now, only one thing is clear: We have repeatedly warned of the shadow government operating at cross purposes to the legitimate authority and behind its back. Now this anti-Constitutional underground is out in the open. More, as has often been the case in our history, it is claiming its actions are lawful. But there is nothing further from the law than these actions. Under the law, a state of emergency can only be declared by an act of the Supreme Soviet, and only strictly in agreement with the legitimate authorities of the localities where the emergency is to be declared. Attempts to legalize an unlawful action after the fact is nothing more than a deception of the public at home and abroad. A parliament cannot make responsible decisions under the rumble of tanks and machine guns."

"If the President of the country is not well enough to perform his duties, he must himself, immediately and freely, under conditions monitored by democratic institutions, inform the people of this and order the procedure for the transfer of power himself. Although I have not had personal contacts with Gorbachev for a long time, I am still certain that his physical and mental state would not deprive him of the ability to perform his functions and executed powers. The natural fatigue that the President experiences given the weight on his shoulders would hardly prevent him from making coherent statements on television and in the press, which he has never refrained from doing, even before his ill-fated vacation."

"Therefore, it can only be a question of someone else, not him, preventing him from taking this opportunity, and preventing him by force. He is being blocked by these same midnight coup plotters, the majority of whom he himself has promoted to the heights of power."

"This can only be a question of an outrageously illegal, anti-Constitutional removal of the lawful President, actions not subject to rights and morals. The group which has seized power is now trying to 'bless' the actions with the name of the President. They are trying to create the illusion that they are defending his interests and the succession of power. ..."

"I maintain that regardless of possible statements still to come from Gorbachev and the junta that has replaced him, the President is not sick. Rather, the junta's actions show symptoms of a chronic ailment that perestroika had tried to heal; a deliberate plot behind the scenes, in secret from the people; the removal of disliked leaders by unlawful methods and under false pretexts; hypocrisy and a double standard in dealing with the people; the projection of an enemy image and the setting of popular masses against disliked or inconvenient persons. ..."

This is what I said and wrote in the hours before the storm in Russia's parliament, when all its defenders, all the advocates of lawful authority—along with our President—were threatened by something far worse than attacks in *Sovietskaya Rossiya* or the CPSU's newspaper *Glasnost.*

After Gorbachev's fortunate release from arrest in the Crimea, he was asked by one journalist at the press conference in Moscow to comment on my personal statement of August 20. How did Gorbachev answer the journalist's question? He said that he had not read my statement, but if I had really said that, it should be on my conscience.

Well, let it be on my conscience. He ought to have analyzed recent events. He had so little idea of what was going on around him that I could simply not be free of all suspicion.

As a man, as a father, as a husband, finally as his former comrade-at-arms, I lived through the 72-hour nightmare of Gorbachev's confinement in the comfortable palace jail of Foros.[10] He was a prisoner of the junta. But when he returned and spoke at the press conference, I saw that he was still a prisoner—of his own nature, his conceptions, and his way of thinking and acting. And now I am completely certain that none other than Gorbachev himself had been spoon-feeding the junta with his indecisiveness, his inclination to back and fill, his fellow-travelling, his poor judgment of people, his indifference towards his true allies, his distrust of the democratic forces, and his disbelief in the bulwark whose name is the people—the very same people who had changed thanks to the perestroika he had begun.

That is the enormous personal tragedy of Mikhail Gorbachev, and no matter how much I empathize with him, I cannot help but say that it almost led to a national tragedy.

...

In the final analysis, the people who defended the President were those he had betrayed, mistrusted or seen as enemies: Boris Yeltsin, the people of Russia and Moscow, the democratic movements and parties, his former comrades. And in this, despite the tragedy of the situation, I take enormous personal satisfaction, because the outcome of the August events confirmed the correctness of my chief principle: only the policy that is morally right will be victorious; only the political idea which takes human freedom as the measure of all things is invincible.

For some—and I would like to believe that they are very few—these were days of shame. For others, the majority, they were days of glory and great happiness achieved through common effort. And now I know that the people, armed only with the faith that they are right, carried the victory.

The plotters took many things into account, except the most important: the years of perestroika had rid us of fear, and we were different people now. And since we were different and they had remained the same, they could not conquer us. I am certain that the end of the coup will be the beginning of a new country, a new community of proud, strong and free people and a new world community.

For during these days, I was convinced anew how many of us there are in the world, and how we are united in the thirst for honor, dignity and truth.

...

NOTES

9. A reference to the Soviet-American summit in Malta, where conservatives believed Gorbachev had made compromises—Trans.

10. Gorbachev was detained at his dacha in the town of Foros in the Crimea—Trans.

61   *Inside Gorbachev's Kremlin*

YEGOR LIGACHEV

...

The real drama of perestroika was that the process of self-cleansing of our society begun in the depths of the Communist Party, not only slowed down, but was, I would say, distorted. In place of the old corrupt elements that for decades had been festering in the body of the Communist Party and the society at large, suddenly, in the space of a year or two, came even more horrible and more absolutely corrupt forces that stifled the healthy start made in the Party and the country after April 1985. Like the rapidly multiplying Colorado beetles, which in a moment eat up all the green potato shoots in a field, these proliferating parasitic forces quickly gobbled up all the sprouts of perestroika. As a result, the country, which had risen up to renew itself, lost its balance and faltered. And now we see the country already falling into the abyss of crisis.

What are these forces? What is their nature? Who is behind them, and why did they attain such free range at the time that the Communist Party, which had begun the self-cleansing process, was bound hand and foot like Gulliver, virtually deprived of the opportunity to wage an active political struggle?

To comprehend fully the bitterness of the cup from which our nation has drunk, we must investigate calmly and thoroughly how perestroika was born, how it began, developed, and ... disintegrated.

...

... I think that Gorbachev at first underestimated the social consequences of the destructive work of press, television, and radio. But the role of the media in the destabilization of the Baltics was very clear, as in the popular front press Lithuania, Latvia, and Estonia became battering rams, shaking the pillars of socialism and the Union state. *Pravda* warned of this while Viktor Afanasev was still in charge there, one of the few editors of national papers who was not within Yakovlev's sphere of influence. (This is why no effort was spared in the successful effort to get rid of Afanasev.)

Many people warned that the Baltics, and Lithuania in particular, were being used as a testing ground for destructive radical models. Unfortunately, neither Gorbachev nor the Politburo as a whole listened to those warnings. I was clear even then that glasnost and democracy were being used by certain radicals to incite social tensions, disorient the public consciousness, and destabilize the state. In the meantime, the perestroika we had created in 1985 was acutely in need of civil consensus and national unity. To keep the Party and country from falling apart, to prevent anarchy, we had to manage the mass media in a new way—not through *diktat*, but through comradely work and discussions, bearing in mind the socialist pluralism of newspapers, magazines, and television programs. But the radical publications were running amok with their attacks. It's hard to recall a Politburo meeting at which media questions did not appear. They were raised by almost all the members of the Politburo, especially Ryzhkov, Kryuchkov, and Lukyanov, and the secretaries of the Central Committee, with the exception of Yakovlev and Medvedev.

The Central Committee began to receive letters from people outraged by publications insulting our Party, army, and veterans. Naturally, it was impossible not to react to such letters. Sometimes Gorbachev himself would express outrage at certain articles or programs. But every time, it was nothing more than a tempest in a teapot, all words and not action. Occasionally the Politburo would assign Medvedev to "deal with the situation," but no one ever followed up on this, and Medvedev never reported his results. I think—no, I am certain—that this policy was well known to the captains of the right-radical press and was an inspiration to them.

The situation was made even more acute by the fact that at all the Central Committee plenums of that period, at all the meetings of workers, peasants, teachers, and industrialists, there was very loud and strong criticism of the media. Rereading the transcripts of those plenums today, I am amazed by the positions that Gorbachev took. He either did not notice the criticism, or interpreted it as an attempt on someone's part to evade the scrutiny of society and the press. The general secretary was making a serious mistake. A dictatorship of the right-wing mass media clearly was on the way—propaganda terrorism in which there could be no talk of diversity of ideas. On a single day, as if reacting to a starter's gun, five or six of the leading Moscow publications, along with TV and Radio Mayak, and with the powerful support of foreign stations, let loose a coordinated wave of attacks against all their foes in a destabilizing propaganda campaign.

People who called themselves democrats were giving off dictatorial signals and striving to monopolize minds, a dangerous tendency that threatened genuine democracy. But Gorbachev underestimated it, and in the final analysis, the inevitable occurred. The evil genie let out of the bottle attacked its liberator. The radical press treacherously spoke out against Gorbachev at the most difficult and most critical moment of perestroika.

It took Gorbachev two years, until the October 1990 Central Committee plenum, to put on the agenda the question of "responsibility of the mass media" for "trying to impose one-sided, subjective views and passing them off as the opinion of the people." He justly accused the media of "abusing glasnost in order to incite trouble." In the long time it took him to reach this conclusion, perestroika, the process of democratization, and all of society had been dealt a hard blow.

The increasingly harsh criticism of the radical media from all segments of society, particularly the Party, forced Alexander Yakovlev to provide a theoretical underpinning for the destructive activity of the newspapers and magazines he protected. And so appeared the mysterious thesis that the press and television are merely a mirror reflecting life: as life is, so are the media. Yakovlev actually said at one Politburo meeting: "The main goal of the mass media is to reflect what is happening in life, in society. No wonder they are this way today."

Everyone buzzed in outrage, and the hostile reception forced Yakovlev to be quiet. But the question remained: How could Yakovlev, who had been in charge of ideology for many years at the Central Committee, speak of "mirroring" as the main function of the media? Everyone, including Yakovlev himself, knew very well that the press and television were the mightiest levers in forming public opinion.

This was my first encounter with Yakovlev's astonishing ability to call white black and black white.

...

By spring 1990, when the threat of an all-encompassing crisis hung over the country and many of the things I had warned about had unfortunately come to pass. ... I used the right of a Communist guaranteed by the bylaws—I wrote a letter to the Central Committee. I cite it without cuts.

To General Secretary of the CPSU Central Committee, Comrade Gorbachev, M. S.

After painful thought, I decided to appeal to you, Mikhail Sergeyevich, with questions on the situation in the CPSU.

In the first three years of perestroika the situation in society changed for the better and the Party's authority increased. Then a retrograde movement began. Now, as many say with anxiety, the country has reached a limit. There is a real threat to the unity of the Soviet federation, to the unity of the CPSU. Our society, which tends to have historical optimism, peace, and quiet, is being overwhelmed with uncertainty, torment, and interethnic conflict. There are thousands of refugees in the country. Great mistakes were made in the implementation of economic reform, discipline and responsibility have fallen, and the lives of many people have grown worse. Forces contrary to socialism are at large in society.

The CPSU Central Committee receives resolutions, letters, and telegrams from Party organizations, work collectives, groups, and individual citizens in which, while supporting the policy of perestroika, Soviet people express profound anxiety and great pain for our Motherland and the Communist Party. I have formed the same impression from my meeting with work collectives. People are constantly asking each of us, and what do we tell them?

I always felt and continue to feel—and I am not alone in this—that the main force that is capable of bringing the country out of this acute situation and to implement reform in society are the CPSU and the soviets. But only if the Party is united and organized and its policies respond to the interests of the working class and the laboring masses. Only in that case can it preserve its political leadership.

In my opinion, the great danger lies in the fact that we allowed the weakening of the Party. That, I believe, is the mistake of the political leadership, the Politburo Central Committee. Of course, the burden of the past has its effect on the Party's authority—the severe consequences of Stalinism and the stagnation period and the fact of moral corruption of some leaders.

Even now there are factions, groups, and opposition tendencies within the Party. Based on the Democratic Platform, the revisionists (who call themselves radicals) are trying to transform the CPSU from within into a parliamentary party, removing it from organization work with the masses and in work collectives. Entire groups of Communists not only participate in, but lead nationalistic, separatist organizations.

An avalanche of lies is falling on the Party. So many worthy Communists, leaders, prominent representatives of science, culture, and literature have been slandered in recent times. The Soviet Army and the security agencies are subjected to constant attacks and slander.

Under the flag of democracy and glasnost, the ideological and moral pillars of society are being washed away. The destructive work of the opposition forces coincides with the hostile forces from outside. They have set as their goal the breakup of socialism in the USSR, after Eastern Europe, to ruin the social transformation along the lines of scientific socialism, and switch our country to the tracks of capitalist development.

As for the mass media, along with the great creative work that they are doing, some publications, television studios, and radio programs openly trample our past and present, inciting tension in society, hushing up the positive processes of perestroika, and paying no attention to the daily work of millions of Soviet people. There is no pluralism of opinion; this is dictatorship.

And there is a lot of talk about this, including at the Central Committee plenums and Politburo sessions and in the USSR Supreme Soviet, but the situation is not improving. It goes no farther than an exchange of opinion.

In connection with the decision of the Lithuanian Supreme Soviet to leave the USSR, the situation in the Soviet federation has grown more acute and the tendency toward separatism in the other Union republics has increased. State and international interests are being pushed into the background.

All the issues I have listed have been raised frequently by many Central Committee members at plenums. It cannot be said that I am writing about the problems of the unity of the Party for the first time, suddenly, or unexpectedly. I have spoken about them openly and honestly at the Central Committee plenums, at meetings of the first secretaries of the Union republics' Party Central Committees, at Territory and Province Party committee meetings, and at the Politburo. Letters and resolutions come to the Central Committee in which Communists and Party committees criticize the Politburo of the Central Committee for inconsistency. They express the opinion of the Party masses, the workers, and demand increased struggle against destructive forces.

Throughout the Party, along with democratization and strengthening ties with the masses, there was the goal of purging the ranks of those who hold positions of revisionism, social democratism, and nationalism. Otherwise the Party may break up. And then the CPSU can expect the fate of the Communist Party of Lithuania. Why are we delaying? Naturally this work must take place strictly within the framework of the bylaws of the CPSU and USSR Constitution.

I feel that this is the time to examine the political situation in the Party at the Central Committee plenum. If we turn to history, we see that the current moment was examined collectively at plenums under Lenin. We must convene an extraordinary CPSU Central Committee plenum. The Party's goals in strengthening its unity and the unity of the Soviet state could be discussed there. We had agreed at the Politburo to send a letter on this issue to the Party organizations. I am certain that that is not enough.

Among other issues, I feel we must pay attention to the question of particular political importance, the participation of the working class and the peasantry in government agencies and Party committees. As you know, things have reached the point that only one worker each from Moscow and from Leningrad was elected as a people's deputy of the RSFSR. Another urgent matter is an open and direct talk and a decision on increasing the influence of the Party on Communists working in the mass media.

The Party expects an analysis of the events in Eastern Europe from the Central Committee. The socialist community is falling apart and NATO is growing stronger. The German question is a priority. I think that in a historical plane, this is a temporary setback for socialism and I am convinced that the Communist idea will be victorious.

You know me and my character, Mikhail Sergeyevich, and you must understand that I had to write this letter. The situation demands immediate action. The Party and the Motherland are in danger, I would say in great danger. The possible breakup of our federation would be a world shock, an irreparable blow against socialism and the international Communist and workers' movement.

I am convinced that an examination of these questions at a Central Committee plenum would be of great benefit.

I would ask you to bring my letter to the attention of the comrades of the Politburo and the Central Committee of the Party.

Respectfully yours,
Ye. Ligachev
17 March 1990

Subsequent events fully confirmed the analysis made in this letter. If Gorbachev had yielded to the demands from local Party committees and convened a Central Committee plenum to discuss the situation in the Party and in the country, it is quite possible that the developments could have been controlled and a profound crisis avoided. Alas, the plenum was not convened. Despite the loud pronouncements about perfecting internal Party democracy, the members of the Central Committee were not shown my letter. It simply fell into a crevasse.

That was Gorbachev's method. Under Stalin, you would have lost your head for a letter like that. Under Khrushchev, you would have been fired. Under Brezhnev, you would be made an ambassador to Africa. And under Gorbachev, you were simply ignored.

…

… The dissent at the plenums stemmed from Central Committee members' belief that extreme radicalization was diverting perestroika from its original path. With all their political experience, they could see who was rushing Gorbachev and why, and they foresaw the consequences of that haste.

If Gorbachev had marched in step with these realists, we would be much farther along today. We would not have landed in this crisis and political destabilization, and we would not have to go backward to restore foolishly disrupted contractual economic ties. And I have no doubt that the Party would not have been removed from economic life.

Instead, the Central Committee's unwillingness to turn perestroika into the "great leap" was presented to Gorbachev as a danger of a coup. It was clear that the radicals' clamor of "conspiracy" was an artifice, a treacherous attempt to lead the Party and society's sound forces far away from the real danger: nationalist separatism and anti-Communism. …

…

…The widespread opinion that the top political leadership was not in the know about certain events is deeply mistaken. The Politburo had virtually exhaustive information on all situations of conflict—political, economic, financial, interethnic.

I remember someone saying to me about Gorbachev, "Mikhail Sergeyevich is a president who wants to go down in history as a clean man, whom no one can accuse of dictatorship."

Perhaps this concern about his "historical image" did sometimes keep Gorbachev from taking decisive, necessary, but unpopular measures. As a result, problems grew, contradictions mounted, and crises escalated. And in the long run, this line led to a slowdown in perestroika. But having analyzed a large number of facts and conversations with Gorbachev, I have come to the conclusion that it was also a tactical measure of a special kind.

Gorbachev is one of those politicians who takes decisive measures when the situation is overripe; he waits for the apple to drop. He always worried about how the country and the world would accept the solutions he offered for some conflict; that's natural in politics. But I wouldn't say he was overly concerned about using unpopular measures—like any politician, he considered this, but it did not predominate. When a conflict situation came to a peak, when the thunder rolled—then Gorbachev would begin to act. He preferred reproaches for being too late to attacks for making mistakes. Being late is not as dangerous as being wrong for a political reputation, at least at first. Besides, intervening after the fact creates the image of a "savior" who comes to straighten out a situation. As for the colossal losses, human and material, caused by the conflict, which could and should have been avoided, those were brushed over, and stress was laid on "clearing up the consequences."

Yes, Gorbachev was often forced to fix his own mistakes. "Someone" overradicalized the development of the economy, trying in 1988 to introduce market relations, and by running too far ahead led to catastrophic disruption of economic ties and a decrease in production and problems in monetary circulation ... and then the president proposed rational measures to get out of the crisis. "Someone" did not appreciate the dangers of nationalism, let it emerge, and as a result the very existence of our state was threatened ... and only then did Gorbachev make desperate, if noble efforts to save the Union.

This list of mistakes and corrective measures could be extended, for after 1988, the policies of perestroika turned into "chasing its own tail," and the country gradually slipped toward the brink. The guilt lay with the tactic of being late: that "someone" was Gorbachev himself.

We can't say he didn't know the situation or was ignorant of the dangers. Gorbachev and all of us were warned many times, and fierce fighting was going on over these questions at the plenums and in the Politburo. The most important moments of that struggle—over the economy, Party unity, and nationalism are reflected in this book. But Gorbachev was under the influence of the radicals.[19] They called themselves the "foremen of perestroika,"[20] but they were actually its gravediggers.

...

Whether intentionally or not, the West happened to give powerful propaganda support to the radical forces, who wanted to turn perestroika into a "great leap."

This in fact led to destruction, the collapse of a great superpower. A whole complex of factors was at work here: ideological rejection of socialism, geopolitical considerations, and so on.

However, I want to stress that the West was deceived. The radicals could not offer a real movement toward progress for the country. Moreover, having taken power in a few local soviets on the wave of anti-Communist and anti-Soviet speculation, they managed to discredit themselves in just a few months. They were helpless when it came to solving practical questions, and managed to set people against them, even those who had supported them in the West. People who had called themselves democrats turned out to be leaders with a monopolistic turn of mind. They showed themselves unable to accept pluralistic thinking, going so far as to ban alternative newspapers. They began selling off Russia's national wealth for the sake of instant gratification. But it could not have been otherwise: if you "scratch our pluralists," in Alexander Solzhenitsyn's words, you will quickly find that virtually all had made their careers in the stagnation period by hailing "developed socialism."

And turncoats, ideological "defrocked priests," as you know, are the least dependable people. Having betrayed their faith once, they will continue switching and lying forever.

...

As we know, our country's economy approached the year 1985 very short of breath; everyone understood that it was being consumed by disease, but no one suspected how serious it was. And so, after performing a kind of X ray of the economic organism with the help of glasnost, society discovered that the economy was gravely ill, the main reasons for the illness being the command methods of leadership and the suppression of economic initiative and independence.

We then set about developing the economic strategy of perestroika and determined the first steps to overcome stagnation as quickly as possible. The nation soon felt a change for the better. There is no particular need to go into detail: 1985–87, when housing construction accelerated and store shelves began to be filled, is still well within people's memories.

What happened to the reform? Why did the economy take a nosedive and then break into a tailspin? Two diametrically opposed points of view dominate public discourse on the causes of what happened. The so-called radicals (the right wing), to whom I have given much attention in this book, submit that the socialist system of structuring society, which does not yield to renewal, is to blame for everything. There is also another viewpoint, which holds that we were led to the brink of the abyss not only by the scope and complexity of the accumulated problems but also by the gross errors made by the leaders of perestroika. They gave in to these same radicals and rashly destroyed the planned economy and existing economic ties before conditions could be created for the transition to economic management methods.

Is the answer in the crisis of the system, or in the blunders and mistakes of the leaders of perestroika?

SUCCESSES AND ERRORS

I am not one of those who consider perestroika to be a Pandora's box, the focus of all evils and ills. But neither do I agree with those who contend that the misfortunes that befell the country are the inevitable accompaniments of renewal. ...

...

It is well known from history that a planned economy is advantageous in concentrating vast forces and resources in the resolution of key national problems. I will make the immediate reservation that the system of planning, or large-scale state programs, is not exclusively characteristic of socialist economies, as some politicians of various ranks—including, strangely enough, professors of economics—hotheadedly contend. The planning of such programs is accepted in all developed countries of the world. In the United States, for example, two of the most impressive examples of this type are the state programs for the development of the high-tech industry: NASA and SDI, the Strategic Defense Initiative. This is to say nothing of the programs of a social nature—for example, the struggle with the drug trade.

There is also no dearth of achievements in the history of our country testifying brilliantly to the advantages of state planning. So it was in the period of industrialization in the 1930s, the conquering of space in the 1950s and 1960s, and the creation of the world-class western Siberian oil and gas complex in the 1960s and 1970s. No reasonable person can deny the economic advantages to be gained from planning; attempts to discredit the planning system have been perfidious indeed. I would go so far as to say that the planned economy, adopted for the first time on a large scale in the USSR, is an achievement of universal human significance; this principle of managing the processes of development is now used all over the world (as is, by the way, the state system of social protection for working people created in our country).

However, command-administrative methods have in many ways distorted the principle of a planned economy, have taken them to the point of absurdity. Those at the top started planning from on high not special programs, not overall directions of development, but literally everything, up to and including the entire distribution of resources and wages. The economy, squeezed by innumerable instructions, started to choke. But the greater the scarcity of resources, the stricter its planning became—although this was no longer planning but willful administrative invasion of the sphere of production.

We realized this very quickly after 1985, as we planned to correct the situation by freeing the national economy from the center's petty guardianship, gradually bringing the share of state planning down to rational limits and giving planning back its primary essence, the large-scale management of material, financial, and labor resources in the interests of society as a whole. Properly understood, centralized planning can be compared to the creativity of an architect who designs a building. The mechanisms and work methods used to erect the structure are the problems of the builders.

...

But the opponents of socialism have proclaimed the above-mentioned distortions of planning the inevitable attributes of the social system and have made it their goal to destroy the planning system completely for the sake of an absolute economic freedom—which does not exist anywhere in the world.

There is one more collapsed item of received wisdom: erroneously understood social justice, which not infrequently turned into primitive egalitarianism.

We discussed this question with particular thoroughness at the Politburo as we prepared for the 27th Congress. What is the true essence of the concept of social justice? The collective answer differed noticeably from the previous crude egalitarianism. Yes,the essence of social justice is contained in the fundamental law of socialism: to each according to the quantity and quality of this work. However, such a definition is insufficient. It must be supplemented with the right of the collective to dispose of its product and the income from its property, if this property is earned by its own honest labor. There is only one criterion, but an unshakable one: the legality of earnings, the social benefit of labor.

This departure from former egalitarianism was a fundamental matter; it was also directed toward the future and gave people room for initiative. The main thing was that a high labor income was rehabilitated in the eyes of society. The rest was a matter of "technique"; we still had to work out the fairest taxation, etc.

I am bitter that this important, fundamental move forward defining the general strategy of perestroika was simply ignored by the new political forces that emerged in the social arena to seize power. Trying to break down an open door, they attributed the old definition of social justice to the Communist Party. As a counterbalance, they advocated the idea of the so-called differentiation of incomes, the division into poor and rich. Publications even appeared to the effect that in any population of living creatures, including the human population, only 4 percent of individuals are active, while the remainder are only the "biological mass," obliged to service those who are the most enterprising. And if these 4 percent are very well off, then the remainder will be just the tiniest bit better off, too.

In a word, they proposed letting the moneychangers and Pharisees back into the temple. Is this social justice? Is this what the people wanted from perestroika? Ideologies of such changes gradually forced out the original economic strategy and in the final analysis brought the country to economic collapse. ...

...

Destatification was in many respects reduced to privatization—in other words, to turning the means of production over to private ownership. This was not a matter of a variety of forms of ownership but of a type of ownership—private—new for our society. After decades, we are returning the country to what the October Revolution eliminated. Translated into language accessible to everyone: Instead of renewing and improving socialism, the system was to be replaced. ...

...

My personal position on the question of private ownership of the means of production is well known. It corresponds to the main original slogan of perestroika, in whose development I participated: More democracy, more social-ism! And yet the establishment of private ownership, the introduction of hired la-bor, and the buying and selling of land contradict the Party's programmatic stat-ute about the socialist option and a Communist future. And adding "labor" to the concept of "private ownership" does not save the situation. One can assume that dragging in private ownership is a concession to the West, to get economic and political aid. Even though plenty of declarations that this is not the case have been made to placate society, the West clearly is counting on the introduction of pri-vate ownership to lead our country to a rejection of socialism. With this prospect in mind, it is even agreeing to some political "sacrifices."

...

Quite a few politicians in the West make economic aid to our country condi-tional on a series of demands, including the introduction of an unregulated mar-ket and private ownership of the means of production. There are those among them who simply hope to turn the Soviet Union into a raw-materials appendage of the West. In other words, we are talking about the openly expressed class nature of Western policy.

...

The fact that some circles in the West, and in our country as well, are trying to replace the problem of forming a regulated market with the problem of introduc-ing private ownership in the USSR is somewhat offensive. The thesis that perestroika is impossible without private enterprise has heated up political pas-sions. It opens up the possibility of changing the social system, and such a course of events naturally leads to social and political instability.

In time, it became clear that preparations were made in advance for the procla-mation of the "sacred principle of private ownership." For this it was necessary first to impair and then to destroy the national planned economy. This task, in turn, was begun with a propagandistic blow to the headquarters, the centers of administration, under the pretext of attacking the "command-administrative sys-tem." ... but what is the "command-administrative system"?

The question was soon illuminated: what was intended was a blow against everything central, from the State Planning Committee to the armed forces. Everything that cemented the great power as a state, as a single whole, was de-clared to be the "command-administrative system," subject to demolition. ...

...

I have no doubt that our leading economists, who are proposing that we re-duce the national economy and break it up into smaller units, to place our stakes on small and medium-sized enterprises in every way possible, understand very well that in fact this goes against the world trend of development, and sidetracks our country from the main road of progress. They understand very well that it throws us back decades, if not a whole century. But these scholars have turned into the most active of politicians; they are motivated not by scholarly or patriotic concerns but by mercenary political advantage. What they passed over in silence in 1988–89 they proclaimed openly in 1991: capitalization, the creation of a social stratum of entrepreneurs based on private ownership. It is this strictly political aim that has been placed at the cornerstone, not economic revival. What is more, its achievement requires that the potential already created must be shattered, that a crisis be created in the country.

...

I take full responsibility for declaring that demands for the immediate dissolution of collective and state farms to create private farming on the basis of private ownership will lead to famine in our country, as experience has already confirmed. In effect, what they want to do is utilize in reverse the same device that Stalin used in the early 1930s, when an artificially created famine was used to liquidate individual farms and institute universal collectivization. Now they crave the opposite version: to create famine artificially again and, after blaming the collective farms for it, to dissolve them forcibly.

And once again it will be the people who have to pay for these political intriguers.

...

In my view, what was most immoral was the fact that both the creators of the "500-Day" Program and many other supporters of private ownership also supported the movement toward separatism and the disintegration of the Soviet Union in the ensuing ideological battle. Under conditions of state instability, ethnic conflicts, and even civil war, it is, of course, easier to attempt a replacement of the social system. Political ambitions and love of power turned out to be higher than patriotism, higher than the age-old interests of the state.

NOTES

ABOUT THE AUTHOR: **Yegor Ligachev** was a member of the Politburo under Mikhail Gorbachev and became one of his leading critics and orthodox opponents.

19. In the spring of 1991, speaking in Byelorussia, Gorbachev justly criticized the radicals by saying that "someone" had given the radicals full freedom, tying the hands of the sound forces in the Party, and now he was putting things in their real place.—AUTHOR

20. "Foreman of perestroika" was a phrase coined in the perestroika era, often used ironically, to describe those in Gorbachev's team who were promoting the new line, or prominent liberal intellectuals who supported Gorbachev's policies.—TRANS.

62 *Conclusion*

GAIL W. LAPIDUS
& ALEXANDER DALLIN

Mikhail Gorbachev's years in the Kremlin—from March 1985 to December 1991—witnessed one of the most astounding developments of this century: an effort to reform the Soviet system that culminated in its collapse. If there is general agreement on its importance, there is considerable debate over how to explain it, how to appraise it, how to compare it with other instances of contemporary transitions from authoritarianism, and how to assess what it portends for the future.

PERESTROIKA—SUCCESS OR FAILURE?

Whether we view the whole experience of *perestroika* as a success or a failure depends very much on the criteria we apply. In terms of Gorbachev's objectives—as a strategy for in-system reform, and as an all-Union project—it clearly failed: It resulted in the destruction of the communist system and in the break-up of the Soviet Union.

If, however, *perestroika* is judged as a vehicle for the transition, albeit unintended, from a communist regime to a noncommunist one; for the gradual opening up of a closed society and for integrating the Soviet Union and its peoples into the global community; for the achievement of self-determination for the constituent nations of the Soviet Union and for the countries of Central and Eastern Europe; then the course of events that we witnessed under Gorbachev—however halting and zigzagging–was essentially the only way these transformations could have been achieved peacefully. Any scenario other than gradual liberalization from above, initiated and sponsored by the ruling Party's leadership and intended as an effort to improve the system, would surely have provoked bloody repression or civil war. Gorbachev's special skills lay in forging the coalition that was necessary to launch the process and then sustaining it for some years. Ironically, it was precisely the formidable power of the general secretary, the rules of Party discipline, and the habits of obedience inculcated over generations that served to inhibit, for several years, serious challenges to his policies.

Whether or not the whole process could have occurred more gradually, over a more extended period of time, thereby creating more favorable economic and political conditions for the post-Soviet evolution of the region, does of course remain a matter of bitter contention. Inevitably, so radical and rapid a transformation came at a high price. The sudden and unexpected unraveling of the Soviet system left in its wake a mass of problems and conflicts, with often tragic consequences ranging from personal to national insecurity and from personal to national impoverishment.

It also left in its wake innumerable obstacles and impediments to the emergence or consolidation of democratic regimes in the fifteen successor states. Some may manifest elements of democratic norms without fully developing democratic systems. Quite possibly, a number of them will, for shorter or longer periods of time, turn toward authoritarian or repressive regimes. But none of this would mark a return to the totalitarian regime they had known in Soviet times. There is no road back to the past.

TRANSITION, FRAGMENTATION, SEQUENCING

The process of liberalization and democratization initiated by the Gorbachev leadership shared many features with other transitions from authoritarian rule in Latin America, southern Europe, and Eastern Europe. As in a number of other cases, deepening cleavages within the political elite amid a growing perception of system crisis triggered a shift of power to a reformist segment of this elite, which moved to consolidate its position by appealing to social forces previously excluded from political roles. Elite-initiated reform was progressively radicalized as a variety of newly empowered actors used the novel opportunities for political mobilization to expand and transform the agenda.[1]

At this point, the Soviet case substantially diverges from the more familiar patterns of transition. A first and fundamental difference lay in the nature of the actors who emerged to fill the newly created political space. As a result of the thoroughgoing destruction of autonomous organizations by the Soviet regime in earlier years and the amorphousness of social structures that resulted from the socio-occupational leveling of the Soviet era, *perestroika* did not trigger the emergence, or reemergence, of a vibrant civil society with effective political parties, trade unions, business associations, or other groups mediating between state and society (except, to a limited extent, in the Baltic states, which had been incorporated into the Soviet Union more recently than the rest). Although a great number of sociopolitical groups and movements did emerge, they tended to be neither cohesive, nor well organized, nor well endowed, nor were they all-Union in scope.

Indeed, with the weakening of the "command-administrative system," the Union republics became the main arenas for political activism. Precisely because of the way the Soviet state had organized and managed ethnicity, the process of democratization and the unintended delegitimation of the Soviet system challenged its imperial features, spawning national movements that pressed for the sovereignty of their former republics. Not only were the key actors different; their goals were as well. Initially, many of these movements supported the broader reformist cause, but ultimately their agenda was independence and not transition. Democratization and marketization became entwined in the Soviet case with pressures for something akin to decolonization, calling into question the very survival of the Union "center."

Thus, in the Soviet case, the state that initiated the transition ceased to exist as a consequence of it and was replaced by fifteen new actors. One transition was replaced by fifteen autonomous transitions. Moreover, many of the newly independent states themselves faced uncertain or contested identities and boundaries. If a critical precondition for successful democratization is established boundaries and identities, as had been argued in earlier literature, such propitious circumstances could not be found either in the Soviet Union or in most of its successor states.[2]

An additional major difference between the Soviet (and post-Soviet) and other transformations related both to the scope of the tasks and to their sequencing. As the new states came into existence, they faced the urgent challenge of simultaneous state- and nation-building—the creation of new identities and the institutions, attitudes, and values that went with them—tasks even more daunting than the challenges faced by transitions elsewhere in the modern world.

At the same time, political institution-building had to take place in a context of economic crisis as a result of the cumulative effects of the Soviet legacy, the Gorbachev reforms, the attainment of independence, and in some instances civil unrest. By 1991 the old economic arrangements in the Soviet Union were shattered, but neither new economic strategies nor new institutions had yet been created. Because of the virtual fusion of political and economic power in Soviet-type systems, political democratization was closely entwined with economic reform. But the transformation from a command economy to a market economy had no precedents to build on, nor any body of theory to offer guidance. Moreover, the unpredictable consequences of the interactions of political and economic reform carried with them the risk of serious destabilization.

Furthermore, all the new states of the region—and especially Russia and Ukraine—were burdened by bloated military-industrial complexes commanding massive economic resources and considerable political clout, which were a major obstacle to both political and economic reform. To build or reorganize armies and security services, to scale down defense enterprises and related activities—from ICBMs to research laboratories—to cope with the legacy of Soviet nuclear weapons and massive environmental devastation had to rank near the top of the new states' agendas.

The task of state-building also encompassed creating new institutions to formulate—and implement—security and foreign policies. International relations among the successor states opened a wholly novel chapter that required them all to define their national interest and their relations to each other and to the outside world. Faced by multiple insecurities, including contested borders, territorial irredenta, fractious ethnic minorities, and the shadow of Russia's presence and hegemonic past, their largely inexperienced elites were taking on enormous tasks.

Notwithstanding many challenges common to all, the situation in which Russia found itself differed fundamentally from that of the other newly independent states. To a greater or lesser degree, the other fourteen republics gained something from the dissolution of the Union, be it the recovery of national languages and cultures or international recognition. For Russia, the breakup constituted a profound trauma, involving the loss of territories that had been part not only of the Soviet Union but also of the pre-1917 Russian empire, of Russian populations now outside the borders of the Russian state, and of superpower status. Adapting to its new, diminished role was a painful challenge to Russia's self-image and vision, with far-reaching repercussions for Russian politics.

FROM EUPHORIA TO SOBRIETY

The end of the Soviet Union was bound to create unexpected and unprecedented opportunities for the fifteen successor states, but the euphoria of independence quickly yielded to the new realities of multiple constraints. And with the passage of time, an observer is struck not only by the new departures that the disintegration of the Soviet system made possible and by the difficulties stemming from the new environment in which the newly independent states were obliged to function but also by the profound impact of the various legacies that the Soviet Union bequeathed to its successors.

Although the whole region experienced what amounted to a revolution, the very term "revolution" belies the fact that underneath the drama of novelty there remained a number of stubborn continuities. There were, first of all, the legacies of Soviet institutions. Sometimes with a change of name, sometimes with a redefinition of functions, the major governmental structures, down to the local level, remained. So too did many features of the Soviet economic system, including the high level of economic interdependence created by extreme divisions of labor, now disrupted by new borders and currencies.

There were likewise remarkable continuities in personnel. This was not so surprising, perhaps, if one considers that there was no pool of potential officialdom outside the all-embracing party-state. Here and there (for instance, in western Ukraine and the Baltic states) some former dissidents came into office, but the bulk of officials remained; former Party secretaries moved over into state functions; enterprise managers became directors of joint-stock companies; unless they retired, police officials and army officers either remained in their familiar services or joined one of the burgeoning private security organizations.

To be sure, significant variations emerged among the different republics. Thus, in Central Asia (except perhaps for Kyrgyzstan) the old elites remained virtually intact; this was somewhat less true in Russia, the Baltic states, Georgia, or Armenia. And former communist officials—from Leonid Kravchuk to Algirdas Brazauskas and from Gennadi Burbulis to Geidar Aliev—varied enormously in the "learning" they had undergone and in their degree of adaptation to the new times and new environment. Noncommunists likewise varied in what they stood for; suffice it to think of Andrei Sakharov and Vladimir Zhirinovsky as contrasting examples of the genre.

Most of those who continued in office and many citizens outside of official structures also shared significant and persistent attitudes. Most widespread perhaps was the habit of dependence on the state—a natural phenomenon after generations of Soviet experience but one with costly consequences. Many of them likewise shared ideas of social justice, attitudes toward authority, and an ambivalence about the West.

Finally, officialdom revealed deeply ingrained habits of bureaucratic behavior and style of work. Inevitably vestiges of intolerance and of an imperial mentality persisted. In many instances, elements of the old and the new would uneasily compete and coexist within the same person; there was no better example of this than Boris Yeltsin himself. It would take time to forge a post-Soviet generation.

Even the formal independence of the successor states is often qualified by the continuing Russian presence in what is now called the "near abroad," including a sizeable Russian diaspora in the newly independent states of the region as well as Russian dominance in an economic system that had been developed over more than half a century without much regard for territorial boundaries within the USSR. More ominously, Russian military units continued to operate abroad, from Moldova to Abkhazia and the Afghan border.

CHALLENGE TO WESTERN POLICY

These unanticipated and complex processes present the West with unprecedented dilemmas. The end of the cold war, the major accords on arms control, and the prospects for integrating the Soviet Union into the world economy had been exhilarating outcomes of the Gorbachev reforms. Understandably, it has been difficult to adjust to a harsher reality.

Among the many challenges that Western policymakers face, none is more important than to distill and articulate the conceptual underpinnings of their policy toward the region. That is a precondition for a steadiness of course, avoiding panic as well as gloating, across the peaks and vales of unexpected developments that this region is sure to produce in the years ahead.

How deeply should, or can, the West be engaged in what happens in these fifteen new states, for moral as well as for economic and political reasons? How should it sort out the conflicting pulls for and against giving priority to a relationship with Russia rather than some of the other successor states—let alone with their neighbors in the international system? How much economic, financial, and technical assistance can and should be provided, in what form and on what conditions? How should the West balance personal and cultural sympathies with geopolitical anxieties? These are but some of the questions that need to be sorted out.

Transforming the former Soviet Union has turned out to be a much more difficult and protracted process than anyone had envisaged only a few years ago. The West must recognize that it cannot simply turn away. If the future of that region matters—as it does, even in the limited perspective of U.S. security, markets, and well-being—Westerners must understand that we are willy-nilly participants in the struggles and dialogs within and among these societies. Their outcomes are affected by what we say and do as much as by what we fail to say and fail to do. By the same token, their words and their behavior are bound to affect Western responses and policies. That interdependence can become a lock or an embrace, but it is the reality from which all must start.

NOTES

1. The classic reference on transition theory is Guillermo O'Donnell and Philippe C. Schmitter, eds., *Transitions from Authoritarian Rule* (Baltimore: Johns Hopkins University Press, 1986), 4 vols. For a stimulating discussion and a review of the literature, see Philippe C. Schmitter with Terry Lynn Karl, "The Conceptual Travels of Transitologists and Consolidologists," *Slavic Review* (Spring 1994).

2. See, in particular, Dankwart Rustow, "Transitions to Democracy," *Comparative Politics* 2 (1970), 337–363.

ABOUT THE BOOK
AND EDITORS

Now fully revised and updated, this reader provides a well-rounded view of the conflicting debates and trends that led to the collapse of the Soviet Union.

In this revised edition, Alexander Dallin and Gail W. Lapidus have brought together Soviet documents and commentary as well as outstanding Western analyses dealing with developments in Soviet politics, economy, society, culture, and foreign policy from 1985 through 1991.

The collection covers the full spectrum of views—skeptical and enthusiastic, ideological and pragmatic—offered by journalists, politicians, observers, and participants. Introductory and concluding material by the editors provides the essential context to help students understand the myriad opinions put forth on the last years of the USSR and on where the region's future may lie.

Alexander Dallin is Raymond A. Spruance Professor of International History and director of the Center for Russian and East European Studies at Stanford University. **Gail W. Lapidus** has been professor of political science at the University of California–Berkeley and chair of the Berkeley-Stanford Program in Soviet and Post-Soviet Studies. She is now senior fellow at the Institute for International Studies at Stanford University.